The **Rough Guide** to

Andalucía

written and researched by

Geoff Garvey and Mark Ellingham

with additional contributions by

Pau Sandham and Chris Stewart

NEW YORK · LONDON · DELHI

www.roughguides.com

Contents

Andalucian cuisine insert following p.264

Semana Santa insert following p.392

Moorish Andalucía insert following p.584

◄◄ Feria de Abril, Sevilla ◄ Casares

Introduction to
Andalucía

Andalucía is the southernmost territory of Spain and the part of the Iberian peninsula that is most quintessentially Spanish. The popular image of Spain as a land of bullfights, flamenco, sherry and ruined castles derives from this spectacularly beautiful region. The influences that have washed over Andalucía since the first paintings were etched on cave walls here more than twenty-five thousand years ago are many – Phoenicians, Carthaginians, Greeks, Romans, Visigoths and Vandals all came and left their mark. And the most influential invaders of all, the Moors, who ruled the region for seven centuries and named it *al-Andalus*, have left an enduring imprint on Andalucian culture and customs.

The heartland of Andalucía is the fertile valley of the mighty **Río Guadalquivir**, flowing across the region from its source in the Cazorla mountains in the northeast through the magnificent cities of Córdoba and Sevilla, before draining into the marshes and wetlands of the Doñana national park and the Gulf of Cádiz. North of this great artery rise the undulating hills of the **Sierra Morena**, from where was gouged the mineral wealth – silver, lead and tin – sought by successive waves of invaders from Phoenicians to Romans. The **Moors**, who arrived in the eighth century, were more interested in harvesting Andalucía's natural wealth and turned the region into an orchard rich in olives, citrus fruits, almonds, saffron, figs and vines – still the major products of the land today. In 1492 the Christian reconquest, after centuries of struggle, finally succeeded

4

in wresting Spain from its Moorish occupiers, the victors symbolically planting their flags on the towers of the Alhambra, the emblematic monument of Andalucía.

The **Moorish legacy** is the most striking feature of Andalucía today, not only in the dazzling historical monuments such as those of Sevilla, Córdoba and Granada but also in the whitewashed houses of many of its smaller medieval towns such as Ronda or the flat-roofed villages of Las Alpujarras. The Moorish love of water is to be seen in the pleasure gardens of the Alhambra, and the typical Andalucian patio – tiled plant-bedecked courtyards often with a central fountain – is another Arab legacy as are the ubiquitous wrought-iron window grilles which lend character to any village street. The dances and music of **flamenco**, whilst probably not of Moorish

▶ Traditional Andalucian dress

Fact file

• Andalucía's **land area** of 90,000 square kilometres is about the size of Ireland or Indiana. With a population of seven million, it is the second largest of Spain's seventeen autonomous regions, with its own administration and parliament based in the regional capital, Sevilla.

• Physically, Andalucía is a land of stark contrasts. To the west the **dunes** and **wetlands** of the Coto de Doñana national park comprise the largest roadless area in western Europe, whilst in the east the province of Almería has Europe's only **desert**. The province of Granada has the Iberian peninsula's **highest peak**, the 3483m Mulhacén.

• Andalucía's **economy** is based on tourism and agriculture, the main products of which – sherry, olive oil and *jamón serrano* (cured ham) – are prized throughout Spain.

• Despite its sunny image Andalucía contains an area with the **highest rainfall** on the Spanish peninsula, the natural park of **Grazalema**.

• Love it or hate it, Andalucía is devoted to the **bullfight**. This multi-billion euro business employs thousands of workers both in the rings and on the ranches where the fearsome *toro bravo*, a beast descended from an ancient species of fighting bull, is raised. In the poverty-ridden backstreets of Sevilla or Málaga the route to fame in the *corrida* is a fabulous temptation for young men (and sometimes women) and big name *toreros* are idolized and wealthy.

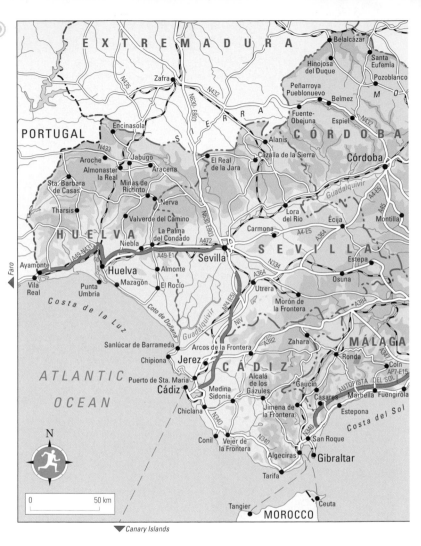

Faro

N

0   50 km

Canary Islands

origin, display the soul of Andalucía and can be an electrifying spectacle when dancers in brilliantly coloured dresses drill their heels into the floorboards in a frenzy of emotion or, in *cante jondo* (deep song), turn the art form into a blues-style lament. The Muslim influence on speech and vocabulary, a stoical fatalism in the face of adversity, and an obsession with the drama of death – publicly displayed in the spectacle of the bullfight – are also facets of the modern Andalucian character. Contrastingly, the *andaluzes* also love nothing more than a party, and the colour and sheer energy of the region's countless and legendary **fiestas** – always in traditional flamenco costume

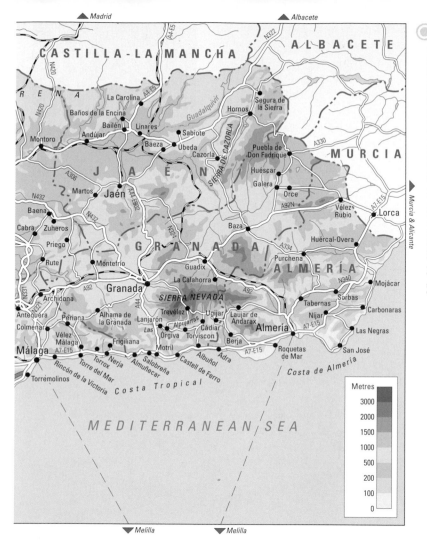

worn with pride – make them among the most exciting in the world. The **romerías**, wild and semi-religious pilgrimages to honour local saints at country shrines, are yet another excuse for a jamboree.

Despite the region's abundant natural wealth, poverty is widespread, a legacy of the repressive **latifundia** landholding system of large estates with absentee landlords. The Christian monarchs who ousted the Moorish farmers doled out the conquered land to the Church, the military orders and individual nobles. These new proprietors often had little interest in the land nor personal contact with those who worked their estates, often leaving an overseer in charge, and an atmosphere of resentment built up towards the wretched pay and miserable conditions that this system entailed. It is perhaps not surprising that many inhabitants emigrated to find work in northern Spain or abroad or that anarchism found many converts among the desperate *braceros* (farmhands) of Andalucía before the Spanish Civil War. Two percent of the landowners still possess fifty percent of the land today, and in the 1960s alone a million Andalucians left their native region to seek a better life elsewhere.

▼ Jamón

Whilst life for many in the countryside remains hard, new industries, particularly tourism, have had a major impact on the region's **economy**. Apart from the petrochemical industry around Algeciras, mining in Huelva and aircraft manufacture in Sevilla, Andalucía has little heavy industry and those not employed in agriculture are usually working in fishing or tourism. One growth industry of recent years is servicing the population of mainly northern European emigrants who have come to the south of Spain to live, retire or do business. Now numbering a third of a million, these expatriates have funded much building and development particularly along the coastal strip of the Costa del Sol, earning this zone its new nickname, the "California of Spain".

▼ Interior patio, Sevilla

Ancient Andalucía

Andalucía's rich and varied history has resulted in a great number of ancient sites, many unique in Europe. The dolmens at **Antequera** and the third-millenium BC settlement at **Los Millares** in Almería are remarkable vestiges from the prehistoric age. Roman sites are scattered across the region, but the excavated towns at **Baelo Claudia** near Tarifa and **Itálica** near Sevilla plus a fascinating necropolis at **Carmona** are worth making an effort to get to.

Two "lost" cities in superb locations are **Mulva**, in the hills of the Sierra Morena to the northeast of Sevilla, and **Ocuri**, atop a bluff to the north of Ubrique in Cádiz. One sensational discovery of recent years is the Roman villa at **Almedinilla**, complete with a spectacular cascade feature in its dining room.

Where to go

Andalucía's manageable size makes it easy to take in something of each of its elements – inland cities, extensive coastline and mountainous sierras – even on a brief visit.

The region's eight provinces take their names from the **provincial capitals**, which are both compellingly individual cultural centres and vibrant cosmopolitan beehives in their own right. The most important is **Sevilla**, Andalucía's stylishly exuberant capital city, home of *Carmen* and all the clichés of the Spanish south with beautiful *barrios* (quarters), major Christian and Moorish monuments, fine museums and extraordinary **festivals** at Easter and at the April *feria*.

Close behind comes **Granada** whose Alhambra palace has a fair claim to being the most sensual building in Europe, whilst at **Córdoba**, the exquisite Mezquita, a former mosque, is another breathtakingly beautiful building left behind by the Moors. Coastal **Málaga** boasts a fine Moorish fort and

▼ Mezquita, Córdoba

a new museum stuffed with artworks by its most famous son, **Picasso**, and further down the coast sea-locked **Cádiz** is one of the most atmospheric cities of the south and Andalucía's seafood capital. Whilst they do not always attract the attention lavished on their more immediately appealing neighbours, the cities of **Huelva**, **Jaén** and **Almería** also all have sights well worthy of a visit. Inland, small-scale towns and villages, once grand, now hardly significant, are an Andalucian speciality. **Baeza** and **Úbeda** in Jaén are remarkable treasure-houses of Renaissance architecture, while **Ronda** and the **Pueblos Blancos** (White Towns) to the west are among the most picturesque hill villages in Spain.

Not that Andalucía is predominantly about cities and monuments. Few places in the world can boast such a wealth of **natural wonders** in so compact an area. The 400km-long Río Guadalquivir, which crosses and irrigates the region, reaches the sea at the dune-fringed beaches and *marismas* (wetlands/marshes) of the **Coto Doñana National Park**, Europe's largest and most important wildlife sanctuary. To the east and towering above Granada are the peaks of the **Sierra Nevada National Park**, snowcapped for most of the year, and only thirty or so kilometres from the sweltering coastal beaches. Nestling in the folds of the same mountains are the valleys of the **Alpujarras**, a wildly picturesque region dotted with dozens of mountain villages, many of them little changed since Moorish times. Further east come the gulch-ridden badlands and lunar landscapes of Almería's **deserts**, sought out by film-makers and astronomers for the clearest skies in Europe.

Andalucía's rural zones are a paradise for hikers and naturalists and the Sierra Nevada and Las Alpujarras are excellent places for **trekking**, as are

◄ The Alhambra, Granada

Offbeat Andalucía

Among the more bizarre things to see in Andalucía are a self-styled "pope" who has built a huge new "Vatican" near Utrera in Sevilla province and a rosary museum at Aroche in Huelva that displays beads once owned by the famous (and infamous). Other curiosities include a nineteenth-century English-designed housing estate in the middle of the city of Huelva, a still-functioning sulphur spa at Carratraca in Málaga once used by Lord Byron, and a Communist village run on Utopian principles at Marinaleda in Sevilla. Andalucía's oldest inn dating from the thirteenth century, complete with highwayman's cell, is located at Alfarnate in the rugged Axarquía district of Málaga whilst Spain's first donkey sanctuary is to be found at Rute in the south of Córdoba province.

the densely wooded hills of the **Sierra de Cazorla** and the **Sierra de Morena** – including the latter's less well-known offshoot, the **Sierra de Aracena**, to the north of Huelva. The region also has a score of other *parques naturales* (natural parks), all located in areas of great natural beauty and detailed throughout the *Guide*.

On **the coast** it's often easy to despair. Extending to the west of **Málaga** is the **Costa del Sol**, Europe's most developed coastline, with its beaches hidden behind a remorseless density of concrete hotels and apartment complexes. This is Andalucía's summer playground, famous for its in-your-face brashness and the unlimited nightlife on offer at every resort. Despite the fact that many places such as **Torremolinos** have given themselves a thorough makeover with new theme parks and improved facilities, the Costa del Sol's appeal is not to everyone's taste. Thankfully though, even here

◀ Windsurfing

The olive and its oil

Spain is the world's largest producer of olive oil, an enormous quantity of which is harvested in Andalucía. Vast areas of the provinces of Sevilla, Córdoba and especially Jaén are given over to the orderly lines of trees, many a thousand years old and more. The finest extra-virgin oils have near-zero acidities, the mark of the crème de la crème of the oil world, and these qualities have gained the product a reputation as a vital aid to health – Spaniards' markedly low susceptibility to conditions such as coronary disease is attributed to their olive-oil-rich, low-cholesterol diet.

In these days of energy conservation the olive is also coming into its own as a major provider of electricity. The waste squeezed fruit from the production process used to be turned into dried-out "briquettes" by farmers to throw on to the fire in winter. This has now been taken a stage further and the many millions of tons of waste that were formerly dumped is now being transformed into fuel to supply two power generating stations in Córdoba and Jáen – and more are in the pipeline.

the other Andalucía is still to be found if you're prepared to seek it out: go merely a few kilometres inland and you'll encounter the timeless Spain of high sierras, white villages and wholehearted country fiestas. Alternatively, travel further both east and west along the coast and you'll find some of the best beaches in all Spain: the **Costa de la Luz** to the west, where Atlantic breakers wash the white-sand strands of **Tarifa**, **Conil de la Frontera** and **Isla Cristina**; in the centre at the less frenzied resorts of **Nerja** and **Almuñecar** on the **Costa Tropical**; and to the east along the **Costa de Almería** where appealing resorts like **San José, Agua Amarga and Mojacár** all hark back to pre-Costa del Sol tranquillity.

Wherever you go in Andalucía you can't fail to notice the *andaluzes'* infectious enthusiasm for life. This is always ebulliently evident in the countless celebrations, **ferias** and **fiestas** that happen almost daily at one town or village or another throughout the summer months. But at other times too, and even in the smallest towns there will always be good food, drink and a surprising range of nightlife and entertainment to be enjoyed. And there are few greater pleasures than joining the regulars at a local bar to wind down over a glass of **fino** (dry sherry from Jerez) while nibbling **tapas** – Andalucía's great titbit invention.

When to go

In terms of climate the question is mainly one of how much heat you can take. During the **summer** months of July and August temperatures of over 40°C (104°F) on the coast are normal and inland they can rise even higher in cities such as Sevilla, generally reckoned to be the hottest in Spain. The solution here is to follow the natives and get about in the relative cool of the mornings and late afternoons, finding somewhere shady to rest up as the city roasts in the midday furnace. The major resorts are busy in July and packed in August (the Spanish holiday month) when prices also are at their highest.

Better times to visit are the **spring** months of April, May and early June when lower temperatures combine with a greener landscape awash with wild flowers. The **autumn** is good, too, although by late October much of the coastal landscape looks parched and the resorts have begun to wind down; in hilly and mountainous areas, however, such as the sierras of Cazorla, Nevada and Aracena and the high valleys of Las Alpujarras, the splendours of autumn can be especially scenic. The **winter** months – particularly December and January – can often be dismal and wet as well as cold at high altitude, although the past decade, when the extended drought of the 1990s was followed by some unusually wet winters, has tended to throw the normal weather patterns into confusion. The winter, of course, is a good time to visit the museums and monuments of Sevilla, Málaga, Córdoba and Granada when they are far less crowded and – should you be

▲ Olive trees in spring

lucky with the weather – the cities themselves can look wonderful, too. The desert province of Almería sees only one day of rain a year on average and in winter has many days of perfect crystal visibility.

Average daily temperatures (C/F)

	Feb	Apr	Jun	Aug	Oct	Dec
Almería						
av. max temp	16/61	20/68	26/79	29/84	23/73	17/63
av. min temp	8/46	12/54	18/64	22/72	16/61	9/48
Cádiz						
av. max temp	16/61	21/70	27/80	30/86	23/73	16/61
av. min temp	9/48	12/54	18/64	20/68	16/61	9/48
Córdoba						
av. max temp	16/61	23/73	32/90	36/97	24/75	14/57
av. min temp	5/41	10/50	17/63	20/68	13/55	5/41
Granada						
av. max temp	14/57	20/68	30/86	34/93	22/72	12/54
av. min temp	2/36	7/45	14/57	17/63	9/48	2/36
Huelva						
av. max temp	18/64	22/72	29/84	32/90	25/77	17/63
av. min temp	7/45	11/52	16/61	18/64	14/57	7/45
Jaén						
av. max temp	14/57	20/68	30/86	34/93	22/72	12/54
av. min temp	5/41	10/50	17/63	21/70	13/55	5/41
Málaga						
av. max temp	17/63	21/70	28/82	30/86	24/75	17/63
av. min temp	8/46	11/52	17/63	20/68	15/59	9/48
Sevilla						
av. max temp	17/63	23/73	32/90	36/97	26/79	16/61
av. min temp	6/43	11/52	17/63	20/68	14/57	7/45
Tarifa						
av. max temp	17/63	20/68	24/75	27/80	23/73	17/63
av. min temp	11/52	13/55	17/63	20/68	17/63	11/52

34

things not to miss

It's not possible to see everything Andalucía has to offer in one trip – and we don't suggest you try. What follows is a selective list of the region's highlights from outstanding buildings and natural wonders to vibrant festivals and tasty food. They're arranged in five colour-coded categories which you can browse through to find the very best things to see and experience. All highlights have a page reference to take you straight into the guide, where you can find out more.

01 **Nerja beach** Page **137** • Stunning beaches are to be found all along Andalucía's coastline, and Nerja's sandy strips, with their wonderful setting, offer some of the region's best.

02 Mezquita, Córdoba

Page **431** & *Moorish Andalucía* **colour section** • Nothing can prepare you for the beauty of Córdoba's medieval mosque, one of the greatest Islamic buildings of all time.

04 Alhambra, Granada

Page **533** & *Moorish Andalucía* **colour section** • One of the most sensual palaces ever built, the magical Alhambra is the supreme legacy of Islamic Spain.

03 El Rocío
Page **382** • On the edge of the Doñana national park and surrounded by wetlands this village's church holds a venerated image of the Virgin, the focus of one of the most extraordinary pilgrimages in Spain.

05 Sherry
Page **275** & *Andalucian cuisine* **colour section** • Andalucía's great wine comes from the "sherry triangle" towns of Jerez, El Puerto de Santa María and Sanlúcar de Barrameda, each with plenty of bodegas to visit.

06 **Parque Natural Sierra de Cazorla** Page **509** • Andalucía's largest natural park is a vast area of rugged mountains and forested valleys inhabited by a feast of wildlife including ibex, wild boar, golden eagles and griffon vultures.

08 **Hiking** Page **567** • Andalucía is prime hiking territory and the walks around Spain's highest mountain, the Mulhacén, can be both challenging and rewarding.

07 **Seafood** Page **57** • An *andaluz* passion, the freshest and tastiest fish and shellfish are to be found in all coastal regions.

09 **Medina Azahara** Page **447** & *Moorish Andalucía* **colour section** • The ruins of Caliph Abd ar-Rahman III's palace-city, named after his favourite wife az-Zahra, evoke the splendour of the Cordoban caliphate.

11 **Alcázar, Sevilla** Page **304** • This fabulous Mudéjar palace decorated with dazzling *artesonado* ceilings, tiles and stuccowork is one of the glories of the city.

10 **Écija** Page **351** • Famed for its dazzling collection of colourful Baroque church towers, Éjica also has some fine mansions and an excellent museum.

12 Sierra de Grazalema

Page **203** • The pretty white village of Grazalema lends it's name to the surrounding *parque natural* where soaring limestone peaks are swathed in forests of oak and fir.

13 La Corrida

Page **71** • The bullfight has been a popular event in Andalucía since it was given its modern form in eighteenth-century Ronda.

14 Plaza Vázquez de Molina, Úbeda Page **498**

• Along with nearby Baeza, Úbeda has a cornucopia of ravishing Renaissance buildings and this square, at its heart, is one of the most beautiful in Andalucía.

15 Parque Nacional de Coto de Doñana Page **378**

• The vast wilderness of Spain's biggest wildlife reserve is home to the endangered Spanish lynx, imperial eagle and wild horses.

16 Museo Bellas Artes, Sevilla Page **316**

• An eighteenth-century former convent provides a magnificent setting for Sevilla's fine arts museum, filled with major works.

17 Mini Hollywood Page **630** • Clint Eastwood, Yul Brynner and Steve McQueen have all faced gunfighters on the streets of Mini Hollywood in the Almerian desert, where the film sets of many famous westerns are preserved.

18 Semana Santa, Málaga Page **94** & *Semana Santa* **colour section** • Holy Week is the most important date in the religious calendar and is celebrated in every town and village, while cities such as Sevilla, Granada, Córdoba and Málaga stage spectacular processions.

19 Gibraltar Page **172** • This colonial hangover with its pubs, sterling currency and Barbary apes makes a bizarre contrast with the rest of Andalucía.

20 **Jamón** Page 410 & *Andalucian cuisine* colour section • Delicious, mouthwatering ham is one of Andalucía's specialities.

21 **Flamenco** Page 658 • The soul of Andalucía, flamenco dance, music and song are widely performed and express the *alegría y dolor* (happiness and pain) of *andaluz* life.

22 **Museo Picasso, Málaga** Page 101 • Málaga's most famous son has a spectacular new museum in the heart of the old quarter displaying hundreds of his works.

23 **Cabo de Gata, Almería** Page 615 • The Cabo de Gata lighthouse stands at the southern tip of the Cabo de Gata natural park, home to a great variety of birdlife including storks, egrets and magnificent pink flamingos.

25 The Albaicín Page **544**
• Granada's atmospheric old Moorish quarter stands on the Sacromonte hill and its sinuous alleys and cobbled streets are a delight to explore.

24 Cádiz Page **236** • Steeped in history, sealocked Cádiz is one of the great cities of the Spanish south and serves up the best seafood in Andalucía..

26 Baelo Claudia Page **225** • Many civilizations have left their mark on Andalucía, including the Romans, who raised the fishing town of Baelo Claudia on the coast near Cádiz.

27 Las Alpujarras

Page **571** • This dramatically beautiful area of woodland, gushing mountain streams and ancient villages, is a rambler's delight.

28 Cathedral, Sevilla

Page **298** • The world's largest Gothic church is a treasure house full of artistic riches. Its astonishingly beautiful Moorish minaret, the Giralda, is now its bell-tower and can be climbed for a stunning view.

29 Castillo de Santa Catalina, Jaén

Page **486** • Formerly an impregnable Moorish fort, this monument now houses Andalucía's most spectacularly sited parador.

30 Encierro

Page **187** • No village fiesta is complete without an *encierro*, when a fierce *toro bravo* roams the streets looking for an encounter with anyone who thinks they're brave enough.

31 **Ronda** Page **188** • Ringed by mountains and perched astride the yawning El Tajo gorge, irresistible Ronda is one of the most dramatically sited towns in Andalucía.

32 **Tapas** Page **57 &** *Andalucian cuisine* **colour section** • Dine Andalucian style, sampling plates of delicious tapas in a variety of bars.

33 **El Chorro** Page **112** • The Garganta del Chorro (El Chorro gorge) is a spectacular natural wonder with the Camino del Rey (a walkway pinned to the gorge's limestone walls) one of it's most arresting features.

34 **Jardín de la Concepción, Málaga** Page **106** • Among many magnificent gardens in Andalucía, Málaga's Jardín Botanico de la Concepción is a spectacular natural wonder.

Basics

Basics

Getting there

The quickest and most convenient way of getting to Andalucía is to fly. From the United Kingdom and Ireland flights take around two and a half hours, and the lowest-priced air fares are cheaper than tickets for the long train or bus journey alternatives. There are also direct ferry services from Plymouth to Santander and from Portsmouth to Bilbao if you have the time for the drive or bus or train journey across Spain to reach the south. With a two-hour flight to Madrid you also have the option of taking Spain's super-high-speed train, the AVE, which covers the 400km to Sevilla in just 2hr 20min.

From North America a number of airlines fly direct to Madrid, many with onward connections to Málaga and Sevilla. Occasionally, however – and especially if you're coming from Canada – you may find it cheaper to route via London, picking up an inexpensive onward flight from there. **From Australia or New Zealand** there are no direct flights to Spain; the quickest route is via Asia to London or Madrid, picking up an onward flight to Andalucía.

Air fares always depend on the season, with the highest being around Easter and June to the end of September, when the weather is best; they drop during the "shoulder" seasons of October and May – also good times to visit the Spanish south – and you'll get the best prices during the low season, November to March (excluding Christmas and New Year when prices are hiked up and seats are at a premium). Note also that flying at weekends ordinarily adds £35/$60 to the round-trip fare; price ranges quoted below assume midweek travel.

You can often cut costs by going through a **specialist flight agent** – either a consolidator, who buys up blocks of tickets from the airlines and sells them at a discount, or a **discount agent**, who in addition to dealing with discounted flights may also offer special student and youth fares and a range of other travel-related services such as travel insurance, rail passes, car rentals, tours and the like. Some agents specialize in **charter flights**, which may be cheaper than anything available on a scheduled flight, but again departure dates are fixed and withdrawal penalties are high. For some of the popular holiday destinations, such as the Costa del Sol, you may even find it cheaper to pick up a **package deal** from one of the tour operators listed below and then find your own accommodation when you get there.

If Spain is only one stop on a longer journey, you might want to consider buying a **Round-the-World (RTW)** ticket. Some travel agents can sell you an "off the shelf" RTW ticket that will have you touching down in about half a dozen cities; others will have to assemble one for you, which can be tailored to your needs but is apt to be more expensive. Figure on £950/$1500 for an RTW ticket including Spain.

Booking flights online

Many airlines and discount travel **websites** offer you the opportunity to book your tickets online, cutting out the costs of agents and middlemen. Good deals can often be found through discount or auction sites, as well as through the airlines' own websites.

Online booking agents and general travel sites:

Ⓦ **www.cheapflights.com** Bookings from UK and Ireland only. Flight deals, travel agents, plus links to other sites.

Ⓦ **www.cheaptickets.com** Discount flight specialists.

Ⓦ **www.deckchair.com** Bob Geldof's online venture, drawing on a wide range of airlines.

Ⓦ **www.etn.nl/discount.htm** A hub of consolidator and discount agent web links, maintained by the non-profit European Travel Network.

Ⓦ **www.expedia.com** Discount air fares, all-airline search engine and daily deals.

Ⓦ **www.flyaow.com** Online air travel info and reservations site.

Ⓦ **www.gaytravel.com** Gay online travel agent, concentrating mostly on accommodation.

Ⓦ **www.geocities.com/Thavery2000/** Extensive list of airline toll-free numbers (in the US) and websites.

Ⓦ **www.hotwire.com** Bookings from the US only. Last-minute savings of up to forty percent on regular published fares. Travellers must be at least 18 and there are no refunds, transfers or changes allowed. Log-in required.

Ⓦ **www.lastminute.com** Original UK site (with links to its international versions) that offers good last-minute holiday package and flight-only deals.

Ⓦ **www.priceline.com** Name-your-own-price website that has deals at around forty percent off standard fares. You can't specify flight times (although you do specify dates and the tickets are non-refundable, non-transferable and non-changeable).

Ⓦ **www.skyauction.com** Bookings from US only. Auctions ticket and travel packages using a "second bid" scheme. The best strategy is to bid the maximum you're willing to pay, since if you win you'll pay just enough to beat the runner-up regardless of your maximum bid.

Ⓦ **www.smilinjack.com/airlines.htm** Lists an up-to-date compilation of airline website addresses.

Ⓦ **www.sydneytravel.com** Australian discount air tickets agents.

Ⓦ **www.travel.com.au** Australian website with good range of discounted air fares.

Ⓦ **www.travel.yahoo.com** Incorporates a lot of Rough Guide material in its coverage of destination countries and cities across the world, with information about places to eat and sleep etc.

Ⓦ **www.travelocity.com** Destination guides, hot web fares and best deals for car hire and accommodation. Provides access to the travel agent system SABRE, the most comprehensive central reservations system in the US.

Ⓦ **www.travelshop.com.au** Australian website offering discounted flights, packages, insurance, online bookings.

Flights from the UK and Ireland

There are numerous flights from the UK and Ireland to Andalucía throughout the year, mostly serving the Costa del Sol. Cut-price packages and **charters** generally tend to be the least expensive. The latter are usually block-booked by package holiday firms, but even in the middle of August they're rarely completely full and spare seats are often sold off at discounts.

Cut-price airlines – such as easyJet, bmibaby, Ryanair and Flybe – are just as inexpensive, offering **no-frills flights** from airports throughout the UK and Dublin. Prices start from as little as £30 one-way from London to Málaga but it's advisable to book as far ahead as possible, as these airlines have limited cheap seats on each flight and regular seats are more than twice as expensive, especially in high summer. Tickets can be bought over the phone or slightly discounted on the Internet. As well as Málaga, budget airlines now operate scheduled services to Sevilla, Almería, Granada and Jerez.

Spain's national airline, Iberia, and British Airways have the widest range of **scheduled flights**, including regular services to Sevilla and Málaga from Heathrow and Gatwick. British Airways also link many regional airports to its London flights to southern Spain. Iberia flies only direct to Málaga from London but direct flights from Manchester and Birmingham to Barcelona and Madrid link up with connecting flights to Málaga. From Dublin, Iberia flies to Madrid and Barcelona (with the same onward connections as above) while Aer Lingus does the same route plus flights to Málaga (April–Oct only). There are no direct scheduled flights from Belfast to Spain: most routeings are via London or Birmingham.

A typical high-season scheduled **fare** from London to Málaga costs from £190, though special offers can take the price as low as £100 so it's worth checking out their websites for these. Fares from Dublin to Málaga with Aer Lingus in high season are around €360, including tax, and €300 in low season; again, special offers booked online can reduce prices. For non-direct flights via London, fares on Aer Lingus, BA and Iberia are basically the same.

Package holiday deals, too, can be worth looking at, especially if you book early, late or out of season. While the cheaper packages may restrict you to some of the worst parts of the coast, remember that there's no compulsion to stick around your hotel. Get a good enough deal and it can be worth it simply for the flight, with transfer to a reasonably comfortable hotel laid on for a night or two at each end. Bargains can be found at virtually any high street travel agent.

City breaks are often available to several Spanish cities, with Sevilla and Granada the most popular destinations in Andalucía. Most operators give you the choice of staying at some very attractive hotels (not just the three- and four-star run-of-the-mill places). Flying from London, Manchester, or Belfast prices start at around £350 for three days (two nights) for both destinations; city breaks **from Dublin** start at around €400. Adding extra nights or upgrading your hotel is possible, too, usually at a fairly reasonable cost. The prices normally include return flights and bed and breakfast in a centrally located two- or three-star hotel. Again, ask your travel agent for the best deal and check the addresses below.

Fly-drive deals are well worth considering, too, as a combined air ticket and car rental arrangement can be excellent value. There are also some very good (and very attractive) deals available in **villas and apartments**, especially from companies who specialize in off-the-beaten-track farmhouses and the like. Several companies also offer a range of *casas rurales*, or more upmarket tours based around Andalucía's historic paradores (for more on accommodation see p.53). Other specialist companies offer a wide range of **activity or cultural holidays** ranging from trekking and mountain-bike holidays to wine and yoga.

Airlines

Aer Lingus UK ☏0845/084 4444, Republic of Ireland ☏0818/365 000; ⓦ www.aerlingus.ie.
Bmibaby ☏0870 264 2229, ⓦ www.bmibaby.com.
British Airways ☏0870/850 9850, Republic of Ireland ☏1890/626747; ⓦ www.ba.com
easyJet ☏0905/821 0905, ⓦ www.easyjet.com.
Flybe ☏0871 700 0123, ⓦ www.flybe.com.
GB Airways ☏0870/850 9850, ⓦ www.ba.com.
Iberia UK ☏0870/609 0500, Republic of Ireland ☏0810/462 000, ⓦ www.iberia.com.
Monarch Airlines ☏08700/40 50 40, ⓦ www.monarch-airlines.com.
Ryanair ☏0906/270 5656, Republic of Ireland ☏1530/787 787, ⓦ www.ryanair.com.

Flight and travel agents

Air Travel Advisory Bureau ☏0870/737 0021, ⓦ www.atab.co.uk. Cheap charter flights to Spain; also does scheduled flight deals.

Air 2000 ☏0870/850 3999, ⓦ www.firstchoice.co.uk. Charter arm of First Choice Holidays.
Aran Travel International Galway ☏091/562 595, ⓦ ireland.iol.ie/~arantvl/aranmain.htm. Good value flights to all parts of the world.
AVRO plc ☏020/8715 4440, ⓦ www.avro.co.uk. UK specialists in charter and scheduled flights.
Flightbookers ☏0870/814 0000, ⓦ www.ebookers.com. Low fares on an extensive selection of scheduled flights.
Joe Walsh Tours Dublin ☏01/872 2555, Cork ☏021/4277 959, ⓦ www.joewalshtours.ie. General budget fares agent.
Lee Travel Cork ☏021/4277 111, ⓦ www.leetravel.ie. Flights and holidays.
Opodo ⓦ www.opodo.co.uk. Online flight search and bookings agency backed by nine major European airlines.
Rosetta Travel Belfast ☏028/9064 4996, ⓦ www.rosettatravel.com. Flight and holiday agent.
STA Travel ☏0870/1600599, ⓦ www.statravel.co.uk. Specialists in low-cost flights and tours for students and under-26s, though other customers welcome.
Trailfinders ☏0845/058 5858, ⓦ www.trailfinders.com. One of the best-informed and most efficient agents for independent travellers.
USIT ☏01/602 1904, ⓦ www.usit.ie. Student and youth specialists for flights and trains.

Tour operators

Andalucian Adventures ☏ & ⓕ01453/834 137, ⓦ www.andalucian-adventures.co.uk. Painting, walking and yoga holidays in Córdoba province and Las Alpujarras.
Andalucian Painting Holidays ☏01382/553736, ⓦ www.langeart.co.uk. Painting holidays with Scottish artist based in the pretty Málaga hill village of Ojén.
Dance Holiday Company ☏0870/286 6000, ⓦ www.danceholidays.com. Flamenco, salsa and Argentinian tango holiday courses in Sevilla and Granada.
Earthwatch ☏01865 318838, ⓦ www.earthwatch.org/Europe. Assist on archeological digs – on the two-week ones volunteers will be trained to excavate, map, clean and categorize fossils and remains.
Exodus Travels ☏020/8675 5550, ⓦ www.exodus.co.uk. Walking and cycling in Andalucía.
Explore Worldwide ☏0870/333 4001, ⓦ www.explore.co.uk. Walking holidays in the Sierra Nevada.
Headwater Holidays ☏01606/720033, ⓦ www.headwater-holidays.co.uk. Trekking and painting holidays in the Alpujarras and Zuheros.
Hotels Abroad ☏0845/330 2500, ⓦ www.hotelsabroad.com. Operator with a wide range

of bed and breakfast and hotel accommodation throughout Andalucía – from small hotels and rustic farmhouses to luxurious country manors.

Individual Travellers ☎0870/0921002, ⊛www .indiv-travellers.com. Farmhouses, cottages and village houses all over Spain.

Keytel International ☎020/7616 0300, ⊛www .keytel.co.uk. Official UK agents for the paradores in Spain.

Kirker Travel ☎0870/112 3333, ⊛www .kirkertravel.com. Short breaks and holiday packages in Andalucían towns and cities.

Limosa Holidays ☎01263 578143, ⊛www .limosaholidays.co.uk. Birdwatching tours to the Strait of Gibraltar. See the great spring and autumn migrations accompanied by knowledgeable guides.

Martin Randall Travel ☎020/8742 3355 ⊛www.martinrandall.com. Small group cultural tours to Sevilla and elsewhere, led by experts on art, archeology or music.

Mountain Bike España ☎01494/870486, ⊛www.mountbik-espana.co.uk. Small company organizing guided mountain-bike tours around the mountains and natural parks close to Málaga.

Peng Travel ☎845/3458345, ⊛www.pengtravel .co.uk. Naturist holidays near Garrucha (Almería) and Estepona (Málaga).

Ramblers Holidays ☎01707/331133, ⊛www .ramblersholidays.co.uk. Walking and hiking holidays throughout Spain, including Andalucía.

Rustic Blue ☎958 76 33 81, ⊛www.rusticblue .com. Alpujarras-based company specializing in rural and activity holidays (rambling and horse trekking) and renting traditional village houses.

Sherpa Expeditions ☎020/8577 2717, ⊛www .sherpa-walking-holidays.co.uk. Trekking in the Sierra Nevada and the Alpujarras.

Spain at Heart ☎01373/814222, ⊛www .spainatheart.co.uk. Holidays, self-catering villas and apartments in rural and city locations throughout Andalucía.

Travellers Way ☎01527/559000, ⊛www .travellersway.co.uk. Tailor-made holidays and city breaks in Andalucía.

Waymark Holidays ☎01753/516477, ⊛www .waymarkholidays.co.uk. Walking holidays in Andalucía.

Winetrails ☎01306/712111, ⊛www.winetrails .co.uk. Wine-based tours of Andalucía.

By rail

Rail passengers have the choice between crossing over to the continent by boat from the English south coast or taking the Eurostar from Waterloo International in London. Both options involve changing trains in Paris (and stations, from Nord to Austerlitz via Metro line #5). Booking a **train-boat combination** to Paris and on to Spain means going to Charing Cross Rail Station in London (no phone calls) who can make you a booking. Once in Paris you need to purchase your own SNCF ticket on to Spain or you can do this in advance through Rail Europe. The hassle-free way to do all this is by booking through European train specialists **Rail Canterbury** (see below) who will book you a train-boat ticket through to Andalucía. From London Victoria Station to Málaga, with a place in a six-berth couchette compartment, it takes a gruelling 37hrs, and costs around £350 return.

The faster and currently cheaper alternative is to take the **Eurostar** from London to Paris, and a sleeper from there to Madrid, changing stations for the last leg down to Andalucía. A typical journey to Málaga from London takes around 27 hours using the Eurostar to Paris. The current return fare (including a reclining aircraft seat for the overnight from Paris to Madrid) costs £257 for non-weekend travel (add £28 for a place in a four-berth couchette). It's also worth noting that the further ahead you book the cheaper it is. Tickets are bookable directly with Rail Europe (see below) or Spanish Rail Service (see p.48). Special offers can reduce fares from London–Málaga to as low as £215 return (including a place in four-berth couchette compartment) and the latter company should be able to advise on these. If you plan to travel extensively in Europe by train, you might consider buying a rail pass. Details of these are given on p.47.

Travelling by car, the fastest option is the Eurotunnel service via the Channel Tunnel. The alternative is one of the time-honoured ferry crossings. **Eurotunnel** operates trains 24 hours a day, running cars, motorcycles, buses and their passengers between Folkestone and Coquelles, near Calais up to four times an hour (one an hour midnight–6am) and taking around 35min. It's possible to turn up and buy your ticket at the toll booths (after exiting the M20 at junction 11a), though at busy times booking is advisable, and note that increased security means that you must arrive at least 60min before departure. **Rates** (see website for details) depend on the time of day, time of year and length of stay (the cheapest ticket is for a day-trip, followed by a five-day return) and whatever offers are current for your intended dates. It's cheaper to travel between 10pm and 6am, while the highest fares are reserved for weekend departures and returns in July and August.

The alternative is the **ferry** or **hovercraft** links from Dover or Folkestone to Calais or Boulogne. With more time you might want to consider one of the ferries to Caen, Le Havre, Cherbourg or St Malo (from Portsmouth) or even Roscoff (from Plymouth). Ferry **prices** vary according to the time of day and year, and according to the size of the vehicle. One of the operators on the Dover–Boulogne route currently offering highly competitive prices for a standard car and up to five passengers is SpeedFerries. Based on the budget airlines principle of the later you leave it to book the higher the price, fares are ranged between £54 and £118 open return all year. Note that, like the budget airlines, there are penalties if you want to change your travel plans at the last minute. Foot passengers should be able to cross for about £18 one-way or £36 open return but without a booking the price can increase if the boat is nearing capacity.

Rail and ferry companies

Eurostar ☎0870/160 6600, ⓦwww.eurostar.com.
Eurotunnel ☎0870/535 3535, ⓦwww
.eurotunnel.com.
Hoverspeed ☎0870/240 8070, ⓦwww
.hoverspeed.co.uk.
Northern Ireland Railways ☎028/9066 6630,
ⓦwww.nirailways.co.uk.
Rail Canterbury ☎01227/45 00 88, ⓦwww
.rail-canterbury.co.uk.
Rail Europe ☎0870/5848 848 (passengers),
☎0870/5300003 (cars), ⓦwww.raileurope.co.uk.
RENFE (Spanish railways) ⓦwww.renfe.es.
Sea France ☎0870/571 1711, ⓦwww.seafrance
.com.
SpeedFerries ☎0870/220 0570, ⓦwww
.speedferries.com.

By ferry

Apart from sailings to France (see above), there are two direct **ferry** sailings to Bilbao

and Santander on Spain's north coast from Britain. See below for company addresses, or contact your local travel agent for the ticket and sailing details; alternatively check out the ferries' website at ⓦwww.seaview .co.uk. From Bilbao and Santander the most direct route to the south is via Burgos to Madrid (240km), then the A4-E5 *autovía* which enters Andalucía at the Despeñaperros pass (another 335km) in Jaén from where, for example, Málaga is a further 300km.

The ferry from **Plymouth to Santander** is operated by Brittany Ferries, takes 24 hours and runs on Mondays and Wednesdays during the summer (April to mid-Sept) and Wednesdays and Sundays the rest of the year. A return ticket for a small car and two adults can cost anything from £485 in low season to £790 in high season. Foot passengers pay around £55–165 return (depending on season) and everyone has to book some form of accommodation; a Pullman seat is cheapest at £5 and two-berth cabins are available for £65–85. Tickets are best booked in advance through any major travel agent or via company websites.

P&O operates a thrice-weekly ferry service from **Portsmouth to Bilbao**. The journey takes approximately 35hrs (check website for sailing days). Return fares for a car and two passengers work out at between £540 and £935 (according to season), with foot passengers paying £211–325; there are frequent special offers (phone or visit website). Cabins are included in these prices. Note that this sailing is significantly cheaper for motorcyclists than for cars, especially if you can find one of the frequent discounts from motorcycling publications.

Note also that both routes are often closed for a couple of weeks in January for maintenance.

Ferry companies

Brittany Ferries ☎0870/901 2400 Republic of Ireland ☎021/277 705, ⓦwww.brittanyferries.com.
P&O European Ferries ☎08705/202020,
ⓦwww.poferries.com.

By bus

Travelling by **bus** from the UK to Andalucía involves a long, tiring journey and can work out more expensive than the cheapest flights. The main bus routes go via the Channel Tunnel and are operated by **Eurolines** linking up with Iberbus/Linebus and Julia in Spain. There are two **routeings** to Andalucía: one goes to Sevilla via Paris, Salamanca and Mérida; the other (the Costa del Sol route) goes via Paris and Madrid. The Costa del Sol bus currently leaves London (with pickups in Canterbury and Dover) on Mon, Wed & Fri at 6.30am arriving in Málaga 36hrs later. There are stops at Jaén, Granada, and the major Costa del Sol resorts en route to the terminus destination of Algeciras. Booking at least four days in advance, **fares** are around £119 one way and £192 return to reach any destination in Andalucía. In both Britain and Spain tickets are bookable through most major travel agents and on the Internet (see below); Eurolines also sells tickets and through-transport to London at all British National Express bus terminals.

Bus operators

Eurolines ☎ 0870/514 3219, ⓦ www.eurolines .co.uk. Tickets can also be purchased from any Eurolines or National Express agent ☎ 0870/580 8080, ⓦ www.nationalexpress.com.

Flights from the US and Canada

There's a fair variety of **scheduled** and **charter flights** from most parts of North America to Madrid, often with connections on to Sevilla, Granada or Málaga. Occasionally, however – and especially if coming from Canada – you'll find it cheaper to route via London, picking up an inexpensive onward flight from there (see "Flights from the UK and Ireland" for details). If Spain is part of a longer European trip, you'll also want to check out details of the Eurail Pass, which must be purchased in advance of your arrival. Flight fares quoted in the following sections assume midweek travel and include tax (around $50 or Can$40–55).

From the US, **Iberia** flies direct to Madrid from New York, Miami and Chicago, and has the advantage that it offers connecting flights to almost anywhere in Spain, often very good value if booked with your transatlantic flight. **Several US airlines** fly direct from the East Coast to Madrid. Finally, you might check out **Air Europa**'s New York–Madrid flights,

which are less frequent, but very competitively priced.

Good deals can be found on **routeings via other major European cities** with the airlines of those countries: KLM via Amsterdam, Lufthansa via Frankfurt, TAP via Lisbon, or British Airways via London, for example. Remember though, that you may be better off continuing with a locally purchased flight (see p.29), or overland (especially if you plan to buy a rail pass). The widest range of deals is on the New York–London route, served by dozens of airlines. Competition is intense, so look for bargains, especially out of season. At the time of writing the major carriers were offering the following round-trip **fares** to Madrid: from New York $615/925 (low/high season); from Chicago $720/1100; from LA $855/1520; and from Miami $695/990. With special promotional offers, round-trip fares can drop as low as $300 from New York and $500 from LA. Flying time is around seven hours from New York to Madrid.

There are no nonstop flights **from Canada** to Spain. However, you should be able to find a fairly convenient routeing using a combination of airlines – most likely via another European capital – from any of the major cities. West of the Rockies you're probably best off either flying Vancouver–London and continuing on to Madrid or an Andalucian destination from there, or alternatively getting a flight from one of the US cities mentioned above.

At the time of writing APEX round-trip **fares** to Madrid start at around Can$1695 in the high season from Toronto or Montreal, and Can$1590/2250 from Vancouver.

Package tours may not sound like your kind of travel, but don't dismiss the idea out of hand. Many agents can put together very flexible deals, sometimes amounting to no more than a flight plus car or rail pass and accommodation; if you're planning to travel in moderate or luxury style, and especially if your trip is geared around special interests, such packages can work out cheaper than the same arrangements made on arrival. Companies generally expect you to book through a local travel agent, and since it costs the same you might as well. A number of American outfits offer tours that focus on Andalucía. For the most part they boil down to two basic formulas: escorted historic city tours, making a circuit of Granada, Córdoba and Sevilla; and accommodation-only packages on the Costa del Sol. Some operators allow you to build your own itinerary with a few nights in each of various cities. Any way you slice it, though, going with a tour company will land you in fairly expensive hotels, in the neighbourhood of $100 a night per person – even more if you're staying in paradores (see p.54). In addition, a few worldwide American companies organize biking and trekking trips in Andalucía, which cost at least as much as city tours due to all the logistics involved.

Airlines

Air France US ☎1-800/237-2747, ⊛www .airfrance.com; Canada ☎1-800/667-2747, ⊛www.airfrance.ca.
American Airlines ☎1-800/433-7300, ⊛www .aa.com.
British Airways ☎1-800/247-9297, ⊛www .ba.com.
Continental Airlines ☎1-800/231-523-3273, ⊛www.continental.com.
Delta Airlines ☎1-800/221-1212, ⊛www.delta .com.
Iberia ☎1-800/772-4642, ⊛www.iberia.com.
Lufthansa US ☎1-800/645-3880; Canada, ☎1-800/563-5954, ⊛www.lufthansa.com.
Northwest/KLM ☎1-800/447-4747, ⊛www .nwa.com.
TAP Air Portugal ☎1-800/221-7370, ⊛www .tap-airportugal.pt.

Flight agents, consolidators and travel clubs

Airtech ☎212/219-7000, ⊛www.airtech.com. Standby seat broker; also deals in consolidator fares and courier flights.
Council Travel ☎1-800/781-4040, ⊛www .counciltravel.com.
Nationwide US organization specializing in student/ budget travel. Flights from US only.
STA Travel ☎1-800/781-4040, ⊛www.sta-travel .com. Worldwide specialist in independent and student travel.
Travel Cuts Canada ☎1-888/359-2887, US ☎1-800/592-2887, ⊛www.travelcuts.com. Canadian student-travel organization.
Travelers Advantage ☎1-877/947-8747, ⊛www.travelersadvantage.com. Discount travel club requiring annual membership; three-month trial membership available for nominal fee.
Travelocity ⊛www.travelocity.com. Online consolidator.

Package and tour operators

Abercrombie & Kent ☎1-800/554-7016, ⊛www.abercrombiekent.com. Several packages, including Granada and Sevilla.
Backroads ☎1-800/GO-ACTIVE, ⊛www .backroads.com. Biking and/or hiking tours of Andalucía. Also offer combined Spain/Portugal cycling tours.
Contiki Holidays ☎1-888-CONTIKI, ⊛www .contiki.com. Spain and Portugal coach tours for 18- to 35-year-olds, with stops in Sevilla and Granada.
EC Tours ☎1-800/388-0877, ⊛www.ectours .com. Offers a variety of tours including pilgrimages, museums and wine and gourmet tours.
Elderhostel ☎1-877/426-8056, ⊛www .elderhostel.org. Specialists in educational and activity programmes, cruises and homestays for senior travellers.
Escapade Tours ☎1-800/356-2405, ⊛www .isram.com. City breaks and multi-city packages.
Globus and Cosmos ☎1-800/221-0090, ⊛www.globusandcosmos.com. Coach sightseeing tours, with stops in Andalucía as part of larger trips in Spain or tours combining Spain and Portugal and Morocco.
M.I. Travel ☎1-888/427-7246, ⊛www .mitravel-melia.com. Historic tours and packages.
Petrabax ☎1-800/634-1188, ⊛www.petrabax .com. Coach tours and arrangements for independent travellers.
Sun Holidays ☎1-800/387-0571 or 416/789-1010, ⊛www.sunholidays.ca. City packages and parador tours.

Flights from Australia and New Zealand

There are no direct flights to Spain from Australia or New Zealand, but changing planes once or twice can get you there within 24 hours via Asia or 30 hours via the US – not counting time spent on stopovers. Flights via Asia are generally the cheaper option.

Most regular return economy **fares** to Spain cost between Aus$2100 in the low season and Aus$3300 in the high season from eastern Australian gateways. From Perth and Darwin expect to pay Aus$100–200 less than this if you're travelling via Asia, or Aus$400 more if routeing via the US. Fares from Auckland cost between NZ$2500 in the low season and NZ$3100 in the high season.

Alternatively, you can find a **rock-bottom return fare** to Amsterdam, London or another European hub city with the likes of Garuda or Sri Lanka Airlines for around Aus$1600/NZ$1850 low season, and then either pick up a cheap charter flight (see p.28) or travel overland by bus (see p.31) or rail (see p.30). However, with the high living and transport costs in northwestern Europe, this rarely works out any cheaper.

The cheapest **scheduled** flights **from Australia** are via Asia and there are several airlines that fly into Barcelona and Madrid. The lowest fares are offered by Japan Airlines (to Madrid, with an overnight stop in either Tokyo or Osaka included in the fare) – from Aus$1800 in the low season to Aus$2900 in the high season. Mid-range fares are with Thai Airways and Air France via their respective gateway cities of Bangkok and Paris for Aus$2000–3000. A little more expensive, at Aus$2200–3200, but faster – with only a short refuelling stop or quick change of planes in Singapore – are Singapore Airlines' flights to Madrid.

Travelling from **New Zealand** to Spain via Asia, Thai Airways and Alitalia (both via Sydney) have through fares from Auckland to both Madrid and Barcelona and Japan Airlines (JAL) has flights to Madrid – all with either a transfer or overnight stop in their carrier's home city – for NZ$2500–3100 (low/high season). Qantas (via Sydney and Bangkok) and Singapore Airlines (via Singapore) also fly to Madrid, but are more expensive at NZ$2300–3000.

Organized tours may seem a little expensive but are well worth it, especially if your time is limited, if you're unfamiliar with the the country's customs and language, have special interests or you just don't like travelling alone. Adventure tours are also worth considering, especially if you want to cover a lot of ground or get to places that could be difficult to reach independently.

Airlines

Air France Australia ☎02/9244 2100, New Zealand ☎09/308 3352; ⓦwww.airfrance.fr.
Garuda Australia ☎02/9334 9970, New Zealand ☎09/366 1862, ⓦwww.garuda-indonesia.com.
Japan Airlines (JAL) Australia ☎02/9272 1111, New Zealand ☎09/379 9906; ⓦwww.japanair.com.
Qantas Australia ☎13/13 13, ⓦwww.qantas.com.au; New Zealand ☎0800/808 767, ⓦwww.qantas.co.nz.

Singapore Airlines Australia ☎13/10 11, New Zealand ☎0800/808 909; ⓦwww.singaporeair.com.
Thai Airways Australia ☎1300/651 960, New Zealand ☎09/377 3886; ⓦwww.thaiair.com.

Travel agents

Flight Centre Australia ☎02/9235 3522, ⓦwww.flightcentre.com.au; New Zealand ☎0800/243 544, ⓦwww.flightcentre.com.au.
Holiday Shoppe New Zealand ☎0800/808 480, ⓦwww.holidayshoppe.co.nz.
Northern Gateway Australia ☎1800/174 800, ⓦwww.northerngateway.com.au.
STA Travel Australia ☎1300/733 035, ⓦwww.statravel.com.au; New Zealand ☎0508/782 872, ⓦwww.statravel.co.nz.
Thomas Cook Australia ☎13 1771, New Zealand ☎09/379 3920; ⓦwww.thomascook.com.au.
Trailfinders Australia ☎02/9247 7666, ⓦwww.travel.com.au.

Packages and tours

Adventure World Australia ☎02/8913 0755, ⓦwww.adventureworld.com.au; New Zealand ☎09/524 5118, ⓦwww.adventureworld.co.nz. Agents for a vast array of international adventure travel companies that offer small-group tours, including Explore's 15-day trek through the High Alpujarras, staying in *hostales* and *pensiones* along the way.
Australian Pacific Touring Australia ☎1800/675 222, New Zealand ☎09/279 6077; ⓦwww.aptours.com. Escorted tours and independent travel.
Australians Studying Abroad Australia ☎1800/645 755, ⓦwww.asatravinfo.com.au. Guided 22-day study tours, focusing on Spain's art and culture; some courses can be credited towards Australian tertiary awards.
CIT Australia ☎02/9267 1255, ⓦwww.cittravel.com.au. City tours and accommodation packages, plus bus and rail passes and car rental.
Contiki Holidays Australia ☎02/9511 2200, New Zealand ☎09/309 8824; ⓦwww.contiki.com. Frenetic tours for 18–35-year-old party animals.
Explore Holidays Australia ☎02/9423 8080, ⓦwww.exploreholidays.com.au. Accommodation and package tours.
Ibertours Australia ☎03/9670 8388 or 1-800/500 016, ⓦwww.ibertours.com.au. Escorted and independent tours to rural and urban areas in Andalucía.
Walkabout Gourmet Adventures Australia ☎03/5159 6556, ⓦwww.walkaboutgourmet.com. Classy food-and-wine walking tours in Spain.

Red tape and visas

Citizens of all EU countries (plus Norway, Iceland, Liechtenstein and Switzerland) need only a valid national identity card to enter Spain for up to ninety days. Since Britain has no identity card system, however, British citizens have to take a passport. US, Canadian, Australian and New Zealand citizens do not need a visa for stays of up to ninety days but this must be for tourism or study purposes only and not for work. Visa requirements do change so it's always advisable to check the current situation before leaving home.

Recent changes to the EU immigration rules mean that EU nationals (and citizens of Norway, Iceland, Liechtenstein and Switzerland) no longer need apply for a residence permit to **stay longer**, as a valid passport or identity document now acts as a permit. This entitles EU citizens to reside as employees, self-employed or students; retired people or those of independent means will still have to apply for a residence permit. The British embassy in Spain (ⓦwww.ukinspain.com) has useful general information for EU citizens.

US citizens can apply for one ninety-day extension, showing proof of funds, but this must be done from outside Spain. Other nationalities will need to get a special visa from a Spanish consulate before departure (see below for addresses).

Foreign embassies and consulates in Andalucía

Australia c/Federico Rubio 14, Sevilla ☎95 422 09 71.
Canada Edificio Horizonte, Plaza Malagueta 3, Málaga ☎95 222 33 46.
Ireland Galerías Santa Mónica, Avda. Los Boliches 15, Fuengirola ☎95 247 51 08.
New Zealand No representation in Andalucía; affairs handled by Australia.
UK Edificio Eurocom, Block Sur, c/Mauricio Moro Pareto 2, Málaga ☎95 235 23 00; The Convent, Main Street, Gibraltar ☎350/45440.

USA Avda. Juan Gómez 8, Edificio Lucía 1º-C, Fuengirola ☎95 247 48 91; Paseo de las Delicias 7, Sevilla ☎95 423 18 85.

Spanish embassies and consulates abroad

Australia ⓦwww.embaspain.com; 15 Arkana St, Yarralumla, ACT 2600 ☎02/6273 355; 24th Floor, St Martin's Tower, 31 Market St, Sydney NSW 2000 ☎02/9261-2433; 4th Floor, 540 Elizabeth St, Melbourne, VIC 3000 ☎03/9347 1966.
Canada ⓦwww.embaspain.ca; 74 Stanley Ave, Ottawa, ON K1M 1P4 ☎613/747-2252; 1 Westmount Sq #1456, Ave Wood, Montréal, PQ H3Z 2P9 ☎514/935-5235; Simcoe Place, 200 Front St #2401, Toronto, ON M5V 3K2 ☎416/977-1661.
Ireland 17a Merlyn Park, Ballsbridge, Dublin 4 ☎01/269 1640.
New Zealand contact the consulate in Sydney.
UK 39 Chesham Place, SW1X 8SB ☎020/7235 5555; Suite 1a, Brook House, 70 Spring Gardens, Manchester M2 2BQ ☎0161/236 1213.
USA 545 Boylston St #803, Boston, MA 02116 ☎617/536-2506; 180 N Michigan Ave #1500, Chicago, IL 60601 ☎312/782-4588; 1800 Bering Drive #660, Houston, TX 77057 ☎713/783-6200; 5055 Wilshire Blvd #960, Los Angeles, CA 90036 ☎213/938-0158; 2655 Le Jeune Rd #203, Coral Gables, FL 33134 ☎305/446-5511; 2102 World Trade Center, 2 Canal St, New Orleans, LA 70130 ☎504/525-4951; 150 E 58th St, New York, NY 10155 ☎212/355-4080; 1405 Sutter St, San Francisco, CA 94109 ☎415/922-2995; 2375 Pennsylvania Ave NW, Washington DC 20037 ☎202/452-0100.

Health

As an EU country, Spain has free reciprocal health agreements with other member states but to claim this you will need to carry an EHIC card (see below). Even so, and especially for non-European travellers, some form of travel insurance is still all but essential; with it, you should be able to claim back the cost of any drugs prescribed by pharmacies. European policies generally also cover your baggage/tickets/money in case of theft, as long as you get a report from the local police.

In January 2006 the E111 form entitling you to free or reduced-cost emergency health treatment throughout the EU was replaced by the EHIC card (**European Health Insurance Card**). This can be obtained by collecting a form and information booklet from any UK post office. You can also **apply online** at ⊛www.dh.gov.uk /travellers or by phone (☎0845 606 2030). In Eire information about and how to obtain the card is available on ⊛www.ehic.ie. The card allows the bearer to obtain essential medical treatment in all 25 EU states plus a number of affiliated European countries but is invalid for "medical tourism" where getting medical treatment is the main purpose of your trip.

No **inoculations** are required for Spain, though if you plan on visiting or journeying on to North Africa, typhoid and polio boosters are highly recommended. The worst that's likely to happen to you is that you might fall victim to an upset stomach. To be safe, wash fruit and avoid tapas dishes that look several days old.

For minor complaints go to a **farmacia** – they're listed in the phone book in major towns and cities (although they are easy to spot in any town centre by their – generally illuminated – green cross) and virtually every village has one. Pharmacists are highly trained, will give advice (often in English), and can dispense many drugs which would be available only on prescription in most other countries. They keep usual shop hours (9am–1.30pm & 5.30–8pm), but some open late and at weekends, and a rota system keeps at least one open 24 hours. The rota is displayed in the window of every pharmacy, or in local newspapers under "Farmacias de guardia".

In more serious cases you can get the address of an English-speaking doctor from the nearest relevant consulate, or, with luck, from a *farmacia*, the local police or Turismo. If you have special medical or dietary requirements, it is advisable to carry a letter from your doctor, translated into Spanish, indicating the nature of your condition and necessary treatments. In emergencies dial ☎091 for the Servicios de Urgencia (Emergency Services), or ☎061 for an ambulance, or look up the Cruz Roja Española (Red Cross), which runs a national ambulance service. Treatment at hospitals for EU citizens in possession of the EHIC card is free; otherwise you'll be charged at private hospital rates, which can be very expensive. Accordingly, it's essential to have comprehensive travel insurance.

Insurance

Even though EU health care privileges apply in Spain, you'd do well to take out an insurance policy before travelling to cover against theft, loss and illness or injury. Before paying for a new policy, however, it's worth checking whether you are already covered: some all-risks home insurance policies may cover your possessions when overseas, and many private medical schemes include cover when abroad.

In **Canada**, provincial health plans usually provide partial cover for medical mishaps overseas, while holders of official student/teacher/youth cards in Canada and the US are entitled to meagre accident coverage and hospital inpatient benefits. Students will often find that their student health coverage extends during the vacations and for one term beyond the date of last enrolment.

After exhausting the possibilities above, you might want to contact a specialist travel insurance company, or consider the travel insurance deal we offer (see box). A typical **travel insurance policy** usually provides cover for the loss of baggage, tickets and – up to a certain limit – cash or cheques, as well as cancellation or curtailment of your journey. Most of them exclude so-called dangerous sports unless an extra premium is paid: in Andalucía this can mean horse riding, windsurfing, skiing, trekking, ballooning, hangliding and mountaineering. Many policies can be chopped and changed to exclude coverage you don't need – for example, sickness and accident benefits can often be excluded or included at will. If you do take medical coverage, ascertain whether benefits will be paid as treatment proceeds or only after returning home, and whether there is a 24-hour medical emergency number. When securing baggage cover, make sure that the per-article limit – typically under £500 equivalent – will cover your most valuable possession. If you need to make a claim, you should keep receipts for medicines and medical treatment, and in the event you have anything stolen, you must obtain an official statement from the police.

Rough Guides travel insurance

Rough Guides has teamed up with Columbus Direct to offer you **travel insurance** that can be tailored to suit your needs.

Readers can choose from many different travel insurance products, including a low-cost **backpacker** option for long stays; a **short break** option for city getaways; a typical **holiday package** option; and many others. There are also annual **multi-trip** policies for those who travel regularly, with variable levels of cover available. Different sports and activities (trekking, skiing, etc) can be covered if required on most policies.

Rough Guides travel insurance is available to the residents of 36 different countries with different language options to choose from via our website – ⓦwww.roughguidesinsurance.com – where you can also purchase the insurance.

Alternatively, UK residents can call ☏0800/083 9507; US citizens should call ☏1-800 749-4922; Australians should call ☏1 300 669 999. All other nationalities should call ☏+44 870 890 2843.

Information, maps and websites

The Spanish National Tourist Office (SNTO; ⓦwww.tourspain.es) produces and gives away an impressive variety of maps, pamphlets and special interest leaflets. The Junta de Andalucía (the regional government; ⓦwww.andalucia.org) also promotes tourism throughout Andalucía.

SNTO offices abroad

If you can, visit one of the SNTO's offices before you leave and stock up, especially on city plans, as well as province-by-province lists of hotels, *hostales* and campsites.

Australia The Spanish National Tourist Office (SNTO), 1st Floor, 178 Collins St, Melbourne, VIC ☏03/9650 7377 or 1/800 817 855.

Canada ⓦwww.tourspain.toronto.on.ca; 2 Bloor St West, 34th Floor, Toronto, Ontario M4W 3E2 ☏416/961-3131.

New Zealand Contact the office in Australia.

UK ⓦwww.tourspain.co.uk; 22–23 Manchester Square, London W1U 3PX ☏020/7486 8077.

USA ⓦwww.okspain.org; 666 Fifth Ave, New York, NY 10103 ☏212/265-8822; San Vincente Plaza Bldg, 8383 Wilshire Boulevard, Suite 956, Beverly Hills, CA 90211 ☏323/658-7188; 845 North Michigan Ave, Suite 915-E, Chicago, IL 60611 ☏312/642-1992; 1221 Brickell Ave, Suite 1850, Miami, FL 33131 ☏305/358-1992.

Information offices

Throughout Andalucía you'll find Junta de Andalucía (regional government) tourist offices – called **Turismos** – in virtually every major town (addresses are detailed in the *Guide*) and from these you can usually get more specific local information and useful maps (now sold by most at a nominal charge). They vary enormously in quality of service, but while generally extremely useful for local information, don't expect them to know anything about what goes on outside their patch. They are often supplemented, particularly in popular tourist destinations, by separately administered provincial or municipal tourist offices.

Turismo and tourist office hours are usually Mon–Friday 9am–1pm and 3.30–6pm, Saturday 9am–1pm – but there are wide variations across the region and you can't always rely on the official hours, especially in more out-of-the-way places, where offices are known to close without notice or (especially around holiday periods) not open at all. On the other hand, the major coastal resorts often have enthusiastic offices staying open all day, often until nine or ten at night in season.

Maps

In addition to the maps in this book and the various free leaflets available, you'll probably want a reasonable **road map**. This can be bought in Spain, where you'll find a good selection in most bookshops (*librerías*) and at street kiosks or petrol stations. Among the best are those published by Editorial Almax, which also produces reliable indexed street plans of Sevilla and Granada. The best single map for Andalucía is the annually updated *Michelin Andalucía* (1:400,000), which includes a plan to get you in and out of Sevilla, the region's only serious traffic headache. It's widely available from bookshops in Spain and abroad. This has recently been complemented by the equally excellent larger scale *Michelin Costa del Sol* (1:200,000) covering not only the coast between Algeciras and Almería but a considerable way inland too, taking in significant chunks of the provinces of Cádiz, Málaga, Granada and Almería. Alternatives are the rip-proof/waterproof *Rough Guide Andalucía Map* (1:650,000/1:150,000) and the 1:200,000 German *Andalusien* (Marco Polo; map detail in Spanish) which, to gain a larger scale, bizarrely lops off the provinces of Huelva and Almería plus the Cazorla Natural Park. Other alternatives are 1:300,000 RV (Reise und Verkehrsverlag) *Andalucía*, distributed in the UK by Roger Lascelles and by Plaza y Janés in Spain, as well as the less detailed Firestone and Rand McNally.

The most comprehensive **city street plans** are the somewhat unwieldy *Planos Callejeros* by Editorial Everest, which cover all the major towns and cities in Andalucía and have street indexes; they are obtainable from most *librerías*, but outside Sevilla the free maps handed out by most tourist offices serve just as well. For Sevilla, the best street plan is the pocketable *La Guía Verde*, generally available from city bookshops; the fold-out *Falkplan Sevilla* is also good. For other major cities the *callejeros* (street directories) produced by Editorial Argival are comprehensive and pocket-sized.

Serious **hikers** can get more detailed maps from the offices and stores listed in the city "Listings" sections of the *Guide*. All the provincial capitals have a **CNIG** (National Geographical Information Centre), which stocks the full range of **topographical maps** issued by two government agencies: the IGN (Instituto Geográfico Nacional) and the SGE (Servicio Geográfico del Ejército). The maps are available at scales of 1:200,000, 1:100,000, 1:50,000, and even occasionally 1:25,000. The various SGE series are considered to be more up to date and accurate by those in the know, although no Spanish maps are up to the standards that British or North American hikers are used to. The relevant CNIG offices, or their commercial equivalents where IGN and SGE maps can be bought, are listed in the Sevilla, Córdoba, Granada, Málaga and Cádiz "Listings" sections at the end of each city account; the local Turismo will provide addresses for the others should you need them. If you are likely to be passing through Madrid, La Tienda Verde, c/Maudes 38 ☎91 534 32 57, ⊛www.tiendaverde.org, has all the maps mentioned above and many more, and is willing to do business by post.

A Catalunya-based company, Editorial Alpina (⊛www.editorialalpina.com), produces 1:40,000 or 1:25,000 **map/booklet** sets for many of the mountain and foothill areas of interest, including a three-part series covering the Sierra de Cazorla in Jaén and excellent new maps for the Sierra Nevada National Park (Granada province) and the Cabo de Gata Natural Park (Almería province). The maps can be purchased online and the useful background books that accompany them (with details of flora and fauna and trekking routes) are published in both Spanish and English. Penthalon is another publisher with a range of guides in Spanish covering many of Andalucía's major walking areas. These are on sale in many bookshops. Other guidebooks dealing with hikes in specific areas are noted in the text where appropriate and in the "Books" section (p.698).

Internet map sources include Netmaps, a Barcelona-based firm which has a website (⊛www.netmaps.es, with a page in English) where you can buy a wide selection of different types of maps. Another (Spanish only) web-based source is at ⊛www.verdinet .com/mapas; here you can purchase detailed maps (including SGE maps) with postal costs included, ⊛www.multimap .com is useful for journey planning and has street plans of most major towns and cities in Andalucía.

Map outlets

UK and Ireland

Blackwell's Map and Travel Shop 53 Broad St, Oxford OX1 3BQ ☎08165/792792, ⊛www .bookshop.blackwell.co.uk.

Easons Bookshop 40 O'Connell St, Dublin 1 ☎01/873 3811, ⊛www.eason.ie.

Heffers Map and Travel 20 Trinity St, Cambridge, CB2 1TJ ☎01223/568 568, ⊛www.heffers.co.uk.

Hodges Figgis Bookshop 56–58 Dawson St, Dublin 2 ☎01/677 4754, ⊛www.hodgesfiggis .com.

John Smith and Sons 57–61 St Vincent St, Glasgow G52 4PJ ☎0141/221 7472, ⊛www .johnsmith.co.uk.

The Map Shop 30a Belvoir St, Leicester LE1 6QH ☎0116/2471400, ⊛www.mapshopleicester.co.uk.

National Map Centre 22–24 Caxton St, London SW1 ☎020/7222 2466, ⊛www.mapsnmc.co.uk.

Newcastle Map Centre 55 Grey St, Newcastle upon Tyne NE1 6EF ☎0191/261 5622, ⊛www .newtraveller.com.

Ordnance Survey Ireland Phoenix Park, Dublin 8 ☎01/802 5300, ⊛www.osi.ie.

Ordnance Survey of Northern Ireland Colby House, Stranmillis Ct, Belfast BT9 5BJ ☎028/9025 5755, ⊛www.osni.gov.uk.

Stanfords 12–14 Long Acre, London WC2 9LP ☎020/7836 1321, ⊛www.stanfords.co.uk.

The Travel Bookshop 13–15 Blenheim Crescent, London W11 2EE ☎020/7229 5260, ⊛www .thetravelbookshop.co.uk.

USA and Canada

Adventurous Traveler Bookstore PO Box 64769, Burlington, VT 05406 ☏1-800/282-3963, ⊛www .adventuroustraveler.com.

Book Passage 51 Tamal Vista Blvd, Corte Madera, CA 94925 ☏1-800/999-7909, ⊛www .bookpassage.com.

Elliot Bay Book Company 101 S Main St, Seattle, WA 98104 ☏1-800/962-5311, ⊛www .elliotbaybook.com.

Forsyth Travel Library 226 Westchester Ave, White Plains, NY 10604 ☏1-800/367-7984, ⊛www.forsyth.com.

Globe Corner Bookstore 28 Church St, Cambridge, MA 02138 ☏1-800/358-6013, ⊛www.globecorner.com.

Map Link Inc 30 S La Petera Lane, Unit 5, Santa Barbara, CA 93117 ☏1-800/962-1394, ⊛www .maplink.com.

Rand McNally ☏1-800/333-0136, ⊛www .randmcnally.com. Around thirty stores across the US; dial ext. 2111 or check the website for the nearest location.

The Travel Bug Bookstore 2667 West Broadway, Vancouver V6K 2G2 ☏604/737-1122, ⊛www .swifty.com/tbug.

Ulysses Travel Bookshop 4176 St-Denis St, Montréal ☏514/843-9447, ⊛www.ulysses.ca.

World of Maps 118 Holland Ave, Ottawa, Ontario K1Y 0X6 ☏1-800/214-8524, ⊛www.worldofmaps .com.

Australia and New Zealand

Mapland 372 Little Bourke St, Melbourne ☏03/9670 4383, ⊛www.mapland.com.au.

The Map Shop 6 Peel St, Adelaide ☏08/8231 2033, ⊛www.mapshop.net.au.

Mapworld 173 Gloucester St, Christchurch ☏0800/627 697, ⊛www.mapworld.co.nz.

Specialty Maps 58 Albert St, Auckland ☏09/307 2217, ⊛www.specialitymaps.co.nz/maps.

The Travel Bookshop 175 Liverpool St, Sydney ☏02/9261-8200.

Andalucía on the Internet

Spain and Andalucía are represented pretty strongly on the **Internet**, with sites in both English and Spanish offering information on most conceivable subjects. Andalucía's provincial capitals all have their own websites and many small towns and villages are starting them up too; all are fairly easy to find. In addition many major tourist attractions such as the Alhambra in Granada have sites,

and these are listed in the relevant sections of the *Guide*. The websites detailed below are useful starting points, and most contain numerous links to more detailed areas.

Andalucía Online ⊛www.andalucia.com. Wide-ranging general site with links to all kinds of information from hotels, villas and restaurants to beaches, bullfighting and business opportunities.

Andalucía There's Only One ⊛www.andalucia .org .The official tourism site of the Junta de Andalucía with piles of visitor-useful info and links.

Andalunet ⊛www.andalunet.com. Extensive Sevilla site with lots of useful city information including the Semana Santa procession routes.

Costa del Sol Online ⊛www.costasol.com. Another site that aims to draw together the Costa's commercial sites, along with a directory of property listings and even a few country walks.

El Índice ⊛www.elindice.com. Very useful Barcelona-based search engine which allows you to search Spanish sites by subject.

El Mundo ⊛www.elmundo.es. Spain's right-of-centre daily newspaper is *El País's* main competitor and allows free access to its news pages.

El País Digital ⊛www.elpais.es. Digital version of Spain's major newspaper and a most impressive – and largely free access – site it is too.

Hotel Search ⊛www.hotelsearch.com. Extensive, though not exhaustive, list of Spanish accommodation in English with more detail on upmarket places. Features customer comments (often hostile) to which hotels post their responses.

Interbook ⊛www.libreriainterbook.com. Major Spanish online bookstore, offering more than a million titles.

Paginas Amarillas ⊛www.paginas-amarillas.es. Spain's Yellow Pages online with very useful eating and accommodation sections. In Spanish only.

Sherry ⊛www.sherry.org. The story of Andalucía's great wine with explanations of how it's made, the different styles, and *bodegas* to visit.

Si Spain ⊛www.sispain.org. Posted by the Spanish Embassy in Ottawa, this is the largest – and best – Spain-oriented English-language site on the Web, bringing together reams of information on all aspects of Spanish culture, politics, history and tourist information.

Sierra Nevada Ski Information ⊛www.cetursa .es. Details of weather conditions, snow type and real-time images from the slopes near Granada (in Spanish but easy to follow).

Soccer Spain ⊛www.soccer-spain.com. English-language news, views, fixtures and results from the Spanish football world. *Marca*, the leading Spanish sports paper, also has a good Spanish-language site ⊛www.marca.es.

Spanish Search Engines ⓦwww
.searchenginecolossus.com. Choose the Spain entry
on this site for a comprehensive list of Spanish search
engines including many regional and local ones.
Spanish Tourist Office ⓦwww.tourspain.es.
General information board for the whole of Spain with
useful links.
Spanish Wine ⓦwww.filewine.es/english.
Comprehensive guide to Spanish wines.
Sur in English ⓦwww.surinenglish.com. The site
of Málaga's main daily newspaper covers the latest
stories taken from its Spanish edition plus lots of other
background gen. For Spanish readers its regular site
ⓦwww.diariosur.es is also good.

Todo la Prensa ⓦwww.prensaescrita.com/
andalucia. Useful Spanish-language site with links to
every daily newspaper published in Andalucía.
Todo Sobre España ⓦwww.red2000.com.
Extensive site with details on all aspects of Spain
from bullfights, bars and beaches to fiestas, food and
flamenco.
Train timetables and fares ⓦwww.renfe.es.
RENFE's (Spanish railways) online schedules include
full route details, times and fares.
Yahoo! Spain ⓦwww.es.yahoo.com. Spanish
cousin of Yahoo's main search engine which is
excellent for digging out things Hispanic.

Costs, money and banks

Although still thought of as a budget destination, hotel prices in Spain have
increased considerably over recent years, and if you're spending a lot of your time
in the cities of Andalucía you can expect to spend almost as much as you would
at home. However, there are still few places in Europe where you'll get a better
deal on the cost of budget accommodation or simple meals and drink.

On average, if you're prepared to buy
your own picnic lunch, stay in inexpensive
hostales and hotels or youth hostels, and
stick to local restaurants and bars, you
could get by on £25–30/US$45–54 a day
per person sharing accommodation, but
we're talking absolute basics here. If you
intend to upgrade your accommodation,
experience the city nightlife and eat fancier
meals then you'll need more like £50–
60/$90–108 a day. On £60–80/$108–145 a
day and upwards you'll be limited only by
your energy reserves – though of course if
you're planning to stay in four- and five-star
hotels or any of Andalucía's magnificent
paradores, this figure won't even cover your
room.

Room prices vary considerably according to season. In the summer you'll find
that for rooms without en-suite bath there's
little below €20 (£14.50/$26) single, €30
(£21.50/$39) double, and for en-suite facili-
ties €30 single, €45 double (£32/$58). Note
that in provincial capitals such as Sevilla or

Granada and popular coastal areas prices
can be much higher. That said, travelling in
country areas especially out of high season
can turn up some real bargains. **Campsites**
start at around €2.50 (£1.75/$3) a night per
person (€4–6 in some of the major resorts in
high season), plus a similar charge for a tent
and any vehicle.

The cost of **eating** can vary wildly, but in
most towns there'll be restaurants offering
a basic three-course *menú* meal (including a beer or glass of wine) for somewhere
between €6 and €9 (£4.30–6.50/$7.75–
11). As often as not, though, you'll end up
wandering from one bar to the next sampling
tapas without getting round to a real sit-
down meal – this can be tastier though
rarely any cheaper (see "Eating and drinking"
p.57). Drink, and wine in particular, costs
ridiculously little: £5/$9 will see you through
a night's very substantial intake of the local
vintage, though again, cruising some of the
swankier city and coastal bars could easily
treble this.

If you're going to be making use of **public transport** in Andalucía this will add to your costs, although prices compare well with the rest of Europe. Most of the journeys you'll be making will rarely be longer than 250km (the distance between Sevilla and Granada) and unless you plan to travel daily your **transport** budget should not prove a major expense. Sevilla to Granada, for example, on the cheapest regional train currently costs around €18 one-way (£13/$23.50), €33 for a return (£23.50/$42), or €16.50 one-way and €31 return by bus (often faster than the train). **Urban transport** almost always operates on a flat fare of €0.75–1.50 (50p–£1/$0.90–1.80).

All of the above, inevitably, is affected by where you are and when. The larger cities such as Sevilla and Granada, as well as the tourist resorts, are invariably more expensive than remoter areas; and prices are hiked up, too, to take advantage of special events like Semana Santa. Despite official controls, you'd be lucky to find a room in Sevilla during Easter week or the April *feria* at less than a third above the usual rate. As always, if you're travelling alone you'll end up spending much more (around two thirds) than you would in a group of two or more – sharing rooms saves greatly. An ISIC **student card** is worth having – it'll get you free or reduced entry to many museums and sites as well as occasional other discounts.

One thing to look out for on prices is the addition of sales tax – **IVA** (pronounced "iba") – which may come as an unexpected extra when you pay the bill for food or accommodation (currently seven percent for hotels and restaurants, sixteen percent for other goods and services), especially in more expensive establishments. Normally restaurants will include this in the price but hotels and *hostales* often leave out the tax (especially in phone or email bookings) to make the price seem more attractive. "*¿Está incluido el IVA?* " ("Is sales tax included?") is what you should ask.

Money and the exchange rate

Spain is one of twelve European Union countries that use the **euro** (€). All prices in this book are given in euros and are correct at the time of going to press. Since the introduction of the new currency there have been many complaints in Spain (along with several other euro nations) about unjustified price increases and the practice of "rounding up" prices (*redondeo*) when converted from the old currency, pesetas.

The euro is a decimal currency comprised of 100 centimos (cents). Euro coins are issued in **denominations** of 1, 2, 5, 10, 20 and 50 cents and 1 and 2 euro; euro notes come in denominations of 5, 10, 20, 50, 100, 200 and 500 euro. Note that many hotels, restaurants and other businesses – fearing fraud – now refuse to accept the 500 (and sometimes the 200) euro notes.

At the time of writing the **exchange rate** for the euro was around €1.45 to the pound sterling (or £0.68 to one euro) and €0.82 to the dollar. For the latest rates check out ⓦ www.xe.com.

Travellers' cheques and credit cards

Probably the safest way to carry your funds is in **travellers' cheques**, though most Visa, Mastercard (Access) or British **bank cards**, and US cards in the Cirrus or Plus systems, can also be used for withdrawing cash from ATMs (*cajeros automáticos*) in Spain: even Andalucía's smaller villages are getting ATMs now. Check with your bank to find out about these reciprocal arrangements – the system is highly sophisticated and all Spanish machines now give instructions in a variety of languages. Some cities such as Sevilla and Granada also have **cash-exchange machines** where you feed in your pounds or dollars and the machine issues euros. Bear in mind that ATMs are not always reliable and may swallow your card, making it advisable to think about using ATMs when the bank is open: at least then you stand a chance of someone being able to help if things go wrong.

Leading **credit and charge cards** are recognized, too, and are useful for such extra expenses as car rental and buying petrol, as well as for cash advances at banks. All upmarket hotels and restaurants will also accept this method of payment, and quite a few budget places are starting to do so too. American Express and Visa,

Lost and stolen cards

To cancel lost or stolen credit cards, call the following numbers:
American Express ☏915 720 303
Diners Club ☏915 474 000
Mastercard ☏900 971 231
Visa ☏900 974 445

which has an arrangement with the Banco de Bilbao Vizcaya Argentaria (BBVA), are the most useful; Mastercard is less widely accepted.

Changing money

Spanish **banks** and **cajas de ahorros** (savings banks) have branches in all but the smallest villages, and most of them should be prepared to change travellers' cheques (albeit occasionally with reluctance for certain brands, and almost always with hefty commissions). Banco Central Hispano, BBVA and La Caixa are three of the most efficient, with numerous branches; all change most brands of travellers' cheques, and give cash advances on credit cards; commissions at La Caixa and Banco Central Hispano are generally the lowest.

Banking hours are generally Mon–Fri 8.30am–2pm, and a few open Sat 8.30am–1pm, although precise times can vary from bank to bank. Outside these times, it's usually possible to change cash at larger hotels (generally bad rates, but low commission) or with travel agents, who may initially grumble but will eventually give a rate with the commission built in – useful for small amounts in a hurry.

In tourist areas you'll also find specialist **casas de cambio**, with more convenient hours (though the rates vary), and most branches of El Corte Inglés, a major department store found throughout Spain, have efficient exchange facilities open throughout store hours (until late evening) and offering competitive rates and generally a much lower commission than the banks, though they're worse for cash. American Express offices, which don't charge any commission on their own travellers' cheques, can also be useful, and there are branches in Málaga, Sevilla and Granada.

Wiring money

Having money **wired** from home using one of the companies listed below is never convenient or cheap, and should be considered a last resort. It's also possible to have money wired directly from a bank in your home country to a bank in Spain, although this is somewhat less reliable because it involves two separate institutions. If you go this route, your home bank will need the address of the bank branch where you want to pick up the money and the address and telex number of the Madrid head office, which will act as the clearing house; money wired this way normally takes two working days to arrive, and costs around £25/$40 per transaction.

Money–wiring companies

Thomas Cook Britain ☏01733/318 922, Northern Ireland ☏028/9055 0030, Republic of Ireland ☏01/677 1721, US ☏1-800/287-7362, Canada ☏1-888/823-4732; ✆www.thomascook.com.
Travelers Express MoneyGram Australia ☏1800/230 100, Canada ☏1-800/933-3278, New Zealand ☏0800/262 263, Republic of Ireland ☏1850/205 800, UK ☏0800/018 0104, US ☏1-800/955-7777; ✆www.moneygram.com.
Western Union Australia ☏1800/501 500, New Zealand ☏0800/270 000, Republic of Ireland ☏1800/395 395, US and Canada ☏1-800/325-6000, UK ☏0800/833 833; ✆www.westernunion.com.

Youth and student discounts

Various official and quasi-official **youth/student ID cards** soon pay for themselves in savings. Full-time students are eligible for the International Student ID Card (ISIC), which entitles the bearer to special air, rail and bus fares and discounts at museums, theatres and other attractions. For Americans there's also a health benefit, providing up to $3000 in emergency medical coverage and $100 a day for 60 days in hospital, plus a 24-hour hotline to call in the event of a medical, legal or financial emergency. The card costs £6 in the UK; $22 for Americans; Can$16 for Canadians; Aus$16.50 for Australians; and NZ$21 for New Zealanders.

You have to be 26 or younger to qualify for the **International Youth Travel Card**, which costs £7/US$22 and carries the same

43

benefits. All these cards are available in the UK from STA; in the US from Council Travel, STA, Travel Cuts and, in Canada, Hostelling International (for addresses, see p.29 for the UK, p.32 for the US and p.34 for Aus/NZ); in Australia and New Zealand from STA or Campus Travel.

Several other travel organizations and accommodation groups also sell their own cards, good for various discounts. A university photo ID might open some doors, but is not as easily recognizable as the ISIC card, although the latter is often not accepted as a valid proof of age, for example in bars or clubs.

Getting around

Most of Andalucía is well covered by both bus and rail networks. For the majority of journeys between major towns – excepting Cádiz, Sevilla and Córdoba where lines have been upgraded – buses tend to be faster than trains. On shorter or less obvious routes buses also tend to be quicker and will normally take you closer to your destination; some train stations are several miles from the town or village they serve and you've no guarantee of a connecting bus – these instances are noted throughout the Guide.

Approximate train and bus journey **times** and **frequencies** can be found in the "Travel details" at the end of each chapter, and local peculiarities are also pointed out in the text. Car rental may also be worth considering, with costs among the lowest in Europe. If your trip to Spain is part of a wider European tour, then it may be worth investing in a rail pass, such as the InterRail ticket.

By bus

Buses will probably meet most of your transport needs, especially if you're venturing away from the larger towns. Many smaller villages are accessible only by bus, almost always leaving from the capital of their province. Service varies in quality, but on the whole the buses are fast, reliable and comfortable enough, with prices pretty standard at around €5 per 100km. The only real problem involved is that many towns still have no main bus station, and buses may leave from a variety of places (even if they're heading in the same direction, since some destinations are served by more than one company). Where a new terminal has been built, it's often on the outer fringes of town.

As far as possible, departure points are detailed in the *Guide*. One thing to bear in mind when comparing a long-distance journey by train or bus is the latter's pervasive DVD and video culture. Movies start rolling as you leave the bus station and a surreal audio backdrop of Wild West gunfights, war battles or screaming police sirens may not ideally complement the scenic delights outside the window; many of the bigger bus companies are now installing headphone systems similar to those used by airlines.

One important point to remember is that all public transport, and the bus service especially, is drastically reduced on **Sundays and holidays** – it's best not even to consider travelling to out-of-the-way places on these days. The words to look out for on timetables are *diario* (daily), *laborables* (workdays, including Saturday) and *domingos y festivos* (Sundays and holidays).

By train

Andalucía's **train** network varies dramatically in its efficiency and operation and whilst lines and services such as those running between Cádiz, Sevilla and Córdoba (with

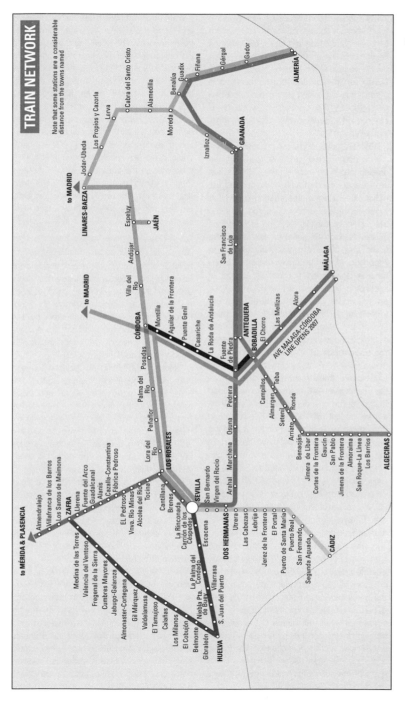

TRAIN NETWORK

Note that some stations are a considerable distance from the towns named

the Málaga–Córdoba line soon to join them) have recently been upgraded to modern European standards and faster **TRD** (Trenes Regionales Diésel) trains have been introduced on journeys between Sevilla, Málaga, Córdoba, Granada and Almería, services in other areas lag a long way behind and can be tortuously time-consuming; worth bearing in mind especially when planning longer journeys.

RENFE, the Spanish rail company, operates a complicated variety of train services divided into three main sections. **Cercanías** are local commuter trains in and around the major cities. **Regionales**, roughly equivalent to buses in speed and cost, run between the provincial capitals stopping at towns en route, although Regional exprés and Delta trains can cover longer distances. **Largo recorrido** (long distance) express trains have a bewildering number of names; in ascending order of speed and luxury, they are known as Diurno, Intercity (IC), Estrella (often just signified by a star *), Talgo, Talgo P(endular), Talgo 200 (T200) and Trenhotel. Anything above Intercity can cost more than twice as much as standard second class on an Intercity. A growing number of super-high-speed trains from Madrid such as the impressive **AVE** (tren de Alta Velocidad Española) run on a dedicated track connecting the capital with Córdoba, Sevilla and (in 2007) Málaga. Costing just under double the normal second class fare, these trains have cut travelling times dramatically for those who can afford it, with Madrid to Sevilla, for example, now taking 2 hours and 20 minutes compared with 6–9 hours on slower trains. RENFE is so confident of its performance that if arrival is more than five minutes later than scheduled you get your money back.

In recent years many bona fide train services have been phased out in favour of buses operated jointly by RENFE and a private bus company. This is particularly the case when the connection is indirect or when the train departure is at an inconvenient time. On some routes the **rail buses** outnumber the conventional departures by a ratio of four to one. Prices are the same as on the trains, and these services usually leave from and arrive at the bus stations/stops of the towns concerned.

Train information is available from stations and Andalucía has a useful **timetable** published jointly by RENFE and the Junta de Andalucía detailing *regionales* trains throughout the region. Entitled *Horarios de Trenes Regionales*, it's available from town and city stations and tourist offices. Make sure the one you are given is current as it is updated twice-yearly. Alternatively, you can ring the centralized RENFE information and reservation number on ☎902 240 202 – though you'll need to speak reasonable Spanish – or look on the Internet at ⓦwww.renfe.es (English version available). Most RENFE train tickets can be booked in advance from **Britain** through Spanish Rail Service (see "Rail Contacts" p.48).

Tickets and fares

RENFE offers a whole range of **discount fares** of 25–40 percent for those over sixty, disabled travellers, children aged four to twelve years and groups of more than ten. Return fares are also discounted by ten percent on *regionales* (valid for fifteen days) and twenty percent on *largos recorridos* (valid for sixty days).

Tickets can be bought at stations between sixty days and fifteen minutes before the train leaves, from the *venta anticipada* window, or in the final hour prior to departure from the *venta inmediata* window. Don't leave it to the last minute, however, as there are usually long queues. There may also be separate windows for *largo recorrido* (long-distance) trains and *regionales* or *cercanías* (locals). If you board the train without a ticket the conductor may charge you up to double the normal fare; if you don't have the cash, they'll call the police. If you do get on a train without a ticket it's always best to find the conductor first and explain, rather than wait to have them find you.

Most larger towns have a much more convenient RENFE office in the town centre as well, which sells **tickets in advance** and has schedule pamphlets – many of these are listed in the *Guide* under the relevant towns.

You can also buy tickets at travel agents which display the RENFE sign – they should have a sophisticated computer system that can also make seat reservations (£2.50/$3.50), which are obligatory on *largo recorrido* trains; the cost is the same as at the station.

You can change the departure date of an electronically issued, reserved-seat, long-distance (*largo recorrido*) ticket up to one hour before your originally scheduled departure with a penalty of 10 percent of the ticket price. If you want to cancel the same sort of ticket you'll be entitled to an 85 percent refund of the ticket price, provided you do so at least half an hour before departure.

Rail passes

Rail passes are only worth considering if you plan to travel extensively around Spain or are visiting the country as part of a wider tour of Europe. There are a number of different passes available. Some such as the Eurail pass have to be bought before leaving home, others can only be bought in the country itself. RENFE also offers its own passes, available in advance from selected agents or from RENFE offices in Spain. One thing to be aware of is that even with a pass, you'll sometimes be charged a **supplement** (see box) that is often almost the same as the ordinary ticket, which is galling after you've splashed out on the pass in the first place.

Euro Domino pass

British and Irish citizens might consider purchasing the **Spanish EuroDomino** Pass from Rail Europe (see overleaf), or some travel agents before arrival. The passes are available for between three and eight days' unlimited travel within a one-month period. There is a discounted youth price for those under 26, and a half-price child (age 4–11) fare. Prices for under/over 26s are three days (£71/84), five days (£108/129), eight days (£163/195). Booking online from Rail Europe saves you a £6 booking fee. Most high-speed train supplements are also included in the price. Individual passes can be bought for any of 28 European and North African countries, and you can buy as many separate country passes as you want.

Spain Flexipass

North American and Australasian travellers can buy a **Spain Flexipass**, roughly the equivalent of the Euro Domino pass. The North American version, available for both first and second class, allows three days' unlimited travel in a two-month period for US$215/165 (first/second class), with the option of buying up to seven additional rail days at US$35/30 per day. North Americans considering a combination of rail and car travel might also be interested in the Spain Rail 'n' Drive pass, valid for three or more days' rail travel and two or more days' car hire in a two-month period. Prices vary according to the number of travel days, style of car, and number of adults sharing it. See overleaf for details of where to buy the Spain Flexipass and the Rail 'n' Drive Pass.

The Australasian Spain Flexipass is issued for travel on a certain number of days within a two-month period and available in second-/first-class versions: 3 days cost (Aus$/261/336, NZ$327/419); 5days (Aus$454/513, NZ$471/583); and ten days (Aus$613/748, NZ$831/993).

Note that with all these passes you may also be stung for surcharges (see below).

InterRail pass

InterRail passes are only available to European residents, and you'll be asked to provide proof of residency before being allowed to purchase one. They come in over–26 and (cheaper) under-26 versions, and cover 28 European countries (including Turkey and Morocco) grouped together in zones:

A   Republic of Ireland/Britain
B   Norway, Sweden, Finland
C   Germany, Austria, Switzerland, Denmark

Pass supplements

Note that **InterRail** and **Eurail** passes are valid on all RENFE trains except EuroMed, but that there is a **supplement** payable for travelling on the fastest trains. The apparently random nature of these surcharges can be a source of irritation, so it's better to know what you're letting yourself in for by reserving a seat in advance, something you'll be obliged to do in any case on some trains.

D Czech & Slovak Republics, Poland, Hungary, Croatia
E France, Belgium, Netherlands, Luxembourg
F Spain, Portugal, Morocco
G Italy, Greece, Turkey, Slovenia plus some ferry services between Italy and Greece
H Bulgaria, Romania, Serbia and Montenegro, Macedonia

The passes are available for 22 days (one zone only) or one month and you can purchase up to three zones or a global pass covering all zones. You can save £6 by booking via the InterRail website ⓦwww.inter-rail.co.uk. InterRail passes do not include travel between Britain and the continent, although InterRail Pass holders are eligible for discounts on rail travel in Britain and Northern Ireland and cross-Channel ferries.

Eurail Passes

A **Eurail Pass** is not likely to pay for itself if you're planning to stick to Spain, but is definitely worth considering if you're doing a fair amount of train travel in other European countries. The pass, which must be purchased before arrival in Europe (and cannot be purchased by European residents), allows unlimited free first-class train travel in Spain and 16 other countries and is available in increments of 15 days, 21 days, 1 month, 2 months and 3 months.

Details of prices for these passes (and those mentioned above) can be found on ⓦwww.eurail.com, and the passes can be purchased from one of the agents listed below.

Rail contacts

In the UK and Ireland

Rail Europe (SNCF French Railways) ☎0870/5848 848, ⓦwww.raileurope.co.uk. Discounted rail fares for under-26s on a variety of European routes; also agents for InterRail, Eurostar and Euro Domino, and sells rail passes for Spain.
Spanish Rail Service ☎020/7224 0345, ⓦwww.spanish-rail.co.uk. Information and booking for RENFE train services. Can also book through tickets from UK to Spanish destinations.

In the US and Canada

CIT Rail ☎1-800/CIT-RAIL or 212/730-2400, Canada ☎1-800/361-7799, ⓦwww.cit-rail.com. Eurail and Europass.
DER Travel ☎1-888/337-7350, ⓦwww.dertravel.com/rail. Eurail, Europass and individual country passes.
Europrail International Canada ☎1-888/667-9734, ⓦwww.europrail.net. Eurail, Europass and individual country passes.
Online Travel Eurail ☎1-800/660-5300 or 847/318-8890, ⓦwww.eurorail.com. Europass and individual country passes for Spain and other countries.
Rail Europe US ☎1-877/257-2887, Canada ☎1-800/361-RAIL, ⓦwww.raileurope.com/us. Official North American Eurail Pass agent; also sells Europass, multinational passes and most single country passes.
Scan Tours ☎1-800/223-7226 or 310/636-4656, ⓦwww.scantours.com. Eurail and many other country passes.

In Australia and New Zealand

CIT World Travel Australia ☎02/9267 1255 or 03/9650 5510, ⓦwww.cittravel.com.au. Sells Eurail and Europass.
Rail Plus Australia ☎1300/555 003 or 03/9642 8644, ⓦwww.railplus.com.au; New Zealand ☎09/303 2484. Sells Eurail and Europass.
Trailfinders Australia ☎02/9247 7666, ⓦwww.trailfinders.com.au. All Europe passes.

By car

Whilst getting around on public transport is easy enough, you'll obviously have a great deal more freedom with your **own car**. Major roads are generally good with EU funds backing more new highways and upgrades of minor ones, and traffic, while a little hectic in Sevilla, is normally well behaved – though Spain does have one of the highest incidences of traffic accidents in Europe. But you'll be spending more, even with a full car; **petrol prices** (particularly diesel) are lower than in Britain (but still almost double US prices), and in the larger cities you'll probably want to pay extra for the security of a hotel with parking, or be forced to stay on the outskirts.

Vehicle crime is rampant – never leave anything visible in the car, and in major cities such as Sevilla and Málaga, empty it if the car is to be left on the street overnight.

Needless to say, remove any visible stickers bearing the rental company's name or logo and check that all locks are fully functioning when you take delivery. Another hazard to be aware of is break-ins when parking at out-of-the-way beauty spots or isolated attractions such as caves. If the road or car park has evidence of broken window glass it's a sure sign that thieves are frequent visitors and you'll need to park elsewhere and ensure that any valuables are safely locked away.

Tow trucks or *gruas* are now big business in most Spanish towns and cities, as the municipalities attempt to control **illegal parking**. In all towns and cities check carefully where you park – look out for the tow-truck symbol on street signs and study the time regulations carefully – and if you return to find your car gone it will usually be in the pound with the only way to retrieve it a stiff fine (currently €45–90 depending on the town or area). No excuses will be accepted and without payment in cash (or a stamped receipt from a local bank stating you have paid) you won't get your vehicle back. Enquiring at any police station, tourist or government office, or decent hotel should produce the address of the pound. It's also a towable offence to park on a taxi rank, and take care when parking along yellow painted kerbs, particularly in narrow streets; everyone does it but if a wide vehicle cannot get by and the police are called then the car on the yellow side gets the ticket and may be towed. You're more likely to find a parking space in summer if you plan to arrive in the larger towns and cities during the siesta period (roughly 2–5pm) when many inner-city workers vacate their parking spaces to drive home.

Andalucía still has a great number of staffed garages where, when buying **petrol** (*gasolina*), you'll need to know the terms Super (four-star leaded), *gasoil* (diesel) and *sin plomo* (unleaded). Credit cards are accepted by most stations although quite a few on the Costa del Sol now refuse to accept cards without a passport confirming identity.

Drivers and the law

Most foreign **driver's licences** are honoured in Spain – including all EU, US, Canadian, Australian and New Zealand ones – but an International Driver's Licence (particularly if your UK licence is pre-1986) is available from motoring organizations like the AA or RAC (or their equivalents in other countries) and is an easy way to set your mind at rest. If you're bringing your own car, it's no longer compulsory to have a green card and a bail bond, though many insurers still advise travellers to bring one. A **green card** will prove to the Spanish authorities the extent of your insurance cover. Always check current requirements with your insurer in plenty of time before leaving home. You must always carry two hazard triangles (of the legally correct size), an offical first aid kit and a set of spare bulbs; this regulation also applies to hire cars.

Spanish **road signs** are often badly sited – either too near or too far from the junctions and other potential hazards they indicate; the signing of the new Costa del Sol motorway (the Autopista del Sol) seems purposely intended to entice confused drivers onto this toll highway resulting in vehicles then having to pay the toll to get off it. Away from main roads you yield to vehicles approaching from the right, but rules are not too strictly observed anywhere. **Speed limits** are posted – maximum on urban roads is 50kph (30mph), other roads 90kph (55mph) or 100kph (60mph) on roads where there is an *arcén*, or hard shoulder; the limit on *autopistas* or motorways is 120kph (75mph). On the main highways speed traps are common. If you're stopped for any violation, the **Spanish police** have the power to levy stiff on-the-spot fines. The Policía Local (urban police) are fairly lenient in applying the law, especially when it comes to such offences as not wearing a crash helmet on a motorcycle, but the Guardia Civil traffic police, who have responsibilty for the main national routes (*carreteras nacionales*) and *autovías* (semi-motorways), are a very different matter and have a mean reputation. For traffic infringements they will usually levy an on-the-spot fine, which can range from €300 to €600, before letting you go on your way, especially since as a foreigner you're unlikely to want, or be able, to appear in court. If you are cautioned, polite acceptance is the best policy, as antagonizing them can lead to other offences being tacked on to the original infringement (such as not carrying a warning triangle or lacking a first-aid kit). If you wish to contest the fine write the words *garantía, no es pago y no está conformé* on the citation in the space provided and sign it. This leaves the way open to contest the ticket later – but if you decide to do so you'd be wise to seek legal advice. However, you'll still need to pay up on the spot (foreigners get a 20 percent reduction for this "prompt payment") and failure to do so can mean the impounding of your vehicle and documents until you do. If you haven't got the cash on you the police will obligingly accompany you to the nearest bank or *cajero automático* (cash machine).

Vehicle rental

Renting a car lets you out of many of the hassles of travelling around by bus and train, and Andalucía is one of the cheapest places in Europe to do this. There's usually a choice of companies in any major town or city, with the biggest ones – Hertz, Avis and Europcar – represented at the airports as well as in town centres. Local companies – such as Larios Car Hire in Málaga (see "Car Rental Agencies" next column) – can often offer excellent value for money. You'll need to be 21 (and have been driving for at least a year), and many companies levy a surcharge (around €3 per day) on drivers under 25. Prices start around €30 (£20/$36) per day for a small car (less by the week; special rates at the weekend).

Fly-drive deals with Iberia and other operators can be good value if you know in advance that you'll want to rent a car. The big companies all offer schemes, but you'll often get a better deal through someone who deals with local agents. Sun Cars, Holiday Autos and Málaga Car Hire are among the best, substantially undercutting the large companies. If you're going in high season, it's best to try and book well in advance.

Car Rental Agencies

In the UK

Autos Abroad ☎0870/066 7788, ⒲www.autosabroad.com.

Avis ☎0870/606 0100, ⒲www.avis.co.uk.

Budget ☎0800/181181, ⒲www.budget.co.uk.

Europcar ☎0845/722 2525, ⒲www.europcar.co.uk.

Hertz ☎0870/844 8844, ⒲www.hertz.co.uk.

Holiday Autos ☎0870/400 0000, ⒲www.holidayautos.co.uk.

Málaga Car Hire ☎020/8398 2662, ⒲www.malagacarhire.com.

National ☎0870/536 5365, ⒲www.nationalcar.co.uk.

Sun Cars ☎0870/500 5566, ⒲www.suncars.com.

Thrifty ☎1494/751600, ⒲www.thrifty.co.uk.

In Ireland

Argus ☎01/490 4444, ⒲www.argus-rentacar.com.

Atlas ☎01/844 4859, ⒲www.atlascarhire.com.

Autos Abroad ☎0870/066 7788, ⒲www.autosabroad.com.

Avis Northern Ireland ☎028/9024 0404, Republic of Ireland ☎01/605 7555; ⒲www.avis.ie.

Motoring organizations

In the UK and Ireland

AA UK ☎0870/600 0371, ⒲www.theaa.com; **Ireland** ☎01/617 9988, ⒲www.aaireland.ie.

RAC UK ☎0800/550 055, ⒲www.rac.co.uk.

In the US and Canada

AAA USA ☎1-800/aaa-help, ⒲www.aaa.com. Each state has its own club – check the phone book for local address and phone number.

CAA Canada ☎613/247-0117, ⒲www.caa.ca. Each region has its own club – check the phone book for local address and phone number.

In Australia and New Zealand

AAA Australia ☎02/6247 7311, ⒲www.aaa.asn.au.

AA New Zealand ☎09/377 4660, ⒲www.nzaa.co.nz.

Budget Republic of Ireland ☎ 0903/277 11, ⓦ www.budget.ie.
Cosmo Thrifty Northern Ireland ☎ 028/9445 2565, ⓦ www.thrifty.co.uk.
Europcar Northern Ireland ☎ 028/9442 3444, Republic of Ireland ☎ 01/614 2888; ⓦ www .europcar.ie.
Hertz Republic of Ireland ☎ 01/676 7476, ⓦ www .hertz.ie.
Holiday Autos Republic of Ireland ☎ 01/872 9366, ⓦ www.holidayautos.ie
Sixt Republic of Ireland ☎ 1850/206 088, ⓦ www .irishcarrentals.ie.

In the US and Canada

Alamo ☎ 1-800/522-9696, ⓦ www.alamo.com.
Auto Europe US ☎ 1-800/223-5555, Canada ☎ 1-888/223-5555; ⓦ www.autoeurope.com.
Avis US ☎ 1-800/331-1084, Canada ☎ 1-800/272-5871, ⓦ www.avis.com.
Budget ☎ 1-800/527-0700, ⓦ www .budgetrentacar.com.
Enterprise Rent-a-car ☎ 1-800/325-8007, ⓦ www.enterprise.com.
Europe by Car ☎ 1-800/223-1516, ⓦ www .europebycar.com.
Hertz ☎ 1-800/654-3001, Canada ☎ 1-800/263 0600; ⓦ www.hertz.com.
National ☎ 1-800/227 7368, ⓦ www.nationalcar .com.
Thrifty ☎ 1-800/367-2277, ⓦ www.thrifty.com.

In Australia

Avis ☎ 02/9353 9000, ⓦ www.avis.com.
Budget ☎ 1300/362 848, ⓦ www.budget.com.au.
Dollar ☎ 02/9223 1444, ⓦ www.dollarcar.com.au.
Hertz ☎ 03/9698 2555, ⓦ www.hertz.com.au.
Thrifty ☎ 1300/367 227, ⓦ www.thrifty.com.au.

In New Zealand

Apex ☎ 0800/93 95 97, ⓦ wwww.apexrentals.co.nz.
Avis ☎ 09/526 2847 or 0800/655 111, ⓦ www .avis.co.nz
Budget ☎ 09/976 2222, ⓦ www.budget.co.nz.
Hertz ☎ 0800/654 321, ⓦ www.hertz.co.nz.
Thrifty ☎ 09/309 0111, ⓦ www.thrifty.co.nz.

In Andalucía

Atesa ☎ 902 100 101, ⓦ www.atesa.es. Major national Spanish company with branches throughout Andalucía.
Almería Almericar ☎ 950 23 49 66, ⓦ www.almeri -car.com. Local company based at Almería airport.
Málaga Larios Car Hire ☎ 95 109 20 69, ⓦ www .larioscarhire.com.
Sevilla ATA S.A. ☎ 95 422 09 57.

By motorbike, moped and scooter

Seeing Andalucía on two wheels is an attractive proposition, especially away from the coast, and most of the major tourist resorts have companies where you can rent **motorbikes, mopeds and scooters**. The smaller bikes and mopeds are ideal for pottering around for a day or two, but don't regard them as serious transport. Inland Andalucía is very mountainous and mopeds simply won't go up some of the steeper hills, even with only one person aboard. For serious touring or exploration you'll need at least 100cc to cope and probably 150cc and more if you're going to be carrying baggage or a passenger.

To **rent a motorbike** (€20–30 a day, cheaper by the week) you have to be 14 to ride a machine under 75cc and 18 for one over 75cc. Crash helmets are compulsory and there's a stiff on-the-spot fine if you're caught not wearing one. Note that mopeds and motorbikes are often rented out with insurance that doesn't include theft – always check with the company first. You will generally be asked to produce a driving licence as a deposit. When renting, check the bike thoroughly before riding off as many are only cosmetically repaired and if you break down it's often your responsibility to return the machine. It's wise to get a phone number from the rental company in case it does collapse miles from anywhere, or you lose your ignition key. Bike repairs after a spill could leave you with a massive bill so make sure that you are adequately insured, both in the rental agreement and by your own travel insurance – many of these schemes specifically exclude injuries sustained while riding motorcycles. Málaga-based Larios Car Hire, who operate from the main bus station (see "Car Rental Agencies"), are a reliable company who rent out a range of bikes and will deliver to the airport to meet your plane.

By bicycle

The Spanish are keen **cycle** fans, but their interest is mainly in racing, and active cycling, perhaps in view of the terrain and high summer temperatures, is largely restricted to racing club members. However, taking your own bike can be an inexpensive and flexible way of getting around, and the saddle of a bicycle offers an incomparable view of the region and guarantees contact with locals that the average visitor could never meet. Do remember, though, that peninsular Spain is one of the most **mountainous** countries in Europe and that Andalucía contains its two highest peaks, so you'll need to be a hardy hill-climber. In searing fierce summer **heat**, attempting to scale the hills becomes an endurance test: seasoned cycle tourists advise starting out at dawn and covering the main part of the day's schedule by mid-morning, before the temperature peaks. That leaves the rest of the day for sightseeing, picnicking around riverbanks or dipping in the often pleasant village pools, before covering a few more kilometres in the cooler hours before sunset.

Most *hostales* and hotels have somewhere safe for **overnight storage** and you should not leave your bike on the street overnight in either Málaga, Sevilla or Granada; elsewhere there should be no problem, but take a strong lock or chain. There are **bike shops** in the larger towns and parts can often be found at auto repair shops or garages – look for Michelin signs. **Cars** tend to honk before they pass, which can be alarming at first but is useful once you're used to it. Do not cycle two-abreast on any road, especially at night, as there have been a number of serious accidents when drivers – unused to dealing with cycles – have collided with the cyclist on the outside. Touring guides to the better areas can be found in good bookshops – in Spanish, of course. See "Books" (p.696) for books on cycling in Spain.

Transporting your bike

Transporting your bike there should present few problems. Most **airlines** are happy to take them as ordinary baggage provided they come within your allowance (though it's sensible to check first to avoid any nasty surcharge surprises at the check-in desk); crowded charters may be less obliging. Deflate the tyres to avoid explosions in the unpressurized hold.

Spanish long-distance **trains** are also reasonably accessible, though bikes can only go on a train with a guard's van (*furgón*) and must be registered – go to the *Equipajes* or *Paquexpres* desk at the station. If you're not travelling with the bike you can either send it as a package or buy an undated ticket and use the method above; be aware, though, that this can often mean a few days' wait if (as often happens) the bike gets delayed en route. For travel inside Andalucía the *cercanías* (local trains) will often allow you to take your bike on board outside the rush hours, but this is at the discretion of the guard. Buses have no set policy on carrying cycles and again it will usually depend on your powers of persuasion with the driver and how full the bus is.

Bike rental

In many of the coastal resorts you'll find basic pedal bikes for rent; they're reasonably cheap for a few hours' exploration and child seats are sometimes available too. Some of these outlets are also starting to rent out mountain bikes for more serious jaunts, and these are detailed throughout the *Guide*.

By plane

Both Iberia and the smaller, slightly cheaper Aviaco operate an extensive network of **internal flights**. While these are quite reasonable by international standards, they still work out to be very pricey, and are only really worth considering if you're in an extraordinary hurry and need to cross the entire peninsula.

Accommodation

Reasonably priced rooms are still widely available in Andalucía, and in almost any town you'll be able to get a simple double for around €25–35, a single for €20 or less. Rooms with en-suite bath or shower start at just above these prices. Only in major resorts and a handful of "tourist cities" (such as Granada or Sevilla) will you have to pay more.

We've detailed where to find places to stay in most of the destinations listed in the Guide, and given a price range for each, from the most basic rooms to luxury hotels. As a general rule, all you have to do is head for the cathedral or main square of any town, invariably surrounded by an old quarter full of accommodation possibilities. In Spain, unlike most countries, you don't seem to pay any more for a central location (this goes for bars and cafés, too), though you do tend to get a comparatively bad deal if you're travelling on your own as there are relatively few single rooms. Much of the time you'll have to negotiate a reduction on the price of a double.

In fact, it's always worth **bargaining** over room prices since although they're officially regulated this doesn't necessarily mean much. In high season you're unlikely to have much luck (although many places do have rooms at different prices, and tend to offer the more expensive ones first) but at quiet times you may get quite a discount. If there are more than two of you, most places have rooms with three or four beds at not a great deal more than the double room price – a bargain, especially if you have children. Also many hotels will often add up to two beds to a double room for a reasonable supplement and often smaller country establishments will not charge at all.

The one thing all travellers need to master is the elaborate **variety** of types and places to stay. Below is a breakdown of the options.

If you have any **problems** with your room – overcharging, most obviously – you can usually produce an immediate resolution by asking for the *libro de reclamaciones* (official complaints book). By law all establishments must keep one and bring it out for regular inspection by the authorities. Although little is ever written in them they are worth using and, as the pages are numbered, difficult to tamper with. Add your home address, too, as you are entitled to be informed of any action taken, including – but don't count on it – compensation. Most establishments

Accommodation price codes

All the establishments listed in this book have been given **price codes** according to the following scale. The prices quoted are for the cheapest available double room in high season; effectively this means that anything in the ❶, and most places in the ❷, range will be without private bath, though there's usually a washbasin in the room. In the ❸ category and above you will probably be getting private facilities (except in major tourist cities such as Sevilla and Granada, where prices are higher). Remember, though, that many of the budget places will also have more expensive rooms including en-suite facilities.

Note that in the more upmarket *hostales* and *pensiones*, and in anything calling itself a hotel, you'll pay a tax (IVA) of seven percent on top of the room price.

❶ Under €25
❷ €25–35
❸ €35–45
❹ €45–65
❺ €65–80
❻ €80–100
❼ €100–130
❽ €130–160
❾ Over €160

prefer to keep them empty, thus attracting no unwelcome attention from officialdom which, of course, works in your favour. You can also take your complaint to the nearest tourist office, who will, if possible, attempt to resolve the matter while you wait.

Consult the "Language" section (p.703) for how to ask for accommodation and specify your needs.

Fondas, pensiones, hostales and hoteles

Least expensive – and most basic – of all accommodation possibilities are **fondas** (mostly identifiable by a square blue sign with a white F on it, and often positioned above a bar), closely followed by **casas de huéspedes** (CH on a similar sign), **pensiones** (P) and, less commonly, **hospedajes**. Distinctions between all of these are rather blurred, but in general you'll often find food served at both *fondas* and *pensiones* (some of which may offer rooms only on a meals-inclusive basis). *Casas de huéspedes* – literally "guesthouses" – were traditionally for longer stays; and to some extent, particularly in the older family seaside resorts, they still are. A variation on these are *casas particulares*, or unlicensed guesthouses, where the householder decides to let the odd room. Particularly common in holiday resorts where they soak up the overflow in high season, they are often a welcome option if things get tight. However, as Spain upgrades its tourist facilities, both *fondas* and *casas de huespedes* are gradually disappearing and, along the *costas* particularly, they are very rare.

Slightly more expensive but far more common are **hostales** (marked Hs) and **hostal-residencias** (HsR). These are categorized from one to three stars, but even so prices vary enormously according to location – in general the more remote, the less expensive. Most *hostales* offer good functional rooms, usually with private shower, and, for doubles at least, they can be excellent value. The *residencia* designation means that no meals other than perhaps breakfast are served.

Moving up the scale you finally reach **hoteles** (H), again star-graded by the authorities (from one to five). One-star hotels cost no more than three-star *hostales* –

sometimes they're actually less expensive – but at three stars you pay a lot more, and at four or five you're in the luxury class with prices to match. Near the top end of this scale there are also luxury hotel chains as well as the state-run **paradores** (Ⓦwww.parador.es): beautiful places (although there are some recently built exceptions), often converted from castles, monasteries and other minor Spanish monuments. If you can to splash out, these are almost all wonderful (the best ones in Andalucía are detailed in the *Guide*), despite a reputation amongst Spanish critics for offhand service. Even if you can't afford to stay, the buildings are often worth a look in their own right, and usually have pleasantly classy bars and restaurants and cafés, open to nonresidents.

Outside all of these categories you will sometimes see **camas** (beds) and **habitaciones** (rooms) advertised in private houses or above bars, often with the phrase *camas y comidas* ("beds and meals"). If you're travelling on a very tight budget these can be worth looking out for – particularly if you're offered one at a bus station and the owner is prepared to bargain with you.

Rural tourism and villas turísticas

There has been a significant growth in **rural tourism** over recent years, encouraged by the *Junta de Andalucía*, in an attempt to spread the wealth of tourism away from the coast and into the less prosperous hinterland. As well as working out cheaper than staying on the coast or in the cities, this can be a great way to discover the most beautiful and unspoilt tracts of Andalucía.

There are several Spanish guides to rural accommodation in farmhouses and villages, among which are the *Anuario de Turismo Rural* (Ediciones Susaeta, Madrid) and the *Guía de Alojamiento Rural* (El País/Águilar), which are both easily comprehensible with photos of each property. Both are available from most Spanish bookshops. A central organization for Andalucía, the **Red Andaluza de Alojamientos Rurales**, Apartado 2035, 04080 Almería (☏950 26 50 18, Ⓦwww.raar.es; English spoken), takes bookings and produces a free brochure with photos and descriptions of rural properties for rent. All the *casas rurales* on their books are listed on the main website but you'll need to send an email for further information. They also have details of rooms at farmhouses and village *casas particulares* (guesthouses). Many of these places encourage longer lets, but out of high season you can often get away with a single night (or two). The **Asociación de Hoteles Rurales de Andalucía**, c/Cristo Rey 2, 23400 Úbeda (℡953 75 58 67, ⓦwww.ahra.es; English spoken), does a similar job for small rural hotels and also has a free brochure. **Rural Andalus**, c/Montés de Oca 18, 29007 Málaga (℡95 227 62 29, ⓦwww.ruralandalus.es), is another organization and lists over 500 rural properties throughout Andalucía.

Villas turísticas are rural hotels or groups of free-standing dwellings set up and run by the regional government. Built in scenic locations, they often use the vernacular architecture of the region. Technically they are self-catering apartments but usually they have all the facilities, including reception, restaurant and room service, that you'd find in a four-star hotel. They would normally be in category ❺ of our price code.

There are also **casas rurales** (rural houses), a scheme established along the lines of the French *gîtes*. Accommodation at these can vary from bed and breakfast at a farmhouse to a rental cottage. Many are mentioned throughout the Guide and local Turismos have details of others in their respective zones.

Youth hostels and refuges

Albergues Juveniles (youth hostels) are a possible option, especially in Andalucía's major towns, and we've detailed the most useful of these in the *Guide*. Most have been extensively refurbished and now stay open all year – the rest operate just for the summer (or spring and summer) in temporary premises – although in towns they can be inconveniently located. Andalucía's nineteen year-round hostels are affiliated to Inturjoven, the region's official youth hostel organization, and a leaflet with details of the locations of these, their facilities and tariffs can be obtained from any *albergue* or the Inturjoven office, c/Miño 24, 41011 Sevilla

(℡95 427 70 87, or central reservations 902 51 00 00, ⓦwww.inturjoven.com). While Andalucía's hostels are pretty lenient when it comes to annoyances such as curfews, be warned that the most popular places are often block-reserved by school groups, or by hostellers who have booked months ahead, and also demand production of a YHA card (though this is generally available on the spot if you haven't already bought one from your national organization). At €9.25–14 per person depending on the season (over 26s pay about a third above these rates), you can quite easily pay more than you would sharing a cheap double room in a *hostal*. That said, many of the newer youth hostels, such as those in Málaga, Córdoba, Granada and Almería are almost like hotels (with double rooms and en-suite bath or shower), and make for a pleasant stopover.

In isolated mountain areas the Federación Andaluza de Montañismo, Camino de Ronda 101, 18003 Granada (℡958 29 13 40, ⓦwww.fedamon.com), runs a number of **refugios**: simple, cheap dormitory-huts for climbers and hikers, generally equipped only with bunks and a very basic kitchen.

Youth hostel associations

In England and Wales

Youth Hostel Association (YHA) ℡0870/770 8868, ⓦwww.yha.org.uk. Annual membership £15.50; under-26 £10; lifetime £200.

In Scotland

Scottish Youth Hostel Association ℡0870/155 3255, ⓦwww.syha.org.uk. Annual membership £6, for under-18s £2.50.

In Ireland

Irish Youth Hostel Association ℡01/830 4555, ⓦwww.irelandyha.org. Annual membership €20, under-18s €10, family €40, lifetime €100.
Hostelling International Northern Ireland ℡028/9032 4733, ⓦwww.hini.org.uk. Annual membership £13, under-18s £6, family £25, lifetime £75.

In the US

Hostelling International-American Youth Hostels ℡301/495-1240, ⓦwww.hiayh.org. Annual membership for adults (18–55) is $28, for

seniors (55 or over) $18, and for under-18s free.
Lifetime membership $250.

In Canada

Hostelling International Canada ☎1-800/663
5777 or 613/237 7884, ⓦwww.hostellingintl.ca.
Membership costs $35, is free for under-18s and you
can become a lifetime member for $175.

In Australia

Australia Youth Hostels Association
☎02/9261 1111, ⓦwww.yha.com.au. Adult
membership rate $52, under-18s, $19.

In New Zealand

Youth Hostelling Association New Zealand
☎0800/278 299 or 03/379 9970, ⓦwww.yha
.co.nz. Adult membership $40, under-18s free,
lifetime $300.

Camping

There are some 130 authorized **campsites**
(*campings*) in Andalucía, predominantly
on the coast. Graded into three classes
according to facilities, they usually work out
at €2.50–6 (£1.75–4/US$3–7) per person
per night depending on season, facilities and
location (the popular beach resorts are the
priciest, rural inland sites much cheaper).
You'll also pay the same again for a tent (but
double this for a family-sized model) and
a similar amount for each car or caravan,
perhaps twice as much for a van. Again
we've detailed the most useful in the text, but
if you plan to camp extensively then pick up
the free *Guía de Camping* published by the
Junta de Andalucía, which details virtually
all of them in map format; it's available from
most Turismos, and in advance from Spanish
National Tourist Offices abroad. A complete
nationwide *Guía de Campings*, listing full
prices, facilities and exact locations, is available from most Spanish bookshops.

Camping outside campsites, aka **wild
camping**, is legal – but with certain restric-
tions. You're not allowed to camp "in urban
areas, areas prohibited for military or touristic
reasons, or within 1km of an official campsite". What this means in practice is that
you can't camp on tourist beaches (though
you can, discreetly, nearby) but with a little
sensitivity you can set up a tent for a short
period almost anywhere in the countryside.
However, it's common courtesy to respect
local sensibilities and whenever possible you
should ask first, especially if it's private land;
if there is a problem with your proposed site,
somewhere nearby will, more often than not,
be recommended.

If you're planning to spend a lot of your
time camping, an **international camping
carnet** may be a good investment, giving a
ten-percent discount on quality campsites. In
the UK and Ireland, the carnet is available to
members of the AA (who will direct you to the
Camping and Caravanning Club below) or the
RAC (£6.50; see p.50 for both). The carnet
is also available for £4.50 (members only)
from either of the following: the Camping and
Caravanning Club, Greenfields House, West-
wood Way, Coventry CV4 8JH (☎024/7669
4995, ⓦwww.campingandcaravanningclub
.co.uk), or the foreign touring arm of the
same company, the Carefree Travel Service (☎024/7642 2024), which provides the
CCI free if you take out vehicle and personal
insurance with them. In the US and Canada,
the carnet is available from home motoring
organizations, or from Family Campers and
RVers, 4804 Transit Rd, Building 2, Depew,
NY 14043 (☎1-800/245-9755, ⓦwww.fcrv
.org). FCRV annual membership costs $25
and the carnet an additional $10. The carnet
serves as useful identification and covers you
for third-party insurance when camping.

Eating and drinking

There are a number of ways to eat out in Andalucía: you can go to a restaurante, cafetería or venta (roadside inn) and have a full meal, or you can have a succession of tapas (small snacks) or raciones (larger ones) at one or more bars. Marisquerías (shellfish bars) and chiringuitos (informal beach restaurants) both specialize in seafood. For more information on tapas refer to the colour insert. As Spain is a major producing country, wine is plentiful and affordable everywhere and the region's bars serve up a wide range of domestic and international beers.

At the less classy *restaurantes*, some *cafeterías* and all *ventas* the best value option is normally the *menú del día*: an economical, filling, three-course meal with a drink. This is often very good value and the more stylish restaurants do their own version called a *menú de degustación* which enables you to try some of the region's best cooking at reasonable cost. Tapas and *raciones* bars tend to be a lot more interesting, allowing you to do the rounds and sample local (often house) specialities.

For a list of food, drink and menu terms, see p.705.

Breakfast, snacks and sandwiches

For **breakfast** you're best off in a bar or café, though some *hostales* and *fondas* will serve the "Continental" basics. Traditionally in Andalucía, it's *churros con chocolate* – long, tubular doughnuts (not for the weak of stomach) with thick drinking chocolate – but most places also serve *tostadas* (toasted rolls) with oil (*con aceite*) or butter (*con mantequilla*) – and jam (*y mermelada*), or egg dishes (*huevos fritos* are fried eggs). Croissants (*cruasán*) are now widely available in most town bars and *cafeterías*, as is the French *pain au chocolat* which transmutes into a *napolitana* on this side of the border. Cold tortilla with a slice of toast (*pan tostada*) also makes an excellent breakfast. Many of the more modern breakfast bars now offer wholemeal bread (*pan integral*) as an option.

Coffee (*café*) and **pastries** (*pastas* or *pasteles*) or doughnuts are available at most cafés, too, though for a wider selection of confectionary you should head for one of the many excellent *pastelerías* or *confiterías*. In larger towns, there will often be a *panadería* or *croissantería* serving quite an array of appetizing baked goods besides the obvious bread, croissants and pizza. For the different ways of ordering coffee see p.63.

Some bars specialize in **sandwiches** (*bocadillos*), and as they're usually outsize affairs in French bread, they'll do for breakfast or lunch. In a bar with tapas, you can have most of what's on offer put in a sandwich, and you can often get them prepared (or buy the materials to do so) at grocery shops. Incidentally, a "*sandwich*" is a toasted cheese and ham sandwich, usually on sad processed bread.

Tascas, bodegas, cervecerías and tabernas

Tascas, **bodegas**, **cervecerías** and **tabernas** are all types of bar where you'll find tapas and *raciones*. Most of them have different sets of prices depending on whether you stand at the bar to eat (the basic charge) or sit at tables (up to 50 percent more expensive – and even more if you sit out on a terrace). **Casinos** are essentially places to drink and relax – quieter and more comfortable than most of the bars – and serve as a kind of club, with locals paying a nominal monthly membership charge. Most small towns have one, and tourists and visitors are always welcome to use the facilities free of charge – worth doing since the membership rule means everybody drinks at reduced prices.

Meals and restaurants

This category is where Spain and Andalucía come into their own; there's simply nowhere else in Europe where you can get a quality three-course meal with wine for what a bowl of soup or a dessert would cost you in an average restaurant in London or New York. This comes from the roadhouse or *venta* tradition along the major highways, where fierce competition for customers has shaved prices whilst upholding standards; and these places – many in business for a couple of centuries – still turn out bargain *menús del día* (daily set menu) for amazingly little.

When eating out, there's a multitude of distinctions. You can sit down and have a full meal in a *comedor*, a *cafetería*, a *restaurante*, a *mesón* or a *marisquería* – all in addition to the more food-oriented bars. Replacing the old-style and now very rare **comedores** (workers' cafés) to some extent are **cafeterías**, which the local authorities now grade from one to three cups (the ratings, as with restaurants, are based on facilities offered – decor, air-conditioning and so on – rather than the quality of the food). These can be good value, too, but their emphasis is more northern European and the light snack-meals served tend to be dull. Food here often comes in the form of a **plato combinado** – literally a combined plate – which will be something like egg and chips or *calamares* and salad, sometimes with bread and a drink included, and generally costing €4–6. *Cafeterías* often serve some kind of *menú del día* as well. You may prefer to get your *plato combinado* at a **bar**, which in small towns and villages may be the only way to eat inexpensively.

Moving up the scale there are **restaurantes** (designated by one to five forks, which relate more to price and facilities than quality), **mesones** (inns) and **marisquerías**. Of the latter two, a *mesón* formerly offered both food and lodging but today they tend to serve traditional local cuisine, whilst *marisquerías* specialize exclusively in shellfish and other seafood and are the most popular places to eat out in Andalucía. **Restaurantes**, which at the bottom of the scale are often not much different in price from *cafeterías* or *ventas*, will also generally have *platos combinados* available. A fixed-price *menú del día*, *menú de la casa*, *menú turístico* or occasionally *cubierto* (all of which mean the same and which are referred to as a **menú** throughout the *Guide*) is often better value: usually three courses including wine (but see "Alcoholic Drinks" below) and bread for around €6–15 depending on location – cities are generally more expensive, rural locations cheaper. Do note, however, that some restaurants only offer their *menú del día* at lunchtimes and in tourist areas many establishments tend not to publicize theirs, hoping you'll select from the more expensive à la carte; it's always worth asking "*hay un menú del día?*". Sunday lunchtime – the day when *andaluz* families traditionally go out for lunch – is another time when the *menú del día* is largely unavailable. If you move above two forks on the *restaurantes* scale, or find yourself in one of the more fancy *marisquerías* (as opposed to a basic seafront fish-fry place), prices can escalate rapidly. However, even here most of the top restaurants offer an upmarket *menú* called a **menú de degustación** (a sampler meal, frequently including wine) which is often excellent value and allows you to try out some of the region's finest cooking for €15–50. For many of the better restaurants listed in this guide we have added a phone number should you wish to **make a reservation**. This does not always mean that booking is essential, although at weekends and holiday periods it is probably advisable to avoid disappointment.

Throughout the guide in the more upmarket places we have tried wherever possible to give main dish **prices**, which enables a quick estimate to be made of the price of a meal for two. If for example, a restaurant's main dishes are listed as costing €9–20, to get an idea of the most economical meal for two, double the lower figure, add in €10 per person to cover first course and dessert, plus at least €10 for a decent bottle of wine, and the total comes to €48. Of course, should you decide to go for the more expensive dishes or a vintage bottle of wine the final total will rise proportionately. To avoid receiving confused stares from waiters, you should always ask for *la carta* when you want a menu; *menú* in Spanish refers only to a fixed-price meal.

In addition, in all but the most rock-bottom establishments customers often leave a small **tip** (*propina*). Andalucians (and Spaniards generally) are judicious tippers, so only do so if the service merits it: the amount is up to you, though five percent of the bill in a restaurant is quite sufficient and ten or fifteen eurocents in a bar. Service is normally included in a *menú del día*. The other thing to take account of in medium- and top-price restaurants is the addition of **IVA**, a seven percent tax on your bill. It should say on the menu if you have to pay this.

In most restaurants your visit will usually be wholly satisfactory, but if you do feel you are being short-changed in terms of quality or service, or if you wish to dispute the bill, a good last resort is to request the **libro de reclamaciones** (complaints book), which every hotel and restaurant is required to have by law (see p.53 for details). If your Spanish isn't up to getting satisfaction the nearest Turismo will usually assist you and may even offer to contact the offending establishment to resolve matters.

Spaniards generally **eat very late** and Andalucians eat later still, so most places serve food from around 1pm until 4 or sometimes 5pm (though no one considers lunch until at least 2pm) and from 8pm to midnight and later (but, again, no one eats before 10pm). Many restaurants close on Sunday evening. If you insist on dining at more familiar hours you'll often be eating alone, with the waiters looking on. The best thing is to try and adjust to the southern style, and in between do what the locals do – keep going on tapas.

What to eat

Our food glossary (see p.705) should give you an idea of what's on offer and help you cope when faced with a restaurant menu. Local specialities are highlighted throughout the *Guide*, too.

If you like **fish and seafood** you'll be in heaven in Andalucía as this forms the basis of a vast variety of tapas and is fresh and excellent everywhere. It's not cheap, unfortunately, so rarely forms part of the lowest priced *menús* (though you may get the most common fish – cod, often salted, and hake – or squid) but you really should make the most of what's on offer. Fish stews (*zarzuelas*) and rice-based paellas (which also contain meat, usually rabbit or chicken) are often memorable in seafood restaurants. Paella comes originally from Valencia and is still best there, but you'll find *arroz marinero*, the Andalucian version, just as good. The coastal strip's obsession with seafood is detailed in the main body of the *Guide*, although Cádiz and the nearby "sherry triangle" of Sanlúcar, El Puerto de Santa María and Jerez deserve top spot for sheer volume and variety. Be aware when ordering fish in

---

Andalucía's top ten restaurants

Andalucía has some of the best restaurants in Spain and quite a few places where you could blow a pretty big hole in your credit card account. However, whilst many recommended in the guide score higher points for cuisine alone, at any of the places below (ranked in no particular order) we feel the welcome, ambience, location and excellent food will all contribute to a memorable meal.

José Vicente Aracena (p.399)
Achuri Cádiz (p.249)
El Chaleco Almuñécar (p.147)
Parador de Málaga-Gibralfaro Málaga (p.108)
El Almejero Garrucha (p.625)
El Bigote Sanlúcar de Barrameda (p.269)
Las Candelas Huelva (p.370)
El Faro de El Puerto El Puerto de Santa María (p.258)
El Roqueo Torremolinos (p.153)
Río Grande Sevilla (p.328)

restaurants that often the price quoted is per kilo or per 100g, and an average whitefish portion will be around 200–300g (don't be afraid to ask the waiter for a price quote when ordering).

Meat is most often grilled and served with a few fried potatoes and a couple of salad leaves, or cured or dried and served as a starter or in sandwiches. *Jamón serrano*, the Spanish version of Parma ham, is superb, and a passion in Andalucía. The finest varieties, though, from Jabugo in the Sierra de Aracena (see p.410) and Trevélez in the Sierra Nevada, are extremely expensive. If you're tempted, they are best appreciated with a glass of *fino* (see p.62). More meat is eaten in inland provinces than on the coast and Córdoba's *rabo de toro* (stewed bull's tail) is renowned. The Sierra de Aracena is also a good place for *setas* (mushrooms) and cooked pork dishes, with *solomillo de cerdo* (pork sirloin) usually outstanding. In country areas bordering the slopes of the Sierra Morena and in the province of Jaén, game is very much a speciality – venison, partridge, hare and wild boar all feature on menus in these parts, as well as fresh trout.

Vegetables rarely amount to more than a few fries or boiled potatoes with the main dish (but you can often order a side dish à la carte). The provinces of Córdoba and Jaén are again the exceptions, and the latter's *pipirrana jaenera* (salad with green peppers and hard-boiled eggs) is only one of a number of hearty vegetable-based dishes to be found in these parts. It's more usual, though, to start your meal with a simple salad or with Andalucía's most famous dish, chilled *gazpacho*. Made from puréed bread and garlic with added peppers, cucumbers and tomatoes, regional variations of *gazpacho* include Córdoba's *salmorejo* (white in colour with more body), Málaga's *ajo blanco* (with almonds and grapes) or Cádiz's *sopa de picadillo* (garnished with *jamón* and hard-boiled eggs).

Dessert (*postre*) in Andalucía tends to be sweet and sticky – another hangover from the region's long Moorish period. The cheaper places will usually offer little variety: nearly always fresh fruit or flan, the Spanish *crème caramel*, often replaced on Andalucian menus by the similar *tocino de cielo*

("heavenly lard") or *natillas* (custard). *Arroz con leche* (cold rice pudding), *crema catalana* (crème brûlée) and *helado* (ice cream) are crème desserts often making an appearance in the more mundane places. Keep an eye out in upmarket restaurants for delicious regional specialities such as *peras al vino* (pears baked in wine with cinnamon) from Málaga, *piononos* (liqueur-soaked cakes) from Granada and *crema de Jerez* (sherry pudding) from Cádiz, as well as *brazo de gitano* (rolled pastry filled with cream), an Andalucía-wide dessert. In more upmarket places the desserts will always be made in house or by a reputable local artisan (or even convent) but in cheaper and out-of-the-way places they often cut corners by offering factory-produced desserts, anathema to most *andaluzes*; "*es casero?*" ("is it home made?") is the question to ask.

Cheese (*queso*) is always eaten as a tapa rather than after a meal in Andalucía. The cheeses of the region don't usually travel beyond their immediate area of production, which offers you the chance to make some interesting discoveries, especially in areas such as Las Alpujarras. The best-known region-wide brand is Córdoba Province's sheep's-milk cheese from Pedroches, although the hard, salty Manchego from neighbouring La Mancha is also common.

Vegetarian eating

Vegetarians have a fairly hard time of it in Andalucía: there's always something to eat, but you may get weary of eggs and omelettes: *tortilla francesa* is a plain omelette, *con champiñones* with mushrooms, while *tortilla española* uses potatoes and onions. In the big cities you'll find vegetarian restaurants and ethnic places which serve vegetable dishes, and these are referred to in the *Guide*. Otherwise, superb fresh produce is always available in the markets and shops, and cheese, fruit and eggs are available everywhere. In restaurants you're faced with the extra problem that pieces of meat – especially ham, which the Spanish don't seem to regard as real meat – are often added to vegetable dishes to "spice them up".

The phrase to get to know is "*Soy vegetariano. Hay algo sin carne?*" (I'm a vegetarian. Is there anything without meat?); you may have to add *y sin mariscos* (and without seafood) *y sin jamón* (and without ham) to be really safe.

If you're a vegan, you're either going to have to compromise or accept weight loss if you're away for any length of time. Some salads and vegetable dishes are strictly vegan, but they're few and far between. Fruit and nuts are widely available, nuts being sold by street vendors everywhere.

Alcoholic drinks

As a major wine-producing country Spain is addicted to the products of the vine. Sherry is Andalucía's great *aperitivo* but there are a wide variety of other beverages as well, and brandy (often referred to as *coñac*) and liqueurs are also very popular.

Wine

Vino (wine), either *tinto* (red), *blanco* (white) or *rosado/clarete* (rosé), is the invariable accompaniment to every meal and is, as a rule, extremely inexpensive. Andalucía's wine-making genius lies elsewhere (see below) and so most table wines are imported from outside the region. One thing worth knowing about Spanish wine is the terms related to the **ageing process** which defines the best wines: *crianza* wines must have a minimum of two years ageing before sale; red *reserva* wines at least two years (of which one must be in oak barrels); red *gran reserva* must have at least two years in oak and three in the bottle. *Vino de Mesa* and *Vino de la Tierra* are the equivalent of France's Vin de Table, and DO (Denominación de Origen)

Wining and dining

One of the great pleasures of eating out in Andalucía is the chance to sample some of Spain's excellent wines. Restaurant **wine prices** compare very favourably with other parts of Europe and in most restaurants and *ventas* you'll often be able to find a decent bottle for under €10. Most establishments usually have an economical house wine too for around half this price or less, (ask for *caserío* or *vino de la casa*) and sometimes this will be served straight from the barrel in a half-litre or litre carafe (*jarra*). This can be great, it can be lousy, but at least it will be distinctively local.

The most common bottled wine in Andalucía is **Valdepeñas**, a good standard wine from the central plains of New Castile (Los Llanos, Viña Albali and Señorío de Guadianeja are good labels). **Rioja**, from the area round Logroño in the north, is one of Spain's classic wines but a lot more expensive (Cune, Faustino I & V, Berberana, Beronia, Marqués de Cáceres, Montecillo, Viña Ardanza, Palacio and Izadi are names to look out for). Another top-drawer, and currently fashionable, region is **Ribera del Duero** in Castilla-León which produces Spain's most expensive wine, Vega Sicilia, besides other outstanding whites (Belondrade y Lurtón) and reds (Pesquera, Viña Pedrosa, Protos and Señorío de Nava). There are also scores of other excellent wines to try from regions such as Catalunya (Bach, Raimat, Torres) which also produces the champagne-like Cava (Codorníu, Freixenet) and the new and pricey Priorat-zone reds which have taken the wine world by storm (Clos Mogador, Alvaro Palacios). Galicia, known for its fragrant whites (Fefiñanes, Fin de Siglo and San Trocado); Navarra (Gran Feudo, Señorío de Sarría, Ochoa); and Valencia (Murviedro, Gandía) are others, and even the once unpromising La Mancha (Santa Rita, Casa Gualda, Estola) is now making a name for itself as a producer of quality wines.

Andalucía's solitary table-wine area of any volume is the **Condado de Huelva**, which turns out reasonable dry whites, which go well with seafood. An interesting new development near Ronda is the foundation of a vineyard geared to the production of quality red wine – something previously thought to be impossible in this climate, and the early vintages have been a great success. There are also many local wines made in the country districts, with some, such as the **costa** wine of the western Alpujarras, and the **Laujar de Andarax** wines of the eastern Alpujarras, always worth trying.

is Spain's version of the French Appellation Contrôlée regulating grape varieties and region of origin.

Dining out away from the larger towns and cities your choice of wine (especially in remoter *ventas*) will be severely limited. One brand of Rioja that seems to find its way into the most out-of-the-way places, however, is Faustino (see previous page) and this is usually a reliable standby to ask for if an establishment has no wine list. Busier *ventas* and restaurants with a healthy reputation, however, usually have well-stocked cellars and will only be too pleased to let you peruse their *carta de vinos*. In Andalucía you will often be asked in restaurants – especially at lunch times in summer – if you would like your wine "con Casera". This is a brand of lemonade (La Casera) which many *andaluzes* use to dilute the wine, turning it into a "spritzer". This combination is also a legitimate bar drink called *tinto de verano* where red wine is mixed with soda or lemonade and makes a great summer refresher. Equally refreshing, though often deceptively strong, is **sangría**, a wine-and-fruit punch which you'll come across at fiestas and in tourist bars.

In a bar, a small glass of wine will generally cost around €0.50–1.50 depending on location (rural bars are usually much cheaper than city places); in a restaurant, if wine is not included in the *menú*, prices start at around €3–5 a bottle in basic establishments but at anywhere with pretensions you're looking at paying at least €8 for a decent bottle and significantly more if you start fancying the vintage stuff. If wine is included, you'll usually get a whole bottle for two people, a *media botella* (a third to a half of a litre) for one. Be on your guard for skinflint establishments which may try to get away with serving you a single glass to comply with the "including wine" offer, thus obliging you to buy a bottle on top. Sadly, many coastal resort restaurants are now tending to cut the "free" wine from their *menús* – although the tradition continues inland – and this seems to have been accelerated since the arrival of the euro currency.

Sherry

The classic Andalucian wine is **sherry** – *vino de jerez* – which is excellent, widely available

and consumed with gusto by *andaluzes*. Served chilled or at *bodega* temperature – a perfect drink to wash down tapas – like everything Spanish, it comes in a perplexing variety of forms. The main distinctions are between *fino* or *jerez seco* (dry sherry), *amontillado* (medium), and *oloroso* (full-bodied) or *jerez dulce* (sweet), and these are the terms you should use to order. Similar in the way they are made – though not identical in flavour – are Montilla and *manzanilla*, which are not fortified with alcohol as is the case with other *finos*. The first of these dry, sherry-like wines comes from the province of Córdoba, and the latter from Sanlúcar de Barrameda, part of the "sherry triangle" along with Jerez and El Puerto de Santa María. More information about these wines is given in the *Guide* under each production centre.

Beer

Cerveza, lager-type beer, is generally pretty good, though more expensive than wine. It comes in 200ml (*botellines*) or 330ml (*tercios*) bottles or, for about the same price, on tap – a *caña* of draught beer is a small glass, a *caña doble* larger. Many bartenders will assume you want a *doble* (especially in tourist areas), so if you don't, say so. Simply asking for *un tubo* (a tube-shaped glass holding roughly half a pint) avoids these complications. Andalucía's main brand is Cruz Campo, produced in Sevilla and now part of the Heineken group, which is also the best beer in Spain, easily surpassing the heavily marketed San Miguel. Cruz Campo is served on draught just about everywhere, although "foreign" brands such as the Castilian Mahou and Aguila or the ubiquitously produced Estrella Dorada are making inroads. Granada's Alhambra beer (particularly the superb Alhambra 1925 special brew) and Jaén's Alcázar – rarely seen outside their home provinces – are others to look out for. A great summer refresher is a beer shandy – "*clara con blanco*".

Spirits and liqueurs

In mid-afternoon – or even at breakfast – many Spaniards take a *copa* of **liqueur** with their coffee (for that matter many

Spaniards drink wine and beer at breakfast, too). One of the best is *anís* (like Pernod) – in its respectable guise, whose coarser brother appears at romerías and fiestas as the often lethally potent *aguardiente* firewater. Slightly more palatable perhaps is *pacharán*, which, as well as being highly popular across the peninsula, is a favourite pre- or post-meal liqueur in Andalucía. Red in hue and made from sloes and *anís*, *pacharán* is best taken "on the rocks" (with a slice of lemon); Zoco is the leading brand. **Brandy** (so-called for legal reasons but also referred to as *coñac*) is another excellent choice and Andalucía is the main centre of production for Spain's leading brands. Produced by the sherry *bodegas*, the distinctive vanilla flavour is imparted by its maturation in old sherry casks. Try Magno, Soberano or Carlos III ("*tercero*") to get an idea of the variety, and Carlos I ("*primero*"), Lepanto and Gran Duque de Alba for a measure of the quality. One "imported" brandy worth looking out for is Mascaró, produced in Catalunya and resembling an armagnac. Most **spirits** are ordered by brand name, since there are generally less expensive Spanish equivalents for standard imports. Larios gin from Málaga, for instance, is about half the price of Gordon's gin. Specify "nacional" to avoid getting an expensive foreign brand. Spain also produces its own fairly indifferent versions of rum, vodka and whisky, the latter of which should be avoided at all costs. The measures of spirits are generous and usually glugged from the bottle into the glass in front of you with deft skill. **Mixed drinks** are universally known as *Cuba libre* or *Cubata*, though strictly speaking this is rum and Coke. Juice is *zumo*; orange, *naranja*; lemon, *limón*; tonic is *tónica*.

Soft drinks and hot drinks

Soft drinks are much the same as anywhere in the world, but local favourites worth trying are *granizado* (slush) or *horchata* (a milky drink made from tiger nuts or almonds), sold from one of the street stalls that spring up everywhere in summer. You can also get these drinks from *horchaterías* and from *heladerías* (ice cream – *helado* – parlours). Although you can drink the **water** almost everywhere, it usually tastes better out of the bottle – inexpensive *agua mineral* comes either sparkling (*con gas*) or still (*sin gas*); Lanjarón from Las Alpujarras, Sierra de Cazorla from the sierra of the same name and Zambra from Córdoba are some of Andalucía's main brands.

Coffee – served in cafés, *heladerías* and bars – is invariably espresso, slightly bitter and, unless you specify otherwise, served black (*café solo*). If you want it white ask for *café cortado* (a small cup with a drop of milk) or *café con leche* (made with lots of hot milk). For a large cup ask for a *doble* or *grande*. Coffee is also frequently mixed with brandy, cognac or whisky, all such concoctions being called *carajillo*. Decaffeinated coffee (*descafeinado*) is increasingly available in many city bars, though in villages and towns you'll only find it in undistinguished sachet form or spooned from a jar at the back of the bar. A great summer refresher is *café helado* (or *café con hielo*): a cup of coffee accompanied by a glass of ice cubes. Pour the coffee onto the cubes – it cools instantly.

Tea (*té*) is also available at most bars, although Spaniards usually drink it black. If you want milk it's safest to ask afterwards, since ordering *té con leche* might well get you a glass of milk with a tea bag floating on top. *Manzanilla* (camomile, not to be confused with the sherry of the same name) is a popular herbal infusion served in most bars; *poleomenta* (mint tea), *tila* (lime) and *hierba luisa* (lemon verbena) are other refreshing herbal possibilities.

Communications

Communications in Andalucía, while improving, are still not up to the standards of northern Europe. Post offices are widely distributed in towns and villages across the region although opening hours in the latter are often limited to a couple of hours in the morning. The phone system is dominated by the European and South American telecommunications giant Telefonica, and the service offered from pay phones and home or business lines is generally good. For emailing home there are plenty of Internet cafés throughout the region.

Mail

Post offices (Correos) are generally found near the centre of towns and are normally open Monday to Friday 8am–noon or 1pm and 5–7.30pm (some also open on Saturday mornings), though big branches in large cities may have considerably longer hours and do not usually close at midday. Except in the cities there's only one post office in each town, and queues can be long: **stamps** (*sellos*) are also sold at *estancos* (tobacconists) – look out for the brown and yellow "Tabac" sign.

You can have letters sent **poste restante** to any Spanish post office: they should be addressed (preferably with surname underlined and in capitals) to "Lista de Correos", followed by the name of the town and province. To collect, take your passport and, if you're expecting mail, ask the clerk to check under all of your names – letters are often filed under first or middle names.

American Express in Málaga, Sevilla and Granada will hold mail for at least a month for customers, and have windows for mail pickup.

Outbound mail is reasonably reliable, with letters or cards taking around five days to a week to the UK, a week to ten days to North America and up to two weeks for Australia and New Zealand.

Phones

Spanish **public phones** work well and have instructions in English (obtained by pressing the language button with a flag symbol). If you can't find one, many bars also have pay phones you can use. Cabins and other phones have been adapted to take the euro but you're best off buying a phone card (*tarjeta telefónica*, available from a *kiosko* or *estanco*) of €6 or €12, which avoids the hassles of finding the right change. One tip is to never buy the €12 cards but only the €6 units, as should the card prove faulty (which happens) you will spend the rest of your life trying to get the company to refund you. All cabins should display instructions in a variety of languages. Spanish provincial (and some overseas) dialling codes are displayed in the cabins. The ringing tone is long, engaged is shorter and rapid; the standard Spanish response is "*dígame*" ("speak to me") often abbreviated to "*diga*" or the even more laconic "*sí*".

For **international calls**, you can use almost any street cabin (marked *teléfono internacional*) or go to a *locutorio*, an office where you pay afterwards. Phoning within Spain is cheaper after 8pm and all weekend for metropolitan and inter-provincial calls. International rates are slightly cheaper between midnight and 8am; the reduced rates apply all day on Saturday and Sunday. If you're using a cabin to call abroad and don't use a phone card, you're best off putting at least €2 in to ensure a connection.

Mobile phones

If you want to use your **mobile phone** in Spain, you'll need to check with your phone provider whether it will work abroad, and what the call charges are. In the UK you may have to inform your phone provider before going abroad to get international access switched on. You are likely to be charged extra for incoming calls when abroad, as the people calling you will be paying the usual rate. If you want to retrieve messages while you're away, you'll have to ask your provider for a new access code, as your home one is unlikely to work abroad. For further information about using your phone abroad, check out ⓦwww.telecomsadvice.org.uk/features/using_your_mobile_abroad.htm.

Unless you have a **tri-band phone**, it is unlikely that a mobile bought for use in the US will work outside the States. For details of which mobiles will work outside the US, contact your mobile service provider. Most mobiles in Australia and New Zealand use GSM, the system used in Spain, and should work fine.

Useful telephone numbers

Alarm call ☎096
Directory Enquiries ☎1003
Domestic Operator ☎1009
International Operator ☎1008 (Europe)
International Operator ☎1005 (rest of world)
Time ☎093
Weather ☎906 365 365

Calling abroad from Spain

To Britain ☎00 44 + area code minus first 0 + number.
To Ireland ☎00 353 + area code minus first 0 + number.
To the US and Canada ☎00 1 + area code + number.
To Australia ☎00 61 + area code minus first 0 + number.
To New Zealand ☎00 64 + area code minus first 0 + number.

Calling Spain from abroad

From Britain ☎00 + 34 + number.
From Ireland ☎00 + 34 + number.
From the US and Canada ☎011 + 34 + number.
From Australia ☎0011 + 34 + number.
From New Zealand ☎00 + 34 + number.

The Internet

The **Internet** has made great inroads into Spanish life and access is widely available at **Internet cafés** (more commonly referred to as *cibercafés* in Spanish), some computer shops and *locutorios* throughout Andalucía. Prices vary; in cities hourly rates can be as little as €1.50, rising to around €5 in some smaller towns and villages. For details of useful websites on Andalucía and Spain, see p.40.

One of the best ways to keep in touch while travelling is to sign up for a free **Internet email** address that can be accessed from anywhere, for example YahooMail or Hotmail – accessible through ⓦwww.yahoo .com and ⓦwww.hotmail.com. Once you've set up an account, you can use these sites to pick up and send mail from any Internet café or hotel with Internet access.

The ⓦwww.kropka.com site gives details of how to plug in your laptop when abroad, phone country codes around the world, and information about electrical systems in different countries.

The media

Your exposure to the local media is mostly going to be in bars or your hotel, where local and national newspapers are usually available for customers, although in many cases these will be one of the several devoted to football. Otherwise, you're rarely far from a kiosk, the larger of which stock all Spanish and – in major cities and along the Costa del Sol – many English-language publications. Spanish TV isn't renowned for its quality and in most bars, restaurants and *ventas* you'll see as much as you're ever likely to want. Surprisingly, radio is more popular than TV in Andalucía and there is a wide variety of stations.

The press

Andalucians, in line with the Spanish generally, are not great devourers of newsprint and none of the Spanish **national papers** has a circulation much above 400,000. The best of these is *El País* – liberal-left, and one of the few with much serious analysis or foreign news coverage; its daily Andalucía supplement is also a good source of information on the region. In the last decade or so the appearance of the centre-right *El Mundo* (also with a daily Andalucía section) has provided competition for *El País* as a serious centrist newspaper and both have good arts and "what's on" listings. The rest are mostly well to the right, notably the dated-format

ABC, solidly old-order with a hard moral line against divorce and abortion, although Barcelona's *La Vanguardia* (available in Andalucía) is centrist and solid.

With a smattering of Spanish by far the most entertaining breakfast read are Andalucía's **regional papers**. Here the scandals and stories from around the parish pump can give the outsider fascinating and often amusing insights into the communities encountered, besides providing handy information on festivals and entertainment. There's always something of interest in most of the local papers but if you're in or around Cádiz the *Diario de Cádiz* – in keeping with the province's liberal traditions – has one of the liveliest readers' letters pages in the region, whilst *El Diario de Sevilla* does a similar job of monitoring Sevilla's pulse. Córdoba's *Córdoba*, Málaga's *Sur* and Granada's *Ideal* are others to look out for. The website ⓦ www.prensaescrita.com/andalucia.php has the web addresses of most of Andalucía's daily papers. Best for keeping up with sport (including foreign football results) are the Madrid **sports papers** *As* and *Marca* and the Catalan *El Mundo Deportivo*, all widely available in Andalucía, which has a phenomenal number of supporters of the Madrid and Barcelona teams.

British newspapers and the *International Herald Tribune* (with a daily insert of Spanish news culled from *El País*) are on sale in most large cities and resorts. The main resort areas have their own English-language publications catering to the vast army of (largely elderly) expats. Along the Costa del Sol, *Sur in English* is a free Friday publication by the Málaga daily, *Sur*, cashing in on the same market; both this and the Spanish edition's small ads section can be good for picking up odd jobs such as bar work and it carries details of local events and entertainment.

TV and radio

You'll inadvertently catch more TV than you expect sitting in bars and restaurants as only the snootiest establishments seem able to function without a set blaring in one corner – usually not being watched or listened to by anybody. On the whole the output is a fairly entertaining mix of ghastly **game** and **chat shows**, **foreign-language films** and

TV series dubbed into Spanish. **Soaps** are a particular speciality, either South American *telenovelas* or home-produced *crónicas rosas* (sentimental tearjearkers) which take up a fair chunk of daytime programming. Well-travelled British, US and Australian exports also feature strongly and hit series such as the UK's *Big Brother* and *Fame Academy* have proved just as popular in their Iberian versions, *Gran Hermano* and *Operación Triunfo*. Live **bullfights** are broadcast throughout most of the summer and no one expresses the slightest quiver of concern that children may be watching. **News programmes**, particularly on the state channels, are comprehensive, with wide coverage given to foreign news and the arts. There are two state channels, TVE1 and TVE2, plus the private Antena 3 and Telecinco. Andalucía also has its own Canal Sur. Canal Plus (often written as Canal+) is a pay-per-view cable company showing mainly films and sport (including Spanish Division One and English Premiership football matches). Most of Andalucía's upmarket hotels are now equipped with **satellite TV** giving access to channels such as BBC World, CNN and Sky. Sports fans are well catered for, with regular live coverage of football and basketball matches – in the **football season**, you can watch two or more live matches a week in most bars or hotel rooms. Since the death of Franco the reaction against any form of censorship has meant that both terrestrial and satellite TV channels broadcast hardcore pornography with little hindrance; in stark contrast to places such as the UK and Ireland the general Spanish attitude is blasé, so don't be surprised to find it on at least one of your hotel's TV channels.

Radio

Andalucians are dedicated **radio** listeners and surprisingly spend more time listening in than almost any other European region. Unlike the TV system, radio has numerous high-quality national and regional, public and private stations broadcasting to a daily audience averaging 16 million people. If you're going to be getting around by car, twiddling the dial will soon give you an idea of what's available on the Spanish broadcasting system, where many Spaniards pick up their daily fix of current affairs, especially on the early-morning and late-evening news programmes. **Stations** to listen out for are the state-owned Radio Nacional de España (RNE; AM) whose excellent classical station RNE 2 plays classical music (with minimal talk) around the clock. For more youthful listeners Onda Cero (FM) and Cadena Cuarenta (FM) are pop stations with big followings. There are a number of **English-language stations** along the Costa del Sol such as Central (FM) and Radio Coastline (FM) with similar middle-of-the-road music and talk formats, and Radio Gibraltar (FM) puts out English news bulletins. If you have a radio which picks up short-wave you can tune in to the **BBC World Service** (⊛ www.bbc.co.uk/worldservice) broadcasting in English for most of the day on several frequencies (12095, 9760, 9410, 7325, 6195, 5975 and 3955 Khz). You may also be able to receive **Voice of America** (⊛ www.voa.gov) and American Forces' stations, especially near to US bases such as Rota in Cádiz.

Opening hours and public holidays

Almost everything in Andalucía – shops, museums, churches, tourist offices – closes for a siesta of at least two hours (and usually three to four) in the hottest part of the day. There's a lot of variation (supermarkets in major towns tend to stay open longer) but basic summer working hours are 9.30am–1.30pm and 5.30–7.30pm. Certain shops (such as El Corte Inglés) stay open all day, and in many city companies there is a creeping movement towards northern European working hours. Nevertheless, you'll get far less aggravated if you accept that afternoons are best spent asleep, or in a bar, or both.

State-owned **museums** and **monuments**, with some exceptions, follow the rule above, with a break between around 1.30pm and 4.30pm. Their summer schedules are listed in the *Guide*; watch out for Sundays (most open mornings only) and Mondays (most closed all day). **Admission charges** vary, but there's usually a big reduction or free entrance if you show an ISIC card. Anywhere run by the Patrimonio Nacional, the national organization which preserves monuments, is free to EU citizens on Wednesday – you'll need your passport to prove your nationality. Most of the sites and museums administered by the Junta de Andalucía are free to EU citizens on production of an identity card (or passport for UK visitors).

Getting into **churches** can present more of a problem. The really important ones, including the majority of cathedrals, operate in much the same way as museums and almost always have some entry charge to see their most valued treasures and paintings, or their cloisters. Other churches, though, are usually kept locked, opening only for worship in the early morning and/or the evening (around 7–9pm). To see them at other times you'll have to find someone with a key. This is time-consuming but rarely difficult, since a *sacristán* or custodian almost always lives nearby and most people will know where to direct you. You're expected to give a small tip, or donation. For all churches "decorous" dress is required, ie no garish beach shorts (some churches also exclude normal shorts and Bermudas), bare shoulders, and so on.

Public holidays

Public holidays can (and will) disrupt your plans at some stage. Alongside the national and regional holidays (see overleaf) there are scores of local fiestas, different in every town and village, but usually marking the saint's day (see below for more on this). Any of them will mean that everything except bars, restaurants and *hostales* and so on locks its doors. August is Spain's own holiday month, when many of the larger inland cities are semi-deserted, and shops and restaurants, and occasionally museums, may close. Be particularly aware of the Feast of the Assumption on August 15 – especially if you are travelling independently. It's the major summer holiday (as is the nearest weekend to it) and it can prove nearly impossible to find a free bed in the more popular coastal and mountain resorts at this time and in plenty of other places, too; similarly, seats on planes, trains and buses should be booked in advance. The same applies to finding accommodation on Good Friday or the rest of Semana Santa (Holy Week) in the major cities. Outside of these periods there is usually no great problem.

Main public holidays

January 1 Año Nuevo (New Year's Day)
January 6 Epifanía (Epiphany)
February 28 Día de Andalucía (Andalucía Day)
Good Friday Viernes Santo
Easter Sunday Domingo de la Resurrección
Easter Monday Lunes de Pascua
May 1 Fiesta de Trabajo (Labour Day)
Early or mid-June Corpus Christi
June 24 Día de San Juan (the king's name-saint)
July 25 Día de Santiago (Spain's patron saint)
August 15 La Asunción (Assumption of the Virgin)
October 12 Día de la Hispanidad (National Day)
November 1 Todos Santos (All Saints' Day)
December 6 Día de la Constitución (Constitution Day)
December 8 La Inmaculada Concepción (Immaculate Conception)
December 25 Navidad (Christmas Day)

Fiestas

It's hard to beat the experience of arriving in some small village, expecting no more than a bed for the night, to discover the streets decked out with flags and streamers, spectacular fireworks lighting up the sky, a band playing in the plaza and the entire population out celebrating the local fiesta.

Everywhere in Andalucía, from the tiniest hamlet to the great cities, will take at least one day off a year to devote to partying. Usually it's the local saint's day, but there are celebrations, too, of harvests, of deliverance from the Moors, of safe return from the sea – any excuse will do.

Each festival has its own particular characteristics but there are facets common to them all. Horses, flamenco, fireworks and the guitar are essential parts of any celebration, usually accompanied by the downing of oceans of *fino* – which is probably why the sherry companies seem to provide most of the bunting. And along with the music there is always dancing, usually *sevillanas*, in traditional flamenco costume, and an immense spirit of enjoyment. The main event of most fiestas is a parade, either behind a revered holy image, or a more celebratory affair with fancy costumes and *gigantones*, grotesque giant carnival figures which terrorize children.

Although these festivals take place throughout the year – and it is often the obscure and unexpected event that proves to be most fun – there are certain occasions that stand out. Easter Week (**Semana Santa**) and **Corpus Christi** (in early June) are celebrated throughout Andalucía with magnificent religious processions. Easter, particularly, is worth trying to coincide with – head for Sevilla, Málaga, Granada or Córdoba, where huge *pasos*, floats of wildly theatrical religious scenes, are carried down the streets, accompanied by weirdly hooded penitents atoning for the year's misdeeds. And just as moving in their own more intimate way are the countless small town and village observances of Semana Santa with smaller processions, traditional customs and sometimes a Passion play.

Among the biggest and best-known of Andalucía's **other popular festivals** are: the Cádiz Carnaval (mid-February); Sevilla's enormous April Feria (a week at the end of the month); Jerez's Feria del Caballo (Horse Fair, April/May); the Romería del Roció, an extraordinary pilgrimage to El Roció near Huelva (arriving there on Whit Sunday); and Málaga's boisterous and good-humoured Feria (mid-August).

The list is potentially endless, and although you'll find more major events detailed below, we can't pretend that this is exhaustive. The Junta de Andalucía publishes an annual **Ferias y Fiestas de Andalucía** guide, available from local tourist offices. Outsiders are always welcome at these festivals, the one problem being that during any of the most popular (though usually not at the small town and village affairs) you'll find it difficult and expensive to find a bed. If you're planning to coincide with a major festival, try and book your accommodation well in advance.

Listed below are some of Andalucía's main fiestas, all worth trying to get to if you're going to be in the area around the time; more are listed under locations covered in the *Guide*. Note that saints' day festivals – indeed all Spanish celebrations – can vary in date, and are often observed over the weekend closest to the dates given.

January

1–2 Día de la Toma – celebration of the 1492 entry of the Reyes Católicos into the city – at Granada.
5 Cabalgata de los Reyes Magos – Epiphany parade at Málaga.
6 Romería de la Virgen del Mar – pilgrimage procession from Almería.
17 Romería del Ermita del Santo – similar event at Guadix.

February

1 San Cecilio – fiesta in Granada's traditionally gypsy quarter of Sacromonte.
Mid-month Carnaval – extravagant week-long

event (leading up to Lent) in all the Andalucían cities. Cádiz, above all, celebrates with fancy dress, flamenco, spectacular parades and street-singers' competitions.

March

5–15 El Puerto de Santa María (Cádiz) celebrates its *carnaval*.
Semana Santa (Holy Week) Following Palm Sunday, this has its most elaborate and dramatic celebrations in Andalucía. You'll find moving and memorable processions of floats and penitents at (in descending order of importance) Sevilla, Málaga, Granada and Córdoba, and to a lesser extent in smaller towns such as Jerez, Arcos, Baeza and Úbeda. All culminate with the full drama of the Passion on Good Friday, with Easter Day itself more of a family occasion.

April

Last week (2 weeks after Easter, usually in April, occasionally May; check with the tourist office). Week-long Feria de Abril at Sevilla: the largest fair in Spain, a little refined in the way of the city, but an extraordinary event nonetheless. A small April fair – featuring bull-running – is held in Vejer.
Last Sunday Romería de Nuestra Señora de la Cabeza at Andujar (Jaén). Three days of celebrations culminate in a huge procession to the sanctuary of the Virgin in the Sierra Morena.

May

1–2 Romería de Nuestra Señora de la Estrella at Navas de San Juan – Jaén Province's most important pilgrimage.
3 "Moors and Christians" carnival at Pampaneira (Alpujarras).
First two weeks Cruces de Mayo (Festival of the Patios) in Córdoba – celebrates the Holy Cross and includes a competition for the prettiest patio and numerous events and concerts organized by the local city council.
Early May (usually the week after Sevilla's fair). Somewhat aristocratic Horse Fair at Jerez de la Frontera.
17 San Isidro Romería at Setenil (Cádiz).
Pentecost (7 weeks after Easter). Romería del Rocío – Spain's biggest: a million often inebriated pilgrims in horse-drawn carriages and processions converge on El Rocío (Huelva) from all over the south.
Corpus Christi (variable – Thursday after Trinity). Bullfights and festivities at Granada, Sevilla, Ronda, Vejer and Zahara de la Sierra. At Sevilla, Los Seises (Six Choirboys) perform a dance before the altar of the cathedral.

Third weekend Romería de Santa Eulalia at Almonaster La Real in the Sierra de Aracena – pilgrimage, fireworks, parades and fandangos in honour of the village's patron saint.

Last week Feria de la Manzanilla, Sanlúcar de Barrameda. Prolonged binge to celebrate the town's major product which is used to wash down huge quantities of seafood whilst watching flamenco and sporting events from beachfront casetas.

June

Second week Feria de San Bernabé at Marbella – often spectacular since this is the richest town in Andalucía.

13–14 Fiestas Patronales de San Antonio at Trevélez (Alpujarras) – includes mock battles between Moors and Christians.

23–24 Candelas de San Juan – bonfires and effigies at Vejer and elsewhere.

23–26 Feria of Alhaurín de la Torre (Málaga) – processions, giants and an important flamenco competition.

30 Conil (Cádiz) feria.

End June/early July International Festival of Music and Dance: major dance groups, chamber orchestras and flamenco artistes perform in Granada's Alhambra palace, Generalife and Carlos V palace.

July

Early July International Guitar Festival at Córdoba – brings together top international acts from classical, flamenco and Latin American music.

9–14 Around feast of San Francisco Solano, Montilla (Córdoba) celebrates its annual feria.

End of July Almería's Virgen del Mar summer fiesta – parades, horse-riding events and usually a handful of major jazz and rock concerts in its Plaza Vieja.

August

First week Berja (Almería) holds its annual fiesta in honour of the Virgin of Gádor.

3 Colombinas at Huelva celebrate Columbus's voyages of discovery with a fiesta.

5 Trevélez (Granadan Alpujarras) observes a midnight romería to Mulhacén.

13–21 Feria de Málaga – one of Andalucía's most enjoyable fiestas for visitors, who are heartily welcomed by the ebullient *malagueños*.

15 Ascension of the Virgin – fair with casetas (dance tents) at Vejer and throughout Andalucía.

15 Noche del Vino at Competa (Málaga) – a riotous wine festival with dancing, singing and endless drinking.

17–20 The first cycle of horse races along Sanlúcar de Barrameda's beach, with heavy official and

unofficial betting; the second tournament takes place exactly a week later.

19–21 Vendimia – grape harvest fiesta at Montilla (Córdoba).

Third week The Algeciras fair and fiesta.

Third weekend Fiesta de San Mamés at Aroche (Huelva) in the extremities of the Sierra de Aracena – unpretentious and great fun, everything a village fiesta should be.

22–25 Feria de Grazalema (Cádiz).

23–25 Guadalquivir festival at Sanlúcar de Barrameda – bullfights and an important flamenco competition.

25–30 Fiestas Patronales in honour of San Agustín at Mojácar (Almería).

September

6 El Cascamorras – annual feria at Baza (Granada) where the Cascamorras or interloper from nearby Guadix attempts to make off with their Virgen and is doused in dirty oil for his pains.

7 Romería del Cristo de la Yedra at Baeza (Jaén) – singing and dancing in the streets.

7–14 Feria de la Moscatel/Feria de Nuestra Señora de Regla at Chipiona (Cádiz). Includes bull-running, flamenco tournaments and much wine-swilling to acclaim the sweet sherry grape grown hereabouts.

8 Romería de Nuestra Señora de los Ángeles at Alajar (Huelva) – lots of colour and horse races to the peak sanctuary of Arias Montano.

8–9 Fiesta de la Virgen de la Cabeza at Almuñecar (Granada).

First/second week Vendimia (celebration of the vintage) at Jerez – starts with the blessing of the new grapes, after which everyone gets sozzled on the old.

6–13 Celebration of the Virgen de la Luz in Tarifa – street processions and horse riding.

First two weeks Ronda bursts into life with a feria, flamenco contests and the Corrida Goyesca, bullfights in eighteenth-century dress.

24–25 Día del Señor (Lord's Day) at Orgiva (Granada) – celebrated with impressive fireworks and processions.

29 Úbeda's (Jaén) Fiesta de San Miguel with a fair and *casetas*.

October

1 Fiesta de San Miguel in Granada's Albaicín quarter and dozens of other towns, including Torremolinos.

6–12 Feria del Rosario – Fuengirola horse-riding events and flamenco.

15–23 Feria de San Lucas – Jaén's major fiesta, dating back to the fifteenth century.

November

1 Todos Los Santos (All Saints Day) Celebrated throughout Andalucía with church services and processions to graveyards.

December

28 Fiesta de los Verdiales/Santos Innocentes

Various towns and villages of Málaga's mountain districts celebrate Spain's equivalent of April Fool's Day with dances, pulsating Moorish-inspired music and outlandish headdress. Good places to see it include Comares, Almogía, Casabermeja in the Axarquía to the east of Málaga and the Venta de San Cayetano, Puerto de la Torre, slightly to the northwest.

Bullfights

Bullfights are an integral part of many Spanish festivals. In Andalucía, especially, any village that can afford it will put on a corrida for an afternoon, while in big cities like Sevilla, the main festivals are accompanied by a week-long (or more) season of prestige fights.

Los Toros (or **La Lidia**), as Spaniards refer to bullfighting, is big business. Each year an estimated 24,000 bulls are killed before a live audience of over thirty million (with many more watching on television). It is said that 150,000 people are involved, in some way, in the industry, and the top performers, the *matadores*, are major earners, on a par with the country's biggest pop stars. There is some **opposition** to the activity from animal welfare groups but it is not widespread: if Spaniards tell you that bullfighting is controversial, they are likely to be referring to practices in the trade. That said, the city of Barcelona recently outlawed bullfighting as did the Canary Islands. In recent years, bullfighting critics (whom you will find on the arts pages of the newspapers) have been expressing their perennial outrage at the widespread but illegal shaving of bulls' horns prior to the *corrida*. Bulls' horns are as sensitive as fingernails, and shaving just a few millimetres deters the animal from charging; they affect the creature's balance, too, reducing the danger for the matador still further.

Notwithstanding such abuse (and there is plenty more), Los Toros maintains its loyal aficionados throughout the country. Indeed, in some areas they are on the rise, with the elaborate language of the *corrida* quite a cult among the young, as the days of Franco's patronage of bullfighting are forgotten, and TV stations pay big money for major events. To **aficionados** (a word that implies more knowledge and appreciation than "fan"), the bulls are a culture and a ritual – one in which the emphasis is on the way man and bull "perform" together – in which the *arte* (art) is at issue rather than the cruelty. If pressed on the issue of the slaughter of an animal, they generally fail to understand. Fighting bulls are, they will tell you, bred for the industry; compared to beasts bred for the abattoir they live a pampered and idyllic life before they are killed; and, if the bullfight went, so too would the bulls.

Whether you attend a *corrida*, obviously, is down to your own feelings and ethics. If you spend any time at all in Spain during the season (which runs from March to Oct), you will encounter Los Toros, at least on a bar TV, and that will as likely as not make up your mind. If you decide to go, try to see the biggest and most prestigious that is on, in a major city, where star performers are likely to despatch the bulls with "*arte*" and a successful, "clean" kill. This happens much less frequently than many aficionados would have you believe and the beginners' fights, or *novilladas*, are often little more than a gruesome repetition of botched jobs. Even in the senior *corridas*, there are few sights worse than a *matador* making a prolonged and messy kill, while the audience whistles its disgust. Established and popular **matadores** include Enrique Ponce, César Rincón, Vicente Barrera, Espartaco, Finito de Córdoba, Sevilla's golden boy Antonio Bareas, the teenage sensation El Juli and, at the opposite end of the age range, the recently retired Curro Romero, who was still wielding the *capote* (cape) at the ripe age of 68. Two recent stars in the headlines are El Cordobés – a young pretender of spectacular technique who claims to be his legendary namesake's illegitimate son – and Cristina Sánchez, the first **woman torero** to make it into the top flight for some time. Although there have been women *matadores* since the eighteenth century, she is the first woman to have been carried shoulder high through the *puerta grande* of Las Ventas, the prestigious Madrid ring – a distinction awarded to few of her male peers. Sánchez's telling comment later was that fighting bulls is easy compared to fighting the macho sexist prejudice she has encountered throughout the whole business, and many leading *matadores* such as Jesulin de Ubrique ("It is unnatural for women to fight, they should be in the kitchen") and Enrique Ponce refuse to appear on the same bill as a woman. This prejudice led to Sánchez retiring in disgust in 1999 at the age of 27, when she found it increasingly difficult to get high-status fights due to the continuing refusal of many big names to share a ring with her. Sánchez's departure, however, has not discouraged others and *malagueña* Mari Paz Vega is the latest woman *torero* – who

has also appeared at Las Ventas – to make waves in this masculine world.

Perhaps the most exciting and skilful performances of all are by mounted *matadores*, or **rejoneadores** as they are known (from *rejón*, "lance"); this is the oldest form of *corrida*, developed at Ronda in the seventeenth century. However, they still dismount to despatch the bull.

A complete **guide to bullfighting** with exhaustive links can be found at ⓦwww.mundo-taurino.org.

The corrida

The **corrida** begins with a procession, to the accompaniment of a *paso doble* by the band. Leading the procession are two *alguacilillos* or "constables", on horseback and in traditional costume, followed by the three *matadores*, who will each fight two bulls, and their *cuadrillas*, their personal "team", each comprising two mounted *picadores* and three *banderilleros*. At the back are the mule teams who will drag off the dead bulls. The ensuing *corrida* takes the form of a drama in three acts or stages (called **suertes**).

Once the ring is empty, the **alguacillo** opens the *toril* (the bulls' enclosure) and the first bull (weighing 500–600kg) appears – a moment of great physical beauty – to be "tested" by the *matador* or his *banderilleros* using pink and gold capes. These preliminaries conducted (and they can be short, if the bull is ferocious), the **suerte de picar** ensues, in which the **picadores** ride out and take up position at opposite sides of the ring, while the bull is distracted by other *toreros*. Once they are in place, the bull is made to charge one of the horses, at which moment the *picador* drives his short-pointed lance into the bull's neck, while it tries to toss his padded and blindfolded (on the right eye) mount. The whole purpose here is to tire and weaken the bull's powerful neck and shoulder muscles, thus forcing him to lower his head – without which (as was discovered at the very outset of the *corrida*) it would be impossibly dangerous to fight and kill on foot. This is repeated up to three times, until the horn sounds for the *picadores* to leave. For most neutral spectators, it is the least acceptable and most squalid stage of the proceedings, and it is clearly not a pleasant experience for the horses, their ears stuffed with rags to shut out the noise of the bull and spectators, and their vocal cords cut to prevent any terrified cries from alarming the crowd.

The next stage, the **suerte de banderillas**, involves the placing of three sets of *banderillas* (barbed darts mounted on coloured shafts) into the bull's shoulders. Each of the three **banderilleros** delivers these in turn, attracting the bull's attention with the movement of his own body rather than a cape, and deftly placing the *banderillas* whilst both he and the bull are running towards each other. He then runs to safety out of the bull's vision, sometimes with the assistance of his colleagues, but occasionally a canny animal will set off in pursuit of his tormentor, often resulting in an undignified leap over the *barrera* to escape the charging horns.

Once the *banderillas* have been placed, the **suerte de matar** begins, and the **matador** enters the ring alone, having exchanged his pink and gold cape for the red *muleta*. He (or she) salutes the president and then dedicates the bull either to an individual, to whom he gives his hat, or to the audience, by placing his hat in the centre of the ring. It is in this part of the *corrida* that judgements are made and the performance is focused, as the *matador* displays his skills on the (by now exhausted) bull. He uses the movements of the cape to attract the bull, while his body remains still. If he does well, the band will start to play, while the crowd *olé* each pass. This stage lasts around ten minutes and ends with the kill. The *matador* attempts to get the bull into a position where he can drive a sword between its shoulders and through to the heart for a *coup de grâce*. In practice, they rarely succeed

in this, instead taking a second sword, the *descabello*, crossed at the end, to cut the bull's spinal cord; this causes instant death. If things get really bad and he can't finish the job with this, then he will instruct one of his *cuadrilla* to end the business with a *puntilla*, a dagger stabbed into the base of the beast's skull. By this time the crowd will be whistling their derision whilst "the whole spectacle of theatre, courage and art is reduced to the level of a knacker's yard", as one commentator vividly described it.

Alternatively, if the audience are impressed by the *matador*'s performance, they will wave their handkerchiefs and shout for an award to be made by the president. He can award one or both ears, and a tail – the better the display, the more pieces the *matador* gets – while if he has excelled himself, he will be carried shoulder high out of the ring by the crowd, through the *puerta grande*, the main door, which is normally kept locked. The bull, too, may be applauded for its performance, as it is dragged out by the mule team.

Tickets for *corridas* in the major city *plazas de toros* start at around €20 for a *sol* seat (see below) rising to €100 and above for the prime seats at prestigious fights in rings such as Sevilla's Maestranza. The cheapest seats are *gradas*, the highest rows at the back, from where you can see everything that happens without too much of the detail; the front rows are known as the *barreras*. Seats are also divided into *sol* (sun), *sombra* (shade), and *sol y sombra* (shaded after a while), though these distinctions have become less relevant as more bullfights start later in the day, at 6 or 7pm, rather than the traditional 5pm. The *sombra* seats are more expensive – not so much for the spectators' personal comfort but because most of the action takes place in the shade. Tickets for *novilladas* (novice fights with young bulls) are much cheaper, costing €10–40, and are often given away free by bars or agents outside the bullring prior to the *corrida* if there hasn't been much demand (which often happens).

On the way in, you can rent cushions – two hours sitting on concrete is not much fun. They also count as something to toss in the ring when there's an especially awful performance – as frequently happens. Beer and soft drinks are sold inside.

Football

To foreigners, the bullfight is easily the most celebrated of Spain's spectacles but in terms of popular support in modern Spain, however, it ranks far below fútbol. If you want the excitement of a genuinely Spanish afternoon out, a football stadium will usually have more passion than anything you'll find in the Plaza de Toros.

For many years, the country's two dominant teams have been Real Madrid and F.C. Barcelona, and these have shared the League and Cup honours more often than is healthy. Recently though, the big two have faced a bit more opposition than usual from clubs like Valencia (champions in 2002), Real Sociedad (from San Sebastián) and new forces Deportivo La Coruña (champions in 2000) and Celta Vigo (both from Galicia).

Sevilla are the main team in Andalucía, but have only recently returned to the top flight following an ignominious three seasons in the Second Division. The other Andalucian First Division sides with pretensions are **Real Betis**, Sevilla's other club who have been outperforming their fierce rival in recent seasons, **Málaga** who returned to the First Division in 1999 after a decade away, and **Cádiz** who rejoined the top flight in 2005 after 14 years in the lower leagues. The region's highest placed teams outside the first division are currently **Xerex** (from Jerez), **Polideportivo Ejido** (from El Ejido in Almería), **Almería**, and **Recreativo Huelva** – the latter Spain's oldest club. See the "Listings" section of each provincial capital for details and grounds of the major teams.

With the exception of a few important games – such as when either of the big two plays Sevilla or the two Sevilla teams play their derbys – tickets are pretty easy to get; they start at around €15 for average First Division games but get close to double this when *Real* or *Barca* are in town. Trouble is very rare: English fans, in particular, will be amazed at the easy-going family atmosphere and mixed sex crowds. And August is a surprisingly good time to catch games since there's a glut of warm-up matches for the new season, often involving top foreign clubs.

If you don't go to a game, the atmosphere can be pretty good watching on TV in a local bar, especially in a city whose team is playing away. Many bars advertise the matches they screen, which, if they have satellite connections, can include Sunday afternoon English League and Cup games.

Music

Andalucía is the home of much Spanish traditional music and you should try to catch as much as you can while in the region. At the numerous fiestas and romerías (see p.68) you can see many of Andalucía's best performers; other likely venues are listed in the body of the Guide.

Traditional **flamenco** (see Contexts, p.658), Spain's most famous sound, is best witnessed in its native Andalucía, and particularly at one of the major fiestas. There are also some specifically flamenco festivals in the summer, most notably at Córdoba, Jerez and around Granada. Clubs and bars which feature flamenco performers tend on the whole to be expensive and tourist-oriented, while the traditional **peñas** (clubs) are often members-only affairs. However, it is possible to find accessible places which cater for aficionados, and in Andalucía itself almost any flamenco guitarist you come across is likely to be extremely good – just watch the cost of the drinks. In recent years, there has been an exciting development in the shape of new flamenco bands, some of which have attempted to introduce jazz, rock and African elements into their music. Names to watch out for are Raimondo Amador, Martirio, rock-fusionist Rosario, Maghreb-roots band Radio Tarifa as well as the more established Ketama and Pata Negra, two bands featured on the recommended Hannibal Records compilation *Los Jovenes Flamencos*.

If you happen to be in the province of Málaga over Christmas you might try and catch the **Verdiales** festival on December 28 at the Venta Puerta de la Torre in the Axarquía (see p.129), located on the A6113 near Almogia. It's a frenetic and exciting form of flamenco played on guitars, lutes, castanets, violins, cymbals and tambourines by groups of musicians called *pandas* which may have their roots in the celebration of the olive harvest in Roman times (ancient ceramic sculptures have been found depicting musicians with similar instruments). *Panda* bands also stage performances in their home villages (Almogia, Montes and Comares) at other times of the year and these are well worth trying to get to. Throughout Andalucía between about December 18 and January 3, look out for performances in local churches of **villancicos**. These are Christmas carols in local style – they can be flamenco, waltz or polyphonic – and are sung by fairly large *coral/rondalla* groups of instrumentalists and vocalists. When they're good they're an extremely beautiful spectacle.

Rock music in Spain may tend to follow British and American trends, but the scene is considerably livelier – and less slavishly derivative – than in almost any other West European country, at its best drawing from a broad range of influences in which traditional Spanish and Latin American rhythms play a major part. There are some excellent home-grown bands and regular gigs in most of the big cities. In Andalucía, the *malagueño* combo Danza Invisible have had some catchy hits and the long list of artists from Sevilla includes Arrajatabla and Kiko Veneno. Veneno's sporadic albums contain clever, literate, utterly Spanish rock songs and come highly recommended.

Thanks to Spain's relatively large expatriate populations, there are also good places to hear **Latin American** and **African** music – again, keep your eye out for posters and check the club and concert listings in the local papers. **Jazz** also has a considerable following, with most of Andalucía's venues located in the cities, although they tend to close down in August; one summer jazz festival of note is that of Almuñecar, held in July and often featuring international big names. Worth checking out, too, is the International Festival of Guitar in Córdoba (early July), where most of the great classical guitarists put in an appearance along with exponents of Latin American and flamenco styles. Among its more adventurous practitioners – merging flamenco (to the outrage of purists) with modern jazz – look out especially for the brilliant *córdobes*, Paco de Lucía.

All of Spain's major music **festivals** are listed on the Internet at Ⓦwww.festivals .com, and Ⓦwww.andalucia.org/flamenco and Ⓦwww.classicalguitarmidi.com/history /flamenco are good sources of information on flamenco with plenty of links.

Trouble, the police and sexual harassment

While you're unlikely to encounter any trouble during the course of your visit, it's worth remembering that the Spanish police, polite enough in the usual course of events, can be extremely unpleasant if you get on the wrong side of them.

Avoiding trouble

Almost all the problems tourists encounter are to do with **petty crime** – pickpocketing and bag-snatching – rather than more serious physical confrontations, so it's as well to be on your guard and know where your possessions are at all times. Sensible **precautions** include: carrying bags slung across your neck, not over your shoulder; having photocopies of your passport and leaving passport and air tickets in the hotel safe; noting down travellers' cheque and credit card numbers; and carrying as little cash and as few valuables as possible – preferably concealed on your person – especially at night in areas such as Granada's Albaicín or the less frequented parts of any city. There are also several ploys to be aware of and situations to avoid as you do the rounds of the city.

Thieves often work in pairs, so watch out for people standing unusually close if you're studying postcards or papers at stalls; keep an eye on your wallet if it appears you're being distracted. Ploys (by some very sophisticated operators) include: the "helpful" person pointing out birdshit (shaving cream or something similar) on your jacket while someone relieves you of your money; the card or paper you're invited to read on the street to distract your attention while your pocket is picked; the move by someone in a café for your drink with one hand (the other hand's in your bag as you react to save your drink).

If you have a **car** don't leave anything in view when you park it. When parked overnight in large towns and cities you'd be wise to remove everything, making sure that a hatchback's boot area is left uncovered. Vehicles are rarely stolen, but luggage and valuables left in cars do make a tempting target and rental cars are easy to spot; see also p.48. At beauty spots, beaches and out-of-the-way attractions, peruse the ground carefully when you park; if it's strewn with broken window glass it's a sure sign that thieves are frequent visitors and you'll need to park elsewhere or take appropriate action.

Looking for **hotel rooms**, don't leave any bags unattended anywhere. This applies especially to blocks where the hotel or *hostal* is on the higher floors and you're tempted to leave baggage in the hallway or ground-floor lobby. And check, if you leave your room windows open while you're out, that there's no possibility of "fishing-rod" crime. This is a new phenomenon where thieves go fishing through even barred windows to "hook" any valuables in sight.

What to do if you're robbed

If you're robbed, you need to go to the police to report it, not least because your insurance company will require a **police report**. Don't expect a great deal of concern if your loss is relatively small – and expect the process of completing forms and formalities to take ages.

In the unlikely event that you're **mugged**, or otherwise threatened, never resist; hand over what's wanted and run straight to the police, who will be more sympathetic on these occasions.

If you have your passport stolen or lose all your money, you can contact your consulate (see p.35) which is required to assist you to some degree.

The police

There are three basic types of **police**: the Guardia Civil, the Policía Municipal and the Policía Nacional, all of them armed.

The **Guardia Civil**, in green uniforms, are the most officious and the ones to avoid. Though their role has been cut back since they operated as Franco's right hand, they remain a reactionary force (it was a Guardia Civil colonel, Tejero, who held the national parliament hostage in the February 1981 failed coup).

If you do need the police – and above all if you're reporting a serious crime such as rape – you should always go to the more sympathetic **Policía Municipal**, who wear blue-and-white uniforms with red trim. In the countryside there may be only the Guardia Civil; though they're usually helpful, they are inclined to resent the suggestion that any crime exists on their turf and you may end up feeling as if you are the one who stands accused.

The brown-uniformed **Policía Nacional** are mainly seen in cities, armed with submachine guns and guarding key installations such as embassies, stations, post offices and their own barracks. They are also the force used to control crowds and demonstrations.

Offences

There are a few offences you may possibly commit unwittingly that it's as well to be aware of.

In theory you're supposed to carry some kind of **identification** at all times, and the police can stop you in the streets and demand it. In practice they're rarely bothered if you're clearly a foreigner on vacation, but given the occasional terrorist and illegal-immigrant clampdowns it would be wise to carry some means of identification even if it's only a photocopy of your passport details.

Nude bathing or **unauthorized camping** are activities more likely to bring you into contact with officialdom, though a warning to cover up or move on is a more probable result than any real confrontation. **Topless tanning** is now commonplace at all the trendier resorts, but in country areas, where attitudes are still very traditional, you should take care not to upset local sensibilities. Many nudist beaches (*playas nudistas*) have been set up along the Costa del Sol and elsewhere and are mentioned in the guide.

If you have an **accident** while driving, try not to make a statement to anyone who doesn't speak English. The Spanish National Tourist Office in your home country can provide a list of the most important rules of the road in Spain; see p.38.

Spanish **drug laws** are in a somewhat bizarre state at present. After the socialists came to power in 1983, cannabis use (possession of up to 8 grammes of what the Spanish call *chocolate*) was decriminalized. Subsequent pressures, and an influx of harder drugs in recent years, have changed that policy and – in theory at least – any drug use is now forbidden. You may see signs in some bars saying "*Porros no*" (no joints), which you should heed. However, in practice the police are not too worried about personal use. Larger quantities (and any other drugs) are a very different matter.

Should you be **arrested** on any charge you have the right to contact your consulate (see p.35). If you've been detained for a drugs offence though, don't expect any sympathy or help from consular officials.

Sexual harassment

Spain's macho image has faded dramatically in the post-Franco years and – despite an alarming level of domestic violence against women – these days there are relatively few parts of the country where foreign women, travelling alone, are likely to feel threatened, intimidated, or noteworthy.

Inevitably, the **big cities** – like any others in Europe – have their no-go areas, where street crime and especially drug-related hassles are on the rise, but there is little of the pestering and propositions that you have to contend with in, say, the larger French or Italian cities. The outdoor culture of *terrazas* (terrace bars) and the tendency of Spaniards to move around in large, mixed crowds, filling central bars, clubs and streets late into the night, help to make you feel less exposed. However, in the darker streets of major cities a woman walking alone at night – especially if she looks in any way foreign – is a potential target. Again we should stress that anything sinister is highly unlikely to happen to you, but it's wise to take as few risks as possible. If you are in any doubt, there are always taxis – plentiful and reasonably priced.

The major **coastal resorts** have their own artificial holiday culture. The Spaniards who hang around in discos here or at fiesta fairgrounds pose no greater or lesser threat than similar operators at home. The language barrier simply makes it harder to know whom to trust. "*Déjame en paz*" ("leave me in peace") is a fairly standard rebuff and the more potent "*¡vete a la mierda!*" ("piss off") should work on those hard of hearing.

Predictably, it is in more **isolated regions**, separated by less than a generation from desperate poverty (or still starkly poor), that most serious problems can occur. We have had two reports over the last fifteen years of women being followed and attacked in remote parts of Andalucía but these are extremely isolated, if worrying, incidents and the overwhelming majority of people you meet will display the dignity and courtesy innate to the region. However, and particularly if you're alone, you do need to know a bit about the land you're travelling around – check with hotel owners, locals or tourist offices.

In some areas you can walk for hours without coming across an inhabited farm or house, and you still come upon shepherds working for little more than the wine they take to their pastures. It's rare that this poses a threat – help and hospitality are much more the norm – but you are certainly more vulnerable. That said, trekking is becoming more popular in Spain as a whole and in Andalucía many women happily tramp the footpaths of the Sierra Nevada, Las Alpujarras and the Sierra Morena. In the south, generally, though, it is worth finding rooms in the larger villages, or, if you camp out, asking permission to do so on private land, rather than striking out alone.

Work

Andalucía has Spain's highest level of unemployment and unless you've applied for a job advertised in your home country, such as au pair work, the only real chance of long-term work in Andalucía is in language schools. If you intend to stay in Spain longer than three months, you'll need a permiso de residencia – see "Red tape and visas" (p.35). A word of warning: although it happens infrequently the police can and may ask for either your passport or residence papers, or both, on the spot, especially out of the tourist season.

European Union citizens may find the EU's website for those planning to live or work abroad within the EU a useful resource; it can be found at ⓦ citizens.EU.int/.

Teaching and translation work

Finding a **teaching job** is mainly a question of pacing the streets, stopping in at every language school around and asking about vacancies. For the addresses of schools look in the Paginas Amarillas (Yellow Pages) under "Academias de Idiomas". Although more schools are beginning to open they tend to be computer-based operations employing very few teachers, so you'll need to persevere if you're to come up with a rewarding position. You'll also need a TEFL (Teaching English as a Foreign Language) or ESL (English as a Second Language) certificate to give yourself any kind of chance.

You could also try advertising **private lessons** (better paid at €10–15 an hour, but harder to make a living at) on the noticeboards of university faculties, British consulates, shop windows, bars and in the small ads magazine *Cambalache* (available from most newsstands), in which advertisements are free. A paid ad in the local newspaper is also a good way of contacting many potential customers for a relatively modest outlay.

Another possibility, so long as you speak and write excellent Spanish, is **translation work**, often working with business correspondence – look in the Yellow Pages under "Traductores". If you intend doing agency work (jobs which are difficult to get outside Madrid and Barcelona), you'll usually need access to a PC with email. Agency work does not pay well (around €0.40 per word) and you'll get more (around €0.70) if you work freelance directly with companies, although then you'll need to pay for a *licencia fiscal* (around €104 annually) and make monthly social security payments (around €200) to work legally.

Temporary work

If you're looking for **temporary work** the best chances are in the bars, restaurants, shops and hotels of the big resorts. This may help you have a good time but it's unlikely to bring in very much money; pay (often from British bar owners) will reflect your lack of official status or work permit. If you turn up in spring and are willing to stay through the season you might get a better deal – also true if you're offering some special skill such as catering and cookery expertise or windsurfing (there are schools sprouting up all along the coast). Quite often there are jobs at **yacht marinas**, too, scrubbing down and repainting the boats of the rich; just turn up and ask around, especially from March until June. As a foreigner you've got little hope of work on the grape or olive harvests – these are jealously guarded seasonal jobs for the region's largely unemployed (for the rest of the year) male population, who are themselves being squeezed out by the *sin papeles* (no papers) immigrant workers forced to suffer even more shockingly bad pay and conditions; these days Andalucía's *temporeros* tend to head for France and the harvests there.

Travellers with disabilities

Spain is not exactly at the forefront of providing facilities for travellers with disabilities. That said, things are steadily improving and there are accessible hotels in each of the major cities and resorts. By law, all new public buildings are required to be fully accessible. The staging of the 1992 Paralympic Games in Barcelona did a great deal towards helping change attitudes and improve facilities throughout Spain; there are also a number of active and forceful groups of disabled people: ONCE, the Spanish organization for the blind, is particularly active, its huge lottery bringing with it considerable power.

Transport is still the main problem, since buses are virtually impossible for wheelchairs – although some of the newer buses now allow wheelchair access – and trains are only slightly better (though there are wheelchairs at major stations and wheelchair spaces in some carriages, especially on the more modern trains such as the AVE between Madrid and Sevilla). Taxi drivers in most towns are usually helpful. The Brittany Ferries crossing from Plymouth to Santander offers good facilities if you're driving to Spain (as do most cross-Channel ferries).

Accessible facilities at cafés, petrol stations and restaurants along the major roads and *autovías* are improving, particularly in coastal areas, but once out of the cities and away from the coast, the difficulties increase. Road surfaces in the mountain regions can be rough, and toilet facilities for disabled travellers are a rare sight. On the **accommodation** front wheelchair access is improving, and in major towns you'll have no problem finding places with facilities within all price brackets; all new hotels now have at least one room fully equipped for the disabled traveller. Outside the major conurbations things tend to be less easy, although the more stars awarded to a place, the more likely it is to have been converted to accommodate disabled visitors. Many places that optimistically claim to be accessible, however, still retain obstacles such as flights of steps at the entrance. An invaluable information source is the **Guía de Hoteles y Pensiones de Andalucía**, published by the Junta de Andalucía. It costs €5.50 and is available from all Turismo offices or from the head office in Marbella (☎95 283 87 85, Ⓦwww.andalucia.org). Updated annually, the guide identifies every hotel and *hostal* in the region which has accessible accommodation with a wheelchair symbol. All bar one of Andalucía's Albergues Juveniles or youth hostels are equipped with disabled accommodation ranging from El Bosque's 3 en-suite rooms to Jerez's 28. If you can afford them, paradores are one answer to the problem of unsuitable accommodation. In Andalucía all except three are wheelchair accessible, and even though most are converted castles and monasteries they still have plenty of room inside to manoeuvre a wheelchair.

There are several **websites** which may prove useful when planning your holiday:

Ⓦ**www.allgohere.com** Database of wheelchair-accessible hotels and airlines.

Ⓦ**www.disabilityresources.org** Comprehensive interactive database with lots of information on travel and other topics.

Ⓦ**www.access–able.com** A site specifically geared to journey planning for elderly and disabled travellers. The section on Spain can be researched by province or city or subject (e.g. hotels, tours and trips, medical services etc.). A US portal.

Ⓦ**www.wemedia.com** Good site for information on travel, and has useful links to other sites dealing with disabled travellers' topics.

Contacts for travellers with disabilities

In Spain

Spanish National Tourist Office See p.38 for addresses. Publishes a fact sheet, listing a variety of useful addresses and some accessible accommodation.

Comité de Representantes de Minusválidos (CERMI) c/Prim 3, Madrid (metro Banco de España). Provides information and sells Braille maps and a wide range of aids for blind and visually impaired people.
ECOM (Federation of Spanish private organizations for the disabled) Gran Vía de las Corts, Catalanas 562 principal, 2a, 08011 Barcelona ☎ 93 451 55 50, ⓦ www.ecom.es. Information on holidays and facilities throughout Spain.
Organización Nacional de Ciegos de España (ONCE) c/Pechuan 1, Madrid ☎ 91 360 1678; c/Calabria 66–76, 08015 Barcelona ☎ 93 325 92 00; ⓦ www.once.es. Sells Braille maps and can arrange trips for blind people; contact for details.
PIMS c/Isla de la Cartuja, Puerta de la Barqueta 41092 Sevilla ☎ 95 446 04 04. Advice centre which can provide information on Sevilla and on Andalucía generally. They also publish a leaflet (in Spanish): *Guía de Turismo Accesible.*
Rompiendo Barreras Travel c/Roncevalles 3, 28007 Madrid ☎ 915 513 622, ⓦ www.rbtravel.es. Spanish travel agency dedicated to disabled travel. Although operating in Spanish they will respond to communications in English.

In the UK and Ireland

Access Travel 6 The Hillock, Astley, Lancashire M29 7GW ☎ 01942/888844, ⓦ www.access-travel .co.uk. Tour operator that can arrange flights, transfer and accommodation in Andalucía and guarantees accommodation standards. ATOL bonded, established ten years.
Disability Action Group Portside Business Park, 189 Airport Road West, Belfast BT3 9ED ☎ 0800/0524040, ⓦ www.disability.org. Information on disabled travel abroad and produces a holiday factsheet.
Holiday Care 7th floor, Sunby House, 4 Bedford Park, Croydon CRO 2AP, ☎ 08451/249971, ⓦ www .holidaycare.org.uk. Provides a free comprehensive travel pack on Spain with details of facilities in hotels, resorts etc. Information on financial help for holidays available.
Irish Wheelchair Association Blackheath Drive, Clontarf, Dublin 3 ☎ 01/818 6400, ⓦ www.iwa.ie. Advice and guidance about travelling abroad with a wheelchair.
RADAR (Royal Association for Disability and Rehabilitation), 12 City Forum, 250 City Rd, London EC1V 8AF ☎ 020/7250 3222, Minicom ☎ 020/7250

4119, ⓦ www.radar.org.uk. Useful website for disabled travel.
Tripscope Alexandra House, Albany Rd, Brentford, Middlesex TW8 0NE ☎ 08457/585641, ⓦ www .tripscope.org.uk. Registered charity providing a national telephone information service with free advice on UK and international transport for those with a mobility problem.

In the US and Canada

Access-Able ⓦ www.access-able.com. Online resource for travellers with disabilities.
Directions Unlimited 123 Green Lane, Bedford Hills, NY 10507 ☎ 1-800/533-5343 or 914/241-1700. Tour operator specializing in bookings for people with disabilities.
Mobility International USA 451 Broadway, Eugene, OR 97401, Voice and TDD ☎ 41/343-1284, ⓦ www.miusa.org. Information and referral services, access guides, tours and exchange programmes. Requires membership (consult website).
Society for the Advancement of Travelers with Handicaps (SATH), 347 5th Ave, New York, NY 10016 ☎ 212/447-7284, ⓦ www.sath.org. Non-profit educational organization that has actively represented travellers with disabilities since 1976.
Travel Information Service ☎ 215/456-9600. Telephone-only information and referral service.
Twin Peaks Press Box 129, Vancouver, WA 98661 ☎ 360/694-2462 or 1-800/637-2256, ⓦ www .twinpeak.virtualave.net. Publisher of a number of useful directories for disabled travellers including one dealing with specialized travel agencies.
Wheels Up! ☎ 1-888/389-4335, ⓦ www .wheelsup.com. Provides discounted air fare, tour and cruise prices for disabled travellers, publishes a free monthly newsletter and has a comprehensive website.

In Australia and New Zealand

ACROD (Australian Council for Rehabilitation of the Disabled), PO Box 60, Curtin ACT floor 1–5 Commercial Rd, Kings Grove 2208 ☎ 02 6282 4333 (also TTY), ⓦ www.acrod.org.au. Provides lists of travel agencies and tour operators for people with disabilities.
Disabled Persons Assembly 4/173–175 Victoria St, Wellington, New Zealand ☎ 04/801 9100, ⓦ www.dpa.org.nz. Resource centre with lists of travel agencies and tour operators for people with disabilities.

Senior travellers

The senior traveller market is well catered for in Spain, especially in the south, where the long summer and mild winters can mean real out-of-season bargains for older visitors who tend to be more flexible in their travel arrangements. Most public museums, galleries and archeological sites offer discounts to senior visitors (usually the same as a student discount) and it is always worth enquiring when purchasing your ticket. Similarily there are deals to be had for the over-60s on the extensive train network (see p.44).

Contacts for senior travellers

In the UK

Saga Holidays ☎ 01303/771111, ⊛ www.saga .co.uk. The country's biggest and most established specialist in tours and holidays aimed at older people.

In the USA and Canada

American Association of Retired Persons ☎ 1-800/424-3410, membership hotline 1-800/515-2299 or 202/434-2277, ⊛ www.aarp.org. Can provide discounts on accommodation and vehicle rental. Membership open to US and Canadian residents aged 50 or over for an annual fee of US $10 or $27 for three years.

Elderhostel ☎ 1/877-426-8056, ⊛ www .elderhostel.org. Runs an extensive worldwide network of educational and activity programmes, cruises and homestays for seniors.

Saga Holidays ☎ 1-800/343-0273, ⊛ www .sagaholidays.com. Specializes in worldwide group travel for seniors. Saga's Road Scholar coach tours and their Smithsonian Odyssey Tours have a more educational slant.

Vantage Deluxe World Travel ☎ 1-800/322-6677, ⊛ www.vantagetravel.com. Specializes in worldwide group travel for seniors.

Gay and lesbian travellers

Gay and lesbian life in Spain has come a long way in the thirty-odd years since Franco's death. To the horror of the church and right-wing groups, same-sex marriages have been legalized and there are strong lobbying movements for same-sex couples to have equal rights; these movements are given greater strength by the suppport of some autonomous governments. The age of consent is 16 – the same as for heterosexual couples. Gay or lesbian couples using hotels and hostales throughout Andalucía should encounter no attitude problems at all.

The largest gay communities in Andalucía are in Cádiz, Sevilla and Torremolinos, and attitudes in all three places, as well as other major cities and resorts, are fairly relaxed. Sevilla and Cádiz in particular have large permanent gay communities and a thriving scene. In Cádiz, Carnaval is a wonderfully hedonistic time to visit.

A variety of gay bars and clubs are detailed throughout the *Guide*. A guide to the Spanish scene worth getting hold of is *Spartacus España*, an offshoot of the international guide series, available in the UK and US. For readers of Spanish *Revista Zero* is the peninsula's leading gay magazine and both this and the Madrid-based *Entiendes* detail gay and lesbian events and entertainment across Spain and are available from news *kioskos*.

Contacts for gay and lesbian travellers

In Andalucía

Federación Colegas (Gay and Lesbian Federation of Andalucía), Plaza de Encarnación 23, 2º B, 41003 Sevilla Ⓦ www.colegaweb.net. Active federation with centres in every province in Andalucía.
Somos (Sevilla Gay, Lesbian and Transsexual Support Group), Plaza del Giraldillo 1, Local A, 41003 Sevilla Ⓣ 954 53 13 99, Ⓦ www.andalucia .com/living/gay. Somos is the main gay and lesbian association in Sevilla; their website gives contact addresses for gay and lesbian associations throughout Andalucía and Spain (go to the link *Enlaces* and then *Asociaciones*).

In the UK

Gay Travel Ⓦ www.gaytravel.co.uk. Online gay and lesbian travel agent, offering good deals on all types of holiday. Also lists gay- and lesbian-friendly hotels around the world.
Madison Travel Ⓣ 01273/202532, Ⓦ www .madisontravel.co.uk. Established travel agents specializing in packages to gay- and lesbian-friendly mainstream destinations, and also to gay/lesbian destinations.

Respect Holidays Ⓣ 0870/770 0169, Ⓦ www .respect-holidays.co.uk. Offers exclusively gay packages to all popular Europan resorts.

In USA and Canada

Damron Ⓣ 1-800/462-6654 or 415/255-0404, Ⓦ www.damron.com. Publisher of the *Men's Travel Guide*, a pocket-sized yearbook full of listings of hotels, bars, clubs and resources for gay men; the *Women's Traveler*, which provides similar listings for lesbians; and *Damron Accommodations*, which provides detailed listings of over 1000 accommodations for gays and lesbians worldwide. All of these titles are offered at a discount on the website.
gaytravel.com Ⓣ 1-800/GAY-TRAVEL, Ⓦ www .gaytravel.com. The premier site for trip planning, bookings, and general information about international gay and lesbian travel.
International Gay/Lesbian Travel Association Ⓣ 1-800/448-8550, Ⓦ www.iglta.org. Trade group that can provide a list of gay- and lesbian-owned or friendly travel agents, accommodation and other travel businesses.

In Australia and New Zealand

Gay and Lesbian Travel Ⓦ www.galta.com. au. Directory and links for gay and lesbian travel in Australia and worldwide.
Gay Travel Ⓣ 1-800/429 8728, Ⓔ parkside@herveyworld.com.au. Gay travel agent associated with local branch of Hervey World Travel; all aspects of gay- and lesbian- travel worldwide.
Tearaway Travel Ⓣ 1800/664 440, Ⓦ www .tearawaytravel.com. Gay-specific business dealing with international and domestic travel.

Travelling with children

Spain is a good country to travel with children of any age; they will be well received everywhere and babies and toddlers, in particular, will be made a real fuss of. There are numerous theme parks and leisure activities specifically aimed at kids mentioned throughout the guide, in particular Mini-Hollywood in Almería. Many tourist attractions and sights have discounts or free entry for children and some cities and resorts produce pamphlets of attractions aimed at kids.

The train company **RENFE** allows children under four to travel free on trains, with 40 percent discount for those between four and twelve years.

Accommodation shouldn't be a problem as *hostales* and *pensiones* generally welcome accompanied children and offer rooms with three or four beds. If you're travelling in elevated regions such as Las Alpujarras and the Sierra Morena, or out of season, however, bear in mind that many *hostales* (as opposed to more expensive hotels) either lack heating systems or often have the most basic sort – and it can get very cold. In these regions *hostales* with efficient heating are detailed in the *Guide*. The wide availability of self-catering options can be appealing for a family holiday and Spain has a good choice of accommodation from seaside apartments to country *casas rurales*. There are also myriad package tour companies that cater specifically for holidays with children and arrange activities for kids of all ages throughout the holiday.

As in other Mediterranean countries children stay up very late in Spain, especially in the summer. It's very common for them to be running around pavement cafés or restaurants and your kids will no doubt enjoy joining in.

As far as babies go, food seems to work out quite well (*hostales* sometimes prepare food specially, or will let you use the kitchen to do so). Disposable nappies (*pañales*, or more colloquially, *dodotis*) and other standard needs are very widely available. Many *hostales* will be prepared to baby-sit, or at least to listen out for trouble. This is obviously more likely if you're staying in an old-fashioned family-run place than in the fancier hotels.

Contacts for travellers with children

In the UK and Ireland

Simply Travel ☎ 020/8541 2280, ⓦ www .simply-travel.com. Upmarket tour company offering villas and hotels in the less touristy parts of Spain. In some destinations they can provide qualified, English-speaking nannies.
Travelling with Children ☎ 0845/2600 892, ⓦ www.travellingwithchildren.co.uk. Website with wide range of tips and information on travelling with kids.

In the US

Rascals in Paradise ☎ 415/921-7000, ⓦ www .rascalsinparadise.com. Can arrange scheduled and customized itineraries built around activities for kids in Spain and other countries.
Family Travel Times ☎ 212/477 5524, ⓦ www .familytraveltimes.com. Organization producing a variety of publications on planning holidays with kids.

Directory

Addresses In Spain addresses are written as: c/Picasso 2, 4° izda. – which means Picasso street (*calle*) no. 2, 4th floor, left-hand (*izquierda*) flat or office; dcha. (*derecha*) is right; cto. (*centro*) centre; s/n (*sin número*) means the building has no number; *bajo* signifies ground floor.

Airport tax You can happily spend your last euros – there's no departure tax.

Birthdays A Spaniard gets two birthdays a year – one is the anniversary of the actual birth whilst the other (and more important one) celebrates the *día del santo* or feast day of the saint he or she is named after; it is unusual – though not uncommon in these days of Kevins, Tamaras and Deborahs appearing on Spanish birth certificates – for anyone in Spain not to be named after a saint.

Contraceptives Condoms (*condones* or *preservativos*) are available from *farmacias*, supermarkets and slot machines in some bars. You should be able to buy most brands of the pill (*la píldora*) over the counter at any *farmacia*; if you encounter difficulties the pharmacist will usually be able to recommend a doctor nearby who will be able to advise. If you take along your EHIC card (see p.36) you won't need to pay for the consultation. Another useful source of help is a private women's clinic which is usually fast and will cost around €30 for a consultation (see under *Planificación Familiar* in Yellow Pages).

Electricity Current in most of Spain is 220 volts AC (just occasionally it's still 110V and such sockets should be labelled): most European appliances should work as long as you have an adaptor for European-style two-pin plugs. North Americans will need this plus a transformer.

Estanco A government licensed store selling tobacco, stamps and matches. Displaying a burgundy and yellow sign saying "TABACOS" they also sell many other items (especially in the larger towns and cities) such as *bonobus* bus passes or carnets of tickets.

Film Movie-going remains a remarkably cheap and popular entertainment. The majority of what's screened is the usual Hollywood fare poorly dubbed into Spanish, but in the cities you will find some films in their original language with subtitles. Look for *voz* or *versión original (subtitulada)*, abbreviated "v.o.", in the listings; "v.e." means *versión español*.

Fishing Fortnightly permits are easily and cheaply obtained from any ICONA (Instituto para la Conservación de la Naturaleza) office – there's one in every big town (addresses from the local Turismo). For information on the whereabouts of the best trout streams and other fishing tips contact the Spanish Fishing Federation (Federación Española de Pesca), Navas de Tolosa 3, 28013 Madrid ☎91 532 83 53, ⓦwww.fepyc.es.

Language courses Most Spanish universities and a growing number of special language schools for foreigners offer courses; the latter tend to have a more modern approach, better facilities, and work with smaller groups. For details overseas contact a branch of the Instituto Cervantes: the London one is at 102 Eaton Square, London SW1 (☎020/7235 0353) or check other addresses on their website ⓦwww.cervantes.es. Many American universities also have their own courses based in Spain. Spanish Directory is a website listing language courses throughout Spain (ⓦwww.europa-pages.com/spain).

Laundries You'll find a few self-service launderettes (*lavanderías automáticas*) in the major cities and some are given in the relevant city "Listings" sections in the *Guide*, but generally they're rare – you normally have to leave your clothes for the full (and somewhat expensive) service wash. Note that you're not allowed by law to leave laundry hanging out of windows over a street. A dry cleaner is a *tintorería*.

Luggage You'll find self-service left luggage *consignas* at most large Spanish train stations. Lockers big enough to hold most backpacks, plus a smaller bag, cost about €2–4 a day; put the coins in to free the key. These are not a good idea for long-term storage, however, as they're periodically emptied by station staff. Bus terminals and some train stations have staffed *consignas* where you present a claim stub to get your gear back; the cost is about the same.

Siesta The mid-afternoon break (normally around 2–5pm) during which most shops, offices and government buildings close. In the age of air-conditioning there has been some movement towards European working hours in northern Spain, but the custom is still strongly adhered to throughout Andalucía, especially during the spring and summer months. This is a good time to arrive in towns and cities if you're seeking a parking space.

Skiing Andalucía's main ski centre is the Solynieve resort in the Sierra Nevada, detailed in the "Granada" chapter or covered on the Sierra Nevada's Ski Information website (ⓦwww.cetursa.es/). The SNTO's *Skiing in Spain* pamphlet is also useful.

Surnames Spaniards use of double-barrelled surnames is a source of constant confusion to foreigners. Women on getting married do not adopt their husband's surnames but continue to use their own name which means that children, when born, are given their father's first surname followed by that of their mother. Thus Miguel de Cervantes Saavedra would use only his father's name (Cervantes) in most situations but his legal name remains the full one.

Swimming pools Most Andalucian towns – and even quite small villages – have a *piscina municipal*, a lifesaver in the summer and yet another reason not to keep exclusively to the coast. They're often landscaped with gardens, quite a few have cafés and there's usually no problem if you want to bring food in. Many of these, along with river swimming spots, are detailed throughout the *Guide*. Several country *ventas* (restaurants) now have pools, too. However, while parents dine inside kids often swim alone unsupervised by anyone; a couple of tragic drownings in recent years have underlined the necessity to keep an eye on children using these pools.

Time Spain is one hour ahead of the UK, six hours ahead of Eastern Standard Time, nine hours ahead of Pacific Standard Time, except for brief periods during the changeovers to and from daylight saving. For Australia, during winter subtract eight hours from Sydney time and in summer subtract 10 hours to get Spanish time; New Zealand is 12 hours ahead of Spain. In Spain the clocks go forward in the last week of March and back again in the last week of October.

Toilets Public toilets are generally reasonably clean but rarely have any paper (best to carry your own). The old-fashioned squat-style WCs are now – thankfully – a rarity. The most common euphemisms are *baño* (literally "bathroom"), *aseos, servicios* (the most used), *retretes* or *sanitarios*. "Señoras" (Ladies) and "Caballeros" ("Gentlemen") or the initials "S" or "C" are the usual signs, though you may also see "Damas" used for women's conveniences and the potentially hazardous combination of "Señoras" ("Ladies") and "Señores" ("Men").

Guide

Guide

1

Málaga and Cádiz

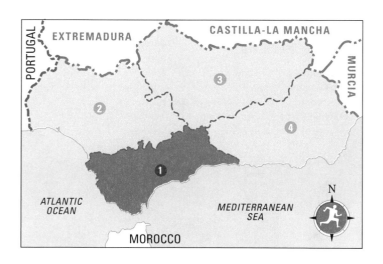

CHAPTER 1 # Highlights

✳ **Málaga** A vibrant city crammed with bars, cafés, museums and a fabulous Moorish fortress. See p.94

✳ **Museo Picasso** With over 180 artworks by Málaga's most famous son, this remarkable museum shouldn't be missed. See p.101

✳ **Parques Naturales** Get away from it all in the natural parks of Sierra de Grazalema, Los Alcornocales and the Parque de El Torcal with its surreal limestone formations See p.125, p.203 & p.210

✳ **Costa del Sol** Despite a downmarket image, there are individual resorts – Nerja, Marbella and Estepona – with plenty of style. See p.149

✳ **Pueblos blancos** The White Towns are picturesque villages of whitewashed houses set amid spectacular scenery. See p.184

✳ **Ronda** Beautiful hill town set astride a yawning gorge with sensational views over the Serranía de Ronda. See p.188

✳ **Cádiz** A beguiling air of genteel decay pervades this old sea town, one of the great cities of the Spanish south. See p.236

✳ **Jerez** Visit a sherry bodega and sample the legendary *aperitivo* at one of the town's numerous tapas bars. See p.270

△ Museo Picasso

Málaga and Cádiz

The Andalucian sun starts singing a fire song, and all creation trembles at the sound.

Federico García Lorca

The smallest of Andalucía's eight provinces, **Málaga** is also its most populous, swelling to bursting point with the sheer weight of visitors in high summer. Although primarily known as the gateway to the Costa del Sol and its unashamedly commercial resorts such as **Torremolinos** and **Marbella**, the province has much more to offer than just its coastline. To most incoming tourists the provincial capital **Málaga** is merely "the place by the airport", but it's also a vibrant city in its own right, with a population of half a million. In the west of Málaga's provincial heartland lies the **Serranía de Ronda**, a series of small mountain ranges sprinkled with gleaming, white-washed **pueblos blancos** (White Towns), of which **Ronda**, located astride the stunningly beautiful Tajo, or gorge, is justly the most famous.

To the north lies the appealing market town of **Antequera** with its remarkable prehistoric dolmens and sumptuous Baroque churches, and from here it's a quick hop south to the natural wonders of **El Torcal**, where vast limestone outcrops have been eroded into a landscape of weird natural sculptures. Another possible trip from Antequera is to the spectacular **El Chorro Gorge**, which, along with the Guadalhorce lake, has become a major climbing and camping centre. Nearby, the saline **Laguna de Fuente de Piedra** is Europe's only inland breeding ground for the greater flamingo, whose flying flocks make a spectacular sight in summer.

The far eastern section of Málaga province is the largely unknown and little-visited **Axarquía** region, an area of rugged natural beauty and once the haunt of mountain bandits. Now the domain of the *cabra hispanica*, a distinctive Iberian long-horned goat, the area's magnificent scenery and earthy villages contrast starkly with the crowded **beaches** to the south.

With a two-hundred-kilometre coastline fronting both the Atlantic and the Mediterranean, **Cádiz** is the most southerly province of Andalucía. The sea has played a large part in the history of the province, and most of Cádiz's dozen or so major conurbations are within easy distance of a beach. Founded by the Phoenicians, the city of **Cádiz** itself makes up for in sheer elegance, atmosphere and sea-girthed location what it lacks in the way of irresistible sights.

After the tumult of the Costa del Sol, the bracing Atlantic winds and broad, white, dune-lined beaches of the **Costa de la Luz** – great stretches of which have so far survived the developers' attentions and which are often deserted – can come as a welcome relief. Resorts such as **Conil**, **Chipiona** and **Sanlúcar de Barrameda** possess a low-key charm, while at the southern tip of the coast, **Tarifa** – also with miles of fine beaches – has become a major windsurfing centre.

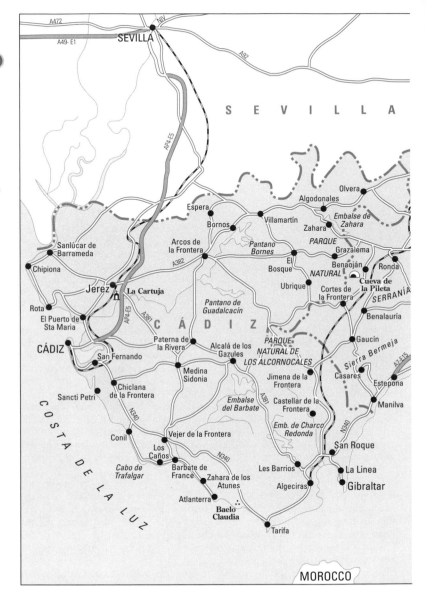

The entire thirty-kilometre stretch between Tarifa and **Algeciras** (Andalucía's main port for sailings to Morocco) has been designated a "potential military zone, placing strict controls on Spanish developments and preventing foreigners from buying up land. Across the Bay of Algeciras, the British colony of **Gibraltar** sits beneath its daunting mountain of rock, regarded uneasily by Spaniards and as a strange, hybrid curiosity to almost everyone else.

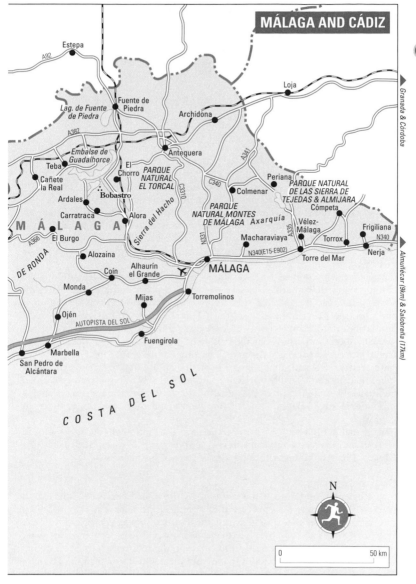

Granada & Córdoba ▶

Almuñécar (9km) & Salobreña (17km) ▶

COSTA DEL SOL

| 0 | 50 km |

N

Inland, Cádiz offers a fascinating variety of landscapes and towns. The mountainous region in its northeastern corner, which it shares with Málaga, is dotted with hill-top White Towns such as **Zahara**, **Olvera** and **Arcos de la Frontera**, while the green oasis of **Grazalema**, the wettest point in Spain, is surrounded by its **natural park**, a paradise for walkers and naturalists. South of here sharp contours give way to rolling hills covered with clumps of walnut trees, pines and Spanish firs, and the ranches around **Medina Sidonia** where *toros bravos* – ominous black fighting bulls – graze in the shade of cork oaks. To the west, vines take over, covering thousands of acres of dazzling white chalk soil, and forming the famous **sherry triangle** between **Jerez**, a fine town in its own right, **Puerto de Santa María** and **Sanlúcar de Barrameda**, the oldest vineyards in Europe.

Málaga

First impressions of **MÁLAGA** are not encouraging. A large and bustling seaport with a population passing half a million, it's the second city of Andalucía (after Sevilla) and also one of the poorest: official unemployment figures for the area estimate the jobless at one in four of the workforce. Yet, though many visitors get no further than the train or bus stations, put off by the grim clusters of high-rises on the fringes, if you penetrate beyond these you will find yourself in one of the most atmospheric and historic cities in Spain. Lorca described Málaga as his favourite town and given a chance it can be a surprisingly attractive place, an impression boosted by the ebullient and big-hearted *malagueños*, among the friendliest people in Andalucía.

Around the traditional fishing villages of **El Palo** and **Pedregalejo**, now absorbed into the suburbs, is a series of small beaches and a *paseo* lined with some of the best fish and seafood cafés in the province. Overlooking the town and port, the Moorish citadels of the **Alcazaba** and **Gibralfaro** give excellent introductions to what you can expect at Córdoba and Granada, and while *sevillanos* loudly proclaim that there is only one Semana Santa worthy of the name, *malagueños* furiously disagree. The processions are celebrated here with great fervour and with much larger floats (*tronos* or "thrones" as they're called here) than those of Sevilla, carried by up to 200 sober-suited males or robed penitents. In mid-August at the peak of the tourist season the town lets rip in its **Feria de Málaga** – one of the wildest and most spectacular fiestas in Andalucía.

Incidentally, **Picasso** was born in Málaga, and although the artist moved away in his early years, you can still visit his birthplace as well as the spectacular **Museo Picasso Málaga** housing a collection of his major works.

Some history

The **Phoenicians** founded the settlement they called Malaka in the eighth century BC, building a fortress on the summit of the hill today dominated by the Alcazaba. Later incorporated into the Roman province of Baetica in the wake of Rome's victory over Carthage, Málaga prospered as a **trading port** exporting iron, copper and lead from mines in the hills near Ronda, as well as olive oil, wine and *garum*, a relish made from pickled fish to which the Romans were particularly partial. After falling to the **Moors** early in the eighth century, Málaga was soon flourishing again as the main port for the city of Granada. Although in the fourteenth century the ruler Yusuf I constructed the Gibralfaro as defence, in 1487 Málaga was taken by Christian forces following a bitter siege, after which the large Moorish population was persecuted and its property confiscated on a grand scale; the city's main mosque was also transformed into a cathedral, and a further twenty into churches. Málaga then entered a period of decline only exacerbated by a revolt of the Moors in 1568 that resulted in their complete expulsion.

It was not until the nineteenth century that real prosperity returned – and then only briefly. Middle-class families arriving from the north invested in textile factories, sugar refineries and shipyards, and gave their names to city streets such as Larios and Heredia, while Málaga **dessert wine** became the favourite tipple of Victorian ladies. Then, in the early part of the twentieth century, the bottom fell out of the boom as the new industries succumbed to foreign competition and the phylloxera bug got to work wiping out the vines. A number of radical revolts leading up to the Civil War also brought the city an unhealthy reputation.

Given its volatile nature it was inevitable that Málaga would be staunchly Republican during the **Civil War**. In the turbulent years leading up to the war and during the conflict itself churches and convents were burned, while in 1937 Italian planes bombed the city, destroying much of its ancient central core, and mass executions of "reds and anarchists" by the conquering Franco forces left enduring emotional scars. This period is vividly described in a contemporaneous account, *Málaga Burning*, by Gamel Woolsey (see "Books" p.693).

The 1960s finally brought an economic lifeline in the form of **mass tourism** and the exploitation of the Costa del Sol. Coastal nightmares, however, barely touch the heart of Málaga. In recent years the town has tried to muscle in on the Costa del Sol tourist boom by projecting itself as a beach resort as well as a cultural centre, and work has been carried out to landscape the beaches and promenades to the west of the harbour as far as El Palo. So far however, all this seems to have had little adverse impact on the city's unique character.

Arrival

From the **airport** (☎ 95 204 88 04), the electric **train** provides the easiest and cheapest way into town (every 30min 7am–11.45pm; €1.10). From the arrivals hall, go up one floor to the Salidas (departures hall), take any exit and then turn right to reach a pedestrian overpass at the end of the airport building. Follow the "Ferrocarril" signs and cross the overpass (baggage trolleys allowed) to the unstaffed station. The kiosk, if open, sells tickets, or use the ticket machine close by; alternatively you can buy a ticket on the train. Make sure that you're on the Málaga platform (the one farthest away and reached by an underpass) and stay on the train right to the end of the line – the Centro-Alameda stop (a 12min ride). From here, you can cross the bridge over the Río Guadalmedina riverbed to the western end of the tree-lined Alameda, effectively the town centre. The #19 **bus** from the airport to the centre departs from a stop outside the arrivals hall (every 30min 7am–midnight), and calls at the main train and bus stations en route. The same journey by taxi to and from the centre of town costs around €10–€15 depending on traffic and takes roughly 15min. For details of getting back to the airport, see "Listings", p.112.

The Ferrocarril stop before Centro-Alameda is RENFE, Malagá's main **train station**, from where it's a slightly longer walk into the heart of town (bus #3 runs from here to the centre approximately every 10min), or you can get on the electric train to Centro-Alameda.

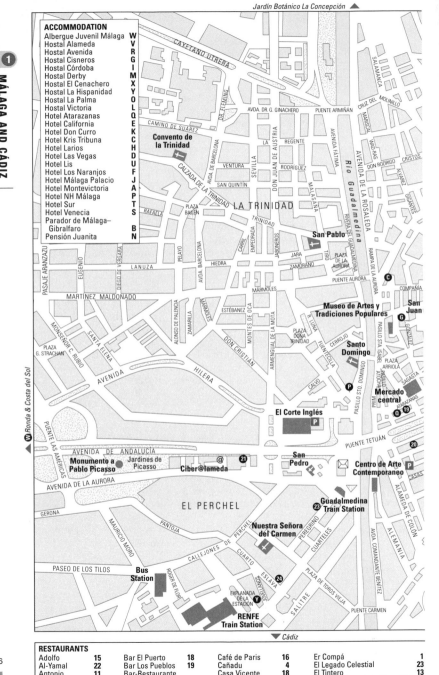

ACCOMMODATION
Albergue Juvenil Málaga — W
Hostal Alameda — V
Hostal Avenida — R
Hostal Cisneros — G
Hostal Córdoba — I
Hostal Derby — M
Hostal El Cenachero — X
Hostal La Hispanidad — Y
Hostal La Palma — O
Hostal Victoria — L
Hotel Atarazanas — Q
Hotel California — E
Hotel Don Curro — K
Hotel Kris Tribuna — C
Hotel Larios — H
Hotel Las Vegas — D
Hotel Lis — U
Hotel Los Naranjos — F
Hotel Málaga Palacio — J
Hotel Montevictoria — A
Hotel NH Málaga — P
Hotel Sur — T
Hotel Venecia — S
Parador de Málaga–
Gibralfaro — B
Pensión Juanita — N

RESTAURANTS

Adolfo	15	Bar El Puerto	18	Café de Paris	16	Er Compá	1
Al-Yamal	22	Bar Los Pueblos	19	Cañadu	4	El Legado Celestial	23
Antonio	11	Bar-Restaurante		Casa Vicente	18	El Tintero	13
Antonio Martín	17	Palacios	24	Cyber@lameda	21	El Vegetariano de la Alcazabilla	9

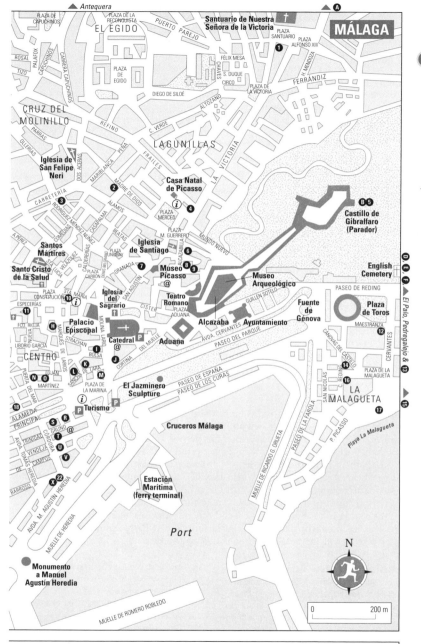

MÁLAGA

La Barraka	8	Parador de Málaga–		Restaurante Tormes	7
La Casa del Angel	2	Gibralfaro	5	Sal Gorda	14
Marisquería Alaska	3	Refectorium	12	Wok out	6
Mesón Gibralfaro	10	Restaurante Arcos	20		

All buses from and to destinations outside Málaga (run by a number of different companies) operate from the one **bus station** on Paseo de los Tilos (T 95 235 00 61), a little northwest of the RENFE station.

Arriving in Málaga by car you face the serious problem of parking; one good-value on-street **car park** (currently €0.70 per day; free at night) is located along the west bank of the Río Guadalmedina (Pasillo del Matadero), below the Alameda. If this is full you'll need to use a pay car park. **Theft** from cars is rampant in Málaga, so remember not to leave valuables inside. Stickers bearing a car rental company's name or logo make the car a magnet for thieves so it would be worthwhile removing these too.

Information

Slightly east of Plaza de la Constitución, the **Turismo**, Pasaje de Chinitas 4 (Mon–Fri 9am–8pm, Sat & Sun 10am–2pm; T 95 221 34 45), can provide full accommodation lists and a larger, more detailed map of the city than the one printed here, and also has lots of information on the Costa del Sol. They stock the monthly *¿Que Hacer?* (*What's On?*), which covers events and entertainment throughout Andalucía, as well as the weekly *Sur in English*, published by Malaga's main daily, *Sur*, which has a useful listings section. An enthusiastic **Turismo Municipal** (Mon–Fri 9am–7pm, Sat & Sun 10am–7pm; T 95 212 20 20) is located in Plaza de la Marina, close to the ferry terminal; it also operates a kiosk (summer only) in Plaza de la Merced as well as two other branches in the arrivals hall at the airport and at the bus station.

One way to get to grips with the city is on an open-topped **bus tour**. This hop-on hop-off service is operated by Malagatour (T 902 10 10 81, W www.malaga-tour.com; €13, tickets valid 24hr), with services leaving the bus station every half-hour (first & last departures 9.15am & 7pm); its many stops include the cathedral, Plaza de la Merced and the Alameda.

Accommodation

Málaga boasts dozens of **fondas** and **hostales**, so budget rooms are rarely hard to come by except during Semana Santa and the August *feria*. Málaga's high season is July and August and outside this period there are some real bargains to be had. Numerous possibilities are to be found in the grid of streets just north and south of the Alameda, which is probably the best place to start looking. The cheapest option is the **youth hostel** (*albergue juvenil*), though this isn't particularly convenient for the centre, as it lies out in the western suburbs. The town's **hotels** are generally poorer value than the *hostales*, but for those who want a little more luxury, we've listed a handful of places slightly further out. Málaga has no **campsite**: the nearest facilities are at Torremolinos heading west (see p.151), and Torre del Mar (see p.128) to the east.

South of the Alameda

Hotel Alameda c/Casas de Campos 3 T 95 222 20 99, W www.hotelalamedamalaga.com. Pleasant hotel upgraded from former *hostal* in high-rise block which lessens traffic noise. Rooms with a/c and TV. ④

Hostal Avenida Alameda Principal 5 T 95 221 77 28. Reasonably priced rooms right on the Alameda but not too noisy. Some rooms en suite. ②–③

Hostal El Cenachero c/Barroso 5 T 95 222 40 88. Clean, quiet, third-floor *hostal* in a quiet street just off the seafront end of c/Córdoba. Friendly proprietors and all rooms en-suite. ④

Hotel Lis c/Córdoba 7 T 95 222 73 00, W www.costadelsol.spa.es/hotel/hotelis. Reasonable-quality hotel offering a/c rooms with bath, TV and balcony. Free overnight parking. ④

Hotel Sur c/Trinidad Grund 13 T 95 222 48 03, W www.hotelsur.com. Quiet, efficiently run hotel with garage; all rooms have a/c, bath and TV. ④

Hotel Venecia Alameda Principal 9 ☎95 221 36
36. Central hotel with good facilities including a/c,
balconies overlooking the Alameda, and satellite
TV. ❻

North of the Alameda

Hostal Cisneros c/Cisneros 7 ☎95 221 26 33.
Pleasant rooms, with and without own bath, and
friendly proprietors. ❸

Hostal Córdoba c/Bolsa 11 ☎95 221 44 69.
Inexpensive, simple rooms in a family-run establishment. ❷

Hostal Derby c/San Juan de Dios 1 ☎95 222 13
01. Very friendly and excellent-value fourth-floor
establishment, on a tiny street north of the Plaza
de la Marina, with some rooms overlooking the
harbour. ❸

Hostal La Palma c/Martínez 7 ☎95 222 67 72.
Pleasant central *hostal* run by a friendly couple.
Some rooms en suite and discounts are sometimes
available. ❷–❸

Hostal Victoria c/Sancha de Lara 3 ☎95 222 42
24. Smart, central *hostal* with good en-suite a/c
doubles and singles with satellite TV. ❺

Hotel Don Curro c/Sancha de Lara 7 ☎95 222
72 00, ⓦwww.hoteldoncurro.com. Central and
comfortable, if rather featureless, hotel where a/c
rooms come with satellite TV. Own car park too. ❼

Hotel Atarazanas c/Atarazanas 19 ☎95 212
19 10, ⓦwww.balboahoteles.com. Central new
three-star hotel with reasonably priced and well-
appointed rooms. Our price code is for the first
three weeks in August outside of which prices fall
by forty percent. ❼

Hotel Kris Tribuna c/Carretería 6, ☎95 212 22
30, ⓦwww.krishoteles.com. Elegant new hotel
offering rooms with satellite TV, room safe and
minibar; one floor is reserved for non-smoking
guests. They cut rates substantially at weekends
and *Rough Guide* readers with this guide can claim
a ten-percent discount. ❽

Hotel Larios c/Marqués de Larios 2 ☎95 222 22
00, ⓦwww.hotel-larios.com. Modern, upmarket
and central hotel inside the shell of an original Art
Deco edifice; satellite TV, room safes and a panoramic rooftop bar are among the features. ❽

Hotel Málaga Palacio Cortina del Muelle 1, ☎95
221 51 85, ⓦwww.ac-hotels.com. This central four-
star with sea view rooms pampers its guests with
free minibar and bathrobes. Facilities include rooftop
pool and gym. Prices drop substantially Mon–Thurs
and they also do weekend special offers. ❾

Hotel NH Málaga Avda. Río Guadalmedina s/n
☎95 207 13 23, ⓦwww.nh-hoteles.com. Málaga's
newest four-star option – part of the nationwide NH
chain – is central and has all the blander attributes

of a corporate hotel aimed mainly at the business
market. Facilities include a gymnasium and sauna,
but no pool. ❽

Pensión Juanita c/Alarcón Luján 8 ☎95 221
35 86. Central and friendly *pensión* on the fourth
floor (there's a lift), offering some en-suites.
Large, multi-bed family rooms also available.
❸–❹

Out of the centre

Albergue Juvenil Málaga Plaza de Pío XII 6
☎95 230 85 00. Pleasantly modern double rooms,
complete with a shared sun-terrace. The #18 bus
(heading west across the river) from the Alameda
will drop you nearby on request. ❷–❸

Hostal La Hispanidad Explanada de la Estación
5 ☎952 31 11 35. Facing the train station this is
a useful option if you've got an early train (or bus)
to catch. The labyrinthine interior has refurbished
en-suite rooms – with a/c and TV – named after
different countries of the Americas, and there are
plenty of eating places nearby. ❹

Hotel California Paseo de Sancha 17, 500m east
of the bullring ☎95 221 51 64, ⓦwww
.costadelsol.spa.es/hotel/california. Charming
small hotel near the beach with a flower-bedecked
entrance. The well-appointed rooms come with a/c
and safes, and it also has its own garage. Buses
#11, #34 and #35 from the Alameda will drop you
outside on request. ❺

Hotel Las Vegas Paseo de Sancha 22 ☎95 221
77 12, ⓕ95 222 48 89. Recently refurbished
modern hotel, 700m east of the bullring and close
to the beach where the a/c rooms have balconies,
many with a sea view. Own swimming pool and
car park too. Buses #11, #34 and #35 from the
Alameda will stop outside. ❻

Hotel Los Naranjos Paseo de Sancha 35, 600m
east of the bullring ☎95 222 43 16 17, ⓦwww
.hotel-losnaranjos.com. Comfortable small hotel
near to the beach. Rooms have balconies (with
sea views from the higher ones), along with a/c,
satellite TV and safes. Parking available. Buses
#11, #34 and #35 from the Alameda can drop you
nearby. ❻

🏃 **Hotel Montevictoria** c/Conde de Ureña 58
☎95 265 65 25, ⓦwww.hotelmontevicto-
ria.com. Sweet little hotel with friendly proprietors
in an elegant villa in the hills above Málaga with
great views over the city. Slightly pricier rooms 104
& 105 have their own terrace. Bus #36 from the
Alameda (ask for the c/Conde de Ureña stop) stops
almost outside. ❺

Parador de Málaga–Gibralfaro Monte de
Gibralfaro ☎95 222 19 02, ⓦwww.parador.es.
You won't get a better panoramic view of the coast

than from this eagle's nest on top of the Gibralfaro hill. Rooms come with a/c and satellite TV and, although it's quite small for a parador, it does have a pool. Well worth calling in for a drink or a meal (see "Eating" p.108). **❼**

The Town

Málaga is bisected by the seasonal Guadalmedina river, which was unsuccessfully landscaped in the 1990s at colossal cost with dismal walkways and reluctant grass. All the major sights lie to the east of this and below the **Alcazaba**. From the **Alameda**, the city's main thoroughfare, the **cathedral**, **Museo Picasso** and a clutch of interesting **churches** all lie within a few minutes' walk. The city has embarked upon a plan to revitalize the *casco antiguo* (old town) by pedestrianizing much of the monumental zone and laying with marble the whole of **c/Marqués de Larios** – a fashionable shopping street – and the focal **Plaza de la Constitución**.

Alcazaba and Gibralfaro castle

Málaga's magnificent **Alcazaba** (Tues–Sun: April–Sept 9.30am–8pm; Oct– March 8.30am–5.45pm; €1.90 or combined ticket for Alcazaba and Gibralfaro €3.15) and Gibralfaro (see below) are an exuberant contrast to the dour fortresses of Castile. At the Alcazaba's entrance stands a **Teatro Romano**, unearthed in 1951 during the construction of the Casa de Cultura, which was recently demolished to allow restoration of its ancient predecessor. The theatre, constructed in the second century BC, is now used as an auditorium for various outdoor entertainments. From here a path winds upwards, lined by the cypresses and flower-encircled arbours so loved by the sybaritic Moors. The citadel too is Roman in origin, and interspersed among the Moorish brick of the double- and triple-arched gateways are recycled blocks and columns of classical marble.

Although the Moors began building on the hill in the 700s, the Alcazaba with its interior palace as we see it today dates from the early decades of the eleventh century and was substantially restored and rebuilt in 1930. It was the residence of the Arab emirs of Málaga, who carved out an independent kingdom for themselves upon the break-up of the Western Caliphate during the same period. Their independence lasted a mere thirty years, but for a while the kingdom grew to include Granada, Carmona and Jaén. Strolling among the restored patios and terraces lined with cypresses, aromatic plants and ornamental pools the impression is of a smaller-scale Alhambra, and traces of stucco decoration surviving on the arches are similar to the artistry to be seen at Medina Azahara near Córdoba.

A recent refurbishment of the palace was intended to provide a home for the town's archeological museum, but political squabbles have seen the jettisoning of this plan and it now seems likely that the archeological collection will be relocated elsewhere (consult tourist offices for the latest information; see p.98).

To reach the Alcazaba without the climb, you can use a **lift** constructed inside the hill itself. With its entrance on c/Guillen Sotelo, directly behind the Ayuntamiento, it transports you effortlessly upwards to emerge in the heart of the palace.

Gibralfaro castle

Above the Alcazaba, and connected to it by a long double wall, is the **Gibralfaro castle** (same hours and entry charges as Alcazaba) reached by climbing a path to the rear of the palace or – and by far the most appealing approach – taking the road to the right of the Alcazaba, then following a path up through gardens, a ramble of towers, bougainvillea-draped ramparts and sentry-box-shaped Moorish wells. You can also approach from the town side, as the tourist coaches do, but this is a rather unattractive walk and not one to be done alone after sundown.

Built by Yusuf I of Granada in the fourteenth century and last used in 1936 during the Civil War, the castle, with its formidable walls and turrets, has, like the Alcazaba, been wonderfully restored and now houses an interesting **museum** dealing with the Gibralfaro's history. Among a collection of military exhibits from all periods there's also a splendid scale model letting you see how the city and Alcazaba complex would have looked in Moorish times. If you're visiting Macharaviaya (p.127), there's a display of seventeenth-century playing cards that were made in the factory there. A walk around the castle's **ramparts** affords terrific views over the city and the complex fortifications of the Alcazaba.

While you're up here, a pleasant place for a **meal** or a **drink** is the nearby *Parador de Málaga–Gibralfaro*, with its terrace overlooking the city (see "Accommodation", p.99). It's reached by following the road leading out of the castle's car park for 500m. If you're feeling lazy, bus #35 from the Alameda Principal in the city centre will drop you by the castle entrance.

The Catedral

Dominating the views from the Gibralfaro is Málaga's peculiar, unfinished **Catedral** (Mon–Sat 10am–6.45pm; €3.50). It lacks a tower on the west front, the result of a radical *malagueño* bishop having donated the earmarked money to the American War of Independence against the British. Despite this curiosity, which has resulted in the building's popular nickname La Manquita ("the one-armed lady"), the cathedral lacks much else of interest. The soaring interior is distinguished only by an intricately carved and naturalistic seventeenth-century *sillería* (choir stall) with outstanding sculptural work – in particular *St Francis* and *John the Baptist* – by Pedro de Mena. However, the **Iglesia del Sagrario** (same ticket and hours as cathedral; also open during services), on the cathedral's northern flank, is worth a look, if only for its fine Gothic **portal**, dating from an earlier, uncompleted Isabelline church. Inside, a restored and magnificent gilded **Plateresque retablo**, which is brilliantly illuminated during services, is the work of Juan Balmaseda. Just along c/Cister from here, you could take a look at the exterior of the house where **Pedro de Mena** – often described as Andalucía's Michelangelo – lived during his years in Málaga; a crumbling place marked by a plaque, it's in a small cul-de-sac named c/Afligidos.

The Museo Picasso

Located just round the corner from the cathedral on c/San Agustín, is the **Museo Picasso Málaga** (Tues–Sun 10am–8pm; permanent collection €6, temporary collection €4.50; combined ticket for both €8; ⓦwww .museopicassomalaga.org) housed in an impressive sixteenth-century mansion – the former residence of the counts of Buenavista – with an elegant patio. A source of enormous pride for the city, the museum was opened by the king and queen in 2003, just over one hundred years after Picasso left Málaga at the age of ten and to where he returned only once for an unhappy, fleeting visit in 1901. In later life he toyed with the idea of "sending two lorries full of paintings" to set up a museum in Málaga but vowed never to visit Spain while General Franco was still alive – Picasso died in 1973 and was outlived by the dictator by two years.

The museum's **permanent collection** consists of 204 works donated by Christine and Bernard Ruiz-Picasso, the artist's daughter-in-law and grandson, while a significant number of limited period loans from the Ruiz-Picassos and major museums make up the **temporary collection**. Whilst not on a par with the Picasso museums in Paris and Barcelona, it does allow you to see some of the lesser-known works that Picasso kept for himself or gave away to his lovers, family and friends – rather harshly described as "the less saleable stuff" by one critic.

Among the highlights are, in Room 2, *Olga Koklova con Mantilla* (a portrait of his first wife, draped in a hotel tablecloth) and a moving portrait of his close-cropped son Paul, painted in 1923. Other rooms have canvases from the breadth of Picasso's career including his Blue, Pink and Cubist periods, as well as sculptures in wood, metal and stone and a few ceramics. Two other influential women who figured prominently in the artist's long and turbulent love life are also the subjects of powerful images: in the temporary collection *Mujer Sentada en un Sillón (Dora)* is a portrait of the beguiling yet tragic Dora Maar, and in Room 8, *Jacqueline Sentada* is a seated representation of his second wife, Jacqueline Roque.

The museum's basement has the unexpected surprise of **archeological remains** revealed during its construction. Substantial chunks of a Phoenician city wall and tower dating from the seventh century BC survive, while from later periods you can view the remains of a Roman *salazones* factory used to produce the famous *garum*, a fish-based sauce and Roman delicacy, and also the remains of the cellar of the sixteenth-century Palacio de Buenavista. A case nearby displays some of the finds unearthed in the excavations including Phoenician, Greek and Roman pottery fragments and a sixth-century BC Egyptian scarab.

The museum also has a good, if cramped, **bookshop** and an equally cramped cafetería, although this spills out onto a pleasant garden terrace in fine weather.

The Picasso museum has taken over the building that previously housed the **Museo de las Bellas Artes** collection, which includes important works by Murillo and Zurbarán. There are plans afoot to relocate this collection in the Aduana (the old customs building on the Paseo del Parque) and either of the tourist offices should have the latest news on this or check their websites.

Casa Natal de Picasso

Picasso's birthplace and family home during his early years, the **Casa Natal de Picasso**, Plaza de la Merced 15, is now the headquarters and museum of the Picasso Foundation (Mon–Sat 10am–8pm & 6–9pm, Sun 10am–2pm; €1). It was during his formative years in Málaga that Picasso's prodigious talent for drawing was first noticed – "When I was a child I could draw like Raphael," he later wrote. "It took me all my life to learn to draw like a child." It was in the cafés around the square that the boy saw the first solid shape that he wanted to commit to paper: *churros*, those oil-steeped fritters that Spaniards dip into their breakfast chocolate.

The recently revamped exhibition space now displays lithographs, etchings and washes by Picasso – mainly with women as the subject matter – while on the stairs are displayed photos of the artist at various stages in his long life. The stairs lead to a reconstructed reception room which has been furnished in the style of the late nineteenth century when Picasso was growing up here. Among the items on display is some embroidered bed linen by the artist's mother, a canvas by his art teacher father and the infant Picasso's christening robe used in the ceremony at the nearby Iglesia de Santiago.

Pasaje de Chinitas

Tucked behind the Plaza de la Constitución, and on the Turismo's doorstep, is one of Málaga's most evocative corners, the **Pasaje de Chinitas**. In the first half of the last century, when Málaga was a thriving industrial town, this narrow white-walled street was filled with *tascas*, or bars, where businessmen would meet to discuss deals over fine wines before slinking off to the *Café de Chinitas* to hear some of the best flamenco in town. In the 1920s and 1930s the fame of this flamenco shrine, now a mundane textile store, grew as it became a noted meeting place of artists and writers, bullfighters and singers. Lorca loved the place and composed a poem in its honour, part of which appears on a plaque fixed to the former café, at the junction with c/Sánchez Pastor:

> In the Café de Chinitas
> Said Paquiro to his brother:
> "I'm more valiant than you,
> more brave and more gitano."

Museo de Artes y Tradiciones Populares and the Centro de Arte Contemporaneo

Just east of the Guadalmedina and housed in a seventeenth-century inn, the entertaining **Museo de Artes y Tradiciones Populares**, c/Pasillo Santa Isabel 10 (Mon–Fri 10am–1.30pm & 4–7pm, Sat 10am–1.30pm; €2), uses the former stables and stores on the lower floor as well as the lodging rooms above to mount displays of arts, crafts and furniture from previous eras. These include a collection of *barros malagueños* – typical painted clay figurines – as well as boats, carriages, farming and wine-making implements and rooms furnished in period style.

To the south of here, following the Río Guadalmedina, is a recently opened **Centro de Arte Contemporaneo** c/Alemania s/n (Sept–June Tues–Sun 10am-8pm; July & Aug 10am–2pm & 5–9pm; free), a modern art museum displaying canvases by American colourist Alex Katz, figurative and installation work by the late Spanish sculptor Juan Muñoz as well as exhibits by US photographic artist Cindy Sherman and her compatriots Ed Ruscha and Peter Halley, among many others. At the time of writing the Málaga city government is planning a substantial enlargement of the museum towards the river and has asked leading architect Rafael Moneo to submit a design for this.

Jardines de Picasso

West of here across the Puente Tetuán and 200m or so beyond the El Corte Inglés department store stands a modern garden, the **Jardines de Picasso**. A memorial garden dedicated to the city's favourite son, in 1978 Spain's first monument to the artist was erected here, a curiously restrained and abstract work by Ramón Calderón. Second thoughts, however, were in a much more monumental vein and Ortiz Berrocal was commissioned to produce something of the size required: a wonderfully intestinal bronze, flanked by two magnificent dragon trees that are fairly remarkable sculptures in their own right. Don't hang around here after dark, however, as the area has a dubious reputation.

Mercado Central

Lying at the heart of an area that bustles with life, the nineteenth-century wrought-iron, Mudéjar-style **Mercado Central** (officially the Mercado Central de Atarazanas, just north of the Alameda on c/Atarazanas, incorporates a little-known architectural gem, largely unnoticed by the daily shoppers. The remarkable fourteenth-century **Moorish arch** on its southern facade was built for Yusuf I of Granada – the ruler also responsible for that other great gateway, the Puerta de la Justicia in the Alhambra – when Málaga was part of the Nasrid kingdom. In those days it formed the entrance to the Moorish arsenal, and the original building's purpose is preserved in the market's present name: Atarazanas in Arabic translates as "the house that guards the arsenal". Note the two coats of arms in the upper corners inscribed in Arabic with the confident proclamation, "There is no Conqueror but Allah. All Praise to Him."

Paseo del Parque

An ideal place for a stroll, especially on summer evenings when the air has cooled, the **Paseo del Parque** is an elegant, palm-shaded avenue laid out at the turn of the twentieth century on land reclaimed from the sea. Along its length are a number of architectural delights as well as a remarkable **botanical garden** containing hundreds of exotic plants and flowers and many varieties of fig, bamboo, jacaranda and yucca trees. Discreet plaques placed at intervals along the esplanade identify the different species. Among the buildings of note are the Neoclassical **Aduana** (the former Customs house) started in 1788, with an austerely impressive patio and, further along, **El Correo**, or the old post office. Don't miss the *paseo*'s star turn a little further on, the exuberant **Ayuntamiento**, a delightful cream and brown Art Nouveau pile, constructed to coincide with the opening of the esplanade. Almost opposite the Correo in the gardens stand the first two of Pimentel's trio of evocative bronzes which are among Málaga's best-loved sculptures: **El Jazminero** (*The Jasmine Seller*) celebrates the men who once sold their trays of blooms throughout the city while the nearby **El Verdialero** pays tribute to the colourful and frenetic Verdiales musicians from the mountains of Málaga to the northeast of the city. The third bronze, **El Cenachero** (*The Fish Seller*), commemorating men who, with their baskets of fish dangling from a yoke, used to be a common sight on the city's streets, is sited behind the municipal tourist office on Plaza de la Marina.

At the Paseo's eastern end you'll come to the **Fuente de Genova**, or Genoa fountain, now encircled by traffic and difficult to appreciate. An Italian Renaissance work, it was captured by pirates during the reign of Carlos V while being transported to its Spanish buyer; when it was finally retrieved, the king awarded it to the city by royal edict.

The English Cemetery

Flanked by carved stone rampant lions, the **English Cemetery**, 150m east of Málaga's bullring (Mon–Fri 9.30am–2.30pm, Sat & Sun 10.30am–12.30pm; contributions welcome) dates from an era when gunboats flying Union Jacks held the world in awe. This did not, however, disturb the Spanish authorities from their post-*Reconquista* custom of denying Christian burial to all "infidels" unlucky enough to die on Iberian turf. British Protestants – who were included in this grouping – suffered the indignity after death of burial upright in the sand below the tide line to their necks. Málaga's expatriate population, which increased during the early nineteenth century, was, understandably, not amused when some of these "shore burials" were washed up on the beach or even seen bobbing on the waves. Thus in 1830 the British consul, William Mark, finally persuaded the authorities to let him found the English Cemetery. In the early days, and to get the place established, it seems that Mark pursued corpses with the zeal of a body-snatcher, hardly waiting for the deceased to expire before carting them off to the new graveyard. Traveller Richard Ford, whose wife's

△ El Jazminero, Paseo del Parque

frailty was his original reason for coming to Spain, became alarmed when Mark began to make overtures. "Hearing of my wife's ill health, he tried all in his power to get me to Málaga to have a pretty female specimen in his sepulchral museum," he wrote to a friend.

The cemetery itself, once an isolated site overlooking the sea but now enveloped by urban sprawl, is still nevertheless a leafy and tranquil oasis. Follow the path from the Paseo de Reding up to the modest red stone **church of St George** where, just before it, stands the sepulchre of William Mark. Further up the hill you'll see the original **walled cemetery** containing the oldest graves, among them a number studded with seashells (an ancient symbol of immortality), marking the passing of child victims of fever and consumption, the scourge of that age.

Alongside the old cemetery's eastern wall the tombstone of Gamel Woolsey, poet and wife of **Gerald Brenan** and author of *Malaga Burning* (see p.693), is inscribed with a poignant message from Shakespeare's *Cymbeline*: "Fear no more the heat o' the sun." In 2001 the remains of her husband were finally placed in a grave alongside hers after lying in a bath of formaldehyde in Málaga University medical school since his death in 1987, as Brenan had specified in his will that he wished his body to be used for medical science. The hospital had no use for the corpse and it took Brenan's friends and admirers over a decade to gain custody of his remains. These were finally interred in the grave and covered with a bucket of earth each from Yegen (see p.587) and Alhaurín El Grande, the two locations where he had spent most of his life. The writer's epitaph is eloquently laconic: "RIP Gerald Brenan, Escritor Inglés, Amigo de España." Many of the other tombstones dotted around the cemetery with their dedications to wives, loyal servants and men of military zeal, most of them in English, make fascinating reading.

Due to funding problems in recent years the cemetery's future has been been thrown into doubt and burials are no longer allowed. A booklet *The English Cemetery at Malaga* by Marjorie Grice-Hutchinson (herself buried here in 2003) gives a detailed history and is on sale, with proceeds going to the cemetery's upkeep.

Nuestra Señora de la Victoria and other churches

Sited on the spot where Fernando and Isabel pitched their tent during the 1487 siege of Málaga, **Nuestra Señora de la Victoria** (Tues–Fri 7am–noon & 4.30–6.30pm; €3), at the north end of c/de la Victoria, is, after the cathedral, Málaga's most prestigious church, where the city's Virgin patron is venerated. The fifteenth-century building was substantially rebuilt in the seventeenth century by the Count of Buenavista, whose remains, along with those of his descendants, lie in an eerie **crypt** decorated with symbolic stucco skeletons and skulls. Above, the main altar's centrepiece is an image of the Virgin in a *camerín* attributed to Pedro de Mena (see p.101).

More central churches with interesting features are the **Iglesia de Santiago** (where Picasso was christened), c/Granada, with an original fifteenth-century Mudéjar tower – note the intricate *sebka* brickwork reminiscent of the Giralda in Sevilla – and the **Iglesia de San Juan**, c/San Juan 3, founded in 1487, with the addition of a curious Baroque tower-portal. The heavily restored interior contains a fine seventeenth-century sculpture of *San Juan* by Francisco Ortiz. Finally, to the north of San Juan, the sixteenth-century **Iglesia de los Santos Mártires**, in the street of the same name, underwent a flamboyant Rococo remodelling a century after construction and is the home church of many of the *cofradías* (brotherhoods) who march in the Semana Santa processions bearing many of the fine images of Christ and the Virgin to be seen in the side chapels.

Jardín Botánico La Concepción

A pleasant trip out of town if you want to escape the centre for a few hours is to the remarkable **Jardín Botánico La Concepción** (guided tours Tues–Sat: April–Sept 10am–6.30pm; Oct–March 10am–4pm; last visit 90min before closing; €3.10), the city's botanical garden 3km out of Málaga at La Concepción. Among the finest in Spain, the gardens were originally designed in the 1850s by Amalia Loring, granddaughter of the British consul, and only purchased in 1990 by Málaga city council, since when they have been converted into the present tropical gardens. Beneath the thirty species of soaring palms, waving pines and lofty eucalyptus, you'll find yellow-flowering acacia, violet-blooming jacaranda and all kinds of exotic blooms trying to steal the show. There are trees of all shapes and continents, such as the Australian banyan with its serpentine aerial roots, giant sequoias, and a variety of bamboos, all to be seen on any one of the five guided itineraries.

To get there by car, take the N331 north out of Málaga, turning off at Km166, and follow signs to the Pantano del Agujero reservoir. You'll eventually see signs for the "Jardín Botánico". Departing from the north side of the Alameda, bus #61 will drop you at the gates on Saturday, Sunday and public holidays, but on weekdays it will drop you at its terminus, leaving a ten-minute walk. Another way of visiting the garden by bus is to use the Malagatour sightseeing bus (see p.98), which has a stop here. A taxi ride to La Concepción will cost about €6 one-way from the centre.

Eating

Málaga has a justified reputation for its splendid signature seafood platter, **fritura malagueña** (fried mixed fish). You'll find many fish restaurants grouped around the Alameda, near the bullring and on La Malagueta seafront, although for some of the very best you need to head out to the suburbs of Pedregalejo and El Palo, served by bus #11 from the Paseo del Parque. On the seafront *paseo* at **Pedregalejo**, almost all of the cafés and restaurants serve terrific fish. Further on, **El Palo** is an even better place to eat, with a beach and fishing huts. Most of Málaga's non-seafood restaurants are hardly in the same league, but we've listed some places where the food is well above average for the price.

To stock up on **picnic** food, your best bet is the Mercado Atarazanas (see also p.108), and for a sweet treat, the nuns at the Abadia (Abbey) of Santa Ana, c/Cister 11 (between the cathedral and the Alcazaba), sell their *dulces* (see box overleaf) between 9am and 1pm. Specialities are coconut and quince cakes. The Convento de las Clarisas does the same at c/Zumaya 1, across the river.

Plaza Merced and cathedral area

Antonio Fernando Lesseps 7. Popular small restaurant serving well prepared *malagueño* dishes with an outdoor terrace in an atmospheric cul-de-sac off the north end of c/Nueva; *menú* for around €12.

Cañadu Plaza de la Merced 21. A vegetarian option serving a good selection of salad and pasta-based dishes accompanied by organic wines and beers.

El Vegetariano de la Alcazabilla c/Pozo del Rey 5, off c/Alcazabilla. Good vegetarian restaurant serving soup, cheese, salads and pasta-based dishes in a cosy atmosphere. Mains €6–8.

La Barraka c/Alcazabilla 9. Decent diner with a few terrace tables and serving up *platos combinados* and an economical *menú* for €7.50 (excluding wine).

La Casa del Angel c/Madre de Dios 29 ✆95 260 87 50. One of the most interesting of Málaga's newer restaurants, sited in an elegant nineteenth-century town house, its walls covered with more than 100 original artworks by big names such as Picasso and Dalí. The eponymous owner is comedy actor Angel Garó who personally supervises the menu, featuring traditional *malagueño* dishes. Main courses priced €15–18.

Marisquería Alaska Plaza San Pedro de Alcántara, off c/Carretería. Good and cheap seafood served at tables under the trees in a charming *plazuela*.

Mesón Gibralfaro Pasaje Chinitas 6. Central and inexpensive restaurant serving *platos combinados*, salads and variety of *jamones* until after midnight.

Restaurante Tormes c/San Agustín 13. Decent meat and fish restaurant with terrace close to the Museo Picasso. They offer a tasty paella (for two) for €18; main dishes €7–14.

Wok Out c/Alcazabilla 14. Economical fast food wok-cooking diner where beef, pork and veggie fry-ups go for €7 a plate, washed down with draught beer.

Alameda Principal and Río Guadalmedina

Al-Yamal c/Blasco de Garay 3 ✆952 21 20 46. Good Arabic restaurant serving up pricey but authentic meat in spicy sauces – *cordero* (lamb) *couscous* is a house special. Good selection of Moroccan wines. Main dishes €10–15. Closed Sun.

Bar El Puerto c/Comisario. Another good *marisquería* a mere shrimp shell's throw away from the Casa Vicente (see below).

Bar Los Pueblos c/Atarazanas, opposite the *mercado*. Simple workers' place, serving satisfying food all day – bean soups and *estofados* are their speciality, while the *gazpacho* is served in half-pint glasses.

Casa Vicente c/Comisario. Lively *marisquería* in a narrow alley on the northern side of the Alameda.

Cyber@lameda Avda. Andalucía 13. This Internet bar (see "Listings", p.112) does a great value *menú* for around €6 (including wine).

El Legado Celestial c/Peregrino 2 at the back of the *Correo*. Delightful vegetarian and vegan self-service restaurant with an Asian slant. Standard charge of €6 and the menu includes a large selection of salads and a dozen or so hot dishes as well as some tempting desserts. Drinks are squeezed juices (their lemon, orange, apple and carrot cocktail is recommended) and teas, but no alcohol.

Restaurante Arcos Alameda 31. Efficient central place behind a garish neon exterior on the south side of the Alameda, towards the Tetuán bridge. Recommended for its all-day *platos combinados* and late-night meals.

Convento dulces

Many convents throughout Andalucía and Spain are in the business of supporting their orders by making **convent dulces**: cakes and pastries that they can sell to the community. Many recipes date back to the Arabs, who used rich combinations of eggs, almonds, sugar and honey to concoct their Moorish goodies. Each convent guards its recipes jealously, and many are so good that they supply local restaurants. The **sherry manufacturers** also had an influence on the development of *convent dulces*, for they traditionally used egg whites to clarify their wines and donated the leftover yolks to the nuns. This is the origin of many egg yolk-based creations such as *tocino de cielo* (Andalucía's richest flan) and *yemas* (sweet cakes), two of the region's most popular pastries.

In most convents you pay your money and are served with the sweets of your choice through a *torno* – a kind of revolving dumb waiter – which means you never see the nun who serves you.

Plaza de Toros and La Malagueta

Adolfo Paseo Marítimo 12 ℡ 95 260 19 14. One of the city's flagship restaurants, with a creative approach (the whole menu changes every four months) to cooking both meat and seafood dishes. There's a *menú de degustación* for around €40 (not available Sat). Closed Sun.

Antonio Martín Paseo Marítimo 16 ℡ 95 222 73 98. One of Málaga's most celebrated fish restaurants, over a century old and the traditional haunt of *matadores* celebrating their successes in the nearby bullring. Expensive, but probably the best in town for *fritura malagueña*. Has a sea-view terrace; main dishes €11–20.

Café de Paris c/Vélez Málaga 8 ℡ 95 222 50 43. One of Málaga's top restaurants for sampling *la cocina malagueña* at its very best. Dining *à la carte* doesn't come cheap but there's a *menú de degustación* for about €35 on weekdays and about €70 at weekends. Closed Sun & Mon eve.

Refectorium c/Cervantes 8, close to *Aceite y Pan* (see above) ℡ 95 221 89 90. Stylish, medium-priced, mainly fish restaurant where the *fritura malagueña*, *urta* (sea bream) and *pez espada* (swordfish) are mouthwateringly tasty. A small bar also serves outstanding tapas; main dishes €10–20.

Sal Gorda Avda. Canovas de Castillo 12. Excellent little *raciones* (and *media raciones*) bar-restaurant serving up a mouthwatering range of seafood and shellfish. Their *arroz marinero*

at €26 (for two) is recommended. Also have outstanding Asturian *sidra* (cider) on draught.

Out of the centre

Bar-Restaurante Palacios c/Eslava 4. Plain, honest food at bargain prices in a vibrant *comedor popular* with friendly waiters; specialities include *jamón iberico*, fish *surtido* and a mean *paella*.

Er Compá c/Compás de la Victoria 24. Pleasant Italian-Spanish owned small *mesón* fronting the church of Nuestra Señora de la Victoria, which offers Mediterranean dishes and a selection of tapas; Spanish-Italian wine list. A couple of nearby *marisquerías* with terraces are also worth a visit: *Noray* next door and *La Cómba* opposite.

El Tintero El Palo. Right at the far end of the seafront, just before the *Club Náutico* (stay on bus #11 and ask for "El Tintero"), this is a huge beach restaurant where the waiters charge around with plates of fish (all costing the same for a plate) and you shout for, or grab, anything you like. *Haute cuisine* it's not, but it's great fun and among the more worthy choices are *mero* (grouper) and *rosada* (rockfish).

Parador de Málaga–Gibralfaro Monte de Gibralfaro ℡ 95 222 19 02. Superior terrace dining with spectacular views over the coast and town, the parador's restaurant specializes in *malagueño* fish and meat dishes. Definitely worth a splurge, or try the *menú* (around €27) for excellent value. Book ahead if you want a table with view. See also p.99.

Drinking

Málaga has a variety of places to **drink**, from bustling breakfast cafés for *churros* and morning coffee to atmospheric bars where you can while away an evening. The best of the breakfast places are clustered around the Atarazanas market, where the daily bustle starts at dawn. **Bars** for more serious drinking – usually with tapas thrown in – are concentrated north of the Alameda and around the cathedral. A number of traditional bars serve the sweet **Málaga wine**, made from muscatel grapes and dispensed from huge barrels; other options include the new, incredibly sweet wine, Pedriot, and the much more palatable Seco Añejo, which has matured for a year.

Cafés

Bar Central East side of Plaza de la Constitución. Cavernous old institution in the centre of town, and one of the city's favourite meeting places with a terrace on the pedestrianized square. Serves tapas and also has an enticing cake counter.

Bar la Nueva Cubana Puerta del Mar 3, a block east of the market. Stylish place with outdoor tables for breakfast coffee and fresh *cruasanes* (croissants) or tea and tempting *pasteles* later in the day. There's another branch at c/Caldería 6, off c/Granada.

Café Lepanto c/Larios 7. This smart central café with an outdoor terrace is the perfect place for afternoon tea or coffee and they cook up a magnificent array of tempting *pasteles* to accompany the beverages.

Casa Aranda c/Herrería del Rey, just east of the market. One of the best of the market cafés, renowned for its excellent *churros*, served at outside tables. There are actually two bars here, one each side of the alley, but owned by the same family and operating as one.

Casa Mira c/Larios 5. This is the place where *malagueños* flock on summer nights for the best ice creams in town.

El Jardín c/Canon s/n, directly behind the cathedral. Nice place for breakfast *café* and *pasteles*, with a fountain, garden and cathedral view fronting outdoor tables. Does *platos combinados* later in the day, and in the evening transforms into a piano bar with a vaguely Viennese ambience.

El Viajero c/Santiago 8, near the Iglesia de Santiago. Relaxed café with a travelling theme; mounts exhibitions on its walls by travel photographers.

Nuestra Señora de la Victoria Hospital Cafetería Plaza Santuario, adjoining the church of the same name and accessed to the left of the church entrance. This café is one of Málaga's best-kept secrets and where – for the price of a coffee – you can sit at a table on a delightful seventeenth-century patio complete with fountain.

Tetería Alcazaba c/San Agustín 21. Cosy Moroccan tearoom almost opposite the Museo Picasso serving a wide range of herbal and Oriental teas. The nearby *La Tetería* at no. 9 is similar and also good.

Tetería Barraka c/Horno 10, close to the Museo de Artes y Tradiciones Populares. Another excellent Moroccan teahouse and confectioner's with an authentic *ambiente marroquí*. The *Tetería Zouk*, c/García Briz 3, slightly west of here, is a similar place with a wide selection of home-made confections.

Bars and tapas bars

Antigua Casa Guardia corner of c/Pastora, on the Alameda. Great old nineteenth-century spit-and-sawdust bar. Picasso was a devotee of their wines, and a photo on the wall shows him toting one of the bar's *jarras*. Try the house *mejillónes* (mussels) or *cola de langosto* (lobster's tail) with Málaga wine.

Antigua Reja (aka Casa Barcenas) Plaza de Uncibay. Lively bar at the northern end of this popular square with a wide tapas and *raciones* range.

Bar la Tosca c/Marín García 12. Popular, city-centre bar with a wide tapas selection and excellent *jamón serrano*.

Bar Lo Güeno c/Marín García 9, off c/Larios. Excellent and atmospheric tapas place; *pincho* (spicy shrimp) and *habas* (broad beans with black sausage) are specials. They've recently added a small restaurant immediately opposite.

Bar Orellana Moreno Monroy 5. Down a small side street off the east side of c/ Marques de Larios close to Plaza Constitución, this is one of Málaga's very best and friendliest tapas bars. House specials include a mouthwatering *palometa* (Ray's Bream).

Bodegas Quitapeñas (aka La Manchega) c/ Marín García 4. Another fine old drinking den; *jibias guisadas* (stewed cuttlefish) is a speciality.

Cafetería Axarquía Alameda Principal 36. Stylish bar near the Guadalmedina bridge with a wide tapas selection and good *fino*. Also does breakfast *chocolate y churros*.

Gambrinus c/Granada 39, north of the cathedral. Popular bar serving a good selection of *raciones* plus international beers.

Irish Times c/Fernando Camino s/n, near the Plaza de Toros. Atmospheric Irish bar with an "authentic" darkwood interior and serving Guinness and whiskeys.

La Casa Belga c/Keromnes 6, just east of the Plaza de Toros. Belgian brasserie and *cervecería* serving tapas with a Belgian slant, all washed down with some of the greatest beers in the world (Belgian, of course).

La Dehesa de Santa María c/Cister 8. Located near the cathedral, this is a branch of a popular tapas bar chain; whilst not up to the standards of the better places in town, with every *tapa* costing under a euro it certainly offers value for money.

Mesón Juan y Mariano c/Granados s/n, off Plaza de Uncibay. Another excellent tapas stop with a tiny restaurant. Try their *ensaladilla malagueño* with potatoes, oranges and cod.

Mesón Las Garrafas c/Mendez Núñez 5, off Plaza de Uncibay. Fine old bar with tiled walls, wooden beams, stacked barrels and good *fino*.

Rincón de Mata c/Esparteros 8. One of Málaga's oldest tapas bars, located in a tiny alley to the west of c/Larios, and decorated with wine bottles. Recommended are the *ensalada tropical* and *calamares rellenos* (stuffed squid).

Rincón de Oliva c/Don Cristián 1. Typical neighbourhood tapas bar round the back of El Corte Inglés with tasty *jamón serrano*.

Siete de Julio Avda. Canovas del Castillo 12, near the Plaza de Toros. Great Basque-run tapas bar, with good restaurant upstairs, taking its name from the start-date of the great festival of San Fermín in Pamplona – celebrated with a vengeance here.

Tapa's Bar Plaza de las Flores s/n. Pleasant new tapas bar with an inviting terrace on a shady square just off the eastern side of c/Marqués de Larios.

Nightlife

You'll find most of Málaga's nightlife northeast of the cathedral around **calles Granada** and **Beatas**, and **Plaza de la Merced** and **Plaza Uncibay**. In the summer months there's also a scene in **Malagueta**, south of the bullring. At weekends and holidays dozens of youth-oriented disco-bars fill the crowded streets in these areas, and over the summer – though it's dead out of season – the scene spreads out along the seafront to the suburb of **Pedregalejo**. Here the streets just behind the beach host most of the action, and dozens of discos and smaller music bars lie along and off the main street, Juan Sebastián Elcano. Málaga's daily paper, *Sur*, is good for local entertainment **listings** and there's a weekly English edition.

Flamenco

Genuine **flamenco** is hard to come by and the few shows there are in Málaga aren't up to much. Many of the *peñas* where it is performed are private, but you could try the venue below for something approaching the real thing. Many flamenco events (generally free) happen in and around the town throughout the year and the Turismo Municipal (see p.98) is the best source of information on these.

Doña Pepa c/Vélez-Málaga 6, two blocks south of the Plaza de Toros. This *bar-restaurante* has a flamenco show at weekends in its main room. Turn up after 10pm.

Nightclubs and music bars

Anden Plaza de Uncibay. Fri & Sat only disco-bar that's open till very late and attracts a wild crowd.

Asúcar Junction of c/Juan de Padilla & c/Lazcano west of Plaza de Uncibay. The place to come for salsa in Málaga.

Bolivia c/Bolivia 97, Pedregalejo. Cocktails and music with a nice summer terrace.

Calle de Bruselas Plaza de la Merced 16. A laid back, largely gay Belgian-style bar with lively terrace that stays open into the small hours.

Cervecería Brow Beer c/Ángel 3 off c/Granada. Bar specializing in a wide variety of world beers. Serious drinkers at midday, youthful revellers at night. Also serves tapas.

Cosa Nostra c/Lazcano 5, slightly west of Plaza de Uncibay. Music bar with mafia-theme decor and regular live bands. Open Thurs–Sun 11pm–6am.

El Cantor de Jazz c/Lazcano 7, west of Plaza Uncibay. Over-thirties hang out at this atmospheric place often staging live jazz by local artists; famed for its great cocktails. Closed Sun.

El Liceo c/Beatas 21. Housed in an old mansion, this is a club popular with Málaga's expatriate set and there's often a lively scene.
El Pimpi c/Granada 62. Cavernous and hugely popular bodega-style bar serving up tasty *vino dulce* by the glass or bottle. A great place to start the evening.
Flor de Lis c/Plaza de la Merced 18. Trendy-chic café-restaurant and *bar de copas* which maintains a chilled out feel both day and night.
Green Village c/Alamos 2, near Plaza de la Merced. *Musica alternativa* club featuring local bands and DJs.
La Botellita adjacent to *Luna Rubia*, Pasaje Mitjana, slightly west of Plaza Uncibay. Wild place packed to the rafters with young local revellers dancing to the tunes of the Spanish top 40. Open till late.
La Chancla The beach, Pedregalejo. One of a rash of bars on the beach; bursts forth at midnight and continues until 3am or later.
Luna Rubia Pasaje Mitjana 4, slightly west of Plaza Uncibay. Wide range of international sounds in a place that's open till dawn.
Morrissey's Irish Pub Plaza del Siglo 3. Hibernian-style bar, popular with a foreign crowd, that occasionally stages live gigs.

Onda Pasadena c/Goméz Pallete 9, slightly north of Plaza de la Merced. Another good place to hear live performances (Tues & Thurs) of jazz and flamenco. Open till the early hours.
Psicodelia c/Madre de Dios 11, off the north end of Plaza de la Merced. Gay bar with eclectic music background.
Puerta Oscura c/Molina Lario 5 near the cathedral. Classical music bar – sometimes with live performers – which also mounts art exhibitions; serves cocktails, ices and baguettes, and opens until 3am.
Ragtime c/Reding 12, Malagueta. Specializing in jazz, blues and rock, often with live performers.
Siempre Asi c/Convalecientes 5, north of Plaza Uncibay. Another late bar playing Spanish rock and techno.
Tortuga Paseo Marítimo, Pedrogalejo 48. With a seafront location this bar has a selection of 40 *chupitos* (shots) and is popular with locals and visitors alike. The nearby *La Caba* is similar.
White c/José Denis Belgrano 19. Slightly cheesy this is one of the few options for midweek clubbing in the old town. Surprisingly good sounds are a mix of R'n'B and hip-hop.
ZZ Pub c/Tejón y Rodríguez 6 north of Plaza Uncibay. Live music at this popular venue on Mon & Thurs and DJs the other nights playing ethnic, funk and rock sounds.

Shopping

El Corte Inglés, Avda. de Andalucía 4, is a great **department store** and their supermarket has a terrific selection of wines and spirits. La Mallorquina, Plaza Felix Saenz (near the market), is also a good place to pick up *malagueño* cheeses, wines, almonds and dried fruit. The main **shopping area** for designer labels and shoes is c/Marqués de Larios together with its surrounding streets. Flamenca, c/Caldería 6 north of the cathedral (@www.flamenka.com), stocks a range of **trajes de flamenco** (costumes) as well as shoes, instruments and flamenco CDs, DVDs and books.

For **books and music**, El Corte Inglés stocks most foreign newspapers and periodicals, though Librerías Prometeo y Proteo, c/Puerta Buenaventura 3, at the eastern end of c/Carretería, is the city's biggest and best bookshop with an excellent selection of flamenco and folk on CD, and English-speaking staff. Candilejas, c/Sta. Lucía 9, north of Plaza Constitución, is another good outlet. Librería de Ocasión, c/Salinas 7, has a selection of English secondhand books, as do Librería Malagueña, c/Mártires 5; Librería Abadía, c/Comedias 16; and Librería Prometeo, c/Carretería 101.

If you're looking for **outdoor pursuits equipment** and advice try the excellent La Trucha, at c/Carretería 100 (☎95 221 22 03), north of Plaza de la Constitucíon, which sells top-brand Spanish walking and climbing boots and can provide information on a variety of courses for rock climbing, hanggliding, canoeing, caving and so on. Cimas Adventure (☎95 221 91 84) is another good shop nearby at c/Carretería 66. IGN **walking maps**, as well as 1:50,000 Mapas Cartografía Militar (military maps), are sold by Indice

(Mon–Fri 8.30am–2pm, ⓦ www.ine.es), c/Panaderos 2 just north of the Alameda Principal.

Listings

Airport Málaga's airport (ⓣ 95 204 88 04) is Andalucía's busiest. See "Arrival" (p.95) for details on transport to and from the airport.

Banks and exchange Numerous places all over town have ATMs/cash machines, especially along c/Marqués de Larios and on the Plaza de la Constitución. El Corte Inglés (see below) will also change currency free of charge.

Car, scooter and motorbike rental Reliable and inexpensive deals are available from Larios Car Hire, c/Roger de Flor 1, at the side of the bus station ⓣ 95 109 20 69, ⓦ www.larioscarhire .com. The same company also rents out a variety of outboard dinghies, boats and trailer-tents.

Consulates UK, Edificio Eurocom, c/Mauricio Moro Pareto 2 ⓣ 95 235 23 00; USA, Avda. Juan Goméz 8, Fuengirola ⓣ 95 247 48 91; Ireland, Galería Santa Monica, Fuengirola ⓣ 95 247 51 08.

Ferries and boat cruises Daily sailings to the Spanish enclave of Melilla in Morocco (7hr). Tickets from Trasmediterranea, Estación Marítima in the harbour, south of Plaza de la Marina (ⓣ 902 45 46 45, ⓦ www.trasmediterranea.es). Cruceros Málaga (ⓣ 95 212 22 88), near the ferry terminal in the port, run cruises four times daily each way to Benalmádena (a 75min trip); there's an onboard bar and glass bottom for viewing marine life. You can return with them or take the bus or train back. One-way €8, return €15 with reductions for kids.

Football Since their promotion to La Liga's first division in 1999, C.F. Málaga have established themselves in the top flight, usually finishing mid-table. Games are at La Rosaleda stadium, Paseo de Martiricos s/n, at the northern end of the Río Guadalmedina. Tickets can be purchased from the stadium (ⓣ 95 261 42 10, ⓦ www.malagacf.es).

Hospital Hospital Carlos Haya, Avda. Carlos Haya, 2km west of the city centre ⓣ 95 239 04 00. A handy 24-hour pharmacy, Farmacia Caffarena is located on the Alameda at no. 2, near the junction with c/Marqués de Larios ⓣ 95 221 28 58.

Internet Navegaweb, c/Molino Lario 11 (daily 10am–10pm), beneath the cathedral's shorter tower with plenty of screens and Pasatiempos, Plaza de la Merced 20 (daily 10am–11pm), are the most central places. On the south side of Avda. Andalucía, near El Corte Inglés. Ciber@lameda at no. 13 also has a good bar-restaurant (10am–11pm; see also "Eating", p.107). Near the Roman theatre Cibercafé Teatro Romano, c/Alcazabilla s/n (10am–midnight), is another tranquil place with plenty of screens while in the Alameda zone Trinitel, c/Trinidad Grund 5, near Hotel Sur (daily 10am–9pm) is another possibility.

Laundry The friendly Lavandería Pizarro, Alameda de Colón 18, to the south of the Puente Tetuán bridging the Guadalmedina, will do a 5kg same-day service wash for €12.

Left luggage There are lockers at the train station (daily 7am–10.45pm), and at the bus station (daily 6.30am–11pm).

Police The Policía Local are at Avda. La Rosaleda 19 ⓣ 95 12 65 00; in emergencies dial ⓣ 092 (local police) or ⓣ 091 (national).

Post office Avda. de Andalucía 1, on the left across the bridge at the end of the Alameda. Mon–Fri 8.30am–8pm, Sat 8.30am–2pm.

Telephones Locutorio at c/Molina Lario 11, near the cathedral (Mon–Sat 9am–9pm; Sun 10am–1pm). However, most international calls are more easily made from cardphone street kiosks. Cards can be purchased from any estanco (state tobacco outlet).

El Chorro Gorge and around

Inland, some 50km north of Málaga, the **Garganta del Chorro** (El Chorro Gorge) is an amazing place. Located to the south of the Embalse del Guadalhorce it's impressive in itself – an immense cleft cut through a vast limestone massif by the Río Guadalhorce – with daunting walls of rock as high as 400m along its three-kilometre length. But the real attraction is a concrete catwalk, **El Camino del Rey**, which threads the length of the gorge hanging precipitously halfway up its side. Built in the 1920s as part of a burgeoning hydroelectric scheme and opened by King Alfonso XIII who walked its whole length and gave it its name,

Walking the Camino del Rey

Walking the **Camino del Rey** catwalk is a risky proposition whichever way you decide to do it, and it should not be attempted if you are of a nervous disposition or are without a very good head for heights. Due to the obvious dangers involved, the safest way to do the Camino is on an **organized trip** with expert climbers Jean & Christine Hofer at *La Campana* (see p.114), who use ropes to ensure maximum safety. A plan to repair the *camino* has been announced (see below) but will not be completed until 2009. Repeated accidents and even deaths recently led Endesa, the electricity company who are proprietors of the structure, to cut access to the Camino del Rey catwalk from the El Chorro (southern) and Embalse (northern) ends. This was intended to prevent hikers from using the catwalk. The middle section, however, is still roughly intact – though in a terrible state of repair – and this can be accessed from the central part of the gorge, although you will have to return the way you came due to the demolition of each end of the catwalk mentioned above.

Many **independent hikers** used to walk through the rail tunnel from El Chorro train station – this is highly dangerous and now pointless as access to the Camino from here is no longer possible without ropes. To reach the catwalk independently you should leave the station and follow the road along the east side of the reservoir for 800m, passing the campsite to your right. You will pass two railway viaducts (the first made of stone, the second of steel); after the second viaduct (above a hydroelectric plant) you can walk up a track into railway tunnel 9 (which has three separate sections) – keep to the right hand (wider) side of the tunnel to avoid passing trains and **do not walk along the line**. Go through tunnels 8 and 7, beyond which, to the left, you will see a narrow concrete footbridge across the gaping gorge – without handrails or parapets – leading to the Camino. If you lose track of which tunnel you are in, always make sure that you can see light at the far end – if not, you have gone too far and should turn back. Once on the Camino, the catwalk can then be followed for about 1.5km to where it has been demolished, forcing you to turn back to descend again. Expert climbers have created access points at each end where the Camino has been demolished, but to get up or down you will need ropes and skills in abseiling. Needless to say, this is no longer a jaunt for adventurous amateurs and unless you have the necessary expertise and equipment you are strongly advised to consult professionals such as Jean and Christine Hofer (who have both and who still take groups along the whole Camino) or give the catwalk a wide berth. A safer way to view the Camino on your own – and a fine **walk** in itself – is to follow the road from the train station, signposted "Pantano de Guadalhorce", reached by crossing over the dam and turning right, then following the road north along the lake towards the hydroelectric plant. After 8km turn right at a junction to reach – after 2km – the bar-restaurant *El Mirador*, poised above a road tunnel and overlooking the various lakes and reservoirs of the Guadalhorce scheme. From the bar (where you should leave any transport), a dirt track on the right, just south of the tunnel entrance, heads towards the gorge. Follow this and take the first track on the right after about 700m. This climbs for some 2km to where it splits into two small trails. The trail to the left leads you to a magnificent viewpoint over the gorge from where you can see the Camino del Rey clinging to the rock face. The right-hand track climbs to an obvious peak, the Pico de Almochon, with more spectacular views, this time over the lakes of the Embalse de Guadalhorce.

it used to figure in all the guidebooks as one of the wonders of Spain. Today it's largely fallen into disrepair and since 2000 it has been officially closed. In 2005 after many false starts it was announced that the *camino* is finally to be repaired and rebuilt as a tourist attraction with the regional, provincial and central governments sharing the cost. The projected finish date is 2009. At present, despite a few wobbly – and decidedly dangerous – sections (one tourist fell to her death in 1998), with random holes in the concrete through which you can see the gorge hundreds of feet below, it's still possible to walk much of its length (see box on previous page). You will, however, need a head for heights, and at least a full day starting from Málaga. If you've neither, it's possible to get a glimpse of both gorge and *camino* from any of the trains going north from Málaga – the line, slipping in and out of tunnels, follows the river for quite a distance along the gorge, before plunging into a last long tunnel just before its head.

If you want to explore the gorge, head for **EL CHORRO**, served by a single daily direct train from Málaga (currently running at 7pm) with two daily trains in the opposite direction (9am & 3pm). There are no bus services from Málaga but there is a **bus** from Álora at 12.30pm (Mon & Fri only), which is served by 10 daily **trains** from Málaga. A taxi from Álora to El Chorro costs about €18. The village is rapidly becoming a centre of outdoor activities for the gorge, particularly rock climbing, and if you want to stay there are a number of **accommodation** options. The village has an excellent shady campsite (T95 249 52 44; W www.alberguecampingelchorro.com) with pool, bar and restaurant reached by heading downhill to your right for 400m after getting off the train. The campsite also offers bunk-beds in its *albergue* (€6) and rents out wood cabins sleeping up to six (❸). A new hostel, *Refugio La Garganta* (T95 249 51 01; ❶), passed on the way to the campsite, has slightly cheaper dorm beds and there's a communal kitchen. *Bar-Restaurante Garganta del Chorro* (T95 249 72 19, W www.lagarganta.com; ❹), at the southern end of the station platform, offers spacious and reasonably priced air-conditioned apartments inside a converted mill; there's also a pool and it has its own **restaurant**. At the opposite end of the station platform there's a grocery shop and a couple of bars, including *Bar Isabel*, which also has a few basic rooms (T95 249 50 04; ❶), plus a couple with bath. For a more tranquil option, follow the signs from the station along a track for 2km to the *Finca La Campana* (mobile T626 963 942, W www.el-chorro.com), a farmhouse set in rural surroundings, with an economical bunkhouse (❶), en-suite cottages with kitchen and two or four beds (❷) and a campsite. The farm has a pool and a small shop where you can hire out climbing equipment and mountain bikes, and they offer climbing and caving courses as well as guided tours along the Camino del Rey. More information on rock-climbing courses as well as guided walks and horse riding in the zone is available from Adventur El Chorro (T95 249 52 18) near the fountain ("El Fuente") in El Chorro; they also sell climbing gear and clothing.

From the station it's about 12km to some attractive lakes and reservoirs, such as the **Embalse del Guadalhorce**. Recent years of prolonged drought have dramatically lowered the water levels, making this area a great deal less attractive than in the past, but the lakes are often swimmable. You can camp along the rocky shores; alternatively, the village of Ardales (see p.117), 4km beyond the lake, has shops, bars, a couple of *hostales* and two daily buses to and from Ronda.

Bobastro

A few kilometres beyond El Chorro, amid some of the wildest scenery in the whole peninsula, lies **BOBASTRO**, the mountain-top remains of a Mozarabic fortified settlement. Famous as the isolated eyrie of colourful ninth-century rebel Ibn Hafsun (see box opposite), the castle was said to be the most impregnable in all Andalucía, but only a ruined **church**, carved into an enormous boulder, remains of the once-great fortress. Situated outside the

Ibn Hafsun

Born near Ronda around 860, **Ibn Hafsun** was a *muwallad* (of mixed Christian-Arab parentage) who, after killing a man, fell out with the Umayyad caliphate at Córdoba and resorted to a life of brigandage. Gathering around him a formidable army, he built his stronghold at Bobastro, and from 880–917 scored a number of spectacular victories over the many Umayyad forces sent to defeat him. At the height of his power Hafsun controlled an area between the straits of Gibraltar in the west and Jaén in the east. His defence of the poor against excessive Umayyad taxation and forced labour further served to increase the popularity of this Robin Hood-style figure, especially among his fellow *muwalladin* who believed they were getting a raw deal from their pure-blooded Arab rulers. After he converted to Christianity in 899, the church at Bobastro was constructed to receive his remains, which were duly interred there upon his death in 917. When Abd ar-Rahman III finally conquered Bobastro in 927, he exhumed the body of Hafsun and hung it on a gibbet outside the Alcázar in Córdoba as a "salutary warning to imitators and a pleasant spectacle to believers (true Muslims)".

original fortified area, and below some cave dwellings of uncertain date, the church is typically Mozarabic in style, its nave and two aisles separated by horseshoe-arched arcades. The transept, and a deep apse chapel flanked by two side chapels, can clearly be seen, making the edifice one of the few identifiable traces of building from the period. Nearby and to the west is the **Cueva de Doña Trinidad** with Paleolithic cave paintings; to see them you'll need to contact the museum at Ardales (see p.117).

You can **get to Bobastro** from El Chorro by crossing the dam from the train station and turning right along the road to *El Mirador* (see "Walking the Camino del Rey" on p.113). After a couple of kilometres a signed turn-off for the *Mesas de Villaverde* restaurant (on the left and easy to miss) indicates a twisting 2km route to another sign (marked "Iglesia Mozárabe") pointing to a slope with steps on the left. Leave any transport here and follow the path for 400m through the pinewoods to the site. Back on the main road and continuing west to just beyond the *El Mirador* restaurant will allow you to view the impressive **dam** at the junction of the two great reservoirs, with the marble table and throne where Alfonso XIII signed the completion of the work on May 21,1921. Across the dam and sited on the banks of the *embalse* is an attractive **hotel**, *La Posada del Conde*, Pantano del Chorro 16 (℡95 211 24 11, 🌐www.laposadadelconde.com; ❺), where some rooms have a view over the "lake"; there's also a good **restaurant**.

Álora

Located by the road to Antequera, 12km south of El Chorro and seen from afar, **ÁLORA** is a sparkling cluster of white-walled dwellings nestling between three rocky spurs topped by the ruins of a Moorish *alcazaba*. On closer acquaintance it's a rather sleepy market town with a severe traffic problem and many narrow, cobbled streets that are tricky to negotiate – which you'll need to do to get a look at the eighteenth-century church of **La Encarnación** (open for services) on the Plaza Baja, or to climb up to the impressive **castle** (daily dawn–dusk), filled with latter-day tombs and burials. Monday is **market** day, when the town becomes a lively mass of stallholders and shoppers. Next to the Encarnación church and housed in a sixteenth-century former chapel is the small **tourist office** (Mon–Fri 10am–2pm, Sat 11am–2pm; ℡95 249 83 80) and **archeological museum** (same hours; €1.50). **Places to stay** include the friendly

Hostal Durán, c/La Parra 9 (☎95 249 66 42; ❸ with breakfast), with a/c en-suite rooms and a **restaurant**, plus the nearby *Casa Parra*, c/La Parra 30 (☎95 249 76 58, ⓦwww.casaparra.com; ❹ with breakfast), with charming en-suite rooms in a restored town house, some with fine views. A good **place to eat** is the nearby *La Candela*, c/La Parra 30, with well-prepared dishes and a *menú* for €7. Álora also has a municipal **swimming pool** on the road towards El Chorro, which you may be glad of if the drought-stricken waters of the nearby lakes are too low for bathing.

Carratraca

Some 2km out of Álora, heading towards Ardales, the scenic MA441 passes the eighteenth-century Baroque **Convento de las Flores**, raised over the site of an earlier *ermita* left behind by Fernando and Isabel in thanksgiving after the town fell to Christian forces in 1484. The small convent **church** is a delight, with restrained frescoes and – on the main altar – a striking image of the Virgin in a *camarín*. The road corkscrews onwards through the hills and some excellent **hiking country** to reach **CARRATRACA**, 5km southeast of Ardales. The town is famous for its **sulphur spa**, now undergoing an extensive refurbishment and set to reopen in the summer of 2006.

Although the baths date back to the days of the Greeks and Romans, it wasn't until the nineteenth century that Carratraca became one of the foremost spas in Europe, and a gathering point for the continent's aristocracy. During its heyday the *balneario* attracted kings, princesses and literary bigwigs such as Lord Byron, Alexandre Dumas and Rainer Maria Rilke. The three casinos, where these socialites used to while away their time between plunges in the stinking, sulphurous waters, which gush from the rocks, are long gone. However, vestiges of the past can be seen throughout; the bath used by Empress Eugénie of France (wife of Napoleon III) is preserved "in perpetuity", the bathrooms are marked with their original signs, and you can visit an "injections room" containing a frightening collection of antique instruments used for propelling the waters into various bodily orifices. When the baths reopen you will be able to sample the hot baths, reputedly more beneficial than the cheaper cold plunge, although the latter is taken in wonderful eighteenth-century, open-air pools surrounded by classical Tuscan columns.

Carratraca's other sights include a Regency-style **Ayuntamiento**, on the edge of the village, formerly the residence of Doña Trinidad Grund, a local benefactor who donated funds for the excavation of the cave near Bobastro which bears her name. She also provided the backing for the curious **bullring** nearby, hacked out of solid rock and scene of the village Passion play during Semana Santa.

Practicalities

Carratraca has one of the most exotic **hotels** in Andalucía: a royal palace built by the tyrannical King Fernando VII early in the nineteenth century to accommodate himself and his retinue while visiting the spa (although he probably never used it). The ⚄ *Hotel El Príncipe*, c/Antonio Rioboó 9 (☎95 245 80 71, Ⓕ95 245 84 68), now occupies the building and is a wonderful old place, with an imposing portal and facade oozing faded grandeur. Currently undergoing renovation, it's scheduled to reopen early in 2006 as a three-star hotel. Just along from the baths, *Casa Pepa* (☎95 245 80 49; ❷) also offers simple **rooms** with and without bath, plus meals for guests. Places **to eat and drink** include *Venta El Trillo*, on the main road as you enter from Álora, with *Bar Venta Martillo* and

Venta El Punto nearby, all of which serve decent *menús*. *Terraza La Cueva*, downhill from the *Hotel El Príncipe*, is a pleasant bar for late-night imbibing that is built into a cave and surrounded by gardens and fountains.

Ardales

At the southern point of the third of the lakes that comprise the Guadalteba–Guadalhorce reservoir, the compact town of **ARDALES** tumbles down the hill below La Peña, a rocky outcrop topped by remains of the Iberian settlement of Turóbriga as well as a Roman fort and ruined Moorish *alcázar*. On the way up to the summit, look out for the fifteenth-century Mudéjar **Iglesia de la Virgen de los Remedios** with its distinctive, partly tiled, tower. When you reach the top, it becomes clear that the tower was the minaret of the former mosque. The interior also has Moorish arches dividing the nave and side aisles, the right of which has the mosque's original *mihrab* oriented towards Mecca. To see the church, call at the house of sprightly octogenarian Señora Asunción Martín, Plaza de la Iglesia 1, opposite, who will effortlessly sprint up the church steps to let you in. A new **Museo de la Historia y las Tradiciones** facing the bridge as you enter the village (Tues–Sat 10.30am–2pm & 5–8pm, Sun 10.30am–2pm; ☎95 245 80 46; €1) has Roman and Moorish archeological finds, sections dealing with local traditions and history, as well as copies of the rock paintings in the nearby paleolithic Cueva de Doña Trinidad (see p.115). The curator will also provide information on visits to see the caves which are currently open for guided tours on Tues, Thurs, Sat & Sun in July and August and Sat & Sun the rest of the year. Because numbers are strictly limited it's advisable to book in advance on the museum's number. If the museum's closed (during the above hours) enquire at the **Ayuntamiento**, set on the wide and animated central Plaza San Isidro, around which most of the activity in Ardales revolves.

The same plaza is also where you'll find a lively **bar** scene – *Bar El Mellizo* is the meeting place for the village's characters but *Bar El Casino* has the best tapas. To **eat** more substantially head for the popular *Mesón Ardales*, c/Cantarranas 2, slightly downhill from the square with a terrace, or, across the bridge at the bottom of the village, to the *Hostal-Restaurante El Cruce*, which serves a good-value *menú* and has en-suite **rooms** (☎95 245 90 12; ❸). *Casa Marcos*, just along the tree-lined main street at c/San Isidro 31, is a *pastelería* renowned for its tasty *roscos de almendras* (almond cakes).

Six kilometres east of Ardales along the MA444 lies the village's scenic "lakeside" **campsite** (actually next to a reservoir), *Camping Parque Ardales* (☎95 211 24 01, ⓦwww.campingparqueardales.com), which also rents out apartments sleeping up to four (❺) and offers a variety of activities including canoeing on the lake. There's no bus to the campsite but a taxi from Ardales will cost about €10 (any of the bars should be able to arrange this for you).

El Burgo and around

A lonely road leaves Ardales for the settlement of **EL BURGO**, 20km southwest. It's a beautifully scenic drive – and a fine three- to four-hour **walk** – through the rugged valley of the Río Turón, which gurgles beneath the heights of the Sierra de Ortegicar to the north and the Sierra de Alcaparain to the south. There's plenty of birdlife, and, halfway along the route, a deserted village with a ruined mill to explore. Until relatively recently, this was bandit country, where travellers needed to be constantly on their guard against robbers and kidnappers. One particularly ruthless *bandolero* named Pasos Largos (Big Steps) worked this stretch in the 1930s and ended his days in a shoot-out with the

Guardia Civil – his memory is still fresh around El Burgo where he was born. El Burgo, when you finally reach it, is a pleasant enough place with another ruined Moorish fort, and makes a good stopover.

The best **place to stay** is ⚜ *Posada del Canónigo*, c/Mesones 24 (☎95 216 01 85, Ⓦwww.laposadadelcanonigo.com; ❹), in a beautifully restored mansion, with friendly owners who can provide you with maps, and organize walks and horse riding in the surrounding hill country (and little-known natural park) of the Sierra de las Nieves. A slightly pricier hotel at the foot of the same street, *La Casa Grande*, c/Mesones 1 (☎95 216 02 32, Ⓦwww.hotel-lacasagrande.com; ❹), has arrived to give the *Posada* some competition but, whilst pleasant and comfortable, it lacks the former's personal touch. Budget rooms – some en-suite – are available at the central *Restaurante Sierra de la Nieves*, c/Comandante Benitez 26 (☎95 216 01 17; ❷). Places to **eat and drink** include the equally central *Bar El Porra* and *Restaurante Sierra de las Nieves*, as well as the restaurant of the *La Casa Grande*; there's also the more upmarket *Venta Yoni*, slightly out of the village on the Yunquera road.

You can also get rooms at **YUNQUERA** itself, 7km to the south of El Burgo and an alternative entry point into the Parque Natural Sierra de las Nieves, where there's another good *hostal-restaurante*: *Asencio*, c/Mesones 1 (☎95 248 27 16; ❷–❸) offering rooms with and without bath. A small **Turismo** at c/Pozo 17 (June–Sept daily 10am–1.30pm; ☎95 248 25 01) has an informative leaflet in Spanish on the sights around the village and walking in the Parque Natural. The village is noted for its local *mosto* (tasty unfermented grape juice), which is best sampled at the delightfully rustic *Bar Antonio Lopez*, c/Antonio 26.

The paved A366 from El Burgo meanders through the valley of the Río Turón and more ruggedly picturesque and uninhabited terrain, eventually climbing to the Puerto del Viento at 1190m. The descent from here crosses valley plains shared by wheatfields and grazing cattle overlooked by brooding, rocky heights until, after 20km, it reaches the suburbs of Ronda (see p.188), passing on the way a well-preserved stretch of **Roman aqueduct**.

Teba

About 15km north of Ardales, the village of **TEBA** spreads itself below a hill crowned by a striking ruined **Moorish castle** (open site) built on Roman foundations. There's a well-preserved dungeon in the castle, but you'll need a torch to find your way around. The castle battlements give wonderful **views** over the surrounding countryside – and you can also glimpse the tempting municipal **swimming pool** close by.

On the plain below the castle, a battle against the Moors took place in 1331 when the forces of Alfonso XI recovered Teba for Christian Spain. In this battle fought Sir James Douglas, who had been commissioned by a dying **Robert Bruce** to carry the Scottish king's heart to the Holy Land "to be carried in battle against the enemies of Christ". Douglas took the long way round, via Spain, and ended up getting involved at the siege of Teba. He wore the royal heart in a silver case around his neck and – at a critical moment in the battle – to spur on his men he threw it into the fray and charged after it to his death. The well-travelled heart was then recovered and taken back to Scotland to be buried in Melrose Abbey, where it was rediscovered in 1996. Near the centre of the village, in the Plaza de España, a block of Scottish granite has been set up to mark Teba's illustrious connection with Robert Bruce and the exploits of Douglas; it was unveiled by one of Douglas's descendants in 1989.

Teba's other main sight is **Santa Cruz Real**, an eighteenth-century Baroque church at the western end of c/San Francisco, with quite a few surprises. The enormous triple-naved interior is divided by lofty Tuscan columns of red marble. Among the church's many treasures, there's a sixteenth-century **gold-plated cross** near the main altar that was given to the castle's church by Fernando and Isabel and is one of only two in the whole of Spain. When the castle was destroyed, the church's valuables were moved here. The **tesoro** (the church's treasure and valuables) contains some beautiful early sixteenth-century vestments embroidered in gold thread also donated (and probably partly made) by Isabel, who was an accomplished seamstress. To see the church, call (preferably 5–6pm) at the adjoining house of the *cura* who will open it up.

The town also has an interesting small **Museo Municipal** (Sat & Sun noon–2pm & 6–8pm; free) located inside the Ayuntamiento on Plaza de la Constitución. It displays artefacts from all periods of Teba's distinguished history including Iberian sculptures from the late first-millenium BC, a fine head of the emperor Tiberius and a superb carved pedestal from the Roman era as well as coins, ceramics and jewellery from the town's Visigothic and Moorish periods. On weekdays, if you call at the Ayuntamiento before 2pm they will open up the museum for you.

You'll find **places to stay** on and around the main thoroughfare c/San Francisco where, at no. 26, the *Hostal Sevillano* (☎95 274 80 11; ❸) has clean en-suite rooms above a **restaurant** with a good-value *menú*. The same street and the nearby Plaza de Andalucía have more places for eating and drinking. Some 3km south of Teba along the old Ronda road an elegant *cortijo* hotel is a step up in price and quality from anything else in Teba: the *Hotel Molino de las Pilas* (☎95 274 86 23, ⓦwww.molinodelaspilas.com; ❺) is housed in a nineteenth-century whitewalled farmhouse with stylish rooms and a restaurant located in the former olive oil mill, whose central feature is a gigantic 120-year-old wooden press.

About 3km to the east of the village lies the small but picturesque Garganta de Teba or **Teba Gorge**, where the oleander-fringed Río la Venta cuts through the limestone hills to join the reservoir. A haven for all kinds of butterflies, there's also plenty of birdlife along the riverbanks and the gorge is a nesting site for the Egyptian vulture and Bonelli's eagle, along with plenty of other varieties such as black kites and choughs. To reach the gorge, descend the unsigned track that leaves the roadside by the bridge over the Río la Venta on the edge of the reservoir.

Antequera and around

Sitting on two low hills in the valley of the Río Guadalhorce, **ANTEQUERA** is an attractive market town with some important ancient monuments and a clutch of fine churches. On the main train line to Granada and at the junction of roads heading inland to Córdoba, Granada and Sevilla, it's easy to get to, and makes a good day-trip from Málaga, which lies 40km to the south. Travelling from Málaga, the bus takes you along the fast but largely uninteresting N331. If you're driving, it's far nicer to take the older, more picturesque road that meanders through **Almogía**, a small hill town with tortuously narrow streets. It's a sleepy place, except on Friday – market day – when the whole place spills over with shoppers. From Antequera itself a couple of enjoyable trips are to the vast **Parque Natural El Torcal** with its marvellous weathered limestone rock formations, and the important flamingo breeding grounds of **Fuente de Piedra**.

Arrival, information and orientation

Antequera's **RENFE station**, Avda. Estacion (☎95 284 32 26), is one kilometre from the centre of town (no bus service). The bus from Málaga brings you closer in, disembarking at the **bus station** (☎95 284 19 57) near the bullring. From here the Alameda de Andalucía and its continuation the c/Infante Don Fernando – the effective centre of town – are within easy walking distance. For information on the town, or help with finding a room, head for the helpful **Turismo Municipal** (April–Sept Mon–Sat 11am–2pm & 5–8pm, Sun 11am–2pm; Oct–March Mon–Sat 10.30am–1.30pm & 4–7pm, Sun 11am–2pm ☎95 270 25 05, ⓦwww.turismoantequera.com) on Plaza San Sebastián alongside the church of the same name. They can also provide information on Torcal and details of houses to rent in the surrounding countryside. A private **tourist office** (Mon–Sat 10am–2pm & 5–8pm, ☎95 270 00 05), which works closely with the above, is located nearby on Plaza Coso Viejo s/n, next door to the *El Angelote* restaurant. **Internet** access is available at Las Americas, c/Encarnación 15, northeast of the Plaza de San Sebastián (daily 9.30am–2.30pm & 4.30–11pm).

Accommodation

You shouldn't have a problem finding a **place to stay**, as demand tends to be low and the generally good-value room prices reflect this. Most hotels have either their own garage (for which you usually pay extra) or can advise on street parking. The nearest **campsite** is at El Torcal (see p.125).

Camas El Gallo c/Nueva 2 ☎95 284 21 04. Very friendly place offering simple spotless rooms (with fans in summer) and equally pristine shared bathrooms. ❶

Hospedería Coso San Francisco c/Calzada 25 ☎95 284 00 14, ⓦwww.cososanfrancisco.com. The former *Pensión Madrona* has had a refit and name change but still provides a friendly welcome with neat en-suite a/c rooms above a restaurant. ❸

Hostal Reyes c/Tercia 4 ☎95 284 10 28. Central en-suite rooms with a/c and TV. ❷

Hotel Casa del Conde de Pinofiel c/ Tercia 10 ☎ 95 284 24 64, ⓦwww.hotelcondepinofiel.com. Antequera's newest hotel occupies a striking eighteenth-century *casa-palacio* with well-equipped rooms situated around an elegant patio complete with Baroque chapel. ❻

Hotel Colón c/Infante Don Fernando 31 ☎95 284 00 10, ⓦwww.antequerahotelcolon.com. This welcoming central hotel is another reliable choice for rooms with a/c and satellite TV. ❸

Hotel Plaza San Sebastián Plaza San Sebastián 4 ☎95 284 42 39. Attractive two-star hotel facing the church of San Sebastián offering well-equipped a/c rooms with satellite TV. ❸

Número Uno c/Lucena 40 ☎95 284 31 34. A relatively new *hostal* with pleasant a/c en-suite rooms with TV, plus a roof terrace above a popular bar-restaurant. ❷

Parador de Antequera Paseo García del Olmo s/n ☎95 284 02 61, ⓦwww.parador.es. A modern parador, to the north of the *plaza de toros*, with well-appointed rooms plus pleasant gardens and pool. ❼

Pensión Toril c/Toril 3 ☎95 284 31 84. This tranquil and pleasant *pensión* has rooms with and without bath arranged around two patios. Free parking. ❷

The Town

A bustling agricultural centre where farmers from the surrounding *vega* come to stock up on everything from tractor tyres to seeding attachments, Antequera has a modern appearance that belies its history. In Roman times Anticaria ("ancient city") seems to have had a substantial population; much later, in 1410, the town was the first in Andalucía to fall to the Christian forces in the *Reconquista*.

Antequera divides into two zones: a **monumental quarter** situated at the foot of the hill dominated by the Alcazaba, and the mainly nineteenth-century **commercial sector** concentrated around the Alameda de Andalucía. This end of town is where modern Antequera works and plays, and there's not much in the way of sights, though the nineteenth-century bullring is worth a look. Probably the most famous sights, however, are the prehistoric **dolmen caves**, on the northern edge of town.

Antequera's annual **feria** happens during the third week in August, a harvest fiesta (*recolección*) with *corridas*, dancing and parades.

The Museo Municipal and San José

At the heart of the monumental quarter, the **Museo Municipal**, c/Coso Viejo s/n (Tues–Fri 10am–1.30pm & 4.30–6.30pm, Sat 10am–1.30pm, Sun 11am–1.30pm; hourly guided tours; €3), is located in a striking eighteenth-century ducal palace. It's just as well that the palace is worth visiting for itself, because the exhibits do little justice to the setting. Largely a hotchpotch of church vestments, silver plate and indifferent paintings, the collection is, however, distinguished by two works of sculpture: a fine first-century AD **Roman bronze** of a youth known as the *Efebo de Antequera*, and an eerily lifelike carving in wood of **St Francis of Assisi** by the seventeenth-century *andaluz* sculptor Pedro de

Mena. More fragments of ancient statuary and tombstones are dotted around the courtyard, and a room on the ground floor devotes itself to the artworks of a modern painter born in Antequera, Cristóbal Toral.

To the east of the museum, on the way to the Alcazaba, the eighteenth-century **Carmelite nunnery of San José** on Plaza de las Descalzas has a good selection of *dulces*. The entrance is behind the small fountain. Inside, asking for a *surtido* (sampler) gets you a bit of everything. You won't see the nun who serves you, but, in a sign of changing times, she may ask you to pay first.

Nuestra Señora del Carmen

The nearby Cuesta de los Rojas climbs steeply to the Postigo de la Estrella, an old postern gate. To the east of this – and not to be missed – lies the seventeenth-century Mudéjar church of **Nuestra Señora del Carmen** (Mon–Sat 10am–2pm & 4–7pm, Sun 10am–2pm; €1.50), whose plain facade little prepares you for the eighteenth-century interior, painstakingly restored to its former glory. The main altar's sensational thirteen-metre-high **retablo** – one of the finest in Andalucía – is a masterly late-Baroque extravaganza of carved wood by Antonio Primo and Diego Márquez, its centrepiece a Virgin in a *camarín* flanked by a bevy of polychromed saints and soaring angels.

The Alcazaba

Further up Cuesta de los Rojas lies the refurbished medieval **Alcazaba**, with its thirteenth-century Islamic fortification, the **Torre del Homenaje** (Tues–Fri 10.30am–2pm & 4.30–6.30pm, Sat & Sun 10.30am–2pm; free). The first fortress to fall to the Christians during the Reconquest of the kingdom of Granada, the ruined Alcazaba now encloses a municipal garden, giving fine views over the town towards the curiously anthropoid **Peña de los Enamorados** (Lovers' Rock) resembling the profiled head of a sleeping giant. The outcrop acquired its name from two lovers (a Christian girl and a Muslim youth) during the Moorish period, who are said to have thrown themselves from the top when their parents forbade their marriage.

Adjoining the Alcazaba, the sixteenth-century **Arco de los Gigantes** preserves stones and inscriptions embedded in its walls that were rescued by antiquaries from the destruction of the Roman town in the same period.

East of the castle, in the spacious Plaza Alta, the sixteenth-century collegiate church of **Santa María** (Tues–Fri 10.30am–2pm & 4.30–6.30pm, Sat & Sun 10.30am–2pm; free) boasts a great Plateresque facade inspired by a Roman triumphal arch. Inside the church – which now serves as a concert hall – you'll also see a superb Mudéjar coffered ceiling.

Antequera's other churches

Walking from the Alcazaba back into the centre you pass a number of churches. The seventeenth-century **San Sebastián** (daily 9.30am–7pm), in the elegant plaza of the same name, possesses a striking brick steeple that dominates the town. Note the carved angels and the tower's weather vane, El Angelote, which has the remains of Antequera's patron saint, Santa Euphemia, in a reliquary hung around its neck. The interior contains some beautifully carved choir stalls, as does the nearby eighteenth-century **San Agustín**, at the start of c/Infante Fernando. At the western end of this street and close to the Palacio Consistorial – a stylish seventeenth-century mansion now functioning as the Ayuntamiento (access to view patio during working hours) – lies the Renaissance church of **San Juan de Dios** (Tues–Fri 7am–9pm, Sun 11.30am–1pm), constructed (or so Richard Ford maintained) almost entirely with stone taken from the demolition of what

△ Antequera

was a perfectly preserved Roman theatre. Slightly further away up a steep climb at the southern end of the town, the Plaza del Portichuelo has the flamboyant Baroque-Mudéjar **Capilla de la Virgen del Socorro** with a double tier of triple arches built to house Antequera's most revered image, Nuestra Señora del Socorro (Our Lady of Succour). The nearby white-walled Baroque chapel of **Santa María de Jesús**, with storks' nests in its belfry, is also worth a look. From a *mirador* behind the churches there are great views towards the Alcazaba and the surrounding hills.

The Plaza de Toros

The western end of town has little in the way of sights, though the nineteenth-century **Plaza de Toros** (museum Sat 6–9pm; Sun 10am–1pm & 6–9pm; free), on the Alameda de Andalucía, is well worth a look – access is usually available to the ring when the restaurant (see "Eating and drinking") is open. This bullring staged its first *corrida* on August 20, 1848, and whatever your views on bullfighting, it's difficult not to pick up on the atmosphere that the old place generates, especially when you view the amphitheatre from the *matador's* position in the centre of the arena.

The dolmen caves

On the town's northern outskirts – an easy one-kilometre walk along the Granada road – lies a group of **prehistoric dolmens** (Tues–Sat 9am–6pm, Sun 9.30am–2.30pm; free), which rank among the most important in Spain. The grandest of these megalithic monuments is the **Cueva de Menga**, its roof formed by massive stone slabs, among them a 180-ton monolith. Dating from around 2500 BC, the columned gallery leading to an oval burial chamber was probably the final resting place of an important chieftain. On the last stone slab of the left wall you'll see some engraved – and probably symbolic – forms; the star, however, is a more recent addition. If you stand just inside the entrance to the Menga dolmen you will be able to see the Lovers' Rock, precisely framed in the portal – something that cannot have been accidental and suggests that the rock may have had some religious or ritual significance. This is underlined by the fact that the sun rises behind the "head" of the rock at the summer solstice and penetrates into the burial chamber.

The **Cueva de Viera**, dating from a century or two later, has better-cut stones, forming a long, narrow tunnel leading to a smaller burial chamber. To the west of here it's possible to make out the quarry on the peak of a nearby hill (topped by a rather incongruous school) from where the stone used to construct the dolmens was hewn before being hauled across the intervening valley.

The third dolmen, **El Romeral** (same hours), is a further 2km down the road on the left behind a sugar factory (easily identified by its chimney). Once you've crossed the train line, the road to it is signed on the left; if it's locked you'll have to return to the Cueva de Menga for the key. Built more than half a millennium later than the other two dolmens and containing dual chambers roofed with splendid corbel vaulting, El Romeral has something of an eastern Mediterranean feel, and bears an uncanny resemblance to the tholos tombs constructed in Crete at around the same time.

Eating and drinking

Antequera, unlike its neighbours on the coast to the south, has little in the way of exciting food or entertainment options. You'll trail past a variety of fast-food places, bars and *heladerías* along the Alameda, but a far better bet, during the day at least, is to head for the many places to eat around the market on Plaza Abastos, catering for the traders and customers who flock in from miles around. Among numerous good places here, the *Hospedería Coso San Francisco*, c/Calzada 25, has a restaurant offering typical dishes of the region with a *menú de degustación* for €15 as well as a bar-cafetería with a hearty and inexpensive *menú* for €7. Good **tapas bars** include the excellent *Bar-Cafetería A La Fuerza*, c/Alameda de Andalucía 32, near the bullring; *Bar Castilla*, c/Infante Don Fernando 40, attached to the hotel of the same name; the nearby *Bar Chicón*, c/Infante Don Fernando 1; and *Bar Lo Güeno*, Plaza Fernández Viagas, slightly east of the Plaza de Abastos.

El Angelote, c/Encarnación, s/n (☎95 270 34 65), is probably the town's best **restaurant** and although mid-priced has a *menú* for €11.50; there's a pleasant terrace too. The slightly more economical *Mesón Papabellotas*, at c/Encarnación 3 just opposite, is another possibility. *Mesón Noelía*, Alameda 12, serves medium-priced *platos combinados* and a good-value *menú*, and has pavement tables – only really appealing once the traffic has died down. A quieter location to sit out is at the *Plaza de Toros*, the bullring's very own restaurant, which offers a medium-priced *menú*, as well as more expensive meals – the bar here is also a good place to stop for lunchtime tapas. *La Espuela*, c/San Agustin 1, a small cul-de-sac off c/Infante Don Fernando, is another excellent mid-priced restaurant with a small terrace and a *menú* for €11. Finally, a couple of good **breakfast bars** are the aforementioned *Bar-Cafetería A La Fuerza* and *Café del Centro* at c/Cantareros 3, slightly north of the main street, where the walls are decorated with photos from Antequera's past.

Parque Natural El Torcal

EL TORCAL, 13km south of Antequera, and 32km north of Málaga, is the most geologically arresting of Andalucía's natural parks. A massive high plateau of eroded grey limestone dating from the Jurassic period, tempered by a lush growth of hawthorn, ivy, wild rose and thirty species of orchid, it's quite easily explored using the **walking routes** that radiate from the centre of the park where the road ends. A **Centro de Recepción** here (daily 10am–5pm; ☎95 203 13 89) gives out maps and general information on the park and its walks, and has audiovisual presentations covering geology, flora and fauna. Try to leave your explorations until the more peaceful late afternoon, when the setting sun throws the natural sculptures into sharp relief.

The best-designed and most exciting **trails** are the yellow and red routes, the former climaxing with suitable drama on a cliff edge with magnificent views over a valley. The latter gives fantastic vantage points of the looming limestone outcrops, eroded into vast, surreal sculptures. Because of the need to protect flora and fauna the red route is in a restricted zone and can only be visited with a **guide** (information on this available from the Centro de Recepción). The **green** and **yellow routes** (waymarked) can be walked without a guide. The green route is the shortest at 1.5km (about 40min if you don't dawdle) while the yellow route takes about 2hrs. In early summer on the popular green route you may find yourself competing with gangs of schoolkids, who arrive en masse on vaguely educational trips, excitedly trying to spot La Copa (the wineglass), El Lagarto (the lizard) and La Loba (the she-wolf) as well as other celebrated rock sculptures. Keep an eye on the skies while you're here for Griffon vultures, frequent visitors whose huge wingspans make a spectacular sight as they glide overhead.

Park practicalities

No buses link El Torcal to Antequera, and it's an arduous 16km hike in high summer; the park is reached by following the C3310 road towards Villanueva de la Concepción and heading down the second signed turning on the right to El Torcal. Without your own transport you might consider a **taxi** (about €18 one-way for up to five). A better value deal is with the **taxi turistico**, which can be arranged through the Turismo at Antequera; for €25 for up to five people a taxi will drop you off at the Centro de Recepción and wait until you have completed the green route before returning you to Antequera. Alternatively renting a taxi for a whole day (€30) allows you to complete the longer yellow route.

Torcal has a **campsite**, *Camping Torcal* (☎95 211 16 08), just off the A3310, 6km south of Antequera, which also has a **restaurant**, supermarket and pool. Camping rough is not allowed inside the park. The Turismo at Antequera can provide information regarding some attractive **casas rurales** to rent in the area.

Laguna de Fuente de Piedra

About 20km northwest of Antequera lies **Laguna de Fuente de Piedra**, the largest natural lake in Andalucía and a celebrated site for observing birdlife. The shallow water-level and high saline content of the lake, and the crustaceans that these conditions encourage, attract a glorious flock of **greater flamingo** each spring, making this Europe's only inland breeding ground for the species. Unfortunately the droughts of recent years and the demands for more water by local farmers cashing in on an asparagus boom in the nearby Sierra de Yeguas have led to the lake almost drying up completely in the summer months, thus placing many of the young flamingo in peril. This resulted in rescue missions being mounted by teams from the Coto Doñana (see p.378) who transferred many young birds back to the wetlands of Huelva. Andalucía's environmental agency is working on a system to prevent this happening again. However, even this has not been sufficient and the drought of 2005 resulted in low water levels surrounding the nesting sites and a reluctance by the birds to breed.

Besides supporting a variety of waders at all times of the year, in winter the lake is often a haven for **cranes**, and the surrounding marshes provide a habitat for numerous amphibians and reptiles. Remember that because this is a sanctuary, the beaches are strictly out of bounds (ruling out swimming) and because many sections are privately owned, limiting access, it's not possible to make a complete circuit of the lake. You're also at a distinct advantage with your own transport, as species such as flamingo often gather at the far end of the lake, up to 7km away.

Practicalities

Easy to get to, the village of Fuente de Piedra is on the **train** route from Málaga to Córdoba, with the lake a ten-minute walk west of the station. There are four daily **buses** from Antequera or Málaga (changing at Antequera) or, with your own transport, take the A343 (direction Sevilla) north, to join the A92 *autovía*, and continue along this for 14km until the signed turn-off. Over the bridge beyond the train station the lakeside **Centro de Visitantes** (Wed–Sun 10am–2pm; ☏952 11 17 15) has displays of the flora and fauna of the lake, and rents out binoculars.

For **rooms**, *Hostal La Laguna* (☏95 273 52 42; ❸), close to the exit from the A92 *autovía*, is an option for en-suite rooms, but the most attractive place to stay is the *Laguna Fuente Piedra* (☏95 273 52 94, ⓦwww.camping-rural.com; ❸ with breakfast), close to the village and overlooking the lake. Accommodation here is in double rooms or fully equipped wood cabins sleeping four to six persons. The grounds are occupied by a **campsite** and there's also a swimming pool and a decent **restaurant** with an economical *menú*. The site also offers a variety of activities including guided walks, mountain biking, caving, canoeing and archery.

East from Málaga: the coast to Torre del Mar

The dreary eastern stretch of the **Costa del Sol** – the beaches within easy distance of Málaga – is a largely unbroken landscape of urbanization and unlovely holiday towns, packed to the gunnels in summer with day-tripping *malagueños*. There are enough places of interest, however, to warrant stopping off en route, before arriving at the unremarkable resort of **Torre del Mar**.

With your own transport it's possible to avoid the Málaga suburbs by using the N340 *circunvalación* (ring road) – picked up on the northern edge of town – which eventually becomes the *autovía* linking Málaga with Nerja. To follow the coastal route described below leave the *autovía* at the Rincón de la Victoria exit (see below). Otherwise, the road heading out of Málaga along the Paseo de Reding (passing the north side of the bullring) traverses the suburbs of Pedragalejo and El Palo, where for most of the summer the beaches are covered with a forest of parasols, before arriving at the small resort of Cala de Moral.

Cueva del Tesoro and Rincón de la Victoria

Just beyond Cala del Moral, a signed road on the left indicates the **CUEVA DEL TESORO** (daily guided visits 10.45am–1pm & 4.45–7pm; €4.25), a spectacular network of underground caves less commercialized than those at Nerja (see p.137). A series of seven chambers, spiked with stalagmites and stalactites, leads to the eighth, the **sala de los lagos**, a Gaudí-esque rock cathedral with natural underground pools. Paleolithic cave paintings were discovered here in 1918 (presently not on view) as well as other prehistoric remains indicating almost continual human habitation. The cave's name (*tesoro* means treasure) derives from the legend that five fleeing Moorish kings took refuge in its depths and stashed a large quantity of gold. The gold is long gone but the cave retains its name.

Two kilometres further on, **RINCÓN DE LA VICTORIA** is a no-nonsense, scruffy sort of place, and another local resort for *malagueño* families. It's a functional spot to swim if you have a day to fill before catching a plane home, but nothing more. A seafood speciality here is *coquinas*, tasty small clams.

Macharaviaya and around

To break the monotony along this strip of coast you could follow a small road north at the featureless suburb of Torre de Benagalbón that winds up into the hills and approaches the hamlet of **MACHARAVIAYA** (from the Moorish Machar Ibn Yahya or "lands of the son of Yahya"). Surrounded by slopes covered with olive and almond trees, the village was expanded in the eighteenth century by the Galvéz family, one of Andalucía's great imperial dynasties. Count Bernardo de Galvéz became governor general of Spanish North America and gave his name to Galveston in Texas after laying siege to the town in 1777. Today, even taking into account its impressive Baroque church (a Galvéz construction), it's hard to believe that this tiny, cobble-paved village was once known as "little Madrid". It was a wealthy place, benefiting from the extensive Galvéz family vineyards as well as a playing-card factory that had a monopoly for supplying cards to the Americas. This was all to end, however, when the phylloxera plague of the 1870s wiped out the vines, the card monopoly lapsed and the Galvéz line died out. The family title died with them, and the last visconte de Galveston is buried in the church crypt among the tombs and alabaster statues of his ancestors.

At the entrance to the village is a rather proprietorial whitewashed brick temple erected by the family in 1786 and, at its centre, the once crumbling exterior of the outsize church of **San Jacinto,** over-restored as part of the Expo 92 celebrations. To gain entry you'll need to get two keys: one from the mayor's house (for the crypt), up a ramp beside the Ayuntamiento opposite, and another (for the church) from the nearby house of Señora Pilar Aponte, c/Elvira 3; as they're both private houses, try to avoid calling at siesta time. Inside the single-nave church, altars dedicated to various Galvéz family members are decorated with fine marble, and inscriptions express the ultimately vain hope that Mass would be said on certain days for their souls *in perpetuum*. Don't miss the eerie crypt behind the church, where a remarkable collection of sombre **alabaster family busts** face each other around an alcove and seem about to start up a gloomy conversation. The great marble tomb of Don José Galvéz, marquis of Sonora and minister for the Indias during the eighteenth-century reign of Carlos III, stands nearby.

Facing the church is the old playing-card factory, now converted into homes. For refreshment, continue uphill along the short alleyway close to the house of Señora Aponte to the simple and friendly *Taberna El Candil*, which serves **tapas** and **raciones** and even full meals, if pushed.

Two kilometres north of Macharaviaya – and approached via a side road to the left at the entrance to the village – the village of **BENAQUE** has a Mudéjar church, **Nuestra Señora del Rosario**, whose tower conserves the minaret of the mosque it replaced. The building has recently been sensitively restored. Just before the church a house on the right was the birthplace of – and is now a **museum** (free, donations welcome) dedicated to – Benaque's most famous son, the modernist poet **Salvador Rueda** (1857–1933). Should you wish to view the disarmingly simple interior, which is more or less as it was when the poet lived here, the key is available from Señor José (Pepe) Cabrera, c/Salvador Rueda 19, just before the bus shelter to the left as you arrive.

Between the two villages is a **place to stay**: the sparkling *Hotel de Macharaviaya* (T & F 95 211 03 99; ❼), which lies off the road to Benaque and is as comfortable a hideaway as you could wish, with well-equipped air-conditioned rooms and a fine pool. Meals are available for guests and the hotel has a non-smoking policy.

If you're looking for a challenging **hike** in these parts it's possible to walk from here across the ridge of the Montes de Málaga west to Olias or alternatively east, to Almayate and the sea, about a two-hour trek in either direction.

Torre del Mar

Back on the main coast road, the chain of localities with "torre" in their names refers to the numerous *atalayas*, or watch towers, which have been used to guard this coast since Roman and Moorish times, many strikingly visible on the headlands. There's little to detain you between Torre de Benagalbón and Almayate – though the latter has a reasonable **campsite**, *Almayate-Costa* (T 95 255 62 89) with limited shade – from where it's only a couple of kilometres to **TORRE DEL MAR**. A line of concrete tower blocks on a grey, pebble beach, this is Torremolinos without the money or fun. Nevertheless, it's a fairly peaceful place and a central promenade area, El Copo, provides a focus for numerous **restaurants and bars** and a rather tame nightlife scene. Good seafood tapas are to be had at *Bar-Marisquería Radar*, Paseo Marítimo 13, close to the *Hostal Don Juan* (see below). Three more tapas bars and *marisquerías* worth seeking out are *El Yate*, *Bar Fernando* and *Bar Toné* in a line with terraces along c/Saladero Viejo, 50m from the tourist office.

If you want to **stay**, the new and central *Hostal Don Juan*, c/Patrón Veneno 14 (T 95 254 58 70; ❹), lies just 30m from the beach and has en-suite a/c rooms with TV. A few doors away the *Hotel Miraya*, c/Patrón Veneno 6 (T 95 254 59 69, W www.hotelmiraya.com; ❺), offers a few more creature comforts. Like everywhere else around here, though, rooms are at a premium in high season, when your best hope will probably be the basic **campsite** *Torre del Mar* (T 95 254 02 24) on the Paseo Marítimo. Otherwise the central and helpful **Turismo**, Paseo de Larios s/n (Mon–Fri 9am–2pm & 6–9pm, Sat & Sun 11am–2pm & 6–9pm; T 95 254 11 04, W www.ayto-velezmalaga.es), may be able to advise; they can also supply a town map. **Internet** access is available at *Cyber Costa del Sol*, c/Blas Infante 4 (daily 9.30am to midnight) close to El Copo (see above). Walkers and readers may want to look up a useful **bookshop**, Pasa Tiempo, c/Infantes 30 (☏95 254 37 03), facing Plaza de la Paz, where a Yorkshire couple – both enthusiastic walkers – keep a wide range of maps.

The Axarquía

If you have your own transport, a trip up into the often spectacularly beautiful region of **La Axarquía** makes a refreshing change from the sun-bed culture of the Costa del Sol. Bounded by the coast, the Sierra de Alhama to the north and, on its eastern flank, the mountainous edge of the province of Granada, this rugged, ham-shaped wedge of territory offers excellent walking country and abundant wildlife, as well as a host of attractive mountain villages that make easy-going stopoffs. Long a breeding ground for *bandoleros* who preyed on traders carrying produce from the coast to Granada, during the Civil War the Axarquía was also a notorious guerrilla encampment whose members fought

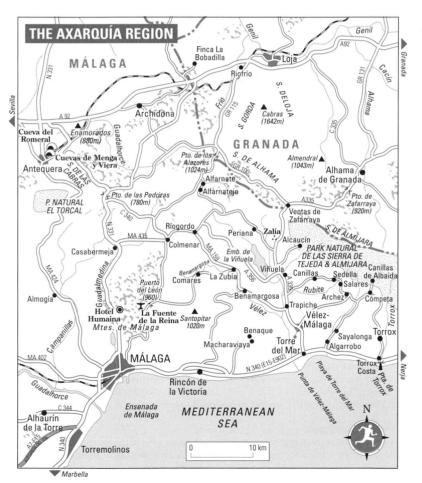

on against Franco's Guardia Civil until the early 1950s: it is only in relatively recent times that the area has become safe for travellers.

The Axarquía is a great place to do some **hiking** and *Walk! the Axarquía* by Charles Davis is a new book of hikes devoted to the region; for Spanish speakers the book by José Luis Clavero Toledo, *Sendas y Caminos de la Axarquía*, details walking routes, refuges and campsites throughout the zone; alternatively, *Walking in Andalucía* by Guy Hunter-Watts has half a dozen hikes to follow in the western Axarquía (see "Books" in Contexts for all three).

Vélez-Málaga

Frequent buses head the 4km inland from Torre del Mar to **VÉLEZ-MÁLAGA**, a bustling market town and supply centre for the region's farmers and capital of the Axarquía. In the fertile valley of the Río Vélez, Vélez-Málaga (often simply referred to as Vélez) was important in both Roman times – under the name of Menoba – and Moorish, when as Ballix-Malaca ("Fortress of Málaga") it had an important role in subduing what has always been a turbulent zone. A number of Phoenician cemeteries and tombs discovered nearby testify to an older pedigree still. When Fernando conquered the town in 1487, the Christian flag was raised on the castle's battlements as the Moors were ejected. This victory, which drove a wedge through the kingdom of Granada, dividing it in two, paved the way for the fall of the Nasrid city five years later.

The town climbs up a slope from the main street, **Avenida Vivar Téllez** – where you'll arrive whether you're travelling by bus or car – towards the **castillo**, as good a place as any to start a tour of the sights. What's left of it clings to a rocky outcrop, which from its dominant position above the white-walled *barrio* of San Sebastián gives good views out over the coast. The castle suffered badly during the War of the Spanish Succession, when the English lost to the French here after a bitter struggle in 1704. Visible from the castle is the sixteenth-century Mudéjar church of **Santa María la Mayor** whose beautiful sectioned tower still holds the minaret of the mosque that preceded it. Inside, Moorish arches separate a triple nave, and there's a fine Mudéjar ceiling. Immediately below the castle another church, **Nuestra Señora de la Encarnación**, has a history reflecting that of Andalucía itself. Beginning life as a Visigoth bishopric, the building was transformed into a mosque during the Moorish period, and back into a church again following the *Reconquista*. The late-Gothic **San Juan Bautista**, on Plaza de España, is also worth a look, featuring an elegant tower and, inside, a superbly naturalistic sculpture, *Cristo Crucificado* by Pedro de Mena.

The restored **Palacio del Marqués de Beniel**, Plaza Palacio 1, is an elegant sixteenth-century mansion – formerly the town hall – which now hosts the International Summer School of the Axarquía covering all aspects of culture, including poetry and theatre as well as flamenco and classical guitar. A prestigious annual **guitar competition** is held here every July, with free concerts taking place in the *palacio*'s delightful patio. The reception desk has details of cultural activities throughout the summer.

Less attractively, Vélez is also one of the last bastions of **cock-fighting** in Europe, and the Sunday fights held in the town in winter pull in crowds of aficionados from miles around to bet on the outcome as the feathers fly.

Practicalities

Vélez-Málaga's **bus station** is on Avenida Vivar Téllez, the main street leading out of town towards the sea. The small **tourist information point** (Mon–Fri

9am–2pm; ☎95 250 68 19), located inside the Ayuntamiento on the central Plaza de las Carmelitas, can provide a town map but the main tourist office is down in Torre del Mar.

Finding **places to stay** isn't usually a problem, except possibly at the end of July when every *hostal* bedroom seems to be twanging furiously as young competitors prepare for the guitar competition. Best of the bunch for simple rooms is the friendly *Casa Los Martínez*, c/Cristo 58, on the main crossroad as you approach the centre from Avenida Vivar Téllez (☎95 250 42 87; ❷). Just across the road, the more expensive *Hotel Dila*, Avda.Vivar Téllez 11 (☎95 250 39 00, ⓦwww.hoteldila.com; ❹), has air-conditioned rooms with bath, while the local **campsite**, *Valle Niza,* on the edge of town (☎95 251 31 81), is a more pleasant option than the one down in Torre del Mar (see p.128).

Many places to **eat and drink** at line the Avenida Vivar Tellez, including the excellent medium-priced *Mesón Los Migueles* at no. 83, serving a variety of fish and meat dishes and a good-value *menú*. There's also a very good restaurant and tapas bar below *Casa Los Martínez*.

North to Alfarnate

A number of good driving **routes** around the Axarquía begin at **Trapiche**, about 3km north of Vélez. One heads northwest along the MA159 towards **BENAMARGOSA**, a village surrounded by citrus orchards and olive groves. You could take a look at its sixteenth-century Gothic-style church of **La Encarnación** before moving on to La Zubia, where a winding road signed on the left climbs dizzily to **COMARES**, an impeccably tidy White Town (or village in this case) spectacularly clinging to the peak of its conical hill. At the highest point of all, beside an attractive cemetery, a ruined Moorish fort – built on Roman foundations – was one of the strongholds of rebel leader Ibn Hafsun (see p.115). In the village is yet another church of **Nuestra Señora de la Encarnación**, this time a sixteenth-century Mudéjar building with a picturesque hexagonal tower, the minaret of the mosque that preceded it. A **mirador** in the focal Plaza del Ayuntamiento gives fine views over the Axarquía. There's a **walking route** around the village's major sights taking in all the above plus an ancient Roman path down the mountain and various Moorish architectural remains; it's waymarked by ceramic footprints embedded in the pavement. En-suite **rooms** are to be had at the *Hotel Atalaya*, c/Encinilla s/n (☎95 250 92 08; ❸), near the entrance to the village (where windows face the barracks of the Guardia Civil rather than the spectacular vista behind). The friendlier *Mirador de la Axarquía* (☎95 250 92 09; ❸), slightly further up the hill as you enter the village, has more en-suite rooms above a restaurant. An altogether more luxurious alternative is 🗡 *El Molino de los Abuelos* (☎95 250 93 09, Ⓔinfo@molino-abuelos.com; ❸–❻; closed Aug), which offers rooms with and without bath plus suites in an enchantingly refurbished eighteenth-century former olive-oil mill on the Plaza del Ayuntamiento. For **eating and drinking** there are bars on the main square and *El Molino de los Abuelos* also has its own very good mid-priced restaurant (main dishes €9–14) located in the former oil pressing room with the ancient equipment still on view. The restaurant of the *Mirador de la Axarquía* (see above) serves regular *venta* food on a pleasant terrace with stunning views and has a good value *menú* for €6. A welcome municipal **swimming pool** is sited between the latter restaurant and the Hotel Atalaya.

Continuing north out of La Zubía the road follows the course of the Río Cueva, finally ascending to **RIOGORDO**, a village with Phoenician and

Roman origins that was a fortified stronghold during the Moorish period. After the *Reconquista* the Moors were replaced by settlers from Castile, the ancestors of the modern inhabitants. The Semana Santa celebrated here is a particularly vivid affair, when local people – dressed for the part – act out the scenes from the Passion, often with bloodcurdling gusto. The village also boasts another attractive municipal swimming pool.

From Riogordo, you have a choice of routes: head east to Alfarnate (see opposite) or west, following a stiff climb, to **COLMENAR**, another brilliant-white hill town and the Axarquía's most westerly outpost. A centre of honey production thanks to the rich variety of flowering plants and shrubs growing in the surrounding hills, the village takes its name from *colmena*, Spanish for "beehive". Among a couple of places to stay here the *Hotel Los Arrieros* (☎95 273 00 37; ❸), 100m out of the village on the Málaga road, is a good bet for en-suite a/c rooms above a decent restaurant. The route from here – via the Puerto del Léon – down to Málaga, twisting through forests of cork oaks and pines forming the **Parque Natural de los Montes de Málaga**, is wonderful, offering during its latter stages stunning **views** over the Costa del Sol. Sixteen kilometres before Málaga, close to a landmark roadside spring named La Fuente de la Reina, there's a delightfully rural **place to stay**, the ⚹ *Hotel Humaina* (☎95 264 10 25, ⓦ www.hotelhumaina.es; ❺), a former hunting lodge (now redundant as no hunting is allowed in the park) tucked away in a wooded valley at the end of a five-kilometre-long track signed from the spring. Friendly staff, comfortable rooms, a small pool and its own good restaurant – together with a chance to spot copious birdlife and animals, such as the wild boar who are frequent visitors to the hotel's rubbish bins in search of nibbles – add up to a memorable hotel. The management can also advise on exploring the waymarked rambling **paths** through the surrounding woods.

Alcaucín and Zálía

Another route out of Vélez heads north from Trapiche and follows the old coach route from Málaga to Granada. At a second fork 8km beyond here, a fast new road – the A356 – skirts the western flank of the Embalse de Viñuela, speeding traffic north towards Casabermeja and the N331 Málaga-Sevilla *autovía*. Taking the right fork along the A355, however, passes a turn-off to **VIÑUELA**, 3km beyond this. Originally a *venta* stop for the traffic heading north and south between Málaga and Granada, the atmospheric old **inn** here, *La Viña*, dates from the eighteenth century and stands opposite the fountain in the narrow main street. A spit-and-sawdust place today, it's usually full on midsummer afternoons of old men arguing around the domino tables and farmhands sheltering from the burning sun. Just down the street, the simple sixteenth-century **Iglesia de San José** (get the key from the neighbour opposite) has a finely worked *Pietà*. For **rooms** on the shores of the nearby Embalse de Viñuela reservoir try the comfortable *Hotel Viñuela* (☎95 253 62 22; ❻), which also has its own **restaurant** and a garden **pool**.

Still following the old road, at the Puente de Don Manuel, a bridge 3km beyond Viñuela, a road cuts off on the right and ascends to the village of **ALCAUCÍN**. On the way up keep an eye to your left where, across a valley, you will be able to make out the ruins of the deserted medieval village of Zálía (see opposite) and, beyond, the Puerto de Zafarraya, a great U-shaped cleavage in the Sierra de Alhama through which passes the ancient route to Granada. Alcaucín itself, perched on the slopes of the Sierra de Tejeda, is a beautiful little village with wrought-iron balconies ablaze with flowering geraniums and a web of narrow white-walled streets reflecting its Moorish origins. As befits a mountain village there are numerous spring-fed fountains, among which the five-spouted Fuente San Sebastián has been restored very much in the Moorish style, complete with *azulejos*.

Continuing north from the Puente de Don Manuel, the A335 heads on towards Granada, passing en route the dauntingly impressive **Zafarraya Pass**, where 30,000-year-old remains found in a nearby cave in 1983 have now been confirmed as the last-known site in Europe inhabited by Neanderthal man. On the way, the road passes the ruins of the fort and the deserted medieval village of **ZALÍA**. Local legend has it that the Moorish village was attacked by a plague of vipers after Patricio, a *malagueño* church minister, arrived in an attempt to convert the inhabitants to Christianity and they spurned him. The more likely explanation is that the population was put to the sword during the uprisings following the *Reconquista*. Throughout most of the Moorish period Zalía's fortress, together with those at Comares and Bentomiz (near Arenas to the south), formed a defensive triangle to control this central sector of the Axarquía region.

Periana, Alfarnatejo and Alfarnate

Pressing on along the C340, joined a short distance beyond the Alcaucín turn-off (see opposite), leads to **Periana**, a noted centre of peach-growing and *anís* production and now the location for a new and attractively sited **Villa Turística** (T & F 95 253 62 22) closed for refurbishment at the time of writing. Accommodation is in traditionally styled chalets, and it makes ideal base for walks in the nearby sierras, now the officially designated **Parque Natural de las Sierras de Tejeda y Almijara**.

Heading on into the Axarquía's more remote extremities, about 3km beyond Periana you'll reach a fork; if you don't want to face a tortuous switchback secondary road, ignore the sign labelled "Alfarnate 15km" and continue along the road signed to Riogordo and Colmenar. A further 4km will bring you to a right turn and an easier route to the village of **ALFARNATEJO** and, a little beyond this, the Axarquía's most northerly conurbation, **ALFARNATE**. Although they lie a mere couple of kilometres apart, it would be difficult to find two places in Andalucía with less in common. Alfarnatejo, the smaller of the two, is staunchly right-wing, while Alfarnate has always been on the left, and, unable to agree or cooperate on anything, they have built up a strong mutual animosity, which even discourages marriages between the two communities. In truth, neither village would win any beauty prizes, though Alfarnate, set on a plain covered with wheatfields, is worth a visit for its attractive church of **Santa Ana**, a sixteenth-century edifice with a graceful Mudéjar tower.

However, Alfarnate's real claim to fame is the thirteenth-century **Venta de Alfarnate** on the village's western edge, which maintains – with some justification – that it is the oldest **inn** in Andalucía. Situated in an isolated spot in the midst of brooding hills, it's not hard to see what attracted the various brigands and highwaymen to the place. Indeed, the interior, as well as being a bar-restaurant, is also a **museum** dedicated to keeping alive the memory of such outlaws as Luís Candelas, who spent a night in the *venta*'s well-preserved prison cell en route to justice in Málaga. By far the most terrifying *bandolero* of all, however, was El Tempranillo, who arrived unannounced one hot day in the 1820s, and, when there were no spoons for him to eat with, ordered the dining clients to eat their wooden ones at gunpoint, cracking their teeth in the process. The place is more civilized these days and its mid-priced restaurant serves a hearty mountain speciality, *huevos a la bestia* (fried eggs with local sausage, ham and black pudding). Places to stay include a fully equipped house (❹) available

△ The *Venta de Alfarnate*

for rent in the village, or a stunning *cortijo* 4km outside, capable of sleeping up to ten for around €600 per week (both ☏ 95 275 92 05 & 95 233 61 99). Keep your eyes peeled in this area for the amazingly agile **cabra hispanica**, the rare Spanish goat; the long-horned male is a spectacular sight as he effortlessly scales almost vertical cliff faces.

East from Torre del Mar: the coast to Nerja

The coast east from Torre del Mar is a nondescript stretch of faceless towns and the occasional concrete resort, dotted with more ancient *atalayas* or watch towers. Inland lie more tempting villages in the **eastern Axarquía** but along the coast the first town of any real interest is **Nerja**, with some fine beaches and a relatively slow pace. Further east, **Almuñécar**, and even better **Salobreña**, are the city of Granada's Mediterranean playgrounds, flanked by numerous coves and inlets where for most of the year you can have a beach all to yourself.

Inland to Cómpeta

Beyond Torre del Mar the coast road climbs slightly to **Algarrobo-Costa**, an unappealing high-rise beach resort. With your own transport it's worth ignoring this – and the bleak stretch of coast that follows – to head inland for some delightful villages in the eastern Axarquía, finally rejoining the coastal road 10km east at Torrox Costa.

From Algarrobo-Costa the MA103 climbs inland for a stretch towards the village of Algarrobo proper. Look out for for some well-conserved **Phoenician**

tombs (signposted on the right) dating from the eighth century BC. Originally these tombs formed part of an extensive cemetery, built of stone blocks and roofed in wood The older inland village of **ALGARROBO** 3km inland, which lent its name to the coastal settlement, is a pleasant enough place, with a charming *hostal-restaurante* (see "Practicalities", overleaf).

Passing through Algarrobo, the road toils on upwards as the fruit orchards of the coastal strip give way to the olive groves and vineyards of the higher slopes. The road then passes **SAYALONGA** 5km further on, a pretty village nestling in the valley of the Río Algarrobo, and then ascends again, twisting and turning for a further 8km until it reaches **CÓMPETA**, a huddle of brilliant-white cubes tumbling down a hillside and surrounded by vineyards. A Moorish settlement in origin, and now discovered by migrants from northern Europe, Cómpeta retains a relaxed atmosphere, and the easy-going villagers don't seem too worried about being swamped by foreigners. The sweet – and potent – **wine** made from the area's muscatel grapes is renowned as the best in the whole province. You can try it for yourself at the *Museo del Vino* on Avenida de la Constitución close to the charming main square, Plaza de la Almijara. Beneath the lofty bell tower (a later addition) of the sixteenth-century church of La Asunción each year on August 15, Cómpeta rolls out the barrels – scores of them – during its annual **fiesta**, the Noche del Vino, when the square is filled with revellers determined to sink as much of the free *vino* as they can hold. Above the plaza to the left, c/San Antonio leads to a shrine with a superb **view** over the valley to the west and the sea beyond.

The road continues for a further 4km north of Cómpeta where it comes to a dead end at the village of **CANILLAS DE ALBAIDA**, something of a mini-Cómpeta, with a place to stay and a couple of decent restaurants (see below).

Practicalities

Cómpeta's new **tourist office** (Wed–Sun 10am–2pm; ☏ 95 255 36 85, ⓦ www .competa.es) is located on the Plaza de la Constitución close to the where **buses** terminate. If you decide **to stay** the only budget possibilities are with unofficial rooms in places dotted around the village – via the tourist office (or their website) is the best way of contacting them. The only other option is the central *Hotel Balcón de Cómpeta*, c/San Antonio s/n, southwest of the main square (☏ 95 255 35 35, ⓦ www.hotel-competa.com; ❹), with comfortable balcony rooms overlooking a pool. In neighbouring Canillas de Albaida, close to the main square, *Posada La Plaza* (☏ 95 255 48 07; ❹ with breakfast) is another option with en-suite balcony rooms with views and a roof terrace. In Algarrobo there's *El Chato* (☏ 952 55 24 03; ❷), a *hostal-restaurante* that's good for an overnight stop or a meal, with excellent local dishes including rabbit, kid and *migas* (fried breadcrumbs).

Back in Cómpeta a good place **to eat** is the economical *Bar-Restaurante Perico* on Plaza Almijara; recommended are the *sopa de berza*, a tasty cabbage and black pudding soup, and *pollo al vino de Cómpeta* (chicken cooked in the local wine). Slightly southwest of the main square *El Pilón*, c/Laberinto s/n, offers more eclectic international cuisine with a lunch *menú* for €10. *Restaurante María*, the restaurant of the *Hotel Balcón de Cómpeta* at the top of c/San Antonio, is another mid-priced possibility, while the restaurant of the *Museo del Vino* in Avenida La Constitución is also good for charcoal grilled meat and fish. *Restaurante Rustico*, on the edge of the village towards Torrox, does very good local dishes and is followed by a string of *ventas* that dot the road towards the coast and make for pleasant lunch stops.

A friendly and informative English **bookshop**, Marco Polo, at c/José Antonio 3 (☎95 251 64 23), just off the main square, stocks walking maps and equipment plus copies of *25 Walks in and Around Cómpeta and Canillas*. Copies of a local magazine, *Market Place*, are also stocked here which includes a useful map of Cómpeta (and many other towns and resorts along this coast). **Internet** access is available at *Cómpeta Webs* (Mon–Sat 10am–2pm & 5–9pm) c/San Antonio 9, near the *Hotel Balcón de Cómpeta*.

Archez, Salares and Sedella

To penetrate further into the Axarquía from Cómpeta you'll need to double back for 2km to the turning north to **ARCHEZ**. Nestling in the foothills of the Sierra Almijara, it's an attractive village with strong Moorish roots. This influence is vividly in evidence at the church of **Nuestra Señora de La Encarnación** (open service times) whose remarkable fourteenth-century tower is the minaret of an earlier mosque. It is one of the best examples from this period, and the *sebka* brickwork and blind arches above are particularly fine. Archez's solitary **place to stay** is the attractive and central *Posada-Mesón Mudéjar*, c/Alamo 6, (☎95 255 31 06, ⊛www.posadamesonmudejar.com; ➍) with en-suite rooms and a restaurant.

The road climbs for another 5km to the brilliant white village of **SALARES**, a centre of olive oil and wine production and one of the most picturesque villages of the Axarquía. Its charms are enhanced by the banning of traffic from its narrow streets, where colourful potted geraniums line the walls and dogs lie prostrate in the afternoon heat. There's a car park at the top of the village; from here, head downhill to the friendly **Ayuntamiento** (Mon–Fri 9am–1pm), where you can pick up a small map. Next door, the church of **Santa Ana** should be your first stop. Just as the church at Archez, this one conserves a fine **minaret** of the mosque it replaced. Inside, a simple interior holds the image of Santa Ana, *patrona* of the village.

The road climbs on to **SEDELLA** 4km away, perched beneath a massive hill terraced with orchards and vegetable gardens. Looming up behind, the Sierra de Almijara is laced with numerous streams and springs that provide necessary irrigation. Apart from winding, narrow streets daubed with liberal amounts of whitewash, there are few sights, though the **Casa Torreón**, an ancient Ayuntamiento with a fine Mudéjar tower topped off by paired arches, is mildly interesting. On the village's northern edge is a pleasant **place to stay**, *Hostal Casa Pinta* (☎95 250 89 55; ➌ with breakfast), with a/c en-suite rooms, fine views, a terrace with pool plus a restaurant with an inexpensive *menú*.

Canillas

Beyond Sedella the road allows fine views over the Vélez and Rubite river valleys to the west. After 6km, there's a basic summer **campsite** signed on the right; to reach it you'll need to leave any transport at the car park below and climb through the woods to the site. A little beyond here, surrounded by slopes of almonds, vines and the olives from which it takes its name, is the large and prosperous village of **CANILLAS DE ACEITUNO**. Gathered below the sixteenth-century church of **Nuestra Señora del Rosario**, Canillas is a relaxing place with plenty of thirst-quenching bars serving tapas dotted along the narrow streets circling the church – *Bar Sociedad* is one to try. If you want to **stay**, the central and excellent-value ⚓ *Pensión Canillas*, c/Placeta 5 (☎95 251 81 02; ➋), has rooms with bath and some equally tempting apartments (€30 per day) sleeping up to four. Just down the street from here lies the village's best

restaurant, *El Bodegón de Juan María*, c/Placeta 6, offering many regional dishes – including their speciality, *chivo al horno* (oven-baked kid) – and a weekday *menú* for €7.

Torrox

To get back to the coast you'll need to retrace your tracks to Cómpeta, and then follow the MA137 as it descends to Torrox and the coast. **TORROX** is a sizeable village some 4km inland from its coastal offshoot, and not without charm. Historically, Torrox reached the height of its prosperity during the Moorish period due to its pivotal role in the silk trade between Granada and cities such as Baghdad and Damascus. Now a permanent haven for colonies of expat Germans and Scandinavians, it has a pretty enough centre, with brilliant white-walled houses clinging to the steep slope on which the town is built.

Back on the coast, **TORROX COSTA** is a depressing concrete corral again favoured largely by German and Scandinavian visitors. In high season – when there's little chance of finding a room or a place for your towel on the overcrowded beach – your best bet is to take a quick look at the remains of a **Roman necropolis and villa** immediately west of the lighthouse, before moving straight on to Nerja.

Nerja and around

Although **NERJA**, 8km along the coast from Torrox, cannot claim to have been bypassed by the tidal wave of post-1960s tourist development, this attractive resort has, nevertheless, held out against Torremolinos-type tower blocks, and its mainly villa and *urbanizaciones* construction has been more in keeping with its origins. Its setting, too, is spectacular, nestling among the foothills of the Almijara range, with a striking seafront **belvedere** flanked by some attractive **beaches**.

Arrival and information

Buses arrive at the stand at the north end of town. It's a five-minute walk south from here to the beach and old town along c/Pintada, at the sea end of which is the helpful **Turismo**, c/Puerta del Mar 2 (daily 10am–2pm & 6–10pm; ☎95 252 15 31, Ⓦwww.nerja.org).

If you'd like to do some **walking** in the area, the Turismo has its own leaflets and at Librería Idiomas almost opposite you can buy individual leaflets detailing walks in the area by local resident and hiker Elma Thompson. Elma is a chirpy Mancunian who – when not struggling with the authorities to keep footpaths open and make them easier to use – offers guided walks from November to May (call for details ☎95 253 07 82).

Accommodation

There's usually no problem finding **rooms** in Nerja except in August, when you should book in advance. The lowest-priced possibilities are in the streets south of the bus station heading towards the sea. If everything's full, one solution is to stay inland at Frigiliana (see p.140), or try renting an apartment. The Turismo can help with information on apartments, and many of the *hostales* listed below have arrangements with *casas particulares* to soak up the overflow. There's a **campsite** *Camping Nerja* (☎95 252 97 14) with good shade, pool, bar and restaurant 4km east of the town close to Maro.

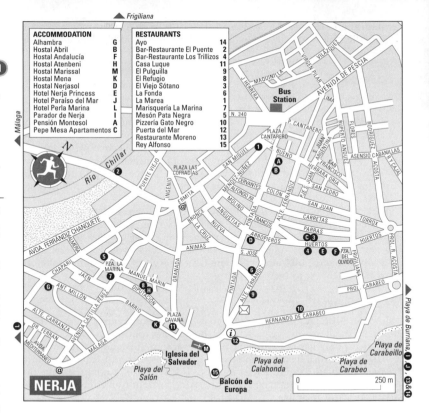

ACCOMMODATION

Alhambra	G
Hostal Abril	B
Hostal Andalucía	F
Hostal Atenbeni	H
Hostal Marissal	M
Hostal Mena	K
Hostal Nerjasol	D
Hotel Nerja Princess	E
Hotel Paraíso del Mar	J
Hotel Perla Marina	L
Parador de Nerja	I
Pensión Montesol	A
Pepe Mesa Apartamentos	C

RESTAURANTS

Ayo	14
Bar-Restaurante El Puente	2
Bar-Restaurante Los Trillizos	4
Casa Luque	11
El Pulguilla	9
El Refugio	8
El Viejo Sótano	3
La Fonda	6
La Marea	1
Marisquería La Marina	7
Mesón Pata Negra	5
Pizzería Gato Negro	10
Puerta del Mar	12
Restaurante Moreno	13
Rey Alfonso	15

NERJA

Alhambra c/Antonio Millón s/n ☎& ⓕ95 252 21 74. Immaculate en-suite rooms, some with sea-facing balcony, in this pleasant *hostal* a little west of the centre. ❸

Hostal Abril c/Pintada 124 ☎95 252 61 67, ⓦwww.hostalnet.com. Sparkling *hostal* with excellent en-suite a/c rooms, lots of cool marble and a friendly proprietor. Also has apartments and studios (❹) sleeping up to four. Free Internet access for guests. ❹

Hostal Andalucía c/Los Huertos 58 ☎95 252 10 58, ⓔhostalandalucia@hotmail.com. Charming *hostal* just east of the centre with spotless en-suite a/c rooms, marble throughout and a *terraza*/solarium on the roof. ❸

Hostal Atenbeni c/Diputación 12 ☎95 252 13 41. Friendly and tidy place offering rooms with bath and fans; close to the Turismo. ❸

Hostal Marissal Paseo Balcón de Europa 3 ☎95 252 66 54 ⓦwww.marissal.net. Bang in the centre of the action, this new *hostal* offers a/c en-suite rooms, many (try for rooms 102–5 or 204–5) with

sea view. Also rents apartments (❻) in same location. ❹

Hostal Mena c/El Barrio 15 ☎95 252 05 41, ⓔhostalmena@hotmail.com. Central rooms with bath, sea views, a/c or fans and a delightful garden at the rear. ❸

Hostal Nerjasol c/Arropieros 4 ☎95 252 21 21, ⓔhostal@hostalnerjasol.com. On a quiet street, with spotless a/c en-suite rooms and a roof patio. They can direct you to a *casa particular* if full. ❹

Hotel Nerja Princess c/Los Huertos 46 ☎95 252 89 86, ⓦwww.hotelnp.com. Excellent small hotel where well-equipped a/c balcony rooms come with satellite TV, minibar and safe. There's a terrace and pool at the rear and the best beaches are nearby. Breakfast included. ❻

Hotel Paraíso del Mar c/Prolongación de Carabeo 22, next door to the parador ☎95 252 16 21, ⓦwww.hotelparaisodelmar.es. Pleasant alternative to the *Parador de Nerja*, where some rooms have a sea-view balcony and Jacuzzi. There's also a pool, gardens, a sauna dug out of the cliff face, and access to the beach. **⑦**

Hotel Perla Marina c/Mérida 7 ☏95 252 33 50, ⓦ www.hotelperlamarina.com. Large, three-star fronting a pebbly beach (there's a better one in the next bay) at the western end of town. Balcony sea-view rooms come with a/c, satellite TV and safe, plus there's a pool, beach restaurant and car park. **⑦**

Parador de Nerja c/Almuñécar 8 ☏95 252 00 50, ⓦ www.parador.es. Modern parador which, despite an exterior resembling an open prison, has a pleasant, plant-filled garden and patio, and a

small park with a bar (worth a visit) overlooking the sea, plus an elevator down the cliff to Burriana, one of Nerja's most popular beaches. The restaurant serves a good-value *menú*. **⑧**

Pensión Montesol c/Pintada 130 ☏95 252 00 14. Friendly *hostal* with en-suite rooms (fans provided) that is more impressive inside than its exterior suggests. **④**

Pepe Mesa Apartamentos c/Los Huertos 33 ☏95 252 41 38, ⓦ www.pepemesa.com. Good-value apartments and studios with kitchenette, satellite TV and rooftop pool. **⑤**

The Town

Nerja's **old town** fans out to the north of the **Balcón de Europa**, a natural palm-lined belvedere which offers magnificent views over the rocky coastline. The tangle of pretty, narrow streets is crowded with visitors all summer long, but the brash shops that service them have yet to suffocate the town's easy-going tranquillity. Nerja's obvious charm has attracted the inevitable colony of migrants – in this case the English – who make their presence felt in the numerous foreign-owned shops and bars. Sights, as such, are few, and once you have strolled along the Balcón and taken a look at the nearby seventeenth-century whitewashed **El Salvador** church (open service times) – which has a fine *Dolorosa* – you should head for the beach or make a short excursion out of town. Nerja's best **beach** is Burriana, an easily walkable kilometre east of the centre. There's also a series of coves within walking distance if you want to escape the crowds.

An entertaining **market** takes place on Tuesday (main market) and Sunday (flea market) mornings and spreads along c/Antonio Ferrándiz (Chanquete), to the east of the centre.

Eating

Restaurant prices in the old town tend to be high and standards indifferent so you'll do better to head further out for good, reasonably priced places. On the western side of town, there are many authentic Spanish restaurants concentrated around Plaza Marina. For **tapas**, three of the best are: *Las 4 Esquinas*, on c/Pintada; *El Chispa*, c/San Pedro 12, which specializes in fried fish; and *Los Cuñaos*, c/Herrera Oria 19, northeast of the centre.

Ayo Burriana beach. Their giant open-air paella fry-up on Sunday lunchtimes (big plate for around €5) is a Burriana institution.

Bar-Restaurante El Puente c/Carretera 4. Decent restaurant with pleasant terrace serving an inexpensive *menú* with vegetarian options.

Bar-Restaurante Los Trillizos c/Los Huertos 38. Budget restaurant offering well-prepared standards with an attractive terrace at the back. Their €7.50 *menú* is probably the best value in town.

Casa Luque Plaza Cavana 2. Good but expensive nouvelle cuisine served up in stylish if rather pretentious surroundings, with a panoramic terrace at the rear. Main dishes €7–14.

El Pulguilla c/Almirante Ferrandiz 26. New location for long-established and

outstanding seafood tapas and *raciones* bar whose quality places it among the best venues in town to eat. Everything sold is straight from the sea and beyond the bar lies a superb terrace. On weekdays they offer a *menú del dia*.

El Refugio c/Diputación 12. Wide choice of fish, *mariscos* and regional dishes in a friendly rustic setting with a reasonable *menú* for around €9 and outdoor tables in the evening.

El Viejo Sótano c/Los Huertos 33. Good mid-priced restaurant with a range of meat and fish dishes as well as some vegetarian options including pastas and salads. Main dishes €8–15.

La Fonda c/Gloria 13 but with an entrance on c/ Almirante Ferrandiz. Upmarket restaurant serving a variety of imaginative fish and meat dishes. *Confit* *de pato con peras al vinagre frambuesa* (confit of duck with pear and raspberry vinegar sauce) is a house special. Main dishes €11–20.

La Marea Plaza Cantarero s/n. Good and modestly priced fish restaurant with terrace, owned by the same proprietors as *La Marina*.

Marisquería La Marina Plaza la Marina s/n. *Marisquerías* don't come any better than this which is why *La Marina* is so popular. Enjoy superb tapas at the bar or mouthwateringly fresh fish (with some great wines) at their restaurant tables or outdoor terrace.

Mesón Pata Negra Plaza La Marina. Authentic regional dishes, and a little more expensive than the other restaurants on this square.

Pizzería Gato Negro c/Hernando de Carabeo 13.

The town's best pizzeria, extremely popular with locals as well as visitors.

Puerta del Mar c/Puerta del Mar 2. Almost next door to the Turismo, this upmarket *marisquería* serves excellent fish and seafood but you pay for the stylish surroundings.

Restaurante Moreno Burriana beach. Nicest out of a cluster of economical eating places at the back of the beach; one of the chefs cooks barbecue-style (in an old boat) outside on the terrace. The fried *sardinas* and paella are excellent.

Rey Alfonso Below the tip of the Balcón de Europa. The best sea view in town, though it can get a bit too briny in hot weather. Plenty of seafood opportunities on a mid-priced menu. Main dishes €9–14.

Bars and nightlife

Most of Nerja's **bars** and **discos** are almost carbon copies of places you'd find in Britain or the States, and are concentrated west of the centre around Plaza Tutti Frutti and along the nearby c/Antonio Millón. There are also numerous bars and restaurants with **live music**, including flamenco. The latter is mainly aimed at tourists although during the September–October Festival de Flamenco (information from the Turismo) you may get the chance to see some memorable performances. The *Guía del Ocio* lists nightlife venues and special events, and is also available from the Turismo.

Bar Cavana Plaza Cavana. One of Nerja's traditional old bars, behind the Iglesia El Salvador; a tranquil place serving food and great for leisurely breakfasts.

Cafetería La Calabella c/Puerto del Mar 8. Excellent little breakfast café close to the Turismo with a terrace overlooking the beach.

Pub Bogey c/Pintada 22. Currently popular music bar on the old town's major thoroughfare.

Pub La Guarida Plaza Tutti Frutti. One of a cluster of music bars on and around this square that thump it out until dawn.

Restaurante Bar-El Colono c/Granada 6, just north of Plaza Cavana. Entertaining free flamenco show.

Listings

Activities Club Nautico de Nerja (☎95 252 46 54), Avda. Castilla Pérez 2, west of the centre, rents out motorbikes and mountain bikes and offers horse riding, diving and sailing tuition plus excursions.
Bookshops There's an English bookshop, W.H. Smiffs, in the small shopping arcade next to the post office on c/Almirante Ferrandiz; they also have an ex-pat noticeboard that often lists job vacancies. Nerja also boasts one of the best second-hand bookshops on the coast, The Book Centre, at c/Granada 30.

Post office c/Almirante Ferrandiz, 50m metres from the Turismo.
Internet access Cafés are located all over town but a couple of the most central are *Zona Cyber*, Plaza Ermita 23, near the bus station (daily 11am–3pm & 6–9pm), and *Med Web Café*, c/Castilla Peréz 21, to the west of centre (daily 9.30am–midnight), which has the best *ambiente* with beers, shakes and snacks while *Europ@web* almost next door is another good place.

Around Nerja

A popular excursion from Nerja is the six-kilometre trip north to **FRIGILIANA**, a pretty Moorish hill village clinging to the lower slopes of

Monte El Fuerte. After the *Reconquista*, Frigiliana became a Morisco settlement where only those Moors who had converted to Christianity were allowed to live. Although a little of the atmosphere of this period survives in the steep, narrow streets, the place is prettified today by the addition of geranium pots and historical plaques.

A new **Turismo**, Cuesta de Apero 10 (Mon–Fri 9am–8pm, Sat & Sun 10am–1.30pm & 4–8pm; ℡95 253 31 26, ⓦwww.frigiliana.org), 50m from the bus terminus, also houses a small **archeological museum** and can provide a useful village map. They also stock more of Elma Thompson's walks pamphlets (see p.137) for this zone. In keeping with the village's status as a tourist draw, some of the restaurants and bars here tend to be overpriced, but if you want to **stay over**, the hospitable *Hotel Las Chinas*, Plaza Capitán Cortés 14 (℡95 253 30 73, ⓦwww.hotellaschinas.cjb.net; ❸), is a good bet for balcony rooms with bath (ask for a room at the rear to avoid street noise). They also have a good restaurant next door. The new *Hotel Villa Frigiliana*, c/San Sebastian s/n (℡95 253 42 21, ⓦwww.frigiliana.com; ❹ with breakfast), is the luxury option and manages to squeeze in a small pool. Two kilometres out of the village along the Torrox road the *Hotel Posada Morisca* (℡95 253 41 51, ⓔposada.morisca@terra .es; ❻) is an attractive small hotel in a rural setting with pool and individually styled rooms. Two kilometres further along the same road *Hotel Los Caracoles* (℡95 203 06 09, ⓦwww.hotelloscaracoles.com; ❺–❻) has fully equipped oddball snail-shell style dwellings with adjacent pool and restaurant. As well as the restaurant next door to *Las Chinas*, good **eating places** are *La Bodeguilla*, c/Chorruelo s/n, an excellent family-run restaurant in the upper village, the nearby *Restaurante Jaime*, c/Amargura 15, and the more upmarket *El Adarve*,

Walks around Frigiliana

One easy walk (roughly 3–4hr) is to follow the 15km dirt track through the foothills of the **Almijara range**, leading from Frigiliana, via the hamlet of Venta del Jaro, to the Axarquía village of Cómpeta (see p.135), which has good facilities and accommodation.

Another circular 8km walk covers the **hill country** to the northwest of Frigiliana. Follow the road north out of the village towards the pleasant refreshment stop of *Venta de Frigiliana* (summer daily 11am–4pm), which you'll reach after 3km. Turn left down the dirt track just beyond the entrance, which leads down the ridge, passing some old cottages and villas. Ten minutes or so further on you'll pass the gates of the Peñones and the Cortijo del Peñon farmhouses on the right. Continue down this track between pine woods and crags until you reach a crossroads, with a walled villa on the far side. Fork sharply left at this point, passing some more old cottages on the right. One of these has a single palm tree, the ancient Moorish sign of welcome. At the first fork, below a large villa, continue left, uphill. The road winds round the villa wall, swings right and crosses the lower Pedregal valley, from where it climbs up the hill to the col on the Loma de la Cruz. Just below the crest of the ridge, where a *carril* (track) comes up from the right, keep straight on up, passing a villa. In front of this villa, a water-cover stamped "SAT no. 7196 Monte Ariza" will confirm that you're on the right road. At the col, go straight across at the cross-tracks marked with red paint and follow the track down and round, keeping left of the fork on the next ridge. This will bring you down past the Casa del Valle, on the left. A little further on, round the bend, you'll see some tumbledown houses on the right; the first of these contains an old olive or wine press which is worth a look. The *carril* now passes through open country, then through *huertas*, rejoining the Torrox road at Casa Fernando. A right and then a left turn will take you to the upper car park on the edge of Frigiliana.

c/Alta 3, which does international and local dishes including its house special *cordero a la miel* (lamb in honey). *Taberna del Sacristán*, Plaza de la Iglesia 12, on the village's main square with a pleasant terrace fronting the church of San Antonio is another good mid-priced option with main dishes costing €7–15. At least six **buses** per day leave for Frigiliana from the bus station in Nerja, the earliest of which gives you enough time to take a walk in the surrounding hills and catch the last bus back at 7.30pm.

Cynics might find the "accidental" discovery in 1957 of the **CUEVAS DE NERJA** (daily July–Aug 10am–2pm & 4–8pm; rest of year closes 6.30pm; Ⓦwww.cuevanerja.com; €6) – neatly coinciding with the arrival of mass tourism – a little suspect. Immediately they were revealed, the series of enormous caverns, scattered with Paleolithic and Neolithic tools, pottery and cave paintings stretching back 30,000 years, became a local, then national, sensation. Nowadays, however, the fairy lights, piped muzak, and cave theatre – which hosts various shows from rock to ballet and flamenco – can't help but detract from the appreciation of a spectacular natural wonder, and the cave paintings are currently not on public view (and possibly never will be). However, you might want to seek out the world's longest known **stalactite** – all 32m of it and verified by the *Guinness Book of Records* – whilst you're probing the depths. A new **Centro de Interpretación** (same hours as cave; free) located near the cave entrance uses dioramas to document the history of the cave and its geology and for more serious explorations (the tourist visit allows access to only one third of the cave's extent) there are fully equipped **speleological tours** in English and Spanish lasting seven hours (€90; ☏95 252 95 20 for details). The **restaurant** at the cave entrance serves a cheap buffet, but can get very busy in high season. A far better place to eat is the restaurant of the refurbished *Hotel al Andalus* (☏95 252 96 48; ❹), down the hill, which serves a good-value *menú* and has a pleasant terrace. From Nerja the caves are an easy but not particularly pleasant three-kilometre walk east along the main coast road; taking a taxi (roughly €5 one-way) or a bus (running approximately hourly) from Nerja bus station is a better alternative.

Further east of Nerja, the coastal road zigzags around the foothills of the Sierra Almijara, climbing above a number of tiny coves. The first settlement, the coastal hamlet of **MARO**, is a sparkling cluster of white-walled houses set above an attractive cove beach. Lying close to the ancient Roman settlement of *Detunda*, the town was revitalized in the eighteenth century by the construction of a sugar factory, now a ruin behind the simple church of Nuestra Señora de las Maravillas, which dates from the same period. There are three **places to stay**. *Hotel Playa Maro* (☏95 252 95 82, Ⓦwww.hotelplayamaro.com; ❺ including breakfast) is a formal hotel at the entrance to the village that also rents out apartments (❻), but *Casa Maro* (☏95 252 96 90, Ⓦwww.hotel-casa-maro.com; ❺), a German-run apartment hotel with sea-view balconies and parrots in the garden, is much the more attractive option; they also have special deals for students. Slightly cheaper sea-view balcony studios – sleeping up to four people – are on offer from *Balcón de Maro*, Plaza de las Maravillas (☏95 252 95 23, Ⓕ95 252 26 08; ❹), near the church. There are numerous **places to eat** around the village and all three of the above hotels have restaurants and bars.

The Costa Tropical (west)

The **Costa Tropical** is the name given to Granada Province's 60km of coastline, much of it refreshingly tranquil after the concrete sprawls along the Costa del Sol; its western stretch, including the attractive towns of **Almuñécar** and **Salobreña**, is most conveniently reached from Nerja.

Beyond Nerja, the N340 passes tracks leading down to inviting coves with quiet **beaches**, a few of which have welcoming bars. One, the Torre Caleta, lies just below the bridge that marks the border of Málaga and Granada provinces. Entering Granada Province, the N340 launches into one of the most panoramic stretches along the whole coast, climbing and twisting inland before running along sheer cliffs high above the jagged coast. Eventually it surfaces at **LA HERRADURA**, a fishing village-resort suburb of Almuñécar, and for anyone with their own transport a good place to stop off and swim. **Rooms**, however, don't come cheap here – the friendly *Hostal La Caleta*, Paseo Andrés Segovia 11 (☎958 82 70 07; ❹), with ensuite a/c rooms with TV, at the eastern end of the seafront, and *Hostal Peña Parda*, Peña Parda Playa (☎958 64 00 66; ❹), where rooms lack a/c or TV, at the western end, are the most reasonable budget options. The new and comfortable *Hotel Almijara*, c/Acera del Pilar 6 (☎958 61 80 53, ⓦwww.hotelalmijara.com; ❻), slightly inland from the sea, is the three-star alternative but lacks a pool. There are also a couple of summer **campsites** with confusingly similar names, of which *Nuevo Camping La Herradura* (☎958 64 06 34) at the extreme western end of the beach is the best. For **food**, good tapas are to be had in the bar of *Mesón El Tinao*, Paseo Maritimo s/n, and full meals in its popular restaurant filled with hanging *jamones*. The seafront *La Parilla*, Paseo Andrés Segovia 39, is another good place specializing in charcoal-grilled meat and fish.

Almuñécar

ALMUÑÉCAR is Granada's flagship seaside resort and, although marred by a number of towering holiday apartments, has made admirable attempts to preserve its *andaluz* character. Founded early in the first millennium BC by the Phoenicians as the wonderfully named Sexi, it possesses ruins both from this and its later Roman and Moorish periods. The town's pebble beaches, it has to be said, are rather cramped and not improved by the greyish sand, but the esplanade, **Paseo Puerta del Mar** (aka Paseo del Altillo), behind them, with palm-roofed bars (many offering free tapas) and restaurants, is fun, and the *casco antiguo*, or old town, is attractive.

Arrival and information

The **bus station** – with frequent connections to Granada and Málaga – is at the junction of Avenida Juan Carlos I and Avenida Fenicia, northeast of the centre. Inconveniently, the **Turismo** (Mon–Sat 10am–2pm & 6–9pm; ☎958 63 11 25, ⓦwww.almunecar.info) is at the opposite end of town (a good ten-minute walk away), near the sea on Avenida Europa. It is, however, located in a striking nineteenth-century neo-Moorish garden mansion and is well worth a look. The Turismo also sells an unlimited **bono turistico** (pass) allowing entry to all the town's monuments (including the Parque Ornitológico) for €3.20. The office should have information on Almuñécar's annual **jazz festival** – now one of the most important in Spain – held in July and often attracting big names. **Internet** access is available at *La Libertad* (daily 10am–midnight), c/Helga Söhnel, at the corner of c/Livry Gargan, behind the Playa Puerta del Mar, and at *Mundo Digital* (Mon–Sat 10am–2pm & 5–11pm) c/Alta del Mar 8, in the old quarter. **Cycles** can be hired by the day from Champion, Paseo de San Cristóbal 3. Following Avda. de Andalucía from the bus station through the old town will take you close to many of the town's *hostales* and *fondas*.

ALMUÑÉCAR

Ship House (800m), Roman Aqueduct (500m) &

ACCOMMODATION		RESTAURANTS & BARS	
Hostal Plaza Damasco	C	Antonio	8
Hostal Rocamar	A	Bar-Taberna El Cortijillo	5
Hostal Tropical	H	El Chaleco	1
Hotel Casablanca	I	Horno de Candida	3
Hotel Goya	E	Jacquy Cotobro	10
Hotel Helios	F	La Trastienda	6
Hotel La Najarra	D	La Última Ola	9
Hotel Almuñécar Playa	G	Restaurante El Capricho	2
Hotel Playa San Cristóbal	J	Restaurante La Muralla	4
Hotel-Hostal Victoria II	B	Restaurante–Mesón Francisco II	7

Accommodation

The pressure on **accommodation** in Almuñécar is not quite as acute as at Nerja.
There are more than enough hotels to cope with the summer crush, whilst good-
value *hostales* encircle the central Plaza de la Rosa in the old town and there are
more to be found just east of here, in the streets off the Avenida de Andalucía.
Almuñécar's **campsite**, *Carambalo* (☎958 63 03 22), is some way inland off the
N340 heading east; La Herradura (see p.143) is perhaps a better bet for camping.

Hostal Plaza Damasco c/Cerrajeros 8 ☎958 63
01 65. Cosy and recently renovated *hostal* just off
the plaza it's named after, offering en-suite rooms
with TV. ❹

Hostal Rocamar c/Córdoba 3 ☎958 63 00 23.
Pleasant French-owned place near the bus station,
offering rooms with bath (but no TV). ❸

Hostal Tropical Avda. Europa s/n ☎958 63 34
58, ⓔatovaga@teleline.es. Near the beach, with
comfortable en-suite rooms. A good deal, considering its position. ❹

Hotel Casablanca Plaza San Cristóbal 4 (aka
Plaza Abderramán) ☎958 63 55 75, ⓦwww
.almunecar.info/casablanca. Excellent family-run

establishment with flamboyant neo-Moorish facade
and interior, offering a/c balcony en-suite rooms
with sea views. In slack times you can often haggle
the price down a bit. ❹

Hotel Goya Avda. Europa s/n ☎958 63 05 50.
Intimate hotel with pleasant a/c rooms opposite the
Turismo and 50m from the Playa de San Cristóbal.
❹

Hotel Helios Paseo San Cristóbal s/n ☎958 63 44
59, ⓦwww.heliosalmunecar.com. Long Almuñécar's leading hotel, the *Helios* has recently been
upstaged by its new neighbour, the *Almuñecar
Playa* (see opposite). This prompted a refurbishment and it's probably the better of the duo,

offering tasteful balcony rooms with sea views, a pool and rooftop solarium. **❼**

Hotel La Najarra c/Guadix 12 ☎95 863 03 91, ⓦwww.hotelnajarra.com. Well-equipped hotel with a/c rooms plus garden pool , tennis courts and easy parking a couple of minutes walk from the Playa de San Cristóbal. **❹**

Hotel Almuñécar Playa Paseo San Cristóbal s/n ☎958 63 94 50, ⓦwww.playasenator.com. The glaring terracotta exterior of this 225-room monster luxury hotel conceals a spectacular atrium lobby with waterfall and plants dangling from the glass roof almost to the floor. Not to everyone's taste, but you get all the frills associated with a four-star hotel, including Internet access and a pool. **❽**

Hotel Playa San Cristóbal Plaza de San Cristóbal 5 ☎958 63 36 12, ⓔjld00005@terra.es. Old-worldly place with a bar full of characters below and a/c balcony rooms with TV above. The eccentric proprietor, an ex-sea captain, constructed the remarkable "ship house" in the north of the town (see p.146). **❹**

Hotel-Hostal Victoria II Plaza de la Victoria 6, off Avda. de Andalucía. Hotel ☎958 63 17 34, hostal ☎958 63 00 22). Decent one-star hotel and (a few doors away) its rather impersonal hostel-style *pensión*. The hotel's rooms come with a/c, bath and TV, whilst the *hostal*'s more basic budget rooms (also en-suite) are clean with balconies overlooking the square. **❸**–**❹**

The Town

Almuñécar's impressive sixteenth-century **Castillo de San Miguel** (April–Sept Tues–Sat 10.30am–1.30pm & 6.30–9pm, Sun 10am–12.30pm; Oct–March Tues–Sat 10am–1.30pm & 5–7.30pm, Sun 10.30am–2pm; €2.10), sitting atop a headland – the Peñon del Santo – which bisects the resort's two bays, replaced the Moorish Alcazaba, itself built on top of an earlier Roman fort, in the time of Carlos V. Distinctive for its massive tower known as La Mazmorra ("the dungeon") this is where, in the Nasrid period, Granada's rulers imprisoned out-of-favour ministers or overweening military commanders whom they saw as a threat. During the *Reconquista* it was taken by Fernando and Isabel in 1489, three years before the fall of Granada itself, and given the name of Almuñécar's patron saint. Held by the French in the War of Independence, in 1808 it was bombarded by the British navy and largely ruined, after which it served as the town's graveyard. This was recently dug up – bones, coffins and all – and relocated in a new cemetery on the outskirts of town, and the castle restored. The interior now houses the town's interesting **museum** containing artefacts and information documenting Almuñécar's distinguished three-thousand-year history.

Below the castle, to the west in the Parque Botanico El Majuelo, a remarkable **Factoría de Salazones** or Roman fish-curing factory has been excavated. The tanks in which the *garum* was prepared are well preserved, and the quality of the famous fish sauce is recorded in the writings of Pliny the Elder. The surrounding botanical garden is extremely peaceful with fine views towards the castillo and walls (open site). Nearby to the south, the **Parque Ornitológico** (April–Sept daily 11am–2pm & 6–9pm; Oct–March daily 11am–2pm & 5–7pm; €2.10) is an aviary filled with a squawking collection of 1500 birds representing 120 international species.

In town, it's well worth stopping off at the small **Museo Arqueológico** (Tues–Sat 10.30am–1.30pm & 6.30–9pm, Sun 10.30am–2pm; €2.10), located above and south of the elegant Plaza Ayuntamiento (officially the Plaza de la Constitución, a name nobody uses) in the Cueva de los Siete Palacios ("Cave of the Seven Palaces"), an ancient structure that may well have been a water reservoir. The museum exhibits – mostly discovered locally – are from the Phoenician, Roman and Moorish periods, including an inscribed seventeenth-century BC **Egyptian vase** which carries not only the oldest piece of written text discovered on the Iberian peninsula, but also the only known reference to the early sixteenth-century BC pharaoh Apophis I, a ruler during Egypt's hazy Hyksos period when foreign usurpers grasped the throne.

△ Ship House, Almuñecar

More ancient remains are visible about 1km out of town along the Río Seco, where there's a first-century two-level **Roman aqueduct** that until recently was part of the town's water supply. With your own transport, you could visit another aqueduct opposite the church in the village of Torrecuevas, which you can reach by following the road north towards Otívar for 3km. Three far more spectacular stretches of aqueduct, however, can be seen by turning left up a road signed "*Casa Minerva*" opposite the Venta Luciano on the same village's southern edge. When you reach the Río Seco turn left – the dry riverbed is driveable – and after 500m beyond orchards on the left you will see three wonderfully preserved spans including one which is double tiered. This visit could be combined with a trip to the restaurant in Otívar (see overleaf).

One remarkable but little-known sight is the astonishing **ship house** built by an ex-merchant sea captain, José-María Pérez Ruiz, at Avda. El Mediterraneo 34, in the northeastern suburb of the town close to the N340 *autovía*. After captaining his ship for thirty years, upon retirement Señor Pérez Ruiz decided to re-create his vessel on dry land – in concrete. When you approach the house you see nothing less than a fifty-metre-long hull towering above the road complete with a bridge (now the captain's lounge and bedroom) sporting radar masts, radio antennae and all flags flying. The "deck" has all the paraphernalia of a real ship, and a swimming pool as well. It's not open to visitors but if you're a guest at señor Pérez Ruiz's hotel (see "Accommodation") you may just get a guided tour.

Eating and drinking

There are countless **places to eat** lined along the Paseo Puerta del Mar, many of them offering cheap if unspectacular *menús*. The town's more interesting

Return to Castillo of the sugar canes

After being trapped in Spain during the Civil War, in the 1950s Laurie Lee revisited some of the places he knew well, one of which was Castillo (a pseudonym for Almuñécar). He describes the pain of this experience in *A Rose for Winter*:

Everything now was as it had been before – though perhaps a little more ignoble, more ground in dust. As I walked through the town time past hung heavy on my feet. The face of a generation had disappeared completely. A few old women recognized me, throwing up their hands with an exclamation, then came running towards me with lowered voices as though we shared a secret. But of the men I had known there was little news, and such as there was, confused. Most of them, it seemed, were either dead or fled. The old women peered up at me with red-rimmed, clouded eyes, and each tale they told was different. My ex-boss, the hotel keeper, who used to pray for Franco in his office, had been shot as a red spy; he had died of pneumonia in prison; he had escaped to France. Lalo, the hotel porter, had been killed on the barricades in Málaga; he ran a bar in Lyon; he was a barber in Jaén. Young Paco, the blond dynamiter of enemy tanks, was still a local fisherman – you could run into him at any time; no, he had blown himself up; he had married and gone to Mallorca. Luíz, the carpenter, had betrayed his comrades and been stoned to death; he lived in Vélez Málaga; he sold chickens in Granada.... In the end I gave up. There was no point in making any further inquiries. Nobody lied deliberately, but nobody wished to seem certain of the truth. For the truth, in itself, was unendurable.

possibilities lie away from the seafront hurly-burly in the *casco antiguo* and beyond. Two outstanding restaurants *Jacquy Cotobro* and *El Chaleco* – both Belgian-run – are located out of the centre but are worth the effort. A couple of decent **tapas bars** are *Bar Madrid* and *Bar Vizcaya* both fronting the Playa San Cristóbal, while for **breakfast** make for the cafés around the Plaza Ayuntamiento in the old town.

Antonio Paseo Marítimo 12 ☎958 63 02 20. Top-class seafront fish restaurant and tapas bar with an excellent *menú* for about €15. Try their *aguacate con gambas* (avocado stuffed with prawns).

Bar-Taberna El Cortijillo Plaza Kelibia 4. Lively tapas bar popular with young locals, in an attractive square with a lively scene on summer nights.

El Chaleco Avda. Costa del Sol 37 ☎95 863 24 02. Slightly out of the way, this is an excellent Belgian-French restaurant with an outstanding kitchen. Among their signature dishes is *conejo a la cerveza con ciruelas* (rabbit with beer and prunes) and you can choose three courses off the menu for €17.50. Closed Sun eve & Mon.

Horno de Candida c/Orovia 3 ☎958 63 46 07. The restaurant of Almuñécar's hotel school is located in an elegant mansion which itself incorporates a remarkable Moorish brick oven (*horno*), now a dining room. The food is outstanding and reasonably priced and there's a wonderful roof

terrace as well. Main dishes €11–15 with a *menú* for €12. Closed Wed.

Jacquy Cotobro Playa Cotobro ☎958 63 18 02. Located on a delightful bay 1km west of the centre and easily reached on foot by following the Paseo San Cristóbal (Paseo de las Flores' western continuation) to its end, this makes a wonderful lunch or evening venue. Belgian chef (and ex-footballer with Standard Liège) Jacques Vanhoren has married the best of his native and Spanish cuisines and all dishes, both fish and meat, are cooked with panache. The desserts – including a celebrated *fondant de tres chocolates* – aren't bad either. The *a la carte* doesn't come cheap, but the *menú de degustación* at €26 is excellent value. Nov–March closed Mon.

La Trastienda Plaza Kelibia s/n. Decent tapas and *raciones* bar also noted for its excellent *roscos* (doughnuts).

La Última Ola Paseo Puerto del Mar 4. This excellent seafront fish restaurant also serves tapas and, pandering to carnivores, squeezes a few meat dishes onto its menu as well. One of its noted dishes is *dorada a la gaditana* (sea bream).

Restaurante–Mesón Francisco II c/Alto del Mar 8. Restaurant offshoot of the great *Bodega Francisco* (see below) run by the proprietor's son. Decent *venta*-style fare with a few regional dishes – *cabrito alpujarreño* (kid) and *chuleta de cordero a la miel* (lamb) are specials – on offer as well. *Menú* for €8.50.

🏃 **Restaurante El Capricho** Otívar, 13km north of town ☎958 64 50 75. Great little country restaurant on the north edge of this hill village that's famed for its *pollo a la manzana* (chicken with apples) and *cordero asado* (roast lamb). For these dishes you'll need to give them at least three hours' notice that you're coming (open lunch & dinner); there are daily buses from Almuñécar's bus station at 2pm & 8.30pm, returning at 4.30 & 7pm.

Restaurante La Muralla c/Ángel Gamay s/n. Excellent *bodega* serving a range of outstanding tapas and meals in their interior room or *al fresco* in a tiny alley. Main dishes €11–20.

Nightlife

Almuñécar's **nightlife** moves at a leisurely pace and centres around the bars and discos circling Plaza Kelibia and Plaza de la Rosa in the old town, and behind the beaches to the eastern side of the Peñon del Santo headland.

Agua Tropic Paseo Velilla s/n at the eastern end of the seafront. Open-air disco with an eclectic taste in sounds, but just the thing on sultry summer nights.

Bodega Francisco c/Real 15, north of Plaza Rosa. Wonderful old bar with barrels stacked up to the ceiling and walls covered with ageing *corrida* posters and mounted boars' heads. The *fino* and *montilla* are both excellent, and the bar offers a wide range of tapas and *platos combinados*. A dining area has recently been added and impromptu flamenco sometimes adds to the fun.

El Convento Plaza Victoria 20. Superb bar next door to the *Hotel Victoria II* and partly housed in a sixteenth-century convent. The second floor stages exhibitions by Spanish and local artists, while the roof terrace is a wonderful place for a drink under the stars.

Aqua Noche Paseo Reina Sofía s/n, behind the Playa Fuente de Piedra at the eastern end of the seafront. One of a number of clubs in this zone that pack them playing flamenco-rock and salsa until dawn and beyond.

Salobreña

The road east from Almuñécar crosses the Río Verde and slowly makes its way upwards, past slopes dotted with almond and custard apple trees until, 13km later, a spectacular vista opens up to reveal **SALOBREÑA**, a White Town tumbling down a hill topped by the shell of its Moorish castle and surrounded by a sea of sugar-cane fields. Comparatively undeveloped, the town is set back a two-kilometre hike from the sea (although there are hourly buses), and is thus less marketable for mass tourism, making it a far more relaxed destination than Almuñécar. Beginning life as a Phoenician city dedicated to Salambo (the Syrian goddess of love), the town retained some importance in Moorish times – as is evidenced by the much restored Alcázar – but then languished in poverty until rescued by more recent prosperity, generated, in part, by its new trickles of tourism.

On the eastern side of town, the **Alcázar** (daily 10am–1pm & 5–8pm; closes 7pm Oct–March; €2.55 including museum below) is worth a look, not least for the fine views from its crenellated towers. Below this, down at the foot of the hill, the sixteenth-century church of **Nuestra Señora del Rosario** (open service times) stands on the site previously occupied by a Moorish mosque. A stone's throw away, the old Ayuntamiento houses the town **museum** (same hours & ticket as the Alcázar) which displays artefacts from all periods of Salobreña's history. There's also an animated **market** each Tuesday and Friday morning in the central Plaza del Mercado, but that's about as far as sightseeing goes.

Practicalities

Buses arrive and leave from the Plaza de Goya, close to the **Turismo**, Plaza de Goya s/n (Mon–Fri 10am–1.30pm & 5–7.30pm, Sat 10am–1.30pm; ☎958 61 03 14, ⓦwww.ayto–salobrena.org), whose town map will help you find your way around; a **kiosk** (same hours) opens in summer on the Paseo Marítimo near El Peñon, the seafront promontory. They also offer guided visits to the old town on Fridays at 6.30pm (July–Sept, €6). The Turismo also has its own bilingual (Spanish and English) book of coastal and hill **walks**, *Rutas y Senderos de Salobreña* (€6), incorporating an ingenious route-finding system making it almost impossible to lose your way. **Internet** access is available at *Ciber Locutorio Salobreña* (daily 11am–2pm & 4–10pm), Plaza Washington Irving, 150m south of the Turismo.

There's usually no problem in finding **accommodation** in Salobreña, even in high season, and the lack of demand is reflected in the low prices. Most of the budget places are on the western side of town. Perhaps the best-value deal is the new French-run *Hostal San Juan* (☎958 61 17 29, ⓦwww.hostalsanjuan .com; ❸) at c/Jardines 1, a couple of minutes walk from the Turismo; situated in a beautifully restored town house with elegant patio, the en-suite rooms come with a/c and TV. Close to Avenida García Lorca, the main avenue winding down from the town to the beach, worthy options for simple rooms include the *Pensión Castellmar*, c/Nueva 21 (☎958 61 02 27; ❷), which has terraces in some rooms, and delightful sea views. Over the road, at no. 21, the similarly priced *Pensión Mari Carmen* (☎958 61 09 06; ❷) is equally nice, with fans in the rooms and some en suites. To the south of here are two more en-suite options: the very pleasant and good-value *Hostal Miramar*, c/Arrabal Villa 37 (☎958 82 85 34; ❷–❸), behind the bar of the same name; and the nearby *Hostal Mary Tere*, c/Fabrica Nueva 7 (☎958 61 01 26, ⓦwww.hostalmarytere.com; ❸), with balcony rooms.

Places to eat are limited, and the best-quality places in town are probably *Restaurante Pesetas*, c/Boveda s/n, near the Alcázar with terrace views, and *La Bodega* (main dishes €11–20), Plaza de Goya, near the Turismo. Both places offer a reasonably priced *menú del día* and serve tapas. Below the Alcázar *Taberna Alhaja*, c/Placeta 6, is an inviting little tapas and *raciones* bar with a laid-back atmosphere; at night it becomes a more drinks-oriented option. *Mesón de la Villa*, Plaza F. Ramirez de Madrid, with a terrace on a palm-fringed plaza not far from the Turismo, is another excellent place for tapas. *Pizzería Betty Blue*, c/Antequera 4, off Paseo de las Flores near the Alcázar, is good for pizzas and has a pleasant terrace with fine views. Down on the seafront, your best bet is one of the many *chiringuitos* lining the shore, among which *El Peñon*, on the promontory from which it takes its name, is extremely popular, although it tends to exploit its location by charging higher prices. The nearby and more reasonably priced *La Bahía* is perhaps a better option. East of these two along the Paseo Marítimo, three more *chiringuitos*, *Tres Hermanos*, *Emilio* and *El Molino*, are also good.

The Costa del Sol

West of Málaga – or more correctly, west of Málaga airport – the real **Costa del Sol** gets going. If you've never seen this level of touristic development before, it can be quite a shock, not least when you see how grit-grey the sands are; you have to keep going, around the corner to Tarifa, before you reach the

The Carretera Nacional N340

The Costa del Sol's main highway, **the N340**, is one of the most dangerous roads in Europe. Nominally a national highway, it's really a hundred-kilometre-long city street, passing through the middle of towns and *urbanizaciones*. Drivers treat it like a motorway, yet pedestrians have to get across, and cars are constantly turning off or into the road – hence the terrifying number of accidents, with, on average, over a hundred fatalities a year. A large number of casualties are inebriated British package tourists who are unfamiliar with left-hand-drive vehicles and traffic patterns. The first few kilometres, between the airport with its various car rental offices and Torremolinos, are among the most treacherous, but worse still is the stretch heading west from Marbella: around thirty accidents a year occur on each kilometre between Marbella and San Pedro.

A new full-scale, four-lane toll motorway replacement – the **Autopista del Sol** – linking Málaga with Sotogrande (south of Estepona) in the west and Nerja to the east, is now complete. Construction of the next phase – stretching from Nerja to Almería and cutting the journey time from Málaga to the Almerian capital to two hours – has now begun but will not be completed for some years.

Meanwhile, if you're using the old N340 don't make dangerous (and illegal) left turns from the fast lane – use the *"Cambio de Sentido"* junctions which allow you to reverse direction. Also be particularly careful after a heavy rain, when the hot, oily road surface sends you easily into a skid. **Pedestrians** should cross at traffic lights, a bridge or an underpass if possible.

golden sands of the tourist brochures. With their faceless 1960s' and 1970s' concrete tower blocks, these are certainly not the kind of resorts you find in Greece or even Portugal. Since the 1980s' boom in time-share apartments and leisure complexes, it's estimated that 300,000 foreigners live on the Costa del Sol, the majority of them retired and British. On the other hand, the cheap package-tour industry – largely responsible for the transformation of the string of poverty-stricken fishing villages that dotted this coast until the 1950s – no longer brings in the numbers it once did, placing the future of purpose-built resorts such as Torremolinos in peril.

Approached in the right kind of spirit, it *is* possible to have fun in **Torremolinos**, and, at a price, in **Marbella**. The sea, at least, is reasonably clean around here, after a lot of work on the sewerage systems. But if you've come to Andalucía to discover the real Spain, keep going at least until you reach **Estepona**.

Torremolinos

The approach to **TORREMOLINOS** – easiest on the electric railway from Málaga or the airport – is a depressing trawl through a drab, soulless landscape of kitchenette apartments and half-finished developments. The town itself, rechristened "Torrie" by English package tourists, is certainly an experience: a vast, grotesque parody of a seaside resort with its own kitsch fascination. This bizarre place, lined with sweeping (but crowded) beaches and infinite shopping arcades, crammed with Irish pubs and real-estate agents, has a large permanent expat population of Britons, Germans and Scandinavians. It's a weird mix, which, in addition to thousands of retired people, has attracted – due to a previous lack of extradition arrangements between Britain and Spain – a notorious concentration of British crooks.

In recent years a dynamic town council has been moving heaven and earth to rid the resort of its "Terrible Torrie" image, and whilst they've stopped short of flattening the concrete monsters overlooking the beach they have made a few commendable improvements. The recently completed seafront promenade, which runs all the way to La Carihuela, can be quite scenic in parts and the maze of alleys in the old town – now largely cleared of their tawdry boutiques and tacky stalls – also have some charm.

Torremolinos will never be Marbella; its whole purpose is geared to giving people a roaring good time, and if that's what you're looking for, there are few places on the coast with as many bars and clubs. Throughout the summer the municipality puts on an infinite variety of free events, including festivals of music, dance and jazz, as well as beach volleyball and football competitions and children's theatre.

Arrival and information

The **train** from Málaga drops you right in the centre of the action, on Avenida Jesús Santos Rein (℡902 24 02 02), a couple of blocks west of the town's main artery, c/San Miguel. The **bus station** (℡95 238 24 19) is a five-minute walk away on c/Hoyo, to the east. The main **Turismo**, on Plaza de la Independencia (Mon–Fri 9.30am–1.30pm; ℡95 237 95 12, ⓦwww.ayto-torremolinos.org), is supported by a number of other **sub offices** (open April–Sept) which open longer hours; the most convenient are located on the seafront at Plaza de las Comunidades Autonomas (daily 10am–2pm & 5–8pm) southeast of the centre, and in the small fishing village of La Carihuela (1km west of the town centre) on the seafront just off Plaza del Remo (daily 10am–2pm & 5–8pm).

Accommodation

Outside August it's usually easy enough to find a **place to stay**, with plenty of economical *hostales* sandwiched between the high-rise horrors, and a couple of very pleasant places a little further out. You may also want to consider escaping to the inland village of Benalmádena Pueblo (see p.154). You'll find a **campsite** (℡95 238 26 02) 3km east of the centre on the main Málaga–Cádiz highway, 500m from the sea. To get there, take the *cercanía* train (get off at Los Alamos) or go by bus (Línea B) from the central Plaza Costa del Sol. The campsite is near *Hotel Los Alamos*.

Central Torremolinos

Hostal Micaela c/Bajondillo 4 ℡95 238 33 10, Ⓔbelen708@hotmail.com. Serviceable rooms with bath, close to the beach. ❸

Hostal Virgen del Rocío II Avda. Isabel Manoja 21 ℡95 237 12 24. The twin to the similarly named *hostal* in Ronda with the same proprietors, this is a neat and friendly *hostal* where en-suite rooms come with TV; Internet access available for guests. ❸

Hotel Picasso Plaza Independencia s/n ℡95 238 76 00, Ⓕ95 238 78 23. Somewhat overpriced upmarket hotel in a quiet plaza. ❺

Hotel Tarik Paseo Marítimo 49 ℡95 238 23 00, ⓦwww.hoteltarik.com. Attractive hotel facing the beach with a garden pool and well-equipped a/c rooms with room safe; a stone's throw from the excellent *Yate El Córdobes* restaurant (see p.153). ❻

Pensión Beatriz c/del Peligro 4, Playa Bajondillo ℡95 238 51 10 Ⓔhostalbeatriz@hotmail.com. Small and good-value *hostal* offering en-suite rooms with a/c, TV and sea view twenty metres from the beach. ❹

The Red Parrot Avda. Los Manantiales 4 ℡95 237 54 45, ⓦwww.theredparrot.com. Bang in the centre, with English proprietors who have given the *hostal* a complete refurbishment; all rooms come with balcony, bath and fans, and the interior patio has a small pool. ❹

La Carihuela

Apartamentos Alegría c/Carmen 23, La Carihuela ℡95 238 02 73 ⓦwww.lacarihuela.com. Charming, two-person seafront studios with kitchen and bath available for minimum stays of two days. ❹

Hostal Flor Blanco Pasaje de la Carihuela 4 ℡95 238 20 71. Friendly *hostal* with clean en-suite

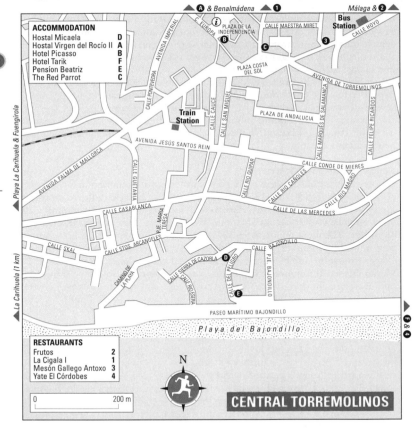

ACCOMMODATION
Hostal Micaela   D
Hostal Virgen del Rocío II A
Hotel Picasso   B
Hotel Tarik   F
Pension Beatriz   E
The Red Parrot   C

RESTAURANTS
Frutos   2
La Cigala I   1
Mesón Gallego Antoxo   3
Yate El Córdobes   4

CENTRAL TORREMOLINOS

rooms, some with partial sea views for the same price (ring ahead to reserve); 50m from the beach in La Carihuela. ③

Hotel Miami c/Aladino 14, west of the centre in La Carihuela ℡95 238 52 55, ⓦwww.residencia–miami.com. One of the most charming hotels on the whole Costa del Sol, this enchanting villa was built by a cousin of Picasso and contains many of the original

designer furnishings. Behind its walls is a garden filled with palms and oleanders and a swimming pool. ④

Hotel Tiburón c/Los Nidos 7, La Carihuela ℡95 238 13 20 ⓦwww.hoteltiburon.com. Attractive small hotel 50m from the beach with pool. All rooms have bath, TV, ceiling fans and sea views and there is Internet access for guests. ⑤ including breakfast.

The Town

To get the flavour of Torremolinos, take a stroll along **Calle San Miguel**, the main pedestrian mall east of the train station. Cutting through the old quarter (which even has a fourteenth-century Moorish tower), the street is lined with garish illuminated signs, tatty amusement arcades and boutiques, and even tattier restaurants serving steak and kidney pie and all its variations. One haven of tranquillity is George's Secondhand Bookshop, on the first floor at no. 28; an excellent source of used paperbacks.

Unlike the street itself, the maze of alleys around c/San Miguel give you a flavour of the old town prior to the tourist invasion and are dotted with bars used by locals. The seafront **promenade** is quite scenic in parts, and runs west all the way to the village of **La Carihuela**, the more elegant (and slightly saner) part of the resort, with a decent beach and a number of good fish restaurants on the seafront. Inland from the centre and close to the N340 autovia, **Aqualand Aquapark** (May–Sept 10am–6pm; €18, kids €12.80) is a water-based playground with chutes, slides and numerous variations on these.

To the west of La Carihuela lies Benalmádena Costa (see p.154), which is the fairly forgettable coastal offspring of the pleasant inland hill village of the same name.

Eating, drinking and nightlife

Hidden away among the many culinary disasters of Torremolinos are a surprising number of excellent **bars** and **restaurants** offering good value for money. At the cheaper end of the scale the sheer competition between outlets is so intense that if you're prepared to walk round, checking a few prices, you can have a decent night out for remarkably little money. For **afternoon tea** or an after-dinner coffee with scrumptious *pasteles* (cakes), head for *Pastelería Lepanto*, c/San Miguel 54, or the equally good *Goyesca* (on the same street at no. 42) whose *tartas de almendras* (almond cakes) are recommended.

Bodega La Guerola c/Las Mercedes 2, at junction with c/San Miguel. A real beehive of a place that's everything a tapas bar should be. It manages to squeeze in a few tables but serious *tapeadores* rest one elbow on the bar.

Bodega Quitapeñas c/San Miguel s/n. Delicious tapas and *raciones* served in a bustling bar with a terrace by the steps at the beach end of c/San Miguel.

Casa Juan Plaza San Gines, off the eastern end of c/Carmen, La Carihuela. Very good fish restaurant and *marisquería*, although the child's picture-book-style menu is probably a mistake. Closed Mon.

El Mesón de la Bodega c/Conde de Mieres 11, near Plaza de Andalucía. Quality tapas haunt run by the same proprietors as *La Bodega* (see below). Specials include *revuelto de ajetes* (young garlic shoots with scrambled eggs) and *morcilla* (blood sausage). There's also a *comedor* for diners.

Frutos Avda. Riviera 80, Los Alamos. Medium-priced, high-quality fish and meat restaurant with a terrace. Closed Sun eve.

La Bodega c/San Miguel 40, near the northern end. Good central tapas bar with small *comedor*. Specials include *boquerones en vinagre* (anchovies) and *ensalada de pulpo* (octopus).

La Cigala I Avda. Los Manantiales 23, 400m north of Plaza Costa del Sol and opposite Supermercado Supersol. Lively *marisquería* with fine fish, waiters who never stop running, and a bargain lunchtime *menú* for €6. They also have a seafront offshoot in La Carihuela.

Mesón Gallego Antoxo c/Hoyo 5 ☎95 238 45 33. Oozing class from the moment you enter, this is an excellent mid-priced Galician restaurant offering dishes and wines from their northwestern homeland, including *merluza a la gallega* (hake) and *tarta de Santiago*. Closed Sun eve.

Restaurante Antonio Plaza del Remo 6, La Carihuela, near the *Hotel Tropicana* ☎95 238 52 10. One of Carihuela's more upmarket restaurants, *Antonio* specializes in superb seafood and fish dishes (*lenguado a la cava* is a speciality), but also serves meat. A legendary dessert trolley offers abundant temptations including the *malagueño* passion *peras al vino* (pears in red wine). Book at weekends. Closed Mon.

Restaurante El Roqueo c/Carmen 35, La Carihuela ☎95 238 49 46. Excellent and friendly mid-priced fish restaurant on the seafront, with a great terrace. Specialities include *fritura malagueña, dorada a la sal* and their *mil hojas* (millefeuille) dessert. Superb tapas at the bar. Closed Tues.

Restaurante La Huerta c/Decano Higueras del Castillo 1, La Carihuela, near the *Hotel Miami*. Great little mid-priced restaurant festooned with plants and vines outside, serving up great fish and meat dishes and especially tasty desserts. Closed Wed.

Yate El Córdobes Paseo Maritimo Playamar, just east of Plaza las Comunidades Autonomas. Great restaurant on the beach with terrace; top notch (and reasonably priced) fish and paella.

Nightlife

When night falls, Torremolinos comes into its own, with a vibrant **nightlife** lifting off in high summer at about 10pm and continuing well beyond dawn, though it's not as wild as in recent years due to the competition of nearby Benalmádena's Puerto Deportivo nightlife zone. Torrie does, however, maintain its thriving gay scene, with calle Casablanca, running west from c/San Miguel, the centre of **gay nightlife** with bars and clubs such as *Men's Club* and *Parthenon* dotted along here and the streets off it. The resort also has a surprisingly decent **flamenco** scene.

Atrevete Avda. Salvador Allende s/n, opposite the *Hotel Pez Espada* in La Carihuela. Salsa venue with two dance floors and a real party atmosphere.
Paladium Avda. Palma de Mallorca 36. Swimming pool, balloons and foam makes this gay (mostly men) club one of the hottest venues in town. March–Oct only.
Kiu Plaza Sol y Mar, Benalmádena. Massive club pulling in crowds from Torremolinos and Málaga which manages to fill three dance floors for most of the summer.
Pepe Lopez Plaza de la Gamba Alegre, ☎95 238 92 84. A tad more commercial and rather pricey, the flamenco here is hardly "puro" but the show is entertaining with a good atmosphere. Mon–Sat €23.

Benalmádena

Beyond Carihuela to the west of Torremolinos, the built-up coastline merges imperceptibly – after 4km – into the neighbouring resort of **BENALMÁDENA COSTA**, with its pseudo-Moorish harbour complex and a seafront lined with bars, restaurants and *chiringuitos*. Hardly an improvement on what has gone before, Benalmádena does have something that its sister resort lacks: a very pleasant hilltop *pueblo*, the original Benalmádena, with a number of inviting places to stay and eat. Three kilometres inland from its coastal namesake, **BENALMÁDENA PUEBLO** also has a charming little **Museo Arqueológico** on Avenida Peralta (Mon–Fri 10am–2pm & 4–6pm; free), displaying finds from around this zone including a beautiful one-and-a-half-metre-high statue of Artemis retrieved from a Roman coastal wreck. There's also a section devoted to the Pre-Columbian peoples of South America.

A greater attraction by far for the majority of visitors to the resort is **Tivoli World**, the Costa del Sol's biggest amusement park (daily 1pm–midnight; July–Aug opens 6pm €4.50), sited between the inland village and the coastal resort on the MA407 and easily reached by train from Fuengirola or Torremolinos (Arroyo de Miel stop); the park has the usual cocktail of rides, restaurants and shows. Opposite the Tivoli World entrance the **Teleférico** (cable car; 10.30am–9pm; one-way €6, round trip €11) ascends to the peak of Monte Calamorro, from where there are panoramic **views** over the Costa del Sol and – in summer – daily displays of falconry. If you choose the one-way fare you have the option of a **walk** back down the mountain along a signed path (a 60–90min trek). On the seafront and close to the Puerto Deportivo, **Sea-Life** (daily 10am–midnight, €9.50, kids €7.50) is the resort's well-presented and ethically slanted marine museum, with displays of the world's fish including a walk-through glass tunnel and a section devoted to sharks.

A **boat cruise** links Benalmádena with Fuengirola and Málaga and there are two to four sailings daily in high summer to and from both places with reduced sailings at other times. Cruises leave from the Costasol Cruceros (☎95 244 48 81 ⓦ www.costasolcruceros.com; €13 round trip, €8 one-way) mooring in the Benalmádena harbour.

Practicalities

Benalmádena Pueblo makes a pleasant alternative to staying in the nearby coastal resorts of Torremolinos or Fuengirola, both of which are easily reached with your own transport. For **rooms**, ⚡ *La Fonda Benalmádena*, c/Santo Domingo 7 (☎ & ℱ95 256 82 73, ⓦwww.fondahotel.com; ❻ with breakfast), is a tranquil oasis with fine views, a pool, and comfortable rooms which are often available at short notice in high season; they also have some apartments in the village for the same price. Nearby, *Hostal La Plazoleta*, Avda. Luis Peralta s/n (☎ & ℱ95 244 81 97; ❺), has pleasant en-suite rooms overlooking a garden behind. A decent budget option is *Habitaciones José Luque* c/Real 19, around the corner from *La Plazoleta* (☎95 244 82 20; ❹), for en-suite rooms with TV.

For **places to eat** in Benalmádena Pueblo find your way to c/Santo Domingo, which links the church of Santo Domingo at the southern end of the village with the Plaza de España to the north. On the plaza facing the church, *El Bodegón del Muro*, c/Santo Domingo 23, is reasonably priced and has a terrace with stunning views over the coast, while *Restaurante Plaza*, on Plaza de España is also good. *La Fonda Benalmádena* (see above) also has the restaurant of the town's hotel school, which is well worth a visit. There's no nightlife as such but an entertaining **music bar** lies in the Jardines del Muro behind the church and stays open till late.

Fuengirola

FUENGIROLA, a thirty-minute train journey from Torremolinos, or a rapid 21km along the old N340 or the new toll *autopista*, is very slightly less developed and infinitely more staid, middle-aged and family-oriented than "Torrie".

Arrival, information and accommodation

Fuengirola's helpful **Turismo** (Mon–Fri 9.30am–2pm & 5–7pm, Sat 10am–1pm; ☎95 246 74 57 ⓦwww.fuengirola.org) can supply a town map and is located at Avda. Jesús S. Rein 6, close to the **train** (☎95 212 80 80) and **bus** (☎95 247 50 66) stations. The town has a number of **Internet cafés**, and *Net & Games*, c/M de Cervantes 17 (daily 10.30–midnight), *Space Call*, c/Capitán 3 (daily 9am–10.30pm), both off Plaza Constitución, and *Cabins@Internet* (daily 9am–midnight), at the junction of the seafront Paseo Marítimo and c/Llano de Espinosa, are three of the most central. Bookworld, Avda. Jesús Santos Rein s/n (opposite the train station) is a good English **bookshop** selling a wide range of titles.

Accommodation is only a problem in August when you'll struggle to find anything at all without a reservation. The friendly *Hostal Italia*, c/de la Cruz 1 (☎95 247 41 93; ❹), is the nicest option around the Plaza de la Constitución for air-conditioned en-suite rooms, or continuing along the nearby c/Capitan would bring you to *Hostal Cuevas*, c/Capitan 7 (☎95 246 06 06; ❹), which also has pleasant a/c rooms with bath. Off the opposite (west) side of the Plaza Constitución, *Hostal Marbella*, c/Marbella 34 (☎95 247 58 02; ❹), is another possibility for air-conditioned en-suite rooms, and on the same street at no. 15, *Hostal Galán* (☎95 246 39 71; ❷–❸) has cheaper but equally decent rooms with and without bath. Moving upmarket, *Hotel Las Piramides*, Paseo Marítimo s/n (☎95 258 32 97, ⓦwww.hotellaspiramides.com; ❾), is a luxury option at the western end of the seafront with its own pool and all the four-star frills.

The Town

Fuengirola's main sights are easily located: on the road west out of town there's the restored but impressive **Castillo de Sohail** (Tues–Fri 10am–3pm, Sat–Sun

10am–5pm; €1.30), a tenth-century fortress built by Abd ar-Rahman III of Córdoba, as well as the scanty remains of a **Roman temple** at the eastern end of the Paseo Marítimo. A recently discovered and extensive Roman villa, **Finca El Secretario** (Mon–Fri 10am–2pm; €1) is another Roman site at the eastern end of town close to the Los Boliches train station on the Fuengirola–Málaga line. Further in, the recently revamped Plaza de la Constitución is officially Fuengirola's centre, but most people are here for the **beach**; a huge, long strand divided into restaurant-beach strips, each renting out lounge chairs and pedal-boats. At the far end is a windsurfing school. A recently opened **Museo de la Historia** in the Parque de España near the bullring (Mon–Fri 10am–2pm; €2) holds a mildly interesting museum documenting the town's development from Phoenician colony and Roman town to the present day.

A popular summer feature located along the N340 on the northwest edge of town is the **Parque Acuatico de Mijas** (daily May–Sept 10am–7pm, €14, reductions for kids and family groups), a water park with all the usual water tubes and chutes. Taking its name from the nearby hill village of Mijas, it is in fact only a few minutes ride from the Fuengirola bus station (frequent buses throughout the summer).

Eating

The streets to the south of the main square (Plaza Constitución) are lined with **restaurants** of a rather depressing similarity. Exceptions are *El Chanquete de Plata*, c/Moncayo 23, preparing decent fish and meat dishes with a €7.50 *menú* and the nearby *Mesón Don Pé*, c/de la Cruz s/n, for mid-price meat dishes (evening only). Plaza Constitución itself has the pleasant *La Plaza*, a good **breakfast**, tapas and late-night drinks bar with a terrace. A charming enclosed square Plaza Yates, just to the west of here and entered via an arch on c/Palang-greros, is a focus for numerous **tapas bars**.

Three of Fuengirola's very best restaurants are slightly outside the normal tourist beat. The first, *Mesón del Mar*, Paseo Marítimo Rey de España, at the extreme western end of the seafront (100m from the landmark *Hotel Piramides*), is delightful, with one of the best seafront terraces in town; specialities include *filete de lenguado con espinacas* (sole with spinach). Some fifty metres inland from here, *Hermanos Alba*, c/Héroes de Baler 4, is an equally good and slightly cheaper option, also with a terrace. A couple of blocks to the north of the Turismo the French ✠ *Restaurante Patrick Bausier*, Rotonda de la Luna (☎95 258 51 20; eve only) has rapidly become one of the town's top dining venues. The eponymous chef turns out a variety of dishes – *ensalada de maigre ahumada* is a speciality – and there's a good selection of Gallic wines with a recommended *menú de degustación* for €22.50. East of here, a little-known gem is *Sol y Sombra*, near the start of c/Maestro Aspiazu, slightly northwest of the Turismo, which serves up a range of fish and meat dishes to a high standard. For more fish, *Bar La Paz Garrido* on the Avda. de Mijas just north of the Plaza de la Constitución serves some of the best-value seafood in town – the *gazpacho* and *cazón* (shark) are recommended. On the central seafront, *Restaurante Portofino*, Paseo Marítimo Rey de España 29, is a mid-priced place serving classy Italian and international dishes. A rare **vegetarian restaurant**, *Vegetalia*, is to be found at the junction of calles Santa Ana and Santa Isabel, to the east of the Turismo off Avenida Santos Rein, serving up a variety of salads and bean-based dishes with a fixed-price buffet for around €7 on weekday lunchtimes (closed Sun & Mon). This is easily reached by taking the train one stop east (direction Málaga) from the centre and getting off at Los Boliches. The same station also lies near another excellent restaurant, *La Langosta*, c/Cano 1, on the seaward side of the line, in a vibrant *barrio* that was formerly the old fishermen's quarter of the town. Nearby on the seafront from here *Los Corales*, Paseo Maritímo, Rey de España 76, is a longstanding family-run place for excellent fresh fish.

Nightlife

Nightlife is centred around the bars, clubs and discos to the west of Plaza Constitución in the streets circling Plaza Yates, and to the north of the harbour where, sharing space with some good *chiringuitos* on the seafront, a fair number of expat singalong bars boom out after sunset with tuneless bellowing in English and Dutch.

El Piso Avda. Condes de Isidro 24 (entry on c/ Estación). Lively *bar de copas* playing flamenco and salsa sounds. There's often live music on Thursdays attracting an enthusiastic crowd.

Havana Café c/Jacinto Benavente s/n. Stylish new bar, with a variety of live music.

Old Town Paseo Maritimo s/n. For late-night drinks or a spot of dancing, this is the pick of the bunch among a line of rather tacky seafront places.

Pihama c/Miguel Cervantes 14. Hip hangout in the old quarter which pulls in a largely local crowd. Fri & Sat only.

Mijas

Often grouped with the more famous White Towns further north (see p.184), the once tranquil hill town of **MIJAS**, a winding eight-kilometre climb into the hills above Fuengirola from where it is served by frequent **buses**, is sited a little too close to the Costa del Sol for its own good, making it an obvious target for bus tours in search of the "typical" Andalucian village. However, despite a host of tacky gift shops and the numbered *burro* (donkey) taxis that transport visitors around the main square, the village retains some of its original character, and there are fine views towards the coast. The ancient **Plaza de Toros** (daily 10am–7pm; €3), which claims – wrongly – to be Andalucía's only rectangular bullring, is worth a look, as is a new **Casa Museo Etnográfico** c/de Los Caños s/n southwest of the main square (daily 10am–2pm & 4–7pm; free) with a collection of artefacts from Mijas's past and a room that stages frequent art exhibitions by the village's amateur artists of whom there are quite a number. Above the square, the ludicrous **Carromato de Max** (daily 10am–7pm; €3), a railway wagon full of junk, claims to house "the smallest curiosities in the world". If items such as Churchill's head sculpted from a stick of chalk, a copy of Leonardo's *Last Supper* painted on a grain of rice, or the shrunken head of a white man retrieved from South American Indians and "certified genuine by the FBI" grab you, then it's well worth the entry fee.

Practicalities

Information and a useful village **map** are available from a friendly **tourist office** (daily 9am–7pm; ☏95 258 90 34, ⓦ www.mijas.es) on the east side of Plaza Virgen de la Peña, the main square, close to where the bus drops you. This office also gives out a free leaflet detailing a number of walks in the surrounding hills and offers free 2–4hr **guided walks** on Wed & Sat at 10am. **Internet** access is available at Mijas Pueblo Call Box (daily 10am–midnight), Pasaje Salvador Cantos Jiménez s/n just off the main square. Should you fancy **staying overnight**, the good value *Hostal La Posada*, c/Coín 47 (☏95 248 53 10; ❷–❹), has a range of room and apartment options. To get there, find your way to Plaza de la Constitución, a small square below the bullring, and ask for directions. Off Plaza de la Constitución, the village's second largest square, ⚸ *Casa El Escudo*, c/Trocha de los Pescadores 7 (☏95 259 12 50, ⓦ www.el-escudo.com; ❺) is a delightful small hotel with charming a/c rooms equipped with TV, minibar and – in rooms 8 and 9 – a terrace with stunning views. *Hotel Club Puerta del Sol* (℡95 248 64 00, Ⓦwww.hotelclubpuertadelsol.com; ❼), is another upmarket option with a/c rooms, restaurant, pool and gymnasium, sited at the entrance to the village coming from Fuengirola.

The village has plenty of **places to eat** and drink. For tapas try *Bar González* or *Casa Pepe* on Avenida Virgen de la Peña, actually the main square. More elaborate meals are on offer at the Basque restaurant *El Mirlo Blanco*, Plaza Constitución 13, near the Plaza de Toros. *La Alcazaba*, on the same square, has great views from its terrace while *Restaurante El Castillo*, Pasaje los Pescadores 2, with terrace, and *El Padastro*, Avda. del Compás 22, are also worth a try. Near Plaza de la Libertad, *Bar La Gamba*, c/San Sebastián 11, is good for *mariscos*, paellas and its signature dish *conejo sierra de mijas* (rabbit). Finally, ⅄ *Restaurante Alarcón*, c/Lasta 1, near the church of Santa Ana in the Barrio Santana in the older part of the village, is an excellent-value little place, worth seeking out for the superb traditional cooking and pleasant roof terrace with fine views.

Marbella and around

Undisputedly the "quality resort" of the Costa del Sol, **MARBELLA** stands in considerable contrast to most of what's come before. Sheltered from the winds by the hills of the Sierra Blanca, it has a couple of excellent **beaches** which first brought it to the attention of the 1960s' smart set. However, don't strain your eyes for celebrities nowadays; the only time the mega-rich motor down from their villas in the hills is to attend a private club or put in an appearance at glitzy places like the *Puente Romano Hotel* on the way to San Pedro, where a beluga caviar starter in the restaurant will cost you the price of a good hotel room.

Marbella's image took a nose dive in the 1970s when British crooks and drug barons began setting up home here, bringing their feuds and rivalries with them. In the late 1980s the authorities became even more exercised by the arrival of Russian and Italian mafia bosses, who controlled their empires from luxury villas and yachts harboured in nearby Puerto Banus. Marbella's notoriety continued throughout the 1990s during the period of rule by the corrupt mayor Jesús Gil y Gil (who avoided a lengthy jail term by dying in 2004) and his GIL political party. A host of unsavoury characters and businesses moved into town and in 2005 Spanish police uncovered Europe's biggest ever money-laundering operation, channelling billions of euros from crime syndicates across Europe through Marbella companies into anonymous "trusts". In an ironic twist of history, there's also been a massive return of Arabs to the area, especially since the late King Fahd of Saudi Arabia built a White House looka-like, complete with adjacent mosque, on the town's western outskirts.

Arrival and information

The **bus** station is a twenty-minute walk north from the centre, at the end of c/Trapiche (℡902 143 144). Buses from Estepona and San Pedro de Alcántara (heading east) and Fuengirola (heading west) still make stops in the centre. Otherwise take buses #2 or #7 from the bus station, which will drop you near to the centre of the old town. Arriving **by car** will land you with the usual parking problem. There are signed pay car parks around the centre and all accommodation places will advise on possible on-street parking places. The **Turismo**, on the north side of Plaza de los Naranjos (Mon–Fri 9am–9pm, Sat 10am–2pm; ℡95 282 35 50), has detailed town maps, and produces a leaflet,

Verano Cultural, detailing the many events held in the town throughout the summer, which often star big names. A second office (same hours) is sited on Glorieta Fontanilla, a roundabout at the eastern end of the seafront.

Internet access is available at *Sky Techno* (daily 8am–1am), Avenida Ramón y Cajal s/n, just east of the Plaza de la Alameda, a tree-lined square to the south of the old quarter, and *American Donats*, Travesía Carlos Mackintosh, on the south side of the Alameda (daily 9am–10pm). To explore the surrounding hill country or merely cruise the coast you can rent **mountain bikes**, scooters and larger machines like Harley Davidsons from Rainbow, Avda. Severa Ochoa 9 (☎95 277 16 99), the main road that enters the town from the east.

Accommodation

All Marbella's budget **accommodation** is in the old town, on or around c/Luna or, a couple of blocks west, along the pretty c/San Cristóbal, the street

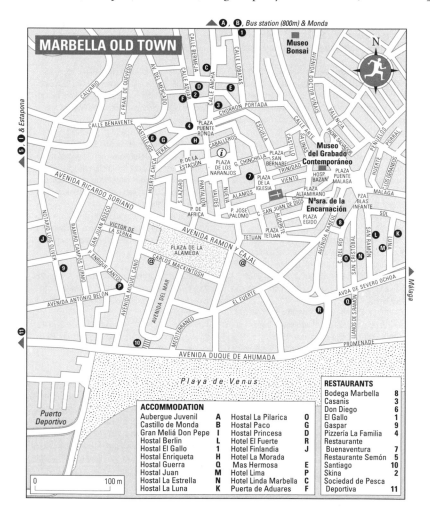

MARBELLA OLD TOWN

RESTAURANTS
Bodega Marbella	8
Casanis	3
Don Diego	6
El Gallo	1
Gaspar	9
Pizzería La Familia	4
Restaurante Buenaventura	7
Restaurante Semón	5
Santiago	10
Skina	2
Sociedad de Pesca Deportiva	11

ACCOMMODATION
Aubergue Juvenil	A	Hostal La Pilarica	O	
Castillo de Monda	B	Hostal Paco	G	
Gran Meliá Don Pepe	I	Hostal Princesa	D	
Hostal Berlin	L	Hotel El Fuerte	R	
Hostal El Gallo	1	Hotel Finlandia	J	
Hostal Enriqueta	H	Hotel La Morada		
Hostal Guerra	Q	Mas Hermosa	E	
Hostal Juan	M	Hotel Lima	P	
Hostal La Estrella	N	Hotel Linda Marbella	C	
Hostal La Luna	K	Puerta de Aduares	F	

0   100 m

of a thousand plants carefully tended by its residents. In-town accommodation ranges between *hostal* and four-star luxury, with precious little in between. Pressure on rooms is tight in July and extremely so in August, when you should book ahead. There's also a very good **youth hostel** (*albergue juvenil*) at c/Trapiche 2 (☎95 277 14 91; under 26 €14, over 26 €18.50), with double rooms (some with bath), pool and plenty of activities.

Castillo de Monda 14km north of Marbella in the village of the same name ☎95 245 71 42, ⓦwww.costadelsol.spa.es/hotel/monda. Stunning hilltop castle converted into a palatial hotel with restaurant and pool. ❼

Gran Meliá Don Pepe c/José Meliá s/n ☎95 277 03 00, ⓦwww.solmelia.es. Reasonably central five-star luxury hotel and part of the Meliá chain, where balcony rooms overlook the sea and facilities include extensive gardens, three pools (one indoor), a gym, sauna, Turkish bath, and tennis courts. The cheapest high-season double costs €417 per night. ❾

Hostal Berlin c/San Ramón 21 ☎95 282 13 10, ⓦwww.hostalberling.com. Sparkling and friendly *hostal*; all rooms come with bath, a/c and satellite TV, and free Internet access is available to guests. The proprietor will collect you from the bus station. ❹

Hostal El Gallo c/Lobatos 44 ☎95 282 79 98. Good value en-suite a/c rooms with TV above a great little restaurant. ❹

Hostal Enriqueta c/Los Caballeros 18 ☎95 282 75 52. Quiet, comfortable *hostal* in an elegant *reja*-fronted building near the Plaza de los Naranjos. En-suite rooms come with TV and ceiling fans. ❹

Hostal Guerra Llanos de San Ramón 2 ☎95 277 42 20. Clean, simple and economical rooms with bath, and some with balcony, near the beach. ❷

Hostal Juan c/Luna 18 ☎95 277 94 7. Good value en-suite rooms with TV and fridge on a tranquil street. ❷

Hostal La Estrella c/San Cristóbal 36 ☎95 277 94 72. Not the warmest of welcomes, but this is a nicely located option in a pleasant street, offering a/c rooms with bath, fridge, TV and some with balcony. ❹

Hostal La Luna c/Luna 7 ☎95 282 57 78. Delightful, spotless *pensión* with balconied rooms around a renovated old patio at the rear; all rooms have bath, fridge, fans and TV. ❹

Hostal La Pilarica c/San Cristóbal 31 ☎95 277 42 52. Pretty and good-value *hostal* in lovely location. En-suite rooms with TV and fridge. ❹

Hostal Paco c/Peral 16 ☎95 277 12 00, ⓦwww.hostalpaco.com. Central *hostal*, where all rooms have bath, fans and TV. ❹

Hostal Princesa c/Princesa s/n ☎95 282 00 49. Close to the Plaza Puente de Ronda, this friendly *hostal* offers neat rooms with and without bath. ❸

Hotel El Fuerte Avda. Severo Ochoa 10 ☎95 286 15 00, ⓦwww.hotel-elfuerte.es. The older and more charming of two four-star hotels with the same name fronting the Playa de Venus. Amenities include beach access, gardens, pool, gym, tennis courts and sauna. The standard high-season double price is around €195 but you'll pay a third more for a face-on sea view. ❾

Hotel Finlandia c/Notario Luis Oliver 12, ☎95 277 07 00, ⓔfinlandia@marbella.com. Pleasant little one-star hotel in a quiet street where rooms – some with balcony – come with TV. Fans are available on request. ❹

🏃 **Hotel La Morada Mas Hermosa** c/Montenebros 16, ☎95 292 44 67, ⓔreservas@lamoradamashermosa.com. Taking its name from the first words of Columbus on sighting the New World ("beautiful place") this is an enchanting small hotel in a restored eighteenth-century town house with elegant a/c rooms. ❻

Hotel Lima Avda. Antonio Belón 2 ☎95 277 05 00, ⓦwww.hotellimamarbella.com. Efficient and central two-star hotel near the harbour where the higher a/c balcony rooms offer sea views. ❻

Hotel Linda Marbella c/Ancha 21 ☎ & ⓕ95 285 71 71, ⓔlindamarbellasl@terra.es. Newish hotel in a central position, with well-appointed rooms and a roof terrace. ❺

Puerta de Aduares c/Aduar 18 ☎95 282 13 12, ⓦwww.puertadeaduares.com. Reasonably priced, stylishly decorated and fully serviced apartments sleeping two or four. ❺

Refugio de Juanar 12km north of Marbella and signed off the A355 ☎95 288 10 00, ⓦwww.juanar.com. Tucked away in the pine forests of the Sierra Blanca, this former hunting lodge of the once-powerful *malagueño* Larios family is now a luxurious, tranquil three-star hotel complete with attractive pool and restaurant. Make sure to do the 3km walk to the Mirador de Juanar with spectacular views over the coast. ❻

The Town

Spared the worst excesses of concrete architecture that have been inflicted upon Torremolinos, Marbella is decidedly tasteful, retaining the greater part of its old town or **casco antiguo**. Slowly, this original quarter is being bought up and turned over to "quaint" clothes boutiques and restaurants, but you can still sit in an ordinary bar in a small old square and look up beyond the whitewashed alleyways to the mountains of Ronda. The resort has three main **beaches** stretching from the easternmost Playa de la Bajadilla and Playa de Venus, both located between its twin harbours and the Playa de la Fontanilla to the west, which gets progressively less crowded the further west you go.

The *casco antiguo*, partially walled, is set back from the sea and hidden from the main road. Here the main sights are clustered in the web of streets surrounding the picturesque **Plaza de los Naranjos**, whose delights are somewhat marred by the invasive terraces of the surrounding restaurants that use it as an open-air dining room. On the plaza (next to the Turismo) is the striking sixteenth-century **Ayuntamiento**, while nearby in Plaza de la Iglesia, is the church of **Nuestra Señora de la Encarnación**. Built in the sixteenth century, it was later remodelled in the Baroque style and has a fine tower as well as, inside, a striking *retablo*. The **Museo Arqueológico** with Neolithic and Roman finds from the surrounding area – including the Roman villa at Río Verde (see p.165) – is currently closed while a new site is found for it; in the meantime a small display of finds from the Roman villa including a maquette and photos is housed in the *Delegación de Cultura*, (Mon–Fri 9am–2pm), Plaza Altamirano s/n, to the east of the Plaza de los Naranjos. The archeological museum's former home – a fine Renaissance hospital founded by Alonso Bazán, then mayor of Marbella – now hosts a mildly interesting **Museo del Grabado Contemporáneo**, c/Hospital Bazán s/n (Tues–Sat 10am–2pm & 6–9pm; €2.50), an engraving museum with works by Miró and Picasso. Northeast of the Plaza de los Naranjos you'll find Spain's one and only Bonsai tree museum, the **Museo Bonsai**, Arroyo de la Represa s/n (daily 10am–1.30pm & 5–8pm; €3), with 150 examples of this arboraceous curiosity.

Eating and drinking

When it comes to food and drink you're better off heading for Marbella's numerous and excellent **tapas bars**, rather than many of the touristy and over-priced **restaurants** around the Plaza de los Naranjos. There are, however, a fair number of good-value eating places within a five-minute walk of the square, and following the Avenida del Mar – lined with Dalí bronzes – towards the sea will lead you to the Puerto Deportivo and another zone filled with bars and restaurants.

Restaurants

Bodega Marbella c/del Río 16, east of the centre. Excellent little bar-restaurant with bags of character, serving a good selection of seafood dishes; the paella is recommended.

Casanis c/Ancha 8 ☏ 95 290 04 50. Mid-priced bistro with a French/Belgian kitchen and plenty of ambience and style. *Confit de patocon lentejas* (duck with lentils) is a house special and main dishes cost €12–22. Closed Sun.

Don Diego c/Haza del Mesón 7. Argentine restaurant serving up charcoal-grilled meats and economical paellas (€10 for two) with a pleasant terrace in a leafy plaza.

El Gallo c/Lobatas 44. Good and popular little neighbourhood restaurant serving up traditional *andaluz* dishes such as *langostino pil pil* (prawns with chilli) and *conejo al ajillo* (rabbit). There's a great value *menú* for €8.

Gaspar c/Notario Luis Oliver 19 ☏ 95 277 90 98. A gem of a restaurant run a by a family from Rioja – which explains the comprehensive wine list. Besides their standard dishes (both fish and meat) you can also order a few plates of *raciones*

△ Marbella

to share. If you have to wait for a table you can peruse the books in the restaurant's library, and impromptu flamenco sometimes happens when *cantantes* (singers) drop in for a meal.

Pizzería La Familia c/Cruz 5, off the Plaza Puente de Ronda. Marbella's best pizzas – along with other Italian dishes – served up in a pleasant atrium dining room.

Restaurante Buenaventura Plaza de la Iglesia 5 ☎95 285 80 69. Scottish chef Gordon Brown fronts the *fogón* at this mid-priced restaurant where *andaluz* dishes are given a creative slant and *colchinillo con puré de membrillo* (suckling pig with quince sauce) is a speciality. The elegant courtyard terrace is made for summer evenings and there's a *menú de degustación* for €48 (excluding wine). Closed Nov.

Restaurante Semón c/Gregorio Marañón s/n ☎95 277 77 96. Top-notch medium-priced Catalan restaurant open lunchtime until 10pm with a good-value lunchtime buffet *menú* for around €16. If you decide to push the boat out you could try the beluga caviar (€160) washed down with a bottle of Vega Sicilia wine (€175). The restaurant also has a delicatessen selling mouthwatering Catalan comestibles. Oct–Jun closed Sun.

Santiago Avda. Duque de Ahumada s/n, near the Puerto Deportivo ☎95 277 23

69. One of Marbella's swankiest and oldest restaurants founded in the 1950s, attracting many from the town's smart set to its seafront terrace. The food matches the hype, however, and as well as noted dishes such as *merluza a la sidra con perlas de tapioca* (hake with a cider sauce) there's a recommended *menú de degustación* for €48 (including wine). A la carte main courses €20–30. Also has an equally outstanding tapas bar. Closed Nov.

Skina c/Aduar 12. Excellent small mid-priced restaurant serving well-prepared meat and fish dishes.

Sociedad de Pesca Deportiva Puerto Deportivo, Local 5. The Marbella fishermen's club should know a thing or two about seafood and they serve up delicious fish and *mariscos* at their restaurant with a terrace in the port. Closed Mon.

Tapas bars

Bar Altamirano Plaza de Altamirano 4, southeast of Plaza Naranjos. Great place for seafood tapas and *raciones*, with tables spread across a small square.

Bar California Junction of c/Málaga & Avda. Severo Ochoa, east of the *casco antiguo*. Excellent *marisco* and *pescado frito* bar, where the *fino* (as proclaimed above the entrance) is as good as the seafood tapas and *raciones*.

Cervecería Simon Avda. Arias Maldonado 1, on the seafront at the western end. Fine tapas at low prices and a pleasant terrace on which to enjoy them. Specials include *chopitos fritas* (cuttlefish) and *patatas bravas*.

El Estrecho c/San Lázaro 12, a narrow alley to the southeast of the Plaza de Naranjos. Excellent and atmospheric little tapas bar with a wide range of possibilities. The nearby *Casa Bar Bartolo* is also worth a visit.

Hogar del Pescador c/Guadalete s/n, on the fishing harbour at the eastern end of the seafront. Good and fresh seafood tapas straight from the sea.

Marisquería La Pesquera Plaza de la Victoria s/n, west of Plaza de los Naranjos. A town favourite for tapas (although its restaurant is somewhat overpriced), with first-class *fino* too. House specials include *cigalitas cocidas* (Dublin Bay prawns) and *almejas marinera* (clams in wine).

Cafés and bars

Atrium c/Gregorio Marañón 11, west of the centre. One of several fashionable outdoor terrace bars in this area frequented by Marbella's well-heeled set. *Gaugin Café* opposite is another cool place for delicious cocktails.

Cafetería Marbella Alameda Gardens, Avda. Ramón y Cajal. Lovely place for breakfast, overlooking the main drag with two shady terraces.

Caprice c/Caballeros 28, near Hostal Paco. Great little bar-café run by a charming French-Argentinian couple serving crepes, salads and pastries during the day and early evening, and cocktails after dark.

El Tonelito c/Pantaleón 4. Popular *cervecería* with a "no music" policy, making it just the place to recover from the night before.

Lepanto Avda. Puerta del Mar s/n, southeast corner of the Alameda. Stylish café just south of the old quarter, which excels in chocolate confectionery creations.

Nightlife

Marbella has one of the liveliest **nightlife** scenes on the *costa*, with action centred around Plaza Puente de Ronda, c/Pantaleón, and Plaza Africa, all in the old town. The main street cutting through the centre, Avenida Ramon y Cajal, and the Puerto Deportivo, the seafront yacht harbour, also pulse with life, although the latter has cooled down in recent years due to complaints about noise and rowdiness by local residents. Nearby Puerto Banús also has a thriving nightlife scene.

Bohemian Plaza Antonio Banderas, Puerto Banús. A popular and vibrant *discoteca* with a blend of house and Latin sounds. When it all gets too much revellers escape to a leafy outdoor terrace with bar and four-poster beds for relaxing.

Club Premiere Plaza de Olivos 2. Lively music venue often staging live gigs ranging from pop to electronica.

Dreamer's Carretera de Cádiz 175, Río Verde. One of the better clubs on the outskirts of Puerto Banús playing a range of techno and house sounds.

Encuadernador c/San Lázaro 3. Popular (beer) drinking bar in a narrow alley southeast of Plaza de Naranjos.

La Abadia c/Pantaleón 1. Popular late-night drinking hotspot playing dance music and with a courtyard to cool down outside.

La Notte Camino de la Cruz s/n, near Plaza Puente de Ronda. Exclusive summer disco-bar with penchant for Latin sounds inside the equally exclusive *Restaurante Meridiana* and much favoured by Marbella's "in crowd".

Morrison's c/Ramón Gómez de la Serna 4, west of the centre. Popular Irish-style music bar playing loud chart hits.

Town House c/Alamo 1. Long-established *bar de copas* with rock/electronica sounds. Open all year, they light a roaring fire in winter.

Around Marbella: Ojén

Eight kilometres north of Marbella lies the charming hill village of **OJÉN**, which makes a pleasant and convenient alternative to the hurly burly of staying in Marbella itself. Although linked with Marbella by frequent buses, it's a much easier base with your own transport. From the picturesque main square, the Plaza de Andalucía with its sixteenth-century church of La Encarnación, the two options for **places to stay** are easily found. The most inviting is *La Posada del Angel*, c/ Mesones 21 (☏95 288 18 08, Ⓦwww.laposadadelangel.com; ❻), a charming small hotel in a restored town house with beautifully furnished rooms and a delightful patio. The enthusiastic proprietors can provide information on walks in the Sierra Blanca to the northwest of the village. The more economical accommodation option is the very welcoming *Hostería de Don Jose*, Paseo del Chifle s/n (℡952 88 11 47, ⓦwww.guadalmina.com/hosteriadonjose; ❹ with breakfast), in the upper village, signed off the main road as you come in, with en-suite rooms, some with terraces and views. A private **information office**, Plaza de Andalucía 1 (daily 10am–2pm, ℡95 288 15 19), can provide a map as well as information on various activities such as walking and mountain biking in this zone.

The village hasn't got much in the way of sights although the **Museo del Vino de Málaga** (daily 11am–3pm & 5.30–9pm; free; ⓦwww.museovinomalaga.net), housed in Ojén's former *anis* distillery just below the main road at the eastern end of the village, is worth a look. Strictly speaking it's as much shop as museum but it does stock many of Málaga's great wines and – as they are out of fashion both in Spain and elsewhere today – provides a tasting opportunity to discover why they were so popular in the nineteenth and early twentieth centuries. Some of the dessert wines are particularly delicate and the *Jarel Moscatel* from a small *bodega* in Cómpeta is a stunner that would grace any dinner table.

For **eating and drinking** the village has many possibilities. There are bars around the main square and restaurants along the main road into the village. For excellent *jamón* and *queso* **tapas** make your way to the diminutive *Bodega de Fernando* down a narrow alley off c/Carreras. The nearby *El Caldero* is also good, but the village's best restaurant is *El Fogón de Flore*, c/Carrera 8, near the church, with a pretty interior patio; flamenco is sometimes staged here at weekends.

San Pedro de Alcántara and around

The road west of Marbella (providing you don't take the toll-charged Autopista del Sol) soon passes – after 7km – the marina and casino complex of **PUERTO BANUS**, where the jet set park up their yachts. An utterly modern resort devoid of any architectural charms, in summer the place presents a bizarre spectacle as crowds of Costa del Sol gawpers come to celebrity-spot, while the bronzed plutocrats attempt to steer their Rolls Royces and Ferraris through the crush to their vessels. If you're determined to see what the fuss is about – or desire to window-shop the numerous designer clothes emporia – a useful tip coming in by car is to use the car park of the El Corte Inglés department store in the *centro comercial* (€0.50 per hour) and walk the five minutes to the gated harbour zone which only vehicles with permits may enter.

Six kilometres further, and about the only place on the Costa del Sol that isn't purely a holiday resort, is the small town of **SAN PEDRO DE ALCÁNTARA**, a none too inspiring place striving to go the way of its neighbour but hindered by the fact that its centre is set back over a kilometre from the sea. The seafront area has recently been landscaped with the almost obligatory palm-lined promenade and some holiday *urbanizaciones*. have been constructed, but this has done little to raise San Pedro's profile. In the town proper, what activity there is centres on the tranquil, palm-fringed Plaza de la Iglesia in the town proper – at its most lively during the Thursday morning **flea market** – but there's not much else to disturb the calm.

There are three remarkable **ancient ruins** in the area (see overleaf) that are definitely worth going out of your way to see and information regarding visits is available from the San Pedro Turismo (see overleaf). However, the visits themselves are organised by the Turismo's **sub office** (Mon–Fri 10am–4pm, Sat 10am–2pm; ℡95 278 13 60), located beneath a huge arch over the main

N340 to the west of the town which is also the meeting point. The visits operate Tuesdays and Fridays at noon and you need your own transport. A guide will rendezvous with visitors at the meeting point and open the sites. The visit is free and lasts approximately two hours.

San Pedro practicalities

The **San Pedro Turismo**, Avda. Marques del Duero 69 – the main street you turn in to when leaving the N340 (Mon–Fri 9am–9pm, Sat 10am–2pm; ☎95 278 52 52) – can supply a map of the town plus information on renting apartments for longer stays. It's also the place to book visits to the ancient sites (see below). A useful secondhand **bookshop**, *Shakespeare*, c/Lagasca 69, one street west from the Turismo, is a place to pick up some reading matter.

Should you require **accommodation**, the new three-star *Hotel Doña Catalina* Avda. Oriental 14, southeast of the church (☎95 285 31 20, ⓦ www.hotasa.es; ❺) has good-value a/c balcony rooms with satellite TV, while the central *Hostal Galea Centro*, Plaza de la Iglesia s/n (☎95 279 98 36; ❹), is a more economical option for air-conditioned en-suite rooms. The friendly *Pensión Avenida*, c/Las Margaritas 19 (☎95 278 31 92; ❷–❸), north of the Plaza de la Iglesia, also has rooms with and without bath above a lively restaurant, and the pricier *Hostal El Molino*, c/Los Geranios 1, almost next door (☎ & ⓕ95 278 65 03; ❹), is a more attractive option with air-conditioned rooms. Other possibilities include the basic *Pensión Armando*, near the Turismo at c/19 Octubre 53 (☎95 278 11 90; ❶), or the nearby *Hostal Acemar*, c/19 Octubre 17 (☎95 278 30 41; ❷).

For **food** the place to head for is Avenida Andalucía to the west of the Turismo and just north of the N340. *El Cid Campeador* at no.13 is the restaurant with pretensions here and offers a good-value lunch *menú* for €9, but along the opposite side of the street a line of terrace restaurants has a great atmosphere in summer. All the places are good, although *Alfredos*, Avda. Andalucía 8, is generally regarded as the best for *cocina casera*, and there's even an Indian restaurant, *Sitar*, here. The nearest place to the seafront, an area dead at night, is the decent fish restaurant *La Pesquera* at the end of the Avenida del Mediterraneo leading to the sea. Halfway along the same road the mid-priced *Restaurante Casa Fernando*, Avenida Mediterraneo s/n, also specializes in seafood and there's a leafy garden terrace to enjoy on summer nights (closed Sun).

Around San Pedro

Four kilometres back along the road east to Marbella are the remains of a **Roman villa** at Río Verde. To get there from San Pedro, pass the turn-off for Puerto Banús and, after crossing the river, take a right before the *Puente Romano Hotel* and follow the signs. Constructed in the late first or early second century, the rooms are decorated with an unusual series of black and white **mosaics** depicting not classical themes or intricate designs as elsewhere, but everyday kitchen equipment. The kitchen utensils are a delight, and the shoes portrayed by the door are evidence of the Roman custom of leaving one's footwear outside the *triclinium*, or dining room. One of the mosaic's Amphorae is so accurately portrayed that its style has helped to date the villa almost precisely. Note also the hanging fowl and fish, ready for the pot.

The sixth-century **Visigothic Christian basilica** of Vega del Mar lies close to the sea at the bottom of the Avenida del Mediterráneo, the main road from San Pedro towards the coast. Take the last road on the right before the beach and you'll come to the railed-off site in the midst of a stand of eucalyptus trees. It's one of the most important Visigothic monuments on the peninsula; the remains enable you to make out clearly a rectangular basilica with a double apse, unique in Spain. Large boulders cemented with lime-mortar were used in its construction along with still-visible brickwork at the corners. A wonderful **baptismal font** is especially well preserved and was deep enough for total immersion, the custom of the time. In and around the basilica is a cemetery of some two hundred tombs (which yielded a wealth of artefacts now in Marbella and Madrid museums), most with the head to the north, the orientation of the church. Note the graves lined with marble, evidence of social stratification even in death.

The third site, the **Roman bathhouse** of Las Bovedas, lies a little way west of here, almost on the beach. Leave any transport at the *chiringuito* and walk the fifty metres along the beach to the site. The substantial remains belong to an octagonal third-century Roman baths. Seven chambers, which would have served as a series of heated steam rooms, surround the well-preserved central bath (parts of the underfloor hypocaust system are visible). Above the central pool was a skylight surrounded by a roof terrace. Because the complex was constructed with a special lime – which, when mixed with sand and pebbles from the beach, set to a granite-like hardness – the building has defied the elements impressively.

Visiting the three sites is only possible through the Turismo (see opposite) but partial viewing of the Roman villa and Visigothic basilica can be had from behind their fences, whilst the Roman baths – which can be seen from the beach – now lie inside a new gated *urbanización* and are inaccessible without a guide.

Estepona

West of San Pedro the A7 toll *autopista* heads inland before turning west, while the coast road is littered with more depressing *urbanizaciones* bearing names such as Picasso or – taking irony to the limit – Paraíso (paradise), each served by its *centro comercial*. Should you feel the urge to stop, **ESTEPONA**, 17km beyond San Pedro, is about the only good bet, a more or less Spanish resort with much of its identity still intact. Lacking the enclosed hills that give Marbella character, it is at least developed on a human scale; the hotel and apartment blocks which sprawl along the front are restrained in size, and there's a pleasant EU blue-flagged beach in town, as well as the Costa del Sol's oldest nudist beach to the west. One feature of note is Estepona's recent opening of four **museums**, all located in the modern Plaza de Toros to the east of the centre.

One of the best, and busiest, times to visit the town is during the first week of July, when the **Fiesta y Feria** brings out whole families of *esteponeros* in their flamenco-style finery and the town is transformed into a riot of colour.

Arrival, information and accommodation

Estepona's **bus station**, on Avenida de España, lies west of the centre behind the seafront. Two hundred metres further west, a **Turismo**, Avenida San Lorenzo 1 (Mon–Fri 9am–8pm, Sat 10am–1.30pm; ☎95 280 09 13), will supply town maps and can help you find a room. **Internet** access is available at *Sh@rk Net*, Avda. de España 3 (daily 10am–10pm), on the seafront near the Correos (main post office). A **street market** is held in the Puerto Deportivo each Sunday morning.

Outside August you should have no problem finding a **place to stay** in Estepona. The nearest **campsite**, *Chullera III* (☎95 289 03 20), lies 8km south of town, just beyond the village of San Luís de Sabanillas. Another option, *Camping Parque Tropical* (☎ & ☎95 279 36 18), is 6km to the north on the N340 (km.162). Set back from the beach in a former tropical garden, it has a spectacular conservatory-pool and restaurant.

Hostal El Pilar Plaza Las Flores ☎95 280 00 18, ©pilarhos@anit.es. Friendly *hostal* on a charming plaza offering en-suite balcony rooms, some a/c. ❸

Hostal Vista al Mar c/Real 154 ☎95 280 32 47. Rather pricey simple rooms without bath at the western end of the central zone. It just about squeezes in a sea view, thus justifying its name. ❸

Hotel Aguamarina Avda. San Lorenzo 32, near the main Turismo ☎95 280 61 55, ©royberhotels@costasol.net. Estepona's best in-town hotel with comfortable rooms but no sea views. It also imposes a silly rule during August forcing you to take lunch or dinner in the hotel restaurant (€10 per person added to room price). ❺ with breakfast.

Hotel Buenavista Paseo Marítimo 180 ☎95 280 01 37, ©hotelbuenavista@infonegocio.com.

Reasonable-value hotel with en-suite sea view balcony rooms with TV and fans. ❹

Hotel Mediterráneo Avda. de España 68, on the seafront to the east of c/Terraza ☎95 279 33 93. Functional but good-value seafront hotel, where rooms have bath, TV and (mostly) sea views. ❹

Hotel Santa Marta Ctra N340, km.166 ☎95 288 81 77, ⓦwww.hotelsantamarta.com. The best deal among a clutch of upmarket hotels lining the beaches to the north of town. ❼

Pensión La Malagueña c/Castillo s/n ☎95 280 00 11, ⓦwww.hlmestepona.com. Comfortable and reliable *pensión*, offering en-suite rooms with TV and fans. ❹

Pensión San Miguel c/Terraza 16 ☎95 280 26 16. Friendly establishment with its own bar, a little west of Plaza Las Flores. All rooms are en-suite and come with fans and TV. ❷

The Town

Estepona is the last stop on the Costa del Sol and one of the most pleasant. The seafront is attractive, with a promenade studded with flowers and palms, and behind this, the older part of the town has some charming corners with cobbled alleyways and two delightful squares, the **Plaza Las Flores** and **Plaza Arce**. Calle Terraza bisects the centre and around this are most of the eating and drinking options, especially along pedestrianized **c/Real**. The **Puerto Deportivo**, to the west of town beyond the lighthouse and near the bullring, is a daintier version of Marbella's nightlife hotspot, with the few bars and clubs becoming really animated only at weekends.

From May onwards, the town's **bullfighting** season gets under way in a modern Plaza de Toros on the west side of town, reminiscent of a Henry Moore sculpture. The building is also home to four new museums (all Mon–Fri 9am–3pm, Sat 10am–2pm; free): the **Museo Etnográfico** (folk museum), **Museo Arqueológico**, **Museo Paleontológico** and the **Museo Taurino** (bullfighting). The folk museum has lots of artefacts from Estepona's agricultural and maritime past; the archeological museum has local finds from the Phoenician, Roman and Moorish periods; the paleontology museum, dedicated to serious research, has a collection of fossils and seashells millions of years old; while the Taurino museum – whatever your position on bull-fighting – gives you some idea of the importance of *taurinismo* in Andalucian culture. There are the usual trophies and photos of past big names as well as (in the centre of the museum itself) the actual *toril* or bull-pen from where the raging bulls are released into the adjoining ring during *corridas*. To get there, take a taxi or walk west along the seafront to the Puerto Deportivo and then turn inland.

The nearby **fish market** is also worth seeing: Estepona has the biggest fishing fleet west of Málaga, and the daily dawn ritual in the port at the western end of the promenade, where the returning fleets auction off the fish they've just caught, is worth getting up early for – be there at 6am, since by 7am it's all over. Afterwards you can head for the animated covered **market**, on c/Castillo, slightly west of Plaza las Flores, also at its best in the morning.

The recently opened **Selwo Adventure Park** (daily 10am–8pm; ⓦwww .selwo.es; €20 adults, €14 kids) is a landscaped zoo 6km to the east of town where the 2000-plus resident animals are allowed to roam in semi-liberty, and there are re-creations of African Zulu and Masai villages, where it's possible to stay overnight in an expensive "African-style" hut (⑥) with the modern additions of TV, fridge and Jacuzzi. To reach the park, there are signed exits indicated from N340 and the Autopista del Sol, plus regular buses from all the major Costa del Sol resorts. Estepona's **nudist beach** and **naturist holiday village**, the Costa Natura (☎95 280 80 65, ⓦ www.costanaturaholidays.com), is located a short bus ride away, 4km west of town, and rents out apartments (⑥) in a complex with bars, restaurant, pool and gardens.

Eating and drinking

Among Estepona's many **places to eat** is a bunch of excellent *freidurías* and *marisquerías*. Worth trying at the foot of c/Terraza is *La Gamba* at no. 25 and further up, at no. 57, *La Palma*. The central c/Real has *Aguilar* at no. 54 with a long list of *raciones*, and to the west of the centre, *Simonito*, Avda. San Lorenzo 6, near the Turismo, is another good choice with an outdoor terrace. ⅀ *La Rada*, Avda. España 4, at the extreme northern end of the seafront, is a lively and excellent fish restaurant and *marisquería* popular with locals. One vibrant place for excellent fish and *mariscos* is the reasonably priced ⅀ *La Escollera* (closed Mon) beneath the lighthouse in the Puerto Pesquero (fishing harbour) adjoining the Puerto Deportivo. In addition to a great tapas bar there's a wonderful sea-view terrace restaurant. Moving upmarket, the **restaurants** are generally less distinguished, although *La Casa de mi Abuela*, c/Caridad 54 to the east of c/Terraza is worth trying for its grilled meats and Argentine steaks, as is *Sabor Andaluz* with well-prepared traditional dishes at c/Caridad 44. On the central Plaza Arce, *Restaurante El Gavilán del Mar* – with a pleasant terrace – is a decent place for seafood and specializes in paellas. Good pizzas and more Argentine steaks are on offer at *Sur*, Plazoleta Ortiz 11, which spreads its tables on this leafy square off the eastern end of the promenade.

Of the town's **tapas bars**, *Mesón Genaro*, c/Lozano 15 (off c/Terraza), and *La Jerezana*, in c/Estremadura nearby, are two of the best. Another good choice, with a distinctly *andaluz* flavour, is *Casa Típico Andaluz,* c/Caridad 55, to the east of c/Terraza; its speciality, called a *plaza de toros*, gets you a little of everything on one plate for around €7. For an after-dinner **ice cream**, *Heladería Vitin* in Plaza Las Flores has the edge, if only for location. The bars in the same plaza are also good places for **breakfast**, or for *churros* try the excellent *Churrería Parrado*, c/Real 116, to the west of c/Terraza (one block back from and parallel to the promenade) – get there before 11am as they sell out early. For picnic supplies, there's a daily **market**; if you're self-catering, you could try the fish market.

When it comes to **nightlife**, Estepona has a range of possibilities. There are the usual **flamenco** burlesques which are best avoided, but *Peña Flamenca* in c/Fuerzas Armadas in the north of town puts on the genuine stuff on Saturday nights at 10pm (the Turismo can provide more information). Nearer the centre, most night-time action takes place along and in the streets around **c/Real** where terrace bars, music places and clubs compete for the custom of a mainly local clientele. **Discotecas** and **music bars** proper are mostly grouped around the Puerto Deportivo, or in town there's *Niagara,* Avda. Juan Carlos, 300m beyond the Turismo on the left.

Casares and around

The greyish coast west of Estepona is punctuated with watch-towers used by peoples as diverse as Phoenicians, Romans and Arabs to protect themselves from pirate attacks. There's little reason to stop along here but one worthwhile detour is to head to **CASARES**, 18km inland from Estepona. One of the lesser known of Andalucía's White Towns, it's a beautiful place, clinging tenaciously – and spectacularly – to a steep hillside below a castle, and attracting its fair share of arty types and expatriates. The village is reputed to take its name from Julius Caesar, who is said to have used the still-functioning sulphurous springs at nearby Manilva to cure a liver complaint. More concrete historical evidence attributes the impressive Alcázar (built on Roman foundations) to the Moorish period, from the ruins of which there are spectacular **views** as far as Gibraltar on clearer days. There's little else in the way of sights, but it's satisfying enough simply to wander around, losing yourself in the twisting and narrow, white-walled streets – another vestige of the Arab period. Flanked by an eighteenth-century church, the central plaza is a good place to sit and have a drink, cooled by breezes off the sierra. The surrounding hill country, richly wooded with cork oaks and pine as well as stands of *pinsapo*, the rare Spanish fir, offers a verdant contrast with the arid plains below and is fine **walking terrain** with plenty of dirt-tracks to follow winding through the folds of the Sierra Bermeja.

With your own vehicle you could return to the N340 and the coast by way of Manilva, reached by continuing through Casares to a junction and turning left (south) along the A377 towards Manilva. This route would allow you to see the remarkably well-preserved **Roman sulphur baths** (open access). To get there follow the signs 3km from Manilva, where the road passes beneath a spectacular viaduct carrying the latest extension of the Autopista del Sol. You'll need to park any vehicle and cross the Río de Manilva using the stepping stones, to follow a track heading inland. Pass the campsite beyond a ford on the right, and the *Bar Álamo* again on the right, and at the top of a rise, the small chapel of San Adolfo. The baths lie a little beyond this. Once at the baths – definitely Roman but now under a rather garish yellow concrete canopy – you'll need to plunge inside to see the original Roman stonework. One dubious souvenir you'll take away from the place is a sulphurous stench, which is guaranteed to cling to your swimwear for weeks. Alternatively, turning right at the junction above would allow you to make a 16km detour to Gaucín (p.186).

Practicalities

Only three **buses** a day (Mon–Sat) leave for Casares from Estepona (11am, 1.30pm & 7pm; return 8.15am, 12.45pm & 4pm; 45min), meaning, if you're without transport, a very brief visit or an overnight **stay**. Should you opt for the latter, the upmarket choice is *Hotel Casares*, c/Copera 52 (☎95 289 52 11, Ⓦwww.hotelcasares.com; ❹), signed from the main square, Plaza de España, where pleasant rooms come with balcony and views. On Plaza de España itself, the budget-priced *Hostal Plaza* (☎95 289 40 30; ❷) has simple rooms with shared bath above a bar.

There are more bars than **places to eat**, but options do include *La Bodeguita de en Medio*, a very good restaurant with a delightful roof terrace on Plaza de España, *Mesón Los Claveles*, c/Arrabal 1, and *La Terraza*, a restaurant just outside the village on the Estepona road, which has great views.

Tourist information is available from a small Museo de Etnohistoria at the top of c/Villa to the south of Plaza de España (☎95 289 44 51, Mon–Fri 11am–2.30pm & 4–6.30pm, Sat 11am–4pm). It can also provide information about activities such as walking and horse riding and has a list of *casas rurales* to rent for longer stays.

On to Gibraltar

Beyond Estepona the scenery takes on a wilder and greener aspect as the Sierra Bermeja yields to the Sierra Almenara. Once across the Río Guadiaro, the road turns inland, offering, as it climbs, distant views of the Rock of Gibraltar, its monumental silhouette often girdled with a halo of cloud. The views of the urban sprawl and towers of the Bay of Algeciras's oil refineries signal that this is also a major industrial zone.

San Roque

SAN ROQUE, 35km south of Estepona in Cádiz Province, was founded in 1704 by the people of Gibraltar fleeing the British who had captured the Rock and looted their homes and churches. They expected to return within months, since the troops had taken the garrison in the name of the Archduke Carlos of Austria, whose rights Britain had been promoting in the War of the Spanish Succession, but it was the British flag that was raised on the conquered territory – and so it has remained. There are few sights, but c/San Felipe, which leads up from the main square to the *mirador*, has some fine *reja*-fronted houses. From the **mirador** you can see the Rock of Gibraltar and the hazy coast of Africa beyond – you'll have to ignore the ugly oil refinery in the foreground. Nearby in the adjacent Plaza de la Iglesia, the **Museo Municipal** (Mon–Fri 8am–3pm; free) inside the Ayuntamiento building has a collection of artefacts documenting the town's previous incarnation as the Roman *Carteia* as well as some powerful works by local sculptor Luis Ortega. The council chamber (which you should ask to see) in the same building has a **banner** given to the earlier Spanish Gibraltar by Fernando and Isabel. On the same square, the eighteenth-century church of **Santa María Coronada** – built over the ancient hermitage of San Roque – has a fine image of the Virgin, also rescued from the Rock in the flight from the British invaders. A handy place for a **snack** or a tapa is *Cafetería Don Benito*, Plaza de Armas 10, adjoining the same square as the museum, with a charming patio and small restaurant.

Practicalities

San Roque's **campsite**, *Camping San Roque* (☎956 78 00 31), is on the N340 highway just east of the town. Far better, though, if you want to stay is **LOS BARRIOS**, 10km to the west, an atmospheric, tranquil place away from the depressing nature of this industrial zone. An elegant palm-lined main street, festooned with plants and flowers in summer, leads to the first **accommodation** option, the pleasant *Hotel Real*, Avda. Pablo Picasso 7 (☎956 62 00 24; ❹), with air-conditioned balcony rooms. Further along, and uphill just beyond a central roundabout, there's a friendly *hostal*, El Semáforo, c/Alhóndiga 5 (☎956 62 01 29; ❶), which has probably the cheapest en-suite rooms in Andalucía. There are plenty of places for **eating and drinking** including the *Hotel Real*'s decent restaurant with a *menú* for around €8 or the terrace restaurant of the bar on the square fronting the roundabout.

La Línea

Obscured by San Roque's huge oil refinery, the **Spanish–British frontier** is 8km south of San Roque at **LA LÍNEA** ("the line"). When Franco closed the frontier in 1969, it was La Línea that suffered most, as workers lost their jobs on the Rock overnight and the town's population dropped by 35 percent. After sixteen years of Spanish-imposed isolation, the gates were reopened in February

1985, and crossing between here and Gibraltar is now routine – except for the odd flare-up when petulant disputes impose long delays on those waiting to cross. La Línea remains in a depressed state, a fact that has pushed many of its people into assisting the Rock's smugglers by warehousing contraband tobacco prior to its distribution throughout Spain. There are no sights as such; it's just a fishing village that has exploded in size due to the employment opportunities in Gibraltar and the industrialized zone around the Bay of Algeciras.

Practicalities

The **bus station** and a friendly **Turismo** (Mon–Fri 9am–3pm, Sat 9am–1pm; ☎956 76 99 50) are both on Avda. 20 Abril, to the south of the main Plaza de la Constitución, a large modern square at the heart of La Línea. The Turismo's leaflet *Campo de Gibraltar* has street maps of both La Línea and Algeciras and they also give out a free *Ruta del Tapeo* (route) leaflet. The closest mainline **train station** is San Roque–La Línea, 11km west of town from where you can pick up a train to Ronda and beyond.

Although La Línea's greater number of hotels make it a better overnight bet than Gibraltar, many of its **hostales** are depressingly grim and not cheap. Accommodation is concentrated around the Plaza de la Constitución. The friendly *La Campana*, c/Carboneras 3, (☎956 17 30 59; ➍) has en-suite rooms with TV and fans. Almost opposite, the slightly cheaper *Hostal-Restaurante Carlos*, c/Carboneras 6 (☎956 76 21 35, ⓦwww.hostalcarlos.com; ➌), is also good value for rooms with bath and TV. Slightly north of here, *Hostal Florida*, c/Sol 37 (☎956 17 13 00; ➋), offers more rooms with bath above a decent restaurant. Cheaper rooms with shared bathroom are available at *Pensión La Perla*, c/Clavel 10 (☎956 76 95 13; ➊), off the north side of Plaza de la Constitución. The upmarket option is *Hotel La Línea de la Concepción*, c/Caireles 2 (☎956 17

Andalucía's Moroccan enclaves

Across the straits from Gibraltar on the north coast of Morocco lie the enclaves of **Ceuta** and **Melilla**, both Spanish territories and officially part of the autonomous region of Andalucía. When they celebrated in 1997 the quincentenary of their founding by the Catholic monarchs Fernando and Isabel, neither King Juan Carlos nor the prime minister José María Aznar saw fit to join in the deliberately low-key festivities – the Spanish establishment acceded to the wishes of Morocco, with which for economic reasons it desires good relations, for minimal observation of the event. This is because Morocco views the territories as China viewed Hong Kong – and as Spain views Gibraltar. Ceuta and Melilla are the remnants of a string of Spanish fortresses built along the coast of North Africa after Andalucía had been reconquered from the Moors. Intended to protect the peninsula from further incursions, they survived into modern times as an anachronism – the United Nations does not even list them as colonies because they were settled long before Morocco existed in its present shape. Their combined populations of 140,000 citizens have the same rights as those on Spain's mainland and vociferously oppose any plans to cede the territories to Morocco.

This opposition has complicated matters for Madrid who see the enclaves as burning up vast amounts of money in grants and subsidies as well as providing an easy entry point for illegal immigrants into Spain and the EU. In line with what is happening in the former Spanish Sahara, Ceuta and Melilla could eventually gain some form of autonomy within Morocco – but so far the inhabitants are unconvinced and the tug of war between Spain and its North African neighbour seems likely to continue for some time yet.

55 66, Ⓦwww.ac-hoteles.com; Ⓢ), fronting the Bay of Algeciras with pool and gym and much better value than anything of the same standard in Gibraltar.

For **eating and drinking**, the *hostales Campana, Carlos* and *Florida* (see above) all have good and economical restaurants. To eat in a more vibrant atmosphere, however, make your way to Plaza Cruz de Herrera, through an arch off the east side of the Plaza de la Constitución. Of the various tapas bars and fast-food outlets here, *La Nueva Mesón Jerezana* does good *fino* and *jamón*. The nearby c/ Real, the main pedestrianized shopping street, offers plenty of reasonably priced bars and cafés – good for breakfast pastries – as well as restaurants. *D'Antonio*, c/Dr Villar 19, just off the north side of the same street, does decent tapas and *raciones*. The popular ⚓ *Bar El Choni*, on Plaza Iglesia at the end of c/Real, is unmissable and serves a wide range of reasonably priced tapas on an animated terrace facing the church. Two of La Línea's best fish restaurants are *La Marina*, Paseo Marítimo s/n, and *Linares*, c/Pavia 4, both northeast of the centre and close to the sea. A more central fish option, *La Pesquera*, Avda. José Meliá 2, the main drag leading from La Línea towards the Gibraltar frontier, serves decent fish and *mariscos* on a terrace with Rock views. For picnic supplies, head for the market, north of c/Real.

Gibraltar

GIBRALTAR's interest is essentially its novelty: the genuine appeal of the strange, looming physical presence of its rock, and the increasingly dubious one of its preservation as one of Britain's last remaining colonies. This enormous hunk of limestone, five kilometres long, two kilometres wide and 450 metres high – a land area smaller than the city of Algeciras across the water – has fascinated and attracted the people of the Mediterranean basin since Neanderthal times, confirmed by the finds of skulls and artefacts in a number of the Rock's many caves.

The Rock (as it is colloquially known) is a curious place to visit, not least to witness the bizarre process of its opening to mass tourism from the Costa del Sol. Ironically, this threatens both to destroy Gibraltar's highly individual society and at the same time to make it much more British, after the fashion of the expat communities and huge resorts up the coast. The frontier opening has benefited most people: Gibraltarians can buy cheaper goods in Spain, a place ironically where twenty percent of them now have second homes, while expats living on the Costas can shop in familiar stores like Mothercare, Safeway and Marks & Spencer. Despite a healthy economy based on tourism, offshore banking and its role as a major bunkering port, the colony has reached yet another crossroads in its tortuous history, and the likely future – whether its population agrees to this or not – is almost certain to involve closer ties with Spain.

Recent discoveries in a cave on the southeast tip of the Rock – flint tools and evidence of camp-fires and cooked meals – are regarded as one of the most important **prehistoric** finds in modern times. The cave appears to have been inhabited by both Neanderthals and homo sapiens, and it's hoped that further excavations will provide vital evidence as to the extinction or amalgamation of our species with the earlier race.

The **Phoenicians** called the Rock "Calpe" and had a fortified naval base here, barring the way to jealously guarded Atlantic trading destinations such as Tartessus. In **Greek** mythology this was the northernmost of the two pillars erected by Heracles. Following the demise of the Roman Empire, the Rock

△ Gibraltar

became the bridgehead for a **Berber** assault on the Visigothic domains of southern Spain. In 711 Tariq ibn Ziryab, governor of Tangier, crossed the straits at the head of an army, defeated the Visigoths and named the Rock "Jabal Tariq" or the Mountain of Tariq, the name – albeit garbled – it still has today.

Gibraltar remained in Moorish hands until taken in 1309 by Guzmán el Bueno, but it was not long before it was recovered. The end finally came when another Guzmán, the duke of Medina Sidonia, claimed it for Spain in 1462. Apart from the raids of Barbarossa, which caused Carlos V to fortify the Rock, Spanish possession was undisturbed until the **War of the Spanish Succession**, when Britain sided with Spain against the French. The outcome of this was the seizure of the Rock in 1704 by the **British** forces whose admiral, Sir George Rooke, gave the inhabitants the choice of swearing allegiance to the Habsburg claimant to the throne – Archduke Charles of Austria – or getting out. Those that left to found San Roque (see p.170) thought their absence would be temporary, but in 1715 the British contrived to have Gibraltar ceded to them "in perpetuity" in the Treaty of Utrecht, no doubt having calculated the military advantages of such a strategic bastion. Despite military and diplomatic attempts by Spain to recover the Rock since, the British have maintained their grip, and Gibraltar played an important strategic role in both World Wars. General **Franco** mounted persistent

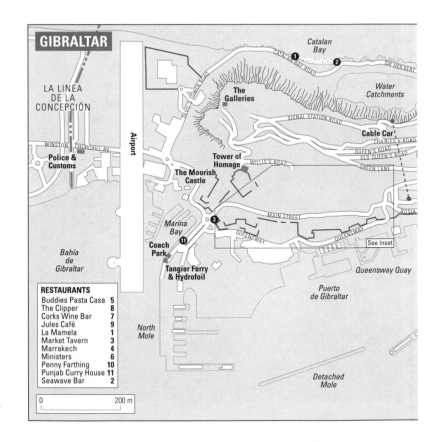

GIBRALTAR

LA LINEA
DE LA
CONCEPCIÓN

Police &
Customs

Airport

The
Galleries

Catalan
Bay

Water
Catchments

Cable Car

Signal Station Road

Charles V Road

Queen's Road

Old Queen's Road

Green Lane

Catalan Bay Road

Sir Herbert

Winston Churchill Av

Devil's Tower Road

Tower of
Homage

Willis's Road

The Moorish
Castle

Marina
Bay

Coach
Park

Tangier Ferry
& Hydrofoil

Main Street

Queensway

Queensway

See Inset

Rosia

Bahía
de
Gibraltar

North
Mole

Queensway Quay

Puerto
de Gibraltar

Detached
Mole

RESTAURANTS

Buddies Pasta Casa	5
The Clipper	8
Corks Wine Bar	7
Jules Café	9
La Mamela	1
Market Tavern	3
Marrakech	4
Ministers	6
Penny Farthing	10
Punjab Curry House	11
Seawave Bar	2

0   200 m

campaigns to get it back and closed the access link with Spain in 1969, a period of enforced isolation that is indelibly etched into the Gibraltarian collective consciousness.

The Rock, it seems, is destined to be a recurring cause of friction between the two nations; in 1988 three **IRA suspects** were gunned down by British agents near the petrol station at the entrance to the town and close to the frontier. The British government – which went to enormous lengths to obscure the facts of the case – produced a version of events much at odds with that of the Spanish police and once more the issue of a "foreign power on Spanish soil" sparked a national debate.

One more curious twist in the colony's history occurred in the spring of 2004 when Gibraltar voted for the first time ever in **European Parliament elections** after being denied the vote by successive British governments wary of the political and diplomatic complexities involved. However, when the Gibraltarians won a victory in the European Court of Human Rights, the British government was forced into a U-turn and somewhat bizarrely Gibraltar's 20,000 voters were appended to the southwest England constituency of Devon and Cornwall, almost 1000 miles away from the Rock – and to where the colony's ballot papers were airlifted once they had been counted. This success has fuelled demands for Gibraltar to have its own Westminster MP, another issue the

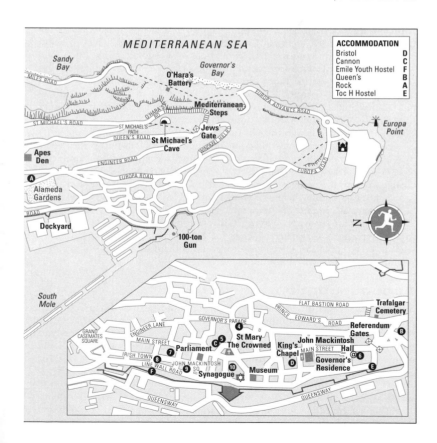

British government would prefer not to think about. For more on the history of Gibraltar, see Contexts, p.645.

Arrival, orientation and information

If you have a car, don't attempt to bring it to Gibraltar – the queues at the border to get in (and out) are often atrocious, and parking on the Rock is limited, due to lack of space. Use the underground **car parks** in La Línea – there's one beneath the central Plaza de la Constitución – instead (it's worth paying for the extra security) and **walk** across. From the frontier, where passport checking is a formality, it's a short **bus ride** (#9, every 15min) or about a ten-minute walk across part of the airport's runway to **Main Street** (La Calle Real), which runs for most of the town's length a couple of blocks back from the port. Most of the shops – cheap, duty-free whisky and tobacco are major attractions with rock-bottom prices due to the non-application of excise duty in the colony – are clustered in and around Main Street, along with nearly all of the British-style pubs and hotels.

The main **tourist office** is housed in Duke of Kent House on Cathedral Square (Mon–Fri 9am–5.30pm; ☎45000, ⓦwww.gibraltar.gi/tourism). There are sub-branches open daily in Casemates Square (Mon–Fri 9am–5.30pm, Sat & Sun 10am–3pm; ☎74982), and in the customs and immigration building at the border (Mon–Fri 9am–4.30pm, Sat 10am–3pm, Sun 10am–1pm; ☎50762). **Internet** access is available at the public library in the John Mackintosh Hall (Mon–Fri 9.30am–10.30pm), at the south end of Main Street, which is also a cultural centre mounting frequent exhibitions. The Gibraltar Bookshop, 300 Main St, is a good source for stocking up on holiday reading and has a good selection of books on the Rock's history. Much of Gibraltar, including restaurants and cafés but with the exception of the cheap booze shops, closes down on Saturday, but the tourist sights remain open, and this can often be a quiet time to visit. Virtually everything closes on Sunday.

The currency used here is the **Gibraltar pound** (the same value as the British pound, but different notes and coins although you'll often find British coins mixed in with your change); if you pay in euros (accepted without problems all over Gibraltar), you generally fork out about 5 percent more; ask for your change in euros if you are on a brief day trip. Gibraltar pounds can be hard to change in Spain or anywhere else. **Banks** with ATMs can be found along Main Street along with *bureaux de change* which stay open longer.

A word of warning **when leaving Gibraltar**: if approached by locals do not carry any packages for strangers across the border back into Spain. What may seem to be a simple carton of cigarettes could contain drugs and – if searched – you, and not they, will suffer the consequences.

Accommodation

Shortage of space on the Rock means that **accommodation** is at a premium, especially in summer, and most of it is not overly inviting. It's really not worth your while searching out a good place to stay unless you have to: your best bet is to visit on day-trips from Algeciras (buses on the hour and half-hour, journey time 30min) or La Línea. The only **budget** accommodation is at the friendly *Toc H Hostel* on Line Wall Road (☎73431; about £6 a person) – though rooms here are none too comfortable, the water is cold and it's almost always occupied by long-term residents. The *Cannon Hotel*, 9 Cannon Lane, near the cathedral (☎51711, ⓦwww .cannonhotel.gi; about £36 a double sharing bath, £45 en suite, including breakfast), is another possibility. Otherwise, you're going to have to pay standard British **hotel** prices: the cheapest are the *Queen's Hotel* on Boyd Street (☎74000, ⓦwww.queenshotel.gi), and the slightly pricier *Hotel Bristol* in Cathedral Square (☎76800, ⓦwww.Gibraltar.gi/bristolhotel), each charging around £50–60 for an interior-facing double (exterior rooms cost more). The flagship *Rock Hotel*, 3 Europa Rd (☎73000, ⓦwww.rockhotelgibraltar .com; cheapest double £160), immediately below the Apes' Den, trades on its imperial connections (rooms are decorated in "colonial style" and come with ceiling fans and a trouser press). At Gibraltar's *Emile Youth Hostel*, Montagu Bastion, Line Wall Rd (☎51106, ⓔemilehostel@yahoo.com), expect to pay £15 a night for a dorm bed (breakfast included) or £34 for a double room sharing bathroom.

No **camping** is allowed on the peninsula, and if you're caught sleeping rough or inhabiting abandoned bunkers, you're likely to be arrested and fined.

Around the Rock

Be on your guard at the frontier for touting taxi drivers who offer "tours of the Rock" – they're generally overpriced (around £7 per person and very rushed. Near the end of Main Street you can hop on the expensive **cable car** (daily 9.30am–6pm, last trip down 5.45pm; £8 each way) which will carry you up to the summit – the **Top of the Rock** as it's logically known. A way to avoid paying the return fare is to walk back down (see below). Entry to this Top of the Rock area for pedestrians is £0.50 but the attractions cost extra (see below). The cable car ascends via the **Apes' Den** halfway up, a fairly reliable viewing point to see the tailless monkeys (Barbary apes) and hear the guides explain their legend. The story goes that the British will keep the rock only so long as the apes remain too; Winston Churchill was superstitious enough to augment their numbers during World War II when they started to decline. The Top of the Rock gives fantastic views over to the Atlas Mountains and the town far below, as well as an elaborate water catchment system cut into the side of the rock. This is also an ideal spot for observing bird migrations between Africa and the Spanish peninsula. From the Top of the Rock it's an easy walk south along St Michael's Road passing another of the apes' dens. Keep a tight grip on your belongings; the unruly primates are prone to stealing tourists' bags and sometimes their cameras – often tossing the items onto rocks a couple of hundred metres below.

Much of the area of the upper Rock has now been designated the **Upper Rock Nature Reserve** (daily 9.30am–7pm; pedestrians £0.50) which you can enter for the pedestrian fee but for which you will need to pay extra to view the attractions described below, plus the **Gibraltar: A City Under Siege** exhibition, housed in a former ammunition store on Willis's Road. An inclusive ticket costing £8 allows entry to all of them.

From the Top of the Rock cable car station a leafy path leads to **Saint Michael's Cave** (daily 9.30am–7pm; inclusive ticket), an immense natural cavern that led ancient people to believe the rock was hollow and gave rise to its old name of Mons Calpe (Hollow Mountain). Used during the last war as a bomb-proof military hospital, the cave nowadays hosts occasional concerts. You can arrange at the tourist office for a guided visit to **Lower Saint Michael's Cave**, a series of chambers going deeper down and ending in an underground lake.

Although it is possible to be lazy and take the cable car both ways, you might instead continue up Queen's Road to visit the fourteenth-century **Tower of Homage** (inclusive ticket). This is the most visible survivor from the Moorish castle, today filled with wax dummies of British soldiers hacking at the stone and doing battle with the Spanish. Further up you'll find the **Upper Galleries** (aka the Great Siege Tunnels; inclusive ticket), blasted out of the rock during the Great Siege of 1779–1782 in order to point guns down at the Spanish lines.

To walk down from the Top of the Rock, you can take the **Mediterranean Steps** at the end of O'Hara's Road – but they're not very well signposted and you have to climb over **O'Hara's Battery**, a big gun emplacement with a very steep descent most of the way down the east side, turning the southern corner of the Rock. You'll pass through the Jews' Gate and into Engineer Road. From here, return to town through the Alameda Gardens and the evocative **Trafalgar Cemetery** (daily 9am–7pm; free) with graves of the Battle of Trafalgar dead and a good line in epitaphs.

Back in town, incorporated into the **Gibraltar Museum** (Mon–Fri 10am–6pm, Sat 10am–2pm; £2), are two beautiful, well-preserved fourteenth-century **Moorish Baths**. Resembling the ancient Roman model, the baths had a cold room and hot rooms heated by a hypocaust. Note the star-shaped skylights, and the pillars used in the construction: one Roman, two Visigothic and four Moorish. Otherwise, the museum's collection is an odd assortment including an incongruous Egyptian mummy washed up in the bay, a natural history display of stuffed birds in glass cases, and a rather dreary military section documenting how the British came to rule the roost here. The museum's star exhibit should be a female skull, dating from around 100,000 years ago and unearthed in 1848 on the Rock's north face. Ironically, because the find was then stored away, it was the later discovery of a skull in Germany's Neander Valley that gave its name to the era we know as Neanderthal, which could just as easily have been termed "Gibraltarian". The museum now retains only a copy, the original having been removed to the research collection of the Natural History Museum in London. Not far away from the museum, and next door to the Governor's Residence, is the sixteenth-century **King's Chapel** (daily 9am–7pm; free) harking back to pre-colonial days. It's a fine old church – now rather marred by the military flags, regalia and wall plaques of Empire – which was formerly the chapel attached to the convent of Franciscan friars (now the Governor's Residence).

Other sites include **Nelson's Anchorage** (Mon–Sat 9.30am–5.15pm; £1 or free with inclusive Rock ticket) on Rosia Road, to the south of the harbour, where a monstruous **100-ton Victorian gun** marks the site where Nelson's body was brought ashore – preserved in a rum barrel – from HMS Victory after the Battle of Trafalgar in 1805. If you have the time to spare you can take a bus (#3 which runs along Line Wall Road and Europa Road – its continuation – with a stop at the Rock Hotel) south to the tip of the peninsula at **Europa point**; however, although on clear days you get fine views across the strait to Morocco and the sight of the odd leaping dolphin there's little else here but a lighthouse, souvenir shop, bus terminal and, interestingly, an impressive mosque donated in the 1990s by King Fahd of Saudi Arabia for the benefit of Muslim immigrants working in Gibraltar. A number of companies run rather pricey daily **dolphin-spotting** boat trips and trips around the bay. Most leave from either Marina Bay or the nearby Queensway Quay. Two established companies operating from Marina Bay are Dolphin Safari (℡71914; £25, children £15) and the cheaper Dolphin World (℡54481000; £20, children £10) but ring first to book a place or ask the Tourist Office (who have a complete list of all companies) to do it for you. Dolphin World offer a money-back guarantee should you not see dolphins.

The best **beach** is at the tiny fishing village of **Catalan Bay**, a characterless stretch of seafront reminiscent of a humdrum British holiday resort whose inhabitants like to think of themselves as distinct from the townies on the other side of the Rock. There's a bus service (#4 from Line Wall Road; every 15m) to Catalan Bay and the other eastern beaches.

Eating and drinking

Eating is a bit of a sad affair in Gibraltar: relatively expensive by Spanish standards, with pub snacks or fish and chips as the norm. Main Street is crowded with dismal touristy places and fast-food outlets, although the tiny *Smiths Fish & Chip Shop*, 295 Main Street, is worth a try. Other budget choices are *Penny Farthing* at 9 King Street, off Cathedral Square, a Lilliputian restaurant with an English menu and, a couple of blocks north of here, *Jules Café*, 30 John Mackintosh Square, is a decent lunch stop with a *menú* for £10.95 (excluding wine) and a pleasant terrace. Off the east side of Main Street decent pasta in all its varieties is served up at *Buddies Pasta Casa*, 15 Cannon Lane, by the cathedral. *Corks Wine Bar*, 79 Irish Town, is a tranquil venue for light meals, and nearby at no. 78 *The Clipper* serves pub grub in a varnished lounge. The *Market Tavern*, Market Place, at the north end of town beyond Casemates Square, serves up traditional "English breakfasts" all day long, and on Casemates Square itself *Rock Fish & Chips*, a friendly Moroccan-run chip-shop, makes an excellent job of the British national dish (eat-in or takeaway). Slightly more tempting is *Ministers Restaurant*, 310 Main Street (southern end), with a pleasant terrace and Spanish-style *platos combinados* costing £6–10. An interesting arrival in the centre of town is the Moroccan ⚓ *Marrakech Restaurant*, 9 Governor's Parade, with a pleasant terrace serving couscous, tagines and other Magrebí dishes with a set *menú* for under £10. *Saccarello's Coffee House* at 57 Irish Town is a local institution and a great place for tea and home-made confectionery.

Further afield, at Marina Bay, try *Biancas*, for reasonably priced seafood as well as pizzas, burgers and salads, or the very good *Da Paolo* which serves a selection of Italian-British-Spanish-style meat and fish dishes. If you're missing a fix of Asian spices the *Punjab Curry House*, Water Gardens, near the Coach Park on the way to Marina Bay, should fit the bill. At Catalan Bay the *Seawave Bar* does decent shellfish *raciones* and good seafood, and the similar *Village Inn* next door is also worth a try. *La Mamela*, at the opposite end of the seafront is more restaurant-style and does fish dishes such as *úrta al coñac* (sea bream) for £9–13 and paella for £6.50 per person. They also do *mariscos raciones* (called "portions" on this side of the border).

Gibraltarian **pubs** mimic traditional English styles (and prices), but are often rowdy, full of soldiers and visiting sailors. For pub food, the *Royal Calpe*, 176 Main Street; *Calpe Hounds* on Cornwall's Lane; *Gibraltar Arms*, 14 Main St; and *The Horseshoe*, 193 Main Street, are among the best, all offering hearty meals. These pubs all have some outdoor seating – a rarity in Gibraltar. For

Gibraltar's sovereignty

Sovereignty over the Rock will doubtless eventually return to Spain, but at present neither side is in much of a hurry. For Britain it's a question of precedent – Gibraltar is in too similar a situation to the Falklands/Malvinas, a conflict that pushed the Spanish into postponing an initial frontier-opening date in 1982. For Spain, too, there are unsettling parallels with the *presidios* (Spanish enclaves) on the Moroccan coast at Ceuta and Melilla – both at present part of Andalucía. Nonetheless, the British presence is in practice waning, and the British Foreign Office clearly wants to steer Gibraltar towards a new, harmonious relationship with Spain. To this end they are running down the significance of the military base, and now only a token force remains – most of these working in a top-secret hi-tech bunker buried deep inside the Rock from where the Royal Navy monitors the sea traffic through the straits (accounting for a quarter of the world movement of all shipping). In financial terms this has cut the British government's contribution to Gibraltar's GDP from 65 percent in the early 1980s to less than 7 percent today, and the figure is still falling.

The majority of the 28,000 Gibraltarians see all these issues as irrelevant in light of their firmly stated opposition to a return to **Spanish control** over the Rock. In 1967, just before Franco closed the border in the hope of forcing a quick agreement, the colony voted on the issue – rejecting it by 12,138 votes to 44 (a poll not recognized, incidentally, by the UN). Most people would probably sympathize with that vote – against a Spain that was then still a dictatorship – but nearly forty years have gone by, Spanish democracy is now secure, and the arguments are becoming increasingly tenuous.

May 1996 saw a change in the trend of internal politics with the **defeat of the Socialist government** of Joe Bossano (following two previous landslide victories) and the arrival in power of a **Social Democrat administration**, led by **Peter Caruana**. However, whilst Caruana had talked of opening up a more constructive dialogue with Spain during the election campaign, once in control he soon began to voice the traditional Gibraltarian paranoia and was re-elected with an increased majority in 2000. His stance caused some dismay in Madrid and London, who were both behind Spain's offer in 1997 to give the colony the status of an autonomous region inside the Spanish state similar to that of the Basques or Catalans. The proposal was rejected out of hand by Caruana who made a speech at the UN castigating Spain's intransigence, and claiming the right of Gibraltar to exercise "self-determination." In the spring of 2002, the **Blair government** – perhaps partly due to the British premier's close relationship with then Spanish leader José María Aznar – moved Gibraltar up the political agenda and it was suggested that a **referendum** on a new power-sharing agreement with Spain could be put to the Gibraltar voters within a year. Scenting what he saw as a sell-out, Caruana began a campaign to kill any idea of ever sharing sovereignty with Spain, and when British foreign secretary Jack Straw made a visit to the colony in May 2002 to promote the idea he was ambushed at the airport and loudly booed by thousands of Union Jack-waving Gibraltarians. Straw later declared that any deal with Spain would have to be sanctioned by the Gibraltar people, a comment that sent shock waves through Spanish diplomatic circles who now feared that Britain would try to renege on the power-sharing deal drafted by Blair and Aznar. When, in July, Straw announced that the Spanish and British governments were in broad agreement regarding how Britain and Spain should share the sovereignty of Gibraltar, Caruana denounced this as an act of treachery and announced that the Gibraltar administration would hold its own referendum on the issue. This duly took place on November 7, 2002 following a month-long campaign which resurrected the old slogan "Give Spain No Hope!" as its theme. The predictable result turned out to be a 99-percent vote against any sharing of sovereignty with Spain, in an 88-percent turnout. When Caruana was again **re-elected** as head of the Gibraltar administration in 2004 this left the

Blair government with no real hope of making progress given its position that the Gibraltarians must approve a deal with Spain. The **new Spanish administration** elected in 2004 and led by José Luis Rodríguez Zapatero has repeated the claims over Gibraltar voiced by all its predecessors and the political stalemate seems set to continue for as long as Britain uses the wishes of the Gibraltarians as a pretext for blocking any change in the colony's status – a policy that infuriates the Spanish government whose former foreign minister, Abel Matutes, stated that the wishes of the residents "did not apply in the case of Hong Kong".

Caruana has regularly been urged by Britain (under pressure from Spain) to crack down on the smuggling of contraband tobacco over the Spanish border and to curb the activities of the Rock's 75,000 "offshore" financial institutions which have mushroomed over the last decade. Many of these companies, Spain claims, are guilty of drugs money laundering besides providing a refuge for Russian mafia money, accusations given some credibilty by the EU's decision to start legal proceedings against a number of them in 1999. In 2005 Gibraltar finance companies were also implicated in the uncovering by Spanish police of a huge money-laundering operation based in Marbella (see p.158). Some Spanish cynics even suggest that it is the certain suppression of these illegal activities once Gibraltar comes under Spanish sovereignty – together with the imposition of excise duties, which would hit cut-price booze, petrol and tobacco sales – that are the real reasons why Gibraltarians are against any deal with Spain. In the hope of applying pressure on the colony, Spain prohibits access to the Rock's airport by non-British aircraft, thus denying an expansion of tourism, and Gibraltar's seaport is not permitted direct communications with any port on the Spanish mainland. The latest cause of rancour between the two administrations is the refusal by Spain to integrate Gibraltar's mobile-phone system into its own – with the result that the Rock's mobiles work all over Europe, except in Spain.

What most outsiders don't realize about the political situation is that the Gibraltarians feel very vulnerable, caught between the interests of two big states; they are well aware that both governments' concerns have nothing to do with their own personal wishes. Until very recently people were sent over from Britain to fill all the top civil service and Ministry of Defence jobs, a practice which, to a lesser degree, still continues – the present governor is Sir Francis Richards, a career diplomat and former head of GCHQ, the British government's intelligence-gathering organization. Large parts of the Rock are no-go areas for "natives", the South District in particular being taken up by military facilities. The withdrawal of British forces has somewhat improved the chronic housing shortage: there's a huge new development in the reclaimed land of the port, and much former army housing has been handed over to the local government.

Locals – particularly on the Spanish side of the border – also vigorously protest about the Royal Navy nuclear-powered and armed submarines that dock regularly at the naval base. Secrecy equally surrounds the issue of whether nuclear warheads and/or chemical and biological weapons are stored in the arsenal, probably deep inside the Rock itself which is honeycombed with 51km of tunnels.

Yet Gibraltarians – sounding at times eerily similar to Ulster Unionists in Ireland – stubbornly cling to British status, and all their institutions are modelled on British lines. Contrary to popular belief, however, they are of neither mainly Spanish nor British blood, but an ethnic mix descended from Genoese, Portuguese, Spanish, Menorcan, Jewish, Maltese and British forebears. **English** is the official language, but more commonly spoken is what sounds to an outsider like perfect Andalucian Spanish. It is, in fact, *llanito*, an Andalucian dialect with the odd borrowed English and foreign words reflecting its diverse origins – only a Spaniard from the south can tell a Gibraltarian from an Andalucian.

1

Onward travel

One of the functional attractions of Gibraltar is its role as a port for **Morocco**. A cata-maran service, the *Tanger Jet*, sails to Tangier on Fridays at 6pm, taking one hour. The return trip from Tangier is on Sundays at 8pm (local time). Tickets cost £20 one way and £35 return for a foot passenger, and £55 single and £110 return for a car. Tickets and updated timetables are available from the agent Turner, 65/67 Irish Town (☏78305, ✉turner@gibtelecom.net). Turner also act as agents for one- and two-day excursions to **Tangier** (sailing from Algeciras or Tarifa) by catamaran operated by FRS (🌐www.frs.es) including a sightseeing tour, lunch and hotel (for the two-day option) costing around €52 for the one day, and €89 for the two-day package. If you're looking for other exotic destinations, at the end of summer the yacht marina fills up with boats heading for the **Canaries**, **Madeira** and the **West Indies** – many take on crew to work in exchange for passage.

Bland Travel, Cloister Building, Irish Town (☏77012, ✉henry@bland.gi; closed Sat & Sun), is the leading travel agent in Gibraltar and can assist with booking British Airways (2 daily) and Monarch Airlines (1 daily) flights to **London** and the latter's (4 weekly) flights to **Manchester**. There are currently no flights between Gibraltar and Morocco.

a quieter drink try the *Cannon Bar* in Cannon Lane beside the cathedral, or the *Piccadilly Garden Bar*, 3 Rosia Rd, just beyond the Referendum Gates (aka South Port).

Algeciras

ALGECIRAS occupies the far side of the bay from Gibraltar, spewing out smoke and pollution in its direction. The last town of the Spanish Mediterra-nean, it was once an elegant resort; today it's unabashedly a port and industrial centre, its suburbs sprawling out on all sides. When Franco closed the border with Gibraltar at La Línea it was Algeciras that he decided to develop to absorb the Spanish workers formerly employed in the British naval dockyards, thus breaking the area's dependence on the Rock.

Most travellers are scathing about the city's ugliness, and unless you're waiting for a bus or train, or heading for Morocco, there's admittedly little reason to stop. However, Algeciras has a real port atmosphere, and even if you're just pass-ing through it's hard to resist the urge to get on a boat south. This is the main port for Moroccan migrant workers, who drive home every year during their holidays from the factories, farms and mines of Northern Europe. In summer, the port bustles with groups of Moroccans in transit, dressed in flowing *djela-bas* and yellow slippers, and lugging unbelievable amounts of possessions. Half a million cross Spain each year, often becoming victims of all levels of racial discrimination, from being ripped off to being violently attacked.

Once you start to explore, you'll also discover that the old town has some very attractive corners that seem barely to have changed in fifty years, especially around the **Plaza Alta**. This leafy square, arguably the town's only sight of any note, lies a five-minute walk from the bus station/port area and if you're killing time provides a much more pleasant place to sit out than around the port. On the square, the eighteenth-century church of **Nuestra Señora de la Palma** and the Baroque chapel of **Nuestra Señora de Europa** – with a fine facade – are worth a look.

Nearer the port, where more impressive but now crumbling edifices echo faded glories, the romantic **Hotel Reina Cristina**, Paseo de la Conferencia s/n, south of the harbour, set in a park and built in the nineteenth century in British colonial style, is a wonderful throwback to the days of the Grand Tour and steam trains. Call in for a drink in their terrace bar and take a look at the plaques behind the reception desk bearing the signatures of famous guests, such as Sir Arthur Conan Doyle, W.B. Yeats, Cole Porter and Federico García Lorca.

Practicalities

The **bus station** is in c/San Bernardo, 250m or so behind the port, beside the *Hotel Octavio*, which has services to and from Tarifa, Cádiz, Sevilla and most other destinations: the bus to La Línea also goes every thirty minutes from here. For Málaga, hourly services leave from Empresa Portillo, Avda. Virgen del Carmen 15, on the waterfront (☎956 65 10 55); from here too, less frequently, are direct connections to Granada and Almería.

Just beyond the bus station is the **train station**, from where the line heads to Ronda and the Bobadilla Junction, where there are connections with Sevilla, Málaga, Córdoba and Granada. The stunningly scenic route to Ronda is one of the best journeys in Andalucía; there are four departures a day.

If you need any information about the town, or want to pick up an accommodation list or map, make for the **Turismo**, c/Juan de la Cierva, on the south side of the train track (Mon–Fri 9am–2pm & 6–8pm; ☎956 57 26 36, ⓦwww.ayto-algeciras.es). **Internet** access is possible at *Locutorio Algeciras*, Avda. Virgen del Carmen 19 (Wed–Mon 10am–2pm & 5–10pm), fronting the harbour.

Accommodation

Regarding **places to stay**, Algeciras has plenty of low-priced *hostales* and hotels in the grid of streets between the port and the train station, and lots of simple *casas de huéspedes* round the market. A good place to start is along c/ Segismundo Moret facing the railway lines by the harbour. Here at no. 4 there's the excellent *Hotel Don Manuel* (☎956 63 46 06, ☏956 63 47 16; ❸) with air-conditioned rooms, or nearby at no. 6, *Casa Sanchez* (☎956 65 69 57; ❶) has rooms with shared bath above a restaurant (see below). There are several possibilities around the corner in c/Duque de Almodóvar, including *Levante* at no. 21 (☎956 65 15 05; ❶) which has clean and economical rooms sharing bath; while along nearby c/José Santacana there's the more comfortable *González* at no. 7 (☎956 65 28 43; ❷) where all rooms come en suite, or the diminutive but pleasant *Nuestra Señora del Carmen* (☎956 65 63 01; ❷) at no. 14, also with en-suite rooms adding a TV. On Plaza Palma, the market square, there's the surprisingly spruce *Hostal Nuestra Señora de la Palma* (☎956 63 24 81; ❷) for more rooms with bath and TV. A very pleasant hotel close to the waterfront is the *Marina Victoria*, Avda. de la Marina 7 (☎956 65 01 11, ☏956 63 28 65; ❹), whose high, air-conditioned balcony rooms overlook the bay with great views towards Gibraltar. Lastly, of course, there's the grand, historic *Hotel Reina Cristina* (see above; ☎956 60 26 22, ✉dir.reinacristina@hotelesglobales.com; ❼) with all mod cons plus indoor and outdoor pools. Algeciras's luxurious **youth hostel**, Ctra. Nacional 340 (☎956 67 90 60, ☏956 67 90 17; €14), with pool, tennis courts and en-suite double rooms, lies 8km west of town on the Tarifa road. Buses heading for Tarifa will drop you outside on request (ask for the "Albergue Juvenil").

On to Morocco

Morocco is easily visited from Algeciras: in summer there are hourly crossings to **Tangier** (daily; fast ferry 1hr 10min, normal ferry 2hr 15min), and at least 10 to the Spanish *presidio* of **Ceuta** (daily; fast ferry 35min, normal ferry 1hr 45min), little more than a Spanish Gibraltar with a brisk business in duty-free goods, but a relatively painless way to enter Morocco. **Tickets** cost €26 (normal ferry) or €28 (fast) one-way to Tangier or Ceuta, and are sold at the scores of travel agents along the waterfront and on most approach roads; they all cost the same, though some places may give you a better rate of exchange than others if you want to pay in foreign currency. Viajes Transafric, Avda. Marina 4 (☏956 65 43 11, ⓦwww.transafric.com), near the port, is a reliable company and will provide up-to-date information on timetable changes. They also do a daily all-inclusive **day-trip** to Tangier by fast-ferry, which includes a guided tour, lunch, and time for shopping, for €48. Wait till Tangier – or Tetouan if you're going via Ceuta – before buying any Moroccan currency; rates in the embarkation building kiosks are very poor. Check the date and time on your ferry ticket, and beware the ticket sellers who congregate near the dock entrance wearing official Ceuta/Tangier badges: they add a whopping "commission" charge. InterRail/Eurail card holders should note that they're entitled to a twenty-percent discount on the standard ferry price: if you have trouble getting this, go to the official sales desk in the embarkation building.

Eating and drinking

The huge number of people passing through the town also guarantees virtually limitless possibilities for **food and drink**, especially around the port/harbour area. Among them, across the railway line from the Turismo, is *Casa Sánchez*, c/Segismundo Moret 6, which has an inexpensive *menú* for €8. A little north of the bus station, the excellent ꭤ *Restaurante Montes*, c/Juan Morrison 27, is more upmarket, but has a great-value *menú* for €8; they also have an equally excellent **tapas** bar lower down the hill on the same street, at the junction with c/Emilio Castelar. More tapas bars are to be found in the streets surrounding the Plaza Alta, where there are more bars, cafés and popular *heladerías*. The daily **markets** are useful places to buy food, as well as vibrant and fascinating to visit; the main one, on Plaza Palma down by the port, is a riot of colour on Saturday mornings.

Ronda and the White Towns

Though Andalucía boasts many pretty *pueblos blancos*, the best known are the group of **White Towns** – unfeasibly picturesque places, each with its own plaza, church and tavern – set in the roughly triangular area between Málaga, Algeciras and Sevilla. At their centre, in a region of wild mountainous beauty, is spectacular **Ronda**, very much the transportation hub and a great attraction in its own right. From Ronda, almost any route north or west is rewarding, taking you past a whole series of lovely little villages, among cherry orchards and vines, many of them fortified since the days of the Reconquest – hence the mass of "de la Frontera" suffixes. Of these, **Arcos de la Frontera**, a truly spectacular White Town perched on a high limestone spur, comes close to Ronda as the best place to spend a few days in the region.

To Ronda from the coast

Of several possible approaches to Ronda from the coast, the route up from Algeciras is the most rewarding – and worth going out of your way to experience.

From Málaga, most of the buses to Ronda follow a rather bleak route, heading along the coast to San Pedro de Alcántara before turning into the mountains along the A376. The train ride up from Málaga is better, with three connecting services daily, the last currently running at 6.05pm.

From Algeciras – a route that goes via **Gaucín** – you can take either the bus or train, or, if you've time and energy, go on a four- or five-day walk. En route, you're always within reach of a river and there's a series of hill towns, each one visible from the next, to provide targets for the day.

Castellar de la Frontera

Heading north out of Algeciras along the A369, after 8km (and just before the turn-off for Castellar below) a turning on the left signed "Casa Convento" leads through expansive woodlands to the enchanting 🛏 *Convento La Almoraima* hotel (☎956 69 30 02, 🌐www.la-almoraima.com; ❻), which is located inside a rehabilitated seventeenth-century convent with a fine Florentine tower and a restaurant in the former cloister. It's surrounded by vast tracts of wooded walking country in the Parque Natural de los Alcornocales (see below), all making it hard to imagine a more serene stopover.

The next turning, about 2km further on, leads to **CASTELLAR DE LA FRONTERA**, a bizarre hill village within a thirteenth-century Moorish castle, whose population was moved downriver in 1971 to a "new" town on the edge of nearby La Almoraima. The relocation was subsequently dropped and a few villagers moved back to their old houses, but many of the dwellings were taken over by retired hippies (mainly affluent Germans). Perhaps not surprisingly, the result wasn't totally successful, and the two groups didn't gel – reflecting this tension, the place today has a brooding, claustrophobic atmosphere. Plans to rebuild the castle as a tourist centre – complete with parador – have been shelved and the Germans remain, their cars and vans parked on the approach roads to the village. There are two **accommodation** options: within the castle walls there's *Casas Rurales de Castellar*, c/Rosario 3 (☎956 23 66 20, 🌐www.tugasa.com; ❹), which has renovated a number of dwellings to rent as self-catering *casas rurales*. The same operation also runs the decent *Restaurante Aljibe*, with a *menú* for around €15. Otherwise *Hostal El Pilar*, c/León Esquivel 4

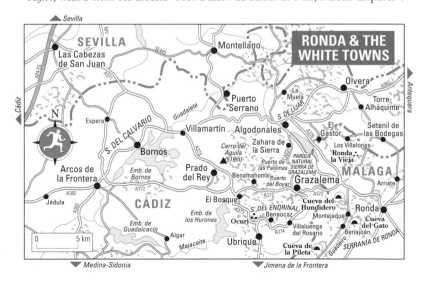

(☎956 69 30 22; ❷), with en-suite rooms lies below in the new town. For **food**, in addition to the *Aljibe* above, there's a *venta* at the start of the road up to Castellar as well as a bar near the entrance to the castle.

Back on the road north the villagers' new home, **NUEVO CASTELLAR**, lies down a turning on the right. It's a rather soulless place with the view from the main square framing the castle – their former home – on the hill above. There are a couple of bars and the *hostal* mentioned above, but not much else to detain you.

Jimena de la Frontera

JIMENA DE LA FRONTERA, 20km north again along the A369, lacks the traumas of Castellar; again, it's a hill town but it's far larger and more open, rising to a grand if ruined thirteenth-century Moorish **castle** with a triple-gateway entrance and round keep. In recent years it has become home to a considerable contingent of British expats who probably feel the need to be within working and shopping distance of Gibraltar. Jimena is also a gateway to the **Parque Natural de los Alcornocales**, a vast expanse of verdant hill country stretching south to the sea and north to El Bosque and covered with cork oaks (*alcornocales*); a haven for large numbers of birds and insects, it's also a paradise for walkers. The tourist offices in this zone should stock a Junta de Andalucía booklet in straightforward Spanish detailing eight **walks** of between 2km and 7km in various parts of the park, the first of which takes in the Tajo de las Figuras Neolithic cave paintings near Benalup de Sidonia (see p.211). *Walking in Andalucía* by Guy Hunter-Watts (see "Books") also describes half a dozen walks in the park, two starting in Jimena. Jimena holds an annual week-long international music **festival** in the second half of July which attracts a wide range of jazz, flamenco, folk and classical artistes, bands and orchestras from Spain and abroad.

In town there are several places to stay including the plush *Hostal El Anon*, c/Consuelo 34 (☎956 64 01 13, ⓦwww.andalucia.com/jimena/hostalanon; ❹), a series of tastefully renovated houses and stables with patio, bar, restaurant and rooftop pool. They can also arrange horse riding in the scenic surrounding countryside. Another option is the charming and friendly *Posada La Casa Grande*, c/Fuentenueva 42, a street off the top of c/Sevilla (☎956 64 05 78, ⓦwww .posadalacasagrande.com; ❷–❸), where rooms are located in three tastefully restored village houses. They also rent out fully equipped apartments (❹) and will accept a one-night stay; keep an eye out for their pet iguana who lives in the hotel's library. A little way out at the train station, *Los Arcos* (☎956 64 03 28; ❸) is another inexpensive *hostal* for rooms with bath. A delightful out-of-town alternative is ⌓ *Cortijo Roman* (☎956 64 05 49, ⓦwww.holidayscortijoroman. com; ❹), a renovated farmhouse turned into apartments ranged around a plant-filled farmyard patio. It's located on the A369, 1.5km north of town.

Jimena's **campsite**, *Camping Los Alcornocales* (☎956 64 00 60), occupies a superb location with great views on the north side of town (reached by following c/Sevilla to its end), and has its own restaurant. Other **places to eat** include *Bar Ventorrillero*, Plaza de la Constitución 2, at the foot of c/Sevilla with a *menú* for around €7, and the equally good *Restaurante Bar Cuenca*, Avenida de los Deportes, on the way into town, which also serves tapas and has a pretty terrace patio at the rear.

Gaucín

Beyond Jimena the A369 climbs for 23km through woods of cork oak and olive groves to reach **GAUCÍN**, just beyond the Málaga border. Almost a mountain village and perched on a ridge below yet another Moorish fort, Gaucín commands tremendous views and makes a fine place to stay. The village has a prosperous air somewhat sustained by a long-standing international community comprised of British and other European emigrants.

The only attraction of any note is the **Castillo del Aguila** (daily 11am–1pm & 4–6pm; free), a Moorish castle reached by a track at the eastern end of the village. From the battlements there are great views across terrain studded with olive, oak and chestnut trees to Gibraltar and even the Moroccan coast beyond on a very clear day. Easter Sunday is always celebrated here with a fiesta and **encierro** (bull run) when beefy fighting bulls career through the streets looking for partying inebriates to get their horns into.

For **accommodation**, *Hostal Moncada* is a good bet (℡95 215 13 24; ❷), with rooms above its restaurant next to the *gasolinera* as you come into the village from Jimena; get a room at the back for a view of the Serranía de Ronda – now somewhat obscured by a new housing development. The more upmarket *Hotel Casablanca*, Teodora de Molina 12 (℡95 215 10 19, ⓦwww .casablanca-gaucin.com; ❽ with breakfast; minimum 2 nights), near the main square, is a charming English-run place with garden, beautiful rooms and stunning views towards Africa. Another upmarket option is the *Hotel Rural Fructuosa*, c/Covento 67 (℡95 215 10 72, ⓦwww.lafructuosa.com; ❻ with breakfast) owned by the restaurant of the same name (see below). For longer stays you can rent one of the expats' houses from Adam Page, c/Lorenzo García 98 (℡95 215 10 93, ⓔadampage@avired.com). He may also be able to put you in touch with some delightful *casas particulares* and is a friendly source of local information.

Places to eat include, as well as the *Hostal Moncada*'s economical terrace restaurant, the equally cheap *Venta Pilar*, down some steps over the road opposite, flanking the swimming pool. Near the centre of the village, the pricier *La Fructuosa* offers delicious traditional cooking, and the nearby mid-priced *La Fuente*, on the main plaza, is also very good, has vegetarian options and operates an **Internet** café. *Venta Socorro*, on the main Ronda road, is another worthy choice and serves up a wide selection of tapas. Excellent tapas are also to be had at *Bar Paco-Pepe* on c/San Juan de Dios, near the centre of the village, which also serves meals.

You can reach Gaucín by **bus**, but perhaps more rewarding is the 13-kilometre walk from its **train station**, not served by buses. The station is actually at El Colmenar, and should you need to rest up before the hike (getting in for 3hr, mostly uphill) there are simple rooms and meals at *Bar-Restaurante Las Flores* (℡952 15 30 26; ❶) or, at the *Hotel Buitreras* (℡95 215 30 70, ⓦwww .hotelbuitreras.com; ❹) on the other side of the tracks. Moving upmarket, an inviting *hotel rural*, *Hacienda la Herriza* (℡95 106 82 00, ⓦwww.laherriza.com; ❼), lies halfway between El Colmenar and Gaucín and comprises a chalet complex in woodland with a pool and restaurant. Horse riding is one of numerous activities on offer. There are several bars along El Colmenar's main street fronting the station and among them *Café-Bar España* is another good place to eat with a *menú* for €7 and, behind *Las Flores*, *Rincon del Cani*, c/Ruiz Zorrilla 2, is another good little place popular with locals. *Las Flores* can also arrange a taxi to Gaucín (about €15) should you chicken out of the hike.

Benarrabá and around

Five kilometres beyond Gaucín a turn off the Ronda road leads to the village of **BENARRABÁ** sited amidst glorious wooded hill country. The very pleasant ⚘ *Hotel Rural Banu Rabbah* (℡95 215 02 88, ⓦwww.hbenarraba.es; ❹) here, adopting the village's original Moorish name, has balcony rooms with stunning views, pool and a decent restaurant and bar. In the village proper, *Bar Barroso*, near the Ayuntamiento, is noted for its **tapas**. Guy Hunter-Watts's book *Walking in Andalucía* (see "Books" in Contexts) has an eleven-kilometre circular **walk** from the hotel which takes in the picturesque hill village of Genalguacil. If you were using this as a staging post on a hiking route to Ronda, there's a useful overnight possibility at La Jimera de Libar (see p.202), from where Ronda is in striking distance.

A couple of kilometres along the A369 beyond the Benarrabá turn-off, a turn on the left (the A373) leads to the village of **ALGATOCÍN** where the attractive *Hotel-Camping Salitre* (☎95 211 70 05, ⓦwww.turismosalitre.com; ❺ with breakfast) is a complex of hotel and cabins in wooded surroundings, and offering all kinds of outdoor activities. Next door, the *Venta Valdivia* is renowned for its *conejo asado* (grilled rabbit) and is a hugely popular Sunday lunch venue.

Twenty kilometres further along the A369 and then the MA536 the village of **JUBRIQUE** is another attractive hill village sited in the midst of more picturesque *serranía* walking country. The main street, c/Algatocín, ascending to its heart has a couple of bars and the inviting *Hotel Taha Baja* (☎95 215 23 76; ❸) with restaurant, which would also serve as a good base.

Ronda

Rising amid a ring of dark, angular mountains, the full natural drama of **RONDA** is best appreciated as you enter the town. Built on an isolated ridge of the sierra, it's split in half by a gaping river gorge (El Tajo, though the river itself is the Guadalévin that drops sheer for 130m on three sides. Still more spectacular, the gorge is spanned by a stupendous eighteenth-century arched bridge, while tall whitewashed houses lean perilously from its precipitous edges.

Not surprisingly, this dramatic and dominant location attracted not only the early Celts, who named it Arunda, but Phoenicians and Greeks as well. Under Rome it became an important military bastion referred to by Pliny the Elder as Arunda Laus ("the glorious"). When the later Moors came to rule the roost here, Medina Runda was transformed and enlarged into the provincial capital of the Tarakuna district. Embellished with lavish mosques and palaces, the town ruled an independent and isolated **Moorish kingdom** until annexed by Sevilla in the mid-eleventh century. It then passed successively through the hands of the Almoravids, Almohads and Merinid Emirate of Morocco before ending up as a fief of Nasrid Granada in 1349. Only after a long and bitter struggle did the town finally fall to Fernando and Isabel in 1485.

Ronda is also notable for having been the birthplace of the **Maestranza**, an order of knights who laid down the rules for early bullfights performed on horseback. During the nineteenth century the town became an increasingly popular destination for Romantic travellers, and even today Ronda has sacrificed little of its enchanting character to the flow of day-trippers from the Costa del Sol, much of its attraction still lying in its extraordinary setting, or in simply walking down by the river, following one of the donkey tracks through the rich green valley. Bird-watchers should look out for the lesser kestrels, nesting in and launching themselves from the cliffs beneath the Alameda park, while, lower down, crag martins can be spotted.

Arrival, information and orientation

The **bus station** is in the north of the Mercadillo quarter on Plaza Redondo, while **trains** pull in a couple of blocks east on Avenida Andalucía (☎95 287 16

73). There's a RENFE office for tickets and timetables at c/Infante 20, near the Plaza del Socorro. Arriving by **car** your best bet is to park as far out as possible (near the train station is usually feasible) and walk to the centre, or head straight for one of the pay car parks (clearly signed).

At the northern end of the Plaza de España, Ronda's helpful and enthusiastic **Turismo** (Mon–Fri 9am–7.30pm, Sat & Sun 10am–2pm; ☎95 287 12 72) has maps and walking information on the Serranía de Ronda (see p.201) plus details of organizations offering guided walks. There's an equally helpful **Turismo Municipal** (Mon–Fri 9.30am–8pm, Sat & Sun 10am–2pm & 3–7pm) opposite the south side of the bullring.

Just north of the Plaza de España is the **Carrera Espinal**, Ronda's main pedestrianized thoroughfare and shopping area. It can be confusing walking around Ronda as many of the streets have **multiple names**: if in doubt, refer to as many maps as possible.

Accommodation

Many of the best **places to stay** in Ronda are in the heart of the Mercadillo quarter, and to the east of the Plaza del Socorro off c/Borrego and its continuations, c/Cristo and then c/Almendra. Upmarket accommodation was once concentrated around the Plaza de Toros, but a number of excellent small hotels have recently sprung up in other parts of the Mercadillo quarter as well as La Ciudad quarter, across the Tajo bridge. Prices increase sharply during Semana Santa and the *corrida goyesca* bullfight festival (usually the first week in Sept) but are otherwise reasonable.

Ronda's **campsite**, *Camping El Sur* (☎95 287 59 39, Ⓦ www.campingelsur .com), with swimming pool, bar and restaurant, lies 2km out of town along the road to Algeciras. You can rent **bungalows** here, too. It's not served by bus, so if you don't fancy the walk, take a taxi (approximately €8).

Budget

Hostal Águilar c/Naranja 28 ☎95 287 19 94. Friendly, family-run *hostal* for a/c rooms with bath and TV. Also has some simpler rooms sharing bath. ❶–❸

Hostal Andalucía c/Martínez Astein 19 ☎95 287 54 50. Pleasant rooms in leafy surroundings opposite the train station, all rooms en suite. ❷

Hostal González c/San Vicente de Paúl 3, east of the centre ☎95 287 14 45. Friendly, family *hostal* with impeccable rooms sharing bath. ❶

Hostal Ronda Sol c/Cristo 11 ☎95 287 44 97. Good-value budget *hostal* for rooms with shared bath, but check what you're offered as two interior rooms (lacking windows) are a bit claustrophobic. ❶

Hotel Arunda I carrera Espinel 120 ☎95 219 01 02, Ⓔ hotelesarunda2@serraniaderonda.com. Pleasant and good-value hotel with a/c rooms and its own garage. ❸

Hotel Arunda II c/José María Castelló Madrid 10 ☎95 287 25 19, Ⓔ hotelesarunda2@serraniader onda.com. Slightly more expensive offshoot of the above, this is equally good with a/c rooms near the train and bus stations. Plenty of parking space in own garage beneath hotel. ❸ with breakfast.

Hotel Colón c/Pozo 1 ☎95 287 43 78, Ⓔ hotelcolon@ronda.net. Charming small hotel with sparkling en-suite facilities and – in rooms 301 & 302 – your own spacious roof terrace. At the lower end of this price bracket. ❸

Hotel Morales c/Sevilla 51 ☎95 287 15 38, Ⓕ 95 218 70 02. Former *hostal* upgraded to a friendly small hotel where en-suite rooms come with TV and a/c. ❸

Hotel San Francisco c/María Cabrera (c/Prim on some maps) 18 ☎95 287 32 99, Ⓦ hotel sanfranciscoronda.com. Intimate small hotel with attractive a/c rooms and own *cafetería*. ❹ with breakfast.

Hotel Virgen de los Reyes c/Borrego 13 ☎95 287 11 40. Congenial two-star hotel offering good-value en-suite rooms with a/c and TV. ❸

🏃 **Los Pastores** 3km outside town along the Algeciras road (A369), on the right with a red sign ☎95 211 44 64, Ⓦ www.lospastores.com. Very pleasant rural option in a Dutch-owned former farmhouse surrounded by fine walking country and offering three en-suite doubles and two more-expensive apartments; breakfast available. ❹

RONDA

N

0   200 m

▲ Málaga & Arriate
▲ Marbella
▲ Algeciras & campsite
▼ Sevilla

ACCOMMODATION

Alavera de los Baños	D
En Frente Arte	E
Hostal Aguilar	C
Hostal Andalucía	D
Hostal González	K
Hostal Ronda Sol	I
Hostal Virgen del Rocío	N
Hotel Arunda I	J
Hotel Arunda II	L
Hotel Colón	M
Hotel Don Miguel	R
Hotel El Juncal	B
Hotel El Tajo	O

Hotel La Casona	H
Hotel La Española	U
Hotel Montelirio	W
Hotel Morales	Q
Hotel Polo	Z
Hotel Reina Victoria	X
Hotel San Francisco	P
Hotel San Gabriel	F
Hotel Virgen de los Reyes	S
Parador de Ronda	T
Pensión La Purisima	A
	G

RESTAURANTS

Alavera de los Baños	5
Bar Luciano	12
Bar-Restaurante Jerez	9
Bar-Restaurante Royal	2
Café-Bar Faustino	4
Casa Santa Pola	7
Don Miguel	6
Doña Pepa	10
Las Capeas	13
Parador de Ronda	1
Pizzeria Da Vinci	14
Restaurante del Escudero	3
Restaurante Las Bridas	8
Restaurante Pedro Romero	11
Tragabuches	

BARRIO PEÑAS
BARRIO PADRE JESÚS
LA CIUDAD
EL MERCADILLO
BARRIO DE SAN FRANCISCO

Train Station
Bus Station

Puente Nuevo
Puente Viejo
Puente de San Miguel
Plaza de Toros
Ayuntamiento
Sta. María la Mayor
Palacio de Mondragón
Museo del Bandolero
Museo Lara
Museo Joaquín Peinado
Alcázar
Puerta Almocábar
Iglesia del Espíritu Santo
Baños Árabes
Palacio del Marqués de Salvatierra
Minarete de S. Sebastián
Casa del Rey Moro
Casa Juan Bosco
Arco de Felipe V
Círculo de Artistas
Mirador El Campillo
Virgen de los Dolores
Posada de las Ánimas
Cvto. Madre de Dios
Ntro. Padre Jesús
Fuente de los 8 Caños
Palacio del Marqués de Parcent

Río Guadalevín
Arroyo de las Culebras

Pensión La Purísima c/Sevilla 10 ☎ 95 287 10 50. Family-run *pensión* with basic but comfortable rooms with and without bath. ②

Moderate to expensive

🏃 **Alavera de los Baños** c/San Miguel s/n ☎ 95 287 91 43, ⓦ www.andalucia .com/alavera. Enchanting, small hotel with compact but elegant rooms, garden, pool and restaurant. ⑥ with breakfast.

En Frente Arte c/Real 40 ☎ 95 287 90 88, ⓦ www.enfrentearte.com. Stylish hotel inside a restored mansion with distinctive and elegant rooms. Breakfast-brunch is included in the price as are self-service soft drinks and beer in the bar. Additional luxuries include a delightful garden pool and games room plus free sauna and Internet access. ⑤

Hotel Don Miguel c/Villanueva 8 ☎ 95 287 77 22, ⓦ www.dmiguel.com. New hotel with comfortable rooms overlooking the Tajo, and a highly recommended restaurant (see p.196). Garage. ⑥

Hotel El Juncal Carretera El Burgo Km1 ☎ 95 216 11 70, ⓦ www.eljuncal.com. Tranquil country hotel in its own grounds offering well-appointed rooms, furnished in contemporary style, and with an excellent garden pool. ⑦

Hotel El Tajo c/Cruz Verde 7 ☎ 95 287 40 40, ⓦ www.hoteleltajo.com. Pleasant traditional hotel with a/c rooms with satellite TV, its own economical restaurant, and a garage. ④

Hotel La Casona c/Marqués de Salvatierra 5 ☎ 95 287 95 95, ⓦ www.lacasonadelaciudad.com. A La Ciudad hotel housed in yet another elegant mansion with all the fittings and fixtures of a four-star hotel: a/c rooms with minibar and safe, plus garden and pool. ⑥

Hotel La Española c/José Aparicio 3, near the Turismo ☎ 95 287 10 52, ⓦ www.ronda.net/usuar /laespanola. Beloved old *fonda* refurbished, reborn (and re-priced) as an attractive small hotel with comfortable if compact rooms, some of which have amazing views towards the Serranía de Ronda. ⑤

Hotel Montelirio c/Tenorio 8 ☎ 95 287 38 55, ⓦ www.hotelmontelirio.com. Spectacularly sited on the edge of the Tajo, this luxury four-star hotel occupies a tastefully renovated *casa palacio* where well-equipped rooms have stunning views. It also manages to squeeze in a small pool and a very good restaurant, the *Albacara*. ⑧

Hotel Polo c/Mariano Soubiron (c/Benitez on some maps) 8 ☎ 95 287 24 47, ⓕ 95 287 24 49. This long-established hotel has stylishly renovated rooms with sparkling bathrooms and elegant fittings. Garage. ⑥

🏃 **Hotel Reina Victoria** c/Jerez 25 ☎ 95 287 12 40, ⓦ www.husa.es. Nineteenth-century retreat for British military visitors from Gibraltar which, although refurbished (and now part of the Husa chain), has a lingering air of decaying grandeur. Ask for one of the corner rooms with a spectacular view over the Serranía de Ronda. Facilities include a pool, gardens and parking. ⑦

🏃 **Hotel San Gabriel** c/José Holgado 19 ☎ 95 219 03 92, ⓦ www.hotelsangabriel. com. Stunning restoration of an eighteenth-century mansion, with beautifully furnished a/c rooms, a billiard room and friendly proprietors. ⑥

Parador de Ronda Plaza de España ☎ 95 287 75 00, ⓦ www.paradores.es. This imposing and relatively new parador teetering on the edge of the Tajo is Ronda's flagship hotel, a superb and tasteful building with luxurious accommodation, pool, terrace bar, restaurant and garage. ⑧

The Town

The town divides into three parts: on the northwest side of the gorge is the largely modern **Mercadillo** quarter, while across the bridge is the old, mazelike Moorish town, **La Ciudad**, and its **San Francisco** suburb. The late eighteenth-century **Puente Nuevo** bridge spans the gorge between them and allows you the chance to peer down the walls of limestone rock into the yawning Tajo and the Río Guadalvín, far below. The bridge has its own **Centro de Información** (Mon–Fri 10am–7pm; €2), housed in a former prison above the central arch, with exhibits documenting the story of its construction and history. Hemingway, in *For Whom the Bell Tolls*, recorded how prisoners were thrown from the bridge to their deaths. Today the bridge and the gorge provide a habitat for a large flock of **chough** (members of the crow family) who glide around the rock cliffs seeking perches.

Casa Del Rey Moro to the Baños Árabes

Crossing the Puente Nuevo into La Ciudad brings you to the somewhat arbitrarily named **Casa del Rey Moro** (House of the Moorish King; daily

Pedro Romero: father of the corrida

Born in Ronda in 1754, Pedro Romero is the father of the modern **bullfight**; previously bulls had been killed only on horseback with a *rejón* or spear, as a patrician pastime. However, Romero was not the first to fight bulls on foot: legend has it that this accolade goes to his grandfather Francisco Romero, who leapt into the ring when an aristocrat had been dismounted by a bull and began to distract it with his hat, delighting the crowd in the process. The hat was changed for the red *muleta*, or cape, and the bullfight was born. Once the *corrida* had been created however, it was Pedro Romero who laid down the pattern for all future contests with his passes and moves, many still in use today, along with the invention of the almost mystical *arte* – the union of animal and man in a form of ballet. In the newly constructed Ronda ring, Romero killed over 5000 bulls and fought into his eighties, passing on to his students his soberly classical Ronda style, which is markedly different from the more flamboyant styles of Sevilla and Córdoba. A statue honouring Romero stands in the Alameda del Tajo.

10am–7pm; €4), an early eighteenth-century mansion built on Moorish foundations, on c/Marqués de Parada (aka c/Santo Domingo). Local legend has it that this was the palace of the Moorish emir Badis, an Arabian Bluebeard, who was reputed to drink his wine from the skulls of the victims he beheaded. From the house a remarkable underground stairway (the Mina) descends to the river at the foot of the Tajo; these 365 steps, guaranteeing a water supply in times of siege, were cut by Christian slaves in the fourteenth century. There's a viewing balcony at the bottom where you can admire the towering walls of rock and the gorge's birdlife but the long climb back up will probably make you wonder if it was worth the stiff entry fee.

Further down the same street is the **Palacio del Marqués de Salvatierra**, a splendid Renaissance mansion with an oddly primitive, half-grotesque frieze of Adam and Eve on its portal together with the colonial images of four Peruvian Indians; the house is still used by the family. Just down the hill you reach the two old town bridges – the **Puente Viejo** of 1616 and the fourteenth-century single-span Moorish **Puente de San Miguel** and nearby, on the southeast bank of the river, are the distinctive hump-shaped cupolas and bizarre glass roof-windows of the refurbished **Baños Árabes** (Mon–Fri 10am–7pm, Sat & Sun 10am–3pm; €2, Sun free). Dating from the thirteenth century and wonderfully preserved, these are truly remarkable structures, with star-shaped windows set in a barrel-vaulted ceiling and beautiful octagonal brick columns supporting horseshoe arches. A channel from the nearby river fed the water into the bath house complex which was formerly surrounded by plant-filled gardens.

Santa María La Mayor and around

At the centre of La Ciudad in Ronda's most picturesque square stands the cathedral church of **Santa María La Mayor** (daily 10am–7pm; €2), originally the Moorish town's Friday Mosque. Externally it's a graceful combination of Moorish, Gothic and Renaissance styles with the belfry built on top of the old minaret. Inside, the church itself is sombre and dull but you can see an arch covered with Arabic calligraphy, and, in front of the current street door, a part of the old Arab *mihrab*, or prayer niche. A little east of the church along the Callejón de los Tramposos stands the **Minarete de San Sebastián**, a tower that survives from a fourteenth-century mosque. Close by and to the rear of the cathedral on Plaza del Gigante, **Museo Joaquín Peinado** (Mon–Sat 10am–2pm & 4–7pm, Sun 10am–2pm; €3) displays the works – influenced by Cézanne and Picasso – of *rondeño* artist Joaquín Peinado. The museum is housed in the Palacio de Moctezuma, a former mansion with two fine patios.

A short distance west from Santa María La Mayor is the most important of Ronda's palaces, the fourteenth-century **Palacio de Mondragón** (Mon–Fri 10am–7pm, Sat & Sun 10am–3pm; €2) on the plaza of the same name. Probably the real palace of the Moorish kings, following the *Reconquista* it was much altered in order to accommodate Fernando and Isabel. Inside, three of the patios preserve original stuccowork and mosaics and there's a magnificent carved wood ceiling; the palace also houses a **museum** covering local archeology and aspects of Moorish Ronda, in particular burial practices relating to the recently discovered cemetery outside the walls (see below). From a restored Mudéjar courtyard there's a fine **view** over the Tajo towards the Serranía de Ronda.

Just north of here at **Casa Juan Bosco** (daily 9am–5.30pm; €1), c/Tenorio 20, you can visit a nineteenth-century mansion stuffed full of heavy mahogany furniture. The house itself is dull and oppressive, but the reconstructed Mudéjar gardens with fountain and mosaics are a delight, offering more great views over the Tajo.

Heading south on c/Armiñan, which bisects La Ciudad, on the left at no. 29 you'll find the **Museo Lara** (daily 11am–7pm; €2.50), containing the eclectic lifetime collection of *rondeño* Juan Antonio Lara, a member of the family who own and run the local bus company of the same name. An avid collector since childhood, Señor Lara has filled the extensive museum with a fascinating collection of antique clocks, pistols and armaments, musical instruments and archeological finds, as well as early cameras and cinematographic equipment. Further along at no. 65, the **Museo del Bandolero** (daily 10.30am–7pm; €3) is largely devoted to celebrating the Serranía's illustrious, mainly nineteenth-century bandits and includes displays of their weapons as well as tableaux and audiovisual presentations. Further along the same street, near the southern end of La Ciudad, are the ruins of the **Alcázar**, once impregnable until razed by the French in 1809 and now partially occupied by a school.

Continuing downhill along c/Armiñan you'll pass the sixteenth-century **Iglesia del Espíritu Santo** (Mon–Sat 10am–1.30pm and 3.30–6pm; €1) with a fine interior, en route to the town's principal Moorish gate, the magnificent **Puerta de Almocábar** leading into the Barrio San Francisco. Deriving from the Arabic *al maqabir* (cemetery) it would have led to the burial grounds which – following the Roman practice – were always located outside the walls. In 1485, the Christian conquerors, led by Fernando, passed through this gate to claim the town. The adjoining arch of **Puerta de Carlos V** was constructed during the reign of Fernando successor, the Habsburg emperor.

El Mercadillo, the Plaza de Toros and Carrera Espinel

When Ronda was retaken from the Moors in 1485, the impoverished governors imposed such heavy taxes on all goods and foodstuffs entering it that the merchants set up their own quarter outside La Ciudad to avoid paying them. This area, **El Mercadillo**, has effectively become the centre of the modern town, and is currently undergoing a prolonged face-lift after years of neglect. Many buildings in and around the focal Plaza de España have undergone renovation, among which is a stylish new parador – the former Ayuntamiento – overlooking the Tajo (see "Accommodation"). A newly constructed path, the **Paseo Blas Infante** at the rear of the parador, can be followed along the edge

△ Ronda's Plaza de Toros

of the Tajo northwards to the Alameda and the *Hotel Reina Victoria* and offers fine **views** towards the Serranía de Ronda.

The *barrio*'s major monument has to be the **Plaza de Toros** (daily 10am–8pm; €5), to the north of the Plaza de España, the oldest, one of the largest and certainly the most venerated bullring in Spain. Opened in 1785, it became the stage upon which the father of the modern bullfight, Pedro Romero, laid down the rules of fighting bulls on foot (see box on p.192). Once you've passed through the elaborate Baroque doorway, it's possible to wander around the arena with its unusual stone barriers and an elegant double tier of seats supported by stone columns. The **museum** gives an illuminating history of the *corrida* or bullfight; besides posters advertising the first *corrida* held here on May 19, 1785, and Pedro Romero's *traje de luces* ("suit of lights"), there are photos of Hemingway and Orson Welles, two regular visitors. Welles's last wish was to have his ashes buried in Ronda and they are now interred on the nearby estate of his friend and one of Spain's greatest *toreros*, the *rondeño* Antonio Ordóñez, whose bronze statue (alongside that of his father) stands near the bullring's Puerta Grande. The artist Goya made a number of paintings here of the *matadores* in action, and each September in a tribute to Goya and Romero the *corrida goyesca* is staged, with fighters garbed in eighteenth-century-style gear similar to those in the paintings.

Along the pedestrianized **carrera Espinel**, the *barrio*'s main thoroughfare, are a number of interesting señorial mansions including, at no. 4, a particularly elegant one now irreverently transformed into a mundane electrical shop. Slightly further along on the right, a shop, Cipriano Ruíz, carrera Espinel 18, sells photos by Ronda's renowned photographer, **Miguel Martín**, who died in 1999 and whose studio (at no. 1) used to be on the opposite side of the street.

He captured the town on film throughout the twentieth-century and also photographed many famous visitors, including film stars and *toreros*, writers such as Hemingway and, more recently, Madonna.

A little way down the same street, picturesque **Plaza del Socorro** opens to the left. Recently pedestrianized it has become a favourite spot with *rondeños*, especially on summer nights, when they gather to chat on the terraces of the numerous bars and restaurants. The northern end is overlooked by the **Círculo de Artistas**, a fine eighteenth-century *casa señorial* mansion and now superbly restored as the town's casino. The doorman will usually not object to you stepping inside to view the building's delightful patio.

Around the Alameda del Tajo

To the north of the Plaza de Toros lies the **Alameda del Tajo**, a pleasant park completed in the early nineteenth century with views towards the Serranía de Ronda. The garden is said to have been laid out at no cost to the local council, the funds raised by fines on those using "obscene language in public, thereby causing a scandal". Continuing in the same direction will bring you to the Carmelite **Convento de la Merced** on Plaza de la Merced, its doors flanked by two great palms. Beyond a doorway at the end of the short street to the left of the church, the nuns sell their *dulces* (mornings and after 5pm): *pan rondeño* and *magdalenas* are two of their specialities.

You could continue along Avenida Fleming (aka c/Jerez) to the **Hotel Reina Victoria**, built by an English company in the first decade of the last century to house British visitors, many of whom came from the military base at Gibraltar. The Austrian poet Rainer Maria Rilke put up here in 1913, and his room (no. 208) – complete with his fascinating framed hotel bill – has been preserved as a museum which the management will allow you to view on request. The hotel's bar has a terrace with stunning views down the Guadiaro river valley to the distant Serranía.

Finally, a couple of blocks in from the Plaza de España is the remarkably preserved inn where Miguel Cervantes once slept, the sixteenth-century **Posada de las Ánimas** (Inn of Souls) on c/Los Vicentes. Today, although this is officially the town's Hogar del Pensionista, or old people's home, the building looks every bit the ancient inn, with a skull and crossbones carved in the keystone above the door, which may have something to do with the building's name. The elderly residents are only too happy to let you see inside. Nearby, the eighteenth-century **Virgen de los Dolores** in the street of the same name is a chapel with a curious porch projecting into the street. Carved on the porch's pillars are some weird, bird-like creatures, as well as others that are part beast, part human, with ropes fastened around their necks. The site of the church was formerly a gallows for condemned prisoners and this strange imagery may be connected with the representation of these unfortunates.

Eating, drinking and nightlife

A great many of Ronda's best **eating and drinking** options are on or around pedestrianized Plaza del Socorro. There are numerous good places for breakfast along carrera Espinel, and a couple of good restaurants in La Ciudad. For **tapas** aficionados there are plenty of quality places to try out. Don't forget to try Ronda's excellent **red wines** from the Cortijo de las Monjas (see p.198), which are served at most of the restaurants opposite. **Nightlife** tends to be provincial and low key, but with a little persistence and luck you may catch some memorable flamenco.

Restaurants

Alavera de los Baños c/San Miguel s/n. Pleasant riverside location for the mid-priced restaurant of the hotel of the same name. A wide range of dishes on offer includes some Moroccan specialities such as *tagine de cordero* (lamb with pears).

Bar Luciano c/Armiñan 42. Pleasant bar-restaurant with a good-value *menú* for around €8.

Bar-Restaurante Jerez Plaza del Teniente Arce. Terraced restaurant, flanking the bullring, serving reasonable *raciones* and *platos combinados*.

Bar-Restaurante Royal c/Virgen de la Paz 42. Good-value tapas bar and restaurant with a €7 *menú*. Some terrace tables front the park.

Café-Bar Faustino c/Santa Cecilia 4. Excellent, economical and atmospheric tapas, *raciones* and *platos combinados* bar that keeps serving till 1am.

Casa Santa Pola c/Santo Domingo 3 ☎95 287 92 08. Impressive restaurant in a former *casa señorial* containing bits of the ninth-century house that preceded it. Spread over three floors, with views over the Tajo, it offers a wide range of local dishes – speciality is *carnes asados* (roasted meats) – and there's a *menú del dia* for €18. On Fri and Sat evenings there's flamenco at 9.30pm.

Don Miguel *Hotel Don Miguel*, Plaza de España ☎95 287 77 22. One of the best restaurants in town, with *rondeño* specialities such as *perdiz estofado* (partridge stew) on the à la carte menu; their unimaginative *menú del dia* for €15.50 is less exciting. The main attraction, though, is the terrace, offering a marvellous view of the Tajo.

Doña Pepa Plaza del Socorro. Decent, family-run restaurant with, on the opposite side of the intervening Pasaje Correos, a separate café-bar serving *bocadillos* and freshly squeezed orange juice.

Las Capeas c/Virgen de la Paz 38. Excellent, inexpensive and friendly little restaurant with strong bullfighting connections (*capea* refers to the bullfighter's cape); well-prepared *platos combinados* and a *menú* for €6.60.

Parador de Ronda Plaza de España. The parador's restaurant has an excellent choice of local and regional dishes such as *perdiz en jugo de naranja* (partridge with orange sauce) and *rabo de toro* (oxtail), many of them appearing on a *menú gastronomico* for around €27.

Pizzería Da Vinci c/Santa Cecilia 1. Range of authentic pizzas (€6–8) and pasta dishes with plenty of vegetarian options.

Restaurante del Escudero Paseo de Blas Infante 1 ☎95 287 13 67. Superb restaurant housed in an elegant mansion with Ronda's best garden terrace offering views towards the Serranía de Ronda. The same proprietors own the *Tragabuches* (see below) but prices here are a good deal more palatable and there's a *menú* for around €15.

Restaurante Las Bridas c/Los Remedios 18. Simple but wholesome home cooking served in a charming patio dating from 1728 (as an engraved stone informs you); *menú* for around €7.

Restaurante Pedro Romero c/Virgen de la Paz 18 ☎95 287 11 10. Excellent, mid-priced restaurant that's a favourite with locals. In winter dining is in the interior rooms surrounded by bullfighting memorabilia *Migas a la rondeña* and *rabo de toro* are two of the signature dishes here, and there's also an economical *menú* for around €16.

Tragabuches c/José Aparicio 1 ☎95 219 02 91. Ronda's most stylish restaurant is named after a celebrated eighteenth-century *rondeño* bullfighter-turned-bandit, and, with an adventurous menu and restrained décor, is worth a splurge. However, with a somewhat unjustifiable price tag of €74, the *menú de degustación* is one of the most expensive in Andalucía. Booking advised. Closed Sun eve & Mon.

Tapas bars

Bar Faustino c/Santa Cecilia 4, off Plaza de Carmen Abuela. Lively place for good-value tapas, *raciónes* and *platos combinados* that stays open until well beyond midnight and has an open-air patio. Closed Mon.

Bodega San Francisco Plaza Ruedo Alameda, close to the Puerta de Carlos V in the Barrio San Francisco. Good tapas bar in this atmospheric *barrio*. The nearby *Casa María* and *Bar Almocábar* across the plaza are also worth a try.

Casa Mateos c/Jerez 6, around the corner from the *Hotel Colón*. Efficient *marisquería* and tapas bar with plenty of seafood possibilities as well as good *jamón* and *queso*.

Casa Romero c/Ríos Rosas 16, south of Plaza del Socorro. Popular tapas and *raciones* bar which also serves *platos combinados*. House specials include *gambas al pil pil* (shrimps with garlic) and *pulpo* (octopus).

El Portón c/Pedro Romero 7, off the west side of Plaza del Socorro. Favourite haunt of bullfighting aficionados; does good *jamón* and *cazón* (shark) tapas and serves an inexpensive *menú*.

La Farola Plaza Carmen Abela 9. Good bar whose specials include *berenejas rebozadas* (aubergine) and *patatas rellenas* (stuffed potatoes).

Patatín Patatán c/Borrego 7, off the east side of Plaza del Socorro. Popular tapas bar with a wide range of specials including *conejo en salsa* (rabbit) and *habas a la rondeña* (broad beans). *La Viña*, next door at no. 9, is also good.

Cafeterías, breakfast bars and heladerías

Bar Relax c/Los Remedios 27. Vegetarian bar-cafetería run by a couple of ex-pat English *señoritas* with a good atmosphere both day and night, and their vegetarian tapas even pass muster with the locals. Salads, juices, fresh soups and a range of vegetarian dishes are on offer, and they throw in some tasty nachos on the house when you buy a jug of one of their cocktails.

Café Alba carrera Espinel 44. Piping hot *churros* and delicious breakfast coffee. If this popular place is too packed, the nearby *Cafetería La Ibense* is a good alternative.

Café de Indias c/Virgen de la Paz 3. Relaxing café serving a variety of coffees, pastries and sweet rolls.

Casino Plaza del Socorro. Housed in the corner of the casino with a pleasant terrace, this is another good place for breakfast snacks.

El Molino c/Molino 6, just north of Plaza del Socorro. Good and friendly place for breakfast croissants and *platos combinados* later in the day; there's a *menú* for around €7.

Rico carrera Espinel 42, south side of the Plaza del Socorro. Nicest *heladería* in town – also good for afternoon tea and, in winter, steaming cups of hot chocolate.

Salon de Té Al-Zahra c/Las Tiendas 19, slightly west of Plaza Carmen Abela. Pleasant Moroccan-style tearoom offering over a hundred different teas and tasty *pasteles* to go with them. Try the *Tunecino* Arab tea or the *Marroqui*. Open 4pm till late.

Sport-Bar Huskies c/Molino, near Plaza del Socorro. Busy small bar where fans gather to watch crucial football games on a huge TV screen.

Nightlife

El Choque Ideal c/Espiritu Santo 9, close to the Puerta de Almocábar. An "arty" bar staging exhibitions plus frequent musical and literary events. The view towards the Serranía de Ronda through panoramic windows is wonderful. Also serves food including economical *bocadillos*. Open till late.

El Grifo c/Virgen de los Remedios 4, near Plaza del Socorro. Stylish late-night drinking bar for cocktails and long drinks, staying open into the small hours.

El Templo c/Jerez 6. Central and popular bar-discoteca with a jazz, rock and folk playlist; shows music videos and occasionally stages live bands. Late 20s-plus age group.

Flamenco at the Museo Lara c/Armiñan 29 ☎95 287 12 63. The atmospheric small theatre in the basement of the museum stages performances (Thurs–Sat, April–Sept; 9.30pm) by the company of celebrated dancer Rocío Vázquez who has a flamenco school in Ronda. Tickets cost €23 which includes a drink and a *tapa*.

Kopas c/Rios Rosas 9, off Plaza Carmen Abela. Relaxed dancing and cocktails club for 30-plusers.

Peña Flamenco Tobalo Plaza los Descalzos ☎95 287 41 77. Housed in the *Bar la Plazuela*, the *peña* puts on live flamenco most Friday nights (not July or August) and welcomes visitors. Ring the night before if possible to save yourself a wasted journey.

Pub Baco c/Molino, at the north corner of Plaza del Socorro. Lively music bar popular with a younger crowd. *Rilke*, c/Cabrera Prim, *Feu*, c/Naranja, and *Siglo XXI*, Plaza Carmen Abela, are similar places nearby.

Listings

Bus companies The following companies operate out of the Ronda bus station: Comes (☎95 287 19 92; Arcos de la Frontera, Jerez & Cádiz), Lara (☎95 287 22 60; Serranía de Ronda villages), Portillo (☎902 14 31 44; Málaga & Costa del Sol resorts), Sierra de las Nieves (☎95 287 54 35; Málaga & Setenil).

Car rental Velasco, c/Borrego 11 ☎95 287 27 82, ⓔrentacarvelasco@terra.es.

Flamenco Ronda has a renowned flamenco school, Escuela Flamenco Pilar Becerra, c/María Cabrera s/n (☎95 287 64 80, ⓦwww .turismoderonda.es), and courses are available for Spanish and non-Spanish speakers, Oct–June.

Internet access *El Molino*, c/Molino 6; *Central Cibercafe*, c/Remedios 26; and *Cafetería Ciber*

Arunda, Avda. Ricardo Navarrete, near the train station.

Maps and equipment Hiking maps of the Serranía de Ronda and Grazalema are available from Comansur, c/Lauria 30 near the bus station and Librería Dumas, c/Jerez 8, near the Plaza de la Merced. Intersport, c/Molino 8 (opposite the *Hotel Polo*), stocks a range of outdoor clothing and walking boots.

Laundry Pressto, c/Mariano Soubirón 17, near the *Hotel Polo*, will wash, dry and fold up to 5kg of clothes on the same day for €9.

Newspapers A variety of foreign newspapers are available from c/Mariano Souviron 5, north of the Plaza del Socorro), who also have fax machines and international phones. *Ronda Semanal* is the town's weekly paper and useful for local news and entertainment.

Outdoor activities Rondanatural, Dolores Iburri 4 (☎95 287 34 96, ⓦwww.rondanatural.com) offer all kinds of outdoor activities in and around Ronda including guided hikes, mountain biking, canoeing, canyoning, and caving. Daily bird-spotting trips (six hours; €34) in the Serranía for beginners and experienced birders are offered by Ornironda (mobile ☎616891359, ⓦwww.spanishbirds.com).

Post office Virgen de la Paz 20, near the Plaza de Toros (Mon–Sat 9am–2pm).

Tours Tajotour makes minibus tours of the Tajo, leaving hourly from the Plaza de España (45min; €10; ☎95 287 75 32).

Around Ronda

Ronda makes an excellent base for exploring the superb countryside in the immediate vicinity or for visiting more of the White Towns, one of the most unusual of which is **Setenil de las Bodegas**, 15km away, with curious cave-like streets. Closer to Ronda lies **Arriate**, famous for its bell-ringers, and the **Cortijo de las Monjas**, the only vineyard in Andalucía producing top-drawer red wines. If you're attracted by ancient ruins and awesome caves don't miss Ronda's Roman predecessor **Ronda La Vieja** or the **Cueva de la Pileta** whose remarkable Stone Age cave paintings are unique on the peninsula. To the west are the temptingly scenic villages of **Benaoján** and **Montejaque**, ringed by rugged limestone heights that hold numerous underground caverns such as the Cueva del Gato, a magnet for cavers.

Arriate and Cortijo de las Monjas

Eight kilometres north of Ronda along the A367, across a plain of olive groves, is the pleasant village of **ARRIATE**. Its fame stems from the Campañeros de la Aurora (Bell-ringers of the Dawn), who rise at dawn every Saturday and tour the streets until 7am singing hymns to the accompaniment of bells, guitars and cymbals. Pausing at the doors of houses who have "pre-booked" numbers from the repertoire, their *salves*, which last ten minutes, cost the most, or they offer a quick cheap blast called a *Pater Noster*. You can get en-suite **rooms** at *Pensión El Chozo*, Avenida Andalucía s/n (☎95 216 53 44; ❷), or there's a pleasant country villa sleeping two with garden and barbecue that can be rented (☎95 216 62 47). The village is served by two daily **trains** to and from Ronda; the station lies on the southern edge of the village.

Three kilometres beyond Arriate along the Setenil road (MA429), a dirt track signed on the right leads to the unique **Cortijo de las Monjas** (currently closed for visits; check with the Ronda tourist offices), a vineyard producing something long believed to be impossible in this climate: a red wine worthy of comparison with the great wines of the north. The vineyard was founded in 1990 by the late Costa del Sol socialite Prince Alfonso Hohenlohe, and French experts were hired to advise on the planting of Gallic vines in the Serranía de Ronda which, with its cold winters and temperate summers, was judged the ideal terrain. The first vintages were favourably received by Spain's wine pundits and the 1995 was so good that it was snapped up within weeks of going on sale. The wines – sold under the Príncipe Alfonso label – are on sale in Ronda at Super Marquez, carrera Espinel 13, or the even better Jamonería Berrocal, further up the same street at no. 112, which stocks some of Las Monjas' rarer vintages as well as Andalucía's best *jamones*.

Setenil de las Bodegas

Seven kilometres north beyond the vineyard turn, **SETENIL DE LAS BODEGAS** is the strangest of all the White Towns, its cave-like streets formed

Walking around Ronda

Walks around Ronda are almost limitless. One of the best is to take the path down to the gorge from the Mondragón palace terrace. In the fields below there's a network of paths and some stupendous views, but look out for several ferocious dogs. One path leads to the **Ermita de la Virgen de la Cabeza**, an ancient and ruined hermitage, and nearby is the **Casa de la Virgen de la Cabeza** where the English artist David Bomberg lived in the 1950s. His dramatic paintings of Ronda and Toledo are now recognized as some of the finest Spanish landscapes. From here, a couple of hours' walk brings you to the main road to the northwest where you can hitch or walk back the 4–5km into El Mercadillo.

from the overhanging ledge of a gorge carved through the tufa rock by the Río Trejo. Many of the houses – sometimes two or three storeys high – have natural roofs in the rock that, in places, block out the sky completely. This was once a major wine-producing centre, since the caves made good wine cellars (bodegas); hence the latter part of the town's name. The phylloxera plague of the nineteenth century destroyed the vines, however, and brought economic ruin in its wake, from which Setenil has only in recent times recovered.

Other sights in Setenil are limited, but if you can get into the church of **La Encarnación** (ask the neighbours or contact the tourist office) – a sixteenth-century Gothic structure – you'll see a fine, twelve-panelled Flemish painting that survived Civil War devastation. The ruins of the nearby Moorish **castillo** are worth a look too, and below the church, the sixteenth-century **Ayuntamiento**, now serving as the **tourist office** (Tues–Sun 10am–2pm & 6–8pm; ☎956 13 42 61, ⓦwww.setenil.com) has a superb Mudéjar *artesonado* ceiling with an inscription dating from September 21, 1484 – the day Isabel and Fernando captured the town. They achieved this triumph only after seven previous attempts (*septem nihil* – seven times nothing) had failed, giving origin to the first half of Setenil's name today.

Good **places to eat** include *El Mirador*, through an arch and uphill from the tourist office with a €7 *menú* and great views, *Bar-Restaurante Dominguez* on the focal Plaza de Andalucía with a pleasant terrace and *Bar-Restaurante Las Flores*, Avda. del Carmen 24, near the river at the opposite end of the town from the church, with more views. To stay, there's also a decent **hotel**, *El Almendral* (☎956 13 40 29, ⓦwww.tugasa.com; ④), on the road just outside town, with a good restaurant downstairs.

Without your own car, the only **public transport** to Setenil is the infrequent bus service from Ronda (Setenil train station is 8km out of the village). Once here it's possible to **walk** the 8km to the ruins of Ronda La Vieja (see below) via the hamlets of Campiña and Venta de Leche.

Ronda La Vieja

Some 12km northwest of Ronda are the ruins of **RONDA LA VIEJA**, the first-century Roman town of Acinipo, set in the midst of beautiful hill country. The ruins (Tues–Sun 9am–5pm; Aug closes 3pm) are reached by turning right (along the MA449) 6km down the main road to Arcos/Sevilla, and following the signs to a farmhouse, where the friendly farmer will present you with a plan (in Spanish) and record your nationality for statistical purposes. Entry to the site, which sprawls away up the hill to the west, is free.

Based on Neolithic foundations, and also an outpost of the Phoenicians, Acinipo reached its zenith in the first century AD as a Roman town. The piles of stones interspersed with small fragments of glittering marble strewn across the hillside once constituted the forum, baths, temples and other edifices of this prosperous agricultural centre, which also had access to iron ore, marble, good building stone and fine potters' clay in close proximity.

Today only an impressive **Roman theatre** – of which just the stage backdrop and some seating survives – alludes to the importance of Acinipo; inscriptions found here tell of crowds flocking to see the chariot races. Immediately west of the theatre, the ground falls away in a startlingly steep escarpment and from here there are fine **views** towards the hill village of Olvera to the north (see p.207). For reasons not entirely clear, Acinipo declined in the third century and, in the fourth, ceded its power in the area to nearby Arunda (modern Ronda). On your way out take a look at the foundations of some recently discovered prehistoric stone huts beside the farmhouse. From here a track leads off towards Setenil de las Bodegas (see p.198).

Cueva de la Pileta

Probably the most interesting trip out from Ronda is to the prehistoric **Cueva de la Pileta** (daily 10am–1pm & 4–6pm; hourly guided tours; final tours leave at 1pm & 6pm; €6.50), set in a deep valley and surrounded by a spectacular wall of white rock. These fabulous caverns, with their remarkable **Paleolithic paintings**, were discovered by a local farmer in 1905 when hunting for guano fertilizer for his fields, and are still supervised by the same family, the Bullóns, one of whom will be your guide. After the usual jokes, as various "cauliflowers", "castles" and a "Venus de Milo" are pointed out among the stalactites and stalagmites en route, the paintings in the depths of the caves, when you reach them, are genuinely awe-inspiring, particularly those in the central chamber.

Etched in charcoal, and red and yellow ochres, they depict an abundance of wildlife including fish, the *cabra hispanica* and a pregnant mare, all painted on walls which bear the scorch marks of ancient fires. Other abstract signs and symbols have been interpreted as having some magical or ritual purpose. The occupation of the caves, and the earliest red paintings, dates from about 25,000 BC, thus predating the more famous caves at Altamira in northern Spain, down to the end of the Bronze Age. The section of the caves (and paintings) open to view is only a small part of a more massive subterranean labyrinth, and archeologists will be kept busy for many years to come documenting this Paleolithic art gallery.

Cave practicalities

To reach the caves **with your own transport,** take the A376 Arcos/Sevilla road northwest from Ronda, turning left after 14km along the MA505 to Montejaque; the caves are a further 12km from the turn-off, beyond Benaoján. By **public transport**, take an Algeciras-bound local train (4 daily; 20min) to the Estación Benaoján-Montejaque; or a bus, which drops you a little closer, in Benaoján. There's a bar at the train station where you can stock up on drink before the hour-and-a-half long (6km) **walk** to the caves. Follow the farm track from the right bank of the river until you reach the farmhouse (approximately 30min). From here a track goes straight uphill to the main road just before the signposted turning for the caves. Alternatively, you could take a taxi from Ronda for around €45 – get the Turismo to arrange the fare – though renting a car for a day could work out cheaper (see "Listings", p.197). Upon arrival wait at the cave entrance; to protect the cave and its paintings a strict **maximum of twenty-five persons** is allowed on each tour and groups larger than four should book ahead (☎95 216 73 43; also useful for confirming opening times). Tours are in Spanish (though the guide may speak some English), and last one hour on average. No photography is allowed in the cave and if you leave your vehicle at the car park, make sure to remove any valuables not locked in a secure boot. And finally, remember to bring a sweater as it can get chilly in the subterranean caverns.

Benaoján, Montejaque and the Cueva del Gato

North of the Cueva de la Pileta the village of **BENAOJÁN** is worth a visit, with a sixteenth-century church built on the site of an earlier mosque (this was a Moorish stronghold well into Christian times). The most central **place to stay** in the village is the upmarket *Molino del Santo*, Bda. Estación (☎95 216 71 51, ⑩www.andalucia.com/molino; ⑨, half-board obligatory in high season), a British-run haven with gardens and pool. A friendly budget alternative is available at the train station where *Albergue La Ermita*, Bda. Estación s/n (☎95 216 75 20; ①) has good-value en-suite rooms. Pricey restaurant **food** is available at the *Molino del Santo*, or the central *Bar Tajillas* has tasty tapas. One place definitely worth seeking out is ✻ *Restaurante El Muelle*, actually on the platform at the train station, 300m out of the village on the Ronda road; dishes include *carnes al horno de lleña* (charcoal grilled meats).

MONTEJAQUE, 3km northeast and cradled between two rocky crags, is also worth a stop, possessing a great, typically Spanish square – with its own

The Serranía de Ronda

Starkly beautiful and offering some of the best walking terrain in Andalucía, the **Serranía de Ronda** is a region of great natural diversity where wooded ravines, awesome crags and vast forests of cork oaks provide abundant habitats for a rich variety of flora and fauna. The remote hamlets are reachable by road, albeit often with difficulty, but the ideal way to travel this region is with a backpack and compass, from which perspective the landscape – with whitewashed villages set among cherry orchards and vines – becomes an enchanting adventure. Both the Ronda tourist offices should have details on the villages and limited accommodation available.

The heart of the Serranía can be reached by a daily **bus** from Ronda operated by Autobuses Lara (Mon–Fri 2.30pm, returning early morning), passing the villages of Parauta, Cartajima, Juzcar (with the comfortable *Hotel del Arriero* ☎952 18 36 60; ③), Igualeja, Pujerra, Alpandeire and Farajan. There's also a very pleasant five-hour **walking route** from Ronda to Cartajima; again, the Ronda Turismo (see p.188) can provide details. The Centro de Iniciativas Turísticas de la Serranía de Ronda, c/Paseo Blas Infante, near the Plaza de Toros (Mon–Fri 10am–1pm; ☎ & ⑥95 287 07 39, ⑩www.serraniaronda.org), has a list of *casas rurales* to rent throughout the Serranía.

The Serranía villages have set up their own **website**, ⑩www.serraniaderonda.org, which provides a comprehensive guide to the *pueblos* of the zone including places to eat, drink, sleep and camp. The best **maps** covering the Serranía are the 1:200,000 *IGN Mapa Provincial de Málaga*, complemented by the 1:50,000 IGN sheet, number 1065. For Spanish readers, the best book on the region is *Rutas por la Serranía de Ronda* by Interguías Clave which clearly describes fifty walks – ranging between 5km and 40km – and has accommodation and background information; it's widely available from bookshops. Alternatively, the Ronda Turismo Municipal's bilingual **walking guide** *10 Rutas Para Senderistas Exigentes* (see p.189), also describes a number of walks in the Serranía.

A walk from Benoaján to Jimera de Libar

There's a fine, none too taxing **walk** from Benoaján to the attractive village of Jimera de Libar, 9km down the railway line linking the two communities. When you've reached Jimera you could take in a well-earned lunch at the *Restaurante Quercus* and return to Benoaján on the afternoon trains (currently leaving Jimera station at 4.48 & 7.51pm; confirm current times with either of the Ronda tourist offices or the *Hote Inz-Almaraz*).

The walk begins from the *Molino del Santo* hotel (see opposite). Turn left from the hotel and head downhill until you come to a stop sign at a level crossing. Turn left along the railway line, cross over a river, and at a second level crossing turn right and cross over the railway track. The road drops before crossing the Río Guadiaro and leads up to a sign marking the official start of the walk. The route from here is fairly straightforward except for a fork just beyond a ruined farm (after 3km), where you should veer left away from the river. At a second fork at a telegraph pole just before Jimera bear right (*not* towards Camino de Huertas Nuevas) to follow the path down to the station of Jimera de Libar. To reach the very good and mid-priced *Restaurante Quercus* (☎952 18 00 41) you need to cross the railway tracks and turn right – the **restaurant** is housed in the former station building actually on the tracks. Overnight **accommodation** is possible in Jimera at the 🛱 *Hotel Rural Inz-Almaraz*, c/Mártires de Igueriben 18 (☎95 218 50 10, 🌐www.serraniaderonda.org/html/hotelinzalmaraz. htm; ❹ with breakfast), which also rents out apartments (❺) and has its own restaurant. The proprietor will also pick up guests from and return them to the train station if you ring. Jimera also has a leafy **campsite** (☎95 218 01 02, 🌐www.rural-jimera. com) close to the train station which also rents out log cabins (❹) and has a pool. A map would be a useful tool to have on this walk (50:000 IGN sheets 1050 & 1064), or it is also well described with its own map in Guy Hunter-Watts' *Walking in Andalucía* (see "Books" in Contexts, p.684).

sparkling white church – fringed with bars, any of which will rustle you up *raciones* if asked; try the friendly *Bar El Rincón*. **Places to stay** include *Palacete de Mañara*, Plaza Constitución 2 (☎95 216 72 52, 🌐www.hotelpalacetedemanara .com; ❹), a charming hotel in a converted *palacio antiguo* with **restaurant** and mini-pool; they can also arrange horse riding, walking and caving excursions. An alternative for longer stays is *Casitas de la Sierra* (☎95 216 73 92, 🌐www .casitasdelasierra.com; ❺) who rent out fully equipped village houses for longer stays and will often agree to a couple of nights' stopover if there are places free.

Returning to Ronda along the direct road from Benaoján (MA555), after 2km you'll pass on the left the *Venta Cueva del Gato* (closed Sun) – famed for its superb *conejo casero* (grilled rabbit). A short distance beyond the *venta* a signed road on the left descends to the new *Hotel Cueva del Gato* (☎95 216 72 96; ❺) with comfortable rooms in a stone building. From here a path leads down to a footbridge across the Río Guadiaro and tunnel beneath the rail line to arrive at the gaping mouth of the **Cueva del Gato**, a cave fronted by an oleander-fringed lagoon (a popular bathing spot). Continue ahead to a viewing platform overlooking a spectacular waterfall gushing out of the cave. Given the close proximity of the Cueva de la Pileta (p.200) it seems likely that this cave, too, may well have been occupied by early humans, but no paintings have so far been discovered. The cave is open to all but to penetrate much further than 50m you'll need ropes, lights and some expertise, or, better still, contact climber Jean Hofer at El Chorro (see p.113) who leads fully equipped explorations of the cave and its dramatic subterranean lakes.

Grazalema, El Bosque and around

Looping through the rocky contours of the last foothills of the Cordillera Subbética mountain range, much of which is covered in pine forest, this route travels first west from Ronda through the verdantly spectacular **Parque Natural Sierra de Grazalema** before exploring yet more picturesque hill villages to the north and east of Ronda. Another great **walking** area, the books by John and Christine Oldfield (*Andalucía and the Costa del Sol*) and Guy Hunter-Watts (*Walking in Andalucía*) both describe a number of walks here (see "Books" p.697).

Grazalema

The A376 winds away from Ronda into the Sierra de Sanguijuela, and forking left after about 16km, along the A372, takes you across the provincial border into Cádiz. Another 17km from the turning, the road arrives at **GRAZALEMA**, the central point of the Sierra de Grazalema, now a protected **Parque Natural**. A pretty white village beneath the craggy peak of San Cristóbal, with lots of sloping narrow streets and window boxes full of blooms in summer, it makes an ideal base for delving into the park. This is also the spot with the country's highest rainfall – and there's quite a bit of snow in winter too – which explains the lush vegetation covering the surrounding area, home to a spectacular variety of flora and fauna. Quite apart from the attractions of the

---

Parque Natural Sierra de Grazalema

Bounded by the towns of Grazalema, Ubrique, El Bosque and Zahara, the **Parque Natural Sierra de Grazalema** is an important mountain wilderness, unique to Andalucía. The limestone mass of the Sierra was formed in the Jurassic and Triassic periods and the close proximity of the range to the sea – which traps many of the clouds drifting in from the Atlantic – has produced a microclimate where numerous botanical species dating from before the Ice Age have survived. The most famous of these is the rare **pinsapo**, or Spanish fir, native only to this area of Europe, which grows at an altitude of between 1000m and 1700m. The high rainfall here, plus the wet, cool summers, are essential to its survival. The Sierra also supports a wealth of **birdlife**: eagles (Bonelli's, booted, and golden), vultures (griffon and Egyptian), as well as various owls and woodpeckers are all common. The streams and riverbanks are the domain of water voles and otters, the latter not popular with a number of fish farms in the area. On the Sierra's higher reaches the magnificent Spanish ibex has been reintroduced to a craggy habitat, and its numbers are increasing.

The best way to appreciate the park is by walking, but to protect wildlife and nesting birds access is restricted to different sections at certain times, and in July and August many routes are closed due to the high fire risk. The park's main **information office** is at El Bosque, Avda. de la Diputación s/n (April–Sept daily 10am–2pm & 6–8pm, Oct–March daily 10am–2pm & 4–6pm; closed Sun afternoon; ☎956 72 70 29), and there are smaller branches in Grazalema and Zahara de la Sierra. The El Bosque office issues access *permisos* (permits; free) and will fax these free of charge to the tourist offices in Grazalema and Zahara de la Sierra. The office also stocks park maps with walking routes, and takes bookings for the Itinerario del Pinsapar, guided walks through the major stands of the pinsapo Spanish fir. In Grazalema, Horizon, c/Corrales Terceros 29 (☎956 13 23 63, ⓦwww.horizonaventura.com), organizes a broad range of outdoor **activities** in the park, including hiking (with English-speaking guides), horse-trekking, mountain bike tours, Land Rover trips and much more. They also conduct a variety of wildlife and bird-watching **excursions** and can even arrange **accommodation** for you.

park the village has its own charm, its simple main square, the Plaza de España, adorned with a pinsapo fir tree and overlooked by the eighteenth-century church of **Nuestra Señora de la Aurora**. Various craft shops have sprung up in the village over the years and one interesting arrival is the Neilson Gallery of Contemporary Art, c/Mateos Gago 50 (Mon–Fri 6–8pm, Sat & Sun noon–2pm & 6–8pm; ⓦwww.neilsongallery.com; free) which mounts an eclectic range of exhibitions.

Practicalities

Grazalema's **Turismo** on the main square, Plaza de España (Tues–Sun 10am–2pm & 4–6pm, July & Aug till 8pm; ☎956 13 22 25, ⓦwww.grazalemaweb.es), can provide information about the park and activities such as horse riding and sells good walking maps. A useful booklet on Grazalema and its sierra, *What to do and see Around Grazalema* (€2) is available from the *Casa de las Piedras* hostal (see below).

The Turismo can also advise on the severely limited budget **accommodation** available. If you're considering a longer stay ask about renting *casas de labranza* (farm cottages), which start at around €35 for two people per day. The only budget place to stay is the hospitable ⚔ *Casa de las Piedras*, c/Las Piedras 32 (☎956 13 20 14; ❶–❸), above the main square, which has rooms with and without bath. Something of a walkers' refuge due to its use by organized groups, the proprietors can provide information on trekking in the area and arrange transport to the start of walks. One of the most attractive of the upmarket alternatives is ⚔ *La Mejorana*, c/Santa Clara 6 (☎956 13 23 27, ⓦwww.lamejorana.net; ❹ with breakfast) housed in an elegant *casa señorial* and reached by following c/Mateos Gago 300m uphill from Plaza de España; it offers charming en-suite rooms (some with great views) plus a pool. Just off the main square, *Hotel Puerta de la Villa*, Plaza Pequeña 8 (☎956 13 23 76, ⓦwww.grazhotel.com; ❼), is a four-star option in a refurbished mansion with restaurant, Jacuzzi, sauna, gym and even a tiny plunge pool. If the latter's opulence seems out of place in such a rustic enclave, the more reasonable *Hotel Peñon Grande*, Plaza Pequeña 7 (☎956 13 24 34, ⓦwww.hotelgrazalema. com; ❹), almost opposite, may be a better choice. Slightly out of the centre, the *Villa de Turística de Grazalema*, 500m along the Ronda road (☎956 13 21 36, ⓦwww.tugasa.com; ❹) has villa-style rooms, with restaurant, gardens and pool; they also rent some detached self-catering apartments sleeping four to eight people (❺).

Grazalema's **campsite**, *Tajo Rodillo* (☎956 13 20 63), is located above the village at the end of c/Las Piedras; its office has literature on the park and will provide information about walks and horse-treks in the Sierra; they also rent out mountain bikes.

The **bars** and **restaurants** on the main square are reasonably priced for *raciones* and *menús*; three places worth singling out are *Cádiz El Chico*, on Plaza de España, the excellent ⚔ *Torreón*, c/Agua 44, just north of it, as well as the very good-value *menú* at the *Casa de las Piedras* (see above). A new arrival, *Restaurante El Pinsapar*, c/Mateos Gago 22, has a good selection of local dishes and a *menú* for €7. For **tapas**, *Bar Zulema* and *Bar Posadilla* on opposite sides of c/Agua – near the Plaza de España – are both popular and good value. The village's **nightlife** warms up in summer and centres around the *Disco de Verano* on Avenida Juan de la Rosa and the bars along c/Agua. If the weather's warm enough, try out the communal **swimming pool**, which is spectacularly sited on the Arcos/Benamahoma road at the village's eastern edge.

△ Parque Natural Sierra de Grazalema

El Bosque

Located on the park's western flank, the village of **EL BOSQUE**, surrounded by slopes of planted pine, is easily reached from Grazalema via a delightfully wooded drive along the A372, which bisects the park. When travel writer Richard Ford passed through here in the 1830s he described it as a "robbers' lair" and counted "fifteen monumental crosses in the space of fifty yards" – victims of the ruthless bandits who preyed on travellers. He advised his readers to make sure they carried a watch to buy off these brigands, preferably one with a gaudy gilt chain, "the lack of which the bandit considered an unjustifiable attempt to defraud him of his right." Today it's a far more peaceful place, although the tranquillity is interrupted in August when nearby summer camps increase the 2000-odd population threefold. El Bosque also has the **head office of the Parque Natural** on Avenida de la Diputación, just off the main square. A new **bus station** on the main road through has connections to all parts of the province and beyond.

El Bosque provides an alternative to Grazalema as a base for visiting the park: for **rooms** there's usually space at *Hotel-Hostal Enrique Carillo*, Avda. Diputación 5 (☏956 71 61 05; ❸), with a/c en-suite rooms, or fractionally pricier accommodation in an adjoining new hotel which adds a pool, minibar and free Internet access. Close by, the aptly named and very comfortable *Hotel Las Truchas*, Avda. Diputacíon 1 (☏956 71 60 61, ⒲www.tugasa.com; ❹), has a **restaurant** where fresh trout features strongly on the menu, often with a slice of *jamón serrano* tucked inside; El Bosque has the most southerly trout river in Europe, the nearby Río Majaceite. Tucked away in the woods behind, another possibility is the *Albergue El Bosque*, a **youth hostel** (☏956 71 62 12, ⒲www.inturjoven.com; under-26 €12, over-26 €16.50), with double and triple en-suite rooms and a pool. To get there, follow the road that bends up behind the *Hotel Las Truchas*.

The village has **plenty of places to eat**, with trout much in evidence. For a great-value meal, head for the trout farm Piscifactoría Acuario, hidden in the woods just beyond the *Albergue El Bosque*; the *Mesón Majaceite* opposite the farm does the freshest trout you can get as part of a €7 *menú*. In the village proper the *Hotel-Hostal Enrique Carillo* has a restaurant but *Venta Julian*, Avda. Diputacion 11, near the bus station, with a pleasant terrace outdoes it for popularity and also has an inexpensive *menú*.

One scenic **walk** along the Río El Bosque is best started from Benamahoma, 4km east: the steep descent is easier this way. Starting from the *El Bujio* bar (a taxi will drop you there if you don't fancy the walk), make for some green gates at the end of the car park. Step through a small stand of eucalyptus to the right of the gates and keep ahead along the left bank of the river. As you follow the river back to El Bosque, there are plenty of opportunities for bird-spotting and picnicking. Benamahoma's **campsite** (T & F956 71 62 75) above the village has plenty of shade, a superb pool and some attractive wood cabin apartments for rent (❹).

Zahara de la Sierra

It's worth going back to Grazalema to take the spectacular CA531 road which climbs to the Puerto de las Palomas (Pass of the Doves, at 1350m the second-highest pass in Andalucía). A little before the pass you'll see on the left an entrance to the forest of the *pinsapo* Spanish fir – this is the start of the Itinerario del Pinsapar walking route (see box p.203). Once over the pass the road embarks on a dramatic descent to **ZAHARA DE LA SIERRA** (or de los Membrillos – "of the Quinces"), today surrounded by olive groves. This is perhaps the most perfect of Andalucía's fortified hill *pueblos*, a landmark for miles around, its red-tiled houses huddled round a church beneath a ruined castle on a stark outcrop of rock. It was once an important Moorish town, and its capture by the Christians in 1483 opened the way for the conquest of Ronda – and ultimately Granada. The heart of the village, which was declared a national monument in 1983, is a cobbled main street which connects the church of **San Juan** and the eighteenth-century Baroque church of **Santa María de la Mesa**, which has a fine *retablo* with a sixteenth-century image of the Virgin. The surviving tower of the twelfth-century **Moorish castle** (free access) – constructed over a previous Roman one – looms over the village and incorporates the remains of an early church. The terrain near to the village has changed dramatically over recent years due to the creation of the Embalse de Zahara y El Gastor **reservoir**, the waters of which now lap the foot of its hill on the northern and eastern flanks.

At the eastern end of the main street, c/San Juan, a Parque Natural **information centre** (daily 9am–2pm & 4–7pm; T956 12 31 14) can provide information on the village and the natural park and acts as a booking office for a number of local *casas rurales* and farmhouses. The village has a number of places **places to stay**: on the main street, *Hotel Marqués de Zahara* (T956 12 30 61; ❸) has balcony rooms, a shady patio, a restaurant serving local specialities and information on renting out *casas rurales* for longer stays. Beyond here, on the road to the castle, the stylish, good-value *Hotel Arco de la Villa* (T956 12 32 30, E9arco.de.la.villa@cadiz.org; ❹) has **rooms** with spectacular views over the nearby *embalse*. Towards the swimming pool on the eastern edge of the village, the *Hostal Los Tadeos*, Paseo de la Fuente s/n (T956 12 30 86; ❸), is another option for rooms with bath and views. Zahara's **campsite** is on the reservoir's shore: *Camping Entre Olivos* (☎956 23 40 44, ⓦwww.entreolivos.net) is located 2km south of the village, reached by following the old Ronda road (C339) and turning off along a signed road to Arroyo Molinos, near the lake, where an artificial beach has been created for bathing and water sports. The campsite has its own restaurant.

For **tapas** there are a cluster of bars around the church of Santa María, and for **meals**, *Mesón Los Estribos*, c/El Fuerte 3 (☎956 12 31 45) near the *Hotel Arco de la Villa*, is a good bet. Both the latter hotel and the *Hotel Marqués de Zahara* have decent restaurants of their own.

Algodonales

Enclosed by the folds of the Sierra de Líjar, **ALGODONALES**, 6km north, is a pleasant enough place with a long, central plaza dominated by the lofty tower of the eighteenth-century Neoclassical church of **Santa Ana**. Although lying a couple of kilometres beyond the park boundary, the village is endeavouring to make itself an activity centre for the park and now has a private **tourist office** (daily 10am–2pm & 5–8pm; ☎956 13 78 82, ⓦwww.al-qutun.com) at the entrance to the village as you come from Zahara. Besides providing information on the park it also offers many activities including hang-gliding, caving, climbing and horse riding. The proprietors run a pleasant **youth hostel** with dormitory rooms (€12 per person) fifty metres away, down the road descending behind the tourist office; they also rent out *casas rurales* nearby, sleeping two (❹). Other places in the village offering **rooms** include the welcoming *Hostal Sierra de Líjar*, c/Ronda 5 (☎956 13 70 65; ❸), just below the main square, which also has a restaurant with a great-value *menú*. Similar rooms are on offer at the *Hostal Alameda* (☎956 13 72 29, ⓦwww.hostal-alameda.net; ❹) on the same square below the church tower.

One place worth a visit in Algodonales is the workshop of renowned **guitar maker** Valeriano Bernal, whose beautiful instruments are sought after by many of the leading classical and flamenco guitarists in Spain. His modest workshop is located at c/Ubrique 8 (Mon–Fri 9am–2pm & 3–6pm, Sat 9am–2pm; ☎956 13 72 80, ⓦwww.valerianobernal.com), a two-minute walk from *Hostal Sierra de Líjar*, whose proprietor can provide directions. Should you want to take a guitar home, prices range from €500 for a student's model to €5000-plus for the virtuoso instrument.

The village's proximity to the main A382 *autovía* means that it has frequent daily **bus** connections with Sevilla, Jerez, Cádiz and Ronda as well as a bus to Zahara (Mon–Fri only) currently running at 7.45am and 1.45pm with the return to Algodonales at 9.15am and 3.15pm. Otherwise a taxi to Zahara will cost you about €20 one way.

Olvera

OLVERA, 18km beyond Algodonales in an area thick with olives (from which the town's name may derive), couldn't look more dramatic – a great splash of whitewashed houses tumbling down a hill below the twin towers of its church and a fine Moorish castle. You can ascend the hill along the town's long main street, C/Llana. The church, **La Encarnación**, is disappointing up close, as it's actually a nineteenth-century version of an earlier, fifteenth-century edifice. More interesting is the somewhat over-restored twelfth-century **Moorish castle** (Tues–Sun 10.30am–2pm & 4–7pm; donations), which formed part of Nasrid Granada's line of defence against the Christian lands; entry is gained through a gate to the side of no. 3 on the plaza (Plaza de la Iglesia) facing the church. There are great views from here over the town and to the surrounding hill villages. The same square also has a small **tourist office** (same hours as castle).

An imaginative development in Olvera is the transformation of the disused rail line – running 34km east to Puerto Serrano through rolling, wooded hill country – into a track for cyclists and walkers, with stations along the route transformed into hotels and *ventas*. Known as the **Via Verde** (ⓦwww .fundacionviaverdedelasierra.com), you can hire a mountain bike for €12 per day from Olvera's dapper station-hotel, the *Hotel Estación Verde*. They will give you a route map and ring ahead to book rooms at your next stop. If you don't want to do the return journey you can deposit the bike in Puerto Serrano. Alternatively you can rent a bike for up to four hours (€9) to do part of the route.

Should you want to use the town as a base for exploring the region with its river, olive groves and stark backdrop of the Sierra de Líjar, **places to stay** include the above-mentioned *Hotel Estación Verde* (mobile ☎661463207, ⓦwww.estacionverdeolvera.com; ❹), which has very comfortable en-suite rooms and its own restaurant. There's also *Hostal Maqueda*, c/Calvario 35 (☎956 13 07 33; phone first; ❹) renting two- to six-person apartments, and nearby at c/Sepulveda 6, *Pensión Medina* (☎956 13 01 73; ❸), has conventional rooms, all en suite. The plusher *Hotel Sierra y Cal*, Avda. Nuestra Señora de los Remedios 2 (☎956 13 05 03, ⓦwww.tugasa.com; ❹), near the centre is also good with comfortable a/c rooms and a pool.

For **food**, *Bar Pepe Raya* on the small square below the church does good tapas in air-conditioned comfort, and you'll find decent tapas, *fino* and a budget *menú* at the friendly *Bar Manolo* in Plaza Andalucía at the foot of the main street. The restaurant of the *Sierra y Cal* hotel also offers a good-value *menú* for €10.

From Ronda towards Cádiz

One truly spectacular White Town route is **from Ronda towards Cádiz** via the appealing villages of **Villaluenga** and **Benaocaz**, the remarkable site of Roman **Ocuris** and the larger settlements of **Alcalá de los Gazules** and **Medina Sidonia**. Following the A376 northwest out of Ronda and turning left along the A372, the route cuts across the Sierra de Grazalema and Los Alcornocales natural parks, winding through rocky hills, deep gorges and dense cork oak forests.

Villaluenga del Rosario

Some 18km beyond the turn-off on the A372 described above, and reached along on a winding secondary road, the tiny village of **VILLALUENGA DEL ROSARIO** is the highest in Cádiz Province. Tucked beneath a great crag, it's a simple place, with narrow streets, flower-filled balconies and pan-tiled roofs, frequently enveloped by mountain mists. In the twilight years of the Nasrid Emirate of Granada and after Ronda had fallen to the Christians in 1485, a now unprotected Villaluenga was conquered and repopulated with settlers from Arcos de la Frontera and Villamartín. Some ancient Moorish wells can be seen dotted along the roadside as you approach. The twentieth-century Civil War was also bitterly fought here when one of the village's two churches was torched: its gutted ruin, located at the top of the village, now serves as the cemetery. Villaluenga's curious **Plaza de Toros**, partly hacked out of the rock, is also worth a look and sees action once a year on October 7, when the feast of the Virgen Del Rosario is celebrated with a *corrida*. The village is famous for its goats' milk cheeses, which can be purchased at the award-winning cheese-maker's shop on the south side of the main road running through.

The village has a couple of **places to stay**, including – in the upper village near the ruined church – the charming *Hotel La Posada*, c/Torre 1 (☎956 12 61 19, ⓦwww.tugasa.com; ④), housed in a beautifully renovated stone-built house above a decent **restaurant**. The budget alternative, with clean and simple rooms above a bar, is the nearby *Fonda Ana María*, c/Mártires 1 (☎956 46 00 43; ①), to the side of the still-functioning church of San Miguel.

Benaocaz

From Villaluenga the road continues through the spectacular Manga de Villa-luenga Pass, an area that has yielded many prehistoric artefacts and dolmens, to the farming settlement of **BENAOCAZ**, another ancient village founded by the Moors in the eighth century. A series of wall plaques around the Barrio Nazari in the upper village provides information (in Spanish) on buildings and locations from this period. A pleasant place to stop over, the village's **Museo Historico** (Sat & Sun 11.30am–2pm & 5–8pm; free; when closed enquire at the Ayuntamiento or *Bar La Palmera* below), at c/Jabonería 7, has lots of historical background on life in the Sierra from prehistoric cave-dwellers to the nineteenth-century *bandoleros*, and its Baroque **church** is built over the former mosque, which used part of the minaret to make its tower. The elegant and recently renovated eighteenth-century Ayuntamiento on the main square, Plaza de la Libertades 1 (☎956 46 14 91), can provide **tourist information** on the village and the surrounding area.

If you want to stretch your legs, there's a fine 6km downhill walk from here to Ubrique along a superbly preserved **Roman road** complete with culverts to protect it from flooding. The start of the route (marked by an information board) is across the road from the bus stop on the main road below the village. If you time your arrival to coincide with the afternoon bus from Ubrique to Benaocaz, this will save you the walk back up the hill.

You can get pleasant **rooms** – and apartments for a longer stay – at *Hostal San Antón*, Plaza de San Antón 5 (☎956 12 55 77, mobile ☎689783906; ④), or at the nearby *El Parral* (☎956 12 55 65; ④), which also squeezes in a small pool. Just outside the village on the Ubrique road *Los Chozos* (April–Sept ☎956 23 41 63, ⓦwww.sierradecadiz.com/loschozos; ⑤) rents out *chozos* (modern versions of traditional circular thatched-roofed dwellings) in a scenic location sleeping two or more.

For **food**, *Bar La Palmera* along the village's main street, c/Fray Domingo, does tapas and both *El Parral* and *Los Chozos* have restaurants. At the other end of the village and opposite the Ayuntamiento, *Bar Las Vegas* also does decent meals with a daily lunchtime *menú*, and serves a vital role as the vendor of daily newspapers for this corner of the Sierra.

Ocuri

Two kilometres west of Benaocaz, close to the junction with the A373, a small road on the right (signed "Consorcio Bahía de Cádiz") leads to the spectacu-larly situated Roman site of **Ocuri**. The road is easy to miss and if you reach the petrol station at the junction beyond it you will need to turn around. Leave any transport at the site **information centre** and **cafetería** opposite the entrance. At the time of writing the site is open weekends only (Sat & Sun 10am–2pm; free), with a guided visit at midday; however, the fence does not present a great obstacle. You should contact the Turismo in Ubrique (see below) to make a visit outside these times.

Once through the entry gate a paved path climbs into the woods for a good kilometre to the site, located on the crest of the hill above. Just before you arrive at the ruins stands a well-preserved (although partly restored) first-century AD **columbarium** tomb with wall niches for burial urns. This is followed by some impressive Cyclopean dry-stone **walls** that date from the site's origin as an Iberian *oppidum*, or tribal settlement, in the pre-Roman era, and the Romans would have had to overcome defences like these during the subjugation of the peninsula in the first and second centuries BC. Once through the walls, you enter the heart of the Roman settlement where the substantial remains of **dwellings**, **baths** and huge **cisterns**, with their mortar linings still intact, surround the ancient **forum**. Archeologists are still busy excavating here and it will be some time before the remains are entirely revealed and understood. On all sides of the site the hill falls sharply away and there are wonderful **views** over the Sierra and the town of Ubrique, far below. There's plenty of shade and lush grass up here and, if you've brought provisions, it's hard to imagine a better place for a picnic.

Ubrique

From Benaocaz the road corkscrews down from the mountainous sierra until the snow-white vista of **UBRIQUE** comes into view below, spreading along the valley of the Río Ubrique with the daunting knife-edged crag of the Cruz de Tajo rearing up behind. Despite this stunning first appearance, on closer contact it's a rather large and dull industrial centre, but the town's bustling prosperity ensures a good variety of places to eat and drink on and around Avenida Dr Solis Pascual, the tree-lined main artery.

A place that has always bred tenacious guerrilla fighters and which fought against the French in the War of Independence (actually defeating a contingent of the Imperial Guard near Gaucín), Ubrique is a natural mountain fortress which was one of the last Republican strongholds in the Civil War. Today, it's a relatively wealthy if unexciting town, surviving largely on its medieval guild craft of **leather manufacturing**, the products of which are sold in numerous shops lining the main street, where most of the bars and restaurants are also gathered. A **Turismo**, Avda. Dr Solis Pascual 19 (daily 10am–2pm & 5–7.30pm; ℡956 46 49 00, @ eoit@ayuntamientoubrique.es), where English is spoken, has information on the town and the zone and can facilitate visits to the Roman site of Ocuri (see p.209). There are two **places to stay**: *Hotel Ocurris*, Avda. Dr Solis Pascual 49 (℡956 46 39 39; ❹), close to the main junction and roundabout as you enter the town from the north, has en-suite rooms with TV whilst at the the opposite end, on the road out to Cortes de la Frontera, the *Hotel Sierra de Ubrique* (℡956 46 68 05, @www.hotelsierradeubrique.com; ❹) is a pleasant new hotel with its own restaurant.

Alcalá de los Gazules

The A375 road from Ubrique towards Alcalá, 44km to the southwest, runs through the **Parque Natural de Los Alcornocales**, with magnificently rugged but sparsely populated mountain scenery. Close to the Sierra de Aljibe to the south, the road skirts the frontier with Málaga and at the junction with the CA503 at the Puerto de Galis the solitary but excellent 🍴 *Venta del Puerto de Galis* is a hunters' favourite and often has game on its menu. Beyond here the road joins the valley of the Río Barbate for the final descent into the White Town of **ALCALÁ DE LOS GAZULES**, the geographical centre of the province of Cádiz. When the Romans were conquering this area early in the second century BC, they tried to divide and rule the Iberian tribes by granting the status of *colonia* to selected settlements – a crucial first step on the way to full Roman citizenship and all the privileges such status could bestow. One such settlement so rewarded was the Iberian Turris Lascutana, as Alcalá then was, and this was an attempt by Rome to win its allegiance away from the Turditanian tribal capital at Hasta Regia near Jerez. A surviving bronze plaque (in the archeological museum in Madrid) records the decree of the Roman governor, Lucius Aemelius Paullus, in 189 BC, which granted Turris possession of the fields and town that they had formerly held as a fief of Hasta. Apart from the winding, narrow streets, little remains of the later Moorish settlement founded by the Berber family the Gazules, who gave their name to the town in the twelfth century when this was a *taifa* state of the kingdom of Granada.

A cascade of white dwellings gathered beneath its ruined Alcázar, Alcalá is a sleepy little place today. In the Plaza Alta in the upper town there's the fifteenth-century Gothic church of **San Jorge**, with an imposing tower, beautifully carved choir and an effigy attributed to Martínez Montañes, but not much else. In the lower town the **Plaza de Toros** has been turned into a *discoteca*, somewhat blasphemously given the surrounding bull-breeding country. Just over the road from the bullring-disco on the c/Paseo de la Playa is *Restaurante Pizarro*, a decent mid-priced **restaurant** with a good-value *menú*. A little further along, the same proprietors run the comfortable *Hostal Pizarro* (☎956 42 01 03; ❷) with en-suite rooms; to stay here you will need to resist attempts to place you in their nearby and more expensive *Hotel San Jorge* (☎956 41 32 55; ❹) where you'll pay extra for air-conditioning and a TV.

Tajo de las Figuras

An alternative route to Medina Sidonia from Alcalá takes you 17km southwest to **Benalup de Sidonia** where the **Tajo de las Figuras** caves have important Neolithic **cave paintings** depicting birds, deer and human figures, perhaps hunters. The caves (Wed–Sun 10am–3pm; free), 7km south of Benalup along the CA212, are signed on the left and the *abrigos*, or rock shelters, some half-a-kilometre distant, can be seen from the road. Park here and go through the gate towards the rock cliffs where you will eventually make out a steel ladder to the main cave above. If closed during this time wait around and the site's guardian (who shelters among the rocks) will eventually emerge to open them up. He can also guide you to another cave nearby with more paintings of animals and human figures (one with a child) and, below this, to some remarkable anthropomorphic

---

Toros Bravos

This part of Cádiz province is bull country and the roads around the towns of Álcala de los Gazules and Medina Sidonia are lined with the ranches of the breeders of fighting bulls destined for bullrings all over Spain. Behind warning signs posted on roadside fences it's often possible to catch a view of the mean, black *toros bravos*, or fighting bulls used in the *corridas*. These magnificent beasts weighing 500 to 600 kilos, the descendants of the *bos taurus ibericus* of ancient times, graze on pastures shaded by olives and holm oaks, and are tended by mounted *vaqueros* who guard them while noting their potential for valour. This is eventually tested in the *tienta* or trial ring, an important first step in deciding whether the bull will die in the *corrida* or the abattoir. The *vaqueros* are always on the lookout for the exceptional bull displaying outstanding bravery and physical construction and these are separated from the herd to be used exclusively at stud, to improve the breed. The bulls that leave these ranches to fight in the ring usually die there, although very occasionally bulls displaying exceptional bravery and spirit will receive the *indulto*, or pardon, to be returned to their ranch of origin for stud.

sarcophagus tombs – some for children – carved into the rocks. You may want to give the guardian a small consideration for his trouble, and it's worth checking current visiting arrangements at the Ayuntamiento in Benalup, c/Cantera s/n (☎956 42 41 29), or the Turismo in Medina Sidonia (see overleaf), to save yourself a wasted journey.

Medina Sidonia

Heading from Alcalá to Medina Sidonia by the direct route along the A381 brings you, after 24km, to a junction with the A390 where you should turn left into the town. Incidentally, this crossroads has a great *venta*, the 🍴 *Ventorillo de Carbón* serving up excellent **tapas** and an inexpensive *menú* and makes an ideal lunch stop.

Following its reconquest by Alfonso X in 1264, **MEDINA SIDONIA**, another ancient hill-top town, was to become one of Spain's most prestigious ducal seats; it supplied the admiral who led the Armada against England. The title of Duque de Medina Sidonia was bestowed upon the family of Guzmán El Bueno for his valiant role in taking the town, a line which continues and is currently led by the firebrand socialist duchess of Medina Sidonia (see p.212). Not unlike the ducal house, the town, depopulated and now somewhat ramshackle, has seen better days, but nevertheless, the tidy narrow cobbled streets with their rows of *reja*-fronted houses still offer glimpses of bygone grandeur.

A good place to begin a look around is the elegant **Plaza de España** dominated by the wonderful Renaissance facade of the seventeenth-century Ayuntamiento. At the top of a steeply climbing road, reached by following directions from Plaza de España, is the impressive **Plaza Iglesia Mayor**, fronted by **Santa María la Coronada** church (daily April–Sept 9.30am–2pm & 4–9.30pm, Oct–March 10.30am–2pm & 4–6.30pm; €2), built over an earlier mosque. Inside, an enormous and exquisite **retablo** depicting scenes from the life of Christ is a stunning sixteenth-century work of craftsmanship in polychromed wood by the *sevillano* school. There's also an imposing sculpted image of *Cristo del Perdón* attributed to Luisa Roldán ("La Roldana") and a fine wood sculpture of *San Francisco de Asís* by Martínez Montañes. The guardian will also point out on request some sixteenth-century benches used by the Inquisition. Medina's importance in Roman times, when it was known as *Asido Caesarina*, is evidenced by some remarkable **Roman sewers** ("Cloacas Romanas"; entry at c/Ortega 10; April–Sept daily Tues–Sun 10am–2pm & 6–8pm, Oct–March Sun only 10am–2pm & 4–6pm; €3.10) buried beneath the town's northern flank. Dating from the first century AD, the extensive stone-built sewers stand over two metres in height, and are a tribute to Roman engineering skills. The same ticket covers entry beneath another building nearby to see a remarkably preserved stretch of paved **Roman road** lying below the town's main street today, c/San Juan. Don't miss the child's game etched into one of the paving stones, which adds a wonderfully human touch. Medina Sidonia also boasts three **Moorish gates** of which the Arco de la Pastora, close to the Jerez road, is the best preserved.

Practicalities

The **Turismo** (April–Sept daily 10am–2pm & 5–9pm, Oct–March Sun only 10am–2pm & 4–6pm; ☎956 41 24 04, ⓦwww.medinasidonia.es), fronting the Plaza Iglesia Mayor, can provide a town map and offers guided visits to the Tajo de las Figuras caves (see p.211), local bull-breeding ranches and the town's monuments.

Medina is unused to tourists but does have **rooms** to suit most pockets. *Pensión Amalia*, Plaza de España 6, near the Ayuntamiento (☎956 41 00 35;

●), has some rooms with bath, or there's *Casa Napoleón* nearby at c/San Juan 21 (☎956 41 01 83; ●), a spotless *pensión* with shared bathrooms that often puts up *matadores* who have come here to train at the local bull-breeding ranches. Photos of famous past guests – dressed to kill in their *corrida* finery – line the walls. East from Plaza de España lies the ✿ *Casa Rural Los Balcones*, c/La Loba 26 (☎956 42 30 33, ⓦwww.losbalcones.turincon.com; ●), a delightful new apart-hotel inside a strikingly elegant nineteenth-century mansion. Comfortable air-conditioned rooms come with kitchenette and fridge, there's a rooftop solarium and guests share a laundry facility. *Hotel El Molino*, c/Al Andalus 1, off Avda. de Andalucía on the east side of town (☎956 41 03 00; ●), has en-suite air-conditioned rooms above a restaurant, but is not so central.

For **food** and **drink** head for the Plaza de España where *Restaurante Cádiz* serves very good regional dishes, has a *menú* for under €10 and does tapas too. Its neighbour, *Bar Ortega*, has fewer pretensions and a *menú* for €5. *Mesón Machín*, Plaza Iglesia Mayor 9, facing the church of Santa María, offers good, mid-priced meals, tapas and *raciones* and has a spectacular view over the town from its terrace. Slightly further out *El Duque*, Paseo Armada Española s/n, is another good mid-priced restaurant with superb views. Medina was noted in Moorish times for its sweets and **pastries**, a tradition continued at Sobrina de las Trejas, Plaza España 7, whose *alfajores* (sugary tubes containing honey, almonds and dried fruit) are delicious.

Arcos de la Frontera

From whichever direction you approach it, your first view of **ARCOS DE LA FRONTERA** – the westernmost of the White Towns – will be fabulous. In full sun the town shimmers magnificently on its great double crag of limestone high above the Río Guadalete. This dramatic location, enhanced by low, white houses and fine sandstone churches, gives the town a similar feel and appearance to Ronda – except Arcos is rather poorer and, quite unjustifiably, far less visited.

Dating from Iberian times and known as Arco Briga to the Romans, Arcos came to prominence as a Moorish town within the Cordoban caliphate. When Córdoba's rule collapsed in the eleventh century, Arcos existed as a petty *taifa* state until its annexation by al-Mu'tamid of Sevilla in 1103. The seizure of Arcos by Christian forces under Alfonso El Sabio (the Wise) in 1264 – over two centuries before Zahara fell – was a real feat against what must have been a wretchedly impregnable fortress.

Each September 29, Arcos's narrow streets echo to the screams of hundreds of children when they run the bulls in the **Feria de San Miguel** honouring the town's patron saint. To see these girls and boys leap up to grab an overhanging balcony, to lift themselves clear of the horns of the rampaging *toro*, is a truly nail-biting sight, and remarkably few seem to get injured.

Arrival, information and orientation

Most of Arcos's monuments are located in the higher old town – where you'll be spending much of your time. The new town has spilled out to the west and east of here at the foot of the crag. The **bus station** is in the new town on c/ Corregidores (☎956 70 49 77), served by the Comes and Amarillo companies, with regular buses to Cádiz and Jerez. **Parking** in the narrow streets of the old town is tricky (although all the hotels have their own arrangements) and you'd be much better off trying to find space on the Paseo de Andalucía or using a pay car park (there's one beneath the Paseo itself). A **Turismo** on the central

Plaza del Cabildo (Mon–Sat 10am–2pm & 4–8pm; ☎956 70 22 64, ⓦwww .ayuntamientoarcos.org) can provide a detailed **map** which you'll need to find your way around the new town. A summer **kiosko** (March–Oct Mon–Sat 10.30am–1.30pm & 5.30–7pm) also operates in the Paseo de Andalucía, reached by following Paseo de los Boliches (left off our map). The Turismo does **guided tours** of the old town every day except Saturday afternoons and Sunday, departing from their office at 10.30am and 5pm (€5, not including admission to churches). A Traditional Patios tour (€5) starts from the same place and on the same days at midday and 6.30pm.

Internet access is currently only available at *Café Cosmopolitan* (daily 10am– midnight), opposite *Café Olé* (see "Eating & Drinking") with a single screen. A useful **minibus** service (Mon–Sat until 9.15pm; €0.81) runs back and forth between Plaza de España in the new town and Plaza del Cabildo in the *casco antiguo* – saving you a climb.

Accommodation

A number of **hostales** providing budget accommodation have recently opened up in the old town, formerly the exclusive preserve of well-heeled travellers staying at a clutch of upmarket hotels. Lower down, the new town has many more options, including a renovated old *fonda* on the main street, c/Corredera. Staying a little out of town, at the **Lago de Arcos**, where there's a *hostal* and the *Lago de Arcos* **campsite** (☎956 70 83 33), is another possibility – though you'll need insect repellent in summer. There's a bus service to the lake (see p.218).

Bar-Pensión Carbonato c/Beatriz Pachecho 42, near the N342 on the west side of town ☎956 70 04 18. A 10min walk from the bus station, the cheapest rooms in town are clean and serviceable, and are set above a bar serving a good-value low price *menú del día*. ❶

Hacienda El Santiscal 3km out of town on the lakeside, beyond the camping ☎956 70 83 13, ⓦwww.santiscal.com. Small country hotel in a beautiful converted *hacienda* with very pleasant a/c rooms and a pool in the grounds. Horse riding available. ❻

Hostal Andalucía Carretera Nacional 342 ☎956 70 07 14. Motel-type *hostal* on the edge of town, a bit too close to the main Jerez road, but offering decent economical rooms with bath, a restaurant and easy parking. ❸

Hostal Mesón de la Molinera Lago de Arcos ☎956 70 80 02, ⓔrumave@teleline.es. Tranquil location on the waterfront with stunning views towards Arcos on its hill top. Chalet-style rooms with bath and terrace, great pool and easy parking. Also has its own bar and restaurant with *menú* for under €10, and the restaurant of the nearby campsite is also good. ❺

Hostal-Bar San Marcos c/Marqués de Torresoto 6 ☎956 70 07 21. Excellent *hostal* in the old town, offering pleasant rooms with bath. The friendly proprietors run a cosy bar-restaurant downstairs with a *menú* for around €8. ❷

Hotel Arcotur c/Alta 1, in the new town ☎956 70 45 25, ⓕ956 70 45 24. Pleasant small hotel run

by the ebullient Sra. Francisca García and offering good value a/c rooms with bath, TV and balcony (some with great views). Also has apartments to rent (❺) and a roof-terrace café for taking breakfast. ❸–❹

Hotel El Convento c/Maldonado 2 ☎956 70 23 33, ⓦwww.webdearcos.com /elconvento. Upmarket hotel in a seventeenth-century former convent whose comfortable a/c rooms – 8 & 9 are recommended – have a spectacular view over the *vega*. Breaksasts are served in a charming courtyard. ❹

Hotel La Fonda c/Corredera 83, in the new town ☎956 70 00 57, ⓕ956 70 36 61. Atmospheric old *fonda* and coaching inn that has been taking in guests for well over a century; now rejuvenated as a friendly one-star hotel where comfortable rooms (numbers 16–19 have terrace) come with a/c, bath and TV. Pleasant bar-restaurant in the converted stables with a *menú* for around €8. ❹

Hotel Los Olivos c/San Miguel 2, in the new town ☎956 70 08 11, ⓦwww .hotelolivosarcos.com. Charming and friendly little hotel near the Paseo de Andalucía gardens, in a superbly restored *casa antigua*. Some of the light a/c rooms have fine views, there's a plant-filled interior patio and there are more views from a rooftop terrace. Car park too. ❺

Hotel Marqués de Torresoto c/Marqués de Torresoto 4 ☎956 70 07 17, ⓦwww .hmdetorresoto.com. Pleasant a/c rooms in a

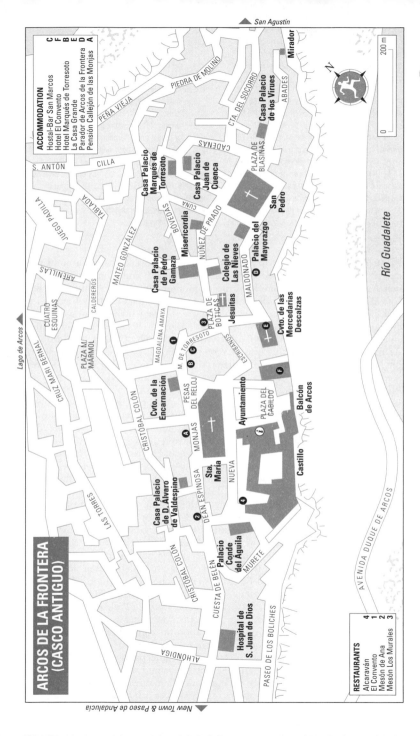

ARCOS DE LA FRONTERA (CASCO ANTIGUO)

Lago de Arcos ▲

▲ *San Agustín*

New Town & Paseo de Andalucía ▼

ACCOMMODATION
Hostal-Bar San Marcos   C
Hotel El Convento   F
Hotel Marqués de Torresoto B
La Casa Grande   E
Parador de Arcos de la Frontera D
Pensión Callejón de las Monjas A

RESTAURANTS
Alcaraván   4
El Convento   1
Mesón de Ana   2
Mesón Los Murales   3

Casa Palacio de los Virues
Mirador
CTA. DEL SOCORRO
ABADES
PLAZA DE BLASINAS
San Pedro
Casa Palacio Juan de Cuenca
Casa Palacio Marqués de Torresoto
CUNA
BÓVEDAS
NÚÑEZ DE PRADO
Misericordia
Palacio del Mayorazgo
MALDONADO
Colegio de Las Nieves
Casa Palacio de Pedro Gamaza
MATEO GONZÁLEZ
Jesuitas
PLAZA DE BOTICAS
Cvto. de las Mercedarias Descalzas
ESCRIBANOS
PIEDRA DE MOLINO
PEÑA VIEJA
S. ANTÓN
CILLA
TABLADA
JUEGO PADILLA
ARENILLAS
CALDEREROS
CUATRO ESQUINAS
PLAZA M. MÁRMOL
CRUZ MARI BERNAL
LAS TORRES
MAGDALENA AMAYA
M. DE TORRESOTO
PESAS DEL RELOJ
Cvto. de la Encarnación
CRISTÓBAL COLÓN
CRISTÓBAL COLÓN
MONJAS
Sta. María
DEÁN ESPINOSA
NUEVA
Ayuntamiento
PLAZA DEL CABILDO
Balcón de Arcos
Castillo
Casa Palacio de D. Álvaro de Valdespino
Palacio Conde del Aguila
MURETE
CUESTA DE BELÉN
Hospital de S. Juan de Dios
PASEO DE LOS BOLICHES
ALHÓNDIGA
AVENIDA DUQUE DE ARCOS

Río Guadalete

N

0   200 m

converted seventeenth-century mansion, the former seat of the marqueses de Torresoto. The delightful colonnaded patio – complete with Baroque chapel – now serves as their restaurant (open to the public). ④

Hotel Peña de Arcos c/Muñoz Vázquez 42, near the Paseo de Andalucía in the new town ☎956 70 45 32, ⓦwww.hotelesdearcos.com. Attractive three-star hotel near the entrance to the town with a/c, rather functional rooms with safe and satellite TV, its own subterranean car park, and a restaurant. ⑤

🏃 **La Casa Grande** c/Maldonado 10 ☎956 70 39 30, ⓦwww.lacasagrande.net. Perched along the same cliff top as the parador, this elegant hotel has beautiful rooms inside a restored *casa señorial* with a columned inner patio and a sensational view from the terrace of their bar across the

river valley. They also offer some more expensive suites. ⑤

🏃 **Parador de Arcos de la Frontera** Plaza del Cabildo ☎956 70 05 00, ⓦwww .parador.es. Perched on a rock pedestal – with reassuringly reinforced foundations to prevent it from sliding over the cliff – this is one of the smaller paradores with elegant balcony rooms to enjoy the view. The delightful patio (open to the public for drinks and afternoon tea) and the "crow's nest" terrace give the best views for miles. Also has a restaurant with a *menú* for around €25. ⑦

Pensión Callejón de las Monjas c/Dean Espinosa 4 ☎956 70 23 02, ⓕ956 70 23 02. Decent if cramped *pensión* for en-suite rooms in the heart of the old town; some slightly pricier rooms come with a/c and terrace. ②

The Town

By far the best thing to do in Arcos de la Frontera is take a stroll around the tangle of narrow streets, lined with a mix of Moorish and Renaissance buildings. At the heart of the **casco antiguo** or monumental quarter is the Plaza del Cabildo, easily reached by following the signs for the parador, which occupies one whole side of it. Flanking another two sides are – behind the Ayuntamiento – the **castle** walls and towers (the castle is privately owned and off limits) and the large fifteenth-century Gothic-Mudéjar church of **Santa María de la Asunción** (Mon–Fri 10am–1pm & 3.30–6.30pm, Sat 10am–2pm, Sun 8.30am for Mass; €1.50), built over an earlier mosque; one side is left open, offering spectacular plunging views to the river valley and the *vega*. Santa María's Plateresque south facade with later additions is a stunning work, although an unfinished bell tower unbalances the whole – the original was destroyed by the Lisbon earthquake of 1755 and the plan was to raise this new one to 58m, second in height only to Sevilla's Giralda. Three years later, however, the money ran out and the tower rested at a relatively feeble 37m. The tower can be visited (€3) and offers views over the town and surroundings. The church's gloomy interior has fine Gothic vaulting as well as a stunning *retablo*, exquisitely carved choir stalls by Pedro Roldán, and a treasury with all the usual collection of church silver and some dubiously attributed artworks.

East of here along c/Núñez de Prado, the Gothic church of **San Pedro** (Mon–Sat 10am–3pm & 4–7pm, Sun 10am–1.30pm; €1), perched precariously on the cliff edge, was rebuilt in the sixteenth century over an original Moorish fort. The later imposing Baroque exterior and tower are in strong contrast to the interior, where a fine sixteenth-century *retablo* documents the life of San Pedro and San Jerónimo and is the oldest in the province. To each side of this are paintings of *San Ignacio* and *La Dolorosa* by Pachecho, the tutor of Velásquez. There's also the rather grisly undecomposed body of San Victor (thankfully behind glass) and an image of the Virgin attributed to La Roldana, the sculptor daughter of Pedro Roldán. You can climb the tower, but you'll need a good head for heights, as there are few guard rails on the top to prevent a nasty fall.

Other monuments in this quarter include the **Palacio del Mayorazgo**, c/Maldonado, with a Renaissance facade, and fine patios within (Mon–Sat 10am–2pm & 5–8pm, Sun 11am–2pm; free), and further east still, the convent of **San Agustín** (daily except Tues 10.30am–1pm & 3.30–6.30pm; free), on the narrow neck of the spur, whose church contains a fine

△ Arcos de la Frontera

seventeenth-century carved wood *retablo* and the town's most venerated image of Jesús Nazareno (Christ bearing the Cross). Nearby, in c/Cuna, there's **Casa Cuna**, formerly the synagogue of the old Jewish ghetto, and further east again in the Plaza de la Caridad lies the **Iglesia de la Caridad** (daily 10.30am–12.30pm & 4.30–6pm; donations), an impressive sixteenth-century church and convent of the Hermanitas de los Ancianos Desamparados (nuns caring for the elderly) built in ornate colonial style with a beautiful patio and stunning carved wood *retablos*.

Back near the church of Santa María, the **Convento de la Encarnación**, c/de las Monjas, is worth a look, though only the church – with a sixteenth-century Plateresque facade – survives. Close by, and back in the Plaza del Cabildo, the **Ayuntamiento** (Mon–Fri 9am–1pm) boasts a superb Mudéjar coffered ceiling, while lower down along the Cuesta de Belén, the fourteenth-century ducal palace **Palacio del Conde de Águila** has the town's oldest facade. At the end of this street, just before it joins the Paseo de Andalucía, the sixteenth-century **Hospital de San Juan de Dios** – a former hospice for travelling pilgrims – incorporates a charming early Baroque church (viewing daily at 9–10am – ring the bell) with a stunning *retablo* in carved pine whose centrepiece is a striking sixteenth-century image of Cristo de la Veracruz, the crucified Christ.

East of town, the A372 road to Ronda leads down to a couple of sandy **beaches** on the riverbank, and to the north of here the Lago de Arcos (actually a reservoir) is a good spot for swimming. The lake is served by five daily buses in each direction (Sun service July & Aug only) leaving from the Plaza de España, below the old town.

Eating and drinking

There's little variety when it comes to **eating and drinking** in Arcos, but a couple of good restaurants are worth seeking out. In addition to the list below, many of the hotels and *hostales* (see "Accommodation") have restaurants of their own.

Alcaraván c/Nueva 1, close to the castle walls. Atmospheric cave restaurant serving tapas and *platos asados* (roasted meats). In April, May, September and October they stage flamenco on Monday nights.

Bar-Restaurante Terraza c/Múñoz Vásquez. Below the old town, in the gardens of the Paseo de Andalucía, this is a pleasant place to sit out and serves a wide variety of inexpensive *platos combinados*.

Café Olé Cerro de la Reina 8, off Plaza de España. New place serving drinks and decent *platos combinados* on a terrace in a revamped plaza.

Café-Bar El Faro c/Debajo del Corral 14, in the new town. Good *platos combinados* and an economical *menú*.

Cafetería Albeniz c/Muñoz Vázquez 10, close to *Bar-Restaurante Terraza* (see above). Good bar for late-night drinks in a town that goes early to bed.

El Convento c/Marqués de Torresoto 7. Mid-priced option in the old town, owned by the hotel of the same name, and renowned for its cooking; there's a *menú* here as well as specialities such as *perdiz en salsa de almendras* (partridge with almond sauce), and a tasty house soup, *sopa de clausura*, with pine nuts and cheese. *Crema de ángel* and *peras al vino* are two recommended desserts. Main dishes €8–15.

Los Faraones c/Debajo del Corral 8. Egyptian Arab restaurant in the new town, offering Spanish standards and tapas as well as some interesting North African dishes, a variety of teas and a €9 *menú*. A similarly priced vegetarian *menú* includes felafel and couscous.

Mesón de Ana c/Dean Espinosa 10. Pleasant little café-bar on the way up to Plaza del Cabildo serving *platos combinados* and lots of snacks.

Mesón Los Murales Plaza de Boticas 1. One of the best low-priced options in the old town, close to the church of San Pedro, and serving an economical *menú* for €7.50. Has a small street terrace.

Nightlife

Arcos locals tend to gravitate to the bars and restaurants for **nightlife**, however, in summer, there are quite a few free outdoor events, such as flamenco (and even rock) concerts and it's worth checking with the Turismo, or perusing the local paper, *Arcos Información,* to see what's coming up. On Thursdays at 10.30pm in July and August there are **flamenco** concerts in the Plaza del Cananeo, close to the Iglesia de San Pedro in the old town. The welcoming *Peña de Flamenco de Arcos* (☎956 70 12 51), Plaza de la Caridad 4, east of the old quarter, also stages regular – and authentic – flamenco, with *actuaciones* (shows) most weekends, normally Saturdays after 10.30pm but ring first (Spanish only) to check. Alternatively, *Disco-Bar Porto Alegre* sets up an open-air **disco** at the lakeside in summer, which gets going after 11pm, and in July and August there are tented **music-bars** ("Las Carpas") below the Paseo de Andalucía, close to the *Bar-Restaurante Terraza.*

The Costa de la Luz

The villages along the **Costa de la Luz** – the "Coast of Light" between Algeciras and Cádiz – are in a totally different class from the resorts along the Costa del Sol.

West from Algeciras the road climbs almost immediately into the rolling green hills of the **Sierra del Cabrito**, a region lashed for much of the year by the ferocious *levante* (east) and *poniente* (west) winds which vie continuously, it seems, for the upper hand. Now cluttered by an inevitable wind farm, from these heights there are fantastic views down to Gibraltar and across the straits to the just-discernible white houses and tapering mosques of Moroccan villages. Beyond, the Rif Mountains hover in the background and on a clear day, as you approach **Tarifa**, you can distinguish Tangier on the edge of its crescent-shaped bay.

Tarifa

TARIFA, spilling out beyond its Moorish walls, was until the mid-1980s a quiet village, known in Spain, if at all, as the southernmost point on the European landmass and for its abnormally high suicide rate – attributed to the unremitting winds that blow across the town and its environs. Occupying the site of previous Carthaginian and Roman cities, Tarifa takes its name from Tarif Ibn Malik, leader of the first band of Moors to cross the straits in 710, a sortie that tested the waters for the following year's all-out assault on the peninsula. Today it's become a prosperous, popular and at times very crowded, resort, following its establishment as Europe's prime **windsurfing** and **kitesurfing** locale (see box p.225). Indeed, according to windsurfing aficionados, Tarifa now ranks alongside Diamond Head in Hawaii and Fuerteventura in the Canaries as one of the top three windsurfing beaches in the world. Equipment rental shops line the main street, and in peak season crowds of windsurfers pack out every available bar and *hostal*. Even in winter, there are windsurfers to be seen, drawn by regular competitions held year-round. Development continues at a rapid rate as a result of this newfound popularity, but for the time being Tarifa remains an attractive place for a stopover.

Arrival, information and orientation

The **bus station** is in the north of town from where the main Algeciras–Cádiz road (c/Batalla del Salado) leads to the walled old town, a five- to ten-minute

Andalucía's bird migrations

Whilst Andalucía's birdlife is fascinating throughout the year, the region also plays host to one of the remarkable spectacles of the natural world, the great **spring and autumn migrations**, attracting an audience of bird-watchers from far and wide. Many birds spend the winter in warmer African climes, a journey that involves a sea crossing – a major challenge for many large birds such as eagles, vultures and storks who rely on the warm air which rises from the earth to keep them aloft. With no thermals over the sea it's essential that they seek out the shortest possible crossing point: the Strait of Gibraltar.

The main "flight path" across the Strait hits land between Gibraltar and Tarifa. Gibraltar (there's an ornithological information centre on the Upper Rock) or the Punta del Carnero (south of Algeciras) are particularly worth a visit when the wind is in the west and anywhere along the main Algeciras–Tarifa road is good when there's an easterly breeze. The birds tend to cross in waves so there will inevitably be times when little is visible and few birds will attempt the crossing in gales or heavy rain. The variety you are likely to see varies from month to month but storks return from Africa in the first months of the New Year. Many black kites, short-toed eagles and other raptors cross the Strait in February and March, but April is the "rush hour" month when huge numbers of honey buzzards are often to be seen aloft and you may even be lucky enough to spot the rare and beautiful black stork.

On to Morocco

Tarifa offers the tempting opportunity of a quick approach to **Morocco** – Tangier is feasible as a **day-trip** on a daily catamaran ferry, normally leaving at 11.30am and 6pm (Fri 7pm), returning at 8.15am or 5.30pm (local time – which is 2hr behind Spanish time in summer, 1hr in winter); check current times with Viajes Marruecotur (see below) or the Turismo. The trip takes 35min, and tickets (around €45 round-trip) are available from the FRS office (Ferrys Rápido del Sur; ℡956 68 18 30, ⊛www .frs.es) in the Estación Marítimo building in the harbour, Viajes Marruecotur, or travel agents along c/Batalla del Salado. If you're planning a day-trip, book a few days in advance.

Catamaran-based one- or two-day **excursions** to Tangier are also available starting at €49.50 for the one-day package which includes a sightseeing tour, lunch and all transport. The two-day version (currently €86) adds a night in a four-star hotel. Details of these and all other ferry information are available from the helpful Viajes Marruecotur, Avda. Constitución 5, near the Turismo (℡956 68 18 21, ⓔmcotur@mcotur.telefonica.es), where English is spoken.

walk. Along this street also you'll find a supermarket, fried fish and *churro* stalls, windsurf equipment shops and many of the larger hotels. The friendly **Turismo** (April–Sept Mon–Fri 10am–2pm & 6–8pm, Sat & Sun 10am–3pm, Oct–March Mon–Fri 10am–2pm & 5–7pm, Sat & Sun 10am–3pm; ℡956 68 09 93, ⊛www.aytotarifa.com; the private ⊛www.tarifainfo.com and ⊛www .tarifaweb.com are also useful) is at the top of the Paseo Alameda, a tree-lined promenade flanking the old town's western wall. They can provide a useful town map – also available from many hotels and *hostales* – and a free tapas booklet to help you discover the best places for a snack and a *fino*.

Accommodation

Tarifa has plenty of **places to stay** although prices tend to be higher than other places along this coast. It's wise to book ahead throughout the year, and especially in August, or whenever there are windsurfing tournaments; we have included a couple of places further out to try if things are tight. The nearest **campsites**, *Río Jara* (℡956 68 05 70) and *Torre de la Peña* (℡956 68 49 03), lie 4km and 7km northwest of town on the Cádiz road respectively. Others nearby include *Tarifa* (℡956 68 47 78) and *Paloma* (℡956 68 42 03). Tarifa's campsites are served by a frequent **bus service** from Avenida Andalucía, just to the north of the Turismo.

Hostal Africa c/María Antonia Toledo 12 ℡956 68 02 20, ⓔhostal_africa@hotmail. com. Charming small *hostal* with clean and simple en-suite rooms and spectacular sea views from a communal terrace. Rooms 5 and 6, with individual balconies, are the ones to go for. ④

Hostal Alameda Paseo de la Alameda 4 ℡956 68 11 81, ⊛www.hostalalameda.com. Pleasant *hostal-restaurante* on the Alameda with sea views and en-suite rooms with bath. ④

Hostal Facundo c/Batalla del Salado 47 ℡956 68 42 98, ⓔh.facundo@terra.es. Reliable and friendly *hostal* for simple rooms sharing bath and en-suite rooms with TV. There's a communal kitchen for guests and a storeroom for surfboards. ③–④

Hostal La Calzada c/Justino Pertíñez 7 ℡956 68 03 66. Popular and friendly *hostal* in the centre of the old town, close by the church of San Mateo, offering rooms with bath. ④

Hostal Tarik c/San Sebastián 32–36 ℡956 68 06 48. Outside the walls in the northern part of town and overlooking the coast, this *hostal* has decent balcony rooms with TV and helpful owners. ⑤

Hostal Villanueva Avda. Andalucía 11 ℡956 68 41 49. Excellent-value *hostal-restaurante* built into the north wall of the old quarter for en-suite rooms with TV. ③

Hotel La Mirada c/San Sebastian 41 ℡956 68 44 27, ⊛www.hotel-lamirada.com. Comfortable hotel outside the walls, but only 3min from the beach.

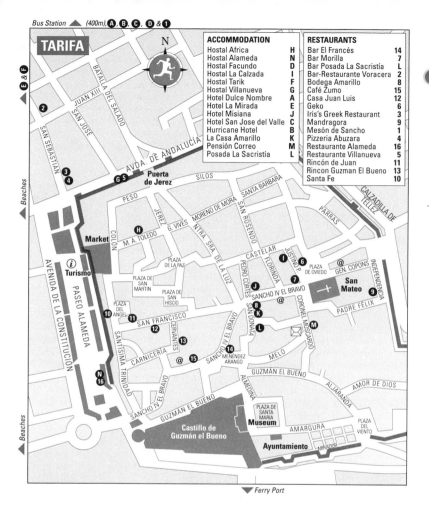

TARIFA

Bus Station ▲ (400m), Ⓐ, Ⓑ, Ⓒ, Ⓓ & ❶

ACCOMMODATION	
Hostal Africa	H
Hostal Alameda	N
Hostal Facundo	D
Hostal La Calzada	I
Hostal Tarik	F
Hostal Villanueva	G
Hotel Dulce Nombre	A
Hotel La Mirada	E
Hotel Misiana	J
Hotel San Jose del Valle	C
Hurricane Hotel	B
La Casa Amarillo	K
Pensión Correo	M
Posada La Sacristía	L

RESTAURANTS	
Bar El Francés	14
Bar Morilla	7
Bar Posada La Sacristía	L
Bar-Restaurante Voracera	2
Bodega Amarillo	8
Café Zumo	15
Casa Juan Luis	12
Geko	6
Iris's Greek Restaurant	3
Mandragora	9
Mesón de Sancho	1
Pizzeria Abuzara	4
Restaurante Alameda	16
Restaurante Villanueva	5
Rincón de Juan	11
Rincon Guzman El Bueno	13
Santa Fe	10

Rooms come with balcony and sea view, satellite TV, a/c and safe. ❹

Hotel Misiana c/Sancho IV El Bravo 18 ☎956 62 70 83, ⓦwww.misiana.com. Stylish hotel where rooms are decorated with modern art and Moroccan furnishings. ❼

Hotel San Jose del Valle Ctra. N340, km70 ☎956 68 71 22, ⓦwww.hotelsanjosedelvalle .com. At the Baelo Claudia junction 15km northwest of town, this reliable hotel often has rooms when everywhere else is full. There's also a decent restaurant below with a good-value *menú*. ❻

Hurricane Hotel Ctra. Cádiz s/n ☎956 68 49 19, ⓦwww.hotelhurricane.com. Set in dense gardens 7km west of Tarifa at the ocean's edge, this American-chic institution has tastefully decorated a/c rooms, fully equipped gym, two pools, stables, windsurfing school and its own restaurant. ❽

La Casa Amarillo c/Sancho IV El Bravo 9. Elegant and reasonably priced rooms in a restored nineteenth-century town house with a/c and cable TV; also has serviced apartments (❺) sleeping two to four with own kitchen. ❹

Pensión Correo c/Coronel Moscardó 8 ☎956 68 02 06. Overpriced but nevertheless charming and reasonably tranquil *pensión* in the old post office offering both simple and en-suite rooms. ❺

Posada La Sacristía c/San Donato 8, off c/ Sancho IV El Bravo. Stylish conversion of a seventeenth-century town house into a boutique hotel with rooms ranged around a central patio. ❼ with breakfast.

The Town

There's great appeal in wandering the crumbling ramparts of Tarifa's old walls, gazing out to sea or down into the network of lanes that surround the fifteenth-century church of **San Mateo** (daily 10am–1pm & 6–8pm; free). Don't be fooled by the crumbling Baroque exterior here, fine though it is; this was added in the eighteenth century and hides, inside, a beautiful late-Gothic church with elegant rib-vaulting in the nave and some interesting modern stained-glass windows. A very helpful leaflet in English will guide you around the church's many features, including a fine crucified Christ by the great eighteenth-century sculptor Pedro de Mena, situated along the right aisle. Nearby, a small seventh-century tombstone confirms that there was a Christian presence here before the Moorish invasion of 711. Further along, the *sagrario* is a stunning Baroque extravaganza in pink and violet, with an enchanting cupola. The church's stirring finale is at the top of the left aisle, where a copy of the original (and now lost) *retablo* contains the early seventeenth-century image of San Mateo by Martínez Montañés, Spain's greatest exponent of wood sculpture.

The restored **Castillo de Guzmán el Bueno** (Tues–Sun 11am–2pm & 5–7pm; €1.80) has great views from its towers and battlements both over the town and across the water towards Morocco. In origin the tenth-century Moorish Alcázar constructed by the great Abd ar-Rahman III, ruler of Córdoba, on the ruins of a Roman fort, this was the site of many a struggle as a strategic foothold into Spain. Known today as El Castillo de Guzmán, the appendage refers to Guzmán El Bueno (the Good), Tarifa's infamous commander during the Moorish siege of 1292, who earned his tag for his role in a superlative piece of tragic drama. Guzmán's nine-year-old son had been taken hostage by a Spanish traitor – surrender of the garrison was demanded as the price of the boy's life. Choosing "honour without a son, to a son with dishonour", Guzmán threw down his own dagger for the execution. The story, a famous piece of heroic resistance in Spain, had echoes in the Civil War siege of the Alcázar at Toledo in 1936, when the Nationalist commander refused similar threats – an echo much exploited for propaganda purposes.

Also worth a look is the charming Plaza de Santa María, behind the castle, where you'll find the Ayuntamiento and a small **museum** (currently closed; check with the Turismo) containing an interesting display of artefacts from the Neolithic, Roman and Moorish periods through to modern times. A **mirador** to the east of the square offers more views of the African coast. The daily covered

---

Whales and dolphins

A popular innovation in Tarifa is **dolphin- and whale-spotting boat trips**, run by two non-profit-making organizations: Whale Watch, Avda. de la Constitución 6 (information ☎956 62 70 13, reservations mobile ☎639 47 65 44, ⓦwww.whalewatchtarifa.net), and FIRMM (Foundation for Information and Research on Marine Mammals; ☎956 62 70 08, ⓦwww.firmm.org), c/Pedro Cortés 3, slightly west of the church of San Mateo. You need to **book in advance** (2 days' notice is preferable; €25 donation for each; children up to 14 €15). The trips last about three hours and if you don't see any dolphins or whales you get a free trip on the next sailing. Whale Watch also runs longer trips to see Orca killer whales.

A more commercial operation, Turmares, with an office on the beach road near the foot of the Paseo de la Alameda (☎956 68 07 41, ⓦwww.turmares.com), also runs whale-spotting trips with a glass-bottomed boat (€24, kids €15).

The straits of death

In Tarifa's cemetery above the town, lines of nameless headstones mark where the dead lie three deep, mostly the remains of unknown Africans washed up on the beach. In recent years the trickle of "wetbacks" eager for a share of European prosperity has turned into a flood, as gangs operating in Tangier offer to get **illegal immigrants** into Spain by evading the Spanish helicopters and coastal patrols. The usual method of transport is *pateras*, flimsy, easily capsized, flat-bottomed fishing boats designed to carry six people. Often packed with as many as thirty – who pay the equivalent of up to €600 each – these fragile craft set out to cross one of the most treacherous stretches of water in the world. Crooked skippers often tip unfortunates into the water too far out from shore and many non-swimmers drown. More often though, the boats themselves don't make it and the toll of bodies washed up along Spanish beaches has risen to alarming levels. Of those that do get safely across the straits, many are picked up by the authorities and held in the detention centre on Tarifa's harbourside, pending extradition. The few that wriggle through the police net face a life as non-citizens without papers, drifting between illegal and low-paid jobs or street-selling. The high death toll seems to have no effect on the numbers willing to take their chances on the open seas and the temptation to migrate seems to be getting ever stronger. In the meantime, Tarifa's gravediggers are kept busy as more of these boat people perish on the way to their promised El Dorado.

market (mornings) – close to the Puerta de Jerez and inside the walls – with Moorish-style arches is worth a visit; when in full swing the bars in the vicinity do a roaring trade. Incidentally, an alcove in the Puerta de Jerez arch itself now displays a large painting of *El Cristo de los Vientos* (Christ of the Winds) by Tarifa's most famous son, the renowned modern artist Guillermo Perez Villalta.

The Beaches

The town **beaches**, separated by a causeway, are the small, popular and sheltered Playa Chica on the Mediterranean side and the Playa de los Lances (aka Playa Grande) facing the Atlantic. Heading northwest from Tarifa, towards the Punta Paloma, you find perhaps the loveliest beaches along the whole Costa de la Luz – wide stretches of yellow or silvery-white sand, washed by some magical rollers. The same winds that have created such perfect conditions for windsurfing can, however, be a problem for more casual enjoyment, sandblasting those attempting to relax on towels or mats and whipping the water into whitecaps.

At **TARIFA BEACH**, a little bay 9km from town, there are restaurants, campsites and a *hostal* at the base of a tree-tufted bluff. There's a windsurfing school here, which acts as the local centre for the sport. Nearby *Hotel Dos Mares* (see overleaf) is another windsurf centre that offers courses and rents out equipment. For more seclusion head for one of the numerous **beach–campsites** on either side (see "Accommodation"), signposted from the main road or accessible by walking along the coast.

Eating, drinking and nightlife

Tarifa has a wide range of **places to eat**, divided between the old town inside the walls and the new town beyond this. In the latter zone it's worth seeking out c/San Sebastián where there are quite a few tempting possibilities. This is another place to try Cádiz's tasty *urta* (sea bream), available all over town.

There's little in the way of entertainment beyond the bars and a couple of *discotecas*. Tarifa's best summer **club** is the open-air *Balneario* fronting the Playa de los Lances, the larger of the town's twin beaches; on windier days there's the indoor *Zoo House*, Plaza de San Hiscio, off c/San Francisco. In summer the town council also puts up *carpas* (disco tents) on the Playa de los Lances beach at the eastern end of town.

Bar El Francés Paseo c/Sancho IV El Bravo 21. A lively French tapas and *raciones* bar with a Gallic slant on such staples as *calamares, rabo de toro* and *tortilla de camarones*. Has a small street terrace.

Bar Morilla c/Sancho IV El Bravo 2. Central bar where *tarifeños* gather to munch early evening tapas while contemplating the old stones of nearby San Mateo.

Bar Posada La Sacristía c/San Donato 8, off c/Sancho IV El Bravo. Relaxing and stylish café-bar beneath the hotel of the same name. They stage live music most nights from June–Sept (including flamenco) and all the furnishings and furniture are for sale. The attached restaurant has a *menú* for €20.

Bar-Restaurante Voracera c/San Sebastián 28. Superb neighbourhood bar-restaurant with tasty tapas and good seafood; *besugo a la espalda* (red bream) is a house special and there's a *menú* (Mon–Fri) for €6.

Bodega Amarillo c/Sancho IV El Bravo 9. Good bodega serving up *raciones* of *cerdo iberico jamón*, plus *calamares a la plancha* (fried squid) and in season *atun del almadraba* (the freshest tuna there is).

Café Zumo c/Sancho El Bravo IV 26b. Good breakfast bar with a selection of fruit and vegetable juices and a variety of breads and healthy snacks.

Casa Juan Luis c/San Francisco 15 ☎956 68 49 00. Despite its proximity to the sea this evening-only place is a shrine to meat, in particular pork in all its Iberian variations. The restaurant, housed in a *casa antigua*, also has a beautiful patio and outdoor terrace. The eponymous owner is a big *toros* fan and the restaurant closes when there's a *corrida*. *Menú* for about €20.

Geko Plaza de Oviedo 1. Fronting the church of San Mateo this is a pleasant little terrace bar serving a variety of economical *raciones*, salads and pasta dishes as well as *bocadillos* and plenty of vegetarian options.

Iris's Greek Restaurant c/San Sebastián 10. Friendly little Greek restaurant with quite a few vegetarian options.

Mandragora c/Independencía 3 ☎956 68 12 91. One of a number of restaurants and tapas bars in town offering dishes from both sides of the straits: in addition to Moroccan couscous and *berenjenas bereber* (aubergine), it does excellent tapas, including *boquerones rellenos* (stuffed anchovies). Main dishes €9–15.

Mesón de Sancho Ctra. Cadíz–Málaga, 6km east of town ☎956 68 49 00. One of the best restaurants in this zone for fish and meat dishes but not cheap. There's a *menú* for around €15.

Pizzeria Abuzara c/San Sebastián 4. Italian owned pizzeria making the best pizzas in town; their menu also has a wide range of meat and seafood possibilities. Pleasant courtyard terrace.

Restaurante Alameda Paseo Alameda 4. Popular restaurant outside the western wall, which does reasonable *platos combinados* and a tasty paella. *Menú* for €9.

Restaurante Villanueva Avda. Andalucía 11. Fine restaurant of the *hostal* of the same name; their *urta* is prepared in five different ways and there's a good-value *menú* for €7.

Rincón de Juan c/San Francisco 22. Attractive fish restaurant whose specialities include *urta* prepared with a variety of sauces.

Rincon Guzman El Bueno c/Cervantes 4. Very good tapas bar and restaurant with a pleasant terrace and lots of choices including a *surtido de pescado frito* (fried fish platter).

Santa Fe Paseo Alameda with entry also at c/Santísima Trinidad 19. Excellent mid-priced French-run bistro with a terrace on the Alameda. They serve up a range of fish and meat dishes accompanied by great (French) wines. Their crepes (served in afternoons with tea or coffee as well as to diners at other times) are mouthwateringly authentic.

Listings

Diving & Surfing courses The Turismo has an extensive list of companies. One company offering diving courses in English are Aventura Marina, Avda. Andalucía 1 ☎956 05 46 26, @www.aventuramarina.org. Surfing and kitesurfing courses (in English) are offered by X-trem @www.tarifaxtrem.com, Tarifa Max Sports @www.tarifamax.net and Kite Surfing @www.kitesurfingtarifa.com.

Horse riding The area around Tarifa is good riding country and horses can be hired from *Hotel Dos*

Surfing on the Gulf of Cádiz

This stretch of Atlantic coast provides some of the best conditions in the world for **windsurfing** and the current rave watersport, **kitesurfing**. International competitions in both sports are held in Tarifa. Board surfing is currently less popular due to the often difficult conditions but on the right day you can still have some great rides. Courses in all water sports are available in Tarifa (see "Listings") and equipment can be rented at numerous shops along c/Batalla del Salado (the Turismo can also supply information). Kitesurf novices are advised to get some instruction (especially regarding potential hazards) before striking out on their own. Below are some of the main beaches with a description of conditions. More information as well as details of courses and companies hiring out equipment is available on ⓦ www.tarifainfo .com/en/surfing.html.

Barbate Sheltered town beach protected by harbour wall. Good option when winds are strong and everywhere else is blown out.

Yerba Buena West-facing beach just beyond Barbate with 200m right-breaking wave off point. Generally needs 2m of swell. North/northeast winds are best. Experienced surfers only.

Caños de Meca South-facing bay approached via pine forest on road from Vejer de la Frontera. Right-breaking wave from point and left-breaking reef breaks. Works on northwest winds. Low tide. Experienced surfers only.

El Palmar West-facing beach with waves from both right and left. Best at mid-to-low tide when waves can reach heights of up to 3m (but is best on 1.5–2m swells).

Conil Good town beach but only works on pushing and dropping tide.

Cabo de Roche (northwest of Conil) Protection from strong east winds. Very fast hollow waves that have tendency to snap boards with no mercy.

La Barrosa (near Sancti Petri) Extensive beach breaks working on same conditions as El Palmar.

Mares (☎ 956 68 40 35, ⓦ www.aventuraequestre. com & ⓦ www.hoteldosmares.com), on the N340, 9km northwest of town, which offers single or multiple-day excursions for around €25 per hour. **Internet** *Bar El Trato*, c/Sancho El Bravo 28, near the castle; *El Navegante*, c/General Copons 1, to the side of the Iglesia de San Mateo; *Ciber*

Pandor@, c/Sancho IV El Bravo 5, fronting the same church.

Laundry A laundry, Girasol, c/Colon 12, slightly east of the Turismo (☎ 956 62 70 37) will wash, dry and fold clothes for collection the same day.

Vehicle and bike rental Speedline, c/Batalla del Salado 10 ☎ 956 62 70 48.

Baelo Claudia

Around the coast from the Punta Paloma to the west of Tarifa and almost on the beach at Bolonia Cove are the extensive ruins of the Roman town of **BAELO CLAUDIA** (June–Sept Tues–Sun 10am–8pm; March–May & Oct Tues–Sun 10am–7pm; Nov–Feb Tues–Sun 10am–6pm; free with EU passport, otherwise €1.50). A recent controversy here has centred on the construction of a "concrete bunker" overlooking the site which is intended to become an information centre and museum. The building – totally out of sync with the site itself and the surrounding landscape – has been the focus of numerous protests by local environmental groups.

Established in the second century BC, the Roman town – rather like modern Zahara and Barbate nearby – became prosperous with the exploitation of tuna and mackerel to make the fish sauce **garum** of which the Romans were passionately fond. The town reached the peak of its prosperity during the first century AD

△ Baelo Claudia

when it was raised to the status of a *municipium* or self-governing township by Emperor Claudius, and the buildings you see today date from this period. Recently reorganized, there are now a series of information boards (in Spanish only) that guide you around the site concluding at the fish factory on the beach.

A tour of the site starts with a look at the bastions of an impressive entry gate in the town's eastern wall. Beyond here a well-preserved rectangular **forum** is best viewed from the platform at the northern end supporting a row of **three temples** to Jupiter, Juno and Minerva, the great gods of imperial Rome. Just west of here is a smaller temple dedicated to the Egyptian goddess, Isis, and directly ahead, occupying the whole south side of the forum, are the remains of the **basilica**, or law court. At the eastern end of this building stood a colossal white marble statue of the second-century emperor Trajan, the head of which is now preserved in the museum at Cádiz (p.243). A replica of the statue now occupies the site. On the forum's eastern flank stood a line of *tabernae* or shops, which seem to have been superseded by the later *macellum* or **market** built to the west of the basilica. The newly restored **theatre**, built into the hillside to take advantage of the slope is also worth a look. The **main street**, the *decumanus maximus*, runs east–west behind the basilica and is crossed to the east of the forum by the *cardo maximus* which cuts through the centre on a north–south axis. You can also see the remains of the public **baths**, once supplied with water from the nearby Sierra de la Plata by three aqueducts.

Probably the most interesting series of buildings stand to the south of the site proper, on the beach. Here has been revealed a **fish factory**, which produced the famous *garum* and you can still clearly make out the great stone vats used to make this concoction – always located as near to the sea and as far away from the town as possible because of the stench. The process involved removing the heads, entrails, eggs, soft roes and blood of the fish, layering these in the vats with salt and brine, and leaving them for weeks to "mature". The resulting mixture was then slopped into Amphorae and shipped all over the empire, particularly to Rome, where the poet Martial droolingly described it as "made of the first blood of a mackerel breathing still, an expensive gift". The mackerel sauce was the Roman equivalent of beluga and they paid the earth for small quantities of it; the tuna-based variety, however, was less of a luxury and much cheaper.

Things may be about to change dramatically here if the governments of Spain and Morocco get EU funding for a **vehicle-carrying train tunnel** connecting Andalucía with Tangier. Bolonia is regarded as the prime site for the entrance on the Spanish side and would tie up with a new rail link to be built between Cádiz and Algeciras. Enjoy the tranquillity while it lasts.

Practicalities

Getting here from the Tarifa–Cádiz road, turn off down a small side road (signed), on the left 15km beyond Tarifa, at a hotel-restaurant named *San José del Vallé* (which serves a good *menú*). You can also walk to Bolonia along the coast from either the Punta Paloma west of Tarifa, or coming from the opposite direction, Zahara de los Atunes (3–4hr), with a couple of natural obstacles en route.

There's a great beach fronting the site, with a scattering of **bars** and **eating places** open in summer. You'll also find a very pleasant **place to stay** at the eastern end of the village: ⚐ *Hostal La Hormiga Voladora,* c/El Lentiscal 15 (☎956 68 85 62; ❹), which has garden rooms with and without bath close to the beach. Nearby *Hostal Lola,* c/El Lentiscal 26 (☎956 68 85 36, ⓦwww .hostallola.com; ❸), is another attractive possibility for rooms with and without bath and has a friendly proprietor. *Hostal Bellavista* (☎ & ⓕ956 68 85 53; ❹), near the turn-off into the village, is another possibility for decent en-suite rooms with TV; they also rent some more expensive apartments. For **food** the restaurant at the latter isn't bad and has a *menú* for around €10, and *Las Rejas,* near the *Hostal La Hormiga Voladora* above, is also worth a try.

Zahara, Atlanterra and Barbate

Eight kilometres north as the crow flies (but a hefty 28km dog-leg by road along the N340), **ZAHARA DE LOS ATUNES** is a small fishing village linked by an infrequent **bus** service with Barbate (see overleaf). Beginning to show signs of development with the construction of the obligatory Paseo Marítimo well in hand – if currently stalled – for the time being it retains the character of a simple, friendly resort with good tapas bars, hospitable people and a fabulous eight-kilometre-long **beach**.

The best of the budget **places to stay** is *Hostal Monte Mar,* c/Peñón 12 (☎956 43 90 47; ❸), bang on the shore and reached by turning right immediately after crossing the bridge into the village and following the road to the end. The friendly owners offer sea-view rooms with bath and balcony, and there are lots of terraces for lounging alfresco. Alternatives include an excellent seafront hotel, the ⚐ *Gran Sol,* at Avda. de la Playa 20 (☎956 43 93 09, ⓦwww .gransolhotel.com; ❼ with breakfast), also with welcoming proprietors and an extension where rooms overlook a garden pool. Of the handful of other places (all of which are usually full in August), the newish *Hotel Doña Lola,* at Plaza Thomson 1, just over the bridge (☎956 43 90 09, ⓕ956 43 90 08; ❼), is bright and swish with a garden pool, while close by, the pleasant *Hotel Almadraba & Almadrabeta,* c/María Luisa 13 (☎956 43 92 74; ❺), with its own restaurant, is another possibility. Out on the road to Atlanterra *Hotel Porfirio,* Ctra. Atlanterra 33 (☎956 44 95 15, ⓦwww.hotelporfirio.com; ❻ with breakfast), is set back from the beach and has a pool and restaurant. A little further along the same road *Hotel Antonio*, c/Atlanterra km1 (☎956 43 91 35, ⓦwww.antoniohoteles. com; ❻–❼), has decent value rooms in its two-star seafront hotel and more luxurious accommodation in the adjoining extension. Zahara's **campsite** *Bahía de la Plata* (☎956 43 90 40) lies 1.5km out of town on the road towards Atlanterra and also rents out bungalows and studios (❻), both with cooking facilities.

Places to eat here include the central *Marisquería Porfirio*, Plaza Tamarón 5, for seafood, and the nearby *Bar Ropiti*, c/María Luisa 6, for meat and fish *platos combinados*. One of the best tapas bars on this stretch of coast is ⚔ *Casa Juanito* at c/Sagasta 7, serving up deliciously fresh seafood; it has now added an equally outstanding restaurant. The restaurant of the *Gran Sol* is also very good and has a daily lunch and dinner *menú* for €15. One mid-priced place a cut above the rest is ⚔ *Antonio*, on the seafront 1km out of town towards Atlanterra (☎956 43 95 42), where fish is king and *atun al horno* and *dorada a la sal* are just two of the house specialities.

South from Zahara a road winds down for 4km to the settlement of **ATLANTERRA**, another hamlet seized upon by developers and, a few kilometres beyond this, to a wonderful **beach**, the Playa Camarinal. Atlanterra itself is rapidly being transformed into a warren of holiday apartments ringed around the bland *Hotel Melia*, part of the luxury hotel chain. Beyond here the road continues for a further 4km passing a few secluded villas circled by lofty palms before coming to a dead end at the **Playa Camarinal** and, a bit further on, the Faro del Punta Camarinal lighthouse. It's a stunning beach, but there are no facilities whatsoever.

BARBATE, next along the coast and linked by a frequent daily **bus** service with Vejer de la Frontera, is an unkempt and rather featureless little town dominated by its harbour and canning industry which processes the tuna caught along this stretch of coast. As the major fishing port in these parts Barbate has some excellent **tapas bars** and **fish restaurants** along its seafront: *Bar Rufo* is

Andalucía and the bluefin tuna

The catch of the **bluefin tuna** is a ritual that has gone on along the Costa de la Luz since ancient times and today still employs many of the age-old methods. The bluefin is the largest of the tuna family, weighing in at around 200 kilos, and the season lasts from April to June as the fish migrate towards the warmer waters of Mediterranean (*el derecho*) to reproduce, and from early July to mid-August when they return to the high seas (*el revés*). Fishing communities dotted along this stretch of Andalucian coast have been taking advantage of this annual abundance of tuna since the Phoenician period and probably long back into prehistory. The methods used to catch the tuna are still referred to by the Moorish name *almadraba* ("place for hitting"), which involved dragging the giant fish ashore in great nets and clubbing them to death. Today the fish are caught at sea by herding and corralling them in a huge net stretched between a circle of boats where they are gaffed – their blood turning the sea crimson – before the weakened fish are then hauled aboard. The biggest market is Japan, and Japanese factory ships can often be spotted waiting offshore in season ready to buy up as much of the catch as they can. Once the tuna are on board, the fish are rapidly gutted, washed, filleted and frozen ready to cross another ocean to be eaten raw as sushi. In recent years tuna numbers have been declining and the season shortening – probably the result of overfishing – much to the concern of the people of Barbate, Conil de la Frontera and Zahara de los Atunes, for whom the catch represents an important source of income for fishermen and a provider of employment in the canning factories nearby.

the best of the cheaper ones, with the slightly pricier *Bar Nani* and the upmarket *El Churrasco* two other places of note. There's a pleasant **walk** (about two and a half hours starting from the west side of the fishing harbour) from here to Los Caños de Meca, through a pine forest and passing the Torre de Tajo (a watchtower once used for spotting invading pirates) with great views, but take care at the cliff edges.

Los Caños de Meca and El Palmar

From Barbate a rolling scenic road winds its way through the verdant pinewoods of the **Parque Natural de Acantilado**. Although Barbate can hardly be recommended for a stopover the natural park does have a wonderful retreat at 🗼 *El Palomar de la Breña* (☎956 43 50 03, 🌐www.palomardelabrena.com; ❺ with breakfast) a superb *hotel rural* with a remarkable dovecote of immense proportions authenticated by the *Guinness Book of Records* as the largest in the world. No longer in use, the dovecote's 8000 nesting places once produced birds for the Spanish Indies fleet who used them to communicate with Spain while out in the Atlantic. The hotel's friendly proprietors are a mine of information on activities in the park and give out a free map detailing walks and mountain bike routes. The hotel is reached via a turn-off from the CA2143, 5km out of Barbate. Precise details of its location can be obtained by ringing ahead (English spoken) or found on the hotel's website.

A further 5km beyond the turn-off for the hotel the road descends into **LOS CAÑOS DE MECA** (served by sporadic **buses** from Barbate to Conil). A small village surrounded by pine groves and a favourite summer escape for *sevillanos*, Los Caños has a long, beautiful beach lined with rocky coves and freshwater springs, marred only by some unfortunate hotel developments on its southern flank. There used to be a hippy colony here and, although this crowd has now gone, some of the laid-back atmosphere lingers, especially among the groups of naturists who swim out to the more secluded coves along the coast. If you want to **stay** – and places tend to be pricey although rates drop dramatically out of high season – you'll find two mid-range hotels on Avenida Trafalgar: the *Hotel Madreselva* at no. 102 (☎956 43 72 29, 🌐www.madreselvahotel.com; ❻ with breakfast), with a pool, and the cheaper and friendly *Hotel Fortuna*, at no. 34 (☎956 43 70 75, 🌐www.hotelfortuna.com; ❹), where en-suite rooms come with balcony, sea view, room safe and TV. Beyond here, at the extreme eastern end of the strand, *Hostal Mar de Frente*, Avda. de Trafalgar 3 (☎956 43 70 25; ❺) has en-suite rooms above the beach with sea views. Inland from the lighthouse *Casa Meca*, Avda. Trafalgar s/n (mobile ☎639613402, 🌐www.casameca.com; ❺) rents out studios and apartments and *Rough Guide* readers with this guide can claim a ten percent discount. Another possibility is *Casa Karen* (☎956 43 70 67, 🌐www.casakaren.com; ❺) 500m east of the turning for the lighthouse and signed down a track for a further few hundred metres; various styles of rooms and apartments (including traditional *chozo* huts) enjoy a garden setting. Just west of town, towards Cape Trafalgar, is a **campsite**, *Caños de Meca* (☎956 43 71 20), with plenty of shade. The central *Camping Camaleón* (☎956 43 71 54) on Avenida Trafalgar is less attractive and further from the beach.

The numerous **places to eat** close to the seafront include *El Caña* on c/ Trafalgar, with a great balcony view of the beach. One place worth seeking is 🗼 *Venta Curro* where the food is excellent and there's a *menú* offering local specialities. Los Caños also has lots of **bars**, lively in season; *El Pirata* at Avda. de Trafalgar s/n sometimes features live music, including jazz. Next door, *La Jaima*, a tented disco, attracts quite a crowd in summer. In the lighthouse zone,

Las Dunas – a big log cabin with *copas* and music – is another popular place worth trying.

The coast road west from Los Caños (taking a left after 5km and continuing for a further 3km) brings you to **EL PALMAR**, a sleepy and isolated seafront settlement popular with surfers and about as peaceful a place as you could wish. This may all be about to change, however, as plans have been announced to build a huge tourist complex, scheduled to be completed in 2007. For the moment, fronting an excellent, if narrow, beach you'll find a few seafood **restaurants** including *Hostal-Restaurant Francisco* (T956 23 27 86, F956 23 27 88; ❺) with delightful balcony **rooms**. Slightly north of here *Hostal Francisco Alferez* (T956 23 21 34; ❹) is a cheaper option for en-suite rooms above a fish restaurant with a €10 *menú*. At the north end of the beach, the friendly *Hostal La Ilusión* (T956 23 23 98; ❺ with breakfast) also has comfortable rooms and a good restaurant beyond an extensive garden. Further north again the friendly *Hostal Café-Bar Reyes* (T956 23 22 11; ❹) is sited just beyond the lighthouse with tidy en-suite a/c rooms above a superb fish restaurant. To rent an **apartment**, contact *La Chanca* (T956 23 22 55 Spanish only; ❻). Set 1km back from the beach there's a very good **camp-site**, *El Palmar* (T956 23 21 61), with a great pool, plenty of shade, restaurant, bar and supermarket, and lots of activities on offer, including trekking, scuba diving, and horse riding.

Vejer de la Frontera

While you're on this stretch of the Costa de la Luz, be sure to take time to head inland and visit **VEJER DE LA FRONTERA**, a classically white, Moorish-looking hill town set in a cleft between great protective hills that rear high above the road from Tarifa to Cádiz. Until relatively recent times the women of Vejer wore long, dark cloaks that veiled their faces like nuns' habits; though still trotted out in many guidebooks, this custom is now virtually extinct outside fiestas. The bus usually makes a stop at two *hostal-restaurantes* on the major road at the foot of the hill – *La Barca de Vejer* (T956 45 00 83, F956 45 10 83; ❸) does superb *bocadillos de lomo* – before toiling up to the *pueblo* proper.

Maintaining a brooding detachment from the world below for most of its history, Vejer has a remoteness and a Moorish feel as potent as anywhere in Spain. Almost certainly a prehistoric hilltop Iberian citadel, Vejer was utilized as a fortress during the **Phoenician** and **Carthaginian** epochs of the first millennium BC to protect coastal factories and fishing grounds from the warlike Iberians of the interior. Dubbed Besipo by the later **Romans**, it was as the **Moorish** town of Bekkeh that Vejer rose to prominence as an important agricultural centre on the western frontier of the kingdom of Granada. Taken by Fernando III in 1250, it was immediately handed over to Alonso Pérez de Guzmán, founder of the ducal house of Medina Sidonia and later hero of Tarifa.

Arrival and information

Arriving by **bus** you're dropped at the Parque de Los Remedios from where you'll need to ascend c/Los Remedios to reach La Plazuela, the effective centre of town. Coming in by **car**, park in the car park at the entrance to the town near the foot of c/Remedios. Sited next to the car park as you enter Vejer, the **Turismo**, Avda. de los Remedios 2 (April–Sept Mon–Sat 9am–3pm & 6–10pm, Sun 10am–2pm; Oct–March Mon–Fri 10am–2pm & 5–7pm, Sat 10am–2pm; T956 45 17 36, Wwww.turismovejer.com), gives out an excellent

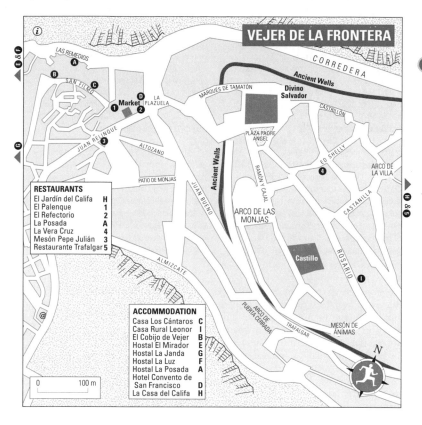

VEJER DE LA FRONTERA

RESTAURANTS

El Jardín del Califa	H
El Palenque	1
El Refectorio	2
La Posada	A
La Vera Cruz	4
Mesón Pepe Julián	3
Restaurante Trafalgar	5

ACCOMMODATION

Casa Los Cántaros	C
Casa Rural Leonor	I
El Cobijo de Vejer	B
Hostal El Mirador	E
Hostal La Janda	G
Hostal La Luz	F
Hostal La Posada	A
Hotel Convento de San Francisco	D
La Casa del Califa	H

free **map** (also available from the *Hotel Convento* when the Turismo is closed).

Both Vejer's **Internet** cafés are a few minutes from the centre. The most tranquil is *Vi@.PC* (10am–8pm), Avda. San Miguel 18, at the foot of c/Juan Relinque. Also out of the centre is *Ciber Sancho IV* (daily 10am–11pm), Arco Sancho 4, near Plaza de España. Discover Andalucía, Avda. Los Remedios 45, near the bus stop (☎956 44 75 75), rents out **mountain bikes** and has information on all kinds of outdoor activities in the area.

Accommodation

Limited accommodation can often make finding a room hard work if you're here for Semana Santa or in July and August. Vejer's **campsite** (☎956 45 00 98, ⓦwww.campingvejer.com) is located below the town on the main N340 road, close to the *La Barca de Vejer* restaurant (see opposite).

Casa Los Cántaros c/San Filmo 14, close to La Plazuela ☎956 44 75 92. Very good and economical *pensión* for rooms with bath. ➋
Casa Rural Leonor c/Rosario 25, near the *castillo* ☎956 45 10 85, ⓦwww.casaleonor.com. This converted Moorish dwelling has comfortable

en-suite rooms with TV, friendly proprietors, and fabulous views towards Morocco from a roof terrace. ➌

El Cobijo de Vejer c/ San Filmo 7 ☎956 45 50 23, ⓦwww.elcobijo.com. Excellent *hostal* created inside a traditional house with delightful flower-filled patio and individual rooms on various levels. The higher priced *Zahara* and *Xauen* (the latter has two fabulous terraces) with own kitchens are the ones to go for. All rooms are a/c, Internet-connected, and have fridges and satellite TV. ⑤–⑥ with breakfast.

Hostal El Mirador c/Calzada de San Lázaro 39, near the bus stop at the entrance to the town ☎956 45 17 13, ✉hostal_el_mirador@wanadoo.es. Clean en-suite rooms with TV. ③

Hostal La Janda Cerro Clarisas s/n, signposted up a side road on the way in ☎956 45 01 42. Another superb *hostal* with light, en-suite rooms with TV. ③

Hostal La Luz Avda. Buenavista, 32 ☎956 45 10 06, ⓦwww.hostaluz.com. Pleasant new *hostal* decorated with artworks throughout and offering en-suite rooms with a/c and TV. Easy parking nearby. ④

Hostal La Posada c/Los Remedios 2, near the top of the hill as you enter the town ☎956 45 02 58, ⓦwww.hostal-laposada.com. Good en-suite rooms

above a restaurant and most with fine views. Has some single rooms too, and rents out apartments (⑤) sleeping up to four. ③

Hotel Convento de San Francisco La Plazuela s/n ☎956 45 10 01, ⓦwww.tugasa.com. Housed in a converted seventeenth-century convent on the smaller of the town's two main squares, this very pleasant and surprisingly reasonable hotel has stylish a/c rooms with TV. Also has own restaurant and *cafetería* (see below). ⑤

La Casa del Califa Plaza de España 16 ☎956 44 77 30, ⓦwww.lacasadelcalifa.com. Stunning hotel created inside a refurbished partly Moorish house, where stylish rooms are decorated with Moroccan lamps and fittings and come Internet-equipped; guests have use of two patios, a terrace with views, library and the price includes buffet breakfast. *Rough Guide* readers with this book are entitled to a ten-percent discount which should be claimed at check-in. ⑤

The Town

Vejer is best savoured by randomly exploring the brilliant-white, labyrinthine alleyways, wandering past iron-grilled windows, balconies and patios, and slipping into one of numerous bars. The **castillo** (daily 11am–2pm & 6–10pm; free), in the heart of the old quarter, is Moorish in origin but underwent substantial rebuilding in the fifteenth century when it was used by the dukes of Medina Sidonia as a summer retreat. Currently occupied by the Boy Scouts (one of whom will show you around and politely encourage you to buy something at their gift shop), the main things to see are a splendid horseshoe arch and some Moorish plasterwork, as well as great views from the terrace. A small **museum** houses finds ancient and not so old discovered in and around the town. To the north of the castle, at the end of c/Ramón y Cajal, the church of **Divino Salvador** (daily 11am–1.30pm & 6.30–8.30pm; free) is a sixteenth-century rebuild of an earlier mosque whose minaret now serves as its tower. The interior is a curious mix of mainly Gothic and Mudéjar styles. From here c/Castrillón descends to the **Plaza de España**, the lovely main square, overlooked by a white-walled Ayuntamiento, and centring on a delightful fountain decorated with nineteenth-century Triana tiles from Sevilla. North of here, **Paseo de la Corredera** offers spectacular views over the countryside to the nearby hill towns of Medina Sidonia and Alcalá de los Gazules. The **Torre de la Corredera** halfway along here was a watchtower used for communicating with those towns.

Eating, drinking and entertainment

Vejer has plenty of places for **eating** and **drinking**. In the old quarter, the *Hotel Convento de San Francisco*'s *cafetería* housed in the old convent's former chapel is one of the best places for **breakfast**. Nightlife is fairly tame, limited to a few bars around town that keep late hours. At the *Peña Flamenca Águilar de Vejer*, c/Rosario (near the castle), you can sample *manzanilla* from the barrel and take in occasional weekend **flamenco** concerts; the Turismo keeps details of upcoming performances. *Bodegas Gallardo* (daily 10am–6pm), on the main Barbate road below the town, welcome visitors to sample and buy the wines and *finos* of the region.

Bar Peneque Plaza de España 27. Traditional local bar built into a cave with tables at the back for munching *raciones* should you not feel like joining in the domino games favoured by regulars.

Café-Bar La Bodeguita c/Marqués de Tamarón 9, uphill from La Plazuela and near the church. Entertaining small tapas place where *pimiento de piquillo* (peppers stuffed with cod) and *albondigas* (meatballs) are specials.

El Jardín del Califa Plaza de España 16. The restaurant attached to the hotel of the same name has a Moroccan chef and serves up a variety of Moroccan and Middle-Eastern inspired dishes on a tree-shaded courtyard terrace. Specialities include *tagines* and spicy Moroccan fish dishes.

El Palenque c/San Francisco 1, in the market. Bistro-style local eaterie with an outdoor terrace noted for its *guisos* (stews) and good fried fish.

El Refectorio La Plazuela. The upmarket restaurant of the *Hotel Convento de San Francisco* is a very good mid-priced place offering many local specialities.

La Posada c/Los Remedios 2. The restaurant of the *hostal* of the same name is a good place for economical *platos combinados* and simple meals.

La Vera Cruz c/Eduardo Shelly 1. Intimate French-run restaurant housed in a sixteenth-century former chapel offering a mix of dishes from both sides of the Pyrenees. *Conejo con ciruelas* (rabbit with prunes) and *dorada relleño al horno* (sea bream) are signature dishes and (Mon–Fri) there's a *menú* for €22.

Mesón Pepe Julián c/Juan Relinque 7, just off La Plazuela. Popular local bar with azulejo-lined walls serving up decent tapas – specials include *chorizo iberico* – and has an economical *menú*.

Restaurante Trafalgar Plaza España 31. One of Vejer's better restaurants with a pleasant terrace on the square for summer eating. Wide range of dishes including *revuelta con morcilla* (scrambled eggs with blood sausage) and *venado con cabrales* (venison with cheese sauce).

Venta Pinto La Barca de Vejer. Down below the town at the road junction with the N340 this is an outstanding mid-priced restaurant with a great range of seafood, fish and game dishes. House specials include *solomillo* (pork loin) and *rape con azafran y langostinos* (monkfish with saffron and prawns) and there's a *menú* for around €17.

Conil

Back on the coast, a dozen or so kilometres further northwest of Vejer de la Frontera, is the increasingly popular resort of **CONIL**. Though this former fishing village appears entirely modern when viewed from the beach, plenty of older buildings survive, and its mainly domestic visitors create a fun, if family-oriented, atmosphere, and throughout the summer, you can also indulge in some very lively nightlife. During the second week in June Conil celebrates the **Semana del Atun de Almedraba** (tuna catch week) when the first half of the tuna season reaches its peak (see box p.228) and the town's restaurants participate in a *ruta gastronomica* offering different dishes prepared with the fish at discount prices (details from the Turismo).

The **beaches** (the central Playa de Los Bateles and Playa de La Fontanilla to the north), Conil's *raison d'être*, appear as a wide bay of brilliant yellow stretching for miles to either side of town and lapped by an amazingly gentle Atlantic. The area immediately in front of town is the family beach: up to the northwest you can walk to some more sheltered coves; across the river to the southeast is a topless and nudist area. The beach here is virtually unbroken until it reaches the **Cabo Trafalgar**, off which Lord Nelson achieved victory but lost his life on October 21, 1805. If the winds are blowing, this is one of the most sheltered beaches in the area. You can get there by road, save for the last 400m across the sands to the rock.

Practicalities

Most **buses** drop you off at the Transportes Comes station on c/Carretera; walk towards the sea and you'll soon pass Conil's helpful **Turismo** (May–Oct daily 8am–2pm & 5.30–8.30pm; Nov–April Mon–Sat 8am–2pm, Sun 8.30am–2pm; ☎956 44 05 01, ⓦwww.conil.org), at the junction of Carretera and c/Menéndez Pidal; a summer office is located in the Torre de Guzmán in the old town (June–Sept daily 10.30am–2.30pm & 6.30–9.30pm). Make sure to pick up their town map and useful booklet *Conil en su Bolsillo*, which details all the town's tapas bars, restaurants and much more. For renting a **scooter** or **mountain bike** – useful ways for getting around and visiting outlying beaches – Conil-Rent (T956 44 15 36, W www.conilguide.de), c/González Sánchez Fuentes s/n, northwest of the main Turismo, is reliable; *Rough Guide* readers with this guide can claim a ten-percent discount. **Cars** can be hired from Crown Car Hire (T956 45 60 03), c/Rafael Alberti 2, fifty metres from the Turismo. **Internet** access is available at the pleasant *Café de la Mar*, c/Carril de la Fuente, near the Torre de Guzmán, with plenty of screens, and also at *Café de la Habana*, Plaza de Santa Catalina s/n, with more limited facilities.

Accommodation

Conil has numerous **hotels and hostales** – August is the only time when you'll struggle to find a bed. This is when you may need to seek out one of a multitude of *casas particulares*, details of which are available from the Turismo. Prices tend to be at their highest in July–August too (the rates we quote), but outside this period they drop by at least a third. Nearby **campsites** include *Fuente del Gallo* (T956 44 01 37; March–Sept) in the *urbanización* Fuente del Gallo, a three-kilometre walk (or taxi ride) to the north of the resort.

Hostal La Posada c/Quevedo s/n, just northeast of Plaza de España T956 44 41 71, W www .laposadadeconil.com. Dapper *hostal* with clean and tidy en-suite a/c rooms with TV – many with sea views – above a good restaurant. ④
Hostal La Villa Plaza de España 6 T956 44 10 53. Economical en-suite rooms above a bar-restaurant in a central square. ③
Hostal Los Hermanos c/Virgen 2 T956 44 01 96. A piece of Conil's history, this wonderful old *fonda* first opened its doors in 1900 but the house dates from the eighteenth century. As a plaque outside informs, the founder of Cadiz's *Carnaval* "Tío de la Tiza" was born here in 1833 (see p.237). Today the friendly owners offer en-suite rooms around a flower-bedecked central patio and also have some fully equipped apartments (④). ③
Hostal Santa Catalina c/Carcel 2, off Plaza Santa Catalina T956 44 15 83, W www.hostal santcatalina.webconil.com. Pleasant small *hostal* with en-suite a/c rooms with TV. ④
Hostal Sonrisa del Mar c/Huerto 3, close to the seafront Paseo del Atlántico T956 44 27 18. Fronting the town beach (Playa de Los Bateles) this seafront *hostal* has balcony a/c rooms with TV and sea views. ⑤
Hostal Torre de Guzmán c/Hospital 5, southwest of Plaza de España T956 44 30 61. En-suite a/c rooms with TV in a relatively new place above a restaurant. ⑤
Hotel Almadraba c/Señores Curas 4, south of Plaza de España T956 45 60 37, W www .hotelalmadrabaconil.com. Taking its name from the annual tuna cull, this is a pleasant new hotel

with stylish well-equipped rooms ranged around a charming patio. It also has its own bar-cafetería and car park. ⑥ with breakfast
Hotel Costa Conil Playa de la Fontanilla T956 45 60 33, W www.hotelcostaconil.com. Modern four-star luxury hotel close to the beach at the eastern end of the seafront. Well-equipped rooms plus pool, bar and restaurant complete the picture. Check their website for discounts. ⑧
Hotel Diufain Cañada del Rosal s/n, Fuente del Gallo T956 44 25 51, F956 44 30 30. Good-value and comfortable balcony rooms in a three-star garden hotel with pool and restaurant a couple of hundred metres behind the beach. ④
🏃 **Hotel Flamenco** Playa Fuente de Gallos T956 44 07 11, W www.hipotels.com. Fronting the Fuente del Gallo beach this elegant 100-roomer is one of the older luxury places set in a tranquil location. Well-appointed rooms have balcony terraces and sea views and there's a bar-restaurant, two garden pools and steps down to a fine strand. ⑤ with breakfast.
Hotel Fuerte Conil Playa de la Fontanilla T956 44 33 44, W www.fuertehoteles.com. Relatively new 250-room luxury garden hotel close to the Playa de la Fontanilla where balcony rooms come with sea views. Facilities include indoor and outdoor pools, tennis courts, diving centre and lots more. ⑨
Hotel Oasis c/Carril de la Fuente 3 T956 44 21 59, E hoteloasisconil@hotmail.com. Pleasant small hotel fronting the town beach (Playa de Los Bateles) where a/c sea-view rooms come with minibar and balconies. ⑤

Conil has lots of good **seafood restaurants** and **tapas bars** along the seafront: *La Bahia*, Avenida de la Playa s/n, and *Casa Manolo* nearby are the town favourites where you should be able to try *ortiguillas* – deep fried sea anemones – a delicious regional speciality. Also worth a try are either of Conil's two outstanding seafood restaurants, *Francisco* (T956 44 08 02) and *La Fontanilla* (T956 44 07 79) side by side on the Playa de la Fontanilla. Beyond the *Hotel Diufain* (see "Accommodation" above) another excellent fish restaurant worth making an effort to get to is ✗ *Restaurante Mirador El Roqueo* (T956 44 33 37; closed Mon), Urbanización Las Palmeras s/n, fronting the beach of El Roqueo. Two restaurants in one, the more formal dining room sits on the street behind the *Mirador* which has a great terrace overlooking the shore below.

Nightlife centres on the music and drinking **bars** to the north of the centre around calles Cádiz and Baluarte and Plaza Santa Catalina. **Las Carpas** is a remarkable all-summer long municipal disco and entertainment complex on the central Playa de Los Bateles, which caters for all ages and tastes from techno to flamenco.

Sancti Petri and Chiclana

Heading north from Conil along the road (not marked on many maps) which hugs the coast brings you, after 18km, to the isolated fishing village of **Sancti Petri** surrounded by marshes and sand bars. The formerly wild stretch of coast that precedes it has been developed into a dismal chain of overspill *urbanizaciones*. Dubbed Novo Sancti Petri by the planners, it's a complex of hundreds of identical avenues lined with featureless tile-roofed dwellings, ugly lamp standards, over-manicured gardens, garish hotels and a golf course designed by Severiano Ballesteros. The old village – just about hanging on to its identity – is still worth a look, however, and harks back to a simpler, less materialistic age.

When you reach it, the village of Sancti Petri (follow signs for the Puerto Deportivo) at the end of a causeway is a place under threat from the encroaching madness to the south and its future remains uncertain. The harbour now contains many more weekend yachts and launches than fishing vessels and, since the tuna-canning factory closed down, there are few jobs. The focal point of the tiny cluster of dwellings is the *Club Náutico de Sancti Petri* where the few fishermen that are left meet up. On Sunday mornings they sell their catch outside the club, and if old Manuel Ramírez is there he'll provide you with some of the freshest oysters and *cañaillas* (murex sea snails) you've ever had for ridiculously low prices. They're best washed down with a beer from the *Náutico*'s bar (they'll also lend you a plate) at a table overlooking the harbour. The bar has recently added an inviting terrace restaurant.

There's a small but nice enough **beach** to the south, where a friendly water sports centre, Novo Jet (T956 49 20 26, Wwww.novojet.net), hires out windsurf boards, kayaks and catamarans and offers courses in scuba diving besides leading guided canoe expeditions around the *marismas* and watercourses of the Parque Natural de la Bahía de Cádiz to the north. Nearer to the *Club Náutico*, Escuela de Vela Zaida (T956 49 64 45) offers sailing and windsurfing courses.

The nearby Cruceros Sancti Petri (mobile T617378894, Wwww.albarco .com) does tourist boat excursions to see dolphins and whales as well as trips (around €7) to the **Castillo de Sancti Petri**, a ruined thirteenth-century castle on an offshore island, where the Phoenicians built an important first millennium BC temple to their god Melkaart which the Romans later turned into a shrine to Hercules. Hannibal was a visitor to the former and Julius Caesar to the latter, and major archeological finds have been discovered which are now on display in the museum at Cádiz.

There are no rooms to be had in Sancti Petri and the nearest place for an overnight stop is **CHICLANA DE LA FRONTERA**, 6km to the east, a pleasant enough place which also serves as a useful road junction, with sporadic buses to Medina Sidonia (see p.212). **Places to stay** include the central *Hostal Villa*, c/Virgen del Carmen 11 (☏956 40 05 12; ❹), with en-suite rooms, and the nearby *Hotel Alborán*, Plaza de Andalucía 1 (☏956 40 39 06, ⓦwww.hotel esalboran.com; ❻), overlooking the river. Beyond Chiclana you emerge into a weird landscape of marshes, dotted with drying salt pyramids, in the midst of which lies the town of **San Fernando** – once an elegant place (and still so, at its centre) but quickly being swallowed up by industrial and commercial suburbs. These extend until you reach the long causeway that leads to Cádiz, an unromantic approach to what is one of the most extraordinarily sited and atmospheric towns of the south.

Cádiz

Cádiz, from a distance, was a city of sharp incandescence, a scribble of white on a sheet of blue glass, lying curved on the bay like a scimitar and sparkling with African light.

Laurie Lee, *As I Walked Out One Midsummer Morning*

Sited on a tongue of land enclosing a bay and a perfect natural harbour, with some fine beaches besides, **Cádiz** has – you would think – all the elements that make for an appealing place to visit. But despite an appealing old town and some fine museums, oddly enough the place seems unable to shake off a brooding lethargy when it comes to entertaining visitors, and the world of tourism has largely passed it by. Once you've got through the tedious modern suburbs on its eastern flank, inner Cádiz, built on a peninsula-island entered via the **Puertas de Tierra** (Land Gates) – a substantial remnant of the eighteenth-century walls – looks much as it must have done in the great days of the empire, with grand open squares, sailors' alleyways and high, turreted houses. Literally crumbling from the effect of the sea air on its soft limestone, it has a tremendous atmosphere – slightly seedy, definitely in decline, but still full of mystique. Above all, Cádiz is a city that knows how to enjoy itself. It has always been noted for its vibrant fiestas: the ancient Roman poet Martial was among the many who commented on the sensuous and swirling dances of the townswomen ("they click their Tartessian castanets with a deft hand"), implying a pre-Moorish origin for flamenco. Although settled after the *Reconquista* with immigrants from the northern city of Santander, Cádiz maintains its Roman reputation for joviality with an **annual carnival** in February, acknowledged to be the best – and wildest – in Spain.

Some history

Founded about 1100 BC by the Phoenicians as Gadir, a transit depot for minerals carried from the mining areas of the Río Tinto to the north, Cádiz has been one of Spain's principal ports ever since, and lays claim to being the oldest city in Europe.

Historically Cádiz served as an important base for the navies of Carthage, Rome and – following a long decline under the Moors – imperial Spain.

Always prone to attack because of its strategic importance, the city's nose was bloodied on numerous occasions, especially by the English. Drake's "singeing of the king of Spain's beard" occurred here in 1587, followed not long after by Essex's ransacking of the port in 1596, and in 1797 Nelson's bombardment.

The city's greatest period, however, and the era from which much of **inner Cádiz** dates, was the eighteenth century. Then, with the silting up of the river to Sevilla, the port enjoyed a virtual monopoly on the Spanish-

¡Carnaval!

Claiming to be saltier than the carnivals of Havana and Río de Janeiro rolled into one, each February Cádiz launches into its riotous **Carnaval**, the most important and wittiest in Spain. Largely a disorganized series of fiestas in origin, it was given its present shape in the late nineteenth century by Antonio Rodríguez Martínez, now known by his nickname El Tío de la Tiza ("Chalky" after the chalk or *tiza* he used in his job) who was improbably employed as a Customs official in the port. He organized the *murgas* or bands – a major feature of Carnaval – into four categories:

Coros These are (recently mixed) groups of about thirty who tour the city on flamboyantly decorated floats singing to the accompaniment of guitars, lutes and mandolins.

Comparsas Groups of around fifteen people who parade on foot with guitars and drums.

Chirigotas Arguably the most popular with *gaditanos*, these are groups of around ten people accompanied on a reed whistle or *pito*, who tour the bars singing hilarious satirical songs about people and events in the public eye.

Trios, Cuartetos, Quintetos These smaller groups not only sing, but also act out parodies and satirical sketches based upon current events as they tour the town in costume.

Illegales Given the city's innate anarchy these bands do not compete officially (see below), but take to the streets for the sheer hell of it with whatever instruments they can lay their hands on. They include whole families, groups of friends and even collections of drunks, staggering about as they attempt to make music.

The above groups provide only the focus, however, for the real Carnaval which takes place on the streets with everyone dressed up in costume and apparently drunk for ten whole days. The "legal" groups compete before judges in the Teatro Falla in between sessions on the streets and are symbolically awarded *un pelotazo* (good shot) for a bitingly witty composition and *un cajonazo* (a box drum) for a bomb. The various groups work at their repertoire for months before, road-testing their compositions during the two weekends prior to Carnaval (but not in costume, which is regarded as bad form) at the warm-up shindigs of the Erizada (hedgehog party) or the Ostionada (oyster party), great street fiestas which feature sea-urchin and oyster tasting.

Attending Carnaval

During Carnaval there are no **rooms** to be had in town at all unless you've made reservations well in advance. One way round this is to see it on **day-trips from Sevilla**, catching an evening train (a couple of hours' journey) and returning with the first train the next day, around 5.30am. These trains are a riotous party in themselves and, packed as they are with costumed carnival-goers from Sevilla, you'd be well advised to get dressed up yourself if you don't want to stand out. The opening and final weekends are the high points of the whole show and for more information see ⓦwww.carnavaldecadiz.com.

American trade in gold and silver: on its proceeds were built the **cathedral** – almost Oriental when seen from the sea – public halls and offices, broad streets and elegant squares, as well as a clutch of smaller churches. This wealth spawned Spain's first modern middle class which, from early on, was free-thinking and liberal, demanding such novelties as a free press and open debate. One historian has claimed that political dialogue in Spain originated along the Calle Ancha, Cádiz's elegant central thoroughfare where politicians met informally.

In the early nineteenth century the city made arguably its greatest contribution to the development of modern Spain, when a group of radicals set up the short-lived Spanish parliament or **Cortes** in 1812 during the Peninsular Wars. The Cortes drew up a Constitution that upheld the sovereignty of the people against the throne and set down a blueprint for a liberal Spain that would take a further century and a half to emerge. Loyal to its traditions, the city relentlessly opposed General Franco during the **Civil War**, even though this was one of the first towns to fall to his forces, and was the port through which the Nationalist armies launched their invasion. Later, when Franco often referred in power to the forces of "Anti Spain" he had in mind the sentiments expressed in the Cádiz Constitution of 1812, ramming home his disapproval by renaming the city's major plazas after himself and other members of the Falangist pantheon. Left-wing Cádiz merely bided its time and now, in the new democracy, these landmarks have regained their original designations. The city's tradition of liberalism and tolerance is epitomized by the way *gaditanos* (as the inhabitants of the city are known) have always breezily accepted a substantial **gay** community here, who are much in evidence at the city's brilliant Carnaval festivities.

Arrival, information and city transport

Arriving by train you'll find yourself on the periphery of the old town, close to the Plaza San Juan de Dios, busiest of the many squares. By **bus** you'll be a few blocks to the north, along the water – either at the Los Amarillos terminal, Avda. Ramón de Carranza 31 (serving Rota, Chipiona, Sanlúcar and resorts west of Cádiz), or a few blocks north again at the Estación de Comes, Plaza de la Hispanidad (serving Sevilla, Tarifa and other destinations toward Algeciras and the rest of Andalucía). Los Amarillos also runs a twice-daily service through Arcos to Ubrique, with a connection there to Ronda – by far the best route. Coming in **by car** you're best off taking accommodation with a garage (all the hotels will assist with parking) or heading for a car park. Two of the most central inside the city walls are by the train station and along Paseo de Canalejas near the waterfront. If you're coming in for a day-trip a useful tip is to park in the huge underground car park of the El Corte Inglés department store (just off the top right of our city map) which is free (but closes at 10pm) and take the bus from outside which goes to the centre.

Information

Timetables as well as general information, a detailed street **map** and a useful *Ruta de Tapas* leaflet are available from the **Turismo**, Avda. Ramón de Carranza s/n (Mon–Fri 9am–7pm, Sat–Sun 10am–1.30pm; ☎956 25 86 46), just north of Plaza San Juan de Dios. On Saturdays starting at 11am they offer a free guided walk around the city. Fifty metres away there's also a useful **Turismo municipal** on the Plaza San Juan de Dios (Mon–Fri 9am–2pm & 4–8pm, Sat & Sun 10am–1.30pm & 4–7pm; ☎956 24 10 01), for maps and information and they produce their own *Ruta de Tapas* leaflet. Their nearby **kiosk** on the same square also opens weekends (Sat & Sun 10am–1.30pm & 4–6.30pm). Throughout the summer the city's theatres and concert venues stage a variety of performances from Beethoven to folk music, dance and flamenco and both tourist offices stock information on these.

It's worth bearing in mind that – in common with several other Andalucian towns – many of Cádiz's streets have multiple names; when in doubt, consult as many maps as possible.

City transport

City buses are a handy way of getting around and a route map is available from the Turismo. A ten-trip Bonobus travelcard (€5.70 from *estancos*, bus kiosks and many newspaper stands) gives you a healthy discount over buying single journey tickets. One way to get to grips with the city is to do an **open-top bus tour** – especially good if you're pressed for time; two competing companies do the same hop-on, hop-off clockwise route around the peninsula. Tour por Cádiz (10am–11pm; €8) and Cádiz Tour (10am–9pm; €10 with a slightly longer route) both have stops at or near Plaza San Juan de Dios, the Cathedral, the Parque Genovés, the Playa de la Victoria and places in between and with the latter company your ticket is valid for 24 hours from the time you board (Tour por Cádiz tickets are valid only on the day of purchase).

Accommodation

In tune with the city itself, much of Cádiz's budget **accommodation** has seen better days. Few places in the old town are either new or comfy, and for more sophisticated lodging you really need to head towards the parador or the Playa de la Victoria. However, many of these crumbling old places are full of character, and efforts are now being made to retain this whilst upgrading the facilities. Except during the Carnaval, and July and August, finding a place to stay shouldn't be a problem. Note that during slack periods many places will drop their prices to fill a room – an amiable haggle is always worth a try.

A good place to start hunting is Plaza San Juan de Dios and the surrounding network of streets, crammed with *hostales* and *fondas*. Calle Marqués de Cádiz also has several budget options, as does the pedestrianized c/Plocia, east of the plaza. More good *pensiones* and *hostales* are a couple of blocks away, towards the cathedral or Plaza de Candelaria and beyond. There is limited upmarket accommodation in and around the centre and we have listed a couple of places further out to try if these are full.

Budget

Casa Caracol c/Suárez de Salazar 4 ☎956 26 11 66, ⓦwww.caracolcasa.com. Friendly backpackers' place with dorm beds (€11 per person) in a large house near Plaza San Juan de Dios. Price includes breakfast, free Internet access and use of kitchen. ❶

Hostal Centro Sol c/Manzanares 7 ☎956 28 31 03, ⓔcentrosol@wanadoo.es. Slightly pricey for what you get, but the en-suite rooms are smart,

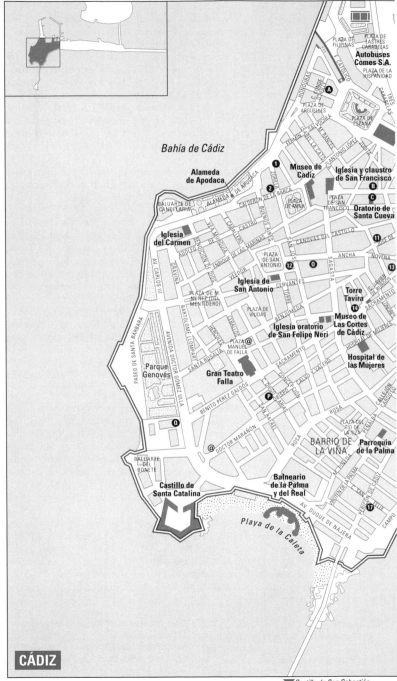

Punta San Felipe ▲

PLAZA DE FILIPINAS

PLAZA DE CASTRES CARABELAS

Autobuses Comes S.A.

PLAZA DE LA HISPANIDAD

C. CATÓLICO

HONDURAS

PLAZA DE ARGÜELLES

PLAZA DE ESPAÑA

TRES CARABELAS

FERMÍN SALVOCHEA

M. FRANCÉS

ANTONIO LÓPEZ

Bahía de Cádiz

Alameda de Apodaca

ZORRILLA

Museo de Cádiz

Iglesia y claustro de San Francisco Ⓑ

ALAMEDA DE APODACA

CALDERÓN DE LA BARCA

BUENOS AIRES

PLAZA DE MINA

PLAZA DE SAN FRANCISCO

Ⓒ

Oratorio de Santa Cueva

BALUARTE DE CANDELARIA

CASTRO

JOSÉ DE

Ⓐ

Ⓑ

Iglesia del Carmen

T. CABALLERO

CÁNOVAS DEL CASTILLO

VEA MURGIA

ENRIQUE DE LAS MARINAS

SAN JOSÉ

ANCHA

NOVENA

Ⓚ

AV. CARLOS III

GRAVINA

ADOLFO

RANCIO DE RÍOS

PLAZA DE SAN ANTONIO

Ⓞ

SAGASTA

Ⓛ

PLAZA DE M. NÚÑEZ DEL MENTIDERO

Ⓜ

Iglesia de San Antonio

CERVANTES

Torre Tavira

C. JAVIER DE BURGOS

SACRAMENTO

BARTOLOMÉ LLOMPART

TORRE

BENJUMEDA

Museo de Las Cortes de Cádiz

Ⓝ

PASEO DE SANTA BÁRBARA

AVENIDA DOCTOR GÓMEZ ULLA

HÉRCULES

CEBALLOS

PLAZA DE VIUDAS

Iglesia oratorio de San Felipe Neri

HOSPITAL DE MUJERES

SANTA ROSALÍA

PLAZA DE MANUEL DE FALLA

@

SACRAMENTO

Hospital de las Mujeres

Parque Genovés

Gran Teatro Falla

BENITO PÉREZ GALDÓS

Ⓟ

OBISPO CALVO Y VALERO

SAN RAFAEL

ROSA

CALLE NUEVA

CALLE DE

SAN JUAN

PLAZA DEL TÍO DE LA TIZA

Ⓠ

@ DOCTOR MARAÑÓN

ROSA

ROSA

BARRIO DE LA VIÑA

Parroquia de la Palma

BALUARTE DEL BONETE

SAN FÉLIX

M. BARRIL

Castillo de Santa Catalina

Balneario de la Palma y del Real

M. DE LA PALMA

PERDÓN DE CÁDIZ

AV. DUQUE DE NÁJERA

Ⓠ

SAN FÉLIX

CAMPO

Playa de la Caleta

▼*Castillo de San Sebastián*

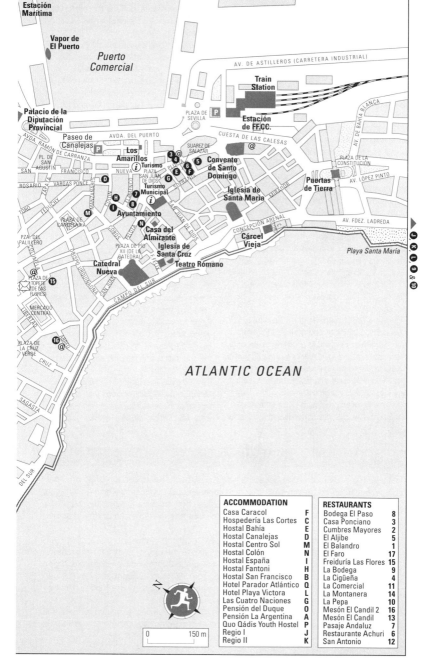

Estación Marítima

Vapor de El Puerto

Puerto Comercial

AV. DE ASTILLEROS (CARRETERA INDUSTRIAL)

Train Station

Palacio de la Diputación Provincial

PLAZA DE SEVILLA

Estación de FF.CC.

CUESTA DE LAS CALESAS

Paseo de Canalejas

AVDA. DEL PUERTO

SUAREZ DE SALAZAR

AVDA. RAMÓN DE CARRANZA

PL. DE SAN AGUSTÍN

Los Amarillos

Turismo PLAZA SAN JUAN DE DIOS

Convento de Santo Domingo

PLAZA DE LA CONSTITUCIÓN

SAN FRANCISCO

NUEVA

AV. LÓPEZ PINTO

ROSARIO

VARGAS PONCE

Turismo Municipal

Iglesia de Santa María

Puertas de Tierra

TORO

PLAZA DE CANDELARIA

Ayuntamiento

AV. FDEZ. LADREDA

PZA. DEL PALILLERO

Casa del Almirante

CONCEPCIÓN ARENAL

Cárcel Vieja

Playa Santa María

PLAZA DE PÍO XII (DE LA CATEDRAL)

Iglesia de Santa Cruz

Teatro Romano

Catedral Nueva

CAMPO DEL SUR

PLAZA DE TOPETE (DE LAS FLORES)

MERCADO CENTRAL

PLAZA DE LA CRUZ VERDE

CRUZ

ATLANTIC OCEAN

SAGASTA

DEL SUR

0   150 m

ACCOMMODATION	
Casa Caracol	F
Hospedería Las Cortes	C
Hostal Bahía	E
Hostal Canalejas	D
Hostal Centro Sol	M
Hostal Colón	N
Hostal España	I
Hostal Fantoni	H
Hostal San Francisco	B
Hotel Parador Atlántico	Q
Hotel Playa Victora	L
Las Cuatro Naciones	G
Pensión del Duque	O
Pensión La Argentina	A
Quo Qádis Youth Hostel	P
Regio I	J
Regio II	K

RESTAURANTS	
Bodega El Paso	8
Casa Ponciano	3
Cumbres Mayores	2
El Aljibe	5
El Balandro	1
El Faro	17
Freiduría Las Flores	15
La Bodega	9
La Cigüeña	4
La Comercial	11
La Montanera	14
La Pepa	10
Mesón El Candil 2	16
Mesón El Candil	13
Pasaje Andaluz	7
Restaurante Achuri	6
San Antonio	12

come with fans and are arranged above a pleasant patio. Has its own café-bar. ❹

Hostal Colón c/Marqués de Cádiz 6 ☎956 28 53 51. Good option for spacious rooms both en suite and sharing bath. ❸

Hostal España c/Marqués de Cádiz 9 ☎956 28 55 00, ⓦwww.pensionespana.com. Rooms with and without bath in an elegant restored nineteenth-century *casa palacio*. En-suite rooms also have TV and fans. ❸

Hostal Fantoni c/Flamenco 5 ☎956 28 27 04. *Hostal* occupying a charming, renovated eighteenth-century house filled with *azulejos* and cool marble. En-suite rooms come with a/c and TV . ❷–❹

Hostal San Francisco c/San Francisco 12 ☎956 22 18 42. Pleasant central *hostal* for rooms with and without bath. Those en suite come with TV and both have fans. ❸–❹

Las Cuatro Naciones c/Plocia 3 ☎956 25 55 39. Clean, unpretentious place with low-priced rooms sharing bath. ❶

Pensión del Duque c/Ancha 13 ☎956 22 27 77. Decent rooms, some with bath and balcony, at this friendly old *pensión*. ❷

Pensión La Argentina c/Conde O'Reilly 1 ☎956 22 33 10, ⓦwww.cadizayto.es/hostalargentina. Simple, cheap and spotless rooms close to Plaza de España. ❶

🏃 **Quo Qádis Youth Hostel** c/Diego Arias 1 ☎956 22 19 39, ⓦwww.infocadiz.com/ Quo_Qadis/Welcome.htm. As eccentric as its name, this is a vibrant place and great if you want to meet people. It has simple doubles, triples, a dorm (€6) and offers all kinds of activities including flamenco, language courses and mountain bike, snorkelling and walking excursions. Prices include breakfast, and there's a restaurant with vegetarian options. ❶

Moderate to expensive

Hostal Bahía c/Plocia 5 ☎956 25 90 61, ⓔhostalbahia@terra.es. By far the nicest *hostal* in this zone, offering rooms with bath, TV and a/c; well worth the price. ❹

Hostal Canalejas c/Cristóbal Colón 5 ☎956 26 41 13. Pleasant two-star hostal in completely restored town house. En-suite rooms come with a/c and TV and there's a pay car park nearby. Avoid the windowless interior rooms though. ❹

🏃 **Hospedería Las Cortes** c/San Francisco 9 ☎956 21 26 68, ⓦwww.hotellascortes .com. Splendid new hotel in a stylishly restored *casa señorial*. Elegant rooms have a/c, minibar and come Internet-connected. Facilities include sauna and gym and there's a *cafetería* and restaurant. Can advise on parking. High season price is Aug only. ❼

Hotel Parador Atlántico Parque Genovés 9 ☎956 22 69 05, ⓦwww.parador.es. Functional, modern parador, somewhat lacking in romance and not particularly welcoming, but with balcony rooms, Atlantic views, an outdoor pool, and garage. ❻

Hotel Playa Victoria Glorieta Ingeniero La Cierva 4 ☎956 20 51 00, ⓦwww.palafoxhoteles.com. If you're seeking a beachfront location this giant four-star hotel fronting the Playa de la Victoria has good facilities including a pool and views (especially from rooms 609–11). ❽

Regio I Avda. Ana de Viya 11 ☎956 27 93 31, ⓕ956 27 91 13. Older of the two Regio hotels behind the Playa de la Victoria; a good two-star place for rooms with bath, a/c and TV. Garage available too. ❻

Regio II Avda. Andalucía 79 ☎956 25 30 08, ⓕ956 25 30 09. Slightly newer (and grander) version of the *Regio* hotel above, and worth the extra. Also has garage. ❻

Boats from Cádiz

Before the decline of passenger ships it was possible to sail to London or South America from Cádiz – today you can go only as far as the Canary Islands. Trasmediterranea, Estación Marítima (☎956 22 74 21, ⓦwww.trasmediterranea.es), currently operates a weekly sailing (Sat 5pm) to **Tenerife** (36hr) and **Las Palmas** (48hr); fares start at around €205 for a shared cabin.

More locally – and for only €3/5 one-way/round trip – you can get a boat to **El Puerto de Santa María**, a forty-minute trip across the bay. Departures are from the Estación Marítima at 10am, midday, 2pm, 4.30pm, 6.30pm and (June–Sept) 8.30pm. The return from El Puerto is at 9am, 11am, 1pm, 3.30pm, 5.30pm and (June–Sept) 7.30pm. The service is run by Motonaves Adriano (mobile ☎629468014, ⓦwww .vapordeelpuerto.com).

Boat trips **around the bay** aboard the *Cabo Leiras* leave from the Estación Marítima at 8pm and (June–Sept) 9.45pm lasting about ninety minutes (☎956 25 00 99). Tickets (€5) are sold on board, and drinks are available at a bar.

The Town

Unlike most ports of its size, Cádiz seems immediately relaxed, easy-going, and not at all threatening, even at night. Perhaps this is due to its reassuring compactness, the presence of the sea making it impossible to get lost for more than a few blocks. Although there are plenty of sights to aim for, including an excellent **museum**, a Baroque **cathedral** and some memorable church art, Cádiz is most interesting for its general ambience and for its **vernacular architecture** – elegant *mirador*-fronted facades painted in pastel shades, blind alleys and cafés, and ancient *barrio* backstreets imprisoned behind formidable fortifications.

Museo de Cádiz

The **Museo de Cádiz**, Plaza de Mina 5 (Tues 2.30–8.30pm, Wed–Sat 9am–8.30pm, Sun 9.30am–2.30pm; free with EU passport, otherwise €1.50), housed in an imaginatively restored Neoclassical mansion just across the square from the Turismo, is an ideal place to start a tour of the city. The ground-floor **archeological collection** (information in Spanish only) includes some fine Phoenician jewellery excavated in the city and bronze figurines from the shrine of the god Melkaart on the island of Sancti Petri. Etruscan artefacts found at the same site hint at sophisticated early trading links. Another Phoenician temple to Astarte/Venus on the site of the modern Bastion of Santa Catalina yielded incense burners (*quemaperfumes* – the only ones found in Spain) with Egyptian decoration and a terracotta head with striking negroid features. Two remarkable fifth-century BC **Phoenician carved sarcophagi** in white marble (one male, the other female) are also unique to the western Mediterranean. It's interesting to observe the fusion of influences here: Egyptian for the sarcophagus, Greek for the depiction of the sculpted images. In the same section there's a display of ancient glassware – some of it of a very high standard – from the Phoenician, Greek and Roman periods.

In the Roman section a **reconstructed boat wreck** displays various amphorae exported from Cádiz to other parts of the empire; they contained *garum* (fish sauce), *salazones* (cured meat and fish), wine and olive oil, and the ship also carried minerals such as copper and lead – all demonstrating the great part played by Spain in making Rome rich. Two enormous anchors nearby, found off Cádiz, attest to the size of vessels that were used. Notable among the Roman statuary is a giant marble sculpture of the second-century emperor Trajan, which prior to excavation stood in the forum of Roman Baelo Claudia at Bolonia (see p.225) near Tarifa. A computer-measured duplicate was made in 2000 and now stands in the basilica at Baelo Claudia.

The second-floor **Museo de Bellas Artes** (fine art museum) is one of the best in Andalucía. The kernel of the collection is a group of twenty-one canvases by **Zurbarán** in Room 2, including a quite exceptional series of saints brought here from La Cartuja, the Carthusian monastery at Jerez, and one of only three such sets in the country preserved intact, or nearly so (the others are at Sevilla and Guadalupe). With their sharply defined shadows and intense, introspective air, Zurbarán's saints are powerful and very Spanish, even the English figures such as Hugh of Lincoln, or the Carthusian John Houghton, martyred by Henry VIII, whom he refused to accept as head of the English Church. Perhaps this is not surprising, for the artist spent much of his life travelling round the Carthusian monasteries of Spain and many of his saints are in fact portraits of the monks he met. Highlights of the many other works on display include, in Room 3, Murillo's *Ecce Homo* and *San Pedro y San Paulo*, as well as his final work, the *Mystic Marriage of Santa Catalina* – during the painting of which he fell from a scaffold to his death – and a *Sagrada Familia* by Rubens. The same room also contains *The Vision of San Félix Cantalicio*, a canvas displaying tenebrist influences by seventeenth-century sculptor, painter, architect and all-round genius, *sevillano* Alonso Cano.

The museum's third floor has an interesting **ethnological collection** divided into two rooms; the first has examples of traditional *artesanía* including ceramics, basketwork, leatherwork and textiles. The second room contains some wonderful **antique marionettes**, part of a section covering the long tradition of Tía Norica, or satirical marionette theatre, in Cádiz. This art form has often been used to pillory the city's rulers and dignitaries, through the "mouths" of its characters taken from the streets – travelling salesmen, waiters, sailors, fishermen, *toreros*, drunks – often in times when overt political activity was dangerous. The city still holds an annual marionette theatre festival. Fascinating though the puppets are behind glass, they need to be brought to life in a show – an idea that awaits an enterprising museum director.

Oratorio de Santa Cueva

A short walk from the museum, on c/Rosario, the eighteenth-century **Oratorio de Santa Cueva** (Tues–Fri 10am–1pm & 4.30–7.30pm, Sat & Sun 10am–1pm; €2) houses three fine Goya frescoes. The church is divided into two dramatically contrasting parts; in the elliptical **upper oratory** beneath an elegant dome are the three frescoes representing the *Miracle of the Loaves and Fishes*, the *Bridal Feast* (either side of the main altar) and the *Last Supper* (above the entrance), an unexpected depiction of Christ and the disciples dining sprawled on the floor, Roman style. The other works here are depictions of biblical scenes by minor artists. In sharp contrast to the chapel above is the **subterranean chapel** containing a sculpture of the Crucifixion whose manifest pathos only adds to the gloom. An eighteenth-century work of the Genoa school, the image is said to have inspired visiting composer Joseph Haydn to write the score of his *Seven Last Words* (of Christ) oratorio. Each Good Friday a sermon on the theme of Christ's last words is preached in the chapel, following which Haydn's work is performed. Somewhat breaking with tradition, spotlights have been added recently to illuminate the lower chapel and a formerly blacked-out lunette has been cleaned, flooding it with light, both inevitably lessening the sculpture's dramatic impact. A small **museum** has been added between the two chapels giving background information – including a display of Haydn's score – on the building's history.

The Catedral Nueva

The huge **Catedral Nueva** (Tues–Fri 10am–1.30pm & 4.30–7pm, Sat 10am–1pm; €4 including museum), so titled because it replaced the former cathedral, Santa Cruz, is one of the largest churches in Spain. Begun in 1722, it took 110 years to finish, and even then the towers – shortened when the money ran out – were completed only in 1853 in an unsympathetic white limestone whose patchwork effect jars with the original sandstone. The time lapse also led to a curious architectural potpourri, strikingly visible on the main facade, where the exuberance of the earlier Baroque below was topped off in a contrastingly sober Neoclassical style. What is more, on closer inspection you'll see that the distinctive "gilded" dome, which appears so impressive from afar, is in fact made from glazed yellow tiles. Sadly, in the latter half of twentieth century the building fell into an advanced state of decay – caused by sea air calcifying the stone – as chunks of the ceiling started falling on the congregation below. A costly programme of restoration over the last few years is now slowly restoring the building to its former grandeur.

Even if you don't normally go for High Baroque, it's hard to resist the attraction of the austere interior, which has more of the architect Vincente Acero's original design. From inside, the soaring 52m-high dome is illuminated by a powdery violet light, the whole, perfectly proportioned building decorated entirely in stone with no gold or white in sight. **Artworks** include a sculpture of *San Bruno* by Martínez Montañés in the chapel of San Sebastián and some other polychromed sculptures including an *Ecce Homo* attributed to Luisa Roldán ("La Roldana"), the daughter of Pedro Roldán. Also worth a look are the wonderful **choir stalls** dating from 1702 which were originally in the Cartuja of Sevilla and moved here upon the latter's Disentailment in 1835. In the **crypt** (same hours) is buried Manuel de Falla, the great *gaditano* composer of such Andalucía-inspired works as *Nights in the Gardens of Spain* and *El amor brujo*. The cathedral's **museum** holds some dubiously attributed paintings as well as a rather tedious collection of ecclesiastical silver enlivened only by a monstrance – an eighteenth-century bejewelled custodia nicknamed the *Millón* (million), a reference to the number of precious gems and pearls set into the work. For a magnificent view over the city you can also climb the **Torre de Poniente** (guided visits daily June–Sept 10am–8pm, Oct–May 10am–6pm; €4) one of the cathedral's twin towers.

Barrio del Populo and Plaza de las Flores

The best view of the cathedral is from the waterfront behind, where the golden dome is perfectly set off by the pastel-tinted facades of the adjacent houses along c/Campo del Sur. To the east of the Plaza de la Catedral fronting the cathedral lies the **Barrio del Pópulo**, a poor, run-down area of narrow alleyways and decaying tenements, a surviving remnant of the thirteenth-century medieval city. Many of its streets are graced by the odd crumbling *palacio*, formerly residences of merchants made wealthy by empire trade, and now split up into residential blocks. One of these, the **Casa del Almirante** on c/Posadilla, is a splendid Baroque pile with an ebullient facade featuring barley sugar and Tuscan columns in rose-tinted Italian marble. At the time of writing there are plans to turn this into a luxury hotel. An ancient, though recently restored as a community centre, seventeenth-century inn, the **Mesón del Pópulo**, c/Mesón Nuevo 11 – at the crook in the street – has the typical layout of these travellers' hostelries with stables below and living quarters above. Calles Sopranis and Santa María – where the Palacio Lasquetty (no. 11) and the church of Santa María are also worth a look – are other good places to sample the typical atmosphere of this quarter.

A couple of blocks to the west of the cathedral lies the **Plaza de las Flores** (aka Plaza Topete), one of the city's most emblematic squares. Fronted by the striking early twentieth-century Correos, the square is a riot of colour most days due to the many flower sellers that have their stalls here. There are a couple of elegant mansions, too: no.1 with a portal decorated with pilasters in the Cádiz Baroque style dates from 1746 and, around the corner in c/Libertad, numbers 15 and 16 are a couple more eighteenth-century mansions with *torres-miradores* or lookout towers. Fronting these two, the whole of Plaza de la Libertad is taken up by the early nineteenth-century marketplace, the **Mercado Central**, a beehive of activity on weekday mornings.

Iglesia de Santa Cruz and other churches

A little further east of the cathedral stands the "Old" Cathedral, the **Iglesia de Santa Cruz** (Tues–Thurs & Sat 10am–1pm & 5.30–8.30pm, Fri 9am–1.30pm

& 5.30–10pm, Sun 10.30am–1pm & 6.15–7.30pm; free). Originally a thirteenth-century church built on top of a mosque, it was almost destroyed by the Earl of Essex during the English assault on Cádiz in 1596, and is effectively a seventeenth-century rebuild with only occasional vestiges such as the entrance arch surviving from the earlier Gothic structure. The sober grey stone interior contrasts with the magnificent seventeenth-century *retablo*, a beautiful work with sculptures by Martínez Montañés, as is the **Capilla de los Genoveses**, its stunning *retablo* of red, white and black Italian marble in dire need of restoration (at the time of writing a programme of work has been announced). Just behind the church is a recently discovered **Teatro Romano** (Roman theatre; daily 10am–2pm; free) dating from the first century BC. Partly cut into by a corner of Santa Cruz and built over by a later Moorish *Alcazaba*, the remaining banks of seats have been restored.

From here you could follow the waterfront west to the **capilla de Santa Catalina** (presently closed), a shrine for Murillo fans. Located on the waterfront close to the c/Capuchinos, this seventeenth-century church was where – during the completion of a commission for the former Capuchin proprietors – the painter fell from a scaffold while finishing the *Mystic Marriage of Santa Catalina* on the high altar *retablo*. He was carried back to Sevilla where he died from his injuries a few days later, and the painting was completed by one of his pupils. Currently this work, together with an *Immaculada* and a stunning *Stigmata of San Francisco*, which also used to hang here, are displayed in the Museo de Bellas Artes (see p.243).

Two churches of note for their paintings and sculptures are the chapel of the **Hospital de las Mujeres** (Mon–Sat 10am–1.30pm; €0.80; ask the porter for admission) on the street of the same name, one of the most impressive Baroque buildings in the city and with a brilliant El Greco of *San Francisco in Ecstasy*; and the **Iglesia y claustro de San Francisco** just east of Plaza de Mina on a tiny square of the same name, with two sculptures of San Diego and San Francisco attributed to Martínez Montañés in its sacristy.

Oratorio de San Felipe Neri and the Museo Histórico Municipal

The eighteenth-century oratory of **San Felipe Neri**, c/San José, to the northwest of Plaza de las Flores (Mon–Sat 10am–1.30pm; €1.20), is one of the most important historical buildings in Spain, evidenced by the number of commemorative plaques from countries as far apart as Chile and the Philippines attached to the exterior. It was here, on March 29, 1812, that a group of patriotic radicals defied the Napoleonic blockade and set up the Cortes, framing a liberal Constitution – the nation's first – which had a major impact on the development of European politics. The church itself, an elegant oval structure, has a double tier of balconies which would once have echoed with the roar of fierce debate, and above which eight *ventanillas* in the dome allow the brilliant light to illuminate the sky-blue decor and the central nave punctuated by seven chapels. The high altar's *retablo* is crowned by a fine *Immaculada* by Murillo.

Next door to the oratory in c/Santa Inés, the **Museo de las Cortes de Cádiz** (June–Sept Tues–Fri 9am–1pm & 5–7pm, Sat & Sun 9am–1pm; free) was set up in 1912 to commemorate the first centenary of the 1812 Constitution. The highlights of the museum are a large Romantic-style mural depicting the events of 1812 together with a number of the original documents of the Cortes, and an enormous eighteenth-century scale model of the city – almost filling a room – made of mahogany and ivory at the behest of King Carlos III. Further north, the Plaza de España is dominated by a rather pompous

△ Catedral Nueva, Cádiz

monument to the Constitution, also set up in 1912 and now crowned with the rather appropriate addition of a crane's nest. *Gaditanos* like to claim that it's the only monument in the world honouring and topped by a book – a representation of the 1812 Constitution.

Just south of the Museo de las Cortes and off c/Sacramento, the **Torre Tavira**, c/Marqués del Real Tesoro 10 (daily 10am–8pm; €3.50), is an eighteenth-century mansion with the tallest tower in the old city, which you can climb to get a great view over the white roofs below and the sea beyond. Many houses had these towers added so that shipowners and merchants could see ships arriving in the port. The tower also holds a camera obscura which gives equally dramatic views, and the rooms below contain historical displays covering Cádiz and its past. A couple of blocks north, the **Calle Ancha** – the historic thoroughfare that is today an attractive pedestrianized shopping street – has another impressive mansion, the nineteenth-century **Casa Mora** at no. 28 (Sat 10am–1pm, consult the Turismo Municipal for other times; free), which has an exquisite patio and is stuffed with porcelain, clocks and furnishings of the period spread over three floors.

Barrio de la Viña

Squeezed between c/Campo del Sur and the Playa de la Caleta to the west of the cathedral lies the **Barrio de la Viña**, the old fishermen's quarter, typically *gaditano* and traditionally renowned for the spirited and sarcastic humour of its inhabitants. Its main street is the c/Virgen de la Palma, close to the eastern end of which lies the tiny **Plaza Tío de la Tiza**, a charming square (filled with terraces for seafood tapas in summer) named after the man who, in the late nineteenth century gave the famous Carnaval the form it has today (see p.237).

The beaches

The western flank of the Barrio de la Viña faces the **Playa de la Caleta**, an over-popular – and often none too clean – beach in a small bay sandwiched between the most impressive of Cádiz's eighteenth-century sea fortifications, the **Castillo de Santa Catalina** and the **Castillo de San Sebastián**, the latter constructed on an islet and reached by a causeway. This is believed to be the site of the ancient Phoenician harbour where, tradition has it, there once stood an impressive temple to the Phoenician god Melkaart. A walk along the seafront here can be wonderfully bracing day or night (when cooling breezes blow in off the Atlantic and many of the monuments are floodlit), with the possibility of a stroll through the Parque Genovés, planted with palms and cypresses as far as the bastion of Candelaria, or onwards to the Alameda Apodaca, another waterfront garden, beyond. The town beach is the **Playa Santa María del Mar**, lying some five hundred metres east of the cathedral.

The city's main beach and the one with all the action – including restaurants and *chiringuitos* – is the **Playa de la Victoria**, 2km of excellent sand, cleaner and usually less crowded than those mentioned above. Getting there is an easy thirty-minute walk from the old town – just find the seafront on the south side of the peninsula and head east – or there's a bus (#7) which starts out from the Parque Genovés and follows the coast as far as the *Hotel Playa Victoria*. The **Playa Cortadura** begins where the Playa de la Victoria ends and it's an altogether less commercialized affair – in fact there are no bars or *chiringuitos* at all. There is one *venta* however, the *Venta La Gallega*, and if you wanted a bracing hour's exercise you could head east from the *Hotel Playa Victoria* and walk the length of the seafront to reach the restaurant, which is actually on the beach. To reach the Playa Cortadura by public transport you can take bus #7 (see above) and walk east from the *Hotel Playa* bus terminus or take the train from the main station; leaving every twenty minutes or so, there are stops at Segunda Aguada (for Playa de la Victoria) and Cortaduras, from where the Playa de la Cortadura is a short walk.

Eating and drinking

Cádiz's best cafés, **tapas bars** and **restaurants** tend to be clustered around its many grand squares, especially Plaza San Juan de Dios, dominated by the delightful wedding-cake facade of the late eighteenth-century Ayuntamiento (whose bells sound the hour with notes from de Falla's *El amor brujo*) and the pleasant Plaza de Mina. Across the old town there are more places to hunt down in and around the adjoining Plaza de las Flores and Plaza de la Libertad, the latter containing the **market**, and the atmospheric **c/Sagasta**, almost bisecting the peninsula north to south, is another place to find more typically earthy watering holes. The old seamen's quarter, the **Barrio de la Viña**, is where *gaditanos* make for on warmer nights to scoff *caballa a la gaditana* (mackerel) and shellfish at economical *marisquerías* in the narrow streets around Plaza Tío de la Tiza and along c/Virgen de la Palma. The city's summer playground, the **Paseo Marítimo** – the long boulevard fronting the Playa de la Victoria – is lively and fun all season, with tapas bars, restaurants and beach *chiringuitos* (*Marimba* and *Marea* are recommended) all doing a roaring trade.

The major squares are also the places to head for **breakfast** snacks, while the most tempting *heladerías* are dotted about the Paseo Marítimo. The *Heladerías Ibense Bornay* chain are renowned for their *batidos* (milk shakes), with *turrón* (nougat) and *pistacho* flavours among the most popular. A great **snack** at any time of the day are *empanadas gallegas* (fish or meat pies), obtained from the only Galician bakery in town, Casa Hidalgo, Plaza Catedral 8, fronting the cathedral.

Restaurants

Bodega El Paso c/San Fernando 2. Friendly and buzzing little restaurant with good selection of cheap *platos combinados* and tapas, a terrace and a €6 *menú*.

Casa Ponciano c/Lazaro Dou. Lively and economical bar-restaurant for tapas, fish and meat dishes; there's also a three-course *menú* for €7.

Cumbres Mayores c/Zorilla 4. Excellent and atmospheric restaurant and tapas bar located in a century-old former brewery where *carne* (particularly Huelva *jamón*) is king. The tapas bar has daily specials and in winter serves up a delicious *berza* – a chick-peas and *morcilla* (blood sausage) based broth.

El Aljibe c/Plocia 25 ☎ 956 26 66 56. A very good restaurant serving up a range of traditional dishes on a menu that changes four times a year. *Chuletas de corzo a la brasa con puré de castañas* (deer with chestnut sauce) is a signature dish. *Menú de degustación* €27 including wine; main dishes €10–15. Closed Sun eve.

El Balandro c/Apodaca 22 (no nameplate outside) ☎ 956 22 09 92. Highly popular venue with a view of the Bay of Cádiz. Wide range of excellent – if pricey – seafood tapas served at the bar or *raciones* and fresh fish and meat dishes on the promenade terrace – a wonderful place to watch the sun set. Main dishes €10–15. Closed Sun eve.

El Faro c/San Félix 15 ☎ 956 21 10 68. In the heart of the Barrio de la Viña, and one of the best fish restaurants in Andalucía. House specialities include *pulpo* (octopus), *merluza* (hake), *urta* (sea bream), and a delicious *arroz marinero* (Andalucian paella). There's a *menú de degustación* for €32 (excluding wine) and a (Mon–Fri) *menú* for €18. Their tapas bar is also well worth a visit (see below).

Freiduría Las Flores Plaza de las Flores. One of the best *freidurías* in town. You can get a takeaway and eat it at the terrace tables of the nearby bar *La Marina* (facing the *correos*), who don't seem to mind – as long as you buy a drink. However, as they have now added their own café-restaurant you may wish to eat inside instead. Another good place is the nearby *Freiduría Europa*, c/Hospital de Mujeres 21 (at the junction with c/Sagasta).

La Bodega Paseo Marítimo 23, on the Playa de la Victoria seafront and close to Cádiz's football stadium, Estadio Ramón de Carranza ☎ 956 27 59 04. Excellent mid-priced restaurant and tapas bar with a wide range of meat and fish dishes.

La Cigüeña c/Plocia 2 ☎ 956 25 01 79. Excellent little restaurant serving up imaginative takes on traditional *andaluz* standards in a dining room decorated with works by local artists. The desserts are outstanding (try their *mousse de chocolate con*

turrón) and there's a 7-plate *menú de degustación* for €28.50 (excluding wine); main dishes €12–15. Closed Sun.

La Comercial c/José de Toro 8 ☎ 956 21 19 14. Smart and stylish upmarket restaurant specializing in a creative approach to traditional *andaluz* dishes. Standard *menú* for around €20 or there's a *menú de degustación* for around €30.

La Montanera c/Sacramento 39. Good place for carnivores in this fish-crazy city. The lamb dishes, especially, are excellent, and check out the dish of the day.

La Pepa Paseo Marítimo 14, beyond the *Hotel Playa Victoria*. Terrace restaurant at the eastern end of the Paseo Marítimo serving excellent fish and rice dishes. Their *arroz fenecio (de antes de Cristo)* is supposed to be based on an ancient Phoenician recipe and includes rabbit and *cabrillas* (giant snails).

Mesón El Candil 2 c/Abreu 7. When the owners of the restaurant listed below decided to go separate ways neither would give up the name. This version is a very pleasant restaurant with a charming terrace on a small square and the chef has been fronting the *fogón* for 35 years so he should know by now how to prepare the house special, *pescado plancha a la Pepe*. Meat is also on offer and there's a *menú* for €6.

Mesón El Candil Javier de Burgos 19. Solid *gaditano* fish and seafood restaurant with a pleasant ambience. Often stages flamenco at weekends.

Pasaje Andaluz Plaza San Juan de Dios. Friendly diner with outdoor terrace and a range of economical *menús* offering meat and fish dishes.

Restaurante Achuri c/Plocia 15 ☎ 956 25 36 13. One of the oldest places in the city and very popular with *gaditanos*, so it can be hard to find a table. Excellent Basque- and *andaluz*-inspired dishes at reasonable prices. *Chipirones en su tinta* (squid in ink), *bacalao al la andaluza* (cod) and *pargo al brandy* (sea bream) are recommended. Also has an excellent tapas bar. Closed eves Sun–Wed.

San Antonio Plaza San Antonio 9 ☎ 956 21 22 39. Good mid-priced typically *gaditano* restaurant offering a variety of local meat and fish dishes. Mains €11–20.

Tapas bars

Bahía Avda. Ramón Carranza 29. Wonderful old harbourfront bar that does excellent *fino* and delicious *guisos* – tapas in sauce; there's no frying here. Try the *costillas de cerdo* (pork ribs) or *papas aliñas* (potatoes in sauce).

Bar El Faro c/San Félix 15. Tapas bar of the renowned restaurant (see above), and probably the best in town. A stand-up place where the *finos* are first rate, the service is smooth and the seafood tapas are mouthwateringly delicious. House specials include *tortillitas de camarones* (shrimp in batter) and *tostaditas de pan con bacalao* (cod).

Bar Manteca Corralón de los Carros 66, near c/San Félix. Great old place in the Barrio de la Viña run by a retired *torero* and decorated with bullfighting memorabilia. Excellent *fino* and *oloroso*. House specials include *chicharrones* (pork crackling) and *lomo* (cured pork loin). *El Pescador*, opposite, is another good place.

Bar Terraza Plaza de la Catedral. Facing the cathedral and founded in 1952, this is a superb tapas bar and fair-priced fish restaurant with a very pleasant terrace. The nearby *Cervecería La Catedral* also does tasty fish tapas and *raciones*.

Bar Zapata Plaza Candelaria, at the corner with c/Zapata. Atmospheric little bar with an excellent selection of *jamón* and *chorizo* tapas and wines.

Casa Lucas Plaza Cruz Verde, west of the market. Charming tiny bar in an ancient town house. Serves hearty *arroz* (paella) at lunchtimes and such house specials as *atún encebollado* (tuna) and *merluza* (hake).

Cervecería Gaditana c/Zorilla. Fine bar – the tasty *montaditos* (or titbits) are wonderful; try the salmon and Roquefort and their *bombita* (baby bomb), a ball of potato with onion and tuna fish.

Cervecería-Marisquería Aurelio c/Zorilla 1, near Plaza Mina. Vibrant and outstanding seafood tapas bar with excellent *manzanilla*. Founded by the legendary Aurelio, who sold shellfish outside the entrance for many years, specials include *merluza rebozada* (hake) and *ortiguillas* (fried sea anemones). They'll also serve you a great fish supper at tables in a side room.

El Garbanzo Negro c/Sacramento, at the junction with c/Londres (aka c/Alcalá Galiano) near the Mercado Central. A lively place serving up very good *salmorejo* (gazpacho Córdoba style) and a range of tapas; also functions as a *copas* bar at night.

El Nuevo Almacen c/Barrié 17, northeast of the Torre Tavira. Charming little shop/bar with tasty tapas selection. The *puntas de solomillo en salsa de vino* (pork loin in wine sauce) is a mini-meal in itself. Their delicatessen sells fine *jamones* , cheeses and wines of the region. Closed Sun.

La Perola & Cia c/Canovas del Castillo 34, southwest of the Santa Cueva chapel. Modern tapas and *raciones* bar with a younger *ambiente* and serving over seventy different tapas.

Marisquería Joselito c/San Francisco 38. Venerable old (recently modernized) haunt and one of a chain of tapas bars, but none the worse for that. There's a sister branch just around the corner (with a pleasant terrace), facing the port on Avda. Ramón Carranza. House specials include *salpicón de mariscos* (seafood cocktail) and *gambas al ajillo* (garlic prawns).

Merodio Plaza Libertad 4, fronting the market. One of the city's best-loved old bars, which gets riotous during Carnaval and really buzzes on Sunday lunchtimes. Specializes in *erizos de mar* (sea urchins) in season, as well as shellfish.

Mesón Las Americas c/Ramón y Cajal 1. Good tapas and *raciones* bar near Plaza de España, specializing in Argentinian meat dishes. Closed Sun.

Taberna La Manzanilla c/Feduchy 18, north of Plaza Candelaria. Wonderful atmospheric eighteenth-century *bodega* serving the odd tapa in addition to excellent *manzanilla* served from huge butts. The proprietor will show you his cellar with some classic vintages if you ask. The nearby *El Cañon* (junction of c/Feduchy & c/Rosario) is another good tapas place.

Cafés, bars and heladerías

Bazar Inglés c/San Pedro 18, near Plaza de San Francisco. Atmospheric bar in a converted nineteenth-century store (hence the name). Often has flamenco on Thurs night (after 10.30pm).

Café-Bar La Marina Plaza de las Flores. With a terrace on this delightful square, this makes an excellent breakfast stop or, later in the day, a place for a quiet coffee or *aperitivo*.

Cafetería-Heladería Andalucía Plaza de las Flores. Popular place for coffee and ice cream.

La Canela de la Baluarte Baluarte de Candelaria, Alameda Marqués de Comillas s/n, near the peninsula's northern tip. Vibrant café-bar which doubles as a cultural centre with film evenings, poetry and literature readings, live music (Wed) and flamenco (Sun).

La Colonia Alameda s/n, fronting the gardens near the sea slightly north of the Turismo. Wonderful little bar, with garden terrace, done out in surrealist style by noted local painter Luís Quintero. Friendly proprietors serve up potent cocktails; in summer try the *horchata* (tiger nut milk) laced with rum.

San Francisco Uno Plaza San Francisco 1. This pleasant bar with a terrace on this delightful square is good for breakfast coffee and perfect for late-night liqueurs or even a wine from their extensive list.

Nightlife

Outside carnival and fiesta times, **nightlife** in Cádiz centres around the Plaza de Miña and Plaza de España zones, especially along calles Antonio López, Rafael Viesca, Manuel Rancés and Zurita, but many of these close during July and August. In summer much of the *marcha nocturna* migrates to the Paseo Marítimo, behind the beaches to the east of the centre (c/Muñoz Arenillas, behind the *Hotel Playa Victoria* is the focus), where you'll find most of the bars and clubs. In the winter revellers flock to the **Punta de San Felipe** (there's a less frenetic scene here in summer, too), known locally as La Punta, the peninsula beyond the harbour to the northeast of Plaza de España.

Flamenco is an irregular feature at private *peñas* or clubs, and isn't always that easy to find. We've listed a couple of places below, but check with the Turismo for more, as well as for details of special concerts and festivals at venues such as the Teatro Falla and the Diputación (regional government building) in Plaza de España.

Clubs and bars

Bar Manteca Corralón de los Carros 66 (see also "Tapas bars" opposite). Flamenco often takes place at this atmospheric bar in the heart of the Barrio de la Viña.

Barabass c/Muñoz Arenillas, off Glorieta Ingeniero La Cierva and behind the Paseo Marítimo. In a street packed with clubs and bars which are full to bursting in high summer, this is a fairly big place with 60s decor and a great atmosphere when the dancing gets going. The nearby *El Civi* is a small and pleasant *copas* bar.

Café de Levante c/Rosario, near Plaza de San Agustín. Relaxed bar with an *ambiente cultural*; on Thursdays it stages literary events, live music and even flamenco.

Cambalache c/José del Toro, north of Plaza Candelaria. Laid-back jazz bar which attracts an "arty" crowd. Closed Mon.

El Disparate c/Manuel Rancés, just west of Plaza de España. Big disco-bar with dance floor. There are quite a few other lively places in this street including *El Búnker*.

El Hoyo c/Beato Diego de Cádiz 8, south of Plaza de España. A friendly late-night bar open until after 4am which gets packed out with a youngish crowd partying to the tunes of the 80s and 90s.

El Pay Pay c/Silencio 1, Barrio del Populo. Large café-bar with a long history as a former sailor's hangout. Now renamed and revamped it stages live music, theatre, and poetry readings and there are noticeboards with information on cultural events around the city.

El Poniente c/R. Viesca, near Plaza de España. Busy and upbeat gay scene rendezvous.

Flamenco Paseo Marítimo 14. Forget the name, this bar is home to aficionados of the alternative scene and those wanting to escape the more frenetic scene in nearby c/Muñoz Arenillas. A favourite for watching the sun go down.

Habana Club c/Rosario, near Plaza San Francisco. Stylish bar for late-night drinking.

La Luna c/Dr Zurita s/n, off the southwest corner of Plaza de España. Good late-night music bar.

Malecon Punta de San Felipe. Good, popular salsa club on this frenetic street. A mixed venue appealing to a lively young crowd and featuring showboating salsa dancers who command the dance floor.

Persígueme c/Tinte, near Plaza de Mina. Trendy music bar open Thurs–Sat in summer. It gets very lively at weekends and sometimes stages live bands.

Woodstock c/Canovas del Castillo at the corner with c/Sagasta and Paseo Marítimo 11. A duo of lively bars at each end of the town serving up eighty-plus of the worlds top beers to the accompaniment of rock, blues, jazz and the occasional blast of Celtic pipes. During winter the old town's branch is the most popular; in summer head for the one on Paseo Marítimo which has panoramic windows overlooking the beach.

Flamenco venues

Baluarte Candelaria On the northern tip of the peninsula. This sea bastion is the venue for some wonderfully authentic flamenco concerts by the *Peña Flamenco Enrique Melliza*, staged every Thursday evening from mid-July to late Aug. Entry costs around €10, it gets going about 10.30pm and there's food and drink.

La Cava Taberna Flamenca c/Antonio Lopez 16, near the Plaza de la Mina ☏956 21 18 66, ⓦ www.flamencolacava.com. Tourist-oriented place where the performers are reasonably serious. Shows Tues, Fri and Sat at 10pm; €36 entry includes dinner.

Peña La Perla c/Carlos Ollera s/n ⑦956 25 91 01. Down a tiny street to the right of the Cárcel Vieja (Old Prison), to the east of the cathedral, this vibrant *peña* is open to visitors and is somewhere that flamenco can happen spontaneously on any night of the week. Alternatively, check with the Turismo.

UMEC c/Fernán Caballero, at the junction with c/ Enrique de Marinas (west of Plaza de la Mina). Bar offering flamenco every Thurs night.

Shopping

Quorum, c/Ancha 27, is the best **bookshop** and stocks a decent selection of books in English. Librería Omega, Avda. Ramón de Carranza 31, fronting the port, is also worth a browse. *El Diario de Cádiz* (Ⓦwww.diariodecadiz.es) is the city's daily paper – good for local information, upcoming flamenco concerts and entertainment details. For city and hiking **maps**, see "Listings", below.

For the latest designer **fashions** head for c/Columela running between c/San Francisco and Plaza Flores where many famous-name shops have their outlets. For **food**, there's a daily market, from 7am to midday, inside the Mercado Central, an elegant market building on Plaza de la Libertad. This is a good place to pick up fresh produce, and quite a spectacle in its own right during the mid-morning bustle. Cádiz province is famed for its **wines** and you can buy and learn all about them at Magerit, c/Fermin Salvochea 2, west of Plaza de España (⑦956 22 79 94, Ⓦwww.vinosmagerit.com), whose engaging female proprietor is a Spanish Master of Wine and conducts week-long tasting courses (2hrs per day; €70).

For other shopping, The Taller Ceramico Pascale, c/Santo Domingo 11, near the church of Santo Domingo, is the studio and shop of creative ceramist and tilemaker Pascale Pérez-Stalder who does a modern take on these traditional *andaluz* **handicrafts**. Aguamanil nearby at c/Plocia 21 is another ceramic workshop. Tosso, Plaza Palillero 4, west of Plaza Candelaria, stocks a range of hand-painted *abanicos* (fans) with scenes of Cádiz done by a local artist; the artist will even take commissions – supply a photo of your selected theme and they'll post it to you when ready. Cádiz's branch of the El Corte Inglés **department store** is at Avda. de las Cortes de Cádiz s/n (⑦956 29 71 00), 1.5km east of the train station; buses #5 or #8 from a stop at the eastern end of Avenida del Puerto (close to the train station) will take you there.

Listings

Banks There are ATMs throughout the city centre with several banks around Plaza San Juan de Dios and Avda. Ramón de Carranza (facing the port). The *Hotel Parador Atlántico* (see p.242) will change travellers' cheques and currency outside business hours.

Car rental Atesa, Avda. del Puerto 1, near the harbour ⑦956 26 66 45; Bahía Rent a Car, Plaza de Sevilla s/n near the train station ⑦956 27 18 95, Ⓦwww.bahiarentacar.com; and Crown, c/Plocia 2 ⑦956 22 10 38, Ⓦwww.crowncarhire.com.

Football C.F. Cádiz is the town team based at the Estadio Ramón Carranza, Plaza Madrid, behind the Playa de la Victoria (⑦956 07 01 65, Ⓦwww .cadizcf.com). After languishing for 14 years in the lower leagues, in 2005 the *Submarino Amarillo*

("Yellow Submarine" – the club's nickname from their canary shirts) sailed back into the First Division of *La Liga*. Former Liverpool player (and now big-name Spanish TV football pundit) Michael Robinson is a director. Tickets can be purchased at the ground.

Hospital For urgent medical treatment go to the Urgencias (emergency) department of the Residencia Sanitaria Hospital, Avda. Ana de Viya 21, near the Hotel Playa Victoria (⑦956 00 21 00).

Internet *Ciber La Sal*, c/Doctor Marañon 14, near the *Hotel Parador Atlántico* (daily 10am–11pm); *Ciber-café San Rafael*, Benjumeda 38, near the Teatro la Falla (daily 9.30am–1pm & 5–10.30pm); *Ciberc@i* c/Abreu 9 Bajo, near the market (Mon–Fri

11am–11pm, Sat–Sun 4pm–midnight); *Telefonos Publicos*, Callejón de los Negros 1, near the Turismo (daily 10am–11pm); *Ciber Columela*, c/Columela 2 off Plaza de las Flores (daily 9am–10.30pm); *Novap Computers*, Cuesta de las Calesas 45, near the train station (daily 10am–11pm).

Laundry The very friendly Laundry Europa, c/Santo Domingo 17, near the Convento de Santo Domingo (☎956 25 73 98), is the only place in Cádiz you'll get your clothes washed, dried and folded on the same day. The cost is €3 per kilo.

Maps IGN maps (1:25,000 & 1:50,000) are available from CNIG, Edificio Nereida, Oficina 310 Avda. Ana de Viya 5, behind the Playa de la Victoria (☎956 27 49 56). A detailed city map

is published by Everest and is available from bookshops.

Police In emergencies dial ☎091 for the Policía Nacional (serious crimes) and ☎092 for the Policía Local (theft and petty crime). Both police forces have their headquarters in the Playa de la Victoria zone: the national police are located in Avenida de Andalucía s/n and the local police are in the Avda. José León de Carranza, next to the football stadium.

Post office Plaza de las Flores, near the market (Mon–Fri 8.30am–8.30pm; Sat 9am–2pm). For poste restante, the Lista de Correos stays open Mon–Fri 8.30am–2.30pm, Sat 9am–2pm. A Correo office is open on Sundays in the El Corte Inglés department store (see "Shopping" above).

The Cádiz coast

For an alternative to Cádiz's often-crowded beaches take a trip across the bay to the resorts of **El Puerto de Santa María**, **Rota**, **Chipiona** and **Sanlúcar de Barrameda**. All have fine and spacious beaches and are within day-tripping distance by bus, boat or train as well as being in striking distance for a visit to the inland sherry capital, **Jerez**.

El Puerto de Santa María

Just 10km across the bay, **EL PUERTO DE SANTA MARÍA** is the obvious choice for a brief day-trip from Cádiz, a traditional family resort for both *gaditanos* and *sevillanos* – many of whom have built villas and chalets along the fine **Playa Puntilla** which you'll pass as the boat comes in to dock at the Muelle del Vapor in the estuary of the Río Guadalete. The town itself, some distance from the beach, has an easy-going air and, despite some ugly modern development on its periphery, is surprisingly picturesque with many narrow, white-walled streets and plant-filled balconies, plus an impressive medieval castle, a clutch of *señorial* mansions, some fine churches and Spain's third most prestigious bullring. On the cultural front, El Puerto will always be associated with one of the major Spanish poets of the twentieth-century, **Rafael Alberti**, who was born here in 1902 and died here in 1999; his birthplace at c/Santo Domingo 25 is now a museum (details from the Turismo).

Today one of the three centres of **wine** production (along with Jerez and Sanlúcar) that make up the "sherry triangle", El Puerto de Santa María came to prominence in the eighteenth century as a botanical garden where plants brought from the New World were cultivated for seed. This and other trading enterprises increased prosperity, as demonstrated by the numerous mansions around the town, which was once known as the *ciudad de los cien palacios* (city of a hundred palaces).

Arrival and information

Whether you arrive by bus (the "station" is little more than a couple of bus stops next to the Plaza de Toros), train or *vapor* (see p.242), the helpful **Turismo** at c/Luna 22 (daily 10am–2pm & 6–8pm; ☎956 54 24 13, ⊛www.elpuertosm .es) is handily sited for picking up a free **street map** as well as a *Ruta del*

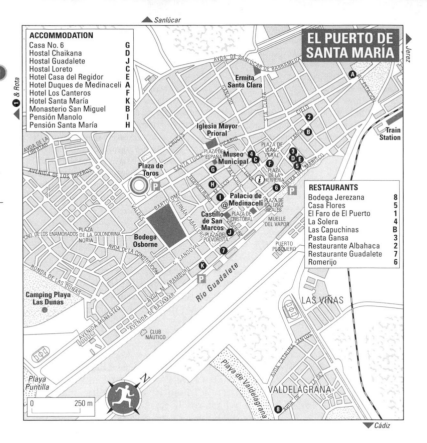

ACCOMMODATION

Casa No. 6	G
Hostal Chaikana	D
Hostal Guadalete	J
Hostal Loreto	C
Hotel Casa del Regidor	E
Hotel Duques de Medinaceli	A
Hotel Los Canteros	F
Hotel Santa María	K
Monasterio San Miguel	B
Pensión Manolo	I
Pensión Santa María	H

EL PUERTO DE SANTA MARÍA

RESTAURANTS

Bodega Jerezana	8
Casa Flores	5
El Faro de El Puerto	1
La Solera	4
Las Capuchinas	B
Pasta Gansa	3
Restaurante Albahaca	2
Restaurante Guadalete	7
Romerijo	6

Tapeo leaflet to find the best tapas bars. From here the heart of the town is within easy walking distance. Many of the main sights (including the Castillo San Marcos) are covered in a free **guided tour** from the Turismo on Tuesdays and Saturdays at 11am. **Internet** access is available at *Ciber Rush*, c/Larga 137 (Mon–Sat 10am–2pm & 5.30–10.30pm, Sun 5–10pm) and *Ciber Bahía* c/Micaela Aramburu 21 (daily 10am–1pm & 5–9pm). For **car hire**, Bahía Rent a Car, c/Misericordia 1 (☎956 87 76 97), is competitive and reliable. The town stages a **cultural festival** each summer (July–Aug) with concerts (mainly classical) taking place on Thursday evenings in the atmospheric Castillo San Marcos; details from the Turismo.

In July and August there are evening **boat trips** around the bay aboard the *Vaporcito*; the ninety-minute cruises sail on Tuesday, Thursday and Saturday evenings, leaving from the ferry quay near the Plaza del las Galeras at 9.45pm; tickets (sold on board) cost €5.

Accommodation

Many visitors come to El Puerto for the day, but should you be tempted to stay – and it makes a great break from Cádiz – there are plenty of **rooms** within easy walking distance of the ferry. Bear in mind that things get tight during August, when you should fix up something as early as possible in the day or ring ahead. If you have problems, ask at the Turismo for assistance; they also keep a list of **apartments** for longer stays.

El Puerto's **campsite**, *Camping Playa Las Dunas* (T 956 87 22 10), just behind the Playa Puntilla, has the advantage of plenty of shade. Take bus #2 from Plaza de Galeras, by the ferry dock.

Casa No. 6 c/San Bartoleme 14 T 956 87 70 84, W www.casano6.com. Rooms in a delightful *casa-palacio* lovingly restored by an Anglo-Spanish couple; en-suite rooms above a gorgeous patio are well furnished and come with fans. They also let two rooftop fully equipped apartments (**7**) with roof terrace. **5** with breakfast.

Hostal Chaikana c/Javier de Burgos 17 T 956 54 29 02, E hostalchaikana@hotmail.com. Small but very comfortable *hostal* near the centre of the action. All rooms have bath, a/c and TV. **4**

Hostal Guadalete (aka *Hostal Sherry*) c/Veneroni 1 T 956 87 09 02. Housed in the crumbling but nonetheless impressive early nineteenth-century Aduana (customs building) this *hostal* offers en-suite rooms with TV and fans. **3**

Hostal Loreto c/Ganado 17 T 956 54 24 10. Pleasant *hostal* with an enchanting patio. Rooms come with or without bath; en-suite ones have ceiling fans, fridge and TV. **3**–**4**

Hotel Casa del Regidor c/Ribera del Río 30 T 956 87 73 33, W www.hotelcasadelregidor.com. Charming new hotel housed in a restored seventeenth-century *casa señorial*. Attractive rooms come with satellite TV and free Internet connection plugs. **6**

Hotel Duques de Medinaceli Plaza de los Jazmines 2 T 956 86 07 77, W www .jale.com/dmedinaceli. A palatial hotel housed in the sumptuous former mansion of the Irish sherry family Terry, this eighteenth-century edifice has been restored to its former glory with a stunning patio, opulent furnishings and rooms decorated with original artworks. There are all the trimmings of a five-star hotel including a pool, sauna and restaurant, plus a magnificent botanical garden in the hotel's grounds (open to the public daily 5–10pm). With friendly and efficient staff, this is already one of the major hotels in Andalucía. Double rooms in high season start at €225. **9**

Hotel Los Canteros c/Curva 6 T 956 54 02 40, W www.hotelloscanteros.com. Central hotel offering a/c rooms with TV and minibar. Light sleepers may be disturbed by nearby music bars. **7**

Hotel Santa María Avda. Bajamar s/n T 956 87 32 11, W www.hotelsantamaria. es. Excellent-value mid-range riverfront hotel in a converted eighteenth-century *palacio* with a/c rooms, restaurant, garage (or there's easy parking by the river) and rooftop pool. **6**

Monasterio San Miguel c/Larga 27 T 956 54 04 40, W www.jale.com/monasterio. One of the best accommodation options in town, set in a sixteenth-century monastery converted into a luxurious four-star hotel complete with patios, pool and rooftop solarium. **9**

Pensión Manolo c/Jesús de Milagros 18 T 956 85 75 25. Pleasant doubles and singles with bath, a/c and TV, above a charming patio. **3**

Pensión Santa María c/Pedro Múñoz Seco 38 T 956 85 36 31. Very welcoming family *pensión*, for clean rooms with and without bath (with a negligible difference in price); not to be confused with the hotel above. **2**

The Town

Arriving by ferry, close to the landing quay you'll immediately spot the fine six-spouted eighteenth-century fountain, **El Fuente de las Galeras**, constructed, as the Latin inscription on it states, to provide galleys leaving for the Americas with water. West of here and a couple of blocks in is the **Castillo de San Marcos** (Mon, Tues & Thurs–Sat 10am–1.30pm, Wed 12–1.30pm; €5, Wed free) on Plaza de Alfonso El Sabio, a thirteenth-century fort built by Alfonso X on the site of a Moorish watchtower and mosque. The towers of the castle bear the stirring proclamations of devotion to the Virgin, a symbol of the victory over the vanquished Moors. So besotted was the king with her that he sang the Virgin's praises in a surviving poetic work, *Las Cantigas*, and renamed El Puerto after her. Inside the fort – today owned by the Luis Caballero *bodega* – Alfonso also constructed a triple-naved **Mudéjar church**, in which the mosque's ancient *mihrab* can still be identified. The current proprietors have long used one of the castle's halls as a sherry *bodega*, stacked with butts. You can take a full tour of the castle, leaving via the *bodega* where they will invite you to taste (and buy) their *finos*.

Following the mostly pedestrianized c/Luna into town from the ferry quay will bring you to the convent of **Las Esclavas de la Sagrada Corazón de Jesús**, a seventeenth-century Baroque church whose *retablo* has fine images of the Virgin and Christ. The church's *azulejo* tile decoration comes from the Triana factory of Charles Pickman at La Cartuja, Sevilla (see p.322), and was made in the early 1900s. Continuing along c/Luna brings you to El Puerto's **Plaza Mayor** (Plaza de España), fronted by the **Iglesia Mayor Prioral** (Mon–Fri 8.30am–12.45pm & 6.30–8.30pm, Sat 8.30am–12.30pm, Sun 8.30am–1.45pm & 6.30–8.30pm; free). A thirteenth-century Gothic edifice, it has suffered much rebuilding and the shell is now largely Baroque, but don't miss its superb Plateresque south entrance. Inside, a richly gilded *retablo* in the capilla de la Virgen de los Milagros holds *La Patrona*, a thirteenth-century image of the Virgin formerly housed in the castle of San Marcos and to which the town is devoted. The church's seventeenth-century images of Christ and San Juan are attributed to the *sevillano* sculptor Pedro Roldán. Note also some fine choir stalls richly carved in walnut and cedar.

A few blocks west lies the **Plaza de Toros** (Tues–Sun 11am–1.30pm & 6–7.30pm; free), one of the largest in Spain (third only to Madrid and Sevilla) and most celebrated by aficionados. Opened in 1880 with a capacity of 15,000, the bullring has hosted all the great names. A mosaic inside the entrance records the words of the legendary *sevillano* bullfighter Joselito, who fought here: "He who has not seen bulls in El Puerto does not know what bullfighting is." The Jesuit college of **San Luís Gonzaga**, two blocks and twenty minutes west of the bullring, conserves the earlier sixteenth-century church of San Francisco where a soaring gilded *retablo* holds two magnificent early seventeenth-century sculptures of San Francisco and San Ignacio by Juan de Mesa.

El Puerto's palacios and the Monasterio de la Victoria

Scattered all over town are the **palacios** left behind by the great eighteenth-century families of El Puerto and decorated with their escutcheons. One block downstream of the ferry dock is the **Palacio Medinaceli**, on c/Amburu de Mora, formerly occupied by the powerful ducal family whose gardens once stretched to the river. The beautiful patio and chapel of the early eighteenth-century **Hospital de San Juan de Dios**, opposite, is also worth a quick look. Other *palacios* worth a look are the enormous eighteenth-century **Palacio Purullena**, c/Federico Rubio 92, northwest of the bullring, a rare example of Spanish Rococo which is finally undergoing restoration after falling into a tragic state of disrepair; **Casa de Vizarrón**, Plaza de Polvorista (slightly south of Palacio Medinaceli), with an elegant escutcheoned doorway; the **Casa de los Leones** (interior daily 10am–2pm & 6–8pm; free), c/La Placilla 2 near the market, with a fine facade and patio; and **Palacio de Aranibar**, fronting the Castillo de San Marcos and now the law court. At c/Palacios 57, just east of Plaza España, a plaque marks the house where Washington Irving lived in 1828 whilst writing *The Conquest of Granada*.

The **Museo Municipal**, c/Pagador 1, just off the Plaza Mayor (Tues–Fri 10am–2pm, Sat & Sun 10.45am–2pm; free), is housed in another mansion, the **Casa de la Marquesa de Candia**, and contains archeological finds from the surrounding area and a selection of fairly awful artworks somewhat alleviated by a few canvases by the poet Rafael Alberti who tried to make it as a painter in his early years.

Finally, another monument tucked away upstream and behind the train station is the poignant **Monasterio de la Victoria** (easily reached via a gate on the

△ El Puerto's Plaza de Toros

train station forecourt), a beautiful sixteenth-century monastery founded by the Medinaceli family for the Mínimos order of friars, which fell into a ruinous state after being sacked by the French during the Napoleonic wars. Only the exterior – with an exquisite ogival portal – may currently be seen, but when the building opens to stage frequent exhibitions (details from the Turismo, see p.253), an equally fine Gothic church and cloister are on view, too.

The beaches

The closest beaches, **Playa La Puntilla** and **Playa Valdelgrana**, are some distance from the town (15min walk or local buses from the ferry dock; Plaza Las Galeras: #1 and #2 for La Puntilla or #35 for Valdelgrana) and are pleasant places to while away an afternoon with lots of lively *marisquerías* and beach bars. For fewer crowds you're better off on the **Playa Santa Catalina** to the west of the Playa La Puntilla; bus #35 (direction Fuenterrabía) from c/Micaela Aramburu near the ferry dock will take you there. If you fancy reaching the beaches under your own pedal power, Bigote, c/Rodrigo de Bastidas 6 (☏956 87 54 18), south west of Plaza de la Noria at the left of our map, rents out cycles and mountain bikes.

Eating and drinking

The best areas in town for **places to eat** are the Ribera del Marisco, a street upstream from the ferry dock lined with a variety of seafood restaurants and bars serving tapas and *raciones,* and the nearby Plaza de la Herrería. You should also try the beaches of La Puntilla and Valdelgrana for a cluster of friendly bars.

Bars, cafés and restaurants

Bodega Jerezana Avda. de la Paz, Valdelgrana seafront. Briny tapas bar and restaurant with a wide range of well-prepared seafood dishes.

Café Central c/Luna 41. Relaxed café for tranquil breakfasts; their *desayuno especial* gets you fresh juice, *café* and *pan tostada* for €2.

Casa Flores Ribera del Río 9. Classic fish and mariscos restaurant. Main courses €10–20.

 El Faro de El Puerto Half a kilometre out, along the Rota road ☎ 956 87 09 52. Outstanding seafood and meat dishes produced under the direction of top chef Fernando Córdoba in this stylish twin establishment of the restaurant of the same name in Cádiz. House specials include *salmonete sobre bereneja* (red mullet) and *rape salteado* (monkfish). Widely regarded as having the best wine-cellar in the province, it also has its own tapas bar, a pleasant garden terrace and a *menú de degustación* for €39.50. Main dishes €12–20. Closed Sun eve.

Las Capuchinas *Monasterio de San Miguel*, c/Larga 27. The *Monasterio* hotel's swish *cafetería* serves up good-value *platos combinados* and its more serious restaurant, *Las Bovedas*, has a *menú* for around €26.

 La Solera c/Ganado 17, next to the *Hostal Loreto* ☎ 956 54 35 62. Delightful if diminutive (booking advised) quality restaurant with fair-priced dishes such as *brocheta de rape con langostinos* (skewer-grilled monkfish). Lunch *menú* for €7.50; main dishes €7.50–10.

Pasta Gansa c/Puerto Escondido 1, near the Ribera del Marisco. A stylish Italian restaurant where diners can enjoy pizzas and risottos at candlelit tables in an attractive patio.

Restaurante Albahaca c/Larga 62 ☎ 956 54 21 64. Superb, welcoming mid-priced restaurant where chef Ramón García looks after his clients with a personal touch. Among a range of meat and fish possibilities the *rapé mozarabe* (monkfish with a pine-nut and almond sauce) and a *solomillo* made with special *carne retinto* from selected beef herds are outstanding. There's a lunchtime *menú* for €9. Main dishes €10–15.

Restaurante Guadalete Avda. Bajamar 14 ☎ 956 85 06 01. An El Puerto institution founded in 1953, this mid-priced restaurant has an elegant main room and prepares a variety of meat and fish dishes. House specialities include *lenguado con fideos* (sole) and *almejas a la marinera* (clams). Mains €10–30.

 Romerijo Ribera del Marisco. This enormous and justifiably popular seafood bar dominates the strip. You can get a takeaway of *mariscos* in a *cartucho* (paper funnel) from their shop and eat it at outdoor tables where buckets are provided for debris and waiters serve beer; the

The sherry bodegas of El Puerto de Santa María

The long, whitewashed warehouses flanking the streets and the banks of the Río Guadalete belong to the big **sherry bodegas**: Luís Caballero, Terry, Osborne and Duff Gordon, the last three founded in the eighteenth and nineteenth centuries by Irish and English families. Osborne (pronounced "Osbornay" in Spanish) and Duff Gordon are now co-owned after a takeover by Osborne, although separate production is maintained. Osborne is also the largest producer of Spanish brandy, and its black-bull logo – long used as a billboard perched on hills throughout Spain – has become a familiar part of the country's landscape.

In sherry circles, El Puerto is noted for a lighter, more aromatic *fino* with more *flor* aroma imparted due to its humid geographical location, close to the sea (see box on p.275 for details of sherry styles). It's easy enough to visit the *bodegas*; Osborne and Duff Gordon, c/Los Moros 7 (visits: in English Mon–Fri 10.30am; in Spanish 11am & midday; ☎ 956 86 91 00; €5); Fernando de Terry, c/Santísima Trinidad 2 (Mon, Tues & Thurs 10am–1.30pm; €5; Wed & Fri guided visit, including stables, at 11am; €11; ☎ 956 85 77 00), with a museum and situated in a beautiful, converted, seventeenth-century convent along with the smaller Gutierrez Colosia, Avda. de Bajamar 40, near the *Hotel Santa María* (guided visits Sat 12.30–1.30pm; information ☎ 956 54 29 36, no booking required). All welcome visitors for tours and tastings, although you'll need to **call in advance** to the first two *bodegas* to book a place. As English is very much the second language of the sherry world, you should have no problems in being understood. Other *bodegas* also do visits and the Turismo can supply a full list with opening hours. The Vinoteca wine shop, c/Micael Aramburu 20, near the ferry dock, stocks all the *finos* of the region.

córtel de mariscos (seafood cocktail) or any of the six types of *langostinos* are delicious. The same firm's *freiduría* restaurant over the road is equally excellent, and a generous *frito variado* (assorted fried fish) easily serves two.

Tapas bars

 Bar Tapia c/Mayorga 7. In a small street opposite the *Pasta Gansa* restaurant, this is an excellent and friendly small tapas and *raciones* bar with a charming summer patio. Specials include *arroz casero* and *mariscos*.

El Grifo c/Luna 19. Entertaining bar which has self-service beer pumps on every (stand-up) table that record how much you've consumed. It also does tapas.

El Brillante c/Dr Múñoz Seca 2 (aka c/Vicario). Slightly north of the Plaza de España, this venerable old tapas bar faces the market and is packed to the gunwales on market day when crowds flock in to feast themselves on the house special, *caracoles* (sea snails).

El Laul c/Avda. de la Bajamar s/n. Diminutive little tapas bar facing the river and 50m downstream from the Galeras fountain. This is one of El Puerto's little-known gems and house specials include *tartar de pargo* (sea bream) and *huevos glaciados con foie* (eggs with pâté).

La Dorada Avda. Bajamar 26, near the ferry dock. Meal-sized and inexpensive *raciones* where the *pescado frito* is superb. *Choco a la plancha* (cuttlefish) is a special. Has a pleasant terrace.

La Galera Plaza de las Galeras, close to the Muelle del Vapor. Good bar for beer and seafood tapas and *raciones* if you're just off, or waiting for, the boat. Has a *menú* for €7.

Nuevo Portuense c/Luna 31. Good and busy central bar with a wide range of seafood tapas and *raciones* (*sardinas empanadas* are a special) and there's a *menú* for around €8.

Sol y Sombra Plaza de Ahuja, facing the bullring. Taking its name from the nearby bullring's seating arrangements, this is often a lively venue – especially on fight days – and prepares good and cheap tapas. House specials include *fideos con almejas* (vermicelli with clams) and paella. It's restaurant is also recommended and does a lunchtime *menú* for €8.50.

Nightlife

Nightlife in El Puerto means just that – in summer many places don't even open until around 11pm. The action centres on the bars along c/Micaela Aramburu near the ferry dock, and the river zone. *Bar 4x4* and *El Niño Perdido* are two of several hectic music bars here that are popular with a younger crowd, while nearby options worth checking out are *La Kama*, *El Rey de Copas* and *Resbaladero*, a disco-bar housed in a converted fishmarket. The stylish, glass-walled *La Doca*, next to the water, is a laid-back late-night music bar; moored just upstream, a floating pontoon music bar, *La Pontona*, with roof terrace is also popular. Further upriver from the ferry dock *Karaoke El Estanque*, Ribera del Río s/n (100m upstream from the Ribera del Marisco), is where locals bellow the night away, and the nearby *La Resaca* is a *Rociero* bar where every night at midnight the lights go down and the El Rocío pilgrims' anthem is sung; this place often stages live flamenco after 10.30pm. The town's most bizarre nightspot is *El Convento*, Avda. Bajamar 30 (fronting the river 500m downstream of the ferry dock), a ruined monastery transformed into a complex of bars and discos, with two patio dance floors in the former cloisters and incense wafting throughout (free entry).

The town centre scene focuses on Plaza de la Herrería with bars like *O'Donoghues*, *Kheops* and *El Recuerdo* in the middle of the action. Just off the plaza to the south, c/Jesús de los Milagros is another drinking zone with *copas* bars *Barsito* and *Totem* attracting plenty of late-night (and early-morning) revellers.

If you're here during July and August you should try to catch a **flamenco** performance staged by two of the town's *peñas*, *El Nitri* and *El Chumi*. They normally take place at 10.30pm on Fridays and Saturdays, are usually memorable and – best of all – are free. Pick up a leaflet from the Turismo.

Rota

Much of the 15km between El Puerto and the town of **ROTA** is taken up by a massive tract of territory occupied by one of the three major **US**

military bases in Spain. Installed in the 1950s as part of a deal in which Franco exchanged strips of Spanish sovereign territory for economic aid and international "respectability", the base is surrounded by a seemingly endless barbed-wire fence bristling with the technological gadgetry of war. Behind the wire it's possible to glimpse farms and whole villages linked by their own bus service along a road system where signs are in English. Huge Ford trucks trundle to and from Rota's harbour from where the base services and supplies the US Sixth Fleet – including nuclear submarines. If you're passing by in your own vehicle, tuning in to the Base radio station – with ads for "ten-pin bowling tournaments" and "World Series DVDs" – will give you even more of the "California in Cádiz" flavour of things here. Long-standing local resentment at this "occupation" occasionally surfaces. Not long ago Bronze Age cave dwellings were found on the territory of the base, but Spanish archeologists were refused permission to carry out investigations. The caves have since been looted by treasure-hunters.

That said, however, the US military population tends to keep to itself, and Rota exudes an affable character very much its own with an attractive *casco antiguo* and some great tapas bars. In season, the resort fairly bounces with life, its excellent **beach**, the Playa de la Costilla, being the main attraction for the crowds who flock here in August.

The town's sights can be seen in under an hour. Highlights in the old quarter include a thirteenth-century castle now housing the Ayuntamiento and Turismo – the frequently remodelled and much-restored **Castillo de Luna** (daily 10am–midday & 5–6pm; free) with a stunning patio. Also worth a look is the sixteenth-century Gothic church, **Nuestra Señora de la Expectación** (known locally as Nuestra Señora de la O; daily 9am–1pm and 6.30–9pm), which hides, behind a box-like exterior, a fine single-naved church with elegant vaulting, magnificent choir stalls depicting the twelve apostles by Diego Roldán and – in the chapel of Jesús Nazareno – a delightful eighteenth-century image of the Last Supper crafted in *azulejos* from Triana in Sevilla (the barely surviving image of Judas has received some rough treatment over the years). If churches are your thing you may also want to take in the **Capilla de San Juan Bautista** (open service times only – try early evening 7–8pm), Plaza Andalucía, near the Turismo, with a spectacular Baroque *altar mayor* by Diego Roldán, one of the finest in the province.

Practicalities

Arriving **by car**, make your way to the seafront *Hotel Duque de Najera* (see below), opposite which is a large public car park from where all the sights and accommodation options are within a few minutes walk. The very helpful **Turismo** is located in the Castillo de Luna, c/Cuna 2 (July–Sept daily 10am–2pm & 6–9pm; Oct–June 9.30am–2pm & 5–7.30pm; ☎956 84 63 45, ⓦwww .turismorota.com), in the old quarter on the town's southern flank. The Turismo has useful **maps** and can help you find a room during the high summer scramble. Rota's **bus station** lies off Plaza del Triunfo, which is a ten-minute walk or an easy bus ride to the centre along c/Calvario.

Accommodation

Places to stay include the excellent *Hostal Macavi*, c/Écija 11, with en-suite rooms off the main Avenida Sevilla, and a mere fifty metres from the beach (☎956 81 33 36; ④), and the nearby and pricier *Hostal Playa*, c/Córdoba 1 (☎956 81 54 09; ⑤), with similar facilities. Perhaps the most interesting room option is ⍗ *Hostal El Torito*, c/Constitución 1, near the Plaza de España (☎956

81 62 73, Ⓦwww.eltoritoderota.com; ❹) a stunningly minimalist new *hostal* which has to rank as one of Andalucía's most original. The a/c rooms (no. 5 with its own terrace is a gem) are ultra-stylish and some more expensive apartments (❺) are equally state-of-the-art. In the same price bracket the nearby ⚓ *Hostal Sixto* (Ⓣ956 84 63 10, Ⓦwww.hostalsixto.com; ❹) is an enchanting small hotel with attractive rooms around a pretty patio or above their nearby restaurant. *Hotel Caribe*, Avda. de la Marina 60 (Ⓣ956 81 07 00, Ⓦwww .hotel-caribe.com; ❼), a couple of blocks inland from these two, has a/c balcony rooms overlooking a pool, and the price includes breakfast and garage space. The town's sleek flagship hotel, the four-star *Duque de Najera*, c/Gravina 2 (Ⓣ956 84 60 20, Ⓦwww.hotelduquedenajera.com; ❾), occupies a remodelled and renovated mansion with pool overlooking the harbour. The nearest **campsite** is *Camping Playa Aguadulce* (Ⓣ956 84 70 78), 9km from Rota along the A491 to Chipiona.

Eating, drinking and nightlife

The modern town fans out from the central Plaza Jesús Nazareno fronting the beach and it's here that you'll find most of the **bars**, **restaurants** and nightlife. Look out for the town's very own speciality, the outstandingly tasty *urta a la roteña* (sea bream in a caramelized onion and tomato sauce). Note also that the *urta* season lasts June–Sept, outside which many restaurants revert to *mero a la roteña* (grouper). Rota's tapas bars tend to be better value than the restaurants, many of which are overpriced and bland. Exceptions include *Mesón Alicantino*, Avda. Sevilla 39 (near the *Hostal Macavi*), for fish and seafood and *Bar–Restaurante La Costilla*, c/Higuereta 68, facing Plaza Jesús Nazareno, a great place to sample the town's signature dish, *urta*. Another place to sample *urta* at its best is at the excellent *Restaurante Sixto*, attached to the *hostal* of the same name (see above) with an inviting terrace. For **tapas** head down atmospheric c/La Mina, a little northwest of the Castillo de Luna, where a number of bars line the pedestrianized street, including the excellent *Emilio* and *El Fresquito*. One bar also worth a look is *Bar Torito*, c/Italia 2, a stone's throw from the chic *hostal* of the same name (see above); less stylistically cutting edge than it's namesake, it's nevertheless a cosy place with tapas, *raciones* and some cool sounds.

Nightlife featuring music bars and a couple of *discotecas* centres on the zone to the north and east of Plaza de Jesús Nazareno, the nearby Plaza de la Cantera at the western end of the old quarter and (late evening) along the Avenida San Juan de Puerto Rico, behind the Puerto Deportivo. Rota's big **festival** is the mid-August Fiesta de la Urta, when all the restaurants in town compete to win the prize for the best *urta*-based dish.

Chipiona

From Rota the road north winds inland behind a coast lined with more golden sand beaches to **CHIPIONA**, 18km away, on a point at the edge of the estuary of the Guadalquivir.

Presenting itself as a modest, straightforward seaside resort crammed with family *pensiones* the town's a great place to spend a few days, except in July and August when its many charms are all but submerged beneath an onslaught of mainly Spanish visitors. Older tourists come here for the spa waters, channelled into a fountain at the fourteenth-century church of **Nuestra Señora de Regla**, which incorporates a delightful Gothic cloister (daily 7–9pm) adorned with seventeenth-century Triana *azulejos*; often they don't open it so try and find a priest or churchwarden to do this for you. The town has a charming **old quarter** on its northern flank, cut through by sinuous, white-walled alleyways. The major thoroughfare here is the pedestrianized c/Isaac Peral (and its continuation c/Miguel Cervantes), lined with shops, bars and some elegant buildings and hotels. But for most it's the twelve kilometres of **beaches** that are the lure; stretching south of the town beyond Spain's tallest **lighthouse** (May–Sept 6–7.30pm, Oct–April 4–6pm; €3) is the long **Playa de Regla**, best avoided in August but where for much of the year it's possible to leave the crowds behind. Northeast, towards Sanlúcar, are sand bars and rocks with fine views towards the Marismas de Doñana and the Guadalquivir estuary.

Practicalities

Maps, **information** and help with accommodation plus a list of tapas bars can be picked up from the **Turismo**, Plaza Juan Carlos I s/n (Mon–Fri 10am–1.30pm & 5–7pm; ☎956 37 71 50, ⓦwww.chipiona.org), in the old quarter, close to the sea. **Buses** to and from Sevilla, Cádiz and Sanlúcar arrive at the central Amarillos bus station on Avenida Nuestra Señora de Regla. Buses to Jerez are operated by Linesur with a station to the east of the centre on Avda. de Andalucía.

Accommodation

Accommodation can be expensive in high summer and in August without an advance reservation you'll struggle to find anything at all and may have to fall back on rooms in *casas particulares* (which also go fast); the Turismo can provide information on these. It's worth noting that outside the July–August period the high-season rates we quote below fall by up to fifty per cent. The **campsite and youth hostal**, *Piñar de Chipiona* (☎956 37 23 21), lies 3km out of town towards Rota; it rents out air-conditioned bungalows with bath (❹ for up to 4 persons) and has a cheap self-service restaurant and pool. Get the Rota-bound bus to drop you off.

Hostal San Miguel Avda. de la Regla 79 ☎956 37 29 76. Comfortable en-suite rooms in a charming 1930s mansion close to the church of Nuestra Señora de la Regla. ❹

Hostal Andalucía c/Larga 14 ☎956 37 07 05. Welcoming central place with a/c en-suite rooms and rooftop solarium. ❹

Hostal Gran Capitán c/Fray Baldomero González 3, close to the seaward end of c/Isaac Peral ☎956 37 09 29. Attractive *hostal* housed in a venerable *casa antigua* – which it is claimed once belonged to Spain's eponymous fifteenth-century military commander – offering a/c en-suite rooms. ❹

Hostal Belén Avda. del Ejército 5 ☎956 37 26 80. Simple and economical rooms sharing bath close to the central c/Miguel Cervantes. ❷

Hostal Naval c/Francisco Lara y Araujo 14 ☎956 37 24 89. Close to the pedestrianized c/Isaac Peral this is a good option for rooms with and without bath. *Rough Guide* readers with this guide can claim a ten percent discount. ❹

Hostal Rompeolas Avda de Jerez 28 ☎956 37 33 58, ⓔhostalesdechipiona@hotmail.com.

En-suite sea-view rooms on the seafront just south of the lighthouse and fronting the Playa de la Regla. It cuts prices by half outside July and August. Nearby on the seafront, the same proprietors have the *Hostal Monserrat* (☎956 37 14 94) and *Hostal Tranvía* (☎956 37 30 19) at Paseo Costa de la Luz 45 and 27 respectively, offering similar deals. ❺

Hotel La Española c/Isaac Peral 4 ☎956 37 37 71, ⓦwww.hotellaespanola.com. Excellent-value and superbly renovated old hotel with many sea-view rooms and whose front door is a mere 20m from the Atlantic breakers; arriving by car here allows the luxury of taking the lift from the hotel's subterranean garage effortlessly to your room. ❹

Hotel Al Sur de Chipiona Avda. de Sevilla 101, facing the church of Nuestra Señora de la Regla ☎956 37 03 00, wwww.hotelalsur.com. Comprising an older, elegant hotel with a new wing – complete with pool and gardens – tacked on, this is the best value of the more exclusive places with well-appointed rooms, all with terrace balcony. July–Aug half-board only. ❼

Eating and drinking

Chipiona has a gratifying range of **restaurants**, all excelling in seafood. For a mid-priced *menú*, try the elegant *La Pañoleta* (the restaurant of the *Hotel La Española*, near the beach), which is very good. Equally tasty seafood is on offer at *Restaurante Peña*, Avda. Sevilla 14, near the lighthouse, a beautiful white-washed building with a shaded terrace. Two superb seafront fish restaurants with shady terraces lie at each end of the tiny Playa de Las Canteras close to the lighthouse. Nearest is ⅔ *Las Canteras*, great for fish (especially *urta* and *dorada*) and *mariscos* and does pretty good chips, too; its neighbour to the north, *Los Corrales*, is also worth a try. North of here again *Bar-Restaurante Repostaero*, c/Dr Tolosa Latour 7, is a boisterous seafood *chiringuito* with a great atmosphere late at night when impromptu flamenco sometimes gets going. In the somewhat lifeless Puerto Deportivo, *Bar-Restaurante Paco* is another outstanding seafood restaurant and tapas bar with a waterfront terrace. For beach lunches *El Dorado Chipiona*, c/Miguel de Cervantes 25 (near the *Hostal Naval* above), is an excellent and popular US-style roast chicken takeaway run by an ex-Rota base serviceman. One out-of-the-centre option is the wonderful *Venta Millan* (☎956 37 40 81), Avda. de Rota 156, just before the roundabout leading to the Rota road, where they cook up tasty *cocina casera*; the price for three courses is €7 and you eat what is prepared on the day, which can be fish or meat.

For more **tapas** and **drinking bars** – some with music – take a stroll along the pedestrianized c/Isaac Peral, where among many others ⅔ *Bar Peña Betica* at the junction with c/Larga is popular. A little further along, at the junction with Plaza Pío XII, *Bar Paquito* is another good tapas venue and at Isaac Peral 14 *Bar La Parra* serves more of the same in an atmospheric *patio andaluz*. South of here along Avenida de la Regla, at no.10 the atmospheric and cavernous bar of the *Bodega Cooperativa Catolico Agricola* is a great place for munching grilled sardines washed down with the cooperative's own *fino*. *La Campana*, Avda. de la Regla 47, is a cosy place for cheap *platos combinados* and has a *menú* for €8. **Flamenco** often takes place at the nearby *Al Compa*, Avenida de Jerez s/n, close to the sea, a cheap restaurant and bar with a good terrace.

Sanlúcar de Barrameda

Like El Puerto de Santa María, **SANLÚCAR DE BARRAMEDA**, 8km beyond Chipiona, is a major sherry town. A substantial place with an attractive old quarter set at the mouth of the Guadalquivir, it is the main depot for **manzanilla** wine – a pale dry *fino* variety with a salty tang – highly regarded by connoisseurs and much in evidence in the bars round here. Sanlúcar is also one of the best places in Andalucía for **seafood**, for which *manzanilla* is the perfect accompaniment.

Although there was a small settlement here in Roman times and the Moors built a fort to guard the vital Guadalquivir estuary from sea raiders, it was after the recapture of the town in 1264 by Alfonso X that Sanlúcar grew to become one of sixteenth-century Spain's leading ports. **Columbus** sailed from here on his third voyage to the Americas and it was also from here in 1519 that Magellan set out to circumnavigate the globe. Decline in the eighteenth century, however, was exacerbated by the War of Independence and the town revived only in the mid-nineteenth century when the duke of Montpensier built a summer palace here. Since then Sanlúcar has grown into the popular resort it is today. During the last week of May the town stages a riotous **fiesta**, the Feria de la Manzanilla,

Sanlúcar's Manzanilla bodegas

The delicate taste of Sanlúcar's distinctive **manzanilla** is created by the seaside environment where the wine is matured, and by not being fortified with alcohol (as happens in Jerez and El Puerto). The humid microclimate necessary for the growth of the dense *flor* (yeast) inside the wine butts is added to by the moist *poniente* wind that blows across the Coto de Doñana, imparting the characteristic saltiness to this driest of all sherries. Sanlúcar is less aggressive than Jerez in its public relations (despite *manzanilla* recently overtaking *fino* sales on the peninsula for the first time), and only a few of Sanlúcar's *bodegas* are open for **visits and tastings**. The town's major producer, Antonio Barbadillo, c/Sevilla 25, near the castle (visits Tues–Sat noon & 1pm; €3; ☎956 38 55 00, ⓦwww.barbadillo.com), which produces seventy percent of all *manzanilla*, also makes *manzanilla pasada*, an exceptional fifteen-year-old wine (as against the normal four for standard *fino*), besides one of Andalucía's best white table wines (Castillo de San Diego) from the same Palomino grape. The only other *bodegas* who welcome visitors are the central Bodegas Hidalgo, c/Banda Playa 24 (visits Wed, Fri & Sat 10am, 11.30am & 12.30pm; €5; ☎956 36 05 16, ⓦwww.lagitana. es), producers of the La Gitana brand, Pedro Romero, c/Trasbolsa 84, east of the Plaza del Cabildo (visits Mon–Sat noon & Mon–Fri 6pm; €6; ☎956 36 07 36, ⓦwww. pedroromero.es), and the tiny Bodega de Velasco, c/Truco s/n, near the market (Mon–Fri 8am–3pm), which is a friendly and intimate family-run place where they'll serve you their La Cigarrera brand *manzanilla* to try (and buy) straight from the butt. They are now part of the larger Bodegas La Cigarrera, Plaza Madre de Dios s/n (near the *Hotel Los Helechos*), who also do organized visits (Mon–Sat 10am–2pm; €2.50; ☎956 38 12 85, ⓦwww.bodegaslacigarrera.com). A *despacho de vinos* (**wineseller**), La Abuela Lola, c/Caballeros 21 near the *Posada de Palacio* (see "Accommodation", opposite), stocks all the major brands and does tastings. The La Cigarrera Bodega, which makes La Cigerra brand, has a shop at c/Bretones 7, near the market, and the Bodegas Hidalgo shop is opposite the Turismo on the Calzada de Ejército.

to celebrate its great wine, which is copiously consumed throughout. In early and late August, the beach is the setting for some exciting **horse races**, a tradition dating from 1845, accompanied by riotous partying by revellers filling the bars and restaurants along the riverfront.

Arrival, orientation and information

Sanlúcar's **bus station** (with services to Chipiona, Cádiz, Sevilla and Jerez) is located between the river and the centre, to the west of the main avenue Calzada del Ejército. Coming in by **car** it's best to avoid the congested central zone and find a parking place along the Calzada del Ejército. Near the top of this avenue the **Turismo**, Calzada del Ejército s/n (Mon–Fri 10am–2pm & 6–8pm, Sat & Sun 10am–2pm; ☎956 36 61 10, ⓦwww.turismosanlucar.com) can provide a detailed street map and a tapas guide. They also offer a guided walking **tour of the town** in English and Spanish (Wed & Fri; €3) which includes a *bodega* visit.

    Internet access is available at *Cibercafe Undernet*, c/Infanta Beatriz s/n, near the *Hotel Guadalquivir* (daily 10am–2.30am), *Haif@*, c/Tartaneros 2, near the Plaza del Cabildo (Mon–Sat 4pm–2am), and *Infociber*, c/Torre de Arena 2, near the Bajo de Guía.

Accommodation

There's a shortage of budget **accommodation** in Sanlúcar, and in August you'll be pushed to find anything at all. This is when a number of

Andalucian
cuisine

The flavours of Andalucian cuisine reflect a dramatic history that has seen waves of traders and invaders attracted to the region's shores. It was the Phoenicians who introduced the olive to Andalucía – which today produces over twenty percent of the world's olive oil – the Greeks brought the vine, and the Moors introduced citrus fruits, almonds and spices. It only remained for Columbus (who sailed from Andalucía) to return from the New World with potatoes, tomatoes and green peppers and the main ingredients of modern Andalucía's cuisine had arrived.

Tapas

Tapas, the small plates of delicious food served up by bars across Spain, are arguably the world's greatest snacks, and Andalucía has the tastiest and broadest range on offer. Dishes are surprisingly cheap, at around €1 or €2 for a standard plate, and for the vast majority of Andalucians, dining out means eating tapas.

The *andaluzes* are passionate about their tapas and tend to eat them with a group of friends – and, as many bars offer a house special, there's usually enthusiastic debate as to the best place for, say, *pulpo gallego* (spicy boiled octopus) or *gambas con gabardinas* (prawns in batter "raincoats"). Normally they'll take in several establishments as part of a **tapeo** (bar tour), ordering just one or two rounds at each. This love of tapas cuts across the board; even King Juan Carlos is rumoured to have visited a particular Sevillano bar, incognito, for its *papas aliñas* (marinated potatoes).

Andalucía's favourite tapas

There are hundreds of tapas possibilities in the bars of Andalucía. Bars in many areas tend to stick to producing their local specialities, but the dishes listed below are standards, justly popular and available across the region.

Jamón Ibérico Mountain-cured ham
Huevos relleños Eggs stuffed with tuna
Boquerones al vinagre Marinated anchovies
Gambas al ajillo Garlic-fried prawns
Garbanzos con espinacas Chickpeas with spinach
Tortilla de patatas Potato omelette
Cazón en adobo Marinated shark
Patatas bravas Potatoes in a spicy sauce
Pollo al ajillo Garlic chicken
Callos Stewed tripe

Gazpacho

One of Andalucía's emblematic dishes is gazpacho soup, habitually served chilled in the heat of the day. It was probably the ancient Greeks who came up with the prototype gazpacho, in the form of a bread and salt soup. The Roman legions later imported it into Spain, adding olive oil, while in the sixteenth century the newly discovered tomatoes and green peppers were added and the classic summer refresher was born. Regional variations on the theme are to be found in Córdoba, where it's called salmorejo, and garnished with ham and chopped hard-boiled eggs; and Málaga, whose ajo blanco substitutes tomatoes with blanched almonds and Muscat grapes.

Pescaíto frito

A major passion along the coasts of Andalucía is pescaíto frito, or quick-fried fish. Served at beach restaurants (*chiringuitos*) or bought as an inexpensive take-away in a paper cone (*cartucho*) from a fried-fish shop (*freiduría*), it's invariably delicious. The fish is always ultra-fresh, allowing it to be served up crisp on the outside whilst remaining mouth-wateringly succulent within. A justly famed dish available everywhere is a *fritura mixta de pescados* (fried white-fish selection) often including shark (*cazón*), whiting (*pescadilla*), plaice (*platija*) and maybe even anchovies (*boquerones*) and whitebait (*chanquetes*), too. If you buy from a *freiduría*, take your *cartucho* to a bar, order a chilled bottle of wine and you've got a feast made in heaven.

Andalucía's top ten tapas bars

Aurelio Cádiz (see p.250)
Bar Juanito Jerez (see p.279)
Bar Orellana Málaga (see p.109)
Bodegas Castañeda Granada (see p.557)
Casa Balbino Sanlúcar de Barrameda (see p.269)
Casa Puga Almería (see p.610)
Cunini Granada (see p.556)
El Faro Cádiz (see p.249)
El Rinconcillo Sevilla (see p.335)
Taberna San Miguel Córdoba (see p.445)

Sherry and tapas: a perfect match

Sherry, or **fino** as it's known in its homeland, is Andalucía's emblematic wine and the perfect partner for tapas. The major area of production is a triangle of land centred on Jerez in the province of Cádiz, although Córdoba province also produces a similar wine called Montilla. There are a variety of *finos* ranging from the darker and nuttier tasting *olorosos* and *amontillados* to the most popular: the dry, light and gloriously refreshing classic sherry exemplified by the Tio Pepe and La Ina brands. One town in the triangle – Sanlúcar de Barrameda – is noted for Manzanilla, a light, dry and delicate *fino* celebrated for its salty tang arising from the seaside location of its vineyards. A celebrated *tapa* is **riñones al jerez**, veal kidneys cooked in a sherry sauce.

Jamón de Jabugo

Andalucía's most celebrated *aperitivo* is the crimson jamón serrano, salt-cured ham from small pigs fed on acorns. The very best *jamón* is the correspondingly expensive *pata negra* (named after the pigs' black hooves), and the most famous curing farms are to be found around the village of Jabugo in the Sierra de Aracena. Trevelez, a Sierra Nevada mountain village is another famous producer of these prized hams that send *andaluzes* into raptures.

Green cuisine

Mixed salads excepted, vegetables are rarely served in restaurants to accompany main dishes. However they are a significant part of Andalucía's tapas lexicon and *espinacas con garbanzos* (spinach with chickpeas) is a tapas classic. In the early summer months *esparragos trigueros* (baby asparagus) is another treat, often stewed with onions, coriander and lemon juice. *Berenjenas fritas* (fried aubergine slices) are another tapas favourite and *huevos a la flamenca* is a wonderful concoction consisting of eggs fried in a terracotta dish and garnished with artichokes, asparagus or peas and invariably a few slices of cured *jamón*.

casas particulares open to mop up the overflow. A handful of these are concentrated along c/Barrameda to the east of Plaza del Cabildo (the continuation of c/de Santo Domingo on our map) and an enquiry in any of the bars or shops along here should soon turn up some possibilities. The Turismo can supply more addresses should you need them, and for longer stays they have information on apartments for rent (minimum three nights), plus *casas rurales* in and around the town.

Algaida Alojamiento Rural Calle 1, no.4 Colonia Monte Algaida, 5km out of town beyond the village of Bonanza ☎956 38 73 72, ⊛www.algaida.org. This friendly rural option offers rooms sharing bath in a large house in a village close to the Guadalquivir estuary. You'll need your own transport and when you ring them they will advise on how to get there. ❸

🏃 **Hospedería Duques de Medina Sidonia** Plaza Condes de Niebla 1 ☎956 36 01 61, ⊛www.ruralduquesmedinasidonia.com. The best address in town is the palace of the dukes of Medina Sidonia, one of Spain's most blue-blooded dynasties. Rooms are airy and tastefully decorated and the patio they surround has a *cafetería* during the day (until 10pm). Rooms run from reasonably priced doubles to luxurious suites with private terrace. ❹

Hotel Doñana c/Orfeón Santa Cecilia s/n ☎956 36 50 00, ⊛www.partner-hotels.com. Functional, bland three-star hotel with views across the river to Doñana from the higher rooms on the west side. ❼

Hotel Guadalquivir Calzada del Ejército 20 ☎956 36 07 42, ⊛www.hotelguadalquivir.com. Modern hotel towering over the thoroughfare leading to the river. Functional rooms are a/c, with vistas from the higher ones, and some have balcony.

Hotel Los Helechos Plaza Madre de Dios 9 ☎956 36 13 49, ⊛www.hotelloshelechos.com. Smart, central hotel in converted former *bodega* with rooms around two charming patios and lots of traditional features. ❹

Hotel Tartaneros c/Tartaneros 8 ☎956 36 20 44, ℻956 38 53 93. Rather dull, old-fashioned and overpriced hotel with a dubious collection of dolls and effigies dotted around the staid interior. ❻

Pensión Blanca Paloma Plaza de San Roque ☎956 36 36 44, ℮hostalblancapaloma@msn.com. Good-value and friendly *pensión* with simple rooms sharing bath in a central position on this small plaza. ❷

Pensión Bohemia c/Don Claudio 5 ☎956 36 95 99. Comfortable en-suite a/c rooms with TV – albeit slightly dark due to windows facing an internal corridor – in a quiet street near the church of Santo Domingo. ❸

Pensión Sevilla c/Bolsa 53 ☎956 36 01 89. Charming and welcoming two-star *hostal* in a splendid old *casa palacio* with en-suite rooms with fridge and TV around an elegant patio. ❸

🏃 **Posada de Palacio** c/Caballeros 11 ☎956 36 48 40, ⊛www.posadadepalacio.com. An elegant converted eighteenth-century *casa palacio* in the Barrio Alto with a delightful patio and tastefully furnished rooms with character. Rooftop terraces, bar and an intimate atmosphere together make this rather special. ❻

The Town

Sanlúcar is split into three distinct quarters, the older and formerly walled **Barrio Alto** on the hill, the **Barrio Bajo** below and the town's former port – the **Bajo de Guía** – 1km away on the river. Many of the monuments are in the higher town, where a good number of sherry warehouses are also to be found, emitting a pleasant hint of sherry into the air.

Barrio Bajo

The **Plaza del Cabildo**, a charming, palm-fringed square ringed with bars and sporting a splendid fountain is a good place to start your explorations. Directly southwest of the square, Plaza de San Roque adjoins the morning **market**, one of the town's great shows when it's in full swing – Saturday mornings are best when burly *señoras* give no quarter in attempting to get their hands on the best fish. Just off this square, the interior of the fifteenth-century **Iglesia de la Trinidad** (Mon–Sat 10am–1.30pm; free) has a fine Mudéjar ceiling. West of here and parallel to c/Bretones at c/Truco 4 lies the curious **Museo del Mar**

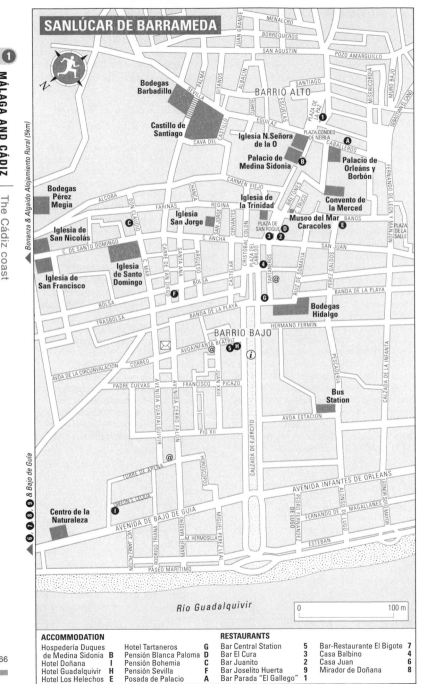

SANLÚCAR DE BARRAMEDA

Bodegas Barbadillo

BARRIO ALTO

Castillo de Santiago

Iglesia N.Señora de la O

Palacio de Medina Sidonia

Palacio de Orleáns y Borbón

Bodegas Pérez Megía

Iglesia de la Trinidad

Convento de la Merced

Iglesia San Jorge

Museo del Mar Caracoles

Iglesia de San Nicolás

Iglesia de Santo Domingo

Iglesia de San Francisco

Bodegas Hidalgo

BARRIO BAJO

Bus Station

Centro de la Naturaleza

Río Guadalquivir

0   100 m

ACCOMMODATION

Hospedería Duques de Medina Sidonia	**B**	Hotel Tartaneros	**G**	
Hotel Doñana	**I**	Pensión Blanca Paloma	**D**	
Hotel Guadalquivir	**H**	Pensión Bohemia	**C**	
Hotel Los Helechos	**E**	Pensión Sevilla	**F**	
		Posada de Palacio	**A**	

RESTAURANTS

Bar Central Station	**5**	Bar-Restaurante El Bigote	**7**
Bar El Cura	**3**	Casa Balbino	**4**
Bar Juanito	**2**	Casa Juan	**6**
Bar Joselito Huerta	**9**	Mirador de Doñana	**8**
Bar Parada "El Gallego"	**1**		

Caracoles (daily 10am–7pm; €1) exhibiting the bizarre lifetime collection of objects retrieved from the sea by eccentric proprietor Garrido García, who resembles a latter-day Long John Silver and conducts tours around his house/ museum with a feral pigeon perched on one shoulder.

East of the Plaza del Cabildo, c/Ancha is the site of a colourful spectacle each August 15, the **fiesta of the Virgen de la Caridad**, when the street is laid with a carpet of colourful "flowers" – actually tinted sawdust – from end to end. A short way along here on the right, the short c/San Jorge contains the sixteenth-century **Iglesia de San Jorge** (Mon–Sat 10am–1pm; free), constructed by English sherry merchants with special permission from the duke of Medina Sidonia, who was keen to encourage their lucrative trade. Inside, a magnificent *retablo* by Juan González de Herrera is topped off by a mounted San Jorge (St George) slaying the dragon. Further east along c/Ancha, the sixteenth-century convent church of **Santo Domingo** (open for 30min viewing prior to service times: Mon–Sat 9.30am & 8pm, Sun 10.30am, 12noon and 8pm) is worth a look, especially for the tombs of a seventeenth-century duke and duchess of Medina Sidonia on either side of the main altar. At the end of the same street lies the church of **San Francisco** (open for services or ring ⓣ956 36 01 26 for appointment) with an elegant facade, built in the sixteenth century by Henry VIII of England – while he was married to Catherine of Aragón – as a hospital for British sailors.

Barrio Alto

The Barrio Alto is reached by following c/Bretones uphill from the Plaza San Roque. Beyond the market to the left the way soon bends right to pass the seventeenth-century **Convento de la Merced** (guided visits 8am–4.30pm). Continuing uphill eventually leads to the neo-Mudéjar **Palacio de Orleáns y Borbón**, a flamboyantly decorated nineteenth-century palace of the dukes of Montpensier, now occupied by the Ayuntamiento with the public library in the gardens. You are allowed to step inside the building's entrance to take a look. Taking a left at the top of this hill will bring you to – on the right – **Plaza de la Paz**, another delightful small square, and, almost opposite, the church of **Nuestra Señora de la O** (Mon–Fri 9am–2pm; also open for daily Mass at 8pm or can be visited on a Turismo tour), Sanlúcar's oldest church founded in the thirteenth century but much altered since and recently restored. The exterior has a fine Gothic-Mudéjar portal depicting lions bearing coats of arms and, inside, there's an impressive *artesonado* ceiling.

The church is connected to the *palacio* of the **duques de Medina Sidonia** (visits Sun 11am & noon; book in advance ⓣ956 36 01 61, ⓦwww.fcmedinasidonia.com; free), whose sixteenth- to eighteenth-century interior, which also houses the family's important historical archive, offers wonderful views over the Coto de Doñana. The duchess of Medina Sidonia still lives here and is one of Sanlúcar's most controversial characters. Known as *la duquesa roja* ("the red duchess"), she has a long history of defending the poor and oppressed of the region – activities that once landed her in jail – and is currently cataloguing the mass of ducal documentation in the family archive. The guided tour of the house and its beautiful gardens takes an hour and proceeds through impressive rooms stuffed with works of Spanish masters such as Roelas, Morales and Goya.

Heading along c/Eguilaz and its continuation c/Sevilla brings you to the semi-ruined fifteenth-century **Castillo de Santiago**, long closed. After years of delay a programme of restoration has finally started to convert the castle into a Museo de Vino (wine museum, scheduled to open at the end of 2006)

The Coto Doñana National Park

Access to the vast, marshy expanse of the **Coto Doñana National Park** (see p.380), on the opposite shore from Sanlúcar, is strictly controlled to protect Europe's largest wildlife sanctuary and a vital wetland for a variety of migrating birds. However, a four-hour **boat cruise** aboard the *Real Fernando* allows visitors to see the park, giving a wonderful introduction to this remarkable area. The boat – which has a *cafetería* on board – leaves from the Bajo de Guía (daily June–Sept 10am & 5pm; March, April, May & Oct 10am & 4pm; Nov–Feb 10am; €15.04, under 12s €7.52, students & senior citizens €10; booking essential on ☎956 36 38 13, ⓦ www.visitasdonana.com). The trips allow two short guided walks led by wildlife experts inside the park where you'll visit a village of *chozas* (traditional Doñana huts) and should see *jabalí* (wild boars), wild horses, flamingos and a profusion of birdlife including buzzards, herons, kites, cranes, eagles as well as stunning wild flowers, depending on your luck and season. In summer it's best to book as early as you can, since the trips are limited to 94 passengers; binoculars (essential) can be hired on board.

Collect your tickets (at least 30min in advance of the sailing) from the Fábrica de Hielo, Bajo de Guía s/n (daily 9am–8pm, ⓦ www.visitasdonana.com) virtually opposite the *Real Fernando*'s jetty. This extravagant exhibition centre in Sanlúcar's old ice factory was created by the National Park authority and contains stunningly unimaginative displays of the park's flora and fauna. The Centro Interpretación de la Naturaleza, almost next door on Avda. Bajo de Guía (Tues–Sun 10am–8pm), is the Junta de Andalucía's effort and has a slightly more interesting exhibition. Viajes Doñana, c/San Juan 20 (☎956 36 25 40), also do **Land Rover-based trips** into the park all year (Tues & Fri; booking essential; €35) starting from the Bajo de Guía at 8.30am and 4.30pm (Oct–April 8.30am & 2.30pm) and covering about 70km in four hours with an expert guide.

documenting the history and development of the sherry and manzanilla zones. A little further along the same street the sherry *bodega* of Barbadillo allows daily public visits (see box p.264). A flight of steps beside the castle leads back down to the Barrio Bajo.

The Río Guadalquivir and Bonanza

A good kilometre walk from the centre (or a €3.50 taxi ride from Plaza del Cabildo or bus #3 or #4 from the Calzada del Ejército), Sanlúcar's shell-encrusted **river beach** – unfortunately marred by a lengthy and rather ugly concrete esplanade – is nevertheless a nice place to while away some time, and is usually quite deserted. The beach is also the setting for some exciting **horse races**, usually held at the beginning and end of August; the Turismo can supply the precise dates.

In summer, private motor boats from the Bajo de Guía, near the *Real Fernando* jetty, will ferry you to the opposite bank for about €6 (make sure to arrange a pick-up time with the boatman if you don't want to be stranded), where the **Coto de Doñana's beaches**, unfortunately not always the cleanest due to pollution from the Guadalquivir estuary currents, provide a change of scene and some bird-spotting possibilities. There are absolutely no facilities, so be sure to take along liquid refreshment and food. There are a number of companies who explore this area by guided tours on **horseback**; Club Equestre La Arboleda (mobile ☎630867672) is one, charging around €20 per hour. The Turismo can provide details of others.

Four kilometres upstream from Sanlúcar, the small port of **Bonanza** is where the sizeable fishing fleet is based, their catch sold at entertaining auctions on the harbourside Mon–Sat at 5pm. This is also the very spot from where Columbus and Magellan set sail on their epic voyages. Fishermen's tales are exchanged at the earthy *Bar Morales* at the harbour entrance or in the more salubrious *Bar de la Campana*, slightly back along the road to Sanlúcar, which serves decent tapas and has a terrace; there's also an excellent restaurant here too, *La Terraza* (aka *Avenida II*, see "Eating and drinking" below). Bonanza can be reached by taxi from the Plaza del Cabildo for €5 or by bus #1 from the top of the Calzada del Ejército.

Eating and drinking

Sanlúcar is renowned for the quality of its **seafood**, and the place to head for is the Bajo de Guía, the old fishing district upstream from where the Alameda meets the river. Numerous **bars** and **restaurants** lining the waterfront have terrace views towards the Coto de Doñana and serve excellent seafood, washed down with *manzanilla*. In the Barrio Bajo, the Plaza del Cabildo has a number of good tapas and breakfast bars, while higher up, Plaza de la Paz is a tranquil little square with various bars serving tapas. *El Rengue*, Avda. V Centenario s/n (at the end of c/San Juan off the right of our map), is a late night *rociero* bar with a great atmosphere that often stages impromptu **flamenco**.

Bar Central Station c/Infanta Beatriz 1, by the side of the *Hotel Guadalquivir*. Original, not-to-be-missed bar created by the train-mad owner of the hotel next door. Features include a steam engine and a full-size reconstruction of a wagon from the old Orient Express with sofa-style seats, lots of polished wood and a gleaming copper tea urn. Ask the bar staff to "*toca el pito*" ("blow the whistle"). In the bar's *cantina*, you can sample *jamón* and *salchichónes* tapas, plus the region's wines, in more conventional surroundings.

Bar El Cura c/Amargura 2, off Plaza del Cabildo. Relatively cheap and cheerful *platos combinados* at this pleasant bar/restaurant. They also do decent tapas.

Bar Juanito Plaza San Roque 18. A popular tapas venue with locals, it's noted for its seafood. The nearby *Bar Clemente* on the same square is another good place.

Bar Joselito Huerta Bajo de Guía s/n, at the upstream end of the strip. Friendly seafood restaurant with a river terrace that is popular with locals. *Almejas* (clams), *cazón con tomate* (shark) and *acedías* (baby sole) are things to try. They also serve good tapas.

Bar Parada "El Gallego" Plaza de la Paz 6. Galician bar which serves excellent *raciones* at economical prices. *Bacalao con tomate* (cod) and *pulpo* (octopus) are good.

Bar-Restaurante El Bigote Bajo de Guía 10 ☎956 36 26 96. Celebrated establishment and one of the "big two" on the waterfront. You can eat great tapas in the lively bar next door or more formally in the restaurant, where the house *arroz de marisco* (seafood paella) and all

fish are outstanding. Don't miss the succulent local *langostinos* (prawns) too. An upstairs dining room offers panoramic views across the river towards the Doñana national park. Main dishes €7–20; reservation advised.

Casa Balbino Plaza del Cabildo 11. Behind an unassuming facade lies one of the best tapas bars in Andalucía. Long established, its walls are hung with faded photos and the obligatory bulls' heads, and the smoothly efficient bar staff will guide you through a daunting tapas menu. The *manzanillas* are outstanding and their *tortillita de camarones* (shrimp in batter) is justly famous. They have added a terrace which somewhat goes against the grain with purists who insist that tapas must be done standing up.

Casa Juan Bajo de Guía 26. Another Bajo de Guía favourite where house specials include *arroz con langostinos* and *rape al cerco* (monkfish). Great terrace with river views.

La Terraza (aka *Avenida II*) Edificio Cofradía de Pescadores in Bonanza, 4km upstream ☎956 38 446 36. On the main road near the port in Bonanza (but easy to miss), a wonderful seafood restaurant and tapas bar, with views from its glassed-in terrace to the Coto de Doñana.

Mirador de Doñana Bajo de Guía s/n ☎956 36 42 05. Outstanding restaurant with a summer terrace overlooking the river. Try their *mi barca Doñana*, white fish in a tomato sauce served in an edible "boat", or *sopa de Galeras*, a special *marisco* soup of which they're deservedly proud. When not busy, the waiters in the tapas bar will be happy to give you a master class in the thirty-plus brands of *manzanilla* on offer. Main dishes €9–20.

Jerez de la Frontera

Encircled by vines planted in the chalky, *albariza* soil, **JEREZ DE LA FRONTERA**, 22km inland from Sanlúcar and 35km from Cádiz, is the home and heartland of **sherry** (itself an English corruption of the town's Moorish name, Xerez) and also, less known but equally important, of Spanish brandy. Once you've penetrated some architecturally bleak suburbs, the town centre possesses a charming *casco antiguo* and a number of elegant, palm-fringed squares, as well as a handful of notable Renaissance and Baroque churches and palaces.

The **Barrio de Santiago**, a fascinating and authentic white-walled *gitano* quarter to the north of the cathedral, contrasts sharply with the great *bodegas* of the sherry houses located in the heart of the town. The sherry dynasties that own these companies (or used to own them, as many have been taken over by international conglomerates) are renowned as some of the biggest snobs in Spain, and take a haughty pride in apeing the traits and customs of the English upper-middle class – their strutting around on polo horses, wearing tweeds and speaking Spanish with an affected accent has earned them the nickname of *señoritos* or "toffs". Jerez's innate sobriety is thrown to the wind, however, during one of the two big **festivals** – the Feria Del Caballo or May Horse Fair (perhaps the most refined – or snooty depending on your viewpoint – of Andalucian *ferias*), and the celebration of the vintage towards the end of September.

Arrival, information and orientation

The **train** and **bus stations** are more or less next door to each other, east of the Alcázar and the town's central square, the Plaza del Arenal. Urban buses, painted lurid lilac, pass the top of the rise outside the station from where Line 10 (which also calls at the bus station) will take you to the centre if you have heavy luggage. Coming in **by car** use the pay car parks signed in the centre or park further out and walk in. There is currently no bus service (although one is planned for 2006: details from Turismo) from Jerez **airport** (7km out of town on the NIV; ☎956 15 00 83) so you need to take a taxi (about €10) to the centre. The **Turismo** (June–Sept Mon–Fri 10am–3pm & 5–7pm, Sat & Sun 10am–2.30pm; Oct–May Mon–Fri 9.30am–3pm & 4.30–6.30pm, Sat & Sun 9.30am–2.30pm; ☎956 32 47 47, ⊕ www.turismojerez.com) is attached to the Convento de Santo Domingo and reached by following the pedestrianized main street, c/Larga north from the centre; it's well stocked with information about the town and can supply a detailed map. To get to grips with the town fairly quickly you could take a guided hop-on-hop-off **bus tour** operated by Tour por Jerez; tickets costing €8 are valid all day (10am–8pm) and there are stops at all the major sights – including Plaza Arenal, the cathedral and the Alcázar – as well as many of the leading bodegas.

Internet access is available at *Ciber Jerez,* c/Santa María 3 (Mon–Sat 10am–11pm), and *Intern@aut@,* c/Bodegas 6 (Mon–Sat 10am–10pm, Sun 3–10pm) both near the market, and *Bar San Pedro,* c/Bizcocheros s/n (Mon–Sat 10am–11pm), near the Convento de Santo Domingo.

Accommodation

There's usually no problem finding rooms in Jerez except during April and May – the town's high season – when Semana Santa, the Festival de Jerez, the World Motorcycle Championship (held at the town's Formula 1 racing circuit) and the Fería del Caballo (May Horse Fair) come one after the other and fill the town to bursting point; make sure to ring ahead if you are planning to visit

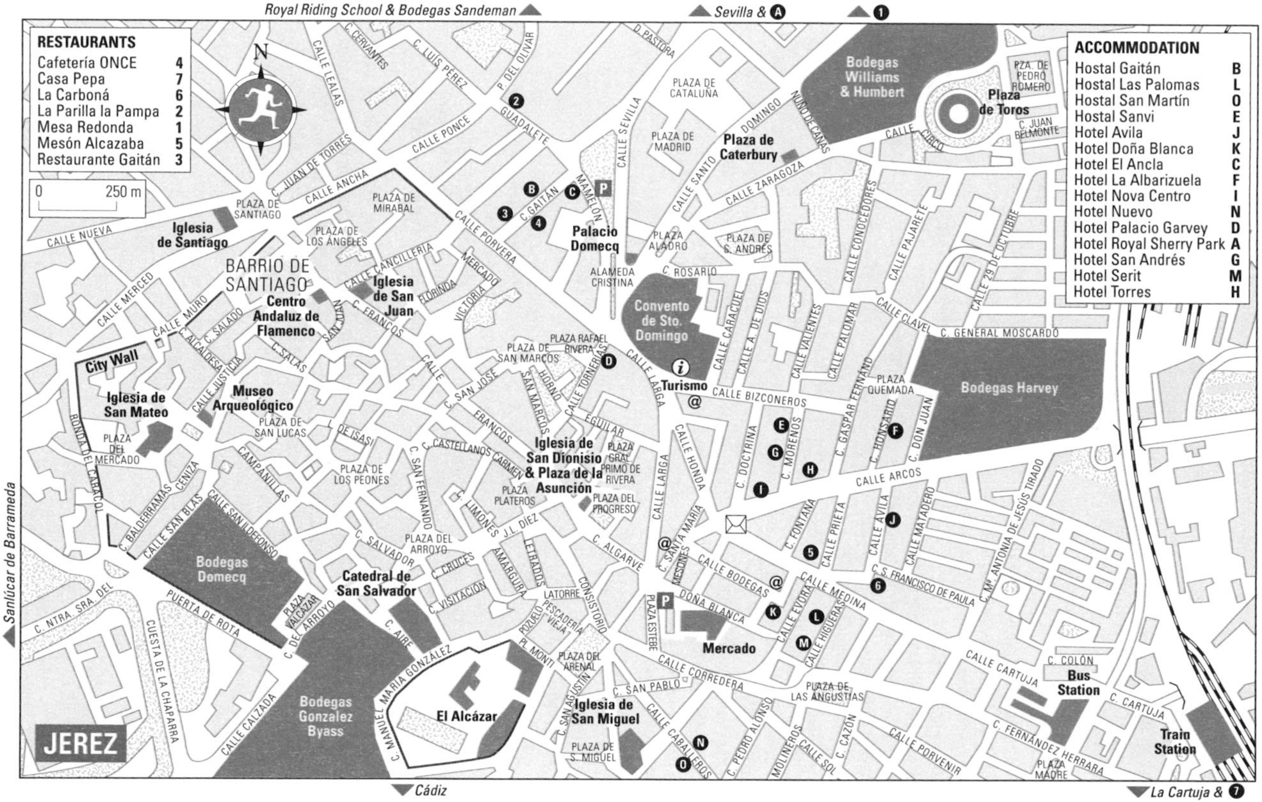

Royal Riding School & Bodegas Sandeman
Sevilla & A
1
RESTAURANTS
Cafetería ONCE 4
Casa Pepa 7
La Carboná 6
La Parilla la Pampa 2
Mesa Redonda 1
Mesón Alcazaba 5
Restaurante Gaitán 3
0 250 m
ACCOMMODATION
Hostal Gaitán B
Hostal Las Palomas L
Hostal San Martín O
Hostal Sanvi E
Hotel Avila J
Hotel Doña Blanca K
Hotel El Ancla C
Hotel La Albarizuela F
Hotel Nova Centro I
Hotel Nuevo N
Hotel Palacio Garvey D
Hotel Royal Sherry Park A
Hotel San Andrés G
Hotel Serit M
Hotel Torres H
N
Bodegas Williams & Humbert
Plaza de Toros
Plaza de Caterbury
Palacio Domecq
Iglesia de Santiago
BARRIO DE SANTIAGO
Centro Andaluz de Flamenco
Iglesia de San Juan
Convento de Sto. Domingo
Turismo
Bodegas Harvey
City Wall
Iglesia de San Mateo
Museo Arqueológico
Iglesia de San Dionisio & Plaza de la Asunción
Bodegas Domecq
Catedral de San Salvador
Mercado
Bodegas Gonzalez Byass
El Alcázar
Iglesia de San Miguel
Bus Station
Train Station
JEREZ
Sanlúcar de Barrameda
Cádiz
La Cartuja & 7

at this time. The high-season prices we quote below are for this April–May period, outside of which rates (especially for hotels) tend to fall by up to fifty percent. Most of the budget **accommodation** is conveniently located within a few minutes' walk of the bus and train terminals. More possibilities are to be found in the streets surrounding the church of San Miguel. Jerez's modern **Albergue Juvenil**, Avda. Carrero Blanco 30 (☎956 14 32 63; under 26 €14, over 26 €18.50), has a fine pool but lies out in the suburbs; bus #9 from outside the bus station will take you there, with a stop closer to the centre on Plaza de las Angustias.

Budget

Hostal Gaitán c/Gaitán 17 ☎956 34 72 71, ℱ956 32 50 05. Tidy little *hostal* close to and owned by the *Hotel El Ancla*; rooms (with and without bath) come with fans. ❷

Hostal Las Palomas c/Higueras 17 ☎956 34 37 73, ⓦwww.hostal-las-palomas.com. Clean, simple rooms sharing bath plus some en suite in a quiet street; fans available. ❷

Hostal San Martín c/Caballeros 28 ☎ & ℱ956 33 70 40. Good place for rooms with and without bath near the church of San Miguel. All rooms come with fans. ❷

Hostal Sanvi c/Morenos 10 ☎956 34 56 24. Sparklingly clean *hostal* with lots of *azulejos* and friendly proprietors offering economical rooms with bath and TV. Garage parking available. ❸

Hotel Nuevo c/Caballeros 23 ☎956 33 16 00, ⓦwww.nuevohotel.com. Attractive and excellent-value hotel set in a lovely nineteenth-century *casa palacio*; rooms come with a/c and TV. ❸

🏃 **Hotel San Andrés** c/Morenos 12 & 14 ☎956 34 09 83, ⓦwww.hotelsanandres. info. Great-value hotel and *hostal* side by side. Charming and friendly, there are en-suite rooms (with a/c and TV) and others sharing bath, plus a pleasant, plant-filled patio. They can advise on parking places nearby. ❷–❸

Moderate to expensive

Hotel Avila c/Avila 3 ☎956 33 48 08, ⓦwww .hotelavila.net. Decent little two-star hotel with a/c rooms and own car park. ❹

Hotel Doña Blanca c/Bodegas 11 ☎956 34 87 61, ⓦwww.hoteldonablanca.com. One of the most central and intimate of the upper-range places with well-equipped a/c balcony rooms with minibar and satellite TV, in a quiet street. Garage. ❼

🏃 **Hotel El Ancla** c/Mamelón 15 ☎956 32 12 97, ⓦwww.helancla.com. Dapper hotel with friendly proprietors. Rooms overlooking the noisy street (quieter at night) are compensated with views of square and fountains; all rooms a/c. ❹

Hotel La Albarizuela c/Honsario 6 ☎956 34 68 62, ℱ956 34 66 86. Very pleasant and newish three-star hotel with comfortable a/c rooms. Don't book ahead if possible as you will be quoted a thirty percent higher rate than their "off the street" customers who pay around €50. ❹

Hotel Nova Centro c/Arcos 13 ☎956 33 21 38, ⓦwww.hotelnovacentro.com. Pleasant, central small hotel whose rooms are equipped with a/c, satellite TV and safe. Parking available. ❺

Hotel Palacio Garvey c/Tornería 24 ☎956 32 67 00, ⓦwww.sferahoteles.net. Beautiful new four-star hotel in the former mansion of the Garvey family, one of the great sherry dynasties in nineteenth-century Jerez. The elegant rooms have modern designer furnishings and come with free minibar, Internet connection, CD-player and satellite plasma TV. The cheapest high season double is €190. ❾

Hotel Serit c/Higueras 7 ☎956 34 07 00, ⓦwww.hotelserit.com. Central hotel with bright, airy rooms equipped with a/c and satellite TV. Car park. ❺

Hotel Torres c/Arcos 29 ☎956 32 34 00, ℱ956 32 18 16. Comfortable hotel with two pretty patios. Recently refurbished rooms – the better ones are off the inner patio – are equipped with a/c and TV, and there's a garage too. ❹

Hotel Royal Sherry Park Avda. Alvaro Domecq 11 ☎956 31 76 14, ⓦwww.hipotels.com. The nearest of the peripheral luxury hotels to the centre, this is a rather bland and modern affair despite an attractive pool, gardens and car park. ❼

The Town and around

Quite apart from the **sherry bodegas** – indisputably Jerez's biggest draw – the town has many sights that warrant a look, not least the gypsy quarter, **Barrio de Santiago**, which is a fascinating place to stroll around. Conveniently, all the major sights and most of the *bodegas* are within just a few minutes' walk of the central, elegant and palm-fringed **Plaza del Arenal**, dominated by a bronze statue of the 1920s dictator Primo de Rivera. However, the square has been a building site for the last few years as Jerez tries to solve its chronic parking problems by constructing the largest underground car park in Andalucía. Whether the car park is the answer to the problem is a matter of fierce local debate, but hopefully the plaza will be restored to its former glory once the work is completed.

The Alcázar

The substantial **Alcázar** (May–Sept Mon–Sat 10am–8pm, Sun 10am–3pm; Oct–April daily 10am–6pm; €1.35 or €3.35 including camera obscura) lies just to the south of the Plaza del Arenal. To reach the entrance, take a right off the southern end of Plaza del Arenal into Plaza Monti, at the end of which you turn left into c/M. María González. The entrance lies uphill on the left. Constructed in the twelfth century by the Almohads, though much altered since, the Alcázar has been extensively excavated and restored in recent years. The **gardens** have received particular attention: the plants and arrangements have been modelled as closely as possible – using historical research – on the original. The interior contains a well-preserved **mosque** complete with *mihrab* from the original structure, now sensitively restored to its original state after having been used as a church for many centuries. There's also a **bathhouse** modelled, by the Almohads, on those of the earlier Romans with cold and hot plunges, as well as impressive walls and towers on the site's outer perimeter. The eighteenth-century **Palacio de Villavicencio** constructed on the west side of the Alcázar's Patio de las Armas (parade ground) houses an entertaining **camera obscura** (same hours) offering views of the major landmarks of the town as well as the sherry vineyards and the sea beyond.

The Cathedral and Plaza de la Asunción

West of Plaza del Arenal, the eighteenth-century **Catedral de San Salvador** (Mon–Sat 11am–1pm & 6–8pm, Sun 11am–2pm; free) was rather harshly dismissed by Richard Ford as "vile Churrigueresque" because of its mixture of Gothic and Renaissance styles, but an elegant façade – largely the work of Vincente Acero – is not without merit. Inside, over-obvious pointing gives the building an unfinished, breeze-block aspect, while, in the sacristy, there's a fine, little-known painting by Zurbarán – *The Sleeping Girl*. The most exciting time to be here is September, when on the broad steps of the cathedral, below the free-standing bell tower – actually part of an earlier, fifteenth-century Mudéjar castle – the wine harvest celebrations begin with the crushing of grapes.

Slightly northeast of here on the corner of c/Salvador is an elegant early eighteenth-century **mansion**, the former home of the Bertemati family and now a convent. The nun on duty in the office at the entrance will allow you inside to view the delightful patio. A little way east, along c/J. Luís Diez, lies the town's most charming square, the **Plaza de la Asunción** (known as Plaza San Dionisio to *jerezanos*), where a sixteenth-century former Ayuntamiento features ornamental statues of Hercules and Julius Caesar on its facade. It's flanked by the fifteenth-century Mudéjar **Iglesía de San Dionisio** (open for services only, generally 7–8 pm) with a graceful bell tower and an interior that underwent some later Baroque alterations.

Barrio de Santiago

Jerez's ancient *gitano* quarter, the Barrio de Santiago, stretches uphill from the cathedral in a maze of narrow lanes and alleys to the church of

1

△ Catedral de San Salvador

Santiago on its northern boundary. Part of the attraction of visiting the *barrio* is its many fascinating churches. The sixteenth-century Gothic **Iglesía de San Mateo**, with a fine *retablo* and superb vaulting over the chapels, is one of a quartet of churches dotted around the *barrio* dedicated to the four Evangelists (saints Marcos, Lucas and Juan, all to the east of San Mateo, are also worth seeking out; all four should be open for services 7–9am & 7–8pm). Nearby, an entertaining *rastro* (**flea market**) takes place on Sundays (Oct–June; 9am-2pm) in Plaza del Mercado fronting the archeological museum, with a more anarchistic extension along the nearby c/Muro fronting the ancient walls.

It's believed that the Phoenicians brought the vine to this area early in the first millennium BC. The Romans shipped wine from here to all parts of their empire, and the Roman settlement of Asido Caesaris may well be the town from which Jerez derives its name, later corrupted to Xerez (pronounced "Sherrish") by the Moors.

British merchants were attracted here in the fourteenth century and, following the expulsions of Moors and Jews in the wake of the *Reconquista*, they established firms that first traded, and later produced, Falstaff's "sack" (probably derived from the Spanish *sacar* – to draw out – referring to the *solera* system, see below). Some of the *bodegas*, or cellars, were founded by British Catholic refugees, barred from careers at home by the sixteenth-century Supremacy Act. The names of the great sherry firms today testify to the continuing love affair of the British with this wine: Britain, along with the Netherlands, still consumes up to seventy percent of all exports.

It's a particular combination of climate, soil and grape variety that gives **sherry wine** its distinctive style. The chalky, white *albariza* soil of the region is the natural habitat for the Palomino sherry grape, and though the resulting wine is fairly ordinary stuff, it's what happens inside the *bodegas* that transforms it into sherry. Here the wine is transferred to oak butts with loose stoppers to let in air. Then the *flor* – a puffy layer of scum (actually yeast) – magically appears on the surface of the wine not only preventing oxidization, but feeding on it too, in the process adding a special flavour and bouquet. It is the subtle nature of the *flor*, the ingredient that cannot be duplicated by competitors, that imparts a different flavour to the sherries of Jerez, El Puerto de Santa Maria and especially Sanlúcar, where it absorbs the salty breezes off the sea, producing the most delicate *fino* of all, *manzanilla*. The *bodegas* of Jerez, unlike in other wine-producing areas, are situated above ground in order to maintain the humid conditions necessary for the growth of this *flor* – helped by sprinkling the sand-covered floors with water.

The final stage in the creation of sherry – but not *manzanilla* – is the fortification of the wine with alcohol (up to fifteen percent in the case of *fino* sherry) before it enters the *solera* system. Because sherry is not a vintage, or yearly, wine it is always blended with older wines through the *soleras* and *criaderas*, as many as six rows of butts placed on top of each other from which the wine is gradually transferred from the topmost to the bottommost over a period of time. This process, mixing the new, younger, wine with the greater quantity of mature, older, wine, "educates" it to assume its character. The wine drawn off at the end for bottling has an even consistency year after year, conveniently with none of the problems of "good" and "bad" years. The classic sherry is the bone-dry *fino*, but variations on the theme include *amontillado* (where the *flor* is allowed to "die" in the butt, imparting a nutty flavour), *oloroso* (produced as *fino* but minus the *flor*) and *cream* – pronounced "cray-am" in Andalucía – a purely British concoction where sweet grapes are blended with *oloroso*.

Museo Arqueológico

Located inside a renovated eighteenth-century mansion, the **Museo Arqueológico**, in Plaza del Mercado (June–Aug Tues–Sun 10am–2.30pm; Sept–May Tues–Fri 10am–2pm & 4–7pm, Sat & Sun 10am–2.30pm; €1.75), is a delight to visit. A plant-filled patio leads to the early rooms dealing with prehistory; upstairs, Room 3 has some curious **Chalcolithic** (early second millennium BC) cylinder-shaped idols with starburst eyes from Cerro de las Vacas, 20km to the north of the town. Room 4 has a wonderfully preserved **Greek** military helmet dating from the seventh-century BC, and found on the banks of the nearby Río Guadalete. This was a time when the early Greeks were colonizing sites all around the Mediterranean, and they evidently expected to meet resistance from the Iberian tribes. Also in Room 4 are finds from the ancient town of **Hasta Regia**, as Pliny, Strabo and Ptolemy referred to Jerez in Roman times. A wide range of Amphorae, funerary stones and sculptures evidence Hasta's importance.

More Roman Amphorae – some stamped with the maker's name – appear in Room 5, once used for the shipping of *garum* (the fish sauce renowned for its quality in these parts; see p.225), olive oil and other products around the Mediterranean. Room 6 has items from the **Visigothic** period and in Room 7 there's an interesting chronological display of **coins** found around Jerez; a good image of the Roman emperor Tiberius (no. 44) is followed by dihrams of rulers Al-Hakam and Abd Ar-Rahman (no. 84) from the period of the Cordoban emirate. Upstairs again, you'll find a **cafetería** with roof terrace, and Rooms 8 and 9, both holding the Moorish and medieval collections, with some fine **Moorish** ceramics, especially a tenth-century **Caliphal bottle vase** with Kufic script, found near Jerez. Before leaving, take a look at the striking works placed around the ground-floor patio. Among them, there's a powerful third- to first-century BC Iberian sculpture of a lion mauling a ram, found nearby, and an intriguing seventh-century Visigothic sarcophagus from La Peñuela carved with curious vegetable, animal and human symbols.

The parroquia de Santiago and the Centro Andaluz de Flamenco

Just west of the museum, along c/Muro, is a bit of the original Moorish **city wall**, which you can follow north to another Gothic church, the fifteenth-century **Iglesia de Santiago**, with wonderfully florid Plateresque portals. Inside, a celebrated sixteenth-century sculpture of the *Prendimiento* – or arrest of Christ – attributed to La Roldana, is the centrepiece of Jerez's Semana Santa processions when it's carried through the streets. On the small square opposite the church stands a bronze bust dedicated to Fernando Terremoto, one of many legendary flamenco artists the *barrio* has produced. You'll come across others dotted around this quarter (there's one of Tío José de Paula behind the church), all testifying to the *barrio*'s great pride in its contribution to Andalucía's musical heritage.

Fronting the Plaza de San Juan, the **Centro Andaluz de Flamenco** (Mon–Fri 9am–2pm; ⓦcaf.cica.es; free) is housed in an elegant eighteenth-century mansion, the Palacio de Pemartín. As one of the founding centres of flamenco song and dance, Jerez has created this library of *flamencología* as well as a sound and vision archive, to preserve the works and performances of past greats in the art; on the top floor, a dance room is used to teach students from all over the world. The staff are welcoming and anyone is free to use the video archive to see performances by flamenco masters past and present – just give them a name and they'll do the rest. There's also a good audiovisual presentation in Spanish, *El Arte Flamenco* (hourly, on the half-hour), which – if you know little about flamenco – will give you a grasp of the basics and an understanding of why it is so important to Andalucians.

The Convento de Santo Domingo, Palacio Domecq and Iglesia de San Miguel

The northern end of the pedestrianized c/Larga – which passes, at the junction with c/Santa María, the old *Café Cena Cirullo*, a fine early twentieth-century building (now the *El Gallo Azul* café), which used to be the great meeting place of Jerez's salon society – is dominated by the august frontage of the **Convento de Santo Domingo** (open for services, generally 7–8pm).

Although badly damaged by fire in the Civil War, it has been diligently restored and, in common with many of the town's other religious buildings, has a curious mixture of styles: in this case Mudéjar, Romanesque and Gothic. The church's seventeenth-century *retablo mayor* is an orgy of gilded wood, with the *Virgen de la Consolación* – the patron of the city, carved in Italian marble – as its centrepiece. At the far end of this square stands the eighteenth-century **Palacio Domecq**, a grand pile erected – and still owned – by the sherry family. Behind an entrance flanked by barley-sugar pillars, an exquisite marble-floored Baroque patio is occasionally open to view. One other church worth a visit is the fifteenth-century Gothic **Iglesia de San Miguel**, just to the south of the Plaza del Arenal. An ornate classical facade added in the eighteenth-century climbs dizzily to a pretty bell tower adorned with blue and white *azulejos*, whilst the interior (Mon–Fri 10.30am–2pm & 3–6pm; free) has a magnificent *retablo* by Martínez Montañés.

The Museo del Tiempo and the Riding School

At the northern end of town, the recently revamped and enlarged **Museo del Tiempo** (aka Museo de Relojes, c/Cervantes 3 (Tues–Sat 10am–2pm & 6–8pm, Sun 10am–3pm; €6), claims to have the largest collection of fully functioning antique clocks and watches in Europe, all chiming on the hour, while nearby, north of the Alameda Cristina, at the **Real Escuela Andaluz del Arte Ecuestre** (Royal Andalucian School of Equestrian Art), Avda. Duque de Abrantes s/n, you can see teams of horses performing to music (Tues & Thurs noon, plus July 15–Oct 15 Fri midday; seats €15–23; information & reservations ☎956 31 80 08, ⓦwww.realescuela.org). Training, rehearsal and visits to the stables (Mon, Wed & Fri 10am–1pm) is a more affordable €8.

La Cartuja

The remarkable Carthusian monastery of **LA CARTUJA** lies 4km along the road out of town towards Medina Sidonia (see p.212) in the midst of lush countryside and surrounded in summer by a sea of sunflowers. The monastery was founded in 1477 and, following great destruction by billeted French troops in 1810, was abolished in 1835 during the Liberal backlash against the church and male religious orders.

After serving as a military barracks for almost a century, La Cartuja was restored to the Carthusians in 1949, since when the handful of monks here have dedicated themselves to restoring and maintaining this beautiful building. The Baroque **facade** you see today – added in the 1660s – is one of the most spectacular in the whole of Spain. Unfortunately, access is restricted to the building's exterior (with a magnificent main doorway), gardens and cloister (daily 9.30am–6pm; free); the church and other parts of the monastery and its artworks may be seen by prior arrangement (details from the Turismo), and then only by "respectably dressed" men wearing *pantalones largos* (long trousers). The monks may bow to pressure, however, and allow women to visit in the near future; again, check with the Turismo.

The Laguna de Medina

If you have transport, you could make another excursion from Jerez to the **LAGUNA DE MEDINA**, a small freshwater lake which – from late August on – attracts a great number of migrating birds returning from northern Europe to Africa. Under the care of ICONA (Instituto para Conservación de la Naturaleza), two paths skirt the lake from where, among a variety of waders, it's possible to spot white-headed duck, spoonbills and the greater flamingo in

The bodegas

The tours of the sherry and brandy processes in Jerez can be a fascinating insight into the mysteries of sherry production, although sampling – nowadays restricted to a couple of tots at the end of a tour – is hardly as much fun as when Richard Ford was here in the nineteenth century and saw visitors emerging "stupefied by drink".

There are a great many **bodegas** to choose from and, with the exception of August when all but a few firms close down, most welcome visitors throughout the year. All those below insist that you **book at least a day in advance** (you can also do this on their website in the case of González Byass); if your Spanish isn't too hot, don't worry, as English is very much the second language in Jerez's sherry fraternities. Below are a selection of *bodegas* offering tours throughout the whole or part of August; should you wish to visit some of the smaller establishments, get hold of a complete list from the Turismo or town centre travel agents. Details of many of these together with visiting times, maps and contact details appear on ⓦwww.sherry.org or on the Turismo's site (see p.270). **Visiting hours** frequently change and it's worth confirming these in advance with the *bodega* or getting an updated list from the Turismo.

The most central *bodega* and one of the two giants of Jerez – whose establishments are almost small towns in their own right – is **González Byass**, c/Manuel González s/n, behind the Alcázar, producers of Tío Pepe *fino* and Lepanto brandy (daily 11.30am, 12.30pm, 1.30pm & 2pm and Mon–Sat 4.30pm, 5.30pm & 6.30pm; Oct–June afternoon visits change to 3.30pm, 4.30pm & 5.30pm. €8.50 visit with wine tasting, €13.50 visit, wine tasting and tapas; ☎956 35 70 16, ⓦwww.gonzalezbyass.es). The González cellars are perhaps the oldest in Jerez and, though no longer used, preserve an old circular chamber, La Concha, designed by Eiffel (of Tower fame). The other major firm is **Domecq**, c/San Ildefonso 3, makers of La Ina sherry and Carlos I brandy (daily Mon–Fri four visits on the hour 10am–1pm; Thurs extra visit at 2pm; Sat March–Oct noon & 2pm, Sat Nov–Feb noon; €6; ☎956 15 15 00, ⓦwww.domecq.es), while others include **Sandeman**, c/Pizarro 10 (June–Sept Mon–Wed visits at 11.30am, 1pm & 2.30pm; €5; ☎956 15 17 00, ⓦwww.sandeman.com), **Williams and Humbert**, Ctra. Nacional IV km641.75 (the Sevilla road; Mon–Fri 9.30am–2pm; €5; ☎956 35 34 06, ⓦwww.williams-humbert.com), and **Harveys** (now part of the Allied-Domecq group), c/Arcos 53 (Mon–Fri 10am–12pm; €5; ☎956 34 60 00, ⓦwww.domecq.es).

Each *bodega* has its celebrity barrels signed by famous visitors – Martin Luther King, Orson Welles, Queen Victoria, Cole Porter and Franco (protected by a glass screen) are some of the big names in the González collection – while a transparent butt (most *bodegas* have one) allows you to see the action of the magical *flor* on the sherry. Nearly all *bodegas* have their own shop too where you can buy the house brands. In town, the Sherry Shop at c/Divina Pastora 1 (top centre of our city map; ☎956 33 51 84) is a friendly and informative place that stocks them all and where you can sample as well. They can also take you on less commercialized visits to some of the smaller *bodegas*. Bodega San Rafael, c/Arcos 4, near the post office, is a similar place.

season. Fringed with reeds and tamarisk trees, the shallow lagoon is also home to numerous frogs, snakes and lizards. Because of its close proximity to the Coto Doñana across the Guadalquivir, many birds – particularly flamingos – use this as an alternative food source, especially if the Doñana's *marismas* are drier than normal towards the end of the summer.

To get there take the C440 out of Jerez for about 11km towards Medina Sidonia; the entrance to the lake area is signposted immediately opposite a cement factory, and there's a small car park.

Eating and drinking

Jerez's booming sherry trade ensures that the town's **restaurants** are kept busy, and a few of these are very good indeed. Befitting the capital of sherry production Jerez also has a range of great **bars** where *fino* – the perfect partner for tapas – can be sampled on its own turf. You can also do as the locals do: buy some takeaway fried fish from a *freiduría* and carry it to a nearby bar. For tapas and snacks head for the atmospheric **Plaza Rafael Rivera** close to the Convento de Santo Domingo, where bars all around the square cater to the clientele seated on their terraces. For **breakfast** and afternoon tea, head for *Cafetería San Francisco*, Plaza Estebe 2, near the market, or its twin *Mesón Reina de León*, c/Latorre 8, slightly northeast of Plaza Arenal. For tapas and tasty *pasteles*, *jerezanos* visit *El Gallo Azul* at the junction of c/Larga and c/Santa María. Another great breakfast bar with a terrace on a leafy square is *Bar Barbiana*, Plaza Eguilar 1, off the west side of c/Larga.

Restaurants

Cafetería ONCE c/Gaitán 10. A napkin's throw from one of the best restaurants in town (the *Restaurante Gaitán*, see below) the spotless, a/c *cafetería* of Spain's powerful charity for the blind has no such pretensions. Instead it serves up the cheapest three-course (including wine) *menú* in town for €5.50 – an excellent deal. Sat–Sun open lunchtimes only.

Casa Pepa Plaza Madre de Dios 14 Good, inexpensive restaurant for meat and seafood dishes with a *menú del día* for around €6. It's a little tricky to find, down a small street between the train and bus stations, so ask if you can't find it.

🏃 **La Carboná** c/San Francisco de Paula 2. Cavernous but wonderfully atmospheric place inside an old *bodega*, specializing in charcoal-grilled fish and meat.

La Parilla la Pampa c/Guadalete 24. Great Argentine restaurant with an excellent-value five-course meal of Argentine specialities (including steaks) – the meat is flown in from South America. Expect around €36 for two.

🏃 **Mesa Redonda** c/Manuel de la Quintana 3, near the *Royal Sherry Park* hotel ☎956 34 00 69. One of the town's best places, this doesn't come cheap, but the food – fish and meat cooked under the direction of noted chef José-Antonio Romero Valdespino – is truly memorable; as is their sherry trifle dessert. House specials include *salteado de solomillo con morcilla* (sautéed pork loin with blood sausage). Main dishes €10–20. Closed Sun.

Mesón Alcazaba c/Medina 19, east of c/Larga. Popular low-priced *platos combinados* restaurant with an attractive patio and offering an inexpensive *menú*.

Restaurante Gaitán c/Gaitán 3 ☎956 34 58 59. Small, attractive upmarket restaurant specializing in Basque and *andaluz* dishes. *Rape en salsa de almendras* (monkfish with almonds) and *cordero al brandy* (lamb) are two specialities, or it has a reasonably priced *menú turistico* for €18. Closed Sun eve.

🏃 **Venta Antonio** Ctra. Jerez–Sanlúcar km5 ☎956 14 05 35. Superb fish and seafood *venta*, five kilometres along the road towards Sanlúcar de Barrameda. Everything is fresh from the sea and whether you take *raciones* in the bar or eat more formally in their airy restaurant you're in for a treat. Noted for its *langostinos* (deep-water prawns) and *tarta de almendras* dessert.

Bars and marisquerías

🏃 **Bar El Poema** Plaza Rafael Rivero s/n. Great and friendly little tapas bar which has won prizes for its tapas: namely *chorizo al vino de jerez* and *el menudo* (cow, lamb and pig's tripe). Three other bars on the same square make this a *tapeadores* heaven.

🏃 **Bar Juanito** c/Pescadería Vieja 4. In a small passage off the west side of Plaza del Arenal, this is the best tapas bar in town, with a menu as endless as the number of excellent *finos* on offer. Specials include *alcauciles* (artichokes), *costillas* (spare ribs) and *fideos* (vermicelli) *con gambas*. Closed Sun.

Bar La Manzanilla c/Veracruz 2, near the market. Atmospheric spit-and-sawdust haunt serving, as its name suggests, *finos* and *manzanillas*. *La Reja*, next door, is another popular place on market days. Closed Sat & Sun eves.

Bar Bereber c/Cabezas 10, near the archeological museum. Venerable old tapas bar in the Barrio de Santiago.

El Arriate c/Francos 43, in the Barrio de Santiago. Flamenco and jazz bar whose amiable proprietor is an aficionado of both traditions; live performances in winter.

El Boquerón de Plata Plaza de Santiago. One of the best *freidurías* in town. *Mesón-Bar La Valencia* on the same square is another good tapas and *raciones* stop.

Freiduría Gallega c/Arcos 5, near the market. Popular bar serving up fried fish and *mariscos* prepared *a la gallega* by proprietors hailing from the northwestern Spanish province of Galicia; eat in or take away.

La Española c/Larga s/n, near the Turismo. Decent bar for tapas, *raciones* and *pinchos* – noted for their tasty *alcachofas* (artichokes).

La Parra Vieja c/San Miguel 9. One of Jerez's oldest tapas bars (over a century in business),

in an alleyway downhill from the Iglesia de San Miguel. Specials include *croquetas de jamón* and *mollejas de cordero* (sweetbreads). They've now added a small mid-priced restaurant too, with an economical *menú*. The nearby *La Marea* at no. 3 in the same street is also worth a call for its excellent fried-fish tapas. Closed Mon.

Las Botas c/Santo Domingo 8, near the Plaza de Toros. Another good tapas venue noted for its *jamones* and *queso* (cheese).

Mesón El Cabildo Plaza del Asunción. Fine little *raciones* bar on this beautiful square. There's a terrace for alfresco eating, and house specials include *solomillo* (pork loin) and *mariscos*.

Nightlife

Much of Jerez's **nightlife** centres around the bars and discos near the bullring and the zone around the Avenida de Mexico to the northeast of here. One place which is very popular with young *jerezanos* is Plaza de Canterbury, c/Nuño de Cañas s/n, almost opposite the Williams & Humbert *bodega*, a renovated plaza pulsing with numerous bars and discos where live music is frequently staged. The local paper *El Diario de Jerez* is a good place to find out about upcoming concerts and festivals.

Bar El Laga Plaza del Mercado, next to the Archeological Museum ☎956 33 83 34. Authentic flamenco bar with recitals and dancing Mon to Sat starting around 10.30pm (admission free) with another show at 12.30am; tapas and *raciones* are served. Tables can be reserved if you want to get a good view.

El Camino del Rocío c/Cádiz s/n, north of Plaza Mamelón. Curious bar that commemorates the memory of the famous pilgrimage to El Rocío – every night. Rocío memorabilia cover the walls, and at midnight the lights go down,

candles are lit and the singing of the *gitano Ave María* begins another night of frenzied flamenco dancing.

Grafton Street c/Zaragoza s/n opposite Plaza de Canterbury. Music bar that packs them in after midnight, especially at weekends. The nearby *Enigma* and *Ritual* are similar places .

La Habana c/Cádiz 181, near the riding school. Popular music bar; one of several along this street.

La Taberna Flamenca Angostillo de Santiago 3. Tucked down the west side of the Iglesia de

Flamenco in Jerez

Given Jerez's great **flamenco** traditions, it's worth trying to hear some of the real thing at one of the many *peñas* (clubs) concentrated in the old gypsy quarter of Santiago, north of the cathedral (be careful in this area after dark). The following are some of the best; turning up at around 10pm at weekends (although they're open at other times, too) should provide an opportunity to hear some authentic performances. Otherwise consult the Turismo, who publish a monthly listings sheet; the Centro Andaluz de Flamenco, who also have details of the special flamenco festivals held in town over the summer; or *El Diario de Jerez* who have a special flamenco listings page on Fridays.

Centro Andaluz de Flamenco Plaza San Juan 1, Santiago ☎956 34 92 65.

Peña Los Cernicalos c/Sancho Vizcaíno 25, south of the church of San Miguel ☎956 33 38 71.

Peña Antonio Cachón c/Salas 12, Santiago ☎956 34 74 72.

Peña La Buena Gente Plaza San Lucas 9, Santiago ☎956 33 84 04.

Peña Tío José de Paula c/La Merced 11, Santiago ☎956 34 30 84.

Santiago. Slightly touristy flamenco Tues–Sat at midday, 4pm, 8pm and midnight. Serves lunch, dinner or tapas during performances.
Los Dos Deditos c/Pescadería Vieja s/n, off Plaza

del Arenal. Relaxed *copas* (drinks and music) bar and one of the very few in the central zone; popular with over 25s. The nearby *Carbonería* is similar.

Travel details

Trains

Algeciras to: Córdoba (1 daily; 4hr 30min); Granada (3 daily; 3hr 30min–4hr); Madrid (2 daily; 11hr; or 6hr 30min with AVE from Sevilla); Málaga (2 daily; 3hr 30min via Ronda); Ronda (4 daily; 1hr 45min); Sevilla (2 daily; 3hr 30min).

Cádiz to: Córdoba (4 daily; 3hr); Granada (via Dos Hermanas; 3 daily; 4hr 30min–5hr); Jerez de la Frontera (13 daily; 40min); El Puerto de Santa María (13 daily; 25min); Sevilla (13 daily; 1hr 50min).

Málaga to: Algeciras (3 daily; 3hr 30min, via Ronda); Antequera (2 daily; 1hr); Córdoba (2 daily; 3hr 30min, via Bobadilla); El Chorro (2 daily; 30min); Fuengirola (every 30min; 14min, via Málaga airport); Granada (1 daily; 2hr 30min); Madrid (2 daily; 6hr); Ronda (3 daily; 3hr, via Bobadilla); Sevilla (4 daily; 3hr–3hr 30min, via Bobadilla); Torremolinos (every 30min; 28min, via Málaga airport).

Buses

Bus times quoted are for the fastest journey times, normally direct. There may be other buses to the same destination which make additional stops at towns and villages en route.

Algeciras to: Cádiz (10 daily; 2hr 15min); Jerez (8 daily; 2hr 15min); La Línea (for Gibraltar: hourly; 30min); Madrid (4 daily; 8hr); Málaga (5 daily; 2hr); Sevilla (8 daily; 3hr 30min); Tarifa (11 daily; 30min).

Cádiz to: Alcalá de los Gazules (2 daily; 1hr 45min); Algeciras (10 daily; 2–2hr 30min); Arcos de la Frontera (6 daily; 1hr 30min).

Chipiona (7 daily; 1hr 30min); Conil (14 daily; 1hr); Granada (4 daily; 4hr 30min); Jerez de la Frontera (20 daily; 45min); Málaga (8 daily; 4hr); Los Caños de Meca (2 daily; 1hr 15min); Madrid (1 daily; 8hr); El Puerto de Santa María (15 daily; 30min); Rota (8 daily; 1hr 15min); Ronda (3 daily; 2hr); Sanlúcar de Barrameda 11 daily; 1hr); Sevilla (14 daily; 1hr 45min); Tarifa (5 daily; 1hr 30min); Vejer de la Frontera (8 daily; 1hr); Zahara de los Atunes (4 daily; 1hr 45min).

Jerez to: Algeciras (8 daily; 2hr); Arcos de la Frontera (17 daily; 40min); Cádiz (23 daily; 50min);

Chipiona (7 daily; 40min); Córdoba (1 daily; 3hr 30min); El Puerto de Santa María (18 daily; 25min); Ronda (3 daily; 2hr 30min); Rota (10 daily; 30min); Sanlúcar de Barrameda (15 daily; 30min); Sevilla (12 daily; 1hr 15min); Vejer de la Frontera (2 daily; 1hr 30min).

Málaga to: Algeciras (12 daily; 2–3hr); Almería (9 daily; 3hr 15min–4hr); Antequera (12 daily; 1hr); Cádiz (5 daily; 4hr); Conil (3 daily; 3–4hr); Córdoba (5 daily; 2hr 30min); Estepona (10 daily; 1hr 40min); Fuengirola (16 daily; 45min); Granada (16 daily; 1hr 30min); Jerez (1 daily; 3hr); La Línea (4 daily; 2hr 30min); Madrid (7 daily; 6hr); Marbella (every 45min; 40min); Motril-Lanjarón (2 daily; 1hr); Nerja (15 daily; 45min); Ríogordo (4 daily; 1hr); Osuna (2 daily; 1hr 30min); Ronda (14 daily; 2hr); Sevilla (12 daily; 2hr 30min); Tarifa (3 daily; 2hr 30min); Torremolinos (every 15min; 20min); Vejer (3 daily; 3hr).

Ronda to: Arcos de la Frontera (5 daily; 1hr 45min); Cádiz (3 daily; 2hr); Grazalema (2 daily; 20min); Jerez (3 daily; 2hr 30min); Málaga (4 daily; 2hr); Marbella (7 daily; 1hr 30min); Olvera (1 daily; 30min); San Pedro de Alcántara (6 daily; 1hr 30min); Setenil (5 daily; 20min); Sevilla (5 daily; 2hr 30min); Ubrique (2 daily; 45min); Zahara (2 daily; 20min).

Rota to: El Puerto de Santa María (9 daily; 20min); Cádiz (8 daily; 45min); Sevilla (3 daily; 1hr 30min); Chipiona (1 daily; 15 min).

Sanlúcar de Barrameda to: Cádiz (9 daily; 1hr); Chipiona (9 daily; 15min); El Puerto de Santa María (9 daily; 30min); Jerez (15 daily; 30min); Sevilla (9 daily; 1hr 30min).

Ferries

Algeciras to: Ceuta (10 daily; 35min–1hr 45min); Tangier (18 hourly; 1hr 10min–2hr).

Cádiz to: Las Palmas (1 weekly on Sat; 48hr); Tenerife (1 weekly on Sat; 36hr); El Puerto de Santa María (5–6 daily; 40min).

Gibraltar to: Tangier (1 weekly: Fri only at 6pm; 1hr).

Málaga to: Melilla (daily except Sun; 7hr); Benalmádena (4 daily each way; 1hr 15min).

Tarifa to: Tangier (2 daily catamaran ferries; 35min).

2

Sevilla and Huelva

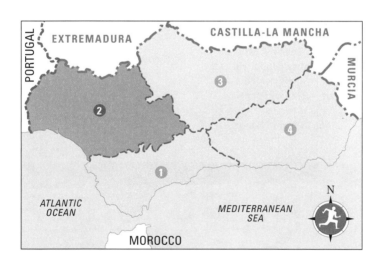

CHAPTER 2 # Highlights

✳ **Costa de la Luz** Huelva's stretch of the Atlantic coast has a string of enjoyable resorts and some of the finest beaches in Andalucía. See p.288

✳ **La Giralda and the Catedral, Sevilla** The city's landmark building and the world's largest Gothic church whose soaring minaret – now the bell-tower – is one of the most beautiful of all Moorish monuments. See p.302

✳ **Alcázar, Sevilla** A Moorish fortress-palace adorned with breathtakingly beautiful stuccowork, tiles and coffered ceilings within, and relaxing gardens without. See p.304

✳ **Tapas bars, Sevilla** The city that invented tapas has some of Spain's very best tapas bars – two not to miss are *Bar Giralda* and *El Rinconcillo*. See p.329

✳ **Semana Santa, Sevilla** The solemn pomp and pagan ecstasy of the Holy Week processions are the most impressive and moving in Spain. See p.338

✳ **Parque Nacional de Doñana** Europe's largest and most important wildlife sanctuary. See p.378

✳ **Sierra de Aracena** A landscape of wooded hills, babbling streams and attractive villages which produce the best cured ham in Spain. See p.399

△ Parque Nacional de Coto Doñana

2

Sevilla and Huelva

With the major exception of the irresistible city of Sevilla, the central and western regions of Andalucía are not much visited – a great pity, as these areas, consisting of the city's province and the neighbouring province of Huelva, are capable of springing a variety of surprises, both scenic and cultural, on those visitors prepared to wander off the beaten track to find them.

Sevilla, Andalucía's capital, has many of the region's most beautiful monuments: the **Giralda** tower, a magnificent Gothic **Cathedral** and a rambling Mudéjar **Alcázar** with fabulous ornamentation are only the highlights of a marvellous architectural feast. Add to these a stunning **Museo de Bellas Artes**, the nearby Roman site of **Itálica** and a number of remarkable Renaissance mansions such as the **Casa de Pilatos**, and you're looking at a stay of at least two days. The most exciting parts of Sevilla, however, are its various **barrios**, each with its own strong character and traditions, and atmospheric places to explore.

East of Sevilla a clutch of smaller towns on the way to Córdoba include Moorish **Carmona**, which possesses a remarkable Roman cemetery, and Baroque **Écija**, with its striking churches and mansions. Also in Sevilla's **Campiña** – the name given to this broad and fertile agricultural plain watered by the Guadalquivir – are the towns of **Osuna** and **Estepa**, both with their own Renaissance architectural gems. To the north, the wooded hills of the **Sierra Morena** offer welcome respite from the intense summer heat, with charming small towns making excellent base-camps for hikes.

The **province of Huelva** stretches from Sevilla to the Portuguese border, and hardly deserves its reputation as the least-visited province of Andalucía. The area boasts the huge nature reserve of the **Coto Doñana National Park**, spreading back from the Guadalquivir estuary in vast expanses of *marismas* – sand dunes, salt flats and marshes. The largest roadless area in western Europe, the park is vital to scores of migratory birds and to endangered mammals including the Iberian lynx, and is home to Andalucía's rumbustious Whitsuntide pilgrimage and fair, the **Romería del Rocío**.

Huelva, the provincial capital, although scarred by its industrial surrounds, tries its best to be welcoming and does have a number of things to see; it also makes a convenient base for trips to local sites associated with the **voyages of Columbus** which set out from here. It was at the nearby monastery of **La Rábida** that the explorer's 1492 expedition was planned and from the tiny port of **Palos de la Frontera** that he eventually set sail to discover a new route to the Indies. The province of Huelva was also the site of ancient **Tartessus**, a legendary kingdom rich in minerals that attracted the Minoans, Phoenicians

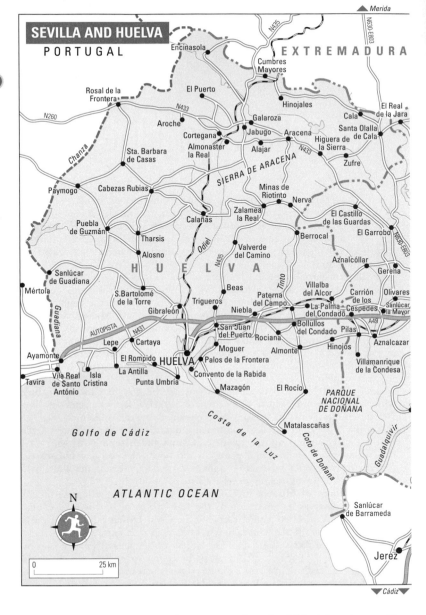

and Greeks in ancient times and is mentioned in the Bible. Minerals are still extracted from the hills to the north of the city – the awesome **Río Tinto Mines** display evidence of the human quest for minerals stretching back over five thousand years.

Some of the most beautiful and neglected parts of this region are even further north, in the dark, ilex-covered hills and sturdy rural villages of the **Sierra de**

Aracena. Perfect walking country, with its network of streams and reservoirs between modest peaks, this is a botanist's dream, brilliant with a mass of spring flowers. You also find here some of the finest *jamón* in Spain, produced from acorn-eating *cerdos ibericos* (black pigs).

While the landlocked province of Sevilla takes its relaxation along the banks of the Guadalquivir, Huelva has a sea coast that harks back to pre-Costa del

Sol tranquillity. This section of the **Costa de la Luz** has some of the finest **beaches** in Andalucía, with long stretches of luminous white sand and little sign of development.

Sevilla

"Seville," wrote Byron, "is a pleasant city, famous for oranges and women." And for its heat, he might have added, since summers here are intense and start in April, but the spirit of the quote, for all its nineteenth-century chauvinism, is about right. What is captivating about the city, as much as the monuments and works of art, is its essential romantic quality – the greatest city of the Spanish south, of Carmen, Don Juan and Figaro, and the archetype of Andalucian promise. *Sevillanos* are world leaders in the art of street theatre too. During **Semana Santa**, for example, sandalled and helmeted Roman soldiers sombrely escort the *paso*, or effigy, of the condemned Christ through the crowded but silent streets, while a couple of weeks later the mood changes dramatically when the city launches into the wild exuberance of the **Feria de Abril** (which also inaugurates the start of the bullfighting season – second only to Madrid's in importance – another *sevillano* passion).

Despite its considerable charm, and its wealth – based on food processing, aircraft production, shipbuilding, construction and a thriving tourist industry – the city lies at the centre of a depressed agricultural area and has an unemployment rate of over twenty percent. The refurbishment of the infrastructure for the 1992 Expo – held to celebrate the 500th anniversary of Columbus's "discovery" of the New World – was intended to regenerate the city's (and the region's) economic fortunes but was not the catalyst for growth and prosperity promised at the time. **Petty crime** in the city is a notorious problem, with bag-snatching often carried out, Italian-style, from passing mopeds. Non-*sevillanos* make much of the city's special breed of thief, *semaforazos*, who break the windows of cars stopped at traffic lights and grab what they can. Avoid leaving anything at all in a car parked on the street overnight; the guarded underground car parks are a possible alternative. However, despite a worrying rise in the number of muggings in recent years, when compared with cities of similar size in northern Europe, violent crime is still relatively rare.

Some history

Sevilla began when ancient Iberian tribes settled on the banks of the Guadalquivir perhaps early in the first millennium BC. The settlement grew into the town now known as **El Carambolo**, whose great wealth derived from the minerals mined in the mountains to the north. The demand for copper, silver and gold lured in the Greeks and Phoenicians, who traded their own ceramics, jewellery and ivory goods. It was the same Phoenicians, or perhaps their successors the Carthaginians, who attacked and then conquered the settlement around 500 BC, subsequently renaming it **Hispalis**, meaning "flat land".

When the **Romans** finally wrested Spain from Carthage the Roman general Scipio founded **Itálica** in 206 on a hill overlooking the river. The final conquest of the peninsula cost the Romans a further two hundred years of dogged campaigning against the ferocious Iberian peoples, and in the latter stages of this struggle, during the Roman civil war, **Julius Caesar** captured Hispalis in 45 BC and renamed it Julia Romula ("Little Rome"). As a leading centre of the Roman province of Baetica (roughly corresponding to modern

On every manhole cover, bus and public building in Sevilla you will see the curious cipher **NO 8 DO**. What looks like a figure 8 is actually the symbol of a twisted skein of wool (*madeja* in Spanish). During the eleventh-century *Reconquista*, Alfonso the Wise, king of Castile, tired of the endless war, made a truce with the Moors. This so angered his excitable son Sancho, that he rebelled against his father and launched a civil war. When the people of Sevilla stayed loyal to Alfonso, the king lauded them with the royal testimonial "**No me ha dejado**" ("You have not deserted me"). In medieval Spanish this came out as "*no ma dejado*" from which the *sevillanos* – long aficionados of word riddles – came up with NO MADEJA DO, soon encrypted as NO 8 DO and swiftly adopted as the city's crest.

Andalucía) the city flourished and nearby Itálica provided Rome with two of its greatest second-century emperors, **Trajan** and **Hadrian**. The city later fell to the Visigoths, whose Christian archbishop **San Isidro** made sixth-century Sevilla into a European centre of learning.

Conquered by the **Moors** in 712, Sevilla briefly became **the capital of al-Andalus**. The Moors left an indelible imprint on the city, not only in its architecture, but also in the Arabic-influenced local dialect, renaming the River Baetis Wadi El Kabir ("great river"), a title it still retains as the Guadalquivir. The **Almohad** dynasty of the twelfth and thirteenth centuries brought great prosperity, and when Sevilla was captured during the *Reconquista* by **Fernando III** in 1248 the city became a favoured residence of the Spanish monarchy, in particular Pedro the Cruel, who was responsible for the construction of the outstanding Mudéjar Alcázar. Religious intolerance racked the city in the wake of the Reconquest, however, and in 1391 the Jewish quarter in the Barrio Santa Cruz was sacked – a harbinger of the banishment of all Jews from Spain, to be proclaimed by Fernando and Isabel a century later.

The fifteenth century also saw, as well as the construction of the **Cathedral**, an event that would catapult the city to the forefront of Spanish affairs – the **discovery of the New World**. Sevilla's navigable river, with access to the Atlantic, made it a natural choice for the main port of commerce with the Americas. In the 1500s, as fabulous wealth poured in from the empire, Sevilla was transformed into one of the great cities of Europe and, with a population of over 150,000, one of the largest.

The **silting up of the Guadalquivir** in the 1680s deprived Sevilla of its port and with it the monopoly of trade with the Americas. The merchant fleet was transferred to Cádiz and the city went into a decline exacerbated by the great **earthquake** of 1755 which, although centred on Lisbon, caused much destruction. The city was further ravaged by the **Napoleonic occupation** of 1810–12 and was largely bypassed by the industrial revolution which permeated slowly from the north. It was only in the later nineteenth century that Sevilla was rediscovered by travellers such as Richard Ford, who declared it to be "the marvel of Andalucía".

Arrival

Sevilla's **airport** (☎95 444 90 00) is 12km northeast of town along the NIV towards Córdoba. From here the Amarillos airport bus (every 30min; €2.30) runs to the Puerta de Jerez, close to the cathedral, stopping at the train station en route. At the time of writing, the regulated taxi fare was €17.61, or €20.72 on Sun or after 10pm, including baggage and up to four passengers carried to any point in the metropolitan area. Check with the driver before setting off and if he does not agree to a fare similar to these, take another taxi. The city's **train station**, Santa Justa (℡902 24 02 02), is some way northeast of the centre, on Avenida Kansas City. Bus #32 will get you from here to the central Plaza de la Encarnación, while bus lines #70 or C1 take you to the main Prado de San Sebastián bus station. A central point for train information and tickets is the RENFE office (Mon–Fri 9am–1.30pm & 4–7pm), off Plaza Nueva at c/Zaragoza 29.

Most **buses** operate from the main bus station at the Prado de San Sebastián (℡95 441 71 11), on the eastern edge of the Barrio Santa Cruz and a short bus-ride from the train station on lines #70 or C1, or from the Torre del Oro on C4. However, services from and to northern Sevilla (including Itálica), Extremadura (provinces of Cáceres and Badajoz), all Huelva province, Madrid and international destinations arrive and depart from the station at Plaza de Armas (℡95 490 80 40) by the Puente del Cachorro, on the river; from here, bus C3 will get you to Puerta de Jerez or the Prado de San Sebastián bus station.

Driving in Sevilla is an ordeal, especially in the narow streets of *barrios* such as Santa Cruz. Your best bet for parking is to find a pay car park (see the city map, p.292), or to choose a hotel with a garage (see the "Accommodation" section, opposite). Otherwise spaces can often be found to the north and east of the Prado de San Sebastián bus station. Many parking spaces are pounced on by touts who demand a fee for "finding" it for you; it's normal to give them €0.50 to €1 but don't pay more or try to cheat them by parking and not paying up – you may return to find a broken wing mirror. If your car disappears off the street it will most likely have been removed from an **illegal parking place**. Follow the instructions on the sticker that should have been placed where your car was, or enquire at the Turismo, police station or any (upmarket) hotel who will assist you in locating the pound.

Information

Sevilla's **Turismo**, just south of the cathedral at Avda. de la Constitución 21 (Mon–Fri 9am–7pm, Sat 10am–2pm & 3–7pm, Sun 10am–2pm; ℡95 422 14 04), can provide good city maps and an excellent free monthly listings guide, *El Giraldillo* (Ⓦwww.elgiraldillo.es), but is often overwhelmed in high season. There's a quieter and very helpful **municipal tourist office** (Mon–Fri 8.30am–9pm, Sat 8.30am–2.30pm; ℡95 422 99 42, Ⓦwww.turismo.sevilla .org) at c/Arjona s/n, next to the Puente de Triana (aka Isabell II) bridge on the east bank of the river, which gives information on the province as well as Sevilla itself. A smaller municipal office just off the northern end of Plaza de San Francisco, Edificio Laredo 19 (same hours; ℡95 459 52 88) is another possibility. The municipal offices also sell the **SevillaCard** which gives you access to all the major monuments and (depending on which version you choose) can include free public transport and tour buses. If your time is limited and you plan to see as much as possible the card should save you money. The cheapest one-day version costs €18; see the tourist office's website for more details. The *Guía Verde Callejero* **street guide**, available from *kioskos* and bookshops, is an invaluable aid to finding your way around the city's more convoluted corners, though it's now facing competition from publisher Everest's more colourful *Guía Callejero de Sevilla*.

Sevilla's best all-round daily **newspaper** is *El Diario de Sevilla*, although the older *El Correo* also sells well; both are good for entertainment listings and local news.

City transport

An enjoyable way to get around Sevilla is by **bike**; see "Listings" (p.343) for rental information. If you're planning on getting around a lot by **bus**, invest in a *bonobus* ticket which gives you ten rides for €5 and allows you to change lines on the same journey for up to an hour; otherwise all bus journeys throughout the city have a flat fare of €1. The *bonobus* is available from Tussam (Sevilla's bus company) street kiosks (there are central ones in Plaza Nueva and Plaza Encarnación), newsstands or *estancos*. A Tussam route map is available from the same kiosks or tourist offices, or on their website ⓦwww.tussam.es. Useful buses are the C1, C3 (clockwise), C2 and C4 (anti-clockwise) lines, which go roughly circularly around the city centre. The main central **taxi ranks** are in Plaza Nueva, the Alameda de Hércules and the Plaza de Armas and Prado de San Sebastián bus stations. The basic charge for a short journey is around €3. Reliable taxi services include Radio Taxi, ⓣ95 458 00 00 and TeleTaxi ⓣ954 62 22 22.

One way to get to grips with the city is on an **open-top bus tour** operated by two companies – Sevirama (ⓣ95 456 06 93) and Sevilla Tour (mobile ⓣ901101081) – and the buses leave half-hourly from the Torre del Oro, stopping at or near the main sites (€12).

A new **metro system** will eventually crisscross the city, the first sections of which – linking the southern suburbs to the Puerto de Jerez and Triana – should be opened by 2008.

Accommodation

Rooms in Sevilla are relatively expensive and during the big festivals you can find yourself paying ridiculous amounts for what is little more than a cell. Out of high season (early summer, Semana Santa and Feria de Abril), however, prices can drop dramatically, and with owners competing for trade, it's worth haggling. For Semana Santa and the April *feria* booking as far ahead as possible is advised. As most hotels and *hostales* regard high season as the two weeks covering Holy Week and the Feria de Abril (sometimes referred to as *temporada extra*) we have quoted the *temporada media* (mid-season) rate below, which applies to the rest of the year barring January and February when prices are at their lowest. It's also worth browsing the websites of the hotels who do frequent special offers especially for the "low season" months of July and August.

By far the most attractive (and priciest) area to stay is the **Barrio Santa Cruz**. You'll find lower-priced options around its periphery (especially immediately north, and southeast towards the bus station). Central and more reasonably priced options are around the churches of **Santa Catalina** and **San Pedro**, and to the south of the **Alameda de Hércules**. Also promising is the area north of the **Plaza Nueva** and the **Maestranza bullring**, especially the streets beyond c/Reyes Católicos towards the Museo de Bellas Artes. Further out still, but walkable from the centre, the solidly working-class *barrio* of **La Macarena** can be a wonderful introduction to the real Sevilla, and there's now a *hostal* over the river in the equally atmospheric **Triana** *barrio*.

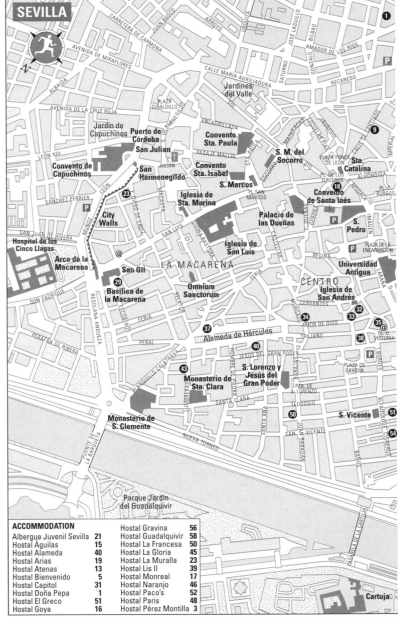

SEVILLA

CARRETERA DE CARMONA

AVENIDA DE MIRAFLORES

JUAN BOSCO

ARROYO

URQUIZA

JOSE LAGUILLO

BILBAO

AMADOR DE LOS RIOS

GONZALO

SATURNO

RECAREDO

CALLE MARÍA AUXILIADORA

Jardines
del Valle

ALBAIDA

AVENIDA DE LA CRUZ ROJA

PLAZA
GIRALDILLO

SOL

ENLADRILLADA

Jardín de
Capuchinos

Puerto de
Córdoba

Convento
Sta. Paula

MADRECO

ESCUELAS PÍAS

LEÓN XIII

San Julián

PASAJE MALLOL

S. M. del
Socorro

PLAZA PONCE
DE LEÓN

Sta.
Catalina

Convento de
Capuchinos

San
Hermenegildo

Convento
Sta. Isabel

PL. DE LOS
TERCEROS

ALHÓNDIGA

SÁNCHEZ PERRIER

LEÓN

JULIÁN

S. Marcos

PL. SAN
MARCOS

Convento
de Santa Inés

PL.
BURGOS

Iglesia de
Sta. Marina

Palacio de
las Dueñas

S.
Pedro

City
Walls

SAN LUIS

GERONA

REGINA

PLAZA DE LA
ENCARNACIÓN

SAN JUAN DE RIVERA

Hospital de los
Cinco Llagas

@

Iglesia de
San Luis

CASTELLAR

Arco de la
Macarena

San Gil

LA MACARENA

Universidad
Antigua

LARANA

DON FADRIQUE

Basílica de
la Macarena

Omnium
Sanctorum

FERIA

CENTRO

Iglesia de
San Andrés

CERVANTES

RESOLANA ANDUEZA

ESCOBEROS

RELATOR

AMOR DE DIOS

PERATÁN DE RIBERA

FERIA

PERAL

Alameda de Hércules

TRAJANO

PL. D.
VICTORIA

BLANQUILLO CALATRAVA

JESÚS DEL GRAN PODER

HOMBRE DE PIEDRA

S. Lorenzo y
Jesús del
Gran Poder

PLAZA DE
GAVIDIA

Monasterio de
Sta. Clara

SANTA CLARA

PZA. DE
S. LORENZO

TEODOSIO

ALFONSO XII

PUENTE DE
LA BARQUETA

Monasterio de
S. Clemente

NUEVA TORNEO

SANTA ANA

JUAN ANTONIO

S. Vicente

SAN VICENTE

SONY

Parque Jardín
del Guadalquivir

PASARELA DE LA CARTUJA

Cartuja

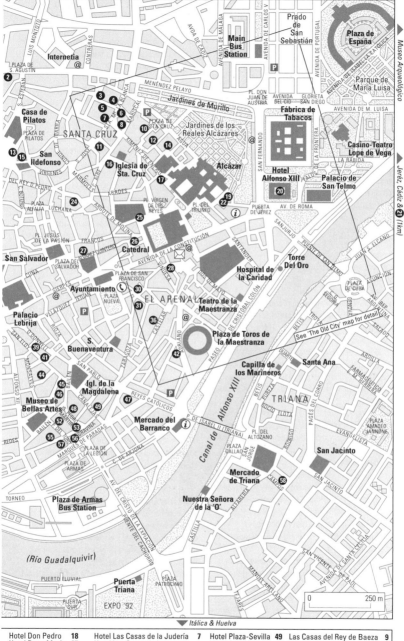

▲ Málaga & Granada

Prado de San Sebastián

Main Bus Station

Plaza de España

Museo Arqueológico ▶

Jeréz, Cádiz & ㉑ (1km) ▶

Parque de María Luisa

Internetia

PLAZA DE S. AGUSTÍN

❷

MENÉNDEZ PELAYO

Jardines de Murillo

Fábrica de Tabacos

AVENIDA DE M. LUISA

Casa de Pilatos

❸ ❹
❺
❼ ❻
❽

SANTA CRUZ

Jardines de los Reales Alcázares

Casino-Teatro Lope de Vega

LA RÁBIDA

PLAZA DE PILATOS

❿

PL. DE STA CRUZ

❶❶

San Ildefonso

❶❸ ❶❺

❶❷ ❶❹

Iglesia de Sta. Cruz ❶❻

❶❼

Alcázar

Hotel Alfonso XIII

❷⓿

Palacio de San Telmo

❷❹

❷❺

PL. VIRGEN DE LOS REYES

PL. DEL TRIUNFO

❶❾
❷❷

PUERTA DE JEREZ

AV. DE ROMA

ⓘ

Catedral

❷❻

❷❼

San Salvador

AVENIDA DE LA CONSTITUCIÓN

Torre Del Oro

Ayuntamiento ❸⓿

❷❽

Hospital de la Caridad

Palacio Lebrija

❸❶

EL ARENAL

Teatro de la Maestranza

S Buenaventura

❸❻

❸❾

❹❶

Plaza de Toros de la Maestranza

❹❹

❹❺

Igl. de la Magdalena

❹❽ ❹❾

❹❷

Capilla de los Marineros

Santa Ana

Museo de Bellas Artes

❺❷ ❺❸

REYES CATÓLICOS

❹❼

TRIANA

❺❺ ❺❻

❺❼

Mercado del Barranco

ⓘ

San Jacinto

Plaza de Armas Bus Station

Mercado de Triana

❺❽

Nuestra Señora de la 'O'

(Río Guadalquivir)

Canal de Alfonso XIII

See The Old City map for detail

Puerta Triana

EXPO '92

0   250 m

▼ Itálica & Huelva

Hotel Don Pedro	18	Hotel Las Casas de la Judería	7	Hotel Plaza-Sevilla	49	Las Casas del Rey de Baeza 9
Hotel Dona María	25	Hotel Las Casas de los		Hotel San Gil	29	Patio de la Alameda 37
Hotel El Paraiso	57	Mercaderes	27	Hotel Sevilla	32	Patio de la Cartuja 43
Hotel Europa	30	Hotel Madrid	53	Hotel Simón	28	Pensión Archeros 4
Hotel La Rábida	36	Hotel Murillo	12	Hotel Zaida	44	Pensión Zahira 41

Sevilla's **youth hostel** is out in the university district to the south of the centre, and the nearest **campsite** (see below) lies some 6km outside the city.

Barrio Santa Cruz and Cathedral area

Hostal Águilas c/Águilas 15 ☎ 95 421 31 77. Small, quiet *hostal* near the Casa de Pilatos. Some rooms with bath. Easy parking. ❸

Hostal Arias c/Mariana de Pineda 9 ☎ 95 421 83 89, ⓦ www.hostalarias.com. Cosy *hostal* with smart if simple rooms – all en suite with a/c and TV – in a quiet pedestrian street. ❹

Hostal Atenas c/Caballerizas 1 ☎ 95 421 80 47, ⓔ atenas@jet.es. A pretty, plant-festooned passage leads to a charming *pensión* decorated with *azulejos*; all rooms with bath and a/c. ❸

Hostal Bienvenido c/Archeros 14, east of c/Santa María la Blanca ☎ 95 441 36 55. Small simple rooms (some en suite), and a nice roof terrace. ❸–❹

Hostal Capitol c/Zaragoza 66 ☎ 95 490 36 24. Pleasant en-suite a/c rooms in an old Art Deco house. ❸

Hostal Goya c/Mateos Gago 31 ☎ 95 421 11 70, ⓕ 95 456 29 88. Good range of simple a/c rooms with bath but lacking TV, in a street with several other possibilities. ❺

Hostal Monreal c/Rodrigo Caro 8 ☎ 95 421 41 66. Decent economical place in the centre of the action for rooms with and without bath. Lots of different styles of room, some with balcony, others with patio view, so ask to see what's available. ❸

Hostal Pérez Montilla Plaza Curtidores 13 ☎ 95 442 18 54. Spotless *hostal* on a tranquil square. Rooms come with and without bath and some have a/c. Quoted prices can drop dramatically when business is slack. ❷–❸

Hostal Picasso c/San Gregorio 1 ☎ 95 421 08 64, ⓦ www.grupo-piramide.com. Comfortable if slightly pricey *hostal* with en-suite rooms ranged around a plant-filled patio. The same proprietors have similar places nearby – see website for details. ❹

Hostal Puerta Carmona Plaza de San Agustín 5 ☎ 95 498 83 10, ⓕ 95 453 39 86. Very pleasant and stylish new *hostal* owned by the proprietors of *Hotel Maestre* in Córdoba. Good modern en-suite rooms with a/c and TV; they will advise on where to park nearby. ❹

Hostal Santa María c/Hernando Colón 19 ☎ 95 422 85 05. Small, simple and friendly place on a busy street in the Giralda's shadow. All rooms en suite with a/c and TV. ❸

Hostal Santa María de la Blanca c/Santa María La Blanca ☎ 95 442 11 74. Friendly small *hostal*

above a shop, through which you gain entry; rooms with and (cheaper) without bath and to turn on the a/c costs an extra €10. ❷

🏃 Hostal Sierpes Corral del Rey 22, northeast of the cathedral ☎ 95 422 49 48, ⓦ www.hsierpes.com. Friendly *hostal* with light and airy en-suite a/c rooms (104 and 306 are particularly spacious) arranged around a central patio. Tricky to reach by car, you can ring them if lost and they'll come and get you. Has own restaurant and garage. ❺

Hostal Toledo c/Santa Teresa 15 ☎ 95 421 53 35. Atmospheric and refurbished *pensión* in the heart of Santa Cruz. All rooms with bath. ❹

Hostería del Laurel Plaza de los Venerables 5 ☎ 95 422 02 95, ⓦ www.hosteriadellaurel.com. Pleasant en-suite rooms above a very good restaurant and tapas bar. Superb location which can get a bit overrun with visitors in high season. ❺

Hotel Adriano c/Adriano 12, ☎ 95 429 38 00, ⓦ www.hoteladriano.net. Close to the bullring, this is a stylish new two-star hotel for rooms with satellite TV and in-room email facility; there's also a roof terrace. ❺

Hotel Alcántara c/Ximénez de Enciso 28 ☎ 95 45 00 95, ⓦ www.hotelalcantara.net. Smart new small two-star hotel close to Plaza Santa Cruz, with attractive a/c rooms. ❺

Hotel Alfonso XIII c/San Fernando 2 ☎ 95 491 70 00, ⓦ www.westin.com. A monument in its own right (see p.309), this has a fair claim to being Sevilla's number-one hotel; the public rooms and patio are stunning but unless you're into pompous decor, a visit to the bar or restaurant might be a better suggestion than overnighting here. The cheapest Internet-booked double room costs €342. ❾

🏃 Hotel Amadeus c/Farnesio 6, near the Iglesia de Santa Cruz ☎ 95 450 14 43, ⓦ www.hotelamadeussevilla.com. Mozart operas and symphonies greet you in the entrance patio of this welcoming hotel – housed in an eighteenth-century *casa señorial* – owned by an aficionado of the great composer. There's a grand piano for use by guests, and the soundproofed and stylish rooms come with a/c, satellite TV and free Internet access. The house is topped off with a stunning roof terrace for breakfast, where there's also a telescope for night-time astronomical contemplations. ❺

Hotel Dona María c/Don Remondo 19 ☎ 95 422 49 90, ⓦ www.hdmaria.com. Located in a mansion a stone's throw from the Giralda tower, the main feature here is the rooftop pool and bar; the rooms are pleasant but ask to see before you commit yourself as a few are not compatible with this price range. **7**

Hotel La Rábida c/Castelar 24 ☎95 422 09 60, ⓦ www.vinccihoteles.com. Refurbished, traditional hotel with a nice patio, lots of marble and good facilities. Rooms in the older part have more character. **8**

Hotel Las Casas de la Judería c/Callejón de Dos Hermanas 7 ☎95 441 51 50, ⓦ www.casasypalacios.com. Stunningly beautiful old mansion transformed into a delightfully serene hotel with pastel-tinted rooms, exquisite patios and a restaurant. Good value for this category. Parking available. **8**

Hotel Las Casas de los Mercaderes c/Álvarez Quintero 12 ☎95 422 58 58, ⓦ www .casasypalacios.com. Converted former *bodega* with delightful patio, roof terrace and great views from some rooms (especially nos. 201–6). Just north of the cathedral and good value for this category. Garage too. **8**

Hotel Murillo c/Lope de Rueda 7 ☎95 421 60 95, ⓦ www.hotelmurillo.com. Traditional hotel in restored mansion with all facilities, plus amusingly kitsch features such as suits of armour, heavy leather chairs and paint-palette key rings. Also rent apartments. **5**

Hotel Simón c/García de Vinuesa 19 ☎95 422 66 60, ⓦ www.hotelsimonsevilla.com. Eighteenth-century mansion with attractive patio and excellent position near the cathedral. Attractive a/c individually styled rooms. **5**

Las Casas del Rey de Baeza Plaza Jesús de la Redención 2 ☎95 456 14 96, ⓦ www.hospes.es. Wonderful new hotel with rooms arranged around an eighteenth-century *corral sevillano*. The plant-bedecked interior patio is charming and stylishly furnished rooms come with traditional exterior *esparto* blinds, a neat finishing touch – and there's a rooftop pool to cool off. **8**

Pensión Archeros c/Archeros 23 ☎95 441 84 65. Pleasant and economical little rooms and a charming plant-filled patio tucked away in a quiet street on the northern edge of the Barrio Santa Cruz. Has more expensive en-suite rooms too. **2**

Plaza Nueva, Reyes Católicos, Museo de Bellas Artes and Triana

Hostal El Greco c/San Vicente 14 ☎95 490 76 08. Comfortable *hostal* offering rooms with and without bath. **3**

Hostal Gravina c/Gravina 46 ☎95 421 64 14, ⓦ www.hostales-sp.com. Friendly, family-run *hostal* with simple rooms sharing bath in a quiet street off c/Reyes Católicos. **2**

Hostal Guadalquivir c/Pagés del Corro 53 ☎95 433 21 00, ⓕ95 433 21 04. If you want to stay across the river in Triana, this is the only budget place you'll find. It's pleasant and friendly, and the en-suite rooms have a/c or fans. **3–4**

Hostal La Gloria c/San Eloy 58 ☎95 422 26 73. Good-value rooms, some with bath, in a wonderful neo-Moorish building above the *Café Zafiro*. **3**

Hostal Lis II c/Olavide 5 ☎95 456 02 28. A couple of blocks east of the Museo de Bellas Artes, this is a clean and simple place with interior patio and rooms with and without bath. There's Internet access (extra charge) for guests. **2–3**

Hostal Naranjo c/San Roque 11 ☎95 422 58 40, ⓦ www.BandBsevilla.com. Welcoming and competitively priced *hostal* offering a/c en-suite rooms with TV and free Internet connection. **3**

Hostal Paco's c/Pedro del Toro 7, off c/Gravina ☎95 421 71 83, ⓦ www.hostales-sp.com. Friendly offshoot of the *Hostal Gravina*, this has small rooms sharing bath, among the cheapest in town. **2**

Hostal Paris c/San Pedro Mártir 14 ☎95 422 98 61, ⓦ www.hostales-sp.com. Good-value *hostal* with lots of facilities, including a/c, in a tiny street near the Museo de Bellas Artes. All rooms en-suite. **4**

Hostal Redes c/Redes 28 ☎95 490 19 46, ⓔ hostalredes@navegalia.com. Clean and tidy *hostal* where all rooms are en suite and fans are provided in summer. Extra charge for a/c. **3**

Hostal Romero c/Gravina 21 ☎95 421 13 53. Basic but efficient *hostal* with another plant-bedecked patio. Rooms sharing bath and en suite (the latter come with TV and fans). **3**

Hotel Bécquer c/Reyes Católicos 4 ☎95 422 89 00, ⓦ www.hotelbecquer.com. Modern, comfortable and central four-star hotel with a/c rooms and lots of facilities. Garage available. **6**

Hotel El Paraiso c/Gravina 27 ☎95 421 79 19. Pleasant small hotel offering a/c en-suite rooms with TV. **4**

Hotel Europa c/Jimios 5 ☎95 421 43 05, ⓦ www.sol.com/hotel-europa. Elegant, traditional and friendly hotel in an eighteenth-century mansion that has comfortable rooms with safes and satellite TV. Garage available. **6**

Hotel Madrid c/San Pedro Mártir 22 ☎95 421 43 06, ⓦ www.hotelmadridsevilla.com. Pleasant family-run hotel offering functional a/c balcony rooms with TV. **4**

Hotel Plaza-Sevilla c/Canalejas 2 ☎95 421 71 49, ⓔ reservas@hotelplazasevilla.com. It's almost worth staying at this comfortable hotel for the stunning Neoclassical facade alone – the work of Anibal González, architect of the Plaza de España. The rather staid interior is another story, however, and the a/c rooms are decent if unexciting. **5**

Hotel Zaida c/San Roque 26 ☎95 421 11 38, ⓦwww.hotelzaida.com. Charming and intimate hotel with a fine exterior and an interior replete with Moorish-inspired decor. All rooms with bath, TV and a/c. Some of the single rooms lack light. ❹

Pensión Zahira c/San Eloy 43 ☎95 422 10 61, ⓦwww.hotelesdesevilla.com. Comfortable a/c rooms with bath but no TV. ❸

Santa Catalina, San Pedro, Alameda de Hércules

Hostal Alameda Alameda de Hércules 31 ☎95 490 01 91, Ⓕp95 490 22 48. Modern but very friendly *hostal* overlooking the tree-lined Alameda. Rooms with bath, a/c and TV. ❸

Hostal La Francesa c/Juan Rabadán 28 ☎95 438 31 07. Quiet, simple rooms with shared bath in pretty little family-run *hostal*. ❷

Hostal Trajano c/Trajano 3 ☎ & Ⓕ95 438 24 21. Good-value rooms with bath and TV at this cosy *hostal*. Fans available. ❸

Hostal Unión c/Tarifa 4 ☎95 422 92 94. One of this zone's best-value *hostales* with en-suite rooms and pleasant management. Extra charge for a/c. ❸

Hotel Casona de San Andrés c/Daoiz 7 ☎95 491 52 53, ⓦwww.casonadesanandres.com. Former nineteenth-century *casa palacio* that's been transformed into a pleasant new hotel. Well-equipped balcony rooms face the square or two interior patios. ❹

Hotel Corregidor c/Morgado 17, off c/Amor de Dios ☎95 438 51 11, ⓦwww.hotelcorregidorsevilla.com. Serene and recently renovated three-star hotel with a nice patio, a/c rooms, garage and everything else you'd expect for the price. ❺

Hotel Don Pedro c/Gerona 24 ☎95 429 33 33, ⓦwww.hoteldonpedro.net. Charming and friendly small hotel housed in a nineteenth-century *casa palacio*. There's an elegant patio and some of the higher rooms come with a generous balcony terrace (€12 supplement). ❺ with breakfast

Hotel Sevilla c/Daóiz 5, fronting the church of San Andrés ☎95 438 41 61, ⓦwww.hotel-sevilla.com. Revamped and refurbished pleasant old hotel with a nice patio, en-suite rooms with a/c and TV plus views onto a pleasant *plazuela* near the church of San Andrés. ❹

🏃 **Patio de la Alameda** Alameda de Hércules 56 ☎95 490 49 99, ⓦwww.patiosdesevilla .com. Old *casa señorial* revamped into an elegant and fair-priced apart-hotel with light and airy balcony rooms, three patios and easy parking. Rooms have kitchen and living room. ❻

Patio de la Cartuja c/Lumbreras 8 ☎95 490 02 00, ⓦwww.patiosdesevilla.com. Unique, stylish

and excellent-value apart-hotel created from an old *corral sevillano*, with balconies around a tiled patio. All rooms have kitchen and living room and there's a garage available too. ❻

La Macarena

Hostal Doña Pepa c/Juan de Vera 20, near Santa Justa train station ☎95 441 36 28, Ⓔhostalpepa@ya.com. Completely renovated *hostal* with good a/c en-suite rooms. Ideal for late arrivals or early departures. ❹

Hostal La Muralla c/Macarena 52 ☎95 437 10 49, Ⓔhmuralla@terra.es. Very pleasant and good-value residential *hostal* facing the medieval walls. All rooms come with bath, a/c and TV. Own car park or easy parking nearby. ❸

Hotel San Gil c/Parras 28 ☎95 490 68 11, ⓦwww.fp-hoteles.com. Luxurious apart-hotel in a beautifully restored early 1900s *palacio*. There's a garden with palms and cypresses, rooftop pool, garage, and an interior decorated with mosaics and *azulejos*; some rooms have a lounge and kitchenette. ❽

Youth hostel and campsites

Albergue Juvenil Sevilla c/Isaac Peral 2 ☎95 461 31 50, ⓦwww.inturjoven.com. Sevilla's leafy if sometimes crowded youth hostel is some way out; take bus #34 from Puerta de Jerez by the Turismo or from Plaza Nueva. Note that they tend not to answer the phone. Under 26 €14, over 26 €18.50.

Camping Sevilla Parque Alcosa ☎ & Ⓕ95 451 43 79. Right by the airport, so very noisy but otherwise not a bad site with restaurant, bar and pool among other facilities. The airport bus will drop you nearby, or take bus #70 from outside the main bus station at Prado de San Sebastián and ask to be dropped at "Parque Alcosa". Alternatively the campsite has its own shuttle-bus service running from a stop in the Avda. de Portugal, slightly south of the Prado de San Sebastián bus station; currently running at 6pm, 8pm & 10pm, it costs €2.

Camping Villsom 10km out of town on the main Cádiz road ☎ & Ⓕ95 472 08 28. Recently overhauled campsite with a pool. Half-hourly buses from c/Palos de la Frontera next to the *Hotel Alfonso XIII* take 20min. Make sure to take the bus signed "Dos Hermanas por Barriadas", which will drop you outside the campsite.

Club de Campo 12km south of the centre in Dos Hermanas ☎95 472 02 50, Ⓕ95 472 63 08. Pleasant, shady site with pool which has the edge on the nearby *Villsom*. Follow the directions for *Camping Villsom* (above) but take bus signed "Dos Hermanas Directo" (direct route), a 20min trip.

The City

The **old city**, where you'll spend most of your time, takes up the east bank of the Guadalquivir. At its heart, side by side, stand the three great monuments: the **Giralda tower**, the **Cathedral** and the **Alcázar**, with the cramped alleyways of the **Barrio Santa Cruz**, the medieval Jewish quarter and now the heart of tourist life, extending east of them. North and west of the barrio is the main shopping and commercial district, its most obvious landmarks the **Plaza Nueva** and **Plaza Duque de la Victoria**, and the smart pedestrianized **Calle Sierpes** which runs between them. To the north of the area enclosed by the

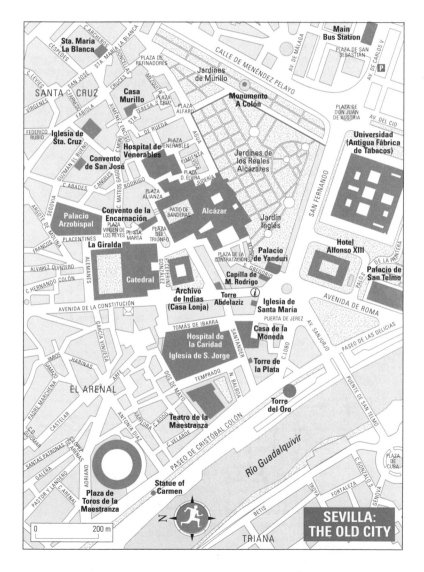

SEVILLA:
THE OLD CITY

0   200 m

medieval walls lies the gritty **Macarena quarter**, from whose church the *paso* of the bejewelled Virgin of Macarena – the most revered in Sevilla – sails forth on the Maundy Thursday of Semana Santa to enormous popular acclaim. Just beyond the walls here in the converted sixteenth-century Hospital de las Cinco Llagas ("Five Wounds of Christ") is the permanent seat of the **Andalucian parliament**.

Across the river is the earthier, traditionally working-class district of **Triana**, flanked to the south by **Los Remedios**, the former business zone and now an upmarket residential quarter. Adjoining this to the south lie the grounds where Sevilla's Feria de Abril is held, and also on this bank, to the north of Triana, lie the remains of the Expo 92 exhibition ground, at Isla de la Cartuja.

The Cathedral and the Giralda

After the Reconquest of Sevilla by Fernando III (1248), the Almohad mosque was consecrated to the Virgin Mary and kept in use as the Christian cathedral. As such it survived until 1402, when the cathedral chapter dreamed up plans for a new and unrivalled monument to Christian glory: "a building on so magnificent a scale that posterity will believe we were mad." To this end

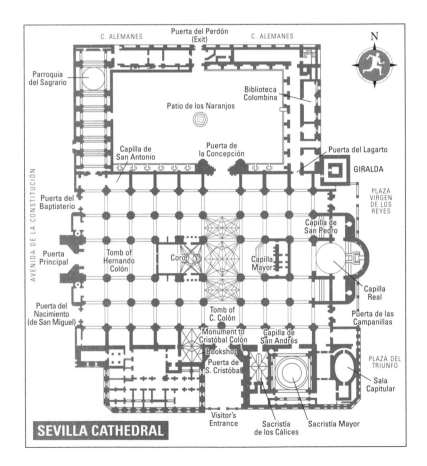

Where lies Christopher Columbus?

The dispute about **Christopher Columbus**'s birthplace – claimed by both Italy and Spain – is matched by the labyrinthine controversy surrounding the whereabouts of his **remains**.

After his death in **Valladolid** in 1506, Columbus was originally buried in that town, but three years later his remains were removed to **Sevilla** and interred at the monastery of Santa María de las Cuevas, across the river on La Cartuja island. Then, when Columbus's eldest son Diego passed away, his remains were buried in the same tomb. After this Columbus's widow declared that she wished to have both bodies transferred to the Caribbean island of **Hispaniola** (modern Haiti and the Dominican Republic), the site of Columbus's first landfall in 1492, for interment in Santo Domingo, capital of Spanish America. Following some bureaucratic resistance and an intervention by the emperor, Carlos V, in 1544 the remains of both bodies were packed into lead coffins and shipped to the island, where they were placed in the cathedral. The remains of Columbus's grandson, Luís, were interred in the same cathedral in 1783.

Later, during repairs to this building, it seems that the coffins were mislaid, then opened, and the names mixed up. It did not take the authorities long to resolve the dilemma of which was which, by having all three sets of remains placed in one coffin. Shortly after 1795, when Spain was forced to cede Santo Domingo to the French, the remains were moved to Cuba and the cathedral in **Havana**, still Spanish territory. When Cuba was lost in 1898 the remains were transported back across the Atlantic and placed in the tomb in Sevilla. The lingering uncertainty lies in the accidental discovery in 1879 of another lead coffin in the cathedral in **Santo Domingo** bearing a silver plate inscribed with Columbus's name. This box of remains then disappeared, and despite the government of the Dominican Republic's claim to have recovered them (now enshrined in a national monument), numerous coffins of bones claiming to be the same have made frequent appearances at auction houses ever since.

Were the correct remains despatched from Santo Domingo to Havana in 1795? Was the discovery of 1879 a fraud? Are the remains in the tomb today really those of Christopher, Diego and Luís? The only certainty in the story is that one member of the Columbus family, at least, was buried in Sevilla's cathedral and has stayed here – Christopher's bookish son Hernando, who wrote a biography of his father and donated his large library to what became the cathedral's Biblioteca Colombina. His tombstone lies in the centre of the pavement towards the main west door, the Puerta Principal, flanked by smaller slabs portraying sailing vessels.

In 2002, science was called on to try to resolve the mystery and a plan was drawn up to subject all the known remains of Columbus family members to DNA testing in the hope that a common genetic code could be established. Initial reports on samples taken from the Sevilla tomb by scientists at Granada university were inconclusive due to the poor condition of the remains, although the tests did indicate that there were matches with other members of the family. A request was then made to test the remains in Santo Domingo which – if this proved negative – would go some way to confirming the authenticity of those in Sevilla. After initially agreeing to this request the government of the Dominican Republic had second thoughts. An announcement by scientists that the Santo Domingo remains are not those of Columbus would be hugely embarrassing for a country where the navigator is a national hero. Thus in early 2005 the republic's government stated that it didn't have sufficient confidence in the reliability of DNA testing to allow the research to go ahead. When the Spanish ambassador announced that Spain would not make an issue of the matter the outcome of this tortuously tangled tale was, for the time being, put on hold, leaving the location of Columbus's remains a mystery for at least a few more years yet.

the Almohad mosque (see box on p.303) was almost entirely demolished, and the largest Gothic church in the world, Sevilla's **Cathedral** (July–Aug Mon–Sat 11am–5pm, Sun 2.30–6pm; Sept–June Mon–Sat 9.30am–3.30pm, Sun 2.30–6pm; ticket valid for Cathedral and Giralda tower; €7, Sun free; ⓦwww .catedralsevilla.org), was completed, extraordinarily, in just over a century (1402–1506). As Norman Lewis said, "it expresses conquest and domination in architectural terms of sheer mass." Built upon the huge, rectangular base-plan of the old mosque whose minaret, the Giralda, now served as the bell-tower, it was given the extra dimension of height by the Christian architects, probably under the direction of the French master architect of Rouen Cathedral. It was previously reckoned to be the third-largest church in the world – after St Paul's in London and St Peter's in Rome – but new calculations based on cubic measurements have now placed it in the number one position, a claim upheld by the *Guinness Book of Records*, a copy of whose certificate is proudly displayed in the church.

Entry to the cathedral is through the **Puerta de San Cristóbal,** on the building's south side where, beyond a reception area displaying minor artworks by Murillo and Zurbarán among others, you enter the church to the west of the portal itself. If you're interested in studying the abundant artworks dotted around the various chapels en route, visit the bookshop by the entrance and obtain a copy of the official *Guide to the Cathedral of Seville*, which deals with them in detail.

Turn right once inside to head east, where you are soon confronted by an enormous late nineteenth-century **Monument to Christopher Columbus** (Cristobal Colón in Spanish), by *sevillano* sculptor Arturo Mélida, which may or may not be the navigator's tomb. It was originally intended to be erected in the Cuban cathedral of Havana, Spain's colony, where it would become a sepulchre for Columbus's remains, but the Spanish-American War – and Cuba's subsequent independence – intervened. As a result the plans were changed and the work was placed here in Sevilla's cathedral. The mariner's coffin is held aloft by four huge allegorical figures, representing the kingdoms of León, Castile, Aragón and Navarra; the lance of Castile should be piercing a pomegranate (now inexplicably missing), the symbol of Granada (and the word for the fruit in Spanish), the last Moorish kingdom to be reconquered.

Moving into the **nave**, first impressions are of the sheer size and grandeur of the place, but as you grow accustomed to the gloom, two other qualities stand out with equal force: the rhythmic balance and interplay between the parts, and an impressive overall simplicity and restraint in decoration. Successive ages have left monuments of their own, but these have been limited to the two rows of side chapels. In the main body of the cathedral only the great box-like structure of the **coro** (choir) stands out, filling the central portion of the nave.

The *coro* extends and opens onto the **Capilla Mayor**, dominated by a vast and fabulous **Gothic retablo** composed of 45 carved scenes from the life of Christ. Begun in 1482 and the lifetime's work of a single craftsman, Fleming Pieter Dancart, this is the supreme masterpiece of the cathedral – the largest and richest altarpiece in the world and one of the finest examples of Gothic woodcarving. Above the central tabernacle, the **Virgen de la Sede** (Virgin of the Chair) is a stunning thirteenth-century Gothic figure of silver-plated cedar. Just to the right, a panel depicts an **image of the Giralda** as it appeared prior to any Renaissance additions.

Before proceeding around the edge of the nave in a clockwise direction it's best to backtrack to the church's southeast corner to take in the **Sacristía de los Cálices** where many of the cathedral's main art treasures

△ Monument to Christopher Columbus

are displayed. Among some outstanding works are a masterly *Santas Justa y Rufina* by Goya, depicting Sevilla's patron saints who were put to death in 287 during the Roman emperor Diocletian's persecution of the Christians. Here also are canvases by Zurbarán, Roelas, Valdés Leal and Jordaens. Behind the **Capilla de San Andres**, which has an exceptional polychromed image of the crucified Christ by Martinez Montañés, lies the grandiose sixteenth-century **Sacristía Mayor** designed in 1528 by Diego de Riaño. It's a prime example of the rich Plateresque style, and Riaño was one of the foremost exponents of this predominantly decorative architecture of the late Spanish Renaissance. Forming a veritable church-within-a-church it induced Philip II to remark to the members of the chapter: "Your sacristy is finer than my Chapel Royal". The sacristy houses more paintings, including a poignant *Santa Teresa* by Zurbarán, and the treasury, a dull collection of silver reliquaries and monstrances. Here also are the **keys** presented to Fernando by the

Jewish and Moorish communities on the surrender of the city; sculpted into the Moor's key in stylized Arabic script are the words "May Allah render eternal the dominion of Islam in this city." Nearby is a polychromed image of Fernando III by Pedro Roldán, one of Andalucía's great eighteenth-century sculptors.

Through a small antechamber here you enter the remarkable oval-shaped **Sala Capitular** (Chapter House), whose elaborate domed ceiling is mirrored in the outstanding geometric marble decoration of the floor. The stone benches provide seats for the members of the chapter. It contains a number of paintings by Murillo, a native of Sevilla, the finest of which, a flowing *Concepción Inmaculada*, occupies a place of honour high above the bishop's throne.

The route continues by proceeding to the southwest corner and the **Puerta del Nacimiento**, the door through which pass all the *pasos* and penitents who take part in the Semana Santa processions, and then turning right (north) along the west wall, passing the **Puerta Principal**. In the northwest corner the **Capilla de San Antonio** contains the *Vision of St Anthony*, a magnificent work by Murillo, depicting the saint in ecstatic pose before an infant Christ emerging from a luminous golden cloud. Try and spot where the restorers joined San Antonio back into place after he had been crudely hacked out of the picture by thieves in the nineteenth century. He was eventually discovered in New York – where art dealers recognized the work they were being asked to buy – and returned to the cathedral. The *Baptism of Jesus* above this is another fine work by the same artist. The nave's north side leads to the **Puerta de la Concepción**, where an altar on the left side has a fine portrayal of the *Virgen de Belén* painted in 1635 by *granadino* artist Alonso Cano. Before exiting here, head for the northeast corner to view the domed Renaissance **Capilla Real** (which is not always open), built on the site of the original royal burial chapel and containing the body of Fernando III (El Santo) in a suitably rich, Baroque silver sepulchre before the altar. The large tombs on either side of the chapel are those of Fernando's wife, Beatrice of Swabia, and his son, Alfonso the Wise. The chapel normally opens for daily services at 8.30am, midday and 5pm. To the left of here, the **Capilla de San Pedro** has a fine seventeenth-century *retablo* by Diego López Bueno with nine Zurbarán scenes depicting the life of St Peter (except for the image of God, which is a later replacement). Also here is the Puerta del Lagarto (Door of the Alligator), so named in commemoration of a stuffed reptile given to Alfonso X by the sultan of Egypt in 1260. A wooden replica now hangs in place of the perished original.

The Giralda and the Patio de los Naranjos

The entrance to the **Giralda** (same ticket as the cathedral) lies to the left of the Capilla Real. Unquestionably the most beautiful building in Sevilla, the Giralda, named after the sixteenth-century *giraldillo* or weather vane on its summit, dominates the skyline and, with its perfect synthesis of form and decoration, is one of the most important examples of Islamic architecture in the world.

The **minaret** – built on a foundation of destroyed Roman statuary – was the culmination of Almohad architecture, and served as a model for those at the imperial capitals of Rabat and Marrakesh. It was designed by the architect of the original mosque, Ahmed ibn Baso, and was used by the Moors both for calling the faithful to prayer and as an observatory. They so worshipped the building that they planned to destroy it before the Christian conquest

Sevilla was one of the earliest **Moorish conquests** (in 712) and, as part of the caliphate of Córdoba, became the second city of al-Andalus. When the caliphate broke up in the early eleventh century it was by far the most powerful of the independent states (or *taifas*) to emerge, extending its power over the Algarve and eventually over Jaén, Murcia and Córdoba itself. This period, under a series of three Arabic rulers from the Abbadid dynasty (1023–91), was something of a golden age. The city's court was unrivalled in wealth, luxury and sophistication, developing a strong chivalric element and a flair for poetry – one of the most skilled exponents was the last ruler, al Mu'tamid, the "poet-king". But with sophistication came decadence, and in 1091 Abbadid rule was usurped by a new force, the **Almoravids**, a tribe of fanatical Berber Muslims from North Africa, to whom the Andalucians had appealed for help against the threat from the northern Christian kingdoms.

Despite initial military successes, the Almoravids failed to consolidate their gains in al-Andalus and attempted to rule through military governors from Marrakesh. In the middle of the twelfth century they were in turn supplanted by a new Berber incursion, the **Almohads**, who by about 1170 had recaptured virtually all the former territories. Sevilla accepted Almohad rule in 1147 and became the capital of this last real empire of the Moors in Spain. Almohad power was sustained until their disastrous defeat in 1212 by the combined Christian armies of the north, at Las Navas de Tolosa in Jaén. Within this brief and precarious period Sevilla underwent a renaissance of public building, characterized by a new vigour and fluidity of style. The Almohads rebuilt the Alcázar, enlarged the principal **mosque** and erected a new and brilliant minaret, a tower over 100m tall, topped with four copper spheres that could be seen from miles round: the Giralda.

of Sevilla, but were prevented from doing so by the threat of Alfonso (later King Alfonso X) that "if they removed a single stone, they would all be put to the sword". Instead the Giralda went on to become the bell-tower of the Christian cathedral. The Patio de los Naranjos (see below), the old entrance to the mosque, also survives intact.

From inside the cathedral you can ascend to the **bell chamber** for a remarkable view of the city – and, equally remarkable, a glimpse of the Gothic details of the cathedral's buttresses and statuary. Keep an eye out, too, for the colony of kestrels which has long nested in the tower – the descendants no doubt of the "twittering, careering hawks" seen by Ford when he climbed up here in the 1830s. Most impressive is the tower's inner construction, a series of 35 gently inclined ramps wide enough for two mounted guards to pass. The Moorish structure took twelve years to build (1184–96) and derives its firm, simple beauty from the shadows formed by blocks of brick trelliswork or *ajaracas*, different on each side, and relieved by a succession of arched niches and windows. The original harmony has been somewhat blemished by the Renaissance-era addition of balconies and, to a still greater extent, by the four diminishing storeys of the belfry – added, along with the Italian-sculpted bronze figure of Faith which surmounts them, in 1560–68, following the demolition by an earthquake of the original copper spheres. The fact that a weathervane blown by the four winds should epitomize the ideal of constant faith, or that this female figure should possess a masculine name ("Giraldillo"), has never seemed to trouble whimsical *sevillanos*.

To reach the cathedral's **exit**, retrace your steps to the Puerta de la Concepción and pass through here to enter the **Patio de los Naranjos**, taking its name from the orange trees which now shade the former mosque's entrance courtyard where ritual ablutions were performed prior to worship. In the centre of the patio a **Moorish fountain** incorporates a sixth-century carved marble font, a surviving remnant of the earlier Visigothic cathedral which was itself levelled to make way for the mosque. Cross to the patio's northern side and the **Puerta del Perdón**, the mosque's original entrance. Although sadly marred by Renaissance embellishments, there remains some exquisite Almohad plasterwork and the original great doors made from larchwood faced with bronze. Minute Kufic script inside the lozenges proclaims that "the empire is Allah's". The pierced bronze door-knockers are copies of the beautiful hand-crafted twelfth-century originals now preserved inside the church (not currently on view).

The Archivo de las Indias and the Ayuntamiento

Should you have been inspired by the Columbus saga after seeing his monument in the cathedral, visit the **Casa Lonja**, opposite the cathedral. Built in the severe and uncompromising style of El Escorial near Madrid, and designed by the same architect, Juan de Herrera, it was the former merchants' commodity exchange (*lonja*), adapted in the eighteenth century to house the remarkable **Archivo de las Indias** (Mon–Fri 10am–1pm; free), a monumental storehouse of the archives of the Spanish empire. Holding over 38,000 documents and files – all in the process of being computerized – from four centuries of Spanish rule, only bona fide researchers can get their hands on the dusty files containing letters signed by Columbus or other luminaries. Casual visitors must make do with an audiovisual presentation (in Spanish) and changing displays that have included Columbus's log and a letter from Cervantes (pre-*Don Quijote*) petitioning the king for a position in the Americas – fortunately for world literature, he was turned down.

Another building worth a visit and sited slightly to the north of the cathedral is the sixteenth-century **Ayuntamiento** at the top of Avenida de la Constitución, with a richly ornamented Plateresque facade by Diego de Riaño, one of the finest in Spain. Substantially enlarged early in the nineteenth century, the building's western exterior facing Plaza Nueva dates entirely from this time and forgoes the exuberant decoration of the original. The interior – decorated with numerous artworks including canvases by Zurbarán and Murillo – is open for guided visits allowing Riaño's star-vaulted **vestíbulo** (entrance hall), the elaborately ornate **Sala de Consistorio** (council chamber) and an **upper Sala de Consistorio** above it, with a ravishing gilded coffered ceiling dating from the time of Philip II, to be seen (Tues, Wed, Thurs visits at 5.30pm, Sat 12noon; closed Aug; free). During the Semana Santa processions Plaza de San Francisco in front of the Ayuntamiento is part of the official route leading to the cathedral, and huge temporary grandstands fill the square providing prime vantage points for the town's dignitaries and their families and friends. The pointed *capirote* hoods worn by the penitent brotherhoods are eerily identical to those worn by the inquisitors of the Spanish Inquisition who, between the fifteenth and eighteenth centuries, sentenced an untold number of "heretics" to death by burning in public *autos da fé*, or trials, held in this same square.

The Alcázar

Rulers of Sevilla occupied the site of the **Alcázar** (April–Sept Tues–Sat 9.30am–7pm, Sun 9.30am–1.30pm; Oct–March Tues–Sat 9.30am–5pm, Sun 9.30am–1.30pm; €5; Ⓦ www.patronato-alcazarsevilla.es) from the time of the Romans. The fortified palace was probably founded in the eighth century on the ruins of a Roman barracks, with the surrounding walls being added in the ninth.

In the eleventh century it was expanded to become the great court of the Abbadid dynasty, who turned the wealth gained from the production of olive oil, sugar cane and dyes into a palace worthy of their hubris. This regime reached a peak of sophistication and decadence under the ruthless al Mu'tamid, a ruler who further enlarged the Alcázar in order to house a harem of eight hundred women, and decorated the terraces with flowers planted in the skulls of his decapitated enemies. Later, in the twelfth and thirteenth centuries under the **Almohads**, the complex was turned into a citadel, forming the heart of the town's fortifications. Its extent was enormous, stretching to the Torre del Oro on the bank of the Guadalquivir. Parts of the Almohad walls survive, but the present structure dates almost entirely from the Christian period following the fall of the city in 1248.

Sevilla was a favoured residence of the Spanish kings for some four centuries after the Reconquest – most particularly of **Pedro the Cruel** (Pedro I; 1350–69) who, with his mistress María de Padilla, lived in and ruled from the Alcázar. Pedro embarked upon a complete rebuilding of the palace, utilizing fragments of earlier Moorish buildings in Sevilla, Córdoba and Valencia. Pedro's works form the nucleus of the Alcázar as it is today and, despite numerous restorations

Visiting the Alcázar

The pressure of visitors to the **Alcázar** has resulted in the introduction of a flow-control system whereby 750 people are allowed in every 20–30min. It's still advisable, however, to visit early morning or late afternoon to savour the experience in relative calm. An official guidebook to the complex on sale at the entrance has detailed maps of the palaces and information on the gardens beyond.

necessitated by fires and earth tremors, offer some of the best surviving examples of **Mudéjar architecture** – the style developed by Moors working under Christian rule. Later monarchs have also left many traces and additions. In the fifteenth century Isabel built a new wing in which to organize expeditions to the Americas and control the new territories; in the sixteenth century Carlos V married a Portuguese princess in the palace, adding huge apartments for the occasion; and under Felipe IV (c.1624) extensive renovations were carried out to the existing rooms. On a more mundane level, kitchens were installed to provide for General Franco, who stayed in the royal apartments whenever he visited Sevilla.

The Patio del León and Patio de la Montería

The Alcázar is entered from the Plaza del Triunfo, adjacent to the cathedral, through the **Puerta del León**, which bears a heraldic image of a lion in fourteenth-century glazed tiles above the lintel. The gateway, flanked by original Almohad walls, opens onto a courtyard – the Patio del León – where Pedro (who was known as "the Just" as well as "the Cruel", depending on one's fortunes) used to give judgement; to the left is the **Sala de Justicia** built by Alfonso XI in the 1340s with exquisite *yesería* (plasterwork) in the Grenadine style and a beautiful *artesonado* ceiling. Beyond, the restored **Patio del Yeso** has more fine plasterwork and the whole patio is the only visible surviving remnant of the Almohads' Alcázar. The main facade of Pedro's palace stands at the end of an inner court, the **Patio de la Montería**, or "hunting patio", where the royal hunt gathered; on either side are galleried buildings erected by Isabel. This principal facade is pure fourteenth-century Mudéjar and, with its delicate, marble-columned windows, stalactite frieze and overhanging roof, is one of the finest features of the whole Alcázar. The castles, lions and other heraldic devices were intended to emphasize the king's power over both Christians and Muslims, but Kufic lettering still proclaims that "There is no God but Allah".

The Salón del Almirante

It's a good idea to look round the **Salón del Almirante** (or Casa de la Contración de Indias), the sixteenth-century building on the right, before entering the main palace. Founded by Isabel in 1503 as an office where personnel could be hired to man expeditions to the New World, this gives you a standard against which to assess the Moorish forms. Many of the early voyages were planned in the first room, the **Cuarto del Almirante**, a name that commemorates Columbus's appointment as Gran Almirante (Senior Admiral), although he probably never used it. Balboa, discoverer of the Pacific, Vincente Pinzón, discoverer of the Amazon, and many other *conquistadores* all spread their maps across tables here and planned the plunder of the Americas. Most of the rooms seem too heavy, their decoration ceasing to be an integral part of the design, and much of the time many of them are closed to public view – as is the whole of the upper floor (except for periodic visits, see below), which provides the residence of the royal family when staying in Sevilla. The only notable exception, architecturally speaking, is the **Sala de Audiencias** (or Capilla de los Navigantes), with its magnificent *artesonado* ceiling inlaid with golden rosettes. Within is a fine early sixteenth-century *retablo* by Alejo Fernández depicting the *Virgin of the Navigators* spreading her protective mantle over the *conquistadores* and their ships – which are so well portrayed that they have been of great assistance to naval historians. Columbus (dressed in gold) is flanked by the Pinzón brothers who sailed with him on his first voyage to the New World, while Carlos V (in a red cloak) shelters beneath the Virgin. In the rear to the left are the kneeling figures of the Indians to whom the dubious blessings of Christianity had been brought by the Spanish conquest. The painting synthesizes the sense of a divine mission – given to Spain by God – prevalent at the time. Beside the altarpiece stands a model of the *Santa María*, Columbus's first flagship. Slightly further along the patio to the right lies the entrance to the **Sala de los Azulejos** containing a display of relatively modern tilework and, beyond, a couple of delightfully serene patios.

The royal apartments, known as the **Palacio Real Alto**, have now been opened for visits when not in use and shouldn't be missed. A temporary desk located in front of the Salón del Almirante sells tickets (an additional €3) for a guided tour lasting about thirty minutes. This takes in the royal chapel, with an exquisite early sixteenth-century **retablo** consisting of painted *azulejos* by Nicola Pisano, the so-called bedroom of Pedro I, with fine early Mudéjar plasterwork and *artesonado* ceiling, and the equally splendid **Sala de Audiencias** – with more stunning plaster and tile decoration – which is still used by the royal family when receiving visitors in Sevilla.

The Palace of Pedro I

Entering the main **Palace of Pedro I**, the "domestic" nature of Moorish and Mudéjar architecture is immediately striking. This involves no loss of grandeur but simply a shift in scale: the apartments are remarkably small, shaped to human needs, and take their beauty from the exuberance of the decoration and the imaginative use of space and light. There is, too, a deliberate disorientation in the layout of the rooms which makes the palace seem infinitely larger and more open than it really is. From the entrance court a narrow passage leads beyond the **Vestibulo**, where visitors removed their outer clothing, straight into the central courtyard, the **Patio de las Doncellas** (Patio of the Maidens), its name recalling the Christians' tribute of one hundred virgins presented annually to the Moorish kings. The heart of the patio has recently been restored to its fourteenth-century original state after being buried under a tiled pavement for four centuries. Archeologists have replanted the six orange trees that once grew in sunken gardens to either side of a central pool, filled with goldfish – as it was in the time of Pedro I – a medieval way of eliminating mosquitos in summer. The court's plaster frieze and dado composed of polychrome *azulejos* (tiles) and doors are all of the highest Granada craftsmanship, and are the finest in the palace. Interestingly, it's also the one location where Renaissance restorations are successfully fused – the double columns and upper storey were added by Carlos V, whose *Plus Ultra* ("Yet still further") motto recurs in the decorations here and elsewhere.

Past the **Salón de Carlos V**, distinguished by a truly magnificent *artesonado* ceiling, are three rooms from the original fourteenth-century design built for María de Padilla (who was popularly thought to use magic in order to

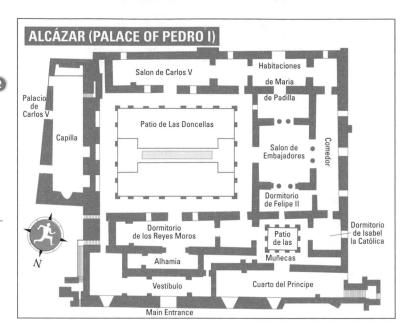

ALCÁZAR (PALACE OF PEDRO I)

Salon de Carlos V

Habitaciones de Maria de Padilla

Palacio de Carlos V

Capilla

Patio de Las Doncellas

Salon de Embajadores

Comedor

Dormitorio de Felipe II

Dormitorio de los Reyes Moros

Patio de las Muñecas

Dormitorio de Isabel la Católica

Alhamia

Vestibulo

Cuarto del Principe

Main Entrance

N

maintain her hold over Pedro – and perhaps over other gallants at court, too, who used to drink her bath water). These open onto the **Salón de Embajadores** (Salon of the Ambassadors), the most brilliant room of the Alcázar, with a stupendous wooden dome of red, green and gold cells, and horseshoe arcades inspired by the great palace of Medina Azahara outside Córdoba. An inscription in Arabic states that it was constructed by craftsmen from Toledo and completed in 1366. Although restored, for the worse, by Carlos V – who added balconies and an incongruous frieze of royal portraits to commemorate his marriage to Isabel of Portugal here – the salon stands comparison with the great rooms of Granada's Alhambra. Note also the original **Mudéjar tiles**, with their Moorish geometric patterns expressing artistically the fundamental Islamic tenet of the harmony of creation. Adjoining are a long dining hall (*comedor*) and a small apartment installed in the late sixteenth century for Felipe II.

Beyond is the last great room of the palace, the **Patio de las Muñecas** (Patio of the Dolls), which takes its curious name from two tiny faces decorating the inner and outer surfaces of one of the smaller arches. The elegant columns in the tenth-century Caliphate style are believed to have come from the ruins of Medina Azahara near Córdoba. Thought to be the site of the harem in the original palace, it was here that Pedro is reputed to have murdered his brother Don Fadrique in 1358; another of his royal guests, Abu Said of Granada, was murdered here for his jewels, one of which, an immense ruby which Pedro later gave to Edward, the "Black Prince", now figures in the British Crown Jewels. The upper storey of the court is a much later, nineteenth-century restoration. On the other sides of the patio are the **bedrooms** of Isabel and of her son Don Juan, and the arbitrarily named Dormitorio del los Reyes Moros (Bedroom of the Moorish Kings).

Palacio de Carlos V and the Alcázar gardens

To the east of the main palace (and reached via a stairway out of the southeast corner of the Patio de las Doncellas) loom the large and soulless apartments of the **Palacio de Carlos V**. Something of an endurance test, with endless tapestries (eighteenth-century copies of the sixteenth-century originals now in Madrid) and pink-orange or yellow paintwork, the apartments' classical style asserts a different and inferior mood. It's best to hurry through to the beautiful and relaxing **Alcázar gardens**, the rambling but enticing product of several eras. Here are the vaulted baths in which María de Padilla was supposed to have bathed (actually an auxiliary water supply for the palace), and the **Estanque del Mercurio**, a pool with a bronze figure of the messenger of the gods at its centre, specially built for Felipe V (1733), who whiled away two solitary years at the Alcázar fishing here and preparing himself for death through religious flagellation. In the gardens proper – and close to an unusual **maze** of myrtle bushes – lies the **pavilion** (*pabellón*) **of Carlos V**, the only survivor of several he built in the gardens. This one, designed by Juan Hernández, was completed in 1543 and has the king's motto *Plus Ultra* displayed on the tiles of the steps leading to the pavilion's entrance.

The gardens are a spacious and tranquil haven to escape the crowds – particularly the Jardín Inglés on the southwest side – and make an ideal place for a picnic. A **cafetería** can be reached via the Puerta de Marchena, to the left of the Estanque del Mercurio, which has a pleasant terrace overlooking the gardens. The way out is via the **Apeadero**, a large coach hall built for Philip V in the eighteenth century, which housed not only the coaches used by the royals, but also legions of servants who slept on the floor. Beyond lies the impressive **Patio de las Banderas** (Patio of the Flags) edged with orange trees and until fairly recently the parade ground of the military barracks surrounding it, now luxury apartments. The flags of the various regiments were assembled here and reviewed by the king prior to battle. Exit from this square to the street, where you emerge on the edge of the Barrio Santa Cruz.

The Barrio Santa Cruz

The **Barrio Santa Cruz** is very much in character with Sevilla's romantic image, its streets narrow and tortuous to keep out the sun, the houses brilliantly whitewashed and festooned with flowering plants. Many of the windows are barricaded with *rejas* (iron grilles) behind which girls once kept chaste evening rendezvous with their *novios* who were forced to *comer hierro* ("eat iron") as passion mounted. Almost all of the houses have patios, often surprisingly large, and in summer these become the principal family living room. Most of the time they can be admired from the street beyond the wrought-iron screen inside the doorway, something the residents don't appear to mind. One of the most beautiful is within the Baroque **Hospital de los Venerables Sacerdotes** (guided tours daily 10am–1.30pm & 4–7.30pm; €4.75), near the centre in a plaza of the same name. Built around the patio and originally a home for infirm clerics, the hospice and church now form a gallery of outstanding artworks. These include **sculptures** by Montañés, Pedro and Luisa Roldán, a painting of the *Last Supper* by Roelas, plus some wonderfully restored **frescoes** by Lucás Valdés and Valdés Leal.

Hotel Alfonso XIII to the Museo Arqueológico

South of the cathedral stand a number of buildings of note: the **Hotel Alfonso XIII**, the **Palacio de San Telmo** and the **Fábrica de Tabacos**, the city's old

A walk around the Barrio Santa Cruz

The Barrio Santa Cruz is a great place for a stroll with no set route to follow. The following **walk** highlights just a few of the *barrio*'s many features.

Starting out from Plaza Virgen de los Reyes, behind the cathedral, the **Palacio Arzobispal** (free access to its patio if open) conceals, behind a Baroque facade, a remarkable staircase made entirely of jasper. Along c/Mateos Gago, *Bar Giralda*, at no. 2, incorporates part of a Moorish *hammam* or steam baths, while over the road and up a bit, at no. 20, is one of Sevilla's institutions, the hole-in-the-wall **bodega of Juan García Aviles**, with its prized gleaming bar counter of Spanish mahogany, well over a century old and one of the few remaining in the city. Juan García passed away in 1996, and the bar has been retitled *Bar La Goleta*, but otherwise it remains as its original owner left it and locals have fixed a plaque to the exterior honouring Juan García's memory and his service to the community. When you've downed a *manzanilla*, continue east and turn right into c/Mesón del Moro where the slightly incongruous *San Marco Pizzeria*, at no. 4, is another establishment operating inside a splendid **Moorish bathhouse**. Further up c/Mateos Gago, a left turn will bring you into c/Guzmán El Bueno where, at no. 10, the charming sisters at the **Convento de San José** will allow you to view some remarkable Mudéjar plaster decoration (its ornate appearance is on a par with the Alcázar) in what was the salon, and is now the chapel, of this former fourteenth-century palace. This street is an especially good one for patio hunting – no. 4, with its plants, *azulejos*, wall-mounted bulls' heads and Roman statuary, is particularly beautiful.

Retracing your steps and following c/Mesón del Moro will bring you – via c/Ximénez de Enciso (a left and then a right) – to c/Santa Teresa where, at no. 8, you'll find the **Casa Murillo** (currently closed for refurbishment). Located in the artist's seventeenth-century home, this house-museum is furnished with contemporaneous artworks, craftsmanship and furniture, but, somewhat disappointingly, none of Murillo's original paintings.

Continuing along this street – note the old grindstones sunk into the wall on the left – will bring you to the delightful **Plaza Santa Cruz** where, until the French burned it down in 1810, stood the church which gave the square (and the *barrio*)

tobacco factory that was also the setting for Bizet's *Carmen*. Further south, but still just ten minutes from the Giralda, lies the **Plaza de España** and adjoining **Parque de María Luisa** (María Luisa park) – laid out in 1929 for an abortive "Fair of the Americas" they are among the most impressive public spaces in Spain. Within the park the **Museo Arqueológico** houses Andalucía's most important archeological collection.

Hotel Alfonso XIII and Palacio de San Telmo

The **Hotel Alfonso XIII**, Sevilla's grandest, is worth a look inside – no one minds as long as you aren't dressed too outrageously. Named after the ill-starred monarch Alfonso XIII who was forced to abdicate soon afterwards, it was built to house important guests attending the 1929 exhibition, and an elegant neo-Baroque facade conceals one of the city's most beautiful patios, best enjoyed over a afternoon tea.

Slightly west of here, the **Palacio de San Telmo** (visits by appointment only; ring ☎95 503 35 00), built as a marine training academy for the Indies fleet and completed in 1734, is another expression of Sevilla's full-tilt Baroque period. During the mid-nineteenth century, it was purchased by the dukes of Montpensier, a member of whose family – the dowager duchess María Luisa – in 1893 presented part of the palace's vast grounds to the city, which became the

its name and in which Murillo was buried. The French consulate appears to see no irony in occupying a building directly overlooking the scene of Napoleonic devastation. The attractive seventeenth-century cross, circled by rose bushes, marks the centre of the original church and was placed here when the plaza was created in 1918. Of three possible directions from here a route east (along calles Mezquita and Doncellas) would bring you to the ancient Gothic-Baroque church of **Santa María La Blanca**, on the street of the same name, which has, built into its south wall in c/de los Archeros, the entrance to the original synagogue, the only surviving architectural remnant of the Jewish quarter. The church's main portal is flanked by Visigothic columns probably from a church pre-dating both the synagogue and the Moorish period, while the interior has lots of *azulejos* from Triana as well as an extravagant filigree stucco ceiling and two artistic gems: a moving *Piedad* (pietà) by the sixteenth-century artist Luís de Vargas, and a stunning *Last Supper* by Murillo, the latter a rare tenebrist work.

In the next street along from the church on the right heading north, the tiny c/Dos Hermanas has, at no. 7, the *Casas de la Judería* hotel – a restored *casa señorial* formerly the residence of the dukes of Bejar – whose beautiful patio is worth a look, perhaps over a drink from the bar. Directly south from Plaza de Santa Cruz are the **Jardines de Murillo**, another peaceful oasis and a place to get your breath back in the midst of shady arbours decorated with Triana tiles. Alternatively, the Callejón del Agua will take you west back towards the town centre where, at no. 6, the **Corral del Agua** restaurant has yet another fine patio quickly followed by the sweet, plant-bedecked c/Pimienta (Pepper Street), thought to take its name from a Jewish spice merchant who once lived here. Turn right along here, at the end turning right again to reach the Plaza de los Venerables where, if you didn't want see the artworks inside the *Hospital de los Venerables*, you could visit the celebrated tapas bars on the plaza, the *Hostería del Laurel* and the *Casa Román*. Otherwise, heading north and then west along c/Jamerdana and the Pasaje Vila returns you to the c/Mateos Gago, just before which (on the tiny c/Rodrigo Caro) there's the *Bodega Santa Cruz*, another – and cheaper – Sevilla tapas institution.

park now named after her. The palace's main facade overlooks Avenida de Roma and has a marvellous Churrigueresque entrance arch topped – in a central niche – by San Telmo (of St Elmo's fire fame), patron saint of navigators.

Nearby, on the northeast side of the Puerta de Jerez traffic junction – a name referring to its former importance as one of the twenty gates in the city's ancient walls – on the corner of c/San Gregorio, lies the small former mosque and now chapel of **Santa María de Jesús**. Converted into a Christian church in 1248, it was frequently visited by Columbus on his trips to the city.

Antigua Fábrica de Tabacos

The **Old Tobacco Factory**, just behind the *Hotel Alfonso XIII* along Avenida San Fernando, was where Carmen – in the nineteenth-century story by Mérimée made into an opera by Bizet – worked as a cigar maker. A beautiful and sensual *gitana,* she falls in love with Don José, a corporal, who deserts his regiment to join her band of smugglers. When Carmen tires of him and transfers her affections to the toreador Escamillo, an insanely jealous Don José stabs her to death outside the bullring where a statue of "Carmen" now stands. Legions of foreign travellers have made pilgrimages to Sevilla in search of their own Carmen. The disillusion of the 1930s Irish traveller Walter Starkie is typical: he said that he had never seen "an uglier collection of women in my life", and was then hounded out of the workshops with a chorus of obscene abuse.

Now part of the university and only open during term time, this massive structure – 250m long by 180m wide – was built in the 1750s and still retains its position as the largest building in Spain after El Escorial. Above the main entrance – facing c/San Fernando – perches a marble angel, a trumpet to its lips, which malicious popular legend has it would only sound when a virgin entered the factory for the first time. The entrance arch below aptly incorporates medallion busts of Columbus (discoverer of the tobacco lands) and Cortés (reputedly Europe's first smoker) – in effect the factory's founding fathers.

The building was divided into residential quarters below with the work areas on the upper – and lighter – level. The entrance leads through a vestibule into the Clock Patio (with fountain) off which, to the left, lies the university's **cafetería,** open to all and offering a wide range of food at budget prices. At its peak in the nineteenth century the factory was also the country's largest single employer, with a workforce of some 10,000 women *cigarreras* – "a class in themselves" according to Richard Ford, and forced to undergo "an ingeniously minute search on leaving their work, for they sometimes carry off the filthy weed in a manner her most Catholic majesty never dreamt of". Production of cigars, cigarettes and snuff – originally ground by 200 donkey-driven rolling mills – continued here until 1965 when its operations were moved to a new factory across the river close to the Puente de Los Remedios.

The Plaza de España and Parque de María Luisa

The **Plaza de España** lies beyond the Avenida del Cid – the latter, incidentally, the site of the Inquisition's *quemadero*, or burning platform, where for three hundred years convicted heretics were put to death; the last witch was burned here in 1781. The vast semicircular complex was designed as the centrepiece of the Spanish Americas Fair which was somewhat scuppered by the Wall Street Crash abroad and political upheavals at home. Designed by Anibal González with theatrical towers, sprinkling fountains, majestic stairways and masses of brick and tile work, its flamboyance would seem strange in most Spanish cities but here it looks entirely natural, carrying on the great tradition of civic display. At the fair, the Plaza de España was used for the Spanish exhibit of industry and crafts, and around the crescent are *azulejo* scenes and maps of each of the provinces: an interesting record of the country at the tail-end of a monied era.

Locals and tourists alike come out to the plaza – crumbling for years but finally undergoing refurbishment – to potter about in the little boats rented out on its tiny strip of canal, or to hide from the sun and crowds amid the ornamental pools and tree-shaded avenues and walkways of the **Parque de María Luisa**. The park is designed, like the plaza, in a mix of 1920s Art Deco and mock-Mudéjar. Scattered about, and round its edge, are more buildings from the fair, some of them amazingly opulent, built in the last months before the Wall Street Crash undercut the scheme's impetus – look out, in particular, for the stylish **Argentina building**, off the Avenida de la Palmera.

The Museo Arqueológico and Museo de Costumbres Populares

Towards the southern end of the park, the grandest mansions from the fair have been adapted as museums, of which the **Museo Arqueológico** (Tues 3–8pm, Wed–Sat 9am–8pm, Sun 9am–2pm; €1.50, free with EU passport) is the most important of its kind in Andalucía. The collection's wide remit, divided among twenty-seven rooms on two floors, spans the period from prehistory to the end of the Moorish age.

Starting in the basement with the prehistoric sections, Room 4 displays a collection of funerary stelae from the Iberian period, while a darkened Room 6 has a unique eighth-century BC bronze **statuette of Astarte-Tanit**, the Phoenician fertility goddess once worshipped throughout the Mediterranean. This room also contains the stunning **Carambolo Treasures** discovered in the Sevilla suburb of Camas in 1958. This remarkable hoard of gold jewellery further fuelled the debate surrounding the whereabouts and existence of the ancient land of Tartessus, known to the Greeks and mentioned in the Bible as Tarshish. The legendary mineral wealth of Tartessus probably indicates a location in the area between Sevilla and the mineral-rich

△ Plaza de España

hills of Huelva, but despite investigations by archeologists for most of the last hundred or so years it has never been found.

Rooms 11 to 24 on the ground floor contain the substance of the **Roman** collection with an interesting display of kitchen equipment in Room 13, including what appears to be a modern-looking fork contradicting the theory that the implement was a medieval invention. The same room also has a fine third-century mosaic from Écija, depicting the god Bacchus being transported on a chariot drawn by tigers. In Room 17 there's a sensitive, second-century **sculpture of Venus** from Itálica, which was imported from Greece. There's yet more statuary in rooms 19 and 20, as well as portrait busts of the emperors Augustus and Nero and local boys Trajan and Hadrian, the latter particularly striking. In a small room off Room 19 you'll find a number of remarkable **bronze plaques** inscribed with the "Lex Irnitana", a rare set of laws illustrating how the Romans – the inventors of jurisprudence – went about ruling their empire. The laws make a fascinating read but are sadly translated only into Spanish. Rubric 72 of the code deals with the freeing of public slaves whilst number 82 relates to the upkeep of roads, tracks, irrigation channels, drains and sewers, all vital to the Roman way of life. The laws are sanctioned by the despotic emperor Domitian, whose name appears at the end of the document

Boat trips on the Río Guadalquivir

A great way to get a different view of Sevilla is to take a **boat trip on the Guadalquivir**. Cruceros Turísticos (T 95 456 16 92, W www.crucerostorredeloro.com) have a quayside office below the Torre del Oro and run an hour-long cruise (every 30min daily 11am–9pm; €14) which takes in all the major riverside sights, including a view of the *Expo 92* site. On Saturdays (May–Oct) they also run a scenic downriver cruise to **Sanlúcar de Barrameda** (see p.263), leaving the Torre del Oro at 8.30am (€27 round-trip). The cruise docks at 1pm at Sanlúcar's Bajo de Guía with its outstanding fish restaurants. A bus departing at 5.30pm returns you to Sevilla, arriving around 7pm. Their **Crucero de Noche** (May–Oct daily 10.15pm; €26.50) cruises the river by night with an on-board fiesta, including an orchestra, entertainers and as much free *sangría* as you can swallow.

To do the river under your own steam, **pedalos** (pedal boats; €8 per hr) can be hired from Acuaterraza (daily noon until sunset; mobile T 679194045) on the east bank of the river near the Puente de Isabel II. They also hire out rowing boats, canoes and motor boats.

dated April 10, 91 AD. A portrait bust of Domitian is displayed in Room 20. Finally, Rooms 26 and 27 display post-Roman finds including early Christian tombstones and Mudéjar ceramic works, among which a fifteenth-century green-glazed **baptismal font** stands out.

Opposite is the fabulous-looking **Museo de Costumbres Populares** (Popular Arts Museum; Tues 3–8pm, Wed–Sat 9am–8.30pm, Sun 9am–2pm; €1.50, free with EU passport) with, inside, an equally fine patio which, despite displays of costumes, implements, furniture, photos and posters describing life in eighteenth- and nineteenth-century Andalucía, feels a bit lifeless. The basement ceramics displays are the highlight, illustrating the regional developments of this craft inherited from the Moors. In spring there are also special exhibitions devoted to Semana Santa and the April *feria*.

Along the river to the Museo de Bellas Artes

Down by the **Río Guadalquivir** the main riverside landmark is the twelve-sided **Torre del Oro** (Tower of Gold), built by the Almohads in 1220 as part of the Alcázar fortifications. It was connected to another small fort across the river by a chain which had to be broken by the Castilian fleet before their conquest of the city in 1248. The tower later saw use as a repository for the gold brought back to Sevilla from the Americas; hence its name. It now houses a small, mildly interesting **naval museum** (Tues–Fri 10am–2pm, Sat & Sun 11am–2pm; €1, free with EU passport), which exhibits charts and engravings of the port in its prime.

The Hospital de la Caridad

One block east of the Torre del Oro is the **Hospital de la Caridad** (Mon–Sat 9am–1.30pm & 3.30–7.30pm, Sun 9am–1pm; €4, W www.santa-caridad.org; entry on c/Temprado), founded in 1674 by Don Miguel de Mañara, who may well have been the inspiration for Byron's Don Juan. According to the testimony of one of Don Miguel's friends, "there was no folly which he did not commit, no youthful indulgence into which he did not plunge . . . (until) what occurred to him in the street of the coffin". What occurred was that Don Miguel, returning from a wild orgy, had a vision in which he was confronted by a funeral procession carrying his own corpse. He repented his past life, joined the Brotherhood of Charity (whose task was to bury the bodies of vagrants and criminals), and later set up this hospital for the relief of the dying and destitute, for which it is still used. Touchingly, whenever a patient dies here, the chapel is closed on the day of the funeral.

Between 1670 and 1674 Don Miguel commissioned a series of eleven paintings by **Murillo** for the chapel, seven of which remain after Marshal Soult looted four of them during the Napoleonic occupation. Murillo always created pictures "made to measure" for the available light, and it's a real treat to see the pictures in the place they were originally intended to hang. Among the surviving works are a colossal *Loaves and Fishes* depicting Christ feeding the Five Thousand, and "a *San Juan de Dios* equal to Rembrandt" as Richard Ford, a fervent Murillo fan, described it. Mañara himself posed as the model for the saint. Alongside them hang two *Triumph of Death* pictures by Valdés Leal. One, portraying the fleeting nature of life, features a skeletal image of Death pointing to the message *in ictu oculi* ("in the blink of an eye"), while the other depicts a decomposing bishop being eaten by worms (beneath the scales of justice labelled *Ni más, Ni menos* – "No More, No Less"). Murillo found this so repulsive that he declared "you have to hold your nose to look at it". The mood of both works may owe a lot to the vivid memory of the 1649 plague that killed almost half the population of the city. The main altar's **retablo** features a superlative *Burial of Christ* carved by Pedro Roldán, and the steps to the left of this descend to a crypt where Mañara is buried.

As you're leaving the Caridad, look out for the **Torre de Plata** (Tower of Silver), a castellated Moorish watchtower, at c/Santander 13. Now visible from just inside a car park, it probably got its name to correspond with the nearby Torre del Oro, although there is no evidence to suggest that it was once coated with silver tiles or was ever a silver store, as local legends have it.

Plaza de Toros de la Maestranza and around

The **Maestranza bullring** (daily 9.30am–7pm, fight days 9.30am–3pm; €4) is the most famous and, for aficionados, the most beautiful bullring in the world. It was completed in the latter half of the eighteenth century to provide a home

Murillo in all his glory

Born in Sevilla in 1618 and orphaned ten years later, **Bartolomé Esteban Murillo** grew up in the home of his brother-in-law. After enrolling as a student under Juan de Castillo he came to the attention of another *sevillano*, Velázquez, who was by then established in Madrid. Murillo studied with Velázquez for three not very happy years in the capital, where he found the social scene oppressive, but was apparently much impressed by the works of the Flemish and Italian schools he saw in the royal collections there.

Once back in his native city Murillo started work in earnest, often using poor *sevillanos* from districts such as La Macarena as his models. In 1682, still at the height of his powers, he was painting an altarpiece for the Capuchin church in Cádiz when he fell from the scaffold, suffering serious injury. He was brought back to Sevilla where he died in the Convent of San José near to his home in the Barrio Santa Cruz.

Downgraded by critics in the nineteenth century for his sentimentalism – a view largely based on the genre paintings of rosy-faced urchins that had found their way across Europe – Murillo's reputation has since been restored. A greater familiarity with the powerful works that remained in Sevilla, such as those in the Caridad, substantiates Ford's proclamation: "At Sevilla Murillo is to be seen in all his glory ... a giant on his native soil."

for the Real Maestranza de Caballería (Royal Equestrian Society). Altered subsequently, it is still one of the finest in Spain and has featured in numerous novels, poems and films – most enduringly in *Carmen*, the opera by Bizet. Once inside the arena, you will see a metal frame in the roof holding a furled canvas. On fight days this is unfurled – not to give spectators more shade but to temper the wind, which often whips up over the river causing the capes of the *matadores* to behave in unpredictable and possibly dangerous ways. The Maestranza's **museum** has the usual posters, prints, photographs and memorabilia. A monument to "Carmen" (see p.311) stands opposite the entrance to the bullring, across the road near the river.

Three blocks downriver – with a dome that's hard to miss – is the new **Teatro de la Maestranza** concert hall and opera house. Built as part of the *Expo 92* improvements, it incorporates the remains of the Artillería ammunition works which previously occupied the site. The rather dominating and uninspired design caused much controversy when it was unveiled because of its detrimental effect on the magnificent view of the city from across the river.

The Museo de Bellas Artes

To the north of c/Reyes Católicos, on the Plaza del Museo and fronted by a formidable bronze statue of Murillo, the **Museo de Bellas Artes** (Tues 2.30–8.30pm, Wed–Sat 9am–8.30pm, Sun 9am–2.30pm; €1.50, free with EU passport), housed in recently modernized galleries in a startlingly beautiful former convent, the Convento de la Merced, ranks second in Spain only to the Prado in Madrid. Founded in the thirteenth century by Fernando III after Sevilla had been taken from the Moors, the building was subsequently remodelled and reached its present form in the eighteenth century. The convent lost most of its own commissioned paintings during the nineteenth-century Disentailment when it was secularized, and it opened as a museum in 1838. You should be aware that the museum has a policy of rotating its collection and not all the works mentioned here may be exhibited. A Sunday morning **art market** takes place in the plaza fronting the museum where local artists and craftworkers sell their work. It starts around 9am and lasts until 3pm.

The downstairs galleries

Among the highlights of an outstanding collection is a wonderful late fifteenth-century sculpture in painted terracotta in Room 1, *Lamentation over the Dead Christ*, by the *andaluz* **Pedro Millán**, founding father of the Sevilla school of sculpture. A marriage of Gothic and expressive naturalism, this style was the starting point for the outstanding seventeenth-century period of religious iconography in Sevilla – a later example, in Room 2, is a magnificent *San Jerónimo* by the Italian **Pietro Torrigiano**, who spent the latter years of his life in Sevilla. Ever his own man, Torrigiano once broke the nose of his contemporary Michelangelo in a quarrel and eventually died at the hands of the Inquisition in Sevilla, condemned for impiety after he had smashed his own sculpture of a Virgin when the duke of Arcos refused to pay the price asked. His *Virgen de Belén* here is another powerful work. This room also has **El Greco**'s portrait of his son, *Jorge Manuel Theotokopoulos*.

Room 3 has a *retablo* of the Redemption, c.1562, with fine woodcarving by Juan Giralte. Originally made for the Convento de Santa Catalina in Aracena, tableaux 6 (the crowning with thorns) and 10 (Mark writing his gospel) are especially fine. There's also a **Velázquez** work here, a portrait of *Don Cristóbal Suarez de Ribera* produced in his teens, betraying sure signs of the master's touch as well as an unparalleled ability to illuminate his figures from within.

A monumental *Last Supper* by **Alonso Vásquez** painted for the monastery of La Cartuja covers an end wall of Room 4, while the grisly terracotta sculpture of the severed head of *John the Baptist* by **Núñez Delgado** may not be something you want to see too soon after lunch. Dated 1591, this work is a prototype of the Baroque images later carried on the *pasos* during Semana Santa. This room also has works by **Pachecho**, one of the protagonists of the Mannerist school and the father-in-law and tutor of Velázquez. His series of canvases for the Convento de la Merced (this building) is represented here by images of *San Pedro* and *San Ramón Nonato*.

Beyond a serene patio and cloister, Room 5 is located in the monastery's former church. The recently restored **paintings on the vault and dome** by the eighteenth-century *sevillano*, Domingo Martínez, are spectacular. Here also is the nucleus of the collection: **Zurbarán's** *Apotheosis of St Thomas Aquinas* as well as a clutch of **Murillos** in the apse crowned by the great *Immaculate Conception* – known as "la colosal" to distinguish it from the other work here with the same name. In an alcove nearby you'll see the same artist's *Virgin and Child*. Popularly known as **La Servilleta** because it was said to have been painted on a dinner napkin, the work is one of Murillo's greatest. In the same room are more Murillos and also works by the early seventeenth-century *sevillano* **Roelas**, including a magnificent *Martirio de San Andrés*.

The upstairs galleries

Room 6 (quadrated around the patio) displays works from the Baroque period, among which a moving *Santa Teresa* by **Ribera** – Spain's master of *tenebrismo* (darkness penetrated by light) – and a stark *Crucifixión* by **Zurbarán** stand out. Room 7 is devoted to Murillo and his school and has a superb *San Agustín y la Trinidad* by the master. In Room 8, eighteenth-century *sevillano* **Valdés Leal** symbolizes the city's enduring fascination with agony and mortality: his depiction of *Fray Juan de Ledesma* wrestling with the devil disguised as a serpent has the brooding intensity of much of his work. There's more sculpture in Room 10, this time by the sixteenth-century **Martínez Montañés**, whose early *Saint Dominic in Penitence* and *San Bruno* from his mature period display mastery of technique. This room also contains works from the **European Baroque**, among which there's an outstanding *La Adoración de los Pastores* (Adoration of the Shepherds) by the Flemish painter Pieter Van Lint and an *Adoración de los Reyes* (Adoration of the Kings) by his compatriot Cornelis de Vos, both connected with the school of Rubens. Also here are more imposing canvases by **Zurbarán**: San Hugo visiting the Carthusian monks at supper (*San Hugo in the Refectory*), *The Visit of San Bruno* to Pope Urban II and the *Virgen de los Cartujos* were all painted for the monastery of La Cartuja across the river. There's also another almost sculptural *Crucifixión* to compare with his earlier one in Room 6.

The collection ends with works from the Romantic and Modern eras where an austere late work by **Goya**, in Room 11, of the octogenarian *Don José Duaso* compensates for some not terribly inspiring works accompanying it. There's also a portrait of the incompetent and indolent ruler *Alfonso XIII* painted in 1929 by Gonzalo Bilbao which tells you all you need to know about this monarchical disaster. The same artist has more works in Room 12 – his *Las Cigarreras* is a vivid portrayal of the wretched life of women in the tobacco factory during the early years of the last century. Room 14 has an evocative image of *Sevilla en Fiestas* dated 1915 by Gustavo Bacarisas and a monumental canvas by José Villegas Cordero, *La Muerte del Maestro*, depicting the death of a *torero*. Purchased by the Junta de Andalucía in 1996, this work serves to underline the continuing importance of the *corrida* in Andalucía's life and culture.

El Centro

El Centro, or central zone, lies north of the cathedral at the geographical heart of the city. It contains the main shopping areas, including **Calle Sierpes**, the city's most fashionable street. Here, too, you'll find many of Sevilla's finest churches, displaying a fascinating variety of architectural styles. Several are converted mosques with belfries built over their minarets, others range through Mudéjar and Gothic (sometimes in combination), Renaissance and Baroque. Most are kept locked except early in the morning, or in the evenings from about 7 until 10pm – a promising time for a church crawl, especially as they're regularly interspersed with tapas bars.

The Casa de Pilatos

Of Sevilla's numerous mansions, by far the finest is the so-called **Casa de Pilatos** (daily 9am–7pm, Oct–Feb closes 5pm; €5 ground floor only, both floors €8, Tues 1–5pm free) in the Plaza de Pilatos, on the northwestern edge of Santa Cruz. Built by the marqués de Tarifa of the Ribera family on his return from a pilgrimage to Jerusalem in 1519, the house was popularly – and erroneously – thought to have been an imitation of the house of Pontius Pilate, supposedly seen by the duke on his travels. In fact it's a harmonious mixture of Mudéjar, Gothic and Renaissance styles, featuring brilliant *azulejos*, a tremendous sixteenth-century stairway and the best domestic patios in the city. After the Civil War the dukes of Medinaceli returned to live here and inaugurated a programme of restoration which has gradually brought the house back to its original splendour.

Entering by the Apeadero (refer to the plan on the back of your ticket), where the old carriages were boarded, and which for most of the year is a riot of magenta bougainvillea, brings you to a gateway leading into the wonderful **Patio Principal**. Here, Muslim elements such as the irregular arches, plaster work and glazed tiles combine with Gothic tracery on the upper balustrades and an Italian Renaissance fountain and columns below. The imposing statues in each corner of the patio are classical originals, of which the **Athene** (bearing a spear) is attributed to the fifth-century BC school of the Greek master, Phidias; the others are Roman. Antique Italian busts of Roman emperors and men of letters such as Trajan, Hadrian and Cicero occupy niches in the arcades.

The **Salón Pretorio** is notable for its coffered ceiling, incorporating the Ribera family's coat of arms. The Roman sculptures – collected in Italy by the sixteenth-century duke of Alcalá – in the nearby Zaquizamí corridor are extremely fine, especially the slumbering Venus and a marble relief fragment, depicting weapons, above. Passing the Jardín Chico (Small Garden), the Chapel of the Flagellation (its central column is supposed to represent the one at which Christ was scourged) and Pilate's "study", you reach the **Jardín Grande**, a verdant oasis with palms, pavilions and a bower, not to mention a wonderful abundance of orange trees. A tradition associated with this garden relates that the first duke of Alcalá obtained from Pope Pius V the ashes of the emperor Trajan, which were then displayed in a vase in the library. Later, a servant is supposed to have dumped them in the garden thinking the urn to be full of dust. The legend grew that an orange tree sprouted up wherever the ashes had fallen.

The **upper floors** (still partly inhabited by the Medinaceli family) are reached from the Patio Principal via the fine, tiled staircase with a gilded, sixteenth-century semicircular dome, but can be seen only by guided tour. The rooms are decorated with various frescoes, canvases by Goya (a tiny bullfighting scene), Ribera and Jordáns, and *objets d'art* collected by the family.

Outstanding here is the **Salón de Pachecho** with the *Apotheosis of Hercules* painted on the ceiling in 1603 by the *sevillano* artist after whom the room is named. As you leave the house, note a rather curious bust of Julius Caesar at the entrance to the toilets. It's a fine portrait and, given the wealth of artefacts the family have hauled back from classical parts, is probably a two-thousand-year-old original deserving a more seemly location.

Churches, convents and monuments in El Centro

Leaving the Casa de Pilatos, a circuit of the churches in the area will take you first via c/Caballerizas to **San Ildefonso**, a fourteenth-century church later rebuilt in the classical style. Inside, behind the altar on the north aisle, there's a **fresco of the Virgin** dating from the original building. The church also has some seventeenth-century wood sculptures by Roldán and a bas-relief, *The Trinity*, by Montañés dated 1609.

Not far away, and still heading in a more or less westerly direction, c/Boteros will bring you to **Plaza Alfalfa**, the forum of Roman Hispalis and a good place for tapas bars. A couple of blocks south of here, along c/Candilejos and c/Muñoz y Pavón, in c/Marmoles are the remains – three enormous columns known as **Los Monolitos Romanos** – once belonging to what must have been a gigantic Roman temple. Continuing north from Plaza Alfalfa, however, along calles Sales y Ferrer and Padre Llop you'll reach the Plaza del Buen Suceso on which lies the **convent** of the same name. Inside, there's a marvellous sculpture of St Anne with the Virgin by Montañés. North again, c/Velilla leads to the Gothic **San Pedro**, with a Mudéjar tower modelled on the Giralda, and where a marble tablet records Velázquez's baptism. Just behind the church on c/Dueñas, the splendid **Palacio de los Dueñas** was the birthplace (marked by a plaque) of another *andaluz* genius, the poet Antonio Machado.

A stroll west from San Pedro along c/Imagen passes the Renaissance chapel of the **Anunciación** on c/Larana, leading to c/Cuna on the left where, at no. 8, stands the eighteenth-century **Palacio Lebrija** (Mon–Fri 10am–1.30pm & 5–8pm, Sat 10am–2pm; €4 one floor, €7 both floors, ⓦwww.palaciodelebrija .com) which has a collection of Iberian and Roman antiquities and some fine Roman mosaics from Itálica built into its three ground-floor patios. A route directly north from here brings you to the tree-lined **Alameda de Hércules**, once a swamp and converted in the sixteenth century into a promenade. The southern end has two pillars taken from a Roman temple to Hercules, which give the promenade its name. Once fashionable, this area went to seed, and until recently was the city's red-light district. New bars and hotels have sprung up here of late, the skin trade has moved on, and with plans in the pipeline to turn the whole square into a pedestrianized zone the Alameda is re-emerging as a vibrant centre of *sevillano* nightlife.

West of the Alameda, on Plaza de San Lorenzo, lies the church of San Lorenzo and, next to it, the modern church of **Jesús del Gran Poder** (daily 8am–1.30pm & 6–9pm; free). In the latter's **retablo** is displayed the much venerated figure of *Jesús del Gran Poder* (Christ bearing his cross) by Juan de Mesa, carved in 1620. This image is borne in procession in the small hours of Good Friday morning.

Plaza de San Francisco and Calle Sierpes

Because of the Muslim origin of its vernacular architecture – which was designed primarily to keep out the sun – Sevilla had no great squares on the European model until relatively recently. Most of the plazas it does possess are the result of palaces and convents being torn down: some, such as the uninspiring Plaza del Duque de la Victoria, site of the *palacio* of the Guzmán family, were created as recently as the 1960s.

In the shadow of the Giralda, the **Plaza de San Francisco**, slightly north of the cathedral, takes its name from the great monastery that once covered much of this and the Plaza Nueva to the west. To the north of here you'll find the true heart of Sevilla, **Calle Sierpes**, where, according to Cervantes – who spent some involuntary time in prison here serving a sentence for his tax debts – "all the social classes of the city come together." This narrow pedestrianized street, today lined with souvenir stores, private clubs and smart *pastelerías*, is a wonderful place to stroll. It's particularly dramatic – though quite uncharacteristic – during Semana Santa, when the brotherhood of El Silencio passes through in total silence in the early hours of Good Friday, watched by an equally hushed crowd lining the route. Look out for Sevilla's most famous *pastelería*, La Campana, at no. 1 (the northern end). At no. 65 a wall plaque indicates the site of the Cárcel Real, or royal prison, where Cervantes was incarcerated. A short way down on the left, in c/Jovellanos, lies the small **Capillata de San José**, one of the best examples of full-blown Baroque in the city with a beautiful gilded *retablo*. Baroque enthusiasts will also want to detour three blocks west of here to take in the massive **Iglesia de la Magdalena**, an eighteenth-century extravaganza containing artworks by Zurbarán and Roldán, which also holds the font where Murillo was baptized. Otherwise, just behind c/Sierpes in the parallel c/Tetuan, a detour will lead you to a wonderful old tiled billboard advertising a 1924 Studebaker car. It's opposite the C&A department store.

Nearby, and to the east of c/Sierpes, the Plaza del Salvador contains the collegiate church of **San Salvador** (Mon–Sat 8.45–10am & 6.30–9pm; free), built on the site of a ninth-century – and the city's first – Friday mosque. Most of what you see today dates from the seventeenth century, with remnants of the mosque preserved in its tower, formerly the minaret, and its patio, originally the ablutions courtyard. Inside, there's a magnificent Churrigueresque **retablo** as well as a number of sculptures, among them the renowned *Jesús del Pasión* by the great master of wood sculpture, Juan Martínez Montañés, who also embellished the church's exterior and whose bronze monument in the plaza outside.

The Barrio Triana

Over the river is the **Triana** *barrio*, a scruffy, lively and not at all touristy neighbourhood, generally believed to have taken its name from the Roman emperor **Trajan** who was born at nearby Itálica. This was once the heart of the city's gypsy community and, more specifically, home of the great flamenco dynasties of Sevilla. The gypsies lived in extended families in tiny, immaculate communal houses called *corrales* around courtyards glutted with flowers; today only a handful remain intact. Triana is still, however, the starting point for the annual pilgrimage to El Rocío (at the end of May), when myriad painted wagons leave town, drawn by elephantine oxen. And one of the great moments of Semana Santa occurs here in the early hours of Good Friday when the candlelit *paso* of the Virgin *Esperanza de Triana* is carried back over the Puente de Triana (Isabel II) to be given a rapturous welcome home by the whole *barrio* assembled on the other side. Triana has long been a centre of **glazed-tile production**, and you'll see plenty of examples of this fine ceramic work as you stroll around the streets.

La Cartuja and the Expo 92 site

Across the river and reached by the Pasarela de la Cartuja (or by buses C1 or C2 from the Prado de San Sebastián bus station or the Puente de los Remedios), a pedestrian bridge constructed for Expo 92, is the fourteenth-century

△ La Cartuja

2

SEVILLA AND HUELVA | Sevilla

La Cartuja (April–Sept Mon–Fri 10am–9pm, Sat 10am–3pm; Oct–March Mon–Sat 10am–8pm, Sun 10am–3pm; €3, free on Tues with EU passport), a former Carthusian monastery.

Founded in 1399 on the site where there had been an apparition of the Virgin in some pottery workshops (*cuevas*) installed here during the Almohad era, the monastery of **Santa María de las Cuevas** was expanded by the Carthusians in the fifteenth and sixteenth centuries with donations from Sevilla's leading families. This was where Columbus lodged on his visits to Sevilla, where he planned his second voyage to the New World, and where for a few years he was buried. The core of the monastery suffered eighteenth-century Baroque additions and was made the headquarters of the notorious Marshal Soult's garrison during the Napoleonic occupation of 1810–12, when the monks were driven out and fled to Portugal. A final indignity was visited on the place when, after Disentailment in 1836, it was

A walk around the Barrio Triana

There are any number of ways to explore Triana, taking time to stop off in some of the wonderful tapas bars on the way (for details see p.333). This particular walk starts out from the Plaza de Cuba, reached by crossing the Puente de San Telmo to the river's western bank. From here head down c/Genova to the Plaza de la Virgen de la Milagrosa. In the centre of this square is a modern statue to **Rodrigo de Triana**, a sailor on Columbus's initial voyage who was the first to set eyes on the New World. In spite of his name, however, more recent research suggests that he hailed not from Triana, but Lepe, in the neighbouring province of Huelva. Determined not to be put off by this academic meddling with their history, the *barrio* erected the sculpture anyway with the laconic "Tierra" ("Land") inscribed on its base, the word an unidentified Rodrigo is presumably yelling as he clings to the mast.

Turning right along c/Troya to c/Betis which fronts the river leads you into the **old docklands area** of Triana, before it was smartened up in the earlier part of the last century and planted with trees. To the right, in c/Gonzalo Segovia, was the gunpowder factory which supplied the vessels of the Indies fleet. An enormous explosion here in 1579 not only destroyed half of Triana but also blew the stained-glass windows out of the cathedral across the river.

In Roman times, clay was collected from this riverbank to make the Amphorae used to transport cereals, wine, oil and pickled fish to the imperial capital – much of the broken pottery piled up in ancient Rome's towering rubbish dump at Monte Testaccio has now been identified as coming from Triana. The same clay also made the bricks for the Giralda and many more of the city's houses and monuments. Behind the *Río Grande* restaurant, which has great terrace views, there are **pedalos** and rowing boats for rent should you want to give the river a closer look.

Further along, a left turn at c/Duarte brings you to Triana's main church of **Santa Ana**, the oldest parish church in Sevilla. Built for Alfonso X in the thirteenth century, it includes many later additions: note, for example, the Mudéjar tower with blocked lobed windows topped by a Renaissance belfry. Should you be able to gain entry – early evening is your best bet – look out for the fine sixteenth-century **retablo** of the *Virgen de la Rosa* and the church's baptismal font – **Pila de los Gitanos** – from which, according to tradition, the gifts of flamenco singing and dancing are bestowed

purchased by a Liverpudlian, Charles Pickman, and turned into the ceramics factory it remained until 1982. The whole complex – including the towering brick kilns and chimney which can be glimpsed from outside the site, and which are now regarded as industrial history – was restored for Expo 92 at enormous cost.

The visit begins at the **Capilla de Afuera** where the chapel's gilded Baroque *retablo* has lost its central effigy of the *Virgen de las Cuevas*, a carved work in cedar and once the monastery's most venerated image. In the chapels of **Santa Catalina** and **San Bruno** (the founder of the Carthusian order) there are fine Triana tiles, and Felipe II used the latter chapel as his oratory when he visited Sevilla in 1570. Apart from a few surviving architectural fragments, the monastery's church is now bare, but maintains a serene dignity after its use as a workshop in the ceramics factory. Off it, the chapel of Santa Ana contains the **tomb of Christopher Columbus** where the navigator's bones rested for 27 years prior to beginning their travels (see p.299). Also here in wall niches are the remains of some fine polychrome tile panels depicting San Juan Evangelista and San Mateo. The **Sacristía** (currently not on view) has the mouldings made by Pedro Roldán where Zurbarán's three masterpieces, *Virgen de los Cartujos*, *San Hugo in the Refectory* and *The Visit of San Bruno to Pope Urban II* (all now

on the newborn infants of the *barrio*. Take c/Pureza (at the church's eastern end) north to no. 53, the **Capilla de los Marineros**, an eighteenth-century chapel now seat of the *Cofradía de Jesús de las Tres Caídas y Nuestra Señora de la Esperanza* (Brotherhood of Jesus of the Three Falls and Our Lady of Hope), one of the major brotherhoods who march in the Semana Santa processions. The chapel's Baroque *retablo* incorporates the figure of the Virgin known as the **Esperanza de Triana** to which the *barrio* is devoted.

Continue north, turning left along calles Rocío and Flota and then right along c/Rodrigo, crossing c/San Jacinto into c/Alfarería, where there are traditional *corrales*. A left turn a short way along here into c/Antillano Campos brings you to *Bar Anselma* (fronting c/Pages), a great old tiled place with occasional impromptu flamenco. Still heading north along c/Alfarería, take a right along c/Procurador and right again to the sixteenth-century church of **Nuestra Señora de la "O"** at c/Castilla 30, with its splendid tiled tower. The interior, as well as holding more ceramics, contains a seventeenth-century sculpture of Jesús Nazareno by Pedro Roldán.

Heading south, with the river on your left, a small alley bears the name Callejón de la Inquisición. This was the site of the former **Castillo de Triana** (Triana Castle), the original residence of the Inquisition until it was forced out by a flood in 1626 or, as Ford colourfully puts it, until "the Guadalquivir, which blushed at the fires and curdled with the bloodshed, almost swept it away as if indignant at the crimes committed on its bank". Almost opposite, *Cervecería Casa Cuesta* is a welcoming old bar with tiled interior serving good tapas. Continuing around the corner you'll come to the spectacular tiled facade of **Ceramica Santa Ana** at Plaza Callao 12. The city's oldest working ceramics factory, over a century old, this is a good place to buy hand-painted Triana pots and tiles. Continuing south brings you to **Plaza Altozano** where there are monuments to the great 1920s flamenco singer Pastora Pavón and Triana's famous *torero*, Juan Belmonte. The latter sculpture by Venancio Blanco nestles against the Puente de Triana – designed by Gustave Eiffel of "tower" fame. Before crossing the bridge back to the centre, take a look at the new market which has been cunningly constructed over **excavations** of the same Castillo de Triana. The exposed remains can be viewed beneath a reinforced glass cover with the market now on top.

in the Museo de Bellas Artes, see p.316), were originally displayed. Here also are some impressive choir stalls by Valencia and Perea dating from the early eighteenth century.

Also off the church are the elegant **Mudéjar cloister**, the centre of Carthusian community life and where there is more tile work, and the **Capítulo de Monjes** (Chapter House) with the sixteenth-century tombs of the Ribeira family and finely sculpted *retablos* made in Italy. Finally, the **refectory**, with more partially tiled walls and a tiled pulpit, retains a beautiful *artesonado* ceiling which was used by the French for target practice. The visit ends with a chance to view Pickman's enormous bottle-shaped kilns close up en route to the *huerta* (market garden) of the former monastery, which is being transformed once again into a tranquil oasis as the recently planted trees mature. Along the garden's northwest wall you can see the pumps which once drew water from the river to irrigate the garden, and from a *mirador* in the reconstructed **Casilla de Santa Justa y Rufina** there is a great **view** over the whole complex to the west, the river and city to the east and, to the north, the rather forlorn and weed-festooned site of Expo 92.

A separate building within the same complex now houses the **Centro Andaluz de Arte Contemporáneo** (same hours and ticket as La Cartuja), which stages rotating exhibitions from a large and interesting collection of contemporary work by *andaluz* artists, including canvases by Antonio Rodríguez de Luna, Joaquin Peinado, Guillermo Pérez Villalta and Daniel Vásquez Díaz whose monumental *Juan Centeno y su cuadrilla* is a striking image of the renowned *torero* and his team.

Expo 92

The staging of **Expo 92** secured a year of publicity and prosperity for Sevilla during which the sybaritic *sevillanos* started to believe their own hype, billing it as the "event of the century". After the fuss died down and the visitors departed, the city was left with a staggering debt of 60 billion pesetas (€360 million), financial scandals, endless recriminations, and a dilapidated site which no one knew what to do with. Plans to turn it into a science park came to nothing and the western side of the complex has now been split between the University of Sevilla and a technological/industrial park. Expo's artificial lake on the east side of the site has been revamped as the focus of the **Isla Mágica** amusement and theme park (April–Nov daily 11am–9pm, later in spring and autumn; €22; *Tarde* or evening-only tickets €15.50; reductions for kids; Ⓦ www.islamagica.es) with rides and attractions (included in ticket price) based on the theme of the sixteenth-century Spanish empire.

The remains of the Expo site lying beyond this and to the south of La Cartuja are mostly a hotchpotch of desolate and weed-festooned buildings, including the Navigation Pavilion celebrating Columbus's voyages, the soaring but now rusting Torre Mirador (which offers the best **view** in the city) plus gimmicks such as the monorail and the Omnimax giant cine screen. Currently closed to the public for some years after the company which took them over went bust and closed down, these may once again be open to visitors if the site finds a new buyer. Should you decide to walk back to the city via the Pasarela de la Cartuja footbridge across the river, look out upstream for the spectacular **Puente de la Barqueta**, another hugely extravagant Expo innovation connecting the city to La Cartuja. Designed by renowned architect Santiago Calatrava, its taut suspension cables resemble the strings of an elongated lyre.

The Barrio Macarena

"The **Macarena**, now as it always was, is the abode of ragged poverty, which never could or can for a certainty reckon on one or any meal a day." Things have changed considerably for the better since Ford was here in the middle of the nineteenth century, and since Murillo used the *barrio*'s beggars and urchins as models for his paintings. Northwest of the Centro and enclosed by the best surviving stretch of the city's ancient walls, Macarena's very unfashionability, along with its solid working-class traditions, have helped prevent its wholesale dismemberment at the hands of speculators and builders. The result today is an area full of character, with many attractive cobbled streets, and quite a few jewels to show off in the way of **churches** and **convents**. The Macarena's pride was further enhanced when it was decided that the barrio would become the home of the newly autonomous **Andalucian parliament** in the converted Renaissance hospital of the Cinco Llagas.

Restaurants

Sevilla is tremendously atmospheric in the evening, packed with lively and enjoyable bars and clubs. That the city has never been particularly noted for its **restaurants** may have a lot to do with its strong tapas tradition (see "Bars

The forgotten brotherhood

The Macarena church of Santa Marina is home to the **Cofradía del Resucitado** (Brotherhood of the Resurrection), the newest of all the brotherhoods who march in the Semana Santa processions. Founded in 1969, it has never been taken to its heart by a citizenry whose apparent lack of interest in this celebration of the Redeemer's return is in marked contrast with the grisly enthusiasm they evidence for each act in the Passion leading up to his death. However, this apathy is the visitor's opportunity, for when El Resucitado leaves Santa Marina at four-thirty in the early dawn of Easter Sunday you'll get a perfect view of the intricate manoeuvres performed by the *costaleros* (porters) to negotiate the two *pasos* – the Risen Christ and the aptly titled Vírgen de la Aurora (Virgin of the Dawn) – through the church's doors, which are normally obscured by vast crowds. And as there are no seats lining the atmospheric c/Sierpes, which is almost impossible to get near during the other processions, you will be able to accompany the *pasos*, the band and the masked, candle-bearing *nazarenos* (penitents) in their all-white tunics along here as the dawn breaks – calling in at nearby bars for a *café* and maybe a *churro* or two.

The procession then passes through a sombre Plaza de San Francisco where the normally packed grandstands are eerily empty. Security is also lax at the cathedral, and with a bit of nimble footwork you should be able to follow the *pasos* through the church and past the enormous monstrance inside to emerge in a sunlit Plaza Vírgen de los Reyes beneath the Giralda tower, where a few *sevillanos* have usually gathered to pay their respects. If you wanted to follow El Resucitado back to Santa Marina it's a great (if slow) meander until they arrive home at about two in the afternoon.

and tapas", p.329). Great though this is, even the most enthusiastic *tapeadores* eventually tire of "plate-pecking" to seek out a place to sit down for a more conventional meal.

Barrio Santa Cruz and Cathedral area

To eat well without breaking the bank, you generally have to steer clear of the restaurants around the major sights and in the **Barrio Santa Cruz**. However, as you're probably going to be spending quite a bit of time here, it's worth listing some of the area's more reasonable options: the streets around the *barrio*'s northern edge (framed by calles Menéndez Pelayo and Santa María la Blanca), make for a good hunting ground.

Café Rayuela c/Miguel de Mañara 9. Pleasant lunchtime venue serving *raciones* and salads at outdoor tables in a pedestrianized street behind the Turismo.

Carmela c/Santa María la Blanca 4. Candlelit outdoor tables at this pleasant restaurant/*tapas* bar; tasty dishes include quiche, *patatas con crema de queso*, and quite a few vegetarian options.

Corral del Agua Callejón del Agua 6 ☏ 95 422 07 14. Very good restaurant where you can eat *cocina andaluza* in a lovely, plant-filled patio. Pricey, but well worth it. There's a *menú* for around €23. Closed Sun.

Doña Francisquita c/Álvarez Quintero 58. Authentic pizzas near the cathedral.

Hotel Alfonso XIII c/San Fernando 2 ☏ 95 491 70 00. The restaurant of the sumptuous hotel has to

be worth a splurge and there's a fair-priced *menu de degustación* for €31. The wonderful patio can also be enjoyed for the price of a beer – or *aperitivo* – from the bar, which comes with a generous ration of tapas.

Kaede Hotel Alfonso XIII c/San Fernando 2. In the gardens of the town's swishest address this is an authentic and entertaining Japanese restaurant. Sushi and sashimi are included on a good-value *menú* for €18, but if you go for the Sapporo beer rather than the *té japonés* (which comes free with the *menú*) you'll substantially increase the bill.

La Albahaca Plaza Santa Cruz 9 ☏ 95 422 07 14. Charming traditional restaurant housed in a converted mansion where three intimate period rooms hung with paintings provide the ambience.

A good place to start a tour around **La Macarena** is the **Plaza de los Terceros**, slightly to the northwest of the Casa de Pilatos. Here you'll find the fourteenth-century Mudéjar church of **Santa Catalina** with a tower modelled on the Giralda and topped off with Renaissance embellishments. The interior (access is difficult but try 6.30–7.30pm) has some interesting Mudéjar features including an elegant panelled ceiling as well as – in the Cristo de la Exaltación chapel (the most easterly on the south side) – a fine sculpture of Christ by Roldán. Within spitting distance of the church (on the corner of c/Gerona) lies another of Sevilla's great institutions, the bar **El Rinconcillo**, founded in 1670 and believed to be the oldest in the city.

Follow c/Sol out of the Plaza Terceros to Plaza San Román where another fourteenth-century Gothic-Mudéjar church, **San Román**, has a fine coffered ceiling. Taking c/Enladrillada along the north side of the church will bring you to the fifteenth-century **Convento de Santa Paula** (Tues–Sun 10am–1pm & 4.30–6.30pm; €2), renowned for its beautiful belfry and church. The church is entered through an imposing fifteenth-century **Gothic doorway** built with Mudéjar brickwork and decorated with Renaissance *azulejos* by Pedro Millán, with ceramic decoration by Niculoso Pisano. Inside there's a sumptuously gilded *San Juan Evangelista retablo* by Alonso Cano with a magnificent central figure of St John by Montañés dated 1637. The convent **museum**, crammed with treasures, is entered through a small patio to the left of the church entrance. Guided tours (in Spanish) are led by one of the convent's 48 nuns who has been given a special dispensation to break the order's vow of silence. The first room has a painting of *San Jerónimo* by Ribera, and, almost as beautiful, a view out onto a seventeenth-century patio cloister. In Room 2 there's a fascinating **maquette** made by Torrigiano before starting on his full-size masterpiece of *San Jerónimo Penitente*, which is now in the Museo de Bellas Artes. Room 3 holds two outstanding, though damaged, painted **sculptures by Pedro de Mena**, a *Virgin* and an *Ecce Homo*. The damage to both works was caused by visits from unruly schoolchildren who pulled off Christ's fingers and knocked both works to the floor. Immediately before the exit there is also a *Crucifixión* by **Zurbarán**. The hard-working sisters are famous for their *dulces* and *mermaladas* (including a tomato jam), which you can buy from their small shop. Facing the convent's entrance, a wall plaque marks a house described in *La Española Inglesa* by Cervantes.

From Santa Paula, head north along Pasaje Mallol to **San Julián**, yet another fourteenth-century church, with a Gothic-Mudéjar portal. Calle Madre Dolores Márquez will then take you the short distance to the **Puerta de Córdoba** (Córdoba Gate) with its horseshoe arch and the best surviving section of the **city wall**. The Almoravids constructed the wall in the early twelfth century, possibly on Roman foundations, and it was further strengthened by the later Almohads as wars against the Christians intensified. This stretch of the fortification – which once spanned twelve gates and 166 towers – owes its survival to the poverty of the *barrio* during the nineteenth century when, elsewhere in the city, it was pulled down to allow expansion.

Follow the wall west until you reach the **Puerta de la Macarena**, the only one of the city's gates to retain its pre-Christian name and reconstructed in the eighteenth century. Just beyond it stands the **Macarena Basilica** (daily 9.30am–2pm & 5–8pm; museum €3) which, despite an apparently Baroque facade, dates from the 1940s. The basilica's importance, however, derives from the revered image of the *Virgen de la Esperanza Macarena* it was constructed to house. Inside the church, to the left, is the solid silver *paso* used to carry the image around the city during the Semana Santa processions. To the right is a second *paso* (the brotherhoods normally carry them in pairs), *Jesús de la Sentencia*, depicting Pilate washing his hands with a fine, but now modestly cloaked, Christ by the seventeenth-century sculptor, Felipe Morales. The *retablo* of the main altar is dominated by a seventeenth-century image of La Macarena, as the Virgin is popularly called by this city of fanatical devotees. Depicted in the trauma of the Passion when her son has been condemned, the work is attributed to La Roldana – largely based on the *sevillano* sentiment that only a woman could have portrayed the suffering of a mother with such intensity. La Macarena's elaborate costume is often decorated with five diamond and emerald brooches bestowed on her by Joselito el Gallo, a famous *gitano torero* of the early part of the last century, and on which he spent a considerable fortune. She didn't return the favours though – he died in the ring in 1920. Despite this mishap, the Virgin is still regarded as the patron of the profession and all *matadores* offer prayers to her before stepping out to do business in the Maestranza. The basilica's treasury **museum** features a rather gaudy display of the Virgin's other jewels and regalia.

Over the road and beyond a small garden lies the sixteenth-century **Hospital de las Cinco Llagas** (aptly, of the Five Wounds Of Christ), one of the first true hospitals of its time and the largest in Europe. Sited outside the walls because hospitals then were places of pestilence and contagion, the restored building is now the seat of Andalucía's autonomous **government** (and many *sevillano* wags drily comment that nothing's changed). The enormous edifice, once capable of holding a thousand beds, is noted for a fine Mannerist facade with a Baroque central doorway of white marble. The interior – including the hospital's impressive former church, now the debating chamber – is open infrequently for public view when the parliament is not sitting (guided tours Mon 5pm & 6pm except Aug; must be booked in advance ☏95 459 21 00; free).

Crossing back to the Puerta de la Macarena, follow c/San Luís to the church of **San Gil** just behind the Macarena Basilica. Badly damaged in the Civil War, the church nevertheless still has a Mudéjar tower and, inside, a timber Mudéjar ceiling. Continuing south along the same street you'll come to the Gothic-Mudéjar church of **Santa Marina**, set back from the road in a *plazuela*. Founded in the thirteenth century, the oldest feature here must be the doorway, dating from around 1300, which has Gothic archivolts, or arch mouldings, with Mudéjar star decoration on the outer band. Another church badly damaged in the Civil War, Santa Marina was in ruins for decades, only spruced up for Expo 92 when the interior was entirely restored. It is now home to the Cofradía del Resucitado (Brotherhood of the Resurrection – see box on p.325).

Back on c/San Luis, the eponymous church of **San Luís** (Tues–Sat 9am–2pm, plus Fri–Sat 5–8pm; closed Aug; free) is a glorious eighteenth-century structure, preserved in 1995 from the demolition hammer after the city government had said they couldn't afford to save it. Public outcry forced a change of heart and the riot of a Churrigueresque facade, topped by glazed-tile domes, has now been restored along with the interior which features a fine fresco by Lucas Valdés on the central dome. The church is also floodlit at night to spectacular effect.

Further along you'll come to the fourteenth-century **San Marcos** in the plaza of the same name. Another fine Macarena church built on the site of an earlier mosque, it has a Mudéjar tower – note the Giralda-style *sebka* brickwork – and a superb Gothic-Mudéjar entrance. Although gutted by fire during the Civil War and since restored, its interior uniquely preserves the original Mudéjar horseshoe arches dividing nave and aisles. At the head of the north aisle there's a seventeenth-century sculpture in painted wood of *San Marcos*, by Juan de Mesa. Cervantes used to climb San Marcos's tower to view the plant-filled and peaceful patio of the convent of **Santa Isabel** just behind the church. You can see why.

Fairly expensive, but there's a *menú* for around €27. Closed Sun.

La Judería c/Cano y Cueto 13 ☎ 95 441 20 52. Popular mid-price restaurant with a tempting *menú* for €17.50. *Revueltos* (scrambled egg dishes) are a speciality here. Main dishes €9–17.

Mesón del Pulpo c/Tomás Ibarra 10. Excellent little Galician restaurant popular with locals. Specializes (as its name implies) in *pulpo a la gallega* (octopus) and there's an excellent value *menú* for €8.

The Río Guadalquivir and Triana

Across the river, **Triana** offers some excellent restaurants. Near the Puente San Telmo, a number of restaurants along c/Salado cater for workers from the Los Remedios business quarter, and along c/Betis close to the water's edge are a number of restaurants with terraces looking out over the city. Around c/García Vinuesa to the west of the cathedral there's an abundance of reasonable *bocadillo* bars and delis for picnic food.

As-Sawïrah c/Galera 5. Superb Moroccan restaurant offering a variety of north African dishes including a delicate couscous and their house special *tajin de cordero con membrillos* (lamb with quinces). Lunch *menú* €12. Closed Sat eve & Sun.
Casablanca c/Zaragoza 50, east of the Maestranza bullring ☎ 95 422 46 98. Smart mid-price restaurant noted for its excellent fish dishes – including *mero con frambuesa* (grouper with raspberries) – but also does meat. Has a small tapas bar which, they insist, King Juan Carlos once visited incognito to sample their *papas aliñás* (marinated potatoes).
El Manijero c/Trastamara 15 (corner with c/Albuera). Excellent and economical neighbourhood bar-restaurant with a tapas and *raciones* bar beyond the entrance and a dining room off this. Fried fish and *solomillo* are their specialities.
Horacio c/Antonia Díaz 9. Moderately priced fish and meat dishes at this pleasant small restaurant near the bullring. *Fabada asturiana* (bean & ham casserole) is a house special.
La Primera del Puente c/Betis 66. One of the city's best options for economical yet generous *raciones* of fish, meat and *mariscos*; sweet talk a waiter to get a frontline table for the spectacular river view from their terrace.
La Sopa Boba c/Torneo 85 ☎ 95437 97 84. Mid-priced, modern and attractive place with a creative approach; specials include *manzana con bacalao y cabrales* (cod with apples and goat's cheese) and *magret de pato en salsa de peras* (duck with pear sauce); also has a *menú* for around €10. Closed Sun eve & Mon.
La Triana c/Castilla 36 ☎ 95 433 38 19. Reasonably priced restaurant with a wonderful terrace for lunch or dinner overlooking the river. Superb service and a *menú* for around €18; house specials include *lomo con salsa de castañas y ciruelas* (pork with chestnut and plum sauce) and *rollitos de pavo* (turkey).

El Faro de Triana Puente de Triana ☎ 95 433 12 51. Sitting atop the western end of the Puente de Triana (aka Puente de Isabel II), the dining room and roof terrace here give amazing river views. Tapas at the bar and *raciones* at the tables consist of fish, meat and *mariscos*.
Mesón Serranito c/Antonia Díaz 11, south side of the Plaza de Toros. Twin restaurant of the one near El Corte Inglés and with similar dishes and *platos combinados* and – due to the location – a line of bulls' heads gazing down from the walls.
Ox's Restaurante c/Betis 61 ☎ 95 427 95 85. Friendly and smart little restaurant renowned for its pricey but authentic Basque fish and meat dishes: *merluza con almejas en salsa verde* (hake with clams) is a signature dish; there's also a good-value *menú del día* for €16.
Poncio c/Victoria 8, in Triana ☎ 95 434 00 10. Excellent mid-priced Triana restaurant with a French-*andaluz* slant to its menu. There's a *menú de degustación* for €43. Closed Sun.
Restaurante Enrique Becerra c/Gamazo 2, east of the bullring ☎ 95 421 30 49. Mid-priced restaurant with a solid reputation for well-prepared *andaluz* dishes such as *cola de toro* (bull's tail) and *corvina al amontillado* (sea bass). Closed Sun and Aug.
Restaurante Japonés Samurai c/Salado 6. Interesting little Japanese restaurant with entertaining versions of Oriental dishes slanted towards Spanish palates; has an economical *menú* for €5.95.
Río Grande c/Betis 70 ☎ 95 427 39 56. One of the best places for a lunchtime feast of traditional meat and fish dishes. Whether you're seated behind panoramic windows or on the terrace, the view across the river to the Torre del Oro and Giralda, illuminated at night, is stunning. There's an all-day €20 *menú*.
Taberna El Alabardero c/Zaragoza 20, just west of Plaza Nueva ☎ 95 456 06 37.

Elegant nineteenth-century *casa-palacio sevillana* with attractive decor and an upmarket clientele. Pricey – and excellent – restaurant upstairs where the *menú de degustación* costs €47; however, a cheaper €15 lunchtime *menú* in the patio bar below comes from the same kitchen.

El Centro, La Macarena, Alameda and Santa Justa

Many parts of the **El Centro** zone still possess a seedy charm, especially in its southern reaches and the remoter bits of **La Macarena**. This is the real Sevilla and you'll have no trouble finding low-priced *comidas* in and around streets such as c/San Eloy which runs into Plaza Duque de la Victoria, as well as all the main arteries of La Macarena. The **Alameda de Hércules** is a formerly dubious area now heading upmarket with new places opening all the time. The streets around the **Santa Justa** train station form another area with plenty of possibilities, and have some of the most economical places to eat in town.

Bar Carlos Alberto c/José Laguillo. Highly illuminated and visible as you emerge from Santa Justa station, this lively diner has perhaps the cheapest *menú* in the city for around €5.

Bar Dueñas c/Dueñas 1, on corner of three streets. Ancient and attractive place to have lunch with delicious home cooking and a *menú* for €7.

Bar Los Niños del Flor c/T. Borges 8, round the side of El Corte Inglés department store in the Plaza Duque de la Victoria. Popular, good-value bar serving a €6 *menú*, but it fills up quickly.

El Ajo Blanco c/Alhóndiga 19, east of Plaza Encarnación. Friendly little bar-restaurant serving up *enchiladas* (tortillas) and a delicious *ajo blanco* (white gazpacho with floating grapes). Also does South American tapas. Closed Aug.

El Pucherito c/Relator 37, off the north end of the Alameda de Hércules. Cheap and friendly restaurant serving up a long list of economical and tasty traditional dishes.

Habanita c/Golfo s/n, a small street off c/Pérez Galdos. Vegetarian dishes with a Cuban slant served on wooden tables in a pleasant diner. Specials include *yuca con salsa mojito* (sweet potato) and *berenjenas Habanita* (aubergine).

Helas c/Gonzalo Bilbao 26. One block south of, and in sight of, Santa Justa train station, this rare Greek restaurant does well-prepared Balkan dishes at decent prices. Offers a good-value 2-person *meze* for €9.90. Closed Mon.

La Yerbagüena c/González Cuadrado 35. Hippy-style place cooking superb organic Latin American food at low prices; also has vegetarian options and a *menú*.

 Lar Gallego c/Gonzalo Bilbao, close to the Santa Justa train station. Excellent little

mid-priced bar-restaurant serving *platos típicós gallegos* – fish and *mariscos* in the restaurant – and equally good tapas at the bar.

Mesón Serranito Alfonso XII 9, behind El Corte Inglés. Cosy little economical restaurant beyond the tapas bar out front, with good fish and meat dishes.

Pando c/San Eloy 47. Lively, stylish and economical tapas and *raciones* restaurant which also does a variety of salads. An ideal lunch stop.

Restaurante Las Piletas c/Marqués de Paradas 28 ⊕95 422 04 04. Diminutive, atmospheric and typically *sevillano* mid-priced restaurant with *tapas* bar (listing 50 possibilities) attached. Specialities include fish and *mariscos* and it has a small outdoor terrace. Main dishes €10–15.

Restaurante Los Gallegos c/Capataz Franco. Friendly and inexpensive Galician restaurant in a tiny alley off c/Martín Villa, serving *gallego* specialities (try their *tarta de Santiago* dessert).

San Marco c/Cuna 6 ⊕95 421 24 40. A few doors away from the Palacio de Lebrija, in an eighteenth-century mansion, this is one of the more affordable of Sevilla's upmarket restaurants, with an international menu and stylish service. Specialities are *pato con aceitunas* (duck with olives) and *cordero a la miel* (lamb with honey). Main dishes €12–20.

Vegetarium c/Santa Angela de la Cruz 37. Newly opened vegetarian restaurant serving pasta-based dishes, salads and imaginative desserts.

Zarabanda c/Padre Tarín 6, off c/Jesus del Gran Poder. Little family restaurant cooking traditional dishes to a high standard. Just the place for a lunch stop.

Tapas bars

A popular saying here is *En Sevilla no se come sino que se tapea* ("In Sevilla you don't eat but *tapear*"). As the city that claims to have invented **tapas**, Sevilla knocks spots off the competition. There is simply nowhere else in Andalucía

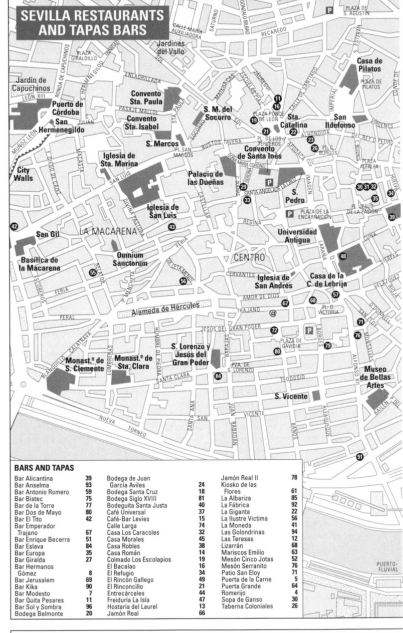

SEVILLA RESTAURANTS AND TAPAS BARS

Jardines del Valle

Jardín de Capuchinos

Convento Sta. Paula

Puerto de Córdoba

San Hermenegildo

Convento Sta. Isabel

S. M. del Socorro

Casa de Pilatos

City Walls

S. Marcos

Sta. Catalina

San Ildefonso

Iglesia de Sta. Marina

Convento de Santa Inés

Palacio de las Dueñas

S. Pedro

Iglesia de San Luis

San Gil

LA MACARENA

Universidad Antigua

Basílica de la Macarena

Omnium Sanctorum

CENTRO

Iglesia de San Andrés

Casa de la C. de Lebrija

Alameda de Hércules

Monast.º de S. Clemente

Monast.º de Sta. Clara

S. Lorenzo y Jesús del Gran Poder

Museo de Bellas Artes

S. Vicente

PUERTO-FLUVIAL

BARS AND TAPAS

Bar Alicantina	39	Bodega de Juan		Jamón Real II	78	
Bar Anselma	93	García Aviles	24	Kiosko de las		
Bar Antonio Romero	59	Bodega Santa Cruz	18	Flores	61	
Bar Bistec	75	Bodega Siglo XVIII	81	La Albariza	85	
Bar de la Torre	77	Bodeguita Santa Justa	40	La Fábrica	92	
Bar Dos de Mayo	80	Café Universal	37	La Giganta	22	
Bar El Tito	42	Café-Bar Levíes	15	La Ilustre Victima	56	
Bar Emperador		Calle Larga	74	La Moneda	41	
Trajano	67	Casa Los Caracoles	32	Las Golondrinas	94	
Bar Enrique Becerra	51	Casa Morales	45	Las Teresas	12	
Bar Eslava	84	Casa Robles	38	Lizarrán	68	
Bar Europa	35	Casa Román	14	Mariscos Emilio	63	
Bar Giralda	27	Colmado Los Escolapios	19	Mesón Cinco Jotas	52	
Bar Hermanos		El Bacalao	16	Mesón Serranito	76	
Gómez	8	El Refugio	34	Patio San Eloy	71	
Bar Jerusalem	69	El Rincón Gallego	49	Puerta de la Carne	5	
Bar Kika	90	El Rinconcillo	21	Puerta Grande	64	
Bar Modesto	7	Entrecárceles	44	Romerijo	4	
Bar Quita Pesares	11	Freiduría La Isla	47	Sopa de Ganso	30	
Bar Sol y Sombra	96	Hostaría del Laurel	13	Taberna Coloniales	26	
Bodega Belmonte	20	Jamón Real	66			

RESTAURANTS

As-Sawïrah	17	Café Rayuela	28	El Ajo Blanco	23	Helas	2	La Judería
Bar Carlos Alberto	1	Carmela	9	El Faro de Triana	89	Horacio	60	La Primera del
Bar Dueñas	29	Casablanca	58	El Manijero	88	Hotel Alfonso XIII	25	Puente
Bar Los Niños del Flor	79	Corral del Agua	83	El Pucherito	55	Kaede	25	La Sopa Boba
		Doña Francisquita	36	Habanita	31	La Albahaca	10	La Triana

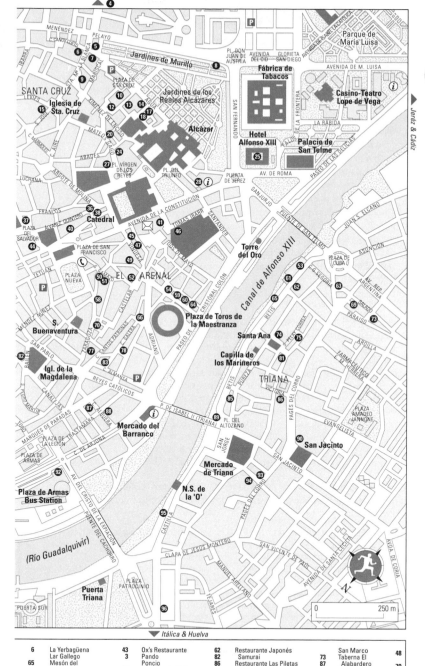

Jerez & Cádiz

Itálica & Huelva

6	La Yerbagüena	43	Ox's Restaurante	62	Restaurante Japonés		San Marco	48
	Lar Gallego	3	Pando	82	Samurai	73	Taberna El	
65	Mesón del	46	Restaurante Enrique	86	Restaurante Las Piletas	87	Alabardero	70
91	Pulpo	54	Becerra	50	Restaurante Los Gallegos	57	Vegetarium	33
95	Mesón Serranito			53	Río Grande		Zarabanda	72

Sevilla's top-ten tapas

The origin of the *tapa* (literally "cover" or "lid") is generally believed to have come from the bartender's generous custom of placing a slice of ham or cheese over the top of a glass of *fino* before serving it to a customer. Many bars in remoter areas still continue this tradition, but most city establishments now charge for the much more elaborate tapas provided. Below is a selection of some of the outstanding taste-treats on offer.

Caracoles – snails.

Chanquetes – tiny fish similar to whitebait; dunked in flour, deep fried and eaten whole.

Cola de toro – bull's tail in a winey sauce.

Espinacas con garbanzos – spinach with chickpeas.

Frito variado de pescado – all kinds of different fried fish. A tapa gets you a piece but most people order the better-value *ración*.

Jamón – slices of cured ham on bread; simple but traditional and delicious.

Pincho moruno – mini meat kebab usually grilled over charcoal.

Puntillitas fritas – tiny baby squid, deep fried.

Revueltos – scrambled egg with a variety of fillings ranging from asparagus to mushrooms and garlic or even all three.

Solomillo al whisky – small pork or beefsteak in a Highland sauce probably made with Spanish grog.

– or even Spain – with such a variety of places to indulge this culinary art. *El tapeo* means eating "on the go" and *sevillanos* do it on their feet, moving from bar to bar where they stand with a *manzanilla* or beer – leaving the seats to tourists – whilst wolfing back fistfuls of whatever tapas take their fancy. Locals tend to drink the cold, dry *fino* with their tapas, especially *gambas* (prawns), but sometimes beer. Another popular tapas partner is a *tinto de verano* – the local version of *sangría* – consisting of wine mixed with lemonade and ice. Finally, don't think that because the servings are small they are always low-priced. Some seafood tapas can be pricey, as can the cured *jamón*, and the plates have a tendency to mount up. Making your way to some of the bars listed below will lead you into areas where tapas outlets tend to congregate, enabling you to make discoveries of your own – an essential part of becoming a *tapeador*.

Barrio Santa Cruz and the Cathedral area

The ancient heart of Sevilla is filled with *tapas* possibilities and has a few of the very best places in town.

Bar Enrique Becerra c/Gamazo 2. Outstanding bar and restaurant (see p.328). House specials: *cazón con patatas* (dogfish), *bocadito de mejillones* (mussels). Closed Sun.

Bar Europa Junction of c/Alcaicería de Loza and c/Siete Revueltas. Fine old watering hole with lots of cool tiled walls plus excellent *manzanilla* and a variety of tapas served on marble-topped tables.

Bar Giralda c/Mateos Gago 1. One of the city's leading bars, in a Moorish bathhouse with arched doorways and lots of *azulejos*, and serving a wide selection of tapas. House specials include *calabacín al horno* (baked courgette) and *cazuela Tío Pepe* (meat stewed with *fino*).

Bar Hermanos Gómez Jardines de Murillo. One of a chain of similar places offering excellent value for money; economical tapas and *raciones* served on a big garden terrace. *Habas con jamón* (broad beans) is particularly recommended.

Bar Modesto c/Cano y Cueto 5. Just about every imaginable tapa including specials such as *punta de solomillo* (pork tenderloin), *coquinas* (clams) and *cañaillas* (murex shellfish). It also serves a good-value €12 *menú*.

Bodega Belmonte c/Mateos Gago 24. A classic place with vibrant ambience and superb tapas – try their tasty *queso de cabra horneado* (baked goat's cheese).

Bodega de Juan García Aviles c/Mateos Gago 20. Also known as *La Goleta*, this ancient and renowned bathroom-sized spit-and-sawdust place serves top-notch *manzanilla* and tapas limited to *jamón* and olives.

Bodega Santa Cruz c/Rodrigo Caro 1. Close to the Hospital de Venerables, serving up generous tapas portions. House specials include *tortilla de bacalao* (cod fish omelette) and *montaditos* (toasted buns with *jamón* or cheese).

Bodeguita Santa Justa c/Hernando Colón 1. Prize-winning tapas outlet with a long list of mouthwatering possibilities including *pinchito de lomo con dátiles y miel* (pork with dates and honey). Also has an economical *menú del dia*.

Café-Bar Levíes c/San José 15. Vibrant tapas bar with terrace on a pleasant small square on the northern edge of the *barrio*. Specials include *solomillo al whisky* (see box opposite).

Casa Morales c/García de Vinuesa 11. Pleasant old bar, founded in 1850, which once served barrelled Valdepeñas wine from great butts (now empty) behind the counter. Today a few simple tapas are served on *tablas* (wooden boards).

Casa Robles c/Álvarez Quintero 58. Fronting the cathedral, this first-rate tapas venue has an equally fine restaurant. House specials are paella and *pez espada al ajillo* (swordfish with garlic).

Casa Román Plaza de los Venerables 1. Ancient and renowned tapas haunt specializing in *jamón* eaten at the bar or at the tables outside. Closed Sun eve.

El Rincón Gallego c/Harinas 21. Tiny outpost of Galicia serving only tapas (which change daily) from this northwest province. House specials include *pulpo a la feira* (octopus with paprika) and *empanada* (Galician pie).

Entrecárceles c/Manuel Cortina s/n. Tiny, century-old bar, on the site of the prison that once housed Cervantes, serving a magnificent, rare (and pricey at around €15) *Fino Imperial* sherry by the glass. Specials include *anchoas con queso* (anchovies

with cheese) and *melva con pimientos* (tuna fish with peppers).

Freiduría La Isla c/García de Vinuesa 13. Great little *freiduría* serving up a wide variety of mouthwatering fried fish and tucked away in the back streets off the south side of Plaza Nueva. The nearby *freiduría El Arenal* on c/Arfe is another excellent place and you should be able to take your *cartucho* of fish into the *El Arenal* bar next door (providing you buy a drink).

Hostaría del Laurel Plaza de los Venerables 5. Historic and popular bar whose superb decor with Triana tiles is complemented by hanging *jamónes* and mouthwatering tapas. House specials are *riñones al jerez* (kidneys in *fino*) and *zarzuelita de mariscos* (shellfish cocktail).

Mesón Cinco Jotas c/Arfe 5. Fans of the famed *jamón iberico* from the Sierra de Aracena have a bar all to themselves. Watch out though – the king of hams doesn't come cheap.

La Moneda c/Almirantazgo 4. Lively haunt owned by a *sanluqueño* (from Sanlúcar de Barrameda), serving up tapas and excellent *manzanilla*. Specials include *langostinos* (king prawns) and *calamares relleños* (stuffed squid). Also has its own attractive little restaurant.

Puerta de la Carne c/Santa María La Blanca 36. Not strictly a tapas bar but a *freiduría* where you can buy a *cartucho* (bag) of delicious fried fish and – with a beer from the bar – eat it out of the paper on a very pleasant terrace.

Las Teresas c/Santa Teresa. Atmospheric, traditional L-shaped bar with cured hams hanging above tiled walls lined with photos of *toreros* and bottles of vintage sherry. Also a nice place to relax over breakfast. Specials include *queso viejo* (mature cheese), *calamares a la riojana* (squid) and a tasty *arroz dominical* ("Sunday rice") served only on the sabbath.

Romerijo Avda. Eduardo Dato 23. If you're a fan of *Romerijo*'s places in El Puerto de Santa María (see p.258) you'll find it no trouble at all to hike ten minutes east from the church of Santa María la Blanca to the Sevilla outpost of their burgeoning empire. The formula's the same here and you buy your shellfish and seafood by weight at the counter and consume with a beer inside or on their terrace.

The Río Guadalquivir and Triana

The streets near the **river** surrounding the Maestranza bullring have always been a prime spot for tapas bars, no doubt to serve the gargantuan appetites of fight fans. Owing perhaps to its *gitano* traditions, **Triana** is another excellent hunting ground for tapas, both on the riverfront along c/Betis, and further into the *barrio*.

Bar Anselma c/Pagés del Corro 49. Fine old place with neo-Moorish facade owned by a *dueña* with many Rocío connections (every night at midnight

the lights are dimmed and the Rocío hymn is sung). If you're lucky you may just catch some of the best impromptu flamenco in town. House specials include *caldereta* (lamb stewed in *fino*), and *pisto* (stewed vegetables). Doesn't open till 11pm. Closed Sun.

Bar Antonio Romero c/Antonia Díaz 19. A real *tapeador*'s bar that is much visited by the Maestranza crowd before and after *corridas*. Specials are *muslo de pato* (duck) and *salmón ahumado con alcaparras* (smoked salmon with capers). They have another bar slightly east of here at c/Gamazo 16.

Bar Bistec c/Pelay y Correa 34. Ancient and hearty Triana hostelry opposite the church of Santa Ana, with outdoor tables in summer. Specials include *cabrillas* (spicy snails), *codorniz en salsa* (quail) and *pan de mi pueblo* (cod *gazpacho*). Closed Wed.

Bar de la Torre c/Zaragoza 10. Excellent tapas – specialities are *gambas con bacon* (prawns with bacon) and *cordero con miel* (lamb with honey), although you may want to pass on their brains in garlic sauce (*sesos en ajillo*). Small diner also has a *menú*.

Bar Jerusalem c/Salado 5. Sevilla's only Jewish eating place is tiny and serves up tapas and *bocadillos*.

Bar Kika c/Pagés del Corro 76. Friendly, no-frills workers' bar with its own Triana clientele and a few tapas. Try their special, *solomillo* (beef in garlic).

Bar Sol y Sombra c/Castilla 151. At the northern end of Triana, this is another favourite with bullfight fans as well as an atmospheric bar in its own right. House specials include *cola de toro* (oxtail), *almejas* (clams) and *cazuela Tío Pepe* (stew with *fino*). Daily 1–3.30pm & 8.30pm–midnight.

Bodega Siglo XVIII c/Pelay y Correa 32. Close to *Bar Bistec*, this solid Triana establishment has pretty tiles, plenty of *corrida* posters and good tapas.

Calle Larga c/Pureza 72. Some of the best tapas in Triana at a neat little bar with a pavement terrace. Try their *calabacines rellenos* (stuffed courgettes), *flamenquines* (pork croquettes) or *costillitas fritas* (ribs).

Jamón Real c/López de Arenas 5. On the Maestranza's doorstep, a "foreign" tapas bar offering delicacies from Sevilla's neighbouring province, Extremadura, including delicious *jamón serrano*.

Jamón Real II c/Pastor y Landero 20. Twin *extremeño* establishment to the one mentioned above serving all the same delicacies. House specials are *jamón de Montánchez* (Spain's other top ham besides Jabugo) and *torta del casar* (delicious Extremaduran ewes' milk cheese). Closed Mon.

Kiosko de las Flores c/Betis s/n, on the river. A Sevilla institution, this *freiduría* has a prime riverside location with fine views. In season you can eat *raciones* at outdoor tables. Specials include *coquinas* (clams).

La Albariza c/Betis 6. Triana bar fitted out like a Jerez *bodega* with butts used as tables. House specials include *tortilla de camarones* (shrimps in batter) and *caña de lomo* (cured pork).

La Fábrica Centro Comercial Plaza de Armas. Original bar with the added feature of its own microbrewery on the premises. Its terrace is popular with a young crowd and they have a variety of tapas as well as an excellent-value *menú* upstairs for around €7.

Las Golondrinas Antillano Campos 26. Charming bar on two floors filled with Triana *azulejos* serving quality tapas. Specials include *caballito de jamón* (ham with fried bread), *punta de solomillo* (sirloin steak) and *alcachofas aliñados* (artichokes). Closed Wed.

Mariscos Emilio (aka Cervecería La Mar) c/Génova 1. Excellent bar specializing in self-service seafood tapas. House specials include *almejas* (clams), *ostras* (oysters) and *cañaíllas* (murex shellfish). Equally good Triana offshoots of the same bar are to be found at c/López de Gomara 18 (with a terrace) and c/San Jacinto 39 (corner with c/San Romero).

Puerta Grande c/Antonia Díaz 33. This bar takes its name from the gate through which successful *matadores* get carried shoulder high. It serves great *fino* along with house specials including *acelgas con pasas* (chard with raisins). There's also a stylish restaurant with *ambiente taurino* and a decent-value *menú* for €18.

Centro, Alameda de Hércules and La Macarena

The **Centro** is the bustling heart of Sevilla in a culinary as well as geographical sense. The zones surrounding four of the *barrio*'s focal landmarks – the Museo de las Bellas Artes, the vibrant artery c/Sierpes, Plaza Alfalfa and the Iglesia de Santa Catalina – provide rewarding hunting grounds for the *tapeador*. The **Alameda de Hércules** used to be the town's red-light district but all that has gone, and it's now become a new focus for tapas bars and nightlife.

Bar Alicantina Plaza del Salvador 2. Famous bar with outdoor tables on a pleasant pedestrianized square, offering excellent, pricey seafood tapas and a celebrated *ensalada rusa*. House specials are *gambas rebozadas* (prawns fried in breadcrumbs) and *huevas de atún* (tuna roe).

Bar Dos de Mayo Plaza de la Gavidia s/n. A popular bar with a good tapas range. Specials include tortilla rellena (*marisco-* or tuna-stuffed omelette) and *tostaditas de bacalao* (cod on toast).

Bar El Tito c/Macarena 8. Close to the Basilica Macarena this is a busy little bar with a good fish and meat tapas range.

Bar Emperador Trajano c/Trajano 10. This tribute to Sevilla's great Roman emperor has lots of brick and beams and offers some good if pricier tapas; house special is *brocheta emperador* (chicken with plums).

Bar Eslava c/Eslava 3, facing the Iglesia de San Lorenzo. Excellent and popular tapas place with low prices and great atmosphere. House specials include *cordero con miel* (lamb with honey), *boquerones relleños* (stuffed anchovies) and *pasteles de verduras* (vegetable pies).

Bar Quita Pesares Plaza Jerónimo de Córdoba 3. Lively bar, run by flamenco *cantaor* Peregil, and serving up decent tapas such as *caña de lomo* (cured pork). Closed Sun.

Café Universal c/Blanca de los Rios 3, off the east side of Plaza del Salvador. Quality tapas in pleasant surroundings with a small terrace; house special is *patatones* (potatoes with various dips). Also does *platos combinados*.

Casa Los Caracoles c/Pérez Galdós, off Plaza Alfalfa. Long-established and friendly bar serving most tapas. House specials include *caracoles* (snails), *espinacas con garbanzos* (spinach with chickpeas) and *navajas* (razorshell clams).

Colmado Los Escolapios Plaza Ponce de León 5. Busy and unusual little place specializing in mouth-watering cheeses as well as fine wines and game. House specials include *cinta de lomo a la salsa de manzana* (pork in apple sauce) and *alcachofas con jamoncítos* (artichokes with *jamón*); also has a terrace.

El Bacalao Plaza Ponce de León 15. This venue is devoted to *bacalao* (cod) in all its manifestations, but they do have other dishes, too. Specials to try are their *tortillas*, *croquetas* and *taquitos* (all cod). Closed Sun.

El Refugio c/Huelva 5, close to Plaza del Salvador. Good-value tapas bar with a wide variety of good-ies, including vegetarian tapas.

 El Rinconcillo c/Gerona 32. Sevilla's oldest bar (founded in 1670), just off Plaza Los Terceros, and full of atmosphere. A meeting place for the city's literati, excellent tapas are often washed down with a *coronel* (colonel), an ample glass of Valdepeñas red. Renowned for its *jamón* and cheese tapas, other specials include *espinacas con garbanzos* (spinach with chickpeas) and *bacalao con tomate* (cod). Closed Wed.

La Giganta c/Alhóndiga 6 (actually in Plaza de Santa Catalina). Taking its name ("The Big Lady") from the city's nickname for the figure of Faith atop the Giralda tower, there are numerous images of her throughout. House special is *tablas de queso gratinado* (various tapas served on bread) but it has a wide tapas range.

La Ilustre Victima c/Dr Letamendi 35. Great tapas and drinking bar with original decor, music and house specials such as couscous and *shoarmas* (kebabs). Opens till late.

Lizarrán c/Javier Lasso de la Vega 14, corner with c/Trajano. Cheap, cheerful and busy bar serving Basque-style *pintxos* (snacks on sticks). There's a wide variety to choose from (€1 each) and when you want to pay, the barman/woman counts up the number of sticks on your plate. It also does meals and has a €8 *menú*.

Mesón Serranito Alfonso XIII 9, behind El Corte Inglés. The bar adjoined to the restaurant (see p.328) is also worth a mention for great-value *tapas*. The house special, *serranito* (*bocadillo* with pork loin and *jamón*) uses the diminutive ironically – it's a meal in itself.

Patio San Eloy c/San Eloy 9. Youthful bustling bar on a busy pedestrianized street with a giant tiled "staircase" at the back where everyone sits to eat their *bocadillos*; options include *salmón ahumado* (smoked salmon) and *montaditos* (titbits on bread) and there's a €6 *menú*.

Sopa de Ganso c/Pérez Galdós 8, close to Plaza Alfalfa. Young, lively vegetarian bar in one of the city's main nightlife zones. On offer are *tagarninas* (a pastie) and *pudín de verduras* (vegetable bake).

Taberna Coloniales Plaza Cristo de Burgos 19. Typical ancient *sevillano* tavern decorated with photos of the town's bygone days; house specials are *salmorejo* and *secreto ibérico*, which is, of course, a secret. Has a very pleasant terrace which you'll need to queue for in summer.

Breakfast, coffee bars and cakes

Sevilla's **breakfast bars** bustle with life on working days, and in the early morning rush hour (8–9am) they're usually packed with standing clients munching *tostadas* (toast with butter or oil) or a few *churros* (fritters) washed down with coffee or hot chocolate. The best are concentrated around the **Centro** and **Macarena**; some to look out for are *Bar Santa Marta*, c/Angostillo 2, in a small square planted with orange trees next to the church of San Andrés,

Convento dulces

Many of Sevilla's *conventos de clausura*, or enclosed orders of nuns, are today a small industry in themselves turning out a spectacular assortment of **dulces**. This took off in a big way in the 1950s, when the pope gave permission for the struggling convents to earn money to support themselves. Some convents take in laundry, others perform tasks such as bookbinding, but most of them turn out the *dulces* which the city's population consumes with a passion equalled only by its contempt for calorie-counting and cholestrol. So skilled have the nuns become in this trade that today they supply many of the city's leading restaurants with their desserts. Among convents only too willing to lead you into temptation are the Convento de San Leandro, Plaza Ildefonso 1, renowned for its *yemas*, a sugar, syrup and egg-yolk concoction, or the Convento de Santa Inés, c/Doña María Coronel 5, near the church of San Pedro, whose speciality is *bollitos* (sweet buns) and *tortas almendradas* (almond cakes). In the heart of Macarena, Santa Paula – more famous for its nineteen varieties of jams and marmalades – also gets into the *dulces* business with another mouth-watering egg-yolk confection, *tocino de cielo* (translated, very inadequately, as "heavenly lard"). When the convent shops are closed you can buy their confections at their jointly owned central store, *El Torno*, in Pasaje de Los Seises, a small vaulted passage off Avda. de la Constitución, opposite the cathedral.

Café Zafiro, c/San Eloy 58, near the Plaza Duque de la Victoria, and the elegantly luxurious *Café del Casino*, Avda. del María Luisa s/n (at the junction with c/Palos de la Frontera) which is open from 11am onwards. Also good is the *Jamaica Coffee Shop*, c/Sagasta 7, just west of Plaza del Salvador, which serves good coffee and a range of teas and confectionery in stylish surroundings. Another new chain to look out for is *Café de Indias* which has become extremely popular with its well-designed decor and good service; central branches include Avda. de la Constitución 34 and – possibly their nicest place – at no.10 on the same street. A place that turns out great **churros** (they're also known as *calentitos*) is *Calentería*, c/Cano y Cueto 7, next to the *Bar Modesto* (see "Tapas bars", p.329).

For the best **cakes** and **pastries** in town, head for the *pastelerías* along c/Sierpes. *La Campana*, at no. 1, is the most celebrated, although many of the others, such as *Ochoa* at no. 45, are just as good. *Horno de San Buenaventura*, at c/García de Vinuesa 10, on the cathedral's doorstep, has two floors where *sevillanos* love to indulge themselves with creamy pastries and *andaluz* classics such as *tocino de cielo*. A popular French-owned *crepería* serving authentic crepes is located at c/Perez Galdos 22, near Plaza Alfalfa. To cool down in Sevilla's intense summer heat the city's favourite **ice cream** maker, *Heladería Rayas*, c/Almirante Apodaca 1 (near the church of San Pedro), has the best selection and there's a terrace, too.

Nightlife

Sevilla has plenty to offer in the way of **nightlife**, from expensive, touristy flamenco shows to atmospheric, tucked-out-of-the-way drinking holes. On summer evenings bar terraces by the river (see p.341) often put on live musical entertainment. Major **concerts** take place in one of the football stadiums (see "Listings", p.343) or in the Auditorio de La Cartuja across the river. La Teatral, c/Velázquez 12, near Plaza Duque de la Victoria (☎95 422 82 29), are the official ticket agents for many concerts. Throughout the summer the Alcázar, the Prado de San Sebastián gardens and other squares host occasional

free concerts. Information on these and most of the above should be available from the Turismo, the local press and the *El Giraldillo* listings magazine.

Flamenco

Flamenco music and dance are on offer at dozens of places around the city, some of them extremely tacky and over-priced. Finding *flamenco puro*, the real thing, isn't easy, possibly because – like good blues or improvised jazz with which flamenco shares an affinity – its spontaneous nature is almost impossible to timetable. Visitor demand for this romantic Spanish art form has resulted in a form of "theatre flamenco", where you can pay to see two shows a night – a far cry from the time when the *gitanos* sang in their *juergas* or shindigs for as long and as often as the mood took them.

The agents of every flamenco "show" or *tablao* will leap to assure you that you're lucky to have alighted on them before rubbishing the competition. Unless you've heard otherwise, avoid these fixed "shows", many of which are a travesty, even using recorded music. If you're here only for a while, however, and are determined to catch something of the flavour of this wonderful art form, we've listed the better places below. Bear in mind that flamenco sessions rarely begin before 11pm.

Various **festivals** such as the Bienal de Flamenco, A Palo Seco (Cante Jondo), Un Verano de Flamenco, as well as concerts staged by the various *barrios*, take place throughout the summer months and are worth keeping an eye out for as your chances of hearing something special are high. They are widely advertised and the Turismo and local press should have details. One place where you are guaranteed to hear some authentic flamenco is in the Triana barrio's annual festival **Velá de Santa Ana** held during the final week in July. There are flamenco performances (free) every night starting around 10 or 11pm in the Plaza del Altozano and along the waterfront c/Betis.

Anselma c/Pages del Corro 49, in Triana. Live flamenco most nights starting around 10.30pm; free.
El Arenal c/Rodo 7, one block south of the Plaza de Toros ✆ 95 421 64 92. Most palatable of the pricey tourist flamenco spots, and run by a former dancer who sees to it that the spectacle doesn't veer too far into burlesque. Tickets for shows at 9pm and 11pm cost a steep €31.50 (including one drink) or, including dinner, €61. If they're not too busy after the first show you can stay to see the second for free.
La Carbonería c/Levíes 18. Excellent bar that often has spontaneous flamenco – Thursday is the best night, but not before 10pm. Once a coal merchant's building (hence the name), this is a large, welcoming place, run by flamenco expert Paco Lira, with its own patio at the back. Tricky to find – slightly to the northeast of the church of Santa Cruz – but well worth the effort.
Los Gallos Plaza de Santa Cruz ✆ 95 421 69 81. Reputable flamenco show using a professional group of singers and dancers who sometimes get close to the real thing, although a nagging feeling persists that the performers are going through the motions. Performances at 8pm & 10pm; entry is €27 and includes one drink.

Café Lisboa c/Alhondiga 43, near the church of Santa Catalina. Music bar staging flamenco on Thursday nights; entry is free.
Casa de la Memoria de Al Andalus c/Ximénez de Enciso 28, in the Barrio Santa Cruz ✆ 95 456 06 70. Cultural centre with fine patio mounting excellent and reasonably priced concerts of flamenco – as well as *raíces* (roots) concerts of music going back to Moorish times – throughout the year. The programme changes monthly so you'll need to ring or pick up a leaflet. Tickets around €11.
Bar El Mundo c/Siete Revueltas s/n (off c/Pérez Galdós), just north of the church of El Salvador. Lively, offbeat bar that stages flamenco guitar, song and dance on Tuesdays. Don't turn up before 11pm. €2 including one drink.
Bar Quita Pesares Plaza Jerónimo de Córdoba, near the church of Santa Catalina. Run by the flamenco singer Peregil, this is a chaotic venue where there's often spontaneous music, especially at weekends. Things get lively around midnight and, more importantly, when the owner is on song. If he isn't, he'll sell you a cassette of an occasion when he was.
El Simpecao Paseo de la O s/n. Triana flamenco bar with a youthful crowd that often erupts into

Sevilla boasts two of the largest festival celebrations in Spain. The first, **Semana Santa** (Holy Week), always spectacular in Andalucía, is here at its peak with extraordinary processions of masked penitents and lavish floats. The second, the **Feria de Abril**, is unique to the city – a one-time market festival, now a week-long party of drink, food and flamenco. The *feria* follows hard on the heels of Semana Santa so if you have the energy, experience both.

Semana Santa

Semana Santa may be a religious festival, but for most of the week solemnity isn't the keynote – there's lots of carousing and frivolity, and bars are full day and night. In essence, it involves the marching in procession of brotherhoods of the church (*cofradías*) and penitents, followed by *pasos*, elaborate platforms or floats on which sit seventeenth-century images of the Virgin or of Christ. For weeks beforehand, the city's fifty-plus *cofradías* painstakingly adorn the hundred or so *pasos* (each brotherhood normally carries two; Christ and a Virgin), spending as much as €350,000 on flowers, costumes, candles, bands and precious stones. The bearers (*costaleros*, from the padded *costal* or bag protecting their shoulders) walk in time to traditional dirges and drumbeats from the bands, which are often punctuated by impromptu street-corner *saetas* – short, fervent, flamenco-style hymns about the Passion and the Virgin's sorrows.

Each procession leaves its district of the city on a different day and time during Holy Week and finally ends up joining the official route at La Campana (off Plaza Duque de la Victoria) to proceed along c/Sierpes, through the cathedral and around the Giralda and the Bishop's Palace. **Good Friday** morning is the climax, when the *pasos* leave the churches at midnight and move through the town for much of the night. The highlights then are the procession of El Silencio – the oldest *cofradía* of all, established in 1340 – in total silence, and the arrival at the cathedral of **La Esperanza Macarena**, an image of the patron Virgin of bullfighters, and by extension of Sevilla itself.

On **Maundy Thursday** women dress in black and it's considered respectful for tourists not to dress in shorts or T-shirts. Triana is a good place to be on this day when, in the early afternoon, **Las Cigarreras** (the *cofradía* attached to the chapel of the new tobacco factory) starts out for the cathedral with much *gitano* enthusiasm.

To see the climax of all the processions, save that of the Resurrection on **Easter Sunday**, there's always a crush of spectators outside the cathedral and along c/Sierpes. However, without a seat (the best of which are rented by the hour and

impromptu flamenco – especially at weekends after 10.30pm. To get there, follow a passage to the river just before the Iglesia de la O on c/Castilla, then turn left along the riverbank for 100m.

Sol Café Cantante c/Sol 5, in La Macarena ☎954 22 51 65. Very good and serious flamenco theatre dedicated to discovering new talent and also staging big-name artists from all over Andalucía. Shows start at 10pm Thurs–Sat and cost €10 including one free drink.

Café Bar La Sonanta c/San Jacinto 31, near the church of San Jacinto in Triana. Good local flamenco bar in this atmospheric *barrio*. Flamenco on Thursdays from 10pm (free) except Jul & Aug.

La Taberna c/Duarte 3, near the Iglesia de Santa Ana, Triana. Long-established bar staging flamenco performances on Fridays from midnight on.

El Tamboril Plaza de Santa Cruz s/n. Tucked into the northeast corner of the plaza, this is another place with a great *ambiente flamenco* where singers often drop in, guitars are strummed, hands start to clap and the magic takes over.

Teatro Central Isla de Cartuja ☎95 446 06 00. Worth checking on this venue in the local press or with the Turismo, as they often stage festivals featuring up-and-coming flamenco talents as well as established performers.

booked up weeks in advance; contact the Turismo for details) or an invitation to share someone's balcony, viewing spots near the cathedral are almost impossible to find. A good place to stand is beneath the Giralda, where the processions exit into Plaza de la Virgen de los Reyes, but even here it gets chaotic. The best way of all to see the processions is to pick them up on the way from and to their *barrios*, which is where you'll see the true *teatro de la calle* – the theatre of the streets.

During Semana Santa the pattern of events changes every day, and while newsstands stock the official programme – *Programa de la Semana Santa* – they quickly sell out. A daily detailed **timetable** is issued with local papers (*El Correo* and *Diario de Sevilla* both do coloured route maps) and is essential if you want to know which processions are where. The ultra-Catholic *ABC* paper has the best background information, and the Turismo's *El Giraldillo* listings magazine prints a brief programme, whilst the banks and bigger hotels tend to produce their own guides. The national *El Mundo* newspaper also puts out an excellent pocket guide with all the routes and *cofradías* tunics listed in colour, and is available from newsstands. A dedicated **website**, ⓦwww.lapasion.net, also has lots of background information and links.

The Feria de Abril

The nonstop, week-long **Feria de Abril** takes place in the second half of the month when a vast area on the west bank of the river, the Real de la Feria, is taken over by rows of *casetas*, canvas pavilions and tents of varying sizes. Some of these belong to eminent *sevillano* families, some to groups of friends, others to clubs, trade associations or political parties. Each one resounds with flamenco singing and dancing from around 9pm until perhaps 6am or 7am the following morning. Many of the men and virtually all the women wear traditional costume, the latter in an astonishing array of brilliantly coloured, flounced gypsy dresses.

The sheer size of this spectacle makes it extraordinary, and the dancing, with its intense and knowing sexuality, is a revelation. But most infectious of all is the universal spontaneity of enjoyment; after wandering around staring, you wind up a part of it, drinking and dancing in one of the "open" *casetas* which have commercial bars. Earlier in the day, from 1pm until 5pm, *sevillana* society **parades** around the fairground in carriages or on horseback in an incredible extravaganza of display and voyeurism with subtle but distinct gradations of dress and style. Each day, too, there are **bullfights** (at around 5.30pm; very expensive tickets in advance from the ring), generally reckoned to be the best of the season.

Discotecas and live music

Earlier on in the evening, Sevilla's **discotecas** attract a very young crowd; the serious action starts after midnight and often lasts till well beyond dawn. For **live music** the bars around Plaza Alfalfa and Alameda de Hércules have the best of the action.

In summer as the town heats up, much of the *movida* (action) switches to the **terrace bars** along the river to the north of the Puente de Triana (aka Puente de Isabel II as far as the Puente de la Barqueta.

Antique Avda. Matemáticos Rey Pastor y Castro s/n, near southern edge of Isla Magica theme park. Popular with Sevilla's *pijo* (yuppie) crowd, this place comes with a transparent dance floor and music that goes from Latin pop to heavier stuff. Open Thurs, Fri & Sat from midnight.

Bestiario Plaza Nueva end of c/Zaragoza. All-day (and night) disco-bar throbbing with manic techno sounds.

Boss c/Betis 67. Cavernous disco which takes off after midnight; has a penchant for house.

Catedral c/Cuesta del Rosario, near the Iglesia del

△ Flamenco

Salvador. Upmarket but attractive smaller disco playing techno, funk and soul. Sometimes has live bands (usually Thurs).

Collage c/Julio César 4, near the Puente de Triana. Cool place with best of Caribbean rhythm: salsa, merengue and bachata.

Faraón c/Trajano 38. Double-floored place done out in Egyptian style. Upper floor for drinking whilst lower floor moves to trance, house and related rhythms. Open Sat & Sun from 7pm; €6 entry includes free drink.

Fun Club Alameda de Hércules 86. Popular weekends-only music and dance bar with live bands. Open Thurs–Sat from 11.30pm.

Holiday c/Jesus del Gran Poder 73, near the Alameda de Hércules. Popular *discoteca* attracting a 30s-plus clientele.

Jazz Bar Naima c/Trajano 47, close to the Alameda. Down-to-earth jazz music bar, this is a popular place which sometimes stages live gigs.

La Reja c/Vargas Campos, just off c/Sierpes. Centre-of-town dance place that has occasional themed nights.

Nu Yor c/Marqués de Paradas 30, near the Puente de Triana. Small disco-bar with Latin (especially Cuban) sounds at weekends and salsa, reggae and flamenco weeknights inside an attractive old building.

Copas and music bars

Copas bars (drinking bars) are scattered all over the centre and many play music. Clusters of good ones are to be found in the Alameda de Hércules and Plaza Alfalfa zones in El Centro, with more gathered to the north of the Maestranza bullring – where there's also a **gay** scene – and along c/Betis in Triana.

Antigüedades c/Argote de Molina 10, near the cathedral. Arty music bar with paintings and sculptures hanging from the ceiling, many the work of the owner.

Azúcar de Cuba Paseo de las Delicias 3 (next door to McDonalds), at the junction with Avda. San Jurjo and near the Puerta de Jerez. A corner of Cuba in Sevilla where the proprietors (from Havana) play salsa sounds accompanied by authentic nibbles. Open daily and till 3am at weekends.

Bar Garlochí c/Boteros 4, one block northeast of Plaza Alfafa. Claims the title as the city's most eccentric bar, a wonderfully kitsch "religious shrine" complete with incense, candles and flying angels. Their sacrilegious Sangre de Cristo crimson cocktail is a must.

Bar Maestranza c/Dos de Mayo 28, near the Maestranza theatre. Pleasant, relaxing bar that fills up on opera and concert nights, often with the musicians and performers themselves.

Bauhaus c/Marqués de Paradas 53, north of the bullring. Bar with resident and guest DJs, techno and electronic music, and light shows.

Bulebar Alameda de Hércules 83. Late-opening bar with a plant-filled terrace facing the Alameda. Often stages theatre, music or other events and serves tapas and *pasteles*.

Café Anibal c/Castilla 98, near the river in Triana. Relaxed music bar inside an ancient Triana mansion with many rooms.

El Barón Rampante c/Arias Montano 3, just off the west side of the Alameda de Hércules. Trendy gay and mixed place with an interesting (and evolving) decor. Good for afternoon coffee and

pasteles or *copas* and cool sounds at night. *El Bosque Encantado*, next door, is also good.

Elefunk c/Adriano 10, near the bullring. Modish *copas* bar with funky *latino* sounds, frequent live bands, and late hours.

La Carbonería c/Levíes 18 (see "Flamenco" on p.337). One of the cities emblematic bars which puts on art shows and different kinds of music including flamenco. Also does decent tapas and *raciones*.

La Imperdible Plaza San Antonio de Padua 9, between the Alameda de Hércules and the river. Vibrant café-bar which puts on fringe theatre, live jazz, poetry readings, short films by local filmmakers (Tues), art and photographic shows and much more. Opens at 9pm; closed Mon.

Sopa de Ganso c/Pérez Galdós 8, in the Alfalfa zone. Music bar serving tapas till late, and with a good selection of vegetarian goodies.

Taberna Anima c/Miguel Cid 80, north of the Museo Bellas Artes. Charming and popular tiled bar (try their *vino caliente*) which doubles up as a vibrant cultural centre; stages art and photo shows all year round.

Trinity Irish Pub c/Madrid s/n, just off Plaza Nueva. For those with a fondness for Guinness this is Sevilla's nearest approximation to a Dublin hostelry. *Flahertys*, c/Alemanes 7, next to the Cathedral is an earthier Celtic venue with big sports screens and pub grub.

Urbano Comix c/Matahacas 5, near the Convento de Santa Paula in Macarena. Popular student bar with zany urban décor for rock, punk and R&B sounds plus live bands, staying open till dawn.

Summer terrace bars

On sultry summer nights it's worth doing what *sevillanos* do and making a beeline for these riverside oases which are the only place to stay really cool in July and August (and often in June and September too). Note that many of these bars stay open only for a season and open up the next under different names and owners.

Alfonso Avda. de la Palmera, at the junction of Paseo de las Delicias and Plaza America in the Parque de María Luisa. Popular terrace bar in the park for cooling off over a long drink. Open from mid-evening to 5am. The neighbouring *Bilindo* and *Libano* opposite are similar relaxing places.

El Capote Next to the Puente de Triana (aka Isabel II). Highly popular riverside bar with outdoor terrace which often stages live bands in summer.

El Chile Paseo de las Delicias, near the Parque de María Luisa. Housed in the old Chile pavilion of the 1929 Fair of the Americas, this a colourful

bar with a pleasant terrace sometimes featuring live music.

El Palenque Triana venue at junction of Avda. Matemáticos Rey Pastor y Castro with Camino delos Descubrimientos, near the Isla Magica theme park. A canopy-covered building housing two summer terrazas, *Tribal* and *Chocolate*.

El Paseo c/Paseo de Colón 2, just opposite the Puente de Triana. Small gay bar playing 1970–90s music.

La Otra Orilla Paseo de Nuestra Señora de la O, near c/Castilla and the Puente del Cachorro. Very attractive riverside bar and *copas terraza*.

Shopping

Sevilla is a great place to **shop**, offering everything from regional crafts and ceramics to chic designer fashions and accessories. Shops – except for the larger department stores such as El Corte Inglés – generally close during the afternoon siesta (roughly 1.30–5.30pm) and stay open until 8 or 9pm.

Ceramics, flamenco and fashion

For typically Andalucian souvenirs, Ceramica Santa Ana, c/San Jorge 31, near the Puente de Triana, has a wide selection of Triana **pots** and **tiles**. Nearby, at Ceramica Rocio-Triana, c/Antillano Campos 8, Rafael Muñiz is a creative potter with a more modern slant who will also create a customized painted tile image (any size) to take home or have sent.

Flamenco dresses to sport during the *feria* or take home are available from Duende, c/San Eloy 29, the nearby Doña Ana, c/San Eloy 14, and Angeles Berral, c/Francos 16, while El Corte Inglés, Plaza Duque de la Victoria, also stocks a wide range leading up to the *feria*; prices start at around €180 but you can sometimes pick up a bargain for half this. Molina, c/Sierpes 11, is another good place to try. Casa Damas, c/Sierpes 61, has a wide range of **flamenco CDs** and books and Compás Sur, Cuesta del Rosario 7, just east of the Iglesia de El Salvador, is another well-stocked little flamenco place.

Toreros get their kit at Pedro Alagaba "Sastrería de Toreros", c/Adriano 39 next to the Maestranza, a fascinating shop specializing in bullfighting attire. Cutting-edge women's **designer fashions** are sold by Purificación García, c/Rioja 13 (off c/Sierpes), while Daniela, c/San Eloy 25 and Cuqui Castellanos, c/Rosario 8, both do imaginative women's shoes. Attractive modern porcelain can be seen at Sargadelos, c/Albareda 17 (off Plaza Nueva), and glassware and candles at Mercedes Marquez, c/Méndez Núñez 7, nearby.

Art and books

Sevilla has a thriving artistic community and many of the **art galleries** are worth a look. The central Galería Margerita Albarrán, c/Mesón de los Caballeros 2 (just off c/Carlos Cañal near Plaza Nueva; 11am–2pm & 6–9pm Tues–Sat), mounts quality exhibitions and has a huge browsable stock of limited edition prints, small sculptures and canvases – many by *sevillano* artists – at very reasonable prices. Other interesting galleries include: La Caja China, c/General Castaños, near the bullring in an elegant building, and Rafael Ortíz, c/Marmoles 12, with international names in painting and sculpture and housed in an attractive old factory, while Pepe Cobo, c/Cardenal Cisneros 5 (just north of the Museo Bellas Artes) is a top-notch gallery selling works by big names such as Warhol and Juan Muñoz. Grabados Antiguos Buril, c/Gamazo 14 near the bullring, sells engravings of provincial, regional and *sevillano* themes.

A wide range of **books** in English (and other languages) is stocked by Vértice, c/San Fernando 33, near the Alcázar, and the Beta chain is also good for guides and maps: central branches include Avda. Constitución 20, Plaza de Gavidia 7 and c/Sagasta 5, just west of Plaza El Salvador. El Corte Inglés, Plaza Duque de la Victoria, stocks English titles and international press. A more comprehensive range of international **newspapers** is stocked by Esteban, c/Alemanes 15, right next to the cathedral.

Markets

Entertaining Sunday **markets** (*mercadillos*; roughly 10am–2pm depending on weather) take place on the Plaza del Cabildo opposite the Cathedral (stamps, coins, pins, ancient artefacts), Plaza del Museo fronting the Museo de las Bellas Artes (various art, tiles and woodcarvings), and Plaza Alfalfa (pets). Calle Feria's longstanding El Jueves Thursday market near the Alameda de Hércules, with secondhand articles and antiques, is another good one. An excellent *artesanía* market, El Postigo, c/Arfe s/n, just west of the cathedral, displays a range of fans, glassware, ceramics, silverware and jewellery with innovative designs made by local craftspeople. Calle Sierpes is a good place for souvenir hunting with lots of quality shops and the nearby Manualidades Cuevas, c/Hernando Colón 5, is a wonderful antique toy shop with lots of surprises.

Listings

Airport information ☏95 444 90 00 for flight information. For flights run by Iberia ring ☏902 400 500.

American Express Plaza Nueva 7 (Mon–Fri 9.30am–1.30pm & 4.30–8pm, Sat 10am–1pm; ☏95 421 16 17). Commission-free banknotes and travellers' cheques exchanged.

Banks and currency exchange Numerous places around the centre, specifically on the Avda. de la Constitución and around Plaza Duque de la Victoria, have ATMs. Bureaux de change can be found on Plaza Nueva but banks are a cheaper option. Banking hours are Mon–Fri 8.30am–2pm. American Express (see above) and the department store El Corte Inglés on Plaza Duque de la Victoria (Mon–Sat 10am–10pm) offer good exchange rates. Most large hotels change notes.

Bike and scooter rental Cyclotour, with stands at the Torre del Oro and in the Parque de María Luisa (from 11am; ☏95 427 45 66), rent cycles for €3/hr or €10 per half-day. They also rent out electric bikes and do guided bike tours of the city. Pedal y Aventura c/Castilla 139, (☏95 433 17 75, ⊛www.pedalyaventura.com) offer guided cycling expeditions to the sierras near the city. Motorbikes, scooters and cycles can be rented from Alkimoto, at c/Fernando Tirado 5, slightly south of the Santa Justa train station (☏95 458 49 27, ⊛www .alkimoto.com); prices for cycles are €8 per day and motorcycles and scooters start at €24 per day. The nearby Renta Moto, c/Padre Méndez Casariego 19 (☏95 441 75 00, ⊛www.rentamoto.net), has similar prices and deals.

Bullfights The main *corridas* are staged during the April *feria*. Tickets from the Plaza de Toros or (with commission) the nearby Impresa Pagés ticket office at c/Adriano 37.

Car rental Avis (☏95 453 78 61) and Europcar (☏95 453 39 14) are located at Santa Justa train station. Good local deals are to be had from Ata S.A. c/Almirante Lobo 2 (☏954 22 09 57), off the Puerta de Jerez.

Consulates Australia, c/Federico Rubio 14 ☏95

422 09 71; for Britain contact Málaga consulate ☏95 235 23 00; Ireland, Plaza Santa Cruz 6, Bajo A ☏95 421 63 61; USA, Paseo de las Delicias 7 ☏95 423 18 85.

Football Sevilla has two major teams playing in Division One. Sevilla FC play at the Sánchez Pizjuan stadium, Avda. Eduardo Dato s/n (☏95 448 94 00, ⊛www.sevillafc.es), on the east side of town. Their fierce rivals Real Betis – the better of the two over recent seasons – play at Estadio Benito Villamarín, Avda. Heliópolis s/n (☏95 461 03 40, ⊛www .realbetisbalompie.es), in the southern suburbs. Pick up schedules from local or national press; you can usually buy tickets at the ground and also at the main Turismo at Avda. de la Constitución 21.

Hospital English-speaking doctors are available at Hospital Universitario Virgen Macarena, c/Dr Marañon s/n (☏95 50 75 00), behind the Andalucía parliament building to the north of the centre. For emergencies, dial ☏061.

Internet There are numerous Internet cafés all around the centre of town and several bars now have screens for Internet access. Almost opposite the cathedral's main entrance, *Seville Internet Center*, c/Almirantazgo 2, on the first floor (daily 9am–10pm; ☏95 450 02 75), is probably the most central. One of the cheapest is *Ciberducke*, c/Trajano 8 (daily 10am–11pm; ☏95 456 34 17). while *Internetia* (daily 10am–1am, ☏95 453 40 03) Avda. Menendez Pelayo, is a modern, spacious place with bar. Other options include *Internet Multimedia Center*, c/Adriano 7 (daily 10am–1am; ☏95 450 25 43), the *E-m@il Place*, c/Sierpes 54, Pasaje de las Delicias (daily 10am–10pm, ☏95 421 85 92), *New Center*, c/Arjona 20 (Mon–Sat 10am–10pm, Sun 3–10pm, ☏95 422 29 05), *@DS Macarena*, c/San Luis 108 (daily 11am–10pm, ☏95 438 06 13), and *Ciber Alcázar*, c/San Fernando 35, facing the Antigua Fábrica de Tabacos (Mon–Fri 10am–11pm & Sat–Sun noon–11pm; ☏95 421 04 01).

Laundry Tintorería Vera, c/Arjona 3, close to the Plaza de Armas bus station (Mon–Fri 9.30am– 1.30pm & 5–8pm, Sat 10am–1.30pm); Lavandería

Sevilla, c/Castelar 2, east of the bullring (Mon–Fri 9.30am–1pm & 5–8.30pm, Sat 10am–2pm); Lavandería Águila, c/Águilas 21, near the Casa de Pilatos (Mon–Fri 10am–8.30pm, Sat 10am–2pm).

Newspapers Sevilla's best all-round daily paper is currently *El Diario de Sevilla*, although the older *El Correo* also sells well; both are good for entertainment listings and local news.

Left luggage There are coin-operated lockers at the Santa Justa train station (€2.40 for 24hr). It's tricky to find, so ask for the *consigna*. The Prado de San Sebastián bus station has a left-luggage office (daily 7am–10pm; €2 per day), and there is another *consigna* at the Plaza de Armas bus station (9am–1.30pm & 3.30–7pm; €3 per day); note that it's not inside the bus station but around the right side of the building by the taxis.

Lost property Oficina de Objetos Perdidos, c/Manuel V. Sagastizábal 3, next to the Prado de San

Sebastián bus station (Mon–Fri 9.30am–1.30pm; ☎95 442 04 03).

Maps and hiking For made-to-measure maps in 1:50,000, 1:100,000 and 1:200,000 scales for a defined area, ring Francisco Marquez, c/Las Cruzadas 7, immediately behind the Plaza de España (☎95 442 03 04), LTC, Avda. Menéndez Pelayo 42 in Santa Cruz (☎95 442 59 64), and Risko, Avda. Kansas City 26, close to Santa Justa train station (☎95 457 08 49), also stocks maps, and has a wide range of outdoor equipment.

Police For emergencies dial ☎092 (local police; less serious matters) or ☎091 (national; violent crime and so on). Central local police stations are at c/Arenal 1 (☎95 459 05 58) and c/Credito 11 (☎95 437 84 96), off the north end of the Alameda de Hércules.

Post office Avda. de la Constitución 32, by the cathedral; also for poste restante (Lista de Correos). Mon–Fri 8.30am–8.30pm, Sat 9.30am–2pm.

Taxis See "City transport", p.291.

North of Sevilla: Itálica and around

The Roman ruins and remarkable mosaics of **Itálica** and the exceptional Gothic monastery of **San Isidoro del Campo** lie some 9km to the north of Sevilla, just outside the village of **Santiponce**, and both are easily reached by bus from the Plaza de Armas bus station in Sevilla (Bay 34; every 30min; Sun every hour), a journey of about twenty minutes. The bus passes the monastery (see below) on its way to the terminus outside the archeological site entrance.

Itálica and Santiponce

Once inside the entrance to **Itálica** (April–Sept Tues–Sat 8.30am–8.30pm, Sun 9am–3pm; Oct–March Tues–Sat 9am–5.30pm, Sun 10am–4pm; €1.50, free with EU passport) a free site map from the ticket office will enable identification of the main features. As you survey the dusty, featureless landscape of the site today it's hard to believe that this was once the third largest city of the Roman world, surpassed only by Alexandria and Rome itself. Itálica was the birthplace of two emperors (Trajan and Hadrian) and was one of the earliest Roman settlements in Spain. Founded in 206 BC by Scipio Africanus after his decisive victory over the Carthaginians at nearby Alcalá del Río, it became a settlement for many of his veterans, who called the place "Itálica" to remind them of home. With a thriving port – now beneath Santiponce – the city rose to considerable military importance in the second and third centuries AD, when it was richly endowed during the reign of Hadrian (117–138). Grand buildings dripped with fine marble brought from Italy, Greece, Turkey and Egypt, and the population swelled to half a million. Itálica declined as an urban centre only under the Visigoths, who preferred Sevilla, then known as Hispalis. Eventually the city was deserted by the Moors after the river changed its course, disrupting the surrounding terrain.

In the Middle Ages the ruins were used as a source of stone for Sevilla, and, from the eighteenth century onwards, lack of any regulation allowed enthusiastic amateurs to indulge their treasure-hunting whims and carry away or sell whatever they found. The duke of Wellington spent some time excavating here during the Peninsular Wars and later the countess of Lebrija conducted her own "digs" to fill her palace in Sevilla with mosaics and artefacts. Somehow, however, the shell of its enormous **amphitheatre** – the third largest in the Roman world – has survived. It is crumbling perilously, but you can clearly detect the rows of seats for an audience of 25,000, the corridors and the dens for wild beasts.

Beyond, within a rambling and unkempt grid of streets and villas, about twenty **mosaics** have been uncovered in what was originally the northern, richer sector of the city. Look for the outstanding Neptune mosaic in the house of the same name, as well as the colourful bird mosaic in the Casa de los Pájaros depicting 33 different species. Towards the baths, in the Casa del Planetario, there's a fascinating representation of the Roman planetary divinities who, in the Roman calendar, gave their names to the days of the week. Finally, the Hadrianic **baths** on the site's western edge are divided into those for men to the centre and right, and those for women to the left.

Itálica today is at the leading edge of archeological technology: advanced X-ray techniques, ground-penetrating radar and infrared aerial photography are being used to gauge the scope of the subterranean remains. So far a large stretch of fourth-century wall has been identified along with what is believed to have been a great religious complex constructed by Hadrian and dedicated to the worship of his adoptive father Trajan.

There's also a well-preserved **Roman theatre** (Tues–Thurs 8am–3pm, Fri–Sat 8am–3pm & 4–7pm, Sun 10–3pm; free) and **baths** in the village of **Santiponce** itself – beneath which lies another sizeable chunk of unexcavated Itálica – a five-minute walk away from the site entrance and signposted from the main road. On the way there you'll pass Santiponce's helpful **tourist office** at c/La Feria s/n (Tues–Sat 8am–3pm, Sun 10am–3pm; Aug Tues–Sat 10am–2pm, Sun 10am–3pm; ☎955 99 80 28; ⓦ www.ayto-santiponce.es). For a meal before or after your visit, the *Ventorrillo Canario* **restaurant** almost opposite the site entrance does good *platos combinados* and is famous for its charcoal-grilled steaks served with *papas arrugadas* – small baked potatoes in *mojo* spicy sauce. Fifty metres away down a side street behind this, *La Caseta de Antonio* is just as good, and the best place for fish or an outstanding paella.

Monasterio Isidoro del Campo

A little over 1km to the south of Santiponce on the road back to Sevilla lies the former Cistercian **Monasterio Isidoro del Campo** (Wed & Thurs 10am–2pm, Fri & Sat 10am–2pm & 5.30–8.30pm, Sun 10am–3pm; €2). Closed for many years, it has now been painstakingly and gloriously restored by the Junta de Andalucía and shouldn't be missed.

Founded by the thirteenth-century monarch Guzmán El Bueno of Tarifa fame, the monastery is a masterpiece of Gothic architecture which, prior to its confiscation during the nineteenth century Disentailment, was occupied by a number of religious orders. Among these were the *ermitaños jerónimos* (Hieronymites) who, in the fifteenth century decorated the central cloister and the Patio de los Evangelistas with a remarkable series of **mural paintings** depicting images of the saints – including scenes from the life of San Jerónimo – as well as astonishingly beautiful floral and Mudéjar-influenced geometric designs. In the sixteenth century the monastery was renowned for its library and in 1569 Casiodoro de Reina made the first translation of the Bible into Castilian Spanish (a copy is on display). But when de Reina and others began to display an overzealous interest in the Protestant ideas of Martin Luther the community fell foul of the Inquisition and was dissolved with some monks being executed and others escaping abroad.

The monastery was then assigned to the non-hermitic main order of San Jerónimo which employed the seventeenth-century sculptor Juan Martínez Montañés to create the magnificent **retablo mayor** in the larger of the complex's twin churches. Depicting scenes from the *Nativity*, the *Adoration of the Kings* and *San Jerónimo* himself, this is one of the greatest works by this *andaluz* master of wood sculpture. In wall niches alongside the *retablo* – and positioned above their tombs – are images of Guzmán El Bueno and his spouse, also by Montañés. Other highlights of this remarkable building include the **Sala Capitular** (chapterhouse) with more wall paintings and **Refectorio** (refectory) with a fine mural of the *Sagrada Cena* (Last Supper) occupying an end wall and displaying more geometric designs worked into the table linen.

To **get here** without your own transport the easiest way to see both monuments (noting the opening hours) is to ask the bus to drop you at the monastery stop ("Parada Monasterio") on the outward journey. When you've seen the monastery you can then cover the 1.5km (a fifteen-minute walk or take a later bus) through the village of Santiponce to the Itálica site entrance, from where buses return to the city.

East from Sevilla

The direct route east by train or car along the valley of the Guadalquivir heading towards Córdoba is a flat and largely unexciting journey. There's far more to see following the A4-E5 route just to the south of this (the one used by most buses), via **Carmona** and **Écija**, both interesting towns. Plenty of buses run along these roads so there's no real need to stay – Carmona in particular is an easy thirty-kilometre day-trip from Sevilla.

Leaving Sevilla the A4-E5 crosses **La Campiña**, a rich and undulating lowland framed between the Guadalquivir to the north and the hills of Penibetic Cordillera to the south. It's a sparsely populated area, its towns thinly spread and far apart – a legacy of post-*Reconquista* days when large landed estates were doled out to the nobility by the crown. The feudal nature of this system of *latifundia* (great estates where the nobles owned not only the towns but also the inhabitants and the serfs on the land) wrought much bitterness in Andalucía, vividly described in Ronald Fraser's book, *Pueblo*.

Carmona

Sited on a low hill overlooking a fertile plain planted with fields of barley, wheat and sunflowers, **CARMONA** is a small, picturesque town which has burst beyond its ancient walls. Founded by the Carthaginians in the third century BC probably on the site of a Turditani Iberian settlement, they named it Kar-Hammon (City of Baal-Hammon) after their great deity – the origin, via the Roman "Carmo", of its present name. A major Roman town (from which era it preserves a fascinating subterranean necropolis), it was also an important *taifa* state in Moorish times. Following the *Reconquista*, Pedro the Cruel built a palace within its walls, which he used as a "provincial" royal residence – it's now the modern parador.

Arrival, information and accommodation

The **bus from Sevilla** will drop you on the Paseo del Estatuto in sight of the Moorish Puerta de Sevilla, a grand and ancient fortified gateway to the old

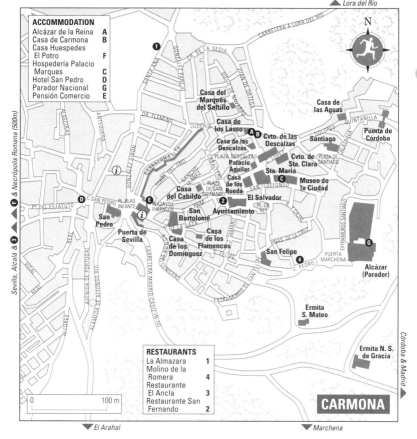

ACCOMMODATION

Alcázar de la Reina	**A**
Casa de Carmona	**B**
Casa Huespedes El Potro	**F**
Hospedería Palacio Marques	**C**
Hotel San Pedro	**D**
Parador Nacional	**G**
Pensión Comercio	**E**

RESTAURANTS

La Almazara	**1**
Molino de la Romera	**4**
Restaurante El Ancla	**3**
Restaurante San Fernando	**2**

CARMONA

0   100 m

town. Located inside the gateway is an efficient **Turismo** (Mon–Sat 10am–6pm, Sun 10am–3pm; ☎95 419 09 55, ⓦ www.turismo.carmona.org). Arriving by **car** use the subterranean **car park** beneath the Paseo de Estatuto (on the left of our map). Parking places also become free along the main c/San Pedro during the siesta period and after 7pm. This is also the halt for **buses from Córdoba and Éjica**.

Carmona has a shortage of **places to stay**, especially in the budget category; if you arrive late in the day during high season you'd be advised to grab what you can. Otherwise, ringing ahead is advised. The cheaper places lie outside the walls, whilst a clutch of more upmarket options all occupy scenic locations in the old town and have their own restaurants and garages. Prices below reflect the *temporada media* (shoulder season) which covers the months of May, September and October. All other periods are low season when (particularly hotel) prices will be significantly cheaper.

Alcázar de la Reina Plaza de Lasso 2 ☎95 419 62 00, ⓦ www.alcazardelareina.com. Rather bland addition to Carmona's luxury hotel list. Fully equipped rooms have Internet access and there's a pool. **⓭**

Casa de Carmona Plaza de Lasso 1 ☎95 419 10 00, ⓦ www.casadecarmona.com. Stylish transformation of a seventeenth-century *casa-palacio* into a serene hotel where rooms are decorated with genuine antiques and artworks. **⓮** with breakfast.

347

Casa Huespedes El Potro c/Sevilla 78 ☎95 414 14 65. The cheapest (and most spartan) option in town with very basic rooms above a restaurant. ❶
Hacienda El Triguero 4km southwest of town along the A392, direction El Viso ☎95 595 36 26, ⓦwww.eltriguero.galeon.com. With your own transport this farmhouse location with en-suite rooms becomes an attractive possibility when places in town are full; also has a pool. Ring ahead before turning up. ❺ inc. breakfast

🏃 Hospedería Palacio Marqués de las Torres c/Fermín Molpeceres 2 ☎95 419 62 48, ⓦwww.hospederiamarquesdelastorres.com. A charming eighteenth-century palace converted into a welcoming new option in the old town. In addition to double rooms there are intriguing dormitories divided into two-bed and four-bed partitioned cubicles (€18 per person) sharing bath. Rates include breakfast. ❹

Hotel San Pedro c/San Pedro 3 ☎95 419 00 87. This pleasant budget place offers a/c rooms with bath and TV. ❹

🏃 Parador Nacional Alcázar Rey Don Pedro ☎95 414 10 10, ⓦwww.parador.es. Despite more recent competition at this end of the market, a superb location, patios and swimming pool ensure that this is still the nicest – and best value – of the luxury places in town. Pay a few euros extra for a room with a balcony. It's worth calling in for a drink at the bar, to enjoy the fabulous views from the terrace. ❽

🏃 Pensión Comercio c/Torre del Oro 56 ☎95 414 00 18. Built into the Puerta de Sevilla gateway, this is a charming small *hostal* with compact a/c en-suite rooms (without TV) around a pretty patio. The terrace overlooks the gate and a good restaurant offers an economical *menú* . ❸

The Town

The majority of Carmona's monuments and churches lie inside the ancient walls. The only site involving a bit of effort to get to is the remarkable **Necrópolis Romana** (Roman cemetery) on the west side of town, a ten-minute walk from the old quarter.

San Pedro and the Puerta de Sevilla

The fifteenth-century church of **San Pedro** (April–June & Sept daily 11am–2pm; Oct–March Mon–Tues & Thurs–Sun 11am–2pm, plus Mon & Thurs 5–7pm; closed July–Aug; €1.20) near the main bus stop, is a good place to start exploring Carmona. With its soaring tower built in imitation of the Giralda and added a century later, San Pedro evokes a feeling of Sevilla – entirely appropriate since the two towns share a similar history, and under the Moors Carmona was often governed by a brother of the Sevillian ruler. Inside, the church has a superb Baroque **sagrario chapel** by Figueroa. Just behind the church at the top of Avda. de Portugal lies a famous fifteen-spouted **fountain**, which has figured in many flamenco songs and poems about the town.

The **old town** – circled by 4km of ancient walls containing substantial Carthaginian, Roman and Moorish elements – is entered by the **Puerta de Sevilla**, an impressive double gateway (tours organized by the Turismo Mon–Sat 10am–6pm, Sun 10am–3pm; €2). Although most of what you see now is of Roman origin there has been a gate of some form here since Iberian times: remains dating back to the late second millennium BC have been found in recent excavations. Through this gate passed the great Vía Augusta on its way from Hispalis (Sevilla) to Corduba (Córdoba). During the Moorish period a fortified *alcázar* was added creating the great bastion that still dominates the town's western flank today.

Inside the walls, narrow streets wind upwards past Mudéjar churches and Renaissance mansions. Follow c/Prim uphill to the **Plaza San Fernando** (or Plaza Mayor), modest in size but overlooked by splendid Moorish-style buildings, including the **Casa del Cabildo** (the old Ayuntamiento). A striking Renaissance facade fronts the town's present **Ayuntamiento** (Mon–Fri 8am–3pm) in the square's southeast corner, which is worth a visit to view in its patio a striking geometric-patterned Roman mosaic with a head of Medusa. Behind the plaza (reached by taking c/Sacramento and turning right along c/Dominguez de Aposanto) there's a bustling fruit and vegetable **market** in an elegant porticoed square.

Santa María La Mayor and the Museo de la Ciudad

Moving east from the Ayuntamiento – along c/ El Salvador, then left into c/Barrera and right along c/Ildefonso – you'll reach **Santa María la Mayor** (Mon–Fri 10am–2pm & 5.30–7.30pm, Sat 10am– 2pm, closed second half Aug; €3), a fine fifteenth-century Gothic church built over the former Almo-had Friday (main) mosque, whose elegant patio it retains, complete with orange trees and horseshoe arches. Like many of Carmona's churches it's capped by a Mudéjar tower, possibly utilizing part of the old minaret. One of

the patio's pillars is inscribed with a Visigothic liturgical calendar, said to be the oldest in Spain. The church's high altar has a splendid Renaissance *retablo* and, in the third chapel to the right, a fifteenth-century triptych by Alejandro Fernández. Slightly east of here and housed in the elegant eighteenth-century Casa del Marqués de las Torres is the **Museo de la Ciudad** (daily except Tues afternoon: June–Sept 10am–2pm & 6.30–9.30pm; Oct–May 11am–7pm; €2.00), documenting the history of the town with mildly interesting displays of artefacts from the prehistoric, Iberian, Carthaginian, Roman, Moorish and Christian epochs. The most entertaining feature is a series of interactive screens in a section dedicated to the role of flamenco in Andalucian culture – enabling you to call up an artiste of your choice and fill the museum with his or her spirited rendition. There's little in the way of bars in this area so the museum's **cafetería** (see "Eating and drinking", overleaf) provides a useful refreshment stop.

The Alcázar and around

Looming above the town's southeastern ridge are the massive ruins of Pedro's **Alcázar**, an Almohad fortress transformed into a lavish residence by the four-teenth-century king – employing the same Mudéjar craftsmen who worked on the Alcázar at Sevilla – but which was destroyed by an earthquake in 1504. It received further architectural attentions from Fernando (after Isabel's death) but later fell into ruin, until it was more recently renovated to become a remark-ably tasteful parador, entered through an imposing Moorish gate. Just west of here along c/Puerta Marchena, the Mudéjar church of **San Felipe** (try service times 7–8pm) is worth a look, if you can gain entry, as it has a fine *artesonado* ceiling inside. Even if you don't get in, an elegant tower and facade are still worth the walk.

To the northeast, beyond and below Pedro's palace, the town comes to an abrupt and romantic halt at the Roman **Puerta de Córdoba**, a second-century gateway with later Moorish and Renaissance additions, from where the old Córdoba road (now a dirt track) drops down to a vast and fertile plain. Following this ancient route for a few kilometres will lead you to a five-arched **Roman bridge** just visible on the plain below. Near to the gate, the church of **Santiago**, at the end of c/Calatrava, is another impressive fourteenth-century Mudéjar building with an elegant brick tower decorated with *azulejos*. Following c/Dolores Quintanilla (and its continuation, c/López) from the Puerta de Córdoba back to the centre, you'll pass by more *palacios* and churches, among them the fifteenth-century **Convento de Santa Clara** (Sat & Sun 10am–1pm), with a *mirador* tower on the left and paintings by Valdés Leal in its church, and beyond the eighteenth-century **Convento de las Descalzas**, the Baroque **Palacio de los Águilar** on the right with a fine facade.

The Roman cemetery

Lying on a low hill outside the walls, as was the Roman custom, Carmona's remarkable **Necrópolis Romana** (guided tours only, English spoken: June–Sept Tues–Fri 8.30am–2pm, Sat 10am–2pm; Oct–May Tues–Fri 9am–5pm, Sat & Sun 10am–2pm; €2, free with EU passport) is one of the most important in Spain. To get there, walk out of town from San Pedro along Paseo del Estatuto and its continuation c/Enmedio, parallel to the main Sevilla road, for about 450m. Here amid the cypress trees, more than nine hundred family tombs dating from the second century BC to the fourth century AD were excavated between 1881 and 1915. Enclosed in subterranean *columbaria* – chambers hewn from the rock – the tombs are often frescoed in the Pompeian style with images of garlands, birds and fruit, and contain a series of niches in which many of the funeral urns remain intact.

Some of the larger tombs, such as the **Tumba del Elefante** (complete with a stone elephant, perhaps symbolic of long life) are enormously elaborate, in preparation for the ceremonies that went with burial and after, when the tomb became a focus for family ritual centred on the dead. Alongside its burial chamber, a bath, pantry and kitchen with chimney as well as stone benches and tables for funeral banquets are wonderfully preserved. Most spectacular is the **Tumba de Servilia**, a huge colonnaded temple with vaulted side chambers and separate *columbaria* for the servants of the family. The tours lead you in gratifying detail round this extraordinary site, pointing out the various types of tombs, together with the **cremation pits** where the corpse would have been burned while members of the family (and hired mourners if they were rich) threw clothes and food into the flames for use in the afterlife. The paths between the tombs were also used in Roman times, and it doesn't take a lot of imagination to visualize a slow procession of grieving relatives and mourners preceded by flute players or trumpeters making their way to the family vault.

The site also has a small **museum**, whose finds from the tombs include gravestones, mosaics and vases. Opposite is a partly excavated second-century **amphitheatre**.

Eating and drinking

There are plenty of places to eat both in the old and new town and you don't need to spend a fortune to eat well. However, a step up in price will allow you to sample some of the best food in the province. In addition to the places below, all the upmarket hotels have their own **restaurants**, often with a reasonably priced *menú*. Carmona has its fair share of **tapas bars** too, and the Turismo have made it easy to do a *tapeadores* tour by producing a free tapas guide and map, called *Des Tapa Carmona*. In the old town it's worth seeking out *Mingalarío*, c/Salvador 1, near the church of El Salvador, which is a fine old bar with excellent tapas. *Bar Goya* c/Prim 42, off the west side of Plaza de San Fernando, *El Tapeo*, almost opposite (which also does a very good-value *menú*), and *Bar Plaza*, on the square itself, are also well worth a try.

Café-Restaurant Sierra Mayor Casa Marqués de las Torres. The bar-restaurant of the Museo de la Ciudad (see opposite) is a decent place for a range of tapas and an ideal lunch stop between monuments.

El Potro *Casa Huéspedes El Potro*, c/Sevilla 78. The restaurant of the *hostal* is a reliable and cheap place to eat and the food is reasonable for the price.

Ferrara Plaza de Lasso 2 ☏95 419 62 00. The restaurant of the *Hotel Alcázar de la Reina* despite being very good and rather swish is very reasonably priced and manages to offer an interesting *menú del día* for €14 (including wine & mineral water).

La Almazara c/Santa Ana 33 ☏954 19 07 76. Slightly out of the centre, this excellent, stylish restaurant and tapas bar in a refurbished old oil mill (*almazara*) offers a *menú* for around €12, and is definitely worth the walk. *Cabrito* (roasted kid) and *cochinilla* (suckling pig) and game dishes are among its specialities.

🏃 **Molino de la Romera** c/Pedro s/n, close to the Alcázar ☏954 14 20 00. With a great

terrace view across the *Campiña* and housed in a former Moorish oil mill, this pleasant restaurant serves up the dishes of the region, has a good value *menú* for around €17.50 (including wine) and its *dulces* are prepared by the nuns of the nearby Convento de Santa Clara.

Parador Nacional Alcázar Rey Don Pedro ☏95 414 10 10. The restaurant of the parador is a model of baronial splendour which can be experienced on a *menú del día* for €27 which includes many local dishes; à la carte is another matter. Main dishes €16–22.

🏃 **Restaurante El Ancla** c/Bonifacio IV, about 500m along the Alcala road ☏954 14 38 04. Out of the centre but well worth the effort, this is a great fish restaurant; there's also an outstanding tapas bar (with a tempting *menú* for around €7).

Restaurante San Fernando c/Sacramento 3 ☏954 14 35 56. Carmona's top restaurant is situated in an ancient *casa señorial* and serves fish (especially *bacalao*), game and meat dishes to a high standard; *menú de degustación* for €24.

Écija

One of the most distinctive and individual towns of Andalucía, **ÉCIJA** lies almost midway between Sevilla and Córdoba, in a basin of low sandy hills. The town is known, with no hint of exaggeration, as *la sartenilla de Andalucía* (the frying-pan of Andalucía) and once registered an alarming 52°C on the thermometer. In mid–August the only way to avoid this heat is to slink from one tiny shaded plaza to another, putting off sightseeing until late in the day. It's worth the effort, since Écija has eleven superb, decaying **church towers**, each glistening with brilliantly coloured tiles. The town also has a unique domestic architecture – a flamboyant style of twisted or florid forms, displayed in a number of fine mansions close to the centre.

The Romans knew Écija as Astigi (the modern inhabitants are known as *astigitanos*), probably the name of an earlier Iberian settlement. It was an important and prosperous olive-growing town, trading the prized Baetican oil all over the empire during the first and second centuries. In the early Christian era Écija became a bishopric, but in Moorish times (now named *Estadja*) sank into relative obscurity as part of the caliphate of Córdoba. Conquered by Fernando III in 1240, it was only in the seventeenth and eighteenth centuries that it staged a recovery, when the prosperity brought by the new *latifundia* – harking back to the great slave-worked Roman estates – encouraged the nobility to build impressive mansions in the town. Following the devastation wrought by the Lisbon earthquake of 1755, Écija's ruined churches were restored at great cost; hence the magnificent collection of the late **Baroque towers** that are the glory of the place today.

The Town

Écija's most important churches and palaces are all within a few minutes' stroll of the once delightful arcaded, and palm-shaded **Plaza Mayor** (Plaza de España), currently a building site due to the construction of a subterranean car park. The town council may be starting to rue ever approving the project, since as soon as earth was broken important archeological evidence (this was also the centre of the ancient Roman and Moorish towns) was revealed that archeologists

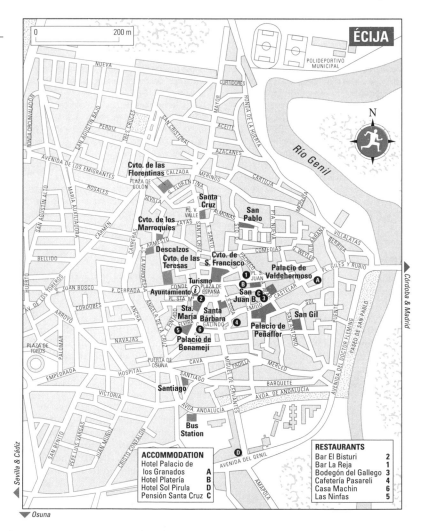

demanded time to investigate. The discovery of a Roman bathhouse in 2001 was later topped by the discovery of a cemetery from the Moorish period containing no less than 2500 burials arranged in neat rows. Despite having acquired some spectacular exhibits for the museum (see below) the price for many – seven years of chaos at the heart of the town – has been too high.

At the western end of the plaza the **Ayuntamiento** has a tourist office (see "Practicalities") and also contains – in the imposing council chamber – a fine second-century Roman mosaic depicting the mythological Dirce being dragged by a bull as a punishment meted out by the two sons of Antiope, Zethus and Amphion – whose mother she had mistreated. Ask in the tourist office for permission to view. An additional feature here is a **camera obscura** (same hours as tourist office; €2.50) providing an effortless way to appreciate Écija's marvellous collection of church towers.

To the west of the Plaza Mayor and just behind the Ayuntamiento, the lyrically beautiful tower of **Santa María** – one of the eighteenth-century rebuilds – overlooks the square. Inside, a cloister displays archeological finds from the surrounding area. Behind this church, on c/Castillo, the magnificent eighteenth-century **Palacio de Benamejí**, with a fine portal in contrasting tints of marble, has been relieved of its former role as an army barracks in order to house the **Museo Historico Municipal** (Tues–Fri 9.30am–1.30pm & 4.30–6.30pm, Sat & Sun 9am–2pm; free). A visit to the museum also provides an opportunity to view this magnificent mansion and its patio, now declared a national monument. The museum's collection of artefacts illustrates the town's history, stretching from Neolithic hunters and gatherers, through the Romans – there's a particularly good section on Astigi's role in the olive-oil trade – to the Moorish and medieval epochs. In 2002 the excavations in the Plaza Mayor unearthed the remarkable **Amazona de Écija** a stunning, over two-metre high first-century AD Roman statue depicting an Amazon resting against a pillar. Of the highest craftsmanship and still bearing traces of ochre paint, the image has become the museum's dramatic focal exhibit and the town's civic icon.

South of here the fifteenth-century church of **Santiago** (Mon–Fri 7–9pm) has a Mudéjar side facade and, inside, a fine *retablo* and stunning *Cristo de la Expiration* (Crucifixion sculpture) by Roldán.

Backtracking to the quarter northwest of the Plaza Mayor, along c/El Conde behind the Ayuntamiento, will bring you to the **Convento de las Teresas**, a fourteenth-century Mudéjar palace which, although not open to the public, has been described as a miniature of the Alcázar in Sevilla with fine Mudéjar stuccowork, *azulejos* and doors. Continuing ahead and then right along c/La Marquesa leads you to the church of **Los Descalzos** with its ornate Churrigueresque facade and fine woodcarvings within, followed just around the corner on c/Saltaderoto by another exquisite belfry belonging to the **Convento de los Marroquíes**. The nuns here are noted for their *bizcochos marroquíes* (almond cookies), sold through a *torno* (9am–1.30pm) and in local shops. Zigzagging north along calles Parda and Bizco allows you to take in the **Convento de las Florentinas**, whose church has a beautiful *retablo* by Roldán. Heading east along c/Pardo and then c/Santa Catalina leads to the church of **Santa Cruz** (Mon 9am–1pm, Tues–Sat 9am–2pm & 6–9pm; free), whose brick tower was once a minaret and carries tenth-century Arabic inscriptions recording the setting up of public fountains. Inside, there are more superb *retablos* and an early Christian sarcophagus, all beneath a lofty cupola. The charming *plazuela* fronting the church has two fine old iron crosses on a plinth, backed in summer by a wonderful avalanche of crimson bougainvillea down the wall behind. The c/Santa Cruz leads back to the Plaza Mayor.

Heading along a narrow street out of the Plaza Mayor's northeast corner, you'll soon spot the ornate belfry of **San Juan Bautista**, perhaps the best of all Écija's Baroque towers. In its churchyard are the substantial ruins of the earlier church destroyed in the eighteenth-century earthquake. Continuing east leads you to the sixteenth-century **Palacio de Valdehermoso**, with a Plateresque facade incorporating Roman pillars and, almost opposite and running along c/Castellar, the enormous eighteenth-century **Palacio de Peñaflor** (May–Sept Mon–Fri 9am–1.30pm, Oct–April Mon–Fri 10am–1pm & 4.30–7.30pm, Sat & Sun 11am–1pm; free), where a magnificent painted curved frontage is complemented by a full-blown Baroque portal topped with twisted barley-sugar columns. Formerly the residence of the marquises of Peñaflor until the line became heirless in 1958, the house was sold to the town council for the nominal sum of 50,000ptas (€300) and now serves as the civic library. The interior has a fine staircase with intricate stuccowork and cupola off a twin-tiered arched central patio. Nearby on c/San Antonio the Gothic-Mudéjar church of **San Gil** (Mon–Sat 10am–1pm; free) is famed for its pencil-slim tower, and has a recently restored interior with an elegant *retablo* in its *sagrario*. Just beyond San Gil more archeological **excavations** are in progress and have so far revealed the foundations of enormous Roman buildings, plus some extremely fine mosaics on view under canopies. The progress of the excavations can be viewed through the surrounding fence.

The nuevas poblaciones of Carlos III

A modern **monument** 20km northwest of Écija, just off the A4-E5 at La Carlota, commemorates one of the more curious episodes in Andalucía's history, when thousands of settlers were attracted from Germany, France, Switzerland and the Low Countries to resettle this corner of Andalucía after disastrous **depopulation** due to the eviction of the Jews and Moors and a plague around 1600. The government also believed that increasing the population would reduce banditry in an area through which passed the *camino real* (royal road), transporting the wealth and bullion of the empire from the port of Cádiz to Sevilla and Madrid. However, when **Carlos III** – urged on by a radical administrator named **Pablo de Olavide** – added a Utopian wish that these colonies should be egalitarian settlements untrammelled by "rank, privilege or parasitic religious orders", he ran into opposition from the landed class of *señoritos*, who were utterly opposed to parting with even the smallest plots of land.

The scheme was eventually set in train nevertheless, and twelve **colonies** were founded, stretching from La Carolina in Jaén to La Luisiana, 160km away near Écija. The foreigners – an application received from Casanova was turned down – soon came, attracted by grants of free land and cattle. But the scheme ran into trouble when many of the Germans were found to be Protestants; this greatly disturbed the Inquisition, who had them expelled. Others, unable to settle in one of the hottest areas of Europe, packed up and left of their own accord. Within two generations most of the foreign colonists had either been assimilated into Spanish stock or had died out. All that remains of this early attempt at social engineering today are place-names on the map, the geometrical layouts of their streets, and the odd German, French or Flemish name listed in the phone books – and now the monument depicting the king and de Olavide bestowing the document of settlement on another colony.

The village of **La Carlota**, as its name indicates, was one of twelve colonies set up by Carlos III in the 1760s. It's a tidy, anonymous place today, but its eighteenth-century **Ayuntamiento** on the main road is worth a look, as is the **coaching inn**, the *Real Casa de las Postas*, opposite, dating from the same period.

Finally, the **bullring**, laid over a Roman amphitheatre on the western edge of town, much impressed a visiting Laurie Lee: "Big, empty, harsh and haunted, for two thousand years this saucer of stone and sand has been dedicated to one purpose, and even in this naked daylight it still exuded a sharp mystery of blood."

Practicalities

Frequent daily **buses** to and from Sevilla and Córdoba stop at the station on Avenida Andalucía. The main **Turismo** is located inside the Ayuntamiento on the Plaza Mayor (Plaza de España) (Mon–Fri 9am–3pm, Sat & Sun 10am–2pm; ☎95 590 29 33, ⊛www.ecija.es) and stocks a useful booklet (in Spanish) detailing the thirty-plus notable buildings throughout the town and can also provide opening hours for the privately owned historic mansions.

Limited **accommodation** options include, to the east of the Plaza Mayor, the basic but charming *Pensión Santa Cruz*, c/Romero Gordillo 8 (☎95 483 02 22; ❷), where you'll need your mosquito repellent for a stay in summer. A step upmarket is the nearby and comfortable *Hotel Platería*, c/Garcilópez 1 (☎955 90 27 54, ⊜hotelplateria@retemail.es; ❹), with modern air-conditioned rooms and its own restaurant. Just east of here the new *Hotel Palacio de los Granados*, c/Emilio Castelar 42 (☎95 590 53 44, ⊛www.palaciogranados .com; ❼) is a beautifully restored eighteenth-century mansion with delightful patios, small pool and rooms decorated with original contemporary artworks. Another option is *Hotel Sol Pirula*, c/Miguel de Cervantes 50 (☎95 483 03 00, ⊛www.hotelsolpirula.com; ❹), south of the centre, which also has decent air-conditioned rooms.

Equally limited are the number of places to eat but there is enough choice to suit most budgets. For **tapas** and **raciones** try *Bar El Bisturi* on the Plaza Mayor or, better, *Bar La Reja* at c/Garcilopez 1, which has a wider choice. For more substantial **meals** *Cafetería Pasareli,* Pasaje Virgen del Rocío, off c/Emilio Castelar, does a budget *menú* for around €7 and has a terrace. Alternatively the *Bodegón del Gallego,* c/A. Aparicio 3, near the Palacio de Peñaflor, is a step up in price but serves fish, shellfish and meat dishes to a high standard and is noted for its *arroz marinero* (seafood paella). Another inviting option is the mid-priced *Casa Machin*, c/Galindo 4, housed in an elegant *casa señorial* where *dorada a la sal* is a house special. Owned by the same proprietors, the nearby and also mid-priced ⋇ *Las Ninfas* is situated inside the Palacio de Benamejí, with a terrace in the palace's courtyard, and *arroz con perdiz* is one of its signature dishes.

From Sevilla to Osuna and Estepa

The A92 *autovía* that leaves Sevilla to cut across the Campiña's southern flank bypasses, after 15km, **Alcalá de Guadaira**, a large satellite town of Sevilla, whose most interesting feature is a twelfth-century Almohad **fortress**, its well-preserved towers and battlements dominating the hilltop above an unkempt park. More appealing are **Utrera**, some 16km further on, with a couple of striking churches, and 14km further, **El Palmar de Troya,** the bizarre "new Vatican" constructed by Andalucía's heretic "pope", the self-proclaimed Gregory XVII. The highlights of this route, however, are the pleasant country town of **Móron de la Frontera** with some fine churches, the ducal town of **Osuna**, 40km beyond **El Arahal**, and its smaller neighbour **Estepa**, just 20km or so east again, both with architectural delights not to be missed. The route terminates at the remarkable communist village of **Marinaleda**, run along Utopian lines.

Utrera and El Arahal

UTRERA, surrounded by olive groves – said to produce the finest green olives in Spain – is a dull, industrial place which is transformed each June during its famous flamenco festival known as the Potaje Gitano, held in the park alongside a ruined Moorish fort. Nearby, the fifteenth-century church of **Santiago** has a fine, if worn, Plateresque west doorway. As you enter the town, on its northeastern outskirts there's also the seventeenth-century pilgrimage church of **Nuestra Señora de la Consolación** with a fine *artesonado* ceiling and

The Mount of Christ the King

South of Utrera along the A394 lies one of the strangest sights in the whole of Andalucía. Across the parched, white fields the amazing towers and domes of the **Palmarian sect's** church of **El Palmar de Troya** dominate the horizon. The story goes that in 1968 the Virgin appeared on this spot to a *sevillano*, Clemente Domínguez, whose faith, the Palmarian church's literature states, was "wavering at the time". She apparently instructed him that he must deal with the "heresy and progressivism" that were destroying the Church of Rome. Miraculous cures, stigmata and numerous conversions were the means chosen by the Virgin to establish her bona fides. Thus convinced, Clemente began his investigations and found that "freemasonry and communism were actually governing the Church" and that Pope Paul VI "was kept under drugs, a prisoner within the walls of the Vatican".

Building work soon started at the "Mount of Christ the King" to create **Vatican II**, while Clemente headed off to Rome to see if he could persuade the erring Church back onto the straight and narrow. It proved a hopeless task and upon his return the Roman pope (and later the "two villains" that succeeded him) was excommunicated and the Holy See of St Peter transferred to Palmar with Clemente installed as the new "pope". During the midst of all these adventures General Franco was posthumously canonized as a saint of the new Church, and Clemente's "battles with Satan" – actually a road accident – left him blind. It only remained for the leader of the new faith to have himself crowned Pope Gregorio XVII in an elaborate ceremony. Rather incongruously, the new pope was also addicted to a racy lifestyle, frequently touring the bars of Sevilla with his papal entourage in tow and indulging in gastronomic bacchanalias that lasted for days, all of which did little to dim his charisma for the Palmarians.

After the complex was attacked by riotous crowds of "true believers" – bussed in by local bishops, claim the Palmarians – high walls had to be erected to protect the growing community inside from belligerent Christians, irate at the frequent ordinations of new priests (from all parts of the globe) and the daily arrival from their convent in Sevilla of the Carmelites of the Holy Face, the new church's order of nuns. When Pope Gregorio died in the spring of 2005 his secretary and designated successor, an Extremaduran lawyer named Manuel Alonso Corral, took over the reins and was enthroned as "Pope Pedro (Peter) II", vowing to continue the "dead pontiff's" mission.

To **visit the complex** (daily 6pm), you'll need to cover all parts of your body – women will be subjected to an obsessive examination by the guards to make sure they are wearing *medias* (tights/pantyhose), without which there is no chance of entry. The impressive building turns out up close to be a hideous mass of concrete and plastered brick. Inside the church the scene is incredible, too, with at least fifty altars – including the main one, often featuring the "pope" himself – simultaneously churning through "Masses", day and night.

glittering gold *retablo*. Should you need a **room**, *Hostal Las Delicias*, c/Abate Marchena 4 (℡95 486 10 12; ➋), has, clean en-suite rooms and is central.

It's hard to believe today, but the pleasant agricultural town of **EL ARAHAL**, 20km northeast of Utrera, has long been one of the revolutionary hot spots of the region. Along with Marinaleda (see p.362), it has led the fight against the abuses and injustices of the great landed estates against the *braceros* or day labourers – one of Andalucía's most enduring social problems. The centre is a pleasant place to stop for a drink, and you could also take a look at the fifteenth-century **Hospital de la Caridad** and the Baroque churches of La Victoria and Santa María. For **rooms**, the comfortable *Hostal El Cordobés* (℡95 584 06 00; ➍) lies 1km along the road south to El Coronil.

Morón de la Frontera

Nine kilometres beyond El Arahal, a turn-off left to the north brings you, after 7km, to **Marchena**, a small town with a fifteenth-century Mudéjar church and some elegant mansions. Taking the southern turn at the same crossroads here allows you to visit **MORÓN DE LA FRONTERA**, 17km to the south. Standing on a hill at the southern edge of the Campiña, this is a charming small town with a couple of impressive churches, as well as a ruined castle. Just below the castle you'll see the Gothic and Renaissance church of **San Miguel**, an impressive pile of honey-coloured stone with a Giralda-style tower and ornate west doorway. Following the street that descends from here to the **Plaza de Ayuntamiento** (the town's main road junction) takes you close to the church of **San Ignacio** (down a street on the left), with another fine Baroque portal.

For **accommodation**, *Hostal Pasqual*, Plaza Ayuntamiento 10, almost on the junction (℡95 585 40 40; ➊), is a simple and friendly place with a few rooms en suite. *Hostal Morón*, c/Suárez Trasierra 6, near the hospital (℡95 485 23 66; ➋), is a more comfortable option, offering rooms with bath and TV. For **eating** and **drinking** there are plenty of bars and restaurants surrounding the main Plaza del Ayuntamiento; one place worth seeking out is *Bar-Restaurante La Campiña*, reached by following c/Luis Daoíz for 50m out of the Plaza del Ayuntamiento, where it's on the left at no.17. They do decent tapas and *platos combinados* and there's a great-value *menú* for €7. Just opposite, *Bar Manolo* is another good bet for beer and tapas.

Osuna

A further 34km along the A92 (or easily reached by the back roads from Móron), little-visited **OSUNA** is one of those small Andalucian towns which are great to explore in the early evening: slow and quietly enjoyable, with elegant streets of tiled, whitewashed houses and some of the finest **Renaissance mansions** in Spain.

Another settlement of obscure Iberian origin, Osuna first came to prominence as the Roman town of Urso, and ten bronze tablets from this period recording the town's statutes are preserved in Madrid's Archeological Museum. In Moorish times the town was of little note and it was during the post-*Reconquista* period, when it became the seat of the dukes of Osuna with enormous territories, that it was embellished with most of the outstanding buildings that make it so attractive today.

Arrival and information

Osuna lies on the Sevilla–Granada line and is served by three daily trains from the provincial capital arriving at the **train station**, Avenida de la Estacion s/n

(☎95 481 03 08), on the western edge of town. The **bus station**, Avda. de la Constitución s/n (☎95 481 01 46), with frequent buses to Sevilla and less frequent services to Málaga and Granada, lies to the southeast of the centre, and is almost as far out. Osuna's **Turismo**, in the Ayuntamiento on the focal Plaza Mayor (Tues–Sat 9.30am–1.30pm & 4–6pm, Sun 9.30am–1.30pm; ☎95 481 57 32, ⓦwww.ayto-osuna.es), can provide a detailed town map and information on the zone.

Accommodation

Accommodation in Osuna is not plentiful, but outside of national holiday periods and the local *fería* (third or fourth week in May) there's usually no great problem finding a place to stay. All the same, it's worth ringing ahead.

Hostal Caballo Blanco c/Granada 1 ☎95 481 01 84. Welcoming and comfortable *hostal* with en-suite a/c rooms with TV in a remodelled old coaching inn. It has an equally good restaurant and large car park at the back. ❹

Hostal Cinco Puertas c/Carrera 79 ☎ & Ⓕ95 481 12 43. Opposite the *Hostal Caballo Blanco*, this has rooms with similar facilities but is not as attractive an option. Parking available. ❸

Hotel El Molino Avda. de la Constitución 4 ☎ & Ⓕ95 481 20 51. Close to the bus station, this recently refurbished and upgraded former *hostal* offers a/c en-suite rooms with TV; also has a good restaurant. ❹

Hostal Esmeralda c/Tesorero 7 ☎95 582 10 73, ⓦwww.hostal-esmeralda.com. A budget option for basic rooms with and without bath. Has own bar-restaurant. ❸

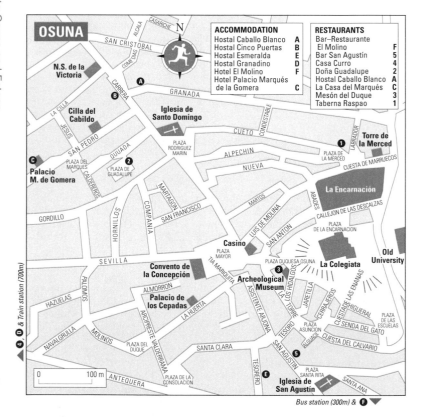

Hostal Granadino Plaza Salitre 1 ☎95 481 00 00. Slightly further away from the centre and south-west of the Plaza Mayor, this is a friendly place for en-suite rooms above a restaurant. ❸

Hotel Palacio Marqués de la Gomera c/San Pedro 20, ☎95 481 22 23, ⓦwww .hotelpalaciodelmarques.com. The town's four-star option, set inside one of the most beautiful *casa palacios* in the country, is a dream. A monument in its own right, this eighteenth-century mansion has a breathtakingly beautiful patio with a Baroque chapel just off it and all rooms are tastefully and individually furnished. Room 7 was used by Franco Zeffirelli when here making a film about the life of María Callas and has a spectacular exterior balcony, while the irresistibly romantic Room 10 is situated in the house's tower. ❻ with breakfast.

The Town

Osuna's major sights are its collection of stunning **Renaissance mansions** within easy walking distance of the Plaza Mayor and, on the hill to the east of the centre, the old university, Collegiata church and the convent of La Encarnación.

Plaza Mayor and the palacios

Before leaving the elegant **Plaza Mayor** in the heart of the town, take a look at the eighteenth-century **Ayuntamiento** here (which now houses the **Turismo**) and, on the west side of the square, the sixteenth-century **Convento de la Concepción** (open service times) with a fine eighteenth-century *retablo*.

The best of the mansions erected by the aristocrats and wealthy landowners are off c/Carrera, running north from the Plaza Mayor, particularly c/San Pedro. Here the **Cilla del Cabildo** (at no. 16) has a superb geometric relief round a carving of the Giralda. Further along, the eighteenth-century **Palacio de los Marqueses de Gomera** is another Baroque extravaganza with undulating ornamentation, balcony and solomonic columns beneath the family crest; it has now been converted into an upmarket restaurant and hotel (see "Accommoda-tion"). Calle de la Huerta, off the Plaza Mayor, has more interesting buildings, including the **Palacio de los Cepadas** (now the palace of justice) with an elegant patio and staircase, and nearby slightly north, on c/Sevilla, the **Palacio de Puente Hermoso**. More *casa palacios* are to be found in calles Gordillo, Sevilla and Compañia (a street off the latter) to the west of the Plaza Mayor.

Old University and Colegiata

Two huge stone buildings stand on the hilltop overlooking the town. The first is the **old university**, now part of the Universidad de Sevilla (patio open term-time Mon–Fri 10am–7pm) with an elegant arcaded Renaissance patio. Founded in 1548 by one of the predecessors of the dukes of Osuna, it was later suppressed by the reactionary Fernando VII in 1820 and only recently recovered its academic status. The other edifice is the lavish sixteenth-century **Colegiata** (guided tours only, English spoken, Mon–Sat 10am–1.30pm & 4–7pm, Sun 10am–1.30pm plus Sept–June 3.30–6.30pm; €2), which should be visited first. This latter is a fine Renaissance building with a damaged Plateresque west doorway caused, so the story goes, by French soldiers in the War of Independ-ence who used it for target practice. Inside, a guide will point out a sumptu-ous gilded *retablo* and the remarkable seventeenth-century *Expiración de Cristo* (Crucifixion) by Ribera – one of the artist's greatest works. Also in the church some exquisite sculptures include a superb *Crucified Christ* by Juan de Mesa, from the same period. More Riberas are to be seen in the **sacristía**, which now holds the church's impressive art collection. His *San Jerónimo*, *San Pedro* and a moving *Martirio de San Bartolomé* are all of the highest quality. The high-point of any visit is the descent to the subterranean depths to view the gloomy

pantheon and chapel of the dukes of Osuna, where these descendants of the kings of León and once "Lords of Andalucía" are buried in niches in the walls. Some of the Renaissance ornamentation is extremely fine, especially the polychromed wooden *Santo Entierro* (burial of Christ), as well as panels from the Flemish school and a fine relief of *San Jerónimo*. The tour ends with the guide pointing out an antique portable **sixteenth-century organ** – one of few to survive from the period.

La Encarnación, Museo Arqueológico and churches

Downhill, opposite the entrance of the Colegiata, is the Baroque convent of **La Encarnación** (same hours as the Colegiata; €2), founded in the seventeenth century by a duchess of Osuna, and where the highlight of the nun-led guided tour is a fine plinth of eighteenth-century Sevillian *azulejos* (from Triana) round its cloister and gallery, depicting curiously secular scenes. After filling up on the tasty convent *dulces* sold here, you could take a walk north, passing the former convent church of **La Merced** with its stupendously carved late Baroque tower and portal by Alonso Ruiz Florindo, and the ruins of Las Canteras, once a hermitage, on c/Camino de las Cuevas. Further along here you'll find the **excavations** of Roman Urso, including a necropolis with tombs quarried from the sandstone, as well as the vague remains of a theatre, fort and a gigantic quarry where the Romans obtained their stone to build the city. Otherwise, the more direct descent to the town takes you past the Torre del Agua, a twelfth-century Almohad tower which houses a small **Museo Arqueológico** (Mon–Sat 10am–1.30pm & 4–7pm, Sun 10am–1.30pm; €1.60) containing finds – and unfortunately many copies of the best items, the originals of which are in Madrid – discovered hereabouts.

Other churches around the town worth seeking out (7–8pm – except Sun – is the best time to find them open) are the sixteenth-century **Santo Domingo**, at the northern end of c/Carrera, a fine Renaissance church with a couple of superb Mudéjar chapels; nearby, **Nuestra Señora de la Victoria** has an impressive Baroque *retablo* by José Mora. To the west of the Plaza Mayor, the **Convento del Carmen**, on the street of the same name, has another stunning sixteenth-century *retablo* in carved wood and, to the south of the same square, the recently refurbished sixteenth-century **San Agustín** has a beautiful single-naved interior and more fine *retablos*.

Eating and drinking

There are food and drink possibilities all over town and many of the accommodation places also have restaurants of their own. One place not to miss is the wonderful **casino** on the east side of the Plaza Mayor; with 1920s Mudéjar-style decor and a grandly bizarre ceiling it's open to all visitors and is an excellent place for a drink (or breakfast) while lounging in armchairs overlooking the square.

Bar–Restaurante El Molino Avda. de la Constitución 4. The fine little restaurant of the hotel of the same name has one of the best-value *menús del día* in Andalucía which comprises three generous courses, a free salad and as much (good) wine as you can drink – all for €6.50.

Bar San Agustín c/San Agustín 15. Good little neighbourhood bar-restaurant offering economical *platos combinados*. Closed Thurs.

Casa Curro Plaza Salitre 5. The town's best tapas and *raciones* bar cooks up a tasty range of seafood and meat dishes. There's a superb restaurant in the back, too.

Doña Guadalupe Plaza Guadalupe 6. In purportedly one of the town's best restaurants the service can be stilted and even the cooking sometimes misses the target. The outdoor terrace is also rather claustrophobic and not a patch on the *Mesón del Duque's*.

Hostal Caballo Blanco c/Granada 1. The *hostal*'s restaurant is very good for *comida casera* serving up dishes such as *potaje de bacalao* (fish soup) and *gachas de osuna* (local gruel) as well as the usual standards. *Menú* for around €15.

La Casa del Marqués c/San Pedro 20. The very good restaurant of the *Hotel Marqués de la Gomera* is on the high side of mid-priced, and with a rather formal dining room you may well prefer their more cheaper courtyard brasserie,

the *Asador del Marqués*, on sultrier nights. Main dishes €12–23.

Mesón del Duque Plaza de la Duquesa 2. Excellent little mid-priced restaurant, with the best terrace in town where at weekends there's often live background music. Wide range of meat and fish dishes including *lomo a la almendra* (pork loin with almonds) and a weekday *menú* for around €8.

Taberna Raspao Plaza de la Merced 7. A very good neighbourhood restaurant for fish and meat tapas and *raciones* with a pleasant terrace on this square.

Estepa

Another delightful Baroque town, **ESTEPA**, 24km east of Osuna, resembles a miniature version of its larger neighbour. Originally a Carthaginian settlement, it took the side of the North African state during the Punic Wars with Rome, and when the victorious Romans finally took the city in 208 BC they found that the citizens had burned their possessions and killed themselves rather than surrender. Repopulated, it eventually became the Roman Ostipo and, later, the Moorish Istabba.

The Town

Close by the central Plaza del Carmen, the eighteenth-century **Iglesia del Carmen** (7–9pm; free) has an exuberant Baroque facade in black and white stone and a stunningly ornate interior, recently restored. Above, in the *ciudad alta*, the **Iglesia de Santa María** (same hours as above) is another impressive church, dating from the twelfth century, with a fine *retablo*. Alongside, the sixteenth-century **Iglesia de la Santa María de la Asunción**, one of Estepa's oldest churches, is currently undergoing restoration as part of a youth employment venture. The Gothic interior has decaying treasures, many rescued from other churches and monasteries. Look out for a fine sculpture of *San Juan Evangelista* by Martínez Montañés. If you can get up to the roof there are great **views** over the town and beyond. Lower down in the *ciudad baja*, you'll notice the elegant **Torre de la Victoria** – all that remains of the convent of the same name. Taking c/Mesones (and its continuation, c/Castillejos) from the Plaza del Carmen back through the town, you pass another fine church, the **Iglesia de la Asunción**, known locally as Estepa's Sistine Chapel due to a splendid painted ceiling depicting scenes from the life of the Virgin. The church was originally the chapel of one of Estepa's best mansions, the **Palacio de los Marqueses de Cerverales** next door, a superb eighteenth-century palace with barley-sugar columns supporting its balcony. One block south, c/Nueva has some of the town's oldest mansions; among them nos. 12 and 14 are good examples. Heading west along c/Cardenal Spinoza (the same street's continuation), at no. 2 take a look at a pair of ancient Visigothic columns built into the doorway of this much later house, a practice all too common in modern Spain where there is a thriving, no-questions-asked, black market in these antiquities.

Practicalities

Estepa's small **Turismo**, c/Aguilar y Carmen 8, just off the Plaza del Carmen 1 (Mon–Fri 9am–2pm; ☎95 591 27 17), can supply a map of the town; next door there's a wonderful porticoed marketplace with an elegant glass canopy. **Rooms** are not plentiful but what there are you'll find along the main Avenida de Andalucía. The best deal is *Hostal Balcón de Andalucía* at no. 23 (T & F 95 591 26 80, W www.balcondeandalucia.com; ❸), where comfortable a/c rooms come with TV, and there's an excellent **pool** at the back. **Places to eat** are also along the Avenida de Andalucía, where the *Hostal Balcón de Andalucía* and *Hostal Rico* at no. 98 both serve decent meals and *menús*. For late-evening **drinks** many of the locals visit *El Jardín*, a charming garden bar in c/Los Vitos near the Plaza del Carmen in the old town.

Marinaleda

Sited 14km north of Estepa, the unassuming agricultural village of **MARINALEDA** seems to have inherited the do-or-die qualities of the early inhabitants of Estepa who resisted the might of Rome. Along with El Arahal to the east, "Red" Marinaleda has become the standard-bearer in the struggle of the *braceros*, or day labourers, against their exploitation by the great landowners. The leader in this struggle is Marinaleda's mayor of 28 years, standing, Sánchez Gordillo, the village schoolteacher and – like the rest of the village almost to a man and woman – a committed communist. He came to prominence as the organizer of a "hunger strike against hunger", but since then has moved on to taking over large estates in the area, by force if necessary. A few years back he occupied a nearby estate belonging to one of Andalucía's major landowners, the duke of Infantado. The scene was vividly described by Michael Jacobs in his book *Andalusia* when he visited the "occupation".

Attached to the post at the entrance of the estate were the words "ESTA TIERRA ES NUESTRA MARINALEDA" ("This land is our Marinaleda"). On the long drive up to the cortijo I passed a group of villagers carrying hoes and rakes, the women dressed in black. They could have been straight out of a communist poster of the 1930s and this impression was reinforced by the political badges they were all wearing. In the middle of all this prowled the leonine and instantly recognisable figure of Sánchez Gordillo wearing a Tolstoyan suit and a red sash. He addressed me in a slow solemn voice with no trace of a smile. I could not help feeling, confronted by such a manner and appearance, that I was in the presence of one of the Messianic figures who toured the Andalusian countryside in the nineteenth century. He talked of the inadequacy of the present agrarian reforms, of the great extent of the Duke of Infantado's properties and of how the land in Andalusia continued to be in the hands of the very few.

The romantic *cortijos* to be seen dotted across the Andalucian landscape – brilliant white pantiled farm buildings surrounded by walls and often shaded by a cluster of elegant palms – have for generations been the focus of the misery of the landless poor, for these are the homes of the landowners, or more often their overseers on whom the day labourers are dependent for what little seasonal work they can get. From the Casa de Cultura at Marinaleda – in reality a workers' club, on the main Plaza de la Libertad – the Sindicato de Obreros del Campo, led by Gordillo, continues to fight for change. The old **Ayuntamiento** – just off the main square and decorated with a mural owing much to Picasso's *Guernica* that denounces militarism and conscription – is a remarkable sight. Despite the ever-present blight of chronic unemployment Marinaleda marches on and has recently constructed an impressive new Casa de Cultura (incorporating a full-size theatre) and Ayuntamiento complex at the east end of the village complete with low-power TV station, communally owned crèche and a secondary school.

One of the village's most established and successful customs is **Domingos Rojos** (Red Sundays), a number of days throughout the year when the council requests that the population – young and old – turn out to do voluntary work (street cleaning, painting, gardening, and the like) in public places. Crime is so low that the village has only one police officer for its 2500 population in comparison with the norm of five or six. And, despite an ambivalent attitude towards Marinaleda by previous and current socialist governments in Madrid, and complete indifference from the rightist Partido Popular administrations, significant tracts of land have been transferred into the ownership of the village cooperative which now controls over a thousand acres. Banners hanging from house balconies proclaim opposition to nuclear testing and landowner exploitation, and each street sign bears the legend "A Utopia building peace". In harmony with these sentiments, in the old Casa de Cultura's lively **bar** on the main square you'll be served up the cheapest tapas, beer and *fino* in the whole of Andalucía. The nearest **accommodation** is in Estepa (see p.361), some 14km away.

West from Sevilla

With your own transport, the fastest – but dullest – way from Sevilla west to Huelva is via the A49 *autovía*. More tranquil and interesting is the A472 which cuts through the area to the west of the city called El Aljarafe by the Moors (the "high lands," actually rather flat), planted with olives, vines and orange trees, and arrives after 8km at **Castilleja La Cuesta**. This village is famous as the place where Hernan Cortés, explorer and conqueror of Mexico, died, but is probably more familiar to most Andalucians, however, as the centre for some of the best **pastries** in the region – Castilleja's delicious cinnamon-coated *tortas* are exported all over Spain.

Ten kilometres beyond Castilleja, between Espartinas and Sanlúcar La Mayor, is *Restaurante Las* Tejas, where at weekends after they've eaten (and drunk) a fair deal, *sevillanos* try out their skill in a bullring behind. Although the *toros* are only calves, some of them can still prove too much for most of these amateur *toreros*. **Sanlúcar La Mayor** itself is a somnolent, rather unexciting place but does nevertheless retain parts of its Roman and Moorish walls and has three Mudéjar churches, the most notable of which is the thirteenth-century **Santa María** – in origin an Almohad mosque – with horseshoe arches, an *artesonado* ceiling and the former mosque's minaret, now the church tower. The olive-planted valley of the Guadiamar comes next, and 14km further on there's a turn-off to the ancient Moorish village of **Carrión de los Céspedes**, also a stop on the train line from Sevilla to Huelva. Once a fief of the Knights of Calatrava, a twelfth-century military order formed to defend the southern frontier of Castile against the Moors, this is still an atmospheric place, retaining many of its Moorish narrow streets. Further west still on the A472, the village of **Manzanilla** looms into view beneath its church tower, followed, 20km beyond Carrión, by the wine-producing town of **LA PALMA DEL CONDADO** off the road to the left. It's highly probable that this terrain, an area first planted with vines by the Greeks, produced the local wine taken on the voyage to the New World by Columbus when he sailed from nearby Palo The wine produced here today is the Condado de Huelva, which hardly ra with Spain's top-drawer vintages, but the dry whites are an excellent partne seafood. With its impressive eighteenth-century Baroque church of **San Bautista** towering over a palm-fringed central plaza, this slow-moving. walled country town makes a good stopping point for a drink of the lo

△ La Palma del Condado

at one of the central bars. If you're tempted to **stay**, the *Hostal Garle* (℡959 40 07 50; ❷), on the junction of the A472, has a/c en-suite rooms over a decent **venta**, or there's *Hostal Los Morenos*, c/Huelva 3 (℡959 40 24 44; ❸), nearer the centre.

Heading south for 6km, **BOLLULLOS DEL CONDADO** is a busy little town filled with **bodegas** and **ventas** (called *bodegones* here) which are big, high-ceilinged places capable of seating over a hundred diners at long trestle tables. A number of them line the main street – *El Postigo* is one worth a try – but another good place worth seeking out is *Bar Oriental*, Avda. Constitución 52, to the west of the main road; they keep excellent *jamón serrano* and there's a small restaurant as well. Once you've tried out the local wine, you could take in some eighteenth- and nineteenth-century **casas señoriales** around the Plaza Mayor (Plaza del Sagrado Corazón) and along c/Cervantes, just off it. On the same square stands the eighteenth-century church of **Santiago**, with a snow-white colonial-style facade and wonderful tower, and an **Ayuntamiento** of the same period with an elegant red stone portal. Unlike many of its neighbours, Bollullos is a prosperous place and its younger set have plenty of venues to let their hair down including an incredible daytime **disco** scene at weekends along c/Cruz de Monteniña (ask for a traffic junction named La Piña) where clubs such as *Camelot*, *Don Piña* and *Café Harley* all fill the street with booming sounds giving customers at the nearby tapas bar *Canasta* a severe headache.

The A483 continues south from Bollullos to El Rocío (see p.382) and the Coto de Doñana.

Niebla and around

Twelve kilometres west from La Palma along the A472, the salmon-pink ancient walls and towers of **NIEBLA** make a spectacular sight. The approach is wonderful, almost a medieval fairy tale come true, for this is a real walled town and looks the part. The Roman **bridge** you cross to reach it – probably built the second century during the reign of Trajan – is remarkably well preserved carried traffic for two thousand years until it was blown up during the Civil has since been meticulously restored.

Little is known about a Phoenician settlement here or the possible Iberian village of the Turditanian tribe which may have preceded it. However, coins found dating from the Roman period gave the town's name as Ilipla, which is probably derived from the Iberian name. Described by the Roman writer Pliny as a fortified city of strategic importance, it was a crucial link in the massive Roman mining operations carried out upriver at the Río Tinto mines. The metals – mostly silver – were moved down the river by barge and then transferred to galleys here for the voyage to Rome and other parts of the empire. A bishopric under the Visigoths, after the Moorish conquest it became successively part of the Almoravid and then Almohad domains until, as an independent *taifa* state, it experienced its greatest period of prosperity during the twelfth century, trading in saffron and raisins. After falling to the Christian forces under Alfonso X in 1262, Niebla was passed around as a fief of various rulers, until in 1369 it came into the hands of the Guzmán dynasty, following which it entered a long period of decline.

The Town

Once inside the two-kilometre-long encirclement of the walls, Niebla's tidy streets of whitewashed houses and small squares are a delight to explore. The Puerta del Socorro leads from the Sevilla–Huelva road to the Plaza Santa María in the heart of the town, dominated by the church of **Santa María de Granada**. The key is available from Señor Juan de Dios, the genial custodian of the Casa de Cultura (itself the former fifteenth-century Hospital de Nuestra Señora de los Ángeles; bar hours 8am–3pm & 5.30pm–midnight) next to the church; he doesn't charge for letting you in to look around the church but it is diplomatic to buy a drink from him in the bar. Entered through a splendid Mozarabic eleven-lobed portal, the original tenth-century church is believed to have been constructed over a Visigothic cathedral, and was used by Christians during the Almoravid period. It was converted into a mosque by the Almohads in the thirteenth century: the *mihrab* now to be seen in the side wall, as well as the elegant tower – its minaret – date from this period. The pillars in the second-floor windows of the tower, incidentally, are believed to have come from the original Visigothic church. Among the artefacts dotted around the austere and much restored Mudéjar-Gothic interior are a couple of Roman altars and the remarkable, stone-carved **Silla Episcopal**, the throne of the Visigothic bishops. Outside the entrance, a **patio** is dotted with remnants of the building's chequered history – various Visigothic, Christian and Moorish stones and pillars.

Of the ruined church of **San Martín** near the town's main gate and sliced through by a road, only the apse, bell tower and a chapel survive. It was built in the fifteenth century on the site of a former synagogue donated in more tolerant times by Alfonso X as a concession to the Jews of Niebla, and before the Inquisition began its grisly work. The locked chapel contains a fifteenth-century sculpture of Christ being scourged.

The town's **four gates** are also worth seeking out, each with its Moorish horseshoe arch and features, as is the **Castillo de Guzmán**, in origin the Moorish Alcázar, but much added to by Enrique de Guzmán in the fifteenth century. It later fell into decay and was ruined after Marshal Soult used it as a barracks for French troops during the War of Independence. Today it stages concerts and theatrical productions over the summer months as part of Niebla's annual festival of theatre and dance.

Practicalities

Niebla's **train station**, on the Sevilla-Huelva line, is served by two trains daily in each direction. The station lies at the end of c/Walabonso, heading downh between the Casa de Cultura and the church of Santa María. You can pick up a map and visitor information at the town's small **Turismo** (Mon–Fri 9am–2pm & 4–6pm, Sat 11am–2pm & 4–6pm; ☎959 36 22 70, ⓦwww.castillodeniebla .com) inside the Castillo. There's a **hostal**, the clean and friendly *Pensión Los Hidalgos*, c/Moro 3 (☎959 36 20 80; ❶), with some en-suite rooms, outside the walls near the Sevilla–Huelva **bus stop**, and nearby you'll find bars and **cafés** and, surprisingly, a couple of **disco bars**. For **tapas**, head for the bars around the Plaza Santa María inside the walled town; here *Café-Bar Santa María* also does meals and a Sunday lunch paella special. The Casa de Cultura serves *tapas* and offers a *menú del día* at weekends. For **restaurants** you'll need to look on the main road outside the walls, where the *Brasería Las Almenas* at c/Padre Marchena 2 (specializing in charcoal-grilled meat dishes) is a decent place, and *Bar Parada* on the road leading out to Huelva is also worth a try. Outside the walls, at the end of a street opposite the main gate, the cavernous *Taberna El Piti*, c/Plaza Pinta s/n, is an entertaining and inexpensive village bar that also serves *platos combinados*.

Dolmen de Soto

Five kilometres beyond Niebla the road crosses the A49 *autovía* and shortly after this a sign on the right indicates a sealed road leading to the prehistoric **Dolmen de Soto** (Mon–Fri 9am–2pm, Sat 10am–2pm; free). Follow the road for about 1km until it winds around to an entry gate on the right. Should you arrive outside the official opening hours this gate is climbable. Inside the gated area you will see a mound (containing the dolmen); another gate giving access to the interior of the dolmen will be locked outside visiting times, but you can see a little through the grille. Discovered in 1923, it dates back to about 2000 BC and consists of a long passage leading to a burial chamber topped by a head-stone estimated to weigh some 21 tonnes. Parts of the walls are engraved with schematic symbols.

Seven kilometres further towards Huelva a turn-off on the left leads to Moguer, one town on the Columbus trail (see p.372).

Huelva and around

Large, sprawling and industrialized, the city of **HUELVA** struggles to present an attractive face to visitors. Still, once you've got past the messy suburbs with their fish canneries, cement factories and petrochemical refineries, the tidy city centre – perched on a peninsula between the confluence of the Odiel and Tinto river estuaries – comes as a pleasant surprise. Huelva's populace escapes the city in summer to enjoy the Atlantic beaches and sea breezes at the resorts of **Punta Umbría** and **El Rompido** across the Río Odiel estuary to the south and southwest.

Huelva was born as Onuba, a trading settlement founded by the Phoenicians early in the first millennium BC (modern inhabitants still call themselves *onubenses*). These early merchant traders were attracted by the minerals in the mountainous areas to the north, and by the time the Carthaginians came to dominate the area in the third century BC Onuba was an established port, conveying these minerals throughout the Mediterranean world. When Spain fell into Roman hands the mining operations at Río Tinto were dramatically expanded to satisfy the empire's insatiable demand for metals such as silver and copper and the city prospered even more. Following Rome's demise the

Visigoths and Moors displayed little interest in mineral extraction; the latter concentrated on dominating the seaborne trade with North Africa.

Huelva's maritime prowess gained for the city its crowning glory when **Columbus** set out from across the Río Tinto to find a new sea passage to India in ships manned by hardy Huelvan sailors. The city enjoyed a boom when the Extremadurans to the north of Huelva – the men who conquered the Americas – used the port as a base for their trade with the new territories overseas, but eventually Sevilla, and later Cádiz, came to dominate the silver and gold routes from the Americas and Huelva was squeezed out. Largely flattened by the Lisbon earthquake of 1755, it is only in the last century that the place has begun to regenerate itself: first as the base for mineral exports from Río Tinto in the early 1900s, and later when Franco established a petrochemical industry here in the 1950s.

Arrival and information

Huelva's **bus station** is at Avda. Dr Rubio s/n (☎959 25 69 00). The Autobuses Damas (🌐www.damas-sa.es) timetable lists all services throughout the province – handy if you're going to be using the town as a base. Frequent trains to Sevilla and three through-trains a day to Madrid leave from the splendid neo-Moorish **train station** (☎902 24 56 14), a short distance southeast of the centre on Avenida Italia. Completed in 1880 at the behest of the Rio Tinto Mining Company, the station is a perfect expression of the burgeoning self-confidence of that period, and is well worth stopping by for a look even if you're not travelling by train.

Coming in **by car**, finding a parking place can often verge on the impossible. The easiest solution is to use a pay car park (see our map): one of the most convenient is sited immediately to the north of the bus station. If you park on the street and are unlucky enough to get towed, call ☎959 54 24 68 or go to the main police station (see "Listings", p.371). Huelva has a drugs problem and theft from cars to support this is rife; be particularly cautious when using car parks outside supermarkets.

The **Turismo**, near the waterfront at Avda. de Alemania 12 (Mon–Fri 9am–7pm, Sat & Sun 9am–2pm; ☎ & ✉959 25 74 03, 🌐www.ayuntamientohuelva.es), has stacks of brochures and timetables, and hands out full accommodation lists and details on current events.

Accommodation

Finding a **place to stay** is usually not a problem this far off the tourist trail, although since most of the town's *hostal* accommodation has closed in recent years there is now little for the budget traveller.

Huelva's **youth hostel** (☎959 25 37 93; under 26 €14, over 26 €18.50) at Avda. Marchena Colombo 14, in the northern suburbs (bus #6 from the b station, or #4 from Plaza de las Monjas), and has en-suite rooms. The to nearest **campsite** is in Punta Umbría, a fifteen-minute bus ride away, wher campsite (see p.372) has a beachfront location.

Hostal Calvo c/Rascon 35 ☎959 24 90 16. Uninspiring, if clean, place for rooms sharing bath. ❶

Hotel Costa de la Luz José María Amo 8 ☎959 25 32 14, ✉959 25 64 22. The best (and cheapest) of the mid-price options where the higher rooms have balcony terraces and come with TV. ❹

Hotel Los Condes Alameda Sundheim ? 28 24 00, ✉959 28 50 41. Comfortabl the museum, with a/c rooms. Garage

Hotel Tartessus Avda. Martín Alon ☎959 28 27 11, ✉hoteltartessos es. Upmarket hotel on the main ? thing you'd expect for the pric garage. ❼

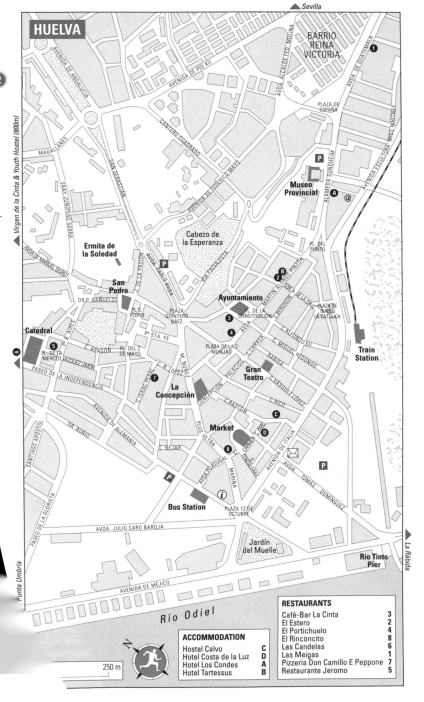

HUELVA

▲ *Sevilla*

BARRIO
REINA
VICTORIA

PLAZA DE
ESPAÑA

Museo
Provincial

PL. DEL
PUNTO

Cabezo de
la Esperanza

Ermita de
la Soledad

San
Pedro

DR.P. BAÑUELOS

Ayuntamiento

PL. DE LA
CONSTITUCIÓN

PLAZA
QUINTERO
BAEZ

Pº STA. FE

Catedral

PLAZA DE LAS
MONJAS

PL. DEL 2
DE MAYO

PLAZA DE
ISABEL
LA CATÓLICA

Train
Station

La
Concepción

Gran
Teatro

Market

Bus Station

PLAZA 12 DE
OCTUBRE

Jardín
del Muelle

Río Tinto
Pier

▲ *La Rábida*

AVDA. JULIO CARO BAROJA

AVENIDA DE MÉJICO

Río Odiel

N

250 m

RESTAURANTS

Café-Bar La Cinta	3
El Estero	2
El Portichuelo	4
El Rinconcito	8
Las Candelas	6
Las Meigas	1
Pizzeria Don Camillo E Peppone	7
Restaurante Jeromo	5

ACCOMMODATION

Hostal Calvo	C
Hotel Costa de la Luz	D
Hotel Los Condes	A
Hotel Tartessus	B

The City

Many of Huelva's key sights are a short walk from **Plaza de las Monjas**, the city's palm-lined main square. Sadly, a wonderful archeological museum has been inexplicably reduced to a third of its size and the fine-arts museum has also been closed for some time. What remains are some interesting churches and a curious British-built quarter, in addition to a couple of notable buildings – the impressive Neoclassical **Gran Teatro**, on c/Vásquez López, and the Art Nouveau **Clínica Sanz de Frutos** (now the Conservatorio de Música), c/Rico 26, both just a short walk from the Plaza de las Monjas.

The Museo Provincial

The best place to start a tour of the city – especially if you're pressed for time – is at Huelva's **Museo Provincial**, Alameda Sundheim 17 (summer Tues–Sat 9am–8pm, Sun 9am–3pm; winter Tues–Sat 9.30am–2pm & 4.30–7pm; free), where an interesting **archeological collection** has exhibits and information about early mining in the north of the province. Inexplicably, many of the museum's most important exhibits are now in storage although a magnificent **Roman water wheel** – used to drain water from the mineworkings at Río Tinto – has been restored to a place of honour next to the entrance. Similarly, the Bellas Artes museum, formerly housed on the second floor, has been replaced by an exhibition space and now seems unlikely to return.

The Barrio Reina Victoria

One of Huelva's more bizarre features is a whole quarter designed by English architects. The **Barrio Reina Victoria** (or Queen Victoria housing estate), east of the museum alongside the Avenida de Guatemala, was constructed by the Río Tinto Mining Company in the early years of the twentieth century to house its British workers. It's a truly weird experience to stroll along the tree-lined avenues flanked by bungalows with rose gardens and semis with dormer windows and mock-Tudor gables – more like Acacia Avenue, Essex, than an Andalucian town. Even the street names have a colonial symmetry about them: Calle A, Calle B and so on. Given the drab uniformity it's little wonder that the present native occupants have attempted to relieve these humdrum northern exteriors with a few primary colours.

Río Tinto pier

The **Río Tinto pier** (Muelle Río Tinto), on the east side of the harbour, is a huge nineteenth-century ironwork structure formerly used to ship out the minerals which arrived by train from the mines to the north. Designed by the British engineer George Barclay Bruce and finished in 1874, the redundant pier's decaying ironwork curves gracefully out into the estuary, and today serves as a boardwalk for loungers and courting couples.

The British workers employed in the mines were also responsible for the importation of **football** into Spain, helping set up Huelva's league club Recreativo in 1889, which is the oldest in the country. It's a pedigree hardly matched by the club's record, however, which has been to languish for most of the last century in the lower leagues, excepting for a purple patch in 2002–3 when they spent a season in the top flight – only to be relegated at its end.

Huelva's churches

The **Catedral de la Merced** (open service times at 7pm), just to the north of Plaza de las Monjas off Paseo de Buenos Aires, was one of the few buildings to survive the eighteenth-century earthquake, resulting in its upgrading to cathedral status which – apart from a brilliant-white Baroque interior and an interesting salmon-pink colonial facade with elegant belfries – it hardly merits. It's worth looking inside at an image of the Virgen de la Cinta (the city's patron) attributed to Montañés.

A more interesting church and one with Columbus connections lies 3km further north along Avenida Manuel Suirot. This is the restored fifteenth-century **Virgen de la Cinta** (daily 8am–6pm; free), a simple white-walled sanctuary set on a low hill overlooking the sea where Columbus is said to have prayed before setting out on his voyage. Inside, beneath the Mudéjar roof, you can see a medieval fresco of the Virgin, a fine altar grille, and a series of 1920s faience tiles by the painter Daniel Zuloaga depicting scenes from the explorer's life. To get there, take the #6 bus from Plaza de las Monjas, and ask for the "Parada de Santa Marta" stop.

Eating and drinking

Most **bars** and **restaurants** are to be found in the streets around the Plaza de las Monjas. For **tapas**, good seafood specialities are on offer at *Marisquería Huelva*, c/Cisneros, alongside the impressive Ayuntamiento in Plaza de la Constitución. Off the southern end of Plaza de las Monjas, *Bar Nueva Abundancía*, c/Vasquez López 45, has another varied selection, plus a €6 *menú*. East of Plaza de las Monjas, *Bar Agmanir*, c/Carasa 9, is a great local bar with outdoor tables and a wide tapas range. Nearby, in the same direction, along c/Berdigón, more tapas are to be had at the friendly *Bar Berdigón* at no. 9 as well as at the atmospheric *Taberna El Condado*, nearby at c/Sor Angela de la Cruz 3, which specializes in Huelva's celebrated *jamón serrano*.

Huelva's best *heladería*, *Ibense Bornay*, c/Concepción 7, near Plaza de las Monjas, does great **ices**, *horchatas* and *granizados*.

Café-Bar La Cinta c/Arcipreste García 9. Down the side of the Ayuntamiento this is a busy little place serving up good tapas and *raciones*. It also does a menú for around €7.

El Estero Avda. Martín Alonso Pinzón 14. Mid-priced restaurant specializing in Andalucian and international dishes. The cavernous interior can feel a bit lifeless if the place is quiet.

El Portichuelo Avda. Martín Alonso Pinzón 1. Pricey but good restaurant. Main dishes €9–15.

El Rinconcito c/Marina 2. Decent tapas and a reasonably priced *menú* – often including paella. Flamenco is staged here (except July & Aug) in an atmospheric room at the back.

Las Candelas 7km from town at the Aljaraque crossroads on the road to Punta Umbría ☎959 31 83 01. An old *venta*, and a step up in class and price from anywhere else in Huelva, this excellent restaurant is recommended for its seafood and is worth making the effort to get to; there's a good-value *menú* for about €15, an extensive wine list and impeccable service. Without your own transport you'll need to get the Punta Umbría bus to drop you or take a taxi. Closed Sun.

Las Meigas Avda. de Guatemala 48 ☎959 27 12 58. Very good upmarket restaurant offering Basque, Galician and *andaluz* dishes (especially seafood) and distinctive desserts – try the *tarta de Santiago*. There's a *menú de degustación* for about €28. Closed Sun eve.

Pizzería Don Camillo e Peppone c/Isaac Peral s/n. Genuine and delicious Italian pizzas, served up east of the Plaza de las Monjas. Closed Wed.

Restaurante Jeromo Plaza de la Merced 6. Attractive little bar-restaurant near the cathedral that offers a lunchtime *menú* for €7.60, including wine.

Nightlife

When it comes to **drinking** and **dancing**, during the summer most *Onubenses* make their way to Punta Umbría (see opposite) and the coast. However, c/ Concepción through to c/Berdigón has numerous bars, *cafeterías*, ice-cream parlours and fast-food joints to cater to those left behind. In term time the university students create their own *marcha nocturna* in the numerous bars and music places along Avenida Pablo Rada, to the north of Plaza de las Monjas. Plaza de la Merced, near the cathedral, and the streets around the Plaza Dos de Mayo slightly southeast provide another focus for their carousals; as a consequence the **bars** here can get quite lively. Huelva's biggest annual **fiesta**, the Fiestas Colombinas, begins on August 3 and lasts for a week, with processions, events, concerts, *corridas* and competitions.

Listings

Banks The major banks, most with ATM cash dispensers, are located along Gran Vía (Avda. Martín Alonso Pinzón), c/Vásquez López and at the bus station. The *Hotel Luz*, c/Alameda Sundheim 26, will change cash and travellers' cheques.

Car rental Auto Alquilar Huelva, in the bus station ℡959 28 31 38; Atesa, inside the train station ℡959 28 17 12.

Hospital Huelva's Hospital General Juan Ramón Jiménez is on the Ronda Norte ring road to the northeast of the centre (℡959 01 60 00).

Internet Internet access is available at *Cyberal@lmeda*, c/Luis Braille 6 (Mon–Fri 9.30am–2pm & 4.30–9.30pm, Sat–Sun 9.30am–9.30pm), near the museum.

Football Recreativo Huelva ("El Recre") is the town team. Tickets and match details are available from the Nuevo Colombino stadium, Avda. del Decano del Fútbol Español s/n (℡959 27 14 62,

ⓦwww.recreativohuelva.com), to the northeast of the centre.

Laundry Odiel, c/Bejar 6, northeast of the bus station.

Left luggage There are lockers at both the train (platform 2) and bus stations.

Markets The more-than-a-century-old Mercado del Carmen to the east of the bus station bustles on weekdays (8am–noon), stacked with fresh landed fish and all the vegetables of the province. There's also a major weekly market on Fridays at the Recinto Colombino, east of the Río Tinto Pier.

Newspapers The local daily *Huelva Información* is good for listings of current events and forthcoming attractions.

Police The policia local (℡959 21 05 68) is at Paseo de la Glorieta s/n, to the northwest of the Turismo.

Post office The main *Correos* is on Avda. Italia s/n (Mon–Fri 8.30am–8.30pm, Sat 9.30am–2pm).

Punta Umbría and El Rompido

PUNTA UMBRÍA, 20km away (hourly buses from the bus station) and sitting astride a finger of land between the Atlantic and the Tinto-Odiel river estuary, is Huelva's nearest – and biggest – seaside resort. English managerial staff from the Río Tinto Mining Company (see p.392) initiated the resort in the 1880s when seeking a place to sojourn by the sea. They constructed the first dwellings here in the British colonial style, quite a few of which survived until the 1970s; these buildings have now gone and the only vestige from this era is the *barrio*'s name, Los Ingleses. Later growth into a seaside town has produced a tidy if uninspiring resort which does, however, have magnificent blue-flag **beaches** flanking the north and south sides of its *punta* (point). It makes a reasonable place to stop over if you don't want to stay in the city; be warned, though, that for the latter part of July and most of August every room will be taken.

Practicalities

The long and sandy beach – lined with some tasteless private villas – leads down to the *punta* where, following the road into town from Huelva (Avenida de Huelva), you'll come to a very helpful **Turismo**, located at the junction with Avenida de Andalucía (July–Aug Mon–Fri 10am–2pm & 6–9pm, Sat 10am– 1pm & 6–9pm, Sun 10am–1pm; Sept–June Mon–Fri 9am–2pm & 4.30–7 Sat 10am–1pm; ℡959 49 51 60), which stocks copious amounts of inform and a useful town **map**. You can't miss the place as it lies just beyond the most peculiar Ayuntamientos in Spain – a bizarre glass and wood st perched on an artificial mudbank, floating in a bath of green water and fronted by a clock tower resembling an oil rig. **Bikes** and **mopeds** can be rented from Moto Bonares (☎959 31 04 71), in an alley behind the Turismo. Turismar (☎959 31 55 26) runs **boat trips** around the estuary and nature reserve of Marismas del Odiel from the Muelle Viajeros quay near the fishing harbour. **Internet** access is available at *Ciberpunt@com* (daily 10am–10pm) Avda. del la Ría 17, fronting the fishing harbour on the north side of the point.

Most **places to stay** are located within a few minutes walk of the Turismo on the east and west sides of the point. Near the harbour on the *punta*'s river flank, there's the friendly *Hostal Manuela*, c/Carmen 8 (☎959 31 07 60; ❹) with en-suite rooms, while the nearby *Hotel Emilio*, c/Ancha 21 (☎959 31 18 00, ⓕ959 65 90 51; ❺) is a slightly more upmarket possibility. On the opposite side of the point, places with an Atlantic sea view include, at Avda. del Océano 95, the excellent value *Hostal Playa* (☎959 31 01 12; ❹) with en-suite rooms 50m from the beach and the nearby *Pensión El Ancla*, Avda. Océano 29 (☎959 31 48 10; ❹) with similar facilities. High-season pressure on rooms could mean that the very pleasant **youth hostel**, Avda. del Océano 13 (☎959 31 16 50; under 26 €14, over 26 €18.50; ❸), with a seafront location and some double en-suite rooms, is the only alternative. The nearest **campsite**, *Camping La Bota* (☎959 31 45 37), lies 6km west, near the hamlet of La Bota; it claims to be Andalucía's first eco-campsite, disposing of rubbish in an environmentally friendly way.

For **food** and **drink**, *chiringuitos* – open-air bars on the seafront serving snacks – are popular, and the resort is full of the usual *freidurías* and *marisquerías*. On the river side of the point *Juanito Coronel*, opposite the fishing harbour, is good for inexpensive fried fish, while the similar *Antonio*, Combes Ponzones s/n, around the corner is also popular. Further along the point *Las Tinajas* is one of Punta Umbría's most celebrated *marisquerías*. On the seaward side, Plaza de la Atlantico, off Avenida del Océano, has the *Restaurante Tiburón*, which is a good choice for seafood with a €7 *menú*, and, just west of here next to the *Hotel Barcelo*, *Camarón* is a popular beachfront *chiringuito*. Close to the youth hostel, *Miramar*, c/Miramar 3, is a welcoming place for *platos combinados* and *fritados variados* with a seafront terrace. On summer evenings the place throbs to a dozen **discotecas** and **bars** strung out along and around the pleasant pedestrianized c/Ancha which cuts through the town on the riverside. On the river itself and downstream from the fishing harbour, *Bar Chimbito*, housed in a old ferry boat, is a popular drinks bar.

El Rompido

For a more peaceful seaside retreat you might want to move further west along the coast – lined with fine beaches and backed by dunes, pinewoods and a protected juniper grove – to **EL ROMPIDO** (served by frequent buses from Huelva). Famous in the past for its oyster beds, it's now a small resort with a few *chiringuitos* and the odd fish restaurant fronting the beaches lining the banks of the Río Piedras estuary. There's another **campsite** here, *Catapum* (☎959 39 01 65), just outside the village as you approach, which in high summer can be a bit grim due to overcrowding.

he Columbus trail

va's greatest source of pride lies with the momentous expeditions of opher Columbus to the New World, the first of which sailed from

Palos de la Frontera (or simply Palos), across the Tinto estuary from the city. When he was unable to get backing for his voyages, Columbus cooled his heels for many years in and around Huelva and the La Rábida monastery until he finally managed to obtain a commission from the king and queen in the spring of 1492. The main sites connected with Columbus – **La Rábida**, **Palos** and **Moguer** – are all within a 30km round-trip from Huelva. Buses running between Huelva and Moguer call at all three locations.

La Rábida

The monastery of **LA RÁBIDA**, 8km from Huelva, can be reached by bus (roughly hourly from Huelva) or, with your own transport, by taking the Mazagón road southeast across the Río Tinto road bridge. At the Punta del Sebo – the tip of land where the Tinto and Odiel rivers meet – there's a **monument** to Columbus donated by the USA. A monster Cubist-inspired statue, sculpted by Gertrude Vanderbilt Whitney in 1929, it has the navigator looking a bit like a cowled boxer on his way to the ring.

Situated amid a forest of umbrella pines (which serve to mask the petrochemical refineries across the polluted river estuary), the small whitewashed Franciscan **monastery** is a surprisingly pleasant oasis once you reach it. Lying at the end of the Avenida de la América, a road linking it with Palos and lined with ceramic pavement tiles marking all the countries of the New World, the monastery may be visited only by guided tour (Tues–Sat hourly 10am–1pm & 4–7pm, Sun 10.45am–1pm & 4–7pm; Ⓦ www.monasteriodelarabida.com; €2.50). Dating from the fourteenth century, the buildings suffered structural damage during the Lisbon earthquake of 1755 and have been extensively restored.

△ La Rábida

The tour begins with the room containing stylized modern frescoes of the explorer's life by distinguished Huelvan artist Daniel Vásquez Díaz. At the building's heart is a tranquil fifteenth-century Mudéjar cloister, opening off the monks' refectory where Columbus would have dined during his many stays here. You will also see the cell where the abbot, Juan Pérez, and Columbus discussed the explorer's ideas. Beyond the cloister, a fourteenth-century **church** contains an alabaster statue of the Virgin and Child to which the mariner and his men prayed before setting sail. Upstairs, above the refectory, lies the **Sala Capitular** (Chapter House) an impressive beamed room with heavy period furniture where Fray Pérez, Columbus and the Pinzón brothers discussed the final plans before the first voyage set sail. On August 3, 1992, the king and the whole Spanish government gathered in this room to mark the 500th anniversary of the event. In other rooms on the same floor you can see models of the three caravels, as well as navigation charts, cases containing various artefacts brought back from the expedition and "team pictures" of the crew. Don't miss the curious **Sala de Banderas**, or Flag Room, where, beneath flags of the various South American nations of the New World, is a casket of earth donated by each. If some of these caskets look a bit roughed-up it's probably due to visiting South Americans who, after reverentially handling the soil of their fatherland, often treat the caskets of their neighbours with some disrespect.

The recently constructed **Muelle de la Carabelas** (Harbour of the Caravels; April–Sept Tues–Fri 10am–2pm & 5–9pm, Sat & Sun 10am–7pm; Oct–March daily 11am–7pm; €3), on the nearby Río Tinto estuary, has impressive full-size replicas of the three caravels that made the epic voyage to the New World. Realistic displays on board reconstruct the grim realities of life at sea, while the surrounding quays are lined with re-creations of fifteenth-century quayside bars and market stalls. In the adjoining **museum** are displays illustrating Columbus's life (including facsimiles of some of his geographical books annotated in a suprisingly delicate hand), video presentations on a giant screen and a *cafetería*.

The monastery's gardens contain an **information office** as well as a pleasant **bar-restaurant** with terrace tables. In summer a tourist **road train** links La Rábida with Palos de la Frontera.

Palos de la Frontera

Four kilometres north along the Río Tinto estuary lies **PALOS DE LA FRONTERA**, a rather featureless village but an important site in the Columbus story. It was from the silted-up bay below the church of San Jorge – then a major harbour and sea-port – that the three caravels, the *Niña*, the *Pinta* and the *Santa María,* set out to reach Asia by crossing the western ocean.

O Palos, no one can equal your glory.
Not Memphis, nor Thebes nor eternal Rome.
Not Athens nor London.
No city can dispute your historical fame!

This modern poem fixed to the exterior wall of the fifteenth-century parish church of **San Jorge** leaves you in no doubt of how Palos views its role in world history. It was here that Columbus and his crewmen attended Mass before taking on water for their voyage from the nearby **La Fontanilla**, a medieval well tarted up in 1992 as the centrepiece of a dismal park to mark the quincentenary. The harbour lay to the west of the fountain in an area now marshland, and it was due to the river's silting up that the decline of Palos set

Probably born in Genoa around 1451 to the son of a weaving merchant, **Christopher Columbus** (in Spanish, Cristóbal Colón) went to sea in his early teens. After years of sailing around the Mediterranean, in 1476 he was shipwrecked off the coast of Portugal and it was in Lisbon – then the world leader in navigation – that Columbus learned the skills of map-making. In 1479 he married into a high-ranking Portuguese family and spent the following years on trading voyages to the British Isles and elsewhere, including in 1482 a journey down the coast of West Africa to **Ghana**, a major source of spices, ivory and slaves. During this time the idea germinated in his mind of attempting to sail west to reach the **Indies** and the Far East, thus shortening the route that Portugal was then exploring around the coast of Africa. He built up an enormous library of ancient and contemporary geographical writings now preserved in Sevilla, all heavily annotated in his own hand. By some optimistic interpretations of these works and a misreading of an Arab geographer, Alfraganus, Columbus seriously undercalculated the earth's circumference, believing that Marco Polo's fabulous island of **Cipangu** (Japan) lay a mere 2400 miles west of the Canaries instead of an actual 10,600.

Trying to find backers, when the Portuguese monarch, still more interested in the African route, demurred, Columbus turned to Spain. In 1486 at Córdoba he presented his plan to reach the gold-rich Orient to Fernando and Isabel, still involved in the protracted and costly war of *Reconquista* against the Moors. Desirous of the gold to boost their fortunes but wary, after consultations with advisers, of Columbus's calculations, they both refused support. Now desperate, Columbus turned to France and then to Henry VII of England, with no success. During his earlier journey from Portugal to Córdoba, Columbus had stayed at **La Rábida** Franciscan monastery. It was to here that he returned frustrated and depressed in the autumn of 1491. The explorer's luck turned when Juan Pérez, the abbot of La Rábida and a former confessor to Isabel, was moved to write to the queen on Columbus's behalf. It was a timely moment. In January of 1492 Granada had fallen, the treasury was empty, and the promise of gold and glory for a resurgent Spain now attracted the monarchs.

Columbus set out from Palos on August 3, 1492, with three small vessels, the *Santa María*, the *Niña* and the *Pinta*, carrying a total of 120 men recruited from Palos and Moguer by the Pinzón brothers. Columbus's discovery of the Atlantic wind patterns ranks alongside his other feats; he sailed via the Canaries to take advantage of the trade winds, but the incredible voyage almost ended in mutiny by crews who believed that they would never find a wind to bring them home. This was avoided when, on October 12, Columbus made landfall on Watling Island (aka San Salvador) in the **Bahamas**. Watched by naked and silent natives he took the island in the name of Spain and gave thanks to God. After leaving a colony of men on **Hispaniola** (modern Haiti) he returned to Palos on March 15, 1493, to enormous acclaim.

Successful as a mariner, Columbus was disastrous as a colonizer, epitomized by his forcing of the native population of Hispaniola into the gold mines in a brutal process that reduced their numbers from a quarter of a million in 1492 to 60,000 fifteen years later. In 1500, Columbus was removed from office as governor and sent back to Spain in chains and disgrace. He was eventually released and made his final voyage in 1502 – a last desperate attempt to find a strait leading to India – but ended up stranded in Jamaica for a whole year after losing his ships to sea worms. Columbus died at Valladolid in 1506, still believing that he had reached the East Indies.

in. The church (Tues–Sun 10am–12 noon & 6.30–7.30pm, or ring ☎959 08 90 outside siesta time for an appointment to view) has a simple, bare-b interior containing some mural fragments as well as a distinctive wrough pulpit – from which the edict was read ordering an initially reluctant F provide ships, crew and provisions for the voyage – and some thirteenth- and sixteenth-century alabaster sculptures of *Santa Ana* and the *Crucifixion*.

On that August morning in 1492 Columbus is supposed to have left the church through its southern Mudéjar **portal** flanked by his captains Martín Alonzo Pinzón and his younger brother Vincente, both from Palos. And it is these native sons that Palos today celebrates, even more than its Columbus connection, claiming that their contribution to the epic voyage has been eclipsed. Indeed, at the time the Pinzón family insisted that Martín – a mariner of great local repute – had planned such a voyage long before Columbus. South of San Jorge on the main street, the house of Martín Alonzo Pinzón at c/Colón 24 survives, and has been converted into a **museum** (daily Mon–Fri 10am–2pm & 5–9pm; free) with reconstructions of daily life, fashions and food from the sixteenth century.

The road north from Palos to Moguer runs through **strawberry fields** (see box) owned by one of the largest cooperatives in Europe, which has brought welcome prosperity to the area. By playing the market, which entails close scrutiny of weather forecasts for northern European customers such as Germany and Britain – sunshine there means high strawberry profits – they decide when is the best moment for picking. Then, loaded with 10,000 kilos of *fresones* apiece, the great refrigerated trucks roll north through the night.

Practicalities

The Ayuntamiento (Mon–Fri 9am–3pm; ☎959 350 100), facing the Plaza Mayor on c/Rábida 3, the main street, can provide tourist **information** and a town map, as well as assistance in viewing the church and museum if these are closed. You'll find **places to stay and eat** close by: *Cafetería Pensión Rábida*, c/Rábida 9 (☎959 35 01 63; ❷), is a good bet for economical en-suite rooms

---

Strawberry Fields

Between of February and May, the strawberry fields surrounding Palos de la Frontera are a frenzy of activity, providing ninety per cent of the strawberries eaten in the whole of Europe. To supply this market tens of thousands of workers are required to do the picking and the packing. Formerly many of these workers came from the Mahgreb, but as the government has clamped down on north African *indocumentados* (illegal workers without papers), the strawberry farms are now recruiting from eastern Europe.

Most of the new hands come from Poland and Romania and almost all are women under thirty on short-term contracts that specify the period of work from February to June, after which they must return to their own country or lose the opportunity to work legally in Spain again. In 2005 12,000 such work permits were issued with the women earning an average of €30 per day. This annual eastern invasion into an area of rural Andalucía has had some dramatic repercussions. Coming from a vastly different cultural background and speaking little or no Spanish, the women are housed in communal cabins/bunkhouses alongside the strawberry orchards. Once work is over they put on their finery and head for the limited nightlife in Palos or, at weekends, the coastal resorts of Mazagón and Punta Umbría. Understandably, this female flood upsets the delicate social balance and local *españolas* are not amused at the prospect of potential *novios* and husbands being enticed from their grasp by glossy northern blondes looking for a good time. The increasing number of weddings ⸱etween the migrants and local men as well as the rising number of divorces caused ⸱cal women say) by men dazzled by Polish charms has led to calls for the invasion ⸱e stopped.

and serves tapas and *platos combinados*; nearby there are pricier rooms with bath at *Hotel La Pinta*, c/Rábida 75 (☎959 35 05 11, ⓦwww.hotellapinta.com; ❹), which also has a restaurant with a *menú* for around €11. The best place to eat, though, is a little further along the same street from the *Pinta* at *Restaurant El Paraiso*, Avda. America 15, offering a wide range of dishes and a great-value *menú* for about €9. With your own transport, another good-value alternative is *Pensión La Niña*, c/Juan de la Cosa 37 (☎959 53 03 60; ❹), on the Mazagón road out of town, which has rooms with bath, air-conditioning and TV.

Moguer

The compact and beautiful whitewashed town of **MOGUER**, 8km north of Palos, also takes pride in its Columbus connection: many of the crew members were recruited here. Quite apart from this, it's a place with plenty to see, and achieved worldwide fame in 1956 as the birthplace of the Nobel prize-winning poet Juan Ramón Jiménez.

Starting from the **Plaza del Cabildo** in the centre – where there's a bronze statue of Jiménez – it's easy to find your way around. First take a look at the elegant eighteenth-century **Ayuntamiento** (free access to patio in mornings when open) on the same square, a quintessentially Andalucian edifice in cream and brown paint described by one art historian as "the finest Neoclassical building in the whole of Huelva Province". For many years it appeared on the now-defunct 2000-peseta banknote.

Close to here in c/Monjas lies the Gothic-Mudéjar **Convento de Santa Clara**. Founded in the fourteenth century, this housed nuns from the order of St Clare until 1898, but is now a **museum** (hourly guided tours Tues–Sat 11am–1pm & 4–6pm; €2). Inside, a Mudéjar cloister leads into the nuns' former quarters which include kitchen and refectory and a large sixteenth-century dormitory. The church possesses a fine *retablo* and some notable alabaster **tombs** of the Portocarrero family, the convent's founders, as well as - at the entry to the choir – a seventeenth-century **diptych** of the Sienese school portraying the Immaculate Conception. Look out for an inscription in the right aisle, which tells of Columbus's visit to offer thanksgiving for his safe return. He is reputed to have spent the whole night in prayer here upon returning from his first voyage in March 1493, in fulfilment of a vow he made in the middle of a terrifying storm. Other parts of the tour take in sculptures by La Roldana, Martínez Montañés and many other beautiful if anonymous works from the fourteenth, fifteenth and sixteenth centuries.

Additional sights in town include the fifteenth-century monastery of **San Francisco**, behind Santa Clara (cloister open daily, church only at service times; free), with its stunning ochre-tinted Mudéjar brick church and from where legions of missionaries were sent out to the New World; its elegant Mannerist patio/cloister can be viewed by entering through the archival museum next door. To the east of the centre **Nuestra Señora de la Granada** (open at service times, try 7.30pm) boasts a scaled-down, whiter version of Sevilla's Giralda tower "which from close up looks like Sevilla's from far away", wrote Jiménez. The house where Jiménez was born, c/Jiménez 5, has been restored as an interesting **museum** (Tues–Sat hourly visits 10.15am–1.15pm & 5.15–7.15pm, Sun 10am–2pm; €1.80) displaying various mementos from the poet's life. On Avenida Hermanos Niño, the road leading towards the Sevilla–Huelva highway, the **cemetery** has the grave of the poet and his wife, Zenobia. His body was returned to the town he loved for burial in 1958 after twenty years spent in exile in Puerto Rico, to where he had emigrated after Franco came to power. The work that most Andalucians remember him for today is *Platero y yo* ("Platero and I"), the story of a little donkey who is a "friend of the poet and children" based on his own donkey, Platero, in whose company he often toured Moguer's streets. Glazed plaques on walls around town mark streets or buildings that occur in the story.

Practicalities

Moguer's **Turismo** (Mon–Fri 9am–2pm & 4.30–7pm, Sun 10am–3pm; ☎959 37 18 98, ⓦ www.aytomoguer.es) lies just off the main square, inside the former castle at c/Castillo s/n, and can provide a basic map and information. **Buses** drop off and leave from c/Coronación to the north of Plaza Cabildo. Arriving by **car**, parking places are hard to find and if you do park on the yellow lines (as the locals do) be aware that if you block narrow streets to wider vehicles you'll receive a ticket. If you're tempted to **stay**, close to the Convento de Santa Clara at the end of c/Monjas there's the delightful and excellent-value *Hostal Pedro Alonso Niño*, c/Pedro Alonso Niño 13 (☎959 37 23 92; ❶), where all rooms come with a/c, shower and TV; get a room overlooking the pleasant patio at the back. Around the corner, the slightly more expensive *Hostal Platero*, c/Aceña 4 (☎959 37 21 59; ❷), has similar en-suite rooms.

For **food**, *Mesón Restaurante Paralla*, Plaza de las Monjas 22, opposite the entrance to Santa Clara, is the best restaurant in town, and serves up excellent regional fish and meat dishes, does tapas and has an inexpensive *menú*. Moguer has some interesting night-time places to eat and drink, including one of the most bizarre bar/restaurants in Andalucía. This is *Mesón El Lobito* on c/La Rábida 31, which includes among its eccentric decor vast numbers of unidentified objects hanging from the ceiling, chickens in cages in a patio, walls completely covered in graffiti (which you're welcome to add to) and a labyrinth of enormous darkened rooms at the back. Wine is sold at crazy (low) prices and fish and meat dishes are served *a la brasa*. There's usually a good atmosphere if you turn up after 10pm.

Disco bars are located along c/San Rafael, three blocks south of Plaza del Cabildo. Moguer holds an annual **Festival de Flamenco** at the beginning of September.

Coto de Doñana National Park

Sited at the estuary of the Guadalquivir, the vast roadless area of the **COTO DE DOÑANA** is Spain's largest wildlife reserve, a world-class wetland site for migrating birds and one of Europe's greatest areas of wilderness. The seasonal pattern of its delta waters, which flood in winter and then drop in the spring, leaving rich deposits of silt, raised sandbanks and islands, give the Coto de Doñana its special interest. Conditions are perfect in winter for ducks and geese, but spring is most exciting: the exposed mud draws hundreds of flocks of breeding birds. In the marshes and amid the cork oak forests behind you've a good chance of seeing squacco heron, black-winged stilt, whiskered tern, pratincole and sand grouse, as well as flamingos, egrets and vultures. There are, too, occasional sightings of the Spanish imperial eagle, now reduced to a score of breeding pairs. In late summer and early autumn, the swamps – or *marismas* – dry out and then support far less birdlife. The park is also home to an estimated 25 pairs of the pardel or Spanish lynx, now in severe peril of extinction (see p.668).

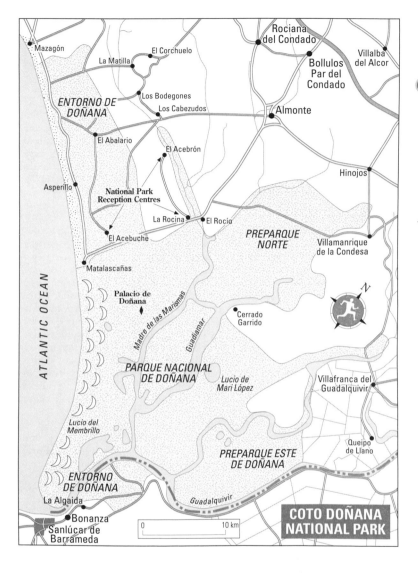

Inevitably, it seems, the park is under threat from development and several lynx have been killed by traffic on the road to the beach resort at **Matalas-cañas**. Even at current levels the drain on the water supply is severe, and made worse by pollution of the Guadalquivir by farming pesticides, Sevilla's industry and Huelva's mines. The seemingly inevitable disaster finally occurred in April 1998, when an upriver mining dam used for storing toxic waste burst, unleashing millions of litres of pollutants into the Guadiamar river which flows through the park. The noxious tide was stopped just 2km from the park's boundary; catastrophic damage was done to the surrounding farmland, with nesting decimated and fish poisoned. One expert has predicted that it will take 25 years for the area to fully recover. What is even more worrying is that the mining dams have not been removed (the mines are a major local employer) but merely repaired. The proposals for a huge new tourist centre – to be known as the Costa Doñana – on the fringes of the park have now been shelved, but worryingly two smaller tourist *urbanizaciones* just to the north of Sanlúcar and near **Mazagón** on the park's western flank have been given the go-ahead, vividly demonstrating that the pressure for development remains. Bitter demonstrations organized by locals who saw the prospect of much-needed jobs in the Costa Doñana development – accompanied by mysterious outbreaks of vandalism against park property – have abated into an uneasy truce. Some experts have proposed that "green tourism", allowing a greater but controlled public access to the park, and thereby providing an income for the local community, is the only way to bring both sides together.

Some history

This area was known to the **Romans** as Ligur, and in the 1990s archeologists were surprised to discover a Roman quayside three kilometres into the *marismas*, showing just how much the area has expanded in the ensuing two millennia. It was Alfonso X, however, who claimed the territory of Las Rocinas as a hunting reserve for the Spanish crown in 1262 during the *Reconquista*. In 1294 his heir, Sancho IV (the Brave), rewarded the "hero" of the siege of Tarifa, Guzmán El Bueno, with the territories of Doñana. The area, still a hunting reserve, remained part of the lands of the dukes of Medina Sidonia – as the Guzmán line became – for the next five centuries, and the park's hunting lodge was named the palace of Dona Aña in honour of the wife of the seventh duke in 1595. The reserve hit a bad patch when it was sold by the Medina Sidonias in 1897 to sherry baron William Garvey, whose company is still operating in Jerez. Garvey turned it into a hunting club and sold off much of the woodland for profit, but saner times followed upon his death in 1909, when people began to realize the unique importance of the area.

In 1957 scientific interest in the park began in earnest and, as a result of concern expressed about proposals to carve a highway across the zone and build tourist developments along its coastline, the **World Wildlife Fund** was set up in 1964. Five years later the Fund persuaded the Spanish government to set up the national park. Since then the Coto de Donaña, now under the management of the National Institute for the Conservation of Nature (ICONA), has expanded to 190,000 acres. The park's administrators then enlisted divine assistance in safeguarding its future when they diplomatically petitioned the brotherhoods to allow the Virgin of Rocío (see p.383) to become the National Park's patron. The brotherhoods graciously acceded to this request and the park's future now seems assured.

Doñana practicalities

Visiting the Coto de Doñana still involves – understandably – a certain amount of frustration. At present the heart of the reserve is still open only to brief, organised bus **tours** (see box opposite). You can also take a boat cruise into the park from Sanlúcar de Barrameda (see p.268).

Day visitors are currently restricted to the **hides** at three access and information centres open to the public. The first of these (moving north from Matalascañas) is the **Centro Recepción del Acebuche** (daily April–Sept 8am–??m, Oct–March 8am–7pm), where there's also an information office

The starting point for **tours of the park** in all-terrain 24-seater buses, and the place to book them, is at the Centro de Recepción del Acebuche, 4km north of Matalascañas towards El Rocío and Almonte, then 1.5km up a signed road on the left. For details of the tours, which need to be booked in advance (April–Sept daily 8.30am & 5pm; Oct–March Tues–Sun 8.30am & 3pm; €21), call in at the centre or phone ahead (daily 9am–8pm; ☏959 44 87 11, English spoken; ⓦwww.parquena-cionaldonana.com). The tour operator, Cooperativa Marismas del Rocío, Plaza del Acebuchal 16, El Rocío (☏959 43 04 32, ℻959 43 04 51), can also provide information and take bookings. Although the Centro has some **binoculars** available for rent (€2.50 per trip), you'd be well advised to bring your own as they are essential. Outside July, August and holiday periods you should be able to get on to the next day's trip, otherwise you'll need to book at least a week in advance. Tours consist of an eighty-kilometre, four-hour trip sampling the park's various ecosystems: dunes, beach, *marismas* and woodland, with the guide pointing out only spectacular species such as flamingo, imperial eagle, deer and wild boar.

If you're a serious ornithologist or naturalist, the tour isn't for you and you should consider a **group booking**, which costs a little more than the daily excursion and lets you create your own itinerary (details from the Centro). The best **map** for the national park is the IGN *Parque Nacional de Doñana* (1:50,000) sold at the Acebuche centre.

(which can supply a useful free map), bookshop, natural history exhibition, a rather tedious audiovisual presentation and a **cafetería**. The five hides adjacent to the Centro overlook a lagoon where marbled teal, purple gallinule, various grebes and – around the trees – azure-winged magpies have all been spotted and where, with luck, you may even glimpse the extremely rare Audouin's gull. You'll need to bring your own binoculars or they can be hired from the centre (€1.50 per hr).

Nine kilometres north, **La Rocina** (daily 9am–3pm & 4–8pm), close to the El Rocío bridge, has a car park, information centre (with more free maps) and a small open-air **museum** with historical reconstructions of life in the *marismas*. Beyond here a 2km route called the "Charco de la Boca" leads to five well-concealed hides in marshland, pine woods and along the riverbank where you might see Cetti's warbler, the spectacular hoopoe, red-crested pochard and herons as well as – in summer – flamingos and a plethora of singing nightingales. A minor road leads 5km west from here to **El Palacio de Acebrón** (same hours) – an impressive former hunting lodge – where there is another car park and information centre housing an ethnographic exhibition dealing with the zone's history and development. A 1.5km marked route threads from the centre, circling a lake mainly through woodland, and offering possibilities to sight the rare hawfinch. This would also make an ideal location for a **picnic** if you've come prepared. It's worth noting that during the Pentecost *romería* (the seventh week after Easter) all three visitor centres are closed.

Back on the main road, the **El Rocío bridge** on the village's southern edge has been described by one naturalist as "the best free bird-watching site in Europe". From this spot, red kite – a common sight here – soaring flocks of whiskered terns, disturbed by the ominous approach of a majestic booted eagle, and migrating greenshank, ruff and sandpiper are all to be seen in season. In high summer, though, the marshes dry out and are grazed by horses while the birdlife is restricted to coot and avocets breeding by the river. The **view** across the marshes towards the village and church of El Rocío from here is superb.

El Rocío

Set on the northwestern tip of the marshes, **EL ROCÍO** – a tiny cluster of white cottages, sandy streets and a church stockade where the most famous pilgrimage-fair of the south occurs annually at Pentecost – is one of the most atmospheric places in Andalucía. As the cowboy-hatted farmers nonchalantly ride horses along the wide sandy streets and tie up at Wild West-style hitching rails in front of their timber cabins, you half expect Clint Eastwood to emerge from a nearby saloon chewing on a cheroot. And this frontier-like feeling isn't altogether accidental, as it was from this area that many of the colonizers of the New World set out, exporting their vernacular architectural preferences with them. In the evening the recently installed street lights do little to undermine the time-warp quality of an area unchanged for centuries.

Centre of the town's Pentecost celebrations, the church of **Nuestra Señora del Rocío** (8.30am–7.30pm; free) was, despite its Baroque appearance, built in the 1960s on the site of a church which collapsed in the eighteenth-century Lisbon earthquake. It holds the venerated image of the **Virgen del Rocío**, a thirteenth-century work in carved wood. Beyond the village's core, ghostly streets of dwellings belonging to the brotherhoods – all with hitching rails and verandahs – stand empty most of the year waiting to be put to service each May–June in the *romería* when the ninety or so brotherhoods use them to house their members.

In the spring, El Rocío is probably the best **bird-watching** base in the area. The *marismas* and pine woods adjacent to the town itself are teeming with birds, and following tracks east and southeast along the edge of the reserve you'll see many species from white stork, herons and egrets to masked great grey shrike and honking wild geese. The Boca del Lobo ("wolf-breath") sewage treatment plant near to the *Hotel Toruño* (see opposite) is an unlikely-sounding bird-spotting location, but vultures and storks are frequent patrons here.

With your own transport another great bird-watching location is the **Cerrado Garrido** (aka Centro José Antonio Valverde; 10am–7.30pm) on the park's northern fringes. To get there from El Rocío follow the signs from the centre of the village, a 30km trip via Villamanrique de la Condesa. Approaching the centre the route traverses the Preparque along unmade tracks and is quite feasible in summer; after heavy rains access may not be possible and you should check with the El Acebuche visitors' centre (see box p.380). Cerrado's visitors' centre has a **cafetería-bar**, as well as telescopes and hides. You'll have plenty of other bird-watching and wildlife-spotting opportunities en route – keep an eye out for purple gallinules in the ditches between the paddy fields. The sunrises and sunsets over the *marismas* at Cerrado Garrido are quite spectacular, too.

Practicalities

A small **tourist office** (daily 10am–5pm; ☎959 44 26 84) is located on the main road, Avenida del Canaliega, where staff can supply a village **map** and lots of information about the national park. They can also advise on **horse riding** treks in the park. The village now has a number of **cash machines** and a bank (sited alongside the *Hotel Rocío Doñana*). There are at least three **buses** a day to and from Sevilla en route to Matalascañas, enabling a stop to be made at the La Rocina or El Acebuche National Park visitor centres (see p.380; make sure to let the driver know you want to be dropped there). Getting to or from Huelva is rather more complicated, requiring a change at Almonte.

The Romería del Rocío

The **Romería del Rocío**, a Whitsun pilgrimage to the sanctuary of the Virgen del Rocío, is one of the most extraordinary spectacles in Europe, with whole village communities and some ninety local "brotherhoods" from Huelva, Sevilla, Málaga and even one from Gibraltar, converging on the village on horseback and in lavishly decorated ox-carts. The event is part pilgrimage and part jamboree as the intense emotions awakened by the two- to four-day journey (not to mention the drinking) often spill over uncontrollably.

The brotherhoods coming from **Sanlúcar de Barrameda** have a special dispensation to follow their ancient route across the heart of the Parque de Doñana which takes them three nights and four days with all the attendant fire risks en route. The army is employed to get them and their carts over the Guadalquivir safely, and the park's rangers set up campsites for them and provide firewood for their great feasts in the woods. Sadly, the rubbish left behind by these large crowds is the cause of many wildlife fatalities as species such as boar choke on the plastic containers they attempt to devour. Throughout the *romería*, which climaxes on the Saturday evening, everyone parties in fiesta costume, while by the time the carts arrive at El Rocío they've been joined by hundreds of busloads of pilgrims.

What they have all come for – apart from the spectacle itself – is the commemoration of the miracle of **Nuestra Señora del Rocío** (Our Lady of the Dew). This is a statue believed to have been found on this spot by a shepherd in the thirteenth century – conveniently after the eviction of the Moors – which, so it is said, resisted all attempts to move it elsewhere. A shrine was built, miraculous healings and events were reported, and El Rocío was suddenly on the map. In the early hours of Pentecost Sunday when many of the revellers either are gripped by religious frenzy or lie prostrate in an alcoholic stupor, the image of the Virgin, credited with all kinds of magic and fertility powers, is paraded before the faithful as she visits each one of the brotherhoods' houses (which lie empty for the rest of the year).

In recent years the sheer size of the Romería has begun to worry the authorities as it has exploded from a few thousand pilgrims in the 1970s to an incredible half a million in the early years of the new century. Despite the whole affair having become a spectacular TV event with arc lamps, amplified music and fireworks, popular enthusiasm is undiminished. The brotherhoods wrestle with each other to carry the Blanca Paloma ("the White Dove" as the Virgin is fondly known) one more time in procession before she's returned to her shrine for another year, and the weary homeward trek begins.

Accompanying one of the brotherhoods on their pilgrimage to El Rocío is a memorable and exhilarating experience. Anyone is entitled to be a pilgrim: just turn up when the processions leave the major villages in the provinces of Sevilla and Huelva in the days leading up to Pentecost, taking with you a sleeping bag and some food and water. The walking is easy with plenty of stops for dancing and liquid refreshment, and the nightly encampments, when folk songs are sung around campfires, are magical.

El Rocío makes a nice **place to stay** – except during the *romería* when rooms (costing a whopping €200–500 per night) are booked up months, even years, in advance. Economical options for en-suite rooms include *Hostal Cristina*, c/Real 58, behind the church (ⓣ959 44 24 13; ❷), and *El Central*, Plaza del Comercio 4 (ⓣ959 44 20 50; ❷) in the centre of the village. *Hostal Isidro*, Avda. Los Ansares 59 (ⓣ959 44 22 42; ❹), on the village's east side is another place for a/c rooms with bath. Upmarket options include the elegant and enormous *Hotel Rocío de Doñana*, Avda. Canaliega 1 (ⓣ959 44 25 75, ⓦwww.rociodonana.com; ❹), for a/c rooms with minibar and Internet access. The best of the more expensive places is *Hotel Toruño*, Plaza Acebuchal

(☎959 44 23 23, ⓔhoteltoruno@eresmas.com; ❺ with breakfast), with comfortable rooms overlooking the *marismas*. The best view is from Room 225 but some of the ground floor rooms (109, 111 & 115) also allow you to spot flamingos, herons, avocets and lots more whilst lying in bed. Three kilometres along the road to Matalascañas another pleasant if pricier option is *Los Mimbrales* (☎959 44 22 37, ⓦwww.cortijomimbrales.com; ❼), a *cortijo* set in a citrus plantation where you can also rent your own villa. There is a mid-priced restaurant and tapas bar in the main building. El Rocío's pricey **campsite** *La Aldea* (☎959 44 26 77, ⓦwww.campinglaaldea.com) lies on the village's northern edge along the Almonte road (A483).

For **eating and drinking** all the hotels and *hostales* above have restaurants – both the *Cristina* and *Isidro* offer economical *menús* – but the more upmarket *Hotel Toruño's* restaurant located opposite the hotel itself is worth the extra, serves fish and organic beef raised in the national park and has a *menú* for €14.50. The other in-town possibility for more elaborate meals is *Aires de Doñana*, Avda. de la Canaliega 1, near the Turismo. There's no *menú* but it's probably worth eating here for the view from their terrace alone, a spectacular panoramic vista over the *marismas* where – in spring – flamingos, spoonbills and herons entertain diners. All El Rocío's eating places tend to close earlier than is normal in Andalucía and start shutting down around 10.30–11pm. Tapas and *raciones* are served at many other restaurants and bars on and around the village's main street – but to eat out on their terraces after sundown you'll need plenty of mosquito protection.

Matalascañas

Birds and other wildlife apart, **MATALASCAÑAS**, a fast-growing beach resort just outside the reserve, is unlikely to excite; with five large hotel complexes, a grim concrete shopping centre and tasteless beachfront developments along a featureless promenade, it looks as if it's just been thrown together (as indeed it has), and it would be difficult to imagine a more complete lack of character. The **beach**, it must be said though, is attractive and you're allowed to use the strand inside the national park, too. You enter by a gate at the eastern end of the village and can walk along the sand (but not into the park proper) with plenty of opportunities for bird-watching; no vehicles or camping are allowed. The least disagreeable part of the resort is reached by continuing straight on at the roundabout on the edge of the town (ignoring signs to Matalascañas centre) along the Avenida de las Adelfas to an area known as **Torre de la Higuera** where, beyond another roundabout, parking area (where the **bus** will drop you) and kiosk, a line of *marisquerías* front the excellent golden-sand beach which also has a few *chiringuitos* (beach restaurants), too. An area of sand dunes here has been transformed into the **Parque Dunar** which you can explore on foot. There are maps of the park at the various entry points near the beach or on the roundabout at the entry to the town. The Parque Dunar Centro de Información also serves as a **tourist office** (Mon–Fri 10am–2pm; ☎959 43 00 86).

Outside July and August (when you'll need to book ahead) comfortable en-suite **rooms** are available in Torre de la Higuera at *Hostal Los Tamarindos*, Avda. de las Adelfas 31 (☎959 430 119; ❹), which also has its own restaurant. In the resort proper rooms with bath are also to be had at the pleasant *Hostal Victoria*, Sector O no. 18 (☎959 44 09 57; ❹), near the concrete *centro comercial*. Other possibilities here include the cheaper *Hostal Rocío*, c/Pintor Greco 60 (☎959 43 01 41; ❷), about 100m from the beach, or the slightly cheaper *Hostal Romero*, Sector M, Parcela 98 (℡959 44 03 45; ❷), both offering rooms with bath. Of the hotels, *Hotel Flamero* (℡959 44 80 08; ❺), at the eastern end of the beach with tennis courts and a pool, is the best value of the bunch. Matalascañas's **campsite** is the sprawling *Camping Rocío Playa* (℡959 43 02 40), 1.5km down the A494 towards Huelva. This site lacks shade and is a little inconvenient without your own transport if you're planning to take regular trips into the fringes of the national park; if you just want a beach, though, it's not a bad option. The Playa de Doñana and its continuation Playa de Mazagón – with two more campsites, *Fontanilla Playa* (℡959 53 62 37; just beyond the parador, see below), and the vast, densely wooded *Doñana Playa* (℡959 53 63 13; also has bungalows, ❹) – stretch the whole distance to Huelva, with fine beaches backed by dunes and hardly another visitor in sight. With your own transport there are a number of access points (with car parks) to tranquil **beaches** such as the signed Playa Questa Maneli between the two campsites. This route is covered at present by three daily **buses** in both directions in summer with a less frequent service the rest of the year.

Mazagón

The small resort of **MAZAGÓN**, 23km west of Matalascañas, makes a preferable stopover with another fine sandy beach and ample restaurants and bars. The village is well served by **buses** from Huelva, Palos and Moguer, and from the centre – where the bus drops you – it's just a short walk to the beach. Outside August, **rooms** are easy to come by; the pleasant *Hostal Álvarez Quintero*, c/Hernández de Soto 174 (℡959 37 61 69; ❷), just off the beach road, is an excellent-value place to try first where en-suite rooms come with air-conditioning. In the village proper other choices include the pricier *Hostal Hilaria*, c/Hilaria 20 s/n (℡ & ℱ959 37 62 06; ❹), which has a/c terrace rooms with bath above a bar, and the nearby and similarly equipped *Hostal Acuario*, Avda. Fuentepiña 29 (℡959 37 72 86; ❹), on a busy central avenue lined with bars and places to eat. The rather elegant *Hotel Albaida* (℡959 37 60 29, ⓦwww.hotelalbaida.com; ❺) east of the centre is the best of the three-star places and has a restaurant. The more central *Hotel Carabela Santa María*, Avda. de los Conquistadores s/n (℡959 53 60 18, ⓦwww.hotelcarabelasantamaria .com; ❹), is also worth considering for good-value well-equipped rooms. For five-star comfort, head for the modern *Parador Cristóbal Colón* (℡959 53 63 00, ⓦwww.parador.es; ❼), 6km east of Mazagón and set among pine woods; with its own decent restaurant, this is a modern addition to the upmarket chain with uninspiring rooms offset by attractive gardens (with pool) leading down to a fabulous beach. Mazagón's **campsite**, *Camping Playa de Mazagón*, Cuesta de la Barca (℡959 37 62 08), lies at the eastern end of the resort above the beach. There are plenty of places for **eating** and **drinking** around the central zone and the beach; in the centre the Avenida Fuentepiña has an economical restaurant, *Las Redes*, below the *Hostal Aquario* (see above), and the nearby *Bar Torre del Oro* is also good for tapas. Two restaurants a cut above the rest are *El Remo*, Avda. de los Conquistadores 123, specializing in seafood at the eastern end of the seafront with a terrace, and *Las Dunas*, Avda. de los Conquistadores 178, at the western end near the yacht harbour.

The N442 road continues west from Mazagón running behind more inviting beaches for 10km before skirting an industrial zone filled with unsightly petrol refineries, beyond which lies the monastery of La Rábida (see p.373) and the city of Huelva (see p.366).

Along the coast to Portugal

The stretch of coast between the Guadiana – which marks the border with Portugal – and Tinto rivers is lined with some of the finest **beaches** in Andalucía and a scattering of low-key resorts that rarely see a foreign tourist. There's no train service, but plenty of buses run along this main route to the frontier, easily crossed by a spectacular road bridge over the Guadiana estuary.

From Huelva the **coast road to Portugal** loops around the Marisma de San Miguel, passing through the dull towns of Cartaya and **Lepe.** The latter glories in a mention by Chaucer (whose father was a vintner) in his *Pardoner's Tale* saying that the potent white wine of Lepe "creepeth subtilly… that whan a man hath dronken draughtes three, and weneth he be at hoom in Chepe, He is in Spaigne, right at the toune of Lepe" – an out-of-body experience no doubt familiar to many modern inebriates. Lepe's main claim to fame today however, is as the butt of hundreds of "did you hear about the man from Lepe…?" jokes, in which the town's supposedly gormless inhabitants are pilloried by the rest of the nation.

Some 5km south of Lepe on the *marismas* of the Río Piedras, the tiny fishing port of **EL TERRÓN** boasts one of the best **fish restaurants** in this area. Located on the harbour, ⚓ *El Ancla* (☏959 38 04 52), which specializes in mouthwatering fried fish and marinated prawns, doesn't come cheap but there's an affordable *menú*. Cheaper options are provided by a couple of tapas and *mariscos* bars on the quayside. If you want to know a bit more about what you've just eaten the nearby Aula Marina **aquarium** (June–Sept daily 5.30–9.30pm, Oct–May daily 12am–2pm & 4.30–7.30pm; €4) has examples of most species to be found in the Mediterranean and Atlantic waters. About 2km down the road from here a **campsite**, *La Antilla* (☏959 48 08 29), may be your best bet if rooms are tight.

The road hits the coast at the **PLAYA DE LA ANTILLA**, a low-key beach resort invitingly peaceful outside high season, if that's what you're seeking. The blue-flag **beach** is good if slightly gravelly, and there's a scattering of *marisquerías* and restaurants to choose from. Many of these line the main street, Avenida de Castilla, a couple of blocks in from the sea. Locals pack the popular *Cervecería Estoril* about halfway down on the right but more formal dining takes place at *Lino*, Avda. de Castilla 2; *Casa Rodri* (c/Adelfa s/n, just off the same street) with an astonishingly good-value *menú* for €5; or the slightly pricier *La Langosta*. *Bar-Restaurante Feria*, Avda. Castilla 16, at the far end, is another excellent place for fish which also serves tapas. For **breakfast** snacks, with a sea view, and evening *platos combinados*, *Café-Restaurante Coral Playa* lies on the seafront close to the *hostales* below. A place worth seeking out in town is *Pizzeria Pavarotti*, Avda. San Francisco 3 (☏959 48 11 19), where a prodigal Italian restaurateur serves up excellent food (the *tagliatelle al salmone* is recommended) and pizzas with as much free *pan de ajo* (garlic bread) as you can put away. To find it head into town from the beach along the Lepe road, turning right (east) along the Avenida El Terrón; the restaurant is on the corner of the second street on the right.

You won't find a room here in August without pre-booking. **Places to stay** cluster around the junction of Avenida Castilla and c/La Parada, which is also where the bus drops you. The nearest to the sea of a line of *hostales* is the dapper *Hostal Azul*, La Parada 9 (☏959 48 07 00, ⓦwww.hostalazul.com; ❹), where balcony en-suite rooms have sea views and there's an attractive roof terrace with loungers. *Hostal Playa*, Plaza La Parada s/n (☏959 48 15 66, ℉959 48 07 26; ❹), has en-suite rooms and is owned by *Bar Parada* on the square opposite, which is a pleasant place for breakfast and snacks. The nearby *Hostal Sol y Mar*

(☎ & ℱ959 48 11 11; ❹) offers a/c rooms with bath and all three places have attractive off-peak price deals. The cheapest room option is the pleasant *Hostal El Álamo*, Avda. Castilla 82 (☎959 48 10 18, ℮hostalelalamo@laantilla.net; ❹ with breakfast), which has rooms with bath and a decent restaurant, too. Otherwise there's a **campsite**, *Luz* (☎959 48 64 54), with a pool, 5km west towards Isla Cristina.

Isla Cristina

The road passes some pretty awful beach development on the western edge of La Antilla as well as, a couple of kilometres further, the newly created coastal nightmare of **La Islantilla,** where a clutch of fairly tasteless upmarket hotels and *urbanizaciones* are flanked to the right of the road by a sprawling 25-hole golf course. A misguided joint venture by Lepe and Isla Cristina to attract the seriously rich, the complex has a conveniently located **Turismo** (daily 10am–2pm & March–Oct 5.30–7.30pm; ☎959 64 60 13), on the left of the through road, with stacks of information on the whole Costa de la Luz. Beyond the **campsites** *Luz* (see above) and *Taray* (☎959 34 11 02), the vista clears to provide a pleasant few kilometres of pine woods and, behind the dunes, more good beaches.

    ISLA CRISTINA, 8km further on, was, as its name implies, once an island but infilling has transformed it into a pleasant resort surrounded by *marismas* and tidal estuaries. For most of the year the town's prevailing atmosphere is one of nonchalant tranquillity, punctuated only in August by the annual invasion of *sevillanos*, who fill its holiday apartment blocks and beaches to bursting point. The commercial centre is concentrated around the **port** which is the second most important in the province and from where shellfish and wet fish are transported overnight on ice to the markets, bars and restaurants of Sevilla, Córdoba and Madrid. At the end of Carretera de la Playa, an avenue shaded by giant eucalyptus trees, the town's fine sandy **beach** somewhat makes up for a drab seafront. Back in town, life revolves around the central **Plaza de las Flores** (officially Plaza del Caudillo, one of several street names from the Franco period tellingly still much in use). The beach is an easy ten-minute walk from here or there's a half-hourly bus (except during the siesta) from the same square. The big event in Isla Cristina is its annual **Carnaval** held in February.

Practicalities

Southeast of Plaza de las Flores (go south along Gran Via Perez and left along c/Madrid) is the **Turismo** (daily 10am–2pm; March–Oct also 5.30–7.30pm; ☎959 33 26 94) on the unnamed square at the eastern end of c/Madrid, which can provide a town map and accommodation list. The **bus station** lies on Avenida de Huelva, a couple of blocks north of Plaza de las Flores, and is served by frequent daily buses from Huelva and Sevilla and (May–Sept) buses to the beach. **Internet** access is available at *Soft Tony*, Paseo de los Reyes 2, east of Plaza de las Flores (Mon–Sat 10.30am–2pm & 5–9.30pm).

    Due to the severe shortage of **accommodation**, if you want to stay – in August especially – you'll have to book ahead. The most central possibility is the very pleasant *Hotel Brisamar*, c/29 de Julio 87 (☎959 33 11 30; ❹) to the east of the Turismo. Seafront options – all near the Playa Central beach the eastern end of the town – include the friendly *Hotel Sol y Mar* (☎959 20 50, ⓦwww.hotelsolymar.org; ❻) right on the beach, and, slightly in' the *Hotel Paraíso Playa*, Carretera de la Playa s/n (☎959 33 18 73, ⓦ .hotelparaisoplaya.com; ❻), which also has a pool. The nearest **camp'**

Giralda (☎959 34 33 18), lies 2km out of town on the La Antilla road, and offers canoeing and sailing.

For **eating** *Restaurante Acosta* on Plaza de las Flores is noted for its fish and *mariscos*, while *Restaurante Reyes*, opposite on the same square, is another good bet for seafood specialities. Along Carretera de la Playa, the avenue leading to the beach, you'll find ⚓ *Casa Rufino* (☎959 33 08 10), an outstanding fish restaurant which does a great *arroz negro de marisco* (rice with squid), a good-value *menú* for about €18 and a house special called a *tonteo* featuring eight different kinds of fish. Another haunt definitely worth seeking out is *Hermanos Moreno*, Avda. Padre Miravent 39, close to the harbour; their fish restaurant upstairs is excellent and everything served in the tapas bar beneath is as fresh from the sea as you can get. **Drinks** are on offer at the town's atmospheric early twentieth-century *casino* on Plaza de las Flores, and at *Puerta del Sol*, on c/Conde del Vallellano south of Plaza de las Flores, which has good tapas and *raciones* and a terrace. For **music bars** – which is about as near to nightlife as Isla Cristina gets – you need to head for the northwest point of the town's peninsula between Plaza de las Flores and the harbour. Here along the narrow, white-walled and cobbled streets of the old fishing quarter is where most of the bars are congregated. You could try *Almadrabera*, c/Dr Gómez Castrero 6, or *Pipirigaña*, c/Diego Pérez Pascual 198, with inside and outdoor patios. There's often **flamenco** staged at *Bar Gonzalo*, c/Romeu 18, a fine old drinking den with a flamenco room at the back close to Plaza de las Flores. A little further away *Peña Flamenco La Higuerita*, Nuestra Señora de los Angeles s/n, around the corner from the *Hotel Brisamar*, is another great flamenco venue; their bar is open daily but check with the Turismo about upcoming performances.

Ayamonte and around

Although the sprawling, slightly scruffy border town of **AYAMONTE** lies only 8km from Isla Cristina, the road has to dogleg 16km around the *marismas* to get there. With **Portugal** now only a few hundred metres away on the opposite bank of the Río Guadiana – and easily visitable – there's a pronounced Portuguese feel to the town, and in the *horario comercial* the streets hum with the conversations of cross-border visitors who come over to do their shopping.

The warren of narrow streets behind the main square, Paseo de la Ribera (and its continuation Plaza de la Coronación) overlooking the harbour, leads up to the old town, with a couple of churches to see. The mildly interesting fourteenth-century **Iglesia de San Francisco** (open service times, try 7–9pm), with a beautiful Mudéjar *artesonado* ceiling, comes first, and, following the same street, c/San Francisco, even further north will bring you to the fifteenth-century **Iglesia de San Salvador** (Mon–Sat 5–8pm; free) with a striking tower which you can climb, when open, for fine views across the river to Portugal. The town's EU blue-flagged **beach** at Isla Canela, 7km to the south, can be reached by half-hourly **bus** (April–Sept) from Paseo de la Ribera.

The beaches

Ayamonte's beaches, the **Playa Isla Canela** and its eastward continuation, the **Playa Punta del Moral**, are excellent places for a bit of basking in the sun, though what was once an attractively wild stretch of coast has undergone a mammoth building programme turning the Punta del Moral into a complex of high-rise holiday apartments and hotels with the gargantuan and tasteless *Hotel ...ts* centrepiece.

The picturesque old fishing village of **PUNTA DEL MORAL** sits on an inlet slightly north of here warily eyeing the concrete monsters dominating the skyline to the south. It's worth seeking out this tiny place for a line of excellent **tapas bars** along its main street. *Bar Simón*, *Chiringuito III* and *El Contrabando* are all good for fresh fish, *raciones* and a wide range of tapas.

Practicalities

Frequent daily buses from Huelva and Sevilla arrive at the **bus station** on Avenida de Andalucía east of the centre. Ayamonte's sleepy **Turismo** (Mon–Fri 10am–1.30pm & 5.30–8.30pm; ☎959 32 18 71, ⓦwww.ayto-ayamonte.ci) is located in an elegant restored mansion known as La Casa Grande, the town's cultural centre, on Plaza del Rosario s/n, a small square slightly to the north of Paseo de la Ribera; they can provide a town map and information, along with details of *casas particulares*. The centre also stages frequent concerts and art shows, details of which are available in a monthly leaflet. The **Internet** café *Todoapc*, Avda. Villa Real de Santo Antonio 6 (daily 10am–9pm), is located on the waterfront facing the fishing harbour.

   Places to stay are limited and rooms can be hard to find, especially in summer; if things become really tight one option may be to cross the Guadiana to the Portuguese side and the town of Vila Real de Santo Antonio on the opposite bank (see below). As you enter Ayamonte from Isla Cristina, opposite the petrol station are two of the best-value options in town: the *Hostal Las Robles*, Avda. Andalucía 121 (☎959 47 09 59; ❷) and, next door, the new and plusher *Hotel Luz del Guadiana* (☎959 32 20 02, ⒻⒻ959 47 16 97; ❹). Both offer pleasant en-suite rooms and those at the latter come with a/c and TV. In the centre, the most economical option is the functional *Hotel Marqués de Ayamonte*, c/Trajano 12, off Paseo de la Ribera (☎959 32 01 26; ❸). *Hotel Don Diego*, Avda. Ramón y Cajal 2 (☎959 47 02 50, ⓦwww.hoteldondiegoayamonte.com; ❻ with breakfast), to the east of the harbour is a step up in price and quality while the town's *Parador Costa de la Luz* at El Castillita overlooking the Río Guadiana (☎959 32 07 00, ⓦwww.parador.es; ❻) is modern and rather bland. Should you wish to splash out, Isla Canela, Ayamonte's beach resort, has a luxury hotel which leaves the parador standing; the 350-room *Hotel Riu Canela* (☎959 47 71 24, ⓦwww .riu.com; ❾) is an extravagant, neo-Moorish parody surrounded by Alhambra-style gardens, fountains and swimming pools. If you want to spend the night in **Portugal** there are quite a few decent room possibilities within a couple of minutes walk of the Vila Real de Santo Antonio ferry quay. The waterfront *Hotel Guadiana*, Avda. da República 94 (from Spain ☎00 351 281 511 482, ⓦwww .hotelguadiana.com.pt; ❺), is an elegant and reasonably priced upmarket choice, whilst *Residencia Villa Marquez*, Rua José Baráo, 61 (from Spain ☎00 351 281 530 420; ❹) is a sparkling place offering a/c en-suite rooms with TV.

   Ayamonte scores well in terms of **eating and drinking**, with many options clustered around the central Paseo (or Plaza) de la Ribera. Slightly west of here *La Casona*, at c/Lusitania 2, offers an inexpensive *menú*, and has a terrace. To the north of here and beyond the elegant Plaza Laguna, *Méson La Vitola*, c/José Pérez Barroso s/n, is a very good economical restaurant serving high-standard fish and meat dishes. On the main square *Cafetería Restaurante Barberi*, Paseo de la Ribera 13, is also worth a try and its café next door has an inexpensive *menú del día*. On the west side of the same square *Mesón Juan Macias*, Paseo de la Ribera 2, is another good place with plenty of *chorizo*- and *jamón*-based dishes. For a pricey blowout, the town's best place – especially for fish – is the mid-priced *Casa Luciano*, c/Palma 2, on the east side of the harbour (☎959 47 01 71).

Nightlife is mainly confined to the summer months when the tourist invasion fills a number of music bars in and around c/Médico Rey García, one block in from the harbour: current hot spots are *A Popa, Sacapuntas, Hangar* and *Acropolis*.

On to Portugal

For a change of scene you can cross over the expansive Río Guadiana to **Portugal** by boat or over the impressive new road bridge. A **ferry** (every 30min until 9pm, Oct–June hourly; €1.10 one way) plies across the estuary and frontier to the busy and pleasant border town of **VILA REAL DE SANTO ANTONIO**, with a riverside promenade lined with popular bars and restaurants. The ferry leaves from the Muelle de Portugal dock in Ayamonte – easily reached by taking the main pedestrianized thoroughfare, c/Lusitania, from the west side of Paseo de la Ribera. **By car** you simply head north out of town along c/Galdames following signs for Portugal and fairly soon you'll be flying effortlessly – and without any border checks whatsoever – high above the river via the magnificent Puente del Guadiana.

Inland to Río Tinto

Of the potential routes to the mountainous north of the province, the westernmost, from near Ayamonte, is the least interesting. Here the road ploughs on endlessly through a dreary landscape dominated by stands of voracious and alien eucalyptus which have sucked the lifeblood from the soil. Far more attractive is the N435 route heading northeast from Huelva city towards Extremadura which offers – with your own transport – an interesting detour to the **mines of Río Tinto** (see box). The **bus** uses the same route to reach Aracena or you could take a **train** which will drop you at Almonaster La Real at the Sierra de Aracena's western end. For visits to the mining area without your own vehicle there are at least three daily **buses** from Huelva to Minas de Ríotinto and Nerva from where there are not-so-frequent daily connections to Aracena and Sevilla. Once clear of Huelva the N435 climbs steadily towards **Trigueros**, a pleasant agricultural village which claims proprietorship over the Neolithic Dolmen de Soto, 8km to the southwest (see p.366). **Valverde del Camino**, 24km north and now by-passed by the arterial road, is a market town noted more for its leather footwear factories than its charm, and the N435 continues a further 10km to where a turn on the right towards the hamlet of **El Pozuelo** allows you to see three **dolmens** from the third millennium BC. Following this minor road for about 2km brings you to a signed road just before a cemetery on the outskirts of the village. Follow this on foot or by car as it loops around the village for a further 2km to reach a rest area and **information board**. Leave any transport here and follow the track on the right which ascends the hill through trees for about 100m to the first dolmen, from where the other two can be seen on hills nearby. The first is the most impressive and has three burial chambers, two with their capstones still in place. The second has four burial chambers, and the last is in ruins. A further six dolmens displayed on the information board are not so easy to spot.

The N435 winds into the wooded hill country of the Sierra Morena until – just beyond Zalamea La Real – a right turn along the A461 leads you into the area of the Río Tinto mines.

Minas de Riotinto and around

Set in an area dramatically scarred by open-cast mineworkings, where the exposed faces of mineral-rich rock are streaked with glinting rivulets of ochre, rust and cadmium, the village of **MINAS DE RIOTINTO**, 6km east of the N435, was created by the Río Tinto mining company in the early twentieth century after they had dynamited its predecessor – complete with Baroque church – which had stood in the way of mining operations.

As you approach it from the west, watch out on the left for the **Barrio de Bella Vista**, or what the locals refer to as the "English colony". This estate of Victorian villas, complete with mock-Gothic Presbyterian church and village green, was constructed to house the largely British management and engineering staff when the mines passed into Anglo-German hands in the nineteenth century. The attitude of this elite to the surrounding village – where the mineworkers lived – is indicated by the estate's high perimeter wall and once-guarded entry gates intended rigorously to exclude "the natives", as they were disdainfully described. In a company policy with racist overtones these "colonialists" were forbidden from living in Bella Vista if they dared to marry a Spanish woman, thus deterring any dangerous interbreeding. In the woods beyond the laurel hedgerows surrounding the church a war memorial records the five names of company staff (management only) who fell in the Great War. To find it, follow a residential road east behind the church for 75m, forking left along a narrow road with a one-way sign; you'll see a small enclosed track running between the grounds of two houses and the monument lies 50m down this path. The estate now houses local people and can be visited as part of the guided tour from the visitor centre at Nerva (see p.393), or you can usually

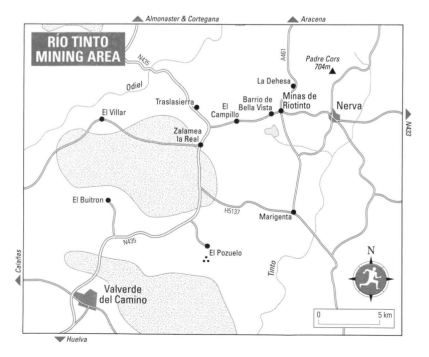

The mines of Río Tinto

The **Río Tinto** (Red River) takes its name from the oxidized iron minerals that flow down from the fissured crags of this strange, forbidding landscape, turning the river blood-red. Evidence of mineral exploitation here goes back at least five millennia – popular tradition asserts that these were the legendary mines of King Solomon, as seen in place names such as Cerro (or hill) de Saloman and Zalamea La Real. More secure historical evidence shows it was the **Phoenicians** (giving the name Ur-yero – "river of fire" – to the Río Tinto) who encouraged exploitation here early in the first millennium BC, during the age of the fabled kingdom of Tartessus from where they acquired the copper to smelt with the tin of Cornwall to make bronze. It was not copper but silver, however, which attracted the **Romans** in the second century BC. Production was dramatically stepped up during the late republic and early empire using remarkable – if brutal – systems to combat flooding, the perennial hazard in deep mining. This they overcame by means of slave-operated *norias,* or water wheels; in some workings as many as eight pairs of these wheels were used in relays to raise water from depths of 100m and more. For the shackled slave miners working with primitive tools by the light of small clay lamps in warrens of cramped, dark galleries (now vividly reconstructed in the Río Tinto mining museum), life must have been wretched. The scale of the Roman operations can be judged from the fifty million tons of visible slag left behind.

After the Romans had gone, the **Visigoths** worked out the Roman shafts but the mines were then run down during the Moorish period – although Niebla built part of its prosperity on its rights of ownership by granting permits. The *conquista* brought further decline in its wake as cheap mineral wealth flooded into Spain from the New World. Loss of empire and hard times induced efforts to restart the industry which, in 1873, resulted in the Spanish government selling the mines to a consortium of British and German bankers. Out of this the **Río Tinto Mining Company** was born, bringing numerous northern Europeans to work here; in 1954 control of the company returned into Spanish hands.

just wander in for a look around. The mining museum (see below) has recently acquired a house in Bellavista and is in the process of turning it into a museum, documenting – with the aid of photos, clothes and furniture – the life of an English family living here at the end of the nineteenth century. It's planned to open in late 2006 (details from the museum).

To continue to the village proper head east along the A461 and turn right following "*centro urbano*" signs. The road leads to a roundabout with palms on its central island, with the former Río Tinto Mining Company's offices (now the Ayuntamiento) to the left. The village's centre lies to the left or east from here while the mining museum is reached by taking a right uphill from the roundabout. **On foot**, from the west side of the same roundabout you can follow a path which ascends through the pine and eucalyptus woods to emerge at the museum.

The mining museum

At the village's western edge on a hill above the Río Tinto company's former offices lies the Río Tinto Foundation's remarkable **mining museum**, Plaza del Museo s/n (daily 10.30am–3pm & 4–7pm; €3). Housed in the company's former hospital, the museum presents an interesting panorama of mining in the area from prehistoric to modern times. The **Roman period** is the best represented, with exhibits illustrating their mining methods, daily life and burial practices in addition to a variety of coins and statuary. A recently opened

Semana
Santa

Nothing can prepare you for the overwhelming spectacle and passion of Semana Santa (Holy Week) in Andalucía. The most important celebration in the Christian calendar, it is at its most moving and intense in this region. Every town and village celebrates the feast in its own way, and a simple candlelit procession with floats of Christ and the Virgin passing through the darkened streets of a small hill village can be just as moving as the big city affairs. It's not all about piety however, as this is southern Spain, home of the fiesta, and in between the processions the bar scene is in full swing day and night – though despite the enormous amount of enthusiasm and preparation, the whole affair can still be cancelled if the weather is bad.

Sevilla, the vibrant, quintessential city of Andalucía, stages the most spectacular Semana Santa celebrations in the world. Its old quarter, the whitewalled Barrio Santa Cruz, provides the backdrop to a week of processions when the whole tragedy of the Passion is replayed with moving ceremony.

Preparing the *paso*

Sevilla's Gothic cathedral is the focus for the fifty-seven **brotherhoods** (*hermandades*) who carry floats (*pasos*) bearing large and elaborately sculpted scenes from the Passion through the streets lined with thousands of onlookers. As each *paso* represents a stage in the drama leading up to the Crucifixion (Palm Sunday, Betrayal by Judas, Judgment by Pilate) they normally process on the same day in Holy Week each year.

Several hundred members of each brotherhood accompany the *pasos* dressed as hooded penitents or **nazarenos**, wearing Ku-Klux Klan-like capes and tall pointed caps which cover the head leaving only narrow slits for the eyes. Many of these *hermandades* have impressive histories and some, such as the oldest of them all, **El Silencio**, date back to the thirteenth century. Each of the *hermandades* spends months preparing for their big day and as this draws near, each brotherhood's images of Christ and the Virgin are meticulously readied in their home church. Finally, the Virgin is draped in beautiful robes and decked out with valuable jewels. Then the whole glittering *paso* is adorned with a dazzling array of flowers.

The role of the *costaleros*

La salida, the moment when the *paso* emerges from the church, is an occasion of great emotion and attracts huge crowds. This is when the skills of the costaleros – the men underneath the *paso* who are carrying it and remain concealed behind a curtain – are put to the test. *Pasos* are built to sway, causing their silver chains and tassles to tinkle, while their canopies rustle and flap in any breeze – all calculated to add to the magic of the occasion – and manoeuvering these delicate yet heavy floats (up to two tons in weight) is a hazardous operation. Its weight also means that it can only be carried for a short distance – usually fifty or so metres – before the *costaleros* have to rest. In fact, each *paso* has two teams of up to forty men, and even though one team rests while the other works, progress is still very slow.

Local variations

Although the processions through the streets to the cathedral or main church are common to all celebrations of Semana Santa, each town and village has its own customs and traditions. On Palm Sunday the Alpujarras village of **Carataunas** starts its Passion week by throwing an image of Judas Iscariot onto a huge bonfire. **Málaga** has the largest *pasos* in Andalucía – many over twenty metres long, weighing six tons and carried by up to two hundred *costaleros* – and is also where a prisoner is freed from the jail on the Wednesday of Holy Week and joins the parade. In the Axarquía village of **Carratraca** a daily Passion play is staged in its bullring, with the villagers – dressed in costume – playing the part of the crowd. At **Baena**, in Córdoba province, the streets resonate to the cacophany of two thousand drums as the processions move around the town. In Sevilla, Málaga and Granada the church authorities allocate each brotherhood a **departure and return time** for the journey to and from their church. If it is more than thirty minutes behind schedule in completing the route, the brotherhood is fined.

La Macarena

The climax of Semana Santa takes place during the early hours of Good Friday, when the candlelit floats depicting the Crucifixion leave their churches at midnight and move through the darkened streets watched by sombre crowds and followed by a band playing traditional dirges. In Sevilla, the image of the Christ on the Cross is accompanied by the most important of the city' Virgins, La Macarena, a stirring seventeenth-century work by Luisa Roldán. The statue's name is taken from her home church and attracts frenzied devotion. As she nears the cathedral, where the air is thick with a pungent cocktail of fragrant orange blossom, incense and burning candle wax, individuals will often step out in front of the *paso* and erupt into an impromptu **lament** delivered in flamenco style (a *saeta*), listened to in silence by the crowd. When it's over, there's a ripple of applause and the *paso* moves on.

Traditions and customs

Depicting the Virgin All the Semana Santa Virgins are portrayed in the trauma of the Passion, grieving for a dead son: many of the statues' tears are in fact priceless diamonds.

Dressing the statue Even though a male sculptor will have carved it, no other man is ever allowed to see an image of the Virgin undressed, so the clothing and preparation of the Virgins is carried out exclusively by senior female members of the brotherhoods.

Procession etiquette When two processions cross each other's paths – inevitable in the major cities – the *pasos* of the Virgin and Christ salute each other in beautifully choreographed movements executed by both teams of *costaleros*. This is a poignant Semana Santa moment and is always applauded by the crowd.

Bollos de cera The processions in major cities deposit tons of candlewax onto the streets during Semana Santa. Children pester the candle-toting penintents along the route for drops of wax which they "snowball" into a *bollo* – a Holy Week souvenir.

section here has a walk-through recons███████████man **mineworking gallery** discovered in the nearby mining ███████████al site cannot be visited as it lies within the zone of the modern mineworkings and is thus dangerous, but the museum has done an excellent job in re-creating it. The section includes a working reconstruction of a *noria*, or **water wheel**, which were worked by slaves and used to drain the mines of flood water. Modern mining is also covered, as well as the geology, flora and fauna of the area. Don't miss the luxurious **wagon of the maharaja**, built in 1892 by the Birmingham Railway Carriage and Wagon Company to be used by Queen Victoria on her proposed visit to India. When this didn't happen it was sold to the Río Tinto company and used for the visit of King Alfonso XIII to the mines. The museum can also provide information on a visit to the old underground mineworkings of Pozo Alfredo. A **cafetería** serves snacks and drinks and its adjoining **shop** sells a wide variety of souvenirs.

In addition, the Río Tinto Foundation's marketing arm, Aventura Parque Minero, runs **train trips**, lasting a couple of hours, through the mining area aboard century-old restored rolling stock – on the first Sunday of each month they use a 120-year-old steam locomotive (daily: Aug 1.30pm & 5pm; June, July & Sept 1.30pm; ring ℡959 59 00 25 for winter/spring timetable; ⓦparquemineroderiotinto.sigadel.com; €9). The same organization also offers combined three-hour visits (reservation required; €15) to the mining area taking in the Corta Atalaya and the Cerro Colorado mines, the Bella Vista Victorian housing estate, the Roman mineworkings and cemetery and the steam engine and mining museums (details from the museum).

Practicalities

Recent closures mean that **accommodation** in the village is limited to the *Hostal Galán,* Avda. de la Esquila 10 (℡959 59 08 40; ❸), around the corner from the museum, with en-suite rooms and a good bar-restaurant below. With your own transport the ⚘ *Cortijo Zalamea* (℡959 56 10 27, ✉lopesigual@eresmas .es; ❺), back off the main N435 close to the village of Zalamea La Real, is as delightful an oasis as you could wish: accommodation is in self-contained cottages, there's a pool and horse riding, mountain biking and walking are some activities on offer. In Río Tinto, the only **eating** options are the restaurant of the *Hostal Galán*, plus, downhill from here, *Restaurante Epoca*, Paseo de los Caracoles 6, for well-cooked *platos combinados*; there is also a *menú*.

La Dehesa and Nerva

Two kilometres northeast of the village, and reached by following the A461 as it heads north towards Aracena, you pass two spectacular open-cast mines: the **Corta Atalaya**; and, with 5000 years of exploitation, the **Cerro Colorado**, set in an awesome landscape of rock cliffs glittering with iron pyrites, copper, silver and gold. From a **viewing platform** by the roadside you can see into the giant elliptical basin of the Corta Atalaya, which at 1200m long and 330m deep is one of the biggest open-cast mines in the world – far below, enormous trucks are dwarfed by the immense walls of rock. Another 2km further on, at **LA DEHESA**, the Río Tinto Company headquarters are backed by a recently discovered **Roman graveyard** featuring a number of interesting tombstones. Alarmingly close to the present mining operations which rumble on in the background, the graveyard is open to the public only on guided tours (see below).

NERVA, 4km east of Minas de Riotinto, is a pleasant little place, its pedestrianized main street fringed with orange trees and overlooked by a splendid red-brick Ayuntamiento with a wonderful minaret-inspired octagonal tower.

△ Roman graveyard, La Dehesa

Opposite there's an extravagant new **Centro de Arte Contemporáneo** (Mon & Sun 10am–2.30pm, Tues–Sat 11am–2pm & 6–9pm; free) honouring Daniel Vásquez Díaz (a Paris contemporary of Picasso), who was born here. In addition to a handful of canvases by Díaz the museum also displays an indifferent collection of works by other *nerveuses* to fill the rather cavernous interior.

There are two daily **buses** (except Sun) to Aracena at 6am and 6.20pm. Nerva also has a pleasant **place to stay**, the friendly, family-run *Hostal El Goro*, c/Reina Victoria s/n (☎ & ⓕ959 58 04 37; ❷), close to the centre, with well-equipped en-suite rooms. *Hotel Vásquez Díaz*, c/Cañadilla 51 (☎959 58 09 27; ❸), is a slightly more upmarket option reached by turning first left into the town coming from Minas de Riotinto. A very good **place to eat** is the central *Bodegón El Sótano*, Avda. de Andalucía 40, near the *Hostal El Goro*, serving tapas as well as fish and meat dishes.

Leaving the mining area by the A461, beyond Campofrío the landscape softens as the road progresses through verdant forests of cork and holm oaks, chestnut and walnut trees towards Aracena.

The almost Martian landscape of much of this zone has attracted scientists from Madrid University and the Astrobiological Institute of NASA, who have begun research into the remarkable microbial life that has developed here in some of the most inhospitable conditions on the planet. The enormous diversity of **eukaryotic life forms** (organisms with genetic cells) able to prosper in the poisonous and highly acidic waters of the Río Tinto mining zone initially astonished experts, who went on to discover here a variety of previously unknown life forms. The researchers hope that the thousands of species of micro-organisms that have evolved here over millennia in the toxic depths of the Red River will provide clues as to how life may have developed and evolved in other parts of the universe.

The Sierra Morena

The longest of Spain's mountain ranges, the **Sierra Morena** extends almost the whole way across Andalucía from Rosal on the Portuguese frontier to the dramatic pass of Despeñaperros, north of Linares. Its hill towns once marked the northern boundary of the old Moorish caliphate of Córdoba and in many ways the region still signals a break today, with a shift from the climate and mentality of the south to the bleak plains and villages of Extremadura and New Castile. The range is not widely known – with its highest point a mere 1110m, it is not a dramatic sierra – and even Andalucians can have trouble placing it. All of which, of course, is to your advantage if you like to be alone.

Visiting the Sierra Morena

The Morena's **climate** is mild – sunny in spring, hot but fresh in summer – but it can get very cold in the evenings and mornings. A good time to visit is between March and June, when the flowers, perhaps the most varied in the country, are at their best. You may get caught in the odd thunderstorm but it's usually bright and hot enough to swim in the reservoirs or splash in the springs and streams, most of which are good to drink. This is an area rich in **wildlife** – including frogs, turtles, lizards, dragonflies, bees, hares and foxes – while bird fanciers should keep an eye out for imperial and booted eagles, as well as goshawks, peregrine falcons and the rare black vulture. In villages such as Cortegana, Zufre and Santa Olalla del Cala the black stork nests on the church towers. The Sierra de Aracena sector of the Sierra has recently been designated as a ZEPA (Zona de Especial Protección a las Aves) in recognition of its importance as a bird sanctuary. The sierra is also home to one of two surviving populations of Spanish lynx on the peninsula, although, with only thirty or so pairs eking out an existence as their forest habitat is gnawed away, you're unlikely to spot one.

Locals maintain that while the last bears disappeared only a short time ago, there are still a few wolves in remoter parts. Of more concern to anyone hiking in the Sierra Morena, however, are the **toros bravos** (fighting bulls), always in fenced-off pastures. Observe signs by roads and tracks depicting a bull and sometimes labelled "*toros bravos*". The thing to do, according to expert advice, is to stay calm, and without attracting the bull's attention, go round. If you even get a whiff of a fighting bull, though, it might well be best simply to drop everything and run.

East–west **transport** in the Sierra (see "Travel Details") is limited but with a little planning most places mentioned below can be reached on public transport. For the zone east of Aracena, specifically the terrain beyond the main N630 in Sevilla Province, bus services are radial and north–south, with Sevilla as the hub. Tracks are still more common in these hills than roads, and rural tourism, which the government of Andalucía is keen to encourage, has so far led to little more than a handful of signs pointing out areas of special interest. The wealth of good **walking country** invites organizing your routes round hikes – if you want to spend any amount of time here. **Cycling**, too, is an option, though you'll need a sturdy bike with plenty of gears, especially on the winding and muscle-taxing hill roads. **Places to stay** are plentiful and most villages run to at least a decent *hostal* and a few now have hotels, too. Rural tourism accommodation has really taken off in recent years and there are also a great number of **villas** and **farmhouses** to rent in lovely settings; the best way to find one is through RAAR (Red Andaluza de Alojamientos Rurales; ☎902 44 22 33, English spoken, ⓦwww.raar.es).

Aracena

Clustered beneath its hill-top medieval castle, the attractive town of **ARACENA** is the highest conurbation in the Sierra Morena as well as the gateway to its own **Sierra de Aracena** to the south and west. Sheltered by this offshoot of the larger Morena range, Aracena is blessed by remarkably sharp, clear air – all the more noticeable, and gratifying, if you've arrived from the heat of Sevilla.

Although traces of Paleolithic occupation of this area have been found, it was only in the Middle Ages that more concrete historical events happened here, namely the passing of this territory into the kingdom of Castile by a treaty of 1267 following a long struggle with Portugal. Once inside the domains of Castile, Alfonso X ceded the zone around Aracena to the Knights Templars to maintain and protect the Sierra. They constructed the castle, one of many erected in this frontier zone, and ruled the roost here until 1312 (see box opposite). Today, the town's main role is as a centre of agriculture and cattle breeding, assisted by the tourist magnet of the **Gruta de las Maravillas** (Cave of Wonders).

Arrival and information

Aracena's new **bus station**, Avda. de Sevilla s/n, lies on the southeast side of town close to the Parque Municipal. For information and a town map, the **Turismo** lies beneath the Gruta de las Maravillas ticket office (daily 10am–2pm & 4–6.30pm; ☎959 12 82 06, ⓦwww.sierradearacena.net). Information on the surrounding Parque Natural Sierra de Aracena y Picos de Aroche is obtainable from an **information centre** in the Cabildo Viejo, Plaza Alta 5 (April–Sept Tues–Sun 10am–2pm & 6–8pm, Oct–March Tues–Sun 10am–2pm & 4–6pm). They can also supply information on the town, including a useful town map. The town's solitary **Internet** café, *Cibercafe Aranet*, c/José Nogales s/n, is located just off the main square, Plaza Marqués de Aracena, on the corner with the market.

Accommodation

Places to stay are limited: the budget option, the simple and friendly *Casa Manolo*, c/Barberos 6 (☎959 12 80 14; ❶), lies below the main square, Plaza Marqués de Aracena, but outside summer make sure to get an exterior

The Knights Templars

A military religious order founded in the twelfth century to protect pilgrims bound for the Holy Land, the **Knights Templars** derived their name from the Temple of Solomon, in Jerusalem. An army of fighting monks in reality, their *raison d'être* became a permanent crusade against the Saracen infidel from their "commanderies" in the Holy Land and western Europe.

For over a century the Templars fought the Muslims for control of Jerusalem and its surrounding territories. A series of defeats culminated in the loss of Acre in 1291, their last Latin outpost in Palestine, and heralded the order's demise. They were also mistrusted by the European monarchs, especially Philip IV of France, who saw the order as a threat to their power. Long accused of being involved in witchcraft due to their interest in the occult, magic and the supernatural as paths to ultimate knowledge, the Templars were persecuted, condemned and executed for heresy by an alliance of monarchs and clerics across Europe. The order was finally dissolved by a bull of Pope Clement V in 1312. In the light of the above it's rather ironic that Aracena's Templar outpost was built on top of one of the most magical and mysterious places in Spain: the Gruta de las Maravillas, of which they must have been completely unaware.

room as the inside ones (which get no sun) can be freezing. More upmarket possibilities include the *Hotel Sierra de Aracena*, Gran Vía 21 (T959 12 61 75, Ehsierraaracena@terra.es; ●), now in need of refurbishment, and the pleasant *Hotel de los Castaños*, Avda. de Huelva 5 (T959 12 63 00, F959 12 62 87; ●), both with heating, garage and many facilities. With your own transport (although it is within walking distance), you could try the *Finca Valbono* (T959 12 77 11, Efincavalbono@wanadoo.es; ●), a rural hotel with pool and restaurant set in thirty acres of scenic woodland, 1km north of town on the road to Carboneras. There are also *casita* stone houses equipped with kitchens sleeping up to four for around €140 per night (min. stay of three nights) and all kinds of activities including hiking and horse riding excursions are on offer. The nearest **campsite**, *Camping Aracena Sierra* (T959 50 10 05), which has a pool, lies 3km along the Sevilla road, then left for 500m towards Cortecconcepción.

The Town

Aracena is a modest but pretty Sierra town, its southern flank rambling up the side of a hill topped by the **Iglesia del Castillo** – or, more correctly, Nuestra Señora de los Dolores – a fine thirteenth-century Gothic-Mudéjar church built by the Knights Templars around the remains of a Moorish castle. The track up to the church begins from the **Plaza Alta**, where there's the unfinished church of **Nuestra Señora de la Asunción** with remnants of Renaissance craftsmanship, flanked by a sixteenth-century *cabildo* or **Ayuntamiento**, the oldest in the province which now houses the Natural Park information centre. The building's imposing main portal is by Hernán Ruíz II and dates to 1563. Slightly northeast of here, the interior of the **Convento de Santa Catalina**, with its fine fifteenth-century Gothic panels, is also worth a look. It was for this convent that the stunning carved wood *retablo* by Juan Giralte, now in Sevilla's Museo de Bellas Artes, was made. The climb to the castle offers good views over the town from an imposing sixteenth-century brick gate complete with belfry, which allows access to the castle area. The church's elegant **Mudéjar tower** was formerly the minaret of the twelfth-century Almohad mosque prior to its destruction by the Templars, and its *sebka*

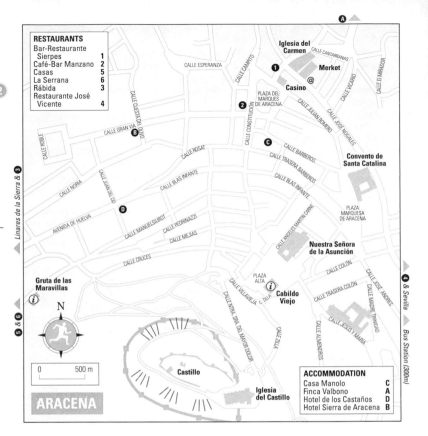

RESTAURANTS
Bar-Restaurante
  Sierpes   1
Café-Bar Manzano   2
Casas   5
La Serrana   6
Rábida   3
Restaurante José
  Vicente   4

ACCOMMODATION
Casa Manolo   C
Finca Valbono   A
Hotel de los Castaños   D
Hotel Sierra de Aracena   B

brickwork ornamentation echoes the Giralda tower in Sevilla. Inside there's an unusual and finely made glazed clay tomb of the sixteenth-century prior, Pedro Vásquez de Miguel.

Aracena's principal attraction is the **Gruta de las Maravillas** (daily 10.30am–1.30pm & 3–6pm; guided hourly visits, half-hourly at weekends €7.50), the largest and arguably the most impressive cave in Spain, discovered, so they say, by a local boy in search of a lost pig. The Gruta lies at the western end of c/ Rosal which you can pick up just south of the Plaza Mayor (Plaza Marqués de Aracena): due to the cave being damaged by the overwhelming number of visitors, a maximum of 35 visitors per tour is now in force. This means that the best **time to visit** is before noon; if you are planning an afternoon visit (the time favoured by coach tours) ring ☎959 12 83 55 and they will advise whether you will be able to gain entry. It can be chilly inside so bring a sweater.

A guide takes you round the cave and the "marvels" are explained in Spanish only (leaflet in English). Although the garish coloured lighting is more Santa's Grotto than geological wonder, the cave is still astonishingly beautiful, and entertaining too – the last chamber of the tour is known simply as the Sala de los Culos (Room of the Buttocks), its walls and ceiling an outrageous, naturally sculpted exhibition, tinged in a pinkish orange light. You might care to ponder why this section of the caves did not appear in the film *Journey to the Centre of the Earth*, much of which was shot here.

In the plaza outside there's a permanent **outdoor museum of contemporary sculpture** with donated works by many noted artists including *Reconocimiento del Vacío* by the famous Basque sculptor Eduardo Chillida, a graceful cube-like structure, and Carmen Perujo's work *Paloma*, sited near the cave entrance

Eating, drinking and nightlife

As Aracena is at the heart of a prestigious *jamón*-producing area, anything with **pork** is highly recommended – you should also try the delicious wild asparagus, mushrooms (Sept onwards) and local **snails** (June–Aug).

Places to eat in town are clustered around the main square, Plaza Marqués de Aracena. *Café-Bar Manzano*, at the southern end, serves great tapas and *platos combinados* and has a terrace, and off the northern end *Bar-Restaurante Sierpes*, c/Mesones 17, housed in an attractive old house serves tapas and – in its restaurant – a variety of dishes plus a *menú* for around €10. For a memorable splurge, head for ✴ *Restaurante José Vicente*, Avda. Andalucía 51 (☎959 12 84 55; closed Fri), where patrons gather to savour the five grades of Jabugo *jamón ibérico* (black-pig ham) under the approving gaze of owner/chef Vicente Sousa. The €18 *menú*, which often includes a mouthwatering *solomillo* (pork loin), is recommended and there is now a new tapas bar as well, *Despensa de José Vicente*, which also sells natural products from the Sierra. Vicente is an expert on the Sierra's *setas* (mushrooms), many remarkable examples of which he keeps in his freezer for use in the kitchen. You can find the restaurant by taking the first right uphill from the *casino* (see below); after about four hundred metres it's on the left opposite the park. At lunchtime (until 4pm), decent alternatives are provided by two restaurants near the entrance to the Gruta de las Maravillas: the excellent *Casas*, Pozo La Nieve 39, and the nearby *La Serrana*, both slightly extravagant with a *menú* at the latter for around €15. More reasonable again is *Rábida*, in c/Chopos, off Avenida Huelva, which has a €8 *menú*. Just up from the restaurants near the caves *Conservas Jabugo S.L.*, c/Pozo de la Nieve s/n, sells the famous *jamones* (hams) and many other products of the Sierra.

For **breakfast** or **evening drinks**, sit with the locals at the outdoor tables of the *casino* bar above the main square, from where you get a wonderful view towards the castle. Finally, for superb *dulces*, the 125-year-old Confitería Casa Rufino, off the main square at c/Constitución 3, is a must; their *tocino de cielo*, *vitoría*s (liqueur-soaked, iced cakes) and *sultanas* (filled coconut cakes) are truly memorable – in the afternoon do what everyone else does, and take your cakes to *Café Manzano*'s terrace.

Nightlife is low-key, but turning left at the end of Gran Vía along c/Juan del Cid will bring you to a few **bars** and a **disco** – *Malh'aman* – frequented by Aracena's younger set. *D'Acuña*, at Gran Vía 20, *Cafetería Bronze*, Gran Vía 5, and *La Moncloa*, one block south on c/Rosal, are other good *copas* bars with a lively atmosphere.

The Sierra de Aracena

With a few days to spare, the rugged villages perched on the hills to the **west of Aracena** make a fine walking tour. Along the route you'll find a number of good places to stay and plenty of tracks to follow through this rich landscape of orange and lemon orchards and forests of cork oaks, chestnut and gum trees. In spring the profusion of flowers is extraordinary: rosemary, French

Minas de Riotinto

lavender, peonies and Spanish irises are most common, and you may also be lucky enough to see the rare brown bluebell and members of the orchid family. You probably won't glimpse the Spanish lynx in one of its last native habitats (outside the Coto de Doñana), but the skies are the place for sightings of black vultures on patrol, and even the occasional imperial eagle, a stirring image as they glide regally above their domain. Black vultures have been reintroduced into the park along with peregrine falcons and on the church towers of Cortegana and Zufre you may be lucky enough to sight the rare black storks that are known to nest there.

If you're coming to the Sierra for a few days and need a base, there are lots of **houses to rent** in scenic locations (see p.396). The **bus service** between Aracena and the villages of Alájar, Almonaster, Cortegana and Aroche currently runs twice daily at 1pm and 5.30pm (not Sun), the latter terminating at Cortegana. There are also four daily buses (Mon–Sat) between Aracena and Galaroza, Jabugo, Cortegana and Aroche at 7.10am, 10.30am (also Sun), 1.15pm (with a change at Cortegana) and 5.30pm (this service is two buses with one calling at Linares, Alájar and Cortegana, the other passing all the rest along the main N432). Similar services return in the reverse direction. All leave from Aracena's new bus station on Avenida de Sevilla s/n near the Parque Municipal.

Linares de la Sierra and Alájar

Leaving Aracena by the minor A470, after about 7km a turn-off left leads to the tiny village of **LINARES DE LA SIERRA**, a fairly simple and impoverished place huddled around its eighteenth-century Baroque church, a typical example of the Sierra style, and curious unpaved bullring plaza. The sandy surface and *barreras* of the latter, behind which the *toreros* dodge the fearsome fighting bulls, seem somewhat eccentric considering that the ring is put to use only a couple of times a year in the village's fiestas. There's no accommodation in the village, but the bar on the square in the bullring/plaza serves tapas and sometimes meals when they're in the mood, and there's also an excellent **restaurant**, *Mesón*

Walking and visitor information in the Sierra

A good **hiking guide** *Sierra de Aracena* by David & Ros Brawn (see "Books", p.696) details twenty-seven clearly described walks in the Sierra ranging between four and fourteen kilometres. An accompanying map for the book is sold separately and all walks also have GPS waypoints identifying key locations en route. *Walking in Andalucía* by Guy Hunter-Watts (see "Books", p.697) has half a dozen clearly described walks in the Sierra de Aracena and, if your Spanish is up to it, it's worth getting hold of *Andar por la Sierra de Aracena* (Penthalon), a walking guide that has seventeen itineraries. Alternatively, the Aracena and Huelva Turismos give out the free *Senderos de la Sierra de Aracena y Picos de Aroche* map listing twenty-three waymarked routes or there is a more detailed *Mapa Guía de la Sierra de Aracena y Picos de Aroche* on sale at the Aracena Turismo. It's also worth enquiring at all the Ayuntamientos along your route, as many of them are now producing their own walking guides, literature and lots of useful local information.

Arrieros, c/Arrieros 2, below the church and off a street to the right, which has a *menú de degustación* for €28 and also does tapas.

A further 4km along the A470, lined with chestnut orchards and great clumps of oregano, a turning on the left descends to **ALÁJAR**, a delightful, cobble-streeted hamlet at the foot of the Peña de Arias Montano. There's another eighteenth-century Baroque church – dedicated to San Marcos – here with the typical spire, besides plenty of places to eat or have a beer, all clustered around the main square. Each September 7 and 8, the village holds a pilgrimage to the hermitage of the **Virgen de los Ángeles** on the Peña de Arias Montano hill, 1km above the village. This involves the young men of the village in the *polleo*, a rite of passage in which they race horses along the narrow streets and then up the steep slope to the shrine. The horses are mercilessly spurred and arrive foaming and bleeding at the top of the climb.

For overnight **accommodation** there's the pleasant *Hotel La Posada*, c/ Emilio González 2, off the west side of Plaza Constitución (☎959 12 57 12, ⓦwww.laposadadealajar.com; ➍ inc. breakfast), which has rooms with bath and heating and also serves food. The proprietors can provide information and maps for walking and mountain biking, and horse trekking is also on offer. One kilometre out of the village in the direction of Santa Ana La Real, *Molino Río Alájar* comprises five superbly equipped cottages available for long and short-tem lets (☎959 59 12 82; ⓦwww.molinorioalajar.com; ➐, price drops for longer stays). For **places to eat**, on the Plaza itself *Bar-Restaurante El Corcho* has, beyond a shop and cobbled floor, a dining room where all the fittings (and even the "glasses") are made from cork. An excellent place for more elaborate but equally inexpensive meals is the *Mesón El Molino*, in a converted old mill with all its original features just up from the main square at c/Alta 9. Follow the street uphill from the main square for 50m, turning left into a narrow alley; the restaurant lies at the end of here.

Peña de Arias Montano

On quieter days the **Peña De Arias Montano**, the rock cliff which towers above the village, is a beautiful leafy spot set among woods of cork oaks, with cold springs surrounding its **shrine**. The Sierra Morena is liberally dotted with these buildings, almost always in isolated spots and dedicated to the Virgin. The site has been hallowed since prehistoric times, and Iberian shamans or priests are reputed to have gained their "second sight" from the

A walk from Alájar to Linares de la Sierra

A fine **walk** (6km) from Alájar to Linares de la Sierra takes in the delightful isolated hamlet of **Los Madroñeros**, whose grassy streets can only otherwise be reached by tractors and off-road vehicles. To find the start of the walk take the street left along the north side of Alájar's church to a *plazuela* (small square) and follow the street downhill to an open area. The path follows the old road, climbing beyond an indicator board (detailing the walk) on the far side. Should you lose the way ask for the *camino antiguo a Los Madroñeros*. Once on the track it soon leads away from the village running between dry-stone walls behind which are cork oaks sheltering *pata negra* black pigs, soon to be turned into the region's prized *jamón*. The settlement of Los Madroñeros is a tranquil haven: a huddle of traditional white-walled dwellings topped by distinctive chimneypots with green grass all around. You'll be lucky to see any inhabitants as they seem to keep a low profile, unlike their numerous cats who will eye you curiously as they sun themselves on rooftops or any convenient flat stone.

The *camino* leads on eastwards away from the village, gently climbing and falling with only one place which may confuse. Just after crossing a stream, about halfway between Los Madroñeros and Linares, you'll come to a deserted semi-ruined farmhouse; the path here isn't immediately clear but you need to go through the gateway of this place to pick up the track on the other side. Soon after this, you reach **Linares**. To return to Alájar you can retrace your route or follow the quiet, scenic road back (the A470). Alternatively you could time your arrival to meet up with Alájar-bound buses (see p.401) passing through about 1.30pm or 6pm. Going in the other direction the Aracena bus currently passes through at 4.15pm.

hallucinogenic *amanita muscaria* mushroom which grows in the woods here – don't experiment yourself though as some species found in these hills can kill in thirty minutes. The sixteenth-century hermitage of the **Virgen de los Ángeles**, filled with ex-votos from pilgrims and distinguished more by the beauty of its setting than for any architectural qualities, is the former retreat of the humanist Benito Arias Montano, confessor and librarian to Philip II, who was born nearby in 1527 and gave his name to the site. The belfry to the side of the church dates from the same period and offers glorious views over Alájar beneath, and the Sierra beyond. A **cavern** below the car park is said to be where magical and religious ceremonies were carried out in ancient times and where Philip II is supposed to have meditated during a visit here – giving it the name Sillita del Rey (The King's Chair), a reference to the huge boulder at the cave's mouth.

The true peace of the place is best appreciated by leaving the visitors' area and heading along the track into the woods of cork oaks where there are plenty of likely picnic spots, and more fine views over the Sierra.

Santa Ana La Real and Almonaster La Real

Six kilometres west of Alájar the modest but pretty white-walled village of **SANTA ANA LA REAL** – with another crumbling eighteenth-century church at its heart – is worth a detour. *Bar Garrafa* is a handy place for refreshment, and a couple of kilometres beyond the village is a convenient **place to stay**, at the junction of the A470 and the N435 – the modern and flower-bedecked *Hostal El Cruce* (☎959 12 23 33; ②), set in fine scenery with a lively tapas bar and popular restaurant. A couple of kilometres north of here, along the N435 to the right, there's a charming and atmospheric Sierra restaurant, *La Abuela* (☎959 50 31 84), near the village of Aguafría. Specialities here include the great *jamones* of the region as well as tasty oven-baked (*al horno*) and barbecued-pork dishes. It's a very popular place, particularly at weekends and other times over the summer, so it may be worth ringing ahead.

Continuing west for another 6km brings you to the main village of this corner of the Sierra, the picturesque **ALMONASTER LA REAL** huddled in a river valley below the peak of the same name, which at 912m is the Sierra's highest summit. A solid and picturesque agricultural centre today, Almonaster has an impressive Moorish past and an important tenth-century **mosque** (daily 9am–7pm; free) on a hill to the south of the town. The mosque may have Roman and Visigothic antecedents, and after it became Christianized in the thirteenth century was little altered, thus preserving its square minaret, the *mihrab* (said to be the oldest in Spain) and beautiful interior of five naves with brick horseshoe arches supported by what are probably recycled Roman columns. It should be open, but if not, ask at the Ayuntamiento, Plaza de la Constitución, for the key. Tacked on to the mosque/church is the village **bullring** where each August a *corrida* is staged during Almonaster's annual fiesta (see box). The mosque's tower is a favourite with the kids of the village at this time, as it provides a free view of the ring.

The village's other main sight is the fourteenth-century Mudéjar-style church of **San Martín** (open service times 7–9pm), whose most notable feature is a superb sixteenth-century Manueline portal, probably Portuguese in inspiration. Also worth a look is the **hermitage of Santa Eulalia**, built over a Roman funerary monument and boasting late-Gothic frescoes depicting the exploits of Santiago the Matamoros (Moorslayer).

Country corridas

Like many other country rings, the **bullring** at Almonaster does not see much action. In fact, the prohibitive cost of mounting a **corrida** with six bulls, three matadores and their retinues often restricts a small village to one *corrida* each year, usually in the middle of its annual fiesta. To see a bullfight at places like Almonaster, however, is to get a fascinating insight into many of the secrets of the *corrida* as, with the ring barely big enough to contain the crowd, bulls and matadores, many of the preparations have to take place outside.

First of all, while the arena is doused from a water tanker, the picadores select their eight-foot-long lances from a couple of dozen leaning against the wall of the ring. When they've chosen, a blacksmith attaches one of three lethal-looking steel points, again selected by the picador. Meanwhile, below the walls of the mosque, the grooms prepare the horses – whose vocal chords are severed so as not to alarm the crowd with their terrified shrieks – by fastening on the *peto* or heavy padding, protection against the bull's ferocious horns. Next the horses' ears are stuffed with oil-soaked rags and securely tied to block out the sound of the crowd and the bull. Finally, they are blindfolded over the right eye, the side from which the bull will attack.

Fifteen minutes before the *corrida* is due to start the village band marches up the hill playing a lively tune before disappearing into the arena. Once inside, they strike up a *paso doble* for the pre-fight parade before the grotesque figure of the helmeted and armoured picador is pushed through the small doorway into the ring and a great cheer goes up from the crowd inside. They are soon yelling "*fuera!*" (away), however, because they don't want the bull too weakened by the lance to be able to put up a decent fight. A few minutes later the trumpets sound and the door opens to allow the picador to exit from the arena. With fresh blood dripping from his lance, the image of this warrior is almost medieval. Big-name *toreros* appear in these village *corridas* because the pay is good, but equally the risks are high. The primitive nature of rings such as the one at Almonaster means a long journey to reach a hospital with adequate facilities should the matador be seriously gored, a factor that has, in the past, proved fatal.

A popular event here in early summer is the **Cruz de Mayo** – a flamenco festival held over the first weekend in May – at which the celebrated *fandangos* of Almonaster are sung and the local women parade in the magnificent costume of the *Serrana* (highlands): colourful flounced dresses and tasselled shoes and shawls, complemented by bouquets of wild flowers. The whole affair provides the participants with an excuse to soak up prodigious quantities of the local *aguardiente* firewater, which is misleadingly described as brandy. If you can't make this one, similar festivals take place in the surrounding villages all through May. In October the village puts on a series of **Jornadas Islamicas** when a *Zoco* (Arab-style market) is set up around the main square and there are lots of cultural activities with an Islamic theme.

Almonaster's **train** station – with infrequent services to Huelva – lies 3km north of the village and is, in fact, nearer to Cortegana. Outside the festival period, finding a **place to stay** is usually no problem. At the entrance to the village *Hotel Casa García* (℡959 14 31 09, ✉hrcasagarcia@aolavant.com; ❹) is comfortable, and the rooms on the front have great views; it also has an excellent restaurant downstairs – try their *tortilla de jamón y espárragos* or *ensalada de pimientos*. Further in, the village's other possibility for en-suite rooms, *Hostal La Cruz*, Plaza El Llano 8 (℡959 14 31 35; ❷), is less expensive, nicely located on a tranquil square, and also has its own restaurant and tapas bar. Perhaps the most entertaining place of all for **food** is the plant-bedecked ⚘ *Las Palmeras* on the road into the village before *Casa García*. Voluble proprietor Alejandro produces everything on the economical *menú* himself, from the tasty *caña de lomo* (cured ham from his own pigs) to the salads from his *huerta*. Nearby, *El Rincón de Curro*, on the Cortegana road a short distance beyond *Casa García*, is a small family restaurant serving up *platos de la sierra: solomillo de cerdo ibérico*

Walks around Almonaster

There are some superb **walks around Almonaster**, following the old cobbled mule paths and village tracks (*senderos*). The paths are well preserved, on the whole – though at times you are forced on to the tarmac road – and are waymarked with paint splashes on trees and rocks. You need sharp eyes to spot the beginning of the paths, below the road, and if you can, you should try to get hold of the *Senderos de la Sierra de Aracena y Picos de Aroche* walks pamphlet which the Ayuntamientos in Almonaster, Cortegana or Jabugo should stock. This is easy to follow with minimal Spanish and has route descriptions and an excellent fold-out survey map. Cortegana also produces its own leaflet, *Senderos de Pequeño Recorrido en el Entorno de Cortegana*, with a good map and covering much the same ground, which is available from the Ayuntamiento. You'd be advised to take along as well a decent 1:100,000 or 1:50,000 map (CNIG sheets 895 & 916 for the latter), just in case you lose the way.

One of the most enjoyable walks, starting from Almonaster, is the **PRA-5** which leads off to the left of the Cortegana road, around 1km out of Almonaster. This takes you through woodland peppered with streams to the hamlets of **Arroyo** and **Veredas** (2hr), where there are bars with food, and on to Cortegana (3hr). Alternatively, if it's just a brief country ramble you're after, follow the sign to Acebuches along the **PRA-5-2** path, under an hour from Almonaster, and again endowed with a small bar.

Another fine walk from Almonaster is to head straight up the hillside northeast of the village along the **PRA-5-1**. This is actually a paved Roman track, presumably built for some kind of quarrying. It takes a couple of hours' strenuous walking to get up to the summit, and, if you're making a day of it, you could continue on to Cortegana or Jabugo.

is a house special. There's not much to do after you've eaten but a *copas* bar, *El Oso Pub*, c/Llana 9 (off the Plaza de la Constitución), is one place to try for a nightcap.

Cortegana

Roughly 2km out of Almonaster the road forks left to **CORTEGANA**, a pleasant and populous *pueblo* spreading along the valley of the Río Carabaña below a heavily restored castle. Built in the thirteenth century during the frontier disputes with the Portuguese, the heavily restored **Castillo** (officially Tues–Sun 11am–2pm & 5–7pm; otherwise enquire at the Ayuntamiento, c/Maura 1, just off the Plaza de la Constitución; €1.50) provided a necessary observation post and today gives fine **views** from its battlements. It is flanked by the fourteenth to fifteenth century **ermita** of Santa María del Castillo whose chapel has been recently refurbished with the addition of some rather tedious modern frescoes. To reach the castle take the Almonaster road – signed from the N433 on the village's eastern edge. After one hundred metres you come to a junction where a driveable road on the left climbs to the castle.

Two churches here are also worth visiting. The **Iglesia del Divino Salvador** (open service times, try 7–9pm) was started in the late sixteenth century but has elements added from much later, such as its bell tower, when the original collapsed in the earthquake of 1755. The interior has a finely worked Baroque pulpit. Built in Gothic Mudéjar style, the church of **San Sebastián** (open service times, try 7–9pm) nearby has interesting Renaissance doors.

Cortegana's big annual knees-up is the Jornadas Medievales **fería** held in the first or second week in August with archery contests, falconry, various tournaments and re-enactments of the storming of the castle walls – accompanied by much music, drinking and dancing. Its other main fería, *Fiestas Patronales,* occurs in early September with *corridas*, processions and concerts.

Practicalities

If you want to **stay** in Cortegana, you could try the excellent *Pensión Cervantes*, c/Cervantes 27, just off the focal Plaza Constitución (☎959 13 15 92; ❶–❷), which has clean and comfortable heated rooms, some en suite; try for a room overlooking a peaceful garden at the rear. Another tempting option for a longer stay is ⚜ *Los Gallos* (☎959 50 11 67, mobile ☎687365754, Ⓦwww .alojamientolosgallos.com; ❹), a leafy and tranquil oasis where you can rent cottages and apartments in and around a restored farmhouse set in spectacular countryside, with gardens and a pool. It lies on the Almonaster road, a couple of kilometres to the southeast, and close to the delightfully rustic (and equally tranquil as there are few trains) Almonaster train station where there's also a great little restaurant (see below). At the start of the road out towards Almonaster and 200m east of the bullring (no. 61 – there's no sign) the friendly *Villa Cinta* (☎959 13 15 22, Ⓦwww.casaruralvillacinta.com; ❹ with breakfast) is another pleasant possibility where rooms are en suite and have stunning views. Another out-of-town possibility is *La Posada de Cortegana* (see the "Walk from Cortegana to La Posada" box overleaf), which can be reached with transport by following a minor road north to La Corte and turning right at a junction just before this village (about 8km).

For **eating and drinking** a number of bars around the centre serve **tapas**: the *casino*, a turn-of-the-twentieth-century institution on the focal Plaza Constitución, is one that also makes a pleasant **breakfast** and morning-coffee stop as it has all the newspapers. The *Café Duende* and neighbouring *El Trueco* on

A scenic **walk** (10km) north from Cortegana follows the valleys of the Arroyo Cara-baña and Río Caliente to *La Posada de Cortegana*, a unique rural hotel and restaurant serving an excellent lunch. The walk leaves Cortegana by c/Sevilla, located behind the church on the southeast side of the village, becoming Callejón Carabaña – a rough track which descends to an *arroyo* or stream. When you meet the main N433 road keep ahead and follow a track to the left heading downhill. Cross a stream (the Arroyo Carabaña) in the valley and follow the path as it heads north along the right bank soon passing a *finca* (house) to the left named Los Molinos. Not far beyond this you'll reach a house at a crossing over the stream run by some friendly New-Agers. Once over the stream continue north for about 3km.

The path zigzags back and forth over the stream always heading north and it isn't immediately obvious where you should and shouldn't cross. However, if you're lucky one of the New-Agers' friendly dogs may accompany you for the exercise and will guide you unerringly along the correct path which they know instinctively. Otherwise it's fairly easy to spot the crossing points as the path soon peters out beyond them and you need only retrace your steps a few metres. Continuing north you will eventually come to *La Posada* (℡959 50 33 01, ⓦwww.posadadecortegana.com; ⑤ with breakfast), a wonderful *hotel rural* comprising log cabins set in woodland with a great terrace **restaurant** making it the high point of the hike. Any of the pork dishes are recommended. Your only problem will be crossing the Arroyo Carabaña to reach it, which, if the water is high, may mean a barefoot wade. Should you decide to stop over they have **rooms** in the cabins, and offer horse riding, mountain biking and a pool. The path, which is signed back to Cortegana, continues behind the restaurant. Follow it for 3km until you reach a road (N433). Turn left along here to return to Cortegana, half a kilometre ahead.

---

the nearby Plaza del Divino Salvador serve tapas and act as hangouts for local youths, which is why they give out information on local events and concerts. The town isn't over-endowed with eating places and for more substantial fare you should head for the reasonably priced *El Aceiton*, Avda. de Portugal 5, where *solomillo de cerdo con castañas* (pork loin with chestnut sauce) is a house special. The nearby *comedor*, *Los Peroles*, at the end of the same street and offering a good variety of *platos combinados*, is another possibility. Both places lie a five-minute walk from the central Plaza Constitución and are reached by following c/Talero (and its continuation) from here to the end and turning right into the Avenida de Portugal. Should you have transport, or just fancy the walk (a couple of kilometres), the delightful *Restaurante El Fogón*, attached to the train station with a tapas bar and *menú* for around €10, is another good place to eat. To save yourself a wasted journey on foot you could ring the nearby *Los Gallos* (see above) to check that it's open.

Aroche

Heading west for 14km along the N433 brings you to **AROCHE**, in sight of the border with Portugal. Perched on a hill dominated by its castle with a fertile plain below, it's a neat little place, with white-walled, cobbled streets, where – because it gets so few visitors – you can be sure of a hearty reception. Aroche was originally the Roman town of Arruci Vetus, but many more ancient vestiges of habitation have been discovered here, including giant prehistoric single standing stones, or **menhirs** (these **Piedras del Diablo** or "Devil's Rocks" are on private land, so if you're interested in seeing them, enquire at the Ayuntamiento, see opposite). Arriving with your own transport take the first

– and fully asphalted – entry on the left into the town coming from Aracena; using the other entry road to the east leads up into a warren of steep cobbled backstreets which are difficult to negotiate.

Once you have made it up the hill to the village, the obvious place to aim for is the Castillo. Constructed by the Almoravids in the twelfth century, the fort was remodelled after the *Reconquista*, but the most bizarre alteration of all was to make the interior into a full-scale **bullring**. A curiosity here are the sallyports – narrow openings in the arena's stone wall – used by the *toreros* to dodge the bull, instead of the normal *barrera* or fence. Note that for **access to all the town's sights**, including the Castillo, you'll need to call at the **Centro de Visitantes** (Fri–Sun 10.30am–2pm & 4–6.30pm; ☏959 14 02 82) up a stepped street to the right of the Ayuntamiento on the main square, Plaza de Juan Carlos I. They also sell copies of *Guía de la Sierra de Aracena y Picos de Aroche*, a useful book with information about all the villages of the sierra. When this is closed the Ayuntamiento can usually help out with information.

In the same building as the Centro de Visitantes, the splendid seventeenth-century former convent of La Cilla incorporating an olive-oil pressing room from the original edifice, is housed the town's **archeological museum** (open same hours as Centro de Visitantes). An interesting collection has numerous finds from the Roman and Moorish periods as well as ceramics and other artefacts from Turóbriga, a first-millenium BC Iberian settlement discovered 3km north of the town (see below).

Just below the castle, the parish church of **Nuestra Señora de la Asunción** was started in 1483 but added a mixture of Mudéjar, Gothic and Renaissance styles before its completion 150 years later. Behind a dour, buttressed exterior, the triple-naved church has a trio of *retablos*: the image of Christ lowered from the cross at the top of the right-hand (or south) nave is by La Roldana; the representation of Christ *nazareno*, bearing his cross, in the *retablo* at the end of the left aisle is a seventeenth-century work by Alonso Cano. Along the north wall nearby, another *retablo* has – below and to the left of Nuestra Señora de Los Remedios, the town's patron – a small and sensitively worked image of the Virgin perched on an inverted half-moon and coiled serpent, another seventeenth-century work by La Roldana. The church's other treasures (only viewable

A walk from Repilado to Los Romeros

Returning to Aracena from Aroche by the N433 takes you through the village of **El Repilado** from where you could make a picturesque five-kilometre **walk** south along the Río Caliente to the charming village of Los Romeros. Leave Repilado by the N433 road towards Cortegana and after crossing the bridge over the river, turn left along the HV-111 going to Los Romeros. Where the road traverses to the east bank of the river, follow the track along the west bank which leads through woods of chestnut and black poplar, and where in spring you'll see a profusion of wild flowers. When the road recrosses the river, use the bridge to gain access to the tiny and picturesque village of **Los Romeros**, a place devoted to *jamón* production (it takes its name from a major ham family). For **accommodation** try *La Silladilla*, a *cortijo* with several refurbished farmhouses and facilities such as a pool (☏959 50 13 50; ⑤). In the village proper the Hermanos Marquéz supermarket (☏959 12 44 50; ⑤) also lets out houses in and around Los Romeros (minimum two nights, sleeping two to four people). *Bodegón Los Romeros* in Plaza del Valle Florido (by the church) does good tapas and *raciones* and has a terrace, while *La Albardería*, a hundred metres up a signed road beyond the church, is a more elaborate but still economical place with a good selection of the sierra's *platos típicos*.

when the *cura* or priest is available due to their value) include the fifteenth-century crucifix of Cardenal Mendoza of Sevilla, the supporter of Isabel, as well as a seventeenth-century Russian icon from St Petersburg.

There are some pretty strange museums in Andalucía, but Aroche's **Museo del Santo Rosario** (Museum of the Holy Rosary), c/Ordoñez Valdes s/n, has to be one of the most eccentric. Located a little downhill to the east of the Ayuntamiento and near the *correo*, the exhibits consist of well over a thousand rosaries donated by such leading religious luminaries as Pope John XXIII and Mother Teresa, in addition to others from *toreros* and soccer players and one each from John F. Kennedy and King Juan Carlos. Those sent in by Richard Nixon and General Franco betray suspiciously little sign of wear.

A pleasant **walk** out of the village starts on the opposite (north) side of the main N433 to the twelfth–fourteenth century Gothic–Mudéjar **Ermita de San Mames**. The track leading to it is signed between the two entry roads to the town. Following this for 2km leads to the *ermita* (Wed–Fri 8am–3pm, Sat–Sun 10am–2pm & 4–7pm; free) a triple-naved church with wall-painting fragments. Next to the church are the extensive and recently revealed remains of the Roman town of **Turóbriga**. Substantial buildings surrounding what appears to be a forum have been unearthed, while further excavations are continuing in the surrounding fields and look set to reveal a substantial ancient conurbation.

Practicalities

For **accommodation**, along the road leading into town there's the small but serviceable *Hostal Picos de Aroche*, Carretera de Aracena 12 (☎959 14 04 75; ➋), where en-suite rooms come with TV.

As regards **eating and drinking** there are a number of good **tapas bars** including the central *Centro Cultural Las Peñas*, c/Real 8, near the church, which has a relaxing bar serving up a great selection – try the *chocos* (cuttlefish). Other possibilities are the popular *Cafetería Las Peñas* – specializing in seafood tapas – on the square near the Ayuntamiento, and the smaller *Cafetería Lalo* above this with its entrance on c/Cilla. More elaborate fare is on offer at *Mesón San Mames*, c/Del Postigo 2, downhill from the main square along c/Dolores Rosada and left after fifty metres. Below the church, along c/Bellido, *Mesón Los Arcos* is another popular tapas haunt. *El Canario*, on the main N433 road at the entrance to the village, is a decent restaurant whose specialities include a wide range of Sierra pork-based dishes.

Jabugo and around

The mere mention of the name of **JABUGO** is enough to make any Spaniard's mouth water, and once you have tasted what all the fuss is about it's easy to understand why. As roadside billboards depicting smiling pigs proclaim, *jamón* is king in Jabugo. To get stuck into ham sampling, when you approach the village from the N433, ignore the sign directing you to the *centro urbano* and continue straight on. You'll pass half a dozen **bars** and **restaurants** all eager to sell you a *bocadillo* stuffed with *jamón de Jabugo* – or even a whole ham should you feel like splashing out. *Bodega Restaurante Jabugo* and *Mesón Cinco Jotas* are probably the best. There are tapas, too, but keep an eye on the prices as the *pata negra* doesn't come cheap.

Ham apart, the village of Jabugo is a sleepy place gathered around a charming square, the Plaza de Jamón, with a central dribbling fountain overlooked by the *casino* – a relaxing place for a beer – and the restored, Baroque **Iglesia de San Miguel**. The nearby Casa Irene is another good source for the pork products of the region.

△ Ham sign in Jabugo

The villages **around Jabugo** – Aguafría, Castaño del Robledo and Fuenteheridos (for the latter two see below and p.411) – all make rewarding destinations for walks amid splendid wooded hills, though all are equally ill-served by public transport and you may well find yourself in for a walk both ways.

Practicalities

Should you want **to stay**, head for the hospitable *Hostal Aurora*, c/Barco 15 (☎959 12 11 46; ❷), running between the *jamón* street and the main square, which has some rooms with bath. For stays of two nights plus, a charming house sleeping two or three people in the heart of the countryside is available; it's located between Jabugo and Castaño del Robledo and to rent it you should ring mobile ☎696 49 61 68 and ask to speak to Carlos or Ana (❹, reductions for longer stays).

For full **meals**, *El Molino de Jabugo*, Plaza de la Constitución 8 (reached by following c/de la Fuente for 200m from Plaza de Jamón), is a charming restaurant housed in an old oil mill; any pork dishes are recommended. *Restaurante Xaúco* (with a *menú*), on the main road at the entrance to Jabugo, is another good bet.

Castaño del Robledo

Four kilometres southeast of Jabugo, but a few kilometres more by road, lies the isolated village of **CASTAÑO DEL ROBLEDO**, which has not one but two outsized churches for its meagre population. Both named Santiago, they attest to a time in the seventeenth and eighteenth centuries when the population here was growing so rapidly that the church of Santiago la Mayor, which was then under construction, had to be enlarged. However, the population declined as quickly as it had grown and the crumbling, cavernous and now little-used church today looks down grimly on the surrounding pantiled roofs. Other remnants from more illustrious days are a number of decaying mansions along the village's narrow, cobbled streets.

The King of Hams

Surrounding Jabugo is a scattering of attractive but economically depressed villages mainly dependent on the **jamón industry** and its curing factory which is the major local employer. Things were little different when Richard Ford passed through here a century and a half ago, describing these mountain villages as "coalitions of pigsties", adding that it was the duty of every good pig to "get fat as soon as he can and then to die for the good of his country".

Sought out by classical writers such as Strabo for its distinctive flavour, and produced since long before by the peoples of the Iberian peninsula, *jamón serrano* (mountain ham from white pigs) is a *bocadillo* standard throughout Spain – the English words "ham" and "gammon" are both derived from the Spanish. Some of the best ham of all, **jamón ibérico** or **pata negra** (both acorn-fed ham), comes from the Sierra Morena, where herds of sleek pigs grazing beneath the trees are a constant feature. In October the acorns drop or are beaten down by their keepers and the pigs, waiting patiently below, gorge themselves, become fat and are promptly whisked off to the factory to be slaughtered and then cured in the dry mountain air. The meat of these black pigs is exceptionally fatty when eaten as pork but the same fat that marbles the meat adds to the tenderness during the curing process. This entails first of all covering the hams in coarse rock or sea salt to "sweat", after which they are removed to cool cellars to mature for up to two years. *Jamón serrano* from mass-produced white pigs is matured for only a few weeks, hence the incomparable difference in taste. At Jabugo the best of the best is then further graded from one to five *jotas* (the letter "J" for Jabugo) depending on its quality – **cinco jotas jamón** comes close to the price of gold.

The king of hams also demands an etiquette all of its own: in bars and restaurants everywhere it has its own apparatus (*la jamonera*) to hold it steady, and carving is performed religiously with a long, thin-bladed knife. The slices must not be wafer-thin nor bacon rashers and once on the plate *jamón ibérico* becomes the classic partner for a glass of *fino*.

On the main square, Plaza del Álamo, just above the smaller church, *Bar La Bodeguita* is a pleasant old place serving decent **tapas**. It has recently been joined on the same square by the mid-priced *El Dornillo*, a surprisingly upmarket restaurant, specializing in *platos típicos* of the region.

Galaroza and Valdelarco

The N433 east from Jabugo rolls along through country filled with dense oak woods surrounded by dry-stone walls, where you may catch a fleeting glimpse of a herd of *cerdos ibéricos*, the celebrated black pigs of the Sierra. **GALAROZA**, encircled by chestnut and fruit orchards, seems awash with water which for much of the year splashes and bubbles in its fountains and along the culverts lining the narrow streets. This may explain its annual Fiesta de los Jarritos during which everyone – including visitors – gets soaked with water when the town goes *agua* mad. September 6 is the date to avoid if you want to stay dry. The village has a striking **Baroque church**, which contains a unique seventeenth-century image of a pregnant Virgin by the sculptress La Roldana.

Good **places to stay** include the excellent *Hostal Toribio*, c/Primo de Rivera 2 (℡959 12 30 73, Ⓦwww.hostaltoribio.com; ❸–❹), with en-suite rooms overlooking the main square, and the more basic *Hostal Venecia* (℡959 12 30 98; ❶), on the main road which has some rooms with bath. More opulent lodgings are to be had at the *Hotel Galaroza Sierra* (℡959 12 32 37, Ⓦwww.hotelgalaroza.com; ❹), an attractive hotel with pool in its own grounds just outside the village on the Jabugo road. They also rent out fully equipped bungalows sleeping up to four (⑤). For **eating and drinking** the decent restaurant *El Encinar*, at the *Hotel Galaroza Sierra* (which also does breakfasts) is worth a try, and on the central Plaza Ayuntamiento, near *Hostal Toribio*, *Casa Castulo* is a recently arrived restaurant serving relatively pricey dishes from the Sierra. *Bar-Restaurante Las Salinas*, Tío Máximo 3, further into the village is another option situated above a disco with the same name. For bars with **tapas** *Bar La Fuente*, Plaza Alcalde Luis Navarro, opposite *Hostal Venecia*, is a humble place with an eccentric proprietor and good economical tapas – try the *jamón con tomate*. *Bar Alonso* on the right as you come in from Aracena also has a decent tapas selection.

A long and winding but very pretty 6km road leads north from just beyond Galaroza to the village of **VALDELARCO**. Set amongst cork oaks, chestnut and almond trees it's an attractive place with a charming main square, Plaza Domínguez. You can also **walk** here from Galaroza along the GR42.1 footpath.

Fuenteheridos

About 5km further east from Galaroza, a right turn brings you almost immediately to **FUENTEHERIDOS**, one of the most picturesque of the Sierra *pueblos* – a huddle of whitewashed dwellings with contrasting red pantiled roofs. The typical tiled Sierra spire of its fine eighteenth-century Neoclassical **Iglesia del Espíritu Santo** hovers above the rooftops.

Accommodation is on offer at *Hostal Carballo*, c/La Fuente 16 (☏ 959 12 51 08, ⓦ www.hostalcarballo.com; ❶–❹), with low-priced singles and a variety of rooms with and without bath. About 100m up from the main square *El Barrio*, c/Esperanza Bermúdez s/n (☏959 12 50 33; ❸), is another place offering en-suite rooms above a decent restaurant. There's also a *Villa Turística* here (☏959 12 52 02; ❺), comprising a somewhat soulless artificial village with one- and two-bedroom chalets, plus restaurant and pool; it's reached by taking the N433 for 1km northwest. The *Bar-Restaurante Biarritz* (see below; ☏959 12 50 88, ⓦ www.biarritzrural.com; ❸–❹) also lets a number of well-equipped cottages and apartments close to the village. A good **campsite**, *El Madroñal* (☏959 50 12 01), lies half a kilometre out of the village towards Castaño Robledo and has plenty of shade.

Fuenteheridos also has good possibilities for **food**. On the main road at the edge of the village, the pleasant *Restaurante La Capellanía* serves up a succulent *solomillo de cerdo ibérico* (pork loin) and has a *menú*. Nearer the centre ⚑ *Bar-Restaurante Biarritz*, c/Virgen de Fuente s/n, just off the main square, where there are plenty of other bars, is a very good restaurant with a weekday *menú* for €5.50 and tasty tapas.

Los Marines, Cortelazor and Cumbres Mayores

Beyond the turn-off for Fuenteheridos and 8km east of Galaroza, **LOS MARINES** is the last village before Aracena, and its prosperity depends on the dense chestnut orchards which encircle it. Some 4km to the north – should your feet be up to it – **CORTELAZOR** is a charming hamlet with a fifteenth-century church, that also registers the province's highest rainfall. Specializing in honey production, it was settled with emigrants from Galicia in the fourteenth century, after the expulsion of the Moors from the Sierra. With transport, you could do a 29km detour for a superb drive north to **CUMBRES MAYORES**, another fine Sierra village with a couple of ancient churches and a magnificent crenellated thirteenth-century **castillo** which dominates the skyline as you approach. Upon closer investigation you'll discover that inside the castle walls there's the ground of the local football team – on match days spectators get a great view of the action from the fort's battlements. Cumbres is another place to sample the region's pork – this time in the *salchichas* (sausages) for which it is renowned. Good-value **rooms** with bath are available at *Pensión Togahilo*, c/ Antonio Machado 47 (☏959 71 00 06; ❷), which also has a **restaurant**.

Zufre and east towards Cazalla

East of Aracena there's more good hiking country – if slightly less wooded – along the northern frontier of Sevilla Province, which traverses the **Parque Natural de Sierra Norte**, a wildlife and nature zone stretching across the north of Sevilla province to the border with Córdoba. The park's comprehensive **website** (Ⓦwww.sierranortesevilla.com) has information on most of the towns and villages in the Sierra, including accommodation, in addition to flora and fauna and lots of useful links.

From Aracena one bus a day (Mon–Sat; 5.30pm), connecting with the bus from Sevilla, covers the 25km southeast to Zufre. If you miss it, you'll have to walk, which takes the best part of a day but can be good in itself. From Aracena you need to pick up the waymarked PRA-44 *sendero* which heads roughly north for 8km to meet the waymarked GR-41. Turn east along this and you'll soon come upon the **Embalse de Aracena**, one of the huge reservoirs that supply Sevilla, dammed by a massive construction across the southern end of the valley. From here a lovely but circuitous seventeen-kilometre route (still following the GR-41) will take you down towards Zufre along the **Rivera de Huelva**. The free **map** (available from the Turismo in Aracena), *Senderos de la Sierra de Aracena y Picos de Aroche*, details the above routes plus others should you want to work out a shorter alternative.

Zufre

ZUFRE, about 25km southeast of Aracena, must be one of the most spectacular villages in Spain, hanging like a miniature Ronda on a high palisade at the edge of a ridge. Below the crumbling Moorish walls, the cliff falls away hundreds of feet, terraced into deep green gardens of orange trees and vegetables. In town, and sharing a charming and leafy *plazuela*, the arcaded **Ayuntamiento** and parish **church** – built of brick and pink stone – are both interesting sixteenth-century examples of the Mudéjar style, the latter built on the foundations of a mosque. In the basement of the Ayuntamiento, too, is a gloomy line of stone seats, said to have been used by the Inquisition. A friendly priest at the house on the other side of the square from the church will usually open it to let you see inside. Zufre's centre, however, is the **Paseo**, a little park with rose gardens, balcony and a bar at one end and a *casino* at the other. The villagers gather round here for much of the day – there's little work either in Zufre or the surrounding countryside, and even the local **bullring**, cleverly squeezed on to a rock ledge above the Paseo, only sees use twice a year: at the beginning of the season in March, and at the town's September *feria*.

Practicalities

The Ayuntamiento, c/Peña 1 in the heart of the village (Mon–Fri 8am–3pm, ☏959 19 80 09, Ⓦwww.zufre.com), can provide **information**. There is also a **hostal**, *La Posá*, c/Cibarranco 5 (☏959 19 81 10; ❷), with decent en-suite rooms. Below the village a road heading south from the A461 signed "La Presa" (reservoir) leads – after a couple of kilometres – to the idyllic 🏕 *La Vicaria* (mobile ☏689 81 84 86, Ⓦwww.lavicaria.net; ❺), an inviting hamlet of fully equipped rural cottages set in rolling woodland. Facilities include a bar-restaurant and free activities such as canoeing on the lake.

Finding **food and drink** in Zufre shouldn't be a problem, as plenty of bars in the warren of Moorish streets above the park serve tapas – seek out *Aleman* and *Benito* on the main Plaza La Quebrada. Just off this square, *Casa Pepa* is a pleasant little country restaurant run by the family who own *Bar Benito*.

Santa Olalla del Cala and El Real de la Jara

There's no bus link between Zufre and **SANTA OLALLA DEL CALA**, 16km to the northeast, but it's not hard to arrange a lift with one of the many locals (try asking in the local bars) who drive the route daily on the way to school and work. If you do choose **to walk**, there's the road or the slightly longer, but infinitely preferable, country route via the waymarked *senderos* PRA-42 and GR-48; pick up the PRA-42 at Calleja del Cementerio, on the edge of Zufre. The latter hike is a memorable experience: a mostly flat route through open country, with pigs and fields of wheat and barley and then a sudden view of the impressive **castillo** – a thirteenth-century Christian construction but incorporating Moorish features – above the town. Below the walls, the fifteenth-century parish **church** has a fine Baroque interior and an image of the *Virgen de los Dolores* by Juan de Mesa.

It's a surprise to find several *hostales* in Santa Olalla, but the town is actually on the main Sevilla–Badajoz road and sees a fair amount of traffic (which somewhat dents its charm), including regular buses between both cities. Now its lifeline, the town is ribboned along the N630 with the castle at the northern end. At the south end **buses** to and from Sevilla stop outside the basic *Bar Primitivo*, at c/Marina 3, as this stretch of the main thoroughfare is named. Nearby there's the friendly *Casa Carmelo*, c/Marina 23 (☎959 19 01 69; ❷), which has en-suite **rooms** with TV. Both places serve **food** and offer economical *menús del día*, with the latter specializing in the region's excellent *jamones* and *salchichas* from the numerous pig farms hereabouts.

Still heading east you enter the **Parque Natural de la Sierra Norte**, a wildlife and nature zone extending across the north of Sevilla province to the border with Córdoba. **EL REAL DE LA JARA**, the next village you reach, has two ruined but impressive Moorish **castillos**. A friendly guesthouse, *Casa Molina* at c/Real 70 (☎954 73 30 53; ❶) has **rooms**, plus there are **places to eat** and a welcome public swimming pool in summer, but no buses. Beyond El Real, the route traverses more hill country for 25km, where it crosses the scenic Embalse del Pintado reservoir. On the banks of the reservoir the remote hamlet of **El Pintado** is a curious settlement with a modern church, a couple of swanky houses surrounded by woodland and a **bar** that sees few customers.

Cazalla and the Central Sierra

The next place of any size, **CAZALLA DE LA SIERRA**, is some 20km further east along a mountainous and lonely route, stunning to look at if you're driving, but a real test on foot. When you finally reach it, Cazalla de la Sierra feels like a veritable metropolis and makes an ideal base for exploring the surrounding Sierra Norte natural park. A charming country town with a number of sights, it's also one of the few places on the Sierra with regular **buses** (daily between here and Sevilla). The town is also served by **trains** (on the Sevilla–Mérida line) but as the station lies 7km east and buses are infrequent, it's best reached by taxi.

An ancient Iberian settlement, Cazalla became the Roman Callentum and later the Moorish Kazalla ("fortified city") from which the modern name

There are some fine spots within easy wandering distance of Cazalla and some of these are listed in a useful booklet (in Spanish) available from the tourist office titled *La Sierra Morena de Sevilla*. A walk of just 5km, for example, will take you southeast to the **Ermita del Monte**, a little eighteenth-century church on a wooded hill above the Ribera del Huéznar.

If you're making southwards for **El Pedroso**, however, you might as well walk from the Cazalla train station, a lovely five-hour route along the banks of the Huéznar, flowing through woods of alder, elm and ash with the occasional weeping willow and a fabulous variety of valley flora and fauna. It's an excellent trout river and a wonderful place to swim, and it can get very crowded with locals during holidays and summer weekends. **To start the trail** from Cazalla station take the road heading east towards Constantina, crossing the rail line. Just after this you'll come to a forest track on the right signed for the "Molino de Corcho", an old water mill. A short way downstream, cross the first bridge, and carry on along the prettier east bank of the river. Cross back at the third bridge and continue past the *Molino del Corcho* itself and on to the Fábrica de Pedroso (an old factory which also has a train station). From here you can follow the road to El Pedroso, or continuing along the river, at a bridge 4km on you should climb up to the road, and follow the A432 from where the village lies 3km east. With planning you could take a northbound train back to Cazalla from El Pedroso (currently running at 4.43pm & 9.09pm).

derives. Its importance in post-*Reconquista* days was as a staging post along the route to Extremadura and the north. The place was noted in Roman times for its vines and wines, a tradition which survives today in the production of *aguardiente* and *anis* (aniseed liqueur), sold in *bodegas* around the town. The Turismo can advise on where to find them if you are interested.

Cazalla's main attraction is the huge fortress-like church of **Nuestra Señora de la Consolación** (open service times, try 7–8pm) at the southern end of town, an outstanding example of *andaluz* mix-and-match architecture begun in the fourteenth century in Gothic-Mudéjar style, with some later Renaissance touches, and finally completed in the eighteenth century. The interior has a fine sixteenth-century retablo and an image of San Bruno by Juan Hernández. Fronting the church's northern door, c/Virgen del Monte – lined with some elegant **casas señoriales** – leads to the market area, a colourful and bustling place on weekdays.

A little out of town, Cazalla's fifteenth-century **Cartuja**, or Carthusian monastery (daily 10am–2pm & 4–9pm; €3), was until recently a near ruin; it's now being gradually and privately restored as an upmarket hotel and arts centre. What remains, particularly a beautiful portal and a cupola of the church with Mudéjar frescoes, is set in picturesque surroundings. To reach it, take the C342 for 3km towards Constantina, turning off along a signposted side road.

Practicalities

You'll find the town's **Turismo** in the Plaza Mayor, next to the church of Nuestra Señora de la Consolación (Tues–Fri 10am–2pm, plus Thurs & Fri 6–8pm; Sat 10am–2pm & 6–9pm, Sun 11am–3pm; ☎95 488 35 62), which can provide information on the area and a useful **map** of the town.

For **accommodation** there is a wide range of options. The best budget choice is *Hostal Castro Martínez*, c/Virgen Monte 36 (☎95 488 40 39; ●), near the main street where some a/c en-suite rooms come with terraces and views. The other economy choice is *La Milagrosa*, c/Llana 29 (☎95 488 42 60; ●), also bang in the centre for rooms with bath. On the same main street there's *Casa Palacio*, c/Llana 2 (T 95 560 02 07, E casapala@terra.es; ④), a slightly upmarket place with three good-value and fully equipped apartments in an elegant mansion (minimum two-night stay). For hotels, head for the *Posada del Moro*, c/Paseo del Moro s/n, a five-minute walk southeast from the Turismo (T 95 488 43 26; ④) where stylish tiled rooms overlook a patio garden and pool. In the same street, a luxurious new arrival is *El Palacio San Benito* (T 954 88 33 36, W www.palaciodesanbenito.com; ⑦–⑨), housed in a magnificent fifteenth-century former hospice of the knights of the Order of Calatrava which gave shelter to pilgrims travelling the Via de la Plata to Santiago de Compostela. All rooms are sumptuously decorated with period furniture and artworks and there's a glittering Mudéjar chapel as well as a bar, library and pool. Out of town and surrounded by rolling hill country, the La Cartuja monastery (see above for directions) has its own atmospheric *Hospedería* (T 95 488 45 16, W www.skill.es/cartuja; ⑥, reductions for stays of two nights plus), an inn with pool and eight elegantly refurbished rooms in what was formerly the monastery's gatehouse. Perhaps the most attractive of Cazalla's accommodations is *Las Navezuelas* (T & F 95 488 47 64, W www .lasnavezuelas.com; ④ with breakfast), offering delightful rooms in a white-walled sixteenth-century *cortijo* and olive mill set among woods and olive groves; it also has a pool and its own reasonably priced restaurant and the owners can arrange horse-riding excursions and advise on trekking routes. The farm is signed on the left, 3km out of town along the road to El Pedroso.

For **eating and drinking** there are numerous bars dotted around the town where tapas are on offer. The central *Bar Torero*, c/Virgen del Monte, near the former Convento de San Francisco, serves up substantial *raciones* and the friendly *Bar Gonzalo*, c/Virgen del Monte 3, in the centre, is an atmospheric place serving *raciones* and a good *menú*. Nearby, *Los Mellis* and the town *casino* next door to each other on the pedestrianized c/Plazuela are more good places for a drink and a tapa. More formal dining takes place at the *Restaurante del Moro*, the excellent mid-priced restaurant of the hotel of the same name (see above) which has a *menú* for around €15. The nearby *Mesón del Moro* in the same street offers a cheaper selection of game and meat dishes of the region. For a late-night drink *Bolera* is a cocktail bar with a pleasant terrace in c/Cervantes, a couple of blocks west of the Turismo.

El Pedroso

EL PEDROSO, 15km south of Cazalla and linked by train with Sevilla, is a pleasant enough little place with a notable Mudéjar church, **Nuestra Señora de la Consolación** (open service times, try 7–8pm) on the central Plaza de España. Inside there are a couple of artistic gems worth seeking out: a seventeenth-century image of the **Inmaculada**, or Virgin, by the great *andaluz* wood sculptor Martinez Montañés and another sculpture of the **crucified Christ** – created around 1500 – by Pedro Millán, the leading early influence on the Sevilla school of sculpture. Pedroso has a small **tourist information office** (daily 9am–3pm, plus Tues & Thurs 5.30–8pm; T 954 88 93 01 weekdays, T 954 88 96 85 weekends) on the same square which can provide a town map, information on a number of pretty walks in the nearby Sierra, and a leaflet in Spanish on the Baroque "treasures" dotted around the other churches here. Another leaflet describes a **tapas tour** of the town's bars, all of which may induce you to extend your visit. Should you wish to **stay the night**, 50m from the train station is the rather swish, friendly and good-value *Casa Montehuéznar*, Avda. de la Estación 15 (T 95 488 90 00, W www.montehueznar.com; ④ with breakfast) and where *Rough Guide* readers can claim a ten percent discount with this guide. The hotel also has a very good restaurant serving up regional dishes including *solomillo* (pork loin) and wild boar and there's an inexpensive *menú*, too. Nearby, and almost facing the train station, an excellent **tapas bar**, the *Serranía*, offers more local specialities such as venison, hare, pheasant and partridge and also has its own *menú*. On the same square as the Nuestra Señora de la Consolación church there's also the town *casino,* a welcoming place serving tapas and *raciones* with a pleasant terrace on the square.

Constantina

Eighteen kilometres southeast of Cazalla – and roughly equidistant from El Pedroso and Cazalla – lies **CONSTANTINA**, an important and beautiful mountain town and the main administrative centre for Sevilla's section of the Sierra Morena. For hikers this is as good a place as any to cut back to Sevilla if you're not counting on continuing across the provincial border into Córdoba. Founded in the fourth century by the Romans during the reign of the emperor Constantine, and named after his son, this was an important wine-producing centre along with nearby Cazalla and sent a wine named *cocolubis* to the imperial capital. The town is a delightful place to wander around, particularly the old quarter, which is dotted with a number of notable eighteenth-century mansions. Topping the hill flanking the western edge of town and high above the streets below, the **Castillo de la Armada** is an impressive medieval fortress surrounded by shady gardens descending in terraces to the old quarter. At the base you'll find the sixteenth-century parish church of **La Encarnación**, once again with a Mudéjar tower – Moorish influence having died hard in these parts – and a splendid, if crumbling, Plateresque portal by Hernán Ruíz, the architect of the cathedral inside the Mezquita at Córdoba and the belfry added to the Giralda in Sevilla. The church's *altar mayor*, a magnificent gilded work by Juan de Oviedo, is also worth a look. Constantina has a public **pool** sited below the castle, very welcome to beat the intense summer heat. With transport you can make a trip to **La Pantalla** – a lake for swimming and fishing – east along the road to El Pedroso. Constantina's **feria**, a rumbustious Sierra affair with horse-riding contests plus drinking, dancing and singing galore, takes place during the last week in August.

Practicalities

There's a **Turismo** cabin (Tues–Thurs 9–2pm, plus Fri 5–9pm; Sat–Sun 9am–2pm; ☎95 588 12 97, ⓦwww.constantina.org) on Avenida Andalucía, near the entry to the town from El Pedroso, who can provide a useful town **map**. When closed this is also to be had from the Ayuntamiento, c/Eduardo Dato 7, near the Encarnación church. Two kilometres out of the town on the El Pedroso road, the El Robledo Centro de Visitantes (Tues–Thurs 10am–2pm, Fri–Sun 10am–2pm & 6–8pm; ☎95 558 15 97) is an **information centre** for the Sierra Norte natural park and has lots of maps, guidebooks and information on walking in the park. There's also a **botanical garden** (same hours) displaying a wide variety of the park's flora.

The cheapest of the **places to stay** is the modern *Albergue Juvenil*, c/Cuesta Blanca s/n, which lies slightly out of the centre, uphill behind a petrol station at the southern end of the town (☎95 588 15 89; under 26 €14, over 26 €18.50) with double rooms and shared showers. Otherwise, the only *hostal* is the central *La Casa Mari Pepa* at c/José de la Bastida 25 (☎95 588 01 58; ❹), where a *casa señorial* has been lovingly transformed into a delightful series of distinctively decorated en-suite rooms. There's also a three-star hotel, *San Blas*, c/Miraflores 4 (☎95 588 00 77, ⓔsanblas.reservas@fp-hoteles.com; ❹), with an elevated location at the northern end of town and a pool.

As regards **eating and drinking**, there are numerous good **tapas bars** along and around c/Mesones, the pedestrianized main street, including *Casino Labradores* at no. 36 and *Bar Bullhy* nearby at no. 30. Others worth seeking out are *La Bodeguita*, Alférez Cabrera 1, and the nearby *Bar Gregorio*, at no.11 on the same street, which lies behind the Encarnación church. Two of Constantina's best places to eat lie near to the Plaza de Toros, at the town's northern end. The first, *El Mesón de la Abuela*, Paseo de la Alameda 39, is good for *carnes a la brasa* (charcoal grilled meats). Slightly further north and arguably the town's best eatery is ⚒ *Cambio de Tercio*, c/Virgen del Robledo 53 (☏95 588 10 80). Taking its name from the stages in a *corrida* and continuing the theme with an amusing entrance imitating a *plaza de toros*, this is also where King Juan Carlos gets his victuals during sessions gunning down the local wildlife (in one of his favourite hunting zones) – they deliver elaborate picnics to him in the field as a photo on one wall demonstrates. There's a lively bar – with its own economical *menú* – in the front and a pleasant room at the back for more formal dining. All is reasonably priced and the *solomillo de cerdo* (pork loin) is excellent.

Lora del Río and Villanueva del Río y Minas

South of Constantina the road descends for 28km through the Sierra de La Cruz until, at the rather dull agricultural town of **LORA DEL RÍO**, it joins the fertile valley of the Guadalquivir. The southern banks of the river from Lora are famous for rearing *toros de lidia*, fighting bulls who greedily graze on the rich river pastures; the Miura family, long renowned among aficionados as supplying the biggest, meanest beasts, has its *ganadería*, or ranch, here.

Heading west towards Sevilla along the C431, the flat and monotonous landscape of the river valley is overlooked 10km further on by the Roman ruins of **Arva**; the site lies 300m east of an old factory building with a prominent brick chimney. Not much is visible yet of the first-century town which lies beneath the olive groves, but if you keep your eyes peeled, on the right of the road you'll see the substantial remains of a bathhouse and an impressive restored stone font.

Some 5km beyond Alcolea del Río a road on the right leads – after 3km – to the old coal-mining town of **VILLANUEVA DEL RÍO Y MINAS**, a starting point for a fine **walk** to the remarkable Roman ruins of Mulva, buried deep in verdant countryside. A fairly humdrum place, Villanueva is a casualty of the Europe-wide depression in the mining industry, and its abandoned pit makes a sad sight on the landscape. You can get **rooms** at the pleasant *Bar-Pensión Reche*, Avda. de la Constitución 179 (☏95 474 78 23; ②) – take the balcony room, if it's available. The home-made *churros* here are recommended for breakfast and they can advise on walking to Mulva.

Heading west from Villanueva, the A431 road arcs south along the Guadalquivir, passing after 13km **Cantillana**, a pleasant town with a couple of Baroque churches, followed by the farming settlements of Villaverde del Río and **Alcalá del Río** – the latter's Renaissance church of Santa María has a stunning *retablo* – before entering Sevilla.

Mulva

The Roman ruins of **MULVA** (ancient Munigua) sit in a dramatic position atop a hill, just to one side of which sits the guardian, protecting the site from plunderers all year round; he will give you a ticket (free) and, if you're lucky, some cool water.

A prosperous city founded by the Romans on top of an earlier Iberian settlement, Munigua's wealth came from iron mining, backed, to judge from the

To **start out** on the 7km trek to Mulva (and in summer make sure you carry water), take the road opposite Villanueva's *pensión* and cross the railway line. Then follow a track which twists around the old colliery – with evocative pitwheel, chimneys and a curiously turreted administration building – down to the river. Head north along the river's east bank and then cross at a low footbridge, known locally as the *puente chico*. Now on the west bank, continue north and pass under the large bridge (*puente grande*) ignoring the sign for Munigua (Mulva) pointing left – this is a longer road route (incidentally only possible with a 4x4). Once under the big bridge follow the track into the hills until you come to a farmhouse, La Palmilla, with green gates (the kindly owners are usually happy to allow you to fill up on water here). The next part of the walk is important, for in the woods beyond here you must take the **left fork** when the track divides. This will eventually lead you – 3km on – to another gate, beyond which the ruins of **Mulva** will eventually appear through the woods, dominating the skyline. For an alternative route back to Villanueva you can return along the road route (mentioned above) which will lead you back to the *puente grande*.

numerous stone olive presses found here, by a flourishing oil industry. Recent excavations have uncovered a suite of **baths** together with some fresco fragments. You can climb the hill to the ruins and explore the **sanctuary** with its phenomenal bulwarking – the heart of ancient Munigua and believed to have been a copy of the great temple of Fortuna at Praeneste near Rome – as well as the forum, dwellings, a mausoleum and walls of this impressive "lost" city.

Travel details

Trains

Huelva to: Almonaster La Real (2 daily; 2hr 45min); Jabugo (2 daily; 2hr 30min); Sevilla (3 daily; 1hr 30min); Zafra (1 daily; 4hr 45min).

Sevilla to: Algeciras (2 daily; 4hr 30min); Almería (4 daily; 5hr–5hr 30min); Cádiz (12 daily; 1hr 50min); Córdoba (AVE 20 daily 45min; 5 daily; 1hr 20min); Granada (4 daily; 3hr–3hr 30min); Huelva (3 daily; 1hr 30min); Jaén (1 daily; 3hr); Madrid (AVE 21 daily 2hr 15min; 12 daily 6–9hr); Málaga (6 daily; 2hr 30min); Osuna (9 daily; 1hr).

Buses

Bus times quoted are for the fastest journey times, normally direct. There may be other buses to the same destination which make additional stops at towns and villages en route.

Aracena to: Alájar (2 daily; 30min); Aroche (4 daily; 1hr); Cortegana/Almonaster (6 daily; 50min); Huelva (2 daily; 2hr); Jabugo (4 daily; 35min); Nerva/Río Tinto (1 daily; 1hr 15min); Sevilla (3 daily; 1hr 15min); Zufre (1 daily; 45min).

Huelva to: Aracena (2 daily, one via Río Tinto; 2hr); Ayamonte/Portuguese frontier (10 daily; 1hr); Granada (1 daily; 4hr); Isla Cristina (15 daily; 1hr); La Antilla (7 daily; 45min); Málaga (1 daily; 4hr); Matalascañas (6 daily; 1hr 15min); Mazagon (12 daily; 40min); Moguer (15 daily; 40min); Palos de la Frontera (15 daily; 30min); Punta Umbría (16 daily; 30min); Sevilla (23 daily; 1hr 15min).

Osuna to: Antequera (4 daily; 1hr 15min); Granada (2 daily; 3hr 15min); Málaga (2 daily; 2hr 30min); Sevilla (12 daily; 1hr 15min).

Sevilla to: Algeciras (8 daily; 3hr 30min); Almería (2 daily; 5hr); Aracena (3 daily; 1hr 15min); Arcos de la Frontera (2 daily; 2hr); Ayamonte (access to Portugal's Algarve – 6 daily; 2hr); Cádiz (13 daily; 1hr 45min); Constantina (5 daily; 1hr 40min); Carmona (34 daily; 45min); Córdoba (12 daily; 1hr 45min); Écija (11 daily; 1hr 15min); El Rocío (5 daily; 1hr 30min); Granada (10 daily; 3–4hr); Huelva (24 daily; 1hr 15min); Jaén (5 daily; 3hr); Jerez (13 daily; 1hr 15min); Málaga (10 daily; 2hr 30min); Madrid (14 daily; 6hr); Marbella (3 daily; 3hr); Matalascañas (5 daily; 2hr); Osuna (12 daily; 1hr 15min); Ronda (5 daily; 2hr 30min); Sanlúcar de Barrameda (8 daily; 1hr 30min).

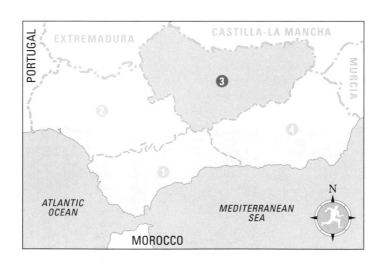

3

Córdoba and Jaén

PORTUGAL

EXTREMADURA

CASTILLA-LA MANCHA

MURCIA

❸

②

④

①

ATLANTIC
OCEAN

MEDITERRANEAN
SEA

N

MOROCCO

CHAPTER 3   # Highlights

* **Córdoba** The city of Córdoba is a feast of museums and palaces, with an old Jewish quarter and some excellent tapas bars and restaurants. See p.424

* **Mezquita, Córdoba** This twelve-hundred-year-old mosque is one of the world's Moorish architectural masterpieces. See p.431

* **Medina Azahara** The ruins of this sumptuous tenth–century Moorish palace evoke the dazzling grandeur of the Córdoba caliphate. See p.447

* **Zuheros** A delightful white village perched on a ridge in the midst of some stunningly picturesque walking country. See p.462

* **Priego de Córdoba** The capital of Córdoba Baroque, this charming town is crammed with fine churches and monuments. See p.464

* **Baños Arabes, Jaén** One of the largest and best-preserved Moorish bath complexes in Spain. See p.484

* **Baeza & Úbeda** The twin Renaissance jewels of Jaén province are filled with a wealth of magnificent monuments in honey-tinted stone. See p.489 & p.495

△ Baños Arabes, Jaén

Córdoba and Jaén

ndalucía's most northerly province, **Córdoba** is horizontally bisected by the Río Guadalquivir. Sited on the river's northern bank, the provincial capital is a handsome city whose outstanding attraction is its twelve-hundred-year-old Moorish **Mezquita**, one of the world's great buildings. In the tangled lanes of the Judería, the old Jewish quarter, that partially surrounds it, the sense of Córdoba's history as the centre of a vast and powerful empire is overwhelming. After the brilliance of the Mezquita the rest of the city, particularly the northern sector of modern Córdoba, can seem like an anticlimax; but persist and you'll discover a host of striking post-*Reconquista* **churches** in addition to a number of elegant **convents and mansions**. Despite a reputation for aloofness and sobriety among its neighbours, Córdoba has some of the most distinctive old **bars** in Andalucía, where taking a drink and a tapa is a particularly unique experience. A few kilometres away there's more lingering Moorish splendour at the ruins of **Medina Azahara**, a once-fabulous palace of the caliphs which is being painstakingly restored.

To the south of the river lies Córdoba's **Campiña**, a rolling landscape of grainfields, olive groves and vineyards, where Montilla, the province's rival to the wines of Jerez, is made. Little visited, the more elevated southern reaches of this area are particularly delightful, with a number of towns and villages such as **Baena**, **Cabra** and **Zuheros** ringed by excellent hiking country. The equally unsung town of **Priego de Córdoba**, further south still, has a clutch of spectacular Baroque churches that are worth a trip in themselves. To the north of the capital, the hardy mining towns in the foothills of the **Sierra Morena** attract even fewer visitors, but there's a rich variety of birdlife here, and the higher slopes are home to deer and wild boar zealously stalked by the hunting fraternity in winter.

The **province of Jaén** has been regarded since Moorish times as Andalucía's gateway – through the **Despeñaperros Pass** – to Castile and the cities of Toledo and Madrid to the north. Although often used as this gateway's doormat and something of a forgotten entity, the region's poorest province has some surprisingly worthy sights. The **city of Jaén** has a fine **Renaissance cathedral** as well as impressive **Moorish baths** but is more often used as a stop on the way to the magnificent twin Renaissance towns of **Baeza** and **Úbeda**. Sharing a similar history, the nobilities of these two conurbations competed in using their sixteenth-century wealth to employ some of the best architects and builders around. These craftsmen, such as the great architect **Andrés de Vandelvira** – whose imprint is everywhere – have left behind a monumental treasure in golden sandstone, one of the marvels not only of Andalucía, but of Spain and Europe as well. The

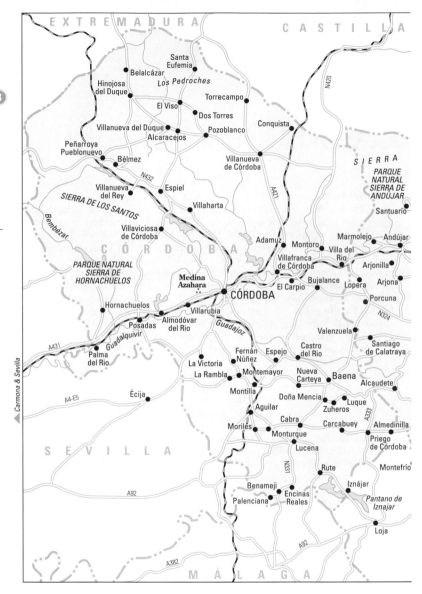

province's mountainous eastern flank now forms the heart of the **Cazorla Natural Park** and cradles the source of the Guadalquivir. Extending northeast from the town of **Cazorla**, the park's vast expanse of dense woodlands, lakes and spectacular crags crowned by eagles' and vultures' nests and patrolled by the agile ibex is a paradise for naturalists and walkers. Its northerly reaches are guarded by many ruined Moorish castles, the

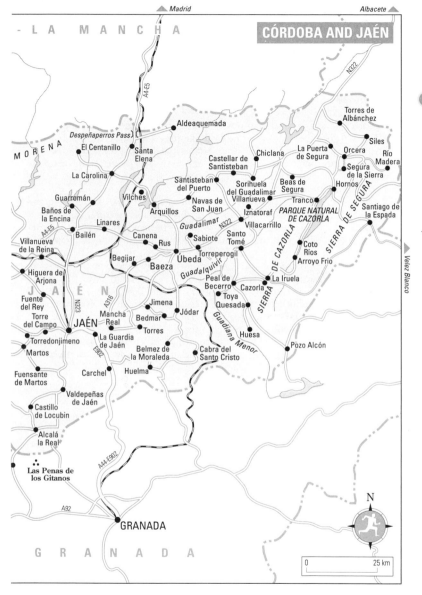

most spectacular of which sits on the hill above the village of **Segura de la Sierra**. The rest is mainly **olive groves**, which cover a vast area of Jaén, and whose exclusive cultivation is the cause of much seasonal unemployment. But there is a beauty in the orderly files of trees, stretching across the red and creamy white hills to the horizon, which seem "to open and close like a fan," as Lorca poetically put it, as you pass.

Córdoba

CÓRDOBA stands upstream from Sevilla beside a loop of the Guadalquivir, which was once navigable as far as here. It is today a minor provincial capital, prosperous in a modest sort of way, but a mere shadow of its past greatness. The city's name – a possible corruption of the Syrian *coteba* or "oil press" – is believed to be of Phoenician origin dating from the time when these merchant venturers sailed up the river to carry away the region's much-prized olive oil.

Córdoba is now principally famous for a single building, the **Mezquita** – the grandest and most beautiful mosque ever constructed by the Moors. It stands right in the centre of the city, surrounded by the Judería, the old Jewish and Moorish quarters, and is a building of extraordinary mystical and aesthetic power. Make for it on arrival and keep returning as long as you stay; its beauty and power increase with each visit.

The Mezquita apart, Córdoba is a city of considerable charm. It has few grand squares or mansions, tending instead to introverted architecture, calling your attention to the tremendous and often wildly extravagant **patios**, yet another Moorish legacy. Filled with pot plants, decorative tiles, tinkling fountains and a profusion of flowers in summer, these shady oases can usually be glimpsed beyond a forged iron *verja* or gate, and are indisputably the best to be seen in Andalucía. They are also actively encouraged and often maintained by the city council, which runs a "Festival of the Patios", usually held during the first half of May. Besides the city's Moorish treasures, there is another Córdoba, to the **north of the old quarter**, an area rarely touched upon by visitors, but with its own rewarding churches and palaces, not to mention bars. In addition to the Patios festival above, the **Cruces de Mayo** celebrations – immediately preceding it – fill the town with lavishly decorated crosses whilst the **Feria de Mayo** during the final week in May is the major fiesta.

Some history

Although archeological finds document an antiquity stretching back to Neolithic times, Córdoba's verifiable history begins with a Bronze Age **Iberian** settlement at the end of the second millennium BC trading on the mineral wealth – silver and copper – brought down from the Sierra Morena to the north. Apparently of little importance during the next millennium, and largely bypassed by the Carthaginian expansion into Spain, Córdoba rose to prominence under **Rome** in the years following the crushing victories against her North African enemy at the end of the third century BC.

Founded as the Roman city of Corduba in 152 BC, Córdoba flourished as the capital of Hispania Ulterior and, foreshadowing its later brilliance, became famous for its poetry as well as its olive oil. Cicero once cracked that Cordoban poetry sounded as if it had got mixed up with the oil due to its guttural style of delivery. Later, after Córdoba had backed the wrong horse in the wars between Caesar and Pompey at the end of the Republic, Caesar sacked the city and an estimated thirty thousand died. When Augustus reorganized Spain in 27 BC, Córdoba's fortunes improved as the capital city of the new province of Baetica, roughly corresponding to modern Andalucía. A brilliant period followed during which the city produced the poets **Lucan** and **Seneca** whilst prosperity – based on oil, wool and minerals – increased.

As Roman power waned in the fifth century the area was overrun first by **Vandals** and then by **Visigoths** before falling to the **Moors** early in the eighth century. In 756 Córdoba became the capital of Moorish Spain and the succeeding three centuries – when the city formed the heart of the Western Islamic

Empire – were Córdoba's golden age, as it grew to rival Cairo and Baghdad as a centre of Muslim art and learning. Though later its political power declined, Córdoba remained a centre of culture and scholarship and was the birthplace of the twelfth-century thinkers Averroës, the great Muslim commentator on Aristotle, and Maimónides, the Jewish philosopher.

After conquest by **Fernando III** in 1236, Córdoba's glory vanished as the city sank into a long and steady decline. Such aspects of civilized life as the elaborate Moorish systems of water supply and sewage disposal fell into ruin and the mosques were turned into churches. Little of the wealth of imperial Spain found its way here, although the city's leatherworkers, silversmiths and *parfumeurs* (all continuing Moorish traditions) achieved some renown in the sixteenth century. Plagues in the next century decimated the population and when Ford arrived in the 1830s he found "a poor and servile city". Córdoba suffered terrible repression in the wars against the **French** as it was to do again in the twentieth century when, during the Civil War, it was captured by the **Nationalists** who carried out brutal atrocities.

Local voters took belated revenge for this in the first post-Franco elections of 1979 when it elected a **communist** council – the only major city in Spain to do so. Befitting its past, Córdoba is now a city of learning once again (the university was re-established in 1971) and its latest faculty is a centre devoted to the study of Muslim history and culture. The town today boasts a progressive air, and has built up a modestly successful economy based upon its agricultural wealth, light industry and tourism.

Arrival and orientation

Córdoba's magnificent new **train station** (☎902 24 02 02) and **bus station** (☎957 40 40 40 for information on routes and operators) complex is located on Plaza de las Tres Culturas, off the Avenida de America to the northwest of the old town. In the adjacent bus station each bus company has its own *ventanilla* (sales window) and beneath the central concourse (and in the subterranean car park) impressive Roman and Moorish excavated remains from the city's distinguished past have been imaginatively incorporated into the new edifice. To reach the centre from the station, pick up the Avenida de los Mozarabes, then veer east onto the broad Avenida del Gran Capitán which will lead you to the old town and the Mezquita, fifteen minutes to the south. Bus #3 from the bus station will take you to the focal Plaza Tendillas, and c/de San Fernando on the old quarter's eastern flank, if you can't face the hike.

Arriving **by car** can be a pain, especially during rush hour in the narrow streets around the Mezquita. Parking is also a major headache, so the best solution is to park your vehicle (stripped of any valuables) for the duration of your stay – the Avenida de la República Argentina on the western edge of the old quarter and across the river in the streets either side of the new *Hotel Hespería* (see "Accommodation") are possible places – and get around the city on foot which is both easy and enjoyable. **Touting** for tips by a range of characters who stand in vacant parking spaces (even if there's a meter) and attempt to coax you into them is now a local tradition and it's normal to give them twenty-five or

Córdoba online

Online information about Córdoba and its monuments and amenities can be found at ⓦwww.ayuncordoba.es, ⓦwww.turismodecordoba.org, ⓦwww.infocordoba.com and ⓦwww.turiscordoba.es.

fifty cents for the favour of "finding" the space for you. If you park illegally your car may well be towed, in which case you'll have to ring ☎957 43 52 32 (Spanish only) or go to the pound, the address of which should be on a sticker on the ground where your car was. If there's no sticker, the nearest hotel should be able to help you locate the pound; all fines must be paid in cash.

③ Information

The city's main **Turismo** (Mon–Fri 9.30am–7pm, Sat 10am–2pm & 5–7pm, Sun 10am–2pm; ☎957 47 12 35) is at the Palacio de Congresos y Exposiciones at c/Torrijos 10 alongside the Mezquita, and has a detailed town plan. Córdoba's municipal tourist office (Turismo Consorcio, ☎957 20 17 74, ⓦwww .turismodecordoba.org) has joined forces with a private company to provide tourist information from four central **kioskos**; one is in the Plaza Campo de los Martires almost facing the Alcázar (daily 9.30am–2pm & 4.30–9.30pm) whilst there's another in the Plaza de las Tendillas in the centre of the modern town (daily 10am–1.30pm & 6–10pm); the others are in the Posada del Potro (see p.438; daily 9.30am–2pm & 4.30–9.30pm) and on the main concourse of the train station (daily 9.30am–2pm & 4.30–7.30pm). The same company also offers guided **walks** around the old city (Paseos por Córdoba; English spoken; €12); the walks start from Plaza de las Tendillas and end up at a typical *cordobés* taverna. You should be aware that Córdoba changes its **monument timetables** more than any other town in Andalucía and these ought to be confirmed with any tourist office. All keep copies of the monthly *Welcome y Olé*, a free bilingual listings magazine detailing the main events. During the May patios festival they also hand out a free guide-map to enable viewing the entries in the competition for best patio. For information on cultural performances and music, make your way to the **Casa de Cultura**, Plaza del Potro 10.

Accommodation

Places to stay can be found all over Córdoba, but the majority are concentrated in the narrow maze of streets around the Mezquita, and if you can resist the urge to lodge on the Mezquita's doorstep, a five-minute walk in any direction leads to some real bargains. On balance Córdoba's *hostales* tend to be better value – and more interesting – than the pricier hotels. Finding a room at any time of the year – except during Semana Santa and the May festivals (the city's high season) – isn't usually a problem, but if you really want to be sure, ring ahead. It's worth bearing in mind also that July and August are the hotel trade's low-season months and the more upmarket places often drop their prices considerably. Where listings below have a garage, unless otherwise stated you will be charged a daily rate for parking (€5–10).

Budget

Fonda Agustina c/Zapatería Vieja 5 ☎957 47 08 72. Charming and spotlessly clean little *fonda*, with basic rooms in a tranquil location. ②

Hostal & Hotel Maestre c/Romero Barros 4 & 16 ☎957 47 53 95 for the *hostal*, ☎957 47 24 10 for the hotel, ⓦwww.hotel maestre.com. Friendly *hostal* with fine patio and attractive en-suite rooms (room 22 has its own terrace); rooms both here and at the nearby hotel

(which are slightly larger) have air-conditioning and TV. They also let a number of nearby apartments (●). *Rough Guide* readers with this guide get free underground parking (except April–May). ②–③

Hostal Alcázar c/San Basilio 2 ☎957 20 25 61, ⓦwww.hostalalcazar.com. Comfortable and welcoming, family-run *hostal* with a nice patio and en-suite a/c rooms with TV. Also has some good-value fully equipped apartments opposite (sleeping up to four) for around €54 per

426

night (minimum stay of two nights). Parking space nearby. ② with breakfast.

Hostal Almanzor c/Corregidor Luís de la Cerda (aka Cardenal González) 10 ☎ & ℱ957 48 54 00. Attractive central place where rooms come with bath, TV and air-conditioning or fans. Some cheaper rooms without bath. Free use of their car park. ③

Hostal Cruz del Rastro c/Cruz Rastro 3 ☎957 48 25 82, ℱ957 47 15 30. Pleasant riverside hostal above a bar-restaurant. The en-suite rooms have a/c and TV, and many have river views. ③

Hostal El Portillo c/Cabezas 2 ☎ & ℱ957 47 20 91, ⓦwww.hostalelportillo.com. Beautiful old *hostal* with an elegant patio and friendly management. Refurbished rooms – many with balconies – come with showers and include a few singles. ②

Hostal La Fuente c/San Fernando 51 ☎957 48 14 78, ⓔinfo@hostalafuente.com. Sparkling *hostal* in a refurbished town house with a delightful patio and pristine en-suite rooms with TV and a/c. Parking nearby. ③

Hostal La Milagrosa c/Rey Heredia 12 ☎957 47 33 17, ⓔlamilagrosa9@hotmail.com. Pleasant *hostal* with a beautiful patio and lots of plants, plus clean and attractive en-suite a/c rooms. ③

Hostal Los Arcos c/Romero Barros 14 ☎957 48 56 43, ⓔayalalosarcos@navegalia.com. Simple rooms (some en suite) with fans in a quiet street behind the Plaza del Potro; charming place with a great plant-filled patio. ②–③

Hostal Luís de Góngora c/Horno de la Trinidad 7 ☎957 29 53 99, ⓦwww.infohostal.com. En-suite rooms with fans in a friendly *hostal* in pleasant location on the northern edge of the Judería. ③

Hostal Plaza Corredera c/Rodríguez Marín 15, ☎957 47 05 81. On the Plaza Corredera (but entry is on c/Rodríguez Marín), this refurbished *pensión* on the wonderful old square has spacious beamed rooms sharing bath and some with great views over the plaza. There are some single rooms, plus a roof terrace above and a bar below for breakfast. Easy parking nearby. ②

Hostal Rey Heredia c/Rey Heredia 26 ☎ & ℱ957 47 41 82. Clean, airy white-walled rooms with fans in a lovely old mansion with plenty of light at the front. Nice patio and staircase and modern communal bathrooms and a couple of slightly more expensive rooms en suite. ②

Hostal Santa Ana c/Corregidor Luís de la Cerda (aka Cardenal González) 25 ☎957 48 58 37. Good upmarket *hostal* with a nice roof terrace and a/c en-suite rooms with TV. There's heating in winter and it has its own garage. ③

Hostal Séneca c/Conde y Luque 7 ☎ & ℱ957 47 32 34, ⓔhostalseneca@eresmas .com. Delightful *hostal* in ancient house with a

stunning patio complete with original Moorish pavement. Rooms with and without bath, and some singles. In summer you'll need to book ahead. ③–④ with breakfast.

Hostal Trinidad c/Corregidor Luís de la Cerda (aka Cardenal González) 58 ☎957 48 79 05. The cheapest rooms in town in a basic but clean, no-frills *hostal*. ②

Pensión Martinez Rucker c/Martínez Rucker 14 ☎957 47 25 62, ⓔreservation@hmrucker.com. A nice patio but the rather spartan rooms aimed at the backpacker market lack hot water (the shared showers have it, though). There are also fridges and a kitchen for use by guests. ②

Moderate and expensive

Casa de los Azulejos c/Fernando Colón 5 ☎957 47 00 00, ⓦwww.casadelosazulejos.com. Stylish small hotel with distinctively furnished rooms, featuring iron bedsteads and artworks, ranged around a leafy patio, itself used for art shows. ⑦

Casa de los Naranjos c/Isabel Losa, 8 ☎957 47 05 87, ⓦwww.casadelosnaranjos.com. In the north of the town near the Plaza de Colón, this is a small two-star hotel with lots of charm and where rooms overlook a leafy patio. ⑤ with breakfast.

Hostal El Triunfo c/Corregidor Luís de la Cerda (aka Cardenal González) 79 ☎957 49 84 84, ⓦwww.htriunfo.com. Traditional hotel-style *hostal* on the Mezquita's east face. Some of the pleasant rooms (on the front) have a Mezquita view, while attic rooms share a rooftop terrace with stunning views over the river and Mezquita. Rooms come with strongbox and there's a good bar and restaurant below. Garage. ④

Hostal Lineros 38 c/Lineros 38 ☎957 48 25 17, ⓦwww.hostallineros38.com. This Moorish extravaganza of a *hostal* has been lovingly created by its friendly proprietors inside an ancient Mudéjar mansion; the furnishings and fittings are all Moorish-inspired, there are arabesques and horseshoe arches everywhere and there's even a *tetería* (4–7pm) in the reception. Some single rooms. ④

Hostal Osio c/Osio 6 ☎957 48 51 65, ⓦwww .hostalosio.com. Charming *hostal* in a refurbished mansion with two fine patios (one a listed monument) and attractive a/c en-suite rooms. The friendly proprietors speak English. ④

Hotel Plateros Plaza Seneca 4 ☎957 49 67 85, ⓦwww.hotelplateros.com. Small hotel housed in an elegant refurbished old mansion on a charming *plazuela*. Pleasant a/c rooms have Internet access and there's a bar below incorporating the ancient house's *bodega* (where the proprietor still makes his own wine) itself using walls which were once part of the ancient Roman

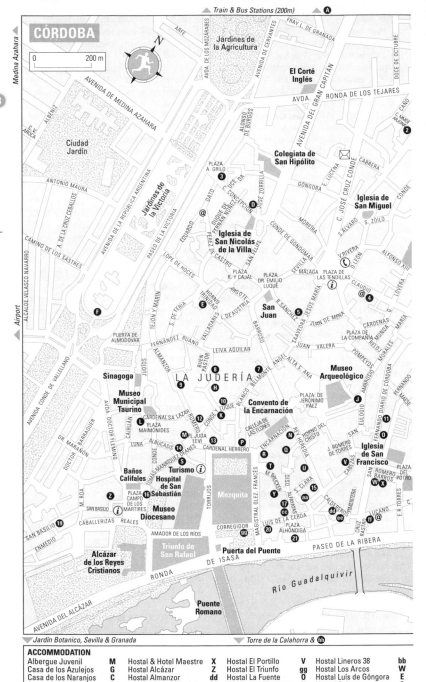

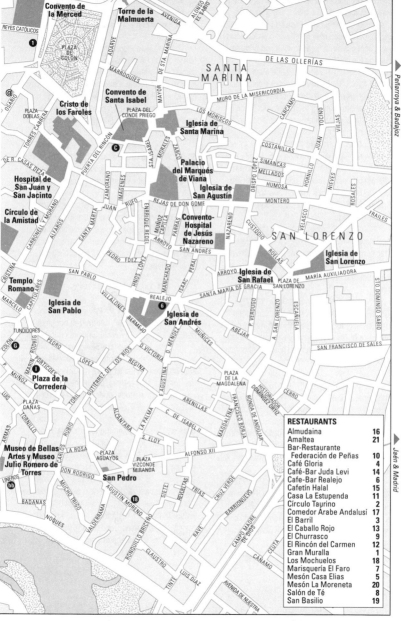

▲ **B** *(Parador)*

► *Peñarroya & Badajoz*

► *Jaén & Madrid*

RESTAURANTS

Almudaina	16
Amaltea	21
Bar-Restaurante Federación de Peñas	10
Café Gloria	4
Café-Bar Juda Levi	14
Cafe-Bar Realejo	6
Cafetín Halal	15
Casa La Estupenda	11
Círculo Taurino	2
Comedor Árabe Andalusí	17
El Barril	3
El Caballo Rojo	13
El Churrasco	9
El Rincón del Carmen	12
Gran Muralla	1
Los Mochuelos	18
Marisquería El Faro	7
Mesón Casa Elias	5
Mesón La Moreneta	20
Salón de Té	8
San Basilio	19

Hostal Plaza Corredera	**I**	Hostal Trinidad	**cc**	Hotel Colon	**A**
Hostal Rey Heredia	**U**	Hotel Albucasis	**H**	Hotel González	**S**
Hostal Santa Ana	**ee**	Hotel Amistad Córdoba	**L**	Hotel Hespería Córdoba	**hh**
Hostal Séneca	**K**	Hotel Andalucía	**D**	Hotel Los Omeyas	**R**
				Hotel Marisa	**P**
				Hotel Meliá Córdoba	**F**
				Hotel Mezquita	**T**
				Hotel Plateros	**J**
				Parador Nacional Arruzafa	**B**
				Pensión Martínez Rucker	**Y**

theatre. The friendly proprietor encourages cycle travellers and can store bikes. ④

Hotel Albucasis c/Buen Pastor 11 ⓣ & ⓕ 957 47 86 25. Charming small hotel with ivy-clad courtyard, spotless en-suite bedrooms and breakfast bar. Garage (€12 per day). ⑤

Hotel Amistad Córdoba Plaza de Maimónides 3 ⓣ 957 42 03 35, ⓦ www.nh-hoteles.com. Four-star hotel (now part of the NH chain) incorporating two eighteenth-century mansions with Mudéjar patio and staircase. Internet access and car park available. ⑦

Hotel Andalucía c/José Zorilla 3 ⓣ 957 47 60 00, ⓦ www.hotelandaluciacordoba.com. Handy hotel for drivers wanting to avoid the Mezquita maze, offering pleasant, en-suite rooms with TV. Give them a ring and they'll tell you how to get there. Relatively easy parking nearby or you can pay to use their garage. ④

Hotel Colón c/Alhaken II, 4, near the train and bus stations ⓣ & ⓕ 957 47 00 17. Modern two-star hotel which is handy for both late arrivals and early departures from the nearby train and bus stations; the old quarter is a 15min walk away. ④

Hotel González c/Manríquez 3 ⓣ 957 47 98 19, ⓔ hotelgonzalez@wanadoo.es. Converted sixteenth-century *casa palacio* with rooms overlooking a brilliant white-walled, geranium-filled patio. It's entered through the hotel's rather tacky souvenir shop. ④

Hotel Hespería Córdoba Avda. de la Confederación s/n ⓣ 957 42 10 42, ⓦ www.hoteles-hesperia.es. Luxurious four-star hotel with great views across the river towards the Mezquita and city from rooms on the front. Features include restaurant, cafetería, pool and rooftop bar (with the same view) and easy access to the town across the pedestrianized Puente Romano. Special offers in July and August. ⑧

Hotel Los Omeyas c/Encarnación 17 ⓣ 957 49 22 67, ⓦ www.hotel-losomeyas.com. Pleasant and airy hotel built around a nice patio but with a severe kitsch problem throughout; rooms come with TV and wall safe and there's parking available. ④

Hotel Marisa c/Cardenal Herrero 6 ⓣ 957 47 31 42, ⓦ www.hotelmarisacordoba.com. You won't get closer to the Mezquita than this. Rather plain hotel where rooms come with air-conditioning (but not TV). Garage. ④

Hotel Meliá Córdoba Jardines de la Victoria s/n ⓣ 957 29 80 66, ⓦ www.solmelia.es. Cordoba's oldest hotel (although it's been rebuilt since) is easy to reach by car along the Avda. de la Republica. Now the Córdoba outpost of the *Meliá* chain of luxury hotels, there's a pool, restaurant, all mod cons and you're a one-minute walk from the Judería. Garage. ⑧

Hotel Mezquita Plaza Santa Catalina 1 ⓣ 957 47 55 85, ⓔ hotelmezquita@wanadoo.es. Atmospheric and central new hotel in a converted sixteenth-century mansion with attractive rooms equipped with satellite TV. ⑤

Parador Nacional Arruzafa Avda. de la Arruzafa s/n, 5km north of town in El Brillante suburb ⓣ 957 27 59 00, ⓦ www.parador.es. Attractive, modern parador with pool, tennis courts, shooting range and views over the city. Worth a trip out for a drink in its gardens. ⑦

Youth hostel and campsites

Albergue Juvenil Plaza Judá Leví s/n ⓣ 957 29 01 66, centralized bookings ⓣ 902 51 00 00, ⓦ www.inturjoven.com. Eighty-one double, triple and four-person rooms with en-suite bath/shower at this modern, relaxed and superbly located hostel make it a prime destination for budget travellers, so you need to book ahead at busy periods. Under-26 €14, over-26 €18.50.

Campamento Municipal El Brillante Avda. Brillante s/n, 2km north on the road to Villaviciosa ⓣ 957 40 38 36. Good site with pool, reached by taking bus #12 from the Puente Romano. Open all year.

Camping Los Villares ⓣ 957 33 01 45. With your own transport, this site is a better option than the *Campamento Municipal*, set in woodland with nature trails and a restaurant. It lies 7km north of the city along a minor road (CP45), just beyond a turn-off for the village of Santo Domingo. Open all year.

The City

The outstanding highlight of any visit to Cordoba and where you'll want to begin your wanderings is the astonishing **Mezquita** in the heart of the old Jewish quarter, **La Judería**. However, just a few streets away from here in any direction the city offers a wealth of fine buildings, churches, monuments and museums, all well worth seeing.

The Mezquita

As in Moorish times, the **Mezquita** (April–Sept Mon–Sat 10am–7.30pm, Sun 2–7pm; Oct–March closes 5pm; €8) is approached through the **Patio de los Naranjos**, a classic Islamic ablutions court with fountains for ritual purification before prayer, which still preserves its orange trees. None of the original ablutions fountains survives, the present ones being purely decorative later additions. Originally, when in use for the Friday prayers, all nineteen naves of the mosque were open to this court, allowing the rows of interior columns to appear as an extension of the trees. Today, with all but one of the entrance gates locked and sealed, the image is still there, though subdued and stifled by the loss of those brilliant shafts of sunlight filtering through. The mood of the building has been distorted a little, from the open and vigorous simplicity of the mosque, to the mysterious half-light of a cathedral.

Nonetheless, a first glimpse inside the Mezquita is immensely exciting. "So near the desert in its tentlike forest of supporting pillars," Jan Morris found it, "so faithful to Mahomet's tenets of cleanliness, abstinence and regularity." The mass of supporting pillars was, in fact, an early and sophisticated improvisation to gain height.

The original architect, Sidi ben Ayub, working under the instruction of Abd ar-Rahman I, had at his disposal columns in marble, porphyry and jasper from the old Visigothic cathedral and from numerous Roman buildings, as well as many more shipped in from all parts of the former Roman Empire. This ready-made building material could bear great weight, but the architect was faced with the problem of the pillars' varying sizes: many were much too tall but the vast majority would not be tall enough, even when arched, to reach the intended height of the ceiling. The long pillars he sank in the floor, whilst his solution for the short pillars (which may have been inspired by Roman aqueduct designs) was to place a second row of square columns on the apex, serving as a base for the semicircular arches that support the roof. For extra strength and stability (and perhaps also deliberately to echo the shape of a date palm, much revered by the early Spanish Arabs), he introduced another, horseshoe-shaped arch above the lower pillars. A second and purely aesthetic innovation was to alternate brick and stone in the arches, creating the red-and-white striped pattern which gives a unity and distinctive character to the whole design. This architectural *tour de force* was unprecedented in the Arab world and set the tone for all future enlargements – excepting the Christian cathedral – of the building. And it was completed within a year of its commencement in 785.

The Mihrab

The mosque's overall uniformity was broken only by the culminating point of al-Hakam II's tenth-century extension – the domed cluster of pillars surrounding the mosque's great jewel, the sacred **Mihrab**. And even here, although he lengthened the prayer hall by a third, al-Hakam carefully aligned the new *mihrab* at the end of the same central aisle which had led to the previous two. The *mihrab* had two functions in Islamic worship: it indicated the direction of Mecca (and hence of prayer) and it amplified the words of the *imam*, or prayer leader. At Córdoba it was also of supreme beauty. As Titus Burckhardt wrote, in *Moorish Art in Spain*:

The design of the prayer niche in Córdoba was used as a model for countless prayer niches in Spain and North Africa. The niche is crowned by a horseshoe-shaped arch, enclosed by a rectangular frame. The arch derives a peculiar strength

Moorish Córdoba and the building of the Mezquita

Córdoba's domination of **Moorish Spain** began thirty years after the conquest – in 756, when the city was placed under the control of **Abd ar-Rahman I**, the sole survivor of the Umayyad dynasty which had been bloodily expelled from the eastern caliphate of Damascus. He commenced the building of the **Great Mosque** (**La Mezquita**), purchasing the site of the former Visigothic Cathedral of Saint Vincent from the Christians. This building which, divided by a partition wall, had previously served both communities had itself been constructed on top of an earlier Roman temple dedicated to the god Janus. Incidentally, some sixth- and seventh-century fragments from the Visigothic church are on display in the cases on the west side of the mosque. Demolishing the church as they built, Abd ar-Rahman's architects, for reasons of speed and economy, incorporated one of the cathedral's original walls – that facing west – into the new structure and this is the reason why the *mihrab*'s prayer wall is not precisely aligned towards Mecca. This original mosque was completed by his son **Hisham** in 786 and comprises about one-fifth of the present building, the first dozen aisles adjacent to the Patio de los Naranjos.

Abd ar-Rahman II

The Cordoban emirate soon began to rival Damascus both in power and in the brilliance of its civilization. **Abd ar-Rahman II** (822–52) initiated sophisticated irrigation programmes, minted his own coinage and received embassies from Byzantium. He in turn substantially enlarged the mosque. A focal point within the culture of al-Andalus, this was by now being consciously directed and enriched as an alternative to Mecca; it possessed an original script of the Koran and a bone from the arm of Muhammad, and, for the Spanish Muslim who could not go to Mecca, it became the most sacred place of **pilgrimage**. In the broader Islamic world it ranked fourth in sanctity after the Kaaba of Mecca, the city of Medina in Saudi Arabia, and the Al Aksa mosque of Jerusalem.

Abd ar-Rahman III

In the tenth century Córdoba reached its zenith under **Abd ar-Rahman III** (912–61), one of the great rulers of Islamic history. He assumed power at the age of twenty-three after his grandfather had killed his father during a period of internal strife and in his reign, according to a contemporary historian, "subdued rebels, built palaces, gave impetus to agriculture, immortalized ancient deeds and monuments, and inflicted great damage on infidels to a point where no opponent or contender remained in *al-Andalus*. People obeyed en masse and wished to live with him in peace." In 929, with Muslim Spain and a substantial part of North Africa firmly under his control, Abd ar-Rahman III adopted the title of "caliph", or successor of the Prophet. It was a supremely confident gesture and was reflected in the growing splendour of Córdoba itself which, with a population approaching (if we take the not always reliable Moorish historians at face value) 500,000, had become the largest, most prosperous city of Europe, and outshone both Byzantium and Baghdad (the new capital of the eastern caliphate) in science, culture and scholarship. At the turn of the tenth century it could boast some 27 schools, 50 hospitals (with the first separate clinics for the leprous and insane), 600 public baths, 60,300 noble mansions, 213,077 houses and 80,455 shops. One of Córdoba's most magnificent buildings during this and later periods would have been the Umayyad palace of the caliphs, of which little except a bath complex remains (see p.439). Extending to the west of the Mezquita from c/Torrijos to the city walls and southwards to the river, the palace was connected to the Mezquita by a secret passage. Built in the ninth century to allow the caliph privileged access to the mosque at all times, traces of this tunnel (not on view) have been found in the building's southwest corner. The construction of a glorious new palace at **Medina Azahara** in the 930s as well as further **development** of the Great Mosque paralleled these new heights of confidence and splendour. Abd ar-Rahman III provided the Mezquita with a new minaret 80m high, topped by three pomegranate-shaped spheres, two of silver and one of gold and each weighing a ton. The minaret was badly damaged in a storm in 1589 and was later used as the core of the sixteenth century Torre del Alminar which replaced it.

Al-Hakam II

The caliph's successor **al-Hakam II** (961–76) was a man from another mould than that of his warrior father, best epitomized by his advice to his own son:

Do not make wars unnecessarily. Keep the peace, for your own wellbeing and that of your people. Never unsheathe your sword except against those who commit injustice. What pleasure is there in invading and destroying nations, in taking pillage and destruction to the ends of the earth? Do not let yourself be dazzled by vanity; let your justice always be like a tranquil lake.

In tune with these sentiments, al-Hakam was a poet, historian and the builder of one of the great libraries of the Middle Ages. This cultured ruler was also responsible for the mosque's most brilliant **expansion**, virtually doubling its extent. After demolishing the south wall to add fourteen extra rows of columns, he employed Byzantine craftsmen to construct a new **mihrab** or prayer niche. This has survived due to having been bricked up following the Christian Reconquest. Only rediscovered in the nineteenth century, it remains complete and is perhaps the most beautiful example of all Moorish religious architecture.

Al-Mansur

Under the vizier-usurper **al-Mansur** (977–1002), who used his position as regent to push al-Hakam's child successor, Hisham II, into the background, repeated attacks were carried out on the Christians in the north, including the daring expedition to Santiago de Compostela in 997, when the pilgrimage cathedral's bells were seized. This **military might** was built on the incorporation of thousands of Berbers from North Africa into al-Mansur's army – a policy that was to have devastating implications for the future when the same Berbers turned on their paymasters and sacked and plundered the city, destroying al-Hakam's treasured library in the process. Within less than thirty years the brilliant caliphate of Córdoba had collapsed in a bloody turmoil as short-lived puppet caliphs attempted to stave off the inevitable.

When he was not away on his military campaigns, al-Mansur gave his attention to further embellishing the Great Mosque. As al-Hakam had extended the building as far to the south as was possible, he completed the final enlargement by adding seven rows of columns to the whole east side. This spoiled the symmetry of the mosque, depriving the *mihrab* of its central position, but Arab historians observed that it meant there were now "as many bays as there are days of the year". They also delighted in describing the rich interior, with its 1293 marble columns, 280 chandeliers and 1445 lamps. Hanging inverted among the lamps were the bells of the cathedral of Santiago de Compostela. Al-Mansur had made his Christian captives carry them on their shoulders from Galicia – a process which was to be observed in reverse after Córdoba was captured by Fernando el Santo (the Saint) in 1236.

from the fact that its central point shifts up from below. The wedge-shaped arch stones or voussoirs fan outwards from a point at the foot of the arch and centres of the inner and outer circumferences of the arch lie one above the other. The entire arch seems to radiate, like the sun or the moon gradually rising over the edge of the horizon. It is not rigid; it breathes as if expanding with a surfeit of inner beatitude, while the rectangular frame enclosing it acts as a counterbalance. The radiating energy and the perfect stillness form an unsurpassable equilibrium. Herein lies the basic formula of Moorish architecture.

The paired pillars that flank the *mihrab* and support its arch were taken from the earlier *mihrab* of Abd ar-Rahman I, their prominent position no doubt a mark of respect by al-Hakam to his great predecessor. The inner vestibule of the niche (which is frustratingly fenced off) is quite simple in comparison, with a shell-shaped ceiling carved from a single block of marble. The chambers to either side, as well as the dome above the *mihrab*, are decorated with exquisite **mosaics** of gold, rust-red, turquoise and green, the work of Byzantine craftsmen supplied by the emperor Nicephorus II at al-Hakam's request. These constitute the *maksura*, where the caliph and his retinue would pray, a fitting monument to this scholarly and sensitive ruler.

The Cathedral and other additions

Originally the whole design of the mosque would have directed worshippers naturally towards the *mihrab*. Today, though, you almost stumble upon it, as in the centre of the mosque squats a Renaissance **cathedral coro**. This was built in 1523, nearly three centuries of enlightened restraint after the Christian conquest, and in spite of fierce opposition from the town council. The erection of a *coro* and *capilla mayor*, however, had long been the "Christianizing" dream of the cathedral chapter and at last they had found a monarch, predictably Carlos V, who was willing to sanction the work. Carlos, to his credit, realized the mistake (though it did not stop him from destroying parts of the Alhambra and Sevilla's Alcázar); on seeing the work completed he told the chapter, "You have built what you or others might have built anywhere, but you have destroyed something that was unique in the world." Some details are worth noting, though, particularly the beautifully carved Churrigueresque **choir stalls** by Pedro Duque Cornejo, created with mahogany brought from the New World. To the left of the *coro* stands an earlier and happier Christian addition, the Mudéjar **Capilla de Villaviciosa**, built by Moorish craftsmen in 1371 (and now partly sealed up). Beside it are the dome and pillars of the **earlier mihrab**, constructed under Abd ar-Rahman II. The mosque's original and finely decorated timber-coffered ceiling was replaced in the eighteenth century by the present Baroque cupolas. Further post-Reconquest additions include the **Capilla Real**, installed by Alfonso X in the thirteenth century, with *azulejo* panels and lobed niches in Mudéjar style, and the early eighteenth-century **Capilla del Cardinal** (Chapterhouse), the *tesoro* (treasury) and *sacristía*, none of which detracts from the building's imposing majesty.

The evocative belfry, the **Torre del Alminar** (currently closed to visitors) at the corner of the Patio de los Naranjos, is built on the site of the original minaret and contemporary with the cathedral addition. The belfry was designed by Hernán Ruíz, who used the earlier tower as a core to support two additional sections more than doubling its height. The climb to the top is a dizzying experience and the **views** over the town and Mezquita itself tremendous. Close by, the **Puerta del Perdón**, the main entrance to the patio, was rebuilt in Moorish style in 1377. It's worth making a tour of the Mezquita's **outer walls** before leaving; parts of the original "caliphal" decoration (in

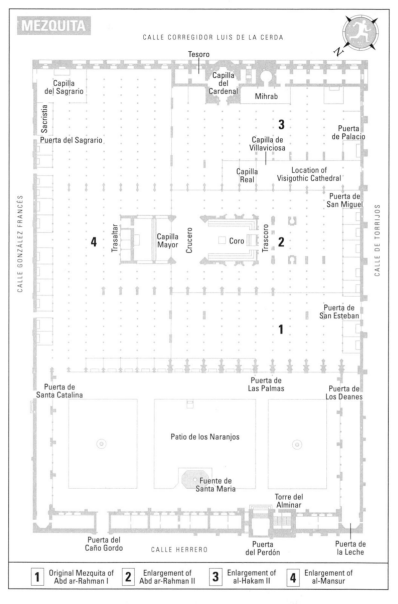

MEZQUITA

CALLE CORREGIDOR LUIS DE LA CERDA

Tesoro

Capilla del Sagrario

Capilla del Cardenal

Mihrab

Sacristía

3

Puerta de Palacio

Puerta del Sagrario

Capilla de Villaviciosa

Capilla Real

Location of Visigothic Cathedral

CALLE GONZÁLEZ FRANCÉS

Puerta de San Miguel

Trasaltar

4

Capilla Mayor

Crucero

Coro

Trascoro

2

CALLE DE TORRIJOS

Puerta de San Esteban

1

Puerta de Santa Catalina

Puerta de Las Palmas

Puerta de Los Deanes

Patio de los Naranjos

Fuente de Santa Maria

Torre del Alminar

Puerta del Caño Gordo

CALLE HERRERO

Puerta del Perdón

Puerta de la Leche

| **1** | Original Mezquita of Abd ar-Rahman I | **2** | Enlargement of Abd ar-Rahman II | **3** | Enlargement of al-Hakam II | **4** | Enlargement of al-Mansur |

particular some exquisite latticework) surrounding the portals are stunning. The west wall along c/Torrijos is the most striking where the **Puerta de San Estebán** was an important side entrance into the original mosque and is the oldest of the doorways, dated by an inscription above it to 855. The **Puerta de San Miguel** is sited in the oldest stretch of wall, and dates from the earlier Visigothic cathedral.

Dating from the time of the *Reconquista*, the **Alcázar de Los Reyes Cristianos** (Sept–June Tues–Sat 10am–2pm & 5.30–7.30pm, Sun 9.30am–2.30pm; July–Aug Tues–Sun 9.30am–2.30pm; gardens only Tues–Sun 8pm–midnight; €4, evening gardens visit €2; free on Fri), a Palace Fortress, was completed in the fourteenth century and now houses a small municipal museum. The original Moorish *alcázar* stood beside the Mezquita, on the site presently occupied by the Palacio Episcopal. After the Christian conquest it was rebuilt a little to the west and used by monarchs – including Fernando and Isabel who were visited here by Columbus in 1486 – when staying in the city, hence its name. That the buildings retain little of their original opulence today is due to their use as the residence of the **Inquisition** for three centuries prior to 1821, and later as a prison until as recently as 1951. The palace underwent extensive Mudéjar rebuilding during the fifteenth century, when the attractive **Moorish-style gardens** were added. One of the glories of Córdoba today with lots of arbours and shady corners, the gardens are dotted with hefty chunks of Roman columns and other masonry all testifying to the city's importance in the Roman era. From the tower's belvedere there are great **views** over the town and river, while the **interior** of the Alcázar has some mildly interesting fifteenth-century royal baths and some fine **Roman mosaics** discovered in the city. The second-century depiction of *Polyphemus and Galatea* is outstanding and the monochrome mosaic beside it is one of the largest complete mosaics in existence. A fine third-century carved sarcophagus – thought to have been made in Rome and sent for the burial of a distinguished person – is also worth a look; a half-ajar portal on the sarcophagus's side indicates that access is open to the person within.

In the gardens across the plaza to the north of the Alcázar are the impressive remains of a tenth-century Moorish *hammam*, or bathhouse, the **Baños Califales**, Campo Santo de Los Mártires s/n (same hours and ticket as Alcázar), constructed in the reign of al-Hakam II. As their name implies, the baths were possibly

△ Alcázar, Córdoba

attached to the Ummayad palace which once covered most of this area. After being scandalously neglected for years when they were used as a playground by kids and graffiti artists and a rubbish dump by almost everyone else, the baths have finally been renovated and protected for posterity. Inside you can see the various bathing rooms, which would have had gradated temperatures, lit by star-shaped windows set in barrel-vaulted ceilings. The baths' western rooms date from the post-califal Taifa, Almoravid and Almohad periods. Travellers to Moorish Córdoba record between three and six hundred bathhouses similar to these throughout the city which would probably not be excessive for a population of half a million inhabitants. The baths – a focal feature of Muslim life – would originally have been surrounded by plant-filled gardens and arbours where bathers could relax and chat. In the afternoon the baths normally passed into feminine hands when a towel would be hung outside to warn absent-minded males of the change of use. See p.439 for visiting a reconstruction of the real thing.

Three hundred metres downriver from the Alcázar lies a new **Jardín Botánico**, Avda. de Linneo s/n (April–Sept Tues–Sat 10am–9pm, Sun 10am–2.30pm plus Thurs & Fri 9pm–midnight; Oct–March Tues–Sat 10am–6.30pm, Sun 10am–2.30pm; €2, free Fri; Ⓦ www.uco.es/jardin-botanico). The gardens are extensive and there are hothouses with more exotic species of succulents, ferns and prickly plants, as well as a rose garden. At the garden's northern end a paleobotanical museum – housed inside a medieval water mill – displays 150,000 specimens of fossil plant life. The nearby arboretum exhibits trees and shrubs from all over the world including in one section samples of Andalucía's own arboreal rarity, the **pinsapo** Spanish fir, transplanted from its only European habitat in the Sierra de Grazalema. Other features include a garden for the visually impaired with a collection of plants recognizable by their aroma and texture and a **cafetería**.

Museo Diocesano

Opposite the Mezquita's west wall on the site of the former Moorish *alcázar* lies the **Museo Diocesano** (Mon–Sat 9.30am–3pm; €1.20). This elegant seventeenth-century building with a fine patio and fountain is now a mildly interesting **museum of religious art**, mainly sculpture. The highlights are in the early rooms where there are some outstanding examples of medieval wood sculpture – a great Spanish tradition. The anonymous thirteenth-century *Virgen de las Huertas* in Room 1 is finely worked, as is a striking fifteenth-century *Calvario Villaviciosá* or Crucifixion. In Room 3, an anonymous early sixteenth-century *pietà* has the agonized expressions of the onlookers beautifully portrayed. The remainder of the museum comprises more wood sculpture from later periods, including an image of *Santo Tomás* by José de Mora as well as tapestries and furniture. Room VI finishes the tour with a vibrant eighteenth-century image of San Miguel Arcángel attributed to La Roldana, the daughter sculptor of Pedro Roldán. On the ground floor, there's a beautiful Baroque **chapel** dedicated to the Virgin (which may be closed).

The Puente Romano and around

The pedestrianized **Puente Romano** is an impressive 250-metre-long span across the Río Guadalquivir probably built during the first or second centuries AD. Inscriptions record repairs to it carried out in Moorish times by the *wali* or governor Al-Samh in the eighth century, and by Al-Hakam II in the tenth, but the structure still retains much Roman stonework.

Guarding the southern end of the Puente Romano is the **Torre de la Calahorra** (daily: May–Sept 10am–2pm & 4.30–8.30pm; Oct–April 10am–6pm;

€4, or €5.20 with multimedia show), a medieval tower that now houses a museum full of hi-tech gimmicks including weird tableaux, a lit-up Alhambra, a model of the Mezquita prior to its Christian alterations and, improbably, a multimedia presentation on the history of man. From the tower you get a wonderful panoramic **view** towards the Mezquita and city beyond.

Standing next to the tower and the bridge is one of the ancient **Moorish water wheels**, the Albolafia. This is the reconstructed sole survivor of a number of mills which crossed the river here and which, besides grinding flour, pumped water to the Alcázar's gardens. So noisy were this wheel's rumblings that Queen Isabel – resident at the Alcázar during a royal visit – had it dismantled when it disturbed her sleep.

The Judería and synagogue

Between the Mezquita and the beginning of the Avenida del Gran Capitán lies the **Judería**, Córdoba's old Jewish quarter. A fascinating network of lanes, it's just as atmospheric as Sevilla's Barrio Santa Cruz, although here too tasteless souvenir shops are beginning to gain ground. Near the heart of the quarter, at c/Maimónides 18, is the **synagogue** (Tues–Sat 9.30am–2pm & 3.30–5.30pm, Sun 9.30am–2pm; €0.30, free with EU passport), one of only three in Spain – the other two are in Toledo – that survived the Jewish expulsion of 1492. This one, built in 1315, is minute, particularly in comparison to the great Santa María in Toledo, but it has some fine stuccowork elaborating on a Solomon's-seal motif together with Hebrew texts in the Mudéjar style, and it also retains its women's gallery. Just south of the synagogue in the *plazuela* named after him is a statue of Maimónides, the Jewish philospher, physician and Talmudic jurist born in Córdoba in 1135.

Nearby is a rather bogus **Zoco** – an Arab *souk* turned into a crafts arcade – on the site of an old mule market. If you're not too impressed by the trinkets on offer, there's a bar and and a pleasant patio to enjoy a drink in. Adjoining this, the small **Museo Taurino** (Bullfighting Museum; Tues–Sat 10am–2pm & 5.30–7.30pm, Sun 9.30am–2.30pm; €3, free on Fri) warrants a look, if only for the kitschy nature of its exhibits: among a number of mounted bulls' heads (some dating from the nineteenth century), two of them were given this "honour" for having killed matadors. Beside a copy of the tomb of Manolete, most famous of the city's fighters, is exhibited the hide of his taurine nemesis, Islero. In addition to Manolete's bloodstained vest from the ill-fated day in 1947, other items on display include eighteenth-century bullfight posters and a series of photos from 1914 depicting a bullfighter being gored and killed.

Finally, close to the Mezquita's northeast corner, you shouldn't miss Córdoba's most famous street, the **Callejón de las Flores**. This is a white-walled alley from whose balconies and hanging pots cascades a riot of geraniums in summer and which, when viewed from its northern end, neatly frames the Mezquita's belfry – the picture that decorates every postcard rack in town.

Plaza del Potro

A short walk east from the Mezquita along c/Corregidor Luís de la Cerda and its continuation, c/Lucano, is the **Plaza del Potro**, one of Córdoba's more historic landmarks. This fine old square is named after the colt (*potro*) which adorns its sixteenth-century fountain. Originally a livestock market dealing in horses and mules, the area once had a villainous reputation, as did the remarkable inn opposite, the **Posada del Potro**, which Cervantes mentions in *Don Quixote*, and where he almost certainly stayed. Sensitively restored, the building, with an atmospheric cattle yard, now houses the Casa de Cultura, municipal education and cultural offices, part of which is used for *artesanía* displays and art and photographic exhibitions, often worth a look.

Slightly southwest of the plaza a glimpse of how Córdoba may have lived in its Moorish heyday is obtainable at the **Hammam Baños Arabes**, c/Corregidor Luis de la Cerda 51 (☎957 48 47 46, ⓦwww.hammamspain.com), a full-scale Moorish bath complex which re-creates the architecture and atmosphere of a medieval *hammam*. Bathers are invited to soak themselves in baths of different temperatures (cold, tepid and hot) with massage and aromatherapy on offer, whilst Arabic music wafts around the complex. Open daily but reservations (by phone is fine) must be made in advance and sessions (lasting 2hr) are available from 10am to midnight; prices start at €18 for a simple bathe and you'll need a bathing suit.

Museo de Bellas Artes and Museo Julio Romero de Torres

On the eastern side of Plaza del Potro, the former Hospital de la Caridad, founded in the sixteenth century, now contains the **Museo de Bellas Artes** (Tues 2.30–8.30pm, Wed–Sat 9am–8.30pm, Sun 9am–2.30pm; €1.50, free with EU passport). Among a fairly unremarkable collection (rendered even more threadbare by the inexplicable disappearance of the Goyas and the best Riberas to Madrid) is an *Immaculate Conception* by Murillo as well as works by Valdés Leal and some dubious Zurbaráns. A couple of interesting drawings by the Victorian British artist David Roberts (in storage at the time of writing) may be displayed and depict the Mezquita's Patio de los Naranjos and the Puerta del Puente as they were at the end of the nineteenth century. The ground floor has a small archeological collection that includes a fine second-century BC **Iberian sculpture** of a she-wolf despatching its victim (another work in storage), as well as a collection of rather humdrum modern sculpture and paintings.

Across the courtyard is a small museum (May–Sept Tues–Sat 10am–2pm & 5.30–7.30pm, Sun 9.30am–2.30pm; Oct–April Tues–Sat 8.30am–2.30pm, Sun 9.30am–2.30pm; €3, free on Fri) devoted to the Córdoban artist **Julio Romero de Torres** (1885–1930), painter of some sublimely dreadful canvases, most of which depict reclining female nudes with furtive male guitar players. Attacked by feminists and dubbed "the king of kitsch" by critics, the *cordobeses*, however, won't have a word said against him. If you wish to decide for yourself, the nightmarish *Cante Jondo* or the raunchy *Naranjas y Limones* (Oranges and Lemons) should be enough to give you the measure of Romero's oeuvre; alternatively, just flick through a catalogue in the foyer.

Probably more rewarding would be a visit to *Bodegas Campos*, just east of here at c/Lineros 32, a wonderful rambling old place where they will allow you to see the cellars – stacked with giant oak *botas* (barrels) – in which the company matures its wine through the *solera* system of blending. You can sample the finished article in their **bar**, and a very good Montilla it is, too.

Plaza de la Corredera

To the north, in an area which was once the *plateros* or silversmiths' quarter, you'll find **Plaza de la Corredera**. A wonderfully ramshackle colonnaded square, rather like a decayed version of Madrid's or Salamanca's Plaza Mayor, it is unique in Andalucía. The square's complete enclosure occurred in the seventeenth century and presented the city with a suitable space for all kinds of spectacles. These have included burnings by the Inquisition as well as bullfights, from which event the tiny Callejón Toril (Bull Pen) on the square's eastern side takes its name. Any other city, you feel, would have transformed this edifice into a monument to civic pride, but sadly the square was neglected for decades and has only recently and belatedly undergone a facelift – cafés and bars have now begun to set up terraces which are becoming popular. Be alert at night, however, as bag snatchers operate in the alleys and streets around here.

Museo Arqueológico

Northwest of the Plaza del Potro, on Plaza de Jerónimo Páez, lies the excellent **Museo Arqueológico** (Tues 2.30–8.30pm, Wed–Sat 9am–8.30pm, Sun 9am– 2.30pm; €1.50, free with EU passport), essential to gaining an understanding of Córdoba's importance as a Roman city in particular, as so little from this period survives above ground today. During the original conversion of the Casa Páez, this small sixteenth-century Renaissance mansion was revealed as the unlikely site of a genuine Roman patio. As a result, it is one of the most imaginative and enjoyable small museums in the country, with good local collections from the Iberian, Roman and Moorish periods.

Following the **prehistoric section** which displays some Iberian sculptures from various sites in the province the visit continues in **Room 3** where you can see evidence of the original Roman building. Highlights here include a large number of finds from the excavation of Córdoba's western necropolis, among which are a number of inscribed first-century gladiatorial tombstones (including the moving exhibit no. 10.681, translated into Spanish). **Room 4** has a fine maquette of the Roman villa of El Ruedo at Almedinilla (see p.469) in the south of the province, incorporating a unique cascade feature in its *triclinium* (dining room). **Room 5** has more exhibits from the Roman period including a superb bronze hermaphrodite from the villa at El Ruedo, and a fascinating carved stone relief depicting the olive harvest. The stairs leading to Room 7 are flanked by fine mosaics including an outstanding one depicting a *quadriga* or four-horse chariot in action. The intricate wooden Mudéjar ceiling here is worth a look too and predates the mansion which was built to incorporate it.

Room 7 contains exhibits from the Moorish period among which is a fine inlaid tenth-century bronze stag – a gift of the Byzantine emperor Constantine VII to Abd ar-Rahman III – and found at the Moorish palace of Medina Azahara (see p.447) where it was used as the spout of a fountain. Also here are a number of fine polychromed ceramic pieces from Medina Azahara. On the **balcony** a collection of wells attests to the Moorish attraction to water – a tradition continued by fountains throughout Andalucía today.

The museum's beautiful double **patio** contains miscellaneous Roman statuary, mosaics and a superb fourth-century Christian marble sarcophagus. Also here is a fine second-century sculpture of Mithras slaying the bull from a mithraeum excavated at Cabra in the south of the province. This conventional image, which was placed in the *retablo* position in the small mithraic cult temples, shows Mithras plunging his dagger into the bull whose blood, initiates believed, gave birth to all living things, hence the dog and the snake trying to get their share. The ever-present problem of evil is portrayed by the symbolic scorpion attacking the bull's vitals.

The rest of the city

Many visitors to Córdoba make a stopover at the Mezquita and then leave without ever discovering the other Córdoba, to the north of the monumental quarter and the Judería, where the city's everyday life is carried on. Here, interspersed among the modern streets – many still built on the ancient grid – are **Gothic churches**, **convents** and **Renaissance palaces** that are little visited but well worth an hour or two. Note that churches are usually locked outside service times: early mornings or evenings (about 7–9pm) are the most promising times to catch them open, perhaps visiting a few tapas bars en route.

Plaza Tendillas and around
Plaza Tendillas is the vibrant centre of modern Córdoba, as it was in Roman times. Dominated by the bronze equestrian statue of El Gran Capitán, a Cordoban general whose Italian campaigns in the late fifteenth century helped to project post-*Reconquista* Spain onto the world stage, the previously traffic-clogged square has recently received a makeover, and its fountains – spurting two metres into the air from the pedestrianized pavement – are a big hit with tourists, children and dogs.

Off the east side of the plaza, along c/Claudio Marcelo, lies the **Templo Romano**, the tortuously reconstructed remains (mostly pillars) of a first-century Roman temple thought to have been of a similar form to the Maison Carrée at Nîmes. Turning left along c/Capitulares from here brings you to the **Iglesia de San Pablo** fronting the street of the same name. A fine Romanesque-Gothic church, dating from the period following the *Reconquista*, it has undergone numerous later modifications including a Baroque facade. Its interior retains a fine Mudéjar dome and coffered ceiling as well as a seventeenth-century sculpture of the Virgin, *Nuestra Señora de las Angustias* (*Our Lady of the Sorrows*), a masterpiece by Juan de Mesa, himself a native of Córdoba.

Northwest from here, on c/Alfonso XIII at no. 14, is the striking **Circulo de la Amistad**, a *casino* founded in 1842, and set inside a former convent. Ask the porter to let you see the marvellous Renaissance **patio**, originally the convent's cloister. Continuing east again, beyond San Pablo lies **San Andrés**, another post-*Reconquista* church and, further on, at the end of c/Santa María de la Gracia, is the Gothic **San Lorenzo**, whose converted Moorish minaret tower, outstanding rose window and triple-arched portico combine to make it the best-looking church in the city. Inside, the apse has some fine fifteenth-century frescoes depicting scenes from the Passion.

Turning north along c/Roelas, passing the nineteeth-century Neoclassical Iglesia de San Rafael, you'll come to another *Reconquista* church, **San Agustín**, in the plaza of the same name. Originally a Gothic church, it was substantially altered in the sixteenth century; inside it has frescoes and another sculpture of the Virgin by Juan de Mesa.

Palacio del Marqués de Viana
Slightly west of San Agustín in Plaza de Gome you'll find the **Palacio del Marqués de Viana** (guided tours Mon–Fri 10am–1pm & 4–6pm, Sat 10am–1pm; €6, patios only €3; last entry 15min before closing), one of Córdoba's finest palaces and seat of the marquises of Viana until the family sold up to a bank in 1981, after which it was opened – apparently just as the family left it – to the public. Started in the fourteenth century, the building has had numerous later additions tacked on, including most of the **twelve outstanding patios**, filled with flowers, the main attraction for many visitors today.

The compulsory guided tour shunts you around a bewildering number of drawing rooms, gaudy bedrooms (one with a telling Franco portrait), kitchens and galleries, linked by creaking staircases, whilst a commentary delivered in machine-gun Spanish (foreign-language room descriptions available) points out a wealth of furniture, paintings, weapons and top-drawer junk the family amassed over the centuries, giving you little time to take anything in.

North of the Palacio de Viana, the fortress-like **Iglesia de Santa Marina** dates from the thirteenth century (with Baroque modifications) and shares the charming plaza of the same name with a monument to the celebrated Cordoban *torero* **Manolete**, who was born in the Santa Marina *barrio* and died in the ring in 1947. At the square's western end, strictly speaking the Plaza del Conde Priego, the fifteenth-century Franciscan **Convento de Santa Isabel** has a delightful patio with an imposing cypress. The *capilla mayor* inside the convent's church has sculptures by Pedro Roldán. The nuns here also sell their home-made *dulces*: the ebullient Hermana Isabel – given a special dispensation from the order's rule of silence to run the shop (usually Mon–Sat 9.15am–12.45pm & 5–7.30pm, Sun 9.30am–1pm) – will serve you.

Calle Conde de Priego leads west to the Puerta del Rincón. By turning right off this after a short distance you enter the simple white-walled Plaza de Capuchinos, the site of **El Cristo de los Faroles** (Christ of the Lanterns), an eighteenth-century sculpture of the Crucifixion which is the centre of much religious fervour. At night, when the lanterns flanking the cross are illuminated, the place has an unearthly, mystical ambience.

North from here are two features – on either side of the Plaza de Colón – worthy of a detour. Close to the northeast corner of this garden-square, the **Torre de la Malmuerta** (Tower of Bad Death) is an early fifteenth-century battlemented tower, once part of the city walls. It takes its name from a crime of passion when a guard posted here is supposed to have killed his adulterous spouse. At the foot of the tower is one of the city's best loved *tabernas*, the *Casa de Paco Acedo* (see p.445), housed in part of a former barracks. The west side of the Plaza de Colón is dominated by the lavishly ornate facade of the eighteenth-century former **Convento de la Merced**, (entry to patio daily 9am–2pm & 5–9pm; free) now the seat of the provincial government, and the biggest and best example of full-blown Baroque in town. Inside is an exquisite Renaissance patio with paired columns, elegant staircases and a central fountain.

Picking up the route south towards the centre, follow c/del Osario until, just before Plaza Tendillas, a left turn brings you into Plaza San Miguel and its charming **Iglesia de San Miguel**, yet another *Reconquista* church founded in the thirteenth century by Fernando III, with a magnificent rose window above the early Gothic entrance. Tucked behind the church lies one of Córdoba's most atmospheric taverns, the **Taberna San Miguel** (see p.445).

Heading back to the Judería you pass another couple of churches: the fourteenth-century **San Nicolás**, at the end of c/Conde de Gondomar, east of Plaza Tendillas, with a spectacular **octagonal bell tower**, and the rather sad **Iglesia de San Juan** in a small square of the same name to the south, where the crumbling minaret of a former ninth-century mosque, complete with elegant horseshoe arches resting on Corinthian pillars, sits precariously beside its later rival.

Eating, drinking and nightlife

Coming from Sevilla or the coast, the nightlife in Córdoba will seem rather tame by comparison. Places start closing at around 11pm and by midnight, the empty streets around the Mezquita, lit by lanterns, have a melancholy air. When they are open, however, many of the city's **bars and restaurants** are among the best in Andalucía and are well worth seeking out.

Restaurants

Córdoba's **restaurants** are on the whole reasonably priced – and quite a few of the upmarket establishments are really excellent. Whilst here be sure to try Córdoba's two most celebrated **dishes**, *rabo de toro* (slow-stewed bull's tail) and *salmorejo* (a hunky *gazpacho* with chunks of ham and egg), available all over town.

Albergue Juvenil Plaza Judá Levi s/n. The youth hostel's *cafetería* (open to all) has some of the cheapest food in town with three-course lunch (2–3pm) and dinner (8.30–9.30pm) *menús* for a bargain €5.15.

Almudaina Plaza Campo Santo de los Martires 1 ☏957 47 43 42. Top-notch restaurant with four stylish rooms in an atmospheric sixteenth-century mansion facing the walls of the Alcázar. Among many fine dishes *pechuga de corniz en salsa* (partridge breasts) is a house special. Expensive (main dishes €15–18), but there's a *menú* for about €21. Closed Sun eve.

Amaltea c/Ronda de Isasa 10 ☏957 49 19 68. Excellent organic restaurant with lots of veggie options run by a charming *cordobésa*. Specialities of the house include couscous, *carpaccio de cecina* (described as cured ham made with beef) and *calabacín con cabrales* (courgettes with strong blue cheese). There are plenty of organic wines and a few special beers too – try the *Alhambra 1925* – along with occasional art exhibitions on the walls. Closed Mon.

Bar-Restaurante Federación de Peñas c/Conde y Luque 8. Moorish-style patio dining room offering a variety of economical *menús*.

Café Gloria c/Claudio Marcelo 15. Attractive eatery done out in Art Deco style with big windows onto the street; offers economical *platos combinados* and a variety of *menús* starting at around €7.

Café-Bar Juda Levi Plaza Judá Levi. Economical *platos combinados* plus ice cream, and there's a pavement terrace on which to enjoy them.

Cafe-Bar Realejo c/Realejo 89. Popular with locals and a good budget option if you happen to be up this end of town; there's a *menú* for around €6.

Cafetín Halal c/Rey Heredia 28. Located in the Islamic cultural centre and serving excellent, inexpensive dishes with many vegetarian options. No alcohol, but their range of fruit cocktails is recommended.

Casa La Estupenda c/San Fernando 39. Solid *casa de comidas* place with a good-value *menú* featuring some vegetarian dishes; pleasant atmosphere with classical music.

Círculo Taurino c/Manuel María de Arjona 1. Excellent, mid-priced, *cordobés* family-run restaurant offering a wide range of local dishes.

Comedor Árabe Andalusí Plaza Abades, off c/Alfayatas. Excellent and economical little North African diner for *shwarma* (shish kebab), felafel, chicken and lamb tagines and couscous. During the day it's also a *tetería* serving over fifty varieties of tea.

El Barril c/Concepción 16. Super efficient tapas and breakfast bar with a small terrace and all-day *platos combinados*. Some vegetarian dishes.

El Caballo Rojo c/Cardenal Herrero 28 ☏957 47 53 75. Beneath the Mezquita's belfry, this is one of Córdoba's choicest restaurants, although a café-style interior lacks intimacy. It prides itself on a Moorish-influenced menu offering such specialities as *cordero a la miel* (lamb in honey) and tasty desserts like *canutillo de almendra* (almond pastry). Expensive (main dishes €13–19) but offers a *menú de degustación* for around €30.

El Churrasco c/Romero 16 (*not* c/Romero Barros) ☏57 29 08 19. The third – and probably the best – of Córdoba's top restaurants, with sumptuously decorated dining rooms and patio, and a long-standing reputation for its *churrasco* (a kind of grilled pork dish, served with pepper sauces). When booking mention that you wish to visit their *Museo del Vino Bodega* (diners only) where you may also choose the wine for your meal. Prices match its reputation (main dishes €11–22), although there's a good-value set *menú* at €24. Closed Aug.

El Rincón del Carmen c/Romero 4. Small, pleasant café-restaurant, with an outdoor patio and restaurant upstairs, serving an inexpensive *menú*.

Gran Muralla Plaza de Colón 29. Excellent, roomy and economical Chinese restaurant hugely popular with locals.

Los Mochuelos c/Agustín Moreno 51. Traditional tapas and *raciones* restaurant with large variety of dishes including *mochuelitos* (spicy meat); plenty of atmosphere, stacked butts, bullfight posters and a pleasant patio.

Marisquería El Faro c/Ricardo de Montís 1, off c/Blanco Belmonte. Small upmarket restaurant with good seafood *raciones* and a decent paella.

Mesón Casa Elías (aka *Mesón El Rey*), c/ Rodríguez Sánchez 5. This big, cheap and cheerful place with a patio makes a good lunch stop for *raciones* or a €6 *menú*.

Mesón La Moreneta c/Corregidor Luís de la Cerda 63 (aka c/González). One of the few worthwhile places to eat near the Mezquita with an attractive patio and a variety of economical *menús*.

Salón de Té c/Buen Pastor 13. To the northwest of the Mezquita's belfry is this very pleasant small Moroccan tea salon with a charming patio offering over fifty varieties, including a special *hierba buena* (mint tea).

San Basilio c/San Basilio 19. Great little neighbourhood restaurant with a pleasant patio, friendly service and a weekday *menú* for €10. House specials include *presa iberica* (pork) and *berenjenas fritas* (aubergine).

Tabernas and tapas bars

The *cordobeses* are proud of their **tabernas** – and with good reason, for few places anywhere can match them for sheer character and variety, not to mention **tapas** – and the municipal tourist office has copies of *La Ruta de las Tabernas de Córdoba*, a route-map of the town's best tapas bars. Remember, too, when ordering *fino* that the equivalent brew here is Montilla and the best way to get up a barman's nose is to ask for any of the wines of Jerez, the product of the upstart province downriver. If you're new to Montilla-Moriles to give it its full title, or have been unimpressed with the insipid concoctions sold abroad under the Montilla name, prepare for a pleasant surprise. Montilla, which vaguely resembles a mellow, dry sherry, is a giant on its native soil, and is considered a healthier tipple by the *cordobeses*; whereas Jerez sherry is fortified with alcohol, here the process is totally natural, leading (they insist) to fewer hangovers. In recent years some of the better bars have been adding small restaurants and these are often excellent places for a more formal meal.

Around the Mezquita and Judería

Bar Caballo Rojo c/Cardenal Herrero 28, facing the Mezquita. The smoothly efficient – and slightly pricier – bar of the famous restaurant has excellent tapas and *raciones* including *boquerones en vinagre* (anchovies in vinegar).

Bar La Cavea Plaza Jerónimo Páez, near the archeological museum. Pleasant little bar with nice terrace where you can knock back a *jarrón* of beer with some excellent tapas. Also serves *platos combinados*. Slightly north of here in c/Ambrosio de Morales there's another branch of the *Sociedad Plateros* chain (see opposite) with more good tapas.

Bar Miguelito Acera Pintada 8, across the river near the Torre de la Calahorra. *Barrio* bar slightly off the tourist beat which is locally reputed for its tapas range and its *gambas* house special. Entertaining *terraza* with babies in prams and nattering clientele.

Bar-Mesón Rafaé c/Deanes 2. North of the Mezquita in the Judería, this pleasant old bar offers a broad tapas range, well-kept Montilla and a reasonably priced *menú*.

Bodega Guzmán c/Judíos 7, close to the synagogue. Cavernous old bar frequented by bullfight aficionados, with a small *taurino* "museum" in its inner sanctum and outstanding *amargoso* Montilla served from a butt behind the bar.

Casa Pepe de la Judería c/Romero 1. Quality, sparkling tapas bar that has expanded into the restaurant business and has a fine terrace. In their stand-up bar, house specials include *salmorejo* and *solomillo de venado* (venison).

Casa Rubio Puerta de Almodóvar 5, in the city wall. Atmospheric and popular local bar with Mezquita-inspired decor, tempting tapas range – try *berenjenas con miel* (aubergine with honey) and *ensaladilla* – and excellent Montilla. Restaurant upstairs. *Casa Bravo*, a few steps away and serving equally good tapas, is also worth a visit.

Casa Salinas Puerta de Almodóvar s/n. Stacked with butts holding its celebrated Montillas, this bar has long-standing flamenco traditions – well-known practitioners often meet up here and impromptu *juergas* can result.

El Olivo Avda. Dr Fleming 25, close to the Plaza Maimonides. Inviting little bar-restaurant with a very pleasant evening terrace which is just the place for enjoying a few tapas.

Around the Plaza del Potro

Bodegas Campos c/Lineros 32. Large *bodega* with great oak barrels (many signed by celebrities including British premier Tony Blair) stacked up in the *sacristía* cellar at the rear. The bar at the entrance sells their own excellent Montilla, there are pricey tapas *on* offer, plus an expensive, highly rated – and rather snooty – restaurant behind.

Taberna El Potro c/Lineros 2, slightly north of Plaza del Potro. Somewhat over-adorned with reproductions of Julio Romero de Torres's "art works" but serving tasty tapas, *platos combinados* and a *menú*.

Bodega Sociedad Plateros c/San Francisco 6. Headquarters of the *Plateros* chain, and in a converted former convent. What started out in 1868 as a mutual benefit society for the workers in Córdoba's silversmith trade eventually branched out into the *bodega* business, presently owning three (reduced from nine in recent years) excellent bars around the city. This bar – now over a century old and serving a wide range of tapas – is light and airy with a glass-covered patio complemented by hanging plants and *azulejos*.

Around and north of Plaza Tendillas

Bar Gaudí Avda. Gran Capitán 22, near El Corte Inglés. Named after the great architect and aptly decorated in Art Nouveau style, this place serves tapas and a wide range of European beers.

Casa del Abuelo Plaza de San Miguel 9, close to the church of San Miguel. Good and ancient tapas tavern popular with students. The house special is *berenjenas fritas* (fried aubergine); *lomo al abuelo* (pork) and *patatas a lo pobre* are also tasty.

Casa Paco Acedo Beneath the Torre de Malmuerta. Fine old bar serving up a superb range of tapas, including *salmorejo* and all kinds of fried fish. The house speciality is a memorable oxtail, the perfect complement to the house Montilla, and best eaten at the tables outside.

Taberna Góngora c/Torres Cabrera 4, northeast of Plaza San Miguel. Welcoming modern bar carrying on the tapas tradition and much favoured by *tapeadores*. Specials include *carne de monte* (cured meats) and *boquerones al limón* (anchovies with lemon).

Taberna San Miguel Plaza San Miguel 1, behind the church. Known to all as *El Pisto* (the barrel) and virtually unchanged for over a century, this is one of the city's legendary bars and not to

be missed. Wonderful Montilla and tapas; *rabo de toro* (oxtail) and *callos en salsa picante* (tripe in a spicy sauce) are big favourites. Closed Aug.

Around Plaza Corredera and beyond

Bar Regina Plaza de Regina, slightly northeast of Plaza Corredera. Century-old bar with plenty of bullfight memorabilia, a nice patio and good tapas, including their noted *patatas bravas*.

Casa El Juramento c/Juramento 6, on east side of Plaza Corredera (go north along c/Toril and turn left). Atmospheric bar with a charming patio and a good tapas selection. House specials include *calamares en salsa* and *revuelto*.

Casa Julián (aka *Casa Castillo*) c/El Realejo 10. Friendly *barrio* bar built around an airy patio, and serving fine Montilla and a hearty *salmorejo*.

Casa La Paloma Plaza Corredera 5. A good and economical bar on this atmospheric enclosed square serving vegetarian dishes, *raciones*, soups and fish.

El Gallo c/María Cristina 6, close to the Roman temple. Fine old *cordobés* drinking hole which has changed little since it opened at the turn of the (twentieth) century. Good tapas selection includes *cangrejo* (crab), *calamares*, *bacalao* (cod), *croquetas* and *gambas rebozadas* (fried prawns). The excellent *amargoso* Montilla comes from their own *bodega* and is reckoned by experts to be the finest there is.

Sociedad Plateros c/María Auxiliadora 25, close to the old city wall on the northeast side of town. Aficionados of the *Plateros* chain will enjoy this cavernous old mini-Mezquita serving up excellent *raciones* and *medias* (half *raciones*). Some way from the centre, it's definitely worth the walk, with a couple of nice churches to see along the way.

Taberna Salinas c/Tundidores 3. Century-old *taberna* with dining rooms around a charming patio and an outstanding range of *raciones*; try their delicious *bacalao con naranja* (cod with orange and olive oil) or *setas en salsa* (mushrooms).

Flamenco, nightlife and discos

Outside Semana Santa and the annual fiesta at the end of May, the city's nightlife centres around bars and restaurants. The only **late-night drinking** you are likely to find is in the north of the city, where the bars in the El Brillante district and around Avenida Tejares, Avenida Gran Capitán and those near the provincial government building in c/Reyes Católicos tend to stay open after midnight. Córdoba's best nonmembership **flamenco** *tablao* is *Tablao Cardenal*, c/Torrijos 10, next door to the Turismo (Mon–Sat 10.30pm; €19, includes first drink; ☎957 48 33 20, ⓦwww.tablaocardenal.com), where you can catch performances by established artists in a pleasant open-air patio, and reserve a table in advance. Also good is *La Bulería*, c/Pedro López 3, near Plaza de la Corredera, open from 10pm every night (performance starts 10.30pm; €11.00, includes first drink; they also serve food). The singer El Calli and his family are the core of the show, and get near enough to the real thing, although corners are sometimes cut when trade is slack. Free flamenco performances are also mounted by the local council in summer and various other concerts are staged at the Gran Teatro, Avda. Gran Capitan 3, and in the Alcázar gardens (details from the Turismos).

In summer the *marcha nocturna* moves out of town to the **El Brillante** suburb (northwest of Plaza de Colón). Here a whole *barrio* of **disco-bares** and music venues line the main road and are jammed to capacity at weekends. For the heart of the action, head for **El Tablero**, a lively plaza. Winter nightlife centres on the **Ciudad Jardín** zone between c/Albeniz (top left of our map) and the bullring a few blocks further west and the streets to the south of c/Antonio Maura, in a quarter with plenty of music and drinking bars favoured by Córdoba's student set. Popular long-standing bars here include *Galía* in c/Alcalde Cruz de Ceballos and the Lilliputian but lively *Salsaya* in c/de los Alderetes.

Conventional **discotecas** are in the centre of town around c/Cruz Conde, north of Plaza Tendillas. *QU*, c/Góngora 10, *Zahira*, c/Conde de Robledo 1, playing Latin and rock until the early hours, and *Paralelo 22* at c/José Cruz Conde 19 just off the Ronda de Tejares are all possibilities. There are also plenty of popular *bares de copas* in this area, among them *Magister Cervecerías Artesanas*, c/Moreira 12, which is huge, old and serves a wide variety of beers, and *Planetario*, c/de Munda, at the junction with c/Reloj to the southeast of Plaza de las Tendillas, a dark, hippyish drinking den. *Jazz Café* c/Espartería s/n, close to the northwest corner of Plaza de la Corredera, is another popular venue staging frequent live jazz performers, while nearby *Soul* c/Alfonso XIII 3, with a wide variety of sounds, is also good. A more spacious disco is *Budú*, on the Carretera de Trassiera – the continuation of Avenida Mozárabes at the top of our city map.

Shopping

Córdoba is known for silver jewellery and embossed leather goods both on offer at many workshops in the streets around the Mezquita; for the former – particularly filigree silver jewellery – try the Zoco in c/de los Judios close the synagogue, while Meryan in the tiny Calleja de las Flores has a wide selection of leather goods.

A remarkable century-old **hat** shop, Sombrería Rusi (founded 1903), c/Conde de Cardenas 1, near the Roman temple, is still making hats by hand on site and stocks a wide range of headwear including the flat-topped *cordobés* style worn by men at fiesta times. Nearby, at Cuesta Lujan 4, Sukia is an entertaining used clothing and retro store with all kinds of accessories and bric-a-brac from the later twentieth century. Almacen Rafael, c/Dr Marañon s/n, to the northeast of the Alcázar, is a well-stocked *bodega* selling most of Córdoba's wines. Stylish jewellery is on sale at Nucra, c/Lucano 22, to the east of the Mezquita, who fabricate their own designs using silver, stone, onyx and ebony. A number of similar shops are located nearby in the same street. Córdoba's branch of the El Corte Inglés department store is on Avenida del Gran Capitán, at the junction with Avenida Ronda de los Tejares.

The twice-weekly **market** sells a wide variety of clothes, food and hardware, and takes place in the El Jardín barrio, along Avenida Gran Vía Parque west of the old quarter, on Tuesday and Friday mornings.

Listings

Banks Numerous banks with ATMs are located along Ronda de los Tejares and Avda. del Gran Capitán. In the Judería there are ATMs in c/Magistral González Francés near the Mezquita and along c/Judería, off its northwest corner.

Bullfights Get details and tickets (the May *feria* has the best *corridas*) from the Plaza de Toros, Avda. Gran Vía Parque ☎957 23 13 69.

Buses and trains Contact Alsina Graells, Estación de Autobuses, Plaza de las Tres Culturas (☎957 27 81 00), for buses to Sevilla, Granada, Málaga, Almería, Cádiz, Jaén and the Costa del Sol. Get details of services to all other destinations from the bus station information desk (☎957 40 40 40). Train information is available from RENFE, Plaza de las Tres Culturas (☎902 40 02 02, ⟨w⟩www .renfe.com).

Car rental Europcar (☎957 40 34 80) and Hertz (☎957 40 20 60) have offices on the train station concourse; Avis, Plaza de Colón 35 ☎957 47 68 62.

Football After five years in the Segunda División, C.F.Córdoba were relegated in 2005 following a poor season. Details and tickets for matches are obtainable from the stadium, El Nuevo Arcángel (☎957 75 19 34, ⟨w⟩www.cordobacf.com), on the east bank of the river.

Hospital Hospital Reina Sofía, Avda. Menendez Pidal s/n (☎957 01 00 00) to the southwest of the centre. Cruz Roja, Avda. del Dr Fleming s/n (☎957 29 34 11); for emergencies dial ☎061.

Hiking maps 1:50,000, 1:100,000 and 1:200,000 maps are available from CNIG (National Geographic Service) branch office: c/Santo Tomás de Aquino 1–6º (☎957 23 35 46). Librería Luque (see "Press and books") is another option.

Internet *Navegaweb* (daily 10am–10pm) inside the Albergue Juvenil (youth hostel; see "Accommodation"); Ch@t, (Mon–Sat 10am–2pm & 5–9.30pm) c/Claudio Marcelo 15, near Plaza Tendillas; *Hostal El Pilar del Potro* (daily 10am–1pm & 5–10pm) c/Lucano 12; *Mundo Digital* (daily 10.30am–2pm), c/del Osario 9, near Plaza de Colón.

Laundry Seco y Agua, c/Dr Marañon 3, slightly northwest of the Alcazár (Mon–Fri 9.30am–1.30pm & 5.30–8.30pm, Sat 9.30am–1.30pm; ☎957 20 35 51), is an efficient *tintorería* who will wash, dry and fold 5kg of clothes the same day for around €14. Telesecco, Ronda de Isasa 10 (☎957 48 33 56), facing the river southeast of the Mezquita, offers a similar service.

Police A local police station is located in Plaza Judá Levi, near the Mezquita (☎957 29 07 60). For emergencies dial ☎092 (local police), ☎091 (national).

Post office The main office is at c/Cruz Conde 15 (just north of Plaza Tendillas) and is also the place for poste restante. Mon–Fri 8.30am–8.30pm; Sat 9am–2pm.

Press and books Córdoba's daily paper, *El Diario Córdoba* (⟨w⟩www.diariocordoba.com), is good for local and provincial news, events and entertainment. For a good selection of books and walking maps try Librería Luque, c/José Cruz Conde 19 (near Plaza Tendillas). English and foreign press is also available from Kiosko Fidela, c/Blanco Belmonte 10, slightly north of the Mezquita.

Travel agents Viajes Halcon, Ronda de los Tejares 8 (☎957 47 10 69), and Rutas y Ocio, c/Manual de Sandoval 4, off the north end of c/José Cruz Conde (☎957 47 06 94), are useful for all kinds of tickets and information.

West of Córdoba

Just a few kilometres from the city is the historic site of **Medina Azahara**, a must for those on the Moorish trail, and with a fascinating eighteenth-century hermitage nearby. Continuing west, along the southern fringes of the Sierra Morena, following the Río Guadalquivir, there's a remarkable castle at **Almodóvar del Río**, a string of charming rural towns and Cordoba province's largest natural park, the **Parque Natural de la Sierra de Hornachuelos**.

Medina Azahara

Some 7km to the west of Córdoba lie the vast and rambling ruins of **Medina Azahara**, a palace and administrative complex built on a dream scale by **Caliph Abd ar-Rahman III**. Naming it after a favourite wife, az-Zahra (the Radiant), he spent one-third of the annual state budget on its construction each year

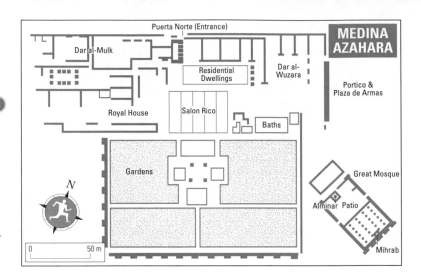

from 936 until his death in 961. Since the first archeological excavations were carried out in 1911, work has been going on more or less continuously to piece together the fragments of this once fabulous creation, which is the reason it is currently only possible to visit a fraction of the excavated site.

The site

The **site** (April–Sept Tues–Sat 10am–8.30pm, Sun 10am–2pm; Oct–March Tues–Sat 10am–2pm & 5–6.30pm, Sun 10am–1.30pm; check winter hours with site; ☎957 32 91 30; €1.50, free with EU passport) is entered by the **Puerta Norte**, the typically Moorish "twisted gate" which forced would-be invaders to double back on themselves, thus making them easy targets. Behind you at this point lies the Dar al-Mulk or royal palace (currently not open to visitors) which is thought to have been the residence of Abd ar-Rahman III. The signed route leads to **Dar al-Wuzara** (House of the Viziers, aka Edificio Basilical), believed to have been the bureaucratic heart of the complex with administrative rooms, archives and a grand salon (with reconstructed horseshoe arches), originally fronted by a patio, now a garden. To the east of here, the route leads to the elegant arched **portico** and the **Plaza de Armas** – formerly a grand parade ground – beyond, still awaiting excavation. The portico is thought to have supported a balcony terrace from where the caliph reviewed his troops. Turning south, you can see the **great mosque** below, one of the first buildings to be constructed on the site, oriented towards the southeast and Mecca. Its ground plan allows you to make out the main entrance, flanked by the base of a minaret (*alminar*), with patio, prayer hall – the floor of which was covered with esparto mats found in the excavations – and *mihrab*. The route now veers west passing the princely baths to the right, presently being painstakingly restored by archeologists repairing washing fountains and marble surfaces, beyond which lay the royal apartments.

For centuries, the site was looted for building materials; parts, for instance, were used in the Sevilla Alcázar and much of the surrounding town served as a quarry for the fifteenth-century construction of the monastery of San

The rise and fall of Medina Azahara

Ten thousand workers and 1500 mules and camels were employed in the construction of **Medina Azahara** in the early tenth century, and the site, almost 2000m long by 900m wide, stretched over three descending terraces above the Guadalquivir valley. Roman masonry was taken from sites throughout Andalucía and reused, whilst vast quantities of marble were shipped in from North Africa. In addition to the palace buildings, the complex contained a zoo, an aviary, four huge fish ponds, 300 baths, 400 houses, weapons factories, two barracks for the royal guard as well as numerous baths, markets, workshops and mosques. Visitors, so the chronicles record, were stunned by its wealth and brilliance: one conference room contained a pile of pure crystals, creating a rainbow when lit by the sun; another was built round a huge shallow bowl of mercury which, when the sun's rays fell on it, would be rocked by a slave, sending sunbeams reflected from its surface flashing and whizzing around the room, apparently alarming guests but greatly amusing the caliph.

Medina Azahara was a perfect symbol of the western caliphate's dominance and greatness, but it was to last for less than a century. **Al-Hakam II**, who succeeded Abd ar-Rahman, lived in the palace, continued to endow it, and enjoyed a stable reign. However, distanced from the city, he delegated more and more authority, particularly to his vizier Ibn Abi Amir, later known as **al-Mansur** (the Victor). In 976 al-Hakam was succeeded by his eleven-year-old son Hisham II but after a series of sharp moves al-Mansur assumed the full powers of government, keeping Hisham virtually imprisoned at Medina Azahara, to the extent of blocking up connecting passageways between the palace buildings.

Al-Mansur was equally skilful and manipulative in his wider dealings as a dictator, and Córdoba rose to new heights of prosperity, retaking large tracts of central Spain and raiding as far afield as Galicia and Catalunya. But with his death in 1002 came swift decline as his role and function were assumed in turn by his two sons. The first died in 1008; the second, Sanchol, showed open disrespect for the caliphate by forcing Hisham to appoint him as his successor. At this a popular revolt broke out and the caliphate disintegrated into civil war and a series of feudal kingdoms. Medina Azahara was looted by a mob at the outset and in 1010 was plundered and burned by retreating Berber mercenaries – splashes of molten metal from this conflagration are still to be seen in the Salon Rico. The ruins slowly disappeared under the earth until archeologists arrived at the site in the early twentieth century. But it was never secure and as late as the 1930s a visiting Gerald Brenan saw stones being carted off to service other buildings. In the 1960s academic study, excavation and reconstruction of the complex began in earnest, and this is set to continue for many decades to come.

Jerónimo (now privately owned) at the end of the track which climbs above the ruins. In 1944, however, excavations unearthed the buried materials from a crucial part of the palace, the **Royal House**, where guests were received and meetings of ministers held. This has been meticulously reconstructed and, though still fragmentary, its main hall, the **Salón Rico de Abd al-Rahman III**, decorated with exquisite marble carvings, must rank among the greatest of all Moorish rooms. Modelled on the Roman basilica, it has a different kind of artistic representation from that found in the palaces at Granada or Sevilla – closer to natural and animal forms in its intricate Syrian Hom (Tree of Life) motifs. Unlike the later Spanish Arab dynasties, the Berber Almoravids and the Almohads of Sevilla, the caliphal Andalucians were little worried by Islamic strictures on the portrayal of nature, animals or even men – the beautiful stag in the Córdoba museum is a good example (see p.440) – and it may well have been this aspect of the palace's artistic decor that led to such

△ Medina Azahara

zealous destruction during the civil war. The reconstructed palace gives a scale and focus to the site, while elsewhere work continues in restoring and rebuilding more ruined structures. Beyond these there are little more than foundations, gardens and the odd horseshoe arch to fuel your imaginings, amid an awesome area of ruins, hidden beneath bougainvillea and rustling with cicadas.

A decade ago biologists from Córdoba University carried out a study of soil samples from the site to gain an understanding of exactly which plants and flowers the Moors had cultivated in the extensive gardens. When the study was completed, planting began in an attempt to reconstruct the gardens of Medina Azahara as accurately as possible. The planted trees, shrubs, plants and herbs are now maturing into a delightful and aromatic garden the caliphs would recognize.

Practicalities

To reach Medina Azahara, follow the Avenida de Medina Azahara out of town, and on to the road to Villarubia and Posadas. About 4km out of town, make a right turn, after which it's another three kilometres to the site. Alternatively, the #01 city **bus** from the stop on the Paseo de la Victoria (almost opposite the *Meliá* hotel) will drop you off at the intersection for the final three-kilometre walk. Ask the driver for the "Cruz de Medina Azahara". A **dedicated bus service** also links the city with the site (daily Tues–Fri 11am, Sat, Sun & hols 10am & 11am; €5 round trip) departing from the same stop as the Córdoba Vision trips. Córdoba Vision runs guided trips to the site (April–Sept Tues–Sat 6pm, Sun 10.30am; Oct–March Tues–Sat 4pm, Sun 10.30am; €10; ☏957 76 02 41, English spoken); buses leave from a stop on the Avda. del Alcázar, below the Alcázar. A **taxi** will cost you about €15 one-way or there's a special round-trip fare of €30, which includes a one-hour wait at the site (details from tourist offices). With your own transport an atmospheric **place to eat** near the site is *Bar-Restaurante El Cruce* – with a leafy terrace and often serving *jabalí* (wild boar) – a 3km climb from the signed junction on the way to the entrance.

Las Ermitas

A scenic signed road climbs for 4km beyond the *Bar-Restaurante El Cruce* to **Las Ermitas** (Tues–Sun 10am–1.30pm & 5.30–8.30pm; Oct–March closes 6.30pm; €1.50), a beautiful jasmine-scented hermitage filled with cypresses, olives and cacti. Here you can see twelve cells dating from the eighteenth century – spaced out around a central shrine – where hermit monks once flagellated themselves in splendid isolation. These hills were inhabited by hermits from the earliest days of Christianity through the Visigothic and Muslim periods and solitaries occupied the hermitage until as recently as 1957. There are dramatic **views** over the valley of the Guadalquivir from the *mirador* of the giant cross, La Cruz del Humilladero.

Almodóvar del Río and around

If you have your own transport, it's possible to continue a further 17km west along the A431 to **ALMODÓVAR DEL RÍO**, where an impressive multi-turreted **castle** (Mon–Fri 11am–2.30pm & 4–8pm, Sat–Sun 11am–8pm; Oct–March closes 7pm; €5, free entry Wed afternoon with EU passport) sits on a hill high above the town dominating the landscape. Dating originally from the eighth century, and significantly expanded by Abd al–Rahman II in the ninth, the fortress underwent many later additions and restorations, most of them following its fall to the Christian army of Fernando III in 1240. Today the castle is privately owned by the Marqués de Motilla. It's easy to find your way up to the castle from the town – a pleasant walk – or, with transport, follow signs and ascend the unpaved track and park by the castle walls. There's little to see in the over-restored interior but there are fine **views** from the battlements over the valley of the Guadalquivir; watch your step as there are no handrails. Almodóvar is served by at least five daily **buses** from Córdoba.

Ten kilometres further west along the A431, a turn on the right (the A2212) leads after 8km to **HORNACHUELOS**, the gateway village to the extensive **Parque Natural de la Sierra de Hornachuelos**, a heavily wooded area on the lower slopes of the Sierra Morena. The park is home to a wide variety of wildlife including the threatened Iberian lynx, as well as deer, wild boar and, in the river valleys, otters. A zone rich in birdlife, Andalucía's second largest colony of black vultures also resides here. On the way through the village a **Turismo** (Fri–Sun 8am–3pm, ☎957 64 07 86) is signed on the right and can provide information on the park as well as a map. Heading into the park along the A2212, two kilometres beyond Hornachuelos and signed on the left, the **Centro de Visitantes Huerta del Rey** (Mon–Fri 10am–2pm & 4–7pm, Sat 10am–7pm; ☎957 64 11 40) is the park's main information centre. It lies in woods beyond the car park, a couple of hundred metres distant. The centre has informative displays on the park's flora and fauna and can provide maps and information on numerous waymarked walking routes. A good-value **place to stay** in Hornachuelos is *Bar-Casa Alejandro* (☎957 64 00 98; ❶), Avda. del Guadalquivir 4, on the village's southern edge; it offers en-suite rooms above an inexpensive bar-restaurant with a daily *menú*.

Continuing west along the A431, at **PALMA DEL RÍO**, a small farming town 20km east of Almodóvar del Río, you can **stay** the night in a converted fifteenth-century monastery. *Hospedería de San Francisco*, Avda. Pío XII 35 (☎957 71 01 83, ℻957 71 02 36; ❻), preserves much of the former monastic tranquillity with a charming cloister, now a patio. The excellent Basque-inspired **restaurant** has a *menú*, or you could have a drink in the monastic bar furnished with stone benches and antique paintings.

South of Córdoba – the Campiña

To the south of Córdoba, and stretching to the mountains of the province's southern border, lies the **Campiña Cordobesa**. A fertile, undulating region of

The Vía Verde

The decline of the railway in this part of Andalucía has had a beneficial knock-on effect for walkers and cyclists. The old line of the *Tren de Aceite* (olive oil train) which was closed in the 1980s has now been transformed into a rambling and biking route linking the towns and villages of Puente Genil, Lucena, Cabra, Doña Mencía, Zuheros and Luque with a further extension planned to the east. Some of the stations along the route have been transformed into bars, restaurants and information centres. There are two outdoor activity centres and at its eastern end the route passes La Laguna del Conde (aka Laguna Salobral), the largest lagoon in the Subbética with a wealth of birdlife and its own information centre. The Centro de Interpretación for the whole project is located in Cabra (see p.455).

wheatfields, olive groves and productive vineyards, it has been renowned since Roman times when the eminent Roman writers Pliny and Martial praised its artichokes, fruit, wool and the excellence of its olive oil. The town of **Baena** keeps up the tradition with an oil so good that it carries an official *denominación de origen* label. Each of the villages of the Campiña has its own interesting castle, church, palace or Roman villa and sometimes a *bodega* – and there are towns such as **Priego de Córdoba**, a Baroque architectural feast and well off the tourist trail, that are undiscovered jewels. The two itineraries described here roughly follow the **bus routes** from Córdoba to Málaga and Granada respectively, making it easy to stop off along the way, as even the smallest villages usually have a *fonda* or *hostal* to provide a **bed** for the night. This opens up the possibility of **walks** exploring some of the Campiña's delightful countryside including – in its lower reaches – the **Parque Natural de las Sierras Subbéticas,** replete with wooded hills and river valleys. Obviously, your own transport – and a little zigzagging and backtracking – would allow you to combine both routes. Many of the tourist offices in this zone stock a free bilingual booklet *La Subbética Senderismo Guide* detailing fourteen walks in the park.

The Ruta del Vino

This itinerary leaves Córdoba by the A4 and, after 14km, forks left along the N331 towards Fernán Núñez, a pleasant hill village a further 14km down the road. Among a number of interesting places along this route are **Montilla**, the centre of Córdoba's wine production, and **Rute**, where *anís*, a far stronger brew, is concocted. The itinerary ends at the beautiful lakeside village of **Iznájar** in the midst of some good trekking country.

Montemayor

Just beyond the village of Fernán Núñez is **MONTEMAYOR**, a charming and typical *campiña* village with a fourteenth-century **castle**. In the centre of its neat little plaza, there's an amusing copy of the Alhambra's fountain of the lions in Granada. More interesting is the sixteenth-century church of **Nuestra Señora de la Asunción** with a beautifully painted stucco *sagrario* and a sixteenth-century carved baptismal font, still used to initiate the newborn of the parish. You'll need to find the priest, Padre Pablo Moyano, to open the church and he may well be in the *casino*, a fine old institution across the square. If you ask, he will also let you see his personal **archeological collection** (official hours daily 9–10.30am & 6.30–8pm; free), kept in a vault beneath the church and for which he is famous for miles around. This enormous accumulation of artefacts includes coins, agricultural implements, grindstones, jewellery and sculpture – most of it from Ulia, as Montemayor was in Roman times – and has been collected on his walks over the years in the surrounding fields. Close to the village on the N331, there are **rooms** at *Hotel El Artista*, Carretera Córdoba–Málaga s/n (☏957 37 50 69, ⓦwww.juanelartista.com; ❸), which is friendly, efficient and has a good-value **restaurant**.

La Rambla

With your own transport, a detour to the right off the N331 on Montemayor's southern edge climbs 4km to the hill-top pottery centre of **LA RAMBLA**. It is famed for the production of spouted drinking jars called *botijos* which, due to their method of fabrication, keep water ice-cold in furnace temperatures. You can buy them at various workshops lining the road into town. The church of the **Colegio de Espíritu Santo** is worth a visit for its fine sculpture of Christ in pine and cedar by the eighteenth-century maestro, Juan de Mesa. Nearby and close to the *parroquía* church of La Asunción is a mildly interesting **Museo de Ceramica** (April–Sept Mon–Fri 10am–2pm & 9pm–midnight; free) detailing the history of pottery in the town.

Montilla

The main N331 presses on into the Sierra de Montilla and endless rows of vines begin to creep across the landscape as you enter Córdoba's **wine-producing region**. The tough Pedro-Ximénez vines planted here have to withstand searing summer temperatures, and send their roots deep down into the whitish-grey *albariza* soil searching for moisture. Eleven kilometres beyond Montemayor, **MONTILLA**, the capital of Córdoba's wine country, comes into view. Hardly the region's prettiest town, you may want to call in, however, to visit one of

Montilla–Moriles: no hangover guaranteed

The Romans and later the Moors (in spite of the Prophet's prohibition) developed the Campiña as a **wine region**. The great wine of Córdoba, **Montilla** (often called Montilla-Moriles, the latter village being its partner in production to the south) has suffered over the years from comparison with the wines of Jerez, with which it shares similar characteristics. The reasons for this are largely historical as, prior to the 1940s, much of Córdoba's vintage was sold to the great *fino* houses of Jerez and eventually marketed as sherry. In 1944 this was made illegal, since when Montilla has been granted its own *denominación*, but the notion that the wines of this region are merely a less expensive alternative to sherry has been a tag that the industry here has found hard to shake off.

The most visual difference in the production of Montilla is the great **tinajas** – huge, earthenware urns in which the wine undergoes its fermentation. These Ali-Baba jars, the direct descendants of the Roman *dolium*, have pointed ends which are buried in the earth inside the *bodegas* and are believed to impart a unique character to the wine. As in Jerez the wine in these great vats also develops a *flor* (a thick layer of yeast) which covers the narrow neck of the urns. Later, the *solera* system (see p.275), during which the wine is aged and blended in oak butts for two years, is used to finish the process. The response you get around these parts should you bring up the subject of comparisons with the *finos* of Jerez is the assertion that Montilla is a natural product, whilst the wines of Jerez need to have their alcohol added. The Pedro-Ximénez grape used for Montilla is baked in the furnace heat of the Campiña sun and produces wines of 16 percent proof which, the *bodegas* here like to claim – unlike that synthetic *jerezano* – never give you a hangover.

the leading **bodegas**, Alvear SA, Avda. María Auxiliadora 1 (visits and tastings Mon–Sat at 12.30pm €2.95 weekdays, €3.95 Sat; shop open Mon–Sat 10am–2pm; ☎957 66 40 14), a picturesque place founded in the eighteenth century. Next door to the *Barril del Oro* (see below), Tonelería Duran is a *despacho de vinos* stocking all the town's (and province's) major wines.

Almost opposite the *bodega*, the *Barril del Oro*, Avda. de Andalucía 22, makes a good place to stop for **tapas**; try their *flamenquines* (stuffed rolls of veal and *jamón serrano*). The excellent Montilla served here comes not from the *bodega* over the road, but is bought in by the *patrón* from his own favourite growers. A very good in-town tapas and *raciones* restaurant is *La Chiva*, c/San Francisco Solano 42, just down the street from the *Hotel Los Felipes* (see below) which also has a weekday *menú* for €7.50. The medium-priced *Restaurante Camachas* (☎957 65 06 58; main dishes €11–20), on the main road at the entrance to the town, is also recommended – specialities here include the delicious *pez espada a la montillana* (swordfish with a Montilla sauce) and *perdiz a la campiña* (partridge) – and there's a good-value *menú* for around €10. If you want **to stay**, rooms are available at the central if rather dour *Hotel Los Felipes*, c/San Francisco Solano 27 (☎957 65 04 96, Ⓦwww.hotel-losfelipes.com; ❸), or the more inviting and nearby *Hostal Bellido* (☎957 65 19 15, Ⓦwww.hostalbellido .com; ❸), a newish place housed in an elegant refurbished mansion. Alternatively, *Hotel Don Gonzalo*, Ctra. Córdoba–Málaga (☎957 65 06 58, Ⓕ957 65 06 66; ❹), is an upmarket option with pool on the A45 (the N331's continuation), to the south of the town.

Aguilar and the Laguna de Zóñar

AGUILAR, 7km further south, perched on top of a hill, is worth a visit to see its wonderful eighteenth-century octagonal plaza of **San José**, probably inspired by the better-maintained one at Archidona in Málaga. The rest of the town is equally charming, its sloping streets lined with white-walled houses, their windows protected by *rejas*, or iron grilles. From the **Torre del Reloj**, a Baroque clock tower and local landmark, there are excellent views over the Campiña. At the top of the Cuesta de Jesús, the sixteenth-century **Santa María del Soterraño** (open service times 7–9pm), with an *artesonado* Mudéjar ceiling, Plateresque doorway and an impressive *sagrario* with a sculpture of Christ in a *camarín* by Donaire Trexo, is Aguilar's best church.

At the foot of this hill, the **Turismo**, Cuesta de Jesús 2 (daily 10am–2pm; ☎957 66 15 67) can provide information on the town and the Sierra Subetica. If you're looking for **accommodation**, the central *Hostal-Restaurante Queen*, c/Pescadería 6 (☎957 66 02 22; ❸), just off the Plaza de San José, has decent a/c en-suite rooms with satellite TV. Aguilar's best **place to eat** is *La Casona*, on the edge of town along the Puente Genil road, with large helpings, reasonable prices and a *menú* for €8.

Some 4km southwest of Aguilar along the A309 and easily walkable, the **Laguna de Zóñar** is the largest of a group of little-known inland salt lakes. Visited in winter by large numbers of **migrating waterfowl**, this time of the year is best for spotting white-headed duck, a species that once almost disappeared but is now on the increase. Other species that can be seen here include red-crested pochard, mallard, great-crested grebe, tufted duck and marsh harrier. In summer there's less to see, although sometimes flamingos fly in from the Fuente de Piedra in nearby Málaga, for a change of scene. There are observation **hides** as well as an **information centre** (April–Sept daily 10am–1.30pm & 5–7pm; ☎957 33 52 52). You can gain access to routes around the lake and the hides when the centre is closed. Other lakes in this group include the Laguna del Rincón, north of Moriles, and the Laguna de Tiscar, north of Puente Genil, both of which, unlike this one, tend to dry up in summer.

Cabra

At Monturque, 9km south of Aguilar, there's a turn-off to Moriles, the other great Montilla name but in truth a dull village, and only to be sought out if you're a wine aficionado. Much more rewarding is the A342 road which heads 12km east from Monturque to **CABRA**, another pleasant Campiña town. Possessing an old quarter with steep, winding streets lined with *rejas* – many holding pots sprouting colourful geraniums in summer – and a number of Baroque mansions, it's a lovely place to wander for an hour or so, or even stop over. At the end of the town, near the castle, the Baroque **Iglesia de la Asuncíon** (☎957 52 01 10 to view), built over a mosque, is surrounded by palms and cypresses. It has a fine portal with twisted marble Solomonic pillars, and inside, an altar of red and black jasper together with fine choir stalls. The church of **San Juan Bautista** (open service times) in the old quarter – Visigothic in origin but much altered since – is reckoned to be one of Spain's oldest, with Moorish and Baroque features added. The *Casa de Cultura*, c/Martín Belda 27, has a small **tourist office** (Mon–Fri 10am–1.30pm & 5–7.30pm, Sat & Sun 11am–2pm; ☎957 52 01 10) who can supply a town map plus information on a host of *casas rurales* to rent in the surrounding sierra; in the same building there's a modest **archeological museum** with local finds from the prehistoric, Visigothic, Roman and Moorish periods. Opposite the tourist office, *Ciberia*, c/Santa Rosalla 5 (daily 11am–2.30pm & 5.30–11.30pm) has **Internet** access. Just to the north of the central Parque Alcantara Romero the town's ancient **Plaza de Toros**, built in 1857, is also worth a look.

On the road leading east out of town towards Priego de Córdoba, there's a wooded picnic and swimming area, **La Fuente del Río**, centred around a natural spring which is the source of the Río Cabra. Seven kilometres beyond this, a road on the left climbs 6km to the **Ermita de la Virgen de la Sierra**, a hermitage sited at an altitude of over 1200m from where there are stupendous **views** west towards the valley of the Guadalquivir, and east to the mountains of the Sierra Nevada. This is also the start point for a hike to Zuheros. Cabra's former railway station, 500m before the Fuente del Río and signed on the left, has been transformed into the **Centro de Interpretación** (Mon–Fri 10am–4pm, Sat–Sun ring ☎957 52 27 77, mobile ☎686319191) for the Vía Verde (see p.452) and has information on walking and cycling (mountain bikes can be hired) along the route; the building also houses a cafetería and **museum** – complete with an original steam engine from the *Tren de Aceite* (oil train) – documenting the history of the line.

Places to stay in Cabra are usually easy to come by; you could try the very friendly ♨ *Pensión Guerrero*, c/Pepita Jiménez 7 (☎957 52 05 07, ☏957 52 03 41; ❸), with en-suite rooms with TV, close to the Parque Alcantara Romero (a tree-lined garden in the centre); it also has its own restaurant for guests. Alternatively, on the outskirts along the A316 heading towards Baena, a newcomer, the *Hotel Fuente Las Piedras* (☎957 52 97 40, ✉fuentelaspiedras@mshoteles .com; ❺ with breakfast) is an upmarket possibility with its own restaurant and tempting garden pool.

There are numerous bars and **places to eat** around the town; the best is *Mesón El Vizconde*, c/Martín Belda 16 (☎957 52 17 02; main dishes €9–25), where the *fritura de pescado* and *merluza con salsa de puerros* (hake in leek sauce) are outstanding; there's also a less expensive *menú* for around €10. *La Despensa Malagueña*, c/José Solis 71, near the Ayuntamiento is another more economical option for *andaluz*, Basque and Italian dishes and there's a *menú* at lunchtime. One of the most remarkable places to visit is Cabra's extraordinary ⅌ *Cervecería Botinero*, Avda. Fernando Pallares 3, off the south end of Parque Alcantara Romero, which stocks an amazing 500 of the world's beers, more than two hundred whiskies, a bewildering number of brandies and over three hundred wines, boasting impressive *reserva* and *gran reserva* vintages dating back to 1927. It also serves some pretty good bar meals to go with them all. The nearby c/Vado del Moro has quite a few **discotecas** (all free) which contribute to the town's surprisingly lively nightlife scene.

Lucena

Surrounded by hills covered with vines and olives, **LUCENA**, 11km down the N331 from Monturque, is a large industrial town that makes its money from furniture production and the manufacture of the great *tinajas*, or earthenware urns, used in the making of Montilla. However, once you've penetrated the rather drab outskirts, Lucena's revamped town centre is not without charm and there are a handful of sights well worth a look. A centre of learning in Moorish times, Lucena fell into Christian hands in 1240 when it was besieged by the armies of Fernando III El Santo, following which event most of its churches and other monuments were erected.

A good place to make for first is the focal **Plaza del Coso** (aka Plaza de España) overlooked by the **Castillo del Moral** whose tower, the Torre del Moral, is the surviving remnant of an earlier castle where Boabdil, the last sultan of Granada, was briefly imprisoned by Isabel la Católica in 1483. The castle now houses the tourist office and an interesting **archeological museum** (entered through the Turismo; same hours; free) which focuses on Lucena's role in Roman times as a centre of *alfarería* (pottery). The town's other major monument is the nearby church of **San Mateo** (daily 7.30am–1.15pm & 7–9.30pm; free) on the Plaza Nueva, a short walk northwest of the castle, housing one of the Baroque glories of the province. The church was started in the fifteenth century over a former mosque and has a superb Mannerist *retablo* and a beautiful eighteenth-century Baroque *sagrario*, with painted stucco cherubs and a feast of decorative detail topped off by a remarkable cupola, all the work of local artist Antonio de Castro.

If you've got an hour to spare other churches also worth a look are the seventeenth-century **Madre de Dios** (daily 10.30am–1pm & 7.30–9pm; free), reached by following c/Las Descalzas north from Plaza Nueva, where you'll find a beautiful patio cloister, and the similarly dated **San Juan Bautista** whose attached hospital – now a home for the elderly – has another picturesque patio lined with green *azulejos*.

This latter church lies at the southern end of town, beside a road leading to the **Sanctuario de Nuestra Señora de Araceli** (daily 8am–9.30pm; free), Lucena's much-venerated 900-metre-high hill-top shrine to the Virgin. The six-kilometre trip is only really worth doing if you've got your own transport, though note that at weekends and in fine weather the car park and small café at the summit are often full to bursting point. The eighteenth-century Baroque shrine has plenty of over-the-top polychrome decor and an image of the Virgin in a *camarín*. Perhaps the best reason for a trip here is the stunning **views** which, weather permitting, allow you to look out over five of Andalucía's eight provinces.

Practicalities

The Castillo del Moral houses a helpful **Turismo** (Mon 9am–2pm, Tues–Fri 9am–2pm & 5–9pm, Sat & Sun 11am–2pm & 6–8pm; ☎957 51 32 82,

@www.turlucena.com) who can provide a town map. For a **place to stay** the former eighteenth-century Convento de Nuestra Señora de la Victoria, the central *Hotel Santo Domingo*, c/Juan Jiménez Cuenca 16 (☎957 51 11 00, @www.husa.es; **⑦**) must rank as one of the most beautiful hotels in Andalucía. The convent's former cloister has been transformed into a stunning patio lounge (where non-guests can enjoy a drink) but the rather sombrely furnished rooms don't pull out quite as many stops as the public areas. A cheaper and good-value alternative is the friendly *Hotel Veracruz*, c/Veracruz 1 (☎957 50 03 00, @hotelveracruz@infonegocio.com; **④**), a couple of blocks north of the Turismo, where rooms come with air-conditioning. The best *hostal* is the welcoming *Hostal Sara*, c/Cabrillana 49 (☎957 51 61 51; **②**), a couple of blocks west of *Hotel Santo Domingo*, which offers a/c en-suite rooms and also has its own restaurant.

Lucena's size and high turnover of business travellers means that there's plenty of choice when it comes **eating and drinking** plus a bevy of good **tapas bars**. A full list of these can be obtained from the Turismo but a couple of decent central ones are *Gambrinus*, c/Montenegro 14, with plenty of *ambiente*, and the nearby *Olympo*, c/El Peso 35, which also has a restaurant. For a more formal meal the *Hotel Santo Domingo* has its own stylish restaurant with a *menú* for around €15, but a more atmospheric choice is *Restaurante Araceli*, Avenida del Parque 10 (reached by following c/El Peso eastwards from Plaza Nueva), offering a variety of dishes including fish, with a *menú* for under €10. The nearby *El Valle*, c/Federico García Lorca 14, is another good neighbourhood restaurant and tapas bar with its own *menú*. For snacks, *El Chollo* on the west side of the central Plaza Del Coso (near the Turismo) does some of the best value *bocadillos* – made to order – in the province.

Rute

The scenic N331 Málaga road continues to **Benamejí**, 20km away, a pleasant agricultural village with a couple of *fondas,* close to the provincial border. However, the more interesting route lies along the road (CP167) which turns off left 8km south of Lucena, heading towards the small town of **RUTE**. Twelve kilometres from the turn, the whitewashed town, sited picturesquely on a hill overlooked by the hazy Sierra de Rute behind, comes into view. Beyond a ruined Moorish castle and a Baroque church, it has few monuments to attract visitors and Rute's fame throughout Andalucía is based on a far more potent allure: the manufacture of a lethal **anís**, the local eau de vie, with springwater from the Sierra and, at its most potent, an undiluted (and illegal) 96 percent proof. The milder *anís seco* at 55 percent is still fierce enough, while the syrupy *anís dulce* (a mere 35 percent) is probably the safest bet. Different variations on the *anís* theme can be tasted at the twenty or so small *bodegas* scattered around the town; *Bodega Machaquita*, Paseo del Fresno 7, is regarded as one of the best.

A guided tour at the **Museo del Anís** (Mon–Fri 8.30am–2pm & 4–7pm, Sat 10am–2pm; free) on the Paseo del Fresno square will tell you all you need to know about the making of *anís* and its history, with a chance to taste and buy at the end. There's a **tourist office** in the Parque Nuestra Señora del Carmen (June–Aug Mon–Fri 10am–2pm, Sept–May 10am–2pm & 4–7pm; ☎957 53 29 29), close to the landmark Anís monument (complete with copper still) on the road through, who can provide a town map.

If you need a **place to stay**, Rute's only options are two hotels sited close to each other at the southern end of the town. The first is the comfortable *Hotel María Luisa*, Ctra. Lucena–Loja 22 (☎957 53 80 96, @www.zercahoteles.com; **④** with breakfast), on the A331 with an excellent garden pool. *Rough Guide*

Save the donkey

One of Rute's more surprising features is a **sanctuary** for ill-treated donkeys. Founded by local draper Pasqual Rovira in 1989, ADEBO (Association for the Defence of the Donkey) is Spain's first-ever donkey refuge, and well worth a visit. Spain's donkey population has shrunk dramatically from over one million fifty years ago to a current 100,000 – most of which are crossbreeds. Only a few hundred remain of the five breeds of pure Spanish *burro* that have existed on the peninsula since pre-Roman times. One of these, the *raza córdobes*, was so renowned in the eighteenth century for its strength that George Washington asked the Spanish king, Carlos III, to send him some for his farm.

Used for centuries as beasts of burden, the **donkeys** often receive brutal treatment at the hands of uncaring owners. Working with scarce resources, and using the meagre profits from the family drapery business, Pasqual and his wife Kika have devoted their lives to ending this cruelty and saving the Spanish breeds – including the *cordobés* – from extinction. They were greatly helped in this when Queen Sofía rang Pasqual in 1999 after reading about his work and offered her support, expressing a wish to visit the sanctuary. This changed everything, and previously sceptical politicians in Córdoba and Madrid became suddenly enthusiastic. For the queen's visit the Guardia Civil constructed an asphalt road up to the sanctuary – plus helicopter landing pad – in three days and the central, regional and local governments financed the construction of a state-of-the-art complex (named the Casa del Burro) to include an expanded sanctuary, donkey history museum and environmental education centre. However, the resulting steel donkey pens are unsuitable, a number of nearby *casas rurales* intended to attract tourists stand uncompleted and a swimming pool – not part of the original plan – has yet to be granted a permit to open. The museum and education centre has so far not been built and its future remains uncertain.

The work of the sanctuary continues though, and both the queen and her husband King Juan Carlos have sponsored donkeys as have the late writer Camilo José Cela, Bill Clinton (remarking that the donkey is the mascot of the Democratic Party) and Fidel Castro. At Christmas 2001, tenor Placido Domingo donated royalties from his version of the popular carol "Arre, borriquito" ("Gee up, donkey") to the centre. The strangest gesture of support, however, came when Madrid composer and animal lover Alfonso Fuster dedicted his new *Symphony for a Donkey* to the centre; it was given its first performance in the spring of 2002 when a full orchestra played it to an audience of sanctuary donkeys assembled outside their stables.

A charming and voluble *cordobés*, Pasqual has a fund of horror stories concerning the animals he's rescued: one poor beast spent five years locked up in a small shed (after arriving at the sanctuary he was christened Mandela) whilst another, a jenny named Alondra, was found abandoned halfway down a ravine with a washing machine tied around her neck. The sanctuary is open daily (9am–noon). To get there, continue uphill from the Museo de Anís in the Paseo del Fresno, following the road for the campsite. The sanctuary (☎957 53 20 32) will provide directions, or enquire at the Turismo (☎957 53 29 29) who can supply a map.

readers with this guide can claim a ten percent discount here. A couple of hundred metres down the road the *Hotel El Mirador* (☎957 53 94 04, Ⓦwww .miradorderute.com; ❹) offers rooms with views over the sierra. For **places to eat** both hotels have their own decent restaurants serving economical *menús*. Other good places in the town include *Restaurante Casa Paco*, c/Blas Infante s/n, near the Anís monument on the main road through, and the nearby *Casa Hernández*, both serving inexpensive *menús del día*. Another good possibility is *Restaurante El Vado*, 6km out along the A331 to Lucena.

After you've eaten it's worth paying a visit to Rute's superb and friendly **flamenco** venue, *Repostería Peña Flamenca*, c/Blas Infante 42 (the main road through), which is a great place to have a drink (they also do tapas) and has a state-of-the-art open-air flamenco terrace and stage at the back. Rute's younger set let their hair down at a number of **clubs** and **bars** along the main road leading out of town, the Carretera de Málaga, close to the *Hotel María Luisa*, and Saturday evenings sees crowds here spilling over the pavements as the popular places fill up.

Iznájar

Reached by following the attractive road A331 from Rute, **IZNÁJAR** is a picturesque, whitewashed farming village, with a spectacular location overlooking a reservoir. Despite the beauty, this is a place of long-standing poverty; it was here in 1861 that peasants, or *braceros*, revolted against the injustices of the landowning class – an uprising that was viciously suppressed.

Of Moorish origin (from the Arabic *hizn*, fort, and *achar*, refuge), Iznájar's ruined **Alcazaba** was constructed in the eighth century, and the church of **Santiago** was added to its interior in the sixteenth. Almost alongside the church, the public library (Mon–Sat 9am–2pm & 5–8pm; Ⓦwww.iznajar.net) can provide **information** and just downhill there's a small **museum** (Mon–Sat 9am–2pm; free) with a display of antique farm implements. From the plaza next to the church there are stunning **views** over the *embalse* and village below. Iznájar's fine hotel and only place to stay is currently closed (check with the Ayuntamiento regarding reopening ☎957 53 40 02). **Camping** for the odd night is allowed on the nearby Valdearenas beach fronting the *embalse*. For **food** you could try *Restaurante Rosi* on the road towards Loja; alternatives are *El Montecillo* near the *gasolinera*, or *El Charcon*, a good bar-restaurant 2km along the Rute road on the left. In summer *Mesón Valdearenas*, a "beach" *chiringuito* on the shores of the *embalse* is also popular.

Twenty kilometres south of Iznájar close to the junction with the A92 *autovía*, a signed entrance on the left indicates a long drive at the end of which lies the grandiose *Finca La Bobadilla* (☎958 32 18 61, Ⓦwww.la-bobadilla.com; ❾), one of the most exclusive hotels in Spain. Surrounded by acres of woodland and built on the model of a "typical" Andalucian village, it has appealed to guests as diverse as Tom Cruise, King Juan Carlos and many Japanese, for whom this is a favourite place to get married. To stay at this Iberian Xanadu will cost you a king's ransom too (currently around €330 per night for the cheapest high-season room, but serious guests take suites), and dinner at the à la carte restaurant – supplied by its own farm on the estate – doesn't come cheap either. Call in for a drink at the bar if you're curious.

The Ruta del Aceite

This itinerary towards Priego de Córdoba, known as the **Ruta del Aceite** (Oil Route), follows the N432 southeast out of Córdoba. It takes in the olive-oil producing region centred on **Baena** before visiting some of the province's most picturesque villages, including Luque and Zuheros.

Espejo and Castro del Río

At **ESPEJO**, 31km to the south of Córdoba, an impressive Moorish castle looms above the white-walled village, vineyards and olive groves spread out below. The fourteenth-century Gothic-Mudéjar **castillo** is the property of the dukes of Osuna, the great ruling family based in Osuna to the southwest, which once owned an enormous tract of Andalucía. The nearby and recently restored Gothic-Renaissance church of **San Bartolomé** dating from the fifteenth and sixteenth centuries, is also worth seeking out for its fine *retablo mayor* by Pedro Romana and its *artesonado* ceiling.

Sited on a low hill on the north bank of the Río Guadajoz, **CASTRO DEL RÍO**, 9km on from Espejo, has a Roman **bridge** spanning the river and a ruined Moorish **castle** built on the foundations of a Roman fort. The village also claims a footnote in Roman history as this is believed to be the place where Pompey's troops rested up prior to their showdown battle with Caesar in 45 BC at nearby Montilla (Munda) which ended the civil war and, briefly, gave Caesar control of the whole Roman world. The **Iglesia de la Asunción**, founded in the thirteenth century with later additions, has a fine if somewhat eroded Plateresque portal, and the **Ayuntamiento** preserves the prison in which Cervantes was locked up for a week in 1568 when, then working as a tax collector, he was falsely accused of fiddling the books. A modern sculpture of Don Quixote, honouring the great writer's literary creation, now adorns the exterior.

Baena

The road continues south into the area geographically known as the Sierra Subbética Cordobesa, a rugged, rambling spur of the Cordillera Betica range in the province's southeastern corner, and now officially designated the **Parque Natural de las Sierras Subbéticas** (ⓦwww.subbetica.org). Beyond Castro del Río the N432 climbs gently through hills covered with olive groves until it reaches Andalucía's most celebrated oil production centre, **BAENA**. Famous for centuries for the high quality of its olive oil, the huge metal tanks for storing the oil can be seen on the outskirts of town. Baena was an important and populous place in the Moorish period, but the town has shrunk as a result of emigration in more recent times. A pleasant and busy place today, on arrival you should aim for the **Turismo**, c/Virrey del Pino 5 (Tue–Sun 10am–2pm & 5–8pm, ☎957 67 17 57) slightly east of the focal Plaza de España, which can supply a useful town map.

The Town

Most of Baena's sights lie in the upper town reached by following c/Juan Rabadan from Plaza de España to the **Plaza de la Constitución**. The eighteenth-century arcaded **almacén**, or warehouse, is now a cultural centre and another part of the same building houses *Mesón Casa del Monte*, a good tapas bar and restaurant (see below).

From the same square, c/Henares leads uphill again to the eighteenth-century **Casa de la Tercia** (Tues–Sat 11am–2pm & 6.30–8.30pm, Sun 11am–2pm; free), an elegant *casa señorial* that contains an interesting **archeological museum** (with much about ancient olive oil production) and the **Museo de Semana Santa**, which covers the history of Baena's Holy Week and its drums. Continuing along c/Henares and veering left brings you to the early sixteenth-century Gothic church of **Santa María** (service times only; try 7–8pm) with a fine portal and a Moorish tower, probably the minaret of a former mosque. The church is a sad testament to the ferocity of the Civil War, during which this beautiful edifice was put to the torch. Ruined and roofless for many years, it has now undergone a substantial restoration which features a magnificent vaulted roof in wood. The fine iron *reja* (altar screen) also survives as a reminder of former days. An image of what was lost, including a precious *retablo*, is preserved in a faded photograph hanging in the sacristy (the Turismo also displays a copy in its entry lobby). Behind the

Baena's oil for connoisseurs

Spain produces, and probably consumes, more **olive oil** than any other country in the world. However, this wasn't always so, and when the Greeks introduced the olive to the peninsula in the first millennium BC, it was regarded with suspicion by the native Iberians who went on using their traditional lard. Only with the arrival of the Roman legions did they begin to acquire a taste for it, and under Roman supervision Hispanic oil became the finest and most expensive in the empire. Later, sophisticated Moorish invaders taught the Iberians better cultivation techniques, as well as culinary and medicinal possibilities. The Moorish, and now Spanish, names for oil and the olive, *aceite* and *aceituna*, are a legacy of this time.

Today, Spaniards are great connoisseurs of quality oil and **Baena** has its own official **denominación de origen**, backed by an official regulatory body, the *Consejo Regulador*, guaranteeing the standards attained by strict methods of production. Baena's finest oil stands comparison with the best in Europe, and *almazaras* (oil mills), such as that operated for several generations by the Núñez de Prado family in the town, take a great amount of care at every stage in the production process. The olives cultivated on the estate are all harvested by hand prior to being ground to a paste on ancient granite stone mills. The "free run" oil – with no further pressure applied – that results from this process is regarded as the *grand cru* of the oil trade and it takes eleven kilos of olives to yield just one litre of such oil. With a markedly low acid content and an unfatty, concentrated flavour, this oil is far too good (and expensive) for cooking and is sparingly used to flavour *gazpacho* – in Córdoba province, *salmorejo* – or tasted on a morsel of bread as a tapa.

The *Núñez de Prado* mill, Avda. de Cervantes 15 (Mon–Fri 9am–2pm & 4–6.30pm, Sat 9am–1pm; ☎957 67 01 41), with parts dating from the eighteenth century, is close to Plaza de España and can be visited, although most of the action takes place between November and February when the harvested olives are pressed. Their shop sells a range of oils including the celebrated *flor de aceite* at bargain prices.

church is the sixteenth-century Mudéjar convent of **Madre de Dios** (open service times 7–8pm), with a fine late Gothic porch, and equally fine *retablo*, *coro* and *artesonados* in its church. A little way northwest of the Plaza de España the **Museo del Olivar** c/Cañada 7 (Tues–Sun 11am–2pm & 5–7pm, ☎957 69 16 41; €2) pays tribute to the history and development of olive oil production in the zone with displays explaining history and production methods plus a chance to sample and buy Baena's famed oils. One section also deals with the modern uses of oil and its by-products – Baena now has a power station fuelled by olive waste.

Besides oil, Baena is also famous for its Semana Santa rituals, which include a **drum-rolling contest** when the streets are filled with the deafening sound of up to 2000 drums being struck simultaneously. From Wednesday to Friday during Holy Week is the time to avoid, unless you have ear plugs.

Practicalities

For the Turismo details, see above. Finding **places to stay** outside the Semana Santa period is not a problem and all budgets are catered for. The central and friendly *Hostal Rincón*, c/Llano del Rincón 13, off Plaza de España (☎957 67 02 23; ❷), has en-suite a/c rooms with a restaurant below. The nearby *Pensión Claveles*, c/Juan Valera 15 (☎957 67 01 74; ❷), has similar air-conditioned rooms with bath, while the equally close and good-value *Hotel Iponuba*, c/Nicolas Alcalá 9 (☎957 67 00 75, ✉iponuba@interbook.es; ❸), is more upmarket with a garage. The elegant, aptly named *Casa Grande*, Avda. Cervantes 35 (☎957 67 19 05, ⦿www.lacasagrande.es; ❻) is a very comfortable – if a touch overpriced

– three-star hotel inside a converted mansion. Perhaps the most attractive budget option is the Ayuntamiento's *Albergue Ruta del Califato*, c/Coro 7 (☏957 69 23 59; ❷), a **youth hostel** close to the church of Santa María in the upper town. Most rooms are doubles (sharing bathrooms) and there are dorms charging €15 per person per bed. Add in spectacular views, a bar-restaurant for breakfast and meals with a €7 *menú*, and it all adds up to a praiseworthy piece of municipal enterprise.

There are plenty of places for **eating and drinking** around the centre; the *Hostal Rincón* (see above) has a *menú* for €7 and the next door *Primero de la Mañana* is an aptly named and good place for **breakfast**. One restaurant a cut above the rest is *Mesón Casa del Monte*, in the upper town on Plaza de la Constitución, facing the Ayuntamiento; *berenjenas con salmorejo* (aubergine soup) is a special and there's a *menú* for around €8. The town's most popular **freidurías**, both on the eastern side of the central Parque Ramón Santaella near the Nuñez de Prado oil mill, are *El Olivo* and *Mesón Los Arcos*, nearby in the corner of the square.

Luque

Seven kilometres beyond Baena, a right turn leads to the attractive village of **LUQUE**, spread out below a daunting rocky outcrop topped by the almost obligatory castle. Dating from the thirteenth century, the ruins of the **Moorish castillo** are worth a look, and beside them is the golden limestone facade of the Gothic-Renaissance church of **La Asunción** with a *retablo* whose central image of San Juan is attributed to Martínez Montañés. There is no accommodation, but for **food** the *Bar-Restaurante La Plancha*, across from the church, is a lively local meeting place, serving up tapas and *raciones* as well as *platos combinados*.

Zuheros

Nestling in a gorge backed by steep rock cliffs some 5km west of Luque, **ZUHEROS** is another stunningly beautiful Subbética village A cluster of white houses tumbles down the hill below a romantic Moorish **castle** built on and into the rock (see below for visiting details). Later Christian additions were made after it fell to Fernando III (El Santo) in 1240 and became a frontier bastion against the kingdom of Granada.

The nearby early seventeenth-century **Iglesia de los Remedios** (open service times 7–9pm) has a fine *retablo* as well as a tower built on the remains of a minaret from an earlier mosque while on the neighbouring small square a **mirador** gives a great view over the surrounding countryside. On the edge of this square and facing *Bar-Mesón de los Palancos* is the village's **archeological museum** (guided visits Sat, Sun & hols on the hour: April–Sept 10am–2pm & 5–7pm; Oct–March 10am–2pm & 4–6pm; otherwise enquire at the *Hotel Zuhayra* or ring ☏957 69 45 45; €2 including guided castle visit), displaying fascinating finds from the Cueva de los Murciélagos (see below) as well as exhibits from the Roman and Moorish periods. A well-presented **Museum of Customs and Popular Arts** (Tues–Sun 11am–2pm & 5–8pm; €2) displaying implements, furniture and decor from bygone days can be found at c/Santo s/n near the *Mesón Atalaya* (see opposite).

In the hills above the village, reached by a paved, four-kilometre road, the **Cueva de los Murciélagos** (guided visits April–Sept Sat, Sun & hols 11am, 12.30pm, 2pm, 5pm & 6.30pm; €4.60; ring ☏957 69 45 45 or *Hotel Zuhayra* for winter hours and to see the cave outside these times) is spectacular and well worth a visit. First explored in 1938, its name means "cave of the bats" and the hour-long tour (bring a sweater) takes in impressive stalagmites, stalactites and awesome rock formations while the guide relates the fascinating story (revealed by recent excavations) of the remarkable **Neolithic cave paintings** and human remains found here.

Practicalities

A small private **tourist office**, c/Horno 3 (Wed–Sun 10am–2pm & 5–8pm; ☎957 69 46 92, Ⓦwww.zuheros.com), is housed inside the *Alúa* sports shop just opposite the castle. Besides providing general tourist information they can also sell walking boots and other equipment and organize outdoor pursuits including rock climbing, caving, canoeing, mountain biking and bird-watching in the surrounding natural park. The office also has information about renting *casas rurales* in the area.

Downhill from the castle there's a charming **place to stay**, the 🏋 *Hotel Zuhayra*, c/Mirador 10 (☎957 69 46 93, Ⓦwww.zercahoteles.com; ❹ with breakfast; ten percent discount for *Rough Guide* readers with this guide), which uses the village's ancient Moorish name and makes a perfect base to explore the surrounding natural park; guests get free use of the village swimming pool. Fully equipped studios and apartments are available to rent at *Señorio de Zuheros*, booked through the tourist office (☎957 69 45 27, Ⓦwww.apartamentoszuheros.com; ❸–❹). For **food** the *Zuhayra* has a very good restaurant with a *menú*, and there are a couple of lively bars for **tapas** and **raciones** – *Bar-Mesón Los Palancos*, facing the castle with its own restaurant, and *Mesón Atalaya*, c/Santo 58, at the eastern end of the village, next to the turn-off to the Cueva de los Murciélagos.

Doña Mencía

Not quite as pretty as some of its neighbours, **DOÑA MENCÍA**, 5km to the west of Zuheros, is a sizeable oil and wine centre lying at the foot of a slope covered with silver-leaved olives, interrupted by the occasional vineyard. On the town's western flank there are the walls and bastions of a fifteenth-century **castle** next to which there's an elegant carved stone **portal**, all that remains of

△ Zuheros

3

an eighteenth-century Dominican monastery destroyed in the Civil War and now incorporated into a new municipal open-air theatre. Off the main square (Plaza Andalucía) at the end of c/Juan Valera is a small **town museum** (Tues–Sat 10am–1pm; ☎957 67 60 20), c/Juan Ramón Jiménez 8, in the former house of the nineteenth-century novelist Juan Valera, whose best-known work, *Pepita Jiménez*, was set in nearby Cabra.

For **rooms**, an excellent and welcoming small *hostal* just off Plaza Andalucía, ⚤ *Casa Morejón*, c/Obispo Cubero 3 (☎957 67 61 69; ❶) offers remarkably economical en-suite rooms around a charming tiled interior patio; it also serves a bargain *menú* for around €7 in its own restaurant. There are a surprising number of wine *bodegas* here, and a clutch of **places to eat** around the pleasant and palm-fringed Plaza Andalucía. Another good place for a meal is the *Mesón la Cantina*, a lively *venta* housed in the town's disused railway station which uses the former platform as its terrace; there's also a good value *menú*. It lies at the junction with the A318 – near the turn off to Zuheros – on the southern edge of town.

Priego de Córdoba and around

PRIEGO DE CÓRDOBA, 20km southeast of Luque and capital of the Subbética, is one of Andalucía's little-known Baroque wonders offering visitors a feast of superb churches and a remarkable fountain, making it an inviting place to stop over. Situated beneath the province's highest mountain, the 1600m La Tiñosa, the northern approach to the town presents a dramatic view of the whitewashed buildings of its old quarter, laid out along the edge of a picturesque escarpment known as the Adarve.

Despite evidence of long prehistoric habitation in nearby caves and a later Roman settlement, it was under the Moors that Medina Bahiga, as Priego was then known, flourished as part of the kingdom of Granada. Following a tug of war between the Moors and Christians during the fourteenth century, in which the town changed hands three times, it finally fell to the Christians in 1341. Recovery from the aftermath of this turbulent era came only in the eighteenth century when, in 1711, Priego became a dependency of the dukes of Medinaceli. An economic resurgence based on the production of silk and textiles poured great wealth into the town and it was during this time that most of the **Baroque churches**, Priego's outstanding attraction today, were constructed or remodelled. In the nineteenth century, though, the industry found it hard to compete with cheap cotton textiles produced in Catalunya and Britain, and a slow decline set in. The Europe-wide slump in textiles in the 1950s and 1960s caused by imports from Asia accelerated the problems and, as factories closed, many people emigrated to seek work elsewhere. Today the remnants of the textile industry, along with farming, are the town's main employers.

The towns and villages surrounding Priego generally lack anything compelling in the way of sights, but two outstanding exceptions are the village of **Almedinilla**, where a remarkable Roman villa has recently been discovered, and, a little further afield, the picturesque town of **Montefrío** and its nearby prehistoric site to the southeast, also well worth a visit.

Arrival, information and accommodation

Buses arriving in Priego will drop you in the central Plaza de la Constitución although the actual bus station is a five-minute walk to the west of the centre on c/Nuestra Señora de los Remedios. There are easy connections with Córdoba, Granada and Málaga.

The town's helpful **Turismo**, c/Carrera de las Monjas 1, effectively the central Plaza Constitución (Mon–Fri 10am–2pm & 4.30–6.30pm, Sat–Sun 10am–3pm; ☎957 70 84 20, ⓦwww.turismodepriego.com), can provide a detailed **map** and has information (also on their website) on *casas rurales* to rent in the surrounding area.

The number of **places to stay** in Priego has increased in recent years, and now includes quite a few very pleasant options. Outside the annual *feria* (first week in September) there's usually no great demand for rooms.

Hostal Las Rosas c/Nuestra Señora de los Remedios 6 ☎957 70 19 71, ⓦwww.hostallasrosas.com. Opposite the bus station this is a sparkling new option with en-suite rooms opening onto three patios. It also has a car park. ❸

🏋 **Hostal Rafi** c/Isabel la Católica 4 ☎957 54 72 69, ⓦwww.hostalrafi.net. In a tiny street east of the main square, this welcoming hostal housed in a *casa señorial* is the best deal in town. Comfortable a/c en-suite rooms come with satellite TV. Has own car park and restaurant. ❷

Hotel Huerta de las Palomas Ctra. Priego-Zagrilla km 3 ☎957 72 03 05, ⓦwww.zercahoteles.com. Four kilometres northwest of town along the CO230, this is a stylish four-star hotel with gym, pool and restaurant in rolling Subbética countryside. It offers lots of activities including mountain biking, tennis and hiking. Ten percent discount for *Rough Guide* readers with this guide. ❻ with breakfast.

Hotel Zahori c/Real 2 ☎957 54 72 92, ⓦwww.hotelzahori.com. In the picturesque Barrio de la Villa, this is a charming new arrival offering excellent a/c en-suite rooms in a refurbished town house. ❹

PRIEGO DE CÓRDOBA

RESTAURANTS

Balcón del Adarve	3
El Aljibe	1
El Virrey	2

ACCOMMODATION

Hostal Las Rosas	G
Hostal Rafi	F
Hotel Huerta de las Palomas	D
Hotel Zahori	B
La Posada Real	C
Río Piscina	A
Villa Turística	E

0   100 m

La Posada Real c/Real 14 ☎957 54 19 10,
ⓦwww.laposadareal.com. Another possibility in
the Barrio de la Villa, this is an attractive, flower-
bedecked little place with cosy, a/c en-suite
balcony rooms. ❸
Río Piscina ☎957 70 01 86, ⓦwww.hotel
riopiscina.com. Newly refurbished hotel on the
eastern edge of town for spacious a/c terrace rooms
overlooking garden pool. Other features include
restaurant, tennis court, gardens and a car park. ❹

Villa Turística Aldea de Zagrilla s/n, three
kilometres beyond the *Huerta de las Palomas*
hotel (above) along the CO230 leading to Zagrilla
☎957 70 35 03, ⓦwww.villaturisticadepriego
.com. Built on traditional lines with lots of Moorish-inspired decor, this country hotel has 52
apartment/chalets sited in gardens where water
features set the mood. Offers a range of outdoor
activities including horse riding and mountain
biking. ❺

The Town

The centre of this tranquil town is the Plaza de la Constitución, an elegant
square fronted by the **Ayuntamiento**, from where all the monuments are
within easy walking distance. By studying the opening times, it should be possible to see most of Priego's main **churches** (all with free entry) in a day. Some
of the lesser visited ones have more restricted hours but are still worth making
the effort to get to. The Turismo can advise on current opening times (which
may change slightly) and also offers free guided tours of the town.

From the Plaza de la Constitución head northeast towards the **Barrio de
la Villa**, the old quarter, which contains most of Priego's principal monuments. A good place to begin is with the austere Moorish **Castillo** (Tue–Sat
11.30am–1.30pm & 4–6pm, Sun 11.30am–1.30pm; free) whose impressive

keep dominates the small Plaza de Abad Palomino. Altered in the thirteenth and fourteenth centuries, the interior is now privately owned but can be visited.

Iglesia de la Asunción

In the square's southeast corner lies the first of the Baroque churches, the **Iglesia de la Asunción** (Tues–Sun 11.30am–1.30pm plus Mon–Fri 6–7.30pm), its modest whitewashed exterior dating from the sixteenth century. The original Gothic building was remodelled in the Baroque style in the eighteenth century by Jerónimo Sánchez de Rueda, an architect who did a similar job on many of Priego's other churches.

It is inside, however, that the surprises begin: an ornate white stucco Baroque interior leads towards a stunningly beautiful carved Mannerist **retablo** with images attributed to Juan Bautista Vázquez. The greatest surprise of all, though, lies through a portal on the left aisle where you enter the breathtaking **sagrario**, one of the masterpieces of Spanish Baroque. Here, a dazzling symphony of wedding-cake white stuccowork and statuary, punctuated by scrolls and cornices, climbs upwards beyond a balcony into a fabulous cupola illuminated by eight windows. The frothy depth of the stucco plaster was achieved by the use of esparto grass to lend it additional strength – a material which has played a remarkable part in the craft history of Andalucía, even found in hats, baskets and sandals discovered in the Neolithic caves of Granada. This recently restored octagonal chapel is the work of Francisco Javier Pedrajas, a native of Priego and one of a number of leading sculptors, carvers and gilders working in the town at this time. The *altar mayor* and the *sagrario* have been declared national monuments.

Barrio de la Villa and Paseo del Adarve

Before taking in more Baroque mastery, the nearby and delightful **Barrio de la Villa** provides a welcome opportunity for a stroll. The ancient Moorish part of the town, a maze of sinuous whitewashed alleys with balconies and walls loaded with pot plants, leads to a number of typical plazuelas. You should eventually stumble on one of the most charming, the **Plazuela de San Antonio**, replete with palms and wrought-iron *rejas*. Behind the Iglesia de la Asunción, c/Bajondillo leads to the **Paseo de Adarve**, a superb, and originally Moorish, promenade with a spectacular **view** over the valley of the Río Salado and undulating groves of olives stretching to the distant hills.

San Pedro and San Juan de Dios

Just to the west of the castillo, the **Iglesia de San Pedro** (Mon–Sat 10.30am–1.30pm) is another Baroque treat with more stucco and a wonderful **altar mayor** in painted wood and stucco with a delightful domed *camarín* (shrine) behind, which holds a stirring image of the *Inmaculada*. The side chapel of the **Virgen de la Soledad**, with another *camarín*, has an image of the Virgin at the centre of its *retablo* by Pablo de Rojas. To the rear of San Pedro, on c/San Pedro de Alcántara, the **Carnicerías Reales**, (Tues–Sat 11.30am–1.30pm & 4–6pm, Sun 11.30am–1.30pm; free) is a sixteenth-century abattoir and meat market with a fine cobbled patio. A short distance west of San Pedro the church of **San Juan de Dios**, with a finely crafted cupola, is an early example of Priego Baroque, completed in 1717.

La Aurora and San Francisco

Moving south along c/Argentina and its continuation c/Álvarez will lead you to the church of **La Aurora**, (Tues–Sun 11am–1pm) yet another Baroque gem remodelled from a former *ermita*, whose exuberant facade, with Corinthian and

Solomonic pillars topped by a Virgin and flanked by exquisite stone and marble decoration, is only a prelude to the interior. This, now restored to its full glory, is a single-naved Baroque explosion in painted wood and stucco descending from the grey and white cornices, with polychromed figures on its ceiling, dome and walls, to an animated and sumptuously theatrical **retablo**. This *retablo* is a glittering amalgam of *vegetal* and geometrical forms, and the crowning achievement of Juan de Dios Santaella, another native Priego talent, born here in 1716. The church is also home to the **Cofradía de la Aurora**, a brotherhood whose sixteenth-century articles of foundation stipulate that they must proceed through the streets in musical procession every Saturday at midnight. Thus, whatever the weather, this band of men, hatted and cloaked, gather behind their banner and a huge lantern to proceed through the streets singing hymns to *La Aurora* (Our Lady of the Dawn) accompanied by guitars, accordions and tambourines.

Just south of here along c/Buen Suceso, the **Iglesia de San Francisco** (Mon–Sat 10am–1pm, Sun 9am–12noon plus Mon–Fri 6–8pm) on an elegant old square, is another late-Gothic church that Santaella had a hand in remodelling and which has recently been restored to its former splendour. Once you've admired the facade and portal (both by Santaella), employing contrasting tones of marble, look inside: the *retablo mayor* is a splendid gilded work by Santaella again. The **chapel of Jesús Nazareno** has a sumptuous gilded and polychromed wood and stucco *retablo* by Pedrajas, the creator of the *sagrario* in the Asunción, and is topped off by another extravagant cupola by Santaella. The altarpiece's central image of *Jesús Nazareno* (Christ bearing the Cross) is a fine work, attributed to Pedro de Mena.

The Fuente del Rey and around

At the southwestern end of the town, and easily reached by following c/Río – a street dotted with many fine Baroque portals – to its end, lies the **Fuente del Rey**, a spectacular sixteenth-century 180-jet fountain (with many later additions) which pours water into a number of basins. The highest of these has a sculpture of a lion struggling with a serpent, whilst the second contains a larger late eighteenth-century depiction of Neptune and Amphitrite, the king and queen of the sea. Amphitrite is clutching the dolphin that returned her to Neptune after her attempted escape, incidentally emphasizing the power of the king, the work's intended ideological message, given that over the border in France, monarchs were losing their heads. There are in fact two fountains here, the second being the **Fuente de la Salud**, to the rear of the plaza, a sixteenth-century Italianate work built on the spot, according to legend, where the conquering Alfonso XI pitched his camp in 1341. One of the most tranquil squares in Andalucía, this leafy area is a wonderful place to relax and get away from it all, which is why there are so many seats.

From just beyond the square you can **walk** to the Ermita del Calvario from where there are fine **views** over the town. Take the steps to the left of the Fuente de la Salud.

Another historic building on c/Río at no. 46 is the birthplace of, and now **museum** (Tue–Sat 10am–1.30pm & 5–7.30pm, Sun 10am–1.30; free) dedicated to, Niceto Alcalá Zamora, first president of the ill-fated Spanish republic from 1931 to 1936. Much of the furniture of this middle-class nineteenth-century family mansion survives intact, and you are free to look around.

The rest of the churches and museums

When you've seen the main churches, there are many more almost as good. Just off the Plaza de la Constitución at the start of c/Río, the **Iglesia de las Angustias** (Sat 11am–1pm) is a charming small church and another work by

Santaella. The interior has a fine cupola with more typically exuberant poly-chromed stucco decoration. Further along c/Río, the **Iglesia del Carmen** (Mon–Tues & Thurs–Sun 7.30–8pm) has a *retablo* by Santaella, probably an early work. Finally, to the west on Carrera de las Monjas, the **Iglesia del Mercedes** (Mon, Fri & Sat 11am–1pm) was an ancient hermitage prior to its remodelling in the latter part of the eighteenth century when it was decorated in Rococo style by Pedrajas, highlighted by the four winged archangels at the scalloped corners. Another stunningly ornate snow-white cupola (which is almost Pedrajas's trademark), is balanced by an elegant *retablo* below. The exterior is an incomplete later addition.

Almost opposite the Iglesia de Mercedes, Priego's **Museo Histórico Municipal** (Tues–Fri 10am–1.30pm & 6–8.30pm, Sat & Sun 10am–1.30pm; free), c/Monjas 9, is housed in an elegant *señorial* mansion with a fine patio. An interesting collection displays finds from the surrounding area dating from the Paleolithic down to the Roman and Moorish periods.

Eating, drinking and nightlife

For **eating and drinking** the bars around the main square are good for break-fast and tapas, and the restaurant attached to the *Hostal Rafi* is especially good with a *menú* for €7.50. The *Hotel Zahori's* mid-priced restaurant (see above) in the Barrio de la Villa is also worth a try. More good **tapas bars** are *Bar Río* at the start of c/Río and *El Telar*, c/Buen Suceso 2, close to the Iglesia de San Francisco. Other **restaurants** are few, but *El Aljibe*, c/Abad Palomino 7, opposite the Iglesia de la Asuncion, is built over a Moorish bathhouse (which you can glimpse through a glass floor in the lower dining room), has some apt Moor-ish inspired dishes and a lunch *menú*; there's also an attractive outdoor terrace. Another good place is *El Virrey*, c/Solana 16, off Plaza San Pedro, preparing a wide range of local dishes and again with another economical *menú*. Priego's most celebrated restaurant is the *Balcón del Adarve*, Paseo de Colombia 36 (☎957 54 70 75; main dishes €10–18), close to the promenade it's named after and part of which it uses as a pleasant terrace; specialities include *rabo de toro* (oxtail) and other dishes of the zone, and there's a *menú de degustación* for €26.

Outside the first week in September when Priego celebrates its annual *Feria Real*, **nightlife** is generally confined to sipping drinks at tables on the Plaza Mayor. However, one interesting diversion is the *Peña Flamenca Fuente del Rey*, c/Río 50, a friendly **flamenco** club where you'll get a warm welcome and, after ten, just maybe some good flamenco.

Carcabuey

Seven kilometres west of Priego and reachable by bus, **CARCABUEY** is a charming place laid out on a hill topped by a ruined castle. The Gothic-Renaissance church of **La Asunción** lower down has a good portal flanked with Solomonic marble pillars, and inside a superb **retablo** with the central figure of Christ attributed to Pedro de Mena and Alonso Cano. It is usually locked, so you'll need to enquire at the nearby houses for the key. For **rooms**, on the nearby main highway 3km towards Cabra, the *Hostal La Zamora*, Ctra. Cabra-Priego, A340 km-62 (☎957 70 42 08, ⓦwww.hostal-lazamora.com; ❷), is a comfortable roadside motel with en-suite a/c rooms above a bar-restaurant with an economical *menú*.

Amedinilla

ALMEDINILLA, 9km east on the Jaén border, is another characteristic Subbética village squatting along the valley of the Río Caicena. Hardly worth a second glance until recently, it has catapulted itself onto the visitor itinerary with the discovery of a remarkable **Roman villa** with unique features as well as a fine **museum**.

Villa Romana de El Ruedo

The villa, officially known as the **Villa Romana de El Ruedo** (Wed–Sun 10am & 2pm, plus Sat 5–8pm; ☎957 70 20 21; €2), is located at the edge of the village close to the main A340 highway. Once inside the entrance you will pass to the left the remains of an ancient **pottery kiln**. This would no doubt have provided the numerous ceramic containers necessary for the substantial oil and grain farming centred on the villa. Beyond this and beneath a canopy lies the villa proper, constructed and inhabited between the first and fifth centuries AD. Laid out around a central patio or **atrium**, with remains of walls well over a metre high, the bedrooms and living rooms – many bearing vestiges of frescoes and laid with mosaic floors – are adjoined by a bath and kitchen as well as bodegas for storing wine, the ruins of an oil mill and warehouses for holding grain. But it is on the north side of the patio in the dining room, or **triclinium**, where the most sensational finds were discovered. In the centre of this room is a well-preserved **podium** upon which diners would have reclined whilst eating. Behind this and set into the wall are the remains of a spectacular artificial **cascade** fed by a diverted nearby stream, unique in Spain and added when the villa was substantially remodelled in the third century AD, providing an aural backdrop to the diners' meals. Also unearthed here were a number of outstanding sculptures; the major work, a bronze figure of Hypnos, in Greek mythology the god of sleep, is now displayed in the Museo Historico (see below).

To the north and east of the villa lie the remains of a **necropolis** that would have served the Roman settlement here, as well as the remnants of numerous other Roman dwellings. In the coming years it is planned to excavate these too, eventually transforming the whole zone into an archeological park. At the moment a **museum–information centre** (same hours), with reconstructions and exhibits discovered during the excavations, is sited opposite the entrance to the villa. You may be lucky enough to coincide with the occasional Saturday or Sunday group visits to the villa which are followed by a typical **Roman meal** – small numbers of visitors to the villa are welcome to join in for free.

Museo Historico

Almedenilla's **Museo Historico** (Wed–Sun 10am–2pm plus Sat 5–8.30pm; ring ☎957 70 20 21 for winter hours; €2) lies on the east side of the village and is housed in a former oil and flour mill, El Molino de Fuente Ribera, whose grindstones were powered by the adjacent Río Caicena. The exhibits are distributed on three floors with the ground floor displaying the mill's grindstones, once used for making olive oil. Taking its theme from this machinery the rest of the room charts the development of olive oil production from Iberian and Roman times to the present day – not losing an opportunity to remind visitors that the oil produced here today is as highly prized as it was in Roman times, carrying its own *denominación de origen*. The second floor is devoted to the **Iberian period**, particularly finds from Cerro de la Cruz, a hill settlement discovered on the crag behind the village by archeologists early in the last century. The remains displayed – pottery, burial goods, weapons and tools – detail a well-planned urban development existing between the fourth century BC and the first century AD. The museum can provide information about guided visits to the Cerro de la Cruz site.

The third floor houses the **Roman collection** with the finds from the Roman villa. Pride of place goes to the sculptures, particularly the fine and superbly restored bronze of the Greek god of sleep **Hypnos**, discovered in the villa's dining room, and a work of exceptional quality. For the Greeks (and the Romans who knew him as Somnus) Hypnos was the personification of sleep and his mission was to lead the soul to a peaceful death, as in a dream. Made from individual casts of bronze later welded together, in his left hand he would have held an opium poppy to induce sleep, and in his right a horn from which he cast the night as he flew across the sky with the aid of wings protruding from his temples. Almost as fine is a bronze **hermaphrodite** depicting the dancing figure staring into a mirror held in its right hand (now lost) which would have reflected the feminine parts thus exciting the masculine side of its androgynous nature. This ancient fascination with dualism – as in life and death, darkness and light, male and female – is undoubtedly the work's underlying message. Other sculptures in stone include a genius of the house, perhaps depicting spring, a partially damaged image of Perseus and Andromeda, and a head of Dionysos. A **maquette** of the Roman villa gives you an idea how it would have looked when in use.

Practicalities

For **eating** and **drinking** in Almedinilla, *Bar-Restaurante La Bodega*, Plaza de España, in front of the Ayuntamiento serves meals at midday with a *menú* for €6, and tapas should be available at other times. Excellent en-suite **rooms** are available in the heart of the village at *Mesón Rural La Era*, Plaza La Era 1 (☎957 70 32 01; ❸) a cunningly re-created copy of an ancient town house which, despite appearances, is completely new. It also has its own bar and restaurant. Should you have any problems gaining access to the Roman villa or museum, call at the Ayuntamiento, Plaza de España s/n (☎957 70 30 85, ⓦwww .almedinillaturismo.org), who should be able to help.

Alcalá La Real and Alcaudete

ALCALÁ LA REAL, 27km east of Priego, is a pleasant country town at the foot of a hill dominated by one of the most impressive Moorish forts in eastern Andalucía. Later reconstructed as the **Castillo de la Mota** (daily July–Sept 10.30am–1.30pm & 5–8pm, Oct–June 10.30am–1.30pm & 3.30–6.30pm; €2), it preserves among its earlier gates the Moorish **Puerta de la Imagen**. After the fort had been taken during the *Reconquista*, Alfonso XI built – and this became the custom – the Renaissance church of **Santa María la Mayor** inside the walls. Designed by the leading architect of the sixteenth century Diego de Siloé and now magnificently restored, its interior floor conserves scores of Visigothic burial niches from an earlier building on the site. Displays in the church's small museum evidence activity on this hill going back to prehistoric times, over 5000 years ago. The fort's imposing **Torre de la Homenaje** also has an interesting small **museum** with great views from the top of the tower. The castle's ticket office doubles as the **Turismo** (same hours; mobile ☎639647796) which can provide information on the town's many other monuments and museums. For a **place to stay** *Hotel Torrepalma*, c/Conde de Torrepalma 2 (☎953 58 18 00; ❹), off the town's main street, Avenida de Andalucía, has comfortable a/c rooms.

    ALCAUDETE, 25km northeast of Priego in Jaén province, tumbles down a hill below yet another impressive Moorish castle, this one dating from the tenth century and with a massive keep. There are a few sixteenth-century churches to see here, too.

Montefrío and the Peña de los Gitanos

One of the more spectacularly sited towns in this part of the country is **MONTEFRÍO**, 24km southeast of Priego (or 32km by road), and just over the Granada border. Cradled between two rocky outcrops, each topped by a church which can be visited, the town has the even bigger Neoclassical **Iglesia de la Encarnación** (daily 10am–2pm & 8–9pm; free) at its heart, with an enormous dome and bizarre acoustics. The most interesting of the hill-top churches is the sixteenth-century **Iglesia de la Villa** (daily 12–2pm; €2.50), a superb building designed by Diego de Siloé, and now converted into a themed museum based on the reconquest of this part of Andalucía from the Moors. The interior has some exquisite **vaulting** and is surrounded by the ruins of the Moorish *alcazaba*; there are fine **views** over the town and beyond from its tower. The church is reached by a bracing climb along the road which ascends beyond the Turismo (see "Practicalities" below).

Nearby, 8km east along the NO26 towards Illora and signposted, is the remarkable Neolithic site of **Las Peñas de los Gitanos**. Six kilometres long and demarcated by limestone outcrops, the site was occupied by Stone-Age people in the third millennium BC. The overhanging rocks and caves were used as shelters by bulls, goats, sheep and other ancient beasts and this food source attracted early humans who would have hunted these animals in groups. These ancient hunters left behind paintings inside the caves (currently not on view), various **stone tombs** – some with carvings of animals and horns – and the remains of later stone and clay dwellings when they became Chalcolithic (copper-age) village dwellers. A detailed leaflet (in Spanish) is available from the Turismo in Montefrío.

To reach the site, park your car at the signed entry road (with locked gate) on the left. Follow the asphalt road for 100m beyond this to a *Prohibido El Paso* sign where you should veer right onto a dirt track, soon crossing large stones. Two hundred metres further, upon reaching a stone quarry, you need to veer left. A further 200m brings you to an open area of grassland with trees in the centre. Continue straight ahead for 300m – passing a ruined dolmen – to a low mound beyond which you will see more dolmens and an information board. Off to the right, Dolmen 23 has another information board and is the best preserved, with a finely worked entrance still intact. If you would like a (free) **guided tour** this can be arranged outside siesta times with the site guardian, Paqui Sanchez (mobile ☎628305337; English spoken), who will meet you at the site.

Practicalities

Montefrío's **Turismo** (Mon–Fri 10am–2pm; ☎958 33 60 04, ⓦwww .montefrio.org) lies just uphill on the left from the Encarnación church and can supply a town map and information. Montefrío's **accommodation** options are severely limited but easily the best is the two-star *Hotel La Enrea*, Paraje de la Enrea s/n (☎958 33 66 62, ⓦwww.zercahoteles.com; ❹ with breakfast; ten percent discount for *Rough Guide* readers with this guide), reached by following the Granada road out of the centre. It's an easy five- to ten-minute walk from the centre and the hotel – a converted nineteenth-century water mill – lies in a picturesque river gorge with comfortable a/c rooms. A number of **casas rurales** are available for rent in and around the town – one is sited on the outcrop just below La Villa church; information is available from the Turismo or by ringing ☎958 31 01 24 (English spoken).

When it comes to **eating and drinking** Montefrío is acclaimed for its *morcilla* (black pudding) and *chorizo*, both excellent at the *Bar Pregonero*, next door to the Turismo. Another good place to try these delicacies is *Bar Uno Más* (or *One More*) facing the Encarnación church. More elaborate meals are to be had at the *Hotel La Enrea*'s good restaurant (see above; main dishes €7.50–12), plus *Mesón Coronichi*, Avda. de la Paz 23, on the Illora road out of town.

North of Córdoba

To the north of Córdoba lies the province's stretch of the **Sierra Morena**, an area rich in scenery and wildlife but poor in sights. Many of the hardy granite villages are casualties of the Europe-wide depression in mining, and the sad air pervading them is possibly why they see few visitors. Persevere into the region's higher reaches, however, and you enter a landscape most frequented by hunters and anglers; outside the winter hunting season, it's ideal rambling territory as well – **Santa Eufemia** is located in richly scenic hill country. This is also another region of the Sierra Morena famed for its *jamón ibérico* or cured ham, and a chance to sample this in the bars and *ventas* along the way shouldn't be missed. For a tour of the area you're at a definite advantage with your own transport and although there are frequent daily buses run by Alsina Graells, López and Ureña, from Córdoba to Peñarroya and Pozoblanco, public transport off the beaten track is minimal.

The main **N432** snaking and climbing north out of Córdoba takes the traffic heading for the towns of Badajoz and Cáceres in Extremadura, to the north. Although this road follows a rail line, there are no longer passenger services. After 44km the road forks just before **Espiel**, a small coal-mining town, and you can follow the **N502 route** towards Hinojosa del Duque and the valley of Los Pedroches.

Towards Hinojosa del Duque and Santa Eufemia

Just before it reaches Espiel, the N502 forks right and crosses a number of wooded valleys and watercourses to **Alcaracejos**, where it joins up with the A420. Turning left at Alcaracejos, the road passes the village of Villanueva del Duque to arrive, 21km further on, at **HINOJOSA DEL DUQUE**, a sombre town with an outsize church. Popularly known as the **Catedral de la Sierra**, the granite Gothic-Renaissance church of **San Juan Bautista** has a fine entrance portal by Hernán Ruíz who designed the belfry for the Mezquita at Córdoba, as well as a superb Gothic interior with a beautiful *artesonado* ceiling. A **tourist office** (Mon–Sat 10am–2pm; ☎957 14 18 31) on the square behind the church stocks town maps and plenty of information on the culture, customs and scenery of the Los Pedroches zone. If you want to **stay**, there's the serviceable *Hostal Ruda*, c/Padre Manjón 2 (☎957 14 07 78; **②**), or the better *Hostal-Restaurante El Cazador*, Avda. Marqués de Santillana 112 (☎957 14 04 43; **③**), on the main A449 road in, coming from Córdoba, with a very good restaurant below. **Food** is also on offer at the central *Mesón Condesito*, c/Brigadier Romero 3, reached by following c/Cristo downhill from just behind the cathedral and taking the first left, which also stocks the region's prized *jamones*. Another option for meals is *Café-Bar Central*, to the side of the cathedral, which does *platos combinados* and has a decent *menú*.

Belalcázar and Santa Eufemia

BELALCÁZAR, 9km north and close to the border with Extremadura, has the ruins of a fifteenth-century **castle** with an impressive keep and a sixteenth-century church of **Santiago** with a fine Plateresque *retablo*. Should you need a **place to stay** there are rooms with bath at *Hostal La Bolera*, c/Padre Torrero 17 (☎957 14 63 00; ❷), which also has a restaurant. However, the better places for **food** are the bars on the main square, Plaza de la Constitución, near the church of Santiago.

Some 28km to the east, **SANTA EUFEMIA** is a picturesque hill village which more than makes up for the journey getting here. Occupying a striking location on a low ridge backed by spectacular crags topped by a ruined eleventh-century Moorish fort, this typical north sierra *pueblo* has an ancient heart where the twelfth-century Gothic-Mudéjar church of **La Encarnación** was one of the south's first post-*Reconquista* churches built in the wake of the victories of Alfonso XI over the Moors. There's some fine **walking country** in the hills surrounding the town, and the Ayuntamiento, Plaza Mayor 1 (☎957 15 82 29), can provide an information leaflet and a map of the village and hands out a booklet of hiking routes (in Spanish), which details a walk taking in the Moorish castle with spectacular views over the Sierra. While you're visiting the Ayuntamiento you should call in at the *Bar Los Monteros* on the same square where you'll get a warm welcome and a free tapa with every drink.

Santa Eufemia also has an excellent-value **place to stay**, ⚜ *Hostal La Paloma*, c/El Calvario 6 (☎957 15 82 42; ❶), where en-suite balcony rooms come with TV and the **restaurant** has a bargain *menú*. Ring ahead if you're coming here in the autumn as rooms are often booked up by the hunting fraternity.

Northeast of Córdoba

The A4-E5 highway which heads northeast out of Córdoba along the valley of the Guadalquivir is the main road to Madrid and one of the great historical highways of Andalucía. Not only was this the bullion route between Madrid and its imperial seaports of Sevilla and Cádiz, but over a millennium and a half earlier, as the Vía Augusta, it formed the vital overland link joining Roman Spain with Gaul, Italy and Rome itself. This route has a number of delightful stopovers including the handsome small town of **Montoro**, an outstanding Moorish castle at **Baños de Encina** and the historic **Despeñaperros Pass**. Transport is easy and **buses** link Córdoba with most places on the route. Montoro, Andújar and Bailén are also served by **trains** on the Córdoba–Linares–Madrid line.

Montoro

MONTORO lies 43km from Córdoba, past the villages of El Carpio and Pedro Abad, and just off the A4-E5. Dramatically sited on an escarpment above a horseshoe bend in the Guadalquivir, the town is a centre of olive-oil production obtained from extensive groves planted in the foothills of the Sierra Morena to the north. A labyrinth of narrow, white-walled streets surrounds the main square, the Plaza de España, dominated by the lofty tower of its Gothic-Mudéjar church, **San Bartolomé**. The interior, behind the red sandstone facade, has a fine *artesonado* ceiling inlaid with mother-of-pearl, recently recovered from under layers of whitewash. A small **tourist office** (Mon–Fri 9.30am–3pm, Sat 10am–1pm, Sun 11am–1pm; ☎957 16 00 89) at no. 8 on the same square can provide basic information. Also here is the sixteenth-century **Ayuntamiento**, an old ducal mansion with a fine Plateresque frontage, and a historic inn – now closed – at no. 19 whose kindly owner will let you in for a look around (avoid siesta time). A narrow street uphill out of the north side of the square leads into an atmospheric old quarter whose main feature is the thirteenth-century church of **Santa María de la Mota**, with some interesting Romanesque capitals, now converted into a small **archeological museum** (Sat, Sun & hols 11am–1pm, outside these times contact the Turismo; free). One other curiosity that also shouldn't be missed is the **Casa de las Conchas** in nearby c/Grajas (no. 17 and signed from the plaza) – the exterior and interior are covered with millions of seashells; the proprietor or his wife will proudly show you around and relate the story behind their 25-year-old obsession.

The narrow main street connects Plaza de España with **Plaza del Charco** (aka Plaza Caridad), which contains the town's main **bars** and two *casinos*, the larger Casino de los Ricos (Rich) and the Casino de los Pobres (Poor), reflecting the bitter class divisions that once existed here and to some extent persist. The former is a fascinating time-warp of a place with an elegant interior patio and, upstairs, the dusty rooms, furnished with drapes, tarnished chandeliers and faded frescoes of flappers, where the town's *señoritos* once held court. Today the dwindling clientele are still the town's right-wingers, and can be overheard reminiscing over their *finos* about the good old (Francoist) days. Both places welcome visitors, but the plaza's liveliest option is *Bar Yepez* where the ebullient proprietor will serve up tapas and fill you in on local information. Slightly uphill from the square lies the eighteenth-century Capilla de San Jacinto, now converted into the **Museo Antonio Rodríguez de Luna** (Sat, Sun & hols. 11am–1pm, or contact the Turismo; free) housing some powerful abstract works by the Montoro-born artist who spent part of his life in Paris and Mexico and died in 1985.

Montoro's other notable monument is the elegant sixteenth-century bridge of **Las Donadas** over the Guadalquivir, paid for by local women who, tradition holds, sold their jewellery to place the town on a more direct, and lucrative, route to the north. Across the bridge, the Cardeña road leading up into the hills offers superb **views** back over the town.

Andújar

Flanked by the mountains of the Sierra Morena which are visible on the northern horizon, the A4-E5 continues to Villa del Río and enters the province of Jaén. Lying some 32km beyond Montoro, **ANDÚJAR** is a sizeable if simple country town which claims to be the world's biggest centre of sunflower-oil bottling. There's also a thriving commercial ceramics industry, as well as a couple of churches worth a visit for their artworks.

The road into the town crosses a fifteen-arched Roman **bridge** spanning the Guadalquivir, which has been considerably restored from Moorish times onwards. The central Plaza de España, a baking furnace in the heat of high summer, contains the impressive Gothic church of **San Miguel** (daily 7.30–8pm; free) with a fine stone tower and Plateresque features, flanked by an equally striking late-Baroque **Ayuntamiento** – recently restored to its full glory – with elegant portals. But the most interesting church is the **Iglesia de Santa María** (daily 7.30–8pm; free) on the plaza of the same name, reached by following c/Feria between the two squares. Built on the site of a former mosque, the free-standing bell tower probably replaced the mosque's minaret and now houses a small tourist office (see below). Inside, a chapel on the left has a fine *Christ in the Garden of Olives* by **El Greco**, a startling surprise in a nondescript country church, highlighted by another painting, an *Inmaculada* by Pachecho, the teacher of Velázquez, in a chapel to the left of the main altar. The superb **reja** which stands before the El Greco is the work of Master Bartolomé of Jaén, who also created the more famous one in the Capilla Real at Granada. The town's **archeological museum** (Tues–Fri 10am–2pm; free) is housed in the striking seventeenth-century Palacio Don Gome, c/Don Gome, to the southeast of Plaza de España, decorated with moustached figures of feathered Indians inspired by the burgeoning Spanish American empire. The collection consists of mainly Roman ceramic exhibits testifying to the town's importance in this field. There are a number of other elegant **Renaissance palaces** within walking distance of the centre and, should you have the time and inclination, the tourist office can provide a map detailing their locations.

Practicalities

The Ayuntamiento on the Plaza Mayor (Plaza de España) or the tourist office next to the Iglesia de Santa María (Mon–Fri 10am–2pm & 6–8pm; ☎953 50 49 59) can provide information and a **town map** which most of the hotels stock as well. Andújar has a number of **places to stay**, the least expensive being the *Hotel-Restaurante La Reserva* (☎953 51 53 40, ℉953 50 19 00; ❸), c/Vendederas 4, to the northwest of Plaza de España, with pleasant en-suites above a bar-restaurant with a good-value €10 *menú*. Alternatives include the slightly more expensive *Hotel Logasasanti*, c/Dr Fleming s/n (☎953 50 05 00, ⓦwww.logasasanti.com; ❹) and the marginally pricier *Hotel Don Pedro*, c/Gabriel Zamora 5 (☎953 50 12 74, ℉953 50 07 85; ❹), to the west and north of the centre respectively.

Plenty of **bars** in town offer **tapas** – *Bar La Tasca* on Plaza de España and *Cafetería Los Naranjos*, c/Guadalupe 4, are both good. For **places to eat** more substantially you could try *Las Perolas*, c/Serpiente 6, a couple of hundred metres northeast of Plaza de España, a *mesón* serving up dishes of the region with an economical *menú*, or the very pleasant *Mesón El Churrasco*, Corredera de Capuchinos 24, to the east of the main square, for excellent tapas and *raciones*. One restaurant that is worth seeking out is the family-run *Restaurante Madrid-Sevilla*, (☎953 50 05 94; main dishes €8–23) Plaza del Sol 4, a little to the east of Plaza de España. Its charming proprietor and chef will not only guide you through his specials – the *flamenquines* and *perdiz* (partridge) and all meat dishes are recommended – but can also provide the recipe for any dish you might want to try at home.

Parque Natural Sierra de Andújar

A wonderful thirty-kilometre drive into the **Parque Natural Sierra de Andújar** to the north of Andújar along the A1208 leads to the thirteenth-century hermitage of **Nuestra Virgen de la Cabeza**, one of the most revered of Andalucía's shrines. To break the journey, on the way up there are three decent **tavernas** – *El Tropezon*, *El Toledillo* and *Los Pinos*. Once you arrive, there's not much left of the ancient building, which was destroyed in the Civil War when two hundred Guardia Civil officers seized the shrine, declaring their support for Franco's rebellion. Bombarded for eight months by Republican forces, the sanctuary was eventually set alight and the guards captured on May 1, 1937. (Pre-democracy Spanish guidebooks felt obligated to append an emphatic exclamation mark to the eight months the siege lasted and the more sycophantic compared it to Numancia and Sagunto, two of the great Spanish sieges of Roman times – thus turning the episode into a symbol of fascist heroism.) The distasteful rebuild flanked by equally bleak Guardia Civil monuments was carried out during the Franco period, but the famous *romería* – in which brotherhoods and pilgrims converge on the shrine from all over Andalucía and Spain on the last Sunday in April – carries on undaunted. There's a decent **hostal** here which would provide a base for exploring the surrounding countryside of the natural park; *Hostal Virgen de la Cabeza* (☎957 10 21 65; ❷) has rooms with bath and an economical **restaurant**. Alternatively the tourist complex *Los Pinos* (☎953 54 90 23, ⓦwww.complejolospinos.com; ❸), 13km from Andújar and mentioned above, has rooms and *apartamentos rurales* or cottages (both ❻) in a pleasant setting with a pool and restaurant. Three kilometres down a track heading east from here (signed "La Jandula") *Villa Matilde* (☎953 54 91 27, ⓦwww .infoandujar.com/villamatilde; ❷) is another pleasant rural retreat offering

△ Virgen de la Cabeza

rooms with or without bath in a converted villa with a pool and its own restaurant that also caters for vegetarians. There's also a **campsite**.

Baños de la Encina

Just beyond Andújar the A4-E5 turns away from the Guadalquivir valley to head northeast to **Bailén**, a dull farming town where Napoleon's troops suffered a crushing defeat in 1808, but with little to stop for. From here it pushes on for another 45km to Andalucía's border with La Mancha at the Despeñaperros Pass (see below) and Madrid. Other **possible routes** from this junction lead south to the city of Jaén, or east to Baeza and Úbeda via Linares.

Some 6km after Bailén a left turn leads to the sizeable village of **BAÑOS DE LA ENCINA**, which has one of the most impressive Moorish castles in Andalucía. Crowning a low hill above the village, the tenth-century **Alcázar** is a magnificent sight with its fourteen square towers and enormous keep spaced out along a crenellated curtain wall. Built by al-Hakam II of Córdoba, the fort was completed in 967, no doubt to control the rugged and mountainous territory to the north, the domain of various unruly Iberian clans. Entered through a double-horseshoe arch, where a plaque in Arabic script dates the edifice to year 357 of the *hegira* (967 AD), the fort has an oval ground plan and from the battlements (take care as there are no handrails) there are **fine views** over the village and towards the Sierra de Cazorla to the east and the less impressive reservoir behind.

To visit the Alcázar you need to collect the **key** from the **tourist office**, Callejón del Castillo 1, just off the main square (Mon–Fri 8.30am–2pm, ☎953 61 41 85, ⓦwww.bdelaencina.com). When closed the key is also available from the house of the guardian, the venerable Señor Antonio González Rezeñaz, at c/Santa María 10, the road leading up to the castle entrance. The tourist office can also provide information on walking in the area, a number of caves with prehistoric paintings nearby, and a Bronze Age site at **Peñalosa** where an important Iberian mining settlement is being excavated. On the main square, Plaza de la Constitución, the splendid red stone Gothic-Renaissance church of **San Mateo**, with an elegant octagonal tower, is also worth a look inside to view an exquisite *sagrario*, constructed in ebony and adorned with silver, marble and tortoiseshell, as are the village's narrow, whitewashed streets dotted with a clutch of *señorial* mansions. The **Ermita de Cristo del Llano**, an eighteenth-century hermitage in the upper village and a ten-minute walk from the tourist office, is worth the trek to see this remarkable church attached to a convent. If you call at the convent (preferably outside siesta time) the nuns will allow you to gain entry to view the church and its startlingly beautiful **Baroque camarín** with stellar decoration and stucco polychromed angels and saints climbing to the roof.

For a **place to stay** the elegant *Hotel-Restaurante Baños*, Cerro de la Llaná s/n (☎953 61 40 68, ⓦwww.hotelbanos.com; ④), occupying a hill behind the castle, has good-value balcony rooms, many with stunning castle views (Room 101 has the best). For **food** you can get **tapas** and *raciones* at **bars** on the main square and at the *Bar-Restaurante Mirasierra*, c/Bailén s/n, near the tourist office, which also does full meals. Behind the castle, *Restaurante La Encina*, c/Consultorio 3, serves hearty Sierra dishes and a good-value *menú* and the restaurant of the *Hotel Baños* is another tempting possibility with a weekday €9 *menú*.

La Carolina

LA CAROLINA, 20km further to the northeast, is the most important of the new towns set up by Carlos III in the eighteenth century (see p.354) to protect the bullion route from Cádiz to Madrid. As with the other settlements it was named after a member of the royal family – in this case the king himself – settled with foreign immigrants and laid out on a regular grid-pattern street plan that still survives today. The town's central square, the Plaza del Ayuntamiento, has the imposing, honey-coloured sandstone **Palacio de Pablo de Olavide**, built for Carlos III's radical minister, the force behind the Nuevas Poblaciones idea. De Olavide did not long enjoy the fruits of his labours, however, for the clergy, who were denied access to these new towns, wreaked their vengeance by denouncing him to the Inquisition. Arrested in 1776, he was divested of his property and confined to a convent in La Mancha subject to whatever penances the monks thought appropriate. He subsequently escaped to France. Flanking the *palacio*, the parish church of **La Concepción** contains a fine Baroque image of the *Virgen de las Angustias* in alabaster. The square is linked by a thoroughfare to an impressive tree-lined avenue entered via a gateway bearing images of Carlos III, at the far end of which lies the municipal **swimming pool**.

There are a number of **places to stay**: the friendly *El Retorno*, c/Sanjurjo 5 (☎953 66 16 13; ❶), a few blocks north of the focal Plaza de España, has en-suite rooms and would do for a night, or you could try the more luxurious *La Perdiz* (☎953 66 03 00, ⓦ www.nh-hoteles.es; ❻) – not be confused with the uninviting *Orellana Perdiz* nearby – on the main A4-E5 highway (km-268) at the edge of town. Even if you're not staying, it's worth knowing that for the price of a drink in the bar you can use their pleasant garden swimming pool.

El Centanillo

A minor road out of La Carolina winds 20km northwest into the hills and ends up at the tiny mountain hamlet of **EL CENTANILLO**, about as far off the tourist trail as it's possible to get in Andalucía. Situated in densely wooded hunting country, *Bar La Entrada* (❷) on the edge of the village, used by the shooting fraternity in winter, should have a **room**, although this establishment does have an eccentric streak – their decent restaurant always seems to have fresh *venado* (venison) on the menu even outside the legal hunting season. There's plenty of good **walking** country around El Centanillo; you could try tracing the Río Grande to its source (about 8km) or, more ambitiously, and with a map (CNIG sheet 862), trekking west along the Sierra de los Calderones to the valley of the Río Jándula bordering the province of Ciudad Real.

The Despeñaperros Pass

Two kilometres beyond La Carolina, slightly before the village of Navas de Tolosa, a huge roadside **monument** marks the site of the important battle that took place in 1212 between the Christian armies under Alfonso VIII and the Almohad forces.

The Moors suffered a crippling defeat, opening the way for the Reconquest of Andalucía. The monument depicts the Christian monarchs as well as the shepherd, an apparition of St Isidore in disguise, who, according to Christian belief, guided them through the well-defended Sierra Morena, thus enabling a surprise attack on the Moorish army who fled after defeat through the Despeñaperros Pass. This event, in fact, gave the pass its name – meaning the "overthrow of the dogs" (or Moors).

The **Despeñaperros Pass**, 14km further on, is the dramatic gateway between Andalucía and La Mancha and the only natural breach in the 500-kilometre length of the Sierra Morena. This narrow defile, flanked by daunting crags and slopes covered with dense pine woods, was for centuries the main point of entry into Andalucía from the north and many travellers have left vivid

Don Quijote and the Despeñaperros Pass

Cervantes would have been familiar with the route through the **Despeñaperros Pass**, connecting La Mancha with Sevilla and Córdoba, where he lived both as a child and in later life. The brooding and threatening nature of the pass – probably greater before it was blasted to make room for road widening and the rail line – appealed to him, for he used it in two of the most memorable scenes in the adventures of **Don Quijote** and Sancho Panza. The centre of the pass is where Don Quijote ran mad and played "the desperate, the raving, the furious lover", in order that Sancho could convey news of this penance to his fantasized Lady Dulcinea del Toboso, in reality a slatternly country lass named Alonza Lorenzo:

Observe the landmarks, and I will try to remain near this spot," said Don Quijote. "And I will even take the precaution of climbing the highest of these crags to look out for you on your return. But your surest way of not missing me, and not getting lost yourself, will be for you to scatter some of the broom that is so plentiful around here. Scatter it at intervals as you go till you get out to open country. The sprigs will serve as landmarks and signs for you to find me by when you come back, just like the thread in Theseus's labyrinth.

This botanical link with the world of Quijote is still strong when, in early summer, the clumps of brilliant yellow flowers are everywhere. About 1km further on, the **Venta de Cardenas** was the inn which the deluded knight errant imagined to be a castle. When the morning after a night's hospitality the innkeeper demanded payment, Quijote refused with the explanation that knights never paid for their accommodation and made his exit. Sancho, however, was not so lucky and was given a violent tossing in a blanket to teach him a lesson. The old *venta* apparently survived until the nineteenth century, when it was seen by Borrow. However, it was subsequently demolished and a characterless hotel now stands on the site. But it's still a stopover on this major transportation route and the lines of articulated lorries parked outside belong to the truck drivers who use this inn today, the successors of the muleteers, drovers and carriers of Cervantes's time.

accounts of arriving in the lush promised land of the south after traversing the dry and arid plains of La Mancha (from the Moorish *manxa*, or parched earth). George Borrow, however, also related the sense of foreboding due to the pass's evil reputation "on account of the robberies which are continually being perpetrated in its recesses". Ford, when going the other way, described the land beyond the pass as where "commences the *paño pardo*, the brown cloth, and the *alpargata*, or the hempen sandal of the poverty-stricken Manchegos".

Jaén

Surrounded by olive groves and huddled beneath the fortress of Santa Catalina on the heights above, **JAÉN**, the provincial capital and by far the largest town in the eponymous province, is an uneventful sort of place. Derived from the Arabic *Geen*, meaning a stop on the caravan route, the modern town is more northerly than Andalucian in its appearance and character, doubtless stemming from its resettlement with emigrants from the north following the *Reconquista,* and the subsequent long centuries spent as the front-line bulwark of Christian Spain against Moorish Granada. At the centre of an area impoverished by lack of economic development and chronic unemployment, while you would hardly want to go out of your way to get here, the city makes an easy place to stop over en route to destinations such as Baeza, Úbeda and Cazorla to the northeast. And, given a chance, it has a surprising number of worthwhile sights, including a fine cathedral, the largest Moorish baths in Spain, some elegant old churches and mansions and an important museum.

Some history

Although the area around the city is liberally dotted with Iberian settlements, it was probably as the Roman settlement of *Auringis* that Jaén was born. A centre noted for its **silver mines** and settled by the Moors shortly after the conquest of 711, to judge by the number of mosques it must have been a thriving place. The Moors also made use of the **hot springs** that had been known to the Romans and utilized them in the construction of several baths. Fernando III's Christian forces captured the city – then part of the newly founded Nasrid kingdom of Granada – in 1246 and made its ruler Ibn al-Ahmar (aka Muhammad ibn Yusuf ibn Nasr) into a vassal, obliged to pay annual tribute. It was from Jaén, two and a half centuries later, that the final assault on Boabdil's Granada was launched. The city then entered into a slow decline which gathered pace in the seventeenth and eighteenth centuries and led many of its citizens to emigrate to the imperial colonies, evidenced by towns with the same name in countries as far apart as Peru and the Philippines. Although Jaén's strategic importance played a part in the War of Independence, the economic disruption caused brought further decline in its wake, from which the city never really recovered. The situation is not much improved today and in a survey carried out by the *Junta de Andalucía*, the city and province registered the largest percentage of Andalucía's population describing themselves as living in poverty (61 percent). The survey also showed that a quarter of all the province's citizens live on an income of less than €100 a month.

Arrival and information

Jaén's **bus station** (☎953 25 01 06) is on Plaza Coca de la Pinera, just off the Paseo de la Estación. There are frequent daily services to and from Úbeda and Baeza and, less often, Cazorla. The **train station** (☎953 27 02 02) is a bit further out, at the end of Paseo de la Estación, and a good ten-minute walk (or an easier ride on bus #19) from the centre. There are train connections to Córdoba and Madrid. Arriving **by car** either use the signed pay car parks around the centre or consult where you're staying; even if they don't have a garage they should be able to advise. The streets around the bullring to the east of the centre usually have parking spaces. The **Turismo**, c/Maestra 13, slightly north of the cathedral (Mon–Fri 10am–7pm, Sat–Sun 10am–1pm; ☎953 24 26 24), has lots of information on the town, while inside the striking nineteenth-century Diputación Provincial building fronting Plaza de San Francisco the **provincial tourist office** (Mon–Fri 8am–3pm; ☎953 24 80 00) has information on the province.

Jaén on the Internet

Information on Jaén and its monuments and amenities as well as the province generally can be found on the provincial government's official site at ⓦ www.promojaen.es, and on the Ayuntamiento's site at ⓦ www.aytojaen.es.

It's worth noting (and applauding) that **admission** to all Jaén's monuments – barring the new audiovisual attraction in the Castillo de Santa Catalina – is free.

Accommodation

Places to stay in town are limited and relatively expensive. The few budget-priced places in the centre are around the cathedral and Plaza de la Constitución. Mosquitoes can be a real problem in the town during the high summer season when places with air-conditioning come into their own.

Hostal Estación RENFE Estación de Tren ☎953 27 47 04, @hostalrenfe@amsystem.es. The RENFE's own *hostal* at the front of the station is rather swish with comfortable a/c rooms with TV, and cuts down your chances of missing that train. **❸**

Hostal La Española c/Bernardo López 9 ☎953 23 02 54. Housed in the former *casa-palacio* of a local count, this haphazardly run place offers basic accommodation; some rooms en suite and singles without bath. **❸**

Hostal Martín c/Cuatro Torres 5 ☎953 24 36 78. Off the south side of Plaza de la Constitución, this is a budget option with clean rooms sharing bath. **❷**

Hotel Europa Plaza de Belén 1 ☎953 22 27 00, @www.husa.es. Perhaps the best of the more upmarket places in the centre, where decent a/c rooms come with safe and satellite TV. Also has a breakfast bar and garage. **❹**

Parador Castillo de Santa Catalina Castillo, 3km above the town, ☎953 23 00 00, @www.parador.es. For a truly memorable experience you could stay in one of the most spectacularly sited hotels in Spain. The comfortable rooms all have fine balcony views with a sheer drop to the valley below, and facilities include a pool, restaurant, bar and ample parking. **❼**

Hotel Xuen Plaza Deán Mazas 3 ☎953 24 07 89, @953 19 03 12. Off the west side of the Plaza de la Constitución, this is a reasonable option with comfortable a/c rooms. **❹**

The Town

Most of Jaén's sights lie within a few minutes' walk of the rather characterless main thoroughfare, the **Paseo de la Estación**. This cuts through the heart of the city from north to south linking the train station with the Plaza de la Constitución, the major hub of activity. The *paseo* is interrupted only by the Plaza de las Batalles, a square dominated by a grotesque sculpture commemorating the battles of Nava de Tolosa (against the Moors) and Bailén (against the French).

The Catedral and around

Jaén's massive and magnificent **Catedral** (Mon–Sat 8.30am–1pm & 5–8pm, Sun 10.30am–1pm & 6–8pm; museum Mon–Sat 10.30am–1pm & 6–8pm; church free, museum €1.80), lying to the west of the Plaza de la Constitución, dwarfs the city. Begun in 1492 after the demolition of the great mosque which had previously occupied the site, the cathedral was not completed until 1802. A number of architects turned their hand to the project during this period, including the great Andrés de Vandelvira whose imprint is on most of the building as it looks today. The spectacular **west facade**, flanked by twin sixty-metre-high towers framing Corinthian pillars and statuary by the seventeenth-century master, Pedro Roldán, is one of the masterpieces of Andalucian Renaissance architecture. Inside, the overall mood of the building is more sombre, with bundles of great Corinthian columns surging towards the roof of the nave. Fine sixteenth-century **choir stalls** have richly carved images from the Old Testament as well as a number of grisly martyrdoms. The dim side chapels also have some interesting artworks, among them an eighteenth-century *Virgen de*

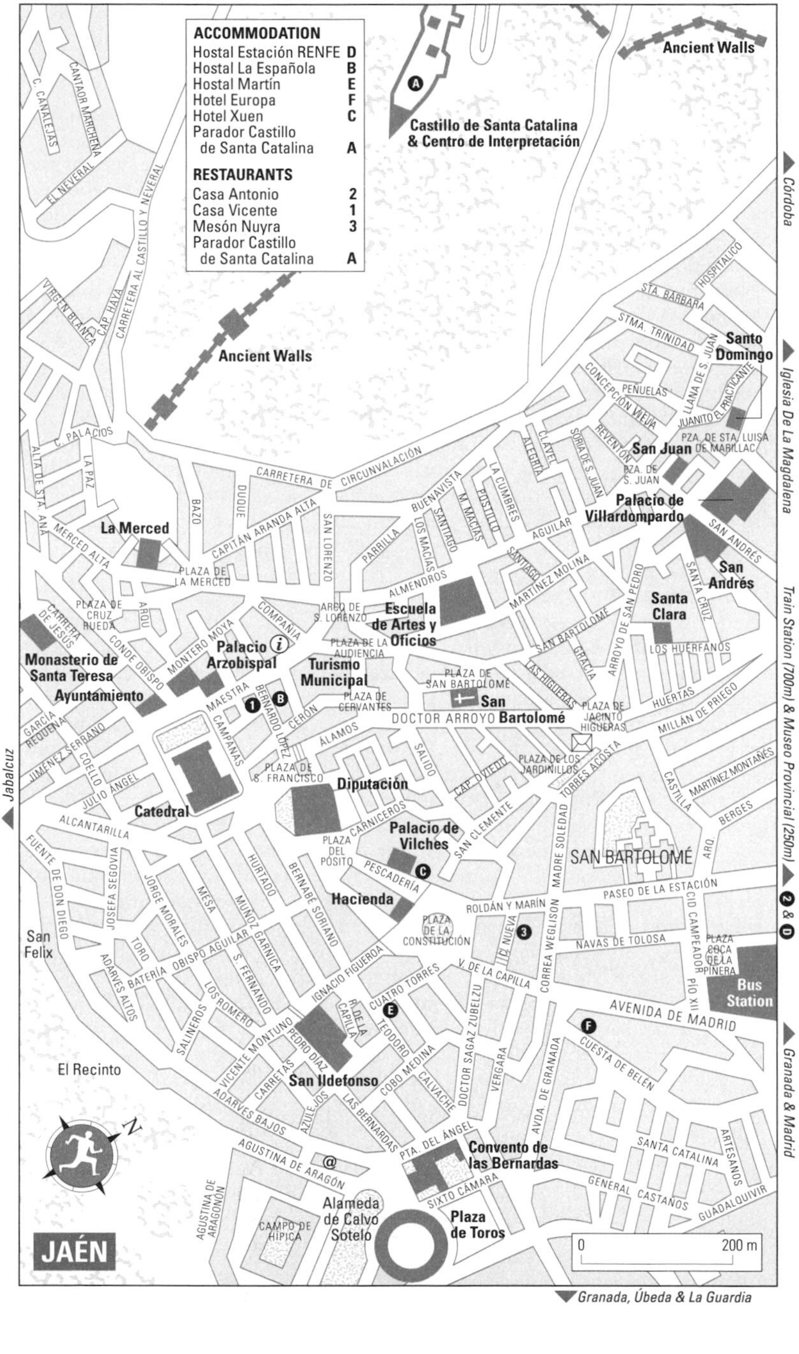

ACCOMMODATION
Hostal Estación RENFE D
Hostal La Española B
Hostal Martín E
Hotel Europa F
Hotel Xuen C
Parador Castillo de Santa Catalina A
RESTAURANTS
Casa Antonio 2
Casa Vicente 1
Mesón Nuyra 3
Parador Castillo de Santa Catalina A
Castillo de Santa Catalina & Centro de Interpretación
Ancient Walls
Ancient Walls
Córdoba
Iglesia De La Magdalena
Train Station (700m) & Museo Provincial (250m)
2 & D
Granada & Madrid
Granada, Úbeda & La Guardia
Jabalcuz
Santo Domingo
San Juan
Palacio de Villardompardo
San Andrés
Santa Clara
La Merced
Escuela de Artes y Oficios
Palacio Arzobispal
Turismo Municipal
Monasterio de Santa Teresa
Ayuntamiento
San Bartolomé
Diputación
Catedral
Palacio de Vilches
Hacienda
SAN BARTOLOMÉ
Bus Station
San Felix
El Recinto
San Ildefonso
Convento de las Bernardas
Alameda de Calvo Sotelo
Plaza de Toros
CAMPO DE HÍPICA
CARRETERA DE CIRCUNVALACIÓN
CARRETERA AL CASTILLO Y NEVERAL
DOCTOR ARROYO
PASEO DE LA ESTACIÓN
AVENIDA DE MADRID
AVDA. DE GRANADA
MADRE SOLEDAD
CORREA WEGLISON
ROLDÁN Y MARÍN
NAVAS DE TOLOSA
CUESTA DE BELÉN
SANTA CATALINA
GENERAL CASTAÑOS
GUADALQUIVIR
AGUSTINA DE ARAGÓN
ADARVES BAJOS
PLAZA DE LA MERCED
PLAZA DE SAN BARTOLOMÉ
PLAZA DE LA CONSTITUCIÓN
PLAZA COCA DE LA PIÑERA
PLAZA DE LOS JARDINILLOS
PLAZA DE CERVANTES
PLAZA DE S. FRANCISCO
PLAZA DEL PÓSITO
0 200 m
JAÉN

las Angustias (Our Lady of the Sorrows) by José de Mora in the fifth side chapel to the right. The church fills up on Fridays (11.30am–1pm) when the **lienzo del Santo Rostro** is ritually removed from its coffer behind the high altar. This Byzantine cloth icon bearing a likeness of Christ is believed locally to be the napkin with which St Veronica wiped his face en route to Calvary. Long queues form to kiss the icon (preserved behind glass) and the attending priest wipes it with a handkerchief after each devotee.

The sacristy **museum** displays works by artists of the region as well as the Tenebrario, a fifteen-armed candlestick by Master Bartolomé de Jaén who also made the magnificent *reja* in the Capilla Real at Granada. Two fine seventeenth-century sculptures by Martinéz Montañés, *San Lorenzo* and *Cristo Nazareno*, are also on display.

Near the cathedral the fifteenth-century **Palacio del Condestable**, c/ Martínez Molina 24, has a beautiful patio and interior decoration by Moorish craftsmen from the kingdom of Granada. The elegant portico of the seventeenth-century **Palacio de los Vilches**, c/Pescadería (and now occupied by a bank), once fronted Jaén's central Plaza Mayor before the present, featureless Plaza de la Constitución replaced it. A short distance east of the cathedral the fifteenth-century (in origin) church of **San Ildefonso** (daily 9.30am–noon & 5.30–9pm; free) is an impressive amalgam of Gothic, Mannerist and Neoclassical styles and worth a look, as is the striking facade and exquisite cloister of the beautiful seventeenth-century convent and church of the **Convento de las Bernardas**.

The Baños Árabes

The main cluster of the city's other sights lies to the north of the cathedral, along c/Martínez Molina in what was formerly the old Moorish quarter. The most interesting of these is the **Baños Árabes** (Tues–Fri 9am–8pm, Sat & Sun 9.30am–2.30pm; free), a remarkable Moorish *hammam* or baths, and the largest to survive in Spain. Originally part of an eleventh-century Moorish palace, the baths fell into disuse after the *Reconquista* and were used as a tannery. In the sixteenth century the Palacio de Villadompardo, now the **Museo de Artes y Costumbres Populares** (arts and crafts museum) was built over them. They were rediscovered early last century and in the 1980s were painstakingly restored. Recent modifications now lead you into the baths over a glass floor allowing views of the Roman and Moorish remains which surround the complex. The various rooms (cold, tepid and hot) have wonderful brickwork ceilings with typical star-shaped windows, and pillars supporting elegant horseshoe arches. An underground passage (now closed) connected the baths with the centre of the Moorish palace, on top of which was built the Monastery of Santo Domingo (see opposite). The **museum of arts and crafts** (same hours) contains a fascinating and well-presented folk history of the province on three floors using artefacts, clothing, toys, ceramics, photos and audiovisual aids. A recent addition here is the **Museo Internacional de Arte Naïf** (same hours) with works by (mainly) Spanish and some international artists.

The baths are flanked by the **Palacio de los Uribes**, a sixteenth-century mansion, on the northern side, whilst the church of **San Andrés** (service times or ring ☏953 23 74 22 to view), which contains a fabulous altar screen depicting the *Holy Family* and the *Tree of Jesse* by Maestro Bartolomé of Jaén, here working on his home patch, lies just to the south. Slightly west of here, the ancient post-*Reconquista* church of **San Juan**, (daily 8am–3pm & 5–8pm; free) in the Plaza de San Juan, has an elegant Romanesque tower and, inside, a fine sixteenth-century sculpture of the Crucifixion by Sebastián de Solís. A couple of streets north, the c/Santísima Trinidad leads to a path which climbs, ruggedly in parts, to the castle of Santa Catalina, a much shorter route than the three-kilometre-plus road. The path starts from the *Bar Sobrino Bigotes*.

Santo Domingo, La Magdalena and around

Standing on c/Santo Domingo, north of San Juan, the **Monastery of Santo Domingo** (patio can be viewed Mon–Fri 8.30am–2pm; free), erected over a Moorish palace, was originally a fourteenth-century Dominican monastery and later became Jaén's university; later still it was a seat of the Inquisition, before being transformed in more recent times into the office of the provincial historical archive (Archivo Historico). From its earlier incarnations a fine sixteenth-century **portal** by Vandelvira and a beautiful **patio** with elegant twinned Tuscan columns survive. The building is closed to visitors, but you can gain access to view the patio by ringing the intercom outside.

A little further north still, the **Iglesia de La Magdalena** (daily 9am–12.30pm & 5.30–8pm; free), the oldest in Jaén, was built over a mosque, the minaret of which is now its bell tower, and a patio at the rear preserves a pool used in Moorish times for ritual ablutions. In the cloister you can still see a few Roman tombstones used in the construction of the original Moorish building; this quarter was also the centre of the ancient Roman town. Inside, the church has a superb **retablo** by Jacobo Florentino depicting scenes from the Passion.

Two more interesting churches can be seen on the way back to the cathedral zone. The first, on c/Huérfanos to the southeast of the Palacio de Villadompardo, is the **Convento de Santa Clara** (open service times, try 7–9pm), with a fine choir and sixteenth-century Ecuadorian sculpture of *Cristo debambú*. South of here on the Plaza de San Bartolomé, the sixteenth-century **San Bartolomé** (daily 6.30–8pm; entry through the sacristy), has a fine Mudéjar *artesonado* ceiling, Gothic ceramic font and an outstanding *Expiration of Christ* by José de Medina.

The Museo Provincial

The **Museo Provincial** at Paseo de la Estación 27 (Tues 2.30–8.30pm, Wed–Sat 9am–8.30pm, Sun 9am–2.30pm; free) is worth a visit for its remarkable collection of Iberian stone **sculptures**, among the most important in Spain. Recently housed in a separate building to the side of the museum (ask at the admission desk for directions) these remarkable objects were found near the town of Porcuna, close to the province's western border, and date from the fifth century BC. One is of a magnificent bull, whilst another is a strange fragment – titled *grifomaquia* – depicting a struggle between a man and a griffon. All the works betray the artistic influence of the classical Greek world on the fertile Iberian imagination. The strange fact revealed by the archeological excavations when these works came to light is that they had been deliberately broken a short time after their execution and then laid in a long trench. No satisfactory explanation for this has yet been put forward. More sculptures are being put on show each year as they are uncovered by archeologists, and it's intended that this will eventually become the major museum for Iberian art in Spain.

Items on display in the main building include Phoenician jewellery and ointment phials, Greek vases, as well as Roman mosaics and sculpture, including an outstanding fourth-century **sarcophagus** found near Martós depicting seven miracles of Christ including the transformation of water into wine. A new addition here is a complete full-scale walk-in replica-reconstruction of the remarkable fourth-century BC Iberian necropolis **tomb** at Toya near Cazorla. Room 7 deals with Jaén's significant **Moorish period** and has lamps and stoneware as well as a whole jugful of money – dirhams and califalas – that someone buried and never came back to collect. This room also has some fine **ceramics** which verify the Moorish origin of the green glazed plates and vases, still the hallmark of the pottery of Jaén province. A Visigothic section has examples of jewellery, vases and metalwork from this hazy period in Spanish history.

Upstairs, the **Museo de Bellas Artes** starts out with some interesting medieval wood sculpture before quickly degenerating into a hotchpotch of fairly awful stuff from the nineteenth and twentieth centuries, although there are a few laughs, not to mention a large number of steamy nudes. The tedium is somewhat relieved by a recently acquired engraving by Picasso and some interesting works by Manuel Angeles Ortiz, a native of Jaén who was a great friend of both Picasso and García Lorca.

Castillo de Santa Catalina

The **Castillo de Santa Catalina**, dominating the crag which rises behind the city, was in origin a Moorish fortress constructed in the thirteenth century by Ibn al-Ahmar. After the Reconquest, the castle was much altered and today part of it has been stylishly converted into a modern parador, and little of the Moorish edifice now survives. What does remain has recently been reconstructed as a **Centro de Interpretación** (daily: April–Sept 10am–2pm & 5–9pm; Oct–March 10am–2pm & 3.30–7.30pm; €3), housing in the fort's five towers a series of hi-tech interactive audiovisual gadgets explaining the building's history.

The dungeon beneath has an entertaining hologram reconstruction of a prisoner telling his story and there's a 3D cinema with a film on the history of Jaén. A number of secret passageways connected the Moorish fortress with the town below and a few of these have been discovered.

A path from the parador car park leads to the older and ruined part of the edifice at the castle's southern end where a *mirador* beneath a huge, whitewashed cross gives a **spectacular view** of the city laid out below your feet and dominated by the massive cathedral. Beyond, Jaén's wealth and misery, the endless lines of olive groves, disappear over the hills into the haze. Nonresidents are welcome to use the parador's bar and restaurant.

△ Castillo de Santa Catalina

If you don't fancy the three-kilometre, near-vertical hike to reach the castle, you can take a taxi (about €5 one way) from Plaza Coca de la Piñera by the bus station.

Eating, drinking and nightlife

Jaén tends to shut down after dark and in the absence of much nightlife you'll probably compensate by **eating and drinking**. In the centre, the best place to find food is on the east side of Plaza de la Constitución. Here, the tiny c/Nueva has a whole crowd of **tapas** bars and places to eat; *Mesón Río Chico* and *La Gamba de Oro* are both good. Above the west side of the Plaza de la Constitución, you'll find *Bar del Posito*, a popular tapas and *raciones* venue on Plaza Deán Mazas with outdoor tables. More bars for tapas around the centre include *Manila*, c/Maestra 4, north of the cathedral, or, a couple of streets away, the cosy *Tasca Los Amigos*, c/Bernardo López, where there's good *jamón* and *morcilla* (blood pudding); the nearby *Bar 82* is also worth a visit. One street south, on c/Arcos del Consuelo, *El Gorrión* serves cheese tapas and *La Catedral* is popular with a younger crowd.

A good **breakfast** stop is *Cafetería Yucatán*, up a flight of steps off the Plaza del Posito, with a terrace; later in the day it also serves economical *platos combinados*. Other pleasant breakfast bars also serving snacks later in the day are the efficient and friendly *La Colombiana*, c/Cerón 6, slightly north of the cathedral, where fifteen types of coffee are on offer, and the tranquil *Café de Indias*, c/Bernabe Soriano 25, slightly southwest of Plaza de la Constitución.

Restaurants

Casa Antonio c/Fermin Palma 3, north of the bus station ☏953 27 02 62. Top culinary choice in town, this place has innovative *jiennense* and Basque-inspired dishes on offer such as *perdiz escabechada* (partridge in wine); there's a *menú de degustación* for about €45.

Casa Vicente c/Francisco Martín Mora, off c/Maestra ☏953 23 22 22. Housed in a superbly restored old mansion with a delightful patio, this is another of Jaén's best restaurants; specialities include *pastel de carne de caza* (game pie) and *cordero mozárabe* (spiced lamb) and there's also a *menú de degustación* for around €36.

Mesón Nuyra Pasaje Nuyra s/n, off c/Nueva. For less expensive fare this restaurant serves up some good fish and meat dishes.

Parador Castillo de Santa Catalina To feast in baronial splendour you'll need to climb – or take a taxi – to this spectacularly located restaurant inside the parador. Dining is in a re-created medieval banqueting room and although service can be a bit fussy, the cooking is excellent and many local specialities – such as *morcilla* (blood sausage) and *pipirrana* (*jamón* and vegetable salad) – are offered on a good-value *menú*, costing around €25.

El Mirador Ctra. de Jabalcuz km-7.9 ☏953 24 36 58. A popular haunt with *jiennenses* – especially on Sundays – this great family-run restaurant offers excellent local dishes, an economical *menú* and fine views from its terraces (closed Mon).

Nightlife

The night-time *movida* takes place in the **drinking bars** of the Barrio de San Ildefonso to the east of the cathedral centring on c/Hurtado, where the friendly *Bar Azulejo* at no. 8 is located inside a *casa señorial* and gives a free tapa with every drink. *Trujal*, *Santuario* and *77* on the same street are also worth a try. *El Hortelano* and *Cuatro Escinas* in the adjacent Plaza de San Ildefonso, and *Iroquai* along c/Las Bernadas slightly east, are other good places nearby. More serious **nightlife** takes place along the lower end of the Paseo de la Estación towards the train station, where a couple of tame discos and some music bars cater for the city's teenage set. A couple of places offering a slightly maturer alternative in the same area are *Chubby Check*, c/San Francisco Javier

7, which often stages live **jazz**, and *Café Latino*, c/Santa Alicia 3, which puts on live **salsa**.

Listings

Banks Numerous places with ATMs are located along the town's two main thoroughfares, the Paseo de la Estación and the Avda. de Madrid.

Car rental Europcar (☎953 26 60 11) and Atesa (☎953 25 59 63) both have offices in the train station, Plaza Jaén por la Paz s/n.

Football Following a few lean years, Real Jaén are currently treading water in the Segunda B division of the lower leagues. They play at the Estadio Nuevo de la Victoria, Avda. Granada s/n (☎953 22 39 38, ❺www.realjaen.com), south of the centre.

Hospital The city's main hospital is Hospital Ciudad de Jaén, Avda. Ejército Español s/n, northwest of the Plaza de las Batallas (☎953 29 90 00). For emergencies dial ☎061.

Hiking maps 1:50,000, 1:100,000 and 1:200,000 maps are available from CNIG (National Geographic Service) branch office: Plaza de la Constitución 10 ☎953 22 18 32.

Internet *Cyber Cu@k* Adarves Bajos 24 (daily 5.30–11.30pm; ☎953 19 06 16).

Markets A vibrant weekly market takes place on Thursdays in the *recinto ferial* at the end of Avda. de Granada, east of the bullring.

Newspapers Jaén's daily paper, *Jaén* (❺www.diariojaen.es), is a good source of information on both the town and province, and has details of entertainment and special events.

Police Plaza Santa María, in the Ayuntamiento building fronting the cathedral (☎953 21 91 00). In an emergency dial ☎091.

Post office Plaza Jardinillos, near the Convento de Santa Clara (Mon–Fri 8.30am–8pm, Sat 9.30am–2pm).

Taxis These congregate outside the bus station on Plaza Coca de la Piñera and in Plaza de San Francisco near the cathedral. You can ring for one on ☎953 22 22 22.

Around Jaén

Two good day-trips from Jaén are to **La Guardia de Jaén**, 10km southeast, and **Martos**, 24km to the west, both with impressive hill-top forts. La Guardia isn't too difficult a journey without your own transport, with three daily buses on weekdays, whilst Martos has hourly buses with a skeleton service on Sundays. Also worth a visit if you are likely to be travelling to Baeza with your own transport is **La Laguna**.

La Guardia

Reached along a minor road which branches off the main A44-E902 to Granada, **LA GUARDIA** is a charming white-walled village gathered beneath its ruined eighth-century **castillo** (collect the key from the Ayuntamiento in the village) which contains elements of previous Iberian, Roman and Visigothic fortifications. Behind its walls the castle precincts also hold the ruined church of **Santo Domingo**, originally part of a Dominican monastery founded in 1530, and a major work by Andrés de Vandelvira, who was also responsible for the cathedral at Jaén. The arcades around the patio (or cloister) and a central fountain are all that remains of the monastery, whilst the sanctuary, nave and transept crossing give some idea of what a fine construction the church must once have been. At the edge of the village on Monte Salido, a small hill, are some rock-cut Visigothic **graves** where numerous artefacts were found, now on display in the museum at Jaén.

Martos

Along the A316 to the west of Jaén, and surrounded by endless olive groves, it doesn't take long to realize why **MARTOS** is Spain's number-one producer of olives. The ruins of a Moorish fortress, *La Peña*, on a great rock outcrop that towers over the small town, are a vivid reminder of the great struggles of the *Reconquista* when the Moorish forts of Jaén became the front line against hostile Christian incursions, and the scene of bitter battles and sieges. This one fell to Fernando III on St Marta's Day in 1225, thus giving the town its present name. In the old quarter with its narrow, winding streets the church of **Santa María de la Villa** is thirteenth-century, constructed soon after the victory, although it underwent substantial rebuilding in the fifteenth and later centuries. The interior has an outstanding Baroque *retablo* as well as a fine early Christian sarcophagus dating from the fourth century. The fifteenth-century church of **Santa Marta** with its Isabelline entrance and the former sixteenth-century prison, now the **Ayuntamiento**, graced by another fine portal, are also worth a look.

If you want **to stay**, *Hostal Fernando IV*, c/Lope de Vega 19 (☎953 55 15 75; ❹), is central, pleasant and has rooms with bath. For **eating and drinking** there are numerous tapas bars around the centre and a surprisingly good restaurant is to be found at the bus station, Avda. Moris 3, with a terrace which, on summer nights, becomes a lively social hub.

La Laguna

A former *hacienda* or olive-oil estate and mill, purchased in 1992 by the Junta de Andalucía, the complex of **La Laguna** now houses the impressive **Museo de la Cultura del Olivo** (April–Sept daily 10.30am–1.30pm & 4.30–7pm, Oct–March 4–6.30pm; ⓦwww.museodelaculturadeolivo.com; free), dedicated to the history and development of Jaén's great wealth earner, describing the history of the olive and production methods used since Roman times. The patio garden has examples of olive species from all over the world. Another part of the complex houses the province's hotel and catering school, and the mid-priced **restaurant**, where the trainee chefs serve up their creations, is the *hacienda's* former chapel, with a stunning domed ceiling. The adjoining **hotel**, *La Laguna* (☎953 77 10 05, ⓦwww.haciendalalaguna.com; ❺), has pleasant air-conditioned rooms with TV and their mini-suites add in a Jacuzzi. La Laguna is aptly located in a sea of olive groves 2km down a signed left turn off the A316 just before the village of Puente del Obispo, 8km short of Baeza.

Baeza

Campo de Baeza, soñaré contigo cuando no te vea.
Fields of Baeza, I will dream of you when I can no longer see you.

Antonio Machado (1875–1939)

Fifty kilometres from Jaén along the winding A316, **BAEZA** is a tiny, compact and provincial country town with a perpetual Sunday air about it. Sited on the escarpment of the Loma de Úbeda, both Baeza and the neighbouring town of Úbeda have an extraordinary density of exuberant **Renaissance palaces**, richly endowed churches and magnificent public squares which are among the finest in Spain.

Important in Roman times as Beatia, Baeza was later a Visigothic bishopric and then a prosperous commercial and agricultural centre under the Moors. After a prolonged and bitter struggle the town fell to the Christian forces in 1227, and *hidalgos* or nobles were granted estates in the surrounding countryside with orders to defend this frontier zone. The power of these noble houses was so untrammelled that they were soon warring among themselves for control of the town (a favoured place of battle being Baeza's Alcázar – until Isabel had it demolished). It was later, in the sixteenth century, however, that Baeza embarked on its most prosperous period. The nobility, made rich by farming and textile production, endowed the town with numerous striking Renaissance buildings as the population expanded.

Arrival and information

The nearest **train station** to Baeza is **Linares–Baeza**, 14km away and served by frequent trains from Sevilla, Córdoba and Granada (buses connect with most trains, or it's a €15 taxi ride), where you'll find fronting the station a good *hostal* and restaurant, *Las Palmeras* (☎953 69 89 79; ❸). Otherwise, you're dependent on buses, and all services (around fourteen daily) between Jaén and Úbeda, 9km further east, call in at Baeza. The **bus station** (☎953 74 04 68), officially at Paseo de Elorza Garat 1, is actually at the end of c/San Pablo and along the Paseo Arca del Agua. Baeza's **Turismo** in the sixteenth-century former **Audiencia**, or appeal court, on the Plaza del Populo (Mon–Fri 9am–2.30pm, Sat 10am–1pm; ☎953 74 04 44), can supply maps and information as well as a *Ruta del Tapeo* booklet and details of guided tours of the town. **Internet** access is available at the central *Speed Informatica*, Plaza de la Constitución 2 (Mon–Sat 10am–2pm & 5–9pm), *Cyberway*, Plaza de la Constitución, Portales Alhondiga s/n, on the opposite side of the same square (daily 11am–2pm and 5–11pm), and *Micro Ware*, c/Portales Tundidores 13, facing the Paseo de la Constitución.

Accommodation

The town has a decent range of **places to stay**, some of which are architectural gems. There's usually no problem finding rooms in Baeza except during the summer *feria* in mid-August and even then you should have no trouble if you ring ahead.

Hostal El Patio c/Conde Romanones 13 ☎953 74 02 00, ☎953 74 82 60. Wonderfully shabby Renaissance mansion set around a courtyard, decorated with mangy mounted bulls' heads and a central fountain. Some slightly pricier rooms have bath. ❶–❷

Hotel Baeza c/Concepción 3 ☎953 74 81 30, ⓦwww.trhhoteles.com. Well-equipped a/c rooms partly housed in a stylishly converted Renaissance monastery with a glassed-in patio. They do frequent cut-price deals so it's worth giving them a ring. ❺ with breakfast.

Hotel El Alcázar Paseo Arca del Agua s/n ☎953 74 00 28. Decent if unadorned rooms (there's no TV) with bath above a restaurant. ❷

Hotel Fuentenueva c/del Carmen ☎953 74 31 00, ⓦwww.fuentenueva.com. Delightful and friendly small hotel housed in a stylishly refurbished nineteenth-century town house with *cafetería* and garden plunge pool. Ultra-modern rooms come with minibar, safe, satellite TV, Internet connection and power shower or Jacuzzi.

Rough Guide readers with this guide can claim a ten percent discount. ❺

Hotel Juanito Paseo Arca del Agua s/n ☎953 74 00 40, ⓦwww.juanitobaeza.com. The service can be a bit sniffy, but there's a top-notch restaurant downstairs and the well-equipped rooms come with a/c and TV. Insist on a west-facing room at the back or a high room on the front to avoid the smell of the *gasolinera* next door. ❸

Hotel Puerta de la Luna c/Pintada Alta s/n ☎953 74 70 19, ⓦwww.hotelpuertadelaluna .com. Beautiful four-star hotel situated in a refurbished seventeenth-century *casa palacio*. Features include two charming patios, restaurant, gym and a small pool. Comfortably furnished tiled-floor rooms are airy and well equipped, and it has its own car park. Room prices drop by 30 percent Sun–Thurs. ❼

Hotel Santa Ana c/Santa Ana Vieja 9 ☎953 74 07 65, ⓦwww.palacetesantana.com. Charming hotel with stylish a/c rooms in a striking stone-built sixteenth-century *casa señorial*. ❹

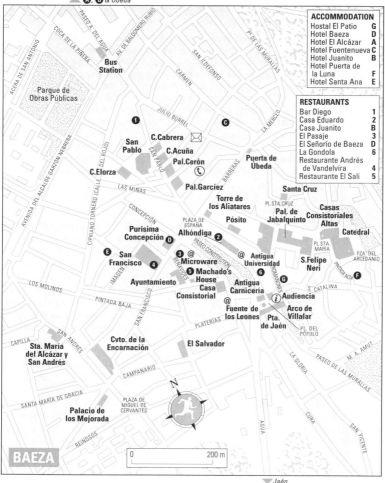

The Town

Most of Baeza's main attractions lie within a few minutes' walk of the pleasant central joined squares of **Plaza de España** and the larger **Paseo de la Constitución**. There are no charges to enter any of the monuments but you may offer the guardian a small *propina* (tip).

Paseo de la Constitución

On the eastern side of the bar-lined *paseo* is **La Alhóndiga**, an elegant porticoed sixteenth-century corn exchange and, almost opposite across the gardens, the arcaded eighteenth-century **Casa Consistorial**, or old town hall, which once fronted the old market square. At the southern end of the *paseo*, you'll find the **Plaza de los Leones** (also called the Plaza del Populo), a delightful cobbled square enclosed by Renaissance buildings. A central fountain incorporates

Walks around Baeza

There are some nice **wandering routes** in town: heading up through the Puerta de Jaén on the Plaza de los Leones and along the Paseo Murallas/Paseo Antonio Machado takes you round the edge of Baeza and gives good views over the surrounding plains. **El Abuelo**, a house on the Paseo de Don Antonio Machado, is noteworthy for its garden sculpture and towering wrought-iron work. It's the first house past the modern bronze bust of the poet Antonio Machado – who was a frequent walker here – looking out over the olive groves. You can cut back to the Plaza de España via the network of narrow, stone-walled alleys – with the occasional arch – that lies behind the cathedral.

Going further afield, near El Abuelo, some tracks lead down to the plain. Take the right-hand fork and after about 45 minutes you'll come to the route of a former rail line now used as a road for farm vehicles. This offers scope for easy walks across country.

Roman lions and a statue – which locals believe is Imilce, the Iberian wife of the Carthaginian general, Hannibal. The fountain is overlooked by some remarkable buildings including the **Antigua Carnicería** (old slaughterhouse), bearing the arms of Carlos V, and beside the arch at the far end, the Audiencia housing the Turismo (see p.490). Also here, on a rounded balcony flanking the double arch of the Arco de Villalar and the Puerta de Jaén, the first Mass of the Reconquest is reputed to have been celebrated. The Puerta de Jaén was a memento (or rebuke) left by Carlos V to the town which had opposed him, and commemorated the Germanic ruler's procession through here in 1526 en route to marry Isabel of Portugal.

Palacio de Jabalquinto and the Antigua Universidad

The stepped street behind the Plaza de los Leones ascends (via c/Romanones and c/Juan de Ávila) to another cluster of monuments including the finest of Baeza's palaces, the **Palacio de Jabalquinto** (patio Mon–Fri 9am–2pm), now a seminary, with an elaborate "Isabelline" front (showing marked Moorish influence in its stalactite decoration). Built in the fifteenth century by the Benavides family, the tranquil interior patio has a double tier of arcades around a central fountain and a superb Baroque **staircase** with fine carving. Next to this palace, the **Antigua Universidad** or old university (patio daily 10am–2pm & 5–9pm) was founded in 1538 and, after functioning for nearly three centuries as a centre of study and debate, its charter was revoked in 1824 during the tyrannical reign of Fernando VII. From 1875 the buildings were used as a school until, in 1979, the building once again became a centre of higher learning albeit as a summer school for the University of Granada. The interior has an elegant patio and, next to a sixteenth-century lecture hall, the preserved **classroom** (ask the guardian to open it up) used by the great *sevillano* poet and writer Antonio Machado when he served as a teacher here from 1912 to 1919. This experience must have provided much of the material for his most famous prose work, *Juan de Mairena*, the observations on life and culture of a fictional schoolmaster.

A little to the north of here in Plaza Santa Cruz, the remarkable church of **Santa Cruz** (Mon–Sat 11am–1pm & 4–7pm, Sun 12–2pm; free) is Baeza's oldest, built shortly after the Reconquest in the thirteenth century, although later much restored. Converted from an earlier mosque, the church betrays a combination of late Romanesque and early Gothic architectural styles. The austere, white-walled interior has slender stone columns as well as some four-teenth- and fifteenth-century frescoes, and the preserved arch of the *mihrab*.

At c/Arcos de las Escuelas 2, near the north end of c/Romanones, stands one of Baeza's more eccentric attractions – a shop (Mon–Sat 8.30am–10pm) ostensibly selling local ceramics. Once you've penetrated the shelves of pots and a bottling plant for mineral water behind, you'll enter a studio that has a series of remarkable **marble replicas** of Baeza's famous buildings, including the Ayuntamiento and the Palacio Jabalquinto. Created in eye-straining detail by the shop's self-taught owner, the replicas are well worth a look.

The Cathedral

To the east of Santa Cruz along the Cuesta de San Felipe, the **Plaza de Santa María** is another of Baeza's glorious squares, with a few welcome, shade-providing trees, fronted by a nucleus of fine Renaissance buildings. The rather squat sixteenth-century **Catedral de Santa María** (daily 10.30am–1pm & 5–7pm; church free, museum €2) dominates the square and inside has a fine nave by Andrés de Vandelvira which is, in many ways, a scaled-down version of his cathedral at Jaén. Like several of Baeza's and Úbeda's churches, the cathedral also has painted *rejas* by Maestro Bartolomé, a local craftsman who was respon-sible for some of the finest examples of this uniquely Spanish contribution to Renaissance art. His work enclosing the choir, with its depictions of a Virgin and Child accompanied by angels and cherubs, is stunning. In the Gothic **clois-ter**, part of the old mosque – which the church replaced – has been uncovered, but the cathedral's real novelty is a huge silver *custodia* cunningly hidden behind a painting of St Peter which whirls aside for a one euro coin. To the east of the cathedral, and beyond Plaza de Arcediano, a narrow street leads to a *mirador* with a fine **view** over the olive groves in the valley of the Guadalquivir towards the distant Cazorla mountain range beyond.

Adjoining the cathedral on the north side is the old Renaissance **Casas Consistoriales Altas** (town hall) with Plateresque features, formerly the palace of the Cabrera family who have another mansion in the town. In the centre of the **Plaza de Santa María** is a sixteenth-century fountain erected by the same family, with pilasters and crude caryatids supporting the arms of Felipe II. Beyond this are the graffiti-covered walls of the sixteenth-century seminary of **San Felipe Neri** where students record their names and dates in bull's blood – a traditional way of celebrating graduation. The building now houses the International University of Andalucía.

The Ayuntamiento and more churches

West of the Paseo de la Constitución, in c/Benavides, the magnificent **Ayuntamiento** was originally the Palace of Justice and prison. Completed in 1559, its richly ornamented facade is exuberantly Plateresque with elegant balconies, coats of arms and, above, a phalanx of gargoyles decorating the cornice. Inside, the main hall upstairs (viewing Mon–Fri 9am–2pm) has a fine coffered ceiling. At the end of the street and facing the same edifice is the charming (privately owned) little **house of Antonio Machado**, marked with a plaque, where the poet lived for most of his time in Baeza.

The nearby c/San Francisco passes the exterior of the **Hospital of the Purísima Concepción** with an elegant Renaissance facade. Adjoining it is the ruined convent of **San Francisco**, designed by Vandelvira and badly damaged during the War of Independence. Sections of both buildings have now been converted into a hotel, banqueting hall and restaurant. At the end of this street and then right along c/San Andrés – lined with ancient *casas señoriales* – lies the early sixteenth-century church of **San Andrés** (open service times, 7–9pm) with an elegant Plateresque facade and *sagrario* off the left aisle by Vandelvira.

Renaissance palaces

Heading north from the Plaza de España, pedestrianized c/San Pablo has a number of interesting Renaissance palaces, many with impressive facades, dating from the sixteenth century. You'll pass the Gothic **Palacio Garcíez**, with a fine patio, the **Palacio Cerón** and the **Casa Acuña**. The best of all is the **Casa Cabrera**, with an elegant Plateresque facade incorporating a double window and frieze over the entrance. In a street to the west of here, the fifteenth-century Gothic church of **San Pablo** (open service times, 7–9pm) has an image of **Christ** by Roldán, and in c/Biedma, behind the church, you'll find the **Casa de los Elorza**, which is also worth a look.

Eating and drinking

For **tapas** and **raciones** there are plenty of places in and around Paseo de la Constitución and the adjacent Plaza de España. The atmospheric *Bar Cafetería Mercantil* overlooking the latter is the town's most popular haunt, well over a century old and once patronized by Antonio Machado; the terrace is a great place for **breakfast** and eavesdropping on local gossip – in winter there's a dining room upstairs. Other good tapas bars to seek out are *Arcediano*, c/Barbacana s/n, off the east side of Plaza de España and *Pedrito Guadalquivir* and *Mibel*, neighbours at c/San Pablo 42 & 44, to the north of Plaza de España with adjoining terraces.

For picnickers, the *Alacena de la Loma*, c/San Pablo 33 (actually a passage on the left off it), serves good **takeaway** roast chicken. Alternatively, all kinds of local provisions are on offer at *Alimentación Cantos*, c/San Pablo 10, just off Plaza de España; delicacies include local *jamón*, *ciervo* (cured venison), *jabalito* (wild boar) as well as Jaén's top olive oils. Teatime treats are to be had nearby at *Pastelería Martínez*, c/San Pablo, next to the Palacio Cabrera, a pleasant **café** serving delicious pastries made on the premises

Bar Diego c/San Pablo 33. Down a passage off c/San Pablo this pleasant little place has a nice terrace, does economical *platos combinados* and offers the town's cheapest *menú* (€8, lunch and dinner).

Casa Eduardo Portales Mercadores, Paseo de la Constitución. Good restaurant with an attractive portico terrace overlooking the main square. Specials include *merluza hojaldrada* (hake in pastry) and there's a *menú* for €12. Main dishes €9–16.

Casa Juanito Paseo Arca del Agua s/n. Attached to the hotel of the same name, Baeza's most celebrated restaurant has walls covered with photos of the great and the good who have dined here, and a superb *menú de degustación* for €33. Signature dishes include *paté de perdiz*, *cabrito al horno* (roast kid) and *lomo de orza* (pork loin). Main dishes €13–21. Closed Sun eve.

El Pasaje c/Benavides 3. A reliable place with a pleasant terrace offering a variety of fish and meat dishes – *ensalada de perdiz* (partridge) and *pierna*

de choto (kid) are specials – with a *menú* for around €10. Closed Mon.

El Señorío de Baeza c/Concepción 3. The restaurant of the *Hotel Baeza* is popular with *baezanos* and offers a good-value *menú* incorporating local dishes such as *pipirrana* (*jamón* and vegetable salad) for around €15. Its *Little Italy* bistro offers a more economical Italian-based menu that includes salads, pasta and pizzas.

La Gondola Portales Carbonería 7, on the Paseo de la Constitución. Slightly pricey but decent place serving up local dishes and salads on their portico terrace with a weekday lunchtime *menú del día* for €12. Main dishes €13–20.

Restaurante Andrés de Vandelvira c/San Francisco 14 ☎953 74 81 72. Baeza's other noteworthy restaurant is installed in the restored ruin of Vandelvira's once-magnificent sixteenth-century convent, which is worth a look, even if you don't intend dining; the convent's former patio/cloister has been fitted with a temporary roof to create a banqueting hall, and the restaurant lies beyond

this. The rather narrow dining room is pleasant and signature dishes include *gallina de pepitoria* (chicken fricassee), *trucha* and *atun escabechada* (marinated trout or tuna). Main dishes €13–16. Closed Sun eve & Mon.
Restaurante El Sali c/Cardenal Benavides 15.

Opposite the Ayuntamiento, the very good *Restaurante Sali* has a weekday *menú* for around €10 and tables outside so you can feast your eyes on this beautiful building. *Rabo de toro* (oxtail) and *cochinillo ibérico* (suckling pig) are two specialities. Main dishes €9–18. Closed Wed.

Nightlife

There's occasional **flamenco** at the *Peña Flamenca*, c/Romanones 6; ask the Turismo for details of performances. Baeza's solitary **disco** is *Al-Bacara* with a pleasant terrace, 100m down the Jaén road out of town. Two *copas* bars worth seeking out are *Burladero*, c/Barbacana, almost next door to the *Bar Arcediano* (see above) and *Café Central*, Obispo Narvaez 19, which often stages live music including jazz on Thursdays (except July & Aug). Baeza's lively annual **feria** takes place during the second and third weeks in August and is a wonderfully rural affair with processions of *gigantones* (carnival giants), fireworks and an enormous funfair on the edge of town.

Úbeda

Little is known of **ÚBEDA**'s previous incarnation as the Roman town of Betula, and it was only in the Moorish period that Obdah, as it became, grew into a prosperous and important centre endowed with walls and a castle. Following the Christian victory over the Moors at Navas de Tolosa in 1212, the Moors from Baeza moved into the city, feeling it provided a more secure refuge against the Christian forces. Despite this, Úbeda was taken a week later and, although an interlude of further freedom for the Muslim occupants was purchased from the Christian armies with massive donations, the town fell conclusively to Fernando El Santo in 1234. As happened in Baeza, numerous noble families were then established by the king and built their mansions in the town. These haughty "lions of Úbeda", as they styled themselves, were soon warring amongst each other, the Arandas fighting the Traperas, and the Molinas against the Cuevas. The fighting got so bad at one point that in 1503 Fernando and Isabel ordered the destruction of the town's walls and towers, to enable the unruly aristocrats to be kept in check. Twelve of these noble families are represented by the twelve lions on the town's coat of arms.

In common with Baeza, it was in the sixteenth century, as a producer of textiles traded across Europe, that Úbeda's fortunes reached their zenith and members of the same noble families came to hold prominent positions in the imperial Spanish court. This was the age of the houses of **Cobos** and **Molinos**, two families who, linked by marriage, dominated the town's affairs. They were also responsible for employing **Andrés de Vandelvira** as their principal architect, whose buildings are the glory of Úbeda today. This prosperity, however, was shortlived and the town declined in the seventeenth century as sharply as it had flourished in the sixteenth, which explains its architectural unity and lack of any significant Baroque edifices. Úbeda is a moderately prosperous provincial town today, its main source of income coming from tourism, the manufacture of farm machinery and sodium sulphates, as well as the more traditional olives and ceramics, and carpets and baskets made from esparto grass.

Arrival and information

The main **bus station**, c/San José s/n, lies to the west of the centre beyond the Hospital de Santiago; there are currently 14 buses a day from Jaén (all stopping en route at Baeza). **Linares–Baeza** is the nearest **train station**, about 15km from Úbeda (connecting buses for most trains, except Sun; a taxi costs around €15).

Úbeda's **Turismo** (Mon–Fri 9am–8pm, Sat–Sun 10am–2pm; ☎953 75 08 97) is located in the elegant Palacio del Marqués del Contadero, c/Baja del Marqués s/n. They can provide a detailed map and, if you are visiting in the May–June period, a leaflet on Úbeda's annual International Festival of Music and Dance, which attracts big names from the fields of flamenco, rock, opera, jazz, blues and ballet. Librería Tres Culturas, c/Rastro 17, near the Plaza de Andalucía, is a good **bookshop** selling walking maps and guides for this zone and the Sierra de Cazorla. **Internet** access is available at *Cibernetworld*, c/Niño 22 (daily 11am–2pm & 4.30–10pm), close to the Parque de Vandelvira to the west of the old quarter, and *Cibercentro*, slightly further out at c/Picasso 14 (daily 11am–2.30pm & 4.30–11pm).

Accommodation

You'll find plenty of budget **places to stay** within walking distance of the bus station, in the modern part of town. The *casco antiguo* (old quarter) now has a great choice of more upmarket places, some in stunning ancient palaces and mansions. Úbeda's high season is in April and May and thus hotel (but not *hostal*) rooms tend to be significantly cheaper in July and August.

Hostal Miguel Avda. Libertad 69 ☎953 75 20 49. Úbeda's cheapest *hostal* is a ten-minute walk away from the centre in the north of town, offering decent en-suite a/c rooms with a good and inexpensive restaurant below. Just around the corner the friendly *Hotel Dos Hermanas*, c/Risquillo Bajo 1 (☎953 75 21 24) is similarly priced and also good. **②**

Hostal Sevilla Avda. Ramón y Cajal 9 ☎953 75 06 12. Reasonable place with comfortable, en-suite and a/c rooms. **②**

Hostal Victoria c/Alaminos 5 ☎953 79 17 18. Comfortable refurbished *hostal* offering pleasant, a/c en-suite rooms with TV. Own car park too. **②**

Hotel Alvar Fáñez c/Juan Pasquau 5 ☎953 79 60 43, ⓦwww.alvarfanez.com. Newish hotel in a reconstituted Renaissance *casa palacio* arranged around an elegant patio. The slightly sombre rooms are nevertheless comfortable and there's a restaurant and good tapas bar. **⑦** with breakfast.

Hotel La Paz c/Andalucía 1 ☎953 75 08 49, ⓦwww.hotel-lapaz.com. This decent mid-range hotel has a/c balcony rooms with TV. **④**

🏃 **Hotel María de Molina** Plaza del Ayuntamiento s/n ☎953 79 53 56, ⓦwww.hotel-maria-de-molina.com. In the heart of the old quarter, this hotel is housed in a magnificent sixteenth-century *casa palacio* with a superb patio. Rooms come with a/c, safe and satellite TV, and

some have balconies. Very good value for this category; rooms fall in price Mon–Thurs. They also let a number of apartments for almost the same rates as rooms. **⑥**

Hotel Ordóñez Sandoval c/Antonio Medina 1 ☎953 79 51 87. Following the example of the Marquesa de la Rambla (see below), proprietor Amalia Perez Ordóñez has opened part of her family's nineteenth-century mansion as a hotel. There's a cloistered central patio and the three en-suite guest rooms are tastefully furnished in grand style. Free parking. **⑥** with breakfast.

Palacio de la Rambla Plaza del Marqués 1 ☎953 75 01 96, ⓔpalaciorambla@terra.es. In the old quarter, this upmarket *casa palacio* is owned by the Marquesa de la Rambla. The lavish interior – with palatial rooms set around a stunning Renaissance patio designed by Vandelvira – contains valuable furnishings and artworks, which is why you have to use an entryphone to get in. Price includes breakfast – brought to your room if you wish. Closed mid-July to mid-August. **⑥**

🏃 **Parador Condestable Dávalos** Plaza de Vázquez de Molina 1 ☎953 75 03 45, ⓦwww.parador.es. On arguably the most beautiful plaza in Andalucía, Úbeda's parador is housed in a fabulous sixteenth-century Renaissance mansion, with some of the well-appointed rooms overlooking the square. Call in for a drink if you're not staying. **⑧**

ÚBEDA

N

Potters' Quarter

RESTAURANTS
El Gallo Rojo	3
El Olivo	4
El Seco	6
Mesón Gabino	1
Mesón Navarro	5
Pintor Orbaneja	2
Restaurante Marqués	7

ACCOMMODATION
Hostal Miguel	A
Hostal Sevilla	I
Hostal Victoria	J
Hotel Alvar Fáñez	E
Hotel La Paz	B
Hotel María de Molina	F
Hotel Ordóñez Sandoval	G
Palacio de la Rambla	H
Parador Condestable Dávalos	D
Rosaleda de Don Pedro	C

0   100 m

REDONDA DE MIRADORES

Hospital de los Honrados Viejos del Salvador

Capilla del Salvador

Palacio de D. Francisco de los Cobos

Palacio de Mancera

Antiguo Pósito

Sta. María de los Reales Alcázares

Puerta del Losal

Oratorio de San Juan

Casa de Los Manueles

San Pablo

Casa de Los Salvajes

Palacio del Condestable Dávalos

Palacio de las Cadenas

Casa Montiel

Casa Mudéjar

Ayuntamiento Viejo

Palacio de los Cobos

Puerta de Granada

Iglesia de San Lorenzo

Pal. Guadiana

San Pedro

Santa Clara

Casa de las Torres

San Nicolás

Iglesia de la Trinidad

Casa del Caballerico Ortega

Palacio de los Bussianos

Torre del Reloj

Palacio Rambla

Hospital de Santiago

Parque de Vandelvira

Bus Station

Madrid   *(1km)*

Linares & Bailén

Baeza & Jaén   *Granada*

Rosaleda de Don Pedro c/Obispo Toral 2
☎953 79 51 47, ⓦwww.rosaledadedonpedro.
com. Efficient three-star hotel with well-
equipped rooms with satellite TV and a small

pool in their terrace garden at the rear. It has its
own restaurant, a library for guests plus garage.
Prices drop by fifteen percent in August. Garage.
❺

The Town

Some 9km east of Baeza and built on the same escarpment overlooking the
valley of the Guadalquivir, Úbeda looks less promising when you reach it.
Don't be put off, though, for hidden away in the old quarter is one of the finest
Renaissance architectural jewels in the whole of Spain, and perhaps even in
Europe. **Guided visits** of the monumental quarter are organized by Artificis
(ⓦwww.artificis.com) and Atlante who do a theatrical tour (in Spanish) using
actors to bring to life historical events in the town's history; details of both tours
are available from the Turismo (see p.496).

The Plaza de Vázquez de Molina

Follow the signs for the "Zona Monumental" and you'll eventually reach the
Plaza Vázquez de Molina, a magnificent Renaissance square at the heart of
the old town. Most of the buildings around this square were the late sixteenth-
century work of Andrés de Vandelvira, the architect of Baeza's cathedral and of
numerous churches in both towns. At the western end he built the **Palacio de
las Cadenas** (or "chains", which once decorated the facade) for the secretary of
Felipe II, Juan Vázquez de Molina, whose family arms crown the doorway of a
beautiful classical facade. The interior, these days occupied by the Ayuntamiento,
features a superb double-tier arcaded patio. To see this you'll need to go to the
back of the building and the Ayuntamiento entrance where the security guard
will allow you a peep.

△ Palacio de las Cadenas

Back on the Plaza Vázquez de Molina, opposite the Palacio de las Cadenas, and between the lions marking the edge of the mansion's domain, lies the church of **Santa María de los Reales Alcázares**, built on the site of a former mosque. Behind the facade, topped by a double belfry, an elegant Gothic cloister encloses what was once the ablutions patio of the mosque. The church contains another fine *reja* by Maestro Bartolomé of Jaén depicting the Tree of Jesse. At the side of the church, as you move east, is the entrance to the sixteenth-century **Cárcel del Obispo** or bishop's prison, which was formerly a convent and is now used as the courthouse. Opposite this is the **Palacio de Marqués de Mancera**, another stately Renaissance edifice with an elegant tower. Adjoining this building and fronting the plaza is the **Antiguo Pósito** or old granary, which later served as a prison and now houses the police station. Close by is a **statue** honouring Vandelvira, the architectural genius who made it all possible. Across the square again, the **Palacio del Condestable Dávalos**, which Vandelvira had a hand in designing, is the former dwelling of the chaplain of the church of El Salvador. This elegant building now houses what must be the most impressive parador in Andalucía. Above the door two angels support the arms of the first chaplain, Déan (Dean) Fernando Ortega Salido, who was also responsible for its construction. A stunning arcaded interior patio now serves as the hotel's bar, and is best contemplated over a cool drink.

Chapel of El Salvador

At the eastern end of the Plaza Vázquez de Molina, Vandelvira erected the **Capilla del Salvador** (Mon–Sat 10am–2pm & 4.30–7pm, Sun 10.45am–2pm & 4.30–7pm; €3), Úbeda's finest church and one of the masterpieces of Spanish Renaissance architecture. Although executed by Vandelvira, he was in fact working to a design created in 1536 by Diego de Siloé (architect of Málaga's and Granada's cathedrals) but typically added his own flourishes. The church was originally the chapel of the mansion – which later burned down – of Francisco de Cobos y Molina, secretary of state to Carlos V and one of the most powerful men of his time. This remarkable building is almost unique in Spain for being built within a very short period (1540–1556) with hardly any later alterations. It also preserves many of its interior furnishings. The exterior **facade** has a carving of the Transfiguration of Christ flanked by statues of San Pedro and San Andrés with a wealth of Plateresque detail. Above the north door around the corner, Vandelvira has placed an image in the tympanum which is almost his trademark – Santiago the Moor slayer, used in Baeza and on the hospital of Santiago in the north of the town.

Entry to the church is via the doorway on the south side. The single naved interior with a beautiful cupola has a brilliantly animated *retablo* on the high altar representing the Transfiguration with a sensitively rendered image of Christ by Alonso de Berruguete who studied under Michelangelo; this is the only part of the altarpiece completely to survive the Civil War. The **reja** fronting the altar is yet another fine work by Maestro Bartolomé de Jaén. In the **sacristy** (all Vandelvira's work) there's a photograph of a statue by Michelangelo given to Francisco de Cobos by the state of Venice, which alas was another Civil War casualty.

Behind El Salvador, and beyond the sixteenth-century **Hospital de los Honorados Viejos del Salvador** (another Vandelvira work), Úbeda comes to a sudden halt at a **mirador** with fine views over a sea of olive groves backed by the Sierra de Cazorla.

The Casa de las Torres and Palacio Vela de los Cobos

To the west of the Plaza Vázquez de Molina along calles Orbaneja and Luna y Sol lies the **Casa de las Torres** (Mon, Wed–Fri 8am–2.15pm, Tues 4–6pm), a sombre building with two enormous keeps, framing an ornate Plateresque facade. Now an art school, when it is open you can view the building's elegant double-tiered patio.

Just behind Plaza Vázquez de Molina, the Plaza del Ayuntamiento has the **Palacio Vela de los Cobos**, another impressive building by Vandelvira dating from the middle of the sixteenth century, with an interesting corner balcony and an elegant facade topped off by a delightful arcaded gallery. This is one of the few palaces that can be visited but prior application must be made to the Turismo. Incidentally on the west side this square, Plaza del Ayuntamiento, Juan Martínez Tito, one of the famous Tito brothers, a noted group of Úbeda potters (see opposite), has his workshop, which is well worth a look.

Oratorio de San Juan de la Cruz and San Pablo

To the north of Plaza Vázquez de Molina (easily reached along c/Francisco de los Cobos), the **Oratorio de San Juan de La Cruz** is where San Juan (St John of the Cross), an accomplished poet and mystic, died of gangrene in 1591. The original monastery was damaged in the Civil War and little of it survives, although a small **museum** (daily 11am–1pm & 5–7pm; €1.20) preserves memorabilia from the saint's lifetime as well as his writing desk and the cell in which he died. At the end of c/San Juan de la Cruz facing the monastery, the **Plaza del Primero de Mayo** (formerly the Plaza del Mercado) is a charming acacia-lined square with a bandstand at its centre marking the site of the fires of the *autos-da-fé* that were once carried out here on the orders of the Inquisition. The Town Council presided over these grisly events from the superb arcaded sixteenth-century **Ayuntamiento Viejo** on the square's western side. Dominating its northern flank is the idiosyncratic **Iglesia de San Pablo** (Mon–Wed 11am–12noon, Thurs–Sat 11am–1pm, Sun 11am–1.30pm, plus Mon & Sat 5–8pm; free), incorporating various Romanesque, Gothic and Renaissance additions and crowned by a Plateresque tower. It boasts a thirteenth-century balcony (a popular feature in Úbeda), and a superb portal. The interior has a fine capilla by Vandelvira (chapel of Camarero Vago) as well some intricate carving in the Capilla de la Mercedes and more superb *rejas*.

Around Plaza del Primero de Mayo

Calle Horno Contado, which leaves Plaza del Primero de Mayo at the southeast corner, has two more palaces you might want to see: a short way down on the right, the **Casa de los Manueles** has a fine facade and, a little further down on the left, the fifteenth-century **Casa de los Salvajes** (savages) is named after the two figures clothed in animal skins supporting the arms of its founder, Francisco de Vago. In reality they are probably natives of the imperial colonies, from whose exploitation much of this conspicuous wealth was derived. Off the north side of the square in c/Cervantes the **Casa Mudéjar** at no. 6 is a fine fourteenth-century building whose elegant Mudéjar **patio** has pointed horse-shoe arches. It houses a small **archeological museum** (Tues 3–8pm, Wed–Sat 9am–8pm, Sun 9am–3pm; free).

Calle Melchor Almagro, leaving the square on the north side of San Pablo, has another mansion, the wonderful Plateresque **Casa Montiel**, and, further along, a sixteenth-century Carmelite convent.

The Potters' Quarter

Leaving the Plaza del Primero de Mayo by the c/Losal in its northeast corner leads to the **Puerta del Losal**, a magnificent thirteenth-century Mudéjar gate with a double-horseshoe arch which was formerly one of the main entrances to the old walled town. Through the arch you enter c/de la Merced soon arriving at Plaza Olleros (Potters' Square), marked by an enormous pot on a plinth. Leading off this square, c/Valencia is the old **potters' street** where the workshops of Úbeda's main ceramic craftsmen are located. Alfarería Tito, c/Valencia 22, is one of the friendliest, where the renowned ceramic artist Paco Tito has his workshop and museum and will usually will give you a demonstration on the potter's wheel. Nearby in the yard is the kiln, where the system used to fire the pots – many glazed and tinted with Úbeda's traditional deep green – is one inherited from the Moors; once the wood is burning, olive stones are introduced into the fire which creates smoke and soaks up oxygen producing superior results in both colour and glaze. There are only six of these traditional kilns left in the whole of Spain and three are in this street. The museum/gallery upstairs is devoted to Paco's more ambitious works including statuary, huge Amphorae and a completely ceramic (and fully functioning) bathroom. Nearby are the workshops of other potters – including Juan and Antonio Almarza, and Góngora – all famous throughout Spain. Paco Tito's equally well-known brother, Juan, also has a workshop on the Plaza del Ayuntamiento, near the Turismo (see p.496).

Plaza San Pedro and Calle Real

Starting out from the Plaza San Pedro (to the west of the Plaza del Ayuntamiento) there are a number of other important sights to see in the northwest of the town. On the Plaza San Pedro itself, the thirteenth-century **Convento de Santa Clara** contains a patio with a fine Gothic-Mudéjar multi-lobed portal. The convent also sells its home-made *dulces* – tasty cakes, biscuits and pastries. Just south from here along c/Narvaez at no. 11 the privately-owned **Casa Museo Quesada** (daily 11am–2.30pm & 6–8pm; €1) is housed in a sixteenth-century mansion filled with period artefacts from other houses around the town. Heading west from Plaza San Pedro you come to another mansion, the **Palacio de la Rambla**, sited at the end of c/Medina. The facade is another graceful work by Vandelvira, and the interior is now an upmarket hotel (see "Accommodation" p.496). Otherwise, across the square, the church of **San Pedro** with a noteworthy portal leads into c/Pascua where, on the junction with c/Real, stands the impressive tower of the **Palacio del Conde de Guadiana**, one of the most striking of all Úbeda's palaces. The tower is, in fact, a seventeenth-century work and the richly ornamented balconies are a delight.

Turning into **Calle Real** brings you to the heart of the old town's commercial centre and its former main shopping street. Many establishments are now deserting this area for new premises in the modern town but a few of the more traditional traders are still here. Pedro Blanco at no. 47 is still making and selling goods made from traditional esparto grass, a versatile material used in the area since ancient times. Although much of the business is devoted to supplying the olive oil industry with collecting and extracting baskets, the firm also makes carpets, bags and all kinds of accessories. Heading north along here brings you eventually to the **Plaza de Andalucía**, an unremarkable square overlooked by the **Torre del Reloj**, a remnant of the thirteenth-century ramparts, crowned with a later sixteenth-century temple.

Just to the north of the Plaza de Andalucía at the start of c/Trinidad is the **Iglesia de la Trinidad** (daily 7.20–8.30pm), an eighteenth-century – and unusually for Úbeda – Baroque building. Further along c/Trinidad, it's back to the Renaissance with the **Palacio de los Bussianos**, attributed to Vandelvira. Taking the next right after this, c/Redondo, and then first left into c/Condesa you pass the **Casa de Caballerizo Ortega**, a sixteenth-century Plateresque mansion. Calle Condesa continues to the church of **San Nicolás** (daily 8.30–9.30am; free), which, although fourteenth-century, has a fine Renaissance west portal by Vandelvira. The sober interior is relieved by a profusely decorated but incredibly sinister "sculpted" **chapel of Déan Ortega** by Vandelvira whose effect is only partially offset by a life-size, plastic choirboy. The *reja* (iron screen) fronting it by Álvarez de Molina is another fine example of the art.

Five minutes west of the Iglesia de la Trinidad along c/Obispo Cobos, and worth every bead of sweat getting there, is Vandelvira's huge **Hospital de Santiago** (Mon–Fri 8am–3pm & 4–10pm, Sat–Sun 11am–3pm & 6–10pm; free). Perhaps the scale put him off, for the exterior decoration is untypically restrained, and its austere dignity has led to the building being described as "Andalucía's Escorial". Commissioned by Bishop Cobos y Molina and begun in 1562, the flight of steps at the entrance is flanked by more "lions of Úbeda", beyond which Vandelvira has inserted his trademark – Santiago the Moor slayer – above the arch. The equally restrained interior has a patio with columns of Genoa marble and a staircase with stunning vaulting, in addition to a striking chapel – all further evidence of Vandelvira's mastery.

Eating, drinking and nightlife

Most reasonably priced **restaurants** are in the modern part of town, along the Avenida Ramón y Cajal. At no. 2, *Restaurante El Olivo* serves cheap *platos combinados* and also has a *menú*. At the end of this street and close to the junction with the Avenida de la Libertad, *El Gallo Rojo*, c/Torrenueva 3, set back from the road, is one of the town's better restaurants, with local specialities, a *menú* for €12 and outdoor tables in the evening. Just north from here along c/Virgen de Guadalupe, *Pintor Orbaneja* at no. 5 does *platos combinados* and excellent tapas. On the northern edge of the old quarter, in c/Fuente Seca near the Puerto del Losal, *Mesón Gabino* is a good place for tapas and *raciones*, in a converted old cellar; its mid-priced restaurant also does decent fish dishes and a house special is a tasty *solomillo* (pork loin); there's a *menú* for €16.

In the old quarter, the popular *Mesón Navarro*, Plaza del Ayuntamiento, behind the Palacio de las Cadenas, is one of only a handful of restaurants (main dishes €6–12) and also has a tapas bar. Further west at the junction of calles Rastro and Rivas, *Bar La Paloma* is another good tapas haunt. Nearby, *Restaurante Marqués*, Plaza Marqués de la Rambla 2, is now run by the *Hotel María de Molina* (see "Accommodation"), and serves up a good-value *menú* often featuring *merluza con almejas y esparragos* (hake with clams), and has a terrace on this square which allows you to contemplate the *Palacio de la Rambla*'s elegant exterior. A number of other restaurants attached to hotels in this zone are also worth considering: the mid-priced *Rosaleda de Don Pedro* and *Alvar Fáñez* both offer *menús del día* starting at €12. One restaurant in this zone a cut above the norm is *El Seco*, c/Corazón de Jesús 8, close to the Plaza del Ayuntamiento; it is noted for its tasty *potaje carmelitano* (chickpea, leek and cod soup) but also does excellent meat and game dishes and there's a *menú* for €13. Otherwise, if you want to dine in the old quarter and in style it has to be the expensive *Parador Condestable Dávalos*, although superbly prepared regional dishes are available on a good-value lunchtime *menú campaña* for €17.50.

Nightlife is limited but does exist. The main *movida* zone lies to the north of the bus station, in and around c/Picasso. Popular music bars on this street include *Toscana* and *Bogart* which go on till late. Just to the east of here *Taberna Doce Leones*, c/Torrenueva 17 is a modish Irish bar selling over fifty brands of beer. The **flamenco** *tablao* El Marqués, c/Santo Domingo s/n near the *Palacio de la Rambla* hotel, mounts flamenco performances each Saturday (10pm; €18) and entry includes tapas and the first drink. Flamenco performances are often staged in the Hospital de Santiago throughout the summer and the Turismo should have details. Úbeda's big **fiesta** is the *Día de San Miguel* on September 29, when carnival giants, fireworks and a flamenco festival honour the town's patron saint.

Towards Cazorla

From Úbeda, the next destination for most travellers is the spectacular **Cazorla Natural Park** (officially titled the Parque Natural de Cazorla, Segura y Las Villas), a wilderness area filled with deep ravines and wooded valleys and which, in its mountains, gives birth to the mighty Río Guadalquivir. The park's towering rock cliffs are the preserve of the acrobatic ibex, whilst the valleys and gorges swarm with birdlife and are home to unique pre-Ice Age plants. From Úbeda there are two **routes into the park**. The more conventional one, taken by the bus, is via the small town of Cazorla, located on the park's southern edge and the main gateway to it. Another route, however, skirts the park's western flank and allows visits to a number of interesting sights – including the picturesque hill villages of **Sabiote**, with a castle and Renaissance mansions, and **Iznatoraf**, with its distinctive Moorish feel – before turning into the park close to the small town of Villanueva.

Into the Park via Sabiote, Villacarillo and Iznatoraf

Leaving Úbeda by the N322 brings you first to Torreperogil, 8km east and – unusually for Jaén province – a centre of wine rather then olive production. A turning here leads to the pretty hill village of **SABIOTE**, 4km distant, a cobble-streeted place still girdled by much of its medieval walls and with a pedigree dating back to Roman times. The sixteenth-century church of **San Pedro Apostól** at its heart has a fine, if worn, Plateresque facade. At the foot of c/Castillo, which has a couple of striking Renaissance mansions (one is now a hotel, see below), the ruined **Castillo** dates back to Roman times, although the Moors made subsequent alterations. More modifications were added during the Renaissance period by Francisco Cobos of the noble house based at Úbeda, and it's thought that he drafted in his architect Andrés de Vandelvira to carry them out. The elegant cloister of the sixteenth-century Carmelite convent (7–8pm; free) is also worth a look. Sabiote has an excellent **place to stay**: the ⌘ *Palacio de Manillas* c/Castillo 1 (☎953 77 30 90, ⊛www.palaciolasmanillas.com/datos; ⑤) is a wonderful sixteenth-century palace sensitively transformed into a very comfortable hotel with bar and good-value **restaurant**. Even if you're not a guest, the friendly proprietor, Manolo Cabrera, will give you a map of the village and is a fount of information on its monuments and history.

Villacarillo and Iznatoraf

VILLACARILLO, 20km further along the N322, is a fairly featureless town surrounded by olive groves but with an impressive Renaissance **Church of the Asunción** by Vandelvira (July–Sept daily 10.30am–1.30pm & 7.30–9pm, Oct–June 7.30–9pm; free), whose major interior features are some spectacular **domes** with sixteenth-century paintings. About 6km after this, a road on the left snakes dizzily upwards to the spectacularly sited hill-top village of **IZNATORAF**. At the end of the climb, the village is clustered around a pleasant Plaza Mayor with a Renaissance arch and the great stone church of **Santo Cristo** dominating its eastern end. After you've wandered around the narrow Moorish streets, many decorated with colourful geraniums in summer, and had a look over the ruins of its walls and castle, don't miss the spectacular **views** over the valley of the Río Guadalimar towards the bordering province of Albacete from a *mirador* perched above the cliff at the village's northern edge.

Not quite 2km beyond the turn-off for Iznatoraf and before Villanueva del Arzobispo, a road leaves the N322 on the right for Tranco and the Cazorla Natural Park. Take note of the signs warning you that there is limited petrol to be had in the park – a full tank would be a wise precaution. Some 7km from the turn-off the road joins the densely wooded valley of the newly born Guadalquivir, a mere stream compared to the mighty torrent which flows through Sevilla over 200km downstream. After a further 14km the road arrives at Tranco on the banks of the Embalse del Tranco (reservoir) which is described in the main account of the park below.

Into the Park via Peal de Becerro and Cazorla

The bus route to Cazorla heads southeast from Úbeda, passing through olive country and crossing the Guadalquivir before turning off the main road to the village of **PEAL DE BECERRO**. The village spreads over a low hill beneath the crumbling towers of its medieval fort. With your own transport, you can take a minor road out of the village 4km southwest to **Toya**, where there's an important Iberian underground tomb. Should you want to **eat** or **stay**, two accommodation options lie within a hundred metres of the Ayuntamiento (see below). *Hostal-Restaurante Juanito* (☎953 73 07 16; ❷), Avda. Constitución 32, has tidy en-suite rooms, and the nearby *Hotel Al-Andalus* (☎953 71 64 80, ⓦ www.halandalus.com; ❹), Carrera Santo Tomé 5, which is the slightly plusher option. Both places have decent restaurants. Continuing the loop around to Cazorla would enable you to take in a remarkable **Roman villa** near to Quesada which has superb mosaic pavements.

Toya's necropolis and Bruñel's Roman villa

In 1909 a large rectangular underground stone tomb was discovered by a farmer near the hamlet of **Toya**, the former Iberian settlement of *Tugia*. Unfortunately, the family cleared the tomb – used from the fifth to the second century BC – of a whole treasure house of artefacts which they then sold. Some fine Greek vases were later recovered, and testified to this remote tribe's sophistication and trading contacts with the Mediterranean world. The totally intact stone-built **necropolis** is impressive and the largest of its kind in Spain. The tomb is located a few kilometres outside Toya, but first you'll need to visit the *Policía Local* office inside the Ayuntamiento at the centre of the town to get the key (in return for the deposit of a passport); they will also clarify directions. From the Ayuntamiento you should head west along the Hornos de Peal road, forking left at a signed road for Toya just outside the town. Three hundred metres before the village of Toya a signed lane on the right leads to the site. A full-scale walk-in replica of the tomb has recently been constructed inside the Museo Provincial in Jaén (see p.485)

To reach the **Roman villa** at **Bruñel**, set off south from Peal along the A315 in the direction of Quesada. A couple of kilometres before the village (which you will see on its hill in the distance) a road on the left is signed for the Roman villa. Once on this road keep going for 2km until you reach (on the left) a white house with a green gate named Villa Josefina. Here you must collect two keys (ask for "Las llaves para la villa romana por favor"). When you have collected the keys turn left and keep ahead past the house along a dirt road. Follow this for about a kilometre until, at the top of a rise by a ruined building to the left, you will see the site entrance opposite. The keys unlock the outer and inner fence gates.

Once inside the site you can appreciate why it was decided to locate the villa here as it enjoys fine views towards the mountains of the Sierra de Cazorla. The villa – possibly the country seat of an important official or farming family – was a substantial affair based around a large atrium with another atrium to the side. The **mosaics** are delightful, all the more so because you will most likely have them all to yourself. The images of animals, particularly a wonderful mosaic featuring ducks, are of the highest quality as is a powerful image of what is thought to be the sea goddess Tethys, wife of Oceanus. Coin evidence has dated the original building here to the mid-fourth century AD and this was substantially enlarged in even grander style later in the same century with the addition of a new peristyled courtyard surrounded by a series of spacious rooms. In the final phase of its existence the villa appears to have been abandoned following a fire and in the middle of the sixth century a double-apsed early Christian basilica was constructed on top of the remains, the walls of which dominate the site today. Fortunately many of the mosaics survived both events, although, and rather surprisingly, they are not protected from the elements in any way.

After you've re-locked the site and returned the keys, continuing along the same road from the Villa Josefina will let you follow the A322 to Cazorla, some 7km distant.

Cazorla

The small town of **CAZORLA**, 15km beyond Peal at an elevation of 900m, huddles towards the top of a valley which runs from the rugged limestone cliffs of the Peña de los Halcones. This rocky bluff, with its wheeling buzzards and occasional eagle, marks the southwestern edge of a vast, protected area, the **Parque Natural de Cazorla**, containing the sierras of Cazorla and Segura and the headwaters of the Río Guadalquivir.

Today the gateway town for visitors to the natural park, little about the attractive town today would lead you to believe that Cazorla had been around for over two thousand years, but not only were there significant Iberian and Roman settlements here, this was also the see of one of the first bishoprics of early Christian Spain. Under the Moors it was a strategic stronghold and one of dozens of fortresses and watchtowers guarding the Sierra. Taken after a bitter struggle in 1235, during the *Reconquista*, the town then acted as an outpost for Christian troops. Nowadays, the two castles that dominate the village testify to

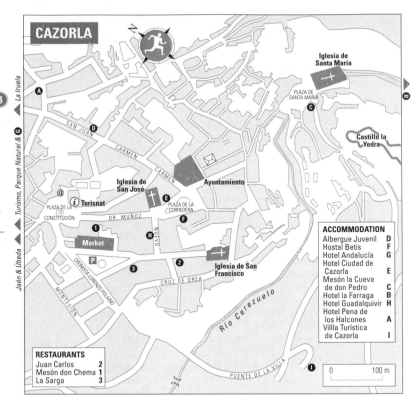

CAZORLA

Iglesia de
Santa María

PLAZA DE
SANTA MARÍA

Castillo la
Yedra

SAN JUAN

CARMEN

CARMEN

Iglesia de
San José

Ayuntamiento

PLAZA DE LA
CORREDERA

DR. MUÑOZ

Turisnat

PLAZA DE LA
CONSTITUCIÓN

Market

CRONISTA LORENZO POLAINO

Iglesia de San
Francisco

CRUZ DE OREA

MONTESIÓN

Río Cerezuelo

PUENTE DE LA VILLA

ACCOMMODATION

Albergue Juvenil	D
Hostal Betis	F
Hotel Andalucía	G
Hotel Ciudad de Cazorla	E
Mesón la Cueva de don Pedro	C
Hotel la Farraga	B
Hotel Guadalquivir	H
Hotel Pena de los Halcones	A
Villa Turística de Cazorla	I

RESTAURANTS

Juan Carlos	2
Mesón don Chema	1
La Sarga	3

0   100 m

its turbulent past; both were originally Moorish but later altered and restored by their Christian conquerors.

Arrival and information

The main road climbs between concrete blocks of flats, disgorging you into the busy Plaza de la Constitución. Arriving **by car**, you should take a right here downhill to the **car park**, as trying to find a place to park anywhere else can be futile, especially in high summer. Up to four **buses** a day (currently Mon–Fri at 7am, 12noon, 4pm & 5.30pm) go from Úbeda to Cazorla. The same buses leave Baeza half an hour earlier and there are also buses from Jaén and Granada. Alsina Graells (Ⓦ www.continental-auto.es), the main bus operator, has a ticket office next to the fountain on the Plaza de la Constitución, where the bus drops you.

In the Plaza de la Constitución is a privately run **tourist office**, Turisnat (daily 10am–1pm & 5.30–8pm; ☏ 953 72 13 51, Ⓦ www.turisnat.org). The staff are friendly but the office exists to promote Land Rover excursions, photo safaris and the like, though they do sell the Alpina map series covering the Cazorla park (see p.509). The town's official **Turismo** (April–Sept Wed–Sun 10am–2pm; ☏ 953 71 01 02, Ⓦ www.cazorla.es) on Paseo del Santo Cristo 19, 100m north of Plaza de la Constitución, can provide a useful town map; they also have a **roadside kiosk** (July–Aug) on the way into town at c/Hilario

Marco s/n, near the bullring, which opens the same hours, and weekends as well. Both can also provide details on all aspects of the park and activities. **Internet** access is available at *Parra Multistore* (daily 10am–2pm & 4–9pm), Plaza de la Constitución 12, next to the Alsina Graells office.

Accommodation

Outside August, finding a **place to stay** is usually no problem, as most visitors are either en route to, or are leaving, the park. Cazorla's **campsite**, *Camping Cortijo* (☎953 72 12 80), is located beyond the Castillo de la Yedra, 1km from the centre; to get there, follow the Camino San Isicio from the Plaza de Santa María. It's worth noting that outside the high summer months it can get quite chilly here in the evenings and whilst all the hotel rooms have heating, not all the *hostales* do, so enquire if you think this may be a problem.

Albergue Juvenil Plaza Mauricio Martínez 6 ☎953 72 03 29, @www.inturjoven.com. Cazorla's tidy youth hostel, housed in a former convent, has some double rooms and a pool, and is reached by following c/Juan Domingo (reached via steps) from Plaza de la Constitución. Under 26 €14, over 26 €18.50.

Apartamentos San Pedro Carretera de la Sierra s/n, La Iruela, 2km out of Cazorla heading into the park ☎953 72 00 15, @www.hotelsierradecazorla .com. Pleasant apartments sleeping from two to six. All are fully equipped and come with kitchen, TV, washing machine and heating, and there's a small pool too. You are also permitted to use the facilities at the nearby *Hotel Sierra de Cazorla*. ⑤

Hostal Betis Plaza Correderra 19 ☎953 72 05 40. Friendly proprietor and good-value accommodation for rooms with and without showers (same price); rooms at the rear (nos. 101–4) have great views. ①

Hotel Andalucía c/Martínez Falero 42, at the north end of town ☎953 72 12 68. A 5min walk from Plaza de la Constitución, this is a serviceable small hotel offering decent en-suite rooms with TV. ③

Hotel Ciudad de Cazorla Plaza de la Correderra 8 ☎953 72 17 00, @www.rlhoteles.com. The modern exterior of Cazorla's newest hotel caused a ruckus when it was unveiled, while inside functional a/c rooms come with minibar and safe, some have terraces and there's a circular pool at the back. ⑤ with breakfast.

Hotel de Montaña Riogazas 7km south of Cazorla along the road to El Chorro and Nacimiento del Río Guadalquivir ☎953 12 40 35, ℗953 71 00 68. An appealing country option in the Sierra de Cazorla with rooms inside a *casa forestal* with pool and restaurant. ④

Hotel Guadalquivir c/Nueva 6 ☎ & ℗953 72 02 68, @www.hguadalquivir .com. Charming and friendly small hotel in a central location offering en-suite a/c rooms with fridge and TV. ③

Hotel Peña de Los Halcones Travesía Camino de la Iruela, reached by continuing along the road beyond the *Albergue Juvenil* ☎953 72 02 11, @los.halcones@wanadoo.es. Decent three-star hotel with a/c rooms plus restaurant and pool (when filled). Own garage and car park. ⑤

Hotel Sierra de Cazorla 2km outside Cazorla, in the village of La Iruela ☎953 72 00 15, @www.hotelsierradecazorla.com. Modern and good-value luxury hotel set in scenic surroundings, with balcony rooms, restaurant, bar and great pool. Has own walks guide for guests. ⑤

Mesón La Cueva de Juan Pedro Plaza Santa María ☎953 72 12 25, @www.cuevajuanpedro .com. Rustic and friendly restaurant that also offers en-suite rooms with bath (②) and excellent studio apartments nearby with kitchen, TV and terrace (③).

Molino La Farraga Camino de la Hoz s/n, 5min from Plaza Santa María ☎953 72 12 49, @www.molinolafarraga.com. An enchanting *casa rural* in a densely wooded garden location above the valley of the Río Cerezuelo with cosy en-suite rooms, pool and friendly proprietors. ⑤ with breakfast.

Parador El Adelantado 25km away in the park ☎953 72 70 75, @www.parador.es. Somewhat featureless modern building made attractive by its wonderful setting and a swimming pool. Make sure to get a room with a view. It has its own bar and restaurant. ⑦

Pensión Taxi Travesía de San Antón 7 ☎953 72 05 25. Up steps opposite the bus stop in Plaza de la Constitución, this is a friendly budget option and has a good-value *comedor*. En-suite rooms have a/c, heating and TV. ②

Villa Turística de Cazorla Ladera de San Isicio s/n, reached by crossing the bridge over the river below Plaza de la Constitución ☎953 71 01 00, @www.villacazorla.com. Most attractive of the upmarket in-town places, with a series of self-contained, a/c chalets with terraces plus communal pool and restaurant. It also has its own car park. ⑤

The Town and around

A few minutes' walk south from the Plaza de la Constitución along the main c/Dr Muñoz leads to the **Plaza de la Corredera** (or *del Huevo*, "of the Egg", because of its shape). This is the traditional meeting place for the *señoritos*, the class of landowners and their descendants who, through influence and privilege, still lay claim to the most important jobs and mould local destiny. The Ayuntamiento is here too – a fine Moorish-style palace off the far end of the plaza. The arrival of the *Hotel Ciudad de Cazorla* on the square's east side caused a controversy in the town because of its jarring architectural style.

Beyond Plaza de la Corredera, c/Gómez Calderón (passing the Ayuntamiento) is one of a labyrinth of narrow, twisting streets descending to Cazorla's liveliest square, the **Plaza de Santa María**. This takes its name from the sixteenth-century cathedral church of **Santa María**, designed by Andrés de Vandelvira, which was damaged by floods in the seventeenth century and later torched by Napoleonic troops. Its impressive ruins, now preserved, and the fine open square with a Renaissance fountain form a natural amphitheatre for concerts and local events as well as being a popular meeting place. The square is dominated by **La Yedra**, the austere, reconstructed tower of the lower of two Moorish castles. It also houses the **Museo de Artes y Costumbres** (Tues 3–8pm, Wed–Sat 9am–8pm, Sun 9am–2.30pm; free), a notable folklore museum. There's a fine **view** from just above the plaza of the castle perched on its rock.

Some 2km up the road heading into the park from Cazorla, the village of **LA IRUELA** has the other ruined Moorish **fortress** perched on a daunting but picturesque rock peak which must have been a wretched struggle for the Christian troops to subdue. It was later rebuilt by the Templars. There's also another ruined church here, Santo Domingo, attributed to Vandelvira. The village has a number of upmarket hotels (see p.507).

Eating, drinking and nightlife

You'll find several bars serving up good tapas around the Plaza Santa María, where for more substantial **eating** there's also the rustic *Mesón La Cueva de Juan Pedro* which has been in the Muñoz family for over a century and offers authentic local food – *conejo* (rabbit) is recommended – cooked on a wood-fired range plus a *menú* for around €10. On Plaza de la Corredera, *Bar Las Vegas* does good sit-down tapas and *raciones* including tasty *revueltos*. Between here and Plaza de la Constitución left off c/Muñoz – and down some steps – *Mesón Don Chema* is a good choice for *platos combinados*, offering many local specialities. Continuing down the same steps to the market square leads to the rather swish ♣ *La Sarga*, (☎953 72 15 07) Cazorla's top – and very good – restaurant preparing regional dishes with flair; *lomo de jabalí en salsa de castañas* (wild boar with chestnut sauce) is one of a number of game options prepared here, and there's also a *menú de degustación* for around €24. At the southern end of the same square, *Juan Carlos* (☎953 72 12 01) is similar but slightly cheaper, serving up delicious trout and game dishes with a *menú* for around €12. Two restaurants attached to accommodation places (see "Accommodation" p.507) are also worth considering: *Pensión Taxi* has a good-value all-in *menú* for €9 and, moving upmarket, the *Hotel Cuidad de Cazorla* does its own popular *menú* (including wine) for around €14.

A few of Cazorla's excellent **tapas bars** provide the route for an entertaining bar crawl between the town's three squares. On Plaza de la Constitución you'll find what many locals believe to be the best in town, *Bar Sola*, and the nearby and the equally bustling *Bar Rojas*. Plaza Corredera has the popular ♣ *Bar La Montería* (try its famous *plato olimpico* for €5 which gets you a selec-

Wild and relatively unspoiled country, with grand panoramas west over the olive plains of Jaén, begins at the edge of Cazorla, and if you choose to base yourself here, you can make a number of good **day-trips**.

Just over an hour's walk away (head up behind the fountain on Plaza Santa María, then pick up the mule track which skirts the hill topped by the ruined upper castle of Cinco Esquinas) is the intriguing sixteenth-century **Monasterio de Monte Sion**. One of the brothers who worked on its reconstruction remains there (summer only), and will proudly show you round his isolated domain, particularly the monastery's chapel with restored frescoes. Be prepared to step back into the Middle Ages – as exemplified by the scourges hanging over the beds in the cells used for retreat. Another hour's walk beyond the cloister to the south will bring you to the base of **Gilillo**, highest point in the southwest of the park, with a yawning gorge to the right.

You can follow the main path over a pass from here to a dilapidated *casa forestal* and then down to **Cañada de las Fuentes**, source of the Guadalquivir, within another two hours. Alternatively – and a more feasible day-walk – you might bear left at the saddle onto a trail descending towards Cazorla town through the canyon of **Riogazas**. This path ends in a jumble of tractor tracks after an hour, after which you must pick your way down through the various water courses for another hour and a half. This five-hour walking day allows ample time for dawdling, but unfortunately many of the pools in the stream on the descent are either difficult to get to or on private property. A good **map** such as the *Alpina Sierra de Cazorla* map would be a useful aid to staying on the right track on all the above hikes.

A popular trip **by car** is to the **source of the Guadalquivir** river, in the mountains to the south of Cazorla. When you reach the source you'll find the infant river innocently bubbling from beneath a rock as it begins its seven-hundred-kilometre journey to the Atlantic. To get there, take the road out to La Iruela and then follow the signs for La Cañada de las Fuentes, around a 25km journey.

tion of all their tapas) and the earthier *Bar Niño* offering fresh seafood. On the same square and near the Ayuntamiento, *Bar Rincón Serrano* has a pleasant terrace with oleander tree, and specializes in *jamón*. Plaza de Santa María has *Bar Julián* where the delicious *callos* (tripe) and *caracoles* are only a couple of the many dishes popular with locals who fill its lively terrace in summer. The daily **market** in Plaza del Mercado (below c/Dr Muñoz) is a good place to gather ingredients for picnics in the park.

Cazorla has a low-key **nightlife** scene with one **discoteca**, *La Leyenda*, on the Úbeda road on the edge of town; **music bars** include *Pub El Barco*, c/Escuelas 12, and *Liberty*, c/Hilario Marco 4, both a little way north of Plaza de la Constitución. *El Escondite*, Plaza Consuelo Mendieta s/n, at the southern end of the car park below Plaza Constitución, is another popular music bar where, when the mood takes them, the clientele even start dancing. On May 15, Cazorla honours its patron, San Isicio, with a vibrant **romería** preceded the night before by **La Hoguera** (bonfires). In mid-September there's the **fiesta de Cristo del Consuelo**, with fairgrounds, fireworks and religious processions.

The Cazorla Natural Park

The **Cazorla Natural Park** – or Parque Natural de Cazorla, Segura y Las Villas to give its official name – is not as lofty as the Sierra Nevada (the highest peaks are 2000m), but outdoes it for beauty, slashed as it is by river gorges and largely covered in forest. The best **times to visit** are late spring and early autumn. The winters can be uncomfortably wet and cold, and roads are often closed due to snow. In summer, although walking is pleasant before noon, the climate tends to be hot and dry.

Inside the park **public transport** is scarce and currently there are just two daily buses running between Cazorla and Coto Ríos, 39km into the park. Distances between points are enormous, so to explore it well you'll need a car or be prepared for long hikes; otherwise day-trips to the outskirts of the park are possible. However, a number of **campsites** – both *camping libre* (free camping) and official sites – dotted around the park make walking tours possible. The **Turismo** at Cazorla (see p.506) will provide a complete list and map of campsites within the park.

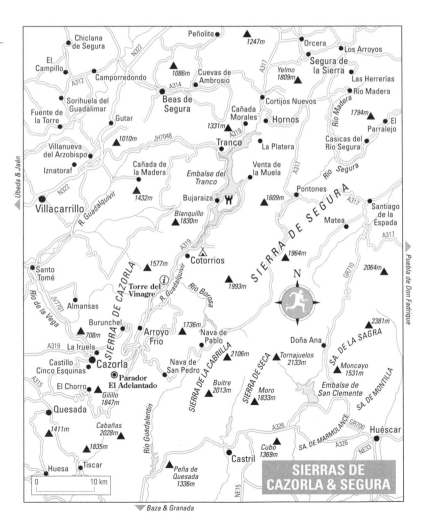

Places to stay – hotels, apartments, villas and wood cabins – are to be found throughout the park, many of them very attractive indeed if getting away from it all is what you're after. Be aware, however, that while for most of the year you should be able to find accommodation with ease, they all tend to fill up in August, when ringing ahead is strongly advised.

Judging from the number of *cabra hispanica* (Spanish mountain goat), deer, *jabalí* (wild pig), birds and butterflies that even the casual visitor is likely to spot, the Cazorla reserve is fulfilling its role handsomely. Ironically, though, much of the best wildlife viewing will be at the periphery, or even outside the park, since the wildlife is most successfully stalked on foot and walking opportunities within the park itself are somewhat limited. There are, in fact, only three **signposted tracks**, all pitifully short. One leads from the Empalme de Valle to the Puente de las Herrerías via the Fuente del Oso (2km one-way); another of about 1.7km curls round the Cerrada (Narrows) del Utrero near Vadillo-Castril village; the best-marked segment, through the lower Borosa gorge (see below), is also a mere 1.7km long. Good **hiking guides** for the park include Guy Hunter-Watts' *Walking in Andalucía*, which details five walks in the park of between five and nineteen kilometres, or, for Spanish readers, *Senderos de Pequeña Recorrido – Parque Natural de Cazorla* by Justo Robles Alvarez describing fifteen walks of 3–22km (see "Books" p.696 for both). Take a good map (see below) when using either of these guides. Before heading into the park, it's worth stopping at the private **tourist office**, *Turisnat*, in Cazorla (see p.506). Both they and the Torre del Vinagre Centro de Interpretación (see p.513) should have copies of the 1:40,000 **map and guide packs** titled *Mapa y Guía Excursionista* (Editorial Alpina). This series splits the park in two parts: *Sierra de Cazorla* (covering the southern zone) and *Sierra de Segura* (the central and northern sectors). These are now the most accurate maps available on the park and detail *senderos* (footpaths), mountain bike routes, refuges, campsites and hotels. The accompanying booklet (in Spanish or English versions) has useful background information on the park's flora and fauna as well as villages, and includes half a dozen described walks.

Arroyo Frio, Torre del Vinagre and Coto Ríos

Two daily (Mon–Sat only) **buses** link Cazorla town with **Coto Ríos** – where there's a campsite and accommodation – near the middle of the park via Torre del Vinagre: one currently running at 6.30am, the other at 2.45pm; there's also a 6.30pm bus on Saturday. Return buses from Coto leave at 8am and 4.15 pm. Taking the early departure allows you to do the classic **walk along the Río Borosa** as a day-trek (see box on p.513; confirm all the above times in Cazorla to avoid being stranded). The road into the park passes Burunchel and climbs over the Puerto de las Palomas with spectacular views before descending into the valley of the Guadalquivir. A little further on there's a turning for the scenically sited **parador** which, with your own transport, would allow you to stop off for a drink; they also offer a good-value set *menú* for lunch and dinner which sometimes includes the excellent local river trout served *a la cazuleña* (with *jamón serrano* and almonds).

Arroyo Frio

The road into the park soon passes the hamlet of **ARROYO FRIO** where the tourist complex of *Los Enebros* (☎953 72 71 10, ⊛www.lfhoteles.com; ➒) has a campsite, hotel and restaurant and rents out freestanding wood cabins; there's

△ Sierra de Cazorla

also a wide variety of activities on offer such as mountain biking, canoeing and guided walks. Close by, *Hotel Cazorla Valle* (☎953 72 71 00, ⓦwww.cazorlavalle .com; ❹ with breakfast) is another hotel renting out rooms and apartments, with a similar list of outdoor activities and its own restaurant and pool. In the centre of the village the *Hotel Montaña* (☎953 72 70 11, ⓦwww.hmontana.com; ❺) is a straightforward affair with restaurant, bar and pool. At the village's southern end the *Picadero El Cortijillo* riding school (mobile ☎690697850) provides tuition and hires out **horses** for guided half-day or full-day treks. Some 4km out of Arroyo the *Monte Piedra Aparthotel* (☎ & ⓕ953 71 31 45, ⓦwww .campingchopera.com) has great views, pool, restaurant and good-value rooms (❹) and apartments sleeping up to six (€70 per night) that are available for daylets outside high summer, when you're looking at one week minimum.

Torre del vinagre
The Río Borosa walk (see box below) begins at **TORRE DEL VINAGRE**, 9km from Arroyo and 34km from Cazorla, where there is a visitors' centre, the **Centro de Interpretación Torre del Vinagre** (daily: April–Sept 11am–2pm & 5–8pm; Oct–March 11am–2pm & 4–6pm; ☎953 71 30 45). Packed with motoring tourists in high summer, this has informative exhibits on the park's ecology as well as a disturbing number of stuffed animals and mounted ibex

The Río Borosa walk

The Río Borosa walk is one of the most popular walks inside the park and follows the Río Borosa upstream. From the visitors' centre at Torre del Vinagre, cross the road and take the path to the side of the Jardín Botánico. When you reach an electricity pylon turn left onto a downhill track. After passing a campsite and sportsfield on the left cross a footbridge over the river and turn right, aiming for a white building peeping above the trees. Soon you'll pass a small campsite (with an open-air bar in summer) and about a kilometre from the footbridge you'll come to a car park at a *piscifactoría* (trout hatchery).

From here follow the path as it crosses back and forth over the Borosa, swift and cold even in summer. After some 6km a signposted footpath diverges to the right; this also marks the beginning of the Cerrada de Elías **gorge**. Two or three wooden bridges now take the path back and forth across the river, which is increasingly confined by sheer rock walls. At the narrowest points the path is routed along planked catwalks secured to the limestone cliff. The walk from Torre del Vinagre to the end of the narrows takes about two hours.

Here the footpath rejoins the track; after another half-hour's walk you'll see a turbine and a long metal pipe bringing water from two **lakes** – one natural, one with a small dam – up the mountain. The road crosses one last bridge over the Borosa and stops at the turbine house. When you get to the gate, beyond which there's a steeply rising gully, count on another full hour up to the lakes. Cross a footbridge and start the steep climb up a narrow track over the rocks below the cliff (at one point the path passes close to the base of the palisade – beware falling stones). At the top of the path is a cavernous amphitheatre, with a waterfall in winter. The path ends about halfway up the cliff, where an artificial tunnel has been bored through the rock; walk through it to get to the lake.

Allow three and a half hours' walking time from Torre del Vinagre for the whole route, slightly less going down. It's a very full day's excursion but you should have plenty of time to catch the afternoon bus back, which currently passes the visitors' centre at around 4.30pm, but it would be a good idea to confirm this before starting out. This walk is clearly detailed on the Editorial Alpina **map** (see p.511).

and deer heads in a rather dismal hunting museum – including one bagged by General Franco (from which the nameplate has mysteriously disappeared) who was a frequent visitor here. Next to the centre a **botanical garden** (daily 11am–2pm & 4–7pm) has living specimens of the park's flora. The centre also offers tours of the park by Land Rover, as well as horse and mountain bike excursions.

For **accommmodation**, a couple of kilometres before Torre del Vinagre, *Hotel Noguera de la Sierpe* (☎953 71 30 21, ⓦwww.lfhoteles.com; ⓞ with breakfast) is one of a string of relatively upmarket hotels close to the road and is housed in a converted *cortijo* with views over a lake and the Guadalquivir valley. Frequented in winter by the hunting fraternity the *patrón* is a hunting fanatic and images of his exploits plus trophies (including a stuffed lion) litter the foyer and public rooms. They also rent out some self-catering *casas rurales* overlooking the lake (ⓞ), and there's a pool and horse stables. More economical accommodation is available at Coto Ríos (see below).

Coto Ríos

Some 5km on from Torre del Vinagre, **COTO RÍOS** is a pleasant village with a river beach on the Guadalquivir. There's a **campsite** here, the shady *Camping Chopera de Coto-Ríos* (☎953 72 19 05), plus two others – *Fuente de Pascala* (☎953 71 30 28) and *Llanos de Arance* (on the opposite bank; ☎953 71 30 36) – just to the north. A couple of kilometres back towards Torre del Vinagre you'll find good-value **accommodation** at the ⚶ *Hotel La Hortizuela* (☎ & ⓕ953 71 31 50, ⓦwww.hotellahortizuela.com; ⓞ), a delightfully serene hideaway down a signed track on the left with garden pool and restaurant. Slightly closer to Coto Ríos, the marginally cheaper *Hotel Mirasierra* (☎ & ⓕ953 71 30 44, ⓦwww.hotel-mirasierra.com; ⓞ), is comfortable with air-conditioned rooms and serves excellent trout in its restaurant. Some 6km further along the Tranco road from Coto Ríos, ⚶ *El Hoyazo* (☎953 12 41 10) has excellent value en-suite rooms with TV (ⓞ) as well as some equally good-value and fully equipped self-catering bungalows (ⓞ) with a communal pool. Nearby, and slightly before the Parque Cinegético (below), the lakeside *Hotel Paraíso de Bujaraiza* (☎953 12 41 14, ⓦwww.paraisodebujaraiza.com; ⓞ with breakfast) is a small, friendly and good-value hotel with comfortable rooms, pool, restaurant and plenty of greenery. It's worth noting that there are no further campsites or places to stay until Tranco.

Eight kilometres beyond Coto Ríos, keeping to the river's west bank, at the southern end of the Embalse del Tranco reservoir, is the **Parque Cinegético**, a wildlife park which eventually hopes to include specimens of all the park's fauna including ibex and mouflon, although at present you'll be lucky to see some rather bewildered deer and the odd wild boar from the viewing balcony. To reach the viewing areas, park at the entrance and walk a good kilometre through the woods (many Spaniards head back to their cars when they realize this) to get to the first viewing hide. Early morning and evening are the best times to see the animals not struck down by midday torpor.

Tranco and the north of the park

The road continues along the west bank of the river, passing more picnic spots and *ventas* along the way, en route to **TRANCO**, 21km north, where the Guadalquivir is dammed to create a reservoir, the Embalse de Tranco. The island in the centre of the lake contains the ruined castle of **Bujaraiza**, all that remains of the village of the same name which disappeared beneath the waters when the dam was created. Apart from a few holiday villas, a lakeside bar, and **campsite** at *Montillana* (℡953 12 61 94), 4km north of the village, Tranco has little to detain you. A couple of places **to stay** beyond here are, after 3km down a turning on the right, the attractive and friendly lakeside *Hotel Los Parrales* (℡953 12 61 70, Ⓦ www.swin.net/usuarios/jcg; ④) with a pool and, 4km further, *Hotel Losam* (℡953 49 50 88, Ⓔ hotel-losam@terra.es; ②), a functional and modern roadside place with a decent restaurant serving a *menú* for €7.50.

Hornos

From Tranco, the road heads north and circles around the northern end of the reservoir before turning into the valley of the Río Hornos from where you can glimpse the village of **HORNOS**, perched on a daunting rock pinnacle beneath the tower of its Moorish castle. When you reach it, the village has an isolated air with plenty of Moorish atmosphere. Its narrow, white-walled streets are perfect for meandering, and the castle is worth a look, although once you've got up close there isn't much to it apart from the tower. The pleasant Plaza Mayor is overlooked by a solid fifteenth-century church, the **Iglesia de la Asunción**, the interior of which is bare of features, but a *mirador* through a door at the back has wonderful **views** over the reservoir, flanked by the heights of the Sierra de Segura. The waters, which lapped the foot of the outcrop below, have receded dramatically in recent years – a symptom of Andalucía's chronic and continuing drought. A stretch of the village's ancient walls is still intact, complete with a horseshoe-arched Moorish gateway.

A pleasant **walk** can be made from Hornos along the reservoir's eastern banks to the hamlet of **La Platera** where there are cottages to rent for longer stays (mobile ℡646810252; ④) and the hill of Montero, with views along the reservoir, 4km beyond. The rock faces above the pine-covered slopes are home to a variety of plants, including yellow-flowered flax and throatwart. Common bird species in this area include azure-winged magpies, kestrels and sparrowhawks, but you will be extremely lucky to see the **Lammergeier** or bearded vulture in this, its only breeding habitat in Spain outside the Pyrenees; the species is now down to a mere handful of breeding pairs as the carrion these scavengers rely on has diminished. The vultures are known as *quebrantahuesos* (bone-breakers) in Spanish, after their practice of hoisting the leg bones of victims high into the air and dropping them onto a rock below – nearly always the same one – splitting them open to allow the birds to extract the marrow.

Places to stay in Hornos include the welcoming *Hostal El Cruce* (℡953 49 50 35; ②), where en-suite rooms come with air-conditioning and TV and whose garden terrace **restaurant** is hard to miss as you enter the village. They also rent **apartments** in the village (⑤) and have free mountain bikes for guests. More rooms with bath are available at *Hostal El Mirador* (℡953 49 50 19; ②) towards the centre, with fine balcony **views** over the Embalse de Tranco; the proprietor also rents out apartments for longer stays. *Raisa Apartments*, on the right as you enter from Cazorla (℡953 49 50 23), is another place for en-suite air-conditioned rooms (②) and apartments (③) with a restaurant below. The best **place to eat** is probably on the *Hostal El Cruce's* terrace, although for a change of scene the central *Restaurante Raisa*, at c/Enmedio 5, about 30m from the church, is also pretty good for Sierra dishes.

Río Madera

If you are seeking a dreamy end-of-the-world location to hole up for a couple of days, few places could better fit the bill than **RÍO MADERA**, a hamlet at the end of a densely wooded road some 20km to the east of Hornos.

Surrounded by woods of beech, oak, pine and poplar, intermingled with clumps of sweet-scented wild thyme and lavender, the river valley is located in the midst of some magnificent hiking country. What makes the place even more attractive, however, is a welcoming **place to stay**, the 🏠 *Hospedería Río Madera* (☎953 12 62 04; ❷) a small country bar-restaurant and hotel which has some good rooms with heating and TV and some well-equipped apartments (❸). The proprietor also stocks hiking maps and books, speaks some English, and there's a good **bar–restaurant** offering many dishes from the Sierra with a *menú* for €15 (including wine). There's a small **shop** behind the hotel where food and hiding snacks can be purchased.

To get there, follow the (signed) Río Madera road from Hornos. There's only one tricky bit where you reach an unsigned junction: here you need to turn right (along the A317) and then left after 100m along a road that *is* signed (direction Siles). This route is clearly shown on the *Sierra de Segura* map (see p.511) and the same map has many tracks and footpaths marked in this zone, enabling you to create your own hiking routes. Give the *Hospedería* a ring if you get lost and they will endeavour to set you right.

Segura de la Sierra

Scenic though Hornos is, it is overshadowed in every sense by the Cazorla park's most spectacularly sited village, **SEGURA DE LA SIERRA**, 20km to the northeast. With a romantic castle crowning an almost conical 1100-metre-high hill top, beneath which the tiered village streets seem in danger of collapsing into the olive groves far below, it's a landmark for miles around. Segura's top-notch **olive oil** (including an organic variety) is famed throughout Spain, for which it has a coveted *denominación de origen* label (one of only four in the whole country); not always easy to get hold of in the village itself, the *almacen* near the church should have a few bottles, or enquire at the tourist office (see below) who now have their own small shop selling products of the Sierra.

Once you've managed to climb the road which snakes up to it and passed through the medieval gate, Segura is a warren of narrow streets left behind by its former Moorish occupants. But its history goes back much further, perhaps as far as the Phoenicians who, local historians claim, called it Tavara. Greeks, Carthaginians, Romans and Visigoths came in their wake, until the last of these were prised out of this mountain eyrie by the invading Moors who constructed the castle they called Saqura. When it fell to the Christian forces under Alfonso VIII during the thirteenth century, the fort became a strategic outpost on the frontiers of the kingdom of Granada, whose borders were framed by the Guadalquivir and Segura river valleys.

The **castle** – now somewhat over-restored after being torched by French troops during the War of Independence – can be visited daily (Wed–Sun 10am–2pm & 6–9pm; free). On your way up to it you can take in views over the country for miles around, including an amusingly primitive rectangular **bullring** below. Once inside the walls, climb the tower for more magnificent **views**. The village's other major monument is the **Baños Arabes** (same hours as castle), a splendid Moorish bathhouse off the central Plaza Mayor. Inside, three well-preserved chambers are illuminated by overhead light vents and contain elegant horseshoe arches. To reach the baths follow a descending street to the right-hand side of the parish church of Nuestra Señora Collado which brings you to a superb Moorish double arch in a preserved tower of the ancient walls. The baths are facing this. Near the church there's also a fine Renaissance **fountain** which bears the arms of Carlos V. Incidentally a waymarked footpath, the GR147, leaves the double arch for Río Madera, a downhill none-too-challenging fifteen-kilometre hike.

Practicalities

There are no bus services to Segura. The village's **tourist office** (daily 10.30am–2pm & 6.30–8.30pm; ☎953 48 02 80) lies to the right before the arch at the top of the street leading into the village. The nearest **campsite** is *Camping El Robledo* (☎953 12 64 69), 4km east of Cortijos Nuevos, passed on the road from Hornos. If you need to cool down, there's a pleasant **swimming pool** on the road leading to the castle.

A number of places to stay have recently opened in the village. The most attractive choice is the welcoming 𝒥 *Los Huertos de Segura*, c/Castillo 11 in the upper village (☎953 48 04 02, ℮antonpeer@arrakis.es; ❹) where comfortable studios come with kitchenette and terrace or balcony and fine views. The other two possibilities are located in the tiny c/Postigo, above the church. One, *La Mesa Segureña* (☎953 48 21 01, ⓦwww.lamesadesegura.com; ❹) rents well-equipped studios and apartments, while *El Mirador Messia de Leiva* (☎953 48 08 06, ⓦwww.messiadeleiva.com; ❹) has similar places. Among Segura's **places to eat** are the restaurants attached to *La Mesa Segureña* and the *El Mirador Messia de Leiva* accommodation options (see above) in c/Postigo. Both prepare dishes from the Sierra and the *Mesa Segureña* probably has the edge for quality, with a daily *menú* for €10. At the entrance to the village *Restaurante Peñalta* (main dishes €5–15) is another possibility with a great view from its terrace.

Moving on from the park

With your own transport, you can avoid backtracking to Cazorla and take an alternative and attractive route out of the park heading south from Hornos along the A317 through the **Sierra de Segura** to **Pontones** and **Santiago de Espada**, on the border with Granada. There are plenty more campsites signed along this route and both Pontones and Santiago – try the friendly *Hotel San Francisco* (☎953 43 80 72; ❹) – have hotels and *hostales*. The same road continues to Puebla de Don Fadrique where there is another decent hotel-restaurant, *Puerta de Andalucía* (☎958 72 13 40; ❸), on the main road through. From here you have a choice between the routes to Granada and Almería. The Granada route via the cattle town of Huéscar, following the A330, takes in the interesting towns of Baza and Guadix and provides an opportunity en route to see the remarkable prehistoric discoveries at Orce (see p.628); otherwise the A317 heads across the deserted but picturesque wheatfields of Granada province's eastern panhandle towards Vélez Blanco (see p.627) with its prehistoric caves, and eventually hits the coast near the Almerian resort of Mojácar (see p.622).

Travel details

Trains

Córdoba to: Algeciras (1 daily; 4hr 30min); Granada (1 daily; 4hr 30min); Jaén (1 daily; 1hr 30min); Madrid (13 daily; 4–6hr; AVE 20 daily; 1hr 45min); Málaga (2 daily; 3hr 30min); Ronda (1 daily; 3hr); Sevilla (AVE 20 daily; 45min; 6 daily; 1hr 20min;).
Jaén to: Córdoba (1 daily; 1hr 30min); Madrid (4 daily; 4hr 30min–6hr); Sevilla (1 daily; 3hr).

Buses

Bus times quoted are for the fastest journey times, normally direct. There may be other buses to the same destination which make additional stops at towns and villages en route.

Baeza to: Granada (8 daily; 2hr 30min); Jaén (14 daily; 1hr); Úbeda (14 daily; 20min).

Cazorla to: Granada (3 daily; 1hr 30min); Úbeda (6 daily; 45min); Jaén (4 daily; 2hr).

Córdoba to: Almería (2 daily; 5hr); Algeciras (2 daily; 5hr); Cádiz (2 daily; 3hr); Écija (5 daily; 1hr 15min); Granada (9 daily; 2–4hr); Jaén (7 daily; 1hr 30min); Madrid (6 daily; 4hr 30min); Málaga (5 daily; 2hr 30min); Sevilla (12 daily; 1hr 45min).

Jaén to: Almería (2 daily; 4hr 30min); Almuñecar (1 daily; 2hr 45min); Baeza/Úbeda (14 daily; 1hr/1hr 30min); Cazorla (2 daily; 2hr); Córdoba (8 daily; 1hr 30min); Granada (14 daily; 1hr 30min); La Guardia (3 daily; 20min); Madrid (5 daily; 6hr); Málaga (4 daily; 4hr); Martos (13 daily; 30min); Sevilla (4 daily; 3hr).

Úbeda to: Baeza (14 daily; 20min); Cazorla (6 daily; 45min); Córdoba (3 daily; 2hr 30min); Granada (7 daily, all calling at Baeza; 2 direct, 6 via Jaén; 2–3hr); Jaén (14 daily; 1hr 15min); Sevilla (3 daily; 3hr).

Granada and Almería

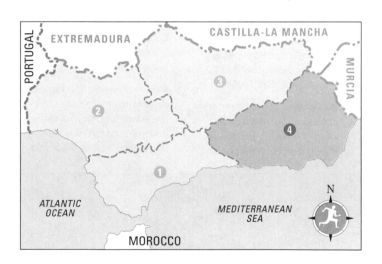

CHAPTER 4

Highlights

✳ **The Alhambra** One of the world's great monuments and the pinnacle of Moorish architectural splendour in Spain. **See p.533**

✳ **The Albaicín** Granada's ancient, atmospheric Moorish quarter. **See p.544**

✳ **Capilla Real** Stunning Gothic chapel built to house the remains of Isabel and Fernando, conquerors of Moorish Granada. **See p.548**

✳ **Las Alpujarras** A wildly picturesque mountain region dotted with traditional villages and many other vestiges of a Moorish past. **See p.569**

✳ **Los Millares** This third millennium BC settlement with a remarkable necropolis is one of the most important prehis-

toric sites in Europe. **See p.592**

✳ **Alcazaba, Almería** One of Andalucía's finest Moorish forts dominates the provincial capital. **See p.604**

✳ **Parque Natural de Cabo de Gata** Desert plants and volcanic hills are the features of this natural park edged with coastal resorts where the beaches are often deserted. **See p.615**

✳ **Mojácar** Attractive "sugar cube" village on a rocky hill with a lively beach resort below. **See p.622**

✳ **Mini Hollywood** The Almería deserts have provided the backdrop for many Westerns and some of the movie sets can still be visited. **See p.630**

△ The Alhambra

Granada and Almería

There is no more convincing proof of the diversity of Andalucía than its eastern provinces: **Granada**, dominated by the Spanish peninsula's highest mountains, the snowcapped Mulhacén and Veleta peaks of the Sierra Nevada; and **Almería**, a waterless and, in part, semi-desert landscape.

For most visitors, the city of **Granada** is not only the highlight of its province but one of the great destinations of Spain, as the home of Andalucía's most precious monument, the exquisite Moorish **Alhambra** palace and gardens. The city preserves, too, the old Moorish quarter of Albaicín and gypsy *barrio* of Sacromonte – places filled with the lingering atmosphere of this last outpost of Muslim Spain – as well as a host of Christian monuments, including the beautiful Capilla Real, with the tombs of Fernando and Isabel, Los Reyes Católicos, who finally wrested the kingdom from Moorish rule. Granada is also an atmospheric place to be during **Semana Santa** (the Easter week of floats and processions), and a place of literary pilgrimage through its associations with Spain's greatest modern poet, Federico García Lorca.

South of Granada rear the peaks of the **Sierra Nevada** and its lower slopes, **Las Alpujarras**, a series of wooded valleys sprinkled with attractive white-washed villages. This is wonderful country for walks and wildlife, with ancient cobbled paths connecting many of the villages, among them **Yegen**, one-time base of author Gerald Brenan, and **Trevélez**, Spain's highest village, famed for its snow-cured *jamón serrano*. The province makes the boast that you can ski in the Sierra Nevada's snowcapped peaks in the morning and swim on the coast in the afternoon. And so you could, if you really wanted to: the resorts of **Almuñecar**, **Salobreña** and **Castell de Ferro**, along the **Costa Tropical**, all have fine beaches and less development than the Costa del Sol.

There's less of interest west and east of Granada. To the west, **Alhama de Granada** is a delightful spa on a scenic back road to Málaga. To the east, amid a landscape of dusty hills covered with clumps of esparto grass, lies **Guadix**, famous for its cave dwellings hacked out of the soft tufa rock, and the red stone Renaissance castle of **La Calahorra**. Beyond here, Granada's panhandle extends past the ancient country town of **Baza** to a lonely landscape of rolling sierras where small farms and isolated villages watch over fields of wheat, fruit orchards and pasture.

The **province of Almería** is a strange corner of Spain. Inland it has an almost lunar landscape of desert, sandstone cones and dried-up riverbeds; on the coast, with a few exceptions, it's relatively unspoilt, with development thwarted by sparse water supplies. As Spain's hottest province, the beach resorts are worth considering during what would be "off-season" elsewhere, since Almería's summers start well before Easter and last into November. In midsummer it's

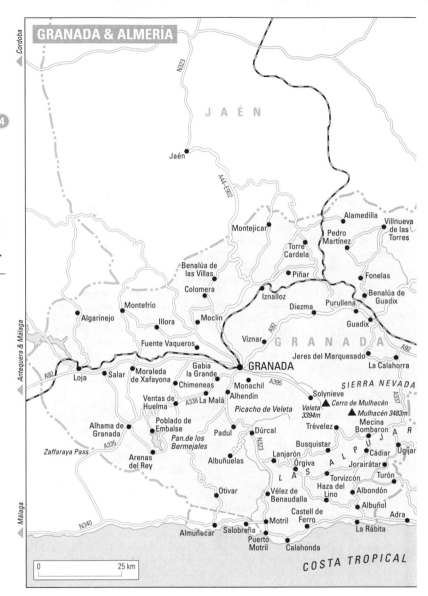

J A É N

Cordoba

N323

Jaén

A44-E902

Alamedilla

Villnueva
de las
Torres

Montejicar

Pedro
Martínez

Torre
Cardela

Benalúa de
las Villas

Piñar

Fonelas

Colomera

Iznalloz

Benalúa de
Guadix

Montefrío

Diezma

Purullena

Algarinejo

Illora

Moclin

A92

Guadix

Fuente Vaqueros

Viznar

G R A N A D A

A92

Jeres del Marquesado

La Calahorra

Antequera & Málaga

A92

Loja

Salar

Moraleda
de Xafayona

Gabia
la Grande

GRANADA

A395

SIERRA NEVADA

A337

Chimeneas

Monachil

Solynieve

Cerro de Mulhacén

Ventas de
Huelma

A338 La Malá

Alhendín

Picacho de Veleta

Veleta
3394m

Mulhacén 3483m

Mecina
Bombaron

Alhama de
Granada

Poblado de
Embalse

Padul

Dúrcal

Trévelez

A

R

Zaffaraya Pass

A335

Pan.de los
Bermejales

Busquistar

P

U

J

Cádiar

Ugijar

Arenas
del Rey

Albuñelas

Lanjarón

Órgiva

A

S

Jorairátar

Turón

L

Torvizcón

A

S

Otivar

Vélez de
Benaudalla

Haza del
Lino

Albondón

Málaga

Castell de
Ferro

Albuñol

Adra

N340

Motril

La Rábita

Almuñecar

Salobreña

Puerto
Motril

Calahonda

C O S T A   T R O P I C A L

0   25 km

incredibly hot – frequently touching 35°C in the shade – while all year round there's an intense, almost luminous, sunlight.

The provincial capital and port, **Almería**, enjoyed a brief period of prosperity under the Moors but has been a bit of a backwater ever since, overlooked by the largest castle the Moors built in Andalucía, the **Alcazaba**, below whose walls is a cave quarter, still populated by gypsies.

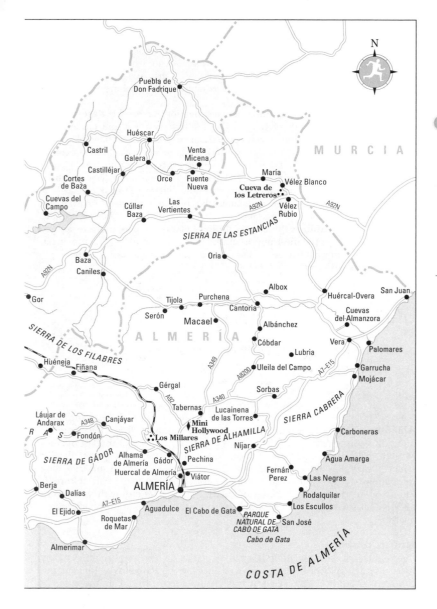

Almería's best **beaches and resorts**, the least developed of the Spanish Mediterranean, lie to the east of the capital. One of the nicest, the small resort of **San José**, lies inside the **Cabo de Gata Natural Park**, a wildlife and wetland area that is home to some interesting desert plants as well as a breeding ground for enormous flocks of **flamingos** in summer. Heading north, **Las Negras**, **Agua Amarga** and **Carboneras** are all attractively low-key places fronting a crystal-clear blue sea where there are sandy strands that see few visitors. North again, things liven up at **Mojácar**, Almería's most fashionable resort, an ancient hill-top village that has spawned an enjoyable seafront quarter. To the west of Almería city a dismal sea of plastic tents – *invernaderos* – covers the **plain of Dalías** from the hills to the coast: a bonanza of drip-irrigation agriculture where exotic vegetables are force-grown to supply northern European markets all year round.

Inland, to the northeast of Almería, begins the most remarkable **desert landscape** in Europe: badlands of twisted gulches, dry riverbeds and eroded hills that have long attracted film producers. Much of *Lawrence of Arabia* was shot here, along with scores of spaghetti westerns, whose sets have been preserved at **Mini Hollywood**, near Tabernas: a fun visit, especially if you have kids to entertain. This weird scenery also shelters some interesting villages such as **Níjar**, a long-established ceramics centre, and the cliff-top **Sorbas**.

The province of Almería also maintains relics of a rich prehistoric past, when the rains were regular and the landscape verdant. In the northeast, near the village of **Vélez Rubio**, is the **Cueva de los Letreros**, whose prehistoric cave paintings are among the most important in Spain, while north of the provincial capital, in the Almerian reaches of Las Alpujarras, is the exceptional archeological site of **Los Millares**.

Granada

Los dos ríos de Granada	Granada's twin rivers
Bajan de la nieve al trigo . . .	Tumble down from the snow to the wheat . . .

Federico García Lorca

The city of **GRANADA** has one of the most dramatic locations in Spain, poised below a magnificent backdrop of the snowcapped peaks of the Sierra Nevada. It's the perfect setting for a near-perfect edifice, the extraordinary **Alhambra** – the most exciting, sensual and romantic of all European monuments. It was the palace-fortress of the Nasrid kings, rulers of the last Spanish Muslim realm, and in its construction Moorish art reached a spectacular yet serene climax. The building, however, seems to go further than this, revealing something of the whole brilliance and spirit of Moorish life and culture. It should on no account be missed – and neither should the city, with its network of Moorish streets, panoply of Christian monuments and atmospheric gypsy quarter.

Some history

Before the arrival of the Moors, Granada's mark on history was slight. An early Iberian settlement here, Elibyrge, was adapted by the **Romans** as Illiberis, but although its fertility was prized, it was greatly overshadowed by the empire's provincial capital at Córdoba. Later, after the region had come under **Visigothic** control in the sixth century, the old Roman town, centred on the modern-day Albaicín, grew a **Jewish suburb**, Garnatha, on the south slope of the Alhambra hill. Popular tradition has it that friction between this Jewish settlement and the Christian town led to the Jews assisting the **Moors** to take the city shortly after the invasion of 711.

The Moors adapted the name to Karnattah, and for three centuries it was an important city under the control of the Cordoban caliphate and, when this fell in 1031, under the Almoravid and Almohad Berber dynasties of Sevilla. When, however, Almohad power crumbled in the thirteenth century as the Christian *Reconquista* gathered momentum, an astute Arab prince of the **Nasrid** tribe, which had been driven south from Zaragoza, saw his opportunity to create an independent state. The kingdom, established in the 1240s by **Ibn al-Ahmar** (aka Muhammad ibn Yusuf ibn Nasr), was to outlast the vanished al-Andalus by a further two and a half centuries.

Nasrid Granada was always a precarious state. Ibn al-Ahmar proved a just and capable ruler but all over Spain the Christian kingdoms were in the ascendant. The Moors of Granada survived only through paying tribute and allegiance to Fernando III of Castile – whom they were forced to assist in the conquest of Muslim Sevilla – and by the time of Ibn al-Ahmar's death in 1273 Granada was the only surviving Spanish Muslim kingdom. It had, however, consolidated its territory, which stretched from just north of the city down to a coastal strip between Tarifa and Almería, and, stimulated by Muslim refugees, developed a flourishing commerce, industry and culture.

Over the next two centuries, Granada maintained its autonomy by a series of shrewd manoeuvres, its rulers turning for protection, as it suited them, to the Christian kingdoms of Aragón and Castile and the Merinid sultans of Morocco. The city-state enjoyed its most confident and prosperous period under **Yusuf I** (1334–54) and **Muhammad V** (1354–91), the rulers responsible for much of the existing Alhambra palace. But by the mid-fifteenth century a pattern of coups and internal strife became established and a rapid succession of rulers did little to stem Christian inroads.

In 1479 the kingdoms of Aragón and Castile were united by the marriage of Fernando and Isabel and within ten years had conquered Ronda, Málaga and Almería. The city of Granada now stood completely alone, tragically preoccupied in a **civil war** between supporters of the sultan's two favourite wives. The Reyes Católicos made escalating and finally untenable demands upon it, and in 1490 war broke out. **Boabdil**, the last Moorish king, appealed in vain for help from his fellow Muslims in Morocco, Egypt and Ottoman Turkey, and in the following year Fernando and Isabel marched on Granada with an army said to total 150,000 troops. For seven months, through the winter of 1491, they laid siege to the city. On January 2, 1492, Boabdil formally surrendered its keys. The Christian Reconquest of Spain was complete.

There followed a century of repression for Granada, during which Jews and then Muslims were treated harshly and finally expelled by the Christian state and Church, both of which grew rich on the confiscated property. The loss of Muslim and Jewish artisans and traders led to gradual economic decline, which was reversed only temporarily in the seventeenth century, the period when the city's Baroque monuments – La Cartuja monastery and San Juan de Dios hospital – were built. The city suffered heavily under **Napoleonic occupation**, when even the Alhambra was used as a barracks, causing much damage, and, although the nineteenth-century Romantic movement saw to it that the Alhambra suffered few more such violations, the sober *granadino* middle class have been accused repeatedly since of caring little for the rest of their city's artistic legacy. Over the last century and a half, they have covered over the River Darro – which now flows beneath the town centre – and demolished an untold number of historic buildings to build avenues through the centre of the city. Things have hardly changed and in recent years the Andalucian parliament has had to block a preposterous plan by the city council to cover much of the Alhambra hill with a luxury housing estate – the bulldozers had actually begun digging.

Lorca described the *granadinos* as "the worst bourgeoisie in Spain", and they are regarded by many other Andalucians as conservative, arrogant and cool, like a colony somehow transplanted from northern Spain. A strong small-shop-keeper economy – which discouraged industrial development – and a society where military and clerics were dominant inhibited innovation and liberal ideas through the early part of the twentieth century. This introverted outlook perhaps contributed also to the events of the **Civil War**, one of the greatest stains on the city's name. In 1936, following Franco's coup, a fascist bloodbath was unleashed during which an estimated seven thousand of the city's liberals and Republicans were assassinated, among them poet and playwright **Federico García Lorca**. The poet deserved better from his native city, of which he had written, "The hours are longer and sweeter here than in any other Spanish town… Granada has any amount of good ideas but is incapable of acting on them. Only in such a town, with its inertia and tranquillity, can there exist those exquisite contemplators of water, temperatures and sunsets."

Arrival and orientation

The **train station** lies a kilometre or so out on the Avenida de Andaluces, off Avenida de la Constitución; to get into town take bus #11 which runs a circular route: inbound on the Gran Vía de Colón and back out via the Puerta Real and Camino de Ronda. Buses #3, #4, #6, and #9 also run between the station and Gran Vía.

The city's **main bus station**, Carretera de Jaén s/n (☎958 18 54 80), is some way out of the centre in the northern suburbs, and handles all services, including those to the Sierra Nevada but not to Viznar. The bus station is served by the #3 bus which leaves from outside and will drop you in the centre on Gran Vía Colón near the cathedral (a fifteen-minute journey). If you're heading for the Albergue Juvenil (youth hostel) you should take bus #10 from the bus station.

Central Granada is often choked with more traffic than its streets are able to bear, and finding on-street parking can be a nightmare. If you do arrive **by car**, you're best off leaving it in a car park or garage for the duration of your stay. Underground car parks (*parking subterráneo*) are located at Puerta Real (down the right-hand side of the post office), La Caleta near the train station, and on c/San Agustín beneath the municipal market off the west side of Gran Vía near the cathedral. Long-term free street parking places are often to be found along Carrera del Genil and the Paseo del Salón slightly southwest of the centre, but you should strip your car of any contents. If your vehicle disappears it's probably been hauled away from an illegal parking spot by the *Grúa* (tow-truck). Contact the Turismo, any police station or upmarket hotel who will assist you in locating the pound.

Flights into Granada's **airport**, 17km to the west of the city on the A92 *autovía*, are served by ten (eight Sat & Sun) daily buses into town (€3 one-way); nine daily buses (eight Sat & Sun) also run out to the airport from a stop on the east side of Gran Vía opposite the cathedral. Check with the bus operator (☎958 13 13 09) for the latest timetable. A taxi will cost about €18–22.

Practically everything of interest in Granada, including the hills of **Alhambra** (to the east) and the **Albaicín** and **Sacromonte** (to the northeast), is within easy walking distance of the centre. The only times you'll need a local bus or taxi are if you're arriving or leaving on public transport, since both the bus and train stations are some way out. **Gran Vía** is the city's main street, cutting its way through the centre along a roughly north–south axis between the Jardines del Triunfo and **Plaza Isabel la Católica**. It forms a T-junction at its southern end with **c/Reyes Católicos,** which runs east to the **Plaza Nueva** and west to the **Puerta Real**, Granada's two focal squares.

Information and tours

The city's **Turismo** c/Santa Ana 2 (Mon–Fri 9am–7pm, Sat 9am–2pm & 4–7pm, Sun 10am–2pm; ☏958 22 59 90) is located up steps to the right of the church of Santa Ana, off Plaza Nueva. They have a branch in the Alhambra's ticket office (open same hours as the monument). There's a good and less frenetic **Turismo Municipal** at Plaza Mariana Pineda 10 (Mon–Fri 9am–8pm, Sat 10am–7pm, Sun 10am–3pm; ☏958 24 71 28), east of Puerta Real, which also stocks information on the province of Granada. From April to September **kiosks** on Plaza Nueva and Plaza Bib-Rambla also give out maps and information. An **information office** (Mon–Fri 10am–2pm & 4.30–8pm) inside the Ayuntamiento on Plaza del Carmen is another source of city maps and transport information. A detailed city **map** (€1.20) can be obtained from a machine in the central Plaza Isabel La Católica, near the cathedral.

If you're pressed for time a way to get around the city is by hop-on hop-off **open-top bus tour**; City Sightseeing Granada (☏902 10 10 81) buses and microbuses run daily from the Palacio de Congresos to the Alhambra with stops along the route at the Plaza Nueva, cathedral and La Cartuja plus the Albaicín and Sacromonte. Tickets (€10) are valid for 24hrs from the time of purchase.

An officially approved **guided walking tour** taking in the city's major sights (including the Albaicín but not the Alhambra) is operated by Cicerone Granada (mobile ☏600412051, 🌐www.ciceronegranada.com; €10, under-14s free; no booking necessary). The walks take place in all weather, last around 2 hours and leave from the Ayuntamiento in the Plaza del Carmen daily at 10.30am (English & Spanish) with an extra walk (Spanish only) on Saturdays at 8pm.

Accommodation

Finding **a place to stay** in Granada usually isn't a problem, except during Semana Santa (Easter week) and the month of August. However, if you want to be certain of finding rooms at some of the more popular options it's wise to ring ahead. There are plenty of *pensiones* and *hostales*, a frequent turnaround of visitors, and prices are no higher than elsewhere in Andalucía. It's also worth remembering for winter or early spring visits that many of the cheaper options don't have heating and nights can be very chilly here.

Most visitors want to be as close to the Alhambra as possible, and there are a couple of pricey options up inside the walls. Unless you book these ahead, however, you'll have to content yourself with streets such as the Cuesta de Gomérez, which ascends towards the Alhambra from the Plaza Nueva, itself a focus for many hotels. The zone surrounding the cathedral is also a good hunting ground for rooms and other attractive options are to be found in the streets between the picturesque Plaza de Bib-Rambla and Plaza de la Trinidad in the university area.

Granada online

Information on Granada, its monuments and amenities can be found at 🌐www .granadatur.com, 🌐 www.turismodegranada.org, 🌐 www.granada.org, 🌐 www .granadainfo.com, 🌐www.andalucia.org and 🌐www.albaicin-granada.com.

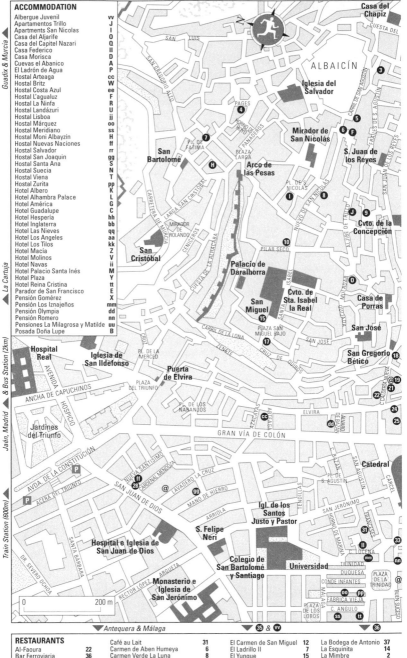

ACCOMMODATION

Albergue Juvenil	vv
Apartamentos Trillo	J
Apartments San Nicolas	I
Casa del Aljarife	O
Casa del Capitel Nazari	Q
Casa Federico	II
Casa Morisca	D
Cuevas el Abanico	A
El Ladrón de Agua	P
Hostal Arteaga	cc
Hostal Britz	W
Hostal Costa Azul	ee
Hostal L'agualuz	F
Hostal La Ninfa	R
Hostal Landázuri	U
Hostal Lisboa	jj
Hostal Márquez	oo
Hostal Meridiano	ss
Hostal Moni Albayzín	H
Hostal Nuevas Naciones	ff
Hostal Salvador	rr
Hostal San Joaquin	gg
Hostal Santa Ana	S
Hostal Suecia	N
Hostal Viena	T
Hostal Zurita	pp
Hotel Albero	K
Hotel Alhambra Palace	L
Hotel América	G
Hotel Guadalupe	C
Hotel Hesperia	hh
Hotel Inglaterra	bb
Hotel Las Nieves	qq
Hotel Los Angeles	aa
Hotel Los Tilos	kk
Hotel Macía	Z
Hotel Molinos	V
Hotel Navas	ii
Hotel Palacio Santa Inés	M
Hotel Plaza	Y
Hotel Reina Cristina	tt
Parador de San Francisco	E
Pensión Gomérez	X
Pensión Los Iznajeños	mm
Pensión Olympia	dd
Pensión Romero	nn
Pensiones La Milagrosa y Matilde	uu
Posada Doña Lupe	B

RESTAURANTS

Al-Faoura	22	Café au Lait	31	El Carmen de San Miguel	12
Bar Ferroviaria	36	Carmen de Aben Humeya	6	El Ladrillo II	7
Bar La Mancha Chica	10	Carmen Verde La Luna	8	El Yunque	15
Bar-Restaurante Sevilla	27	Casa Blas	17	Horno de Santiago	26
		Casa Cepillo	33	Juanillo	1

La Bodega de Antonio	37
La Esquinita	14
La Mimbre	2
La Ninfa	16
Lago de Como	11

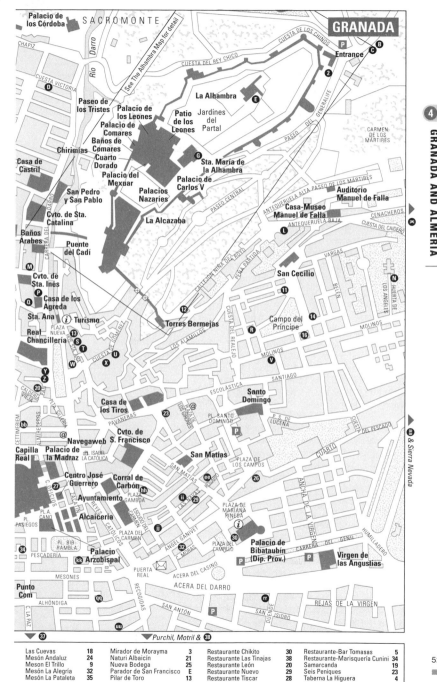

Las Cuevas	**18**	Mirador de Morayma	**3**	Restaurante Chikito	**30**	Restaurante-Bar Tomasas	**5**
Mesón Andaluz	**24**	Naturi Albaicín	**21**	Restaurante Las Tinajas	**38**	Restaurante-Marisquería Cunini	**34**
Mesón El Trillo	**9**	Nueva Bodega	**25**	Restaurante León	**20**	Samarcanda	**19**
Mesón La Alegría	**32**	Parador de San Francisco	**E**	Restaurante Nuevo	**29**	Seis Peniques	**23**
Mesón La Pataleta	**35**	Pilar de Toro	**13**	Restaurante Tiscar	**28**	Taberna La Higuera	**4**

The **Bono Turístico** (City Pass) gives you access to eight of the city's monuments including the Alhambra, Capilla Real, Catedral and La Cartuja for €22.50. Valid for a week it's a plastic card that you swipe through the gates at any of the monuments listed. You can enter once only and will have a specified time for visiting the Palacios Nazaríes of the Alhambra. The Bono also includes ten bus journeys and should you stay a minimum of two nights in a double at any of the thirty or so hotels that are part of the scheme (details from either Turismo) this will entitle you to one Bono Turístico free. Cards can be purchased from the ticket offices of the Alhambra and the Capilla Real, as well as the Caja General de Ahorros bank at Plaza Isabel la Católica 6 during business hours, but here you will incur a commission charge of €2. They can also be ordered by phone (℡902 10 00 95) or online (@www.granadatur.com or @www .cajagranada.es), in which case you will need to collect them on arrival in Granada.

Attractive location though it is, **budget** accommodation in the atmospheric Albaicín quarter – with a couple of honourable exceptions – hardly exists and most places here are at the upper end of the market often in attractive, converted mansions or, on the edge of Sacromonte, a cave hotel. **Self-catering accommodation** (minimum stay two nights) is also an option: we've listed a couple below but for a wider choice visit @www.granadahotel.com. With your own transport, staying in one of the pleasant **rural villages** to the south of the city is also an option and we've included a couple of attractive possibilities in and around the villages of La Zubia and Monachil.

Around Plaza Nueva and towards the Alhambra

Hostal Britz Cuesta de Gomérez 1 ℡958 22 36 52, @www.lisboaweb.com. Small, welcoming, very comfortable and well-placed *hostal* near the Plaza Nueva. Some rooms en suite. ❸–❹

Hostal Landázuri Cuesta de Gomérez 24 ℡958 22 14 06, @www.hostallandazuri.com. Pleasant, good-value rooms, some en suite, plus its own restaurant, bar and a roof terrace with a view of the Alhambra. Some single rooms. ❸

Hostal Santa Ana c/Hospital de Sta. Ana 8 ℡958 22 58 20. Elegant new *hostal* inside a restored 200-year-old mansion. Attractive en-suite rooms come with a/c and TV. ❸

Hostal Viena c/Hospital de Sta. Ana 2 ℡958 22 70 75, @www.hostalviena.com. Efficient, friendly, Austrian-run *hostal* in a quiet street. The a/c rooms come with and without bath, and it has its own car park. If this place is full, try their nearby *Hostal Austria* (same phone number). ❸–❹

Hotel Macía Plaza Nueva 4 ℡958 22 75 36, @www.maciahoteles.com. Centrally located hotel, offering comfortable, a/c rooms, most overlooking the square, with Internet connection. *Rough Guide* readers with this guide can claim a ten percent discount. ❺–❻

Hotel Plaza Plaza Nueva 2, entrance on side street ℡958 21 52 73, @www.hotelplazanueva.com.

Elegant hotel in a refurbished nineteenth-century building. Some slightly cheaper rooms look onto a central patio rather than the plaza. ❽

Pensión Gomérez Cuesta de Gomérez 10, ℡958 22 44 37. Simple but convenient guest-house with basic rooms, some single; charges extra for showers. ❷

Cathedral area

Casa Federico c/Horno de Marina 13 ℡958 20 85 34, @www.casadefederico .com. Enchanting boutique hotel in a refurbished traditional town house with individually styled and well equipped wood-beamed a/c rooms. A roof terrace – for breakfasting and drinks – has spectacular views. ❹

Hostal Arteaga c/Arteaga 3 ℡958 20 88 41, @hostalarteaga@hotmail.com. Central and economical *hostal* offering en-suite a/c rooms with TV in a quiet street. ❷

Hostal Costa Azul c/Rosario 5 ℡958 22 22 98, @www.hostalcostaazul.com. Friendly, central, small *hostal* for pleasant en-suite rooms with heating and a/c. Has own restaurant and free Internet. It also rents out some luxurious apartments (❻) nearby, complete with basement spa. *Rough Guide* readers with this guide can claim a fifteen-percent discount on apartments or free breakfast at the *hostal*. ❸

Hotel Inglaterra c/Cetti Meriem 4 ☎958 22 15
59, ⓦwww.nh-hoteles.com. Three-star hotel with
comfortable, a/c rooms with satellite TV, Internet
and minibar in a stylishly modernized building. Car
park available. ❼

Hostal Lisboa Plaza del Carmen 27 ☎958 22
14 13, ⓦwww.lisboaweb.com. Modern, clean and
comfortable *hostal* bang in the centre. Many rooms
are en suite and it provides fans in summer. ❸

Hostal Salvador c/Duende 6 ☎958 26 19 55,
ⓦwww.casasalvador.net. Small and comfortable
hostal in a quiet pedestrianized street. All rooms are
en suite with a/c and TV, and rooms 303 & 304 come
with terrace. There's a decent restaurant too. ❸

Hotel Hesperia Plaza Gamboa s/n ☎958 01 84
00, ⓦwww.Hesperia-granada.com. Stylish new
luxury hotel in a beautiful old mansion with delightful patio. The rather staid rooms are less inviting,
but an interesting tariff structure has frequent
special offers which can reduce rates by up to sixty
percent; ring or check website for details. ❽

Hotel Los Tilos Plaza de Bib-Rambla 4 ☎958 26
67 12, ⓦwww.hotellostilos.com. Plain, two-star
hotel on this atmospheric square. Decent rooms
have TV, but make sure to request one on the exterior as the interior rooms are gloomy. Rooms 401
& 402 or 301 & 302 with Alhambra views are the
ones to go for. Parking nearby. ❹

Hotel Navas c/Las Navas 24 ☎958 22 59 59,
ⓦwww.hoteles-porcel.com. Elegant and central
small hotel on a quiet street with a/c rooms, which
have safe, minibar and satellite TV. Own garage. ❺

Pensión Los Iznajeños c/Lucena 1 mobile
☎679708951. Very friendly and good-value family
pensión with spotless rooms in a tiny street just off
Plaza de la Trinidad. ❶

Pensión Olympia c/Álvaro de Bazán 6 ☎958 27
82 38. Central, basic but clean *pensión* with pleasant proprietors. ❶

Plaza de la Trinidad and around the university

Hostal Márquez c/Fábrica Vieja 8 ☎958 27 50
13, ⓔhosatl-marquez@ozu.es. Recently refurbished *hostal* with some rooms en suite, a few
singles and all with a/c. The lobby is dominated by
a snarling boar's head bagged by the *patrón*. Parking spaces. ❷–❸

Hostal Meridiano c/Angulo 9 ☎ & ☏958
25 05 44, ⓔhostalmeridiano@telefonica
.net. Friendly and efficient *hostal* offering bright a/c
rooms with and without bath. There's free Internet
access available to guests, and they can assist
with parking. ❷–❸

Hostal Nuevas Naciones Plazoleta de Triviño
1, off c/San Juan de Dios, ☎958 27 05 03,

ⓔhnuevasn@wanadoo.es. Neat, tidy and friendly
place with recently refurbished en-suite, a/c and
heated rooms complete with TV. ❸

Hostal San Joaquin c/Mano de Hierro 14 ☎958
28 28 79. A great, rambling old place with simple
and en-suite rooms (some with a/c and TV) and
charming patios; probably the best deal in this
area. ❸

Hostal Zurita Plaza de la Trinidad 7 ☎958 27 50
20. Welcoming *hostal* where immaculate balcony
rooms come with and without bath, and all have TV
and a/c. Garage. ❷–❸

Hotel Las Nieves c/Alhóndiga 8 ☎958 26 53 11,
ⓦwww.hotellasnieves.com. Reliable and central
mid-range hotel west of Plaza Bib-Rambla offering
spacious well-equipped balcony rooms above, and
with own bar-restaurant below. ❻

Hotel Reina Cristina c/Tablas 4, close to Plaza
de la Trinidad ☎958 25 32 11, ⓦwww.hotel
reinacristina.com. Modern and welcoming hotel
inside an older building – with fine patio – where
Lorca spent his last days before being seized by the
fascists. Twin-bedded rooms tend to be larger and
also has its own good restaurant and garage. ❼

Pensión Romero c/Sillería 1, corner of Plaza de
la Trinidad ☎958 26 60 79. Charming family-run
pensión with spotless if basic rooms, many with
balconies overlooking this delightful square. ❶

Pensiones La Milagrosa y Matilde c/Puentezue-
las 46, slightly southwest of Plaza de la Trinidad
☎958 26 34 29. Two serviceable *pensiones* under
the same ownership; their cheaper rooms (which
you need to ask for) are good value. Some rooms
en suite. ❷

Albaicín, Sacromonte and north of the centre

Apartamentos Trillo c/Aljibe de Trillo 26
☎958 22 78 43, ⓔfuimus@hotmail
.com. Five 2–4 person apartments in a refurbished
and traditional *casa andaluza* with well-equipped
balcony rooms, charming patio, garden and Alhambra views. ❺

Apartments San Nicolas Plaza San Nicolas 3
☎ & ☏958 22 90 90, ⓦwww.granadainfo.com
/nicolas/index.htm. Self-catering a/c apartments
with views of the Alhambra, pretty shared garden
with fountain and pond, cleaning service and car
park. Minimum two-night stay. ❺

Casa del Aljarife Placeta de la Cruz Verde 2
☎ & ☏958 22 24 25, ⓔaljarife@granadainfo.
com. Charming small upmarket *hostal* in a restored
sixteenth-century house, near the heart of the
Albaicín; three beautiful en-suite rooms and patio,
plus free use of Internet. Free collection from train
station or airport. ❻

Casa del Capitel Nazari Cuesta de Aceituneros 6 ☎958 21 52 60, ⓦwww .hotelcasacapitel.com. Beautiful sixteenth-century *palacio* transformed into an enchanting small hotel with attractively furnished wood-ceilinged rooms overlooking a triple-tiered patio; room 22 has an Alhambra view. Own restaurant too. Special offers in July–Aug & Jan–Feb can cut prices significantly. Parking nearby. ⓺

Casa Morisca Cuesta de la Victoria 9 ☎958 22 11 00, ⓦwww.hotelcasamorisca .com. Stunningly romantic small hotel inside an immaculately renovated (for which it won an award) fifteenth-century Moorish mansion with exquisite patio below the walls of the Alhambra in the Albaicín; there are re-created Moorish furnishings throughout (though the splendid Mudéjar wooden ceilings are original), and room 15, with Alhambra views, is the one to go for. Exterior rooms cost more. Easy street parking outside. ⓻

Cuevas el Abanico Verea de Enmedio 89, near the Casa del Chapiz ☎ & ⓕ958 22 61 99, ⓦwww .el-abanico.com. Fully equipped and stylishly renovated en-suite cave-dwellings with kitchen, available for a minimum stay of two nights. ⓸

El Ladrón de Agua Carrera del Darro 13 ☎958 21 50 40 ⓦwww.ladrondeagua.com. Beautiful hotel inside a restored sixteenth-century Mudéjar *palacio* with lots of exposed brick, understated furnishings and a charming patio. Some rooms have Alhambra views. ⓺

Hostal L'agualuz Plazoleta del Comino ☎958 22 68 27, ⓦwww.bbgranada.com. Delightful bed and breakfast place with individually styled en-suite rooms in an Albaicín *carmen* with leafy garden. Significant price reductions in late July and Aug. ⓸ with breakfast.

Hostal Moni Albayzín Plaza San Bartolomé 5 ☎958 28 52 84, ⓔ hostalalbayzin@hotmail.com. This is the Albaicín's first budget *hostal* and it's a cracker. The proprietors provide a hearty welcome and the en-suite rooms – with TV and a/c – are spotless. The roof terrace has views of the Alhambra and Sierra Nevada and guests have use of fridge and washing machine. Also rents some good-value (⓸) fully equipped apartments nearby. ⓷

Hotel Palacio Santa Inés Cuesta de Santa Inés 9 ☎958 22 23 62, ⓦwww .palaciosantaines.com. Sumptuous eleven-room hotel in a beautiful, restored sixteenth-century Mudéjar mansion on the south side of the Albaicín with Alhambra views – especially from rooms 31–34. The nearby and equally delightful *Carmen de Santa Inés*, Placeta de Porras 7, off c/San Juan de los Reyes ☎958 22 63 80, is owned by the same proprietors and occupies an equally attractive restored Moorish *carmen*. ⓻

Inside and around the Alhambra

Hostal La Ninfa Campo del Principe s/n ☎958 22 79 85, ⓕ958 22 26 61. On one of the nicest squares in town, this place – with an exterior studded with multicoloured stucco flowers – is easy to find. The interior offers pleasing white-walled, en-suite rooms with individual furnishings, a/c and TV. The rooms with *cama de matrimonio* (double bed) are significantly cheaper than those with two beds. ⓸

Hostal Suecia Huerta de los Ángeles 8 ☎958 22 77 81, ⓕ958 22 50 44. Charming, good-value small *hostal* – with some rooms en suite – in a quiet, leafy area below the Alhambra with garden terrace to eat breakfast. Rooms have heating but no TV. Easy parking. ⓷–⓸

Hotel Albero Avda. Santa María de La Alhambra 6 ☎958 22 67 25, ⓦwww.hotelalbero.com. This excellent-value, attractive and friendly small hotel lies on the new access road to the Alhambra to the south of the centre. Sparkling a/c balcony rooms come with TV and there's easy parking. Ring if you have problems finding them and they will advise (English spoken). ⓷

Hotel Alhambra Palace Peña Partida 2–4 ☎958 22 14 68, ⓦwww.h-alhambrapalace.es. On the Alhambra hill and a 5min walk from the palace entrance, this opulent Belle Époque hotel in neo-Moorish style offers every service you would expect for the price, except a pool. The cheapest high-season room costs around €167. The bar's terrace (open to the public) has dramatic views over the city. Car park. ⓽

Hotel América Real de la Alhambra 53 ☎958 22 74 71, ⓦwww.hamericagranada.com. Charming, small hotel in the Alhambra grounds, bang opposite the parador, so you can get an early march on the queues and take a siesta midday. You pay for the location rather than creature comforts (a/c rooms but no TV) and prices have risen steeply (and unjustifiably) here. ⓻

Hotel Guadalupe Paseo de la Sabica ☎958 22 34 23, ⓦwww.hotelguadalupe.es. Smart three-star hotel a stone's throw from the Alhambra's entrance. Some of the well-equipped a/c rooms have views towards the Alhambra. June–Aug sees rates drop thirty percent. Easy parking. ⓺

Hotel Los Angeles Cuesta Escoriaza 17 ☎958 22 14 23, ⓦwww.hotellosangeles.net. Attractive three star hotel on a leafy, quiet avenue in walking distance of the Alhambra. Recent enlargement has removed the garden, but the pool remains. All rooms come with terrace balcony and there's a car park. ⑥

Hotel Molinos c/Molinos 12 ☎958 22 73 67, ⓦwww.eel.es/molinos. Little over 4m wide, this place is listed in the *Guinness Book of Records* as the narrowest hotel in the world. Pleasant a/c en-suite balcony rooms, and a friendly owner. Prices drop by 30 percent Mon–Fri. ⑤

🏃 **Parador de San Francisco** Real de la Alhambra ☎958 22 14 40, ⓦwww .parador.es. Without doubt the best hotel in Granada – a converted fifteenth-century monas-tery (itself created from a Nasrid palace) in the Alhambra grounds. Alas, this top-of-the-range parador is also the most expensive in the city with the cheapest rooms costing around €245; rooms to go for are nos. 209–16, with views of the Alhambra and Generalife. Booking is advised at least four months ahead in summer or over Easter. Non-guests can call in for a drink on the terrace bar. Car park. ⑨

Posada Doña Lupe Avda. Generalife-Alhambra s/n ☎958 22 14 73, ⓕ958 22 14 74. Rambling and potentially inviting place on the Alhambra hill blighted by a student hostel atmosphere (toilet paper and towels are doled out at check-in); there are numerous permutations of prices, some exception-ally cheap. Many rooms are en suite and there's a *cafetería* and small swimming pool. Easily reached by the Alhambrabus from Plaza Nueva. ❶–❸

Out of town: La Zubia & Monachil

Balcón de Cumbres Verdes Cerro del Caballo, La Zubia, 8km south of Granada, ☎958 89 10 58, ⓦwww.hotelcumbresverdes.com. Fifteen minutes from the city centre, this is a pleasant rural hotel in rolling countryside beyond the village of La Zubia. Rooms come with kitchenette and there's a pool. ④

Hotel El Balcón de Cumbres Verdes c/Alayos 174, in the village of Cumbres Verdes beyond La

Zubia ☎958 89 20 62, ⓦwww.balcondecumbres .com. Not to be confused with the similarly named place above, this is another charming place in the foothills of the Sierra Nevada. Traditionally but comfortably furnished rooms have satellite TV and there's a pool plus a decent restaurant over the road. ⑥

El Molino de Rosa María Serrano Avda. del Río 23, Monachil, 11km southwest of the city ☎958 30 19 14, ⓦwww.molino-rosa-maria-serrano .com. Very pleasant rural hotel in this pretty village a mere 10min from the city centre with attractive rooms and its own restaurant. ④

Youth hostel and campsites

Albergue Juvenil Avda. Ramón y Cajal 2, off the Camino de Ronda ☎958 00 29 00, ⓦwww .inturjoven.com. If you arrive late, this is handy for the train station: from there, turn left onto Avda. de la Constitución and left again onto the Camino de Ronda – it's the large white building by a sports stadium (Estadio de la Juventud); from the bus station take bus #3 to the cathedral and then bus #11, which will drop you outside. Recently reno-vated with lots of facilities, all rooms are en-suite doubles, the staff are friendly but the food is insti-tutional. An excellent alternative is the new hostel at Viznar, in the hills above the city (see p.553). Under-26 €14, over-26 €18.50, ❸.

Camping Reina Isabel 4km along the Zubia road to the southwest of the city ☎958 59 00 41. With a pool, less noise and more shade than the site below, this makes a pleasant rural alternative and – with your own transport – the city is within easy reach.

Camping Sierra Nevada Avda. de Madrid 107, northwest of the centre and 200m south of the bus station ☎958 15 00 62. Easiest reached from the centre on bus #3, this is the most convenient city site, and – with a pleasant pool – probably the best too.

The Alhambra

The Sabika hill sits like a garland on Granada's brow,
In which the stars would be entwined
And the Alhambra (Allah preserve it)
Is the ruby set above that garland.

Ibn Zamrak, vizier to Muhammad V (1362–91)

One of the most sensual architectural creations in the world and the greatest treasure of Moorish Spain, the **Alhambra** sits on a hill overlooking the city it has captivated for seven centuries. There are three distinct groups of buildings on the Alhambra hill (known as Sabika to the Moors): the **Casa Real** (Royal Palace or Palacios Nazaríes), the palace gardens of the **Generalife**, and the

The overwhelming number of visitors to the **Alhambra** (daily: April–Oct 8.30am–8pm; Nov–March 8.30am–6pm; last admission 1hr before closing time; €10) during high season makes it imperative to turn up as early as possible. Only 8100 daily **tickets** are issued, three-quarters of which are issued in advance only (see below) by the Banco Bilbao Vizcaya y Argentería (BBVA), Plaza Isabel la Católica 1, in the centre, which you are strongly advised to use. The remaining tickets can be purchased at the entrance (ticket office opens 8am) but be prepared for lengthy queues in spring and summer. Tickets have sections for each part of the complex (the Alcazaba, Palacios Nazaríes and Generalife) which must be used on the same day. They are also stamped with a half-hour **time slot** during which you must enter the Palacios Nazaríes (once inside you can stay as long as you like): any waiting time can be spent in the Alcazaba or at one of the numerous cafés dotted around the complex. Note also that the Museo de la Alhambra (see p.541) and the Museo de las Bellas Artes (see p.541), both in the palace of Carlos V, have different hours to those of the Alhambra. It's worth pointing out too that only the palaces, museums and Generalife gardens require a ticket to gain entry – the rest you are allowed to wander freely around.

You can **book in advance** through the BBVA (☎902 22 44 60, from abroad ☎00 34/915 37 91 78; Visa or Mastercard only, €0.88 commission) a minimum of one day or a maximum of one year ahead. Tickets purchased this way state whether they are for 8.30am–2pm or 2–8pm (Nov–March 2–6pm) sessions and you must enter between the stated times (once inside you may stay as long as you wish). You'll need your booking reference and passport to collect your tickets from any of the 2800 BBVA branches in Spain (at least a day before the visit) or the Alhambra ticket office. In high season there may be a queue at the latter, so arriving at least an hour before your session starts is advisable. They can also be reserved at ⓦwww .alhambratickets.com.

The Alhambra is also open for floodlit **night visits** of the Palacios Nazaríes (March–Oct Tues–Sat 10–11.30pm, ticket office 9.45–10.15pm; Nov–Feb Fri & Sat 8–9.30pm, ticket office 7.45–8.15pm; €10). Themed **guided visits** (in Spanish; Sept–June; €5) also allow visitors to view parts of the complex (many in the process of restoration) not normally open to the public. A leaflet on them, *Programa de Visitas Guiadas*, is available from the Alhambra ticket office. To check any changes in opening times, admission charges or booking procedures visit the Alhambra's website ⓦwww .alhambra-patronato.es where the latest **information** is posted.

The ticket office entrance to the Alhambra brings you into the complex at the eastern end, near to the Generalife gardens. However, your time slot for entering the Palacios Nazaríes (usually up to an hour ahead) means that it makes sense to **start your visit** with the Alcazaba, at the Alhambra's opposite (western) end. To get there from the entrance, walk up the short avenue lined with cypresses to a three-way fork, taking the signed path to the Alhambra. Cross the bridge over the "moat" following signs to the Alcazaba and Palacios Nazaríes. You will eventually pass the gates of the *Parador de San Francisco* (right) and the *Hotel América* to enter the Calle Real. Continue alongside the palace of Carlos V to pass through the Puerto del Vino where our account begins (see p.536).

Alcazaba. This last, the fortress of the eleventh-century Ziridian rulers, was all that existed when the Nasrids made Granada their capital, but from its reddish walls the hill top had already taken its name: Al Qal'a al-Hamra in Arabic means literally "the red fort".

The first Nasrid king, Ibn al-Ahmar, rebuilt the Alcazaba and added to it the huge circuit of walls and towers which forms your first view of the castle. Within the walls he began a palace, which was supplied with running water by diverting the Río Darro nearly 8km to the foot of the hill; water is an integral part of the Alhambra and this engineering feat was Ibn al-Ahmar's greatest contribution. The Casa Real was essentially the product of his fourteenth-century successors, particularly **Muhammad V**, who built and decorated many of its rooms in celebration of his accession to the throne (in 1354) and conquest of Algeciras (in 1369). Also within the citadel stood a complete "government city" of mansions, smaller houses, baths, schools, mosques, barracks and gardens.

After their conquest of Granada, **Fernando and Isabel** lived for a while in the Alhambra. They restored some rooms and converted the mosque but left the palace structure unaltered. As at Córdoba and Sevilla, it was their grandson **Emperor Carlos V** who wreaked the most insensitive destruction. He demolished a whole wing of rooms in order to build yet another grandiose Renaissance palace. This and the Alhambra itself were simply ignored by his successors and by the eighteenth century the Royal Palace was in use as a prison. In 1812 it was taken and occupied by **Napoleon's forces**, who looted and damaged whole sections of the building, and on their retreat from the city tried to blow up the entire complex. Their attempt was thwarted only by the action of a crippled soldier (José García) who remained behind and removed the fuses; a plaque honouring his valour has been placed in the Plaza de los Aljibes.

Two decades later the Alhambra's "rediscovery" began, given impetus by the American writer **Washington Irving**, who set up his study in the empty palace rooms and began to write his marvellously romantic *Tales of the Alhambra* (on sale all over Granada – and good reading amid the gardens and courts). Shortly after its publication the Spaniards made the Alhambra a **national monument** and set aside funds for its restoration. This continues to the present day and is now a highly sophisticated project, scientifically removing the accretions of later ages in order to expose and restore meticulously the Moorish creations.

Approaches to the Alhambra

The standard approach to the Alhambra is along the Cuesta de Gomérez, a narrow, semi-pedestrianized road which climbs uphill from Plaza Nueva. The only vehicles allowed to use this road in daytime are taxis and the **Alhambrabus** (line #30), a dedicated minibus service (daily 7am–10pm, every ten minutes; €0.95) linking the Plaza Nueva with the Alhambra palace. To approach the Alhambra **by car** use the signed route heading from Puerta Real along the Paseo del Salón and the Paseo de la Bomba to the Alhambra's car park on the eastern edge of the complex.

Should you decide to walk up the hill (a pleasant twenty-minute stroll from Plaza Nueva), after a few hundred metres you reach the **Puerta de las Granadas**, a massive Renaissance gateway topped by three pomegranates which became the city's symbol (*granada* is the fruit's Spanish name). Beyond the gate the path on the right climbs up towards a group of fortified towers, the **Torres Bermejas**, parts of which may date from as early as the eighth century (see p.543 for other sights on this route). The left-hand path heads through woods of closely planted elms and past a huge terrace-fountain (courtesy of Carlos V), eventually reaching the main gateway of the Alhambra in Moorish times, the **Puerta de la Justicia.** A magnificent tower that forced three changes of direction, making intruders hopelessly vulnerable, it was built by Yusuf I in 1348 and preserves above its inner arch the Koranic symbol of a key (for Allah, the opener of the gates of Paradise) and, over the outer arch, an outstretched hand whose five fingers represent the five Islamic precepts: prayer, fasting, alms-giving, pilgrimage to Mecca and the oneness of God. A Moorish legend stated that the gate would never be breached by the Christians until the hand reached down to grasp the key. To reach the ticket office continue uphill for 400m.

Leaving the Alhambra, a lovely alternative route down to the city is the Cuesta de los Chinos, and its continuation the Cuesta del Rey Chico, which descends beneath two arches to the right of the *La Mimbre* restaurant near the Alhambra's ticket office. It winds gradually down, passing beneath the Alhambra's northern walls, to the Río Darro and a terrace of riverside cafés.

❹ The Alcazaba

Having made your way from the ticket office, go through the **Puerta del Vino** – named from its use in the sixteenth century as a wine cellar – and across the Plaza de los Aljibes you are confronted by the walls of the **Alcazaba**, the earliest, though most ruined, part of the fortress. Quite apart from filling in time before your ticket admits you to the Palacios Nazaríes, this is an interesting part of the complex and one where you can get a grip on the whole site.

Once inside, thread your way through remnants of the barracks to the Alcazaba's summit, the **Torre de la Vela**, named after a huge bell on its turret which until recent years was rung to mark the irrigation hours for workers on the *vega*, Granada's vast and fertile plain. The views from here are spectacular: west over the plunging ravine of the Darro with the city and the *vega* beyond, and north towards the Albaicín and Sacromonte hills, with the Alhambra itself behind and the snowcapped peaks of the Sierra Nevada forming a backdrop. It was on this same parapet at 3pm on January 2, 1492, that the Cross was first displayed above the city, alongside the royal standards of Aragón and Castile and the banner of St James. Boabdil, leaving Granada for exile in the Alpujarras, turned and wept at the sight, earning from his mother Aisha the famous rebuke: "Do not weep like a woman for what you could not defend like a man." The visit route continues via the **Jardín de los Ardaves**, a delightful seventeenth-century garden laid out along the fort's southern parapets with creepers, fountains and sweet-scented bushes.

To gain access to the palace you need to recross the **Plaza de los Aljibes** (where there's a very welcome drinks kiosk). In Nasrid times this area was a ravine dividing the hill between the Royal Palace on one side, and the Alcazaba on the other. Following the *Reconquista* the ravine was filled in to hold two rainwater cisterns (*aljibes*) and the surface above laid out with fortifications. During the construction of Carlos V's palace in the sixteenth century, the area was cleared of these structures to create a parade ground, the rather desolate form it retains today. The underground **cisterns** can now be seen only as part of a guided visit (see box p.534). Follow the arrows indicating the Palacios Nazaríes (Nasrid Palaces) to reach the royal palace. Fronting the entrance to the palace a **Sala de Presentación** has a small exhibition – with some informative maquettes – detailing the development of the Alhambra.

The Palacios Nazaríes

It is amazing that the **Palacios Nazaríes** has survived survived, for it stands in utter contrast to the strength of the Alcazaba and the encircling walls and towers. It was built lightly and often crudely from wood, brick and adobe, and was designed not to last but to be renewed and redecorated by succeeding rulers. Its buildings show a superb use of light and space but they are principally a vehicle for ornamental stucco decoration. This, as Titus Burckhardt explains in *Moorish Culture in Spain*, was both an intricate science and a philosophy of abstract art in direct contrast to pictorial representation:

> With its rhythmic repetition, [it] does not seek to capture the eye to lead it into an imagined world, but, on the contrary, liberates it from all pre-occupations of the mind. It does not transmit any specific ideas, but a state of being, which is at once repose and inner rhythm.

Burckhardt adds that the way in which patterns are woven from a single band, or radiate from many identical centres, served as a pure simile for Islamic belief in the oneness of God, manifested at the centre of every form and being.

Arabic inscriptions feature prominently in the ornamentation. Some are poetic eulogies of the buildings and builders, others of various sultans – notably Muhammad V. Most, however, are taken from the Koran, and among them the phrase "Wa-la ghaliba illa-Llah" (There is no Conqueror but God) is tirelessly repeated. It's said that this became the battle cry of the Nasrids upon Ibn al-Ahmar's return from aiding the Castilian war against Muslim Sevilla; it was his reply to the customary, though bitterly ironic, greetings of *Mansur* (Victor).

The palace is structured in three parts, each arrayed round an interior court and with a specific function. The sultans used the **Mexuar**, the first series of rooms, for business and judicial purposes. In the **Serallo**, beyond, they would receive embassies and distinguished guests. The last section, the **Harem**, formed their private living quarters and would have been entered by no one but their family and servants.

The Mexuar

The council chamber, the main reception hall of the **Mexuar**, is the first room you enter. It was completed in 1365 and hailed (perhaps obsequiously) by the court poet and vizier Ibn Zamrak as a "haven of counsel, mercy and favour". Here the sultan heard the pleas and petitions of the people and held meetings with his ministers. At the room's far end is a small **oratory**, one of a number of prayer niches scattered round the palace and immediately identifiable by their angular alignment to face Mecca.

This "public" section of the palace, beyond which few would have penetrated, is completed by the Mudéjar **Cuarto Dorado** (Golden Room), redecorated under Carlos V, whose Plus Ultra motif appears throughout the palace, and the **Patio del Cuarto Dorado**. This latter has perhaps the grandest facade of the whole palace, for it admits you to the formal splendour of the Serallo.

The Serallo

The **Serallo** was built largely to the design of Yusuf I (1333–54), a romantic and enlightened sultan who was stabbed to death by a madman while worshipping in the Alhambra mosque. Its rooms open out from delicate marble-columned arcades at each end of the long **Patio de los Arrayanes** (Myrtles) with its serene fountain and pool flanked by clipped myrtle bushes. At the court's northern end is the **Sala de la Barca**, with a fine copy of its original cedar ceiling (destroyed by fire in the nineteenth century), and beyond this the fortified **Torre de Comares**, two floors of which are occupied by the royal throne room.

This room, known as the **Salón de Embajadores** (Hall of the Ambassadors), is the palace's largest and most majestic chamber. It was where the delicate

Wa-la ghailiba illa-Liah
"There is no Conqueror but God"

(stylized inscription from the Alhambra)

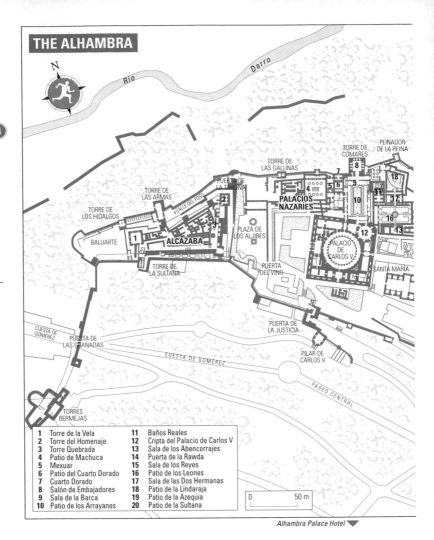

THE ALHAMBRA

1	Torre de la Vela	**11**	Baños Reales
2	Torre del Homenaje	**12**	Cripta del Palacio de Carlos V
3	Torre Quebrada	**13**	Sala de los Abencerrajes
4	Patio de Machuca	**14**	Puerta de la Rawda
5	Mexuar	**15**	Sala de los Reyes
6	Patio del Cuarto Dorado	**16**	Patio de los Leones
7	Cuarto Dorado	**17**	Sala de las Dos Hermanas
8	Salón de Embajadores	**18**	Patio de la Lindaraja
9	Sala de la Barca	**19**	Patio de la Azequia
10	Patio de los Arrayanes	**20**	Patio de la Sultana

0   50 m

Alhambra Palace Hotel ▼

diplomacy with the Christian emissaries would have been transacted – the means by which the Nasrid dynasty preserved itself – and as the sultan could only be approached indirectly it stands at an angle to the entrance from the Mexuar. It is perfectly square, with a stunning wooden dome, a superb example of *lacería*, the rigidly geometric "carpentry of knots" domed roof, and with a complex symbolism representing the seven heavens of the Muslim cosmos. The walls are completely covered in tile and stucco decoration and inscriptions, one of which states simply "I am the Heart of the Palace". It was here, symbolically, that Boabdil signed the terms of his city's surrender to the Reyes Católicos, whose motifs (the arms of Aragón and Castile) were later worked into the dome. Here, too, so it is said, Fernando met with Columbus to discuss his planned voyage to find a new sea route to India – the trip which led to the discovery of the Americas.

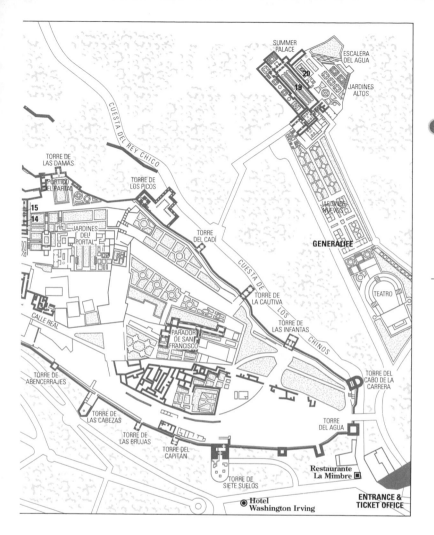

Carlos V tore down the rooms at the southern end of the Patio de los Arrayanes. From the arcade there is access (frequently closed) to the gloomy **chapel crypt** (*cripta*) of his palace; it has a curious "whispering gallery" effect, whereby words whispered on one side of the crypt can be heard quite clearly on the opposite side.

The Harem
The visit route continues to the **Patio de los Leones** (Court of the Lions), which has become the archetypal image of Granada, and constitutes the heart of the harem section of the palace. It was this area that moved Washington Irving to write in his *Tales of the Alhambra*:

It is impossible to contemplate this scene, so perfectly Oriental, without feeling the early associations of Arabian romance, and almost expecting to see the white arm of some mysterious princess beckoning from the gallery, or some dark eye sparkling through the lattice. The abode of beauty is here as if it had been inhabited but yesterday.

The stylized and archaic-looking lions beneath its fountain probably date, like the court itself, from the reign of Muhammad V, Yusuf's successor; a poem inscribed on the bowl tells how much fiercer the beasts would look if they weren't so restrained by respect for the sultan. The court was designed as an interior garden and planted with shrubs and aromatic herbs; it opens onto three of the finest rooms in the palace, each of which looks directly onto the fountain.

The most sophisticated rooms in this part of the complex, apparently designed to give a sense of the rotary movement of the stars, are the two facing each other across the court. The largest of these, the **Sala de los Abencerrajes**, has the most fabulous ceiling in the whole Alhambra complex: sixteen-sided, supported by niches of astonishing stalactite vaulting and lit by windows in the dome. Based on Pythagoras's theorem, the whole stupendous design – with a final and deft artistic flourish – is reflected in a fountain on the floor. Its light and airy quality stands at odds with its name and history, for it was here that Abu al-Hassan, Boabdil's father, murdered sixteen princes of the Abencerraj family, whose chief had fallen in love with his favourite, Zoraya. The stains in the fountain are popularly supposed to be indelible traces of blood from the severed heads thrown into it – but are more likely to be from rust.

△ Patio de los Leones

At the far end of the court is the **Sala de los Reyes** (Hall of the Kings), whose dormitory alcoves preserve a series of unique paintings on leather. These, in defiance of Koranic law, represent human scenes. They were probably painted by a Christian artist in the last decades of Moorish rule and were once thought to portray images of the Nasrid rulers – hence the room's name.

The second of the two facing chambers on the court's north side, the **Sala de las Dos Hermanas** (Hall of the Two Sisters), is more mundanely named – from two huge slabs of white marble in its floor – but just as spectacularly decorated, with a dome of over 5000 honeycomb cells. It was the principal room of the sultan's favourite, opening onto an inner apartment and balcony, the **Mirador de la Daraxa** (Eyes of the Sultana); the romantic garden patio below was added after the Reconquest.

Beyond, you are directed along a circuitous route through **apartments** redecorated by Carlos V (as at Sevilla, the northern-reared emperor installed fireplaces) and later used by Washington Irving. Eventually you emerge at the **Peinador de la Reina** (Queen's Pavilion), which served as an oratory for the sultanas and as a dressing room for the wife of Carlos V; perfumes were burned beneath its floor and wafted up through a marble slab in one corner.

From there, passing the **Patio de la Lindaraja** added in the sixteenth century (though the basin of its marble fountain was taken from outside the Mexuar), you come to the **Baños Reales** (Royal Baths), wonderfully decorated in rich tile mosaics and lit by pierced stars and rosettes once covered by coloured glass. The central chamber was used for reclining and retains the balconies where singers and musicians – reputedly blind to keep the royal women from being seen – would entertain the bathers. At present, entry is not permitted to the baths, though you can make out most of the features through the doorways.

The visit route exits via the exquisite **Portico del Partal** with a tower and elegant portico overlooking a serene pool. What appears no more than a garden pavilion today is in fact the surviving remnant of the early fourteenth-century Palace of the Partal, a four-winged structure originally surrounding the pool, the Alhambra's largest expanse of water. The **Jardines del Partal** lie beyond this and the nearby turnstile brings you out close to the entrance to the Palace of Carlos V.

The Palacio de Carlos V

Entering the **Palacio de Carlos V** strikes a totally different mood to what has gone before. The architecture of the palace with its rigid symmetries and dour exterior could not be more different than that of the Nasrid palaces. The building is dominated by its interior circular courtyard, where bullfights were once held. The palace itself was begun in 1526 but never finished – the coffered ceilings of the colonnade were added only in the 1960s before which the Ionic columns had projected into open sky – as shortly after commissioning it, Carlos V left Granada never to return, his plan to turn the city into the seat of the Spanish monarchy forgotten. Despite seeming totally out of place, however, the edifice is a distinguished piece of Renaissance design in its own right – the only surviving work of Pedro Machuca, a former pupil of Michelangelo. Lorca once referred to the stylistic clash between the two palaces as symbolic of "the fatal duel that throbs in the heart of each of Granada's citizens".

The palace's lower floor houses the **Museo de la Alhambra** (Tues–Sat 9am–2.30pm; €1.50, free with EU passport), a wonderful collection of artefacts that visitors are often too jaded to take in after the marvels of the Moorish palace outside. As well as fragments of sculptured plaster arabesques saved from the Alhambra and a splendid ceramic collection, look out for some outstanding fourteenth- and fifteenth-century Nasrid paintings and equally stunning carved wood panels and screens. The rare and beautiful fifteenth-century **Alhambra Vase** (Jarrón de las Gacelas) is the museum's centrepiece. Almost a metre and a half in height, and made for the Nasrid palace from local red clay enamelled in blue and gold with leaping *gacelas* (gazelles), it is the ceramic equal of the artistic splendours in the palace.

On the upper floors of the palace is a **Museo de Bellas Artes** (Tues 2.30–8pm, Wed–Sat 9am–8pm, Sun 9am–2.30pm; €1.50, free with EU passport), a cavernous gallery whose paintings and sculpture might command more attention elsewhere. At the time of writing the museum had closed for a year to carry out a major reorganization, but when it reopens most of the works described here should again be on view. In Room 1 there's a fine sixteenth-century woodcarving of the *Virgin and Child* by Diego de Siloé. Room 4 is dedicated to the works of Alonso Cano, the seventeenth-century *granadino* painter and sculptor. His *Virgin and Child* and *San Bernadino de Siena* panels are outstanding, as are the sculptures of *San Antonio* and the head of *San Juan de Dios*, the latter made with some assistance from Granada's other great sculptor, Pedro de Mena. Room 5 has more examples of the Andalucian sculptural tradition, with a brace of *Dolorosas* matched by a pair of *Ecce Homos*, a fervent theme of the region's artists reflected in the *pasos* carried during the Semana Santa processions; the *Ecce Homo* by Diego de Mora is the better of the two, whilst his more famous brother José de Mora has the finer *Dolorosa*. The later rooms, devoted to paintings from the nineteenth and twentieth centuries, are fairly forgettable, but look out for a small watercolour by nineteenth-century British artist David Roberts depicting the *Puerto del Vino*.

It's worth noting that both the above museums are prone to loan out exhibits or remove items into storage to free up space for exhibits on loan from other museums. In the basement of the Palace is one of the three official Alhambra **bookshops** (Librería de la Alhambra) with a wide variety of texts and postcards relating to the monument; the others are next to the ticket office at the entrance and along the Calle Real.

The Convento de San Francisco

Behind Carlos V's palace are the remnants of the town (with a population of 40,000 during the Nasrid period) which once existed within the Alhambra's walls. The main street, c/Real, today lined with tedious tourist shops, guides you east towards the Generalife, and on the way it's worth looking into the fifteenth-century **Convento de San Francisco**. Built by Fernando and Isabel on the site of another Moorish palace, this is now a parador whose marvellous plant-filled patio, dominated by a soaring cypress projecting above the roof, preserves part of the chapel where the Catholic monarchs were buried – commemorated by a marble slab – before being removed to the cathedral. It's tricky to find, and you'll need to ask for directions at the hotel's reception. At the rear of the parador, there's a restaurant and a very pleasant terrace bar, both open to nonresidents.

The Generalife

Paradise is described in the Koran as a shaded, leafy garden refreshed by running water where the "fortunate ones" may take their rest under tall canopies. It is an image which perfectly describes the **Generalife**, the gardens and summer palace of the Nasrid rulers. Its name means literally "garden of the architect" and the grounds consist of a luxuriantly imaginative series of patios, enclosed gardens and walkways.

By chance, an account of the gardens during Moorish times, written rather fancifully by fourteenth-century Moorish historian, poet and palace vizier Ibn Zamrak, survives. The descriptions that he gives aren't all entirely believable but they are a wonderful basis for musing as you lounge around by the patios and fountains. There were, he wrote, celebrations with horses darting about in the dusk at speeds that made the spectators rub their eyes (a form of festival still indulged in at Moroccan *fantasías*); rockets shot into the air to be attacked by the stars for their audacity; tightrope walkers flying through the air like birds; men bowled along in a great wooden hoop, shaped like an astronomical sphere.

Today, even devoid of such amusements, the gardens remain deeply evocative, above all, perhaps, the **Patio de la Sultana** (aka Patio de los Cipreses), a dark and secretive walled garden of sculpted junipers where the sultana Zoraya was suspected of meeting her lover Hamet, chief of the unfortunate Abencerrajes. The trunk of the seven-hundred-year-old **cypress tree** (marked by a plaque) is where legend says their trysts took place and where the grisly fate of the Abencerraj clan was sealed. Nearby is the inspired flight of fantasy of the **Escalera del Agua** (aka Camino de las Cascadas, a staircase with water flowing down its stone balustrades. At its base is a wonderful little **Summer Palace**, with various decorated belvederes.

If you're looking for a lunchtime **place to eat** or a refreshing drink between palaces and museums, the shady terrace of *Restaurante La Mimbre* is one of the best-value places on the hill (see "Eating and Drinking", p.551).

Other sights on the Alhambra hill

From the Puerta de las Granadas, taking the right-hand path uphill leads, in its higher reaches, to the **Casa Museo Manuel de Falla**, c/Antequerela s/n (guided visits Mon–Sat 10am–2pm; €2), the former home of the great Cádiz composer. The tiny house has been re-created to appear just as he left it in 1939 – with piano, domestic clutter, medicine bottles by his bed (he was a life-long hypochondriac), and stacks of books – before quitting fascist Spain for an exile spent in Argentina where he died in 1946. The walls and surfaces are dotted with mementoes and gifts from friends – including a series of sketches by Picasso – and the pleasant garden with its bench and vista is where the composer relaxed ("I have the most beautiful panoramic view in the world" he wrote to friend). A summer café here opens 8.30pm–1am. Occasional concerts of de Falla's works are performed in the nearby **Auditorio de Manuel de Falla**, Paseo de los Mártires s/n, on Saturday evenings and Sunday mornings throughout the year (details from the Turismo). Beyond at the end of an avenue is the **Carmen de los Mártires** (Mon–Fri 10am–2pm & 5–7pm; Sat & Sun 10am–7pm; closed Aug; free), a turn-of-the-twentieth-century house set in a delightfully tranquil garden filled with grottoes, statues, and follies as well as peacocks and black swans. Part of the grounds is currently being transformed into a botanical garden.

Just opposite the de Falla Museum, the terrace of the exclusive neo-Moorish **Alhambra Palace Hotel** (open to the public providing you're decently dressed) with fine **views** over the city is a great place for a drink. Ask at the reception desk to see the hotel's charming **theatre**, also in pseudo-Moorish style and where on June 7, 1922, an evening of poetry and song launched the career of a youthful Federico García Lorca (the guitarist Segovia appeared on the same bill). Just to the north of here on the Paseo del Generalife, the nineteenth-century **Hotel Washington Irving** is another of Granada's hotels with many historical associations. The hotel – run down and in serious need of attention – closed its doors in 2001 but it is to be hoped that such an important part of Granada's modern history will at some point be rehabilitated. In 1928, *New York Times* journalist Mildred Adams met Federico García Lorca here for the first time and fell under his spell. The poet sat down at the hotel's battered, out-of-tune piano in the lobby and sang her a ballad about the arrest and death of a local flamenco singer. "In gesture, tone of voice, expression of face and body, Lorca himself was the ballad," she wrote later.

The rest of the city

If you're spending just a couple of days in Granada it's hard to resist spending both of them in the Alhambra. There are, however, a handful of minor Moorish sites in and around the run-down medieval streets of the **Albaicín**, the largest and most characteristic such quarter to survive in Spain. After the delights of Moorish Granada it takes a distinct readjustment and effort of will to appreciate the city's later Christian monuments – although the **Capilla Real**, at least, demands a visit, and Baroque enthusiasts are in for a treat at the **Cartuja**.

The Albaicín

Declared a World Heritage Site by UNESCO in 1994, the **Albaicín** stretches across a fist-shaped area bordered by the Río Darro, Sacromonte hill, the old town walls and the winding Calle de Elvira (which runs parallel to the Gran Vía). From the centre, the best approach is from the Plaza Nueva and along the Carrera del Darro, beside the river. Coming from the Alhambra, you can make your way down the Cuesta de los Chinos – a beautiful path and a short cut. Following the walking route into the Albaicín described below is pleasant and takes in many of the most notable sights. To save your legs, **buses #31 and #32** from Plaza Nueva can take you to Plaza del Salvador in the heart of the *barrio*, and Plaza San Nicolás, near the famous *mirador*. Roughly one bus per hour (#34) deviates from this route to take in the adjoining *barrio* of Sacromonte.

Plaza Nueva and Cuesta De Gomérez

Before starting out from the **Plaza Nueva**, take a look at the square itself. It was constructed just after the *Reconquista* as a new focus for the city, and soon served as the site of an act of stunning Christian barbarity: a bonfire of 80,000 books from the former Muslim university. The square's elegant sixteenth-century fountain, the **Pilar del Toro**, is the last known work by the eminent Renaissance architect Diego de Siloé.

Flanking the plaza's north side is the austerely impressive **Real Chancillería** (Royal Chancery), built at the same time as the square, and now the law courts. Beyond its monumental entrance lies an elegant two-storeyed **patio** designed by Diego de Siloé with marble Doric columns and a staircase with stalactite ceiling.

On the opposite side of the square, the **Cuesta de Gomérez** leads up to the Alhambra. It's here that most of Granada's renowned guitar manufacturers are gathered. Behind the windows of these places – Casa Morales at no. 9 is one of the most famous – you may catch sight of a major concert or flamenco

---

Personal security in the Albaicín

There has been an increasing number of **thefts** from tourists in the Albaicín in recent years, often by drug addicts to fund their addiction. The preferred method is bag snatching, and is rarely accompanied by violence. However, don't let the threat put you off visiting one of the city's most atmospheric quarters; applying a few common-sense measures should ensure that you come to no harm.

Firstly, do not take any valuables (including airline tickets and passports) or large amounts of cash with you when visiting the Albaicín and keep what you have on your person, not in a bag. If your bag is snatched don't offer resistance – the thief will be concerned only with making a speedy getaway. Some people use their bag as a "decoy", even stuffing it with rubbish. Finally, and especially at night, keep to well-lit streets where there are other people around.

musician trying out a new instrument; they are not averse to giving the shop's customers a free concerto or two.

Santa Ana and the Baños Árabes

Perched over the Darro at the Plaza Nueva's eastern end is the sixteenth-century church of **Santa Ana** (open service times 6–7.30pm) whose elegant bell tower is the converted minaret of the mosque it replaced. The church's interior has flamboyantly decorated Baroque side chapels and a fine *artesonado* ceiling. Following the river's northern bank along the **Carrera del Darro**, glance back to where the river disappears from sight under the city and "moans as it loses itself in the absurd tunnel" as the young Lorca put it.

A little way up at no. 31 are the remains of the **Baños Árabes** (Tues–Sat 10am–2pm; €1.50, free with EU passport), a marvellous and little-visited Moorish public bath complex. Built in the eleventh century, the sensitively restored building consists of a series of brick-vaulted rooms with typical star-shaped skylights (originally glazed) and columns incorporating Roman and Visigothic capitals. When Richard Ford was here in the 1830s he found it being used as a wash-house by the local women because "one of the first laws after the conquest of the Catholic sovereigns was to prohibit bathing by fine and punishment". To get an idea of what a **Moorish bathhouse** was like when functioning, one has been re-created just behind the church of Santa Ana. At *Hammam*, c/Santa Ana 16 (reservation required ☏958 22 99 78; bath €9), you can wallow in the graded temperatures (cold, tepid and hot) of the traditional bath surrounded by marble pavements, mosaic wall decor and plaster arabesques. There's also a pleasant *tetería* (tearoom) upstairs too. See "Listings", p.561 for more of these bathhouses.

Casa de Castril: the Museo Arqueológico

At Carrera del Darro no. 43 is the **Casa de Castril**, a Renaissance mansion with a fine Plateresque facade and doorway, which houses the city's **Museo Arqueológico** (Tues 2.30–8pm, Wed–Sat 9am–8.30pm, Sun 9am–2.30pm; €1.50, free with EU passport), with its interesting exhibits of finds from throughout the province. Rooms 1 and 2 cover the Paleolithic and Neolithic periods, among which are some remarkable artefacts from the **Cueva de los Murciélagos** near Albuñol. In this fourth-millennium BC Neolithic cave, alongside a dozen cadavers arranged in a semicircle around that of a woman, were found some modern-looking esparto grass sandals and baskets, as well as a **golden diadem**. Room 3 has some interesting reconstructions of social life and culture in the Bronze Age and one exhibit shows how copper weapons and tools were manufactured using primitive moulds. Room 4 contains the Iberian and pre-Roman collection with some fine examples of early lapidary work, including a hefty carved stone bull, stone vases and outstanding alabaster vessels. The finds from the necropolis at **Punté Noye** near Almuñecar (the Phoenician Sexi) suggest a large colony here trading as far afield as Egypt and Greece from where the vases (some bearing pharaonic titles) were imported. The Roman section in Room 5 has a striking third-century bronze statue of a man in a toga as well as some interesting **early Christian lamps** from the fourth century.

Pride of place in the **Moorish section** (Room 7) is a fourteenth-century **bronze astrolabe**, demonstrating the superior scientific competence of the Arabic world at this time. The instrument was adopted by the Arabs from ancient Greece and used for charting the position of the stars in astrology, precisely orienting the *mihrab* of the mosques towards Mecca, determining geographical coordinates as well as trigonometry and converting Muslim dates into Christian ones. Its transmission from the Arab to the Christian world made possible the voyages of discovery to both east and west. More Moorish symmetry is evident in the designs on the vases, wooden chests and Amphorae also displayed here.

Further along the Darro and the Casa del Chapiz

Alongside the Casa de Castril, c/Zafra has a Moorish house, the **Casa Zafra**, with a pleasant patio and pool, whilst close by again is the convent of **Santa Catalina de Zafra**, housed in a sixteenth-century Mudéjar palace. The nuns here are renowned for their convent *dulces* and will gladly supply you (through a *turno*) with their speciality, *glorias* (almond cakes); they're open daily except in August. At the top of the same street, **San Juan de los Reyes** is another church – the first established in Granada after the *Reconquista* – built around the courtyard of a former mosque whose minaret, with characteristically Moorish *sebka* decoration, now serves as a belfry.

Continuing along the Darro you'll eventually come to **Paseo de los Tristes** (aka Paseo del Padre Manjón), a delightful esplanade beside the river overlooked by the battlements of the Alhambra high on the hill above, a great spot for a drink and especially so at night when the Alhambra is floodlit. There are several attractive bars fronting the river.

Two streets off here also contain **Moorish houses**: c/del Horno de Oro (no. 14) and, two streets further along, Cuesta de la Victoria (no. 9). The street after this, the **Cuesta del Chapiz**, climbs left into the heart of the Albaicín, passing first, on the right, the **Casa del Chapiz**, in origin a Moorish mansion – with a charming patio – and today reclaimed as a school of Arabic studies. The **Camino del Sacromonte**, just beyond it, heads east towards this *barrio*'s celebrated caves where, after sundown, the *gitanos* will attempt to entice you in for some raucous but often dubious flamenco (see box).

The Cuesta del Chapiz eventually loops around to the Plaza del Salvador where the church of **San Salvador** (daily 10.30am–1pm & 4.30–6.30pm; €1)

Sacromonte: Granada's gitano quarter

Granada has an ancient and still considerable **gitano** (gypsy) population, from whose clans many of Spain's best flamenco guitarists, dancers and singers have emerged. Traditionally the gypsies inhabited cave homes on the **Sacromonte hill**, and many still do, giving lively displays of dancing and music in their *zambras* (shindigs). These were once spontaneous but are now blatantly contrived for tourists, and are often shameless rip-offs: you're hauled into a cave, leered at if you're female, and systematically extorted of all the money you've brought along (for dance, the music, the castanets, the watered-down sherry…). Which is not to say that you shouldn't visit – just take only as much money as you want to part with. Turn up mid-evening; the lines of caves begin off the Camino de Sacromonte, just above the Casa del Chapiz (centre top on our city map). When the university is in session, the cave dwellings are turned into **discos** and are packed with students at weekends.

For revelations of a different kind wander up to Sacromonte a little earlier in the day and take a look at the old **caves** on the far side of the old Moorish wall – most of them deserted after severe floods in 1962. There are fantastic views from the top. Sacromonte now has its own museum, the **Centro Interpretación del Sacromonte**, Barranco de los Negros s/n (April–Oct Mon–Fri 10am–1pm & 5–9pm, Sat–Sun 11am–2pm; Nov–March Mon–Fri 10am–2pm & 4–7pm, Sat–Sun 11am–7pm; €4), depicting the life and times of the *barrio*. In this area and Sacromonte generally it would also be wise to heed the warnings on personal security mentioned in the box on p.544.

is built on the site of a mosque of which the **courtyard** – with whitewashed arches and Moorish cisterns – is beautifully preserved. Diego de Siloé, the architect of the sixteenth-century church, which was badly damaged in the Civil War, converted the mosque's original **minaret** into its tower.

Plaza Larga and the Mirador De San Nicolás

From San Salvador, c/Panaderos leads into **Plaza Larga**, the busy heart of the Albaicín, with a concentration of restaurants and bars. The nearby c/Agua has more **Moorish dwellings**: take a look at nos. 1, 37, 28 and 19. A busy little **market** is held in Plaza Larga on Saturday mornings selling the usual fruit and vegetables as well as potted plants and bootleg DVDs.

From here the obvious route is to the **Mirador de San Nicolás** with its justly famous panoramic **view** of the Sierra Nevada, the Alhambra and Granada spread out below. To get there from Plaza Larga, go through the Arco de las Pesas, an old arch in the west corner, and turn sharply left up Callejón de San Cecilio. When you reach it, the fifteenth-century church of San Nicolás is of little note but the nearby **aljibe** (fountain) is a Moorish original, one of many in the Albaicín to survive from the time when every mosque – there were more than thirty of them – had its own.

Below the *mirador*, c/Nuevo de San Nicolás descends into c/Santa Isabel la Real, passing, on the right, the early sixteenth-century convent of **Santa Isabel** (Tues, Thurs & Fri guided visits 10am & 11.30am; free) with a superb patio. The **convent church** has a superb Plateresque doorway and, inside, a fine Mudéjar ceiling, and holds sculptures by Pedro de Mena and José Mora. The convent was partly constructed within a fifteenth-century Nasrid palace – part of which was the adjoining **La Daralhorra** (Mon–Fri 10am–2pm; free) of which only the patios and some arches survive. This was the residence of Aisha, the mother of the last king of Granada, Boabdil.

Plaza de San Miguel Bajo and San José

Calle Santa Isabel drops into one of the Albaicín's most delightful squares, **Plaza de San Miguel Bajo**, lined with acacia and chestnut trees. The church of **San Miguel** on its eastern side is another sixteenth-century work by Diego de Siloé, built over yet another mosque, and preserves its original thirteenth-century *aljibe* (fountain) where the ritual ablutions would have been performed before entering. The square also has a clutch of good bars, whose terraces are extremely popular at night; *Bar Lara* serves the potent barrelled *costa* wine brewed in the Alpujarras. The opposite end of the plaza leads to the **Mirador del Carril de la Lona** with its views over the western side of the city. You could also detour north from here – climbing uphill beyond the walls – to the church of **San Cristóbal**, which has another fine **view** of the Alhambra from its own *mirador*.

One final church worth taking in on the way back to the centre is **San José** (open service times 7–9pm), reached by following calles San Miguel and San José from Plaza San Miguel. This is another sixteenth-century conversion from a ninth-century mosque, whose minaret forms its belfry. Its interior has a superb gilded Mudéjar coffered ceiling and octagonal dome.

Slightly south of the church on the Cuesta de San Gregorio, you could take a look at the **Casa de Porras** with its Plateresque facade and, opposite, the **Carmen de Cipreses**, one of the most picturesque garden-villas in the Albaicín. At the bottom of here, Plazoleta San Gregorio gives access, along c/Cárcel Alta, to Plaza Nueva. Alternatively, you could head west to the nearby calles Calderería Nueva and Calderería Vieja which have been transformed into a vibrant and delightful "Little Morocco" with food shops, restaurants and excellent teahouses serving a wide variety of refreshing teas, infusions and pastries – *As Sirat* and *Al-Faquara* on c/Calderería Nueva are recommended – (see "Eating, drinking and nightlife").

Other Moorish remains

A further group of Moorish buildings are located just outside the Albaicín. The most interesting of them, and oddly one of the least known, is the so-called **Palacio de la Madraza** (Mon–Fri 8am–10pm; closed August; free), a vividly painted building opposite the Capilla Real. Built in the early fourteenth century at the behest of Yusuf I – though much altered since – this is a former Islamic college (*medressa* in Arabic) and retains part of its old prayer hall, including a magnificently decorated **mihrab**. Note that the hours change here when it is used for exhibitions.

Slightly south of here lies the **Corral del Carbón**, a fourteenth-century *caravanserai* (an inn where merchants would lodge and, on the upper floors, store their goods) which is unique in Spain. A wonderful horseshoe arch leads into a courtyard with a marble water trough. Remarkably, the building survived intact through a stint as a sixteenth-century theatre – with the spectators watching from the upper galleries – and later as a charcoal burners' factory, the origin of its present name. The building is a little tricky to find: it lies down an alleyway off the c/de los Reyes Católicos, opposite the **Alcaicería**, the old Arab silk bazaar, burned down in the nineteenth century and poorly restored as an arcade of souvenir shops.

An impressive Mudéjar mansion, the **Casa de los Tiros**, stands on c/Pavaneras, just behind Plaza de Isabel Católica. This was built just after the *Reconquista* ended and has a curious facade adorned with various Greek deities and heroes as well as a number of *tiros* (muskets) projecting from the upper windows. Above the door is a representation of the sword of Boabdil which the family who lived here claimed they held in custody. The interior – which is worth a look – now houses the mildly interesting **Museo Casa de los Tiros** (Tues 2.30–8.30pm, Wed–Sat 9am–8.30pm, Sun 9am–2.30pm; free) exhibiting documents, furniture, engravings and photos from the city's past.

Capilla Real and Centro José Guerrero

The **Capilla Real** (Royal Chapel; daily: April–Sept 10.30am–1pm & 4–7pm; Oct–March 10.30am–1pm & 3.30–6.30pm; €3) is Granada's most impressive Christian building, flamboyant late Gothic in style and built ad hoc in the first decades of Christian rule as a mausoleum for Los Reyes Católicos, the city's "liberators". Before entering, note the stone frieze above the entrance which romantically alternates the initials of the two monarchs. Isabel, in accordance with her will, was originally buried on the Alhambra hill (in the church of the San Francisco convent, now part of the parador) but her wealth and power proved no safeguard of her wishes; both her remains and those of her spouse Fernando, who died eleven years later in 1516, were placed here in 1522. Isabel's final indignity occurred in the 1980s, when the candle that she asked should perpetually illuminate her tomb was replaced by an electric bulb – after many protests the candle was restored. But, as with Columbus's tomb in Sevilla, there is considerable doubt as to whether any of the remains in these lead coffins – so reverentially regarded by visiting Spaniards – are those of the monarchs at all. The chapel and tombs were desecrated by Napoleon's troops in 1812 and the coffins opened and defiled.

△ The Capilla Real

The monarchs' **tombs** in a plain underground crypt below are as simple as could be imagined: Fernando and Isabel, flanked by their daughter Juana ("the Mad") and her husband Felipe ("the Handsome"), rest in lead coffins placed in a plain crypt (a not easily spotted "F" marking that of the king on the left of the central pair). The smaller coffin to the right is that of the infant Príncipe de Asturias who died before reaching the age of two. Above them, however, is an elaborate Renaissance monument, with sculpted effigies of all four monarchs – the response of their grandson Carlos V to what he found "too small a room for so great a glory". The figures of Fernando and Isabel are easily identified by the rather puny-looking lion and lioness at their feet. Popular legend has it that Isabel's head sinks deeper into the pillow due to the weight of her intelligence compared with that of her husband; this is not without some truth as Fernando was never much more than a consort. Carved in Carrera marble by the Florentine Domenico Fancelli in 1517, the tomb's **side panels** depict the Apostles and scenes from the life of Christ and are especially fine. The Latin inscription at the monarchs' feet is brutally triumphalist in tone: "Overthrowers of the Mahometan sect and repressors of heretical stubbornness." The tomb of Joana and Felipe, a much inferior work, is by Ordóñez.

In front, dating from the same period, is an equally magnificent **reja**, or gilded grille, the work of Maestro Bartolomé of Jaén, and considered one of the finest in Spain. Its outstanding upper tier has scenes from the life of Christ and a Crucifixion. The altar's striking **retablo** is by Felipe Vigarny dated 1522, depicting in one scene San Juan being boiled in oil; beneath the kneeling figures of Fernando and Isabel – sculptures possibly by Diego de Siloé – are images depicting events close to both their hearts, Boabdil surrendering the keys of Granada for him, the enforced baptism of the defeated Moors for her.

In the capilla's **Sacristy** are displayed the **sword of Fernando**, the **crown of Isabel**, and the banners used at the conquest of Granada. Also here is Isabel's outstanding personal collection of **medieval Flemish paintings** – including a magnificent **El Descendimiento** (Descent from the Cross) triptych by Dirk

Bouts. Also here are other important works by Memling, Bouts and van der Weyden – as well as various Italian and Spanish paintings, including panels by Botticelli, Perugino and Pedro Berruguete.

South of the chapel, along c/Oficios, stands the **Centro José Guerrero** (Tues–Sat 10am–2pm & 5–9pm, Sun 11am–2pm, ⓦ www.centroguerrero.org; free), a new museum dedicated to the city's most famous modern artist and brilliant colourist José Guerrero (1914–91). Influenced early on by Cubism and later by Miró, in 1950 Guerrero moved to New York where he became a leading exponent of American Expressionism, before returning to Spain in 1965. The museum displays arresting works from all his major periods of artistic development.

The Catedral

For all its stark Renaissance bulk, Granada's **Catedral**, adjoining the Capilla Real and entered from a door on Gran Vía (April–Sept Mon–Sat 10am–1.30pm & 4–8pm, Sun 4–8pm; Oct–March Mon–Sat 10.45am–1.30pm & 4–7pm, Sun 4–7pm; €3), is a disappointment. It was raised on the site of the Great Mosque, with work commencing in 1521 – just as the royal chapel was finished – but it was then left uncompleted until well into the eighteenth century. The main west facade by Diego de Siloé and Alonso Cano is worth a look, however. It still carries a provocative inscription honouring Primo de Rivera, founder of the fascist Falange Party, added in the Franco period, and, significantly for Granada today, never removed.

Inside, the church is pleasantly light and airy due to its painted stonework and twenty giant pillars which push the central dome to a height of over thirty metres. The Capilla Mayor has figures by Pedro de Mena of Fernando and Isabel at prayer, with, above them, oversized busts of Adam and Eve by Alonso Cano, who also left quite a bit of work in the other chapels and is buried in the crypt – a marble and bronze plaque next to the main door honours him.

In the eighteenth-century **sagrario** there are more works by Cano as well as a fine *Crucifixión* by Martínez Montañes. In the side chapels are a triumphant sculpture of *Santiago* (St James) in the saddle, by Pedro de Mena (Capilla de Santiago) and an **El Greco** *St Francis* (Capilla de Jesús Nazareno).

The University Quarter: San Juan and San Jerónimo

North of the cathedral, ten minutes' walk along c/San Jerónimo, the Renaissance **Hospital de San Juan de Dios** is well worth a visit. It was founded in 1552 by Juan de Robles (Juan de Dios) as a hospital for the sick and a refuge for foundlings, and its elaborate facade has a statue by José de Mora depicting the saint on his knees and holding a cross, which popular legend says is how he died. The hospital itself still functions and you'll have to pass the entrance hall to reach two marvellous **patios**. The outer and larger one is a beautiful double-tiered Renaissance work with a palm at each of its four corners and a fountain in the centre; the inner patio – with orange trees in the corners here – has delightful but deteriorating frescoes depicting the saint's miracles. Next door, the impressive church, a Baroque addition, has a Churrigueresque *retablo* – a glittering, gold extravaganza by Guerrero.

Close by lies a little-known jewel: the sixteenth-century **Convento de San Jerónimo** (Mon–Sat 10am–1.30pm & 4–7.30pm, Sun 11am–2pm; €3), founded by the Catholic monarchs, though built after their death. This has a further exquisite pair of Renaissance **patios** (or cloisters in this context), the largest an elegant work by Diego de Siloé with two tiers of 36 arches. The **church**, also by Siloé, has been wonderfully restored after use as cavalry barracks and has fabulous eighteenth-century frescoes, another monumental carved and painted *retablo*, and, on either side of the altar, monuments to "El Gran Capitán" Gonzalo de Córdoba and his wife Doña María. The remains of this general, responsible for many of the Catholic monarchs' victories, may lie in the vault beneath, but the Napoleonic French were here too and, as Ford noted not much later, had "insulted the dead lion's ashes before whom, when alive, their ancestors had always fled." The church is little visited, and in late afternoon you may hear the nuns singing their offices in the railed-off choir loft above. A small shop at the entrance sells the convent's marmalade and *dulces*.

A short walk away along c/de la Duquesa and left into Plaza Universidad lies the old **University building** – now the Law faculty – founded by Carlos V with a Baroque portal flanked by twin barley-sugar pillars; no one minds if you step inside to view the patio. In the same square the eighteenth-century **Iglesia de Santos Justo y Pastor** has an impressive facade and, inside, an elaborately decorated cupola and gilded *retablo*.

Just behind this church, with its entrance on c/San Jerónimo, the **Colegio de San Bartolomé y Santiago** is a sixteenth-century university college with an elegant patio, off which is a students' *cafetería* which they don't mind sharing with visitors. Slightly further out, to the north along the Ancha de Capuchinos, the **Hospital Real** (Mon–Fri 9am–1pm), a magnificent Renaissance building designed by Enrique Egas and formerly known as the Hospital de los Locos, was founded by the Catholic monarchs and finished by Carlos V. As its former name implies, it was one of the first lunatic asylums in Europe, though it now houses the main library of the University of Granada. Inside, a beautiful arcaded patio and some fine *artesonado* ceilings are worth a look.

La Cartuja

Granada's **Cartuja** (Mon–Sat 10am–1pm & 4–8pm, Sun 10am–noon & 4–8pm; Nov–April closes 6pm; €3), on the northern outskirts of town, is the grandest and most outrageously decorated of all the country's lavish Carthusian monasteries. It's a ten- to fifteen-minute walk beyond the Hospital Real; alternatively, bus line #8, going north along Gran Vía, passes by.

The monastery was founded in 1516 on land provided by "El Gran Capitán", Gonzalo de Córdoba (see above), though the building is noted today for its heights of Churrigueresque-inspired Baroque extravagance – added, some say, to rival the Alhambra. The **church** is of staggering wealth, surmounted by an altar of twisted and coloured marble described by one Spanish writer as "a motionless architectural earthquake". There are Bocanegra paintings and a seventeenth-century sculpture of the *Assumption* by José de Mora.

The **sagrario** drips with more marble, jasper and porphyry and has a breathtakingly beautiful gilded and frescoed **cupola** by Antonio Palomino, while the **sacristía** pulls out yet more stops with another stunning painted cupola and fascinating sculptural features influenced by the art of the Aztec and Maya civilizations encountered in the New World. Here also are fine sculptures of *San Bruno* by José de Mora in a side niche, and an *Inmaculada* by Alonso Cano.

Eating, drinking and nightlife

Granada is quite a sedate place, at least compared to Sevilla or Málaga, and if it weren't for the university, you sense the city would go unnaturally early to bed. However, on a brief stay, there's more than enough to entertain you, with some decent restaurants and plenty of animated bars, especially in the zone between **Plaza Nueva** and **Grand Vía**, the plazas of the **Albaicín** quarter,

One of the ghosts that walks Granada's streets and plazas is that of Andalucía's greatest poet and dramatist **Federico García Lorca**. Born in 1898 at Fuente Vaqueros, a village in the *vega*, the fertile plain to the west of the city, he moved to Granada eleven years later. But it was his childhood spent growing up on the family farm, where he soaked up both the countryside and the folklore of its people, that was to have an enduring influence on his work.

Lorca published his first book of essays and poems while still at university in Granada, in 1918. It was in 1928, however, that he came to national prominence with *El Romancero Gitano*, an anthology of gypsy ballads. This success led to a trip to New York in 1929 where he spent a year at Columbia University ostensibly learning English, but actually gathering material for the collection of poems, *Poeta in Nueva York*, published after his death.

He returned to Spain in 1931 at the advent of the Spanish Republic and was given a government grant to run a travelling theatre group, *La Barraca* (the cabin). From this period the poet's major works for the stage – *Bodas de Sangre* (Blood Wedding) and *Yerma* – emerged.

In July 1936, on the eve of the Civil War, Lorca went back to Granada for the summer. This visit coincided with Franco's coup and control of the city was wrested by the Falangists, who initiated a reign of terror. Lorca, as a Republican sympathizer and declared homosexual, was hunted down by fascist thugs at the house of a friend, now the *Hotel Reina Cristina*. Two days later he was murdered in an olive grove near the village of Viznar. His body was never found.

It has taken the city a long time to accord Lorca the recognition he deserves, partly because of his sexual inclinations, and mainly through guilt concerning the way he died. If you have an interest in tracing the locations of his life, the most important are detailed below. More avid followers should get hold of the excellent *Lorca's Granada* by Ian Gibson, his biographer.

Huerta de San Vicente

West of the centre is the **Huerta de San Vicente** (July–Aug Tues–Sun 10am–2.30pm; April–June & Sept–Oct Tues–Sun 10am–12.30pm & 5–7.30pm; Nov–March Tues–Sun 10am–12.30pm & 4–6.30pm; €1.80, Wed free; guided tours every 45min; ⓦwww. huertadesanvincente.com), an orchard where the poet's family used to spend the summer months. It spreads back from c/de la Virgen Blanca, behind *Los Jardines Neptuno Flamenco* nightclub; to get there take the southbound bus #4 from Gran Vía or Plaza del Carmen (direction Palacio de Deportes), or a taxi.

The **house** – now restored and opened as a museum – is set in the centre of what is now the largest rose garden in Europe, the **Parque Federico García Lorca**, the city's belated tribute. When the Lorcas had it, the five-acre holding was planted with vegetables and fruit trees. Then a tranquil rural plot on the city's edge, it has since been enveloped by ugly urban sprawl and it's hard to square the scene today with the poet's description of a "paradise of trees and water and so much jasmine and night-shade in the garden that we all wake up with lyrical headaches". The light and airy rooms contain some of their original furniture including, in Lorca's bedroom, his work desk, bed, a poster of the *Barraca* theatre company and the balcony (from outside, the furthest left of the three) looking towards the Sierra Nevada, which inspired one of his best-known poems, *Despedida* (Farewell):

Si muero, dejad el balcón abierto.
El niño come naranjas. (Desde mi balcón lo veo.)
El segador siega el trigo. (Desde mi balcón lo siento.)
Si muero, dejad el balcón abierto!

If I die, leave the balcony open.
The child eats oranges. (From my balcony I see him.)
The harvester scythes the corn. (From my balcony I hear him.)
If I die leave the balcony open!

In a *hornacina* or wall niche outside is the tiny image of San Vicente placed there by Lorca's father – and where it has remained ever since – when he bought the house in 1925 and changed its name to that of the saint.

Fuente Vaqueros and Valderrubio

In this village I dreamt my first ambitious dreams. In this village one day I will merge with the earth and flowers . . .

Lorca's birthplace in the tranquil farming village of **Fuente Vaqueros**, 17km west of Granada, is the site of the **Lorca Museum** (July–Aug Tues–Sun 10am–2pm; Sept–May Tues–Sun 10am–1pm & 4–6pm; guided visits on the hour; €1.80; ☎958 51 64 53). The house lies just off the village's main square on c/Poeta García Lorca. Now a charming shrine to Lorca's memory and watched over by the amiable director Juan de Loxa (a poet himself), the museum is stuffed with Lorca memorabilia, manuscripts and personal effects. It also has a fleeting video fragment of Lorca on tour with the Teatro Barraca – the only piece of cinema film to capture the poet and his engaging smile. An impressive new theatre, the Teatro Lorca, has been constructed opposite the house.

After you've seen the house, pay a visit to the parish church (open service times 7–9pm) at the end of the street opposite, where Lorca's mother took him regularly as a child. Although the church has been heavily reconstructed since, the old stone font can still be seen where Lorca – or "Federico" as he is known to all the world here – was baptized.

From Granada, **buses** operated by Ureña run to the village from the Avda. de Andaluces fronting the train station; the weekday outward service leaves on the hour (except 10am) from nine in the morning, with the return also hourly (except 11am); it's a twenty-minute trip and the last bus returns to Granada at 8pm. Should you want **to stay**, there are en-suite a/c rooms at the friendly *Hostal-Restaurante Moli-Lorc* at c/Ancha Escuelas 11 (☎958 51 63 48; ❷) next to the church, and a decent place **to eat**, *Restaurante Genil*, 2km out of the village on the Chauchina road with a good-value *menú*. On Saturday mornings a lively **market** fills the street fronting the church.

The Lorca family also had a house 4km to the northwest in the pleasant village of **Valderrubio**. Each year the Lorcas moved here at harvest time (Lorca's father was a wealthy landowner) and the infant Lorca spent many summers playing in surrounding fields. The house at c/Iglesia 20 (which remained in the Lorca family until 1986) has been opened to the public as a **museum** (Wed–Sun 10am–1.30pm; €1) and is signed from the main road into the village.

Viznar

The village of **Viznar**, 10km northeast of Granada, will always be linked with the assassination of Lorca in August 1936. After his arrest in Granada, he was held for two days at a farmhouse called La Colonia before being taken to a bleak gully (*barranco*) nearby and shot. A poem of Lorca's seemed eerily prescient about his own end:

I realized I had been murdered.
They searched cafés and cemeteries and churches,
they opened barrels and cupboards,
they plundered three skeletons to remove their gold teeth.
They did not find me.
They never found me?
No. They never found me.

From the centre of the village the road towards La Fuente Grande passes the site of **La Colonia** (later demolished), near to a white-walled cottage. From here, the road curves around the valley to the **Parque Federico García Lorca**, a sombre monumental garden marking the *barranco* and honouring all the Civil War dead. Climb the steps to the garden and veer left up more steps: the site of Lorca's murder was here, beneath a solitary olive tree. After the killing – he was shot with three others – a young gravedigger threw the bodies into a narrow trench. The supposed site is marked by a granite memorial.

Viznar is served by **buses** run by Martín Perez (☎958 15 12 49) from Granada's Arco de Elvira terminal on the Plaza del Triunfo at the northern end of Gran Vía (Mon–Fri 2.45pm and 8pm, Sat 1.30pm, returning Mon–Fri at 7.45am and 4pm, Sat 8.30am; no service Sun; €0.75). The village also has a superb **youth hostel** (☎958 54 33 07; tends to fill up so ring ahead; under-26 €14, 26+ €18.50), complete with a swimming pool open to all.

whose streets make for enjoyable (if confusing) evening wanderings, around the **Campo del Príncipe**, a spacious square with outdoor eating and drinking, at the foot of the west slopes of the Alhambra hill, and along the **Carrera del Darro**. Granada's discos – mostly dismal teenage hangouts – are concentrated along the **c/Pedro Antonio** to the west of the centre, which turns into one big disco at weekends. For serious drinking into the early hours head out to the bars along calles Gran Capitán, San Juan de Dios and Pedro Antonio de Alarcón in the university zone.

The monthly *Guía de Granada* (€0.90 and available from newspaper kioskos) has **listings** for most of what's happening on the cultural and entertainment front though it tends to be less up-to-date than the city's rather staid daily paper, *Ideal*, which has a more reliable entertainment guide, particularly in its weekend editions.

Restaurants

Granada is not noted for the quality of its **restaurants**, and service and standards even at the best places often leave a lot to be desired. That said, good-value food is to be found all over town, and there are a number of places worth paying a bit more for, too. Beware, of course, the inevitable tourist traps, particularly around the Plaza Nueva and on the Alhambra hill. It's worth remembering that you can also get substantial meals at many of the bars listed in the following section.

Plaza Nueva and cathedral area

Al-Faoura c/Calderería Nueva, just off c/Elvira. Juices and crepes to the accompaniment of classical music. They also do a wide range of teas – try their *"té Pakistani"* or *"té Al-Faoura"*.

Bar-Restaurante Sevilla c/Oficios 12 ☎958 22 12 23. One of the few surviving prewar restaurants this place is steeped in literary history and Lorca spent many happy hours here. There's a *menú* for €36 and, in the evenings, tables outside with a view of the *capilla*. Main dishes €10–18. Closed Mon.

Café au Lait Callejón de los Franceses 31. Laid-back French-style café-bar with pleasant palm-shaded terrace. It serves a good-value breakfast (€2.25 complete with domestic or foreign newspapers) and later does pizzas, tapas and *menús del día* from €8.

Las Cuevas c/Calderería Nueva. Crepes, *dulces arabes*, *tagines* and pizzas cooked in a wood-burning oven make this a popular place with locals. There's a small terrace facing San Gregorio church.

Mesón Andaluz c/Cetti Meriem 10 ☎ 958 22 73 57. Pleasant, slightly pricey restaurant with a renowned *fritura mixta* (fried fish platter) and *menú* for €10. The *Nueva Bodega*, almost opposite and under the same proprietors, serves more economical fare with a *menú* for €7.20.

Naturi Albaicín c/Calderería Nueva 10. Imaginative vegetarian cooking – fine salads, spinach-stuffed mushrooms and the like – served up with New Age music and green magazines; quality makes up for often slow service. Has €7 *menú*. Take tea or coffee after at the nearby teahouses.

Nueva Bodega c/Cetti Meriem 9. Good-value local *bodega* that serves up basic tapas, *bocadillos* and *platos combinados* with a *menú* for €7.

Pilar de Toro c/Hospital de Santa Ana 12 ☎ 958 22 38 47. Stylish, medium-priced bar-restaurant inside a former seventeenth-century *casa señorial* with exterior *terraza*, elegant patio bar (serving tapas) and, upstairs, a mid-priced restaurant with its own leafy and secluded patio. Main dishes €9–15.

Restaurante León c/Pan 3. Long-established economical Cordoban restaurant serving many *carne de monte* (game) dishes and *migas* (fried breadcrumbs); offers an economical *menú* for €7.

Samarcanda c/Calderería Vieja 3. Excellent Lebanese restaurant (with quite a few vegetarian options) and the best of the few places in "Little Morocco" where it's worth having a full meal.

Albaicín

Bar La Mancha Chica c/Nueva de San Nicolás 1. Simple place with an outdoor terrace serving *platos combinados*.

Carmen de Aben Humeya c/Cuesta de las Tomasas 12. Superb Alhambra views from the terrace of this *bar–cafetería* serving tea and *pasteles* in the afternoon, and salads, meat and fish dishes in the evenings. Main dishes €8.50–14.50.

🏃 **Carmen Verde La Luna** Camino Nuevo de San Nicolás 16 ☎ 958 29 17 94. Beautiful garden terrace restaurant with a breathtaking view of the Alhambra. Ring for a front-line table. The mid-priced cooking matches up to the vista, and specials include *berenjenas rellenos*, *bacalao*

albaicinero (cod with almond sauce) and *cordero Verde Luna* (lamb with prune sauce). Good wine list. April–Sept Wed–Sun 8–11pm only. Main dishes €11.50–17; *menú de degustación* €29. Reservation advised.

Casa Blas Plaza San Miguel Bajo 15. Hearty working mens' (and womens') food like *costillas* (ribs) and *ciervo* (deer) feature here, along with many *andaluz* classics; has an inviting terrace on this pleasant square.

El Ladrillo II Plazoleta de Fatima This place specializes in *barcos* (boats) of fried fish, served at economical prices on tables beneath the stars – all of which make the climb worthwhile. Their newly opened offshoot *Ladrillo III*, around the corner at c/Agua del Albaycín 20, is another superb little restaurant with wonderful roof patio and a *menú* for around €7.

El Yunque Plaza San Miguel Bajo 3. Probably the best of this square's bar-diners, owned and run by a noted *flamenco cantaor*, Antonio, and his wife – who was a well-known dancer in her time. House specials include *pollo en salsa de almendras* (chicken in almond sauce) and *lomo alpujarreño* (pork loin). They have inside seating on the adjacent corner if it's chilly or wet.

Juanillo Camino del Monte 81. Well-known low-priced restaurant in Sacromonte serving typical no-nonsense but well-prepared *raciones*, paella and other rice dishes with great views of the Alhambra. Take the bus from Plaza Nueva if you can't face the hike.

🏃 **Meson El Trillo** Callejón del Aljibe del Trillo 3 ☎ 958 22 51 82. Enchanting little mid-priced restaurant in an Albaicín *carmen* offering Basque-influenced cuisine: *bacalao al pil-pil* (salted cod with garlic) is a signature dish. It has outdoor tables on a delightful garden patio shaded by pear and quince trees.

Mirador de Morayma c/Pianista García Carrillo 2 ☎ 958 22 82 90. Situated in a gorgeous Albaicín *carmen* (villa and garden) with a fine view of the Alhambra, *granadino* specialities here include *tortilla de Sacromonte* (sweetbread and vegetable omelette) and the desserts are made by the sisters at the Convento de Santa Catalina. Main dishes €10–20; good-value *menú* for €30. On Tuesday evenings they stage a flamenco concert. Closed Sun eve.

🏃 **Restaurante-Bar Tomasas** Carril de San Agustín 4, just below the Mirador de San Nicolás, ☎ 958 22 41 08. Mid-priced summer restaurant serving *cocina andaluz* in a huge and beautiful *carmen* with a stunning terrace view of the Alhambra. *Ajo blanco* (white *gazpacho*) is a speciality. You can also nurse a drink here if you don't want to eat. Closed Sun and (July–Aug) midday. *El Agua*, nearby to the south at c/Aljibe del Trillos 7, is a similar place – with more Alhambra views – specializing in fondues.

Taberna La Higuera Horno de Hoyo 6. Economical and highly popular place with a broad terrace under a huge fig tree (*higuera*). Try the squid (*chipirones*) which come in their ink.

Plazas Bib-Rambla and Trinidad

Casa Cepillo Plaza Pescadería 8 – a marketplace linking the two squares. Cheap *comedor* with an excellent-value *menú* for €7.50; the soups are especially good here.

Bar Ferroviaria c/Lavadero Tablas 1, off c/Tablas. This is in fact a pensioners' club for former railway workers but don't let that put you off. Behind the anonymous exterior you'll find an amazingly cheap *menú* (currently €5) that attracts workers and students for miles around; if the paella is on, it's your lucky day. Open daily 1.30–8pm (lunch 1.30–4.30pm). Closed Aug.

La Bodega de Antonio c/Jardines 4, south of Plaza Trinidad. Atmospheric, mid-priced seafood *bodega* with a mouthwatering *pulpo La Bodega* (octopus on a bed of artichokes) for €10.50.

Mesón La Pataleta Plaza Gran Capitan 1. Very good mid-priced restaurant renowned for its barbecued meat dishes. Main dishes €13–21.

Restaurante Las Tinajas c/Martínez Campos 17, to the southwest of the centre ☏958 25 43 93. One of Granada's top-notch restaurants offering a range of *granadino* dishes as well as some northern Spanish specialities. Recommended here are *berenjenas rellenas de setas* (aubergine stuffed with wild mushrooms) and *rape mozárabe* (monkfish). There's also a *menú* for around €35. Closed July & Aug.

Restaurante Tiscar c/Cardenal Mendoza 22, at the junction with c/San Juan de Dios. Popular and economical restaurant in the university district serving a range of *platos combinados* and an economical *menú* for €6 (including wine).

Restaurante-Marisquería Cunini Plaza Pescadería 14 ☏958 25 07 77. A gleaming, marble-topped bar serves standing customers with high-quality fish tapas and *raciones* and there's a pricier and equally excellent small seafood restaurant behind (for which reservation is advised).

Plaza Mariana Pineda and the south central area

Horno de Santiago Plaza de los Campos 8 ☏958 22 34 76. Central mid-priced restaurant offering classic *granadino* fish, meat and game dishes

cooked with finesse. There's a *menú* for about €36. Closed Sun & Aug.

Mesón La Alegría c/Moras 4. Atmospheric local *mesón* noted for its meat dishes *a la parrilla* – cooked by yourself on a table hotplate. It also has a pleasant street terrace.

Restaurante Chikito Plaza del Campillo 9 ☏958 22 33 64. Fronted by four towering plane trees, and formerly the *Café Alameda* where Lorca, Falla and the *Rinconcillo* group met. Literary lights from abroad such as Kipling and H.G. Wells all visited the bar's corner table (*rincón*). More recently it's where soccer ace Maradona used to come for his steaks. Today's restaurant – with outdoor terrace – is one of Granada's better ones for à la carte, but the medium-priced *menú* is unexciting. Main dishes €8–20. Closed Wed.

Restaurante Nuevo c/Navas 25. Good budget restaurant with economical *platos combinados* and *menús*.

Seis Peniques Plaza de Padre Suárez. Quite a good little bar-restaurant with a small terrace facing the Casa de los Tiros; serves a decent *menú* for around €8.

Alhambra and Campo Del Príncipe

El Carmen de San Miguel Plaza Torres Bermejas 3 ☏958 22 67 23. One of Granada's top places to eat with a fabuluous terrace looking out over the city. An innovative approach (occasionally overdone) to *andaluz* cuisine is illustrated by a signature dish, *conejo relleno de langostinos escabechados con ostras y limón* (rabbit with prawns and oysters). Main dishes €13–20, *menú de degustación* for €45. Closed Sun.

La Esquinita Campo del Principe s/n. The plaza's best place for reasonably priced *cocina andaluz* is renowned for its fried fish with a €10 *menú*.

Lago de Como Campo de Príncipe 8. Slightly cheaper than *La Ninfa*, this two-storeyed Italian restaurant is more routine but is also more likely to have a table.

La Mimbre Paseo del Generalife s/n, near the Alhambra's entrance. With a delightful terrace shaded by willows (*mimbres*) this is one of the best restaurants on the Alhambra hill. The food is good but they are sometimes overwhelmed in high season. Decent *menú* for around €17.50, which you may need to ask for. Main dishes €9–20.

La Ninfa Campo del Príncipe. Popular Italian restaurant that puts out tables on this pleasant plaza, and is often full to bursting at weekends. The *ensalada primavera* is a must for your first course and the desserts are pretty good too.

Parador de San Francisco Alhambra ☏958 22 14 40. The parador's restaurant is one of the best in an upmarket chain often noted for its blandness. It boasts fine views and offers a varied and not-too-bank-breaking *menú* for around €27.

Out of the centre

🏃 **Ruta del Veleta** Carretera de Sierra Nevada 136 (Cenes de la Vega), ☏958

48 61 34. Three kilometres out of town along the Sierra Nevada road, this is currently Granada's top restaurant. The cooking is outstanding, as is the wine list. Try their *caldaretas de arroz con boga-vante* (lobster) or *cordero segureño* (lamb with rosemary). If you're going to be up in the Solynieve ski resort (see p.568) they have an offshoot there, too. Main dishes €10–22; *menú de degustación* €45.

Tapas and drinking bars

Granada's proximity to the Sierra Nevada brings a coolness to the city that carries over into its imbibing and its nightlife. In the **bars** here you're just as likely to find locals ordering a glass of *rioja* as soon as the beloved *fino* of the rest of Andalucía. One local wine which the *granadinos* do cherish, though (and which you shouldn't miss), is *vino de la costa* (coast wine – ironically made in the mountains of the Alpujarras); amber in colour, fairly potent, but relatively easy on hangovers, it's the ideal partner for a tapa.

The **bars** recommended below are mainly for drinking, though most serve tapas and *raciones* and you could happily fill up and forget about going to a restaurant. The city has quite a reputation for its **tapas**, which are more elabo-rate than is usual in Andalucía and in most bars one comes free with each drink – a laudable trait in a city generally regarded as penny-pinching by most *anda-luzes*. It's worth noting that the Turismo produces a glossy free *Rutas de Tapas* **pamphlet**, which has maps and recommendations for places in both Granada and its province.

Plaza Nueva and cathedral area

Al Pie de la Torre c/Pie de la Torre s/n. Close to the foot of the cathedral's tower this is an atmos-pheric little bar for tasty tapas with an intimate small restaurant behind for fish and meat dishes (main dishes €12–17).

Bar Bareto El Sol c/San Matias 29, to the south-east of the Corral de Carbón. New and friendly bar featuring world music sounds with some interest-ing vegetarian tapas.

Bar Reca Plaza de la Trinidad, corner with c/Infan-tes. Lively tapas venue on a leafy square which fairly hums at lunchtime and in the early evening.

Bar Sabanilla c/San Sebastián 14. Not easy to find, just off the northeast corner of Plaza Bib-Rambla, down a passageway behind an unmarked door, this bar claims to be the oldest in Granada (it certainly looks it) and stays open till late. It's a basic, poky place, run by two friendly women who offer a free tapa with every drink. The barrel-led *costa* wine here (from the Alpujarra village of Albondón) is recommended.

🏃 **Bodegas Castañeda** c/Almireceros 1, at the corner of c/Elvira, across Gran Vía from the cathedral. One of the city's oldest bars, much refurbished and prettified but still an attractive first

stop of an evening. Good tapas include generous paté and cheese boards (*tablas*), *montaditos* (small open sandwiches), baked potatoes and *gazpacho*. A lethal house special is the *Calicasas* cocktail, which seems to include just about everything behind the bar.

Bodegas La Mancha c/Joaquín Costa 10, around the corner from *Bodegas Castañeda*. Monumental spit-and-sawdust establishment (slightly more refined after refurbishment) hung with hams, and with great wine vats stationed behind the bar like rockets on a launch pad. Tasty tapas on offer include *jamón serrano*; they also sell excellent hot and cold *bocadillos* to eat in or take away.

Café-Bar Oliver Plaza Pescadería 12, slightly northwest of the Plaza de la Trinidad. Good *raciones* bar featuring a popular (with the *granadino* smart set) outdoor terrace.

Casa Enrique Acera de Darro 8, near the Puerta Real. Fine daytime or early-evening haunt with a wide tapas selection. Specializes in *jamón iberico* and *chorizo* from Salamanca. Wide-ranging wine list.

Casa Julio c/Hermosa, off Plaza Nueva. A pocket-sized boozers' bar lined with fine old *azulejos* that nonetheless turns out some excellent fried seafood tapas. Try also the fried *berenjenas* (aubergine) which are a treat.

El Rinconcillo Plaza Nueva, next to *Pilar de Toro* restaurant. Friendly Lilliputian bar with lively *terraza* serving good tapas and *raciones*.

Hannigan and Sons c/Cetti Merriem s/n, near the *Taberna del Irlandés*. Independent Irish house whose owner *is* named Hannigan. The usual range of beers and stouts are on offer and the place has an airy feel to it with a snug, decorative stained glass and the only wooden floor in town. If you throw your cigarette ends on it Tony Hannigan will chuck you out; confusingly for locals, every other bar in town encourages you to do just that.

La Bodeguilla de al Lado c/Tendillas de Sta. Paula 4, just north of the cathedral. Pricey but authentic tapas (from ancient family recipes) in a cosy bar where the charming female proprietor is an authority on Spanish wines. Closed July–Aug.

La Trastienda c/Cuchilleros 11, on a small plaza just off c/Reyes Católicos. Plush little drinking den hidden behind a shop selling wine, cheese and ham. Once you've negotiated your way around the counter it's surprisingly cosy in the back.

Nueva Bodega c/Cetti Meriem 9, off Gran Vía. Good-value *bodega* which serves up basic tapas and *bocadillos* downstairs and a *menú* for €5.95 upstairs.

Taberna del Irlandés c/Almireceros 7, just north of the cathedral. Vibrant and rather too-popular-for-its-own-good little "Irish" bar – with well-kept stout – run by ebullient hibernophile Manolo. A good deal more authentic than most of the region's synthetic Irish theme pubs.

Taberna Salinas c/Elvira 13, slightly west of Plaza Nueva. Solid drinking taverna with lots of tapas and twelve international beers on draught.

Albaicín

Al Sur de Granada c/Elvira 150, near to the Moorish Puerta de Elvira arch. Great modern little bar-shop serving delicious cheese, ham and *salchichón* tapas. Each drink comes with a generous free tapa of its own and they often stage exhibitions of work by local artists.

Bar Aixa Plaza Larga. Welcoming bar with terrace tables serving up well-prepared tapas and *raciones*. Try their *migas* (breadcrumbs) stir-fried with crispy pork fat and green peppers or fresh anchovies.

Bar Caracoles Plaza Aliatar, slightly northeast of the Iglesia del Salvador. Popular and atmospheric tapas place, famous for its *caracoles* (snails).

Bar Lara Plaza San Miguel Bajo. A fine bar which puts out tables on this picturesque Albaicín square, and serves tapas, *platos combinados* and an excellent *costa* wine.

Paprika Cuesta de Abarqueros 5, close to *Al Sur de Granada* (above). Very popular place with a younger international crowd serving Asian-inspired tapas and informal snacks accompanied by laid-back sounds including jazz. Has a pleasant summer terrace.

Rincón del Aurora Plaza San Miguel Bajo 7. Another good bar with outdoor tables on this square. Try the *fritura* (fried fish) or *carne al la Rondeña*.

Campo del Príncipe and Carrera del Darro

Ajoblanco c/Palacios 17, close to the church of Santo Domingo. Charming, cosy bar with artistic cheese and pomegranate tapas.

Bar Candela c/Sta. Escolástica 1. A mixture of students and neighbourhood artists fill this Basque bar every night. Serves *jamón*, cheese and *chorizo* tapas.

Café-Bar Ocaña Plaza del Realejo 1, north of Campo del Príncipe. Bustling neighbourhood bar serving up great *bocadillos* with a very spicy tomato relish. The nearby *El Jergón*, off the same square's north side at Cuesta del Realejo 10, is also worth a visit and has a few vegetarian options on its tapas list.

Rabo de Nube Paseo de los Tristes 1 (aka Paseo del Padre Manjón). One of many terrace bars on this plaza – at the far end of the Carrera del Darro – and a wonderful place to sit out at night with a drink whilst gazing up at the Alhambra's illuminated battlements. This place serves *tablas* (paté and cheese boards) and pizza. The bar mounts frequent art and photo shows and the city council often puts on concerts in the plaza during the summer.

Taberna de Baco Campo de Principe 22. Economical Peruvian-run diner with tasty tapas including a celebrated *pastela* (Peruvian corn, beef and tomato pie).

University zone

Anaïs Café c/Buensuceso 13. Very pleasant literary-themed bar lined with books and newspapers and run by an ebullient Catalan.

Bar Lax c/Veronica de la Magdalena 31, a couple of blocks west of Plaza de la Trinidad. Pleasant Swedish bar serving – amongst others – salmon tapas and smorgasbord and with a small terrace on which to enjoy them.

Chupitería c/Pedro Antonio Alarcon 69. Popular shots bar that has a hundred selections listed on a board. If you can't choose one they'll make up your own poison. A dubious bonus here is that each shot purchased gets you a token that can be exchanged for prizes: 20 tokens gets you a T-shirt and 25 some underwear, but by then you'll be too smashed to know.

La Tertulia c/Pintor López Mezquita 3, slightly northeast of the bus station. Argentinian bar with some tapas and live tango on Tuesday nights (when they also have tango classes at 8pm).

Breakfast bars, tearooms and ice cream

Granada's **breakfast bars** set the city up for work in the mornings and to watch the best of them dishing up *pan tostada*, *chocolate* and *cafés exprés* with production-line efficiency is an entertainment in itself. The show begins all over town around 8am and lasts about an hour. You'll soon spot the best places – they're very busy – but a typical one is *Café Bib-Rambla* on the plaza of the same name which also serves up delicious *churros*. More leisurely breakfasts are to be had at *Café au Lait* and in the beautiful patio of *Pilar de Toro* on Plaza Nueva (see restaurant listings for both) where toast and coffee come surprisingly cheap considering the location. Late or early travellers might appreciate *Café Bar Ochando*, by the train station on Avenida de los Andaluces, open 24 hours and serving a good breakfast. For sit-down **cakes and pastries** later in the day, in the Albaicín you could try *Casa de los Pasteles* in Plaza Larga, or in the centre *Cafetería Lisboa*, at the corner of c/Elvira and c/Reyes Católicos, which turns out its own range of mouthwatering confections.

In the "Little Morocco" district in and around the calles Calderería Nueva and Calderería Vieja a large number of **teterías** or **teahouses** have sprung up to become a colourful part of the city's social scene. However, so many have climbed on the bandwagon in recent times that service and standards in some leave a lot to be desired. The friendly, Moroccan-run *As-Sirat* ("bridge between earth and paradise"), c/Calderería Nueva 5, is one of the oldest and offers eighty-plus teas in its Moorish-inspired interior. Nearby at no. 11 *Dar Ziryab* is another option which often stages live concerts of Middle-Eastern and North African music; its cultural centre offers classes in guitar and Maghrebi music. At the top of the hill, the multistoreyed *Pervane*, Calderería Nueva 24, is popular with a younger crowd. Also worth a try are *Kasbah* at the foot of Calderería Nueva, and *Tetería Tuareg*, c/Corpus Cristi 5, just off the foot of c/Calderería Vieja, where a cave-like interior recesses into candlelit gloom and teas are served along with *crepes* in summer and *pasteles* in winter. A more recent arrival here is *Repostería Morisca*, c/Calderería Vieja 12, a bakery selling Moroccan cakes, pastries and pies – try their *pastela*, a delicious spicy chicken- and egg-filled filo pastry.

The undisputed queen of Granada's **ice-cream** parlours is the popular *Los Italianos*, opposite the cathedral at Gran Vía 4, with excellent home-made ices: their *cassata* is recommended. The *helados* at *La Perla* (Plaza Nueva 16) are almost as good, and they certainly have the better location; try their refreshing *horchata* in summer. Both places also serve up the refreshing summertime *blanco y negro* – iced coffee with cinnamon-flavoured ice-cream. The *Café Football Heladería*, Plaza María Pineda, is another pleasant place, with tables on this leafy square; they also do good breakfast *churros* here.

Discobares and discotecas

Conventional **discotecas** aren't too popular with the restrained *granadinos*, though the university guarantees a bit of action during term time and particularly at weekends; **c/Pedro Antonio de Alarcón**, to the west of the centre, is where the action is and the stretch between Plaza Albert Einstein and Obispo Hurtado is the main focus. There are, as everywhere in Spain, a fair scattering of **discobares** – drinking bars with loud sound systems, trendy decor and a fashion-conscious clientele. Granada has a lively **gay scene** and visiting any of the gay and lesbian places mentioned overleaf is a good introduction to the scene.

4

Angel Azul c/Lavadero de Tablas 15, west of Plaza Trinidad. Along with the nearby *Tic Tac* (c/Horno de Haza 19) this is the most gay of Granada's gay bars with lots of action at weekends (Spanish language skills not required).

Babylon c/Silleria (between Plaza Nueva and Gran Vía). Reggae club – and popular pick-up venue – much favoured by US students.

Camborio Camino del Sacromonte s/n, Sacromonte. Fashionable *discobar* housed in a cave which is especially lively at weekends from about 4am. Other similar late-night venues run along the same street and are lots of fun in the early hours.

Entresuelo c/Azacayas, off Gran Vía. Popular *discobar* frequented by many of the city's English-language teachers. Also has twice weekly transvestite show.

Fondo Reservado c/Santa Ines 4, northeast of Plaza Nueva. Funky gay and straight bar with a hilarious drag show every weekend.

Granada 10 c/Carcél Baja 10, off Gran Vía near the cathedral. Small and popular central *discoteca* inside a beautifully restored retro cinema – which is what it still is before the dancing starts. Worth seeing a film first just to wallow around in its marvellously decadent gold lamé sofas.

La Estrella c/Cuchilleros near Plaza Nueva. Congested, smokey *discobar* with great sounds.

La Sal c/Santa Paula 11, off the west side of Gran Vía. Originally a lipstick lesbian dance bar, but now attracting gay males too.

Patapalo c/Naranjos 2, near the Puerta de Elvira. Stylish *discobar* appealing to a younger crowd.

Peatón Pub c/Socrates 25, off c/Pedro Antonio de Alarcón. Rock bar popular with a student crowd. Other lively places nearby include *Babel*, *Van Gogh* and *Genesis*.

Planta Baja Horno de Abad, off Carril del Picón and slightly northwest of Plaza de la Trinidad. Long-established *discobar* – garage is big here – now in a new home.

Quilombo c/Carril de San Cecilio 21, uphill from the Campo del Principe. With a pool table and big dance floor that get busy from around 3am. Sometimes stages live music.

Son c/Joaquín Costas 3, slightly west of Plaza Nueva. Ultra-cool two-level bar with older salsa scene upstairs and younger heavy-metal scene in the smokey (not tobacco smoke) downstairs.

Live music, theatre and dance

Like many cities of Andalucía, Granada lays claim to the roots of **flamenco**, though you'd hardly believe it from the travesties dished up these days in the gypsy quarter of Sacromonte (see box on p.546). The bus-'em-in "flamenco shows" on offer in the city aren't much better, either, being geared firmly to the tourist trade. However, up in the Albaicín there is one genuine *peña* (club; see below), with consistently good artists and an audience of aficionados, and we also list a number of other places that are reasonably authentic. Generally more rewarding are the **festivals** held throughout the year, such as the city's Theatre Festival at the end of May, or the International Music and Dance Festival at the end of June, during which you may just be lucky enough to see a performance under the stars in the Alhambra. Information on these events is available from any tourist office and tickets are sold at a kiosko on Acero del Casino, close to the post office on Puerta Real. Other concerts by folk, rock and flamenco artistes are staged throughout the year in locations such as the **Corral del Carbón** or Moorish patios in the Albaicín. Watch out for street posters, check listings in the local daily paper *Ideal* or the monthly *Guía de Granada*. There's also an annual **jazz festival** in October or November – the Turismo will have details.

Flamenco

Bar-Restaurante La Zeta c/Pages 10, Albaicín, a couple of blocks northwest of Plaza Larga (☎958 29 48 60). Stages frequent flamenco shows.

El Niño de los Almendras c/Muladar de Doña Sancha, at the junction with c/La Tiña and southeast of Plaza San Miguel Bajo, Albaicín. This tiny, unsigned bar – done up inside to resemble a cave – is owned by the flamenco singer of the same name. Only open Fri nights (starts around midnight), but there's unforgettable flamenco when it happens.

Los Faroles Sacromonte. Almost at the very end of the line of "caves" – ask anyone for directions as it's well known – this is a good place for a lunch-time or evening drink, with a view of the Alhambra from its terrace. The genial owner is a fount of information on flamenco and the impromptu real thing often happens here after dark.

Peña Platería Patio de los Aljives 13, Albaicín (☎958 21 06 50). Private club devoted to the celebration of Andalucía's great folk art. Flamenco is performed most nights (Thurs or Fri are your best chances; entry €7), and visitors are generally welcomed so long as they show a genuine interest and aren't in too large a group. You'll need to speak some Spanish and use a bit of charm. Closed Aug.

Jazz

Echevaria c/Postigo de la Cuna 2, a tiny alley off c/Azacayas which is off the east side of Gran Vía.

Jazz/flamenco bar which gets quite lively. Wed, Thurs and Sun nights only.

Jazz Café Bohemia c/Santa Teresa 17, west of Plaza de la Trinidad. Relaxed jazz bar with cool sounds and walls lined with photos and memorabilia.

Picaro c/Varela 10, near Plaza Mariana Pineda. Cool jazz bar with live bands two or three times a week (look for bright orange posters plastered to phone booths all over town). Not the chicest of *ambientes* but the music can be great and the crowd is always hip and fun.

Shopping

For clothing **accessories** and **jewellery**, Ocho y Media, c/San Matías 15, north off Plaza Mariana Pineda, sells a small but tasteful collection of local designer bags, jewellery and shawls. Artesanía El Suspiro, at Cuesta de Gomérez 45, on the way up to the Alhambra, has an interesting range of *granadino* **ceramics**, tiles and marquetry as well as *andaluz* foodstuffs and books on Granada-related themes. Castellano, meanwhile, c/Almireceros 6, between c/Elvira and Gran Vía, also caters to **food** and **drink** shoppers by being the best place to buy *jamón serrano* and also stocks regional wines and brandies. La Casa de Los Tés, c/Calderería Vieja s/n, sells herbs and spices, incenses and exotic teas plus foreign imports like peanut butter and veggie pâtés. La Alcena de Salinas, c/Almireceros 5 (near Castellano above), sells a wide range of wines and local deli products. La Oliva, c/Rosario 9, close to Plaza Mariana Pineda, is a wonderful shop specializing in the *gastronomía* of Andalucía (olive oil, wines, cheeses, honey) and the (English-speaking) owner will encourage you to sample before you buy. La Alcena, c/San Jerónimo 3, on the cathedral's north side, is a similar place specializing in the region's olive oil, wines and cheeses (try the *queso de almendras* made with almonds). Granada's branch of the El Corte Inglés department store is on the Acera del Darro, to the south of Puerta Real.

The main – and ultramodern – **market** is in Plaza San Agustín, just north of the cathedral (Mon–Fri early until 1.30pm). For a wide range of Moroccan/traditional Spanish fruits and groceries try c/Calderería Nueva and neighbouring c/Calderería Vieja. Encarni II is a recommended general store in the latter and La Tienda is an excellent health food store (at no. 8) in the former. Metro, c/Gracia 31, off c/Alhóndiga, to the southwest of Plaza de la Trinidad, is the best international **bookshop** with a wide selection of titles on Granada and Lorca, plus it has walking maps. Librería Atlantida, Gran Vía 9, has a wide selection of books, including a good array on aspects of Granada. **Foreign press** is sold by the kioskos in Plaza Nueva and Puerta Real. Festival Discos, c/San Sebastian 10, off the northeast corner of Plaza Bib-Rambla, is an excellent **CD** shop, stocking a wide range of Spanish music.

Listings

Airport Granada airport (☎958 24 52 00) handles domestic flights to Madrid and Barcelona, details from Iberia (☎958 24 52 37), as well as international and budget flights from the UK. Buses to the airport by Autocares González (☎958 49 01 64; nine on weekdays, eight

weekends; €3 one-way) run to the airport from a terminus by the Palacio de Congressos (with a central stop on Gran Vía near the Cathedral) and take 30min.

Banks Numerous banks and ATMs are available along c/Reyes Católicos and Gran Vía.

Bathhouses Following in the footsteps of Hammam (see p.545) a number of similar bathhouses have opened based on the principle of a traditional *hammam* using Moorish-inspired decor and providing services such as massage. A good one is Aljibe Baños Árabes, c/San Miguel Alta 41, southwest of Plaza de la Trinidad (T958 52 28 67; reservation required), charging €12.50 for a basic soak.

Bullfights Held in season at the Plaza de Toros, Avda. Dr Olóriz, in the northern suburbs (T958 27 24 51).

Bus departures See "Arrival" for details of the bus terminal. For information on bus services and current timetables check with the companies, which are all – except for the service to Viznar – based at the bus station. Alsina Graells (T958 18 50 10, Wwww.alsinagraells .es) for Almería, Alpujarras (high and low), Córdoba, Jaén, Málaga, Motril, Úbeda, Sevilla and the coast. Empresa Autedia (T958 40 06 01, Wwww .maestra-autedia.com) for Baza and Guadix. Autocares Bonal (T958 46 50 22) for Veleta and the north side of Sierra Nevada.

Camping and hiking equipment Deportes de Aire Libre, c/Paz 20, just southeast of Plaza de la Trinidad (T958 52 33 61), is a good outdoor pursuits shop selling climbing, camping and trekking gear. Armería, c/Mesones 53 (off the same plaza), is similar.

Car rental ATA, Plaza Nueva (T958 22 40 04) are a reliable local outfit who undercut the big boys. Atesa, Avda. Andaluces s/n, near the train station (T958 28 87 55, Wwww.atesa.es), has reasonable deals with national back-up.

Consulates UK, Carmen de San Cristóbal, Ctra. de Murcia s/n (T958 22 47 24).

Football C.F. Granada are another of Andalucía's clubs plodding along in the basement divisions of the football league. After a few dismal seasons, the club is desperately trying to regain its Segunda División "B" status. The stadium, Nuevo los Cármenes (T958 25 33 00, Wwww.granadacf .com), lies northwest of the Hospital Real.

Hiking maps Maps of the Sierra Nevada and Las Alpujarras can be obtained from the Turismo,

though for a more specialist selection try Cartografica del Sur, c/Valle Inclán 2, southwest of the train station in the university zone (T & F958 20 49 01), which sells a wide range, including military maps. The CNIG (National Geographic Institute), c/ Divina Pastora 7, by the Jardines del Triunfo (T958 29 04 11), also sells 1:50,000 and 1:25,000 maps. See also the Metro bookshop.

Hospital Cruz Roja (Red Cross), c/Escoriaza 8 (T958 22 22 22), or Hospital Clinico San Cecilio, Avda. Dr Olóriz, near the Plaza de Toros (T958 02 03 00). In an emergency call T061.

Internet *Net*, Plaza de los Girones 3, near the Casa de Los Tiros (Mon–Fri 9am–11pm, Sat & Sun 10.30am–11pm; T958 22 69 19), is Granada's most efficient online operation. They have another branch at c/Buen Suceso 22, close to Plaza de la Trinidad. Other central Internet cafés open daily include *Navegaweb*, c/Reyes Católicos 55 (daily 10am–11pm, T958 21 05 28), *Punto Com*, Plaza de la Trinidad 2 (daily 10am–midnight, T958 53 56 01), *Seven*, c/Lavadero de la Cruz 23 (Mon–Fri 10.30am–11pm, Sat & Sun 5.30–10pm) and *Madar Internet*, c/Calderería Nueva 12 (Mon–Fri 10am–midnight, Sat & Sun noon–midnight; T958 22 94 29).

Laundry Lavandería Duquesa, c/Duquesa 24, near the church of San Jerónimo (Mon–Fri 9.30am–2pm & 4.30–9pm, Sat 9.30am–2pm; T958 28 06 85), is very efficient and will wash, dry and fold 4kg the same day for €10. Lavandería La Paz, c/La Paz 19, just west of Plaza de la Trinidad, has similar hours and prices.

Left luggage There are lockers at both train and bus stations as well as a *consigna* (left luggage office) at the latter.

Police For emergencies dial T091 (national) or T092 (local). The Policía Nacional are located at c/Duquesa 15 off Plaza de la Trinidad (T958 27 83 00). The Policía Local station is in the Ayuntamiento building on Plaza del Carmen (T958 24 81 00). There is also a property lost-and-found section in the same building (T958 24 81 03).

Post office Puerta Real: Mon–Fri 9am–8pm, Sat 9am–2pm.

West towards Málaga: Alhama de Granada

Travelling from Granada to Málaga by bus will take you along the fast but dull A92 *autovía*, which crosses the *vega* to the west of the city. With your own transport and time to spare, a more interesting and scenic route passes through the delightful but little-visited town of **Alhama de Granada** and traverses the spectacular **Zaffaraya Pass**, descending into Málaga by way of the ruggedly beautiful **Axarquía** region.

Leave Granada by the route for Motril and the coast, along the N323 – but avoid the *autovía*. At Armilla, 4km southwest of the city, follow the A338 which branches right, towards the village of **La Malá** (which has a fine roadside *venta*), and, 10km beyond, **Ventas de Huelma** where *Luciano* is another excellent *venta* stop. From here the road twists and climbs into the Sierra de la Pera and, after descending to the lakeside village of **Poblado del Embalse** – where there's a good **campsite**, *Los Bermejales* (☏958 35 91 90), with pool and restaurant – continues through a rich landscape of bubbling streams and rocky gulches overlooked by hills planted with olives, to Alhama de Granada, 14km further.

Alhama de Granada

Scenically sited along a ledge overlooking a broad gorge or *tajo* created by the Río Alhama, the spa town of **ALHAMA DE GRANADA** is one of the unsung gems of Granada province and makes a wonderful overnight stop. It has a couple of striking churches in a well-preserved old quarter, and its baths, dating back to Roman and Moorish times (Al Hamma in Arabic means "hot springs"), still draw in numerous visitors to take the waters. They were greatly treasured during Moorish times, and the Spanish expression of regret "¡Ay de mi Alhama!" was the cry of sorrow attributed to Abu al-Hacen (the Mulhacen after whom the Sierra Nevada peak is named) when he lost the town in a crucial battle here against the Christian forces in 1482. It was this loss that severed the vital link between Granada and Málaga (and hence North Africa), foreshadowing the end of eight centuries of Moorish rule. Settlement started here much earlier, however, and the ancient Iberian town on the site was referred to by the Romans as Artigi.

The Town

Most of Alhama's sights are within a short walk of Plaza de la Constitución, the main square fronted by bars and restaurants. At the square's northern end there's a ruined and now privately owned **Moorish castle** with the unfortunate addition of nineteenth-century crenellated battlements. Heading east alongside the castle, the sixteenth-to-eighteenth-century **Iglesia del Carmen** (8–9.30pm) is Alhama's prettiest church, overlooking the **Tajo** and fronted by an old fountain where the farmers water their donkeys on sultry summer evenings. Just off to the right here, with its back to the Tajo, is Artesanía Los Tajos, c/Peñas 34, selling local ceramics as well as some remarkable traditional clay water-whistles called *canarios*. Once used by local shepherds and goatherds, they make an ear-splitting racket, as the proprietor will eagerly demonstrate.

To reach the other monuments backtrack slightly to c/Baja Iglesia which leads up to Plaza los Presos, passing en route (up a ramp to the left) the **Casa de la Inquisición**, which may have nothing to do with the Inquisition at all but is noted for a fine Plateresque facade. The town's main church, **La Encarnación** (Tues, Thurs & Sat noon–2pm; €1), dominates the Plaza de los Presos, a pleasant little square with a central fountain. Donated by Fernando and Isabel after the conquest of the town from the Moors, the church was completed in the first half of the sixteenth century by some of the major architects of the time – among them Enrique Egas and Diego de Siloé, the designers of the Capilla Real and cathedral at Granada. Siloé was responsible for the striking and massive

4

Richard Ford and the Handbook for Spain

Very few books have been written about Spain that do not draw on **Richard Ford** and his 1845 *Murray's Handbook for Spain* – arguably the best, the funniest and the most encyclopedic guidebook ever written on any country.

Born in 1796 into a family of means, Ford studied law but never practised and in 1824 married Harriet Capel, the attractive daughter of the earl of Essex. When she received medical advice to seek a warmer climate for her health, Ford – inspired by Irving's recent publication of the *Conquest of Granada* – took his family off to Spain where they lived for three years, wintering in Sevilla and spending the summers living in part of the Alhambra in Granada.

Ford spent most of his time traversing the length and breadth of the country – but particularly Andalucía – on horseback, making notes and sketches. It's hard to believe that all this was not meant for some literary purpose, but it was only back in England – and six years after his return – when publisher John Murray asked him to recommend someone to write a Spanish travel guide, that Ford suggested himself.

His marriage now broken, he settled in a Devon village in a house to which he added many Spanish features (including some souvenirs from the Alhambra) to work solidly for nearly five years on what became the *Handbook for Spain* (see "Books" p.688). When Murray and others took exception to the final manuscript's often caustic invective, he was advised to tone it down and a revised – but still gloriously outspoken – edition finally appeared in 1845 to great acclaim. Curiously, although he became *the* resident expert on Spain, he never returned to the country which had put him on the literary map.

Ford's blind spots, such as British prejudice against Baroque architecture (the more extravagant styles of which he dismissed as "vile Churrigueresque"), are often irritating, and High Tory attitudes sometimes verging on jingoism, added to a splenetic francophobia, often threaten to tip over into the worst kind of churlishness. However, the author's enduring fascination with Spain and all things Spanish – he personally introduced *amontillado* sherry and Extremaduran *jamón serrano* into England – allied to a crisp writing style and a dry wit, invariably save him, and some of his passages are still hilariously funny and related with a wry irony. His description of the hostelry at Alhama is typical:

The *posada* at Alhama, albeit called *La Grande*, is truly iniquitous; diminutive indeed are the accommodations, colossal the inconveniences; but this is a common misnomer, *en las cosas de España.* Thus Philip IV was called El Grande, under whose fatal rule Spain crumbled into nothing; like a ditch he became greater in proportion as more land was taken away. All who are wise will bring from Málaga a good hamper of eatables, a bota of wine, and some cigars, for however devoid of creature comforts this grand hotel, there is a grand supply of creeping creatures, and the traveller runs risk of bidding adieu to sleep, and passing the night exclaiming, *Ay! de mi, Alhama.*

Renaissance belfry which towers above the town. The restrained interior has an impressive *artesonado* ceiling and the *sacristía* has fifteenth-century vestments with embroidery attributed to Isabel herself.

Opposite the church, on the same square, is an ancient **posito** (granary) dating from the thirteenth century but incorporating parts of an earlier synagogue. Just downhill from here the sixteenth-century **Hospital de la Reina**, c/Vendederas s/n (open daily except Sun & Mon), was the first building of this kind to be built in the kingdom of Granada. Leaving the square to the right of the church along c/Alta Iglesia takes you past the misleadingly named **Casa Romana** on the right, an eighteenth-century mansion believed to have been constructed on the site of a Roman villa. The same street returns to the Plaza Mayor.

Alhama's only other site of note is a well-preserved first-century BC Roman **bridge** at the edge of the town, close to the A338 to Granada, a short distance along the road to the *balneario* (baths). Beyond here, a (signed) twisting road leads 1km to the **baths** which give the town its name. Although little remains of the Roman baths seen by Ford in the nineteenth century, elements of the Moorish *hammam* survive and can be seen by enquiring at the *Hotel Balneario* (guided visits daily 2–4pm; €1) whose staff will conduct you into the depths to see some astonishing Moorish arches and the odd stone inscribed in Latin.

Practicalities

The **Turismo**, at Paseo Montes Jovellar s/n (April–Sept Mon–Fri 10am–2pm, Oct–March Mon–Fri 9.30am–3pm; ☎958 36 06 86, ⓦwww.turismodealhama .org), below the Plaza de la Constitución can provide maps and information on walking in the area.

On the **accommodation** front things have improved immeasurably since Ford was here (see box opposite) and the dreaded *La Grande* is no more. If you want to stay, outside August there's usually no problem fixing up a room at ⚸ *La Seguiriya*, c/Las Peñas 12 (☎958 36 08 01, ⓦwww.laseguiriya.com; ❹ with breakfast; reductions for longer stays), a charming *hospedería rural* and restaurant fifty metres uphill off the main square. Housed in an eighteenth-century house with fine views over the Tajo, the friendly proprietor is a retired flamenco *cantante*, and the en-suite rooms are appropriately named after flamenco styles. They also offer various outdoor activities including hiking, canoeing and mountain biking. Just up from the main square and housed in a refurbished old *casa palacio*, *Hospedería Casa Sola*, c/Alta de Mesones 17 (☎958 35 01 12; ❸ with breakfast), is a possible alternative. A cheaper option is *Hostal San José*, Plaza de la Constitución 27 (☎958 35 01 56; ❷), right on the main square, with some en-suite rooms. On the square in the lower town, a pleasant new arrival is the sparkling *Hostal Ana*, Ctra. de Granada 8 (☎958 36 01 08; ❸), for a/c en-suite rooms with TV. An attractive rural alternative is the *Hotel El Ventorro*, 3km out of town on the Málaga road (take the turn-off for Játar),

△ Alhama de Granada

fronting a lake (℡958 35 04 38; ❹ with breakfast) with a decent restaurant. Continuing further along the Málaga road, the *Hotel Los-Caños de la Alcaicería* (℡958 35 03 25; ❹ with breakfast) lies 10km from town with rooms above a restaurant; features include a pool, its own bullring and outdoor activities. A more upmarket option is the spa hotel *Balneario de Granada* (℡958 35 00 11, ⓦwww.balnearioalhamadegranada.com; ❻), at the baths 1km off the road into town from Granada which, although situated in dense pine woods, has the ambience of a sanatorium.

The main square, Plaza de la Constitución, has plenty of **places to eat** with terraces – *Mesón Diego* is worth a try for the usual standards – but the town's best restaurant is that of *La Seguiriya* (see above) where specials include *lomo con ciruelas pasas* (pork with prunes) and *atún a la roteña* (tuna). *Bar Ochoa* (off the main square and slightly uphill from *Hostal San José*) serves up tasty **tapas**. Down in the lower town *Mesón Raya*, next door to *Hostal Ana*, is a popular restaurant and has a daily €7 *menú*. Alhama has a **swimming pool** with shade just out of town along the Málaga road.

Towards the Zaffaraya Pass

South of Alhama, the A335 climbs towards Ventas de Zaffaraya – passing a great value *venta*, San Marcos La Alcaicería, 10km out – cutting through a rich agricultural area where tomatoes, cereals and other vegetables are grown. The spectacular **Zaffaraya Pass**, which slips through a cleft in the Sierra de Tejeda and was part of the old coach route, provides a dramatic entrance into the Axarquía region of Málaga Province, with superb **views** to the distant Mediterranean. Roughly 6km beyond the pass lies the deserted medieval village of **Zalía**, after which the road continues to **Vélez-Málaga** and the coast.

The Sierra Nevada National Park

Southeast from Granada rise the mountains of the **SIERRA NEVADA**, designated Andalucía's second **national park** in 1999, a startling backdrop to the city, snowcapped for most of the year and offering skiing from November until late May. The ski slopes are at **Solynieve**, an unimaginative, developed resort just 28km away (40min by bus). Here, the direct car route across the range stops, but from this point walkers can make the relatively easy two- to three-hour trek up to **Veleta** (3394m), the second highest peak of the range and the second-highest summit on the Spanish peninsula.

Before the road was constructed in the 1920s few *granadinos* ever came up to the sierra, but one group who had worn out a trail since the times of the Moors were the *neveros* or icemen, who used mules to bring down blocks of ice from the mountains, which they then sold in the streets. Their route to Veleta can still be followed beyond **Monachil**, to the southeast of the city, a pleasant village on the Río Monachil, which is well worth a visit. There's a nice place to stay (see p.533) and Ride Sierra Nevada (℡958 50 16 20, ⓦwww.ridesierranevada.com), in the centre of the village, organize all kinds of outdoor pursuits in the zone including mountain biking, horse riding, climbing and hiking in the spectacular Los Cahorros gorge; they can also provide information on renting *casas rurales* and cave dwellings for longer stays. The village is connected by frequent buses to Granada running from the terminal at the Paseo del Salón. The main A395 road, though, has been a mixed blessing for the delicate ecosystem of the Sierra, and the expanding horrors of the Solynieve ski centre, which was chosen to hold the 1995 World Ski Championships (subsequently cancelled due to lack of snow and then held in 1996), has only made things worse.

The best general **map** of the Sierra Nevada and of the lower slopes of the Alpujarras is the one co-produced by the Instituto Geográfico Nacional and the Federación Española de Montañismo (1:50,000). Not far behind is the Editorial Alpina's Sierra Nevada (1:40,000) map which has the bonus of a booklet (with an English edition) describing fourteen hikes in the Sierra as well as useful background information on the zone. The CNIG's 1:25,000 sheets are more detailed for trekking purposes, and all three can be obtained in Granada (see "Listings" p.561).

Inside the park, to report any **emergencies** such as forest fires, stranded hikers or personal injuries there's a coordinated emergency service contactable on ☎112; the park's Guardia Civil unit can be reached on ☎062. Weather forecasts (in English) are available on ☎906 36 53 65.

Solynieve and the Veleta/Mulhacén ascent

Throughout the year Autocares Bonal runs a **daily bus** from Granada to the Solynieve resort and, just above this, to the *Albergue Universitario* (see p.568). It leaves Granada bus station at 9am, returning from the *Albergue Universitario* at 4.30pm (and passing Solynieve 10 minutes later). For the winter service (Oct–March) ring the bus company (see Granada "Listings") or check with any Turismo. Tickets to Solynieve (€7 round trip) should be bought in advance at the bus station, although you can pay on board if the bus is not full.

The route leaves Granada via the Paseo del Salón (with a bus stop should you wish to pick it up here) where two wagons stand as a memory to the tram service which, from the 1920s until 1970, used to ascend as far as Güejar Sierra. Beyond Pinos de Genil the road begins to climb seriously and, after 28km, the ski resort of **Solynieve** appears.

With **your own transport** take the Acera del Darro south from the Puerta Real and follow the signs for the Sierra Nevada. Once on the ascent to the mountains the road is dotted with alpine-style **eating places** which do good business in season. Some 16km out, a signed turn on the right leads – after 3km – to *Camping Ruta del Purche* (☎958 34 04 07) the only **campsite** in these parts, with a restaurant and pool and which also rents out en-suite log cabins (●). After some 17km you could make a stop at the **Balcón de Canales** with fine views over the Río Genil and its dam. At the 22km mark and signposted just off the road is the **"El Dornajo" Sierra Nevada National Park Visitors' Centre** (daily 10am–2pm & 4–6pm; ☎958 34 06 25, ⓦwww.mma.es/parques),

---

The Sierra Nevada's flora and fauna

The Sierra Nevada is particularly rich in **wild flowers**. Some fifty varieties are unique to these mountains, among them five gentians, including *Gentiana bory*, the pansy *Viola nevadensis*, a shrubby mallow *Lavatera oblongifolia*, and a spectacular honey-suckle, the seven- to ten-metre high *Lonicera arborea*.

Wildlife, too, abounds away from the roads. One of the most exciting sights is the *Cabra hispanica*, a wild horned goat which you'll see standing on pinnacles, silhouetted against the sky. They roam the mountains in flocks and jump up the steepest slopes with amazing agility when they catch the scent of the walker on the wind. The higher slopes are also home to a rich assortment of **butterflies**, among them the rare Nevada Blue as well as varieties of Fritillary. **Bird-watching** is also superb, with the colourful hoopoe – a bird with a stark, haunting cry – a common sight.

which sells guidebooks, maps and hats (sun protection is vital; see below), has a permanent exhibition on the park's flora and fauna, provides hiking information (English spoken), and rents out horses and mountain bikes. The centre also has a pleasant **cafetería** with a stunning terrace **view** beyond the ancient tram parked in a garden behind.

Solynieve

SOLYNIEVE ("Sun and Snow", aka Pradollano) is a hideous-looking ski resort – worse than usual – and regarded by serious alpine skiers as something of a joke. But with snow lingering so late in the year (Granada's Turismo should be able to advise on the state of this, or contact Sierra Nevada Club's interactive phone line on ☎958 24 91 19 or visit ⓦwww.sierranevadaski.com) it has obvious attractions for *granadinos* and others determined to ski in southern Spain. From the middle of the resort a lift takes you straight up to the main ski lifts, which provide access to most of the higher **slopes**, and when the snow is right you can ski a few kilometres back down to the *zona hotelera* (the lifts run only when there's skiing). There are plenty of places to rent gear. If you intend to ski (or walk) here be sure to double your **skin protection** as this is the most southerly ski centre in Europe with intense sun at high altitudes. Visiting Solynieve in high summer is a surreal experience as it's almost a ghost town with only the odd shop or bar open and a vast, central plaza – teeming with crowds sporting multicoloured ski-suits in winter – eerily empty.

The Turismo at Granada can advise on **places to stay** at the resort (many hotels open only during the ski season) or contact the Sierra Nevada Club (☎958 24 91 11, ⓦwww.sierranevada.es). The cheapest accommodation is the modern and comfortable *Albergue Juvenil*, c/Peñones 22 (☎958 48 03 05, ereservas.itj@junta-andalucia.es; open all year), on the edge of the ski resort, where you can get good-value double (April–Oct; ❸) and four-bed studios and apartments, all en suite. They also rent out skis and equipment in season when room prices increase significantly. Other places in the resort proper are incredibly **expensive** in season, with even the cheapest doubles priced in our ❺ category. Heading higher, 3km away in isolated Peñones de San Francisco is another attractive option: the *Albergue Universitario* (☎958 48 01 22, ⓦwww.nevadensis.com; ❷ with breakfast; ❹ in ski season), just off the main road where the bus drops you, has bunk rooms, doubles and a restaurant. It's a stunning location for exploring the national park but without transport extremely isolated, which may, of course, be just what you're looking for. The bus (which only runs beyond the ski resort in summer) turns around at the *Albergue* and this marks the start of the Veleta ascent.

The Capileira road, Veleta and Mulhacén

The ascent of **Veleta** is a none-too-challenging hike rather than a climb but should only be attempted between May and September – unless you're properly geared up – but even then you'll need warm and waterproof clothing. From the parador the **Capileira-bound road** – now permanently closed to traffic to protect the Sierra's delicate environment – actually runs past the peak of Veleta. Recently asphalted – somewhat removing the sense of adventure from the trek – it is perfectly, and tediously, walkable (bikes are allowed but it's a fierce climb). However, most hikers follow the well-worn shortcuts between the snakes the road is forced to make. With your own transport it's possible to shave a couple of kilometres off the total by ignoring the no-entry signs at the car park near to the *Albergue Universitario* and continuing on to a second car park further up the mountain from which point the road is then barred. Although the peak of

Ruta Integral de los Tres Mil

The classic **Ruta Integral de los Tres Mil**, a complete traverse of all the Sierra's peaks over 3000m high, starts in Jeres del Marquesado on the north side of the Sierra Nevada (due south of Guadix) and finishes in Lanjarón, in the Alpujarras. It's an exhausting three- to four-day itinerary described in detail in Andy Walmsley's book *Walking in the Sierra Nevada* (see "Books" p.698). For any serious exploration of the Sierra Nevada, essential equipment includes a tent, proper gear and ample food. It's a serious mountain where lives have been lost so come prepared for the eventuality of not being able to reach (or find) the refuge huts, or the weather turning nasty.

the mountain looks deceptively close from here you should allow two to three hours to reach the summit and one and a half hours down. Make sure to bring **food and water** along as there's neither en route and a picnic at the summit is one of the best meals to be had in Spain, weather permitting.

With a great deal of energy you could conceivably walk to Capileira, though it's a good 30km, there's nothing along the way and temperatures drop pretty low by late afternoon. En route, an hour beyond Veleta, you pass just under **Mulhacén** – the tallest peak on the Iberian peninsula at 3483m. The climb is two hours of exposed and windy ridge-crawling from the road, and with a sudden, sheer drop on its northwest face. There is a gentler slope down to the Siete Lagunas valley to the east.

Las Alpujarras

The N323 road south from Granada to Motril crosses the fertile *vega* after leaving the city and then climbs steeply until, at 850m above sea level, it reaches the **Puerto del Suspiro del Moro** – the Pass of the Sigh of the Moor. Boabdil, last Moorish king of Granada, came this way, having just handed over the keys of his city to the Reyes Católicos in exchange for a fiefdom over the Alpujarras. From the pass you catch your last glimpse of the city and the Alhambra. The road then descends and beyond Padul crosses the valley of Lecrín planted with groves of orange, lemon and almond trees, the latter a riot of pink and white blossom in late winter. To the east, through a narrow defile close to Béznar, lie the great valleys of **Las Alpujarras** – "the Switzerland of Spain" as Ford described them – first settled in the twelfth century by Berber refugees from Sevilla, and later the Moors' last stronghold.

Walkers' guides to the Alpujarras are now beginning to mushroom and useful recent publications include Charles Davis's *34 Alpujarras Walks*, Jeremy Rabojohns' *Holiday Walks in the Alpujarras* and *GR142: Senda de la Alpujarra* (in Spanish) by Francisco Jiménez Richarte; there are also half a dozen Alpujarras treks in *Andalucía and the Costa del Sol* by John and Christine Oldfield and an equal number in Guy Hunter-Watts' *Walking in Andalucía* (see "Books" in Contexts for details of all these publications).

Some history

The valleys are bounded to the north by the Sierra Nevada, and to the south by the lesser *sierras* of Lujar, La Contraviesa and Gador. The eternal snows of the high *sierras* keep the valleys and their seventy or so villages well watered all summer long. Rivers have cut deep gorges in the soft mica and shale of the

LAS ALPUJARRAS

Láujar de Andarax

Bayárcal

C-331

Alto de
San Juan
3781m

Cherín

Hirmes

Lucainena

Laroles
Mairena

GR431

Mecina
Alfahar

Ugíjar

Emb. de
Benínar

Turón

Valor

Yegen

A348

Cojáyar

Múrtas

Arroyo de Valor

Yátor

Jorairáto

N

Cerro
Vacares
3149m

Mulhacén
3483m

Siete
Lagunas

Las
Angosturas

Mecina
Bombarón

Cádiar

A345

Albondón Albuñol

Pico
Veleta
3394m

Prado
Llano
2579m

Bérchules

GR421

Juviles

Cástaras

SIERRA DE LA CONTRAVIESA

Trévelez

Busquístar

Capileira

Pórtugos

Mecina
Fondales

Almegíjar

Torvizcón

A348

Albondón Albuñol

High road to Granada
permanently
closed to vehicles

Pitres
Ferreirola

Solynieve

Caballo
3013m

Bubión
Pampaneira

Los
Tablones

Carataunas

Albondón Albuñol

PARQUE NATIONAL

DE SIERRA NEVADA

Sopórtujar

Órgiva

Pico de
la Carne
1886m

Monachil

2079m

Cáñar

Guadalfeo

L451

Vélez Benaudalla & Motril

Monachil

La Zubia

Cumbres
Verdes

Lanjarón

A348

Lanjarón

1524m

Nigüelas

Dílar

Suspiro
del Moro
860

Padul

Dúrcal

Lecrín

Restábal

Saleres

Piños del
Valle

N-323

Guájar
Alto

Guájar
Faragüit

Albuñuelas

Granada

10 km

0

upper mountains, and over the centuries have deposited silt and fertile soil on the lower hills and in the valleys; here the villages have grown, for the soil is rich and easily worked. The intricate terracing that today preserves these deposits was begun perhaps as long as two thousand years ago by **Visigoths** or **Ibero-Celts**, whose remains have been found at Capileira.

The **Moors** carried on the tradition, and modified the terracing and irrigation in their inimitable way. They transformed the Alpujarras into an earthly paradise, and there they retired to bewail the loss of their beloved lands in al-Andalus. After the fall of Granada, many of the city's Muslim population settled in the villages, and there resisted a series of royal edicts demanding their forced conversion to **Christianity**. In 1568 they rose up in a final, short-lived revolt, which led to the expulsion of all Spanish Moors. Even then, however, two Moorish families were required to stay in each village to show the new Christian peasants, who had been marched down from Galicia and Asturias to repopulate the valleys, how to operate the intricate irrigation systems.

Through the following centuries, the villages fell into poverty, with the land owned by a few wealthy families, and worked by peasants. It was one of the most remote parts of Spain in the **1920s**, when the author Gerald Brenan settled in one of the eastern villages, Yegen, and described the life in his book *South from Granada*, and things changed little over the next forty-odd years. During the **Civil War**, the occasional truckload of Nationalist youth trundled in from Granada, rounded up a few bewildered locals, and shot them for "crimes" of which they were wholly ignorant; Republican youths came up in their trucks from Almería and did the same thing. In the aftermath, under Franco, there was real hardship and suffering, and in the **1980s** the region had one of the lowest per capita incomes in Spain, with – as an official report put it – "a level of literacy bordering on that of the Third World, alarming problems of desertification, poor communications and high under-employment".

Ironically, the land itself is still very fertile – oranges, chestnuts, bananas, apples and avocados grow here, while the southern villages produce a well-known dry rosé wine, *costa*. However, it is largely the recent influx of **tourism** and foreign purchase of houses and farms that has turned the area's fortunes around, bringing pockets of wealth and an influx of new life to the region.

The so-called **High Alpujarras** – the villages of **Pampaneira**, **Bubión** and **Capileira** – have all been scrubbed and whitewashed and are now firmly on the tourist circuit, as popular with Spanish as foreign visitors. Lower down, in the **Órgiva area**, are the main concentration of expatriates – mainly British, Dutch and Germans, seeking new Mediterranean lives. Most seem to have moved here permanently, rather than establishing second homes (though there are houses for rent in abundance), and there's a vaguely alternative aspect to the new community, which sets it apart from the coastal expats. In addition to property owners, the area has also attracted groups of British New Age travellers. The locals, to their credit, seem remarkably tolerant of the whole scene.

Approaches to the Alpujarras

From Granada, the most straightforward **approach to the Alpujarras** is to take the Lanjarón turning – the A348 – off the Motril road. Coming from the south, you can bear right from the road at Vélez de Benaudalla and continue straight along the A346 to Órgiva, the market town of the western Alpujarras. There are several **buses** a day from both Granada and Motril, and one a day from Almería, to Lanjarón and Órgiva. One operated by Alsina Graells (℡958 18 54 80) direct to the High Alpujarras, via Trevélez as far as Bérchules, leaves the main Granada bus station at noon and 5.15pm daily: in the other direction it leaves Bérchules at 5.20am or 5.05pm, passing Trevélez half an hour later, to arrive in Granada at 8.45am or 8.45pm respectively. There's also a service from Granada to Ugíjar in the Low Alpujarras, via Lanjarón, Órgiva, Torvizcón, Cádiar, Yegen and Valor, currently departing at 8.30am and 6pm; this takes a little over four hours to the end of the line. The return journey from Ugíjar currently runs at 5.45am and 3pm. There are also nine buses daily between Granada and Órgiva (three via Lanjarón) and vice versa, and three daily buses link with Pampaneira, Bubión, Capileira and Pitres.

Lanjarón

LANJARÓN has known tourism and the influence of the outside world for longer than anywhere else in the Alpujarras due to the curative powers of its **spa waters**. These gush from seven natural springs and are sold in bottled form as mineral water throughout Spain. Between March and December, when the spa baths are open, the town fills with the aged and infirm and the streets are lined with racks of herbal remedies, all of which imparts a rather melancholy air. This might seem good reason for passing straight on to the higher villages, though to do so would be to miss out on some beautiful local walks, and a town centre that, now a new bypass has removed much of the traffic, grows on you. Should you wish to try a cure at the **Balneario**, a basic soak will cost about €12 with add-ons for massage, mud baths, pressure showers and all kinds of other alarming-sounding treatments such as *drenajes linfáticos* and *pulverizaciones faríngeas*.

Like so many spa towns Lanjarón is Roman in origin, though today the place is largely modern, with a ribbon of buildings flanking its pleasant, tree-lined main thoroughfare, split into three sections running west to east: Avenida de Andalucía, Avenida de La Alpujarra and c/Real. Below this, and beyond the town's new bypass, marking Lanjarón's medieval status as gateway to the Alpujarras, is a Moorish **castle**, now dilapidated and barely visible. It was here on March 8, 1500, that the Moorish population made its final heroic stand against the Christian troops under the command of Fernando. Pounded by artillery, hundreds died as the town was taken. A ten-minute stroll reveals its dramatic setting – follow the signs downhill from the main street and out onto the terraces and meadows below the town.

Lanjarón puts on a stirring **Semana Santa** – one of the best in the province, and worth going out of your way to see if you're in the area.

Practicalities

Lanjarón has no tourist office but Union Travel, Avda. de Andalucía s/n, operates a municipal **information kiosk** (Mon–Tues & Thurs–Sun 10am–2pm & 4.30–8.30pm; ☎958 77 02 82), opposite the Balneario on the right coming in from Granada, which can provide basic information. Midway along the main street is the Alsina Graells **bus terminal** (☎958 77 00 03). **Internet** access is available at Cyberplay Lanjaron, Avda. de Andalucía 30, near the La Caixa bank (daily except Wed 6pm–midnight).

Accommodation

Due to the Balneario, there's no shortage of **places to stay** in town, most along the main road. In high summer it's essential to book ahead, while in winter many places close in January and February. Also note that evening temperatures stay low here well into late spring; the places listed opposite in category ❸ and above have central heating.

Bar Galvez c/Real 95 ☎958 77 07 02. Cheapest rooms in town above a bar with good-value meals. ❶

Hostal El Dólar Avda. de Andalucía 5 ☎958 77 01 83. Pleasant, simple and inexpensive *hostal* with mountain-view en-suite rooms and friendly proprietor. Open April–Nov only. ❶

🏃 Hotel Castillo Alcadima c/Francisco Tarrega 3, down a signed turn-off from the main street ☎ 958 77 08 09, ⓦwww.alcadima.com. Not to be confused with the *Hotel Castillo Lanjarón* next door, this excellent hotel is not only the cheaper option but has the best pool and best restaurant terrace in town. Many of the comfortable rooms have stunning balcony views towards the castle and guests may use a small gym. They also have a number of two-bedroomed family suites. ❹–❺

Hotel El Sol Avda. de La Alpujarra 30 ☎ & ⓕ958 77 01 30, ⓦwww.hotelelsol.com. Good-value choice if you're here in winter or early spring as there is reliable heating in these apartments. Guests also have use of sauna and Jacuzzi. ❹

Hotel España Avda. de La Alpujarra 42 ☎ & ⓕ958 77 01 87, ⓦwww.lanjaron.biz. Grand-looking, good-value hotel near the Balneario which has played host to such luminaries as García Lorca and Manuel de Falla in its time. Friendly staff, good rooms, own bar and restaurant plus a pool. Spring and autumn offers here get you full board for €28 per person. ❹

Hotel Miramar Avda. de Andalucía 10 ☎ & ⓕ958 77 01 61. For a step up in price you can enjoy the relative luxury of the town's top hotel where a/c rooms come with safe and (some) a balcony. It also has a bar, restaurant, pool, garden and garage. ❺

Hotel Nuevo Palas Avda. de La Alpujarra 24 ☎ & ⓕ958 77 01 11, ⓦwww.hotelnuevopalas.com. Pleasant hotel with a/c rooms, rooftop pool, gym and – in the bar – pool tables. ❹

Hotel Paris Avda. de La Alpujarra 23 ☎958 77 00 56, ⓕ958 77 03 74. A charming and very good-value recent arrival to the main street; rooms come with TV and there's a good-value restaurant and pool. ❸

Venta El Buñuelo 1km from the centre along the Órgiva road ☎958 77 01 81. Refurbished and revitalized roadside *hostal-restaurante* where en-suite rooms come with great views and there's easy parking. ❷

Eating and drinking

Plenty of **bars and restaurants** line the Avenida de Andalucía and many of the hotels and *hostales* have good-value meals and tapas, too – especially the hotels *España* and *El Sol*. Best choice for dining out, however, has to be the terrace restaurant of the *Hotel Castillo Alcadima* which is a pretty well perfect place to while away a summer evening with a superb terrace view of the castle and a *menú* for €13. *Bar Galvez* (see "Accommodation") is a good choice if you're on a tighter budget. At the main street's eastern end *Café-Bar Health*, c/Señor la Expiración s/n is a new arrival serving breakfasts and full meals with many vegetarian options and often has live music in the evenings. Continuing out of town brings you to *Venta El Buñuelo* (see above), another place for good low-priced *alpujarreño* cooking with a weekday *menú* for €7. The more expensive *El Club* at Avda. de Andalucía 18 specializes in Alpujarran dishes with a *menú* for €10. For seafood, try *Los Mariscos*, Avda. de Andalucía 6, also with a €10

Walks from Lanjarón

The countryside and mountains around Lanjarón are spectacularly beautiful. Wander up through the backstreets behind the town and you'll come across a track that takes you steeply up to the vast spaces bordering on the Reserva Nacional de la Sierra Nevada.

For a somewhat easier day's **walk** go to the bridge over the river just east of town and take the sharply climbing, cobbled track which parallels the river. After two to two and a half hours' walk through small farms, with magnificent views and scenery, a downturn to a small stone bridge lets you return to Lanjarón on the opposite bank. Allow a minimum of six hours for a leisurely expedition. The town produces a **leaflet** – *Turismo Activo in Lanjarón* – detailing more walks, which should be available from the information kiosk.

menú. Nearby, the justly popular *Jamones Gustavo Rubio*, Avda. de Andalucía 38, is worth a visit for its excellent tapas bar behind a shop selling the wines, *jamones* and other local products.

On the Avenida de Andalucía's main "square", midway between the Balneario and the church, lies Lanjarón's celebrated *churrería*, claimed by some to sell the best home-made potato crisps in Andalucía, opposite which are a couple of good ice-cream parlours. Almost next door to the *churrería*, *Noche Azul* is a popular **nightclub**.

Órgiva (Órjiva)

Heading east out of Lanjarón brings you after 7km to a turn-off for Las Barreras, notable for a new **campsite**, *Puerta de la Alpujarra* (☏958 78 44 50) with its own shop, bar and restaurant and panoramic views; it also rents out wood-cabin bungalows (❹) sleeping up to four. Three kilometres further lies **ÓRGIVA**, the market centre of the western Alpujarras. It's a lively little town, with a number of good bars and hotels, and an animated **Thursday market**, when everyone from miles around turns up with something to sell or buy, a drum to beat, a guitar to strum and a bowl to fill with euros. The contrast between the time-worn *campesinos* and their pack-mules, and some of the foreign New Age travellers who seek their indulgence and charity, is as bizarre as anything this side of Madrid. Many of the New Agers here inhabit a **tepee village**, *El Beneficio*, on the edge of town where a polyglot community of mainly northern Europeans and their offspring endure freezing winters under canvas.

Órgiva's other sights line the main street: the sixteenth-century Baroque **church** of Nuestra Señora de la Expectación, whose towers add a touch of fancy to the townscape, and a crumbling Moorish **palace** that today houses various shops.

Órgiva comes to life with its **annual fiesta** on September 24 and 25 when the population doubles as prodigal sons and daughters all return to join in the fun. A more eccentric festival is the **Dia del Señor** on the second Thursday before Easter. Opening with a terrifying salvo of rockets, this fiesta went disastrously wrong a few years back when the bank's windows were blown in. On the Friday morning all the town's womenfolk attack the church until they are able to make off with the effigy of El Señor (Christ), which is then paraded around town accompanied by great displays of emotion – not to mention more rocketry.

Practicalities

Daily **buses** from the Alsina Graells stop on Avenida González Robles, run east across the Alpujarras to Ugíjar, and up to all the High Alpujarran villages; the latter service is the Granada bus, which passes through Lanjarón at 9.45am and 7.30pm and Órgiva thirty minutes later. If you're **driving**, note that Órgiva is the last stop for filling up before Cádiar or Ugíjar. Viajes Eolo, c/González Robles 6 (☏958 78 55 89), is a useful source of travel and other information for this zone and also offers **car rental** at competitive rates with delivery to Málaga or Granada airports; it can also arrange **taxis** to and from the same airports. **Internet** access is available at the nearby *Ciber Ocio*, c/González Robles 13 (daily 10am–2pm & 6–10pm) and there's a useful noticeboard for locals and visitors in the nearby wholefood shop Herbolario La Alacena; both places are over the road from the *Pensión Alma Alpujarreña* (below).

Órgiva has a fair choice of **accommodation**. Just beyond the traffic lights at the town's main intersection, the pretty, economical and friendly *Pensión Alma*

Alpujarreña (☎958 78 40 85, Ⓦwww.hostalalma.com; ❷) has rooms (some single) with and without bath, plus a restaurant beneath a vine trellis. Good en-suite rooms are also on offer at *Hostal Mirasol*, c/González Robles 3, on the way in from Lanjarón (☎958 78 51 59; ❷); they also have a slightly more upmarket hotel (❸) next door. Slightly further out from here the new *Hotel Puerta Nazari*, Carretera Tablate Albuñol s/n (☎958 78 49 52, Ⓦwww.puertanazari.com; ❹ with breakfast) is a more luxurious option with a/c balcony rooms and its own bar-restaurant. Near the main junction, the charming ⚘ *Casa Rural El Molino*, c/González Robles 12 (mobile ☎646616628, Ⓦwww.casaruralelmolino.com; ❹ with breakfast), is the most attractive in-town option offering excellent rooms in a refurbished old olive mill, with pleasant patio and pool. An inviting place to stay with your own transport is the rural *Hotel Taray* just over a kilo-metre along the A348 south of the town (☎958 78 45 25, Ⓦwww.hoteltaray .com; ❺); it's surrounded by lovely gardens with a superb pool and has a decent restaurant. The town's **campsite**, *Camping Órgiva* (☎958 78 43 07) 2km south of the centre beyond the *Hotel Taray*, has a pool and also rents out cabins (❷), bungalows (❹), *casas rurales* (sleeping up to six; ❻) and a tree house; it has its own restaurant and pool and can advise on walking routes and renting horses in the nearby Sierra de Lújar.

For **eating** and **drinking**, good places include *Agustín*, at the top of the town in c/Alcalde Jesús Moreno, for tapas, and the nearby and economical *Baraka*, c/Estación 12, a pleasant small Moroccan café and *tetería* offering felafel, cous-cous, tagines and a variety of teas. Near the church, *Bar Santiago*, in c/García Moreno, has a wide selection of beers and wines plus you get to choose your own (free) tapa with each drink – a bonus for vegetarians. *La Almazara*, almost next door to the *Pensión Alma Alpujarreña*, does freshly made pizzas plus more elaborate fare and has a garden terrace. Close by and on c/Gonzáles Robles, *Braserie El Patio* serves up excellent tapas and has good-value lunch and dinner *menús*. On the way out of town towards Torvizcón, *Bar Mirasierra* is where a certain (now famous, but then unknown) writer wrote most of his work about life on a nearby Alpujarras hill farm; it's a fine airy place serving up decent tapas and *raciones*. For full meals the *Pensión Alma Alpujarreña* (see above) has a decent kitchen and serves a good-value *menú* for €8.50. The *Hostal Mirasol* (see above) also does good tapas and offers a rather *menú* for €7.50 inside or on their terrace, and the restaurant of the *Hotel Taray* (see above) is also worth a try. For coffee and cakes there's *Café Galindo Plaza* on the square, and *Pastelería Gerardo*, c/Lora Tamayo 20 (near *Bar Mirasierra* above), sells excellent confectionery and is renowned for its fresh-from-the-oven bread.

The High Alpujarras: Órgiva to Capileira

From Órgiva, you can reach the High Alpujarran villages by car or bus, or you could walk – the best way to experience the region. There is a network of paths in this zone, though to avoid getting lost it's wise to equip yourself with a compass and the *Instituto Geográfico Nacional/Federación Española de Montañismo* 1:50,000 **map**, which covers all the territory from Órgiva up to Berja. A reasonable knowledge of Spanish is also invaluable.

At their best, Alpujarran **footpaths** are remnants of the old Camino Real, the mule routes which crossed Spain, and are engineered with cobblestones, and beautifully contoured, alongside mountain streams, through woods of oak, chestnut and poplar, or across flower-spangled meadows. In their bad moments they deteriorate to incredibly dusty firebreaks, forestry roads or tractor tracks, or (worse) dead-end in impenetrable thickets of bramble and nettle. Progress is

High Alpujarras hikes: the highlights

Rewarding **hikes** in the High Alpujarras include:

Pitres to Mecina Fondales: Twenty minutes' hike to Mecina Fondales, and then a good hour-plus from neighbouring Ferreirola to Busquístar.

Busquístar toward Trevélez: One hour's hike, and then two-plus hours of road walking.

Pórtugos toward Trevélez: Two hours, meeting the tarmac a little beyond the end of the Busquístar route.

Trevélez to Berchules: Four hours, with the middle two hours on a dirt track.

Trevélez to Juviles: Three hours, including some sections of firebreak.

slow, gradients are sharp and the heat (between mid-June and Sept) is taxing. Over the past few years part of the path network through the High Alpujarras has been upgraded as the final section of the **European long-distance footpath** that begins in Athens and ends in Algeciras. Designated as footpaths E4 or GR7 in Spain, the full route is now waymarked (in theory – you'll still need a good map where the posts are missing or misplaced) with red and white ringed posts and each village along the route – 23 of them between Lanjarón and Bayárcal – should carry a special symbol on its nameplate. Maps detailing the footpath should be available from tourist offices and Ayuntamientos along the route.

Cañar, Soportújar and Carataunas

Following the high road from Órgiva, the first settlements you reach, almost directly above the town, are the isolated but pretty **CAÑAR** – at the end of a sinuous 5km drive off the main road – and **SOPORTÚJAR**, a maze of picturesque white-walled alleys bridged by numerous *tinaos* (see box, opposite). Like many of the High Alpujarran villages, they congregate on the neatly terraced mountainside, planted with poplars and laced with irrigation channels. Both have **bars** where you can get a meal, and Soportújar can provide excellent-value en-suite **rooms** for the night; ask at the friendly *Bar Correillo* (☏958 78 75 78; ❷) on c/Real (behind the church); they will also do *platos combinados* on request. Perched precariously on the steep hillside, both villages share a rather sombre view of Órgiva in the valley below, and on a clear day the mountains of North Africa over the ranges to the south. Each village has a sixteenth-century church, both of which fell into a terrible state of disrepair at the end of the last century, and both of which, thankfully, have now been refurbished and saved.

Just below the two villages, the tiny hamlet of **CARATAUNAS** is particularly attractive, and puts on a lively start to its Semana Santa on Palm Sunday, when an effigy of Judas is tossed on a bonfire.

The Poqueira Gorge

Shortly beyond Carataunas the road swings to the north after passing the turnoff to the Buddhist monastery of Osel Ling (see p.578), and you have your first view of the **Gorge of the Poqueira**, a huge gash into the heights of the Sierra Nevada. Trickling deep in the cleft is the Río Poqueira, which has its source near the peak of Mulhacén. The steep walls of the gorge are terraced and wooded from top to bottom, and dotted with little stone farmhouses. Much of the surrounding country looks barren from a distance, but close up you'll find that it's rich with flowers, woods, springs and streams. A trio of spectacular

Alpujarran architecture

Alpujarran **village houses** are unlike any others in Spain – though they are almost identical to Berber houses across the straits in the Rif mountains of Morocco, where many of the Moorish refugees settled. They are built of grey stone, flat-roofed and low; traditionally they are unpainted, though these days *cal* (whitewash) – a luxury until recent times – is increasingly common. The coarse walls are about 75cm thick, for summer coolness and protection from winter storms. Stout beams of chestnut, or ash in the lower valleys, are laid from wall to wall; on top of these is a mat of canes, ilex or split chestnut; upon this flat stones are piled, and on the stones is spread a layer of **launa**, the crumbly grey mica clay found throughout the area, which is made waterproof when pressed down.

The *launa* must – and this maxim is still observed today – be laid during the waning of the moon (though not, of course, on a Friday) in order for it to settle properly and thus keep rain out. Gerald Brenan wrote in *South from Granada* of a particularly ferocious storm: "As I peered through the darkness of the stormy night, I could make out a dark figure on every roof in the village, dimly lit by an esparto torch, stamping clay into the holes in the roof."

Another feature peculiar to the Alpujarras are the **tinaos**, a kind of portico or bridge that enables access from a dwelling in one row to another in an upper or lower row. In summer, time is passed on the roof terrace or *terrao*, especially once the sun has cooled in early evening. Bubión, Capileira and Pitres all have good examples of the traditional architectural style.

---

villages – Pampaneira, Bubión and Capileira – teeter on the steep edge of the gorge among their terraces. They are, justifiably, the most touristy villages in the region and a bit over-prettified, with craft shops and the like, but nonetheless well worth it as is some walking on the local mule paths. A number of fine **walking routes** are detailed with maps in *Landscapes of Andalucía and the Costa del Sol* (see Books in Contexts).

Pampaneira and the Tibetan monastery

PAMPANEIRA, the first of the Poqueira villages, is a neat, prosperous place, and a bit less developed and spoilt than its neighbours. Around its main square are a number of bars, restaurants, *hostales* and craft shops, one of which, just down the hill, is a weaving workshop that specializes in traditional Alpujarreño designs. For **rooms**, near to the **bus stop** there's the homely *Hostal Pampaneira* (☏958 76 30 02; ❷) at c/José Antonio 1, with some en-suite rooms and, for a bit more comfort, the *Hostal Ruta del Mulhacén*, Avda. de *alpujarra* 6 (☏958 76 30 10, ⓦwww.rutadelmulhacen.com; ❸), which has balcony rooms with bath and central heating.

Off the main square (see below) at the heart of the village *Hostal Barranco del Poqueira* (☏958 76 30 04, Ⓔjamonesnarciso@yahoo.com; ❹) is another decent place offering en-suite rooms with terrace and TV, plus fine views. If you have difficulty locating it enquire at *Restaurante Narciso* on the square. For **food** the *Hostal Pampaneira* has its own (good) restaurant, while also worth considering is *Casa Julio*, up some steps nearby. On the main square, the leafy Plaza de la Libertad, *Bar Belezmín* is one of the village's best places to eat with a menu filled with hearty local dishes; the nearby *Casa Diego* is another possibility with a terrace and *menú* for €9.

Also on Plaza de la Libertad you'll find Nevadensis (Tues–Sat 10am–2pm & 5–7pm, Sun & Mon 10am–3pm; ☏958 76 31 27; ⓦwww.nevadensis .com; English spoken), a private, efficiently run **information centre** for the

National Park of the Sierra Nevada. As well as providing information, they sell large-scale topographical maps of the zone, walking guidebooks and a leaflet in English (€1.50) detailing a trekking route through the Poqueira valley. They also organize themed guided walks in all seasons and offer organized activities and excursions including mountain biking, climbing, canyoning, hiking, and cross-country skiing. If you're thinking of a longer stay, this is also where you can pick up a list of hostels, village houses, and farmhouses for rent throughout the Alpujarras.

Above Pampaneira, on the very peak of the western flank of the Poqueira gorge in a stunning location, is the small Tibetan Buddhist **Monastery of Osel Ling** (Place of Clear Light) founded in 1982 by a Tibetan monk on land donated by the communities of Pampaneira and Bubión. Three years later, in 1985, a baby born to Spanish parents in Granada was recognized by the Dalai Lama as the reincarnation of the former head lama – one Yeshé – and the youth is currently undergoing training under the Dalai Lama in the Himalayas. The simple stone-built monastery complete with stupas and stunning **views** across the Alpujarras welcomes visitors between 3 and 6pm daily; lectures and courses on Buddhism are held regularly and facilities exist for those who want to visit for periods of retreat in simple cabins dotted around the site (☎958 34 31 34 for details). The monastery is reached by a track on the left – signed "camino forestal" – 1km east of the turning to Soportujar. Should you encounter difficulty locating it, enquire at Nevadensis (see above) or *Rustic Blue* (see Bubión account below) who will set you right.

Bubión

BUBIÓN is next up the hill, backed for much of the year by snowcapped peaks. Lacking the focus of a main square, it's probably the least attractive of these high villages but – perhaps because of this – it certainly seems the most peaceful. The tranquillity may not last long, though, if the property developers have their way and already there is quite a bit of building taking place on the lower slopes. Towards the end of August, Bubión celebrates its **Fiestas Patronales** with music, dance, fireworks and copious imbibing.

Plentiful **accommodation** includes a fancy apart-hotel built along traditional lines, the *Villa Turística de Bubión*, Barrio Alto s/n (☎958 76 39 09, ⓦwww .villabubion.com; ❺), where detached dwellings come with four-star facilities including a restaurant and a small pool. Less ostentatiously, there's a comfortable *pensión*, *Las Terrazas*, Plaza del Sol 7 (☎958 76 30 34, ⓦwww.terrazasalpujarra .com; ❷), with en-suite rooms with views. *Los Tinaos*, downhill at c/Parras s/n (☎958 76 32 17, ⓦwww.lostinaos.com; ❸–❹), offers some excellent apartments which come with garden terrace, kitchen, satellite TV and fine views. Signs around the village will lead you to cheaper rooms in private houses and more apartments for longer lets.

For **food** a couple of bars serve up tapas and *raciones*, and a very good restaurant, *La Artesa*, at c/Carretera 2, turns out *alpujarreño* specialities with a *menú*. *Teide*, just over the road, is another good place for solid mountain cooking. The restaurant of the *Villa Turística* (see above) is also worth a try, and is noted for its *plato alpujarreño* consisting of *papas a lo pobre*, fried eggs, ham, *longaniza* and *morcilla* (both sausages). Also of note is the pleasant *Monfi Café Morisco*, c/Pérez Ramón 2 in the lower village, serving teas and a North African inspired menu featuring couscous on a charming terrace; it also has **Internet** screens.

A private **information office**, Rustic Blue (Mon–Fri 10am–2pm & 5–7pm, Sat 11am–2pm, ☎958 76 33 81, ⓦwww.rusticblue.com; English spoken), at the entrance to the village on the right, is a useful source of local knowledge and stocks maps and walking guides to the area as well as organizing week-long guided treks and horse-riding tours. It can also provide information on renting apartments and houses (minimum seven days) throughout the Alpujarras. The village has a number of ranches for **horse riding** in the Alpujarras, offering a couple of hours (around €25) or one- to five-day trips in groups

△ Bubión

with a guide; the friendly *Rancho Rafael Belmonte* (☏958 76 31 35, ⓦwww
.ridingandalucia.com) at the bottom of the village near Rustic Blue, *Cabalgar*,
c/Ermita s/n (☏958 76 31 35) or Dallas Love (☏958 76 30 38) are the places
to contact. La Boutik de la Montaña, c/Alcalde Juan Perez Ramón 3, just below
the main road, is a good place to get hold of **climbing** and **trekking** gear and
clothing.

Capileira

CAPILEIRA is the highest of the three villages and the terminus of the road
– Europe's highest, but now closed to traffic – across the heart of the Sierra
Nevada from Granada. A picturesque and tranquil place, except in high summer
when it is deluged with visitors and coach tours, Capileira makes a fine walking
base from which to explore the Poqueira Gorge, or you could even strike out
for Trevélez about five hours to the northeast.

Just downhill from the kiosko (see "Practicalities") lies the village's
museum (Tues–Sun 11.30am–2.30pm; €1), containing displays of regional
dress and handicrafts as well as various bits and pieces belonging to, or
produced by, Pedro Alarcón, the nineteenth-century Spanish writer, born
in Guadix, who made a trip through the Alpujarras and wrote a (not very
good) book about it. On the Sunday prior to August 5, Capileira embarks
on its annual **romería** to the summit of Mulhacén and the *ermita* of the
Virgen de las Nieves.

Practicalities

There are daily **buses** to Capileira from Granada (see "Travel details", p.634).
Buses out of Capileira to Órgiva and Granada currently leave at 6.30am,
4.15pm and 6.15pm. The kiosko (daily 9am–2pm & 5–8pm) at the centre of
the village near where the bus drops you sells newspapers, large-scale walking
maps, hands out a free village **map** and acts as an **information** office.

Among several **places to stay**, on the way into the village on the right *Hostal
Atalaya* (☏958 76 30 25; ❷ with breakfast) has pleasant en-suite rooms with
views. Just beyond the kiosko where the bus drops you, 🛉 *Mesón-Hostal Poqueira*,
c/Dr Castilla 11 (☏ & ⓕ958 76 30 48; ❷), has good-value en-suite heated
rooms, with terrace and TV, plus – in its restaurant – one of the best-value set
menús in the mountains. *Hostal Paco Lopez* (☏958 76 30 11; ❷) also near the bus
halt has pleasant en-suite rooms with balcony views plus a few bargain apartments (❸) nearby. Continuing uphill along the same road the more upmarket
Finca Los Llanos (☏958 76 30 71, ⓦwww.hotelfincaloslllanos.com; ❺) has traditional-style rooms in a garden setting with pool. *Ruta de Las Nieves* (☏958 76 31
06; ❷–❹) higher up the same road has rooms with bath and heating and a few
good-value apartments. Some 500m beyond this (and signed up a track on the
left), another delightful hideaway, *Cortijo Catifalarga* (☏958 34 33 57, ⓦwww
.catifalarga.com; ❹), has charming rooms inside a traditional *alpujarreño cortijo*,
along with fabulous views. Should you desire even more solitude then continue
along the mountain road for a further 3km, turning right along a signed track
to *Cortijo Prado Toro* (☏958 34 32 40, ⓦwww.pradotoro.com; ❻), at an altitude
of 1500m with spectacular views and where there is very comfortable accommodation in restored mountain dwellings.

All the above have **restaurants** or tapas bars attached, and places like *Paco
Lopez*'s restaurant offer good value *menús* for around €10. *Restaurante El Tilo*, on
the focal Plaza Calvario in the lower village, is a decent place for *platos combinados* or watching-the-world-go-by drinks on its tranquil terrace shaded by a lime
tree. Downhill from here *Bodega La Alacena*, Callejon de las Campanas s/n, is a

popular option for ham and cheese tapas and its shop also sells local products. Near the museum (see above) *Casa Ibero*, c/Parra 1 (open all day weekends, weekdays open evenings only), is the place to find vegetarian dishes among the couscous (recommended), Indian and other adventurous concoctions emerging from its kitchen. Close to *Hostal Paco Lopez*, one place with an interesting ambience is the *Panjuila*, Barranco de Poqueira 24, where in addition to a *menú* filled with *alpujarreña* specialities, there's often the possibility of flamenco performances, especially at weekends.

The Poqueira Gorge

Capileira is a handy base for easy day walks in the **Poqueira Gorge**. For a not-too-strenuous ramble, take the northernmost of the three paths below the village, each of which spans bridges across the river. This one sets off from alongside the Pueblo Alpujarreño villa complex and winds through the huts and terraced fields of the river valley above Capileira, ending after about an hour and a half at a dirt track within sight of a power plant at the head of the valley. From here, you can either retrace your steps or cross the stream over a bridge to follow a dirt track back to the village. In May and June, the fields are tended laboriously by hand, as the steep slopes dictate.

A number of reasonably clear paths or tracks also lead to **Pampaneira** (2–3hr; follow the lower path to the bridge below Capileira), continuing to **Carataunas** (a further 1hr, mostly road) and **Órgiva** (another 45min on an easy path) from where – if you time it right – you can get a bus back.

In the other direction, taking the Sierra Nevada road and then the first major track to the right, by a ruined stone house, you can reach **Pitres** (2hr), **Pórtugos** (30min more) and **Busquístar** (45min more). Going in the same direction but taking the second decent-sized track (by a sign encouraging you to "conserve and respect nature"), **Trevélez** is some five hours away. More skilled, equipped and ambitious climbers may wish to attempt the summit of **Mulhacén**, the peninsula's highest peak at 3483m, achievable in a day from Capileira, but perhaps more sensibly done over two days with an overnight stop at the *Refugio Poqueira* (☎958 34 33 49; open all year but book in advance) at the head of the Poqueira valley.

Further along the High Route to Trevélez and Cádiar

The High Route continues east from Pampaneira through **Pitres** and **Pórtugos** before making a great loop to Trevélez, Spain's highest permanent settlement. From there, the road drops down to a junction, with a crossing to **Torvizcón**, on the south side of the Alpujarras, and east to the valley and village of **Cádiar**.

Pitres

PITRES is far less picturesque and less developed than the trio of high villages to its west and, like its equally unpolished neighbour, Pórtugos, offers more chance of rooms during high season. All around, too, spreads some of the best Alpujarran walking country.

Currently the only en-suite room option here is the *Hotel San Roque*, c/Cruz 1, on the east side of the village (☎958 85 75 28; ❹), offering pleasant rooms with (on the south side) views. Nearby on the opposite side of the road, the *Refugio Los Albergues* (☎958 34 31 76; ❶) is an old Civil War hostel rustically refurbished to provide dormitory beds (there's one double room; ❶), but outdoor toilets. It's signposted from the main road, but if you get lost ask for Casa Barbara (Hauck), the name of the friendly German who runs it. There's use of a library and kitchen to cook organic veg from an extensive garden. Pitres's **campsite**, the *Balcón de Pitres* (☎958 76 61 11; March–Oct), lies in a stunning position just out of town to the west, with a swimming pool and great views; it also rents out a few *casas rurales* (phone for details). Its charming little **restaurant** serves Alpujarran specialities such as *solomillo de cerdo* (sirloin of pork) and *cordero rellena* (stuffed shoulder of lamb). You may also be lucky enough on Saturday or Sunday nights here to stumble on an authentic and memorable mountain flamenco session.

For **food**, you have a choice between the bars on the village's main square and the campsite (above) or, on the village's eastern edge, the *Hotel San Roque* with its own restaurant. Near to here, *El Jardín* (March–Sept) is a British-run restaurant with garden terrace, great views and an eclectic vegetarian *menú*.

Pórtugos, Mecina Fondales, Ferreirola and Busquistar

PÓRTUGOS is equally rustic and its centre has a couple of **places to stay**, including the pleasant *Hostal Mirador* (☎958 76 60 14; ❷), on the main square with en-suite rooms and its own decent **restaurant**. Don't bother with the *Hotel Nuevo Malagueño* on the main road, whose rooms and restaurant are overpriced.

Down below the main road are a trio of villages – **MECINA FONDALES**, **FERREIROLA** and **BUSQUÍSTAR** – which along with Pitres and Pórtugos and a couple of smaller settlements formed a league of seven villages known as the **Tahá** (from the Arabic "Tá" meaning obedience) under the Moors. These are among the most unspoilt of the Alpujarra *pueblos* where you can find plenty of examples of typical regional architecture (see box on p.577). Ferreirola and Busquístar – the latter a huddle of grey *launa* roofs – are especially attractive, as is the path between the two, clinging to the north side of the valley of the Río Trevélez. You're out of tourist country here and the villages display their genuine characteristics to better effect.

For **accommodation**, Mecina Fondales has the very pleasant upmarket *Hotel Albergue de Mecina* (☎958 76 62 41, ⓦwww.hoteldemecina.com; ❺), a delightful hideaway with an excellent garden pool – and passed on the Tahá walk (see box) – where you can also hire horses and mountain bikes. The hotel has its own restaurant, but the best place for **food** here is at the French-run ⚡ *L'Atelier* (☎ & Ⓕ958 85 75 01), a restaurant specializing in vegetarian/vegan cuisine, located in the old village bakery at c/Alberca s/n. Booking is advised at weekends.

Nearby Ferreirola has the delightful Scandinavian-run *Sierra y Mar*, c/Albaycin 3 (☎958 76 61 71, ⓦwww.sierraymar.com; ❹ with breakfast), with fine views and where the owners – enthusiastic walkers – will advise on routes in the area; guests also have use of a kitchen to prepare their own food. To get there, take the road to the right of the fountain out of the main plaza.

Another option hereabouts is the recently refurbished inn, the *Alcázar de Busquístar* (☎ & Ⓕ958 85 74 70; ❹), which lies just uphill from the church in Busquístar, has one of the best views in the Alpujarras, a decent **restaurant** with vegetarian possibilities and squeezes in a pool. It's also well sited for a hike up to Trevélez and beyond and the proprietor, a *montañero* (hill climber), can advise on this and other trekking routes in this zone. Another good option for tapas and *raciones* here is *Bar Paco*, just below the main road as you pass through the village.

A circuit of the Tahá villages – with many fine stopping places for a picnic – is a good introduction to the Alpujarras, offering opportunities to appreciate both typical architecture and landscape within a compact area. The following walk around the **Southern Tahá** is an easy two-hour hike, although you'll probably want to take the diversion down to the picturesque Trevélez Gorge which adds another half-hour or so; allow three hours for the full circuit. There's little shade on parts of the route, so avoid the afternoon sun in summer. Remember that the second (uphill) part of the walk is the most strenuous.

The route starts in **Pitres**. Follow the narrow path, which begins as a concrete driveway curving behind *Restaurante La Carretera* (on the main road to the right as you enter the village) and descends southwards – veering left – to **Mecinilla**, which is soon visible below; you should be aiming for the left of the church tower. Ignoring turnings, after fifteen minutes or so, you emerge in the upper part of the village (Mecilla). Cross the main Pitres–Ferreirola road into the lower village (Mecinilla), following the road past the *Hotel Albergue de Mecina* (with a decent tapas bar and restaurant) and the church on the left. Just after the *Bar El Aljibe* (on the left), go through a gap and take an immediate right. After a drinking fountain (marked "1964"), turn left; continue downwards through the narrow streets, eventually leaving the village beneath a *tinao* (see box p.577). Initially following the edge of a ravine, the path continues downwards through orchards (crossing the road once but continuing clearly a little to the right) until reaching the maze of narrow, white streets that make up **Mecina–Fondales** – this should take another half-hour or so. Take your time here, partly as it's one of the most peaceful and least spoilt villages, but also as the maze of streets makes it easy to get lost and the vociferous dogs zealously guarding their patches can be off-putting; ask for directions if you can.

From here, for the **shorter route**, take the Camino Real towards Ferreirola, a well-maintained mule track leaving the centre of the village heading east. For the **longer route**, head to the wash area known as "La Fuente" in the village's southeast corner – veer downhill to the left from the road to pass beneath an elaborate *tinao* topped by a vine trellis – to reach the five-basined wash place. From here take the track descending towards the river, bearing left where there's any confusion. After a while the gushing waters become audible below, and the path emerges high above the gorge with the Trevélez bridge visible ahead. Immediately before the bridge, turn left up a small path which crosses the Río Bermejo, before climbing steeply over rocks (ignore the right-hand fork) and continuing uphill to **Ferreirola**.

In Ferreirola, head for the church square; close by is another wash place. Take the path rising north alongside it which, after another steepish climb, leads to **Atalbéitar**. The path actually emerges on the road below the village from where you turn left to continue the walk, but first you should visit Atalbéitar, another unspoilt hamlet, well off the usual tourist trail. Leaving the village, passing a lifeless oak tree and rubbish container on the right, turn left as the road bends to the right and follow this track in the direction of Pitres (now visible above) past a few houses. The path twice briefly joins the "road" (more of a dirt track); each time, take the path to the left where the road bends right. Leaving the track the second time, just before it joins the "main road", the path first skirts the Bermejo Gorge but then drops sharply to cross the river – some welcome greenery here hides the bridge until you're close to it. Across the river, the path climbs to an *acequia* (irrigation channel); turn right here and continue along the wooded path, past the *Albergue*, till emerging on the main road slightly to the east of **Pitres**.

Trevélez

The cut into the mountain made by the Río Trevélez – sadly, rather polluted on its lower reaches – is similar to the Poqueira, but grander and more austere. **TREVÉLEZ** village stands on a flank at the end of the ravine and its altitude – this is Spain's highest conurbation – makes it a cool place even in high summer when many of the inhabitants continue to don sweaters and coats. It's built in traditional Alpujarran style, with a lower and two upper *barrios* overlooking a grassy, poplar-lined valley where the river starts its long descent. The upper *barrios* (*alto* and *medio*) are probably the most pleasant places to stay as the lower (*barrio bajo*) is more touristy and filled with stalls and shops selling *jamones*, crystals, earrings and herbal remedies all attracting streams of visitors, especially at weekends. There are fine walks in the valley and you can swim, too, in a makeshift pool by the bridge.

Trevélez is traditionally the jump-off point for the high **Sierra Nevada** peaks (to which there is a bona fide path) and for treks across the range (on a lower, more conspicuous track). The latter begins down by the bridge on the eastern side of the village. After skirting the bleak Horcajo de Trevélez (3182m), and negotiating the Puerto de Trevélez (2800m), up to which it's a very distinct route, it drops down along the north flank of the Sierra Nevada to Jerez del Marquesado.

In late spring and summer (when the mountain snows have retreated) you might want to try a trip on horseback to **Las Siete Lagunas**, a spectacular collection of mountain lakes in a valley on the upper slopes of the mighty Monte Mulhacén. It's a five-hour journey each way and you spend a night on the mountain at an altitude of 3000m; you'll need your own sleeping bag and it's possible to pitch a tent at Siete Lagunas, although this is not essential. The highpoint of the trip is the sun rising above the Sierra de Gador in the east. The trips are organized by Rutas de Caballo Virgen de Las Nieves, c/Puente s/n, in the *barrio alto* (☎958 85 86 01; Spanish only) and cost €70 per person (meals included). They also do shorter trips (a couple of hours or a half-day; €10 per hr). Note that a little Spanish would help (although this is not a major problem) and that no insurance cover is provided, so check your policy.

Practicalities

The village is well provided with **places to stay**, in both the lower and upper squares, and with *camas* advertised over a few bars; if you are susceptible to low temperatures, outside July and August you may want a place with efficent heating. In the *barrio medio* the pleasant and welcoming *Hostal Fernando*, c/Pista del Barrio Medio s/n (☎958 85 85 65; with heating; ❷), offers rooms with bath and great terrace views (from some rooms); it also lets out some excellent-value apartments with kitchen and terrace (❸). Beside the Ayuntamiento in the *barrio alto*, the ⚓ *Hotel La Fragua*, c/San Antonio 4 (☎958 85 86 26, ⓦwww .hotellafragua.com; ❷–❸), is probably the most luxurious of the village places with pine-furnished, en-suite, heated rooms with more fine views; there's also an excellent and good-value restaurant. It's a popular place with walking groups so may be worth ringing ahead. In the *barrio bajo Hostal Regina*, Plaza Francisco Abellán 12 (☎958 85 85 64, Ⓔhregina@supercable.es; ❷–❸), has heated rooms, some with bath and views, and the friendly *Hotel Restaurante Alvarez* (☎958 85 85 03; ❸) next door is also good. Also in the lower *barrio, Hostal Mulhacén*, Ctra. Ugíjar s/n (☎ 958 85 85 87; with heating; ❷–❸), 100m along the Juviles road from Plaza Francisco Abellán, is another pleasant possibility for rooms with and without bath, and offers more great views down the valley. Perhaps the most attractive place of all to stay in this zone is out of

Moorish Andalucía

The arrival of the Moors from North Africa in the eighth
century ushered in one of the most brilliant periods in
Spanish architectural history. Over the next seven hundred
years they constructed a vast array of imposing edifices
– from fortresses and watchtowers to palaces and mosques –
particularly in the Moorish heartland of Andalucía, culminating
in the astonishing Alhambra in Granada. Moorish influence
extended beyond great monuments, however, into other
areas of local life, from irrigation to domestic architecture.
Andalucía today would be a very different place indeed
without the contribution of the Moors.

Andalucía's Moorish monuments

The Mezquita see p.431 ◄

The **Mezquita** or Great Mosque of Córdoba is the architectural apex of the Cordoban Caliphate and one of the great buildings of the Middle Ages. From its commencement in 784 it grew in magnitude and magnificence climaxing in the tenth century with the addition of a spectacularly ornate **prayer niche** (mihrab) by the caliph al-Hakam II and a near doubling of its size by his successor al-Mansur.

Medina Azahara
see p.447 ▼

The Cordoban Caliphate's other remarkable architectural legacy is the palace-fortress of **Medina Azahara**, sited on a low hill to the west of the city and with outstanding views over the valley of the Guadalquivir. Built in the tenth century by the cultured ruler Abd ar-Rahman III, and named after his favourite wife, this edifice epitomised the confidence, power and splendour of the Cordoban court. In 1944 excavators revealed the remains of a royal palace and in its main room – the **Sálon Rico de Abd al-Rahman III** – they found exquisite carvings in marble depicting the Syrian Hom (Tree of Life) motifs. Painstakingly reconstructed in the years since, this magnificent room finally gives some credence to the descriptions of gaping wonder recorded by medieval visitors to the caliph's palace.

The Giralda see p.302 ▶

In the eleventh-century Andalucía fragmented into rival kingdoms, allowing successive waves of Moorish invaders to move into the power vacuum. One of these, the ultra-fundamentalist **Almohads**, left behind a number of remarkable buildings. First and foremost is the **Giralda** tower in Sevilla, the surviving minaret of the Friday mosque which was later demolished to construct the cathedral. At 100m high with elaborate *sebka* brickwork panels adorning its exterior walls, the tower is similar to minarets from the same era erected in Marrakech and Rabat in Morocco. Started in 1184 under the architect Ahmed ibn Baso, it was completed twelve years later and has become symbolic of Sevilla.

The Alhambra see p.533 ▼

The pinnacle of Moorish architectural splendour in Spain was achieved in the sunset years of Nasrid-ruled Granada, the last outpost on the peninsula to fall to the Christians. Dominating the city from its hilltop location, the **Alhambra** is the finest example of a medieval Islamic palace and one of the world's greatest buildings. Constructed between 1230 and 1354, it is a treasurehouse of craftsmanship where subtle use of space, light and water are employed to add lustre to the complex's architectural splendour. From marble, pillared arcades to magnificent domes with stalactite and honeycomb decoration to exquisite stuccowork with endlessly repeated stylized inscriptions proclaiming that "There is no conqueror but God", the genius of the design is breathtaking.

The Generalife see p.542

In the Alhambra's gardens, the **Generalife**, the architects pulled off a further tour de force with an oasis of peace away from the cares and intrigues of the palace. Here, among jasmine scented arbours and groves of juniper, myrtle and cypress, the emirs were able to relax in elegant pavilions surrounded by the sound of water tumbling in fountains and cascades. The intention was to create an earthly reflection of paradise and in the Alhambra and Generalife they surely came as close to achieving this as any civilization before or since.

The Moorish legacy

Grand monuments may be the Moors' most obvious legacy, but they also had a profound effect on other aspects of Andalucian life. From domestic architecture and their advances in irrigation to the introduction of new crops including almonds, rice, saffron, oranges and lemons, the changes they made are the very things that today are seen as quintessentially Andalucian.

Alcázar, Córdoba

When the Moors first set eyes on the region it was the plentiful rivers that they found the most wondrous aspect of their new domain. Irrigation, started by the Romans, was thus extended and upgraded with hundreds of **water wheels** (nurias) mounted on all major rivers while mountainous districts such as Las Alpujarras and Almería were criss-crossed with **water channels** (acequias) bringing irrigation to formerly inaccessible areas and even deserts. The Moors also loved to employ water as a decorative, inspiring and contemplative feature in their houses, palaces and public squares. Often this meant pumping the water from a source far below, as was done with the **Patio de los Leones** fountain in the Alhambra. The fountains and cascades in squares and courtyards throughout Andalucía today continue this tradition.

The Moors' influence on domestic architecture had a fundamental influence not only in Andalucía but also, ultimately, throughout Europe. A Roman invention in essence, the **patio** was developed by the Moors into a sanctuary away from the hustle and bustle of the streets outside. The *carmen*, meanwhile, is a **walled garden** version of the patio that was added to urban villas; many examples are still to be seen in the Albaicín quarter in Granada. Into the mountainous Las Alpujarras south of Granada, the Moors imported another form of architecture: clay-roofed dwellings with a *tinao* or bridge enabling access from one building to another and a *terrao* or **roof terrace**.

Tinao in Mecinilla, Las Alpujarras

Central to the Moorish way of life was the practice of bathing in public *hammams* or **bathhouses**, and Roman-style baths with gradated temperatures and the hypocaust (under-floor heating) were a common feature. This civilized practice was regarded as un-Christian by the Church, and one of the first acts of the Catholic conquerors was to prohibit bathing on pain of fine or punishment. Washing infrequently and wearing garments until they stank thereby became a mark of Christian piety meaning that bathhouses were closed down or – as happened with Granada's bathhouse in the Albaicín – turned into wash-houses. Among the numerous examples that survive, those in Jaén are the largest and best preserved.

town at the *Alcazaba de Busquístar* (☎958 85 86 87, ⓦwww.alpujarralcazaba .com; ❻), a tranquil hideaway some 5km south along the GR421 road which descends along the east side of the ravine to meet the A348. This apart-hotel has traditional-style Alpujarran dwellings (no. 411 is recommended) with *launa* roofs and fine views, plus a restaurant and pool; horse riding, mountain biking and trekking are some of the activities on offer. Heating comes from a *chimenea* (wood burning stove) that you feed yourself. Trevélez's **campsite** (☎958 85 87 35) lies 1km out along the Órgiva road and is officially open all year, although you can expect arctic conditions in midwinter. It also rents out some heated cabins (❷).

Among **places to eat**, besides the very reasonably priced *Hotel La Fragua* (see above), are *Casa Julio*, Plaza de la Iglesia, also in the *barrio medio*, and the *Río Grande*, off the east side of Plaza Francisco Abellán in the *barrio bajo*, both serving up good, solid mountain food. The great-value *Mesón Haraicel*, in c/Real just above the same square in the *barrio bajo*, offers tasty tapas and *raciones* in its bar and the nearby *Restaurante Alvarez* attached to the hotel of the same name (see above) is another place serving well-prepared *alpujarreño* dishes. A little way out along the Ugíjar road, *Piedra Ventana* is another popular eating place. A trio of good **tapas bars** worth seeking out are *Bar Rosales* (near *Hostal Fernando*), *Bar Cerezo* and *Bar Fuente de la Panedería*, all in the *barrio medio*.

Trevélez's celebrated **jamón serrano** is justifiably a local passion and can be tried, along with many other specialities, at the bars above and also at *Mesón del Jamón*, which has an attractive terrace above the Plaza de la Iglesia in the *barrio medio*. Another *jamón* specialist is *Mesón Joaquín*, at the entrance to the village in the *barrio bajo*, where beneath a ceiling hung with hams, regional specialities are served including *habas con jamón* (beans with ham), *plato alpujarreño* (mixed fry-up with blood pudding, *jamón* and egg) and *trucha* (river trout) with *jamón*; there's also a €7 *menú*. These famous *jamones dulces* sent Richard Ford into raptures when he passed through Trevélez on horseback in the 1830s: "No gastronome should neglect these sweet hams. Very little salt is used; the ham is placed eight days in a weak pickle, and then hung up in the snow." A good place to buy and try *jamón* is at Jamones Jiménez, 50m before the bridge.

Birdwatching in the High Alpujarras

This corner of the Alpujarras is an excellent place for **birdwatching**, particularly in late spring. Quiet roads, an abundance of footpaths and dirt tracks make access easy. At this time of the year, most of the species associated with the upland areas of southern Spain can be found in the Poqueira Gorge (p.576) and the Trevélez River Valley. Above the village of Capileira, a walk from the end of the metalled road in areas clear of pine woods can turn up sightings of southern grey shrike, rock thrush, black-eared wheatear and the striking black-eyed race of northern wheatear as well as Ortolan bunting. Higher up, in autumn, honey buzzards can occasionally be seen heading for the Straits of Gibraltar and winter quarters in Africa. Higher still, the alpine accentor is to be spotted around mountain huts.

The more wooded parts of the Trevélez Valley have booted eagle, buzzard, raven and the short-toed treecreeper, whilst lower down, near Pitres, Scops owl and red-necked nightjar can be heard at dusk, and in late summer bee eaters congregate for their migration south. Throughout these areas golden eagle, crag martin, black redstart and rock bunting are also to be seen and, with a little more persistence and patience, the members of the warbler family – Dartford, spectacled, selodius and Bonelli's – can be turned up in suitable habitats.

South to Torvizcón

South from Trevélez, you can head by road or by footpath to Almegíjar and Torvizcón. On foot, it is around 15km: a very pleasant walk, lined with masses of wild flowers and fragrant herbs in spring and early summer.

Start by following the road down the valley from Trevélez in the direction of Juviles. At the junction after 7km, ignore the road going east to Juviles and take the turn on the right signed to Cástaras. Follow this road, passing through Cástaras after 6km, to join the GR413 shortly beyond, which then makes a winding 12km descent into Torvizcón.

TORVIZCÓN is another robust Alpujarran village with cobbled streets and whitewashed houses stacked up the northern slopes of the Sierra de la Contraviesa. **Rooms** are available at *Pensión Moreno*, Plaza del Arroyo 4 (☎958 76 40 06; ❷), a friendly, family-run place near the main square which serves food (€10 *menú*) accompanied by local *costa* wine made in a bodega on the premises.

East to Juviles, Bérchules and Cádiar

Heading east from Trevélez, either by vehicle or on foot, you come to **JUVILES**, a great centre of silk production in Moorish times, and today an attractive village straddling the road. At its centre is an unwhitewashed, peanut-brittle-finish church with a clock that's slightly slow (like most things round here). The villagers don't appear to have taken to their renovated plaza with its jarring ornamental fountains, lamp-standards and trees in brick boxes, and in the evening people still promenade in the road, knowing that there will be no traffic. Juviles also takes its share of the **jamón** business and a large attractive building on the main road as you exit towards Ugíjar houses Jamones de Juviles S.A. (🖰www.jamonesdejuviles.com), a curing factory for this *alpujarreño* delicacy. Ring the doorbell indicated at the entrance and you will be invited inside to taste their fine hams, which can be bought whole or in smaller cuts. The atmospheric *Bar Fernández* on the main street, does inexpensive **meals** and for **rooms** *Pensión Tino* (☎958 76 91 74; ❷), on the same road at the western end of the village, has en-suites above a bar, views and a pretty, flower-filled terrace.

BÉRCHULES, a high village of grassy streams and chestnut woods, lies just 6km beyond Juviles, but a greater contrast can hardly be imagined. It is a large, abruptly demarcated settlement, three streets wide, on a sharp slope overlooking yet another canyon. There's a handful of **places to stay**: *La Posada* (☎958 85 25 41; ❷), on the central Plaza Victoria, is a friendly place for rooms with and without bath and serves meals (including vegetarian options) at their bar just around the corner. Nearby, *Alojamiento Rural La Tahoma*, c/Baja de la Iglesia s/n, which (as the street name tells you) is just below the church (☎958 76 90 51; ❷), offers excellent-value apartments with kitchen, *salón* and TV, and one-night stays are possible. Also in the village, the new *El Mirador de Bérchules*, Plaza de Zapata 1 (☎958 85 25 23; ❸) has more good-value apartments with terrace and views. En-suite rooms are also available at the pleasant but pricier *Hotel Bérchules*, Carretera s/n (☎958 85 25 30, 🖰www.hotelberchules.com; ❸), with its own restaurant, sited on the road into town from Juviles. Good **tapas** and **raciones** are to be had at *Bar Vaqueras*, on Plaza Victoria. On the same square there's also an excellent grocery – a godsend if you're planning on doing any walking out of here, since most village shops in the Alpujarras are primitive. More elaborate **meals** are found at the popular *Cafetería El Mirador* attached to the accommodation place of the same name (see above) and at *Bar Cuatro Vientos* on the edge of the village near the *Hotel Bérchules* (see above); despite a drab exterior there's a large bar serving up decent tapas and a good-value *menú* for €7. They've even got a few rooms above (☎958 76 90 39; ❷), all en suite.

CÁDIAR, just below Bérchules and the central town – or "navel" as Gerald Brenan termed it – of the Alpujarras, is more attractive than it seems from a distance. Local life centres on its main square, fronted by a sixteenth-century stone church, and a regular series of events are worth coinciding with if possible: a colourful produce **market** takes place on the 3rd and 18th of every month, sometimes including livestock, and from October 5 to 10 the **Fuente del Vino** wine and cattle fair takes place, turning the waters of the fountain literally to wine. There are quite a few *hostales* and *camas* if you're looking for **places to stay**, and one of the best deals is at *La Ruta de la Alpujarra* (☎958 76 80 59, ℻958 76 88 05; ❸), sited near the petrol station as you arrive from Bérchules, where spacious rooms come with fully equipped kitchenette. Slightly further back along the same road, the large new apart-hotel *La Para del Suerte* (☎958 76 89 00; ❷) has some remarkable-value apartments with terrace balconies. The same family also owns the inexpensive *Hostal Montoro*, c/San Isidro 20 (☎958 76 80 68; ❶), near the central plaza and with heated rooms. Another excellent place definitely worth seeking out is *El Cadi*, c/Real 21, facing the church (☎958 76 80 64; ❶–❷) with nicely refurbished en-suite rooms behind a drab exterior. If you're looking for something a little more special, the upmarket apart-hotel ⚘ *Alquería de Morayma* (☎958 34 33 03, Ⓦwww.alqueriamorayma.com; ❺), 2km out of town along the A348 towards Torvizcón, is a typical Alpujarran *cortijo* in 86 acres of farmland with tastefully decorated rooms and houses (sleeping up to four; ❻) in a lovely setting with friendly proprietors; facilities include a good restaurant (open to non-guests) and pool, and activities such as trekking, cycling and horse riding are also on offer.

For **food**, the restaurants of *La Para de la Suerte* and *La Ruta de la Alpujarra* (see above) both have decent restaurants with economical *menús* or there are tapas and *raciones* to be had in the latter's bar or in other bars on and around the main square. The restaurant of *El Cadi* is a better bet though, serving up *alpujarreño* specialities on a good-value *menú* for €8 – and they've got an impressive selection of wines to wash it down with.

The eastern and southern Alpujarras

Cádiar and Bérchules mark the end of the western Alpujarras, and a striking change in the landscape; the dramatic, severe, but relatively green terrain of the Guadalfeo and Cádiar valleys gives way to open, rolling and much more arid land. The villages of the **eastern Alpujarras** display many of the characteristics of those to the west but as a rule they are poorer and less visited by tourists. There are attractive places nonetheless, among them **Yegen**, which Brenan wrote about, the market centre of **Ugíjar**, a remarkable museum at **Jorairátar** and, down on the southern slopes, the *costa* wine-producing villages of **Albuñol** and **Albondón**.

Yegen and Mecina Bombarón

YEGEN, some 7km northeast of Cádiar, is where **Gerald Brenan** lived during his ten or so years of Alpujarran residence (see box overleaf). Brenan connections aside, Yegen is one of the most characteristic of this zone's villages, with its two distinct quarters, cobbled paths and cold-water springs. It has a couple of **places to stay**, one of which, *Bar La Fuente*, opposite the fountain in the square (☎958 85 10 67; ❶–❷), has en-suite rooms and an apartment to let (❹) and serves **tapas** and **raciones** in a bar dotted with Brenan memorabilia and photos. The

Gerald Brenan's autobiography of his years in the Alpujarras, **South from Granada**, is the best account of rural life in Spain between the wars, and also describes the visits made here by Bloomsburyites Virginia Woolf, Bertrand Russell and the arch-complainer Lytton Strachey who attributed his Iberian ailments to "crude olive oil, greasy tortillas and a surfeit of *bacalao*" and proclaimed when he got home that "Spain is absolute death". Disillusioned with the strictures of middle-class life in England after World War I, Brenan rented a house in Yegen and shipped out a library of 2000 books, from which he was to spend the next eight years educating himself. Since only a handful of the inhabitants of Yegen were literate, the reserved, lanky stranger was regarded as an exotic curiosity by the villagers. With glazed windows in only two dwellings, no doctor, electricity or telephone and no road to the outside world, Yegen's rustic isolation together with its characters, traditions, superstitions and celebrations provided the raw material for his great work. Towards the end of his stay he became involved in a number of scandals and, after getting a young teenage girl pregnant, moved to the hills of Churriana behind Torremolinos, with his wife, US writer and poet Gamel Woolsey. Here he died in 1987, a writer better known and respected in Spain (he made an important study of St John of the Cross) than in his native England. The contribution he made to informing the world about the Alpujarras, its history and culture, is recorded on a plaque fixed to his former home, now the **Casa de Brenan**, just along from the fountain in Yegen's main square.

proprietor can provide a leaflet of walks (in Spanish; one route is named after Brenan) around the village. There are more en-suite rooms at *El Tinao* (℡958 85 12 12, ✉loranne123@hotmail.com; ❷) on the main road through.

Heading east out of the village, the more luxurious *El Rincón de Yegen* (℡958 85 12 70; ❸) has heated rooms with TV, apartments (❹) sleeping up to four for longer stays, a pool and a good mid-priced **restaurant** – try the *bacalao con pimientas* (cod with peppers) – with a weekday €10 *menú*. Slightly before this, *Alojamientos Las Eras* (℡ & ℻958 85 11 91, ⓦwww.grupoei.com/laseras; ❸) rents out fully equipped apartments with TV and terrace. One **bar** worth finding your way to in Yegen's *barrio bajo* (lower quarter) is *Bar Muñoz*, on c/Iglesia, where on cooler nights locals gather around the fireplace to enjoy *jamón serrano* cured on the premises by the proprietor; if someone decides to unhook one of the guitars from the wall, sessions of singing can continue late into the night.

From Yegen there's an easy 4km **walk** up to the hamlet of **Mecina Bombarón**, along one of the old cobbled mule paths. This starts out from the old bridge across the gorge and is easy to follow from there, with Mecina clearly visible on the hill above. In the village (also reachable by road) the *Casas Blancas* rural **hotel** (℡ & ℻958 85 13 70, ⓦwww.casasblancas.org; ❹) is a pleasant place to stay, where studio rooms come with TV, kitchen and sun balcony. The new *Apartamentos Altas Vistas* next door is owned by a branch of the same family with similar prices and is also good. For **food** there's *Casa Joaquín*, just below the church where you should insist on having the *menú del día* rather than the more expensive fare they may try to foist on you.

Válor, Ugíjar and Jorairátar

Six kilometres beyond Yegen, and sited between deep ravines, **VÁLOR** is a charming and sleepy hamlet, a fact which belies its history as a centre of stubborn resistance in the sixteenth-century revolt by the Moors against the "insults and outrages" of the Christian ascendancy. These events are "celebrated" in the annual **Fiestas Patronales** in mid-September when the whole story

– including battles between Moors and Christians – is colourfully re-enacted in the main square. Should you wish to stay, en-suite **rooms** are available at the comfortable *Hostal Las Perdices* on the road through (☎958 85 18 21; ②) with – as its name implies – a good **restaurant** noted for its partridge dishes. On the main road on the village's eastern edge the *Balcón de Válor* (☎958 85 18 21, Ⓦwww.balcondevalor.com; ②) has good value en-suite rooms with TV and a pool behind. The tranquillity here doesn't seem to have been disturbed by the arrival of the *Aben Humeya* disco-pub (down a street almost opposite the *Hostal Las Perdices*) which, besides serving up good **tapas** and *platos combinados*, puts on weekend karaoke sessions.

UGÍJAR, 6km on from Válor, is the largest community of this eastern sector, and an unassuming, quiet market town. There are easy and enjoyable walks to the nearest villages – up the valley to Mecina-al-Fahar, for example – and plenty of **places to stay**. Try the comfortable *Hostal Pedro*, c/Fábrica de Sedes s/n (☎958 76 71 49; ②), which has en-suite heated rooms with TV, or the nearby *Hostal-Restaurante Vidaña* (☎ & Ⓕ958 76 70 10; ②) on the Almería road which has good-value en-suite rooms above a **restaurant** with outdoor terrace and a good-value *menú* for €7. Two **tapas bars** to seek out are *Bar La Peña* on the corner of the main road by the church, serving a bargain *menú* for €7 (their *sopa de picadillo* is delicious) and where a huge tapa comes with every drink, and *Bar Progreso*, just a few metres away up a side street. About 150m beyond the church in the direction of Lanjarón, *Info-Ugíjar* (☎958 76 70 72) is a small **Internet** café. **Buses**, which stop in the central plaza, run onwards to Almería (3hr). Slightly west of Ugíjar a road heads north to Laroles to join the A337, which climbs over Puerto de la Ragua pass (p.600), descending beyond to the spectacular castle of La Calahorra (p.599) on the northern slopes of the Sierra Nevada.

With your own transport you may wish to detour 10km to **JORAIRÁTAR** to take in the remarkable **Museo Historico de las Alpujarras** (daily 1–8pm; free; ☎958 85 31 14, Spanish only). Occupying two floors of an enormous building, the museum is a labour of love devoted to the disappearing traditions and way of life of the people of the Alpujarras. Spread over numerous rooms, highlights include a reconstructed kitchen kitted-out as it would have been a hundred years ago, a school room complete with period desks, books and maps, plus a host of paraphernalia. When you arrive in the village, a charming place in itself, make for the *barrio alto* (upper village) and ask for the house of the museum's guardian, Señora Angelita Martínez, and her husband Juan Soría who will give you an enthusiastic tour (a little Spanish would be an advantage).

To get to Jorairátar from Ugíjar, take the A348 in the direction of Cádiar, turning off (after some five kilometres) along the SE29 to reach the village.

The southern ranges

The tiny hamlets of the **southern Alpujarras** have an unrivalled view of the Mediterranean, the convexity of the hills obscuring the developments and acres of growers' plastic that mar the coast. There are few villages of any size, as there is little water, but the hills host the principal **wine-growing** district of the Alpujarras. For a taste of the best of this *costa* wine, try the *venta* at **HAZA DEL LINO** (Plain of Linen) on the western edge of the Sierra de la Contraviesa; the house brew is a full-bodied rosé. Also worth a look on the village's northern edge is an enormous chestnut **tree**, reputedly the oldest in Andalucía.

ALBUÑOL and ALBONDÓN to the east are other scenic centres of wine production. The local wines can be tasted only at Albondón, however, where various **bodegas** are located along the main street. Much of the *costa* wine drunk in Granada comes from Albondón and excellent stuff it is, too. If you want to buy, take your own container, or be prepared to have it served to you in a rinsed-out cola bottle. Just outside Albuñol, along the Rambla de Angusturas (and signposted), is the Neolithic **Cueva de Los Murciélagos**, which produced the remarkable esparto baskets, sandals and jewellery now exhibited in the museum at Granada. The cave can be visited but there's not an awful lot to see.

The Almerian Alpujarras

From Ugíjar the A348 toils eastwards and, once across the Río de Alcolea, enters the province of Almería where the starker – but no less impressive terrain – gradually takes on the harsh and desiccated character of the deserts that lie ahead. There are still the odd oases to be found, however, in **Láujar de Andarax** and the spa of **Alhama de Almería** and, just beyond the latter, a remarkable prehistoric site, **Los Millares**.

Laroles and Bayárcal

If you're in no hurry to reach Láujar a scenic detour along the A337 and AL612 through the hamlets of Laroles and Bayárcal offers a chance to see some of the National Park's magnificent upland terrain, and the possibility of overnighting at two attractive bases for exploring an area rich in trekking possibilities and on the route of the E4 (marked GR7 on Spanish maps) pan-European footpath. At **LAROLES**, 12km from Ugíjar, the *Refugio de Nevada*, c/Mairenas s/n (℡958 76 03 20, ℻958 03 38; ❸), has comfortable en-suite heated rooms with TV and stunning views, and they also rent out some slightly more expensive fully equipped apartments; **food** is available at their own good restaurant or at the nearby village bars, and the attractive village swimming pool is sited at the rear of the building. On the village's western edge there's a decent **campsite**, *Puerto de las Espinas* (℡958 76 02 31), with a good pool. Five kilometres further (via a short cut just outside Laroles) in **BAYÁRCAL**, the *Posada de los Arrieros* (℡950 52 40 01, ℻952 46 31 74; ❹) is a wonderful stone-built mountain hotel, and well equipped to withstand the winter snows that engulf it until well into spring. There are comfortable heated en-suite rooms and Swiss-style chalets nearby sleeping up to four persons. Use of their **bunkhouse** is also possible (own sleeping bag required; ❶). The hotel's **restaurant** – serving hearty *alpujarreño* specialities – is recommended and has a good-value *menú*. Built on the site of an old muleteers' inn on this important commercial route between the Alpujarras and Almería, there are spectacular **walks** to be made from the hotel including one to the Puerta de la Ragua, which at 2000m is Andalucía's highest pass. Information on this and other walks in the area is available from the hotel's friendly English-speaking staff who are enthusiastic hikers. The cool temperatures at this altitude (even in August) make walking in this area pleasant all summer, although you still need to protect yourself from the sun.

Láujar de Andarax

It was at **LÁUJAR DE ANDARAX**, 16km east of Ugíjar, at the source of the Río Andarax, that Boabdil, the deposed Moorish king of Granada, settled in 1492 and from where he intended to rule the Alpujarras fiefdom granted to him by the Catholic monarchs. But Christian paranoia about a Moorish resurgence led them to tear up the treaty and within a year Boabdil had been shipped off to Africa, an event which set in train a series of uprisings by the

Alpujarran Moors, ending in their suppression and eventual deportation, to be replaced by Christian settlers from the north.

The **Río Andarax's source** is at the town's eastern edge – signposted (*nacimiento*) – and is a pleasant and shady spot, with a restaurant, the *Mesón El Nacimiento*, serving hearty *platos combinados* at lunchtime, beside the falls. If you're here on a Sunday you'll find the falls a hive of activity as families pour in to make barbecues at a line of purpose-built "barbies" under the trees. In Láujar's centre the **Plaza Mayor** has a seventeenth-century four-spouted fountain – one of many dotted around the town – and an elegant late eighteenth-century **Ayuntamiento**, where you can pick up a street map. This will enable you to find four crumbling seventeenth-century **palacios** as well as an impressive Mudéjar-style seventeenth-century church of **La Encarnación**, which contains a sculpture of the Virgin by Alonso Cano. The eastern panhandle of the Sierra Nevada National Park lies 15km to the north of Láujar and a National Park **information office**, the Centro de Visitantes (Thurs–Sun 10.30am–2.30pm & 4–6pm,) is located on the edge of the town as you come in from Ugíjar.

For a good **walk** in this area, follow the road forking right on the western edge of the town which climbs into the wooded slopes of the Sierra Nevada, where there are forest tracks east towards the abandoned lead mines, and west to the mountain villages of **Paterna del Río**, a spa with a sulphur spring, and Bayárcal (see above), higher still. On these lower slopes of the Sierra Nevada covered with ilex and pine, you may be lucky enough to spot the *cabra hispanica*, or wild Spanish goat, as well as eagles and a variety of other birdlife, plus the odd wild boar.

Láujar is the centre of a burgeoning **wine industry**, and although smoother and slightly less potent than the *costa* wines further west, the brew is just as palatable. The Cooperativo Valle de Láujar, on the main road 2km west of town, was founded in 1992 and is beginning to commercialize these wines both within Spain and abroad. At their small shop (Mon–Sat 8.30am–noon & 3.30–7.30pm) you can taste and buy their four good reds as well as whites and a rosé, and their *digestif* made from grape juice, coffee and *anís*, plus cheeses and other local produce.

Should you decide **to stay**, Láujar offers two good-value *hostales*. The friendly *Hostal Fernández* on c/General Mola 4 adjoining the main square (☎950 51 31 28; ❷) has rooms with and without bath, plus a lovely salon and terrace with views over the valley, in addition to a superb **restaurant** with a daily *menú* for €10 washed down with local wine. West along the main street, *Hostal Nuevo Andarax*, c/Canalejas 27 (☎950 51 31 13; ❷) has more en-suite rooms above a bar-restaurant. Alternatively, the *Hotel Almirez*, on the main road at the western edge of town (☎ & ℱ950 51 35 14, ⓦ www.hotelalmirez.com; ❸), has en-suite balcony rooms with TV, plus its own restaurant.

East to Alhama de Almería

The road east of Láujar de Andarax passes a series of unremarkable villages, surrounded by slopes covered with vine trellises, little changed since Moorish times and little visited today. Among them is **FONDÓN**, with a **campsite** (☎950 51 42 90) and whose church tower was the minaret of the former mosque, and **PADULES**, 11km beyond Láujar, where the municipal swimming pool might prove a greater lure in the baking heat of high summer. The prettier village of **CANJÁYAR**, 4km further on, also has a swimming pool, and becomes a centre of frenetic activity during the autumn *vendimia*, when the grapes are gathered in. At other times it reverts to a sleepy hamlet beneath its small church. There's a **hotel** here, *La Piscina* (☎950 51 10 50; ②), signed off the main road through, with (as its name tells you) a large pool and decent and economical terrace **restaurant**.

The road then trails the course of the Andarax river valley through an arid and eroded landscape, skirting the Sierra de Gádor before climbing slightly to **ALHAMA DE ALMERÍA**, 16km further on. This is a pleasant spa town, dating back to Moorish times, and most of its visitors are here to take the waters – hence the rather incongruous three-star *Hotel San Nicolás*, c/Baños s/n (☎951 64 13 61, ℗950 64 12 81; ④), sited on the location of the original baths. If you want a cheaper **place to stay** – and Los Millares (see below) is a reason why you might – the unsigned *Pensión Chiquito*, c/Pablo Picasso 5, near the church (☎950 64 02 31; ②), has very pleasant a/c en-suite rooms with TV. The only **places to eat** are a couple of *raciones* bars along the main street or at the restaurant of the *Hotel San Nicolás*. Alhama also has a delightful municipal **swimming pool** with plenty of shade, close to a magnificent **cascade** tumbling down rocks at the western end of the town. It's worth noting that there is **no public transport** from here or the provincial capital to the Los Millares site, although the 5km distance is walkable at a push or you could take a taxi (about €5 one-way).

Los Millares: the Chalcolithic settlement

Leaving Alhama by the Almería road, after 5km the road passes a signed turn-off leading to the remarkable pre-Bronze Age settlement of **LOS MILLARES**, one of the most important of its kind in Europe. Situated on a low triangular spur between two dried-up riverbeds, this was exposed in 1891 during the construction of the Almería-to-Linares railway line that passes below the site today. Two Belgian mining engineers, Henri and Louis Siret, who were also enthusiastic amateur archeologists, took on the excavations at the turn of the twentieth century, funding them from their modest salaries. What they revealed is a Chalcolithic or Copper Age (the period between the Neolithic and the Bronze Age) **fortified settlement**. It dates from c.2700 BC and was occupied until c.1800 BC, when both stone and copper but not bronze were used for weapons and tools. Whilst it is not entirely clear who the occupants were

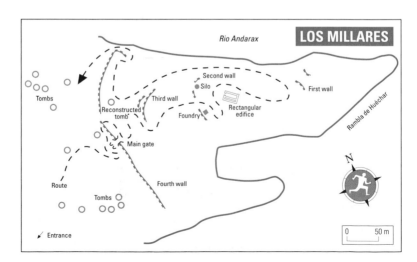

– possibly emigrants from the eastern Mediterranean or perhaps an indigenous group – the settlement they left behind is exceptional. Spread over twelve acres it consists of four sets of defensive walls, with a number of advanced fortlets beyond these, as well as an extraordinary cemetery with over one hundred **tombs** which are without equal in Europe.

Looking over the barren landscape that surrounds the site today, it's hard to believe that five thousand years ago this was a fertile area of pine and ilex forests, inhabited by deer and wild boar. The nearby Río Andarax was then navigable and the inhabitants used it to bring copper down from mines in the Sierra de Gádor to the west. The population – perhaps as many as two thousand – not only hunted for their food but bred sheep, goats and pigs, grew vegetables and cereals, made cheese and were highly skilled in the manufacture of pottery, basketwork and jewellery, as is evidenced by the finds now in museums in Almería and Madrid.

Excavations are continuing at the site and information boards (in English and Spanish) have been set up at various points; a map on the wall of the entrance office shows **walking routes** outside the site which take in dolmens and ten forts related to the Los Millares settlement discovered in the surrounding hills. The most impressive of the forts (with fine **views** over the Los Millares site), *Fortin Uno* (Fort One), lies up a track on the opposite side of the road from the site entrance and the site guardians will advise how to reach it.

The site

A tour of the **site** (Wed–Sun 10am–2pm plus June–Sept Wed–Sat 6–9pm; free; ring to confirm opening hours ☎950 01 11 31 or mobile ☎677903404; the Almería Turismo can also advise) begins with the outermost of four exterior **walls** which were constructed successively further west as the settlement expanded across the escarpment in the latter part of the third millennium BC. An impressive structure 4m high when built, the fourth (and last) wall was lined with outward-facing bastions or towers, and at 310m is the longest wall known in Europe from this period. Its layout bears a striking similarity to a wall of the same epoch at the early Cycladic site of Halandriani on the island of Síros in Greece, suggesting a possible link with the Aegean. The **main gate**, towards the centre, is flanked by barbicans or watch towers, beyond which a walled passage gave access to the settlement.

A little way north of here are the remains of a primitive **aqueduct** which cut through the wall to carry water from a spring near to the village of Alhama into the populated area. Fifty metres east of the main gate remains can be seen from the third wall. Close to here also are the remains of a number of circular **huts** – one of which has been partially reconstructed – in which the inhabitants of the site lived. Six to seven metres in diameter with pounded earth floors, they consisted of cavity stone walls filled with mud and pebbles, with a roof probably made from straw. Inside the huts the excavators found remains of hearths as well as grindstones, pottery and a variety of utensils.

Moving east again, beyond the second wall lies a primitive **foundry** where the copper ore was crudely smelted by means of fire and bellows before being hammered into the required form. Moulds arrived only in the later Bronze Age. Further north, on the line of the wall, lies a **silo** used for storing grain. Behind this wall are the foundations of a **rectangular edifice**, 32m in length, whose function is as yet unknown. The settlement at first appeared to lack a hierarchical social structure due to the overall similarity of the huts, but after the discovery of this building – much larger than the rest – some have speculated that it could have served as a form of council chamber or even a royal palace.

The remains of the first wall, enclosing what may have been the citadel, lie further back still and excavations here recovered many of the patterned, bell-shaped vases to be seen in the museum at Almería.

The necropolis

Retracing your steps to the outer (or fourth) wall will bring you to one of the reconstructed tombs, part of the ancient **necropolis**. This "beehive" tomb, originally sited outside the third wall, was encompassed by the later fourth wall. It is one of more than a hundred tombs (the rest lie west of this wall), and the typical structure of a low corridor punctuated by perforated slate slabs leading to a domed burial chamber bears a striking resemblance to tholos tombs of a similar date from the Aegean, particularly southern Crete. It has been suggested that early Cretans (for whom the bull was religiously significant) may have found their way here and that the importance of bulls and bullfighting on the Iberian peninsula may owe something to this link. Present academic thinking, however, tends towards the idea that the civilization here was of local origin.

More tombs, most in a collapsed state, in which clan members were buried together with their possessions such as arms, tools and what appear to be ceramic idols (suggesting the existence of a cult), lie beyond the outer wall. Originally, and again as in the Aegean, the tombs were covered with an earth mound or tumulus. Try to resist climbing over them as many are in a fragile condition and the importance of this site for posterity is hard to overstate.

Guadix, Baza and La Calahorra

An alternative route from Granada to Almería – via the N342 and A92 and covered by Empresa Autodía buses from the main bus station – runs close to **Viznar** (where Lorca was assassinated, and **Purullena** 30km further, a centre of ceramic production. The town's pottery output is on show at colourful roadside stalls, where there's also a good-value **pensión** with restaurant, *El Caminero*, Avda. Andalucía 30 (☎958 69 01 54; ❷). The road drives on to **Guadix**, a crumbling old Moorish town with a vast and extraordinary cave district. For those with transport, the route also offers the opportunity for a detour to the impressive Renaissance castle of **La Calahorra**.

To the northeast, the A92N *autovía* speeds traffic from Guadix towards Lorca and Murcia, and there is a possible stop at the pleasant market town of **Baza** beyond which the road pushes on through a sparsely populated landscape for the 70km between here and the towns of Vélez Rubio and Vélez Blanco.

Guadix

Sited on the banks of the Río Guadix, in the midst of a fertile plain, **GUADIX** is a ramshackle, windblown sort of town, often coated in the red dust which gusts in from the surrounding hills. It's not a particularly attractive place and if it were not for its remarkable cave district there would be little reason to stop.

An ancient settlement dating back to Paleolithic times, it became the Roman town of Julia Gemella Acci in 45 BC, established by Julius Caesar as a base for exploiting seams of silver in the surrounding hills. Following a period of decline during the Visigothic era, the conquering Moors revived its fortunes, renaming the town Guadh-Haix ("River of Life"), and it rapidly grew in size, soon becoming a rival for Granada. It was renowned for its poetry, and bards such as Ibn Tofayl sang the praises of Guadix's beauty and its valley. It was also during the Moorish period that the town developed an important silk industry, whose mulberry trees can still be seen along the river. More recently, industrial development was based upon the production of esparto grass products and cutlery. Guadix endured terrifying atrocities during the Civil War, which Gerald Brenan vividly described in *South from Granada*.

Arrival and information

Guadix is not a large place and, if you arrive at the **bus** station (frequent services to and from Granada and Almería), to the southeast of the centre off Avenida Medina Olmos, it's easy enough to set your sights on the walls and cathedral – around five minutes' walk. The **train station** (4 services daily to and from Granada and Almería) is on the northeast side of town, 1.5km out along Avda. de Buenos Aires (the Murcia road). A small and helpful **Turismo** (Mon–Fri 9am–3pm; ☎958 66 26 65) along the Avda. Mariana Pineda (aka Ctra. de Granada), not far from the cathedral, will provide a useful town **map**, or many of the kioskos around the centre will sell you a small fold-out version. **Internet** access is available at *Habana Café Internet*, Plaza de la Constitución 4, near the cathedral.

Accommodation

Should you want a **place to stay** overnight, the *Hotel Mulhacén*, Avda. Buenos Aires 41 (☎958 66 07 50, ☎958 66 06 61; ❸), is near the centre and functional. The slightly higher priced *Hotel Comercio*, c/Mira de Amezcua 3 (☎958 66 05 00, ✉hotelcomercio@moebius.es; ❹), an elegant and refurbished turn-of-the-twentieth-century hotel, is easily the best place in town. Rooms here come with a/c, minibar, room safe and TV and clients get free use of a spa and sauna.

If you're taken with the idea of cave life there's a chance to experience it for a night in the cave district at the spotless cave *Hostal Chez Jean & Julia*, c/Ermita Nueva 67 (☎958 66 91 91, mobile ☎689369800), where you have a choice of a double room (❷ with breakfast) or your own en-suite cave apartment (sleeping up to four; ❺) with salon, kitchen and washing machine. It's near the cave museum (see below) and to find it make your way there and give the proprietors a ring for directions (English spoken). Another possibility is the cave hotel *Pedro Antonio Alarcón* (☎958 66 49 86, ⓦwww.cuevaspedroantonio.com; ❹), on the other side of town beyond the train station; this is a more luxurious complex of nineteen caves with pool, gardens and restaurant; it lies a couple of kilometres from the centre along Avenida de Buenos Aires.

The Town

Guadix's old quarter is still largely walled, and the circuit includes an imposing Moorish gateway, the Puerta San Turcuato. Within, it's dominated by the red sandstone towers of its sixteenth-century **Catedral** (Mon–Sat 10.30am–1pm & 4–6pm; €2) – circled on Saturdays by a lively **market** – built on the site of a former mosque. This has been much hacked around and embellished over the years and the exterior is eighteenth-century Corinthian, the work of Vincente Acero. The sombre, late-Gothic interior was designed by Diego de Siloé, based on that of the cathedral at Málaga. Its best feature is the superb Churrigueresque choir stalls by Ruíz del Peral. Civil War reminders from both sides of the conflict include the defaced and destroyed heads of the saints on the carved marble pulpit and, near to the entrance, two plaques recording the names of local priests "killed by Marxism".

Just across from the cathedral entrance, beneath an arch, stands the elegant **Plaza Mayor**, an arcaded Renaissance square which was reconstructed after severe damage in the Civil War. A right turn in the stepped street (c/Santisteban) at the far end of the square leads up to the Renaissance **Palacio de Peñaflor**. Nearby in the Placeta de Santiago the whitewashed church of **Santiago** (daily 6.15–8pm; free), another work by de Siloé, has an imposing Plateresque entrance and, inside, a beautiful *artesonado* ceiling.

Next to the Peñaflor mansion, a former theological seminary alongside the sixteenth-century church of **San Agustín** gives access to the conclusively ruined ninth-century Moorish **Alcazaba**. At the time of writing the town council had purchased both the disused seminary and the Alcazaba and a major programme of rebuilding and restoration has begun. When this has been completed in late 2006, the Turismo will be able to advise on the new visiting times. From the Alcazaba's battlements there are **views** over the cave district of Santiago (see below) and beyond towards the Sierra Nevada.

The cave district

South of the Alcazaba and sited in a weird landscape of pyramidal red hills, the **Barrio de las Cuevas** or cave district still houses some 10,000 people (most of whom, and contrary to popular belief, are not *gitanos* or gypsies), and to take a look round it is the main reason for most visitors stopping off.

The quarter extends over a square mile or so in area, and the lower caves, on the outskirts, are really proper cottages sprouting television aerials, with upper storeys, electricity and running water. But as you walk deeper into the suburb, the design quickly becomes simpler – just a whitewashed front, a door, a tiny window and a chimney – and the experience increasingly voyeuristic. Penetrating right to the back you'll come upon a few caves which are no longer used: too squalid, too unhealthy to live in, their whitewash faded to a dull brown. Yet right next door there may be a similar, occupied hovel, with a family sitting outside, and other figures following dirt tracks still deeper into the hills.

Be aware that offers to show you around the interior of a cave will often be followed by a demand for substantial sums of money when you emerge. A **Cueva Museo** (Cave Museum; Mon–Sat 10am–2pm & 4–6pm, Sun 10am–2pm; €1.40), Plaza Padre Poveda, opposite the church of San Miguel (aka Iglesia de las Cuevas) – and signed along c/San Miguel heading south from the centre – is the easiest way to get an understanding of cave culture. Sited in a series of rehabilitated cave dwellings, it documents the history and reality of cave living with audiovisual aids and reconstructed rooms. On the way to the museum you will pass a private cave museum on your left (Museo de la Alcazaba; Mon–Fri 10am–1.30pm & 5–8.30pm, Sat & Sun 11am–2pm; €2) which – although friendly and mildly interesting – is not worth the entry fee and is mainly a front for selling the wares of the *alfarería* (pottery) opposite.

Eating, drinking and nightlife

For food the **restaurant** of the ✻ *Hotel Comercio* is the best in town – the *perdiz* (partridge) dishes are recommended – with a good-value *menú* for €11. Another decent option, *Boabdil*, c/Manuel de Falla 3, with great salads and good tapas, is to be found halfway between the cathedral and the Turismo, turning right off Avda. Mariana Pineda. For cheaper meals head for the Plaza de Naranjos, a stone's throw east of the cathedral. Here among a bunch of popular eating places *Cafetería Cart Luis* does **tapas**, **raciones**, hamburgers and a cheap *menú*. *Restaurante-Bar El Albergue* at Avda. Medina Olmos 48, close to the bus station,

Fiesta de los Cascamorros

Guadix and Baza are linked by old rivalries that are kept alive in the annual **Fiesta de los Cascamorros** on September 6–9. At the outset of this festival a man dressed as a jester and carrying a sceptre walks from Guadix to Baza in an attempt to retrieve an ancient image of the Virgin, over which the two towns have disputed ownership since the sixteenth century. However, to retrieve the sacred image from the church, he must remain unblemished and so, as he nears Baza, a huge reception committee awaits him armed with drums of used engine oil at the ready.

Needless to say, he is coated from head to toe in the stuff within seconds of crossing the city limits – as are a whole crowd of the Virgin's protectors – and the oily mass then squelches its way to the Plaza Mayor where, amidst the tolling of church bells, the mayor (from the safety of a balcony) proclaims that Guadix has blown it yet again, after which the town lets rip on a three-day binge of celebration.

is reasonable, too. Not much happens in Guadix by way of **nightlife** but the *Café Jazz* in the basement of the *Hotel Comercio* is a good place for a drink or two and sometimes stages live concerts of modern jazz.

Baza

BAZA, 44km northeast of Guadix along the A92N, is another old Moorish town, well worth a detour if you have time and transport. Approached through an ochre landscape dotted with weird conical hillocks covered with esparto grass, the town is slightly smaller than Guadix, with a web of streets encircling its ancient central plaza. As with many towns in these parts, it has a history dating back well into prehistoric times. A prosperous Iberian settlement here named *Basti* produced the remarkable *Dama de Baza* sculpture (see p.598) and the town remained a considerable centre under the Romans, and later, like Guadix, a focus of silk production under the Moors; it was especially renowned for its silk prayer mats. Taken by Christian forces in 1489 after a long siege, the town has had a less-than-glorious past few centuries, in part due to trouble from earthquakes, which have crumbled away most of the old Moorish Alcazaba. Like Guadix, Baza also has a **cave quarter**, albeit less touristic, on the northern side of town, close to the bullring.

Heading on from Baza, possible destinations include the Cazorla Natural Park, to the north, or the Almería coast via the A92N *autovía* with the option of a detour to Orce, the site of sensational finds concerning early humans in Spain, and the prehistoric cave paintings at Vélez Rubio.

Arrival, information and accommodation

The **bus station** (with frequent connections to Guadix) is located on Avenida Reyes Católicos to the west of the centre, and an easy five-minute walk to the Plaza Mayor. In the Plaza Mayor's Museo Arqueológico (see overleaf) a **tourist office** (Mon–Fri 9am–2pm, Sat 11am–2pm; ☎958 86 13 25) will provide you with a good town map. When this office is closed, maps are also available from the reception of the Ayuntamiento on the opposite side of the Plaza Mayor.

There are limited **places to stay** in Baza, but demand is usually low outside festival periods. The only central options are the very comfortable *Hotel Anabel* (☎958 86 09 98; ❸), about four blocks east of the Plaza Mayor at c/María de Luna s/n. and, in the same area, *Hostal Avenida*, Avda. José de Mora 26 (☎958 70 03 77; ❷), with bargain-priced a/c en-suite rooms with TV above a bar.

Continuing to the end of c/José de Mora and taking a right leads to the welcoming *Hostal Casa Grande*, Ctra. de Ronda 28 (☎958 70 27 32; ❷), offering immaculate en-suite rooms with a/c, heating and TV. It has its own very good restaurant with a *menú* for €7 next door.

The Town

The impressive Renaissance collegiate church of **Santa María** – and its eighteenth-century brick tower – leads you to the pedestrianized Plaza Mayor. Built over an earlier mosque, the church's elegant **Plateresque main door** – attributed to Diego de Siloé – is worth a look and inside there's an interesting marble pulpit and elegant vaulting. On the corner of c/Arco de la Magdalena and fronting the Plaza Mayor is Confitería Emilio Castellaño, which opened its doors in 1857 and has been in the same family for five generations – and the sixth has recently been born. The shop maintains much of its period interior and is still turning out delicious *pasteles* made to the same recipes as a century ago. On the opposite side of the Plaza Mayor a small **Museo Arqueológico** (Mon–Fri 9am–2pm, Sat 11am–2pm; free) preserves finds from the town's ancient past, including a copy of the *Dama de Baza*, a magnificent life-size fourth-century BC Iberian painted sculpture unearthed in 1971 in a necropolis on the outskirts of the town. The original is now in Madrid, where it is exhibited alongside the century-later *Dama de Elche*, another iconic work of Spain's early artistic tradition. On the charming Plaza Santo Domingo, to the southeast of the Plaza Mayor, is the town's old theatre, the turn-of-the-twentieth-century Teatro Dengra. Despite being converted into a cinema, it retains many of the antique fittings from its earlier incarnation, including boxes and scarlet velvet seats, and is worth a peep.

A few minutes' walk to the east of Plaza Mayor, following c/Cabeza then turning left along c/del Agua, are the **Baños Árabes**, a tenth-century Moorish bath complex – one of the oldest surviving in Spain. The town council recently purchased the baths from a private owner and a programme of restoration is now under way with the complex due to open to the public in 2006. Consult the tourist office for the latest information. Close to the baths the **Iglesia de Santiago** (service times only, try 7–8pm), Plaza de Santiago, is a fine sixteenth-century church built over a former mosque and inside has a magnificent Mudéjar *artesonado* coffered ceiling in nave and apse.

Eating and drinking

There are plenty of places for **eating** and **drinking** in Baza, including the excellent *La Curva*, c/Corredera 3 (☎958 70 00 02), a few blocks southeast of the Plaza Mayor, a mid-priced restaurant renowned for its ham and seafood. *Mesón Siglo XX*, c/Solares 5, slightly west of here, is the kind of splendid local restaurant that Andalucía excels in; an all-female kitchen cooks up a range of local delicacies including great soups, stews and a tasty paella, and the *menú* is a gift at €7. *Mesón los Moriscos*, c/Cava Alta 3, 100m north of the church of Santa María, lives up to its name and dishes up fine tapas and *platos combinados* in a mini-Alhambra inspired dining room. A cluster of pleasant **tapas bars** – some with terraces – lie slightly west of the Plaza Mayor at the end of c/Serrano, with *Bar Perdiz* and *La Solana* good possibilities. Just south of here, *Bar Los Canteros*, in Plaza Arcipreste Juan Hernández, is another good place for seafood and meat *raciones* with a pleasant terrace. *La Bodega*, beneath two lofty plane trees and next to the fountain and church in the charming Plaza Santo Domingo, to the southeast of the Plaza Mayor, also has tables to sit out and serves a free tapa with every drink. The terrace of the *casino* on the west side of the Plaza

Mayor is a great place for a leisurely **breakfast** and they also serve up tapas later in the day.

La Calahorra

Continuing southeast of Guadix along the A92 to Almería, the spectacular domed Renaissance castle of **La Calahorra** heaves into view at the 16km point. A turn-off to the right takes you the 4km to the village of the same name, where, on a hill above it, this brooding red stone monster was constructed in 1509–12. Its architect was Italian and its owner, one Rodrigo de Mendoza, was the bastard son of the powerful Cardinal Mendoza, who did much to establish Isabel on the throne. Rodrigo, created marquis of Zenete by Isabel, acquired a taste for the Renaissance during an Italian sojourn, and ordered the castle as a wedding gift for his wife, María de Fonseca. The bleak situation proved unattractive both to them and to their descendants, however, and it was rarely used.

The privately owned castle is open to the public on Wednesdays only (10am–1pm & 4–6pm; €3); outside these times access is possible by visiting c/de los Claveles 2 in the village (☎958 67 70 98; avoid siesta time), home of the guardian, Antonino Tribáldoz who was born in the castle. Once inside you'll be able to view an exquisite Renaissance **patio** – the last thing you'd expect behind such a dour exterior. The doorways, arches and stairway of this two-storey courtyard are beautifully carved from Carrara marble. Some of the palace's rooms have finely crafted *artesonado* ceilings and there's also a curious women's prison. Leave your vehicle at the bottom of the boulder-strewn track leading up to the castle and walk up to avoid severe damage to the underside of your hire car.

△ La Calahorra

Should you wish **to stay**, rooms are available at the comfortable *Hospedería del Zenete*, Ctra. La Ragua 1, the road leading into the village (☎ & ℱ 958 67 71 92, ⓦ www.hospederiadelzenete.com; ❺), a four-star hotel with great views of the castle from most rooms (make sure to request this). One plus point about staying here is that if you ring at least 24 hours ahead they will arrange a visit to the castle for you. The hotel's **bar-restaurant** is good for tapas and formal meals and has an economical *menú*. Further along the same road *Hostal-Restaurante La Bella*, Crta. de Aldeire 1 (☎ 958 67 70 00, ℱ 958 67 72 41; ❷), in the village proper, is the budget option and offers a/c rooms with TV above a **restaurant** with a decent weekday €8 *menú*.

From La Calahorra, a lonely but scenic road – the A337 – toils south to the **Puerto de la Ragua**, at 1993m Andalucía's highest all-weather pass. The hairpin climb offers spectacular views back over the plain of the Hoya de Guadix and the rose-tinted La Calahorra castle. When you reach the pass – where it can be chilly even in high summer – you'll find a pleasant **refuge** with comfortable bunk accommodation and a restaurant. To be certain of a bed, ring ahead (☎ 958 34 51 62, English spoken; ❶). Antonio Mesa, the friendly warden, can provide details of fine **walks** in the vicinity, plus horse riding and (in winter) cross-country skiing, both available at the refuge. Beyond the pass the road forks, offering alternative descents to the Alpujarras villages of Válor or Ugíjar to the west, and Láujar de Andarax in the east. Forking left towards Láujar would bring you to Bayárcal and the superb mountain hotel *Posada de los Arrieros* (see p.590).

Towards Almería

East beyond La Calahorra, the A92 crosses the border into Almería and passes by **FIÑANA**, with another castle, this time Moorish and in a more ruinous state. If you have time, the walk up to the castle – along stepped streets – is picturesque and the ancient **mezquita** (mosque; when closed a partial view can be had through a small window in the door) and sixteenth-century church of **Nuestra Señora de la Asunción**, with elegant Mudéjar wooden ceiling, are also worth a look. To see these monuments – plus a Moorish bathhouse – call at the Ayuntamiento in the central Plaza de la Constitución on weekdays before 2pm; they can also supply a town map. Some 25km further on there's a turn-off for **GÉRGAL**, with another well-preserved fortress and, on the highest summit of the Sierra de los Filabres behind, an observatory housing one of the largest telescopes in Europe, sited here by a German–Spanish venture to take advantage of the almost constantly clear skies (see p.631). The A92 gradually descends into the valley of the Río Andarax – where you could detour to the prehistoric site of Los Millares (see p.592) – which it follows for the final 15km to Almería.

Alternatively, following the A340 towards Almería, a little beyond the village of Rioja (where you should leave the *autovía* following signs for Pechina) and 7km kilometres before Almería, a turn on the left to the village of **PECHINA** offers the possibility of a stay at the charming and tranquil *Balneario de Sierra Alhamilla* (☎ 950 31 74 13, ⓦ www.gratisweb.com/sierra_alhamilla; ❹), a refurbished stone-built eighteenth-century bishop's palace constructed on the site of a Roman baths. A variety of curative treatments and massages (extra charge and available to nonresidents) are on offer in the bathing complex beneath the hotel where hot springs provide the water source. Breakfast is served in the former chapel and there's also a pool and restaurant. Next door, the *Bar Restaurante Sierra Alhamilla* (☎ 950 16 02 75; ❹) rents out fully equipped apartments above its bar-restaurant.

Almería

Cuando Almería era Almería	When Almería was Almería
Granada era su alquería	Granada was but its farm.

Traditional Almerian couplet

ALMERÍA is a pleasant and largely modern city, spread at the foot of a stark grey hill dominated by a magnificent Moorish fort. Founded by the Phoenicians and developed by the Romans, who named it Portus Magnus, it was as a Moorish city – renamed al-Mariyat (The Mirror of the Sea) – that Almería grew to prominence. The sultan Abd ar-Rahman I began the building programme soon after the conquest, in 713, with an arsenal beside the port, and the great **Alcazaba**, still the town's dominant feature, was added, in the tenth century by Abd ar-Rahman III, when the city formed part of the Cordoban caliphate.

The splendours created here by the Moors – most of which have been lost – inspired the popular rhyme at the beginning of this section, contrasting this early prosperity with the much later glories of Nasrid Granada. After the collapse of Moorish Córdoba, Almería's prosperity was hardly affected and, as a principality or *taifa* state, it became the country's major port, famed for its exports of silk, as well as a pirates' nest feared around the adjacent coasts. This period ended when the city fell to the forces of Fernando in 1490 and the Moors were expelled. Their possessions and lands were doled out to the officers of the conquering army, forming the basis for the *señoritismo* which has plagued Almería and Andalucía throughout modern times. Predictably, there followed a prolonged decline over the next three hundred years, reversed only by the introduction of the railway and the building of a new harbour in the nineteenth century, as well as the opening up to exploitation of the province's vast mineral wealth, particularly iron, lead and gold.

The Civil War interrupted this progress. The city's communist dockworkers gave staunch backing to the Republic, at one point in 1937 causing Hitler to order that the city be shelled from offshore by the German fleet. It was one of the last cities to fall to Franco's forces in 1939, after which many suicides took place to avoid the fate planned for the most bitter enemies of the new order.

Although still the centre of one of the poorest zones in Europe, Almería today is seeking a more prosperous future based upon intensive vegetable production in the surrounding *vega*, in tandem with gaining a greater share of Spain's tourist economy. Whilst even its most devoted admirers wouldn't describe it as a beautiful place, the provincial capital deserves more visitors than it gets. Enjoying something of a recent renaissance, the city has sunk enormous funds into smartening up the town centre which has areas with considerable charm. Add to this a handful of fascinating sights and a friendly welcome in some great bars and restaurants, and you may be induced to give it a bit longer than the customary one-night transit.

Arrival, orientation and information

Almería's **bus station** (☎950 26 20 98) and **train station** (☎902 24 02 02) have been combined into a striking new Estación Intermodal, Carretera de Ronda s/n a couple of blocks east of the Avenida de Federico García Lorca, with the bus terminals and train platforms side by side. The splendid old stone, brick and steel nineteenth-century **neo-Moorish train station** at Plaza de la Estación s/n, beside the new edifice, is worth a look, and is possibly going to be revamped as a cultural centre. Almería's relatively new **airport** (☎950 21 37 00), 8km east from the city along the coast, handles scheduled budget services

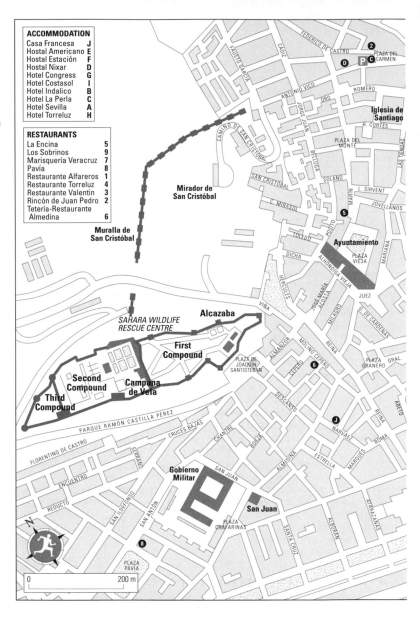

from the UK and other parts of Europe. For airport buses and details of onward travel, see "Listings", p.611, and "Travel details", p.634.

The **Avenida de Federico García Lorca,** formerly an unsightly dry river-bed but now dramatically transformed into a stately avenue with palms, fountains and newsstands, bisects the city from north to south. Most of the action takes place to the west of this artery, where you'll find the **old town** and, to the

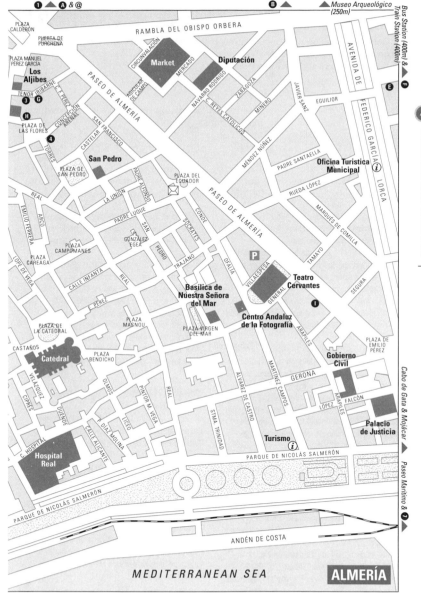

Museo Arqueológico
(250m)

Bus Station (400m) &
Train Station (400m)

Cabo de Gata & Mojácar

Paseo Marítimo &

PLAZA
CALDERÓN

PUERTA DE
PURCHENA

RAMBLA DEL OBISPO ORBERA

PLAZA MANUEL
PÉREZ GARCÍA

Los
Aljibes

TENOR IRIBARNE

PLAZA DE
LAS FLORES

Market

Diputación

PASEO DE ALMERÍA

CIRCUNVALACIÓN

MONTE DE
CAMPO

MERCADO

NAVARRO RODRIGO

C. REYES CATÓLICOS

ZARAGOZA

MINERO

JAVIER SANZ

EGUILIOR

AVENIDA DE

FEDERICO GARCÍA LORCA

CONCEPCIÓN
ARENAL

C. T. PÉREZ

SAN FRANCISCO

CASTELAR

San Pedro

PLAZA DE
SAN PEDRO

TORRES

REAL

EMILIO FERRERA

LOPE DE VEGA

PLAZA
CAREAGA

PLAZA
CAMPOMANES

ARCO

PADRE ALFONSO

LA UNIÓN

PADRE LUQUE

SAN

GONZÁLEZ
EGEA

PEDRO

TRAJANO

SÓCRATES

PLAZA DEL
ECUADOR

PASEO DE ALMERÍA

MÉNDEZ NÚÑEZ

PADRE SANTAELLA

RUEDA LÓPEZ

Oficina Turística
Municipal

MARQUÉS DE COMILLA

TAMAYO

SEGURA

CALLE INFANTA

REAL

F. PÉREZ

PLAZA
MASNOU

ÓFALA

VILLAESPESA

GENERAL

Teatro
Cervantes

Basílica de
Nuestra Señora
del Mar

PLAZA VIRGEN
DEL MAR

Centro Andaluz
de la Fotografía

ARÁPILES

PLAZA DE LA
CATEDRAL

CASTAÑOS

Catedral

VELÁZQUEZ

CIPRÉS

PLAZA
BENDICHO

OLMOS

DUENDE

PINTOR M. VEGA

REAL

ÁLVAREZ DE CASTRO

MARTÍNEZ CAMPOS

GERONA

PLAZA DE
EMILIO
PÉREZ

Gobierno
Civil

FALCÓN

LÓPEZ

ARÁPILES

C. HOSPITAL

CALLE ALICANTE

DÍAZ MOLINA

LICEO

STMA. TRINIDAD

Turismo

Palacio
de Justicia

Hospital
Real

PARQUE DE NICOLÁS SALMERÓN

PARQUE DE NICOLÁS SALMERÓN

ANDÉN DE COSTA

MEDITERRANEAN SEA

ALMERÍA

north, the **Puerta de Purchena**, a busy traffic junction where six thorough-fares meet, effectively marking the centre of the modern city.

The **Turismo** (Mon–Fri 9am–7pm, Sat & Sun 10am–2pm; ☏950 27 43 55), at Parque Nicolás Salmarón s/n (junction with c/Martínez Campos) and fronting the harbour, has a good city map (€0.60). The friendly **Oficina Turís-tica Municipal**, Avda. Federico García Lorca s/n (Mon–Fri 9am–7pm; Sat

Almería online

Online information on Almería, its monuments and amenities and the province in general can be found at Ⓦwww.almeria-turismo.org, Ⓦwww.almeriacultura.com, Ⓦwww.indalia.es and Ⓦwww.andalucia.org.

9am–2pm; ☎950 28 07 48), has lots of information on the town and province, including a good map and a free tapas-bar guide.

Accommodation

Rooms are generally easy to come by at any time of the year and there are concentrations of *hostales* and hotels around the focal Puerta de Purchena. Note that *hostal* rates here tend to be higher than elsewhere in the province.

Casa Francesa c/Narváez 18 ☎950 23 75 54. Basic but clean *fonda* a couple of blocks west of the cathedral. Rooms share bath. ❷

Hostal Americano Avda. de la Estación 6 ☎950 25 80 11. Nothing special and rather pricey, but rooms are en suite and it's convenient if you arrive late or plan to leave early. ❸

Hostal Estación c/Calzada de Castro 37 ☎950 26 72 39. Sited close to the train and bus stations with decently furnished en-suite rooms and garage parking. ❸

Hostal Nixar c/Antonio Vico 24 ☎ & Ⓕ 950 23 72 55. Decent-value en-suite rooms with a/c and TV in a quiet street; ask for the higher floors, which are airier. ❸

Hotel Congress c/Tenor Iribarne s/n ☎950 23 47 09, Ⓦwww.amhoteles.com. Good-value three-star hotel in the heart of the old town with attractive rooms and decor plus an underground garage reached by a car-lift. Breakfast included in room price Fri–Sun. ❹

Hotel Costasol Paseo de Almería 58, ☎950 23 40 11, Ⓦwww.hotelcostasol.com. Central and comfortable hotel with spacious rooms; some on the front have terrace balcony. ❺

Hotel Indalico c/Dolores R. Sopeña 4 ☎950 23 11 11, Ⓦwww.hotelindalico.com. Traditionally furnished three-star hotel with well-equipped rooms and garage close to the Avda. Federico García Lorca. ❻

Hotel La Perla Plaza del Carmen 7 ☎950 23 88 77, Ⓦwww.githoteles.com. The city's oldest hotel

has pleasant a/c rooms with satellite TV; some at the rear can be rather cramped, so check what you're offered. Rates cut by 25 percent Sun–Thurs. ❻

Hotel Sevilla c/Granada 25 ☎950 23 00 09. Welcoming, modern, small hotel with en-suite rooms equipped with a/c and TV. ❹

Hotel Torreluz Plaza Flores 2 ☎950 23 43 99, Ⓦwww.torreluz.com. The town's leading hotel contains both two-star and four-star options in the same complex. Aimed at the corporate sector, the rather staid rooms underline this. Weekend deals (in the four-star hotel) cut rates by 25 percent. ❹ & ❻

Youth hostel and campsite

Albergue Juvenil Almería c/Isla de Fuerteventura s/n ☎950 26 97 88, Ⓦwww.inturjoven.com. Almería's swish and friendly youth hostel has 150 double-rooms and some singles, all en suite. It lies on the east side of town next to the Estadio Juventud sports arena; take bus #1 from the junction of Rambla del Obispo Orberá and Avda. F. García Lorca (top right corner of our map). Under 26 €14, over 26 €18.50, ❸.

Camping La Garrofa ☎950 23 57 70. The nearest campsite to town – 5km west, on the coast at La Garrofa – is easily reached by the buses to Aguadulce and Roquetas de Mar (where there's another, giant site).

The Town

Almería's most impressive monument, the formidable **Alcazaba**, is probably the best surviving example of a Moorish military fortification. It can be reached by following any of the narrow streets which climb the hill west of the cathedral, aiming for the entrance below the walls in the Plaza Joaquín Santisteban, at the end of c/Almanzor. The city's other sights pale by comparison, though it is worth taking time to look over the **cathedral** and the **Puerta de Purchena** area.

The city **beach**, southeast of the centre beyond the rail lines, is long but crammed for most of the summer. For a day-trip, the best options are Cabo de Gata or San José, both easily accessible by bus.

The Alcazaba

The **Alcazaba** (Tues–Sun 9am–8.30pm, closes 6.30pm Nov–March; €1.50, free with EU passport) was begun by Abd ar-Rahman III of Córdoba in 955 and was just one part of a massive building programme which included a great mosque and city walls. During the eleventh century when the city enjoyed a period of prosperous independence, between the fall of the Cordoban caliphate and its capture by the Almoravids, the medina (walled city) here contained immense gardens and palaces and housed some 20,000 people. It was adapted after the *Reconquista* by the Catholic monarchs but severely damaged during a great earthquake in 1522. A programme of restoration in recent years has begun to reverse the centuries of crumbling decay.

Through the **Puerta Exterior**, a zigzagged entrance ramp – a traditional Moorish architectural feature to make attack precarious – leads to the **Puerta de la Justicia**, the gateway to the first of the Alcazaba's three great compounds. Halfway up the ramp to the right is the **Tower of Mirrors**, a fifteenth-century addition, where mirrors were employed to communicate with ships approaching the port below.

The first compound

The first compound is the largest of the three. Now filled with delightful gardens and aromatic plants, it was originally designed as a military camp and an area in which the populace could seek protection when under siege. A **well** in the centre of this area raised water from a depth of 70m to supply the site. At the eastern end of the enclosure, the **Saliente Bastión** was a lookout point over the town below, and the sea beyond.

Below the north side of the compound, the **eleventh-century wall** (Muralla de San Cristóbal) descends the hill; it originally formed part of a great complex of walls, not only surrounding the city but also dividing it internally. Above the wall, which divides the first and second compounds, is the **Campana de Vela**, a bell erected during the eighteenth century to announce ships sighted nearing the port, or to summon soldiers to their battle stations.

The second compound

The second compound accommodated the Moorish kings, when resident in the city, and at other times served as the governor's quarters. In the eleventh century, when Almería was the wealthiest, most commercially active city of Spain, the buildings here were of unparalleled brilliance. Their grandeur was even reputed to rival the later court of Granada, but the ruins that remain today make a valid comparison impossible.

What you can see, however, are the remains of **cisterns**, the old **mosque** – converted into a chapel by the Reyes Católicos – and once palatial dwellings, but sadly no sign of the magnificent stuccowork said to equal that of the Alhambra, the last remnants of which were sold off by the locals in the eighteenth century. The **Ventana de Odalisca**, a *mirador* window in the compound's northern wall, is a poignant reminder of lost glory. A legend attached to this concerns an eleventh-century Moorish slave-girl, Galiana, the king's favourite, who fell in love with a prisoner and arranged to help him to escape. But the guards discovered them in the attempt and the prisoner threw himself from this window into the valley below, whilst Galiana died of a broken heart a few days later. Recent archeological excavations here have uncovered Moorish bath-houses and other structures.

This compound has a self-service **cafetería** on its east side.

The third compound

The third and highest compound demonstrates the starkly contrasting style of the conquering Christians. When they took the city, the Catholic monarchs found the fortress substantially damaged due to an earthquake a couple of years before. They therefore built walls much stronger than the original Moorish structure, to cope with both potential future earthquakes and the recent innovation of artillery. Triangular in form, this upper fort is guarded by three semicircular towers built of ashlar masonry, both features at odds with the earlier Moorish design.

To the right, the **Torre del Homenaje** (Tower of Homage) bears the crumbling escutcheon of the Catholic monarchs and looks out over the **Patio de Armas** (Courtyard of Arms) where the guard would be assembled. From the **Torre de Pólvora** (Gunpowder Tower) and the battlements (take care as there are few handrails) fine views are to be had of the coast and of Almería's *gitano* cave quarter – the Barrio La Chanca – on a low hill to the west.

The Mirador de San Cristóbal and Wildlife Centre

The hill-top **Mirador de San Cristóbal**, which can be seen from the Alcazaba, has more fine views over the town and the coast, and can be visited by following c/Antonio Vico west from the Puerta de Purchena. Adjoining the *mirador* is a chapel with a huge figure of Christ, erected in 1928 over the site of an earlier chapel founded by the Templars after the Christians, under Alfonso VI, took the city, briefly, in 1147. The open-air chapel's altar at the rear of Christ's statue has been completely hacked apart and the walls covered with graffiti – a telling comment on Spain's rapid transition to a secular state. The **sunsets** to be seen from both here and the Alcazaba are legendary.

North of the *mirador* and Alcazaba – and visible from both – is a curious-looking farm, where you can often see gazelles sprinting around. This is the **Sahara Wildlife Rescue Centre**, a research organization studying and breeding animals in danger of disappearing from their natural habitat. The centre can be visited only by prior application (the day before is usually fine) to their office at c/General Segura 1 (☎950 28 10 45), off the south end of the Paseo de Almería.

The Catedral

Located in the heart of the old quarter, the **Catedral** (Mon–Fri 10am–4.30pm, Sat 10am–1pm; €2) is another building with a fortress look about it. Begun in 1524 on the site of the great mosque – conveniently destroyed by the 1522 earthquake – it was designed in the late-Gothic style by Diego de Siloé, the architect of the cathedral at Granada. Because of the danger of attack in this period from Barbarossa and other Turkish and North African pirate forces, the corner towers once held cannons. The threat was real and not long after its construction the cathedral chapter is recorded purchasing guns, muskets and gunpowder.

Like many of Andalucía's cathedrals, it was never completely finished and it may be that the city's inhabitants had no great affection for this austere giant, preferring instead their more intimate parish churches. The **exterior** is of little interest apart from a curious, pagan-looking relief of a garlanded radiant sun on the eastern wall – that is, facing the rising sun. Echoing the Roman Sol Invictus, or unconquerable sun, its appearance on the church has been put down to a sixteenth-century bishop with masonic leanings, but its true significance will probably never be known. Appropriately, as the province with the highest sun-hours statistic in Spain, Almería now uses the image as its official logo.

The cathedral is entered through the Puerta Principal, an elegant Renaissance doorway flanked by buttresses. Within, the sober Gothic **interior** is distinguished by some superb sixteenth-century choir stalls carved in walnut by Juan de Orea.

△ Almería's Catedral

Just behind this, the **retrochoir** is a stunning eighteenth-century altar in contrasting red and black jasper. Behind the Capilla Mayor (or high altar) with some elegant and sinuous vaulting, the Capilla de la Piedad has a painting of the *Annunciation* by Alonso Cano and *Immaculate Conception* by Murillo, whilst the Capilla de Santo Cristo – next door to the right – contains the sixteenth-century sculptured tomb of Bishop Villalán, the cathedral's founder, complete with faithful hound at his feet. Further along again, a door (often closed) leads to the sacristy and a rather uninspiring Renaissance cloister – relieved by a small garden with palms and orange trees. The church also contains a number of fine **pasos** of the Passion carried in the Semana Santa processions at Easter; among these, *El Prendimiento* (the Arrest of Christ) is outstanding.

Around the old town

West of the cathedral stands the seventeenth-century church of **San Juan** (open service times, 7–8pm), built over a tenth-century mosque. Inside, the church's southern wall preserves the *mihrab* (or prayer niche) of the original building. Next to this, there's another niche that would have contained the wooden pulpit used for readings from the Koran.

Further west lies the **Barrio de Chanca**, an area of grinding poverty occupied by *gitanos* and hard-pressed fisherfolk which has hardly changed since Brenan vividly described it in his *South from Granada*; there are some occupied cave dwellings here, too, but it's not a place to visit alone at night. East towards the port, on c/Hospital, the eighteenth-century **Hospital Real** has an elegant

Neoclassical facade and, inside, a beautiful marble-tiled patio usually containing a few prostrate patients on hospital trolleys. Like many others in Spain, this is a still fully functioning infirmary two and a half centuries after it was built.

A couple of blocks east of the cathedral, and housed in an eighteenth-century former Dominican convent with a stunning patio, the **Centro Andaluz de la Fotografía**, c/Conde Ofalía 30 (Mon–Fri 10am–2pm & 4–9pm, Sat 7–10pm; free), is Andalucía's first photo museum, often staging interesting exhibitions. To the north of the cathedral the **Plaza Vieja** (officially Plaza de la Constitución) is a wonderful pedestrian square which – because of its restricted entrance – you would hardly know was there. It contains the **Ayuntamiento**, a flamboyant early twentieth-century building with a pink and cream facade, and a monument to citizens put to the firing squad in 1824 for opposing the tyrannical reign of Fernando VII. This square has bags of potential and elsewhere would be full of restaurants and nightlife; at present, though, it's a rather melancholy place after dark.

Around the Puerta de Purchena

Further sights are located within a couple of minutes' walk of the **Puerta de Purchena**, which takes its name from a Moorish gate – long gone – where al-Zagal, the city's last Moorish ruler, surrendered to the Catholic monarchs in 1490.

On the west side of the junction, at the end of c/Tenor Iribarne at c/de los Aljibes 20, are some well-preserved eleventh-century Moorish water cisterns – known as **Los Aljibes** (Mon–Fri 9.30am–2.30pm; free). The **Calle de las Tiendas** (the continuation of c/de los Aljibes) – the oldest street in the city – was formerly called Calle Lencerías (drapers' street) and in the nineteenth century was Almería's most fashionable shopping thoroughfare. Some of the street lamps survive from this period, although the place has now become rather seedy.

A little further down you'll arrive at the **Iglesia de Santiago,** dating from the same period as the cathedral, and built with stone from the same quarry. A fine Plateresque portal incorporates a statue of Santiago slaying the Moors as well as the coat of arms of the all-powerful Bishop Villalán, the cathedral's founder.

Finally, across the Paseo de Almería, the main street which leaves the Puerta de Purchena from its southern side, a colourful daily **market** at the end of c/Aguilar de Campo is also worth a look.

Museo Arqueológico and Centro de Arte

When Almería's **Museo Arqueológico** (Tues 9am–2pm guided visits only (in Spanish); Tues–Sat 2.30–8.30pm, Sun 9am–2.30pm; free) closed in 1993 due to dangerous structural faults, few believed that it would be over a decade before the treasures inside would be put on view again. After much local and national criticism the city demolished the old building and built an impressive new museum on the same site. At the time of writing the collection was being installed in its new home, located at Ctra. de Ronda 13 off the east side of Avda. Federico García Lorca, and is due to open in early 2006 (details from either tourist office). On view will be the important collection of artefacts from the prehistoric site of **Los Millares** (see p.592), plus interesting Roman and Moorish collections, including some fine Moorish ceramics.

Near to the train-bus station an impressive recently constructed **Centro de Arte** (Mon 6–9pm, Tue–Fri 11am–2pm & 6–9pm, Sat 6–9pm, Sun 11am–2pm; free), Plaza Barcelona s/n, has a collection of modern art (mainly paintings) and often stages exhibitions by famous names.

Eating, drinking and entertainment

Almería has a surprising number of interesting and good-value places to **eat and drink**. Most of the best eating options are to be found around the Puerta de Purchena and in the web of narrow streets lying between the Paseo de Almería and the cathedral. For seafood there are a number of places in the Barrio de los Pescadores, the old fishing quarter at the western end of the commercial port and more in the zone behind the beach on the city's eastern flank. On the **nightlife** front, the city's music bars can be lively and in summer there are late-night marquees on the beach.

In August the city holds its annual music and arts **festival**, the Fiesta de los Pueblos Ibéricos y del Mediterráneo, with concerts and dance events, many of them free, taking place in the squares and various other locations throughout the city (details from either tourist office). Tacked on to the end of this is the Festival de Flamenco with big-name artists performing on a stage set up in the atmospheric Plaza de la Constitución. During the last week of the month, the city's main annual fiesta, the Romería de Augusto, also takes place with lots of street parties and spectacular processions with carnival giants. Details of the exact dates for all these again are available from the tourist office.

For **breakfast**, there are plenty of bars and **pastelerías** along the Paseo de Almería, and more still along Avenida Federico García Lorca. For **afternoon tea** or coffee with delicious pastries head for *La Dulce Alianza*, Paseo de Almería 8, near the Puerta de Purchena, a century-old *pastelería* with a terrace.

Restaurants and tapas bars

The best place for early-evening **tapas** is around the Puerta de Purchena, where the whole town turns out during the evening *paseo* to see and be seen. Places around the cathedral and old town are more lively at lunchtime.

Around Puerta de Purchena

Restaurante Alfareros c/Marcos 6, slightly north-east of the Puerta de Purchena. Wonderful cheap place to eat, packed at lunchtime with people in town for the market, with an excellent-value *menú* for €9.

Bodega Aranda Rambla del Obispo Orbera 8, near the Puerta de Purchena. Great tapas bar which fairly hums at lunchtimes when local professionals come to grab a bite. In former days this was the "sordid" *pensión* where a penurious Gerald Brenan put up in 1921 (sleeping 6 to a room) while waiting for a letter with money from England – which never came.

Bodega Las Botas c/Fructuoso Pérez 3, just south of the Puerta de Purchena. Great tapas place with hanging *jamón serrano* shanks and upturned sherry butt tables; excellent *fino* and *manzanilla* (served with a free tapa) goes well with the house special, *merluza en escabeche* (marinated hake).

Bodega Ortega c/Obispo Orbera 5, almost opposite the *Aranda* (see above). Great old rambling tapas bar decorated with bullfight posters where a friendly proprietor serves up seafood tapas made with fish fresh from the nearby market.

La Encina c/Marín 16 ☎950 27 34 29. Excellent little mid-priced restaurant serving tapas in its bar at the front and creative and innovative fish and meat dishes in a cosy restaurant at the rear (where a feature is a Moorish well found during the restaurant's refurbishment); *menú de degustación* for €30.

Peña Taurina Almeriense c/Regocijos 23, north of the Puerta de Purchena. Great old bar where *corrida* aficionados gather to talk about fights past, present and to come, looked down on by historical photos and paraphernalia.

El Quinto Toro c/Reyes Católicos 6. Top-notch atmospheric tapas bar taking its name from the fifth bull in the *corrida* (reputed to always be the best). Friendly service and mouth-watering *patatas a lo pobre*. They have recently opened up *El Quinto Toro II* slightly southeast of here at the junction of c/Javier Sanz with c/Padre Santaella. The same people also run the good beer bar *Cervecería La Estrella*, Plaza del Carmen 12, off the Puerta de Purchena.

Rincón de Juan Pedro Plaza del Carmen ☎950 23 58 19. One of the town's pricier restaurants, serving top-quality Almerian specialities. On a budget, stick to the good-value *menú* for around €9 which includes wine.

Restaurante Torreluz Plaza Flores 1. Close to the hotel of the same name, this is a very good mid-priced restaurant with a creative bent. There's a *menú de degustación* for €35.

Restaurante Valentin c/Tenor Iribarne 19 ☎950 26 44 75. Owned by the same people as *Bodega Las Botas*, this is a stylish mid-priced restaurant and tapas bar noted for its seafood; it has a *menú de degustación* for €34. Closed Mon.

Tetería-Restaurante Almedína c/Paz 2. Very friendly little Moroccan-run *tetería* which serves full meals later in the day including couscous and chicken and lamb *tagines*. On alternate Saturday nights they stage live concerts of flamenco and north African music.

Around the cathedral

Bar Bahía de la Palma c/Mariana, next to Plaza Vieja. Good lunchtime tapas stop. Recorded flamenco music is the accompaniment to the drinking here and some evenings they even put on live sessions.

Bodega Montenegro Plaza Granero, just west of the cathedral. Delightful neighbourhood bar, stacked with barrels. Once they've got over the initial novelty of seeing a foreigner walk through the door, they serve up great local wines and seafood tapas.

Bodega del Patio c/Real 84. At the southern end of c/Real, this is another wonderful old Almerian *bodega*, little changed for decades.

Bodega El Ajoli c/Padre Alfonso, slightly south of the Iglesia de San Pedro. On the same street as the *Bodega Ramón*, this tapas and *raciones* bar also has outdoor tables. Specializes in pork dishes – ordering their *surtido* gets you a bit of everything.

Bodega Ramón c/Padre Alfonso, slightly south of the Iglesia de San Pedro. Good tapas and *raciones* bar on a pleasant street, with tables to sit out at.

Casa Joaquín c/Real 111, near the port. Fine and popular tapas bar which buzzes with contented imbibers most evenings. All tapas and *raciones* are excellent, especially the seafood.

Casa Puga Corner of c/Lope de Vega and c/Jovellanos. With marble-topped tables and walls covered with *azulejos*, this is another outstanding tapas bar – founded in 1870 – with a great atmosphere and loyal clientele; try their *pescado frito*.

Barrio de los Pescadores and the beach area

Los Sobrinos Cuesta de Muelle 32. Facing the port, this place serves up fish dishes and is a slightly cheaper place than the *Pavía* (below).

Marisquería Veracruz Avda. Cabo de Gata 119, between the youth hostel and the seafront. Excellent and popular seafood and fish restaurant serving a wide range of seafood and shellfish.

Pavía Plaza Pavía 10. Fine fish and seafood served on tables in the square in summer.

Nightlife and flamenco

Most of Almería's **nightlife** takes place in the beach resorts to the west of the town. However, if you're determined to party, head for the bars in the streets around the Plaza Masnou near the cathedral, and c/San Pedro south of the Puerta de Purchena, which attract big night-time crowds, especially at weekends. The *Irish Tavern*, Plaza González Egea, just west of c/San Pedro, is the best of the town's twin Hibernian bars and has tables outside on a pleasant terrace. The *Geographic Café*, at the junction of calles Marqués de Comilla and General Tamayo off the east side of the Paseo de Almería, is an atmospheric music bar with travel-themed decor.

To move the night-time *marcha*, or scene, away from the residential area in summer, the city council erects a line of **discoteca marquees** at the start of the Paseo Marítimo, near the beach. At around 3am these places start to get quite wild. At other times of the year the focus moves back into town and the streets around c/Trajano off the Paseo de Almería where **music bars** *Godard*, *Underground*, *Desatino* and *Vhada* are popular. On the Paseo de Almería at no. 56 *Molly Malone* is a popular bar housed in the elegant old *casino* with a theatre behind; their outdoor terrace is a great place for a drink on summer nights.

For **flamenco**, the only genuine establishment is *Peña El Taranto,* taking its name from the *taranto*, Almería's dramatic and clamorous contribution to the flamenco canon. Based in the Moorish Baths, near the Puerta de Purchena, this

Getting to Morocco

There is a **daily boat to Melilla** on the Moroccan coast throughout the summer (less often out of season), a six-hour journey, but one which cuts out the haul to Málaga or the usual port for Morocco, Algeciras. In summer (June–Sept) a high-speed vessel does the trip in four hours. For information and tickets contact the *Compañía Tras-mediterránea* (☏902 45 46 45, ⓦ www.trasmediterranea.es), Parque Nicolás Salmerón 19, near the port. The daily six-hour route to Nador (south of Melilla) is operated by *Ferrimaroc* (☏950 27 48 00, ⓦ www.ferrimaroc.com) who have an office in the port.

club holds regular concerts (except in August) and their good-value tapas bar is always worth a visit.

Listings

Airport Local buses make the journey from the centre every half-hour between 7am and 9pm; take lines #14 or #20 labelled "El Alquián" from the junction of the Avda. Federico García Lorca and c/Gregorio Marañón (one block above the top right corner of our map).

Banks The major banks, most with ATMs, are along the Paseo de Almería and close at 2pm; there is also an ATM at the airport.

Books and newspapers Papelería Goya, Paseo de Almería 8, has a good book selection on the town and province. Almería's main daily paper is *La Voz de Almería* (ⓦ www.lavozdealmeria.com), a useful source for local and provincial news as well as entertainment listings at weekends.

Buses Schedules and tickets are available from the bus station (see p.601). For more information see "Travel details", p.634.

Car rental Europcar, at the airport ☏950 29 29 34, ⓦ www.europcar.es or Alva, Rambla Alfareros 11, north of Puerta de Purchena (☏950 23 77 47, ⓦ www.alva.es), for a cheaper local alternative.

Football Almería supports two teams, both founded in the 1980s. U.D. Almería (☏950 22 87 06), playing in the third division, are currently the more successful of the two, whilst their fierce rivals Polideportivo Almería (☏950 24 56 42) are toiling in the lower leagues. Both play matches at the Estadio Municipal, Avda. Torrecardenas s/n, in the northern suburbs.

Hiking maps Librería Cajal, c/Navarro Rodrigo 14, just south of the market, stocks walking guides and maps. Nearby Picasso, c/Reyes Católicos 16 is a similar place.

Hospital The main infirmary is Hospital Torrecárdenas (☏950 01 60 00) in the northeastern suburbs.

Internet *Cyber*, inside the Estación Intermodal (train-bus station; Mon–Sat 10am–11pm), is Almería's most central Internet café. An alternative is *Cyber-Café Europa* (daily 9am–11pm) Hermanos Pinzón 49, near the archeological museum.

Left luggage There are coin-operated lockers at the Estación Intermodal (train-bus) station for €3.

Police Contact the Policia Municipal c/Santos Zárate 11, off the north end of the Avda. Federico García Lorca, to report thefts or lost property (☏950 62 12 05). In case of emergency dial ☏092 (local police) or ☏091 (national).

Post office Plaza Cassinello 1 (Mon–Fri 9am–8pm, Sat 9am–1.30pm), near Plaza del Ecuador, off Paseo de Almería.

Trains Tickets and schedules are available from the train station (see p.601) and the RENFE office at c/Alcalde Muñoz 7, behind the church of San Sebastián near the Puerta de Purchena. For more information see "Travel details", p.634. There are direct services to Guadix, Granada and Baeza as well as longer-haul destinations such as Madrid (via Linares).

West of Almería: the Costa Tropical

Almería's best beach resorts lie on its eastern coast, the Costa de Almería, between the city and Mojácar. On the so-called **Costa Tropical**, west of the city, the nearest beaches such as **Aguadulce**, **Roquetas de Mar** and

Almerimar are overdeveloped and the landscape is dismal, backed by an ever-expanding plastic sea of *invernaderos*, hothouses for cultivation of fruit and vegetables for the export market (see box opposite). Beyond Adra things improve, and smaller resorts such as **La Rábita**, **Castell de Ferro** and **Calahonda** make tolerable places to stop.

From Almería to Adra

This section of coast is certainly not an unspoilt paradise; indeed, no one comes here for the beaches. The one half-decent reason for a stop in these parts is if you're a **bird-watcher**, in which case the inland salt lakes may well appeal.

AGUADULCE, 13km west of Almería, is the oldest of the city's local resorts, with a palm-lined promenade that does its best to offset the miserable concrete boxes flanking it. There's a reasonable beach, the usual *costa* nightlife, and some fairly expensive accommodation, full all summer.

The next place along, **ROQUETAS DE MAR**, used to be another old fishing port, though its remaining whitewashed core is now submerged by an ugly conglomeration of hotels and beach emporia. On the plain behind the resort, plastic greenhouses compete fiercely with developers for land and this must be the only place in Spain where agricultural land is more profitable than tourist development – a couple of acres sells for many thousands of euros. The centre of the cultivation is the boom town of **EL EJIDO** (see box opposite), 30km inland from Roquetas de Mar along the arrow-straight A7-E15.

Some relief from the tedium can be found 5km to the south of Roquetas, where **Las Marinas** is a good place for spotting **birdlife**. A saline marsh fringed by tamarisks, it attracts greater flamingos, little egrets and avocets, and, in winter, the white wagtail. The lake is reached by turning left beyond the *Urbanización Roquetas de Mar*. A road joins this to a second area at **Punta Sabinar**, 1km south, consisting of beach, sand dunes and salt marsh with possible sightings of crested larks, great grey shrikes and fantailed warblers.

Almerimar, Adra and around

ALMERIMAR is a long 18km from Roquetas, through the plastic-covered desert – and not much relief when you eventually arrive. A rather tasteless conglomeration of *urbanizaciones* – with more being assembled – crowd around a dismal yacht harbour where the local *plasticultura* billionaires park their floating assets alongside craft from the four corners of the Mediterranean. Less interested in attracting foreign package tours, this is the "glitz" resort for the nouveauriches of El Ejido, and the place where these agricultural tycoons can indulge in conspicuous consumption. Tacky shopping arcades with neo-Moorish facades, overpriced restaurants and three golf courses – one designed by Gary Player – complete the picture.

It's a relief to join the main A7-E15 heading west, although not for long because you soon arrive in **ADRA**, another place with nonexistent charms. "The last king of the Moors, the unfortunate Boabdil, stayed in Adra immediately before leaving Spain for good. If he sighed when leaving Granada, he would have sighed even more had Adra in the fifteenth century been anything like it is today." Few would argue with Michael Jacobs's comments on this seedy industrial port in his book *Andalusia*. The best that can be said for it is that the planners have considerately sited the **bus station** on the seafront near the harbour, thus allowing for a speedy and relatively painless getaway. Should you be stuck for a place to stay (and rooms can be tight along this coast in high season) the good-value *Hostal Los Olivos*, Ctra. Almería 6, on the road into the

West of Almería, and stretching from beneath the hills of the Sierra de Gador to the sea, lies the **Campo de Dalías**, a vast plain of salt flats and sand dunes which has become a shining sea of *plasticultura* – the forced production of millions of tons of tomatoes, peppers, cucumbers, strawberries and exotic flowers. This industry has wrought quite a revolution in impoverished Almería, covering a once-barren wilderness with a shimmering sea of 64,000 acres of polythene canopies (producing 20,000 tons of plastic waste annually) propped up by eucalyptus supports.

The boom is all due to the invention of drip-feed irrigation and it has led to phenomenal increases in the year-round production of crops, allowing cheap tropical fruit and flowers to fill the supermarket shelves of northern Europe throughout the year. The appliance of biological engineering now means that Campo de Dalías's farmers can produce vegetables to almost any specification – "name your size" tomatoes, red peppers with large cavities for stuffing or lettuces without coarse outer leaves which look green even under fluorescent supermarket lights. The future of the miracle, however, may be precarious. Scientists have serious worries about the draining of the province's meagre water resources through the tapping of countless artesian wells – many as deep as 100m. A plan hatched by the Partido Popular government in 2002 to solve this problem by diverting water from the Río Ebro in northern Spain met with outraged resistance from the inhabitants and farmers of the Ebro delta and the plan was dropped by the incoming PSOE regime in 2004. The Almerian farmers have now placed their hopes in the construction of a mammoth seawater desalination plant at Carboneras.

The centre of the *plasticultura* zone is **El Ejido**, a conurbation that has multiplied from a modest population of two thousand, twenty years ago, to some fifty thousand today, making it second in the province only to the capital itself. Like some Wild West town, El Ejido has grown up for a dozen kilometres along the main highway with little or no planning restraints and with the free market in almost total control. The bonanza has lured in peasants from all over Spain and beyond, and many *andaluzes* who formerly worked in the factories of Barcelona and Germany have come home with their savings and bought plots. El Ejido's wealth explosion has also funded a football team – Polideportivo Ejido – which has charged up the divisions and is currently holding its own in Division Two with games against the likes of Real Madrid and Barcelona now a real possibility. More depressingly, the high demand for workers willing to toil in the terrible conditions has led to the arrival of 10,000 **immigrants** (mostly illegal) from Morocco and other African countries, who have built squalid shanty settlements on the edges of town. Despite the threat of high fines if farmers are found to be using these "*sin papeles*" (without papers) workers, many farmers still take the risk and the authorities often turn a blind eye.

The lack of facilities for this enormous population growth – now being belatedly investigated by the authorities – has led to serious problems and the social cost has been high: the suicide rate has risen sharply as those who don't make the easy money anticipated get deep into debt, and the twelve- to fifteen-hour days worked in jungle humidity all year long inside the *invernaderos* (plastic tents) often lead to breakdowns. Besides illness and alcoholism, gambling and drug addiction are also taking their toll. Early in 2000 simmering local resentment at the immigrant "invasion" erupted into violence when a two-day riot followed the fatal stabbing of a local woman who had resisted an immigrant (and mentally unstable) thief intent on taking her bag. The furious townspeople attacked the shops, bars and support centres of the immigrant population, setting some hostels ablaze and covering others with racist slogans. It took six hundred of the Guardia Civil to quell the disorder and the government's interior minister described it as "a disgrace for Spanish society". In the years since this event some resources have been channelled into improving facilities for the immigrants but a brooding tension between the two communities remains.

town coming from Almería (℡ & ⓕ 950 56 70 00; ❸) with hotel-style facilities, usually has rooms.

Some 16km inland from Adra is the solid farming town of **BERJA**, the capital of *Alpujarra Baja*, surrounded by vineyards and fruit orchards, with a considerable Roman and Moorish past (there's an impressive ruined *alcazaba* in the suburb of Villavieja) and a lively daily market. Nearby **DALÍAS**, another pleasant farming village, is founded upon the ruins of Roman Murgis.

Adra to Motril

Things start to look up along the coast to the west of Adra, and there are attractions inland, too. From La Rábita a scenic secondary road, the A345, heads up into Las Alpujarras, passing by the *costa* wine villages of Albuñol and Albondón.

Güainos Bajos and Castillo de Baños

Around 5km west of Adra, **GÜAINOS BAJOS** fronts a pleasant and small beach. A further 10km along – and over the provincial border in Granada – you reach **LA RÁBITA**, another place that might invite a stop, although its charms are somewhat compromised by more invasive plastic greenhouses creeping over the surrounding hills. Enclosed in a rocky creek, it has a reasonable beach (though it is often litter-strewn after the weekend onslaught), as well as a clutch of **rooms** places, bars and restaurants.

CASTILLO DE BAÑOS, 13km west of La Rábita, takes its name from a nearby *atalaya* or watchtower and is another possibility for a stopover with a decent beach and a good **campsite**, *Camping Castillo de Baños* (℡958 82 95 28, ⓦ www.doncactus.com), with plenty of shade but surrounded by more plastic tents.

Castell de Ferro and beyond

CASTELL DE FERRO, 6km on from Castillo de Baños, is by far the best of the resorts along this stretch of coast and even preserves remnants of its former existence as a fishing village. Dominated by another hill-top *atalaya*, it's quite sheltered and has a couple of wide, if pebbly, **beaches** to the west and especially east, although the town beach fronting the small assemblage of bars, restaurants and *hostales* is less inviting. Among the **places to stay** (all on the seafront Plaza de España), the friendly *Hostal Bahia* (℡958 65 60 60; ❷) is outstanding value and has seaview rooms with terrace, with the *Costa del Sol* (℡958 65 60 54; ❸), offering rooms above a decent restaurant, a good second choice. Of Castell's four **campsites**, *Camping Las Palmeras* (℡958 65 61 30), the westernmost of the bunch, is the one to go for, with shade, plenty of space and access to the beach. For **meals**, *Restaurante La Brisa* does **raciones** plus a good and inexpensive *menú*, as do most of the places along the seafront.

The coast road east again from here skirts the foothills of the Sierra de Carchuna where **CALAHONDA** is another small resort with a good beach, the Playa de Carchuna, often full to the gunwales in summer. In the centre, the fish restaurant *El Ancla* is the best of the eating places, and a pleasant beach bar and *chiringuito*, *El Farillo*, is to be found by an old watchtower at the western end of the strand. Next comes the unremarkable **TORRENUEVA**, where there's a reasonable beach but little else to stop for, before the road crosses a dreary plain planted with sugar cane, to the north of which lies the large and ugly chemical and industrial town of **MOTRIL**, and to the south its equally unappealing port-resort. The beaches to the west of Motril are described in Chapter One.

The Costa de Almería

The **Costa de Almería**, east of Almería, has a somewhat wild air, with developments constrained by lack of water and roads and by the confines of the **Parque Natural de Cabo de Gata**, a protected zone since 1987. If you have transport, it's still possible to find deserted beaches without too much difficulty, while small inlets shelter relatively low-key resorts such as **San José**, **Los Escullos**, **Las Negras** and **Agua Amarga**.

Further north is **Mojácar**, a picturesque hill village, which has grown a beach resort of quite some size over the past decade. It is easiest – and most speedily – approached on the inland routes via Nijar (the A7-E15) or the "desert" road (N340A) through Tabernas and Sorbas.

Almería to Mojácar

The coast between Almería and Mojácar is backed by the **Sierra del Cabo de Gata**, which gives it a bit of character and wilderness. **Buses** run from Almería to all the main resorts, though to do much exploring, or seek out deserted strands, transport of your own is invaluable. The heat is blistering here throughout the summer, and you should bear in mind that during July and August Natural Park accommodation is at a premium – try and book ahead if possible.

El Cabo de Gata and Las Salinas

Heading east along the main AL12, a turn-off to the right, 3km beyond the airport, heads south to **EL CABO DE GATA**. This is the closest resort to the city with any appeal: a lovely expanse of coarse sand, best in the mornings before the sun and wind get up. Six buses a day (four on Sundays) run between Almería and El Cabo, making an intermediate stop at Retamar, a retirement/holiday development.

Arriving at El Cabo, you pass a lake, the **Laguna de Rosa**, a protected locale that is home to flamingos and other waders. Nearby there's a **campsite**, *Camping Cabo de Gata* (☎950 16 04 43). In the village itself there are plentiful bars, cafés and shops, plus a fish market. The seafront has a rather listless air and no places to stay meaning that for **rooms** you'll need to head inland to the friendly but pricey *Hostal Las Dunas* (☎950 37 00 72, ℗950 37 72; ❹), 100m back from the beach at c/Barrionuevo 58, offering a/c en-suite rooms with TV. The three-star *Hotel Blanca Brisa*, c/Las Joricas 49, on the edge of town (☎950 37 00 01, ⓦwww.blancabrisa.com; ❺ with breakfast) is not a great step up in price.

Just south of the village is another area known as **Las Salinas** – The Salt Pans – and it is exactly that, with a commercial salt-drying enterprise at its southern end. In summer **flamingos** and other migrants are a common sight here (see box), so take binoculars if you have them – just before dusk is a good time. The natural park authorities have now installed **hides** here (signed off the road). The hills of salt are a striking sight in the bright sun, too, and the industry here has a pedigree dating back to the Phoenicians who first controlled the seawater which entered through the marshes to create pools for the extraction of salt in the first millennium BC. The park authorities like to cite the modern industry as an example of resource extraction and environmental conservation working hand in hand. Certainly the flamingos seem perfectly happy with the arrangement.

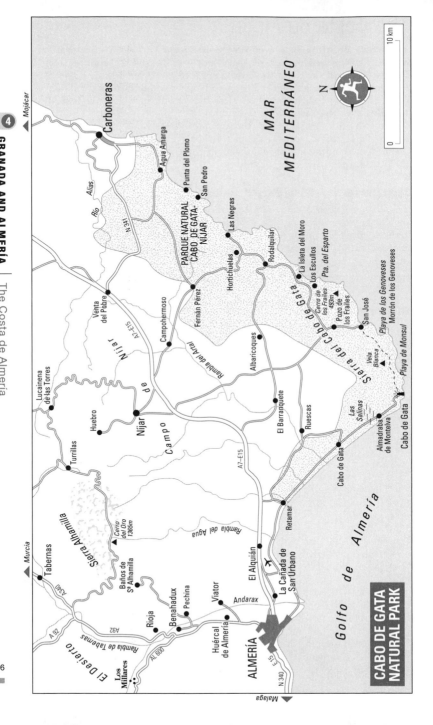

MAR MEDITERRÁNEO

N

0   10 km

Mojácar

Carboneras

Agua Amarga

Punta del Plomo

San Pedro

N 341

PARQUE NATURAL CABO DE GATA-NÍJAR

Las Negras

Rodalquilar

La Isleta del Moro

Los Escullos

Pta. del Esparto

Cerro de los Frailes 493m

Pozo de los Frailes

San José

Playa de los Genoveses

Morrón de los Genoveses

Vela Blanca

Playa de Monsul

Hortichuelas

Fernán Pérez

Campohermoso

Venta del Pobre

Río Alías

AL-E15

Níjar

Campo de Níjar

Rambla del Atzal

Albaricoques

El Barranquete

Ruescas

Las Salinas

Almadraba de Montelva

Cabo de Gata

Sierra del Cabo de Gata

Lucainena de las Torres

Huebro

Turrillas

Sierra Alhamilla

Cerro del Oro 1365m

Baños de Sª Alhamilla

Rambla del Agua

A7-E15

Cabo de Gata

Retamar

Golfo de Almería

Murcia

Tabernas

A 92

A340

El Desierto

Los Millares

Rambla de Tabernas

AL 600

Rioja

Benahadux

Pechina

Viator

Andarax

Huércal de Almería

El Alquián

La Cañada de San Urbano

ALMERÍA

N 340

Málaga

CABO DE GATA NATURAL PARK

Parque Natural de Cabo de Gata

Protected since 1987, the 71,500 acres of the **Parque Natural de Cabo de Gata** stretch from Retamar to the east of Almería across the cape to the Barranco del Honda, just north of Agua Amarga. The Sierra de Gata is volcanic in origin and its adjacent dunes and saltings are some of the most important wetland areas in Spain for **breeding birds** and **migrants**. At Las Salinas alone more than eighty species can be sighted throughout the year, including the magnificent pink flamingos as well as avocet, storks and egrets during their migrations. And there have been rarer sightings of Andouin's gull, as well as Bonelli's eagle and eagle owls around the crags.

Other **fauna** include the rare Italian wall lizard (its only habitat in Spain), with its distinctive green back with three rows of black spots, as well as the more common fox (sporting its Iberian white tail tip), hare and grass snake. Among the **flora**, the stunted dwarf fan palm is Europe's only native palm and the salt marshes are home to a strange parasitic plant, the striking yellow-flowering Cistanche phelypaea, which feeds on goosefoot.

The best times for sighting the fauna here are at **dawn and dusk** as, with temperatures among the highest in Europe and rainfall at 10cm a year the lowest, energy has to be conserved. Cabo de Gata village has a park **Oficina de Información** at Avda. Miramar 88 (daily 10am–2.30pm & 5.30–9pm; ☎950 38 02 99, ⊛www.cabodegata-nijar.com) which also rents out mountain bikes and has information on walking; there's another office in San José. Any hiking in the park is greatly assisted by using the Editorial Alpina 1:50.000 *Cabo de Gata Nijar* map which accurately marks trekking routes, tracks and campsites.

Almadraba de Montelva and the Cabo de Gata lighthouse

Four kilometres to the south of El Cabo village, just beyond Las Salinas, four **ALMADRABA DE MONTELVA**, more a continuation than a separate place, but altogether more pleasant for hanging around. You'll find a few bars and a couple of **restaurants** here: the seafront *La Almadraba* is the friendlier and more down-to-earth, whilst the nearby *Hotel Restaurante Morales* (☎950 37 01 03, ⊛www.hotellassalinas.com; ⑦) has a terrace and prices to reflect it; its kitschy hotel also has some pricey rooms.

Another 4km south, past a hill known as the Pico de San Miguel, the **Faro de Cabo de Gata** (lighthouse) marks the cape's southern tip. In the lighthouse car park a **Parque Natural information cabin** (June–Oct daily 10am–2pm & 6–8pm; Oct–May Sat & Sun 10am–3pm) has maps and information on the park. There's also a friendly tapas bar here, *El Faro*, serving up tasty locally caught fried fish and paella, as well as a *mirador* from where you can get a great view of the rock cliffs and – on clearer days – a sight of Morocco's Rif mountains.

Beyond the lighthouse a track leads to two of the finest **beaches** in the province, and to the resort of San José beyond. This track is closed to cars, which is all to your advantage for it makes for a fine walk through the Natural Park. Starting out as a paved road, climbing up from the lighthouse, this soon degenerates into a dirt track, passing prickly pear cactus plantations grown for their fruit, and access tracks to the wonderful fine sand beaches of **Monsul** (6km out) – with freshwater springs and a track west to the even more secluded Media Luna cove – and further east, **Los Genoveses** (10km from the lighthouse). A couple of kilometres further, and beyond another spur, you'll sight the sea and the resort of San José.

To reach San José **by car**, you'll need to double back to El Cabo de Gata and follow the signed road further inland.

San José

The attractive little resort of **SAN JOSÉ** (served by three daily buses from Almería) has a sandy beach in a small cove, with shallow water, while more fine beaches lie within walking distance. Only a few years ago it was almost completely undeveloped, though things are changing, with a rash of apartments and a new yacht harbour.

If you've followed the walk from the lighthouse to San José (see previous page) and want to continue along the coast there's another **track**, running 12km north to Los Escullos and La Isleta. To start the walk take the road north out of San José, along which you'll shortly come to a turn-off along a dirt track on the right that heads around a hill – Cerro del Enmedio – towards the coast. The track branches at various points and you'll have to decide whether

△ San José

to follow the coastal tracks (which can be impassable) or the surer inland route. The first track off to the coast provides access to a beautiful and secluded cove. Further on, the route skirts the 500m-high Cerro de los Frailes, beyond which lie the inlets of Los Escullos and La Isleta.

Information

On San José's main street, Avenida de San José, near the centre of the village you'll find the official **Centro de Información** for the Natural Park (daily 10am–2pm & 5–8pm; ☎950 38 02 99, ⊛www.cabodegata–nijar.com) which has lots of information on activities such as guided walks and horse treks in the zone; they also have a complete list of accommodation and information on apartments to rent which may be a cheaper option for a longer stay. **Internet** access is available at *Bla Bla Bla* (daily 9am–midnight), Pasaje Curry, close to the Centro de Información. Near the main street's central junction, and up some steps almost opposite the *Hostal Costa Rica*, David the Bookman (Sat–Thurs 10.30am–1.30pm & 5–9.30pm) is a good source of paperback **books** in English and will exchange any books you wish to offload. **Horses** can be hired for exploring the park from the *Hotel Cortijo El Sotillo* (see below). Alpha (☎950 38 03 21, ⊛www.alphabuceo.com) is a PADI-certificated **diving centre** located in the Puerto Deportivo (yacht harbour) for courses in snorkelling and scuba diving. Along Avenida de San José there's a **bank** with ATM cash machine, plus a couple of well-stocked **supermarkets** for picnic supplies.

Accommodation

Rooms can be hard to come by even outside high season (July & August), and during this period many places want stays of at least 5 days (applying a surcharge for shorter durations). During high season it's essential to ring ahead and advisable at other times of the year, too. San José's good **campsite**, *Camping Tau* (☎950 38 01 66; April–Oct), is reached via a signed road on the left as you enter the village.

Albergue Juvenil c/Montemar s/n ☎950 38 03 53, ⊛www.alberguesanjose.com. Reached by same road leading to the campsite (above) this privately run youth hostel has 86 places divided between rooms sleeping from two to eight persons. It is usually booked solid at Easter and in August. €10 per person

El Cortijo Sotillo Ctra. San José s/n ☎950 61 11 00, ⊛www.elsotillo.org. To the left on the main road in and a kilometre from the centre, this is a refurbished eighteenth-century ranch-house converted into a four-star country hotel with elegant rustically furnished rooms, restaurant, bar, pool, tennis courts, and horses for hire. ❼

Hostal Agades Agidir c/Córdoba s/n ☎950 38 03 90, ⓕ950 38 00 06. A hotel in all but name, this is a very pleasant option for a/c en-suite balcony rooms plus garden pool, bar and restaurant. Sited on the right-hand side of the main road as you come in (a five-minute walk from the village). ❺

Hostal Aloha c/Cala Higuera s/n ☎950 38 04 61. Close to the sea, this place offers fairly basic en-suite balcony rooms but has the bonus of a superb palm-fringed pool. ❸

Hostal Brisa del Mar c/Ancla s/n ☎ & ⓕ950 38 04 31. Over the road from *Las Gaviotas*, (below) this is a new arrival with bright and airy en-suite a/c rooms with TV and terrace balcony. ❹

Hostal El Paraiso II c/Córdoba s/n ☎950 38 03 80. Located on a street running behind the *Hostal Agades Agidir*, this is a friendly budget option for rooms with and without bath and also has a few with their own terrace. ❸–❹

Hostal Las Gaviotas c/Córdoba s/n ☎950 38 00 10, ⊛www.hlasgaviotas.com. Almost next door to *Hostal Agades Agadir* this is a more economical (and downmarket) option for en-suite rooms with a/c and TV. ❹

Hostal San José c/Las Olas s/n ☎950 61 10 80, ⊛www.servimar.net. Perched on a hill overlooking the harbour, this is an upmarket *hostal* with a/c en-suite rooms equipped with kitchenette and balcony terraces with fine sea views. ❺

Hostal Sol Bahía c/Correos 5 ☎950 38 01 14, ⓕ950 38 03 06. Near the main junction in the centre of the village, *Hostal Sol Bahia*, is one of the better-value central places, offering spacious a/c en-suite balcony rooms with TV. ❹

Hotel Doña Pakyta c/Correo s/n ☎950 61 11 75, ⓦwww.hotelpakyta.com. One of the swishest places in town at the western end of the bay offering light and airy terrace balcony rooms with stunning sea views. ⑧ with breakfast.

Hotel La Posada de Paco c/Correo s/n ☎950 38 00 10, ⓦwww.laposadadepaco.com. On the main street and slightly east of the main junction, this is a stylish small hotel with pool and a/c terrace rooms with satellite TV. ⑥ with breakfast.

Eating and drinking

For **food and drink** there are numerous bars and restaurants on the central Plaza de Génova and facing the nearby beach on c/del Puerto Deportivo, offering everything from fast food and pizzas to excellent fresh local fish. Try the *salmonetes* (red mullet fried with garlic) at *La Cueva*. Next door to the latter, the equally good *El Tempranillo* does a tasty *besugo* (red bream with parsley and garlic) and treats its clientele to some excellent – and cheap – Láujar wines from the Almerian Alpujarras. Just around the corner from these two and overlooking the Puerto Deportivo, the *Taberna del Puerto* is another good – if slightly pricier – place for fish and has a small terrace. Near the main junction, *Bar-Restaurante El Emigrante* (the restaurant of *Hostal Sol Bahía* above) prepares good fish and *platos combinados* and has a *menú* for €10. For a splurge, the zone's only place with any pretensions is *La Gallineta*, 4km back along the entry road at El Pozo de Fraires (☎950 38 05 01; main dishes €9–20; closed Mon); it offers sophisticated meat and fish dishes in a stylish traditional house beside a restored Moorish waterwheel.

Los Escullos and La Isleta

Next along this rugged coastline is the isolated but developing **LOS ESCULLOS**, 8km north by road, with a good if rather pebbly beach and a formidable ruined fort, the eighteenth-century **Castillo de San Felipe**. The pleasant beachfront *hostal-restaurante*, *Casa Emilio* (☎950 38 97 61; ④), offering a/c en-suite rooms with terrace balcony has been joined by the new *Hotel Los Escullos* (☎950 38 97 33, ⓦwww.hotelescullos.com; ⑥) which has air-conditioned rooms with TV. There's also a **campsite**, *Camping Los Escullos* (☎950 38 98 11), set back from the sea with limited shade. **LA ISLETA**, 2km beyond, is another fishing village which is slowly expanding, but it still manages to retain a sleepy atmosphere and has a rather scruffy pebble beach, although there's a better one – Playa la Ola – to the east backed by a car park. A **hostal**, *Isleta del Moro* (☎950 38 97 13, ⓕ950 38 97 64; ③), overlooks the harbour, has reasonably priced en-suite rooms plus a decent **bar–restaurant** serving tapas and a good-value *menú* for around €10. The nearby 🗲 *Bar-Restaurante La Ola*, set back from the beach with a shady terrace, is another excellent little bar-restaurant for seafood tapas and *raciones*.

Rodalquilar

The road north of here climbs over the cliffs above Isleta and heads inland before descending to a pleasant valley, passing after 4km the desert hamlet of **RODALQUILAR** surrounded by scrub, palms and cactuses. There's a **Natural Park information office** (May–Sept daily 10am–2pm & 6–8pm, Oct–March Sat & Sun 10am–3pm; ☎950 38 97 42) opposite the church in the centre, and on the village's eastern edge the attractive desert **inn** *Hotel Rodalquilar* (☎950 38 98 38, ⓦwww.hotelrodalquilar.com; ⑦ with breakfast) has attractive rooms arranged around a sunken courtyard; a restaurant, pool, sauna and gym are just a few of the facilities on offer. Next door to here the *El Ajillo* is a very good mid-priced restaurant (main dishes €10–17) and also rents out modern stylish rooms at its own adjoining hotel (☎950 38 97 20, ⓦwww.posadaelajillo.com; ⑥). Rodalquilar is served by a single daily **bus** from Almería.

Las Negras and San Pedro

LAS NEGRAS, 5km further, is situated in the folds of a beautiful cove, with an *atalaya*, or watchtower, sited on the edge of the village as you approach. There's a pebbly beach, a few **bars** – including the pleasant *La Manteca* on the seafront which stays open all year – and a decent **restaurant**, *La Palma*, which overlooks the beach. A **campsite**, *La Caleta* (☎950 52 52 37), set in a tranquil location with its own bay, is reached via a 1km road just outside the village on the way in. For **rooms**, the friendly and excellent-value *Hostal Arrecife*, c/Bahia 6 (☎950 38 81 40; ❸), close to the *estanco* (see below), has a/c en-suite sea-view terrace rooms with TV. More possibilities aren't difficult to spot in summer as many shops and bars post signs offering accommodation to let. Another option for longer stays (five nights plus in high season) is the collection of **apartments and chalets** (❹–❺) in coastal and country locations rented out by *Estanco Piedra García* (☎ & ☎950 38 80 75, ⓦwww.lasnegras.com), the main street tobacconist and information office whose proprietors speak English.

For a change of beach the *estanco* should be able to arrange for someone to row you up the coast to the ruined village of **SAN PEDRO**. If you can't find an oarsman, you'll have to walk – no bad hike when it's cool – to visit the village with its caves and ruined castle; it lies 4km north on a poor track. The place was inhabited until a few years ago when the mainly elderly residents upped sticks to Las Negras, which had acquired a road, leaving their houses – sometimes occupied by north European pseudo-hippies – to crumble. If you are feeling really energetic, you could walk 7km on from here along the coast to Agua Amarga, via another pleasant beach at **Cala del Plomo**. If you attempt these walks in summer remember to take along drinking water as there is none to be had en route or at San Pedro.

Agua Amarga

AGUA AMARGA stands just before the Natural Park's northern boundary and is a delightful little fishing village cut off from the surrounding world by a long road and a lack of accommodation. To reach it from Las Negras (a route not served by public transport) you'll need to head inland to the village of **Fernan Pérez**, from where a new road heads east for 11km to reach the small resort.

Most of the summer visitors here are Italians who rent a tasteful crop of villas. The excellent, fine sand **beach** has outlets renting windsurf boards and canoes, and there are a number of bars and restaurants backing it. The PADI-certificated Centro de Buceo, c/Aguada s/n behind the beach (☎950 13 82 13) offers courses for beginners and experienced scuba divers.

Should you wish **to stay**, there's the friendly French-run *Pensión Family* on c/La Lomilla (☎950 13 80 14, ⓔriovall@teleline.es; ❺ with breakfast) set back from the south end of the beach, where en-suite rooms are complemented by a small pool, garden and restaurant offering a good-value €16 *menú*. Alternative accommodations include the *Hotel Las Calas*, c/Desagüe s/n, fronting the beach at the southern end of the village (☎950 13 80 16, ⓦwww .hotellascalas.com; ❻), offering pristine rooms with terrace and sea view, and, on a rise behind *Pensión Family*, *Hotel El Tío Kiko* (☎950 13 80 80, ⓦwww .eltiokiko.com; ❾ with breakfast), a luxury boutique hotel with terrace sea-view rooms arranged around a pool. *Hostal-Restaurante La Palmera* (☎950 13 82 08, ⓔhrlapalmera@terra.es; ❺ with breakfast) has en-suite rooms behind the beach. For longer stays (2 nights plus) renting a fully equipped sea-view **apartment** from the friendly *Casas Requeña*, c/Aguada s/n (☎950 13 82 02 Spanish, mobile ☎659266688 English; ❺), is another possibility. All the hotels and *hostales* above have their own **restaurants** and another place well worth a visit for seafood is the beachfront *chiringuito Los Tarahis* near *Pensión Family*.

Carboneras

Leaving the Natural Park behind, **CARBONERAS**, 11km north of Agua Amarga, is a larger but easy-going fishing port with an average beach only slightly marred by the shadow of a massive cement factory around the bay. The town congregates round a pleasant little park (Parque Andaluz) and the sixteenth-century **Castillo de San Andrés**, built – along with a line of watch-towers to the west – to protect this stretch of coast from invaders. A stone's throw east of the castle a **Turismo**, c/del Mar s/n (daily 9am–2pm & 6–9pm, ☎950 13 60 52), can supply a town map and accommodation list. The seafront Paseo Marítimo promenade has a few **tapas** bars, while pleasant a/c en-suite **rooms** are to be had at the *Café Bar La Marina* (☎950 45 40 70; ❸), c/General Mola 1, close to the Parque Andaluz, or the nearby and seafront *Hostal-Restaurante Sol y Playa*, Paseo Marítimo s/n (☎950 45 40 78; ❹), both with rooms above good restaurants.

Towards Mojácar

North of Carboneras lies a succession of small, isolated coves, backed by a characteristically arid Almerian landscape of scrub-covered hills and dried up *arroyos*, or watercourses. The **Carboneras–Mojácar road** itself winds peril-ously – and scenically – through the hills and offers access to some deserted grey-sand beaches before ascending to the Punta del Santo with fine views along the coast. The descent from here brings you to the **Playa de Macenas**, another pleasant beach with wild-camping possibilities. There are a couple more beaches – **Costa del Pirulico** is a good one with a beach *chiringuito* – before the urban sprawl of Mojácar takes over.

Mojácar and around

MOJÁCAR, Almería's main and growing resort, is split between the ancient hill-top village – **Mojácar Pueblo** – sited a couple of kilometres back from the sea, a striking town of white cubist houses wrapped round a harsh outcrop of rock, and the resort area of **Mojácar Playa** which ribbons for a couple of miles along the seafront.

In the 1960s, when the main Spanish *costas* were being developed, this was virtually a ghost town, its inhabitants having long since taken the only logi-cal step, and emigrated. The town's fortunes revived, however, when the local mayor, using the popularity of other equally barren spots on the Spanish islands and mainland as an example, offered free land to anyone willing to build within a year. The bid was a modest success, attracting one of the decade's multifari-ous "artist colonies", now long supplanted by package holiday companies and second-homers. A plush 80-room hotel has opened in the village as well as a parador fronting the beach, and there's a burgeoning foreign jet set which lives here for half the year and migrates in summer, all of which has rapidly down-graded Mojácar's obvious charms.

Mojácar Pueblo

Mojácar's hill-top settlement goes back at least to prehistoric Iberian times, and became prominent during the Roman period when Pliny described it as one of the most important towns of *Baetica* – as the Roman province was called. Coins found from this era give the Roman name as *Murgis*, which the later

Moors adapted to *Muxacra*. The village's **main fountain** (the Fuente Mora) – signed to the right off the road climbing towards the centre – has been newly restored with lots of marble and geraniums and was where thirty years ago veiled women still used to do the family washing. A plaque nearby relates how keen the Moors were to hang on to their hill-top eyrie when challenged by the *Reconquista*. First declaring loyalty to the Reyes Católicoss the Moorish mayor, Alabez, then stated that if the Catholic monarchs wouldn't accede to the request to be left in peace, "rather than live like a coward I shall die like a Spaniard. May Allah protect you!" The monarchs were impressed and, for a time at least, prudently granted Alabez's wish.

An ancient custom, no longer practised but parodied on every bangle and trinket sold in the tourist shops, was to paint an **indalo** on the doorways of the village to ward off evil. This symbol – a matchstick figure with arms outstretched, holding an arc – comes from the six-thousand-year-old Neolithic drawings in the caves at Vélez Blanco to the north, and anthropologists believe that it is a unique case of a prehistoric symbol being passed down in one location for numerous millennia.

Indalos apart, sights in the upper village are limited to strolling around the sinuous, white-walled streets, looking at the heavily restored fifteenth-century church of **Santa María**, and savouring the view over the strangely formed surrounding hills and coast to the north from the **mirador** in the main square, Plaza Nueva. After which it's either a tour of the boutiques and souvenir shops, a seat on the terraces of drinking dens with names like *Gordon's Bar* and *Time and Place*, or a crawl around noisier disco pubs such as *Budu*, *Lapu Lapu* or *La Muralla*.

Practicalities

The **Turismo** (Mon–Fri 10am–2pm & 5.30–7.30pm; Sat 10.30am–1.30pm, ☎950 61 50 25, ⓦwww.mojacarviva.com) is located just below Plaza Nueva – you'll need their free **map** to negotiate the maze of narrow streets – with the **post office** in the same building and an ATM next door. Places **to stay** include a handful of small *hostales*, all with some en-suite rooms, including the good-value *Casa Justa* at c/Morote 5 (☎950 47 83 72; ❷), behind the church. Just off the main square, *Hostal Arco Plaza* (☎950 47 27 77, ⓕ950 47 27 17; ❹) is the next best deal for rooms with bath and TV. Another alternative slightly east, is the friendly *Pensión El Torreón*, c/Jazmín 4 (☎ & ⓕ 950 47 52 59; ❹), which has charming if pricey rooms sharing bath. On the way into town, the more upmarket but good-value ⚑ *Mamabel's* at c/Embajadores 3 (☎ & ⓕ950 47 24 48, ⓦwww.mamabels.com; ❻) has beautiful, individually styled en-suite rooms (no. 1 is a dream), some with stunning view, and a restaurant. The grand *Hotel El Moresco* (☎950 47 80 25, ⓦwww.arturocantoblanco.com; ❻), despite its pool, comes second best. Mojácar's **campsite** *El Quinto* (☎950 47 87 04) lies 2km below the village along the Turre road.

Places to **eat and drink** tend to be a bit pretentious and most of the over-priced restaurants are best avoided. The tapas bars around the main square are worth a try, and the nearby *Rincón de Embrujo*, with a terrace on the plazuela fronting the church, does inexpensive *platos combinados*. Internationally slanted fare is on offer at *Siglo XXI*, c/Enmedio 24, with a *menú* for €8. Moving upmarket, another place for carefully prepared Spanish standards is the mid-priced *Casa Minguito*, with an inviting terrace on the leafy Plaza Ayuntamiento at the heart of the village, next to the town hall. Nearby, ⚑ *El Palacio*, Plaza del Cano s/n, (June–Sept dinner only, ☎950 47 28 46) is one of the pueblo's two best-value restaurants with a reasonably priced menu and wine list, creative dishes such as *mero a la naranja* (grouper with orange sauce) and a wonderful roof terrace for alfresco dining. An equally memorable meal is on offer at *Mamabel's* (see above) where a good-value €19 *menú* – often featuring couscous and paella – can be enjoyed with vertiginously spectacular views from their terrace.

There's not much **nightlife** in the hill village but late-night drinking goes on at *Budu Pub* and the nearby *Pub La Muralla*, both on c/Estación Nueva north of the church, and at the oddball *El Loro Azul*, off the nearby Plaza Fronton.

Mojácar Playa

Down below on the seafront, **Mojácar Playa** is refreshingly brash: an excellent beach with warm and brilliantly clear waters, flanked by lots of fine beach bars and discotecas, **rooms for rent**, several hotels and hostales, and a good campsite, *El Cantal de Mojácar* (℡950 47 82 04). The beach resort's focal point is an ugly Centro Comercial, at the intersection – known locally as *El Cruce* – of the seafront highway with the road leading inland to Mojácar Pueblo. Hourly **buses** from the beach up to Mojácar Pueblo run from a stop outside the Centro Comercial, or you can pick them up at various stops along the seafront. Just south of here **Internet** access is available at *Indal-futur*, Paseo del Mediterráneo 293 (Mon–Fri 9am–2pm & 5–10pm, Sat & Sun 11am–2pm & 6–11pm; ℡950 61 51 56). The Turismo's **map** (see above) also covers the coastal strip and is a useful aid to getting your bearings.

Among the **places to stay**, the sprawling seafront *Hotel El Puntazo* on the Paseo del Mediterráneo s/n, 1km south from *El Cruce* (℡950 47 82 29, ⓦwww .hotelelpuntazo.com; ❽), is an obvious landmark. In the same zone *Hotel Sal Marina* (℡950 47 24 04; ❺) has very pleasant a/c balcony rooms with sea views and drops prices by 30 percent outside August. Another hotel nearby doing similar price cuts is *Virgen del Mar* (℡950 47 22 22, ⓦwww.hotelvirgendelmar .com; ❺), a three-star place with sea-view balcony a/c rooms with TV. Nearby, the simpler *Hostal Bahía* (℡951 47 80 10; ❸) has en-suite rooms ranged around a charming patio. Next door, *Hotel Marazul* (℡950 47 84 36, ⓦwww.mar-azul .net; ❻) rents out fully equipped sea-view studio apartments sleeping up to three; here also prices are almost halved outside high summer. Another reasonable option is *Rancho del Mar*, Playa del Desgargador, 700m north of *El Cruce* (℡950 47 86 15, ⓦwww.hotelranchodelmar.com; ❺). Not far from here the friendly *Hotel-Restaurant Provenzal*, Paseo del Mediterráneo 393 (℡950 47 83 08; ❺ with breakfast), has sea-view a/c rooms with TV. Mojácar's nondescript parador, the modern *Parador de Mojácar* (℡950 47 82 50, ⓦwww.parador.es; ❼), with pleasant gardens and pool, also fronts the beach.

Food along the seafront is dismal, overpriced and standards fall markedly in high season; the sterile parador restaurant has nevertheless a reliable €25 *menú*. A kilometre further south *Restaurante Bogavante*, Paseo Mediterraneo 85, facing the Playa de las Ventanicas, is a rare exception to the general dross and serves up a tasty *menú* on its terrace for €10. Other places worth a try on the seafront in this zone are *Albatros*, close to the *Hotel El Puntazo* (see above) on the seaward side of the road, and *Sal Marina* attached to the hotel of the same name; both do good fish and paella. A kilometre further south the frill-obsessed *Omega* and its even frillier neighbour *Casa Egea* are a couple of other reliable seafront places.

Nightlife spreads all along the beach strip and it's fun just to stroll and see what's on offer. The sassiest of the discos is *Pascha*, and its beachfront neighbour *Goa*, near *El Cruce*, is similar. Another popular dance joint is *Viva Mojácar*, half-way along the road between the hill village and the coastal strip.

North from Mojácar

North from Mojácar, there's a clutch of resorts – none of them much to write home about – and a few last sights of interest, before the road crosses Andalucía's border into Murcia. Inland, two small towns are worth an excursion: at **Vélez Rubio**, there's a cave with important **prehistoric paintings** depicting the *indalo* (see p.623), whilst at neighbouring **Vélez Blanco** there's a fine Renaissance **castle**. Although both are served by a single daily **bus** from Almería, transport of your own will make these detours much more rewarding.

Garrucha and Vera

North from Mojácar, and served by occasional buses, **GARRUCHA** is a lively, if undistinguished, town and fishing harbour with a sizeable fleet. When this comes home to port with its catch in mid-afternoon the ensuing auction at the port-side market is wonderfully entertaining. The fleet also lands a good supply of the seafood – the prawns are renowned – served at the numerous **fish restaurants** lining the seafront harbour promenade, El Malecón. The most celebrated place in town is the outstanding 🔆 *El Almejero*, (☎950 46 04 05; main dishes €10–20) with its attractive terrace actually fronting the Puerto Pesquero harbourside, where the fish is landed – if what's caught doesn't meet their exacting standards they don't open. All the fish dishes are recommended (especially their renowned *arroz caldoso* – fish and rice soup) and there's an excellent tapas bar attached, too – try the mouthwatering *calamares* and *boquerones fritos*. Should you wish **to stay**, pleasant en-suite rooms are available at *Hostal-Restaurante Cortés*, Paseo Marítimo 200 (☎950 13 28 13, Ⓦwww .hostalcortes.net; ❹), overlooking the promenade and excellent beach.

From Garrucha, the road heads 9km inland, skirting the estuary of the Río Almanzora, to **VERA**, a small farming town with a fortified sixteenth-century church, **La Encarnación** with four huge towers, and a Renaissance **Ayuntamiento**, as well as a couple of **hostales** of which *Hostal Regio* on c/Ancha 4–6 (☎950 39 09 89; ❸) with comfortable en-suite rooms is the best; their decent restaurant also does good tapas and offers a good-value €10 *menú*.

North along the coast

The town of **CUEVAS DE ALMANZORA**, 6km north of Vera, has a well-preserved sixteenth-century Gothic castle built to defend the settlement from piracy, and a handful of Guadix-style cave dwellings where evidence of habitation by Neanderthal and Cro-Magnon man was found nearby. The castle – the splendidly restored **Castillo del Marqués de Los Vélez** – now houses a interesting archeological museum and the **Museo Campoy** displaying artworks by Picasso, Miró, Toral and Vásquez Díaz among others (both Mon–Fri 10am–2pm; free).

Slightly back from here, there's a road which returns you to the coast and the village of **PALOMARES**, of nuclear notoriety (see box overleaf). The rather curious feature of this otherwise dull hamlet is a church tower which resembles – with its rounded cone – an atom bomb. Near to where you rejoin the coast, Vera's **Parque Aquatico** (daily 10.30am–7.30pm; €13, kids €8) is a fun place to kill a couple of hours, especially if you're towing kids; it's got all the usual water features, and they allow you to take your own picnic inside.

Three kilometres on from Palomares, **Villaricos** is a humdrum resort with an uncomfortable black pebble beach. North again from here, the road cuts between the sea and the **Sierra Almagrera**, riddled with mine workings. The old mining settlements beyond these hills, in a landscape of scrub and desert

Palomares and the H-bombs

Palomares was once at the centre of one of the world's biggest nuclear scares. Here, on January 17, 1966, an American B-52 bomber collided with a tanker aircraft during a midair refuelling operation. Following the collision, three ten-megaton **H-bombs** fell on land and a fourth into the sea, just off the village. Those that fell in the fields were recovered quickly, though one had been damaged, causing radioactive contamination nearby. Fifteen US warships and two submarines searched for many weeks before the fourth bomb was recovered. On March 19, thousands of barrels of plutonium-contaminated soil were transported by the USAF for disposal in South Carolina. Nobody has ever convincingly explained how the incident happened, nor is it known why the bombs didn't explode, for the damaged bomb had actually lost its safety catch.

cactuses, are eerie, godforsaken places where any strangers are regarded with suspicion. Back on the coast, **POZO DEL ESPARTO**, 12km from Villaricos, has a reasonable pebble beach with plenty of shade, and quite a few places where wild-campers can pitch their tents. Another 4km on, **SAN JUAN DE LOS TERREROS** straddles the seafront behind a narrow beach flanked by characterless *hostales* and mushrooming *urbanizaciones* and holiday apartments. Just to the north of here, however, the coast road passes a number of temptingly isolated coves and inlets with small beaches, before Andalucía's border with Murcia is reached.

Vélez Rubio and the Letreros cave

Inland from Vera, a rambling 60km detour along the A7-E15 and A327 will bring you out at the town of **VÉLEZ RUBIO**, surrounded by sierras, olive groves and fields of cereals. It's no great shakes as towns go (Vélez Blanco is a better proposition for an overnight stop), but the **Turismo** (Tues–Sun 9.30am–2pm & 5.30–7pm; ☏950 41 25 60, ⓦwww.losveleturismo.org), housed in the town **museum**, c/Carrera del Carmen 19 (same hours), can provide information and a town map. The museum, itself located inside the eighteenth-century Hospital Real, contains an interesting collection of artefacts and ceramics from prehistoric to Moorish times and includes a section on the ancient cave paintings in this area.

The main monument of note here is the magnificent Baroque church (Almería province's biggest) of **La Encarnación** (Tues–Sun 10am–1pm & 5–8pm; free) on the plaza of the same name. Constructed in the eighteenth century, this has an imposing carved façade which includes, above the entrance, the arms of the marquises of Villafranca y Vélez, who built it. Inside, the main altar has a superbly detailed, 20-metre-high carved wood **retablo**.

What makes a trip here really worthwhile, however, is to see the prehistoric cave paintings of the **Cueva de los Letreros**, 4km out of town. To get there take the A317 north until you reach a petrol station on the left, next to which is a signed turning to the cave. Visits to the cave are now only possible with a guide who will meet visitors (daily July–Sept noon & 6pm, Oct–June noon & 4pm; €2.50) at the information kiosk near the campsite on the opposite side of the road to the petrol station. Any queries, or in case of bad weather, should be directed to the guide, Señora Milagro Navarro, on mobile ☏617882808 (some English spoken). The tourist offices in Vélez Rubio or Vélez Blanco will be able to detail any changes to this arrangement.

The cave or *abrigo* (rock shelter) is sited beyond a secure fence on the side of the hill behind the petrol station, a good kilometre's walk. Once through the gate of the compound you will be able to see remarkably fresh-looking red and brown sketches of human figures, birds, animals, astronomical signs and not very well-preserved *indalos* (see p.623) which have been dated to around 4000BC and are amongst the oldest representations of people and animals together. Unfortunately the local practice of touching the *indalos* and throwing water on the paintings in order to make them clearer has not helped their preservation, but what remains is still stunning.

Vélez Blanco

Nestling at the foot of a rocky outcrop, the whitewashed village of **VÉLEZ BLANCO**, 6km north of its neighbour, is a smaller and more attractive conurbation. Atop the hill is an outstanding **Renaissance castle** – an extension of the original Moorish *alcazaba* – built by the marquises of Vélez Blanco in the early years of the sixteenth century. It is today something of a trompe l'oeil, with an empty shell behind the crenellated battlements: a gutting that took place as recently as 1904, after the castle was sold off by the impecunious marquis for 80,000ptas (€500) to an American millionaire, George Blumenthal, who tore out the whole interior including the **Patio de Honor** – a fabulous courtyard carved in white marble by Italian craftsmen – and shipped it off to the United States. After service as this plutocrat's Xanadu, it has since been reconstructed inside the Metropolitan Museum of Art in New York. The castle's interior, much of it now supported by steel girders, has fragments of the original decoration and, given the Met's reluctance to return its dubiously acquired prize exhibit, there are now plans to carry out a complete reconstruction of the original using marble from the nearby quarries of Macael. A book on sale in the small shop at the entrance – *El Castillo de Vélez Blanco* by Alfonso Ruiz García – has an image of the reconstituted patio in the New York Met, plus a watercolour of what it looked like *in situ*. Make sure to take in the fine **views** from the tower, the Torre del Homenaje. If you can't get in during normal hours (July–Sept daily 11am–2pm & 5–8pm; Oct–June Sat, Sun & hols 11am–2pm; €1), call ☎950 41 50 27 or mobile ☎607415055, or enquire at the Ayuntamiento (☎950 61 48 00) on c/La Corredera, or at *Bar La Sociedad* for Julio El Pata, the guardian. At the opposite end of the town, the sixteenth-century **Convento de San Luís**, also built by the Vélez family, has a fine chapel (currently closed to visitors) which was damaged during the Civil War.

Practicalities

The Almacen del Trigo **information office** (Tues–Sat 10am–2pm & 4–6pm, Sun 10am–2pm; ☎950 41 53 54) at the far end of the town (follow the signs), has information on Vélez and the surrounding Parque Natural de la Sierra de María (see overleaf). For a **place to stay** in Vélez Blanco, the *Hostal La Sociedad*, c/Corredera 14 (☎950 41 50 27; ❷), is central and friendly for pleasant en-suite rooms with TV, or moving upmarket there's the elegant and good-value ⚲ *Casa de los Arcos*, c/San Francisco 2, near the information office (☎950 61 48 05, ⓦwww.casadelosarcos.net; ❹), a beautifully restored eighteenth-century *casa señorial* overlooking a gorge. This hotel also organizes daily guided visits to the Letreros cave which are open to non-guests. A **campsite**, *Pinar del Rey* (☎950 52 71 02), lies on the edge of town towards Vélez Rubio, close to the Letreros cave. For **meals** the *Hostal Sociedad*'s owners, *Bar Sociedad* over the road, serve decent tapas and *raciones* on their lively terrace. More formal meals and good local cooking are on offer at *Restaurante El Molino*, up some steps opposite a tiled fountain at the west end of the main street, with a charming patio terrace (the fresh trout is good here). *Mesón Antonia* near the castle entrance with a *menú* for around €8, and the nearby *Barbacoa María Fernández*, c/Al'qua-sid 10, are other good little local places to eat.

Sierra de María

Walkers – and those in need of greenery after endless desert landscapes – may be tempted to continue northwest from Vélez Blanco along the A317 to María, a small town set among pine woods and, incidentally, the highest settlement in Almería, which is also the jumping-off point for the **Sierra de María**, a recently declared Natural Park. This little-known area is visited mainly by Almerían and Murcian weekenders seeking cooler air, trees and (in winter) a rare glimpse of snow. **MARÍA** itself is unremarkable, but its setting beneath rocky crags is quite dramatic and there's a pleasant central plaza fronting its church, the scene of a lively Saturday market. For decent en-suite **rooms**, head for *Hostal-Restaurante Torrente*, c/Camino Real 10 (☎950 41 73 99; ❸), on the main road, which also serves **meals** and has a good-value lunchtime *menú*. Just off the main highway, *Hotel Sierramaría*, c/Paraje la Moratilla s/n (☎950 41 71 26, ⓦwww.hotelsierramaria.com; ❹), is an altogether plusher affair with its own restaurant. Just outside the town towards Orce and then off the road to the left, a scenic hour's **walk** leads to the Ermita de la Virgen de la Cabeza. To do more serious walking – and you're in largely virgin territory here – good maps will be required, although a number of waymarked routes ranging from eight to fifteen kilometres have already been completed inside the park, such as the *Ruta de Gabar*, a scenic 8km circular hike around the 1500m peak of Gabar, the park's highest. While in the park keep an eye out for **griffon vultures** which have been reintroduced after disappearing in the 1940s and are now breeding successfully. Information about walking trails, the park's *refugios* (mountain huts) and on the park in general is available from a **visitors' centre** (Fri–Sun 10am–2pm & 6–8pm; ☎950 52 70 05), 2.5km beyond María on the Orce road. Although it seems to have been designed mainly for kids, the centre's interactive displays will appeal to those with an interest in flora and fauna.

Orce

Beyond María the SE35 soon enters an extensive plain covered with wheatfields and stretches arrow-straight and apparently endlessly to the distant mountains. In high summer this plain is a cauldron beneath vast cloudless skies and you'll be lucky to meet another vehicle. Apart from a couple of godforsaken hamlets and the occasional wheeling eagle overhead hunting for prey, there are few features to punctuate this desolate but beautiful panorama. The landscape takes on a doubly dramatic aspect when you realize that one and a half million years ago this plain was a great lake visited by elephants, hippos, rhinos, water buffaloes, musk oxen, giant bears and ferocious hyenas as well as lions, leopards and lynxes. Early humans were known to have been in the area as early as 500,000 years ago but recent finds seem to have pushed this back by an astonishing additional one million years which, if scientifically confirmed, would make it the earliest appearance of primitive humans on the continent of Europe by a long way. These Stone Age arrivals probably came from Africa and lived on a diet of wild plants and carrion supplemented by fracturing the craniums and bones of the dead beasts to extract the brains and marrow – they had not yet developed the technology to take on and hunt big game.

When you finally reach it, the dusty and impoverished little settlement of **ORCE** hardly lives up to the self-styled billing – now proclaimed on all its literature – as *Cuna de la Humanidad Europea* (Cradle of European Man). The heart of the village is a tree-lined main square, Plaza Nueva, fronted by the Ayuntamiento and in one corner the village's main bar, *Bar Molina*. This institution is a hangout for the largely unemployed male population, and on searing summer afternoons it draws its curtains and turns on the fans, while the whiskery clientele get down to serious games of dominoes.

Just behind the main square (with a rear entrance onto it) lies the **Casa Palacio de los Segura**, c/Tiendas 18, a sixteenth-century *casa señorial* with an elegant tower. This now houses a **tourist office** (Tues–Sun 9am–2pm & 4–7pm; ☎958 74 61 71, ⓦwww.orce.es) and the **Museo de la Prehistoria** which exhibits the Orce discoveries. As well as impressive animal remains from the periods of the finds there are displays (in Spanish) reconstructing the lifestyle of these early humans. The star exhibit is a copy (the original is under lock and key in the Ayuntamiento) of the small million-and-a-half-year-old **fragment of human skull** that has brought worldwide celebrity to Orce. Whilst not accepted conclusively by many experts, its discoverers claim it belonged to a child of unknown sex which is thought to have been devoured by a great hyena. Various free leaflets on the finds in Spanish and an informative book on the excavations, *El Hombre de Orce*, are on sale. Archeologists and paleontologists working in the area are now fairly sure that the skull fragment is not human but local politicians – who have turned the whole issue into a matter of civic pride and tourist income – have made it heresy to say so. However, the same experts are convinced that the dating *will* eventually be confirmed due to crucial evidence turned up in 1998–99 of human artefacts around 1.4 million years old; finding genuine human remains, they believe, is only a matter of time.

Orce's only other sights of note lie just off the main square. The first is the eleventh-century **Moorish alcazaba** (Tues–Sun 9am–2pm & 4–7pm; free) with an impressive tower – the Torre del Homenaje – whilst the other, opposite across a square, is the eighteenth-century **Iglesia de Santa María** (open service times 7–9pm) with a fine *retablo*.

A wonderful **place to stay** in Orce is at the ⚚ *Cuevas de Orce*, Ctra. de María s/n (☎958 74 62 81, ⓦwww.cuevasdeorce.com; ❻), passed on the way into the village coming from María which is, as its name tells you, a **cave hotel**. Cosy en-suite cave dwellings come with kitchen and amusing cave bathrooms. The village's best **place to eat** is *Mesón La Mimbrera*, (☎958 74 61 48) just off the main square which does tasty game and regional dishes with a lunchtime *menú* for €8. Along the Galera road, 1km out of Orce, the green valley of the Río Galera contains the Manantial de Fuen Caliente, a beautiful natural pond filled with fish which has become the local **swimming pool**, complete with *cafetería*.

At Cúllar Baza, 23km southwest of Orce along routes SE34 and A330, you can pick up the A92N *autovía* heading towards Granada, 130km distant.

Inland Almería

An alternative way of reaching the coast to the east of Almería is to take a trip through the weird lunar landscape of Almería's distinctive desert scenery. There are two possible routes: via **Níjar** along the A7–E15 *autovía* to Carboneras, or via the more interesting **Tabernas** and **Sorbas** route (along the N340A) to Mojácar. The latter more northerly route, described below, passes by Almería's old western film set, **Mini Hollywood**, and a detour off this road can also be made to the pottery centre of **Níjar**. A visit to the underground caves of **Sorbas** is also a great adventure.

The road to Tabernas

The main road to Tabernas heads north out of Almería along the valley of the Río Andarax and forks right at Benhadux – along the A340 – passing the village of **Rioja** before it enters a dramatic brown-tinged-with-purple eroded landscape which looks as if it should be the backdrop for a Hollywood western. Some 10km past Rioja, in a particularly gulch-riven landscape, at Mini Hollywood you discover that someone else had the same idea first.

A visit to **MINI HOLLYWOOD** (April–Nov daily 10am–9pm, Dec–March Sat–Sun 10am–7pm; €17, under 12s €9) is hard to resist – especially if you're travelling with kids – although better value if timed with one of the daily shows. The old film set's most famous production was a *Fistful of Dollars*, a connection that its publicity flyers never tire of repeating. Once inside, you'll see a main street overlooked by a water tower, which you may just recognize from the 1960s classic, or from *The Good, the Bad and the Ugly*, another film made here along with countless other spaghetti and paella westerns. You can wander into the *Tombstone Gulch* saloon for a drink, and in summer there are daily "shows" (noon, 5pm and 8pm), when actors in full cowboy rig and blasting off six-guns stage such epics as the capture, escape and final shooting of Jesse James, whilst in between the saloon stages shows of cancan girls flaunting their frillies. There's also a somewhat incongruous **zoo** – with birds, reptiles and big cats prowling depressingly small cages – plus a **pool** and numerous **fast food** outlets. Regular **buses** (from Almería's Intermodal bus-train station) link the city with Mini Hollywood, but not the places mentioned below.

Further along the road towards Tabernas, on the left, is **Texas Hollywood** (April–Oct daily 9am–8pm; show at 2.30pm; €12.50, kids €7.50), the location for *Once Upon a Time in the West* among other productions, where a couple of less commercialized film sets in a much more spectacular setting

△ Mini Hollywood

have an Indian village complete with wigwams, a Mexican town and a US cavalry frontier fort as well as camels and buffaloes. A kilometre or so east on the same road, a third site, **Western Leone** (similar hours and prices to the one above), offers more sets used in the making of many Sixties' and Seventies' westerns including a ranch used in the making of *Once Upon a Time in the West.*

As well as the landscape and cheap labour costs, the film-makers were also drawn to the same unpolluted crystalline air which has lured astronomers here, and to the north of Tabernas, at Calar Alto in the Sierra de Filabres, a series of high-powered telescopes to study the heavens have been installed. The **Hispano–German observatory**, an 18km climb into the mountains north of Tabernas, and marked on the *Michelin Andalucía* map, is open for free guided visits (in Spanish and with a slide show) on Wednesdays at 3pm. Ring ahead to book a place on the visit (☎950 23 09 88).

Tabernas

Surrounded by torrid desert scrubland, **TABERNAS** lies at the foot of a hill dominated by an impressive-looking **Moorish castle** where Fernando and Isabel ensconced themselves during the siege of Almería. Unfortunately, closer inspection reveals it to be mainly ruined and there's little to hang around for, except a drink, in the searing summer heat. Just beyond the village a road on the left – followed after 1km by a right turn towards the hamlet of Senés – leads to the **Centro Solar**, one of Europe's biggest solar energy fields, where row upon row of mirrors reflect the powerful sunlight and generate energy. Still at the development stage, it's hoped that when the system is commercially viable it could power massive desalination plants to regenerate the desert. If you have your own transport and are looking for **food** the *Venta Compadre* on the N340, just beyond Tabernas, is an excellent stop for a hearty *menú*. Four kilometres beyond Tabernas on the left the *Hospedería del Desierto* (☎950 52 53 08, ⊛www.hospederiadeldesierto .com; ❸–❺) is a desert *hostal*-hotel with palms, yuccas and cactuses filling its gardens, where there's also a pool.

Across the Sierra Alhamilla

Beyond Tabernas there are more dramatic landscapes – badlands with naked ridges of pitted sandstone, cut through by twisted and dried-up riverbeds, all of which vary in colour from yellow to red and from green to lavender-blue depending on the time of day and the nature of the stone. After 9km a road on the right opens up the possibility of a wonderfully scenic trip south to Níjar **across the Sierra Alhamilla**.

This road climbs through more Arizona-type landscape, first to the hamlet of **Turrillas**, and then turns east to **LUCAINENA DE LAS TORRES**, a cluster of white boxes surrounding its red-roofed church. Here, a narrow main street leads up to the church, fronted by the tiny Plaza del Ayuntamiento, on which stands a good **place to eat**, *Mesón La Plaza*, a fine little country hostelry – try their *conejo con almendras* (rabbit with almond sauce). Two kilometres outside the village along the Níjar road an appealing **place to stay** is the *Cortijo los Baños* desert hotel (☎950 52 52 50, ⊛www.cortijo-al-hamam.com; ❺ includes breakfast & dinner) housed in a refurbished mid-nineteenth century spa where shiatsu massage, yoga and guided hikes are all available to guests. The hotel's restaurant is vegetarian using organic produce grown in their own *huerta*. Beyond Lucainena the road snakes over the rugged Sierra Alhamilla to descend into Níjar, 16km to the south.

NÍJAR is a neat, white and typically Almerian little town, with narrow streets in its upper Moorish quarter designed to give maximum shade. Now firmly on the tourist trail due to the inexpensive handmade **pottery** manufactured in workshops around the town and sold in the shops along the broad main street – Avenida García Lorca – and c/Real to the west, it still retains a relaxed and tranquil air. Little remains of the Moorish fort here but the pottery tradition – dating back to when the Moors held sway and including attractive traditional patterns created with mineral dyes – lives on, as exhibits in the museum at Almería clearly demonstrate. The town is also known for its **jarapas**: bed-covers, curtains and rugs made from rags. The more authentic potters are located in the **barrio alfarero**, along c/Real running parallel to the main street, where the *talleres* (workshops; open 10am–2pm & 4–7pm) of Gongora, Granados, El Oficio and the very friendly and cheaper Angel y Loli (at no. 54) are located. Also here, off the bottom of the street in a bullishly named studio-shop called La Tienda de los Milagros, is resident English ceramic artist Matthew Weir (married to an *almeriense*) who has a more modernist approach. His wife is a skilled producer of *jarapas* and textiles in her own right.

Practicalities

In the upper town, on the Plaza La Glorieta, a gift shop doubles as an **information office** (daily 10am–9pm; ☎550 36 01 23) and can provide literature on the town and region.

There are a number of small **hostales** for staying over, of which the best for en-suite rooms is *Montes* (☎950 36 01 57; ❶) at Avda. García Lorca 26; they also serve a *menú*. At the top of the same street *Hostal-Restaurant Asensio* (☎950 36 10 56; ❸) is another accommodation possibility. Other places along the main street serving **meals** include *Casa Pedro*, Avda. García Lorca 6, which does

---

"Blood Wedding"

An event that happened at Níjar in 1928 inspired one of Lorca's most powerful plays, *Bodas de Sangre* (*Blood Wedding*). A young woman named Francisca was about to marry a man named Casimiro at a farmhouse near Níjar. She was an heiress with a modest dowry and a reluctant bride, he a labourer pressured by his scheming brother and sister-in-law to make this match and thus bring money into the family. A few hours prior to the wedding taking place, Francisca eloped with her cousin, with whom she had been in love since childhood, but who had only realized his feelings when confronted with the reality of losing her. They were swiftly intercepted by Casimiro's brother, who shot her cousin dead. His brother was convicted of the murder, whilst Casimiro, the groom, was unable to overcome his humiliation and, it is said, never looked upon Francisca or even her photograph again. Francisca never married and lived as a recluse until her death in 1978.

Lorca avidly followed the story in the newspapers and had a knowledge of the area from time spent in Almería as a child. An interesting afterword is told by the writer Nina Epton, who, on a visit to San José in the 1960s, was dining at the house of a wealthy Spanish *señoron*, or landowner, while a group of farm labourers waited outside on a long bench, no doubt for payment. In her book *Andalusia* she describes what happened when eventually she accompanied Don José, her host, to speak to the men:

Among them was a wizened old man called Casimiro whom I would not have looked at twice before I was told that a dramatic incident in his youth had inspired Federico García Lorca to take Casimiro for his model of the novio in "Blood Wedding".

excellent tapas (the *chorizo al vino* is recommended) and *platos combinados* and has a small terrace. There are more **tapas** and **raciones** bars in the upper town beyond the church where, on Plaza La Glorieta, *El Pipa* also does meals and *Bar La Glorieta* – with an elevated terrace – is a pleasant place for a nightcap.

Sorbas and the Paraje Natural de Karst en Yesos

Continuing 18km east from the turn-off to Lucainena de las Torres along the N340A, this corner of Almería has one last dramatic sight in **SORBAS**, an extraordinary place, surrounded by more moonscapes, whose cliff-top houses overhang an ashen gorge, best seen from the main road. Like Níjar, it is reputed for its **pottery** – although the designs are less original – which is sold at a trio of inconspicuous *alfarerías* (workshops, one of which still has its original Moorish oven) in the lower part of the village, near a white-walled church and signed from the main square, Plaza del Ayuntamiento. This tidy little place is also on the tourist trail, especially on Thursdays when trippers flock in from Mojácar for the weekly **market** in the same plaza.

The main pull for visitors to these parts, though, is the astonishing scenery in the surrounding **Paraje Natural de Karst en Yesos** (just south of town and signed from the main N340A), where around six million years ago water erosion carved out subterranean chasms full of stalagmites and stalactites. Guided visits to the caves are a two-hour adventure – with helmets and lights and not a little scrambling and squeezing – organized by the Turismo (April–Oct visits daily on the hour from 10am–1pm & 3pm–8pm, ⓦ www.cuevasdesorbas.com; €11, kids €7). A couple of more-challenging explorations lasting 3–6hrs are also on offer (see website for details). Above ground, the water's action has created flat-topped, volcano-like protrusions and deep gorges. These are visible from the main N340A, but for a closer look take the minor A8203 towards Los Molinos del Río Aguas east of Sorbas. At the crest of a hill, a track to the left leads to a peak above the gorge, where sweeping circular views extend over the lunar landscape as far as the snowcapped peaks of the Sierra Nevada; it's a great place to watch the sunset. Alternatively, you could follow the track descending through the tumbledown but picturesque hamlet of **Los Molinos** to follow the course of the dried-up river gorge.

Practicalities

Sorbas's small **Turismo** is at c/Terraplén 9, just off the main N340A on the way into town (daily 11am–2pm & 5–8pm, ⓣ950 36 44 76, ⓦ www.sorbas.org). Their town map will guide you around a number of faded *señorial* mansions, including the seventeenth-century erstwhile summer retreat of the duques de Alba. The Turismo lies 50m uphill from the **Centro de Visitantes** (daily 11am–2pm & 5–8pm; ⓣ950 36 44 81) for the Karst en Yesos caves.

Should you wish **to stay**, *Hostal Sorbas* (ⓣ950 36 41 60; ❸), on the right as you enter the town from Tabernas, has neat and tidy en-suite rooms. **Food** is available at *Cafetería Caymar* on Sorbas's main square, Plaza del Ayuntamiento, which does tapas and *raciones* and offers **Internet** access; for more elaborate fare visit their upmarket offshoot next door, *Restaurante El Rincón* (ⓣ950 36 41 52), which prepares regional specialities with flair. On the main road to the east of town – where you'll get the best view of the cliff-top houses – the *Café-Bar El Chacho* does substantial *platos combinados*.

To reach Sorbas from Níjar you could retrace your path back over the **Sierra Alhamilla** (there's a 4km short cut to the N340A from Lucainena) or, for a bit of variety, follow the A7-E15 east for about 23km, turning off along a minor road (the A8203) for the final 10km to Sorbas.

Cóbdar and around

If you find this surreal desert landscape to your taste – and it's surprising how it begins to grow on you – with transport you might like to try a trip starting 16km west of Sorbas, where a turn-off on the right heads into relatively uncharted territory, first north along the A8200 to Uleila del Campo and the continuing beyond here to Cóbdar and the surrounding mountain villages in the **Sierra de los Filabres**. For 35km the scenic road winds upwards past abandoned *fincas* and pastures of wild thyme, with occasional splashes of green and plenty of opportunities for bird and butterfly spotting. When you get there, **CÓBDAR** turns out to be a neat little village of parallel white streets perched on a towering outcrop of reddish rock, where the friendly locals will be bemused, but pleased, to see you. Extraction of marble from this rock – which was also the quarry used by the Moorish builders of the Alhambra – is the main source of income for the surrounding towns and villages but mars parts of the landscape further north where man-made, volcano-like craters and umber-tinted landslides dominate the views. Most of the villages in the sierra have **bars** serving tapas or *raciones* and at **Albánchez** – 6km north of Cobdar – there's a decent **hostal**, *Amanacer* (☎950 12 23 23; ②).

Travel details

Trains

Almería to: Granada (4 daily; 2hr 10min); Guadix (4 daily; 1hr 15min); Madrid (2 daily; 6hr 40min–8hr 40min); Sevilla (4 daily; 5hr–5hr 30min).
Granada to: Algeciras (3 daily; 3hr 30min–4hr); Almería (4 daily; 2hr 10min); Córdoba (1 daily; 4hr 30min); Guadix (4 daily; 1hr 10min); Madrid (2 daily; 6–8hr); Málaga (1 daily; 2hr 30min); Ronda (3 daily; 2hr 45min); Sevilla (4 daily; 3hr–3hr 30min).

Buses

Bus times quoted are for the fastest journey times, normally direct. There may be other buses to the same destination which make additional stops at towns and villages en route.

Almería to: Agua Amarga (1 daily; 1hr 15min); Aguadulce (daily every 30min; 20min); Almerimar (5 daily; Cabo de Gata (via Retamar; 6 daily; 30min); Carboneras (4 daily; 1hr 15min); Córdoba (2 daily; 5hr); Garrucha (3 daily; 1hr 15min–1hr 45min); Granada (12 daily; 2hr 15min); Guadix (9 daily;1hr 30min); Jaén (1 daily; 4hr 30min); Láujar de Andarax (2 daily; 1hr 15min); Las Negras (2 daily; 1hr 15min); Málaga (10 daily; 3hr 15min–4hr); María (1 daily; 2hr 45min); Mojácar (5 daily; 1hr–1hr 45min); Madrid (4 daily; 7hr); Mini Hollywood (4 daily; 30min); Níjar (2 daily; 45min); Roquetas de Mar (daily every 30min; 25min); Rodalquilar (1 daily; 1hr 45min); Sevilla (2 daily; 5hr); San José (3 daily; 1hr); Sorbas (3 daily; 1 hr); Santa Fe de Mondújar/Los Millares (2 daily in each direction; 30min); Tabernas (6 daily; 35 min); Úbeda (1 daily; 4hr 15min); Vélez Blanco (1 daily; 2hr 30min); Vélez Rubio (1 daily; 2hr 15min).
Granada to: Almería (10 daily; 2hr 15min); Almuñecar (10 daily; 1hr 30min); Baeza/Úbeda (7 daily; 2hr 30min); Cazorla (2 daily; 1hr 30min); Baza (8 daily; 2hr); Cádiz (2 daily; 5hr); Córdoba (8 daily; 2–4hr); Guadix (12 daily; 1hr); Herradura (5 daily; 1hr 45min); Jaén (12 daily;1hr 30min); Madrid (10 daily; 5–6hr); Málaga (17 daily; 1hr 30min); Montefrío (2 daily; 1hr 30min); Mojácar (2 daily; 3hr 30min); Motril (9 daily; 1hr); Nerja (4 daily; 2hr); Salobreña (10 daily; 1hr); Sevilla (9 daily; 3–4hr); Sierra Nevada/Alpujarras: the following all pass Lanjarón and Órgiva, a 1hr trip from the city; current departure times from Granada to other villages are: 8.30am & 6pm to Ugíjar (also passing Albondón, Cádiar & Yegen); 10.30am, noon & 5.15pm to Berchules (also passing Pampaneira, Bubión, Capileira, Pitres, Busquistar & Trevélez); 1pm to Berja.

Ferries

Almería to: Melilla (1 daily April–Sept, less frequent rest of year; 6hr or 4hr with high-speed ferry May–Sept); Nador (1 daily April–Sept; 6hr).

Contexts

Contexts

History

As the southernmost region of the Iberian peninsula, Andalucía has manifested throughout its history a character essentially different from the rest of Spain. Due to the variety of peoples who came and settled here, the region has always had an enriching influence on the territories further north. This meeting place of seas and cultures, with Africa only nine miles off the coast of its southern tip, brought Andalucía into early contact with the sophisticated civilizations of the eastern Mediterranean and a long period as part of the North African Moorish empire. The situation was later reversed when Andalucía sent out explorers to the New World and became the gateway to the Spanish American empire.

Prehistory

The first Europeans of whom we have knowledge lived in Andalucía. A recent series of spectacular discoveries at **Orce**, seventy miles east of Granada, rocked the archeological world as the date for the **arrival of early humans in Europe** was pushed back from c.700,000 years ago to perhaps a million years before this, making Orce – if the findings are scientifically confirmed – the earliest known site of human occupation in Europe by a long way. Arriving from Africa and crossing the straits by swimming or on rafts these Stone Age people colonized an area of now vanished lakeland near Orce. Here they hunted hippos, hyenas, mammoths and vultures and made tools from flint. Evidence of occupation by Stone Age societies stretching back some 400,000 years was already known about from discoveries at nearby **Venta Micena** where early inhabitants hunted elephant and rhino and left behind tools and camp fires. Archeologists will now get to work on filling in the gaping prehistorical record between these two sites. Some of the earliest **human fossils** found on the Iberian peninsula were unearthed inside the **Gibraltar** caves with evidence of **Neanderthals** dating from around 100,000 BC. In the Paleolithic period, the first **homo sapiens** arrived on the Iberian peninsula from southern France, settling around the Bay of Biscay as well as in the south. They were cave dwellers and hunter-gatherers and at the Pileta and Nerja caves in Málaga have left behind remarkable **cave paintings** depicting the animals that they hunted. During the later Neolithic phase, a sophisticated material culture developed in southern Spain attested to by the finds of esparto sandals and baskets as well as jewellery in the **Cueva de los Murcilélagos** in Granada.

Subsequent prehistory is more complex and confused. There does not appear to have been any great development in the cave cultures of the north. Instead the focus shifts south – where **Neolithic colonists** had arrived from North Africa – to Valencia and **Almería**. Cave paintings have been found in rock shelters such as those at **Vélez Blanco** dating from around 4000 BC. Here also, not long afterwards, **metalworking** began and the debate continues as to the cause of this dramatic leap forward: a development by the indigenous inhabitants or the arrival of "technicians" – evidenced by many trading artefacts such as ivory and turquoise – from the eastern Mediterranean. The fortified site of **Los Millares** (c.2700 BC), in the centre of a rich mining area in Almería, with its Aegean-style "bee-hive" tombs is one of the most important remains from this era. In the same period, **dolmens** were being built such as those at **Antequera**, a building style which spread from here throughout the peninsula and into Europe. This dolmenic culture also influenced a ceramic style, typified by bell-shaped artefacts and giving rise to the name **Beaker folk**. More developments occurred in the same area of Almería about 1700 BC when the **El Argar** civilization started to produce bronze and worked silver and gold, trading across the Mediterranean. This culture fanned out across the south between 1700 and 1000 BC and, during the first millennium BC, the **Iberian civilization** fully established itself.

Tartessus and the Iberians

The **kingdom of Tartessus** appeared early in the first millennium BC and typifies the great strides forward being made by the Iberians of the south. Both the Bible (which names it Tarshish) and Greek and Latin texts refer to this important kingdom and trading centre. It was probably sited on the estuary of the Río Guadalquivir on the border of Huelva and Sevilla provinces; its precise location has yet to be identified, although its prowess as a producer and exporter of bronze, gold and silver as well as a creator of sophisticated **jewellery** is apparent from the finds displayed in Sevilla's archeological museum. The Tartessians were also a literate people but nothing of their literature survives apart from scattered inscriptions which have thus far defied translation. In the mid-sixth century BC Tartessus incurred the wrath of the rising power of Carthage through its friendship with the Greeks and not long after this appears to have been destroyed by them.

The Iberians at other centres in the south also developed sophisticated cultures based upon agriculture, stockbreeding, fishing, mining and iron production. When the Romans came into contact with them in the third century BC they found a literate people with written laws, and a vibrant culture which included music and dance. Their skills in the plastic arts – an enduring flair throughout the peninsula's history – are displayed in artefacts such as the splendid **Dama de Baza**, a dramatic fourth-century BC painted terracotta statue of a woman, discovered at Baza in Granada. The Iberian skill with masonry and stone sculpture can be seen at the necropolis at **Toya** in Jaén province, and other remarkable works from the fifth century BC are in the museum at Jaén itself.

The first colonists

The southern coast attracted colonists from different regions of the Mediterranean. The **Phoenicians** – founders of a powerful trading empire based in modern Lebanon – established the port of Gadir (Cádiz) about 1100 BC. This was obviously connected with their intensive **trading operations** in the metals of the Guadalquivir valley carried from Tartessus where they may even have had a factory. Their wealth and success gave rise to a Spanish "Atlantis" myth, based around Huelva. Besides metals, the Phoenicians also came for the rich fishing along the southern coast which stimulated industries for salting and preserving the catch. The salt itself was gained from beds such as those at the **Cabo de Gata** – still in commercial operation – in Almería. Other operations, such as the **purple dyeing industry**, for which the Phoenicians were famous, exploited the large stocks of murex shellfish in coastal waters. The coastline of Andalucía is dotted with Phoenician **settlements** from this time such as those at Malaka (Málaga), Sexi (Almuñecar) and Abdera (Adra). Market rivalry also brought the **Greeks**, who established their trading colonies along the northeastern coast – the modern Costa Brava – before penetrating southwards into the Phoenician zone. They were encouraged by the Tartessians, no doubt in an attempt to break the Phoenician economic stranglehold on the region.

When the Phoenicians were incorporated into the Persian empire in the sixth century BC, however, a former colony, **Carthage**, moved into the power vacuum, destroyed Tartessus and ejected the Greeks from the south. Carthage then turned the western Mediterranean into a jealously guarded trading monopoly, sinking ships of other states who attempted to trade there. This she tenaciously held on to, as the rising power of Rome forced her out of the central Mediterranean. In the course of the third century BC, Carthage built up Spain into a new base for her empire, from which to regain strength and strike back at her great rival. Although making little impact inland, the Carthaginians occupied most of Andalucía and expanded along the Mediterranean seaboard to establish a new capital at Cartagena ("New Carthage") in Murcia. The mineral wealth of Andalucía, particularly **silver**, was used to finance the military build-up as well as to recruit an enormous army of Iberian mercenaries. Under Hannibal they prepared to invade Italy and in 219 BC attacked Saguntum (modern Sagunto), a strategic ally of the growing Roman Empire. This precipitated the **Second Punic War**, bringing Roman legions to the Spanish peninsula for the first time. Heading south from modern Catalunya, the coastal towns were successively conquered and the **end of Carthaginian domination** of Spain was sealed in 206 BC at the battle of Ilipa (Alcalá del Río), just north of Sevilla. When Cádiz fell the following year, Rome became master of the southern peninsula and **Itálica** (near Sevilla) was founded as the first Roman city in Spain. A new and very different age had begun.

Romans and Visigoths

The **Roman colonization** of the peninsula was far more intense than anything previously experienced and met with great resistance from the Celtiberian tribes of the north and centre, although much less so in Andalucía where the Turditanian people, tired of Carthaginian oppression, welcomed the invaders. In the final years of the Roman republic many of the crucial battles for control of the Roman state were fought out in Spain, ending with Julius Caesar's victory at Munda, south of Córdoba, in 45 BC. After Caesar's assassination, his successor Augustus reorganized Spain into three provinces, the southernmost of which became **Hispania Baetica**, roughly modern Andalucía, with **Corduba** (Córdoba) as its capital.

In this period Spain became one of the most important and wealthiest centres of the Roman Empire and Andalucía was its most urbane heartland. Unlike the rugged and fractious Celtiberians further north, the sophisticated Iberians of the south had their own municipal traditions and took easily to Roman ideas of government. Indeed, their native languages and dialects had disappeared early in the first century AD as Latinization became complete. For four centuries Andalucía enjoyed a **"Golden Age"** with unprecedented prosperity based on the production of olive oil, wool, grain, wine and the highly prized garum fish sauce made at centres such as **Baelo Claudia** near Tarifa. Another important development was a massive expansion of mining at **Río Tinto** in Huelva. During this period, Baetica supplied **two Roman emperors**, Trajan (one of the greatest) and his adopted son Hadrian, along with the outstanding writers Seneca and Lucan. The finest monuments of the period were built in the provincial capital at Córdoba, and cities such as Cádiz, Itálica, Málaga and Carmona, linked by a network of superb roads and adorned with temples, baths, amphitheatres and aqueducts, were the equal of any in the empire.

In the fourth and fifth centuries, however, the Roman political framework began to show signs of **decadence and corruption**. Although the actual structure didn't totally collapse until the Muslim invasions of the early eighth century, it became increasingly vulnerable to **barbarian invasions** from northern Europe. Early in the fifth century AD, the Suevi (Swabians), Alans and Vandals swept across the Pyrenees leaving much devastation in their wake. The Romans, preoccupied with attempts to stave off Gothic attacks on Italy, bought off the invaders by allowing them to settle within the imperial borders. The Suevi settled in Galicia, the Alans in Portugal and Murcia, whilst the **Vandals** put down roots in Baetica, providing the origin of Andalucía's name. The resulting wars between the invaders only served to weaken further Rome's grip on the peninsula as a burgeoning Christian Church – its first Spanish council was held at Iliberis (Granada) – gained more influence over the population.

Internal strife was heightened by the arrival of the **Visigoths** from Gaul, allies of Rome and already Romanized to a large degree. The triumph of Visigothic strength in the fifth century resulted in a period of spurious unity, based upon an exclusive military rule from their capital at Toledo, but their numbers were never great and their order was often fragmentary and nominal, with the bulk of the subject people kept in a state of disconsolate servility and held ransom for their services in times of war. Above them in the ranks of the military elite there were constant plots and factions – exacerbated by the Visigothic system of elected monarchy and by their adherence to the heretical Arian philosophy. When **King Leovigild** attempted ito impose this creed on Andalucía in the mid-sixth century, the region revolted with the king's son Hermenegild at its head, but the insurrection was brutally crushed. In 589 **King Recared** converted to Catholicism which for a time stiffened Visigothic control, but religious strife was only multiplied: forced conversions, especially within the Jewish enclaves, maintained a constant simmering of discontent. The Visigoths precariously held on to their domain for a further century as plots and counterplots surrounded the throne. This infighting led indirectly to the Moorish invasions of Andalucía when **King Witiza**, who died in 710, was thwarted by a usurper, Roderic, duke of Baetica, from handing over the throne to his son, Achila. Once **King Roderic** had installed himself on the throne the embittered family of Witiza appealed to the Muslims in North Africa for assistance to overthrow him. The North Africans, who had long eyed the riches of Andalucía with envy, now saw their opportunity.

The Moorish conquest

In contrast to the long-drawn-out Roman campaigns, **Moorish conquest** of the peninsula was effected with extraordinary speed. This was a characteristic phenomenon of the spread of Islam – Muhammad left Mecca in 622 and by 705 his followers had established control over all of North Africa. Spain, with its political instability, its wealth and fertile climate, was an inevitable extension of their aims. In 711 **Tariq**, governor of Tangier, led a force of 7000 Berbers across the straits and routed the Visigoth army of King Roderic on the banks of the Río Guadalete close to Jerez. Two years later the Visigoths made a last desperate stand at Mérida and within a decade the Moors had conquered all but the wild mountains of Asturias. The land under their authority was dubbed **al-Andalus**, a fluid term which expanded and shrank with the intermittent gains and losses of the Reconquest. It was Andalucía, however, that was destined to become the heartland of the Moorish ascendancy and where the Moors were to remain in control for most of the next eight centuries.

The Moorish incursion was not simply a military conquest. The Moors (a collective term for the numerous waves of Arab, Syrian and Berber settlers from North Africa) were often content to grant a limited autonomy in exchange for payment of tribute; their administrative system was tolerant and easily absorbed both Spanish Jews and Christians, those who retained their religion being known as "Mozarabs". This **tolerant attitude** was illustrated when the Moorish army reached Córdoba where they found the large Visigothic church of St Vincent, now the fabulous Mezquita. Unlike previous invaders, they did not sack or burn the heathen temple but purchased half of it to use as a mosque whilst the Christians continued to use the other half for their own services.

Al-Andalus was a distinctly Spanish state of Islam. Though at first politically subject to the eastern caliphate (or empire) of Baghdad, it was soon virtually independent. In the tenth century, at the peak of its power and expansion, Abd ar-Rahman III asserted total independence, proclaiming himself caliph of a new **western Islamic empire**. Its capital was **Córdoba** – the largest, most prosperous and most civilized city in Europe. This was the great age of Muslim Spain: its scholarship, philosophy, architecture and craftsmanship were without rival and there was an unparalleled growth in urban life, trade and agriculture, aided by magnificent irrigation projects. These and other engineering feats were not, on the whole, instigated by the Moors who instead took the basic Roman models and adapted them to a new level of sophistication. In **architecture** and the **decorative arts**, however, their contribution was original and unique – as may be seen in the astonishingly beautiful monuments of Sevilla, Córdoba and Granada.

The Cordoban caliphate (and the emirate that preceded it) created a remarkable degree of unity, despite a serious challenge to their authority by the rebel leader **Ibn Hafsun** from his Bobastro fortress (north of Málaga) in the latter years of the ninth century. But its rulers were to become decadent and out of touch, prompting the brilliant but dictatorial **al-Mansur** to usurp control. Under this extraordinary ruler Moorish power reached new heights, using a professional Berber army to push the Christian kingdom of Asturias-León back into the Cantabrian mountains and sacking its most holy shrine, Santiago de Compostela, in 997. However, after al-Mansur's death the caliphate quickly lost its authority and in 1031 disintegrated into a series of small independent kingdoms or **taifas**, the strongest of which was Sevilla.

Internal divisions meant that the *taifas* offered less resistance to the Christian kingdoms which were rallying in the north, and twice North Africa had to be called upon for reinforcement. This resulted in two distinct new waves of Moorish invasion – first by the fanatically Islamic **Almoravids** (1086) and later by the **Almohads** (1147), who restored effective Muslim authority and left behind one of Moorish Spain's most elegant monuments, the **Giralda** tower in

Sevilla. However, their crushing defeat by the Christian forces under Alfonso VIII in 1212, at the battle of **Las Navas de Tolosa** in Jaén, marked the beginning of the end for Moorish Spain.

The Christian Reconquest

The **Reconquest** of land and influence from the Moors was a slow and intermittent process. It began with a symbolic victory by a small force of Christians at Covadonga in the region of Asturias (718) in northern Spain and was not completed until 1492 with the conquest of Granada by Fernando and Isabel. Covadonga resulted in the formation of the tiny Christian **kingdom of the Asturias**. Initially just 25km by 19km in area, it had by 914 reclaimed León and most of Galicia and northern Portugal. At this point, progress was temporarily halted by the devastating campaigns of al-Mansur. However, with the fall of the Cordoban caliphate and the divine aid of Spain's Moor-slaying patron saint, the avenging Santiago (St James the Apostle), the Reconquest moved into a new and powerful phase.

The frontier castles built against Arab attack gave name to **Castile**, founded in the tenth century as a county of León-Asturias. Under Fernando I (1037–65) it achieved the status of a kingdom and became the main thrust and focus of the Reconquest. In 1085 this period of confident Christian expansion reached its zenith with the capture of the great Moorish city of Toledo. The following year, however, the Almoravids arrived by invitation from Sevilla, and military activity was effectively frozen – except, that is, for the exploits of the legendary **El Cid**, a Castilian nobleman who won considerable lands around Valencia in 1095, thus checking Muslim expansion up the eastern coast.

The next concerted phase of the Reconquest began as a response to the threat imposed by the Almohads. The kings of León, Castile, Aragón and Navarra united in a crusade which resulted in the great victory at Las Navas de Tolosa. Thereafter Muslim power was paralysed and the **Christian armies** moved on to take most of al-Andalus. Fernando III ("El Santo", the saint) led Castilian soldiers into Córdoba in 1236 and twelve years later into Sevilla. By the end of the thirteenth century only the Nasrid **kingdom of Granada** remained under Muslim authority and this was to provide a brilliant sunset to Moorish rule in Andalucía. Its survival for a further two centuries whilst surrounded by its Christian enemies was due as much to skilful diplomacy as to payment of tribute to the monarchs of Castile.

Two factors should be stressed regarding the Reconquest. First, its unifying religious nature – the **spirit of crusade**, intensified by the religious zeal of the Almoravids and Almohads, and by the wider European climate (which in 1085 gave rise to the First Crusade). At the same time the Reconquest was a movement of **recolonization**. The fact that the country had been under arms for so long meant that the nobility had a major and clearly visible social role, a trend perpetuated by the redistribution of captured land in huge packages, or **latifundia**. Heirs to this tradition still remain as landlords of the great estates, most conspicuously in Andalucía where it has produced wretched conditions for the workers on the land ever since. Men from the ranks were also awarded land, forming a lower, larger stratum of nobility, the **hidalgos**. It was their particular social code that provided the material for Cervantes in Don Quixote.

Any spirit of mutual cooperation that had temporarily united the Christian kingdoms disintegrated during the fourteenth century, and independent lines of development were once again pursued. **Castile** emerged as the strongest over this period: self-sufficiency in agriculture and a flourishing wool trade with the Netherlands enabled the state to build upon the prominent military role under Fernando III.

Los Reyes Católicos

Los Reyes Católicos – the Catholic Monarchs – was the joint title given to **Fernando V of Aragón** and **Isabel I of Castile**, whose marriage in 1479 united the two largest kingdoms in Spain. Unity was in practice more symbolic than real: Castile had underlined its rights in the marriage vows and Aragón retained its old administrative structure. So, in the beginning at least, the growth of any national unity or Spanish – as opposed to local – sentiment was very much dependent on the head of state. Nevertheless, from this time on it begins to be realistic to consider Spain as a single political entity.

At the heart of Fernando and Isabel's popular appeal lay a **religious bigotry** that they shared with most of their Christian subjects. The **Inquisition** was instituted in Castile in 1480 and in Aragón seven years later. Aiming to establish the purity of the Catholic faith by rooting out heresy, it was directed mainly at Jews (despite Fernando's half-Jewish parentage) – resented for their enterprise in commerce and influence in high places, as well as for their faith. Expression had already been given to these feelings in a pogrom in 1391; it was reinforced by an edict issued in 1492 which forced up to 400,000 Jews to flee the country. A similar spirit was embodied in the reconquest of the Nasrid **kingdom of Granada**, also in 1492. During this long campaign Gonzalo Fernández de Córdoba, "El Gran Capitán," developed the Spanish army into a formidable force that was set to dominate the battlefields of Europe for the next century and a half. As Granada was the last stronghold of Muslim authority, the religious rights of its citizens were guaranteed under the treaty of surrender. Then the policy was reversed and forced mass conversions were introduced. The subsequent and predictable rebellions – particularly violent in **Las Alpujarras** – were brutally put down and within a decade those Muslims under Christian rule had been given the choice between conversion or expulsion.

The year 1492 was symbolic of a fresh start in another way: it was in this year that **Columbus** sailed from Huelva to make the **discovery of America,** and the papal bull that followed, entrusting Spain with the conversion of the American Indians, further entrenched Spain's sense of a mission to bring the world to the "True Faith". The next ten years saw the systematic conquest, colonization and exploitation of the **New World**, with new territory stretching from Labrador to Brazil, and new-found wealth pouring into the royal coffers. The control of trade with the New World was carried on through **Sevilla** where the Casa de Contración (House of Trade) was established in 1503. The city rapidly grew into one of the great cities of Europe during which it enjoyed two centuries of commercial monopoly. Paradoxically, Andalucía as a whole benefited little from this wealth which was appropriated by the crown for its foreign campaigns and by absentee landlords. Over the succeeding two centuries the region languished as a backwater and the poverty of the peasants led many to emigrate to the

△ Fernando and Isabel

New World in order to better themselves, at the same time turning much of the region into a vast, unpopulated desert.

The Habsburg Age

Carlos I, a Habsburg, came to the throne in 1516 as a beneficiary of the marriage alliances of the Catholic monarchs. Five years later, he was elected emperor of the Holy Roman Empire as Carlos V (**Charles V**), inheriting not only Castile and Aragón, but Flanders, the Netherlands, Artois, the Franche-Comté and all the American colonies to boot. With such responsibilities it was inevitable that attention would be diverted from Spain, whose chief function became to sustain the Holy Roman Empire with gold and silver from the Americas. It was only with the accession of **Felipe II** in 1556 that Spanish politics became more centralized and that the notion of an absentee king was reversed.

This was a period of unusual religious intensity: the **Inquisition** was enforced with renewed vigour, and a "final solution" to the problem of the Moriscos (subject Moors), who continued to adhere to their ancient traditions and practised Muslim worship in secret, resulted in a decree banning Arabic dress, books and speech. The result was another rising of Moriscos in Las Alpujarras which was fiercely suppressed with Muslims being forcibly deported to other parts of the country. Felipe III later ordered the expulsion of half the total number of Moriscos in Spain – allowing only two families to remain in each Alpujarran village in order to maintain irrigation techniques. The **exodus** of both Muslim and Jew created a large gulf in the labour force and in the higher echelons of commercial life – and in trying to uphold the Catholic cause, an enormous strain was put upon resources without any clearcut victory. Despite being a golden literary and artistic age, politically and economically the seventeenth century was a disaster for Spain. Lurching progressively deeper into debt, she suffered heavy defeats on the battlefield as her possessions in the Netherlands and France were lost, and recurring financial crises and economic stagnation engendered a deepening mood of disillusionment. **Andalucía** shared in this decline, exacerbated by the tendency of the mercantile classes to involve themselves only in entrepôt trade which left most of the profits in the hands of other countries. There was also no stimulus given to industrial production by the custom of merchants retiring from commerce and investing their profits in land, which created a landed gentry weighed down by honours and titles whose lifestyle came to be looked upon as being incompatible with commerce.

The Bourbons

The **Bourbon dynasty** succeeded to the Spanish throne in the person of Felipe V (1700); with him began the **War of the Spanish Succession** against the rival claim of Archduke Charles of Austria, assisted by British forces. As a result of the Treaty of Utrecht which ended the war (1713), Spain was stripped of all territory in Belgium, Luxembourg, Italy and Sardinia, but Felipe V was recognized as king. **Gibraltar** was seized by the British in the course of the war. For the rest of the century Spain fell very much under the French sphere of influence, an influence that was given political definition by an alliance with the French Bourbons in 1762. This Gallic connection brought the ideas of Enlightenment Europe into the peninsula and during the reign of Carlos III (1759–88) a number of radically minded ministers attempted to deal with the nation's chronic problems. Along with a more tolerant attitude towards the **gypsies**, who had become victims of racial abuse and hostility, the king's minister, Pablo de Olavide, began an imaginative, if ultimately unsuccessful, scheme to **repopulate the Sierra Morena** in Andalucía with foreign immigrants (see p.354).

Contact with France also made involvement in the **Napoleonic Wars** inevitable and led eventually to the defeat of the Spanish and French fleet at the **Battle of Trafalgar** off the coast of Cádiz in 1805. Popular outrage was such that the powerful prime minister, Godoy, was overthrown and King Carlos IV forced to abdicate (1808). Napoleon seized the opportunity to install his brother, Joseph, on the throne, whilst French armies and generals ransacked and stole much of the country's artistic heritage.

Fierce local resistance in the form of guerrilla warfare was accompanied by armies raised by the various local administrations. Thus it was that a militia put in the field by the junta of Sevilla inflicted a resounding defeat on a French army at **Bailén** in Jaén in 1808, which forced Joseph, the "intruder king", to flee back across the border. This resistance was eventually backed by the muscle of a British army, first under Sir John Moore, later under the duke of Wellington, and the French were at last driven out in the course of the **War of Independence** (Peninsular War). Meanwhile, the **American colonies** had been successfully asserting their independence from a preoccupied centre and with them went Spain's last real claim of significance on the world stage. The entire nineteenth century was dominated by the struggle between an often reactionary monarchy and the aspirations of liberal constitutional reformers.

Seeds of Civil War

Between 1810 and 1813, whilst the war raged on across the peninsula, an ad hoc Cortes (parliament) meeting in **Cádiz** had set up a **liberal constitution** which stipulated a strict curtailment of the powers of the crown with ministers responsible to a democratically elected chamber. The first act of the despotic Fernando VII on being returned to the throne was to abolish this, and until his death in 1833 he continued to stamp out the least hint of liberalism. But the Constitution of 1812 was to remain a "sacred text" for a future democratic Spain, besides introducing the word "liberal" to Europe's political vocabulary. On Fernando's death, the right of succession was contested between his brother, Don Carlos, backed by the Church, conservatives and Basques, and his infant daughter, Isabel, who looked to the Liberals and the army for support.

So began the **First Carlist War**, a civil war that divided Spanish emotions for six years. Isabel II was eventually declared of age in 1843, her reign a long record of scandal, political crisis and constitutional compromise. Liberal army generals under the leadership of General Prim effected a coup in 1868 and the queen was forced to abdicate, but attempts to maintain a Republican government foundered. The Cortes was again dissolved and the throne returned to Isabel's son, Alfonso XII. The military began increasingly to move into the power vacuum left by the weakened monarchy. The **pronunciamiento** – whereby an officer backed by military force "pronounced" what was in the best interests of a city or region – was born in this period and was to plague the country into modern times.

The **nineteenth century in Andalucía** mirrored Spain's national decline. The loss of the American colonies had badly hit the region's trade, and this was compounded by the phylloxera plague from the 1870s onwards which wiped out most of the vineyards, brought the sherry industry to its knees, and fuelled the growth of strikes in the cities and popular uprisings on the land as the economy deteriorated. Parodoxically, this century also did more than any other to bestow on Andalucía the image it has held ever since. Writers, artists and travellers of the **Romantic Age** saw in its bullfights, flamenco, bandits and beguiling women a world of gaiety and colour, epitomized in the operas *Carmen* and *The Barber of Seville*, both works from this period.

The years preceding World War I merely heightened the discontent, which found expression in the growing **political movements** of the working class. The Socialist Workers' Party was founded in Madrid after the restoration of Alfonso XII, and spawned its own trade union, the UGT (1888). Its anarchist counterpart, the CNT (Confederación Nacional de Trabajo), was founded in 1911, gaining substantial support among the oppressed peasantry of Andalucía.

The loss of **Cuba** in 1898 emphasized the growing isolation of Spain in international affairs and added to economic problems with the return of soldiers seeking employment where there was none. In Andalucía a regionalist movement known as **Andalucismo** was born demanding land reform and greater Andalucian autonomy. A call-up for army reserves to fight in **Morocco** in 1909 provoked a general strike and the "Tragic Week" of rioting in Barcelona. Between 1914 and 1918, Spain was outwardly neutral but inwardly turbulent; inflated prices made the postwar recession harder to bear.

The general disillusionment with parliamentary government, together with the fears of employers and businessmen for their own security, gave **General Primo de Rivera** sufficient support for a military coup in 1923. Coming himself from Jerez de la Frontera, the paternalistic general backed the great **Ibero-American Exhibition of 1929** at Sevilla which, it was hoped, would calm the agitation for radical change by promoting a "rose-coloured" image for the troubled region; its most immediate effect was to bankrupt the city. Dictatorship did result in an increase in material prosperity, heavily assisted by a massive public works policy, but serious political misjudgments and the collapse of the peseta in 1929 made Rivera's voluntary resignation and departure into exile inevitable. The legacy of this dictatorship was to reinforce a belief on the Right that only a firm military hand would be capable of holding society together, and many of those who served in Primo de Rivera's administration were to back the Franco regime in the next decade. The victory of anti-monarchist parties in the 1931 municipal elections forced the abdication of the hopelessly out of touch King Alfonso XIII, and the **Second Republic** was declared.

The Second Republic

The Second Republic, which lasted from 1931 to 1936, was ushered in on a wave of optimism that finally some of the nation's fundamental ills and injustices would be rectified. But the government – a coalition of radicals, socialists and leftist republicans – struggling to curb the power of vested interests such as the army, the Church and the landowning class, was soon failing to satisfy even the least of the expectations which it had raised. Moreover it lost support when it got involved in activities identified with earlier repressive regimes when, as happened at the village of **Casas Viejas** (modern Benalup de Sidonia) in Cádiz, it ordered the troops to open fire on a group of starving workers who had been the victims of a lockout by the local landowner and who were attempting to raise the area in an anarchist revolt.

Anarchism was gaining strength among the frustrated middle classes as well as among workers and peasantry. The **Communist Party** and left-wing **socialists**, driven into alliance by their mutual distrust of the "moderate" Socialists in government, were also forming a growing bloc. There was little real unity of purpose on either left or right, but their fear of each other and their own exaggerated boasts made each seem an imminent threat. On the right the **Falangists**, basically a youth party founded in 1923 by **José Antonio Primo de Rivera** (son of the dictator), made uneasy bedfellows with conservative traditionalists and dissident elements in the army upset by modernizing reforms.

In an atmosphere of growing confusion, with mobs fighting on the streets and churches and monasteries being torched whilst landed estates were taken over by those impatient for agrarian reform, the left-wing Popular Front alliance won the general election of **February 1936** by a narrow margin. Normal life, though, became increasingly impossible: the economy was crippled by strikes, the universities became hotbeds for battles between Marxists and Falangists, and the government failed to exert its authority over anyone. Finally, on July 17, 1936, the military garrison in Morocco rebelled under **General Franco**'s leadership, to be followed by risings at military garrisons throughout the country. It was the culmination of years of scheming in the army, but in the event far from the overnight success its leaders almost certainly expected. Airlifting his troops into Sevilla by means of German transport planes, Franco ensured that the south and west quickly fell into Nationalist hands, but Madrid and the industrialized north and east remained loyal to the Republican government.

The Civil War

The ensuing **Civil War** was undoubtedly one of the most bitter and bloody the world has seen. Violent reprisals were taken on their enemies by both sides – the Republicans shooting priests and local landowners wholesale, the Nationalists carrying out mass slaughter of the population of almost every town they took. Contradictions were legion in the way the Spanish populations found themselves divided from each other. Perhaps the greatest irony was that Franco's troops, on their "holy" mission against a godless "anti-Spain", comprised a core of Moroccan troops from Spain's North African colony.

It was, too, the first modern war – Franco's German allies demonstrated their ability to wipe out entire civilian populations with their bombing raids on Gernika and Durango in the Basque country, and radio proved an important weapon, as Nationalist propagandists offered the starving Republicans "the white bread of Franco".

Despite sporadic help from Russia and thousands of volunteers in the International Brigades, the Republic could never compete with the professional armies and the massive assistance from Fascist Italy and Nazi Germany enjoyed by the Nationalists. As hundreds of thousands of refugees flooded into France, General Francisco Franco, who had long before proclaimed himself head of state, took up the reins of power.

Franco's Spain

The early reprisals taken by the victors were on a massive and terrifying scale. Executions were commonplace in town and village, and upwards of two million people were put in concentration camps until "order" had been established by authoritarian means. Only one party was permitted and censorship was rigidly enforced. By the end of World War II, during which Spain was too weak to be anything but neutral, **Franco** was the only fascist head of state left in Europe, and responsible for sanctioning more deaths than any other in Spanish history. Spain was economically and politically isolated and, bereft of markets, suffering – almost half the population were still tilling the soil for little or no return. The misery of the peasantry was particularly acute in Andalucía and forced mass emigrations to Madrid and Barcelona and Europe beyond.

When General Eisenhower visited Madrid in 1953 with the offer of huge loans, it came as water to the desert, and the price, the **establishment of American nuclear bases** such as those at Rota near Cádiz and Morón de la Frontera, was one Franco was more than willing to pay. Once firmly in the US camp the Franco regime (administered by the so-called *tecnocratas* group of ministers) rapidly transformed Spain into a market economy and in the late Fifties the country joined the International Monetary Fund, the International Bank for Reconstruction and Development and the OECD in quick succession. However belated, economic development was incredibly rapid, with Spain enjoying a growth rate second only to that of Japan for much of the 1960s, a boom fuelled by the tourist industry, the remittances of Spanish workers abroad and the illegality of strikes and industrial action at home.

Increased **prosperity**, however, only underlined the political bankruptcy of Franco's regime and its inability to cope with popular demands. Higher incomes, the need for better education, and a creeping invasion of Western culture made the anachronism of Franco ever clearer. His only reaction was to attempt to withdraw what few signs of increased liberalism had crept through, and his last years mirrored the repression of the postwar period. Franco finally died in November 1975, nominating **King Juan Carlos** as his successor.

The new Spain

On October 28, 1982, *sevillano* Felipe González's Socialist Workers' Party – the PSOE – was elected with massive support to rule a country that had been firmly in the hands of the right for 43 years. The **Socialists** captured the imagination and the votes of nearly ten million Spaniards with the simplest of appeals: "for change". It was a telling comment on just how far Spain had moved since Franco's death, for in the intervening years change seemed the one factor that could still threaten the new-found democracy.

Certainly, in the Spain of 1976 the thought of a freely elected left-wing government would have been incredible. **King Juan Carlos** was the hand-picked successor of Franco, groomed for the job and very much in with the army – of which he remains official commander-in-chief. His initial moves were cautious in the extreme, appointing a government dominated by loyal Francoists who had little sympathy for the growing opposition demands for "democracy without adjectives".

To his credit, however, Juan Carlos recognized that some real break with the past was now urgent and inevitable, and set in motion the process of **democratization**. He legitimized the Socialist Party and, controversially, the Communists. When elections were held in June 1977, the centre-right **UCD** Christian–Democrat party gained a 34 percent share of the vote, the **PSOE** (Spanish Socialist Workers' Party) coming in second with 28 percent, and the Communists and Francoist Alianza Popular both marginalized at 9 percent and 8 percent.

It was almost certainly a vote for democratic stability rather than for ideology. The king, perhaps recognizing that his own future depended on the maintenance of the new democracy, lent it his support – most notably in February 1981 when a tragicomic Civil Guard colonel named Tejero stormed the Cortes brandishing a revolver and, with other officers loyal to Franco's memory, attempted to institute an **army coup**. But the crisis, for a while, was real. Tanks were brought out onto the streets of Valencia, and only three of the army's ten regional commanders remained unreservedly loyal to the government. But as it became clear that the king would not support the plotters, most of the rest affirmed their support. Juan Carlos had taken the decision of his life and emerged with immensely enhanced prestige in the eyes of most Spaniards.

The new political system had successfully dealt with the first real challenge to its authority and following these events Spanish democracy – even in army circles where most of the old guard were gradually pensioned off – now became firmly institutionalized. And in the fourteen-year rule of the charismatic **Felipe González** (always known as "Felipe") and the PSOE the system found, at least until the Nineties' slide into the political mire and defeat, a party of enduring **stability** and to the left of exasperating **moderation**.

The nation's progressive disillusion with González's government in the Nineties as it became enveloped in sleaze and scandals saw the rise to prominence of **José-María Aznar** as leader of the **Partido Popular** conservatives (a merger of the UCD and Alianza Popular). A former tax inspector, Aznar's dogged criticism of the PSOE government's incompetence and corruption finally won the PP a narrow **victory** in the 1996 elections, following an equally narrow defeat in 1993. Problems for both major parties ensued from this indecisive result, however, for Aznar had to fix a precarious deal with the Basque and Catalan nationalist parties (whom he had described as "greedy parasites" on the hustings) in order to have a workable parliamentary majority, whilst the PSOE's avoidance of the expected crushing defeat was proclaimed as a vindication by González – who hastily dismissed ideas of retirement. This merely delayed the inevitable and, unable to make any significant impact on changing public opinion and with his party still in turmoil, early in 1998 **González** finally **resigned** from the leadership of the party he had led in government and opposition for 23 years.

González was replaced as PSOE leader first by his former transport minister, **José Borrell**, and then – following Borrell's resignation when linked with a financial scandal – the distinctly uncharismatic **Joaquín Almunia**. Paunchy and balding, Almunia cut little ice with the Spanish electorate, not helped by his refusal to criticize the record of his mentor González. In an attempt to forestall a seemingly inevitable electoral defeat, early in 2000 Almunia stitched up a deal with the PSOE's bitter arch rival, the ex-communist Izquierda Unida (United Left) party, thinking that their combined votes could overturn a likely Aznar victory. However, many of the rank and file on both sides were unhappy about this "shotgun marriage" (each has long blamed the other for Franco's victory in 1939) and the disorganization on the ground was reflected in their leaders' lack of a coherent policy.

The outcome of the March 2000 **general election** was a stunning **victory for Aznar** and the PP in which – for the first time since the death of Franco – the right were in power with an overall majority, and no longer dependent on the whims of nationalist coalition partners. It seems that the great majority of the electorate were not willing to risk the economic gains of Aznar's period in office, while many on the left didn't bother to turn out to support a leftist coalition which smacked more of political opportunism than a government in waiting. Joaquín Almunia, the architect of this crushing defeat for the left, resigned on election night.

At the party convention that followed, and bearing parallels to Tony Blair's elevation to the Labour leadership in Britain, the PSOE's old guard were swept aside and delegates elected a relatively unknown young politician, **José Luis**

Rodríguez Zapatero – a member of the moderate socialist "Nueva Via" (new way) group within the PSOE – as their new leader. After an unpromising start in which he struggled to get to grips with both Aznar and the party's powerful regional "barons", Zapatero embarked on a strategy of owning up to the PSOE's past mistakes, in particular distancing himself and the party from the sleazier activities of the González years. This seemed to go down well with public opinion and Zapatero's improved performance against Aznar in the Cortes (Spanish parliament) gave the party some hope of mounting a successful challenge to the ruling Partido Popular government in the elections to be held in 2004.

In 2001 José María Aznar – ever an enigma to those around him – announced that he would not be leading the PP into the next general election and that it must seek a new leader. As leader designate (to take over following the election) the party chose Aznar's nominee, the less prickly, cigar-puffing Mariano Rajoy, minister for the interior and deputy prime minister. Despite the highest level of **unemployment** in the EU and a **general strike** in June 2002, caused by opposition to labour law and social security reforms intended to free up the labour market and slash social security benefits, the opinion polls showed solid public support for the Aznar administration. The government was tested again, however, by the sinking of the oil tanker **Prestige** off the coast of Galicia in November 2002. Its inadequate and disorganized reaction to one of Europe's biggest ecological disasters brought a torrent of media criticism. However, throughout 2003 the government ploughed development funds into the heartlands of its support (as well as the areas affected by the *Prestige* oil spill) whilst urging the electorate to back the party that had brought steady economic growth and low inflation. This strategy appeared to have worked and early in 2004 all the indicators suggested the following March general election would be a comfortable victory for the ruling PP and its new leader, Rajoy.

Then, on March 11, and three days before polling day, a series of **bombs exploded on rush-hour commuter trains** travelling into Madrid, killing 192 people and injuring almost two thousand others. The nation was thrown into shock at the most savage attack seen in Spain since the Civil War. Despite the discovery by police within hours of a van connected to the bombings containing detonators and a Koranic audiotape, the PP leadership decided that the Basque terrorist group ETA had to be the culprits. This was a high-risk tactic for the government but it seemed convinced that by pinning the responsibility on ETA it would deflect attention away from its support for the Iraq war (90% of Spaniards had been against it) just long enough for the votes to be counted. No mention was to be made of any possible link with Islamic militant groups and at the same time the blaming of ETA would conveniently vindicate Aznar's hardline stance against Basque terrorism and separatism.

For the three days prior to the election the heavily state-influenced media and Spanish diplomats around the world attempted to peddle the "ETA is responsible" line. But soon doubts began to surface and in the hours before the polls opened the electorate seems to have become highly suspicious of the government's tactic of using ETA as a scapegoat to save its skin, believing that the attack – as was subsequently proved – was the work of **Islamic terrorists** and a retaliation for Spain's participation in the unpopular Iraq war.

The nation turned out in force (turnout went up by a crucial eight percent over the 2000 poll) to give its verdict and Zapatero and the **PSOE an**

unexpected victory. Two million new young voters already angered by the government's mishandling of the *Prestige* oil spill and Aznar's unwavering support for the Iraq war seem to have been pivotal to the final result. In Catalunya and the Basque country the government's duplicity backfired spectacularly. The Catalans voted overwhelmingly for socialist and Catalan nationalist candidates, reducing the PP to a fringe party, and there was a similar fall in support in the Basque regions. The lies and distortion accusations hurled at the Partido Popular following the election result only intensified when it was revealed that the outgoing government had hired a specialist company to destroy all computer records dealing with the bombings before leaving office.

The first act carried out by Zapatero as government leader was to announce the immediate **withdrawal of Spanish troops from Iraq**, an election promise. This aligned him firmly with the German and French governments in Europe to whom Aznar had been hostile, but incurred the displeasure of US President George W. Bush, illustrated by Zapatero's call to the White House to congratulate the president on his 2004 re-election which went unreturned. Bush has since let it be known that Zapatero will never set foot in the White House so long as he is president.

In his first year in office Zapatero's record has been competent if unspectacular. He has still to define a coherent strategy capable of meeting Spain's economic and constitutional problems. The **economy** – driven by tourism, a burgeoning construction industry and consumer spending – has dark clouds on the horizon as unemployment figures again start to edge upwards. This is partly explained by Spain losing out to the new east European members of the EU as multinational companies quit the peninsula (at the rate of one a month) to cut costs by moving production to low-wage economies such as Poland, Hungary and the Czech Republic. The bureaucracy and red tape surrounding business start-ups, an education system that fails to provide students and redundant workers with new skills, added to an almost total lack of government support for new enterprise and innovation, are yet more contributors to Spain's problems. One Catalan business leader recently suggested that if these issues were not addressed urgently Spain would rapidly become a "country of waiters and waitresses". But there are problems in the tourist sector too, as tourist revenue declines due to escalating domestic prices and stiff competition from low-cost holiday destinations around the Mediterranean such as Turkey, Croatia and Tunisia. More worrying still is the fact that as a result of EU enlargement Spain – until now the largest recipient of EU aid – is set to lose around €7 billion in annual grants.

On the wider political stage the consensus across Spanish politics on Spain's role in **Europe** means that, while the nation is no longer as starry-eyed about the EU as it was two decades ago when it joined the then EC, most citizens are acutely aware of the benefits that have flooded into the country as a result of huge EU grants funding important infrastructure projects as well as subsidies channelled to the pivotal farming sector under the Common Agricultural Policy. Ideologically, a significant majority of Spaniards still identify strongly with European integration and see their participation at the launch of the **single currency** and the replacement of the peseta with the **euro** in 2002 as yet another landmark in the country's move into the European mainstream. This longstanding commitment was further underlined when Spain voted "yes" in a referendum on the **European Constitution** early in 2005, the first member state of a now 25-strong EU to do so.

Modern Andalucía

Andalucía shared in the progressive decentralization of power in Spain throughout the post-Franco period and in 1980 became an **Autonomous Region** with a regional government based in Sevilla exercising a large amount of control over its own destiny for the first time. Largely because of its enduring social problems, Andalucía remained a socialist bulwark for the PSOE throughout the eighties – the so-called *sartenilla* (frying pan) of the south which traditionally "fries" the right-wing votes further north. However, whilst the government's reluctance to grasp the nettle of fundamental change, especially in the area of land reform, lost it some support in the 1993 elections, the region's enduring, if increasingly sceptical, commitment to Felipe González ensured the PSOE's narrow election victory over the emergent Partido Popular. The **elections of 1996** followed a similar pattern and Andalucía confounded the polls to turn out once more for "Felipe" (himself a *sevillano*) which, whilst not enough to bring about another socialist victory, crucially denied Aznar an overall majority of seats in the Cortes (parliament). The *sartenilla* (Andalucía returns 62 members to the Madrid parliament, more than any other autonomous region) had cooked the northern votes yet again. But the tide was turning and in the **general election of 2000** there was a significant shift in voting patterns away from the left and towards Aznar and the PP which contributed significantly to the right's victory. In the **poll of 2004** Andalucía shared in the national fury at the PP government's attempts to shift the blame for the Madrid bombings onto ETA and they turned out once more to vote for Zapatero and the PSOE increasing the number of votes for the Socialist Party by almost three million over the 2000 figure.

Despite a more fickle attitude to voting (or abstaining) in general elections that allowed the PP to win a majority in Andalucía, in the 1996, 2000 and 2004 elections to Andalucía's **regional government** southern voters repeatedly balloted to maintain this in the hands of the left, where it has been since the Sevilla parliament was inaugurated in 1982. This has been due in no small part to the PSOE's leader in Andalucía, **Manuel Chaves**. A canny and popular politician and president of the autonomous government since 1990, he has presided over a revolution in Andalucía which has seen rapid growth in tourism, a vast improvement in communications and the eradication of poverty in large parts of the region.

Still, and contradicting the sunny image presented to most of its visitors, chronic economic and social problems remain, and not for nothing is Andalucía known as the "workhouse of Spain". The regional **unemployment** level is among the European Union's highest at an alarming 18 percent (compared with 12 percent for Spain as a whole), and earnings per head are a third lower. Recently, efforts have been made to remove some of the serious obstacles to economic progress with radical improvements in the region's infrastructure and above all communications with the rest of the country and Europe. The **Expo 92** world fair in Sevilla brought new road and rail links aimed at providing faster connections with Madrid and Barcelona whilst a start was made on upgrading the internal links between the provinces of Andalucía as well. Additional funding from the EU – until recently Spain received the highest share of its regional aid budget – has upgraded airports and roads and created industrial parks, and more investment is in the pipeline for the first decade of the new century. However, serious structural problems remain and the task of training and retraining workers in new skills has hardly begun.

The **sovereignty of Gibraltar** continues to be an important issue in Spanish and Andalucian politics and, whilst viewed less urgently in London, the British – at Spain's bidding – have pressured the Gibraltar authorities into clamping down on the twin scourges of drug and tobacco smuggling and money laundering which have exploded in the colony over the last decade. A recent proposal by the Spanish government to share sovereignty over Gibraltar for one hundred years, after which the colony would revert to Spain, received a predictable blast of abuse from the inhabitants of the Rock and its political leaders, and an inscrutable silence from London. A referendum held in 2002 by the Gibraltar governing council produced a 99 per cent vote against any deals with Spain and Gibraltar's current leadership remains uninterested in any negotiations with their Iberian neighbour except on its own narrowly defined terms – such as opening the Rock's airport to international flights in addition to those from London – and there is currently no sign of the deadlock being broken.

The position of Andalucía's 200,000 **agricultural workers** on the land, who face nine months' unemployment each year and depend on patronage from the great landowners for work during the other three, remains unresolved, despite the PSOE government having introduced a minimal unemployment benefit scheme in the 1980s. Vastly increased land improvement grants from the European Union have further enriched the landowners, enabling them to mechanize their farms, whilst the *braceros* or landless day-labourers get nothing and have fewer job opportunities as a result. Industries such as fishing have also been affected by EU regulations limiting the size of catches to conserve dwindling fish stocks, with the consequent rise in unemployment in port towns throughout Andalucía.

All this has compelled a greater dependence on **tourism**, a sector which despite predictions of a downturn has remained buoyant, providing much needed, if seasonal, jobs. This success has produced its own problems as many flock to the coast in search of work leaving a mere twenty percent of the population in provinces such as Almería inhabiting the hinterland. The Junta de Andalucía regional government has now stepped up its "rural tourism" campaign to attract visitors inland in order to channel some of the tourist income away from the coast. Another area now receiving long-overdue attention is the region's **education system**, which has so far largely failed to provide the vocational courses necessary to train the skilled workers essential to drive a modern economy. Although prospects look brighter than ever before as Andalucía strides confidently into the new millennium, it seems that the land which produced Picasso, Manuel de Falla, Federico García Lorca and Juan Ramón Jiménez will have to wait some time yet before all its people can enjoy, as well as endure, their place in the sun.

Chronology

c.25,000 BC ▶ Cave dwellers occupying caves in Málaga province. **Cave paintings** at La Pileta and Nerja.

c.4000 BC ▶ Neolithic colonists arrive from North Africa. Esparto baskets, sandals and jewellery found in the Cueva de Murciélagos near Albuñol in Granada.

c.2500 BC ▶ Los Millares Chalcolithic site flourishes in Almería. Dolmens constructed at Antequera.

c.1100 BC ▶ **Phoenicians** found Cádiz. Remains of later Phoenician settlements at Málaga, Almuñecar and Adra.

C9th–4th BC ▶ Celts settle in the north of Spain. Kingdom of **Tartessus** flourishes around Guadalquivir estuary. **Greeks** establish trading posts along east coast.

C5th BC ▶ **Carthage** colonizes southern Spain. Celto-Iberian culture develops, with Greek influence: statue of La Dama de Baza, necropolis at Toya (Jaén), Iberian stone sculptures made at Porcuna (Jaén museum).

214 BC ▶ Second Punic War with Rome.

210 BC ▶ **Roman colonization** begins. Important Roman cities at Itálica, Córdoba, Cádiz, Carmona and Málaga.

27 BC ▶ Octavian-Augustus becomes first Roman emperor and divides Spain into three parts: Andalucía is named **Baetica**. **Golden Age** and Latinization of Baetica. Mining expanded at Río Tinto.

c.409 ▶ **Vandals** invade southern Spain.

C5th–7th ▶ **Visigoths** arrive and take control of most of Spain including Andalucía. Visigothic cities founded at Mérida and Córdoba.

711 ▶ **Moors** under Tariq invade and defeat Visigothic King Roderic at Río Guadalete, near Jerez. Peninsula conquered in seven years.

718 ▶ Pelayo defeats Moors in a battle at Covadonga in Asturias in northern Spain marking the start of the **Reconquest**.

756 ▶ Abd ar-Rahman I proclaims **emirate of Córdoba.** Great Mosque (**Mezquita**) begun at Córdoba, climax of early Moorish architecture.

928 ▶ Abd ar-Rahman II establishes Cordoban caliphate. **Mozarabic churches** built by Arabized Christians. Construction of palace at

Medina Azahara and extensions to Mezquita in caliphal style.

967 ▶ **Al-Mansur** usurps caliphal powers and forces Christians back into Asturias. Final enlargement of the Mezquita at Córdoba.

1013 ▶ Caliphate disintegrates into **taifas**, petty kingdoms. Medina Azahara palace destroyed by Berber mercenaries. Alcazabas built at Málaga, Sevilla, Carmona, Ronda, etc.

1086 ▶ **Almoravids** invade from North Africa. Philosopher Averroës born at Córdoba (1126). Sevilla becomes new Moorish capital in Spain.

1147 ▶ Invasion by **Almohads** from Morocco; Muslim authority re-established. Almohad minarets include La Giralda and Torre del Oro.

1212 ▶ Almohad advance halted by **Christian victory** at Las Navas de Tolosa (Jaén). **Mudéjar** style emerges through Moorish craftsmen working on Christian buildings: good examples in Sevilla (Alcázar, Casa de Pilatos) and in Córdoba (Capilla Real inside Mezquita).

1236–48 ▶ Fernando III conquers Córdoba and then Sevilla.

1238 ▶ Ibn al-Ahmar (aka Muhammad ibn-Yusuf ibn-Nasr) takes Granada and founds the Nasrid dynasty. Granada's Alhambra palace constructed under Ibn al-Ahmar (1238–73) and his successors.

1262–92 ▶ Cádiz falls to Alfonso X, Sancho IV takes Tarifa.

1479 ▶ Castile and Aragón united under **Fernando and Isabel**. Spanish Inquisition set up in Sevilla. **Sevilla Cathedral** built (1402–1506).

1492 ▶ **Fall of Granada**, the last Moorish kingdom. Discovery of America by Columbus. Expulsion of Jews from Spain.

1516 ▸ **Carlos V** succeeds to the throne and in 1520 becomes Holy Roman emperor inaugurating the **Golden Age**. **Renaissance** reaches Spain. Elaborate early style known as Plateresque, best represented by the Ayuntamiento at Sevilla and the Colegiata at Osuna. Later key figures include Diego de Siloé (1495–1563; Granada, etc) and Andres de Vandelvira (d. 1575; Jaén, Úbeda, Baeza).

1519 ▸ **Magellan** starts global voyage from Sanlúcar de Barrameda; Cortés lands in Mexico.

1556 ▸ Accession of **Felipe II** (d. 1598). Painters and sculptors include: El Greco (1540–1614), Ribera (1591–1652), Zurbarán (1598–1664), Alonso Cano (1601–67), Velázquez (1599–1660), Murillo (1618–82), Roldán (1624–1700), de Mena (1628–88), Martínez Montañes (1580–1649). All are represented in Museo de Bellas Artes, Sevilla.

1587 ▸ Drake carries out raid on Cádiz.

1588 ▸ Sinking of the Armada.

1609 ▸ Expulsion of Moriscos, last remaining Spanish Muslims.

1649 ▸ Great plague in Sevilla wipes out one third of the population.

1700 ▸ War of the Spanish Succession brings Felipe V (1713–45), a Bourbon, to the throne. British seize Gibraltar. **Baroque** develops in reaction to the severity of the High Renaissance and reaches a flamboyant peak in the Churrigueresque style of the C18th: La Cartuja (Granada), Caridad (Sevilla), Écija, Lucena, Priego de Córdoba, etc.

1759–88 ▸ Reign of Carlos III. **Enlightenment** ideas enter Spain. Colonies of Germans, French and Swiss settled in the Sierra Morena.

1808 ▸ French occupy Spain. Liberal constitution declared in Cádiz

(1812). Andalucía divided into eight provinces (1834). Romantic era brings travellers to Spain. English cemetery set up at Málaga (1830). Washington Irving publishes *Tales of the Alhambra* (1832).

1835 ▸ **First Carlist War**. Peasant risings begin throughout Andalucía.

1855 ▸ **Dissolution of monasteries** and confiscation of Church lands.

1874 ▸ **Second Carlist War**. Many of Andalucía's greatest creative artists born in last part of C19th: Antonio Machado (Sevilla)1875; Manuel de Falla (Cádiz) 1876; Picasso (Málaga) and Juan Ramón Jiménez (Moguer) both 1881; guitarist Segovia (Andújar) 1893; Federico García Lorca (Granada) 1898.

1898 ▸ Loss of Cuba, Spain's last American colony.

1923 ▸ Primo de Rivera dictatorship. Ibero-American Exhibition flops in Sevilla (1929). Site now Plaza de España.

1931 ▸ Second Republic.

1936–9 ▸ **Spanish Civil War**. Franco dictatorship begins.

1953 ▸ Franco secures economic aid from US in return for military bases. Costa del Sol opened up to tourist development (1962).

1975 ▸ Death of Franco; restoration of democracy.

1980 ▸ Andalucía votes to become an **Autonomous Region**.

1982 ▸ Sevillano and PSOE leader **Felipe González** elected prime minister. Elections for first Andalucian parliament.

1985 ▸ Frontier between Spain and Gibraltar opens (1985). Spain joins European Community (1986).

1992 ▸ Expo '92 in Sevilla celebrates the 500th anniversary of Columbus's discovery of America. Many striking buildings and bridges constructed in Sevilla and elsewhere to coincide with this event.

1993 ▶ Minority PSOE government returned to power with aid of Catalan Nationalist Party.

1996 ▶ Election of minority Partido Popular (Conservative) government led by José María Aznar.

1998 ▶ Felipe González resigns as leader of PSOE.

1999 ▶ Spain joins ten other EU states to create the European Economic and Monetary Union (EMU) and a **single currency**, the **euro**.

2000 ▶ Emphatic victory by Jose María Aznar's Partido Popular gives the right an overall majority for the first time since the end of the Franco regime. PSOE hangs onto power in Andalucía's **regional elections** but loses its majority.

2002 ▶ Spain's currency, the peseta, is replaced by the **euro**.

2003 ▶ New **Picasso Museum** opens in Málaga displaying major works by the **malagueño** artist.

2004 ▶ Terrorist **bombs** in Madrid dramatically alter the course of the March general election and **José Luis Rodríguez Zapatero** is elected at the head of a PSOE government. In regional elections Andalucía returns a **PSOE autonomous government** with a substantial majority.

Flamenco

lamenco is undoubtedly the most important musical–cultural phenomenon in Spain, and over the past decade or so it has experienced a huge
resurgence in popularity, and a profile that has reached out far beyond its
Andalucian homeland. The sanitized kitsch flamenco, all frills and castanets, exploited as an image of tourist Spain during the Franco period, has been
left far behind by a new age expressing the vitality and attitudes of a younger
generation of flamenco clans.

In the 1980s, the Spanish press hailed **Ketama** (named after a Moroccan
village famed for its hashish) as creators of the music of the "New Spain",
after their first album which fused flamenco with rock and Latin salsa. Since
then they have pushed the frontiers of flamenco still further by recording
Songhai, an album collaborating with Malian kora player Toumani Diabate
and British bassist Danny Thompson. *Blues de la Frontera* (Frontier Blues),
the first disc of **Pata Negra** ("black leg" – the highest quality Andalucian
leg of cured ham – and an everyday term used for anything good), caused
an equal sensation.

This flamenco revival of the 1980s and 1990s is no longer confined to the
purists who kept old-time flamenco alive in their *peñas* or clubs. On radio
and on cassettes blaring from market stalls right across the country you hear
the typical high-pitched treble tones of commercial flamenco singers such as
Tijeritas. The European success of the flamenco-rumba of the **Gipsy Kings**,
a high-profile gypsy group from southern France, has further opened and
prepared the ear of European popular audiences for something more powerful. Rumba, a Latin form, has come back to Spain from Latin America, and
so is known as a music of *ida y vuelta* ("go and return"), one of the many
fusions of the Spanish music taken to the New World with the *conquistadores*
and their descendants, where it has mixed with African and other elements,
before making its way back again. The impetus began at the end of the 1970s,
with the innovations of guitarist **Paco de Lucía** and, especially, the late
great singer, **El Camarón de la Isla**. These were musicians who had grown
up learning from their flamenco families but whose own musical tastes have
embraced international rock, jazz and blues. Paco de Lucía blended jazz and
salsa on to the flamenco sound. Camarón, simply, was an inspiration – and one
whose own idols (and fans) included Chick Corea and Miles Davis, as well as
flamenco artists. Latterly flamenco musicians are to be found playing in many
different contexts, including rock and folk genres – the result is an exciting
and dynamic scene.

Origins

The **roots of flamenco** evolved in southern Spain from many sources:
Morocco, Egypt, India, Pakistan, Greece and other parts of the Near and Far
East. How exactly they came together as flamenco is a source of great debate
and obscurity, though most authorities believe the roots of the music were
brought by **gypsies** arriving in the fifteenth century. In the following century,
it fused with elements of Arab and Jewish music in the Andalucian mountains,
where Jews, Muslims and "pagan" gypsies had taken refuge from the forced

conversions and clearances effected by the Catholic monarchs and the Church. The main flamenco centres and families are to be found today in quarters and towns of gypsy and refugee origin, such as Alcalá del Río, Utrera, Jerez, Cádiz and the Triana *barrio* of Sevilla.

There are two theories about the origins of the name flamenco. One contends that Spanish Jews migrated through trade to Flanders, where they were allowed to sing their religious chants unmolested, and that these chants became referred to as flamenco by the Jews who stayed in Spain. The other is that the word is a mispronunciation of the Arabic words *felag* (fugitive) and *mengu* (peasant), a plausible idea, as Arabic was a common language in Spain at the time.

Flamenco aficionados enjoy heated debate about the purity of their art and whether it is more validly performed by a **gitano** (gypsy) or a **payo** (non-gypsy). Certainly, flamenco seems to have thrived enclosed, preserved and protected by the oral tradition of the gypsy clans. Its power, and the despair which its creation overcomes, has emerged from the precarious and vulnerable lives of a people surviving for centuries at the margins of society. Flamenco reflects a passionate need to preserve their self-esteem.

These days, there are as many acclaimed *payo* as *gitano* flamenco artists. However, the concept of an **active inheritance** is crucial. The veteran singer **Fernanda de Utrera**, one of the great voices of "pure flamenco", was born in 1923 into a gypsy family in Utrera, one of the *cantaora* centres. She was the granddaughter of the legendary singer "Pinini", who had created her own individual flamenco forms, and with her younger sister Bernarda, also a notable singer, inherited their flamenco with their genes. Even the members of Ketama, the Madrid-based flamenco-rock group, come from two gypsy clans – the Sotos and the Carmonas.

Although flamenco's exact origins are obscure, it is generally agreed that its "laws" were established in the nineteenth century. Indeed, from the mid-nineteenth century into the early twentieth, flamenco enjoyed a legendary **"Golden Age"**, the tail-end of which is preserved on some of the earliest 1930s recordings. The original musicians found a home in the *café cantantes*, traditional taverns which had their own group of performers (*cuadros*). One of the most famous was the *Café de Chinitas* in Málaga (see p.103), immortalized by the Granada-born poet García Lorca. In his poem *A las cinco de la tarde* (At five in the afternoon), Lorca claimed that flamenco is deeply related to bullfighting, not only sharing root emotions and passions, flashes of erratic genius, but because both are possible ways to break out of social and economic marginality.

Just such a transformation happened in 1922 when the composer Manuel de Falla, the guitarist Andrés Segovia and the poet García Lorca were present for a legendary *Concurso de Cante Jondo*. A gypsy boy singer, **Manolo Caracol**, reportedly walked all the way from Jerez and won the competition with the voice and flamboyant personality that were to make him a legend throughout Spain and South America. The other key figure of this period, who can be heard on a few recently re-mastered recordings, was **Pastora Pavón**, known as *La Niña de Los Peines*, and popularly acclaimed as the greatest woman flamenco voice of the twentieth century.

In addition to *café cantantes*, flamenco surfaced – as it does today – at fiestas, in bars or *tablaos*, and at *juergas*, informal, private parties. The fact that the Andalucian public are so knowledgeable and demanding about flamenco means that musicians, singers and dancers found even at the most humble local club or festival are usually very good indeed.

△ Flamenco

The art of flamenco

It is essential for an artist to invoke a response, to know they are reaching deep into the emotional psyche of their audience. They may achieve the rare quality of **duende** – total emotional communication with their audience, and the mark of great flamenco of whatever style or generation. *Duende* is an ethereal quality: moving, profound even when expressing happiness, mysterious but nevertheless felt, a quality that stops listeners in their tracks. And many of those listeners are intensely involved, for flamenco is not just a music, for many it is a way of life, a **philosophy** that influences daily activities. A flamenco is not only a performer but anyone who is actively and emotionally involved in the unique philosophy.

For the musicians, this fullness of expression is integral to their art, which is why, for as many famous names as one can list, there are many, many other lesser-known musicians whose work is startlingly good. Not every superb flamenco musician gets to be famous, or even to record, for flamenco thrives most in **live performance**. Exhilarating, challenging and physically stimulating, it is an art form which allows its exponents huge scope to improvise while obeying certain rules. Flamenco guitarist Juan Martín has remarked that "in microcosm it imitates Spanish society – traditional on the outside but, within, incredible anarchy".

There is a **classical repertoire** of more than sixty flamenco songs (*cantes*) and dances (*danzas*) – some solos, some group numbers, some with instrumental accompaniment, others *a cappella*. These different forms of flamenco are grouped in "families" according to more or less common melodic themes. The most common beat cycle is twelve – like the blues. Each piece is executed by juxtaposing a number of complete musical units called *coplas*. Their number varies depending on the atmosphere the *cantaor* wishes to establish and the emotional tone they wish to convey. A song such as a *cante por solea* may take a familiar 3/4 rhythm, divide phrases into 4/8 measures, and then fragmentally subdivide again with voice ornamentation on top of that. The resulting complexity and the variations between similar phrases constantly undermine repetition, contributing greatly to the climactic and cathartic structure of each song.

Songs and singer

Flamenco **songs** often express pain, and with a fierceness that turns that emotion inside out. Generally, the voice closely interacts with improvising guitar (*toque*), the two inspiring each other, aided by the **jaleo**: the hand-clapping *palmas*, finger-snapping *palillos* and shouts from participants at certain points in the song. This *jaleo* sets the tone by creating the right atmosphere for the singer or dancer to begin, and bolsters and appreciates the talent of the artist as they develop the piece.

Aficionados will shout encouragement, most commonly "¡*Olé!*" – when an artist is getting deep into a song – but also a variety of stranger-sounding phrases. A stunning piece of dancing may, for example, be greeted with "¡*Viva la maquina escribir!*" (long live the typewriter), as the heels of the dancer move so fast they sound like a machine; or the cry may be "¡*Agua!*" (water), as the scarcity of water in Andalucía has given the word a kind of glory.

An essential characteristic of flamenco is the singer or dancer taking certain risks, by putting into their performance feelings and emotions which arise directly from their own life experience, exposing their own **vulnerabilities**. Aficionados tend to acclaim more a voice that gains effect from surprise and startling moves than one governed by recognized musical logic. Vocal prowess or virtuosity can be deepened by sobs, gesticulation and an intensity of expression that can have a shattering effect on an audience. Thus pauses, breaths, body and facial gestures of anger and pain transform performance into **cathartic events**. *Siguiriyas* which date from the Golden Age, and whose theme is usually death, have been described as cries of despair in the form of a funeral psalm. In contrast there are many songs and dances such as *tangos*, *sevillanas* and *fandangos* which capture great **joy** for fiestas.

The **sevillana** originated in medieval Sevilla as a spring country dance, with verses improvised and sung to the accompaniment of guitar and castanets (which are rarely used in other forms of flamenco). **El Pali** (Francisco Palacios), who died in 1988, was the most well-known and prolific *sevillana* musician, his

Most popular images of flamenco dance – twirling bodies in frilled dresses, rounded arms complete with castanets – are **sevillanas**, the folk dances performed at fiestas, and, in recent years, on the nightclub floor. "Real" flamenco dance is something rather different and, like the music, can reduce the onlooker to tears in an unexpected flash, a cathartic point after which the dance dissolves. What is so visually devastating about flamenco dance is the physical and emotional control the dancer has over the body: the way the head is held, the tension of the torso and the way it allows the shoulders to move, the shapes and angles of seemingly elongated arms, and the feet, which move from toe to heel, heel to toe, creating rhythms. These rhythms have a basic set of moves and timings but they are improvised as the piece develops and through interaction with the guitarist.

Flamenco dance dates back to about 1750 and, along with the music, moved from the streets and private parties into the *café cantantes* at the end of the nineteenth century. This was a great boost for the dancers' art, providing a home for professional performers, where they could inspire each other. It was here that legendary dancers like **El Raspao** and **El Estampío** began to develop the spellbinding footwork and extraordinary moves that characterize modern flamenco dance, while women adopted for the first time the flamboyant **hata de cola** – the glorious long-trained dresses, cut high at the front to expose their fast moving ankles and feet.

Around 1910, flamenco dance had moved into Spanish theatres, and dancers like **La Niña de los Peines** and **La Argentina** were major stars. They mixed flamenco into programmes with other dances and also made dramatic appearances at the end of comic plays and silent movie programmes. **Flamenco opera** was established, interlinking singing, dancing and guitar solos in comedies with a local flamenco flavour.

In 1915 the composer Manuel de Falla composed the first flamenco ballet, **El Amor Brujo** (Love, the Magician), for the dancer Pastora Imperio. **La Argentina**, who had established the first Spanish dance company, took her version of the ballet abroad in the 1920s, and with her choreographic innovations flamenco dance came of age, working as a narrative in its own right. Another key figure in flamenco history was **Carmen Amaya**, who from the 1930s to the 1960s took flamenco dance on tour around the world, and into the movies.

In the 1950s, dance found a new home in the **tablaos**, the aficionados' bars, which became enormously important as places to serve out a public apprenticeship. More recently the demanding audiences at local and national fiestas have played a part. Artistic developments were forged in the 1960s by **Matilde Coral**, who updated the classic dance style, and in the 1970s by **Manuela Carrasco**, who had such impact with her fiery feet movement, continuing a rhythm for an intense and seemingly impossible period, that this new style was named after her (*manuelas*).

Manuela Carrasco set the tone for the highly individual dancers of the 1980s and 1990s, such as **Mario Maya** and **Antonio Gades**. These two dancers and choreographers have provided a theatrically inspired staging for the dance, most significantly by extending the role of a dance dialogue and story – often reflecting on the potency of love and passion, their dangers and destructiveness.

Gades has led his own company on world tours but it is his influence on film which has been most important. He had appeared with Carmen Amaya in *Los Araños* in 1963 but in the 1980s began his own trilogy with film-maker Carlos Saura: *Boda de Sangre* (Lorca's play, Blood Wedding), *Carmen* (a reinterpretation of the opera) and *El Amor Brujo*. The films featured Paco de Lucía and his band, and the dancers **Laura del Sol** and **Christina Hoyos** – one of the great contemporary dancers, who has herself created a superb ballet, *Sueños Flamencos* (Flamenco Dreams).

Aside from the great companies and personalities of flamenco dance, there are an enormous number of local dancers all over Andalucía, whose dancing brings flamenco to life, and whose moves can be sheer poetry.

unusually gentle voice and accompanying strummed guitar combining an enviable musical pace with a talent for composing popular poetic lyrics. In the last few years dancing *sevillanas* has become popular in bars and clubs throughout Spain, but their great natural habitats are **Sevilla's April Feria** and the annual pilgrimage to **El Rocío**. It is during the Sevilla *feria* that most new recordings of *sevillanas* emerge.

Among the best contemporary singers are the aforementioned **Fernanda** and **Bernarda de Utrera**, **Enrique Morente**, **El Cabrero**, **Juan Peña El Lebrijano**, the **Sorderas**, **Fosforito**, **José Menese** and **Carmen Linares**. However, one of the most popular and commercially successful singers of modern flamenco was the extraordinary **El Camarón de la Isla** (The "Shrimp of the Isle" of León, near his Cádiz home), who died in 1992. Collaborating with the guitarists Paco and Pepe de Lucía, and latterly, Tomatito, Camarón raised **cante jondo**, the virtuoso "deep song", to a new art. His high-toned voice had a corrosive, rough-timbred edge, cracking at certain points to release a ravaged core sound. His incisive sense of rhythm, coupled with almost violent emotional intensity, made him the quintessential singer of the times.

Flamenco guitar

The flamenco performance is filled with pauses. The singer is free to insert phrases seemingly on the spur of the moment. The **guitar accompaniment**, while spontaneous, is precise and serves one single purpose – to mark the *compas* (measures) of a song and organize rhythmical lines. Instrumental interludes which are arranged to meet the needs of the *cantaor* (as the creative singer is called) not only catch the mood and intention of the song and mirror it, but allow the guitarist to extemporize what are called *falsetas* (short variations) at will. When singer and guitarist are in true rapport the intensity of a song develops rapidly, the one charging the other, until the effect can be overwhelming.

The flamenco **guitar** is of lighter weight than most acoustic guitars and often has a pine table and pegs made of wood rather than machine heads. This is to produce the preferred bright responsive sound which does not sustain too long (as opposed to the mellow and longer sustaining sound of classical guitar). If the sound did sustain, particularly in fast pieces, chords would carry over into each other.

The guitar used to be simply an accompanying instrument – originally the singers themselves played – but at the end of the nineteenth century and in the early decades of the twentieth century it began developing as a **solo** form, absorbing influences from classical and Latin American traditions. The greatest of these early guitarists was **Ramón Montoya**, who revolutionized flamenco guitar with his harmonizations and introduced tremolo and a whole variety of arpeggios – techniques of right-hand playing. After him the revolution was continued by Sabicas and Niño Ricardo and Carlos Montoya. The classical guitarist **Andrés Segovia** was another influential figure; he began his career playing flamenco in Granada. Then in the 1960s came the two major guitarists of modern times, **Paco de Lucía** (see overleaf) and **Manolo Sanlucar**.

Solo guitarists, these days, have immediately identifiable sounds and rhythms: the highly emotive **Pepe Habichuela** and **Tomatito**, for example, or the unusual rhythms of younger players like **Ramón el Portugúes**, **Enrique de Melchor** and **Rafael Riqueni**. Flamenco guitar has now consolidated its position on the world's great stages as one of the most successful forms of instrumental music.

Nuevo flamenco

One of flamenco's great achievements has been to sustain itself while providing much of the foundation and inspiration for new music emerging in Spain today. In the 1950s and 1960s, rock'n'roll displaced traditional Spanish music, as it did indigenous music in many parts of the world. In the 1980s, however, flamenco reinvented itself, gaining new meaning and a new public through the music of Paco de Lucía, who mixed in **jazz**, **blues** and **salsa**, and, later, groups like Pata Negra and Ketama, who brought in more **rock** influences. Purists hated these innovations but, as José "El Sordo" (Deaf One) Soto, Ketama's main singer, explained, they were based on "the classic flamenco that we'd been singing and listening to since birth. We just found new forms in jazz and salsa: there are basic similarities in the rhythms, the constantly changing harmonies and improvisations. Blacks and gypsies have suffered similar segregation so our music has a lot in common."

Paco de Lucía, who made the first moves, is the best known of all contemporary flamenco guitarists, and reached new audiences through his performance in Carlos Saura's films *Blood Wedding* and *Carmen*, along with the great flamenco dancers, Cristina Hoyos and Antonio Gades. Paco, who is a non-gypsy, won his first flamenco prize at the age of 14, and went on to accompany many of the great traditional singers, including a long partnership with Camarón de la Isla, one of the greatest collaborations of modern flamenco. He introduced new harmonies, chord structures, scales, open tunings and syncopation that initiated the most vital renaissance of *toque* since Ramón Montoya, a remarkable achievement considering the rigid and stylized nature of this most traditional of forms. He started forging new sounds and rhythms for flamenco following a trip to Brazil, where he fell in love with bossa nova, and in the 1970s he established a sextet with electric bass, Latin percussion, and, perhaps most shocking, flute and saxophone from Jorge Pardo. Paco has also introduced into Spanish flamenco the Peruvian **cajón**, a half-box resembling an empty drawer played by sitting straddled across the top; this reintroduced the sound of the foot of the dancer. Over the past twenty years he has worked with jazz-rock guitarists such as John McLaughlin and Chick Corea, while his own regular band, featuring singer Ramón de Algeciras, remains one of the most original and distinctive sounds on the flamenco scene.

Other artists experimented, too, throughout the 1980s. **Lolé y Manuel** updated the flamenco sound with original songs and huge success; **Jorge Pardo** followed Paco's jazz direction; **Salvador Tavora** and **Mario Maya** staged flamenco-based spectacles; and **Enrique Morente** and **Juan Peña El Lebrijano** both worked with Andalucian orchestras from Morocco, while **Amalgama** worked with southern Indian percussionists, revealing surprising stylistic unities. Another interesting crossover came with **Paco Peña**'s 1991 *Misa Flamenca* recording, a setting of the Catholic Mass to flamenco forms with the participation of established singers such as Rafael Montilla "El Chaparro" from Peña's native Córdoba, and a classical academy chorus.

The more commercially successful crossover with rock and blues, pioneered by **Ketama** and **Pata Negra**, became known, in the 1990s, as **nuevo flamenco**.

This "movement" is associated particularly with the label Nuevos Medios, and in Andalucía, and also Madrid, where many of the bands are based, is a challenging, versatile and musically incestuous new scene, with musicians guesting at each other's gigs and on one another's records.

The music is now a regular sound at nightclubs, too, through the appeal of young singers like **Aurora**, whose salsa-rumba song "Besos de Caramelo", written by Antonio Carmona of Ketama, was the first 1980s number to crack the pop charts, and **Martirio** (Isabel Quinones Gutierrez), one of the most flamboyant personalities on the scene, who appears dressed in lace mantilla and shades, like a cameo from a Pedro Almodóvar film, and sings songs with ironical, contemporary lyrics about life in the cities. In general, the new songs are more sensual and erotic than the traditional material, expressing a pain, suffering and love worth dying for.

Martirio's producer, **Kiko Veneno**, who wrote Camarón's most popular song, "Volando voy", is another artist who has brought a flamenco sensitivity to Spanish rock music, as has Rosario, one of Spain's top woman singers. Other contemporary bands and singers to look out for on the scene include **La Barbería del Sur** (who add a dash of salsa), **Wili Giménez** and **Raimundo Amador**, and **José El Francés**. In the mid-1990s **Radio Tarifa** emerged as an exciting group who started out as a trio, expanded to include African musicians, and whose output mixes Arabic and traditional sounds onto a flamenco base. Flamenco is one of the most powerful popular traditions of music to be found in Europe today, distinguished by its ability to renew itself constantly.

Discography

Many of the recordings recommended here can be obtained from El Mundo Flamenco, 62 Duke Street, London W1 (☎020/7493 0033, ⓦwww .elmundoflamenco.com), who also stock flamenco guitars, videos, books, costumes and shoes and sell the quarterly *Flamenco International* magazine (ⓦwww.flamencointernational.com). Flamenco Lunares (ⓦwww.flamenco .twocatz.com) does a similar job in the USA. Another online operation, Flamenco Store, also sells flamenco CDs, books, dancewear, shoes, guitars and lots more over the Internet (ⓦ www.andalucia.com/flamenco). The Flamenco in Europe website (ⓦwww.flamenco-seiten.de) has lots of links to clubs, schools and magazines Europe-wide. Other useful sites include ⓦ www.andalucia.com/flamenco, ⓦ www.elflamencovive.com and ⓦ www .flamenco-world.com. Using a search-engine such as Google and keying-in "flamenco" should also turn up a wide variety of sites.

Classic flamenco anthologies

Cante Flamenco live in Andalucía (Nimbus, UK).
Early Cante Flamenco – Classic Recordings from the 1930s (Arhoolie, USA).
Magna Antología del Cante Flamenco (Hispavox, Spain; 10 volumes).

Noches Gitanas (EPM, Spain; 4CDs).
Sevillanas: the soundtrack of Carlos Saura's film (Polydor, UK).
Various Flamenco: The Rough Guide (World Music Network).

Individual artists

Camarón de la Isla *Una leyenda flamenca*, *Vivire* and *Autorretrato* (Philips, Spain).
Agustín Carbonell Bola *Carmen* (Messidor, Spain).
Carmen Linares *La luna en el río* (Auvidis, Spain).
Duquende *Duquende y La Guitarra de Tomatito* (Nuevos Medios, Spain).
Federico García Lorca (piano) **y La Argentinita** (Hispavox, Spain).
El Indio Gitano *Nací gitano por la gracia de Dios* (Nuevos Medios, Spain).
Paco de Lucía y Paco Peña *Paco Doble* (Philips, Spain).

Enrique de Melchor *Cuchichi* (Fonodisc, Spain).
José Menese *El viente solano* (Nuevos Medios, Spain).
Moraíto *Morao y oro* (Auvidis, Spain).
Enrique Morente *Negra, si tú supieras* (Nuevos Medios, Spain).
Ramón el Portugués *Gitanos de la Plaza* (Nuevos Medios, Spain).
Tomatito *Barrio Negro* (Nuevos Medios, Spain).
Fernanda et Bernarda de Utrera *Cante Flamenco* (OCORA, France).

Nuevo flamenco and crossovers

Amalgama y Karnataka College of Percussion (Nuba, Spain).
Chano Domínguez *Chano* (Nuba, Spain).
Ray Heredia *Quien no corre, vuela* (Nuevos Medios, Spain).
Jazzpaña (Nuevos Medios, Spain).
Ketama *Canciones hondas* (Nuevos Medios, Spain) and *Ketama* (Hannibal, UK).
Los Jóvenes Flamencos Vol I & II (Nuevos Medios, Spain/Rykodisc, UK).
Martirio *Estoy Mala* (Nuevos Medios, Spain).

Paco de Lucía Sextet *Solo Quiero Caminar* (Philips, Spain), *Live... One Summer Night* (Phonogram, UK), *Almoraima*, and *Siroco* (Polygram, Spain).
Juan Peña Lebrijano y Orquestra Andalusi de Tanger *Encuentros* (Ariola/Globestyle).
Paco Peña *Misa Flamenca* (Nimbus, UK).
Pata Negra *Blues de la Frontera* (Nuevos Medios, Spain/Hannibal, UK).
Radio Tarifa *Rumba argelina* (Música Sin Fin, Spain), *Temporal* (World Circuit).

Getting started

Juan Martín's Guitar Method (United Music Publishers). Self-tuition flamenco guitar course with audio cassette of practice pieces.

La Guitarra Flamenca (Flamenco Vision). Self-tuition guitar course based on three videos.

Jan Fairley

Wildlife

The incredible diversity of natural habitats, flora and fauna to be found in Andalucía makes it one of the most attractive destinations for **wildlife** enthusiasts in western Europe. With 82 protected areas, together accounting for almost 15,000 square kilometres – more than 17 percent of the region – the Junta de Andalucía has shown a dedication to environmental preservation unrivalled in Spain. It also produces a series of leaflets describing the wildlife of Andalucía's protected areas, which can be obtained from Parque Natural offices and Turismos.

Habitats

Andalucía lies at two major **geographical crossroads**: the meeting point of Africa and Europe, and the convergence of the Atlantic Ocean with the Mediterranean Sea at the Strait of Gibraltar. Andalucía also harbours a wide range of topographical and climatic conditions, with altitudes ranging from sea level to near 3500m and precipitation from 170mm to over 2000mm (both the driest and the wettest places in Spain are found here).

In terms of habitats, Andalucía can be divided broadly speaking into coasts, arid lands, inland wetlands and mountains. West of Tarifa, the **Atlantic coast** is characterized by long, sandy beaches and extensive dune systems, while the relatively flat landscape means that the rivers have so little gradient in their lower reaches that they are tidal for many kilometres upstream and generally form great marshes where they meet the sea. The mountains lying behind the **Mediterranean coast**, in contrast, give rise to long stretches of sea cliffs, while rivers here have steeper inclines, are faster flowing and are thus less likely to form great estuarine marshes. The **arid lands** of Almería and eastern Granada, with as little as 170mm of precipitation per year and almost constant sunshine, are one of the driest regions in western Europe, with semi-desert landscapes more appropriate to Morocco.

Throughout Andalucía, a network of **inland wetlands** – permanent or seasonal, freshwater or saline, still or fast-flowing – provides oases for wildlife in a land where there is a pronounced summer drought. Many lie close to the **Strait of Gibraltar**, the primary bird migration route in the western Mediterranean, thus providing refuge for the millions of birds needing to rest and feed en route between Africa and Europe in spring and autumn.

Almost one-fifth of Andalucía is mountain; that is, lies above 1000m. Two great ranges dominate the landscape: the **Sierra Morena**, which separates Andalucía from the rest of Spain, and the **Cordillera Bética**, which runs in a northeasterly direction from Tarifa, continuing out under the Mediterranean to emerge later as the Balearic Islands. The **Sierra Nevada**, at the heart of the Cordillera Bética, possesses the Iberian peninsula's highest mountain – **Mulhacén**, at 3482m.

Plants

More than half of the 8000 **species** of vascular plant known to occur in peninsular Spain and the Balearic Islands are found in Andalucía, including 152 species which are found nowhere else in the world; more than any European country except for Greece. Particular centres of endemism in Andalucía are the arid lands of Almería, the Sierras de Cazorla y Segura, the Serranía de Ronda and the Sierra Nevada.

Perhaps the most important botanical feature of Andalucía, however, is the **pinsapo forests** of the Serranía de Ronda and the Sierra de Grazalema. This tree, *Abies pinsapo*, is a species of fir which is thought to have arrived in Andalucía during the Quaternary (starting 1.6 million years ago), pushed south by the ice sheets, becoming isolated in a few mountain areas when the glaciers retreated. Although only six square kilometres of pinsapo forest remained in 1950, an intensive conservation programme has more than quadrupled this area today.

Mammals

Andalucía is home to 54 species of mammal, the most outstanding of which is the **pardel lynx**, *(lince iberico)* a European relative of the lion and tiger unique to the Iberian peninsula. It is one of Europe's most endangered vertebrates, with a world population now estimated at under 600 individuals, 60 per cent of which live in Andalucía. In 1999 the Worldwide Fund for Nature severely censured the Spanish government for the inadequacy of its plans to protect the lynx. While its natural habitat has been invaded by construction projects, hunters and pesticides, these problems have been compounded by a virus which prevents many adult animals from breeding. The latest statistics suggest the lynx's numbers have fallen even further – perhaps as low as 200 according to one pessimistic study. This collapse of the lynx population was further confirmed at a conference of experts at Andújar in November 2002 which announced that the situation was "catastrophic", adding that unless drastic and immediate action was taken in the next three years the species would be totally extinct in the wild within a decade. When four lynx were found dead in a protected zone earlier in the same year – causing a public outcry – an emergency breeding programme was set up in cooperation with Jerez zoo using abandoned cubs. But when these first attempts at breeding the lynx in captivity failed, a second breeding programme was set up inside the Doñana national park. To the relief of experts and public alike in March 2005 the female of two captive lynxes gave birth to three cubs in the Doñana nursery. The cubs appear to be thriving and it's now hoped that this breakthrough will eventually produce sufficient numbers to replenish the population in the wild. The primary enclaves for this magnificent feline are the Doñana national park and the Sierra Morena.

Genets and **Egyptian mongooses** are also widespread and abundant in Andalucía, although both are thought to have been introduced from North Africa in ancient times, with other common carnivores including wildcats, otters, polecats, beech martens, badgers and weasels. The main stronghold for the **wolf** in Andalucía is the Sierra Morena, which houses up to 75 individuals in small family groups; Sierra farmers angry at the wolf's protected status are now entitled to compensation if their livestock is attacked by wolves. The **Algerian hedgehog**, distinguished from its western European relative by its paler colouring, longer legs and larger ears, is another species of northwest African origin; it has tentatively established itself in a few places on the Iberian

△ Iberian lynx

coast, particularly in eastern Andalucía. The most noteworthy large herbivore of Andalucía is the **Spanish ibex**, the most significant populations inhabiting the Sierras de Cazorla y Segura, the Sierra Nevada and the Serranía de Ronda, with satellite populations recently establishing themselves in some of the nearby ranges. **Mouflon**, originally from Corsica and Sardinia, have been introduced to several areas, notably the Sierras de Cazorla y Segura, as a game species.

Birds

Outstanding among the **wildfowl** of Andalucía is the **white-headed duck**, the western subspecies of which is confined to southern Spain and a small enclave in the Maghreb. Fifteen years ago the Spanish population was on the verge of extinction, but a phenomenal conservation effort has resulted in a population approaching 1000 birds today. Andalucía is also the European stronghold of the secretive **purple gallinule**, distinguished by its long red legs and metallic blue-purple plumage, while the Iberian population of the **collared pratincole** is practically the last one in Europe, a major breeding site being the Guadalquivir marshes.

Crested coots, marbled teal and ferruginous ducks are also virtually unknown as European breeding birds outside Andalucía, while the European stronghold of the greater **flamingo** is the salt lake of Fuente de Piedra, in Málaga, where more than 14,000 pairs have gathered to breed in recent years, relegating the French Camargue to second place. The Spanish **imperial eagle**, Europe's most endangered raptor, is endemic to the Iberian peninsula. The world population of this bird is less than 150 pairs, about a quarter of which are found in Andalucía, primarily in the Doñana National Park and the Sierra Morena. The Sierra Morena also contains the largest European enclave of **black vultures**, numbering over 70 breeding pairs.

Reptiles and amphibians

Some 25 species of **reptile** occur in Andalucía, with noteworthy species including the **chameleon** confined to the coastal areas of Huelva, Cádiz and Málaga, and only found elsewhere in Iberia in the Portuguese Algarve. **Spur-thighed tortoises**, which are globally at risk from habitat loss and collecting, are found in northeastern Almería and Doñana, the only localities in the Iberian peninsula. **Spiny-footed lizards**, endemic to southern and central Iberia and northwest Africa, are extremely common in dry, sandy habitats, the young animals resplendent with bright red tails. By contrast, two much rarer Andalucian lizards are the Spanish algyroides, known only in a small area in the Sierras de Cazorla y Segura, and the Italian wall lizard, surprisingly present at Cabo de Gata, despite having a main area of distribution in Italy and the Balkans.

The peculiar **amphisbaenian**, like a fat pinkish earthworm, occupies an intermediate position between snakes and lizards. Although found throughout Andalucía, this subterranean creature is rarely seen, although it sometimes comes to the surface at night or after heavy rain. Confined to Iberia and northern Africa are the **false smooth snake**, identified by its dark hood, and **Lataste's viper**, distinguished from all other Iberian vipers by its distinct nosehorn, while the beautifully patterned **horseshoe whipsnake** has a similar distribution, but is also found in Sardinia.

Of the fifteen species of **amphibian** which occur in Andalucía, the most noteworthy are the sharp-ribbed salamander, a large warty creature up to 30cm long, which is found only in southern Iberia and Morocco; the tiny, orange-bellied Bosca's newt, confined to western Iberia and thus occurring only in Huelva and northern Sevilla in Andalucía; and the Iberian midwife toad, a southwest Iberian endemic, the males of which carry the egg-strings wound around their hind legs until they hatch.

Butterflies

Andalucía is home to many **butterflies** that occur only in the southern Iberian peninsula and North Africa, including the desert orange tip, Lorquin's and false baton blues, the Spanish fritillary and the Spanish marbled white. Yet others are true Spanish endemics, such as the Panoptes, Nevada and mother-of-pearl blues and the Nevada grayling. Several interesting butterflies are particularly associated with the Andalucian coast, including the extremely rare **Zeller's skipper**, recorded near Algeciras, as well as the more widespread pygmy and Mediterranean skippers. Several large and attractive vagrant species turn up sporadically from across the Atlantic, including the American painted lady, the milkweed, or monarch, and the plain tiger.

When and where to go

The Mediterranean habitats of Andalucía have a climate so mild that a visit at any time of year will be rewarding for **wild flowers**. The arid lands of Almería are best seen in early spring, however, while the alpine flora of the Sierra Nevada and other high mountain regions is not at its peak until summer.

Wetland birds are generally a spring and autumn proposition, although some of the rarer breeding species – purple gallinules, white-headed ducks, crested coots and spoonbills – are perhaps more obvious during the summer. Winter concentrations of wildfowl and waders sometimes number hundreds of thousands, especially in the larger wetlands, such as Doñana. **Raptors** are best seen in late spring and early summer, when the adults must venture out continuously in search of food for their young. By this time too, the short-toed and booted eagles, Egyptian vultures and Montagu's harriers have arrived from Africa. Many of the smaller, colourful birds typically associated with Mediterranean scrub and forest are also summer visitors.

The **carnivores** are virtually impossible to see at any time of year, as most of them are secretive and nocturnal creatures, although the Egyptian mongoose is sometimes encountered trotting through the scrub in broad daylight. Ibex and mouflon are a different proposition altogether, being easily spotted at all times of year and often approached with relative ease.

Summer is best for the **snakes** and **lizards** of the region, although even in the depths of winter they will emerge on sunny days. Alpine **butterflies** generally appear only in late summer, but many species of the milder Mediterranean habitats have two broods a year and can be seen from early spring onwards.

Marismas del Odiel

The **Marismas del Odiel** is an extensive wetland area consisting of a maze of islands, creeks, salt marshes and salinas lying to the west of the Río Odiel where it flows into the Atlantic. Although immediately adjacent to the industrial port of Huelva, this *paraje natural* supports a rich and varied fauna.

More than 200 species of bird have been recorded here, with pride of place going to the 300-odd pairs of **spoonbills**, about 30 percent of the European population, which nest in the grassy marshes of the Isla del Enmedio, one of only three breeding sites in Europe. The Odiel marshes also support large colonies of purple and grey herons and little egrets, as well as hundreds of pairs of little terns and black-winged stilts. Concentrations of up to 2000 **flamingos** are commonplace, particularly during the winter and on migration, when they are often accompanied by large numbers of common cranes, sanderling, avocets and curlews. To the west of the Odiel marshes, the coastal juniper forests of Punta Umbría are an important refuge for chameleons.

Doñana

One of the greatest of all European wetlands, the **Coto de Doñana** truly merits its reputation as a superb destination for wildlife enthusiasts. Spain's premier national park covers 500 square kilometres and is centred on the extensive marshes on the west bank of the Río Guadalquivir. It is almost completely surrounded by a *parque natural* known as the Entorno de Doñana, which acts primarily as a protective buffer zone against industrial pollution from the city of Sevilla and the mines of Huelva, but is also important for wildlife in its own right. A long-feared **disaster** finally occurred in 1998 when an upriver mining dam burst, unleashing millions of tons of toxic waste, threatening the park and its wildlife. At first sight a flat, monotonous landscape, the Doñana marshes are in fact highly diverse, consisting of **vetas**, raised areas which are rarely covered with water, **lucios**, great depressions, sometimes several kilometres long, which retain water until early summer, and **caños**, the reed-fringed channels which wind through the marshes, carrying water in all but the most extreme periods of drought. The coast of Doñana consists of a wide, sandy beach, backed by four parallel fronts of mobile **dunes** which are gradually advancing inland.

The park also contains large areas of *monte*: dense **Mediterranean scrublands**, dominated by species of cistus, halimium, thyme and rosemary. Spring-flowering bulbs include *Dipcadi serotinum*, looking rather like a dull brown bluebell, wild gladioli, irises and trident-shaped asphodels over a metre tall. The *monte* and dune chains also conceal numerous **lagoons**, whilst between the *monte* and the marshlands lies a unique transitional habitat known as the **vera**, its cork-oak studded pastures undoubtedly one of the most diverse ecosystems of the park.

The vertebrate populations of Doñana are almost without parallel in Spain, including eight species of fish, 31 reptiles and amphibians, 29 mammals and 125 breeding birds, with a further 125 species of bird utilizing the park during the winter and on migration. Among the **reptiles**, the most noteworthy species are the chameleon, spur-thighed tortoise, Montpellier and ladder snakes, Lataste's viper, ocellated and spiny-footed lizards, both European pond and stripe-necked terrapins and three-toed skinks, as well as the bizarre, wormlike amphisbaenian, while unusual **amphibians** include stripeless tree-frogs, western spadefoots and sharp-ribbed salamanders.

The list of **mammals** is impressive indeed, topped by the pardel lynx, one of Europe's most endangered mammals, as well as other hunters such as badgers, otters, weasels, mongooses and genets. Wild boar, red deer and the introduced fallow deer are present in considerable numbers, particularly in the *monte*, but the most abundant herbivore is the rabbit, the main prey of the lynx.

Doñana harbours one of the largest populations of Spanish **imperial eagles** in the world (a recent census revealed a minimum of 16 pairs), as well as breeding populations of red and black kites, booted and short-toed eagles and hobbies. Azure-winged magpies, great grey and woodchat shrikes, nightingales, great spotted cuckoos and Scops owls breed in the *monte*, while the venerable cork oaks of the *vera* support mixed colonies of spoonbills, white storks, little and cattle egrets, and purple, grey, squacco and night herons.

The dunes, open grasslands and stunted halophytic vegetation of the dried-out marshes provide suitable nesting areas for lesser short-toed and Thekla larks, red-necked nightjars, stone curlews and pin-tailed sandgrouse, while the marshes support breeding black-winged stilts, avocets, slender-billed gulls, gull-billed, little and whiskered terns, purple gallinules and collared pratincoles, as well as many species of wildfowl, the most significant being large numbers of red-crested pochard, crested coot and marbled teal, with the rare ferruginous and white-headed ducks putting in a sporadic breeding appearance. Many other birds flock to the marshes in winter and on migration, including tens of thousands of greylag geese, pintails, teal, shovellers and black-tailed godwits, as well as lesser numbers of shelduck, wigeon, red-crested pochard, gadwall, common cranes, flamingos and waders.

Bahía de Cádiz

The 100-square-kilometre *parque natural* of the **Bahía de Cádiz** encompasses a wide range of coastal habitats, including sand dunes, stone pine forests, sandy beaches, extensive intertidal salt marshes, abandoned saltpans and small lagoons. Despite the proximity of the 400,000-plus inhabitants of Cádiz itself, the bay is a veritable paradise for **birds**, supporting one of the largest breeding colonies of little terns in Spain, as well as several hundred breeding pairs of black-winged stilts, avocets and Kentish plovers. Its proximity to the European-North African migration route is responsible for a number of more unexpected guests, including arctic skuas, red-breasted mergansers, razorbills and scoters.

The extensive stone pine forests, best preserved at La Algaida, close to Puerto Real on the Bay of Cádiz, are renowned for their **chameleons**, many of which unfortunately meet their maker on the plethora of busy roads which ring the bay.

Acantilado y Pinar de Barbate

With the exception of Gibraltar, the *parque natural* of the **Acantilado y Pinar de Barbate** is the only cliffed section on the Atlantic coast of Andalucía. The sheer walls of **Los Caños de Meca**, plunging over 80m into the sea, are topped by one of the most diverse and best conserved coastal plateau forests on the Andalucian shore, **El Pinar de la Breña**. Stone pines and junipers are interspersed with Mediterranean scrub, hosting barn owls, kestrels and buzzards, as well as a thriving population of chameleons. The isolation of the cliffs themselves has encouraged the establishment of a great colony of **cattle egrets**, numbering over 2500 pairs and unique on the Andalucian coast, as well as breeding peregrines, blue rock thrushes and rock doves.

Sierras de la Plata y Retín

These small sierras lie near the coast between Barbate and Tarifa, close to the town of Zahara de los Atunes, where, in the 1960s, the first **white-rumped swifts** to breed in Europe were observed; curiously, this bird will only rear its young in the abandoned nests of red-rumped swallows.

The **vegetation** is primarily Mediterranean scrub, dominated by Kermes and cork oaks, lentisc, wild olives and dwarf fan palms, forming a mosaic with limestone grasslands that are a riot of colour in spring; some of the more eye-catching species are Spanish iris, Peruvian squill, wild tulip, palmate anemone and star of Bethlehem. Commonly seen **butterflies** include cleopatras, Moroccan orange tips, Spanish festoons and long-tailed blues plus the occasional monarch, a vagrant from North America.

The skies above the Sierras are rarely without the profile of **griffon vultures** riding the thermals – the precipitous cliffs, known locally as *lajas*, support dozens of pairs of nesting griffon vultures – but you can also expect to see Egyptian vultures, Montagu's harriers and peregrines. The Mediterranean scrub is home to a colourful array of smaller birds, including woodchat shrikes, hoopoes, Orphean warblers, rollers and golden orioles, while the drier areas support both great and little bustards, Calandra and crested larks, black-eared and black wheatears and Spanish sparrows.

Playa de los Lances

Close to Tarifa, on the Atlantic coast of Cádiz, lies the *paraje natural* of **Playa de los Lances**, a classic coastal site, comprising a long beach of fine white sands, a ridge of dunes and the marshlands of the ríos Jara and Valle, both of which run parallel to the coast here for several kilometres.

The **beach flora** includes such gems as sea daffodil, cottonweed, southern bird's-foot trefoil and sea medick, while further inland, a mosaic of stone pine forests, dense Mediterranean scrub dominated by lentisc and dwarf-fan palms and dry grasslands covers the plains and hills of the Santuario valley.

Great flocks of **waders** visit the reserve in winter and on migration, the most commonplace being sanderling, dunlin, grey, ringed and Kentish plovers, turnstones, bar-tailed godwits and oystercatchers, as well as hundreds of the rare Audouin's gull. It is a particularly important migration stopover for thousands of white storks and black kites, particularly when bad weather prevents them from crossing the Strait, while ospreys too put in an occasional appearance. Little terns and Kentish plovers both breed in fair numbers on the beach and dunes, while the wealth of piscine life in the rivers and marshes attracts otters, the most characteristic mammal of the reserve.

Punta Entinas-Sabinar

The *paraje natural* of **Punta Sabinar**, which extends along 15km of coast between the resorts of Almerimar and Roquetas in Almería, contains a wide range of habitats, including a sandy beach, littoral dunes clothed with Mediterranean scrub, the saltpan complex of Salinas Viejas and Salinas de Cerillos, and the lagoons of Punta Entinas, all of which are backed by the scarp of Los Alcores, itself a superb example of a raised beach.

Mammals recorded here include the garden dormouse and Mediterranean pine vole, the latter confined to the southern Iberian peninsula, while Lataste's viper is a noteworthy member of the reptilian fauna. But it is the birdlife of the reserve that is truly outstanding, the tally to date numbering almost 200 species.

Among the **breeding birds**, hundreds of pairs of stone curlews and lesser short-toed larks make use of the drier habitats, while the salinas attract post-nuptial concentrations of flamingos of up to 1000 birds, as well as red-crested pochard, cormorants, grey herons and avocets. May is a particularly good time to visit the reserve, affording the chance to see Montagu's harriers, collared pratincoles, Mediterranean and Audouin's gulls, sandwich and whiskered terns, fan-tailed and spectacled warblers and black-eared wheatears. Look out also for woodchat and great grey shrikes, red-necked nightjars, Thekla larks and Marmora's and Dartford warblers in the Mediterranean scrublands.

Cabo de Gata-Níjar

This *parque natural* in southern Almería extends over some 260 square kilometres of the volcanic headland known as **Cabo de Gata** and the steppes of the **Campo de Níjar**. Essentially an arid area with large expanses of semi-desert vegetation, it also includes a wide variety of coastal habitats, ranging from precipitous cliffs over 100m high to dunes, salt marshes and salinas, as well as encompassing the marine ecosystem to a depth of 100m.

The park's sierra itself boasts important formations of **dwarf fan-palm**, Europe's only native species of palm, growing amid lentisc, holly oak,

Mediterranean mezereon and wild olive, as well as extensive steppes dominated by drought-adapted shrubby thymes or the spiny, deciduous shrub *Zizyphus lotus*. Cabo de Gata-Níjar is home to many plants which occur nowhere else in the world, including the **snapdragon** *Antirrhinum charidemi*, known locally as *flor del dragon*, which grows only on volcanic pinnacles in the sierra, as well as the **pink** *Dianthus charidemi* and the **toadflax** *Linaria benitoi*, which flowers only at the onset of the spring rains. Look out too for the short-stalked clusters of mauve-striped white flowers of the endangered lily *Androcymbium europaeum*, also endemic to this part of Spain.

No fewer than sixteen species of **reptiles** and **amphibian** are here, including Lataste's viper, Iberian wall lizards, confined to Iberia, northwest Africa and the western Mediterranean coast of France, and Italian wall lizards, a more easterly species which is found in only a handful of places in Spain. **Butterflies** of interest include desert orange tip and common tiger blue, both essentially African species whose only European populations are found in southern Spain.

Breeding **birds** of the salt marshes include little terns, Kentish plovers, black-winged stilts and avocets, with Cetti's and great reed warblers in the reedbeds. Between June and September, 2000–3000 **flamingos** descend on the coastal areas to feed, particularly when other Andalucian sites have dried out, while wintering and passage birds on the coast include spoonbills, Audouin's gulls, shelduck and red-breasted mergansers. The sierra itself is renowned for its breeding **eagle owls**, **Bonelli's eagles** and **Montagu's harriers**, as well as rufous bushchats and red-necked nightjars, but it is the dry steppes of Níjar that are of supreme ornithological significance, supporting important nesting concentrations of little bustards, stone curlews, black-bellied sandgrouse, lesser short-toed larks and trumpeter finches. Perhaps the most noteworthy bird of Cabo de Gata-Níjar, however, is **Dupont's lark**, an essentially North African species which was only recently discovered as a breeding bird in Europe.

Desierto de las Tabernas

Immediately inland from Cabo de Gata, sandwiched between the sierras Alhamilla and de los Filabres, lies one of the most spectacular landscapes in the Iberian peninsula: the arid lands of the **Desierto de las Tabernas**.

The vegetation of Tabernas consists mainly of **steppes**, dominated either by false esparto grass and *Stipa tenacissima*, or by stunted spiny bushes of *Ziziphus lotus*, the endemic crucifer *Euzomodendron bourgaeanum*, and aromatic thymes, or by salt-tolerant, often succulent, members of the goosefoot family, particularly *Salsola genistoides* and *Salsola papillosa*, both of which are endemic to southern Spain.

These arid lands are home to many plants which are found nowhere else in the world, including the **toadflax** *Linaria nigricans*, the **rockrose** *Helianthemum almeriense*, and the **sea lavender** *Limonium insignis*, which flowers promptly in response to the first rains.

Reptiles are in their element here, the commonest species being ocellated and spiny-footed lizards and ladder snakes. Animals requiring greater humidity in order to survive, such as marsh frogs, natterjack toads, stripe-necked terrapins and viperine snakes, are found only in the seasonal creeks, or ramblas, which thread their way between the eroded hills and plateaux. The Desierto de las Tabernas is also one of the few places where both western and Algerian hedgehogs occur, the latter essentially a northwest African species, established in only a few places on the Spanish coast.

The **birdlife** of Tabernas is extremely diverse, with the soft, eroding cliffs formed by the meanders of the ramblas supporting breeding jackdaws, blue rock thrushes, crag martins, black wheatears, bee-eaters, rollers and alpine and pallid swifts. The steppes themselves support important populations of stone curlews, black-bellied sandgrouse, Thekla larks and black wheatears, as well as being one of the best places in Europe to see trumpeter finches.

Around Tabernas

To the south of the Desierto de las Tabernas lies the 25km-long range of the **Sierra Alhamilla**, where, amid the dry, rocky outcrops, steep gullies and arid grasslands and scrub, you can hope to see little bustards, black-bellied sandgrouse, trumpeter finches, Thekla and Dupont's larks, the latter distinguished by their long, down-curved bills, as well as stone curlews and black wheatears galore.

To the west of Tabernas, in the eastern part of the province of Granada, two great semi-arid depressions also support important populations of steppe birds. The **Hoya de Baza** is largely dedicated to dry cereal croplands today, but nevertheless supports important breeding populations of little bustards, stone curlews, black-bellied sandgrouse and Dupont's and lesser short-toed larks, while the nearby **Hoya de Guadix** is formed predominantly of soft gypsum, carved by flash floods into steep-sided ravines.

Guadix is one of the best areas for observing dry grassland birds in Andalucía, its extensive steppes, cereal cultivations and patches of holm oak scrub providing the perfect habitat for hundreds of little bustards, stone curlews and black-bellied sandgrouse. Montagu's harriers, peregrines and hobbies hunt here by day, replaced by long-eared and eagle owls at dawn and dusk.

Zonas Húmedas del Sur de Córdoba

The **Zonas Húmedas del Sur de Córdoba** is a series of widely dispersed wetlands in the southern part of the province of Córdoba. The six *reservas naturales* – three permanent and three seasonal **lagoons** – which make up the complex have a total area of over ten square kilometres; the reservoirs of Cordobilla and Malpasillo on the Río Genil, both *parajes naturales*, are also sometimes included.

The permanent lagoons are **Zóñar**, **Amarga** and **Rincón**, of which the largest and deepest is the Laguna de Zóñar, up to 8m deep. All are slightly brackish and contain abundant submerged vegetation as well as being surrounded by thick belts of peripheral vegetation – poplars, tamarisks, reeds and reedmace – up to 15m wide in places.

The abundance of submerged vegetable matter supports a wealth of breeding wildfowl, the most noteworthy of which is undoubtedly the **white-headed duck**; these wetlands are the main breeding area in Spain for this diminutive stifftail, with over 45 nesting pairs and winter concentrations of 100-plus birds. Red-crested pochard, pochard, little grebes, purple gallinules, little bitterns, great reed warblers and kingfishers also breed here. In winter and during migration periods, the resident birdlife of the permanent lagoons is swelled by the arrival of large numbers of tufted duck, shovellers, wigeon, teal and pintail, with greylag geese, scaup, shelduck and the rare ferruginous duck also putting in an occasional appearance.

All three permanent lagoons support interesting **reptiles and amphibians**, notably stripe-necked terrapins, grass and viperine snakes, painted frogs and sharp-ribbed salamanders. By contrast, the shallow seasonal lakes of **El Conde o Salobral**, **Los Jarales** and **Tíscar** contain notably saline waters and are surrounded by halophytic vegetation. During the summer these lagoons often dry out completely, such that their ornithological significance is largely concerned with wintering and passage birds. A visit after the autumn rains should turn up black-winged stilts, avocets, grey herons, red-crested pochard, shoveller and wigeon, as well as an occasional greylag goose, flamingo or shelduck. Great bustards are sometimes seen in the dry cereal croplands surrounding the Laguna del Conde o Salobral, while the Laguna de los Jarales, rather surprisingly, supports populations of apparently salt-tolerant natterjack toads, western spadefoots and painted and marsh frogs.

Fuente de Piedra

A little further south, in the north of Málaga, lies the *reserva natural* of **Fuente de Piedra**, a shallow, saline **lagoon** of endorreic origin; that is, it is the result of the accumulation of ground and surface water from the surrounding area and has no outlet. Some 6km long and 2.5km wide, Fuente de Piedra is the largest natural lake in Andalucía.

Salt-tolerant herbs and shrubs surround the lagoon and also thrive on the long banks which traverse the lake. It is these raised areas that support Fuente de Piedra's pride and joy: the largest breeding colony of **flamingos** in Europe, and the only regular nesting site on the continent, apart from the French Camargue. Depending on water levels in the lagoon (if too low the birds are reluctant to breed), in an average year around 14,000 pairs of flamingos raise some 12,000 young at Fuente de Piedra. During the winter, when full, the lake covers an area of some 14 square kilometres, but during the summer it becomes little more than a glistening sheet of dried salts, although pumps installed in recent years ensure that sufficient water remains in the centre of the lake for the young flamingos to fledge. During times of low water, the adult flamingos disperse all over Andalucía in search of food, turning up hundreds of kilometres away at Doñana, the Odiel marshes and Cabo de Gata.

A freshwater channel surrounds the main lagoon, supporting a rich marsh vegetation and attracting **other wetland birds**: at least 20 pairs of marsh harriers, up to 200 pairs of the rare gull-billed tern, a few pairs of the equally rare slender-billed gull, black-winged stilts, avocets, red-crested pochard, gadwall, garganey and great crested and black-necked grebes all breed here. In the winter, look out for common cranes, as well as greylag geese and shelduck among the 50,000 wildfowl present, while in spring the lake becomes a focal point for thousands of black terns on migration.

The cereal fields and Mediterranean scrublands surrounding Fuente de Piedra are worth a look for crested larks, stone curlews, bee-eaters, great grey shrikes, hoopoes and pallid and alpine swifts in the summer.

Lagunas de Cádiz

The **Lagunas de Cádiz**, which are scattered across the hinterland of the Bahía de Cádiz, are renowned for their important breeding populations of white-headed duck, crested coot and purple gallinules, all virtually unknown as European breeding birds outside Andalucía.

The most important lake in the complex is the **Laguna de Medina**, the largest in Cádiz. Like most of the lagoons it is surrounded by a thick belt of emergent vegetation, dominated by reeds, reedmace, rushes and stands of tamarisk, which grades into cereal cultivations interspersed with dense patches of Mediterranean scrub away from the shore. Here spring brings a flush of orchids into bloom, including the exotic sawfly, mirror, yellow bee and bumblebee orchids.

Other **breeding birds** of the Lagunas de Cádiz include black-necked grebes, red-crested pochard, black-winged stilts and Kentish plover, with the reedbeds attracting little bitterns, great reed and Cetti's warblers, marsh harriers and possibly spotted crakes.

The lagoons come into their own in the winter months and during migration periods, when thousands of ducks, coots and geese arrive, including greylag geese, wigeon, garganey, gadwall, pintail and such rarities as marbled teal and ferruginous duck. White storks, purple squacco and night herons, bitterns and little bitterns, spoonbills, flamingos and common cranes can be seen feeding here when the lagoons are full, as well as black and whiskered terns, collared pratincoles and an occasional osprey on migration.

Sierra Morena

The 500km-long ridge of the **Sierra Morena**, which virtually cuts Andalucía off from the rest of Spain, reaches a maximum altitude of only 1110m, comprising for the most part low, rounded hills, clothed with dense forests that are favoured by many animals not found elsewhere in the region.

Within Andalucía much of the Sierra Morena is protected by a series of *parques naturales*. At the western end, bordering Portugal and Extremadura, lie the **Sierra de Aracena y Picos de Aroche**, the **Sierra Norte** and the **Sierra de Hornachuelos**, while the eastern Sierra Morena holds the **Sierra de Cardeña-Montoro** and the adjacent **Sierra de Andújar**. In northern Jaén, the kilometre-deep river gorge of Despeñaperros – the only crossing point between Andalucía and the *meseta* in ancient times – is also a *parque natural*.

The vegetation of the Sierra Morena was originally composed of **Mediterranean forests** dominated by holm, Lusitanian and cork oaks, interspersed with wild olives, cistuses, lentisc, strawberry tree and myrtle; the best-preserved examples are found today in the Sierra de Andújar. Other woodland types are also present, however, such as the magnificent enclave of Spanish chestnuts which thrives around Galaroza and Fuenteheridos, in the Sierra de Aracena, and the rich gallery forests of alders, elms, ashes and willows which line many of the rivers of the Sierra. In the western Sierra Morena, extensive areas of the original Mediterranean forest have been converted to *dehesa* – the evergreen oak "parkland-and-pastures" which dominates much of southwestern Iberia – dedicated largely to cork and charcoal production and the rearing of black pigs, whose succulent, acorn-fed hams are famous worldwide. The *dehesa* grasslands are a riot of colour in spring, some of the more attractive species including Spanish bluebell, wild tulip, star of Bethlehem, tassel hyacinth, asphodels, Spanish iris, Barbary nut, peonies and palmate anemone.

The mammalian fauna of the Sierra Morena comprises good populations of **wild boar** and red and fallow **deer**, as well as all the Andalucian small carnivores: weasels, beech martens, polecats, badgers, mongooses, genets and wildcats, with otters particularly abundant along the Río de las Yeguas, which separates the Sierra de Cardeña-Montoro from Andújar. The Andalucian stronghold for the **wolf** is the eastern Sierra Morena, although it also strays westwards into the Sierra Norte, while the endangered **pardel lynx** is known to occur in the Sierras de Hornachuelos, Cardeña-Montoro and Andujar.

The Sierra Morena is also a superb locality for **birds of prey**, housing important populations of golden, Bonelli's, short-toed and booted eagles, griffon and Egyptian vultures and eagle owls, as well as a few pairs of Spanish imperial eagles. Here, too, you will find the most important population of **black vultures** in Andalucía, nesting in the tops of the ancient cork and holm oaks, with more than 30 pairs in the Sierra de Aracena and 20-plus pairs in the Sierra de Hornachuelos. The Sierra Morena is also the only place in Andalucía with breeding **black storks**.

Sierra Nevada

Almost 80km long and 15–30km wide, the **Sierra Nevada** – designated Andalucía's second **national park** in 1999 – is one of the best-known mountain ranges in Spain, not least for its highest peak, **Mulhacén**, which at 3483m is known colloquially as the "roof" of the peninsula. The southern foothills of the Sierra Nevada, the **Alpujarras**, have an almost tropical climate owing to their proximity to Africa, while the highest peaks – twelve of which are over 3000m – are snow-clad for up to nine months of the year. Composed mainly of mica schist, the Sierra Nevada is very different geologically from the nearby limestone ranges, which may account partly for the large number of endemic species found here.

A botanical enclave of supreme importance, the Sierra Nevada houses almost **2000 species of vascular plant**, more than 70 of which are found nowhere else in the world. Most of the endemic species occur in the highest peaks, forming part of a unique snow-tolerant community whose members include the endangered daffodil *Narcissus nevadensis*, one of the first plants to flower in the spring, the white-flowered Nevada saxifrage (*Saxifraga nevadensis*), the wormwood *Artemisia granatensis*, found only above 3000m, glacier toadflax (*Linaria glacialis*), another endangered species which occurs at similar altitudes, the white-flowered buttercup *Ranunculus acetosellifolius*, distinguished by its arrow-shaped leaves and mauve sepals, and the cushion-forming, pinkish-flowered violet *Viola crassiuscula*.

The Sierra Nevada is also famed for its large number of endemic **butterflies**, including the subspecies of the Spanish brassy ringlet, found only above 2000m; *ssp. nevadensis* of the apollo, which can be seen in late summer at altitudes ranging from 700 to a phenomenal 3000m; and the Nevada blue, which flies between 2100 and 2400m, while the zullichi subspecies of the Glandon blue, perhaps **Iberia's rarest butterfly**, has only been found by a handful of specialists near Pico Veleta. The lower slopes of the Sierra Nevada have Lorquin's and zephyr blues, which also occur in the Sierra Morena.

Even among the larger animals, the diversity is incredible. Within the boundaries of the *parque natural* alone, you could find 35 mammals, 125 breeding birds and 29 reptiles and amphibians. The **Spanish ibex**, which almost became extinct here in the 1930s, now numbers more than 3000 individuals, but the largely treeless terrain is less favourable for other mammals; the pine plantations of the lower slopes support a few badgers, beech martens and wildcats. Breeding raptors include golden, Bonelli's, short-toed and booted eagles, goshawks and peregrines. Several hundred pairs of choughs nest around the high level cliffs, while the alpine grasslands are the only place where alpine accentors – undoubtedly the tamest high mountain birds – breed in the southern half of Spain. The approach into the Sierra Nevada via the Alpujarras will add some of the smaller and more colourful birds to your list, including hoopoes, bee-eaters, woodchat shrikes, black redstarts, black-eared wheatears and blue rock thrushes.

Sierra de María

At the eastern end of the **Cordillera Subbética** in Andalucía lies the *parque natural* of the **Sierra de María**, centred on the almost naked limestone outcrop of María (2045m). The lower slopes support extensive shady forests of aleppo and laricio pine, interspersed with relict Scots pines and small patches of junipers, maples and holm oak: home to wildcats, badgers and red squirrels, as well as eagle owls. Above the tree line you should be able to spot golden, booted and short-toed **eagles** soaring on the thermals, as well as **griffon vultures** recently reintroduced into the Sierra after disappearing in the 1940s and now breeding successfully. Other species to look out for include wallcreepers, peregrine falcons and alpine swifts. An interesting botanical locality, Sierra de María contains several endangered species, including the knapweeds *Centaurea mariana* and *C. macrorrhiza*, both of which are found only here and in the adjacent Sierra del Gigante in Murcia, and *Sideritis stachydioides*, a member of the mint family which is unique to María.

Sierra de María is also renowned for its **butterfly** fauna, particularly at high altitudes, including the Spanish argus, unique to Iberia, an endemic subspecies of apollo (*ssp. mariae*), and the Nevada grayling (also in the Sierra Nevada), represented in Spain by the subspecies *williamsi*; this species is otherwise found only in southern Russia, some 5000km distant.

Sierras de Cazorla, Segura y Las Villas

In the extreme northeast of Andalucía, in the province of Jaén, lies a series of deep valleys separated by parallel limestone ridges running in a northeast-southwesterly direction: the *parque natural* of the **Sierras de Cazorla, Segura y las Villas** (over 2000 square kilometres), the largest protected area in Andalucía. With average annual precipitation exceeding 2000mm, this is one of the rainiest places in Spain, and it is here that the headwaters of the great Río Guadalquivir rise. Originally one of Spain's foremost hunting reserves, the park has lost much of its native vegetation owing to extensive planting with aleppo, maritime and laricio pines, although the latter is a very ancient species which also occurs here naturally. Above the tree line the vegetation is more or less still in a natural state, the predominant plants being stunted laricio pines and junipers and cushion-forming members of the pea family: purple-flowered hedgehog broom, yellow-flowered *Echinospartium boissieri* and white- or pink-flowered mountain tragacanth, as well as the spiny crucifer *Ptilotrichum spinosum*.

The **flora** of the Sierras de Cazorla, Segura y las Villas numbers some 1300 species, including more than 30 endemics, such as the pale blue columbine *Aquilegia cazorlensis* and the cranesbill *Geranium cazorlense*, neither of which was discovered until the 1950s. The stronghold for both species is the peak of Cabañas (2036m).

Other endemics are the insectivorous butterwort *Pinguicula vallisneriifolia*, an endangered species whose bluish-white flowers are only found on damp, shady limestone cliffs, and the smallest Iberian narcissus – a tiny hoop-petticoat daffodil which goes under the name of *Narcissus hedreanthus* – as well as the largest, the 1.5m *N. longispathus*. The carmine-flowered Cazorla violet (*Viola cazorlensis*), a rare species which flowers towards the end of May, also occurs in the nearby Sierra Mágina.

The park is also home to more than 140 species of bird and is an important refuge for **raptors**. Griffon vultures and booted eagles nest in large numbers (the lammergeier, or bearded vulture, is down to a handful of pairs, as well as a few pairs of Egyptian vultures, golden, Bonelli's and short-toed eagles, peregrine falcons, hobbies and goshawks. At dusk look (or listen) out for eagle, Scops and tawny owls in the forests.

Red and fallow **deer** and **mouflon** were introduced as game species during the park's time as a game reserve, but the outstanding large herbivore is undoubtedly the **Spanish ibex**, which inhabits the rocky pastures above the tree line. Unfortunately, in 1987 the Cazorla ibex became infected with mange, which wiped out almost 90 per cent of the population, but it is on the increase again today.

Mammalian **predators** include wildcats, genets, beech martens and polecats, with pardel lynx reputed to frequent the Segura forests, while otters occur on all the major rivers. Greater white-toothed shrews, an endemic subspecies of red squirrel (*ssp. segurae*) and garden dormice provide the main diet for the forest carnivores, since rabbits and hares are both uncommon here. The tiny Spanish algyroides, sometimes called Valverde's lizard, is endemic to the Sierras de Cazorla y Segura, where it inhabits damp rock-strewn habitats; it was only discovered in 1957 and can be distinguished by its coffee-coloured back, usually with a narrow black vertebral stripe, and distinct collar. Other **reptiles** of interest include Lataste's viper, horseshoe whipsnake, ladder snake, amphisbaenian, Bedriaga's skink, Iberian wall lizard and stripe-necked terrapin. The more notable **butterflies** of the park include the mother-of-pearl blue and Spanish argus, both of which are unique to Spain, but they are outshone by an endemic subspecies of the Spanish moon moth (*ssp. ceballosi*), a pale green and bronze beauty, a hand's span across, which occurs only in pine forests in Spain and parts of the French Alps.

Sierra Mágina

At the heart of the Cordillera Subbética lies the *parque natural* of the **Sierra Mágina**, centred on the 2167m peak of Mágina itself. Above the tree line is a landscape dominated by cushion-forming species such as hedgehog broom, junipers and the prickly crucifer *Ptilotrichum spinosum*, domain of Spanish ibex, blue rock thrush, choughs and alpine swifts, while golden and Bonelli's eagles soar overhead.

The middle zone is occupied by fairly humid deciduous **Mediterranean forest**, with Montpellier maple and Lusitanian oak, Spanish barberry and St Lucie's cherry, haunt of wild boar and small predators such as wildcats, beech martens and weasels, although you're more likely to see one of the recently introduced red deer. Short-toed treecreepers, crested tits and goshawks are the most typical birds to look for at this level.

The lowest levels are clothed with the typical **evergreen forests** and scrub of the region, characterized by holly and holm oaks, prickly juniper and Mediterranean mezereon. Although rarely seen, polecats, genets and badgers favour the dense vegetation, with Moorish geckoes, ocellated and Iberian wall lizards, and ladder and Montpellier snakes frequenting the more open areas. Some of the more interesting vascular plants of the Sierra Mágina limestone include the Iberian endemic *Lonicera arborea*, an unusual honeysuckle in that it takes the form of a small tree rather than a climber, the red-berried mistletoe *Viscum cruciatum*, and several southern Iberian endemics: the Cazorla violet *Viola cazorlensis*, the dwarf daffodil *Narcissus cuatrecasasii* and the yellow-flowered, shrubby kidney vetch *Anthyllis ramburii*. The gromwell *Lithodora nitida*, which grows between the cushions of hedgehog broom and *Echinospartium boissieri*, is an endangered species unique to Mágina.

El Torcal de Antequera

In the centre of the province of Málaga, just a few kilometres south of Fuente de Piedra, lies **El Torcal de Antequera**, a remarkable landscape resembling a petrified city, and considered to be one of the best karstic phenomena in southern Europe.

The fluted and scalloped limestone turrets are dotted with **rock-plants** such as the endemic saxifrage *Saxifraga biternata*, Antequera toadflax, which is also found in the Serranía de Ronda, the yellow violet *Viola demetria*, with flowers often only millimetres across, and the glaucous-leaved *Rupicapnos africana*, a bizarre member of the poppy family. Grassy areas between the pillars are a paradise for spring-flowering **orchids**, including many members of the genus Ophrys: yellow bee, bumblebee, brown bee, mirror, sawfly and woodcock orchids, to mention but a few.

From the top of El Torcal, at 1369m, the view over the surrounding countryside is spectacular, as well as offering the possibility of spotting a passing griffon or Egyptian vulture, or short-toed or Bonelli's eagle.

Serranía de Ronda

The westernmost massif of the Cordillera Subbética is the **Serranía de Ronda**, which straddles the borders of Cádiz and Málaga. The eastern part of this huge limestone range coincides with the *parque natural* of the **Sierra de las Nieves**, a formidable landscape riddled with deep gorges and vertiginous cliffs, while the western massifs lie within the *parque natural* of the **Sierra de Grazalema**, one of southern Spain's prime wildlife sites, also renowned for being the rainiest place in Iberia. The vegetation is predominantly Mediterranean evergreen and deciduous woodlands and low scrub, interspersed with extensive dry pastures, nibbled to the roots by wild and domestic herbivores alike, but studded with rocky outcrops where huge flowering clumps of saxifrages, catchflies and stonecrops thrive by virtue of their inaccessibility. More than **1300 species of vascular plant** have been recorded in the Serranía de Ronda, among the more eye-catching being six daffodils, including the endangered *Narcissus baeticus*, seven irises and 27 orchids. Several species are found nowhere else in the world, such as the delicate orange-red poppy *Papaver rupifragum*, the toadflax *Linaria platycalyx* and the endangered *Merendera androcymbioides*, a member of the lily family. The outstanding botanical feature of the Serranía de Ronda, however, is the **pinsapo**; a species of fir which is found nowhere else in the world. Although the largest forests lie in the Sierra de las Nieves, the more accessible examples occupy the northern slopes of Grazalema's Sierra del Pinar.

Over 200 species of vertebrates are known to occur in the Serranía de Ronda, 40 of which are mammals, including several thriving populations of Spanish ibex, roe and red deer and small carnivores such as genets, mongooses, wildcats, badgers and otters. The cave system of Hundidero-Gata houses more than 100,000 **Schreiber's bats** in winter: one of the largest concentrations of hibernating bats in Europe.

The birds of prey are outstanding here, the Serranía being one of the primary breeding areas for **griffon vultures** in Europe. Bonelli's, golden, short-toed and booted eagles are all common here, as well as Egyptian vultures, goshawks, peregrines and eagle owls. The rock-bird community includes choughs, alpine swifts, black wheatears and blue rock thrushes, as well as a colony of the rare white-rumped swift.

Los Alcornocales

Immediately south of the Sierra de Grazalema lies a range of low, forested sand-stone hills that extends almost to Tarifa. Known as **Los Alcornocales**, it houses **one of the largest cork-oak forests** in the world. The vegetation here is a superb example of the original Iberian forests, comprising jungle-like, thick forests of massive Lusitanian and cork oaks and wild olives, some of which are thought to be over 1000 years old. The zone is a large producer of cork for the wine industry and the move towards synthetic stoppers in recent years has worried producers. Laurels and rhododendrons also thrive here, relics of the Tertiary semitropical flora that was once widespread in Europe but has virtu-ally disappeared today as a result of climatic change. These forests are the haunt of the southernmost population of roe deer in Europe, as well as of red deer, genets, mongooses and wildcats. Golden eagles, griffon vultures and eagle owls are the commonest birds of prey, while a handful of black vultures nest in the ancient cork oaks and olives.

Teresa Farino

Books

T he listings on these pages represent a highly selective reading list on Andalucía and matters Spanish, especially in the sections on history. Most titles are in print, although we've included a few older classics, many of them easy enough to find in secondhand bookshops and libraries. We have also included websites below for some publishers whose publications are not widely distributed and where it is possible to order from their website. Where the publisher has more than one entry the website appears in the details of the first publication listed in each section.

Two reliable **specialist sources** in the UK for out-of-print books on all aspects of Spain are Keith Harris Books, PO Box 207, Twickenham TW2 5BQ (☎020/8898 7789, ⊛www.books-on-spain.com), and Paul Orssich, 2 St Stephens Terrace, London SW8 1DH (☎020/7787 0030, ⊛www.orssich.com). For all books in print, publishing details are in the form (UK publisher/US publisher), where both exist; if books are published in one country only, this follows the publisher's name (eg Serpent's Tail, UK). University Press is abbreviated as UP.

General accounts

Introductions

David Baird *Inside Andalusia* (Lookout, Málaga). A book that grew out of the author's series of articles published in *Lookout* magazine. Anecdotal yet perceptive overview of the region with plenty of interesting and offbeat observations and glossy illustrations. The same author's *Back Roads of Southern Spain* (Ediciones Santana, Málaga; ⊛www.santanabooks.com) is a drivers' guide to Andalucía displaying the same erudition.

Ian Gibson *Fire in the Blood: the New Spain* (Faber/BBC, UK). Gibson is a Madrid-based writer, resident since 1978, and a Spanish national since 1984. He is a passionate enthusiast and critic of Spain and the Spanish, both of which he gets across brilliantly in this 1993 book – the accompaniment to a gripping TV series – in all their mass of contradictions, attitudes, obsessions, quirks and everything else. Despite the lack of an

---

The Mercurio literary review

If you're a Spanish-speaker one magazine you should certainly look out for is **Mercurio**, an excellent monthly literary review carrying articles on Andalucía's literary figures past and present – Richard Ford and Ian Gibson have featured (see p.564 and above respectively for both) – as well as reviews of many new books (fiction and non-fiction) dealing with *andaluz* and broader Spanish themes. The best thing of all is that it is free and available from most good bookshops in the region's major towns and provincial capitals – such as Vértice in Sevilla or Proteo in Málaga. If you can't locate a copy, email ⊛revistamercurio@mundofree.com for a list of stockists.

updated edition, it's still hugely readable with strong pieces on Andalucía, but did receive flak from outraged Spanish reviewers.

 John Hooper *Spaniards: A Portrait of the New Spain* (Penguin, UK/US). Excellent, insightful portrait of post-Franco Spain and the new generation by *The Guardian's* former Spain correspondent. Although it has only passing references to Andalucía and is now in need of a further update, along with Ian Gibson's book (above), this is the best possible introduction to contemporary Spain.

Michael Jacobs *Andalusia* (Pallas Athene, UK/US).

Well-crafted, opinionated and wide-ranging introduction to Andalucía. It covers everything from prehistory to the Civil War and manages to cram in perceptive pieces on flamenco, gypsies and food and drink. A gazeteer at the back details major sights. Recently updated, this remains one of the best introductions to the region.

Allen Josephs *White Wall of Spain* (Iowa State UP, US). Intelligent series of essays on the mysteries of Andalucian folk culture from the origins of flamenco to the significance of Semana Santa and bullfights by the former president of the Ernest Hemingway Foundation.

Recent travels and accounts

David Baird *Sunny Side Up* (Santana, Málaga Ⓦ www.santanabooks.com). A shrewdly and humorously observed *homenaje* to the village of Frigiliana in Málaga where Baird, a veteran Costa del Sol writer and journalist, has lived for over thirty years.

Alastair Boyd *The Sierras of the South: Travels in the Mountains of Andalusia* (Collins, UK). A sensitively worked portrait of the Serranía de Ronda which describes one Englishman's continuing love affair with a region he knew as home for twenty years. His earlier *The Road from Ronda* (Collins, UK) is a Sixties' view of the same landscape – the peasants are still struggling.

David Gilmour *Cities of Spain* (John Murray/Ivan R Dee). A modern cultural portrait of Spain which attempts to describe the country's history through portraits of selected cities. Very much in the old tradition, it is a little fogeyish at times but excellent, nonetheless, in its evocation of history, especially on the Moorish cities of Andalucía – though curiously not Granada.

Adam Hopkins *Spanish Journeys: A Portrait of Spain* (Penguin, UK). Published in 1993, this is an enjoyable and highly stimulating exploration of Spanish history and culture, weaving its considerable scholarship in an accessible and unforced travelogue form, and full of illuminating anecdotes.

Norman Lewis *The Tomb of Seville* (Picador, UK). This final work (before his death in 2003) by eminent travel writer Lewis draws on recollections of a journey to Sevilla's cathedral in 1934 to attempt to discover a family tomb. The often hazardous journey, through a Spain on the brink of civil war, is described with the writer's customary panache.

Nicholas Luard *Andalucía – A Portrait of Southern Spain* (Century, UK). English writer and naturalist Luard went off to live in Andalucía with his cookery-writer wife and kids for a decade which spanned the end of dictatorship and the early post-Franco years. The result is a closely observed and well-written account of the passing of the seasons in an isolated valley in the Campo de Gibraltar.

Peter B. Meyer *A True Story About Doing Business in Spain* (Avon Books, UK). This quirkily written tale of a Dutch businessman's adventures setting up enterprises in Spain features encounters with corrupt bureaucracy, knavish builders, yacht and car thieves, shifty lawyers, crooked business partners and a parade of police and politicos straight out of central casting. A sometimes skewed, always fascinating and often hair-raising insider's view of Spanish business life.

Elizabeth Nash *Seville, Córdoba and Granada: a cultural and literary history* (Signal Books, UK/Oxford UP, US). An eloquent, themed and multi-layered exploration of the literary and cultural history of Andalucía's three major cities by the London *Independent*'s Madrid correspondent. Ideal reading for the plane or dipping into along the way.

Chris Stewart *Driving Over Lemons* (Sort Of Books, UK). A contributor to this guide ploughs the same furrow as Luard (above) only this time in Granada, where he describes – often with humour – his move with family to an Alpujarran farmhouse (El Valero) and the

numerous adventures involved in setting up house there. The sequel, *A Parrot in the Pepper Tree* (Sort Of Books, UK), has more stories from El Valero interspersed with accounts of some of the author's earlier adventures as a sheep shearer in Sweden, drummer with rock band Genesis, and greenhorn flamenco guitarist in Sevilla.

Ted Walker *In Spain* (out of print). Until his death in 2004 the poet Ted Walker had lived and travelled in Spain on and off since the 1950s. This is a lyrical and absorbing account of the country and people, structured around his various sorties, a couple of them in Andalucía.

Jason Webster *Duende* (Doubleday UK/Broadway Books US), *Andalus* (Doubleday/Black Swan UK). In *Duende*, author Webster sets off on a Spanish odyssey to learn flamenco guitar, which takes him to Alicante, Madrid and finally Granada with quite a few emotional encounters along the way. *Andalus* relates a journey with an illegal immigrant whose precarious toe-hold in Spain inspires parallels with the current position of Islam on the peninsula. Interestingly told, but a "What the Arabs did for us" approach sometimes grates.

Earlier twentieth-century writers

Gerald Brenan *South From Granada* (Penguin/Cambridge UP) and *The Face of Spain* (Penguin, UK). *South From Granada* is an enduring classic. Brenan lived in a small village in Las Alpujarras in the 1920s, and records this and the visits of his Bloomsbury contemporaries Virginia Woolf, Lytton Strachey and Bertrand Russell. In 2002 the book was made into a film, *Al Sur de Granada* by Spanish director Fernando Colomo. *The Face of Spain*

is a later collection of highly readable travel writings gathered on a trip through Franco's Spain in 1949 with a substantial chunk devoted to Andalucía.

Penelope Chetwode *Two Middle-Aged Ladies in Andalucía* (Century, UK). Poet John Betjeman's wife took to the roads of Andalucía with another middle-aged lady – her horse. A paean to "picturesque poverty", this is southern Spain seen from a quaintly English perspective.

Nina Epton *Andalusia* (Weidenfeld & Nicolson, UK). Sixties portrait of the region by a friend of Gerald Brenan. Contains interesting vignettes on people and places immediately prior to the arrival of mass tourism.

Laurie Lee *As I Walked Out One Midsummer Morning* (Penguin, UK/US), *A Rose For Winter* (Penguin, UK), *A Moment of War* (Penguin/New Press). *Midsummer Morning* is the irresistibly romantic account of Lee's walk through Spain – from Vigo to Málaga – and his gradual awareness of the forces moving the country towards Civil War. As an autobiographical account, of living rough and busking his way from the Cotswolds with a violin, it's a delight; as a piece of social observation, painfully sharp. In *A Rose For Winter* Lee describes his return, twenty years later, to Andalucía, while in *A Moment of War* he looks back again to describe a winter fighting with the International Brigade in the Civil War – an account by turns moving, comic and tragic.

Alfonso Lowe *Companion Guide to the South of Spain* (Companion Guides, UK). A travel classic from the 1970s. Idiosyncratic account of southern Spain often recording an Andalucía long gone – packed with fascinating background.

Rose Macaulay *Fabled Shore* (out of print). The Spanish coast as it was in 1949 (read it and weep), travelled and described from Catalunya to Portugal's Algarve. More focused on culture than people.

James A. Michener *Iberia* (Corgi/Crest). A bestselling, idiosyncratic and encyclopedic compendium of interviews and impressions of Spain on the brink – in 1968 – looking forward to the post-Franco years. Fascinating, still.

Jan Morris *Spain* (Penguin/Prentice-Hall). Morris wrote this in six months in 1960, on her (or, at the time, his) first visit to the country. It is an impressionistic account – good in its sweeping control of place and history, though prone to see everything as symbolic. The updated edition is plain bizarre in its ideas on Franco and dictatorship – a condition for which Morris seems to believe Spaniards were naturally inclined.

Walter Starkie *Don Gypsy* (out of print). The tales of a Dublin professor who set out to walk the roads of Spain and Andalucía in the 1930s with only a fiddle for company. The pre-Civil War world – good and bad – is astutely observed and his adventures are frequently amusing. Like Borrow earlier, he fell for the gypsies and became an expert on their culture.

J. B. Trend *Spain from the South* (Darf, UK). A classic look at the south in the 1920s by a well-travelled Hispanist who intermingles perceptive observations on the region's history, culture and landscape with shrewd and entertaining sketches of the contemporary scene.

Christopher Wawn & David Wood *In Search of Andalucía: the Malaga Seaboard* (The Pentland Press UK/US). Anecdotal history of the Málaga coastline with plenty of interesting background information on curious characters, customs and culture throughout the region.

Older classics

George Borrow *The Bible in Spain* and *The Zincali* (both out of print). On first publication in 1842, *The Bible in Spain* was subtitled by Borrow "Journeys, Adventures and Imprisonments of an English-man"; it is one of the most famous books on Spain – slow in places but with some very amusing stories. *Zincali* is an account of the Spanish gypsies, whom Borrow got to know pretty well and for whom he translated the Bible into *gitano*.

Richard Ford *A Handbook for Travellers in Spain and Readers at Home* (Centaur Press/Gordon Press); *Gatherings from Spain* (Pallas Athene, UK). *The Handbook*, first published in 1845, must be the best guide ever written to any country and stayed in print as a Murray's Handbook (one of the earliest series of guides) well into the last century. Massively opinionated, it is an extremely witty book and in its British, nineteenth-century manner, incredibly knowledgeable and worth flicking through for the proverbs alone. Copies of Murray's may be available in secondhand bookstores – the earlier the edition the purer the Ford. The *Gatherings* is a filleted – but no less entertaining – abridgement of the Handbook produced "for the ladies" who were not expected to be able to digest the original. Also recommended is a new biography *Richard Ford, Hispanophile, Connoisseur and Critic* by Ian Robertson (Michael Russell, UK Ⓔ michaelrussell@waitrose.com); a fascinating read, it illuminates the creation of Ford's great work and places him in the context of the Victorian world of arts and letters.

Washington Irving *Tales of the Alhambra* (originally published 1832; abridged editions are on sale in Granada). Half of Irving's book consists of Oriental stories, set in the Alhambra; the rest of accounts of his own residence there and the local characters of his time. A perfect read *in situ*. Irving also wrote *The Conquest of Granada* (1829; out of print), a description of the fall of the Nasrids.

Anthologies

Jimmy Burns (ed) *Spain: A Literary Companion* (John Murray, UK). A good anthology, including worthwhile nuggets of most authors recommended here, amid a whole host of others.

Lucy McCauley *Travellers' Tales: Spain* (Travellers' Tales Inc., US). A wide-ranging anthology slanted towards more recent writing on Spain; includes strong pieces on Andalucía by many of the authors mentioned in this section.

David Mitchell *Travellers in Spain: an Illustrated Anthology* (Cassell, UK). A well-told story of how four centuries of travellers – and most often travel writers – saw Spain. It's interesting to see Ford, Brenan, Laurie Lee and the rest set in context. Also published as *Here in Spain* (Lookout, Málaga) and widely available at bookshops in tourist areas.

Customs and culture

Carrie B. Douglass *Bulls, Bullfighting and Spanish Identities* (Arizona UP, US). Anthropologist Douglass enters the *corrida* debate by first delving into the symbolism of the bull in the Spanish national psyche, and then examining the bullfight's role in some of the thousands of country-wide fiestas that support it.

Bernard Leblon *Gypsies and Flamenco* (University of Hertfordshire Press). An important and interesting study of the gypsy influences on the origins and development of flamenco by a French expert. Also includes a discography of key recordings.

Timothy Mitchell *Flamenco Deep Song* (Yale, UK/US). Diametrically opposed to Woodall's work (next column), the author sets out to debunk the mystagogy of flamenco purists by arguing that they are shackling the form's development and ends up with an improbable defence of the Gipsy Kings. A well-researched and entertaining read whether or not you accept its iconoclastic premise.

Eamonn O'Neill *Matadors* (Mainstream, UK). Subtitled "a journey into the heart of modern bullfighting" this is part autobiographical travelogue, part sociological study of the role of bullfighting in modern Spain, throwing light on a peculiarly Iberian industry worth a billion dollars annually.

Sarah Pink *Women and Bullfighting* (Berg, UK, US). Based on a doctoral thesis carrying out field research in Córdoba, this analysis of women in the ring also examines the reaction – frequently negative – that this phenomenon attracts from Spanish male society.

Paul Richardson *Our Lady of the Sewers* (Little Brown, UK). Presents an articulate and kaleidoscopic series of insights into rural Spain's customs and cultures, fast disappearing.

James Woodall *In Search of the Firedance: Spain through Flamenco* (Sinclair-Stevenson, UK). This is a terrific history and exploration of flamenco, and as the subtitle suggests it is never satisfied with "just the music" in getting to the heart of the culture.

History

General history

Juan Lalaguna *A Traveller's History of Spain* (Windrush, UK). A lucid – and pocketable – background history to the country which spans the Phoenicians to Franco, Felipe González and the emergence of democratic Spain.

M. Vincent & R.A. Stradling *Cultural Atlas of Spain and Portugal* (Andromeda, UK). A deceptive, coffee-table format belies a formidable historical, artistic and social survey of the Iberian peninsula from ancient times to the present; excellent colour maps and well-chosen photos amplify the text.

Early history to the nineteenth century

Manuel Fernández Álvarez *Charles V* (out of print); **Peter Pierson** *Philip II of Spain* (Thames & Hudson, UK). Good studies in an illustrated biography series.

James M. Anderson *Spain: 1001 Archaeological Sites* (Hale/Calgary UP). A good guide and gazetteer of Spain's archeological sites with detailed instructions of how to get to them.

Henri Breuil *Rock Paintings of Southern Andalucía* (Oxford UP, UK). Published in 1929, this is still the definitive guide to the subject.

J.M. Cohen *The Four Voyages of Christopher Columbus* (Cresset Library, UK) The man behind the myth; one of the best books on Columbus in English.

Roger Collins *Spain: An Archeological Guide* (Oxford UP, UK). Covering around 140 sites, temples, mosques and palaces dating from prehistory to the twelfth century, this book devotes more space per entry to maps, plans and data, making it a more useful vade mecum to the major sites than Anderson's work (above).

Roger Collins *The Arab Conquest of Spain 710–97* (Blackwell, UK). Cogently argued and controversial study which documents the Moorish invasion and the significant influence that the conquered Visigoths had on the formative phase of Muslim rule by a scholar uniquely expert in both fields. Collins's *Visigothic Spain* (Blackwell) is a significant companion volume to the above and his earlier *Early Medieval Spain 400–1000* (Macmillan, UK) takes a broader overview of the same subject.

John A. Crow *Spain: the Root and the Flower* (California UP, US/UK). Cultural/social history from Roman Spain to the present.

J.H. Elliott *Imperial Spain 1469–1716* (Penguin, US/UK). Best introduction to "the Golden Age" – academically respected and a gripping tale.

Maria Cruz Fernández Castro *Iberia in Prehistory* (Blackwell, UK). A major study of the Iberian peninsula prior to the arrival of the Romans which includes extensive coverage of early Andalucian sites such as Los Millares as well as the later Iberian settlements encountered by the Phoenicians and Greeks. This is the first volume of this publisher's important series on the history of Spain from the prehistoric era through to the Civil War.

Richard Fletcher *Moorish Spain* (Weidenfeld & Nicolson/California UP). A fascinating, provocative and highly readable narrative with a suitably iconoclastic conclusion to the history of Moorish Spain. The best introduction to the subject.

L.P. Harvey *Islamic Spain 1250– 1500* (Chicago UP, US/UK). Comprehensive account of its period – both the Islamic kingdoms and the Muslims living beyond their protection.

Henry Kamen *The Spanish Inquisition* (Mentor, US). Highly respected examination of the causes and effects of this grisly institution and the long shadow it cast across Spanish history and development. The same author's masterly *Spanish Inquisition: An Historical Revision* (Weidenfeld & Nicolson, UK) returns to the subject in the light of more recent evidence, while his *Philip of Spain* (Yale UP, US/UK) is the first fully researched biography of Felipe II, the ruler most associated with the Inquisition.

S.J. Keay *Roman Spain* (British Museum Publications/California

UP). Definitive survey of a neglected subject, well illustrated and highly readable.

Elie Kedourie *Spain and the Jews: the Sephardi Experience, 1492 and after* (Thames & Hudson, UK/US). A collection of essays on the three-million-strong Spanish Jews of the Middle Ages and their expulsion by the Catholic monarchs.

John Lynch *Spain 1516–1598* (Blackwell, UK). New interpretation of Spain's rise to empire with plenty of interesting detail on Andalucía's trading role – especially the cities of Sevilla and Cádiz – in the exploitation of the Americas. The same author's *Hispanic World in Crisis and Change 1598–1700* and *Bourbon Spain 1700–1808* (both Blackwell, UK) carry the story forward to the critical crossroads which determined Spain's future for the ensuing century and a half.

Bernard F. Reilly *The Contest of Christian and Muslim Spain* (Blackwell, UK). A fascinating and detailed study of the stresses and strains of the crucial tenth and eleventh centuries when Christians, Muslims and Jews were locked in a struggle for supremacy on one hand and survival on the other, by an acknowledged expert on the subject.

John S. Richardson *The Romans in Spain* (Blackwell, UK). A new look at how Spain came to be a part of the Roman world which also examines the influences that

flowed from Spain to Rome as well as vice versa.

Adrian Shubert *A Social History of Modern Spain* (Routledge, UK). This accomplished first social history of Spain in English documents the turbulent history of post-1800 Spain from a people's perspective. An essential read to understand the origins of modern Andalucía's structural and social problems – such as *latifundismo* – in their Spanish and European context.

Colin Smith, Charles Melville & Ahmad Ubaydli *Christians and Moors in Spain* (Aris & Phillips, UK; 3 vols). A fascinating collection of documents by Spanish and Arabic writers from the Muslim conquest to the Christian supremacy which are intended for the lay reader as well as the academic. The bilingual parallel text (including Arabic) allows you to read firsthand not only the key historical, military and literary accounts but also the invariably fascinating views of Christians and Moors on each other. Recommended.

Chris Stringer & Robin McKie *African Exodus* (Jonathan Cape, UK). If you want to grasp Spain's part in the Neanderthal story, this lively and accessible account by an expert in the field aided by the London *Observer*'s science editor is the book. The account of the last of the Neanderthals hanging on in a cave above the Zaffaraya Pass in northern Málaga only adds to the drama of the landscape on the ground.

The twentieth century

Gerald Brenan *The Spanish Labyrinth* (Cambridge UP, US/UK). First published in 1943, Brenan's study of the social and political background to the Civil War is tinged by personal experience, yet still an impressively rounded account.

Raymond Carr *Modern Spain 1875–1980* (Oxford UP, US/UK) and *The Spanish Tragedy: the Civil War in Perspective* (Weidenfeld, UK). Two of the best books available on modern Spanish history – concise and well-told narratives.

Ronald Fraser *Blood of Spain* (Pantheon, US). Subtitled "The Experience of Civil War, 1936–39", this is an impressive piece of research, constructed entirely of oral accounts. *In Hiding* (Penguin, UK), by the same author, is a fascinating individual account of a Republican mayor of Mijas (in Málaga) hidden by his family for thirty years until the Civil War amnesty of 1969. *The Pueblo* (Allen Lane, UK) is a penetrating and compelling study of the trials and struggles of one Costa del Sol mountain village seen through the eyes of its inhabitants which speaks for much of Andalucía today.

Ian Gibson *Federico García Lorca* (Faber & Faber/Pantheon), *The Assassination of Federico García Lorca* (Penguin, UK) and *Lorca's Granada* (Faber & Faber, US/UK). The biography is a gripping book and *The Assassination* a brilliant reconstruction of the events at the end of his life, with an examination of fascist corruption and of the shaping influences on Lorca, twentieth-century Spain and the Civil War. *Granada* explores Lorca's city by way of a collection of fascinating walks around the town.

Gerald Howson *Arms for Spain: the Untold Story of the Spanish Civil War* (John Murray, UK). One of the most important books of recent times uses recently opened Russian and Polish archives to explain how the Republicans were duped, double-crossed and betrayed by almost every government (including the Nazis who used the profits to finance a clandestine drugs ring) they attempted to purchase arms from – with their avowed ally Moscow one of the major culprits.

Joe Monk *With the Reds in Andalucía* (out of print). One Irishman's account of the optimism, hell, and finally despair, of fighting with the Irish Brigade of the international volunteers during the Civil War.

Paul Preston *Concise History of the Spanish Civil War* (Fontana/HarperCollins), *Franco* (HarperCollins, UK/US), *The Triumph of Democracy in Spain* (Routledge, UK). A formidable expert on the period, Preston has succeeded in his attempt to provide a manageable guide to the Civil War labyrinth – with powerful illustrations. *Franco* is a penetrating – and monumental – biography of the dictator and his regime, which provides as clear a picture as any yet published of how he won the Civil War, survived in power so long, and what, twenty years on from his death, was his significance. *Triumph* presents the absorbing story of the unravelling of the Franco years and the ultimate burial of the past with the election of the 1982 Socialist government.

Leslie Stainton *Lorca – A Dream of Life* (Bloomsbury, UK). A Lorca biography that complements rather than competes with Gibson's works (above). She approaches the poet's life from the perspective of drama and theatre and the work is illustrated with poignant photographs.

Hugh Thomas *The Spanish Civil War* (Penguin/Touchstone). This exhaustive 1000-page study is regarded (both in Spain and abroad) as the definitive history of the Civil War, but is not as accessible for the general reader as Preston's account (above).

Paddy Woodworth *Dirty War, Clean Hands: ETA, the GAL and Spanish Democracy* (Yale UP, UK/US). "Democracy is defended in the sewers as well as the salons" was Felipe González's retort to critics of his dirty and illegal 1980s war against the Basque terrorist organization ETA when the state employed assassination and kidnap squads to play the terrorists at their own game. This important and impeccably researched work analyses what happens when a democracy abandons the rule of law and shows how this shocking policy actually strengthened rather than defeated revolutionary terrorism.

🏃 **Gamel Woolsey** *Málaga Burning* (Pythia Press, US Ⓦ www.pythiapress.com) and, under its original title *Death's Other Kingdom* (Eland, UK). A long ignored minor classic written in the late 1930s and recently reprinted (and retitled) by a US publisher in which the American poet and wife of Gerald Brenan vividly describes the horrors of the descent of their part of Andalucía into civil war. The Eland edition includes an interesting biographical afterword by Michael Jacobs.

Art and architecture

Marianne Barrucand and Achim Bednoz *Moorish Architecture* (Taschen, Germany). A beautifully illustrated guide to the major Moorish monuments.

Bernard Bevan *History of Spanish Architecture* (Batsford UK; out of print). Classic study of Iberian and Ibero-American architecture which includes extensive coverage of the Mudéjar, Plateresque and Baroque periods.

🏃 **Titus Burckhardt** *Moorish Culture in Spain* (out of print). An outstanding book which opens up ways of looking at Spain's Islamic monuments, explaining their patterns and significance and the social environment in which, and for which, they were produced.

Jerrilyn D. Dodds *Al-Andalus* (Abrams, UK/US). An in-depth study of the arts and monuments of Moorish Andalucía, put together as a catalogue for a major exhibition at the Alhambra.

Godfrey Goodwin *Islamic Spain* (Viking, UK/Chronicle Books, US). Architectural guide with descriptions of virtually every significant Islamic building in Spain, and a fair amount of background. Portable enough to take along.

José Gudiol *The Arts of Spain* (Thames & Hudson, UK). Good general introduction to Spanish art covering prehistory to Picasso.

🏃 **Michael Jacobs** *Alhambra* (Frances Lincoln UK/Rizzoli US). If you've fallen under the Alhambra's spell then this sumptuously produced volume with outstanding photographs and expert commentary will rekindle the memory. Authoritatively guides you through the history and architecture of Andalucía's emblematic monument, placing it in its Islamic context, and concludes with a fascinating essay on the hold that the palace has had on later artists, travellers and writers from Irving and Ford to de Falla and Lorca.

David Talbot Rice *Islamic Art* (Thames & Hudson, UK). A classic introduction to the whole subject.

Meyer Schapiro *Romanesque Art* (Thames & Hudson/Braziller). An excellent, illustrated survey of Romanesque art and architecture – and its Visigothic and Mozarabic precursors.

Sacheverell Sitwell *Spanish Baroque* (Ayer, US). First published in 1931, this is interesting mainly for the absence of anything better on the subject.

George Kubler and Martin Soria
Art and Architecture in Spain and Portugal 1500–1800 (Pelican, UK). Provides an alternative to, if not a vast improvement on, the Sitwell book in the previous page.

Anatzu Zabalbeascoa *The New Spanish Architecture* (Rizzoli, UK/US). A superb, highly illustrated study of the new Spanish architecture of the 1980s and 1990s in Barcelona, Madrid, Sevilla and elsewhere.

Fiction and poetry

Spanish fiction

Pedro de Alarcón *The Three-Cornered Hat and Other Stories* (out of print). Ironic nineteenth-century tales of the previous century's corruption, bureaucracy and absolutism by a writer born in Guadix. He also wrote *Alpujarra* (out of print), a not very well-observed tour through the Sierra Nevada.

Miguel de Cervantes *Don Quixote* (Penguin/Signet). *Quixote* (or *Quijote*) is of course the classic of Spanish literature and remains an excellent and witty read, especially in J.M. Cohen's classic Penguin translation or a new version by Edith Grossman (Harper Collins UK/US).

Juan Ramón Jiménez *Platero and I* (out of print). Andalucía's Nobel Prize-winning poet and writer from Moguer in Huelva paints a lyrically evocative picture of Andalucía and its people in conversations with his donkey, Platero.

Antonio Machado *Eighty Poems* and *Juan de Mairena* (out of print). The best-known works in English of this eminent *sevillano* poet and writer. The latter novel draws on his experience as a schoolteacher in Baeza.

Modern fiction

Arturo Barea *The Forging of a Rebel* (out of print). Superb autobiographical trilogy, taking in the Spanish war in Morocco in the 1920s, and Barea's own part in the Civil War in Andalucía and elsewhere. The books were published under the individual titles *The Forge*, *The Track* and *The Clash*.

Arturo Pérez Reverte *The Seville Communion* (Harvill Press, UK). An entertaining crime yarn by one of Spain's leading writers involving a hacker in the pope's computer, a stubborn old local priest up against rapacious bankers eager to bulldoze his church, a number of corpses, and an investigator dispatched by the

Vatican. All is played out against the colourfully described backdrop of Sevilla. *The Dumas Club*, an engrossing tale about a bibliophile's search for a book on black magic, *The Fencing Master*, a political thriller set in nineteenth-century Spain (both Harvill Press), and *The Nautical Chart*, a search for treasure in a galleon sunk off the coast of Andalucía (Harcourt US/Picador, UK), are other translated works by Pérez Reverte. His latest novel, *The Queen of the South* (Picador UK/Penguin US) took the Spanish bestseller lists by storm and relates the story of a woman drug trafficker running narcotics between Morocco and Cádiz.

Plays and poetry

A.J. Arberry (trans.) *Moorish Poetry* (Cambridge UP, UK). Excellent collection of Hispano-Arab verse.

Cola Franzen (trans.) *Poems of Arab Andalusia* (City Lights, US). Sensitively rendered collection of verse by some of the best poets of Moorish al-Andalus.

Federico García Lorca *Five Plays: Comedies and Tragicomedies* (Penguin/New Directions); *Selected Poems* (Bloodaxe Books, UK); *Poem of the Deep Song* (City Lights, US). Andalucía's great pre-Civil War playwright and poet. The first two volumes have his major theatrical works and poems, whilst the latter is a moving poetic paean to *cante jondo*, flamenco's blues, inspired by his contact with *gitano* culture. Arturo Barea's *Lorca: the Poet and His People* is also of interest.

San Juan de la Cruz *The Poetry of Saint John of the Cross* (Penguin, UK). Excellent translation by South African poet Roy Campbell of the poems of this mystical confessor to Teresa of Ávila who died at Úbeda.

Foreign fiction

Tariq Ali *Shadows of the Pomegranate Tree* (Chatto & Windus, UK). Pakistani/British author digs into his Muslim roots to come up with a story about the end of Nasrid Granada seen through the eyes of a well-to-do family.

Douglas Day *Journey of the Wolf* (Penguin, UK). Outstanding first novel by an American writer, given the seal of approval by Graham Greene ("gripping and poignant"). The subject is a Civil War fighter, "El Lobo", who returns as a fugitive to Poqueira, his village in the Alpujarras, forty years on.

Ernest Hemingway *Fiesta/The Sun Also Rises* (Cape/Scribner) and *For Whom the Bell Tolls* (Cape/Scribner). Hemingway remains a big part of the American myth of Spain. *Fiesta* contains some lyrically beautiful writing while the latter – set in Civil War Andalucía – is a good deal more laboured. He also published an enthusiastic and not very good account of bullfighting, *Death in the Afternoon* (Cape/ Scribner).

David Hewson *Semana Santa* (Harper Collins UK/US). A well-crafted whodunnit set against the background of Sevilla's major religious event by a journo-turned-writer. Strong on detail.

Amin Maalouf *Leo the African* (Quartet, UK). A wonderful historical novel, re-creating the life of Leo Africanus, the fifteenth-century Moorish geographer, in the last years of the kingdom of Granada, and on his subsequent exile in Morocco and world travels.

Specialist guides

Phil Ball *Morbo – The Story of Spanish Football* (When Saturday Comes Books, UK Ⓦ www.wsc .co.uk). Excellent account of Spanish football from its nineteenth-century beginnings with the British workers at the mines of Río Tinto to the golden years of Real Madrid and the dark days of Franco, with the ever present backdrop of the ferocious *morbo* – political, historical, regional and linguistic rivalry – that has driven it since. The same author's *White Storm –100 years of Real Madrid* (Mainstream, UK) is more than a history of Spain's legendary team, and in addition to probing the murkier evidence of Real's links with the Franco regime, corrupt Madrid politics, and neo-Nazi supporters, also attempts to evaluate the club's place in the modern Spanish psyche.

Bob and Ruth Carrick *Made in Andalucía – the Arts and Crafts of Southern Spain* (Santana, Málaga Ⓦ www.santanabooks.com). Informative guide to the crafts workshops and artisans of rural Andalucía (the larger towns and provincial capitals are not covered), organized by province with suggested routes enabling tours of a specific area, with maps, directions and contact details for all the artisans and workshops mentioned.

M.J. Gómez Lara & J. Jiménez Barrientos *Guía de la Semana Santa en Sevilla* (Taba Press, Spain). The best guide available to Semana Santa in Sevilla – and a book for which you don't need very much Spanish; all the processions and routes are detailed along with superb illustrations.

David Searl *You and the Law in Spain* (Santana, Málaga). Invaluable, lucid and remarkably comprehensive guide to the Spanish legal and tax system (now in its fifteenth updated edition) and an essential read if you are thinking of buying property, working or setting up a business in Spain.

Charles Teetor *Strolling through Seville* (Iberica, UK/US). More anecdotal version of the below with rather wobbly references to the Civil War.

Christopher Turner *The Penguin Guide to Seville* (Penguin, UK/US). A set of interesting guided walks around Andalucía's capital city.

Hiking and cycling

Justo Robles Alvarez *Senderos de Pequeño Recorrido – Parque Natural de Cazorla* (El Olivo, Spain Ⓦ www .biblioandalucía.com). Well-planned walking guide in Spanish describing fifteen walks in this magnificent park. Good background information on waymarking, flora and fauna, and places to find food and shelter.

J.L. Barrenetxea & K. Muñoz *La Alpujarra en Bici* (Sua Edizioak, Spain). A well-researched guide to getting your bike around the villages and landscape of this stunningly picturesque corner of Andalucía. It forms part of a superb range of regional guides for cyclists, functionally ring-bound, with detailed maps and route contours.

David and Ros Brawn *Sierra de Aracena* (Discovery UK Ⓦ www .walking.demon.co.uk). Excellent walking guide to this magnificent Sierra by two experienced walkers. Covers 27 walks (from 3–14km) with an accompanying map (sold separately) and all routes are GPS waypointed.

Matt Butler *Holiday Walks from the Costa del Sol* (Sigma, UK ⓦ www .sigmapress.co.uk). Holiday walks within reach of a Costa del Sol base, covering the coast from Cádiz province in the west to Granada province in the east. Free Internet updates available.

José Luís Clavero Toledo *Sendas y Caminos por los Campos de la Axarquía* (Editorial Clave, Málaga). Excellent Spanish guidebook to this scenic corner of Málaga Province with loads of background on the region and information on flora and fauna, as well as seventeen clearly described walks.

Ben Cole and Bethan Davies *Walking the Via de la Plata* (Pili Pala Press ⓦ www.pilipalapress.com). Detailed hikers' guide to the alternative *Camino de Santiago* pilgrims' route setting out from Sevilla. Good maps and plenty of info about things to see along the way and where to eat and sleep.

Charles Davis *Costa del Sol Walks* (Santana, Málaga ⓦ www.santana books.com). Well-written guide to 34 walks – between 4 and 8 kilometres – along the Costa del Sol between Nerja and Estepona; each walk has it's own map. The same author's *Walk! the Axarquía* (Discovery, UK) is a reliable guide to this picturesque region describing thirty walks between 5 and 22 kilometres, all GPS waypointed. Davis has also published *34 Alpujarras Walks* (Discovery, UK) with a similar format detailing thirty-four GPS waypointed treks between 4km and 25km. In both the latter books each walk has its own map or there are waterproof 1:40,000 *Axarquía/Alpujarras Tour and Trail* maps

(sold separately) with all walks (and GPS points) marked.

Harry Dowdell *Cycle Touring in Spain* (Cicerone, UK ⓦ www .cicerone.co.uk). Well-researched cycle touring guide which describes eight touring routes of varying difficulty in the north and south of Spain. Plenty of practical information on preparing your bike for the trip, transporting it, and what to take.

Robin Collomb *Sierra Nevada* (West Col, UK). A detailed guide aimed primarily at serious hikers and climbers.

Chris Craggs *Andalusian Rock Climbs* (Cicerone, UK). Introductory guide to one of Andalucía's fastest-growing sports. Has descriptions of all the major climbs plus details of how to get there.

Marc S. Dubin *Trekking in Spain* (Lonely Planet, UK/US). A detailed and practical trekking guide (with maps) by a Rough Guide author moonlighting for the opposition. It has a section on Andalucía's Sierra Nevada.

🏃 **Guy Hunter-Watts** *Walking in Andalucía* (Santana, Málaga). First-rate walking guide to the Natural Parks of Grazalema, Cazorla, Los Alcornocales, Aracena and La Axarquía as well as the Alpujarras and the Sierra Nevada, comprising thirty-two walks between eight and seventeen kilometres in length, each with its own colour map.

Francisco Jiménez Richarte *GR142: Sendero de la Alpujarra* (Iniciativas Líder Alpujarra, SA). Edited by a member of the Andalucía Mountaineers Federation, this guide in Spanish covers the GR142 walking route's Alpujarras section starting at Lanjarón in the west and finishing at Fiñana in the eastern Almerian Alpujarras. It splits the route into 25 sections which can be walked as one journey of 144km over a week or two, or used for single day rambles. Each trek comes with a detailed fold-out map and there are clear route descriptions.

John & Christine Oldfield *Andalucía and the Costa del Sol* (Sunflower Books). This addition to the popular *Landscapes* walking guide series has 23 clearly described walks (with maps) ranging from 5km to 22km in Las Alpujarras, Sierra Nevada, Axarquía and Grazalema, as well as the areas bordering the Costa del Sol.

Jeremy Rabjohns *Holiday Walks in the Alpujarra* (Sigma, UK). Excellent small walking guide by Alpujarras resident Rabjohns describing twenty-four walks between three and twenty-two kilometres in length with clear maps (including many village street maps) and background information. Free updates and corrections available on the Internet.

Alison Raju *Via de la Plata – The Way of St James* (Cicerone, UK). A walker's guide to the lesser-known pilgrim route – much of it following ancient Roman roads – to Santiago de Compostela which started out from Sevilla. Gives clear route directions, plus information on sights en route, places to stay and practicalities.

Guías Penthalon (Penthalon, Spain). Detailed and generally reliable – although some need updating – series of walking guides (in Spanish) to various regions of Andalucía including the Sierra de Aracena and Sierra Nevada.

Interguías Clave *50 Rutas por la Serranía de Ronda* (widely available in bookshops in Andalucía). Fifty walking routes between six and forty kilometres in the Serranía de Ronda are well described with sketch maps. Also has information on refuges and places to find food and accommodation.

Andy Walmsley *Walking in the Sierra Nevada* (Cicerone, UK). Forty-five walks of varying distance and difficulty from three-hour strolls to the seriously arduous Tres Mils (3000m-plus) peaks.

Wildlife

John R. Butler *Birdwatching on Spain's Southern Coast* (Santana, Málaga ⓦ www.santanabooks.com). A guide to the major – and many minor – birdwatching sites of Andalucía including the Costa de Almería, Costa de la Luz and the Doñana national park. The author – who lives in Málaga and leads birdwatching tours – includes maps and the usual bird calendars as well as the highly unusual (and laudable) information concerning sites accessible (the vast majority are) to wheelchair-using and disabled twitchers.

Ernest García and Andrew Paterson *Where to Watch Birds in Southern Spain* (A&C Black, UK). A well-planned guide to bird-watching sites throughout Andalucía with location maps and reports detailing species to be seen according to season.

Frederic Grunfeld and Teresa Farino *Wild Spain* (Sheldrake Press/Sierra Club). A knowledgeable and practical guide to Spain's national parks, ecology and wildlife with a section on Andalucía. Farino is the author of the wildlife section for this guide (see p.667). Particularly recommended.

Heinzel, Fitter and Parslow *Collins Guide to the Birds of Britain and Europe* (Collins, UK). Alternative to the *Collins* (next page). Also includes North Africa and the Middle East.

John Measures *The Wildlife Travelling Companion: Spain* (Crowood Press, UK). Clearly laid-out field guide to specific wildlife areas complete with an illustrated index of the most common flora and fauna.

Peterson, Mountfort and Hollom *Collins Field Guide to the Birds of Britain and Europe* (Collins Reference/Houghton Mifflin). Standard reference book – covers most birds in Spain though you may find yourself confused by the birdsong descriptions.

Oleg Polunin and Anthony Huxley *Flowers of the Mediterranean* (Chatto, UK). Useful if by no means exhaustive field guide.

Food and wine

Nicholas Butcher *The Spanish Kitchen* (Macmillan, UK). A practical and knowledgeable guide to creating Spanish – including *andaluz* – dishes when you get back. Lots of informative detail on tapas, olive oil, *jamón serrano* and herbs.

Bob Carrick *Ventas Within a Short Drive of the Costa del Sol* (Santana, Málaga ⓦ www.santanabooks.com). Useful guide to some of the best *ventas* – Spain's bargain roadside restaurants – within easy reach of the Málaga coast. Widely available at bookshops in major resorts.

Penelope Casas *The Foods and Wines of Spain* (Penguin/Knopf) and *Tapas: the little dishes of Spain* (Pavilion). An excellent overview of classic Spanish and Andalucian cuisine, plus the same author's guide to the tapas labyrinth.

Alan Davidson *The Tio Pepe Guide to the Seafood of Spain and Portugal* (Santana, Málaga). An indispensable book that details and illustrates every fish and crustacean you're likely to meet in Andalucía.

Julian Jeffs *Sherry* (Faber, UK). The story of sherry – history, production, blending and brands. Rightly a classic and the best introduction to Andalucía's great wine.

Jean Claude Juston *The New Spain – Vegan and Vegetarian Restaurants* (Imprenta Generalife, Spain; copies available from Apartado Postal 126, 18400 Órjiva ⓦ www.vegetarian guides.com). Very useful guide to vegetarian restaurants throughout Spain by the owner/chef of a vegetarian restaurant in the Alpujarras. Catering also for vegans, each listing has its own review and there's lots of background information on Spanish veggie websites and magazines plus details of animal-friendly organizations.

Elisabeth Luard *The La Ina Book of Tapas* (Martin/Simon & Schuster) and *Flavours of Andalucía* (Collins & Brown, UK). Once you're hooked on tapas, this is the bible for all classic recipes. The Andalucía volume parades the major dishes of the region province by province.

Maite Manjon *Gastronomy of Spain and Portugal* (Garamond, UK). Useful alphabetical guide to food and drink on the peninsula.

Mark and Kim Millon *Wine Roads of Spain* (HarperCollins, UK/US). Everything you ever wanted to know about Spanish wine and sherry: when it's made, how it's made and where to find it, with lots of useful maps.

John Radford *The New Spain*, *The Wines of Rioja* (both Mitchell Beazley, UK). Lavish coffee-table format disguises *New Spain*'s serious content: a detailed region-by-region guide to Spanish wine with colour maps, bodega and vintage evaluations and fine illustrations. *Wines of Rioja* is a comprehensive vade mecum to the wines and producers in this emblematic Spanish wine region.

🏃 **Jan Read** *Guide to the Wines of Spain* (Mitchell Beazley, UK). Encyclopedic (yet pocketable) guide

to the classic and emerging wines of Spain by a leading authority. Includes maps, vintages and vineyards.

Antonio Zapata *Guía Gastronomica de la Alpujarra* (Junta de Andalucía, Spain). Spanish guide to the eastern, as well as western Alpujarras detailing village restaurants and *ventas* and their specialities. The latter part of the book has numerous *alpujarreña* recipes.

Learning Spanish and living In Spain

Breakthrough Spanish (Macmillan, UK). The best of the tape- and book-linked home-study courses which aims to give you a reasonable fluency within three months. The same series has advanced and business courses.

🏃 **Collins Spanish Dictionary** (HarperCollins UK/US). Recognized as the best single-volume bookshelf dictionary. Regularly revised and updated so make sure to get the latest edition.

🏃 **Get by in Spanish** (BBC Publications, UK; book and cassette). One of the BBC's excellent crash-course introductions which gets you to survival level (bars, restaurants, asking the way, and so on) Spanish in a couple of weeks.

Jonathon Packer *Live and Work in Spain and Portugal* (Vacation Work, UK). Well-researched handbook full of useful information on moving to the peninsula, buying property, seeking work, starting a business, finding schools and lots more.

David Hampshire *Living and Working in Spain* (Survival Books,

UK Ⓦ www.survivalbooks.net). A comprehensive guide to moving to, and setting up home in, Spain. The same publisher's *Costa del Sol Lifeline* by Joanna Styles narrows down the focus for expats on the Costa del Sol.

🏃 **Learn Spanish Now!** (Transparent Language UK/US Ⓦ www.transparent.com). CD-ROM based interactive language course which is a step-change in language learning incorporating all kinds of gadgets and gizmos enabling you compare your pronunciation with a native speaker, take part in conversations, access web-based additional learning resources and play skill-improving interactive games. Works on either Mac or PC systems. The same publisher's *Wordace Spanish Translation Dictionary* provides an entertaining way – via games and puzzles – to improve vocabulary and verb skills and gives model pronunciation. Both recommended.

🏃 **Spanish Dictionary Phrasebook** (Rough Guides). Good pocket-size dictionary that should help with most travel situations.

Language

Language

Language

O nce you get into it, **Spanish** is one of the easiest languages to learn – and you'll be helped everywhere by people who are eager to try and understand even the most faltering attempt. English is spoken, but only in the main tourist areas to any extent, and wherever you are you'll get a far better reception if you at least try communicating with Spaniards in their own tongue. Being understood, of course, is only half the problem – getting the gist of the reply, often rattled out at a furious pace, may prove far more difficult.

The rules of **pronunciation** are pretty straightforward and, once you get to know them, strictly observed. Unless there's an **accent**, words ending in d, l, r, and z are stressed on the last syllable, all others on the second last. All **vowels** are pure and short; combinations have predictable results.

A somewhere between the "A" sound of back and that of father

E as in get

I as in police

O as in hot

U as in rule

C in castellano (standard Spanish) is lisped before E and I, hard otherwise: cerca is pronounced "thairka". However, many parts of Andalucía pronounce this case as an "s" – "sairka" or even "Andalusia".

G works the same way, a guttural "H" sound (like the ch in loch) before E or I, a hard G elsewhere – gigante becomes "higante".

H is always silent

J the same sound as a guttural G: jamón is pronounced "hamon".

LL sounds like an English Y or LY: tortilla is pronounced torteeya/torteelya.

N is as in English unless it has a tilde (accent) over it, when it becomes NY: mañana sounds like "manyana".

QU is pronounced like an English K.

R is rolled, RR doubly so.

V sounds more like B, vino becoming "beano".

X has an S sound before consonants, normal X before vowels.

Z (in castellano) is the same as a soft C, so cerveza becomes "thairvaitha", but again much of Andalucía prefers the "s" sound – "sairvaisa".

A list of a few essential words and phrases follows which should be enough to get you started, though if you're travelling for any length of time, a dictionary or phrasebook is obviously a worthwhile investment. If you're using a dictionary, bear in mind that in Spanish CH, LL, and Ñ count as separate letters and are listed after C, L, and N respectively. For recommended books and tapes on learning Spanish, see the "Books" section.

Useful words and phrases

Basics

Sí, No, Vale	Yes, No, OK	Con, Sin	With, Without
Por favor, Gracias	Please, Thank you	Buen(o)/a, Mal(o)/a	Good, Bad
Dónde, Cuando	Where, When	Gran(de), Pequeño/a	Big, Small
Qué, Cuánto	What, How much	Barato, Caro	Cheap, Expensive
Aquí, Allí	Here, There	Caliente, Frío	Hot, Cold
Esto, Eso	This, That	Más, Menos	More, Less
Ahora, Más tarde	Now, Later	Hoy, Mañana	Today, Tomorrow
Abierto/a, Cerrado/a	Open, Closed	Ayer	Yesterday

Greetings and responses

Hola, Adiós	Hello, Goodbye	¿Habla (usted) inglés?	Do you speak English?
Buenos días	Good morning	(No) Hablo español	I don't speak Spanish
Buenas tardes/ noches	Good afternoon/night	Me llamo...	My name is...
Hasta luego	See you later	¿Como se llama usted?	What's your name?
Lo siento/ disculpéme	Sorry	Soy inglés(a)/ australiano(a)/ canadiense(a)/ americano(a)/ irlandés(a)	I am English/ Australian/Canadian/ American/Irish
Con permiso/perdón	Excuse me		
¿Como está (usted)?	How are you?		
(No) Entiendo	I (don't) understand		
De nada	Not at all/You're welcome		

Hotels and transport

Quiero	I want	(una semana)	(one week)
Quisiera	I'd like	¿Está bien, cuánto es?	It's fine, how much is it?
¿Sabe...?	Do you know...?	Es demasiado caro	It's too expensive
No sé	I don't know	¿No tiene algo más barato?	Don't you have anything cheaper?
(¿)Hay(?)	There is (is there)?	¿Se puede...?	Can one...?
Deme...(uno así)	Give me...(one like that)	¿acampar aquí (cerca)?	camp (near) here?
¿Tiene...?	Do you have...?	¿Hay un hostal aquí cerca?	Is there a hostel nearby?
...la hora	...the time		
...una habitación	...a room	¿Por dónde se va a...?	How do I get to...?
...con dos camas	...with two beds/		
cama matrimonial	double bed	Izquierda, derecha, todo recto	Left, right, straight on
...con ducha/baño	...with shower/bath		
Es para una persona	It's for one person	¿Dónde está...?	Where is...?
(dos personas)	(two people)	...la estación de autobuses	...the bus station
...para una noche	...for one night		

...la estación de ferrocarril	...the railway station	Quisiera un billete (de ida y vuelta) para...	I'd like a (return) ticket to...
...el banco mas cercano	...the nearest bank	¿A qué hora sale (llega a...)?	What time does it leave (arrive in...)?
...el correos/ la oficina de correos	...the post office	¿Qué hay para comer?	What is there to eat?
...el baño/aseo/ servicio	...the toilet	¿Qué es eso?	What's that?
¿De dónde sale el autobús para...?	Where does the bus to...leave from?	¿Como se llama este en español?	What's this called in Spanish?
¿Es este el tren para Sevilla?	Is this the train for Sevilla?		

Numbers and days

un/uno/una	1	ochenta	80
dos	2	noventa	90
tres	3	cien(to)	100
cuatro	4	ciento uno	101
cinco	5	doscientos	200
seis	6	doscientos uno	201
siete	7	quinientos	500
ocho	8	mil	1000
nueve	9	dos mil	2000
diez	10		
once	11	primero/a	first
doce	12	segundo/a	second
trece	13	tercero/a	third
catorce	14	quinto/a	fifth
quince	15	décimo/a	tenth
diez y seis	16		
veinte	20	lunes	Monday
veintiuno	21	martes	Tuesday
treinta	30	miércoles	Wednesday
cuarenta	40	jueves	Thursday
cincuenta	50	viernes	Friday
sesenta	60	sábado	Saturday
setenta	70	domingo	Sunday

Food and drink

Andaluz cuisine reflects its history and climate: many of the spices used, like cumin, coriander and saffron, were introduced by the Moors, and the variety of cold dishes such as gazpacho are intended to cool you down as much as to nourish. The list below should cover most of your needs, and local specialities are mentioned in the body of the Guide. Other things you'll simply see people eating. "Quisiera uno así" ("I'd like one like that") can be an amazingly useful phrase.

Restaurant terms

Almuerzo	Lunch		
Botella	Bottle	La cuenta	The bill
La carta	Menu	Desayuno	Breakfast
Cena	Dinner	Mesa	Table
Cubierto	set of cutlery	Tenedor	Fork
Cuchara	Spoon	Vaso	Glass
Cuchillo	Knife		

Menu terms

al ajillo	in garlic	al horno	baked
asado	roast	alioli	with mayonnaise
a la brasa	(charcoal) grilled	cazuela, cocido	stew
a la Gallego/a	Galician style	cocina casera	home-made
a la Navarra	stuffed with ham	en salsa	in (usually tomato) sauce
a la parilla/plancha	grilled		
a la romana	fried in batter	frito	fried
a la rondeña	Ronda style	guisado	casserole
a la sal	baked in a salt crust	rehogado	baked

Basics

Aceite	Oil	Pan	Bread
Ajo	Garlic	Pimienta	Pepper
Arroz	Rice	Queso	Cheese
Azúcar	Sugar	Sal	Salt
Fruta	Fruit	Verduras/Legumbres	Vegetables
Huevos	Eggs	Vinagre	Vinegar
Mantequilla	Butter		

Soups and starters (sopas y entrémeses)

Ajo blanco	Creamy gazpacho with garlic and almonds	Sopa de picadillo	A type of gazpacho with garnish
		Sopa de cocido	Meat soup
Caldillo	Clear fish soup	Sopa de gallina	Chicken soup
Caldo verde or gallego	Thick, cabbage-based broth	Sopa de mariscos	Seafood soup
Gazpacho	Cold tomato and cucumber soup	Sopa de pasta (fideos)	Noodle soup
Migas	fried breadcrumbs	Sopa de pescado	Fish soup

Salad (ensalada) and starters

Arroz a la cubana	Rice with fried egg and home-made tomato sauce	**Pimientos rellenos**	Stuffed peppers
Ensalada (mixta/verded)	(Mixed/green) salad	**Verduras con patatas**	Boiled potatoes with greens

Fish (pescados)

Anchoas	Anchovies (tinned)	**Mero**	Grouper
Anguila	Eel	**Mojama**	Salted blue-fin tuna
Angulas	Elvers (baby eel)	**Pez espada**	Swordfish
Atún	Tuna	**Rape**	Monkfish
Bacalao	Cod (often salt)	**Rodaballo**	Turbot
Besugo/Dorada	Sea bream	**Salmón**	Salmon
Bonito	Tuna	**Salmonete**	Mullet
Boquerones	Anchovies (fresh)	**Sardinas**	Sardines
Chanquetes	Whitebait	**Trucha**	Trout
Lenguado	Sole	**Urta**	Member of the bream family
Lubina/Baila	Bass		
Merluza	Hake		

Seafood (mariscos)

Almejas	Clam	**Mejillones**	Mussels
Calamares	Squid	**Ostras**	Oysters
Cangrejo	Crab	**Percebes**	Goose barnacles
Centollo	Spider-crab	**Pescadilla**	Small whiting
Chipirones	Small squid	**Pulpo**	Octopus
Cigalas	King prawns	**Puntillitas**	Baby squid
Conchas finas	Large scallops	**Sepia**	Cuttlefish
Gambas	Prawns/shrimps	**Vieiras/Conchas**	Scallops
Langosta	Lobster	**Zamburiñas**	Baby clams
Langostinos	Giant king prawns		

Meat (carne) and poultry (aves)

Albóndigas	Meatballs	**Cordero**	Lamb
Callos	Tripe	**Escalopa**	Escalope
Cabra	Goat	**Faisán**	Pheasant
Carne de vaca	Beef	**Hamburguesa**	Hamburger
Cerdo	Pork	**Hígado**	Liver
Chorizo	Spicy sausage	**Jabalí**	Boar
Chuletas	Chops	**Lengua**	Tongue
Cochinillo	Suckling pig	**Lomo**	Loin (of pork)
Conejo	Rabbit	**Mollejas**	Sweetbreads
Codorniz	Quail	**Morcilla**	Blood sausage

Perdiz	Partridge	Salchicha	Sausage
Pollo	Chicken	Salchichón	Cured salami-type sausage
Pato	Duck		
Pavo	Turkey	Sesos	Brains
Rabo de toro	stewed bull's tail	Ternera	Veal
Riñones	Kidneys		

Vegetables (legumbres)

Aguacate	Avocado	Judías verdes, rojas, negras	Green, red, black beans
Alcachofas	Artichokes		
Berenjenas	Aubergine/eggplant	Lechuga	Lettuce
Champiñones/Setas	Mushrooms	Nabos	Turnips
Coliflor	Cauliflower	Palmitos	Palm hearts
Cebollas	Onions	Patatas (fritas)	Potatoes (chips/french fries)
Espárragos	Asparagus		
Espinacas	Spinach	Pepino	Cucumber
Garbanzos	Chickpeas	Pimientos	Peppers
Guisantes	Peas	Puerros	Leeks
Habas	Broad beans	Repollo	Cabbage
Judías blancas	Haricot beans	Tomate	Tomato
		Zanahoria	Carrot

Rice dishes

Arroz negro	"Black rice", cooked with squid ink	Paella a la catalana	Mixed meat and seafood sometimes distinguished from a seafood paella by being called Paella a la valenciana
Arroz a banda	Rice with seafood, the rice served separately		
Arroz a la marinera	Paella: rice with seafood and saffron		

Desserts (postres)

Alfajores	Honey and almond pastries	Natillas	Custard
		Pastel	cake or pudding
Arroz con leche	Rice pudding	Peras al vino	Pears cooked in wine
Crema catalana	Crème brûlée	Pestiños	Anís or wine fritters
Dulces	tarts or cakes	Polvorones	Almond cakes
Flan	Crème caramel	Tarta de Santiago	pastry tart with almond filling
Helados	Ice cream		
Melocotón en almíbar	Peaches in syrup	Tocino de cielo	Andalucía's rich crème caramel
Miel	Honey	Yemas	Egg-yolk cakes
Nata	Whipped cream (topping)	Yogur	Yogurt

Fruit (frutas)

Albaricoques	Apricots	Melocotónes	Peaches
Chirimoyas	Custard apples	Melón	Melon
Cerezas	Cherries	Naranjas	Oranges
Ciruelas	Plums, prunes	Nectarinas	Nectarines
Dátiles	Dates	Peras	Pears
Fresas	Strawberries	Piña	Pineapple
Higos	Figs	Plátanos	Bananas
Limón	Lemon	Pomelo	Grapefruit
Manzanas	Apples	Sandía	Watermelon

Tapas and snacks

The most usual fillings for *bocadillos* are *lomo* (loin of pork), *tortilla* and *calamares* (all of which may be served hot), *jamón* (York or, much better, serrano), *chorizo*, *salchichón* (and various other regional sausages – such as the small, spicy Catalan *butifarras*), *queso* (cheese), or *atún* (tuna – probably canned). Standard tapas and *raciones* might include:

Aceitunas	Olives	Hígado	Liver
Albóndigas	Meatballs, usually in sauce	Huevo cocido	Hard-boiled egg
		Jamón serrano	Mountain cured ham
Anchoas	Anchovies	Jamón York	Regular ham
Berberechos	Cockles	Judias	Beans
Boquerones	Fresh anchovies	Mejillones	Mussels (either steamed, or served with diced tomatoes and onion)
Calamares a la romana	Squid, deep fried in rings		
Calamares en su tinta	Squid in ink		
		Morcilla	Blood sausage (black pudding)
Callos	Tripe		
Caracoles	Snails, often served in a spicy/curry sauce	Navajas	Razor clams
		Pan con tomate	Bread, rubbed with tomato and oil
Carne en salsa	Meat in tomato sauce		
Champiñones	Mushrooms, usually fried in garlic	Patatas alioli	Potatoes in garlic mayonnaise
Chipirones	Whole baby squid	Patatas bravas	Fried potato cubes topped with spicy sauce and mayonnaise
Chorizo	Spicy sausage		
Cocido	Stew		
Croqueta	Fish or chicken croquette		
		Pimientos	Peppers
Empanadilla	Fish/meat pasty	Pincho moruno	Kebab
Ensaladilla	Russian salad (diced vegetables in mayonnaise)	Pulpo	Octopus
		Riñones al Jerez	Kidneys in sherry
		Salchichón	Cured sausage
Escalibada	Aubergine (eggplant) and pepper salad	Sardinas	Sardines
		Sepia	Cuttlefish
Gambas	Shrimps	Tortilla española	Potato omelette
Habas con jamón	Broad beans with ham	Tortilla francesa	Plain omelette

Drinks

Café	Coffee	Agua mineral	Mineral water
Café solo	Espresso coffee	...(con gas)	... (sparkling)
Café con leche	White coffee	...(sin gas)	... (still)
Descafeinado	Decaff	Leche	Milk
Té	Tea	Zumo	Juice
Chocolate	Drinking Chocolate	Horchata	Tiger-nut drink
Agua	Water		

Alcohol

Cerveza	Beer	Vino	Wine
Champán	Champagne	Fino	Sherry

Glossary

Acequia irrigation channel.

Alameda park or tree-lined promenade.

Albariza type of soil in wine-growing zones with high chalk content enabling retention of moisture.

Alcalde mayor of town or village.

Alcazaba Moorish castle.

Alcázar Moorish fortified palace.

Almohads Muslims originally of Berber stock, who toppled the Almoravids and ruled Spain in the late twelfth and early thirteenth centuries.

Almoravids fanatical Berber dynasty from the Sahara who ruled much of Spain in the eleventh and twelfth centuries.

Artesonado wooden coffered ceiling of Moorish origin or inspiration.

Atalaya watchtower.

Autovía/autopista dual carriageway or highway/motorway or expressway.

Ayuntamiento town hall (also Casa Consistorial).

Azulejos glazed ceramic tiles (originally blue – hence the name).

Balneario spa.

Barrio suburb or quarter.

Bodega cellar, wine bar, or warehouse.

Bracero landless agricultural worker.

Calle street.

Camarín shrine (inside a church) with a venerated image.

Campiña flat stretch of farmland or countryside.

Cante jondo deeply-felt flamenco song.

Capilla mayor chapel containing the high altar.

Capilla real royal chapel.

Carretera highway or main road

Carmen Granadan villa with garden.

Casa forestal woodland hunters' house/hotel

Casa señorial/palacio aristocratic mansion.

Casco antiguo the old part of a town or city.

Cartuja Carthusian monastery.

Casino social and gaming club.

Castillo castle.

Centro comercial shopping centre/mall.

Chiringuito beachfront restaurant.

Churrigueresque extreme form of Baroque art named after José Churriguera (1665–1725) and his extended family, its main exponents.

Ciudad town or city.

Ciudadela citadel.

Colegiata collegiate (large parish) church.

Comunidad autónoma autonomous region with significant powers of self-government. Andalucía is one of seventeen autonomous regions set up following the return to democracy in the 1970s.

Convento monastery or convent.

Converso Jew who converted to Christianity.

Coro central part of church built for the choir.

Coro alto raised choir, often above west door of a church.

Corral type of patio or yard.

Correos post office.

Corrida de toros bullfight.

Cortes Spanish parliament in Madrid.

Cortijo rural farmhouse in Andalucía.

Coto de caza hunting reserve.

Cuesta slope/hill.

Cueva cave.

Custodia large receptacle or monstrance for Eucharist wafers.

Desamortización (Disentailment) nineteenth-century expropriation of church buildings and lands.

Duende to have soul (in flamenco).

Embalse artificial lake, reservoir or dam.

Ermita hermitage.

Esparto grass used for mats, window blinds and olive presses.

Feria annual fair.

Finca farm.

Fogón stove.

Gitano gypsy.

Huerta vegetable garden.

Isabelline ornamental form of late Gothic developed during the reign of Isabel and Fernando.

Jarra wine jug or pitcher.

Jornalero landless agricultural day-labourer.

Judería Jewish quarter.

Juerga (gypsy) shindig.

Junta de Andalucía government of the Autonomous Region of Andalucía.

Latifundio large estate.

Locutorio Telephone office.

Lonja stock exchange building.

Marismas marshes.

Medina Moorish town.

Mercado market.

Mezquita mosque.

Mihrab prayer niche of Moorish mosque facing towards Mecca.

Mirador viewing point (literally balcony).

Monasterio monastery or convent.

Morisco Muslim Spaniard subject to medieval Christian rule – and nominally baptized.

Movida The (nightlife) scene; where the action is.

Mozarabe Christian subject to medieval Moorish rule; normally allowed freedom of worship. Mozarabic is the architectural style evolved by Christians under Arab domination.

Mudéjar Muslim Spaniard subject to medieval Christian rule, but retaining Islamic worship; most commonly a term applied to architecture which includes buildings built by Moorish craftsmen for the Christian rulers and later designs influenced by the Moors. The 1890s–1930s saw a Mudéjar revival, blended with Art Nouveau and Art Deco forms.

Palacio aristocratic mansion.

Pantano reservoir held by a dam.

Parador luxury state-run hotel, often converted from minor monument.

Parroquia parish church.

Paseo promenade; also the evening stroll thereon.

Paso float bearing tableau carried in Semana Santa processions.

Patio inner courtyard.

Piscina swimming pool.

Plateresco/plateresque elaborately decorative Renaissance style, the sixteenth-century successor of Isabelline forms. Named for its resemblance to silversmiths' work (platería).

Playa beach.

Plaza square.

Plaza de toros bullring.

Plaza mayor a town or city's main square regardless of its name.

Posada old name for an inn.

Pueblo village or town.

Puerta gateway, also mountain pass.

Puerto port.

Rambla dry riverbed.

Reconquista the Christian reconquest of Moorish Spain.

Reja iron screen or grille, often fronting a window or guarding a chapel.

Retablo carved or painted altarpiece.

Río river.

rociero Adhering to the traditions of the El Rocío pilgrimage.

Rococo late-Baroque style with a profusion of rock-like forms, scrolls and crimped shells. From the French rocaille – "rock-work".

Romería religious procession to a rural shrine.

Sacristía, sagrario sacristy or sanctuary of a church.

Sacristía (ii), wine cellar in sherry bodega

Saeta passionate flamenco song in praise of the Virgin and Christ.

Sebka decorative brickwork developed by the Almohads (eg, Giralda).

Semana Santa Holy Week, celebrated throughout Andalucía with elaborate processions.

Señoritismo Behaving in a condescending manner; applied generally to rich landowners.

Sevillana rhythmic flamenco dance.

Sierra mountain range.

Sillería choir stall.

Solar aristocratic town mansion.

Solera blending system for sherry and brandy.

Tablao flamenco show.

Taifa small Moorish kingdom, many of which emerged after the disintegration of the Córdoba caliphate.

Tajo gorge

Tetería Arabic tearoom

Trascoro end-wall of the choir.

Torno dumbwaiter used by convents to sell their cakes and pastries.

Urbanización residential housing estate

Vega cultivated fertile plain.

Venta roadside inn.

Yeso/yesería plaster/plasterwork.

Political parties and abbreviations

ETA Basque terrorist organization. Its political wing is the banned Batasuna.

Falange Franco's old fascist party; now officially defunct.

Fuerza Nueva Descendants of the above, also on the way out.

IR Izquierda Republicana, left-wing republican party.

IU Izquierda Unida, broad-left alliance of communists and others.

MC Movimiento Comunista (Communist Movement), small radical offshoot of the PCE.

MOC Movimiento de Objectores de Conciencia, peace group, concerned with NATO and conscription.

OTAN NATO.

PA Partido Andalucista, the Andalucian Nationalist Party

PASOC Partido de Acción Socialista, "traditional" socialist group to the left of the PSOE.

PCE Partido Comunista de España (Spanish Communist Party).

PP Partido Popular, the right-wing party formed by a union of Alianza Popular and the Christian Democrats led by Mariano Rajoy; currently the main oppostion party in the Cortes.

PSOE Partido Socialista Obrero Español (Spanish Socialist Workers' Party). Currently the government party led by prime minister José Luis Rodríguez Zapatero.

UGT Unión General de Trabajadores, Spain's most powerful trade union.

★ **waterproof**

★ **rip-proof**

★ **amazing value**

ROUGH GUIDE MAP

France

1:1,100,000 • 1 INCH: 17.3 MILES • 1 CM: 11 KM

Plastic waterproof map
ideal for planning and touring

ROUGH GUIDES

CITY MAPS
Amsterdam ·Athens · Barcelona · Berlin · Boston · Brussels · Chicago · Dublin
Florence & Siena · Frankfurt · Hong Kong · Lisbon · London · Los Angeles
Madrid · Marrakesh · Miami · New York · Paris · Prague · Rome · San Francisco
Toronto · Venice · Washington DC and more...
US$8.99   Can$13.99   £4.99

COUNTRY & REGIONAL MAPS
Algarve · Andalucía · Argentina · Australia · Baja California · Brittany · Crete
Croatia · Cuba · Cyprus · Czech Republic · Dominican Republic · Dubai · Egypt
Greece · Guatemala & Belize · Iceland · Ireland · Kenya · Mexico · Morocco New
Zealand · Northern Spain · Peru · Portugal · Sicily · South Africa · South India ·
Sri Lanka · Tenerife · Thailand · Trinidad & Tobago · Tuscany · Yucatán Peninsula
· and more...
US$9.99   Can$13.99   £5.99

MAPS

Small print and

Index

A Rough Guide to Rough Guides

Published in 1982, the first Rough Guide – to Greece – was a student scheme that became a publishing phenomenon. Mark Ellingham, a recent graduate in English from Bristol University, had been travelling in Greece the previous summer and couldn't find the right guidebook. With a small group of friends he wrote his own guide, combining a highly contemporary, journalistic style with a thoroughly practical approach to travellers' needs.

The immediate success of the book spawned a series that rapidly covered dozens of destinations. And, in addition to impecunious backpackers, Rough Guides soon acquired a much broader and older readership that relished the guides' wit and inquisitiveness as much as their enthusiastic, critical approach and value-for-money ethos.

These days, Rough Guides include recommendations from shoestring to luxury and cover more than 200 destinations around the globe, including almost every country in the Americas and Europe, more than half of Africa and most of Asia and Australasia. Our ever-growing team of authors and photographers is spread all over the world, particularly in Europe, the USA and Australia.

In the early 1990s, Rough Guides branched out of travel, with the publication of Rough Guides to World Music, Classical Music and the Internet. All three have become benchmark titles in their fields, spearheading the publication of a wide range of books under the Rough Guide name.

Including the travel series, Rough Guides now number more than 350 titles, covering: phrasebooks, waterproof maps, music guides from Opera to Heavy Metal, reference works as diverse as Conspiracy Theories and Shakespeare, and popular culture books from iPods to Poker. Rough Guides also produce a series of more than 120 World Music CDs in partnership with World Music Network.

Visit www.roughguides.com to see our latest publications.

Rough Guide travel images are available for commercial licensing at www.roughguidespictures.com

Rough Guide credits

Text editor: Clifton Wilkinson
Layout: Umesh Aggarwal, Diana Jarvis
Cartography: Jai Prakash Mishra
Picture editor: Simon Bracken, Sarah Smithes
Production: Katherine Owers
Proofreader: David Price
Cover design: Chloë Roberts
Photographer: Demetrio Carrasco
Editorial: London Kate Berens, Claire Saunders, Geoff Howard, Ruth Blackmore, Polly Thomas, Richard Lim, Alison Murchie, Karoline Densley, Andy Turner, Keith Drew, Edward Aves, Nikki Birrell, Helen Marsden, Alice Park, Sarah Eno, David Paul, Lucy White, Joe Staines, Duncan Clark, Peter Buckley, Matthew Milton, Tracy Hopkins, Ruth Tidball; **New York** Andrew Rosenberg, Richard Koss, Steven Horak, AnneLise Sorensen, Amy Hegarty, Hunter Slaton, April Isaacs, Sean Mahoney
Design & Pictures: London Simon Bracken, Dan May, Diana Jarvis, Mark Thomas, Jj Luck, Harriet Mills; **Delhi** Madhulita Mohapatra, Ajay Verma, Jessica Subramanian, Amit Verma, Ankur Guha, Pradeep Thapliyal
Production: Sophie Hewat, Aimee Hampson

Cartography: London Maxine Repath, Ed Wright, Katie Lloyd-Jones; **Delhi** Manish Chandra, Rajesh Chhibber, Ashutosh Bharti, Rajesh Mishra, Animesh Pathak, Jasbir Sandhu, Karobi Gogoi, Amod Singh
Online: New York Jennifer Gold, Suzanne Welles, Kristin Mingrone; **Delhi** Manik Chauhan, Narender Kumar, Shekhar Jha, Lalit K. Sharma, Rakesh Kumar, Chhandita Chakravarty
Marketing & Publicity: London Richard Trillo, Niki Hanmer, David Wearn, Demelza Dallow, Louise Maher; **New York** Geoff Colquitt, Megan Kennedy, Katy Ball; **Delhi** Reem Khokhar
Custom publishing and foreign rights: Philippa Hopkins
Manager India: Punita Singh
Series editor: Mark Ellingham
Reference Director: Andrew Lockett
PA to Managing and Publishing Directors: Megan McIntyre
Publishing Director: Martin Dunford
Managing Director: Kevin Fitzgerald

Publishing information

This fifth edition published April 2006 by **Rough Guides Ltd**,
80 Strand, London WC2R 0RL
345 Hudson St, 4th Floor,
New York, NY 10014, USA
14 Local Shopping Centre, Panchsheel Park,
New Delhi 110017, India
Distributed by the Penguin Group
Penguin Books Ltd,
80 Strand, London WC2R 0RL
Penguin Putnam, Inc.
375 Hudson Street, NY 10014, USA
Penguin Group (Australia)
250 Camberwell Road, Camberwell,
Victoria 3124, Australia
Penguin Books Canada Ltd,
10 Alcorn Avenue, Toronto, Ontario,
Canada M4V 1E4
Penguin Group (New Zealand)
Cnr Rosedale and Airborne Roads
Albany, Auckland, New Zealand
Cover design by Peter Dyer.

Typeset in Bembo and Helvetica to an original design by Henry Iles.
Printed in Italy by LegoPrint S.p.A.
© Geoff Garvey and Mark Ellingham 2006
No part of this book may be reproduced in any form without permission from the publisher except for the quotation of brief passages in reviews.
728pp includes index
A catalogue record for this book is available from the British Library
ISBN 13: 978-1-84353-590-4
ISBN 10: 1-84353-587-4
The publishers and authors have done their best to ensure the accuracy and currency of all the information in **The Rough Guide to Andalucía**, however, they can accept no responsibility for any loss, injury, or inconvenience sustained by any traveller as a result of information or advice contained in the guide.

1   3   5   7   9   8   6   4   2

Help us update

We've gone to a lot of effort to ensure that the fifth edition of **The Rough Guide to Andalucía** is accurate and up to date. However, things change – places get "discovered", opening hours are notoriously fickle, restaurants and rooms raise prices or lower standards. If you feel we've got it wrong or left something out, we'd like to know, and if you can remember the address, the price, the time, the phone number, so much the better.

We'll credit all contributions, and send a copy of the next edition (or any other Rough Guide if you prefer) for the best letters. Everyone who writes to us and isn't already a subscriber will receive a copy of our full-colour thrice-yearly newsletter. Please mark letters: "**Rough Guide Andalucía Update**" and send to: Rough Guides, 80 Strand, London WC2R 0RL, or Rough Guides, 4th Floor, 345 Hudson St, New York, NY 10014. Or send an email to **mail@roughguides.com**

Have your questions answered and tell others about your trip at
www.roughguides.atinfopop.com

Acknowledgements

On our fifth edition grateful thanks must go to Josép Vergés, Angela García and Josefina del Castillo for help in Almería. Special thanks also to Pau for her invaluable assistance in Sevilla and to Chris and Ana Stewart for the lowdown on the western Alpujarras. We are also indebted to Mark Colenutt, Daniela Pittiglio and Gina de los Santos for Sevilla help; to Holli McGuire for Costa del Sol and Cádiz nightlife research; Pamela Lalonde in Granada; Bienvenido Luque in Málaga; and María José Lopez Soler in the Alhambra. A big thank you also goes from Geoff to Han for her untiring help and support in getting the job done.

Valuable assistance on the ground was also rendered by Jean and Christine Hofer in El Chorro, Pasqual Rovira and Quica Caballero Mata in Rute, James Stuart and Carmen Atkins García in Vejer, Vicente Sousa in Aracena, Jean-Claude Juston in Mecina Fondales, Ignacio Muñiz García in Almedinilla, Julie Hetherington and Rafael Calzado Reca in Andújar, Mariano Ortiz in Constantina, Adam & Teresa Page in Gaucín, Paco Moyano & Lola Maiztegui in Alhama de Granada, Angelica Romero in Huelva, Manuel Amigo García in Aroche, Juan Carlos Ábalos Guerrero and Clive Jarman in Zuheros, Jesús García in Benarrabá, Elma Thompson in Nerja, Juan Manuel Pérez in Salobreña, María Angeles Rodríguez in Antequera, Rosa González in Conil, Raquel Ahedo in La Linea, Juan Carlos Raths Aznar in Mojácar, Francisco Serrano in Mijas, Fausia Alui in Granada, Margarita Murillo and José Luis Melero in Sevilla, Angelica Romero in Huelva, Mercedes Galvez in Jaén, Anton Peer in Segura de la Sierra, Raquel Pasqual in Córdoba, Pepe Morales in Punta Umbría and Juan María Luna Moreno in La Axarquía.

Special thanks are also due to Tony Wailey for Civil War background, Bienvenido Martinez Navarro for updates on excavations at Orce, Paul Winstanley for modern art information, Hugh Broughton for architectural suggestions and to Mark Honigsbaum for surfing tips. We were greatly helped with advice on birdspotting from Huw Morgan, Anthony Winchester and Martin Bott. We would also like to thank Olga Velasco and the staff of the Spanish National Tourist Office in London for their help with numerous queries, as well as the staff of the Sherry Institute in London.

Readers' letters

Thanks to all the readers who have taken the time to write in with comments and suggestions (and apologies if we've inadvertently omitted or misspelt anyone's name):

Kathy Abbot, Evangelos Aktsalis, Sue Ashcroft, Mark Ashton, Bill Bain, Derek Barker, David Barnes, Samantha Barton, J Baxter, Anita Beijer & Walter Michels, Amanda Bekker, Frits Blomsma, Rupert Blum, Anne Bodie, Lorenzo Bohme, Sara Bond, Pru Bowen, Peter Bowman, Finola Brady, Ian Broad, Clare Brown, E Bruixot, Jim Burke, Phil Burrows, Jeff Buse, Susan Butcher, Peter Cameron, Iain Campbell Aird, Beatriz Cano, Nicholas Carr, Julyan Cartwright, Loli Cervantes, M Chambers, Harold Chaplin, Leonora Charles, Sarah Christian, Ali & Mike Coleman, Andrew Coleman, Peter Coles, M Conway, Monica Cornelis, Nick Davies, Gina Day, Mauricio de la Guardia, Csilla de Bagota, Claire Demaret, P Drower, Jill Duncan & John Hamilton, Jack Edwards, Lynn Ennis, Simon Evans, Jonas F Ludvigsson, Michael Fahy, Peter Fenn, Heather Fielding, Chris Finley, Hugh Finn, Pat Firth, Paul Fisher, Graham Fletcher, Dennis Forde, Patrick Foreman, Sarah Fradsham, Karen Friedlander, Ed Gallagher, Barry & Audrie Gant, Beltran García Ligero, Becky Gethin, Antonio Gomez, Teresa Goss, Alasdair Graham, Carey Gray, Richard & Megan Greene, Judith Groves, Simon Hancock, Patrick Hannet, Peter Harland, John Harris, Dr & Mrs E Harrison, Rita Hassemeier, Stuart Hastings, Ian Hastings, Victor Henderson, Jennie Holland, Jan Holmes, Clive Holt, Tim Holt & Keith Tennyson, Cherry How, Andrew Howard, Claire Hunt, Ian Watson, David James, Edmund Janowski, Karin Joanidopoulos, Gareth Jones, Kath Jones, Linda Jones, Francisco José Mulero, G K Stocker, David Kelly, Simon Kempf, Sabine Kenis & Dirk Farasijn, Sally Kerr, Alice

Kildsgaard & Lau Mølgård, Andrea Knox, Truusja Kofflard, Lisa Koponen-Wotherspoon, Sophia Lambert, Louise Lambert, Sophia Lambert, David Lanfear, Tricia Langton, David Lant & Katerina Lindop, Brian Lewis, Richard Lovett, Chris Lowe, Derek Marsh, Pam Martin, Nichole Martinson, Stewart Mason, Mike Mason, Andrew Maynard, John McCafferty, David McCann, Elspeth McCreadie, Frank McKell, Ian McNichol, Peter McNulty, Carolyn Melville-Smith, David Meredith, Luis Miguel Aguilera & Aurora Damigo, Annick Milcamps, Juliet Molteno & John Knight, Olivia Montagu, Adam More, A Morrison, Anja Mutic, Aoufe Ní Charbhaill, Gail Nolan, Gary Norman, Peter North, David O'Mahony, Marie & Denis Murphy, Marietta Pantin, Michael Parker, G Patton, Angela Pearman, Jannie Pedersen, Fernando Peire, Myriam Pérez Torres, Professor Peter Golding, Cristina Pignatoro, Frank Pike, Caroline Pilgrim, Gerald Pitcher, William Plumtree, Lisa Portman, Sarah Potter, Geoffrey & Janet Price, Charlotte Proctor, Fiona Rayner, Zena Reedie, Noel Richardson, Maria Richardson, Carmen Ridley, Madeleine Riley, Anita Roberts, Will Roberts, Stephen Roberts, Alan Roberts, Tina Robinson, Adam Rothapel & Isobel Pearce, Harriet Rowland, Andrea Sabina, Lucia Sanou, Louis Sassi, Peter Saunders, Carol Scanlon, Robert Schwartz, Katja Schwieger, Bob Shepherd, Seb Sheppard, Alice Sheppard, Richard Smith, David Smith, Kirsty Smith, Susi Steiner, Nicholas Stokes, Ruth & Andrew Stuber, Peter Swarbrick, Pat Swinbanks, Charles Swinley, Pat Tanumihardja, Jane Taylor, Dawn Taylor, Bill Thomas, Jo Thomas, Rita Thompson, Jill Tideman, Sonia Torres, Bretta Townend-Jowett, R Truman, Menno & Jeannine Van der Meer, Guy Van Vlierden, Michael van Beinum & Kate Foster, Joanne Wainwright, Stephanie Walker & Graham Donachie, Andrew Walker, Alan White, Jane Whittle, Mike Wilson, Carrie Winstanley, Nicola Wright, Antonio Zafra Romero, Luis Zarzuela.

ROUGH GUIDES

Photo credits

All photos © Rough Guides except the following:

Title page
Feria de Abril, Sevilla © aslphoto/Alamy

Full page
Casares © Gavin Hellier/Getty Images

Introduction
Olive trees in bloom © G. Rossenbach/Corbis

Things not to miss
01 Nerja Beach © Geoff Garvey
06 Sierra de Cazorla © David Norton Photography/Alamy
15 Iberian Lynx © Carlos Sanz/VW Pics/Alamy
18 Semana Santa © Geoff Garvey
21 Flamenco dancers © Geoff Garvey
27 Las Alpujarras © Geoff Garvey
30 Encierro © Geoff Garvey
31 Ronda © Gavin Hellier/Alamy
32 Tapas bar © Jochem Wijnands/Alamy

Colour insert Andalucian Cuisine
Tapas bar © Renaud Visage/Alamy
Selection of tapas © Miguel Raurich/iberimage
Marinated anchovies and olives © Renaud Visage/Alamy
White gazpacho © Firebird/Alamy
El Rinconcillo, Sevilla © Miguel Raurich/iberimage
Sherry and olives © Jochem Wijnands/Alamy
Jamón being prepared in a tapas bar © Paul Quayle/Axiom
Spinach with chickpeas © Rick Lew/Getty Images

Colour insert Semana Santa
Semana Santa, Málaga © David Norton Photography/Alamy
Semana Santa procession © Geoff Garvey
Hermandades, Sevilla © Andrea Pistolesi/Getty Images
Costaleros © Geoff Garvey
Carratraca Passion play © Geoff Garvey
La Macarena, Sevilla © Julio Donoso/Corbis

Colour insert Moorish Andalucía
Moorish horseshoe arch © Linda Whitwam/Dorling Kindersley
Striped stone arches in the Mezquita, Córdoba © Geoff Brightling/Dorling Kindersley
Medina Azahara © Geoff Garvey
Inscription in the Alhambra, Granada © Geoff Garvey
Alcázar, Córdoba © Linda Whitwam/Dorling Kindersley
Tinao © Geoff Garvey

Black and whites
p.599 La Calahorra Castle © isifa Image Sevices s.r.o./Alamy
p.644 Engraving of Ferdinand and Isabella © Corbis
p.660 Flamenco dancers © Geoff Garvey
p.669 Iberian Lynx © Carlos Sanz/VW Pics/Alamy

Index

Map entries are in colour.

INDEX

INDEX

Map symbols

maps are listed in the full index using coloured text

– – – – –	National boundary		♦	Point of interest
— – ·· –	Provincial boundary		⊥	Gardens
– – – –	Chapter boundary		⛪	Monastery
	Motorway		🏰	Mosque
	Major road		♜	Castle
	Minor road		✡	Synagogue
	Steps		⊙	Statue
– – – – – –	Footpath		⊠—⊠	Gates
———	Wall		✈	Airport
	Railway		🅿	Parking
●– – – –●	Cable car		⛷	Skiing
— – — –	Ferry route		@	Internet access
———	River		ⓘ	Tourist information
⪥	Mountain pass		⊠	Post office
▲	Mountain peak		ℂ	Phone office
/|\\	Hill shading		◉	Hotel
	Rocks		◼	Restaurant
	Cliff			Building
⚘	Viewpoint			Church/cathedral
⌒	Caves			Park
⟩	Dunes			Forest
⚠	Campsite			Beach
⚲	Lighthouse			Saltpan
∴	Ruin/archeological site